P9-EJJ-540

FOURTH EDITION

Introduction to Private Security

Kären M. Hess
Normandale Community College
Bloomington, Minnesota

Henry M. Wrobleski
Private Security Investigator
and Evaluator

West Publishing Company
Minneapolis/St. Paul ▪ New York
Los Angeles ▪ San Francisco

Production Credits
Cover Photo: Courtesy of Pinkerton's, Inc.
Interior Design: John Edeen
Copyediting: Deborah Drolen Jones
Composition: Parkwood Composition
Index: Christine Hess Orthmann
Photo Credits Follow Index

West's Commitment to the Environment

In 1906, West Publishing Company began recycling materials left over from the production of books. This began a tradition of efficient and responsible use of resources. Today, 100% of our legal bound volumes are printed on acid-free, recycled paper consisting of 50% new paper pulp and 50% paper that has undergone a de-inking process. We also use vegetable-based inks to print all of our books. West recycles nearly 22,650,000 pounds of scrap paper annually—the equivalent of 187,500 trees. Since the 1960s, West has devised ways to capture and recycle waste inks, solvents, oils, and vapors created in the printing process. We also recycle plastics of all kinds, wood, glass, corrugated cardboard, and batteries, and have eliminated the use of polystyrene book packaging. We at West are proud of the longevity and the scope of our commitment to our environment.

West pocket parts and advance sheets are printed on recyclable paper and can be collected and recycled with newspapers. Staples do not have to be removed. Bound volumes can be recycled after removing the cover.

Production, Printing and Binding by West Publishing Company.

10 11 12 13 14 09 08 07 06 05

British Library Cataloguing-in-Publication Data. A catalogue record for this book is available from the British Library.

610 Opperman Drive
P.O. Box 64526
St. Paul, MN 55164-0526

Printed in the United States of America

Library of Congress Cataloging-in-Publication Data

Hess, Kären M.
Introduction to private security / Kären M. Hess, Henry M. Wrobleski, — 4th ed.
p. cm.
Includes bibliographical references and index.
ISBN 0-314-06732-9 (hard : alk. paper)
1. Private security services—United States. 2. Industry—Security measures. I. Wrobleski, Henry M. II. Title.
III. Title: Private security
HV8291.U6H47 1996 95-32862
363.2'89—dc20 CIP

Contents in Brief

Contents in Brief iii
Contents v
List of Figures xiii
List of Tables xv
List of Acronyms and Initials xvi
List of Cases xix
Preface xxi
How To Use This Book xxi
Acknowledgements xxiii

SECTION I
PRIVATE SECURITY: AN OVERVIEW 1

CHAPTER 1 The Evolution of Private Security: A Brief History 2
CHAPTER 2 Modern Private Security: An Overview 28
CHAPTER 3 The Public/Private Interface and Legal Authority 50
CHAPTER 4 Legal Liability 72

SECTION II
BASIC SECURITY GOALS AND RESPONSIBILITIES 93

CHAPTER 5 Enhancing Security through Physical Controls 95
CHAPTER 6 Enhancing Security through Procedural Controls 144
CHAPTER 7 Preventing Losses from Accidents and Emergencies 189
CHAPTER 8 Preventing Losses from Criminal Actions 235
CHAPTER 9 Enhancing Information/Computer Security 273
CHAPTER 10 Enhancing Public Relations 312

SECTION III
WHEN PREVENTION FAILS 337

CHAPTER 11 The Investigative Function 338
CHAPTER 12 Obtaining and Providing Information 357
CHAPTER 13 Testifying in Court 399

SECTION IV
SECURITY SYSTEMS AT WORK: PUTTING IT ALL TOGETHER 419

CHAPTER 14 Loss Prevention through Risk Management 421
CHAPTER 15 Industrial Security 448
CHAPTER 16 Retail Security 474
CHAPTER 17 Commercial Security 524
CHAPTER 18 Institutional Security 567
CHAPTER 19 Other Applications of Security at Work 606

SECTION V
CHALLENGES FACING THE SECURITY PROFESSION IN THE 1990S AND BEYOND 625

CHAPTER 20 The Challenges of Violence in the Workplace 626
CHAPTER 21 Practicing and Promoting Ethical Conduct 649
CHAPTER 22 The Security Professional and Profession 671
CHAPTER 23 A Look to the Future 700

APPENDIXES 723
A Site Security Evaluation 723
B Training Requirements State by State 733
C Academic Programs in Security and Loss Prevention 739

Glossary 751
Answers to Critical Thinking Exercises 764
Author Index 767
Subject Index 775

CONTENTS

Contents in Brief iii
Contents v
List of Figures xiii
List of Tables xv
List of Acronyms and Initials xvi
List of Cases xix
Preface xxi
How To Use This Book xxi
Acknowledgments xxiii

SECTION I
PRIVATE SECURITY: AN OVERVIEW 1

CHAPTER 1
THE EVOLUTION OF PRIVATE SECURITY: A BRIEF HISTORY 2
Introduction 2
Ancient Times 3
The Middle Ages (476–1453) 6
The Eighteenth Century 9
Nineteenth-Century England 13
The Evolution of Private Security in the United States 15
Summary 24

CHAPTER 2
MODERN PRIVATE SECURITY: AN OVERVIEW 28
Introduction 28
Private Security Defined 29
Purpose and Objectives of Private Security 30
Types of Private Security Services and Personnel 31
Proprietary vs. Contract Private Security Services 37
Regulation of Private Security 41
Regulation of Private Investigators 43
Certified Protection Professional (CPP) 44
Summary 46

CHAPTER 3
THE PUBLIC/PRIVATE INTERFACE AND LEGAL AUTHORITY 50
Introduction 50
The Public/Private Interface 50
Legal Authority 54
Historical Friction 56
The Complementary Roles of Private and Public Officers 58
Areas Where Private Security Can Help Public Police 64
Partnerships in Action 67
Summary 68

CHAPTER 4
LEGAL LIABILITY 72
Introduction 72
Law and Liability in the United States 74
Elements of Negligent Liability 76
Common Civil Lawsuits Brought against Private Security 78
The Civil Rights Act—Section 1983 81
Reducing Liability 83
Common Defenses against Civil Lawsuits 88
Surviving a Lawsuit 88
Summary 89

SECTION II
BASIC SECURITY GOALS AND RESPONSIBILITIES 93

CHAPTER 5
ENHANCING SECURITY THROUGH PHYSICAL CONTROLS 95
Introduction 96
Basic Physical Controls 96
The Perimeter 99
The Building Exterior 104
The Building Interior 109
Basic Security Equipment 111
Locks 111
Security Lighting 118
Alarms 119
Surveillance Systems 128
Other Means to Enhance Security through Physical Control 131
The Physical Security System 136
Summary 138

CHAPTER 6
ENHANCING SECURITY THROUGH PROCEDURAL CONTROLS 144

Introduction 144
Shrinkage—A Major Problem and Challenge 145
The First Line of Defense—Hiring Well 147
The Second Line of Defense—Training and Supervising 152
The Third Line of Defense—Access Control 153
Other Procedures to Enhance Security 173
Making Rounds 173
Conducting Routine Searches 174
Transporting Valuables 176
Detecting Employee Theft and Pilferage 176
Insurance and Bonding 179
Summary 180

CHAPTER 7
PREVENTING LOSSES FROM ACCIDENTS AND EMERGENCIES 189

Introduction 189
The Occupational Safety and Health Act 190
Accident Prevention 193
Medical Emergencies 195
Protecting Aainst AIDS and Hepatitis B 196
Hazardous Materials Incidents 197
General Guidelines for Dealing with Emergencies 199
Civil Disturbances, Riots and Strikes 201
Bombs and Bomb Threats 203
Preventing and Protecting Against Loss by Fire 212
Natural Disasters 223
Other Emergencies 226
Summary 226

CHAPTER 8
PREVENTING LOSSES FROM CRIMINAL ACTIONS 235

Introduction 236
The Seriousness of the Problem 236
Criminal and Civil Offenses in Review 238
Crimes of Concern to Private Security 239
Alcohol and Other Drugs in the Workplace 249
Other Crimes 256
Enforcing Proprietary Rights 256
Expelling, Detaining and Arresting 257
The Use of Force 259
Investigating 260
Searching 261

Interviewing and Interrogating 263
The Trend toward Transferring Police Tasks to Private Security 266
Summary 267

CHAPTER 9
ENHANCING INFORMATION/COMPUTER SECURITY 273
Introduction 273
Problem of Information Security 274
Specific Threats 276
Telecommunications 278
Security Measures 280
Computers and Security 282
Computer Crime Defined 283
The Seriousness of the Problem 283
Types of Threats to Computer Security 287
Legislation Related to Computer Crime 293
Security Measures for Computer Systems 295
Investigating Computer Crime 303
Prosecuting Perpetrators of Computer Crimes 305
Summary 305

CHAPTER 10
ENHANCING PUBLIC RELATIONS 312
Introduction 312
Public Relations Defined 313
The Role of Security Personnel in Public Relations 313
Factors Involved in Public Relations 314
Interaction with Individuals 318
Understanding Self and the Image Projected 328
Interaction and Cooperation with the Press and Media 329
Cooperation with Public Police 329
Public Relations and the Promotion of Security 330
Summary 333

SECTION III
WHEN PREVENTION FAILS 337

CHAPTER 11
THE INVESTIGATIVE FUNCTION 338
Introduction 338
Characteristics of an Effective Investigator 338
Responsibilities of Investigators 340
Investigating Accidents 342
Investigating Fires 344

Investigating Complaints of Sexual Harassment 344
Investigating Crimes 347
Specific Crimes and Investigative Responsibilities 349
Computer-Related Crimes 351
Avoiding Lawsuits 352
Summary 352

CHAPTER 12
OBTAINING AND PROVIDING INFORMATION 357
Introduction 357
The Communication Process 358
Listening 361
Nonverbal Communication 363
Barriers to Communication 365
Lines of Communication 365
General Guidelines for Effective Communication 367
Interviewing and Interrogating Techniques 368
Providing Information 374
Taking Notes 374
Writing Reports 378
Characteristics of a Well-Written Report 381
A Reminder: Communications as Public Relations 394
Summary 394

CHAPTER 13
TESTIFYING IN COURT 399
Introduction 399
Testifying in Court—An Overview 400
Before the Trial 401
The Trial 402
Tips for Success 412
Expert Testimony 413
Trends in Decisions and Settlements 414
Summary 415

SECTION IV
SECURITY SYSTEMS AT WORK: PUTTING IT ALL TOGETHER 419

CHAPTER 14
LOSS PREVENTION THROUGH RISK MANAGEMENT 421
Introduction 421

Risks and Risk Management Defined 422
Risk Management: The Total Picture 423
Risk Analysis 428
The Security Survey 430
Selecting Alternatives to Handle Identified Risks 438
Reporting the Results 441
Implementing the Recommendations 441
Evaluating the Security System 442
Summary 443

CHAPTER 15
INDUSTRIAL SECURITY 448
Introduction 448
Industrial Security Responsibilities 449
Types of Industrial Losses 452
Sabotage and Espionage 456
Vulnerable Areas 460
Transporting Goods by Truck, Rail and Ship 461
Special Problems in the Utilities Industry 467
Summary 470

CHAPTER 16
RETAIL SECURITY 474
Introduction 474
Shrinkage 476
Shoplifting 476
Bad Checks 496
Fraudulent Credit Cards 502
Retail Employee Theft 503
Shopping Center/Mall Security 510
Assistance in Enhancing Retail Security 514
Retail Security in the Future 514
Summary 517

CHAPTER 17
COMMERCIAL SECURITY 524
Introduction 524
Financial Institution Security 525
Office Building Security 531
Housing 534
Hotel/Motel Security 538
Public Gatherings and Special Events 546
Movie Industry 550
Recreational Parks 551

Racetracks 552
Airport and Airline Security 554
Mass Transit Security 557
Cruise Ship Security 559
Summary 560

CHAPTER 18
INSTITUTIONAL SECURITY 567
Introduction 567
Hospitals and Other Health Care Facilities 567
Educational Institutions 576
K–12 Programs 577
Colleges and Universities 580
Libraries 590
Museums and Art Galleries 591
Religious Facilities 597
Summary 599

CHAPTER 19
OTHER APPLICATIONS OF SECURITY AT WORK 606
Introduction 606
Parking Lot and Parking Garage Security 607
Courtroom Security 610
Protecting VIPs, Corporate Executives and Political Candidates 612
Protecting Individuals and Business Interests Abroad 618
Summary 620

SECTION V
CHALLENGES FACING THE SECURITY PROFESSION IN THE 1990S AND BEYOND 625

CHAPTER 20
THE CHALLENGES OF VIOLENCE IN THE WORKPLACE 626
Introduction 626
The Extent of the Problem 627
Forms of Workplace Violence 630
Causes 631
Profile of the Perpetrator of Violence 632
Indicators 634
Risk Factors 635
Preventing Workplace Violence 636
Dealing with Violence That Occurs 642

Legal Implications 643
Summary 644

CHAPTER 21
PRACTICING AND PROMOTING ETHICAL CONDUCT 649
Introduction 649
Ethics Defined 650
Developing Personal Ethics 653
Promoting an Ethical Organization 655
Code of Ethics 656
Ethics in Practice 663
Summary 665

CHAPTER 22
THE PRIVATE SECURITY PROFESSIONAL AND PROFESSION 671
Introduction 672
The Place of Private Security in the Organizational Structure 673
Responsibilities of the Security Director 674
Loss Prevention Specialist Responsibilities 675
Administrative Responsibilities 676
Investigative Responsibilities 680
The Security Director as Manager 682
Managerial Responsibilities 683
On Becoming a Security Professional 694
Summary 696

CHAPTER 23
A LOOK TO THE FUTURE 700
Introduction 700
What the Future Holds for Specific Areas of the Security Profession 701
Comments from a Round Table of Experts 703
View from the Joint Security Commission 705
Other Experts Look to the Future 705
Summary 721

APPENDIXES 723
A Site Security Evaluation 723
B Training Requirements State by State 733
C Academic Programs in Security and Loss Prevention 739

Glossary 751
Answers to Critical Thinking Exercises 764
Author Index 767
Subject Index 775

LIST OF FIGURES

3–1 Private Security and Law Enforcement Employment Compared 57
3–2 Private Security and Law Enforcement Spending Compared 58
4–1 Use of Force Continuum 82
5–1 Concentric Layers of Physical Security 97
5–2 Barrier of Light 103
5–3 Measures Used to Protect Against Door Frame Spreading 105
5–4 Standard Security Hinges 106
5–5 Basic Security Equipment at the Three Lines of Defense 112
5–6 Basic Types of Bolt Mechanisms 113
5–7 Typical Sensors 122
5–8 Security Checklist 137
6–1 After-Hours Sign-In/Out Log 156
6–2 Temporary Badge Sign-In/Out Log 157
6–3 Visitor Register Log 159
6–4 Nonbusiness Visitor Access Request 159
6–5 Contract Employee Access Request 160
6–6 Sample Record of Keys in Use 161
6–7 Key-Control Checklist 162
6–8 Sample Reproduction Work Order 167
6–9 Property Pass 168
6–10 Property Sign-In/Out Log 169
6–11 Personal Property Registration 169
6–12 Request for Authorization to Take Pictures 171
6–13 Camera Pass 172
6–14 Sample Search Notification 175
7–1 Sample Bomb Threat Form 209
8–1 Security Checklist 242
8–2 Sample Citizen Arrest Form 260
8–3 Sample Card Listing Suspect's Rights—Miranda Warning 265
9–1 Office Memo Subject: FWD)Computer Virus 292
12–1 Incident Report Log 375
12–2 Incident Report Form 376
12–3 Incident Report Follow-Up Form 377
12–4 Canterbury Downs Report Form 380
12–5 Evaluation Checklist for Reports 390
IV–1 The Interaction of Security Equipment, Procedures and Personnel 420
14–1 The Risk Management Circle 424
14–2 The Risk Management Process 426

14–3 The Risk Cycle 427
14–4 Cost vs. Level of Protection 427
14–5 Basic Security Survey 433
14–6 Illustrated Checklist of Security Measures 434
14–7 Sample Security Survey 435
14–8 The Security Audit Process 444
16–1 Sources of Retail Shrinkage 477
16–2 Check-Cashing Information Stamp 502
16–3 Retail Cash and Cash Records Flow 508
16–4 Sample Employee Termination Statement 510
16–5 Retail Security Checklist 515
17–1 Sample Petty Cash Voucher 534
17–2 Stop Thief 536
17–3 Home Security Educational Materials 537
17–4 Checklist for Fire and Pool Safety 542
18–1 Key and Lock Survey for Hospital Administration 570
18–2 Key and Lock Survey for Education 587
20–1 Fatalities of Women in the Workplace 630
21–1 The Corporate Vision and Operating and Financial Goals of the Wackenhut Corporation 657
21–2 The American Society for Industrial Security Code of Ethics for Members 659
21–3 The American Society for Industrial Security Code of Ethics for Security Officers 662
21–4 The American Society for Industrial Security Code of Ethics for Security Managers 663
22–1 Private Security Vicious Circle 685

List of Tables

2–1 Estimates of Private Security Employment for 1990 40
2–2 Number of Employees to 2000 42
5–1 Detectors—An Interior Space Protection Review 124
5–2 Selection and Application Guide to Fixed Surveillance Cameras—National Institute of Law Enforcement and Criminal Justice 132
7–1 How to Extinguish Specific Types of Fires 221
8–1 Common Symptoms, Signs and Dangers of Drug Abuse 252
8–2 Statutory Arrest Authority of Private Citizens 258
9–1 Summary of National Costs of Computer Crimes 285
9–2 Categories of Computer Crime 286
9–3 Computer Threat Incident Rates 288
9–4 Summary of Computer Crime Victims 288
9–5 Summary of Rates of Computer Crimes 289
10–1 Disability Language for the '90s 322
10–2 Epileptic Seizure or Drug/Alcohol Abuse? 324
12–1 Interviewing Subjects 370
12–2 Interview Questions 372
12–3 Common Abbreviation Used in the Security Profession 379
12–4 Common Homonyms 388
13–1 Brief Review of Common Tactics of Cross-Examination 410
14–1 Detailed Security Checklist for Manufacturing Companies 436
14–2 Example of a Budget for Security 442
16–1 Inventory Shrinkage as a Percentage of Retail Sales 478
16–2 Methods of Detecting Shoplifters 483
16–3 Prosecution Rates 494
16–4 Methods of Detecting Employee Dishonesty 504
16–5 Anticipated Change in the Use of Loss Prevention Systems 517
18–1 Typology of Evolution of Campus Police Systems 581
18–2 A Comparative Analysis of Contemporary Police Models 589
20–1 Violence in the Workplace (Annually 1987–1992) 628
20–2 Victims of Violence at Work Were Less Likely to Be Injured than Persons Victimized While Not Working, 1987–1992 634
21–1 Honesty and Ethics: 1994 Poll 651
21–2 1994 Survey Respondents' Opinion of What Character Traits Should Be Taught in Public School 654
23–1 Growth and Projected Growth of Number of Contract and Proprietary Security Employees 717
23–2 Private Security Revenues/Expenditures, 1993 717

List of Acronyms and Initials

AAA	American Automobile Association
ABA	American Bankers Association
ACH	automated clearinghouse
A.D.	Alzheimer's disease
ADA	Americans with Disabilities Act
ADT	American District Telegraph
AIDS	acquired immune deficiency syndrome
AIR	active infrared
AMC	American Motors Corporation
APA	American Psychological Association
ASIS	American Society for Industrial Security
ATM	automatic teller machine
BAI	Bank Administration Institute
BASs	building automation systems
BEL	building emergency leader
BIR	Brainerd International Raceway
BOCA	Building Officials Conference of America
CAD	computer-assisted design
CAE	computer-aided engineering
CAM	computer-assisted manufacturing
CCTV	closed circuit television
CCVE	closed circuit video equipment
CDC	Centers for Disease Control
CEO	chief executive officer
CEUs	continuing education units
CI	competitive intelligence
CIA	Central Intelligence Agency
CIM	computer-integrated manufacturing
CPCs	continuing professional credits
CPO	certified protection officer
CPP	Certified Protection Professional
CPR	cardio-pulmonary resuscitation
CPTED	crime prevention through environmental design
CSO	Cognizant Security Office
CSR	community service representative
DEA	Drug Enforcement Administration
DIS	Defensive Investigative Service
DISP	Defense Industrial Security Program
D.O.D.	Department of Defense
DPMA	Data Processing Management Association

DTI	drug-testing initiative
EAS	electronic article surveillance
EDP	electronic data processing
EEOC	Equal Employment Opportunity Commission
ELIS	Electronic Information Security
EPIC	El Paso Intelligence Center
EPPA	Employee Polygraph Protection Act
ERE	emergency response employee
ERS	emergency response services
ERT	emergency response team
FAA	Federal Aviation Authority
FBI	Federal Bureau of Investigation
FDC	Front Desk Controller
FDE	forensic document examiner
FinCEN	Financial Crimes Enforcement Network
GSA	General Services Administration
HELP	Housing Enterprises for the Less Privileged
HIV	human immunodeficiency virus
H/M	hazardous materials
HVAC	heating, ventilation and air conditioning
IACP	International Association of Chiefs of Police
IAHSS	International Association for Healthcare Security and Safety
IAVA	interactive video and audio (capabilities)
IBM	International Business Machines Corporation
ICSC	International Council of Shopping Centers
ID	identification
IME	Institute of Makers of Explosives
IMO	International Maritime Organization
INPS	International Network of Protection Specialists
INTERPOL	International Criminal Police Organization
IR	infrared
ISM	*Industrial Security Manual*
IUAM	Indiana University Art Museum
JAG	Jewelry and Gem Initiative
JAMA	*Journal of the American Medical Association*
JSA	Jewelers' Security Alliance
LAN	local area network
LEIU	law enforcement intelligence unit
MASH	mobile army surgical hospital
MBO	management by objective
MBWA	management by walking around
NBFAA	National Burglar and Fire Alarm Association
NCCCD	National Center for Computer Crime Data
NCIC	National Crime Information Center
NCPI	National Crime Prevention Institute
NFPA	National Fire Protection Association
NIAA	National Institute of Alcohol Abuse and Alcoholism

NCSI	North Country Security, Inc.
NIDA	National Institute on Drug Abuse
NIOSH	National Institute of Occupational Safety and Health
NLBA	National Licensed Beverage Association
NRC	Nuclear Regulatory Commission
NSA	no such account
NSF	nonsufficient funds
OPSEC	Operations Security
OSHA	Occupational Safety and Health Administration
OSHAct	Occupational Safety and Health Act of 1970
PA	public address
PBX	private branch exchange
PC	personal computer
PI	private investigator
PIN	personal identification number
PLC	programmable logic controllers
POS	point of sale
POST	Peace Officers' Standards and Training (Board or Commission)
PSE	psychological stress evaluation
PSM	process safety management
PVC	polyvinyl chloride
RF	radio frequency
SIA	Security Industry Association
SKM	security key monitor
STV	Secure Transport Vehicle
TAM	Techniques of Alcohol Management
TSI	theft sensitive items
UAW	United Auto Workers
UCR	Uniform Crime Reports
UL	Underwriters Laboratories
VMX	voice mail system
VTR	videotape recording

LIST OF CASES

Anderson et al. v. Monongahela Power Company and The Allegheny Power System Inc., Cir. Ct., Monongalia County, West Virginia, No. 92-C-483, 1994 341–342

Atamian v. Supermarkets General Corp., 369 A.2d 38 (N.J. Super. 1976) 80

Baggs v. Eagle-Picher Industries, Inc., 750 F.Supp 264 or 957 F.2d 268 (1992) 173

Bowman v. State, 468 N.E.2d 1064 (Ind. App. 1984) 54

Brown v. Jewel Companies, Inc., 530 N.E.2d 57 (Ill. App. 1988) ·77

California v. Greenwood, 486 U.S. 35, 108 S.Ct. 1625 (1988) 277

Caroll v. United States, 267 U.S. 132, 45 S.Ct. 280, 69 L.Ed.2d 543 (1925) 491

City of Hialeah v. Weber, 491 So.2d 1204 (Fla. App. 1986) 62

Cramer v. Housing Opportunities Commission, 501 A.2d 35 (Md. 1985) 83

De Lema v. Waldorf Astoria Hotel, Inc., 588 F.Supp. (D.C.N.Y. 1984) 544

Dent v. May Dept. Stores Co., 459 A.2d 1042 (1982) 487–488

Eastman v. Time Saver Stores, Inc., 428 So.2d 1163 (1983) 495

Florence Trentacost v. Dr. Nathan T. Brussel, 412 A.2d 436 (N.J. 1980) 80

Glide Lumber Products Company v. Employment Division, 741 P.2d 907 (Or. App. 1987) 255

Gonzales v. Southwest Security and Protection Agency, Inc., 665 P.2d 810 (N.M. App. 1983) 689–690

Granite Construction Corp. v. Superior Court of Fresno, 197 Cal. Rptr. 3 (Cal. App. 1983) 75

High Tech Gays v. Defense Industrial Clearance Office, 895 F.2d 563 (1990) 151

Horn v. I.B.I. Security Service of Florida, Inc., 317 So.2d 444 (Fla. App. 1975) 690–691

In re Deborah C., 635 P.2d 446 (Cal. 1981) 265

James T. Hazlett v. Martin Chevrolet, Inc., 1985 WL 9938 (Ohio App. 1985) 255

Kline v. 1500 Massachusetts Ave. Apartment Corp., 439 Fed.2d 477 (1970) 80

Kolosky v. Winn Dixie Stores, Inc., 472 So.2d 891 (Fla. 1985) 81

Kuehn v. Renton School Dist. No. 403, 694 P.2d 1078 (Wash. 1985) 403

Largo Corp. v. Crespin, 727 P.2d 1098 (Colo. 1986) 251

Malorney v. B & L Motor Freight, Inc., 496 N.E.2d 1086 (Fla. 1986) 83

Marshall v. Barlow's Inc., 436 U.S. 307, 98 S.Ct. 1816 (1978) 192

Mest v. Federated Group, Inc., U.S. Dist. Ct. Oakland, CA, No. 8129668-90, 6/89 150

Meyers v. Ramada Inn of Columbus, 471 N.E.2d 176 (Ohio 1984) 80, 544

Miranda v. State of Arizona, 384 U.S. 436, 86 S.Ct. 1602 (1966) 264
Mount Sinai Hosp. v. City of Miami Beach, 523 So.2d 722 (Fla. App. 1988) 62–63
National Labor Relations Board v. St. Vincent's Hosp., 729 F.2d 730 (1984) 55
National Treasury Employees Union v. Von Raab, 489 U.S. 656, 109 S.Ct. 1384 (1989) 256
People v. Haydel, 109 Cal. Rptr. 222 (Cal. 1973) 265
People v. Stormer, 518 N.W.S.2d 35 1 (N.Y. 1987) 266
People v. Virginia Alvinia Zelinski, 594 P.2d 1000 (Cal. 1979) 266, 492
Picco v. Ford's Diner, Inc., 274 A.2d 301 (N.J. Super. 1971) 80
Pittard v. Four Seasons Motor Inn, Inc., 688 P.2d 333 (N.M. App. 1984) 544
Ponticas v. K.M.S. Investments, 331 N.W.2d 907 (Minn. 1983) 147
Ramada Inns, Inc. v. Sharp, 711 P.2d 1 (Nev. 1985) 545
Sheerin v. Holin Co., 380 N.W.2d 415 (Iowa 1986) 83
Sorichetti v. City of New York, 482 N.E.2d 70 (N.Y. 1985) 80
State v. Burleson, Dist. Ct., Tarrant City, TX: No. 032493OR, 1988 291
State in Interest of T.L.O., 463 A.2d 934 (N.J. 1983) 588
State v. Weiss, 449 So.2d 915 (Fla. App. 1984) 545
Taylor v. Centennial Bowl, Inc., 416 P.2d 793 (Cal. 1966) 79–80
Texas State Employment Union v. Texas Department of Mental Health, 7467 S.W.2d 203 (Tex. 1987) 150
Tolbert v. Martin Marietta Corp. 621 F.Supp. 1099 (Colo. 1985) 83
Turner v. General Motors Corp., 750 S.W.2d 76 (Mo. App. 1988) 665
United States of America v. John DeGilio, et al., 538 F.2d 972 (1976) 294
United States of America v. Paul A. Lambert, 446 F.Supp. 890 (1978) 294
United States v. Bice-Bey, 701 F.2d 1086 (1983) 503
United States v. Dockery, 736 F.2d 1232 (1984) 64
United States v. Lyons, W.L. Rept. Vol. III, No. 114 (1983) 545
United States v. Tartaglia, 864 F.2d 837 (1989) 262
Wold v. State, 430 N.W.2d 171 (Minn. 1988) 265

PREFACE

In our modern, industrial, urban society, private security has become such an important and accepted part of life that an understanding of its development, philosophy, responsibility and function is imperative for all. A historical and philosophical perspective of private security will help students to better understand the present stage of private security, its principles, its legal authority and its effect on society in general.

Introduction to Private Security, fourth edition, provides basic information to serve as an overview of the entire field as well as a solid foundation for future courses. The content in each chapter could easily be expanded into an entire book or course, but the basic concepts have been included. This feature alone helps increase the text's usefulness to students and instructors alike.

The text incorporates the major findings and recommendations of the *Report of the Task Force on Private Security* with other current security publications and research, including the Hallcrest Report I and II and the Rand Report.

HOW TO USE THIS BOOK

Introduction to Private Security is more than a textbook; it is a learning experience requiring your active participation to obtain best results. You will get the most out of this book if you first familiarize yourself with the total scope of private security. Read and think about what is included in the Table of Contents. Then follow these steps as you read each chapter:

1. Read the objectives at the beginning of each chapter:
   DO YOU KNOW
   - What the primary goal of private security is?
     Think about your current knowledge on each question. What preconceptions do you hold?
2. Read the chapter (underlining or taking notes if that is your preferred study style).
   Pay special attention to all information that is boxed:

> The primary goal of private security is to prevent losses caused by criminal actions and/or disasters.

The key concepts of each chapter are highlighted in this manner.

3. When you have finished reading the chapter, reread the list of objectives given at the beginning of the chapter to ensure that you are able to give an educated response to each. If you find yourself stumped, find the appropriate material in the chapter and review it.
4. Complete the Application at the end of each chapter. These application exercises provide an opportunity to use the concepts in actual or hypothetical cases.
5. Sections II through IV also provide critical thinking exercises based on actual cases. Read each exercise and select the answer you believe matches how the court ruled. Answers are provided on page 764 just before the indexes.
6. Finally, read the discussion questions and prepare to contribute to class discussion of these questions.

Good reading and good learning.

Acknowledgments

We would like to thank the following individuals for their review of the manuscript and their numerous helpful suggestions: William Bopp, Florida Atlanta University; R. B. J. Campbelle, Middle-Tennessee State University; Jerry Dowling, Sam Houston State University; Robert Fischer, Western Illinois University; James Fyke, Illinois Central College; Ernest Kamm, California State University, Los Angeles; Hayes Larkins, Community College of Baltimore; Donald Mayo, Loyola University; Merlyn Moore, Sam Houston State University; Norman Spain, Ohio University; David Steeno, Western Illinois University; Bill Tillett, Eastern Kentucky University; Robert Camp; Janet McClellan, Park College; Susan Hinds; Robert Ives, Rockford College; and Vincent DeCherchio, Bryn Mawr College.

Thank you to the reviewers of the second edition for their insightful suggestions: Robert Wyatt Benson, Jacksonville State University; Terry A. Biddle, Cuyahoga Community College; Edmund Grosskopf, Indiana State University; Leo C. Hertoghe, California State University at Sacramento; David MacKenna, University of Texas at Arlington; Michael D. Moberly, Southern Illinois University at Carbondale; Mahesh K. Nalla, Northern Arizona University; Robert L. O'Block, Appalachian State University; and Michael J. Witkowski, University of Detroit.

Thank you also to the reviewers of the third edition of *Introduction to Private Security* for their numerous suggestions to make this edition as current and practical as possible: Robert Ives, Rock Valley College; Stephen Jones, Crown Academy; Robert LaRatta, LaSalle University; David MacKenna, University of Texas at Arlington; Michael Moberly, Southern Illinois University at Carbondale; Bill Riley, Albuquerque Technical and Vocational Institute; and Diane Zahm, Florida State University. In addition, we are most appreciative of the contributions prepared especially for this text by Minot B. Dodson, vice president of operations and training of Pinkerton Security and Investigation Services and Michael E. Goodboe, vice president of training, Wackenhut Training Institute.

Yet another valuable contributor to this fourth edition is Waldo Asp, Normandale Community College, who prepared the critical thinking exercises for Chapters 6 through 22.

A special thank you to the National Crime Prevention Institute for the numerous diagrams provided, and to J&B Innovative Enterprises, Inc., which provided security surveys, charts and diagrams.

Finally, thank you to our families and colleagues for their support during the development of *Introduction to Private Security,* fourth edition, to Christine Hess Orthmann for her indexing and preparation of the Instructor's Guide, and to the fine professional staff at West Publishing Company for their invaluable assistance in preparing the manuscript for publication: Robert Jucha, editor; and Amy Hanson, our production editor.

About the Authors

Kären M. Hess

Kären M. Hess, PhD, has written extensively in the field of law enforcement. She is a member of the English department at Normandale Community College as well as the president of the Institute for Professional Development.

Other West texts Dr. Hess has co-authored are *Community Policing: Theory and Practice, Criminal Investigation* (4th edition), *Criminal Procedure, Introduction to Law Enforcement and Criminal Justice* (4th edition), *Juvenile Justice* (2nd edition), *Management and Supervision in Law Enforcement (2nd edition), Police Operations* and *Seeking Employment in Criminal Justice and Related Fields* (2nd edition).

Henry M. Wrobleski

Henry M. Wrobleski, LLB, formerly coordinator of the Law Enforcement Program at Normandale Community College, is a respected author, lecturer and consultant with 40 years of experience in law enforcement and private security. He is also Dean of Instruction for the Institute for Professional Development, holds an LLB degree and is a graduate of the FBI Academy.

Other West texts Mr. Wrobleski has co-authored are *Introduction to Law Enforcement and Criminal Justice* (4th edition) and *Police Operations*.

Both are members of the American Society for Industrial Security (ASIS). Both are also members of the Textbook and Academic Authors Association.

SECTION I

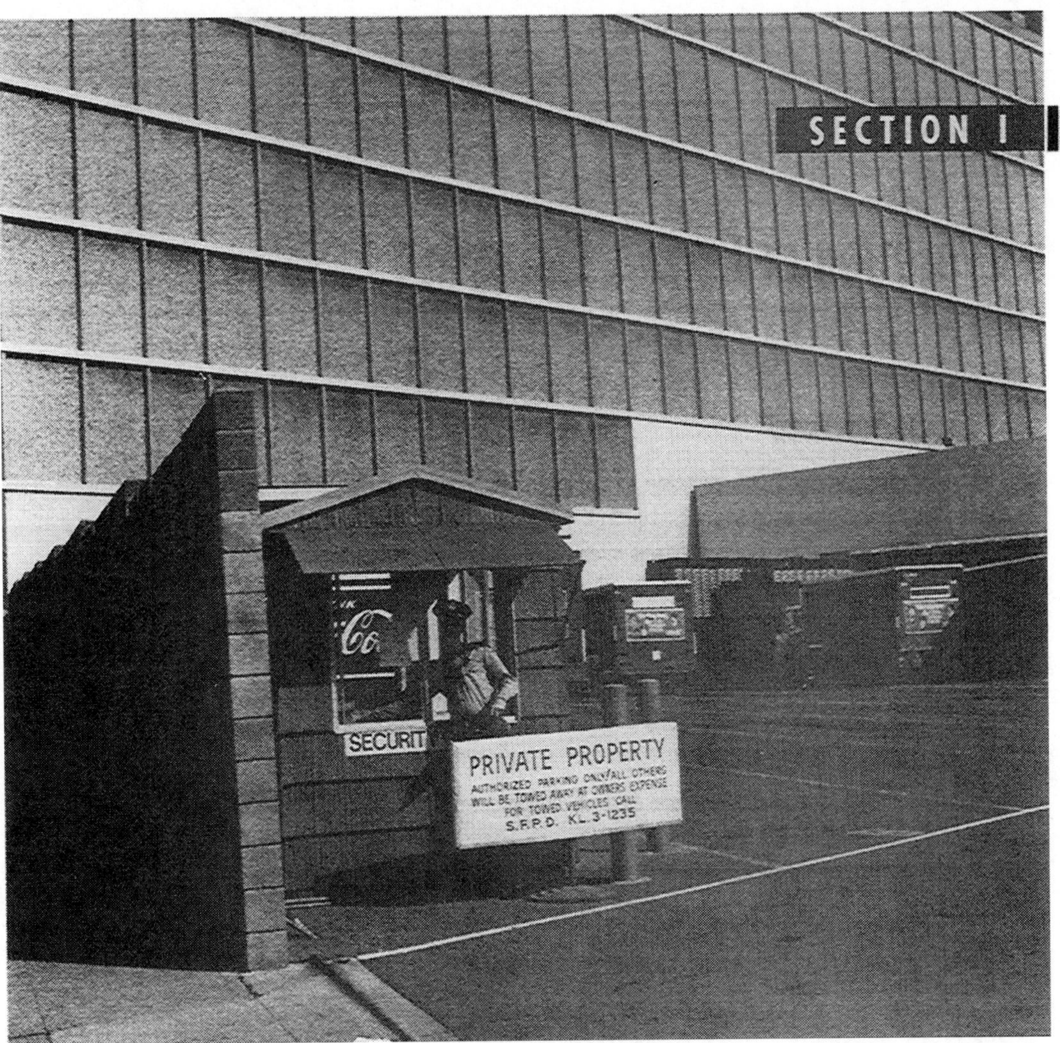

PRIVATE SECURITY: AN OVERVIEW

The chapters in Section I present an overview of the private security profession, beginning with its history and the methods of protection that have evolved from ancient times to the present (Chapter 1). The various aspects of protection being used in private security, the kinds of personnel and services involved and whether they are contractual or proprietary are examined next (Chapter 2). This is followed by a look at the interface of private security and the criminal justice system, the law enforcement component in particular (Chapter 3). The section concludes with an in-depth look at legal liability for those engaged in private security (Chapter 4).

It is within this context that the security professionals of the 1990s will operate. The concepts introduced in this section will be of direct relevance in how the basic security responsibilities are performed (Section II) and what kinds of security systems might be implemented (Section III).

CHAPTER 1

The Evolution of Private Security: A Brief History

Do You Know

- Generally how private security has differed from public law enforcement throughout history?
- What security measures were used in ancient times? In the Middle Ages? In eighteenth-century England? In early colonial America?
- What security measures were established by the tithing system? The Frankpledge system? The Magna Charta? The Statute of Westminster?
- What contributions to private security were made by Henry Fielding, Patrick Colquhoun, Sir Robert Peel, Allan Pinkerton, Washington Perry Brink, William J. Burns and George Wackenhut?
- What role the railroad police played in the evolution of private security?
- What impact the world wars had on the evolution of private security?
- Into what status private security has evolved by the 1990s?

Can You Define These Terms?

assize of arms	parish
Bow Street Runners	private security
feudalism	Statute of West Minister
Frankpledge system	tithings
hue and cry	watch and ward
Magna Charta	

Introduction

Since the beginning of recorded time, people have sought *security*—safety, protection, freedom from fear and danger. They have armed themselves, built barriers around their dwellings and made rules and laws which they have tried to enforce individually, as a group and through others. Reith (1975, pp. 13–15) outlines four phases in the evolution of the quest for security.

First, individuals or small community groups came together in search of collective security, to ease food finding or to satisfy other mutually felt individual needs.

Second, they discovered the need for rules or laws. Historically people believed that passing "good" laws was sufficient; the ruler's army could enforce them.

Third, they inevitably discovered that some community members would not obey the rules. Even the best laws people can devise are useless, and rulers and governments are powerless, if the laws are not obeyed.

Fourth, in one form or another, means to compel the observance of rules were found and established. Sometimes they worked, but frequently they did not. Consequently, more communities have perished because they could not enforce their laws than have been destroyed by natural disasters or hostile aggression.

Reith's main premise is that past civilizations fell because no police mechanism existed between the army of the ruler and the people. Without such a police mechanism to enforce the laws, the country fell into anarchy. When this occurred, armed troops were called in to restore order, but, as a form of force divorced from the law, they could secure only temporary relief. Thus, the dispatching of troops to restore order became: "as often as not, a pouring of oil on flames" (Reith, 1940, p. 105).

Early civilizations relied on a ruler and his army to govern and protect the people. The people of the Middle Ages tried loosely organized experiments with evolving forms of public law enforcement and isolated instances of private security when public law enforcement was ineffective. Not until the nineteenth century did public law enforcement and private security begin to clearly separate. To that point, the history of private security is intertwined with that of public law enforcement. With the acceptance of public police officers, private individuals and organizations began to seek further protection, a means of preventing access to themselves or their property.

> **Private security** evolved from the human desire for additional, individual protection for themselves and their property.

This chapter begins with a discussion of security in ancient times and the Middle Ages. This is followed by developments in security in the eighteenth and nineteenth centuries in England. The chapter concludes with a discussion of the evolution of private security in the United States.

Ancient Times

Throughout history, people have erected physical barriers for security, and certain individuals, notably rulers, have demanded special security.

> In ancient times people relied on physical security measures such as weapons, lake or cliff dwellings, walls and gates.

The objective then, as it is today, was to prevent others from gaining access to them or their property. Lake dwelling was one popular means of achieving security. Healy (1968) describes some 300 such lake sites discovered in

Cliff dwelling ruins of the ancient Pueblo Indians (A.D. 1275) located in Mesa Verde National Park, Colorado.

Switzerland alone, all simple homes, some single units, some entire villages, built with meager tools on sunken pilings. One dwelling on Lake Geneva could house 1,200 people. Access to these lake dwellings was controlled by drawbridges or boats.

Some prehistoric Americans, surrounded by unfriendly tribes, moved into natural caves high on cliffs. Their security came from isolating themselves high in the air with ladders that could be pulled up to make their homes impregnable" (Healy, 1968, p. 1).

The most elaborate security system in ancient times was the Great Wall of China, built 20 centuries ago by Emperor Chin to guard China from the Mongols. Requiring 15 years and half a million workers to build, the Wall was long enough to stretch from New York to Mexico.

Rome also emphasized physical security in the form of broad, straight roads patrolled by legions and bridges controlled by iron gates and guards. Frequently, however, rulers went beyond mere physical controls.

> Rulers often appointed individuals to assist them in enforcing the laws, protecting not only the general welfare (public security), but also the safety of the ruler (private security).

These specially appointed individuals who were not part of the military force were the means by which the famous leaders of the massive predatory migrations in Asia and Europe seized authority and leadership.

The Roman Emperor Augustus recognized that the law enforcement machinery of his administration depended solely on the military force of the

The Great Wall of China, 20 to 30 feet high and 15 to 20 feet thick, served as a defense against invaders. It stretched 1,400 miles between Mongolia and China.

legions. The legions were a dangerous power in that the emperor was forced to depend on their often unreliable will. To remove this power from them and place it on a more secure foundation, he created the following (Reith, 1975):

- The Praetorian Guard, a form of bodyguard police.
- The Urban Cohorts, a form of gendarmerie, or armed police, composed of soldiers with police and military duties.
- The Vigiles, a large body of police-fire fighters.

Members of the Praetorian Guard were scattered throughout Rome and probably wore civilian clothes because of the extreme resistance to military control. The Guard was considered an elite group and, consequently, was not asked to function as riot police. This task fell to the Urban Cohort whose specific function was keeping order among the slaves and controlling unruly citizens. The Praetorian Guard later destroyed its function when it joined the intrigues of the legions, becoming part of the crude, uncontrolled military force that seated and unseated emperors.

The third group Augustus established, the Vigiles of Rome, was assigned the task of fighting the devastating fires frequently occurring in Rome as part of the general disorder. The Vigiles' assignment was extended beyond fire fighting, however, to also include policing, previously carried out by the Urban Cohort. As noted by Folley (1980, p. 39):

> In this sense, we see the establishment of the first *police-fire integrated service*. Their function was to control fires and to exercise police functions

which included the right to arrest thieves and housebreakers as well as to control and suppress riots.

Augustus also organized the city into *wards*, assigning specific groups of Vigiles to specific areas. This is the forerunner of current *precincts*.

THE MIDDLE AGES (476–1453)

Early in the Middle Ages **feudalism** held sway, with the lowliest workers (serfs) laboring for a nobleman who answered to the king. The nobleman provided food and security for the serfs who worked the land, and they provided arms for the king and fought in his wars. Castles with moats and drawbridges afforded additional security.

The Anglo-Saxons brought with them to England the acceptance of mutual responsibility for civil and military protection of individuals. Groups of 10 families, called **tithings,** banded together for security and to provide collective responsibility for maintaining local law and order.

In 1066 England was invaded by the Normans under William the Conqueror. Following this *Norman Conquest*, the tithing system was expanded into the **Frankpledge system** under which the king demanded all free Englishmen to swear to maintain the peace.

> During the Middle Ages the tithing system and the Frankpledge system provided security and collective responsibility for law and order.

Castles surrounded with moats were common during the Middle Ages.

The first significant change in the feudal system occurred in King John's reign when his lords revolted and forced him to sign the **Magna Charta** (1215). This document established the supremacy of law over arbitrary edict, as well as the lords' individual rights and the responsibilities of the state and its subjects.

> The Magna Charta, similar to our Bill of Rights, gave Englishmen "due process" of law.

The Magna Charta contained 63 articles which initially benefited only the barons and other members of the feudal class. Later they became important to all people. Some articles granted the church freedom from royal interference. A few guaranteed the rights of the rising middle class. Ordinary freemen and peasants, although the great majority of England's population, were barely mentioned.

The articles of the Magna Charta established "due process" and became the foundation for modern justice.

The next milestone in the evolution of security and law enforcement was the **Statute of Westminster.** Issued by King Edward in 1285, this statute formalized much of England's practice in criminal justice and apprehension. These rules were enforced for many centuries and influenced our common-law elements of arrest. Under the statute, ordinary citizens were greatly involved in criminal justice: "Not only was it the right of any person to apprehend offenders; there was also a positive duty to drop all work when the hue and cry was raised, and to join immediately in pursuit" (Hall, 1952, p. 166). The preamble to the statute sets forth its basic objective as being "to abate the power of felons" (Critchley, 1967).

> The Statute of Westminster established three practical measures: (1) the watch and ward, (2) hue and cry and (3) assize of arms.

The **watch and ward** provided town watchmen to patrol the city during the night to supplement the traditional duties of the constable during the day (ward). This was the first distinct difference between town and rural policing. Watchmen, stationed at every gate of the walled town between sunset and sunrise, were given power to arrest strangers during darkness and hand them over to the constable in the morning. All men in the town were placed on a roster for regular service. Those who refused to serve were placed in the stocks.

The **hue and cry** revived the ancient Saxon practice for dealing with those who resisted the watchman's arrest. When resistance occurred, the watchman cried out and all citizens pursued the fugitive and assisted in his capture.

Medieval watchmen with cressets and beacon.

To enforce the hue and cry, the Statute of Westminster also established the **assize of arms,** which required every male between ages 15 and 60 to keep a weapon in his home as a "harness to keep the peace." The Statute of Westminster was the only major law regulating policing in England between the Norman Conquest of 1066 and the Metropolitan Police Act of 1829.

The Statute of Westminster marked the end of the first police "system" in England, which pivoted around the part-time constable, the ancient principles of personal service to the community and the power of arrest under common law. Critchley (1967) notes that the preventive aspect of policing was secured by the watch by night and the ward by day, the repressive by the hue and cry and the punitive by presentment to the constable the next morning.

Merchants of England, however, were often dissatisfied with the protection afforded them. Furthermore, the middle class was rebelling against compulsory watch service, insisting on paying deputies to take their places. Unfortunately, the hired deputies frequently did not protect them, forcing the merchants to take matters into their own hands.

> Some merchants hired private police to guard their establishments, to investigate crimes against them and to recover property stolen from them.

One futile attempt to establish a military police force occurred in England in 1655 when Cromwell tried to use his highly trained, efficient, victorious army as a police force to prevent and to repress crime. However, he was defeated by lack of cooperation from all classes of people and by the absence of an effective police mechanism between the people and his troops. The watch and ward, although ineffective, remained the primary means of security and law enforcement until the Industrial Revolution.

Early attempts at security and protection reveal two common themes. First was division into geographic sections and the rotation of duties among the citizens. Second, citizens' dissatisfaction with their duties resulted in the hiring of others to take their place. (Even up to the American Civil War one could hire another to serve in his place.)

With the passing of feudalism and the rise to power of the state church, the **parish*** became the unit of local government in rural areas. The parish annually appointed a person to be constable and act as the law officer. This system of maintaining law and order in rural Britain remained from the Middle Ages until the eighteenth century.

THE EIGHTEENTH CENTURY

Extensive social and economic changes during the Industrial Revolution brought about the mechanization of production systems and resulted in a change from home or cottage industries to large factories located in cities. One primary reason for the shift from cottage work to factories and shops was an effort to control workers' production and inventory in the textile industry. Too much material was being diverted for personal use.

During this same period, famine struck the rural areas, causing thousands to move from the country into the towns to seek work in the mills and factories. As people left the rural areas for jobs in the cities, the problem of protection from crime gained new impetus. But in this rapidly changing time, little was done to stem the tremendous amount of crime that arose in the cities.

In addition, political extremists often sparked angry mobs, and riots occurred frequently. Because the government had no civil police force to deal with mob violence, it ordered a magistrate to read the "Riot Act" which called in the military to quell the riot.

South (1987, pp. 73–76) describes the deterioration of formal social control in the late seventeenth and early eighteenth centuries: "As the formal system declined, provision by private self-interest flourished, strongly encouraged by legislation." The former methods of control simply did not work for an industrialized society.

"By the year 1700," says South (p. 76), "disciplined industrial capitalism was already becoming familiar in certain parts of England, with the time sheet, the time keeper, the informers and the fines. For example, the *Law Book of Crowley's Iron Works* represented an entire civil and penal code, running to more than 100,000 words to govern and regulate the refractory labor force."

*The area defined by the congregation of a particular church.

Midland Works Foundry, Sheffield, England, around 1863.

Rural eighteenth century also used private policing in reaction to increasing rural crime (Critchley, 1967, p. 28):

> The wealthy paid gamekeepers to protect their property and slept with arms near to hand and the middle-class tradesmen formed voluntary protection societies.

> During the eighteenth century private citizens carried arms for protection and banded together to hire special police to protect their homes and businesses. The military was used to suppress riots.

Because of prejudices toward those responsible for upholding the law, no serious reform was advocated until the late eighteenth century. The policy was to encourage law-abiding citizens' participation in criminal justice with rewards and to discourage law-breaking citizens with severe punishments. Consequently, a number of self-help organizations sprang up because, as Romilly (1956, p. 12) wrote, "It had become necessary for every man to trust himself for his security."

Henry Fielding (1707–1754)

In 1748 Henry Fielding, lawyer, novelist and playwright, became Chief Magistrate of Bow Street in policeless London. Sympathetic to the injustices that abounded in the city, Fielding fought for social and criminal reform and defied the law by discharging prisoners convicted of petty theft. He gave reprimands in place of the death penalty and exercised general leniency (Reith, 1975). He wrote and published books and pamphlets about the poor of London and the causes of crime. In these, he called for an understanding and alleviation of their suffering.

Fielding advocated that all magistrates be paid a salary, making them independent of fees and fines as their source of income. He also suggested that magistrates be given power to inflict light sentences when advisable.

At this time the parish constable was so ineffective that thieves and robbers moved freely in the streets, and no one interfered with looting and rioting. Although riots inevitably brought soldiers, it sometimes was not for two or three days. Law-abiding citizens looked after their own safety: "The rich surrounded themselves with armed servants and were comparatively safe and independent. . . . The less affluent saw to it that their houses were protected as strongly as possible by bars and bolts and heavy doors and shutters, and that blunderbusses and pistols were always close at hand" (Reith, 1975, p. 134).

Fielding conceived the idea that citizens might join forces, go into the streets, trace the perpetrators of crime and meet the instigators of mob gatherings *before* they assembled a following and caused destruction.

> Henry Fielding was one of the earliest and most articulate advocates of crime *prevention*.

Fielding selected six honest, industrious citizens to form an amateur volunteer force. With his advise and direction, they "swept clean" the Bow Street neighborhood. Many criminals were arrested, and many others fled from the neighborhood.

Fielding also wrote an ironic novel, *Jonathan Wild: The Story of a Great Man*. The novel depicted the life of an actual person living in eighteenth-century London who was a notorious fence, thief and master criminal. As noted by Fischer and Green (1992, p. 6): "In many ways, Wild's career typified the problems of security—or more specifically theft control—in the eighteenth century."

The basic problem was that during this period receiving stolen property was not considered a crime, even if the person knew the property was stolen. Fischer and Green explain that the common law's ignoring of receiving stolen goods may have resulted from there being a limited amount of movable property to steal and limited opportunities to dispose of such property. The law focused on apprehending offenders rather than recovering stolen property, with the victims of theft left to fend for themselves.

In 1691, during the reign of William and Mary, a statute was enacted making receivers of stolen goods subject to prosecution, but only as accessories rather than as principals in the crime. As noted by Fischer and Green (1992, p. 7): "The weakness of the law and its attitude toward property crimes as much as the lack of effective law enforcement combined to make possible Jonathan Wild's legendary career."

The fact that it was legendary is attested to by the inclusion in a staff report prepared in 1972 for the Select Committee on Small Business of the U.S. Senate of eight pages devoted to his activities. This was more than 200 years after Wild was hanged.

Henry Fielding was succeeded by his blind half-brother, John, who carried Henry's ideas forward. Critchley (1967, p. 33) notes: "The greatness of the brothers as educators of public opinion lies in the single-minded determination with which, over nearly thirty years, they strove to demonstrate to their contemporaries how serious were the dangers which threatened to engulf the nation."

Several years after Henry Fielding's death, the Bow Street volunteer force turned professional and was known as the **Bow Street Runners,** the first detective agency in England. Unfortunately, the practical results of Fielding's preventive ideas achieved in the Bow Street neighborhood were ignored for 30 years.

The Defeat of Pitt's Reform Bill

In spite of isolated successes such as those achieved by Henry Fielding, nationwide hostility against a police force existed in England. The general view was: "Once admit a police force into England, and the long-cherished liberties of Englishmen would be swept away in a reign of terror and oppression" (Critchley, 1967, p. 35).

In the summer of 1780 London was subjected to nearly a week of mob violence during the Gordon Riots and had to be rescued by the army. Shocked and angry citizens called for further strengthening of the already savage criminal law, mobilizing the hue and cry and creating a voluntary association of armed citizens.

In 1785 Prime Minister William Pitt proposed a reform bill to embody all the major proposals of the last 30 years, anticipating Peel's Metropolitan Police Act by nearly half a century. Pitt's Reform Bill provided for establishing a strong police force to act throughout the entire metropolitan area and for a clear separation between law enforcement and the justices. The bill met with widespread hostility by the press, the public and the justices, and it was consequently defeated.

Pitt was able to affect some positive reform through his Middlesex Justice Bill in 1792, which established seven public offices, each with three salaried magistrates and six paid constables.

Patrick Colquhoun (1745–1820)

One of the three paid magistrates appointed under Pitt's Middlesex Justice Bill was Patrick Colquhoun. Like Pitt, Colquhoun was vitally interested in social reform and in expanding and adapting the ideas of Henry Fielding to shape his preventive theory into "the new science of preventive police."

In *A Treatise on the Police of the Metropolis* (1796), Colquhoun presented startling statistics supporting the need for a large police force for London. The preface to the sixth edition of his *Treatise* (1800) stated: "Police in this country may be considered as a new science . . . in the prevention and detection of crimes."

Colquhoun also advocated complete separation of police and judicial powers. His treatise was a landmark in presenting statistics on crime and criminals and in using the statistics to draw up wide-ranging plans.

> Colquhoun compiled statistics on crime and criminals to support his belief that London be considered as a whole and that it have a large police force to prevent crime. He also established a private security force.

As a result of his treatise, a group of West India planters and merchants approached Colquhoun and asked if he would help them with their problem of thefts from ships at the London docks. Colquhoun produced a plan for river police officers organized for watching and unloading West India ships while in port. The plan, financed and implemented by the planters and merchants, saved them £66,000 during the first eight months (Reith, 1975).

Colquhoun's pleas to extend the plan to all ports and to create police forces in all towns were ignored. The possibility of using police to solve the problems of crime and disorder was abandoned by cabinet ministers while at the same time the intensity of the problem increased.

Toward the end of the eighteenth century it became clear that the institutions of headboroughs, tithingmen or petty constables, with a chief constable at their head, was an inefficient system to police a civilized country, especially its metropolis. The weakness of this system, with its divided authority and inefficient staff, was obvious to many.

NINETEENTH-CENTURY ENGLAND

In the beginning of the nineteenth century, inadequate law enforcement over much of England required a further supplementation of security by private enterprise. Industrial firms that employed large numbers of unruly workers established their own police. The railway companies, in particular, employed a private police force to maintain order. Similar forces were hired by the ironmasters of the Tredegar Works in Monmouthshire and Lancashire. For the most part, however, collective responsibility for repression of disturbances, the employment of special constables and the formation of the armed associations remained the major forms of law enforcement until the reforms proposed by Sir Robert Peel.

The Bow Street Runners continued in existence, having for nearly a century provided an alternative to the disreputable private thief-takers. But to stay informed about crime, runners frequented the tavern hangouts of thieves.

Public outcry plus concern over the corrupting influence of the reward system led to a parliamentary investigation in 1828. Bribery and criminal collusion were discovered and the runners were censured. One critic, Charles Dickens, wrote of the runners (Adam, n.d.):

> We are not by any means devout believers in the old Bow Street Police. To say the truth, we think there was a vast amount of humbug about those worthies. Apart from many of them being men of very indifferent character, and far too much in the habit of consulting with thieves and the like, they never lost a public occasion of jobbing and trading in mystery and making the most of themselves.
>
> . . . Although as a preventive police they were utterly inefficient, and as a detective police they were very loose and uncertain in their operations, they remain with some people, a superstition to the present day.

One year after the parliamentary investigation, Robert Peel's new police appeared on the scene.

Sir Robert Peel (1788–1850)

Public opposition to a police department was still strong when Sir Robert Peel became Home Secretary in 1822, more than 30 years after Pitt's Reform Bill was defeated. Peel, however, was more successful. He devoted his early years as Home Secretary to reforming criminal law. By 1826 he had drawn up a plan for establishing a single police system within a 10-mile radius of London's

Sir Robert Peel, father of modern policing (1788–1850).

St. Paul's Cathedral. Ironically, the financial section of London, called the City, was excluded from the plan. In 1827 Sir Robert Peel became a member of a parliamentary committee on criminal matters. This committee's second report, published in 1828, asserted: "The art of crime, if it may be so called, has increased faster than the art of detection."

Based on the committee's report, Peel introduced his "Bill for Improving the Police in and near the Metropolis." Peel, often referred to as the Father of Police Administration, proposed a return to the Anglo-Saxon principle of individual community responsibility for preserving law and order, but also said that London should have a body of civilians appointed and paid by the community to serve as police officers. Parliament agreed and in 1829 organized the Metropolitan Police of London.

> Robert Peel's Metropolitan Police Act created the London Metropolitan Police, whose principal objective was to be prevention *of crime.*

The First Order of the Metropolitan Police read:

> IT SHOULD BE UNDERSTOOD, AT THE OUTSET, THAT THE PRINCIPAL OBJECTIVE TO BE ATTAINED IS THE PREVENTION OF CRIME.
>
> To this great end every effort of the police is to be directed. The security of person and property, the preservation of public tranquility, and all other objects of a Police Establishment, will thus be better effected, than by the detection and punishment of the offender, after he has succeeded in committing the crime.

Included in the handbook for the Metropolitan Police were two objectives that again clearly reflect the preventive nature intended:

1) To prevent crime and disorder, as an alternative to their repression by military force and severity of legal punishment.

2) To recognize always that the test of police efficiency is the absence of crime and disorder and not the visible evidence of police action in dealing with them.

But this emphasis on crime prevention did not last. The public police became more and more occupied with investigating crimes and apprehending criminals, and prevention efforts decreased proportionately. Thus, the need for private security as a means to *prevent* crime continued to exist.

THE EVOLUTION OF PRIVATE SECURITY IN THE UNITED STATES

The American colonists brought with them the English system of law enforcement and its reliance on collective responsibility.

> Constables and night town watchmen were the primary means of security in the United States until the establishment of full-time police forces in the mid-1800s.

Early in the eighteenth century several Societies for the Reformation of Manners appeared, and by the end of the century many moral societies existed, the most prominent of which was the Society for the Suppression of Vice and Encouragement of Religion, founded in 1801. Later in the nineteenth century an "evangelical Police" system developed to watchdog the lower classes with spies and informants and to enforce Puritan propriety.

Out West, the stagecoaches carrying mail, gold, money and passengers were prey to holdups by road agents. The professionals who went up against these road agents rode shotgun on the stagecoaches. Crime was rampant in the West following the Civil War. It was the era of outlaw gangs such as the James Gang and the Wild Bunch. Stage line companies responded by building their own security forces and hiring detective agencies to track down outlaws. Other industries saw the need to form protective services, especially those industries vulnerable to strikes, such as coal and iron mining.

Violence in the West increased with the discovery of gold in 1848. Cities in the East and South fared little better. Even in Washington, DC, members attending Congress had to carry arms. Because transporting goods was so fraught with risk, express companies were formed. In 1850 Henry Wells and William Fargo joined to form the American Express, which operated east of the Missouri River. In 1852 Wells Fargo and Company was established to serve the country west of the Missouri. These companies had their own private detectives and shotgun riders. Also extremely vulnerable were the railroads.

Railroad Police

With the westward expansion in the United States during the 1800s, railroad lines moved into sparsely settled territories that had little or no public law enforcement. Trains were attacked by Indians and roving bands of outlaws who robbed passengers, stole cargos, dynamited tracks and disrupted communications.

> Because of problems of interstate jurisdiction and lack of public police protection, many states passed railway police acts, allowing private railroads to establish proprietary security forces, with full police powers, to protect their goods and passengers.

As noted by Gough (1977, p. 19): "The railroad special agent was a colorful part of the old Wild West. Being able to shoot fast and ride hard were important skills in the late 1800s. In addition to train robbers, there were also station holdup crooks, pickpockets, con men, and bootleggers to contend with. Because of his mission in countering such problems, the railroad special agent of the old West was considered as nearly a duly commissioned law enforcement officer as his modern-day counterpart."

> In many parts of the country, the railroad police provided the only protective services until governmental units and law enforcement agencies were established.

As noted by Dewhurst (1955): "A railroad agent who could hold his own in a gun battle with train robbers was considered an asset to the railroad. In this era of the smoking sixshooters, tact and investigative intelligence placed second to the ability to handle physical contact with those who preyed upon the railroad. . . . It was the general custom simply to hand the newly appointed man a badge, a revolver and a club and send him out to work without further instructions as to the laws or how to enforce them, or even how to make an arrest." Nevertheless, the railroad police made a significant contribution to the evolution of private security. In 1921 the Association of American Railroads was formed to help coordinate mutual problems, particularly those associated with security.

Allan Pinkerton (1819–1884)

Allan Pinkerton was a key figure in the development of the railroad police as well as in the development of contract security forces.

Born in Scotland, he joined the radical Chartist group as a young man and was forced to flee from Scotland or face imprisonment. He and his young wife

Allan Pinkerton, President Lincoln and Major General John A. McClernand photographed at Antietam, Maryland, on October 1862 by Alexander Gardner.

Railroad police are still important in the 1990s. Here a railroad officer and his K-9 patrol the station under New York's World Trade Center shortly after the bombing. The damaged area of the station is shrouded in plastic sheeting.

fled to America, where Pinkerton set up his trade of coopering (making barrels) in Chicago. Soon after, they moved to Dundee, Illinois, where his cooperage became a way station for the underground railroad, a secret network that assisted escaping slaves.

One day Pinkerton accidentally found the hideout of a group of counterfeiters and helped the local sheriff capture them. He eventually sold his shop and was appointed deputy sheriff of Cook County. In 1843 he was appointed Chicago's first detective.

Pinkerton resigned his position in 1850 because of economic pressures and took two private clients, the Rock Island and the Illinois Central railroads. The next year he formed the Pinkerton National Detective Agency. Its slogan was "We Never Sleep," and its logo was an open eye, probably the origin of the term "private eye." His agency concentrated on catching train robbers and setting up security systems for the railroads.

> Allan Pinkerton was the first law enforcement officer hired to protect railroads. He also established the first and currently the largest private security contract operation in the United States.

In 1853, on his way home, Pinkerton was shot in the back by a gunman who darted out of the shadows. Pinkerton's habit of walking with his left hand tucked behind him under his coat saved his life. The two slugs set his coat on fire and shattered the bone five inches from the wrist.

Very early Pinkerton hired Kate Warne, the first woman in the United States to become a detective (Lavine, 1963, p. 33). Warne was so highly thought of that when she died in 1868 of cancer she was buried in the Pinkerton family plot at Chicago Graceland Cemetery.

Pinkerton's services were important to his clients mainly because public enforcement agencies either were inadequate or lacked jurisdiction. When the Civil War broke out in 1861, President Lincoln called Pinkerton to Washington to discuss establishing a secret service department to "ascertain the social, political, and patriotic relations of the numerous suspected people in and about Washington" (Lavine, 1963, p. 33). Using the name E. J. Allen, Pinkerton did intelligence work for the Union army, work which today would be performed by a governmental agency.

In the 1860s and 1870s the Pinkerton National Detective Agency gained national stature by capturing train robbers and bandits. They chased murderous gangs of bank robbers and such notorious criminals as the Dalton Boys, the Hole in the Wall Gang, Jesse James, the Sontags, the Farringtons and the Renos, much as the FBI hunts wanted criminals today. Gough (1977, p. 17) notes: "Pinkerton encouraged the use of burglarproof safes in all railroad express cars. By using such a heavy safe, any outlaws intending to rob the train had to use a large charge of black powder or dynamite to blow it open. The resulting blast's magnitude usually destroyed the contents of the safe, as well as the roof and sides of the express car. Pinkerton also recommended the employment of express guards heavily armed with high-powered rifles." One reason the Pinkerton Agency became so famous was that there was virtually no national enforcement except theirs.

However, during two periods in the Pinkerton Agency's history, it established a poor image. In the last two decades of the nineteenth century and during the Great Depression of the 1930s, the agents worked as strikebreakers and private guards. One notorious case involved an organization of coal miners called the Mollie Maguires. In the late 1870s a Pinkerton man infiltrated the allegedly terrorist organization and 17 men (whom many believed innocent) were hanged as a result of his testimony. In 1892, 300 Pinkerton agents suffered a humiliating defeat by sit-in strikers they sought to dislodge at Homestead, Pennsylvania. They were involved in dozens of similar strikebreaking situations in the 1930s. Finally, after a congressional inquiry into the labor-management relations in 1937, Robert A. Pinkerton, then head of the agency, forbade any member of his agency to ever again accept undercover work involving the investigation of a labor union.

The Pinkerton Agency was not the only agency involved in strikebreaking. During the late 1800s, much controversy surrounded the use of private security agencies. For example, the strike on the Erie Railroads in 1877 was broken when Jim Fisk employed a force of approximately one thousand "thugs" and turned them loose on the strikers, "thrashing and maiming them" (Reith, 1975, p. 95). The use of private security agents as strikebreakers led to bitter confrontations between labor and management, often resulting in injuries and setbacks for labor.

Fortunately, the Pinkerton Agency had seen and learned to avoid the dangers inherent in using private security personnel in strikebreaking situations, and the agency continued to thrive. The company became a public corporation in 1965 and changed its name to Pinkerton's Inc. Currently it employs between thirty-six and forty thousand people and concentrates on security in industry and institutions, security for sporting facilities, investigations of industrial thefts and insurance investigations.

Other Security Advances

In 1853 August Pope patented one of the first electric burglar alarm systems. The system had electromagnetic contacts mounted on doors and windows and then wired to a battery and bell. He sold his invention to Edwin Holmes who took it to New York City and sold alarms to wealthy homeowners. In 1858 Holmes established the first central burglar alarm service in the country. His operation evolved into Holmes Protection, Inc.

Pope also used electrified metal foil and screens still widely used by many alarm companies. In addition, he built the first central communications center wired to bank and jewelry vaults (Kaye, 1987, p. 243).

By the 1870s and 1880s mansions and businesses were being protected against fire with heat sensors. William Watkins established a company called AFA Protection and was first to use such sensors in a central monitoring station. Other companies followed suit, adding burglar systems to the fire protection systems. The use of alarms and detection devices grew to provide protective services through the use of messengers and telegraph lines. By 1889 the use of such alarms and detection devices in industrial and commercial enterprises was well established. In 1901 Western Union consolidated several of these local alarm companies into American District Telegraph Company (ADT) (Kaye, 1987, p. 243).

In 1858 Washington Perry Brink founded Brink's, Inc., as a freight and package delivery service. He began by shuttling trunks and packages around Chicago in a one-horse dray. At first Brink concentrated on transporting goods for travelers passing through Chicago. Abraham Lincoln used Brink's services when he was in Chicago attending a Republican convention.

Bonded courier and express delivery services flourished partly because provisions in the common law made it risky to use employees or servants as couriers (Hall, 1935, pp. 31–32):

> The common law recognized no criminality in a person who came legally into possession of property and later converted it. Apparently it was thought that the owner should have protected himself by selecting a trustworthy person. Since, presumably, this could readily be done, the owner must have been negligent if he delivered his property to a person who absconded with it.

In 1891, Brink's carried its first payroll for Western Electric Company. In the early days Brink's tried to be inconspicuous, using standard buggies and wrapping cash in newspapers or overalls. But in 1917, when "Ammunition" Wheed and his gang killed two Brink's men in a holdup, the armored car was born.

> Washington Perry Brink established armored car and courier services in the United States.

Tozer (1960, p. 90) describes how the armored car, "the bankvault on wheels whose invulnerability had been paid for by the blood of good men" came into being.*

> Its design began on August 28, 1917, as messenger Barton Allen stepped out of a touring car with $9,100 payroll for Winslow Bros. in Chicago. A bandit drilled him in the stomach. A second thug forced the guard from the car, and a third dropped the driver with a single shot. They fled with the loot. Brink's countered by bolting steel panels to the sides and roof of every car.
>
> But they had more to learn. In March, 1926, Paul Jawarski timed the weekly movement of an armored car from Pittsburgh to the Terminal Coal Co. at Coverdale, Pa. Then he mined two sections of its lonely route with lengths of pipe crammed with explosives. . . .
>
> As the three-ton armored car rumbled over the first mine, they threw a switch. The explosion tossed the car into the air. It landed upside down. The gang smashed through the floor and scrambled off with $104,000.

Brink's armored car in 1925.

Following a well-practiced, well-guarded routine, Brinks security officers move bags of silver coins out of the First National Bank of Chicago and into a Brink's armored truck.

> *Some changes made.* Brink's redesigned its cars again. Out went the wooden floors and frames. In went all-steel frames and steel floors. Frames of today's juggernauts are half-inch cold-rolled steel. Outside panels are 12-gauge, high-carbon steel; inner panels are 18-gauge sheet with a stuffing of fiberglass between. The result is a car that can be blown open only by an anti-tank weapon.

Today Brink's handles about half the cash that is transported by courier in the United States.

In 1883 jewelers formed the Jewelers Security Alliance for protection against burglary. Advancements in security continued and accelerated in the twentieth century. In 1909 William J. Burns, a former Secret Service investigator and head of the Bureau of Investigation (forerunner of the FBI), started the William J. Burns' Detective Agency.

> William J. Burns founded the sole investigating agency for the American Banking Association. It grew to become the second-largest contract guard and investigative service in the United States.

For all practical purposes, the Pinkerton's agency and Burns' were the only national investigative bodies concerned with nonspecialized crimes in the country until the advent of the FBI in 1924.

The World Wars and the Depression

Before and during World War I, concern for security intensified in American industry because of fear of sabotage and espionage. Private security forces were used to protect war industries and the docks against destruction by saboteurs. Security services expanded to meet the demands but tapered off after the war, reaching a low point during the depression.

In 1921, a Burglary Protection Council was formed and held its first meeting, the result of which was establishing Underwriters' Laboratories to establish specifications, testing and certification of burglar alarm systems and devices.

The period 1930 to 1947 was, according to Weiss (1987, p. 110), "an important period in private policing history, a time during which private industrial policing went from its highest level of activity to a dramatic decline." He noted that in the 1920s the heavy manufacturing industries had the "financial wherewithal to withstand the scattered resistance of strikers" while being supported by states that declared strikes illegitimate. An article in the *New York Times* (January 8, 1928), for example, labeled Henry Ford as "an industrial fascist—the Mussolini of Detroit" (Weiss, 1987, p. 113).

The depression helped to change that. As noted by Weiss (1987, p. 112): "To deal with the depression crisis, Franklin Roosevelt established the National Recovery Act of 1933, which contained a provision (Section 7A) granting workers the right to organize and bargain collectively, free from employer interference or coercion. A rush to unionization followed." In 1935 the Wagner Act gave "legal force, backed by fines, to labor's right to organize." The result was, as Weiss (1987, p. 113) describes, "the demise of the 'slugging detective' and the ascent of the 'labor relations department.' "

World War II was a significant catalyst in the growth of the private security industry. Before awarding national defense contracts, the federal government required munitions contractors to implement stringent, comprehensive security measures to protect classified materials and defense secrets from sabotage and espionage. The FBI assisted in establishing these security programs. Additionally, the government granted the status of auxiliary military police to more than two hundred thousand plant security guards whose primary duties were protection of war goods and products, supplies, equipment and personnel. Local law enforcement agencies were responsible for training them.

One of the best kept secrets of World War II was "Ultra," an encoding machine invented by the Germans. Its real name was "Enigma," the Greek word for puzzle. With this machine the British could crack every code the Germans invented. Churchill (BBC/CBN) said of it: "Ultra was my most secret source. It gave me knowledge of the enemy's precise strength and disposition. It told me when and how Hitler and his generals would act. Without it the war in the North African desert, the battles in Normandy, and indeed, the victory in the Middle East, would have been long and arduous, costing heavily in Allied lives."

The British were given the machines by the Poles who, due to lax security, stole several of them from a German factory. The "Ultra" was one of the first complex computers ever invented. It gave the British a precise picture of almost all important events taking place behind the German lines. It was, in reality, an eavesdropping device that shortened the war, saved thousands of lives and cut the tremendous costs of a war fought on so many fronts.

According to the British documentary, "Best Kept Secrets," such details as what the British did with the information after it had been decoded, how they extracted it even to make sense from Hitler's last scrambled telephone calls and how Britain fit the information into the total intelligence and made it immediately operational still cannot be told. All this information is secret and will remain so, for to reveal it is an act punishable by life imprisonment.

> The world wars heightened emphasis on security in the government and made industry increasingly aware of the need for plant security.

After World War II, the use of the private security services expanded to encompass all segments of the private sector. According to Shearing and Stenning (1987, p. 9): "Since World War II the phenomenon of private security has been growing exponentially, and continues to do so."

Contemporary Private Security

Increases in government regulations and the inability of the public police to respond to every private need promoted the growth of private security. For example, in 1954 George R. Wackenhut and three other former FBI agents formed the Wackenhut Corporation as a private investigative and contract security firm.

By 1959 the Wackenhut Corporation had more than tripled its business from $300,999 to more than $1 million. In only 20 years Wackenhut established itself as the third-largest contract guard and investigative agency in the country. By 1993, sales figures were calculated at $664 million. Wackenhut has more than 45,000 employees and has spread its operations across the United States, into Canada and to the United Kingdom, Western Europe, Africa, the Middle East, the Far East, Australia and Central and South America ("The Wackenhut Corporation," n.d., pp. 1, 4).

Other businesses began to form their own in-house security services rather than contracting for services from private agencies. However, whether the security personnel were proprietary or contracted, private security provided industry and private businesses with individual protection for persons and homes; guard services for construction sites and business property when they were closed; security services for large shopping centers; advice on internal and external security systems for homes, businesses and factories and private investigations.

The *preventive* philosophy underlying the private security field has influenced other areas as well. Notably, it is influencing architecture and building codes, as noted by C. Ray Jeffery in his classic *Crime Prevention Through Environmental Design* (1972): "Criminal behavior can be controlled primarily through the direct alteration of the environment of potential victims. . . . Crime control programs must focus on crime before it occurs, rather than afterward. As criminal opportunity is reduced, so will be the number of criminals."

Perhaps even more significant, the *preventive* aspect of crime is now being stressed by many public law enforcement agencies, as evidenced by the creation of the National Crime Prevention Institute (NCPI), established in 1971 as a division of the University of Louisville's School of Police Administration. This does not mean, however, that the need for private security officers and measures will lessen. Rather, it means that the full importance of preventive measures has become apparent. The public police will probably never have sufficient personnel to meet private needs, and government regulations regarding security will doubtless continue to proliferate.

> By the 1990s private security has evolved to a multibillion-dollar-a-year business employing more than a million people.

From two hundred thousand plant security guards in World War II to more than one million private security personnel today, the private security force has experienced tremendous growth. With increased technology and needed protection for sophisticated, delicate machinery, private security employment will increase even more rapidly in the future. According to the Hallcrest Report (Cunningham et al., 1985), by 2000 it will employ 1,883,000, an increase of 2 percent.

Mangan and Shanahan (1990, p. 18) suggest: "Private security has emerged as a major player in the safeguarding of Americans and their property."

The Hallcrest Report II (Cunningham et al., 1990) analyzed trends in the security industry based on data collected from 1989–1990 and suggests the following:

- Total private security employment will continue to increase over the decade.
- The average annual growth rate throughout the 1990s for all components of private security will be 8 percent, or double that of public law enforcement.
- Private security employment is growing at twice the rate of national employment.
- Private security is forecast to grow at 2.3 percent annually to the year 2000.

Chapter 23 focuses on a look toward the future as viewed by a multitude of security professionals.

SUMMARY

Private security evolved from the human desire for additional, individual protection and the desire to prevent crimes against one's person or property. In ancient times people relied on physical security such as weapons, lake or cliff dwellings, walls and gates. In addition, rulers appointed individuals to protect the general safety as well as their own personal safety.

During the Middle Ages the tithing system and the Frankpledge system provided security and collective responsibility for law and order. The Magna Charta, similar to our Bill of Rights, gave Englishmen "due process" of law. Also during this period, King Edward issued the Statute of Westminster to "abate the power of felons" by establishing the watch and ward, which provided town watchmen to patrol the city during the night; reviving the hue and cry, which required all citizens to assist in the capture of anyone resisting arrest; and instituting the assize of arms, which required that every male between the ages of 15 and 60 have a weapon in his home. Some merchants hired private police to guard their establishments, to investigate crimes against them and to recover property stolen from them.

During the eighteenth century, private citizens carried arms for protection and banded together to hire special police to protect their homes and businesses. The military was used to suppress riots. Midway through the century, Henry Fielding became one of the first and most articulate advocates of crime prevention. Thirty years later Patrick Colquhoun wrote a decisive treatise using statistics on crime and criminals to support his belief that London be considered as a whole and that it have a large police force to *prevent* crime. He also established a private security force for planters and merchants from West India.

The most important development in nineteenth-century England was the introduction of the Metropolitan Police Act by Robert Peel. It passed, creating the London Metropolitan Police, whose principal objective was to be *prevention* of crime.

In colonial America, constables and town watchmen were the primary means of security until the establishment of full-time police forces in the mid-1800s. Because of problems of interstate jurisdiction and lack of public police protection, many states passed railroad police acts, allowing private railroads to establish proprietary security forces, with full police powers, to protect their goods and passengers. In many parts of the country, the railroad police provided the only protective services until governmental units and law enforcement agencies were established.

Allan Pinkerton was the first law enforcement officer hired to protect the railroads. He also established the first and currently the largest private security contract operation in the United States. About the same time, Washington Perry Brink established armored car and courier services in the United States. In the twentieth century, William J. Burns founded the sole investigating agency for the American Banking Association. It grew to become the second-largest contract guard and investigative service in the United States.

The world wars heightened emphasis on security in the government and made industry increasingly aware of the need for plant security. George R. Wackenhut's corporation, in only 20 years, established itself as the third-largest contract guard and investigative agency in the country. By the 1990s private security has evolved into a multibillon-dollar-a-year business employing more than a million people. The future for private security appears excellent.

Application

1. You have been asked to speak to a college class on "The Evolution of Private Security." What facts will you include in your talk? What will you stress most?

2. You have been asked to speak to a class at the local police academy on the historical role of private security as it related to early public law enforcement. What facts will you include? What will you stress most?

Discussion Questions

1. What features of ancient security systems may still be found in the 1990s?
2. Until recent times, it was felt a ruler and his army could enforce the laws. Why does Reith feel a "police mechanism" is necessary between the ruler and the army?
3. What relationship exists between the ancient assize of arms and our Constitution's Second Amendment right of the people "to keep and bear arms" for the necessity of a "well-regulated militia"?
4. Throughout history there has been hostility to the establishment of public police. Why were people so opposed to an organization that could have benefited them so greatly?
5. In the absence of effective public law enforcement, what parallel functions did the Pinkerton Detective Agency and the railroad police perform?

References

Adam, H. L. *The Police Encyclopedia*. London: Waverly Book Company, n.d. 1:125.

BBC (British Broadcasting Company) and CBN (Canadian Broadcasting Network). "The Importance of Industrial Espionage." *Best Kept Secrets*. 1954 television series.

Critchley, T. A. *A History of Police in England and Wales,* 2d ed. Montclair, NJ: Patterson Smith, 1967.

Cunningham, William C.; Strauchs, John J.; and Van Meter, Clifford W. *The Hallcrest Report II: Private Security Trends 1970–2000*. Stoneham, MA: Butterworth-Heinemann, 1990.

Dewhurst, H. S. *The Railroad Police*. Springfield, IL: Charles C. Thomas, 1955.

Fischer, Robert J. and Green, Gion. *Introduction to Security,* 5th ed. Stoneham, MA: Butterworth-Heinemann, 1992.

Folley, Vern L. *American Law Enforcement*. Boston, MA: Allyn & Bacon, Inc., 1980.

Gough, T. W. "Railroad Crime: Old West Train Robbers to Modern-day Cargo Thieves." *FBI Law Enforcement Bulletin,* February 1977, pp. 16–25.

Hall, J. *Theft, Law and Society*. Indianapolis, IN: Bobbs-Merrill, 1935.

Hall, J. *Theft, Law and Society,* 2d ed. Indianapolis, IN: Bobbs-Merrill, 1952.

Healy, R. J. *Design for Security*. New York: John Wiley and Sons, 1968.

Jeffery, C. R. *Crime Prevention through Environmental Design*. Beverly Hills, CA: Sage Publications, 1972.

Kaye, Michael S. "Residential Security in the Year 2000." In *Security in the Year 2000 and Beyond,* by Louis A. Tyska and Lawrence J. Fennelly. Palm Springs, CA: ETC Publications, 1987.

Lavine, S. A. *Allan Pinkerton: America's First Private Eye*. New York: Dodd, Mead, and Company, 1963.

Mangan, Terence J. and Shanahan, Michael G. "Public Law Enforcement/Private Security: A New Partnership?" *FBI Law Enforcement Bulletin,* January 1990, pp. 18–22.

Reith, C. *Blind Eye of History*. Montclair, NJ: Patterson, Smith, 1975.

Reith, C. *Police Principles and the Problems of War*. London: Oxford University Press, 1940.

Romilly, S. *A History of English Criminal Law and its Administration from 1970,* Vol. 3, *Cross-Currents in the Movement for the Reform of the Police.* London: Stevens and Sons, 1956.

"Security Directors: How Much Are They Earning?" *Security World,* December 1980, pp. 19–27.

Shearing, Clifford D. and Stenning, Philip C. "Reframing Policing." In *Private Policing,* by Clifford D. Shearing and Philip C. Stenning, eds. Beverly Hills, CA: Sage Publications, 1987, pp. 9–18.

South, Nigel. "Law, Profit and 'Private Persons': Private and Public Policing in English History." In *Private Policing,* by Clifford D. Shearing and Philip C. Stenning, eds. Beverly Hills, CA: Sage Publications, 1987, pp. 72–107.

Tozer, E. "Riding with a Million in Cash." *Popular Science,* March 1960, pp. 3–4, 90–91, 246–247.

"The Wackenhut Corporation: A Brief History and Description of Capabilities." Palm Beach Gardens, FL: Wackenhut Corporation, n.d.

Weiss, Robert P. "From 'Slugging Detectives' to 'Labor Relations,' Policing Labor at Ford, 1930–1947." In *Private Policing,* by Clifford D. Shearing and Philip C. Stenning, eds. Beverly Hills, CA: Sage Publications, 1987, pp. 110–130.

CHAPTER 2

MODERN PRIVATE SECURITY: AN OVERVIEW

DO YOU KNOW

- What private security is?
- What major functions are performed by private security officers?
- What the major types of private security personnel are?
- How proprietary private security differs from contractual private security?
- How private security services might be regulated?
- How private investigators/detectives are regulated?
- What the requirements for becoming a private investigator are?
- What a Certified Protection Professional (CPP) is?

CAN YOU DEFINE THESE TERMS?

alarm respondent
armed courier services
armored car services
Certified Protection Professional (CPP)
contract services
courier
guard
hybrid services
licensing
private security services
proprietary services
registration

INTRODUCTION

Private security has come into its own, as evidenced by the development of college degree programs as well as state and national efforts for registering and licensing. It is a multifaceted industry that has made great advances since the day of the lone watchman or the single guard in a guardhouse. The numerous functions performed by private security personnel and the vast array of security equipment and procedures developed in the past decades offer the potential for more security than ever before.

This chapter begins by defining private security and examining the purpose and objectives of private security. This is followed by a discussion of the types of services and personnel that might be used to accomplish these objectives as well as the advantages and disadvantages of using proprietary and contract private security services.

Next the regulation of private security companies and private investigators is discussed. The chapter concludes with an explanation of the requirements to become a Certified Protection Professional (CPP).

PRIVATE SECURITY DEFINED

Before looking at definitions of private security, consider first, definitions of *security*. The government defines security as "the physical measures designed to safeguard personnel, prevent unauthorized access to material, equipment, facilities and documents, and to protect against sabotage, damage, and theft" (Dingle, 1993, p. 75).

Sutherland (1992, p. 59), however, states: "Security, like beauty, is in the eye of the beholder." He contends (p. 61): "The answer to, What is security? is multifaceted. Security is what we believe it to be." Indeed, as will be discussed in Section Three, it is up to management to define security for itself.

Many definitions of *private security* have been formulated to characterize the modern security industry. Among the more comprehensive definitions are the following:

- Private security includes those self-employed individuals and privately funded business entities and organizations providing security-related services to specific clientele for a fee, for the individual or entity that retains or employs them, or for themselves, in order to protect their persons, private property, or interests from varied hazards (*Private Security,* 1976, p. 4).
- The terms private police and private security forces and security personnel . . . include all types of private organizations and individuals, providing all types of security-related services, including investigation, guard, patrol, lie detection, alarm, and armored transportation (Kakalik and Wildhorn, *Rand Report,* Volume 1, p. 3).

On a more philosophical note, Hertig (1993, p. 96) suggests:

> Private security is the invisible empire of criminal justice, largely unseen by the public, whether from the perspective of protective services or career path. Private security is undervalued in criminal justice literature and seldom recognized for the growing importance it plays in society. Similarly, security officers are the forgotten soldiers of this empire, almost totally ignored in the literature and given little in the way of professional standards and training.

This view of private security and private security officers is changing drastically in the 1990s as the field becomes more professionalized and as it is relied upon more heavily to keep our citizens and their possessions safe, as discussed in the next chapter.

> Private security is a profit-oriented industry that provides personnel, equipment and/or procedures to *prevent* losses caused by human error, emergencies, disasters or criminal actions.

As the name implies, private security meets the needs of individuals, businesses, institutions and organizations that require more protection than is afforded by public police officers. The consumer of **private security services** might be any individual or group of individuals, public or private, large or small. Wealthy individuals may hire a private security patrol for their residences; colleges often hire security patrols; a bank, a shopping center, an office building—almost any conceivable business, organization or agency—might use private security services.

Consumers of private security services seek protection against many types of natural and human-made risks, with emphasis on the human-made risks of accidents; theft and pilferage; fraud; employee disloyalty and subversion; espionage; sabotage; strikes, riots and demonstrations and violent crimes (Paine, 1972, p. 36).

Although the duties assumed by private security personnel may vary greatly, most private security officers spend the majority of their time in nonenforcement, nonpolice functions.

Purpose and Objectives of Private Security

The purpose of private security is to protect assets and property and to provide a stable, nonthreatening environment in which employees and visitors of a facility may pursue their work objectives without disruption or harm.

Common objectives of private security include the following:

- To fairly and consistently enforce the policies and procedures regarding general security, access and asset control and employee safety.
- To provide a workplace environment that will attract and retain personnel and protect them from exploitation by external pressures.
- To prevent the compromise and unauthorized disclosure of the company's assets or technology.
- To protect and preserve the company's assets.
- To respond to on-site incidents that threaten the well-being of employees or the organization.
- To report conditions that constitute a breach of sound security or pose a potential security hazard.

> The primary function of security personnel is to prevent loss by (1) gathering information, (2) controlling access to and maintaining order on private property and (3) protecting persons and property against crime and disaster.

In addition, private security personnel may provide valuable public relations services. The specific type of security position an individual holds will determine which functions will be of primary concern.

Types of Private Security Services and Personnel

Security objectives may be met through a variety of services. According to the Hallcrest Report II (Cunningham et al., 1990), the most common security services being provided are contract guards, alarm services, private investigators, locksmith services, armored car services and security consultants. Before looking at specific services, consider how the services might be provided.

The services may be provided by a single individual or by a team of security professionals under the direction of a full-time security manager. They may be the responsibility of individuals on staff, that is, proprietary, or they may be the responsibility of people hired on a contract basis, as discussed shortly.

> The primary types of private security personnel are guards, patrols, investigators, armed couriers, central alarm respondents and consultants.

Private Security Guards

A common and highly visible type of security officer is the private security **guard,** who is usually in uniform and is sometimes armed. Premises may be guarded 24 hours a day, seven days a week; only during the day; only during the night or only during peak periods, such as when sporting events are being conducted.

Security guards control access to private property, maintain order on the premises, enforce the rules and regulations of the employer, protect against loss from fire or equipment failure and help to prevent and/or detect criminal acts on private property, which sometimes involves stopping, questioning and arresting suspects. The amount of crime-related activity varies depending on the particular establishment being guarded.

Security guards are sometimes also responsible for property control, energy conservation, maintaining sign-in logs, opening and closing, escort service and emergency response and support during medical, fire or weather emergencies.

Some security guards are responsible for preventing and/or detecting embezzlement, misappropriation or concealment of merchandise, money, bonds, stocks, notes or other valuable documents. Some security guards protect individuals rather than premises and property. The rising incidence of executive kidnappings and hostage situations has resulted in a dramatic increase in bodyguard service since the mid-1970s. Likewise, escort services increased in demand in the 1980s.

The Hallcrest Report (Cunningham and Taylor, 1985) states that several major corporations are concerned about protecting their chief corporate executives from terrorism or from kidnapping for ransom. This confirms the statement in the Figgie Report (1981) that 40 percent of executives surveyed were concerned about kidnapping, either of themselves or of their families or business associates. Larger companies may carry corporate executive kidnap/

ransom insurance policies or may provide armed bodyguards to protect top executives.

Private Patrol Officers

Patrol has been called the "backbone" of the public police force because it is the primary means of preventing or detecting criminal activity. Private patrol officers perform the same function. Moving from location to location on foot or in a vehicle, they protect the property of specific employers rather than that of the general public. They are, in essence, an extension of public patrol, because many people do not readily differentiate between the vehicles of public police officers and private patrol officers. In other words, the private security patrol officers may prevent criminal activity while en route to an assigned area. As noted in "New Roles for Private Patrols" (1994, p. 11):

> In large and small communities across the country, private security companies are playing a greater role in helping to police communities. Whether called in by private home owners, home associations, co-op shareholders, or block associations, these private patrols do everything from drive-in patrols to picking up mail and newspapers for vacationing homeowners. Specialty services may even include escorting individuals from the car to the front door, along with a complete door and window check.

One reason for this increase in using private patrols is given by Munk (1994, p. 104): "Unimpressed by the security provided by strapped, undermanned and frequently demoralized municipal police forces, frustrated citizens are increasingly turning to the private sector for their protection."

For example, in New York's Upper East Side, residents and businesspeople collaborated to fund a supplemental security operation of some 500 security officers.

Another example is an "elegant" Los Angeles neighborhood which began experiencing drive-by shootings and armed robberies. The neighbors organized and hired a private armed patrol service with extremely successful results, going from a serious crime every week to only one carjacking in the 12 months the patrol service was involved.

According to Munk (1994, p. 106): "Counting both commercial and residential protection, the private protection business is already doing $52 billion a year and is growing at 8% a year."

Security patrols are sometimes also responsible for opening and closing facilities, conducting interior and exterior inspections, checking on facilities and equipment, providing escort service, transporting equipment or documents and responding to alarms.

Some private patrol officers have one employer who is responsible for an establishment with very large premises requiring patrol. Other private patrol officers work for several employers, moving from place to place, sometimes going inside the premises, sometimes not. Some wealthy neighborhoods may employ a private patrol officer to maintain surveillance of the neighborhood and to routinely check homes and property. Likewise, a group of businesspeople or merchants within a neighborhood or within a shopping center may

The Galleria shopping center in Edina, Minnesota, uses security officers to patrol its premises and to assist shoppers.

hire a private officer to patrol their establishments. Many communities have established special patrol service agencies.

Private Investigators

Popular television series have glamorized the vocation of private investigator (PI), but in reality, criminal investigation is only a small part of a private investigator's work.

Private investigators provide services for a fee as independent contractors. It has been estimated that there are five thousand private investigative agencies in the United States, with approximately two hundred thousand employees.

Private investigators' businesses may be structured as individuals doing business as private contractors, as sole proprietorships, as partnerships or as corporations. In addition, many businesses and industries have their own internal (proprietary) investigators. Both private and proprietary investigators serve similar functions.

Law firms frequently hire private investigators to assist in preparing for civil and criminal trials. Insurance companies use private investigators to investigate

This private security investigator is debugging a phone believed to be involved in espionage.

such things as arson, life insurance fraud, large theft claims, workers' compensation fraud, automobile accidents and product liability. Utilities may hire private investigators for a variety of reasons; for example, the telephone company might hire an investigator to look into obscene or threatening telephone calls, pay-phone burglaries, use of illegal telephone equipment or long-distance billing frauds.

Most investigations conducted by security personnel concentrate on such matters as background checks for employment, insurance and credit applications; civil litigation matters on assignment from private attorneys and investigation of insurance or workers' compensation claims. Frequently investigators are brought in to work undercover to detect employee dishonesty, pilferage or shoplifting. As noted by LaRatta (1994, p. 2):

> Good private investigators develop skills which include conducting good surveillance and background checks. The private investigation business also requires the investigator to learn laws, interviewing techniques and investigative techniques.
>
> The best private investigators also possess good verbal and written skills, as well as analytical skills. To be very successful, they must also know where to find information and data and have a "contact bank" of personal resources.
>
> Some private investigation firms provide undercover operatives, polygraph examinations, countersurveillance equipment and services, forensic photography, and bodyguards. Other firms offer investigation and countermeasures for complex forms of white-collar crime.
>
> The "new breed" of investigator in these firms may have background in accounting, data processing, investigative reporting or internal auditing. No longer is the traditional law enforcement/criminal justice background exclusively associated with private investigators.

Many businesses prefer to have their cash transported by armored truck rather than placing their own personnel at risk of being robbed.

Armed Couriers

Most private **armed courier services** use armored cars, vans or trucks, but they may use airlines and trains as well. A **courier** is uniformed and armed to ensure the protection of money, goods, documents or people as they are transported from one location to another. The public police seldom become involved with armed courier deliveries unless there is a high probability that a crime will be attempted during the delivery.

Managers considering using **armored car services** should heed the observation of McGuffey (1993, p. 50):

> Businesses often assume that armored carriers are regulated since they are entrusted with large sums of money. Nothing could be further from the truth.
>
> Some states require licensing for possession of firearms, and Interstate Commerce Commission regulations govern the trucking industry as a whole; however, regulations that ensure the protection of assets simply do not exist.

Brink's, the largest of the armed courier services, has established a credible service record while it carries billions of dollars a day.

> The armored car specialist has been called on to move diamonds, Picasso paintings, the original copy of the Gettysburg Address, 15 tons of rare coins, and special materials for World War II's Manhattan Project—the atomic bomb.

Central Alarm Respondents

Some intrusion detection systems simply sound an alarm when an intrusion is detected, thus relying on an employee or a passerby to notify the police. Other alarm systems are connected directly with police headquarters so the police are automatically notified. However, because the false-alarm rate is greater than 95 percent for many currently used systems, some cities have banned direct connection of alarms to police equipment because so much public effort is expended in responding to these private false alarms. Consequently, private central alarm services, dominated by American District Telegraph (ADT), have become a popular, effective alternative.

According to Mosler's Electronic Systems Division, a central station alarm is:

> A system in which the secured area is directly connected to an alarm panel in a centrally located alarm receiving station via a pair of leased telephone wires. Upon receiving an alarm, the company, which is usually a privately owned organization, will dispatch its guards to the location of the secured area and will also notify the police. Alarm installation of this type can only be U.L.* approved when the protected premises are within 10 minutes traveling time from the central office (*Private Security,* 1976, p. 3).

Given the extremely high percentage of false alarms, such a system improves relationships with the police, but it also poses considerable hazard to the **alarm respondent,** that is, the individual sent to investigate the alarm. An intruder may still be on the premises and may pose a direct threat to anyone answering the alarm. Chapter 5 presents a detailed discussion of the various alternatives available in alarm systems.

Consultants

As noted by Thornton et al. (1991, p. 54):

> A security consultant—whether in-house or outside—is called on to do one or more of the following:
>
> - Assess what types of threats or risks affect the assets to be protected.
> - Render an opinion on the probability of those threats or risks.
> - Recommend a security or loss prevention plan to reduce the probability of those threats or risks.

As private security expands and becomes professionalized, the need for expertise on security problems also expands. This expansion has given rise to a variety of specialists who provide consultation in areas such as electronic surveillance; protective lighting, fencing and barricading; alarm systems; access control; key control and security training. Other individuals have become experts in polygraph examination and psychological stress evaluation (PSE) and may be used as consultants to private enterprise.

Since polygraph ("lie detector") tests were first submitted as evidence in an Illinois court in 1964, their use in law enforcement and in the private sector has been controversial. Some states prohibit use of the polygraph or PSE for employment screening, but many corporate executives and security directors feel such instruments are valuable for screening.

Using the polygraph for preemployment became strictly regulated through the Employee Polygraph Protection Act (EPPA) signed into law by Presi-

*Underwriter's Laboratory sets standards for various appliances and types of equipment.

dent Reagan, effective December 1988. This law, according to Bailey et al. (1989, p. 1):

> . . . prohibits the use of all mechanical lie detector tests in the workplace, including polygraphs, psychological stress evaluators, deceptographs, and voice stress analyzers. . . .
>
> EPPA allows for one type of lie detector test—the polygraph—to be used by private sector employers for certain types of pre-employment screening . . . [including] employers whose primary business is the provision of certain types of security services. . . .
>
> Where the particular employer is the United States government or any state or local government, EPPA does not apply. Government employers may use any lie detector test without complying with any of EPPA's procedures or restrictions. The FBI, the CIA, firms doing sensitive defense work, and companies who manufacture, distribute, or dispense controlled substances are also exempted.

In addition to doing background checks on employees, sometimes using deception detection instruments, consultants also can provide advice on risk management, loss prevention and crime prevention systems design and evaluation; architectural liaison and security ordinance compliance.

The Central Role of Security Personnel

At the heart of sound security are people, security officers and managers. These individuals rely on such security measures as physical controls, discussed in Chapter 5, and procedural controls, discussed in Chapter 6. Whether they do so as employees of the entity seeking the services or as employees of a security agency that contracts out the services is an important management decision.

Proprietary vs. Contract Private Security Services

An important consideration for any security manager is deciding whether loss prevention can be most effectively and efficiently achieved by having one's own security personnel or by hiring an outside agency to supply such personnel.

> **Proprietary services** are *in-house*, directly hired and controlled by the company or organization. In contrast, **contract services** are *outside* firms or individuals who provide security services for a fee. **Hybrid services** combine the two.

Advantages and Disadvantages of Proprietary and Contract Services

Many companies prefer to have their own security personnel because they are likely to be more loyal, more motivated due to promotion possibilities, more knowledgeable of the specific operation and personnel of the organization, more courteous and better able to recognize VIPs and more amendable to training and supervision. In addition, having proprietary security personnel is seen as a status symbol among many employers, and there is usually less turnover.

There are also disadvantages to proprietary security services. The most important are cost, lack of flexibility and administrative burdens. In addition, proprietary security personnel may become *too* familiar with the organization and become ineffective or even corrupt. Also, they may go on strike with the company union members. Because of such reasons, many business executives seek to contract with outside agencies or individuals to receive security services.

Among the most commonly provided contract security services are guard services, private patrol services and investigative services (such as those provided by Pinkerton's, Wm. J. Burns', Wackenhut and Walter Kidde) and armored car and courier services (such as those provided by Brink's, Wells Fargo and Loomis).

One of the most important factors behind the rise in contract services is cost. The Task Force Report on Private Security (*Private Security,* 1976, p. 245) gives the cost as 20 percent less than in-house services, *not counting* administrative savings on such items as insurance, retirement pension, social security, medical care, vacation time and sick days. Supervision, training and administrative functions are all assumed by the contract service.

Another distinct advantage of contract services is their flexibility; more or fewer personnel are available as needs change, and many contract services can provide a wide variety of services and equipment unavailable to in-house security. In addition, contract security personnel are likely to be more objective, having no special loyalty to the "employer" or contractor.

However, contract services are not necessarily ideal. There is a high turnover in contract guards; they are frequently reassigned; there is less job security and personal satisfaction and a conflict of loyalties may develop.

The Task Force Report on Private Security summarizes the major advantages and disadvantages of both proprietary and contract security services (*Private Security,* 1976, pp. 245–46):

Unfortunately, the image of contracted private security officers is not always the best. As noted by Hamit (1991, p. 39): "One of my continuing disappointments as a marketer of contract guard service is how woefully and willfully misinformed the people who purchase such services can be." Hamit believes that most contract security officers are hired to meet insurance needs and that companies hire the lowest-bidding firm. Management may equate these low wages with lack of training or skill. But, they may also feel they are getting more than they are paying for, as seen in the phrase "rent-a-cop." Often clients believe their security officers have enforcement powers that they simply do not have. Hamit concludes: "I am not the only executive in the contract industry to be both bemused and a bit outraged by the expectation that a security officer charged with protecting millions of dollars' worth of your property should be paid at the lowest possible rate."

Proprietary Advantages	Contract Advantages
Loyalty	Selectivity
Incentive	Flexibility
Knowledge of internal operation	Replacement of absenteeism
Tenure (less turnover)	Supervision (at no cost)
Control stays in-house	Training at no cost
Supervision stays in house	Objectivity
Training geared to specific job	Cost (20% less, not counting administrative costs)
Company image improved	Quality
Morale	Administration and budgeting taken care of
Courtesy to in-house personnel	Little union problems
Better law enforcement liaison	Variety of services and equipment
Selection controlled	Hiring and screening (at no cost)
Better communication	Better local law enforcement contacts
	Sharing expertise and knowledge
Disadvantages	**Disadvantages**
Unions	Turnover (extremely high industrywide)
Familiarity with personnel	Divided loyalties
Cost	Moonlighting (may be tired and not alert)
Inflexibility	Reassignment
Administrative burdens	Screening standards (may be inadequate)
	Insurance

This unfortunate situation is also noted by Muntz (1991, p. 26): "Historically, the contract security industry has been plagued with marginal employees, moonlighting, high turnover, low wages, poor supervision, and inadequate training."

The choice between a contractual or proprietary service need not be an either/or situation, as noted by Ledoux (1995, p. 37):

> Managers generally believe they must choose between the cost effectiveness of a security personnel provider and the intangible benefits more often associated with a proprietary force—performance quality, company loyalty, low turnover, and less frequent training demands. . . . Managers may be underestimating the capabilities of a contract guard force and denying their companies potential savings in the process.

The answer is often a combination, with proprietary security in a management role. Performance quality can be obtained by seeking qualified contract security officers—not going for the low bid. Company loyalty is also tied to wages and fair treatment. Says Ledoux (p. 38): "[I]f contract personnel are treated properly, paid appropriately, and provided clear standards and expectations, they will identify with their workplace, regardless of employer, and perform exceptionally." The same can be said of turnover rates (Ledoux,

p. 38): "The turnover rate of contract personnel is directly related to wage rates, benefits, and working conditions."

Olick (1994, p. 9) asks if managers remember the saying, "You get what you pay for." He notes: "It has been determined, time and time again, that this adage is applicable to security officers."

In addition, Arscott et al. (1991, p. 31) contend that contracted services will be most successful if expectations on both sides are clearly defined:

> The contractor must have a clear understanding of staffing requirements, total contract hours, insurance coverage, bonding and licensing requirements, and use of supervisory personnel to provide an accurate bid. Contracts should include rates for all services provided.
>
> Liability also should be addressed. The type of insurance required should be clearly defined, and proof of compliance should be requested.

Vassell et al. (1993, p. 41) caution: "A contract security company depends on proper scheduling for its success." They suggest:

> Armed with site and personnel information, the system [computer program] allows the manager to schedule security officers. It matches officer qualifications and availability to site requirements automatically.

The Hallcrest Report II (Cunningham et al., 1990, p. 196) states: "The proprietary sector continues to be one of the major employers of security personnel, representing more than 25% of all private security employees. In 1990 contract security guards are virtually tied at 35%. Thus, these 2 segments account for almost three-quarters of all employment." The Hallcrest estimates of private security employment for 1990 are summarized in Table 2–1.

The Hallcrest staff predicts that proprietary security will begin to lose ground during the 1990s and that by the year 2000 it will account for only 20

Table 2–1. Estimates of Private Security Employment for 1990

Segment	Employees in 1990	Percent of Total
Armored car	15,000	1.0%
Alarm companies	120,000	8.0%
Contract guards	520,000	34.8%
Private investigators	70,000	4.7%
Consultants/engineers	2,900	0.2%
Locksmiths	69,600	4.7%
Manufacturers and distributors	88,300	5.9%
Other	79,500	5.3%
Proprietary security	528,000	35.4%
TOTAL	1,493,300	100.0%

SOURCE: Reprinted by permission from *The Hallcrest Report II: Private Security Trends: 1970 to 2000*, © 1990 Butterworth-Heinemann, Stoneham, MA.

percent of the employment. The staff also predicts that contract services will maintain its 35 percent and that the most employment gains will be made by alarm companies, manufacturers and services represented in the "other" category.

Hallcrest employment data with the proprietary services omitted are summarized in Table 2–2.

The *manufacturers and distributors* category includes such things as electronic access control systems, safes and vaults, closed-circuit television systems and communications equipment.

As seen in Table 2–2, well over half of private security personnel work for "guard companies."

Regulation of Private Security

Since private security has become "big business," efforts have been made to regulate it. The reasons behind such efforts are fairly obvious (*Private Security,* 1976, Foreword):

> In many large cities, the number of private security personnel is considerably greater than the number of police and law enforcement personnel. Of those individuals involved in private security, some are uniformed, some are not; some carry guns, some are unarmed; some guard nuclear energy installations, some guard golf courses; some are trained, some are not; some have college degrees, some are virtually uneducated.

Although criticism of increased government regulation of business and industry has generally heightened, many favor regulation of private security because of the preceding disparities, and because of the nature of the field itself. First, private security services are important and expensive. Consumers should be assured that they are receiving the services they are paying for. Second, private security personnel come into daily contact with the public as authority figures. Control of these contacts must be ensured. Third, many private security personnel carry weapons that can kill or inflict great bodily harm. Use of such weapons must also be controlled.

Nevertheless, licensing and regulation of security personnel are highly controversial issues. With the national emphasis on *de*regulation, care must be taken not to be overly restrictive. For example, the governor of Ohio vetoed a bill that mandated 120 hours of training for Ohio security officers. The added paperwork and excessive cost of such training was felt to be prohibitive.

After much deliberation by numerous experts in law enforcement and private security, the Task Force on Private Security, organized by a federal government commission, established recommended standards for regulating private security (*Private Security,* 1976, pp. 282–306). Among these standards were recommendations for licensing and registering.

Table 2–2. Number of Employees to 2000

Segment	Employees in 1980	Percent of Total 1980	Employees in 1990	Percent of Total 1990	Average Annual Rate of Growth 1980 to 1990	Employees in 2000	Percent of Total 2000	Average Annual Rate of Growth 1990 to 2000
Armored car	11,500	2%	15,000	2%	3%	16,500	1%	1%
Alarm companies	55,000	10%	120,000	12%	8%	250,000	17%	8%
Contract guards	330,000	59%	520,000	54%	5%	750,000	51%	4%
Private investigators	45,000	8%	70,000	7%	4%	90,000	6%	2%
Consultants/engineers	1,200	0.2%	2,900	0.3%	9%	6,200	0.4%	8%
Locksmiths	45,000	8%	69,600	7%	4%	88,000	6%	2%
Manufacturers and distributors	55,000	10%	88,300	9%	5%	132,000	9%	4%
Other	13,500	2%	79,500	8%	19%	140,000	10%	6%
TOTAL	556,200		965,300		6%	1,472,700		4%

SOURCE: Reprinted by permission from *The Hallcrest Report II: Private Security Trends: 1970 to 2000*, © 1990 Butterworth-Heinemann, Stoneham, MA.

> Regulation of the private security industry should be performed at the *state level** through a regulatory board and staff.† Regulation can be achieved by requiring **licensing** of contract security services and by requiring **registration** of all persons specifically performing private security functions.

The Task Force recommended that the regulatory board consist of representatives from private security, local police departments, consumers and the general public. Various departments are responsible for regulating private security at the state level, including state troopers and state police, departments of public safety, boards of examiners and departments of commerce. These state regulatory bodies should establish licensing and registering requirements and a mechanism for resolving consumer complaints. To fulfill their responsibilities, they should have access to all criminal history record information to check applicants for licenses and registrations.

Basically, the Task Force favors licensing private security businesses and registering "every person who is employed to perform the functions of an investigator or detective, guard or watchman, armored car personnel or armed courier, alarm system installer or servicer, or alarm respondent . . ." (Standard 11.1). Such a procedure would be costly given the vast number of individuals involved; hence the controversy remains. Whether the benefits might justify the cost by eliminating undesirable personnel and professionalizing the private security field has not yet been resolved.

Acting on the recommendations of the Task Force, the majority of states have passed legislation requiring licensing of guards, investigators and alarm systems and setting forth the major qualifications for the license. License requirements often include no felony conviction; U.S. citizenship; a minimum age, experience, education and/or training; a written examination and a licensing period restriction. Additional requirements might include an application fee, being fingerprinted/photographed, a fingerprint check, a check for a criminal record and a check of personal references.

Grounds for revocation of a license include violations of license laws, false statements, felony convictions, dishonesty/fraud, impersonating a police officer, insolvent bond, release of confidential information, failure to render service, violation of a court order, false advertising and incompetency.

Regulation of Private Investigators

Most states and some cities provide some form of government regulation of the formation and operation of private investigation agencies, but only a few states have enacted laws controlling the investigative employees of private

*Standard 9.1.
†Standard 9.2.

contract agencies. In addition, state laws regulating security, private investigators and related enterprises vary in content and application.

> Most states that regulate the private investigative business require the licensing of individuals, partnerships and corporations providing private contract investigative services, and most have established a variety of standards to obtain a license.

The cost of such a license and the provisions for renewing it also vary from state to state.

In addition to state and city statutes and regulations, federal laws such as the Fair Credit Reporting Act affect private investigators and their activities. Although the act was passed originally to regulate and control mercantile credit, insurance, employment and investment agencies, recent interpretations of this law have resulted in its being applied to many facets of the private investigative function. Requirements for a private investigator's license vary from state to state, with some states being much more restrictive than others.

> Requirements for a private investigator's license usually include state residency, U.S. citizenship, training and/or work experience as a police officer or investigator, a clean arrest record, the passing of a background investigation and the passing of an oral or written examination.

Usually applicants must meet all or most of the preceding requirements to obtain a license. In addition, applicants must usually pay an initial license fee and must obtain a specific amount and type of insurance.

In addition to being licensed or registered, many individuals have established their expertise by becoming a Certified Protection Professional.

Certified Protection Professional (CPP)

In 1977 the American Society for Industrial Security (ASIS) organized the Professional Certification Board to grant a designation of **Certified Protection Professional (CPP)** to individuals meeting specific criteria of professional protection knowledge and conduct.*

The CPP program gives special recognition to those security practitioners who have met certain prescribed standards of performance, knowledge and conduct and who have demonstrated a high level of competency by improving

*The following program description (pp. 44–46) is adapted from a brochure provided by the ASIS and is reprinted by permission.

the practices of security management. It also encourages security professionals to continue to develop professionally by requiring continuing education to renew the certification.

The program is administered by a board appointed by the president of the ASIS. Applicants must meet specific experience and education requirements to be eligible to take the written exam.

> A Certified Protection Professional (CPP) has met specific experience and educational requirements and has passed a common knowledge examination as well as an examination in four specialty subjects.

Education and Experience

To be eligible to take the CPP examination, candidates must meet the following basic standards:

Degree		Security Experience		Responsible Charge Experience
None		10 years	and	7 years
Associate	and	8 years	and	6 years
Bachelor's	and	7 years	and	5 years
Master's	and	6 years	and	4 years
Doctoral	and	5 years	and	3 years

Behavior and Endorsement

In addition to meeting the experience and education requirements, candidates must affirm adherence to the CPP Code of Professional Responsibility and be endorsed by a person already certified as a Protection Professional. If these basic requirements are met, the person is eligible to take the written examination.

The Examination

The CPP examination is a one-day objective, multiple-choice test consisting of two parts: a Mandatory test administered in the morning and Specialty Subjects administered in the afternoon. According to the ASIS (1989, p. 4): "The Mandatory or Common Knowledge examination contains 200 questions covering basic knowledge applicable in the field of security and loss prevention. The specialty examinations test knowledge through four optional 25-question examinations, chosen by the candidate from fifteen subjects on security and loss prevention practice in special areas." The Mandatory and Specialty Subject areas are:

- **Mandatory Subjects**
  Emergency Planning
  Investigations

Legal Aspects
Personnel Security
Physical Security
Protection of Sensitive Information
Security Management
Substance Abuse
Loss Prevention
Liaison

- **Specialty Subjects**

Banking & Financial Institutions
Computer Security
Credit Card Security
Defense Industrial Security Program
Educational Institutions Security
Fire Resources Management
Health Care Institutions Security
Manufacturing Security
Nuclear Power Security
Public Utility Security
Restaurant & Lodging Security
Retail Security
Transportation & Cargo Security
Oil & Gas Industrial Security
Telephone & Telecommunications Security

After successfully passing the examination, a person is certified as a Protection Professional. Certification is valid for three years. Recertification is contingent on accumulating nine professional credits. The recertification program is designed to encourage individuals to keep current in new security developments and active in security programs. As of November 1, 1994, the current number of CPPs was 2,816.

The ASIS (1989, p. 1) says: "The Certification of protection professionals benefits the individual practitioner, the profession, the employer and the public. The evidence of competency in security protection furnished by certification will improve the individual, raise the general level of competency in the security profession, promote high standards of professional conduct, and provide evidence to management of professional performance capability."

The ASIS also notes that many companies are now requiring applicants for employment to have a CPP and suggests that this trend will continue as the program becomes more widely known.

Summary

Private security is a profit-oriented industry that provides personnel, equipment and/or procedures to *prevent* losses caused by human error, emergencies, disasters or criminal actions. The primary function of private security personnel is to prevent loss by (1) gathering information, (2) controlling access to and maintaining order on private property and (3) protecting persons and property against crime and disaster. The primary types of private security personnel are guards, patrols, investigators, armed couriers, central alarm respondents and consultants.

Security services may be proprietary or contracted. Proprietary services are in-house, directly hired and controlled by the company or organization. In contrast, contract services are outside firms or individuals who provide security services for a fee. Both arrangements present advantages and disadvantages to the security manager.

Although not all agree, the 1976 Task Force on Private Security recommended that private security be regulated at the state level through a regulatory board and staff that require licensing of contract security services and registration of all persons specifically performing private security functions.

Most states that regulate the private investigative business require the licensing of individuals, partnerships and corporations providing private contract investigative services, and most have established a variety of standards to obtain a license. Requirements usually include state residency, U.S. citizenship, training and/or work experience as a police officer or investigator, a clean arrest record, the passing of a background investigation and the passing of an oral or written examination.

One important step toward the professionalization of private security is the establishment of a Certified Protection Professional program by the American Society for Industrial Security. A Certified Protection Professional (CPP) has met specific experience and educational requirements and has passed a common knowledge examination as well as an examination in four specialty subjects.

✔ APPLICATION

1. Read the following eight statements about the private security officer industry and state whether you think the statement is true or a misconception.
   1. Security officers are private police officers.
   2. The average security officer is a Rambo-like "wannabe cop."
   3. Owners of security companies make huge profits from their low-paid labor force.
   4. All security officers dress like police, and most of them carry guns.
   5. Private security officers are forever making unlawful arrests.
   6. Security companies always fight any proposal that security officers all receive standardized training.
   7. Few security officers stay on the job long. It's just a job to "pass through" to better things.
   8. Most security officers are either stupid or have shady characters.

(From "Common . . . about the Private Security Officer Industry," 1994, pp. 19, 25.)

2. Discuss with a friend what his or her image of a private security officer is, and what rights and restrictions are normally present in carrying out the responsibilities of a private security officer. Then arrange for a similar discussion with a person in public law enforcement and one in private security.

Discussion Questions

1. Is licensing of private security agencies and/or officers an advantage or disadvantage to private security agencies?
2. Why is supervision so important to a private security agency?
3. With or without specific regulations of private security officers in some states, what is the best way to ensure the maximum performance of these officers?
4. Do you think private investigators enjoy more status than individuals in the private security work force?
5. Consult your Yellow Pages. What security listings are given? Is there a listing for *polygraph services? Lie detection services? Surveillance?*

References

American Society for Industrial Security (ASIS). "Certification Procedure and Examination Information for Certified Protection Professional: CPP." Arlington, VA: American Society for Industrial Security, 1989.

Arscott, Robert D.; Lambert, Marc P.; and Revis, Sharon W. "Choosing and Using Contract Security." *Security Management,* June 1991, pp. 31–33.

Bailey, F. Lee; Zuckerman, Roger E.; and Pierce, Kenneth R. *The Employee Polygraph Protection Act: A Manual for Polygraph Examiners and Employers.* Severna Park, MD: American Polygraph Association, 1989.

"Common Misconceptions about the Private Security Officer Industry." *Security Concepts,* November 1994, pp. 19, 25.

Cunningham, William C.; Strauchs, John J.; and Van Meter, Clifford W. *Private Security Trends, 1970 to 2000: The Hallcrest Report II.* Stoneham, MA: Butterworth-Heinemann, 1990.

Cunningham, W. C. and Taylor, T. H. *The Hallcrest Report: Private Security and Police in America.* Portland, OR: Chancellor Press, 1985.

Dingle, Jeff. "Back to the Basics." *Security Technology and Design,* November/December 1993, p. 75.

The Figgie Report on Fear of Crime: Part II. The Corporate Response to Fear of Crime. Willoughby, OH: The Figgie Corporation, 1981.

Hamit, Francis. "Perpetuating the Rent-a-Cop Myth." *Security Management,* June 1991, pp. 39–42.

Hertig, Christopher A. "Who Are the Forgotten Soldiers?" *Security Management,* February 1993, pp. 95–96.

Kakalik, J. S. and Wildhorn, S. *The Private Police.* New York: Crane Russak, 1977 (The Rand Corporation).

LaRatta, Robert. Review of Third Edition of *Introduction to Private Security,* 1994, p. 2.

Ledoux, Darryl T. "Exploding the Myths of Contract Security." *Security Management,* January 1995, pp. 37–39.

McGuffey, Jim. "The Armored Car Quagmire." *Security Management,* November 1993, pp. 50–51.

Munk, Nina. "Rent-a-Cops." *Forbes,* October 10, 1994, pp. 104–106.

Muntz, Alan M. "Contracting for the Right Relationship." *Security Management,* June 1991, pp. 26–30.

"New Roles for Private Patrols." *Security Management,* December 1994, pp. 11–12.

Olick, M. "Contract Security Guard Companies: What to Look For." *Security Concepts,* May 1994, pp. 9, 23.

Paine, D. *Basic Principles of Industrial Security.* Madison, WI: Oak Security Publications, 1972.

Private Security. Report of the Task Force on Private Security, National Advisory Committee on Criminal Justice Standards and Goals. Washington, DC: U.S. Government Printing Office, 1976.

Sutherland, Garrell E. "Answering the Question—What Is Security?" *Security Management,* July 1992, pp. 59–61.

Thornton, William E.; McKinnon-Fowler, Ellen; and Kent, David R. "Stalking Security Statistics." *Security Management,* April 1991, p. 54–58.

Vassell, William C.; Ramsdell, Edward A.; and Tharp, David O. "Bringing Contract Services On-line." *Security Management,* December 1993, pp. 41–45.

CHAPTER 3

The Public/Private Interface and Legal Authority

Do You Know

- How private security officers and public police officers are alike?
- How private security officers differ from public police officers?
- What authority private security officers have? How they are restricted?
- How private security officers compare in numbers with public police officers?
- How private and public security officers might work together?
- What advantages private security offers public police and vice versa?

Can You Define These Terms?

arrest	POST Commission
authority	power
Exclusionary Rule	privatization

Introduction

Security managers must be concerned with their own loss prevention program and the individuals hired to implement it, but they must know how the private "policing" function differs from that of the public police, how they might contribute to public policing efforts and, in numerous instances, how they might benefit from public policing efforts.

They must also be completely familiar with the legal authority they and their employees have and the restrictions on this authority.

This chapter introduces the public/private interface and the legal authority of private security officers. This is followed by a look at the friction that has existed historically between public and private officers. Next the complementary roles of private security and the public police are discussed. The chapter concludes with a look at specific areas in which private security might lessen the burden of the public police and specific examples of successful public/private partnerships in action.

The Public/Private Interface

Loss prevention, security, privacy—such goals are not the sole domain of private security. They have been of concern since recorded time. Recall from

Chapter 1 that the history of public policing and private security is intertwined. According to Shearing and Stenning (1987, p. 15):

> With contemporary corporations as the modern-day equivalents of feudal lords, reigning supreme over huge feudal estates, the search for a historical parallel leads us back beyond frankpledge to more ancient concepts of private peaces and conflicting private authorities. Indeed, the very distinction between private and public takes on a new significance that blurs, and contradicts, its liberal meanings. This is true not only because private "individuals" are engaged in the maintenance of public order but also because more and more public life is nowadays conducted on privately owned and controlled property.
>
> Corporate orders are defended on the grounds that corporations, like any other "persons," have the right to a sphere of private authority over which they have undisturbed jurisdiction. Furthermore, this right is sacrosanct, for to encroach upon it would undermine the very freedoms that are definitive of liberal democracy.

This "right to a sphere of private authority" has long been recognized by governments and by the wide variety of policing mechanisms they have established, with public and private policing continuing to coexist, as noted by Bayley (1987, p. 6):

> Policing has been done under an enormous variety of auspices—national and local governments, revolutionary and nonrevolutionary parties, neighborhoods, churches, landowners, workers, peasants, businesses, and professional associations. Even more interesting, varieties of policing are complexly mixed. . . . Although the proportions in the mixture vary, similar forms appear again and again. In particular, "public" and "private" policing never wholly supplant one another. Indeed, the distinction itself becomes problematic in many circumstances. Public and private police institutions cooperate, sometimes interpenetrate, and often share modes of operation. . . . Policing is a reciprocating engine in that groups regulate individuals but individuals collectively regulate groups.

As noted by the United Way Strategic Institute (1989, p. 3): "There will be a blurring of the boundaries that have traditionally defined the roles of the public sector versus the private sector, as well as individual versus institutional responsibilities."

Shearing et al. (1980, p. 14) describe private policing as a continuum going from one end representing those who have special powers and public accountability to the other end representing no special powers and accountability only to private interests:

> Where on this continuum any given security employee should be placed depends, we believe, not only on who his immediate employer is but also on what legal powers he possesses and to whom he is accountable for the exercise of those powers.

Authority is the right to command, enforce laws and compel obedience. **Power,** in contrast, is the force that can be used to carry out one's authority. To be effective, security officers must have not only the authority to enforce their employer's regulations but also the power to do so. As noted by Bennett and Hess (1996, p. 40):

> Authority and power are alike in that both imply the ability to coerce compliance, that is, to *make* subordinates carry out orders. Both are important to managers at all levels.
>
> They differ in that authority relies on force or on some sort of law or order, whereas power relies on persuasion and lacks the support of law or rule.

Although they are speaking of the relationship between managers and their subordinates, the same relationship can exist between security officers and the public with whom they interact.

Marx (1987, p. 187) lists a series of questions to be asked in determining if policing is public or private:

- Where does the policing occur—in public, private, or mixed space?
- Whose interest is served by the policing—the general public, a private interest, or both?
- What is the function of the policing?
- Who pays for, or sponsors, the policing—public or private interests, or both?
- Who carries it out—regular sworn agents of the state with full police powers, special-purpose deputies with more limited powers, or citizens with no official powers?
- Who controls and directs the policing?
- Where the policing involves data collection and investigation, who has access to the results?
- What popular and self-definitions characterize those doing the policing?
- What organizational form does the policing take?
- To what extent are social control agents linked together in informal networks that transcend their nominal definition as public or private?

Answers to these questions will call attention to certain basic similarities and differences between the private and the public "policing" efforts.

Similarities Between Private and Public Officers

Private and public officers do have many things in common, including wearing a uniform and badge, being trained to compel obedience to their authority and being liable for their actions. Both private and public officers seek to prevent losses from criminal actions and, if such losses occur, to investigate and apprehend the person(s) responsible.

> Private and public police officers may wear uniforms and badges, are trained in compelling obedience and are apt to be sued. Both also seek to prevent crime and to apprehend criminals.

Both public and private officers may receive respect and cooperation from those they work with or may face hostility and aggression. In addition, both

Police officers are usually easily recognizable by their uniform and badge.

Private security officers' uniforms may resemble those of the public police, but their badges are usually distinctive as are their arm badges.

public and private officers have a tremendous influence on the image of those for whom they work. Their every action has an impact on public relations, as discussed in Chapter 10.

Differences Between Private and Public Officers

Four basic differences exist between private and public officers: (1) the financial orientation, (2) the employer, (3) the specific functions performed and (4) the statutory power possessed.

Private Security:

- Profit-oriented enterprise.
- Serving specific private clients.
- To prevent crime, protect assets and reduce losses.
- To regulate noncriminal conduct not under the authority of public police.

Public Law Enforcement

- Nonprofit, governmental enterprise.
- Serving the general public.
- To combat crime, enforce laws and apprehend offenders.
- Statutory authority.

One seldom-discussed difference between the public police and private security officers is that of the corporate culture. It is well established that the police have a culture steeped in tradition and pride. They know what their peers expect of them, and they are usually governed by clear policies and procedures. In contrast, as noted by Hamit (1994, p. 97): "Unlike the police or military, security has no strong traditions to sustain our pride in ourselves and our work." This is an area that will doubtless evolve as the security profession matures.

Other basic differences between private and public officers exist in the authority they have and the restrictions placed on them.

Legal Authority

Because they wear uniforms, often carry weapons and have been placed in a position of authority by their employer, private security officers may appear to have more legal authority than private citizens. This is not always the case, however.

> Private security officers usually have no more powers than private citizens. As citizens, they have the power to **arrest,** to investigate, to carry weapons, to defend themselves and to defend their property or property entrusted to their care.

Often private security officers conduct periodic inspections of personal items such as briefcases, purses and lunch boxes as directed by management and specific policy. Generally, private security officers have no police authority. Their authority does not go beyond that of a private citizen. Nonetheless, because they wear uniforms and may be armed, they are likely to give the *appearance* of authority. In addition, their training and experience makes it more likely that they will be able to exercise this authority.

> Private security officers can deny access to unauthorized individuals into their employers' business or company, and they can enforce all rules and regulations established by their employers. They can also search employees and question them without giving the Miranda warning in most states.

Private security officers *do* have the authority to prevent access of unauthorized individuals into a business or company and to enforce those rules and regulations established by their employer.

In *Bowman v. State* (1983), an Indiana court ruled that private security officers, unlike public law enforcement officials, are *not* required to issue Miranda warnings. Giving warnings, the court observed, is required only in cases involving state action.

Restrictions on Private Security Officers

Laws governing the conduct of private security officers are derived from several sources: tort law, state statutes, criminal law, constitutional guarantees and contract law.

> Private security officers cannot invade another's privacy, electronically eavesdrop, trespass or, in some jurisdictions, wear a uniform or badge that closely resembles that of a public police officer.

Because of actions they must perform in fulfilling their responsibilities, private security officers are more open to civil lawsuits than most other citizens, as discussed in the next chapter.

Many of the restrictions on private security officers come from the tort law of each state. (Tort law defines citizens' responsibilities to each other and provides for lawsuits to recover damages for injury caused by failing to carry out these responsibilities.) Civil liability is discussed in the next chapter.

State and federal criminal laws prohibit security officers from committing crimes such as assault. Other state and federal laws regulate wiretapping, surveillance, gathering information on individuals, impersonating public police officials and purchasing and carrying firearms. For example, in *National Labor Relations Board v. St. Vincent's Hospital* (1977), the U.S. Court of Appeals held that the interrogation of hospital employees by their supervisors in connection with several thefts did *not* constitute coercive action. The court did observe, however, that placing hospital employees who were engaged in union activities under surveillance did violate the National Labor Relations Act.

Although it is well known that the U.S. Constitution places the major legal limitations on police powers, such restrictions are applied only to state activities. However, the distinction between state and private activity is not always clear-cut. This is true, for example, when a private security officer is hired by a public institution or when a private security officer is deputized. In such instances, it is often felt that the constitutional restrictions *do* apply to those private security officers.

Usually private security officers who are deputized or are contracted by a public authority are subject to the same restrictions as public officers. In addition, public police officers who work during off-hours in private security positions are considered to be public law enforcement officers in many states. Consequently, many police departments do not allow their officers to "moonlight" in private security positions. Two states, Connecticut and Kansas, specifically deny a private security license to anyone vested with police powers.

Clearly, the distinction between public and private police is not always black and white, but various shades of gray. In some states shopkeeper statutes and other similar legislation dealing with railroad officers, nuclear facility officers, bank security officers and the like give private security officers greater powers than those of the general public. A few jurisdictions recognize private security officers who have total public police authority based on compliance with certain legal and training requirements.

State laws also regulate the arrest powers of private security officers. In the majority of 31 states surveyed, private security officers can arrest for a misdemeanor. In all 31 states they can arrest for a felony, but in none of the states are they granted police arrest powers.

Other restrictions are placed on private security officers by local ordinances and state statutes that establish licensing regulations. These restrictions vary greatly from state to state.

Finally, most security officers are further restricted by the contract they sign to provide their services to an agency or to an employer.

The similarities in goals and objectives of private and public policing and the differences in their legal authority suggest that in many ways public and private policing efforts are complementary, but they often have not been viewed that way.

Historical Friction

Friction has often existed between the police and private security, as noted by Mangan and Shanahan (1990, p. 19): "Police have traditionally viewed private security employees as inadequately trained and ill-paid individuals who could not find other work but were nevertheless allowed to carry a gun."

Cain et al. (1993, p. 25) note: "The relationship between private security and public law enforcement has been a rocky one."

One source of friction, according to Reibstein (1994, p. 74), is the fact that the police have to follow the U.S. Constitution and private security officers don't. He notes: "Police detectives say it's no surprise that private eyes can solve some tough cases."

Historically, public and private security have seen themselves as being in competition, with private security usually coming out on the "short end of the stick." A police sergeant was quoted as saying (Remesch, 1989, p. 32): ". . . to state that the only difference between a police officer and a security officer is the title 'security,' is like comparing a surgeon to a butcher since they both cut meat." According to Remesch (1989, p. 33):

> Much of the problem centers on the still-evolving nature of the private security industry. Like a grown sibling, the older, wiser, public police officer wants the private police officer to just follow his lead in the path he's traveled a million times. But like the younger sibling who has finally reached the age of maturity, members of private security are saying to their brethren: "We've grown up. Give us some respect."

That private security has, indeed, "grown up" is highlighted by a study by the National Institute of Justice (Cunningham et al., 1991, p. 1):

> Private security is now clearly the Nation's primary protective resource, outspending public law enforcement by 73 percent and employing 2½ times the workforce. . . . Currently spending for private security is $52 billion and private security agencies employ 1.5 million persons. Public law enforcement spends $30 billion and has a workforce of approximately 600,000. The average annual rate of growth in private security is predicted to be 8%, double that of public law enforcement.

> There are now 2½ times as many people employed in private security as there are public police.

These comparisons are illustrated in Figures 3–1 and 3–2.

One way to alleviate friction, according to Hertig (1991), is through education, that is, including courses on private security in criminal justice programs. This suggestion is based on the assumptions that many people entering law enforcement will begin their careers in security and that many law enforcement positions are related more to asset protection than enforcement. Hertig contends (p. 216): "If tomorrow's police officers had a course or two

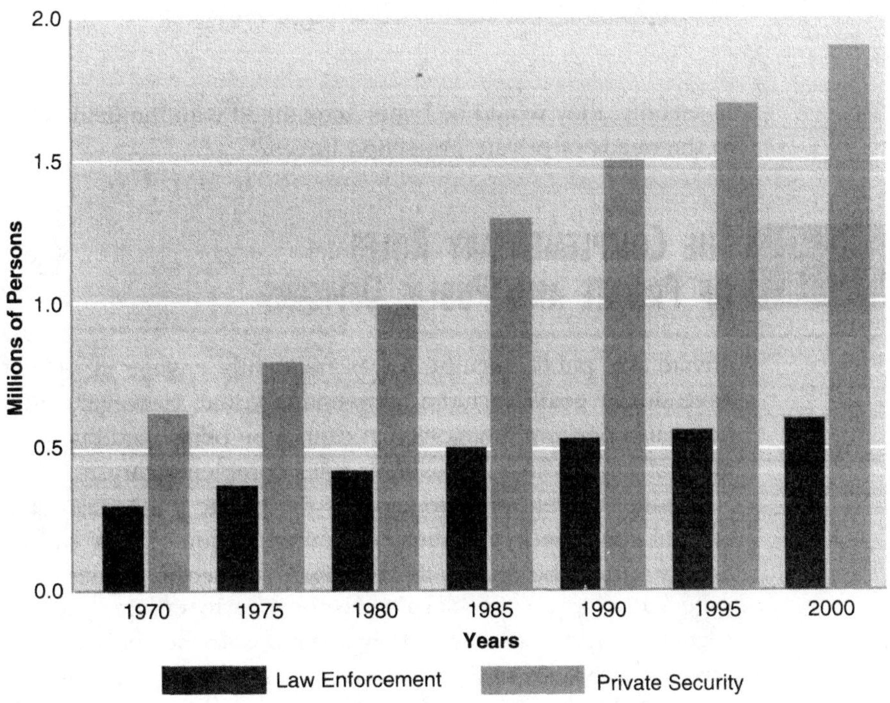

Figure 3–1. Private Security and Law Enforcement Employment Compared

SOURCE: William C. Cunningham et al. *Private Security: Patterns and Trends*. Washington, DC: National Institute of Justice Research in Brief, August 1991, p. 3.

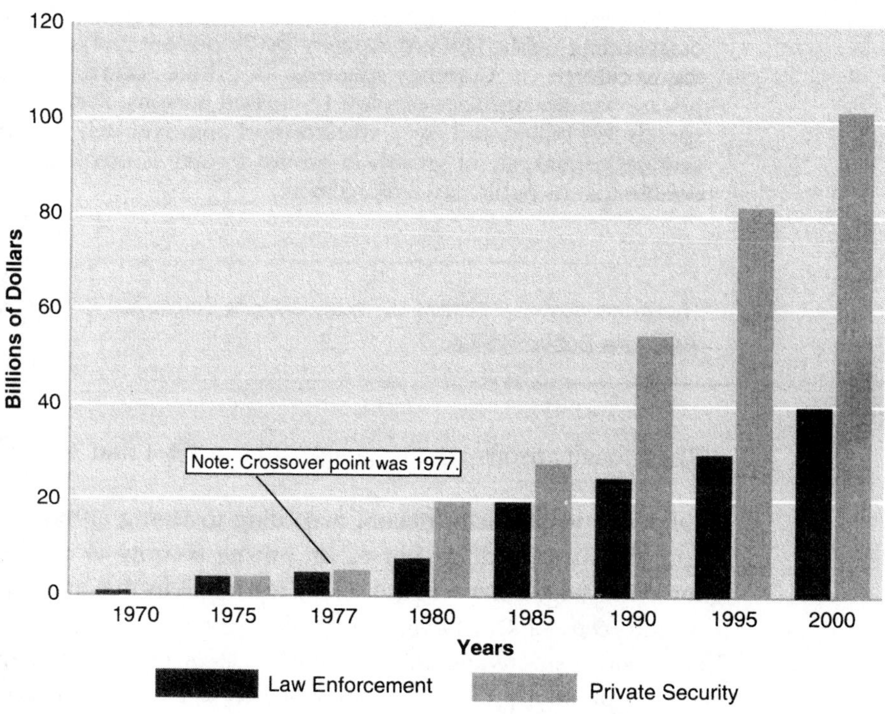

Figure 3–2. Private Security and Law Enforcement Spending Compared
SOURCE: William C. Cunningham et al. *Private Security: Patterns and Trends*. Washington, DC: National Institute of Justice Research in Brief, August 1991, p. 3.

in security, they would be better acquainted with the field and more receptive to the needs of private protection forces."

THE COMPLEMENTARY ROLES OF PRIVATE AND PUBLIC OFFICERS

Private and public security forces frequently engage in similar activities and have similar goals, including preventing crime. However, private security officers also perform functions that cannot be performed by public law enforcement officers, which makes their roles complementary.

Security officers provide services the public police cannot, either because of legal constraints or because of limited resources. Law enforcement officers usually cannot be spared to investigate suspected crimes such as employee pilferage. Nor are they legally responsible to enforce the private rules and regulations of businesses and organizations. In fact, public police officers often have no jurisdiction inside premises until after a crime has been committed.

Promoting cooperative interaction between private and public police officers is of utmost importance, as noted by Charles Connally, chairperson of the American Society for Industrial Security's (ASIS) Law Enforcement Liaison Council at a national conference (Bocklet, 1990, p. 59):

> Many private forces are far ahead of police departments in technology and available security resources. Their training has improved, some meet state standards and experienced retired law enforcement officers are often employed as directors. In fact, security management is becoming a real profession with 200 colleges giving courses, 25 offering BAs, ten offering MAs, and the University of Michigan even starting a doctorate program.
>
> ASIS's major task this year is to develop operational guidelines for the burgeoning security industry to link up with local law enforcement.

Connally noted that 80 percent of the nation's police departments have a dozen or fewer officers and could especially profit from linking up with private security:

> Police can save time and manpower by training private security to gather evidence and do preliminary investigations, become better courtroom witnesses, take crime and accident reports, carry out tedious surveillance procedures, and even giving lectures that police usually do.
>
> Large industrial plants can loan smaller departments listening devices, communications equipment, trucks, rovers, helicopters and planes. And since corporations maintain top-grade lawyers, they might provide useful legal advice on cases as well. The gains in working with private security are multiple.

Although public police officers also seek to prevent crime, a large portion of their time is devoted to enforcing laws, investigating crimes and apprehending suspects. Their presence may serve as a deterrent to crime, but they cannot be everywhere at once. The vital role played by private security in preventing crime was clearly stated 20 years ago in the preface of the Task Force Report on Private Security (*Private Security*, 1976):

> The application of the resources, technology, skills, and knowledge of the private security industry presents the best hope available for protecting the citizen who has witnessed his defenses against crime shrink to a level which leaves him virtually unprotected.
>
> Underutilized by police, all but ignored by prosecutors and the judiciary, and unknown to corrections officials, the private security professional may be the one person in this society who has the knowledge to effectively prevent crime.

In 1978 *The Police Chief*, the official publication of the International Association of Chiefs of Police (IACP), devoted an entire issue to private security. An editorial in that issue by the president of the IACP reiterated the importance of private security in relation to public law enforcement (Shook, p. 8):

> Today, more than ever, private security forces are contributing to the public safety and security. Their omnipresence in business, industry, transportation, and government relieves public police from many of the order maintenance duties that are so vital to the public safety.

Likewise, a key finding of the Hallcrest Report was the need for private security (Cunningham and Taylor, 1985, p. 275):

> Citizen fear of crime and awareness that criminal justice resources alone cannot effectively control crime has led to a growing use of individual and corporate protective measures, including private security products and services and neighborhood-based crime prevention programs. . . . Law enforcement resources have stabilized and in some areas are declining. This mandates greater cooperation with the private sector and its private security resources to jointly forge a partnership on an equal basis for crime prevention and reduction. Law enforcement can ill afford to continue isolating and, in some cases, ignoring this important resource. . . . The creative use of private security, human resources and technology may be one viable option left to control crime in our communities. . . .
>
> As long as law enforcement maintains the posture that they should bear the primary burden for protection of the community, then creative alternative solutions will be limited in the midst of dwindling public resources.

The need for cooperation between public and private officers is summed up by a Los Angeles police sergeant (Munk, 1994, p. 106): "It's like you're in a war with no weapons. . . . Our cars are outdated—some have clocked over 100,000 miles; we've got faulty equipment, a dated communications system." He described a situation when a drug-crazed teenager began attacking passengers on a public bus on his beat and it took him 20 minutes during rush hour to travel the 15 miles to the scene, another 15 minutes before backup arrived and 50 minutes before the transit police arrived. He explained, "It's not that we're lazy, but there aren't enough of us to go around."

In many jurisdictions, the police are simply overwhelmed. According to Reibstein (1994, p. 74), police detectives in California handle two and three times the number of cases they did 15 years ago. In contrast, over that same period the number of private detectives in California has tripled to about 7,500.

Yet the danger exists that a two-tiered patrol system with the police providing services in public areas and private security officers providing services for private employers could divide the rich and the poor. In addition, as noted by Sherman ("Local Police Just Aren't Enough," 1991, p. 14):

> The pitfall [in gated cities] . . . is that eventually everybody is going to be a cliff dweller. . . . They've got to stay inside their very tightly, privately secured places—their homes, their offices, their shopping centers. . . . The middle class is going to become in effect prisoners of private security. They can't leave their own safe places if they don't provide enough support for public police to make public places safe.

To avoid such a situation, given the reality that the United States is the most violent industrialized nation in the world, public/private cooperation is essential. As noted by D'Addario (1992, p. 57): "The potential for violent bloodshed in this country exceeds the likelihood of having cancer, being injured in a traffic accident, or getting divorced. . . . By working together, public and private security can reduce the bloodshed on our streets."

Public/Private Interdependence

Hertig (1993, p. 96) notes:

> [M]any people simply do not understand the connection between public and private security. While it is inaccurate to equate private security with criminal justice or law enforcement, private security often works in conjunction with criminal justice and law enforcement. For example, private security personnel are often the ones who first apprehend and question a suspected criminal.

Marx (1987, pp. 172–173) discusses five forms of "interdependence between public and private police" in undercover work:

- Joint public/private investigations.
- Public agents hiring or delegating authority to private police.
- Private interests hiring public police.
- New organizational forms in which the distinction between public and private is blurred.
- The circulation of personnel between the public and private sectors.

> Public and private officers may work together, may hire or delegate authority to each other or may move from one sector to the other.

Marx gives as an example of joint public/private investigations an FBI-IBM sting involving "perhaps the largest industrial espionage case ever in the United States," the sale of computer secrets in Silicon Valley.

Bocklet (1990, pp. 58–59) describes a joint effort between public and private police in Tacoma, Washington, where drug trafficking was a major problem at downtown intersections. Businesses banded together, taxed themselves, and hired 15 private security guards who became community service representatives (CSRs), patrolling the streets and providing escort services to those who wanted it. They also provided much valuable information about drug trafficking to the public police, serving as "extra sets of eyes and ears" (p. 58). According to an officer involved with the program: "The heavy security presence has driven the druggies out of the downtown area and a better business climate has ensued" (pp. 58–59).

To illustrate public hiring of private police, Marx (1987, p. 178) notes that in 1984: "Approximately 36,000 of the nation's 1.1 million private security guards worked for government. . . . They serve as U.S. marshals in federal courthouses, and guard military bases, nuclear facilities, NASA, and various public buildings, including city halls and public housing projects. They also provide security at airports."

Private sector hiring of public police can be seen in such efforts as trade associations and chambers of commerce cooperating in sting operations. For example: "In operation 'mod-sound' the recording industry contributed

$100,000 to an FBI investigation of pirated records and tapes" (Marx, 1987, p. 178).

New quasi-public or quasi-private organizations include the Law Enforcement Intelligence Unit (LEIU), "founded as a private organization for local and state police to share intelligence files. The private nature of the organization apparently permits the exchange of information that would not otherwise be possible by agents acting strictly in a public capacity" (Marx, 1987, p. 179). Another example is the National Auto Theft Bureau, a private, nonprofit organization that serves as a clearinghouse for law enforcement agencies seeking information on vehicle thefts.

Finally, the exchange of personnel also is occurring frequently, with people using security jobs as stepping-stones into law enforcement and law enforcement officers moonlighting or retiring to go into private security or to become security directors for corporations.

According to Burden (1989, p. 92): "The rent-a-cop business has grown steadily over the past 30 years as the fear of crime and the demand for police service have risen. Today, in some city precincts, there are more moonlighters than on-duty officers on the streets."

Potential Problems with Moonlighting

The practice of public police officers moonlighting is not without its problems. Maxwell (1993) describes a case in which a Miami Beach police officer was injured while moonlighting at a hospital. The question became, "Under what conditions does a police officer's authority cease and the officer become a private citizen able to obtain injury compensation?"

The officer, Gary Lehman, was going out the emergency room door to check the parking lot, one of his specific duties, when he slipped and his right knee gave way. The hospital contended that the officer was an agent of the city and that it should not be liable. The compensation commission, however, found the hospital liable, and the hospital appealed. The case, *Mount Sinai Hospital v. City of Miami Beach* (1988), hinged on determining if the officer was engaged in his primary responsibility as provided in Florida Statutes Section 440.091. This statute states that an injured law enforcement officer "shall be deemed to have been acting within the course of employment" when injured if the officer was discharging his/her "primary responsibility" (that is preventing or detecting crime and enforcing the law) and "was not engaged in services for which the officer was paid by a private employer."

The hospital based its case on the precedent set in *City of Hialeah v. Weber*. This case involved a moonlighting police officer working as a security guard at a lounge who was injured in apprehending individuals slashing car tires at a business across the street. The court held that the moonlighting officer was an employee of the city police department at the time of the injury and hence the city was responsible for compensating him for his injuries.

In *Mount Sinai Hospital v. City of Miami Beach*, the court described a spectrum along which such cases should be judged. At one end is a case where a moonlighting officer is "unequivocally" performing a police function, as in the case of the moonlighting lounge employee who acted to stop a crime being committed in his presence and was not performing a task for which he had been hired by his private employer. Therefore, the City of Hialeah was responsible for the compensation. At the other end of the spectrum was the case of moonlighting officer Lehman who was clearly performing a service for which he was paid by the hospital, not performing a police function. Therefore, the court upheld the ruling of the compensation commission.

Although these two cases present opposite ends of the spectrum for this specific Florida statute, the vast majority of cases are not as clear-cut, falling somewhere along the spectrum and posing much more difficulty for the courts.

To avoid such difficulties, Hamit (1994, p. 79) suggests a rethinking of how things are done:

> The very roles are being redefined by economic and social forces, and we need either to enhance the role of the private sector or to start paying police officers enough that they don't feel the need to go into business for themselves. The only business they should be concerned with is protecting and serving the public that pays them.

Mutual Advantages

The advantages of private police using public police, according to Marx (1987, p. 183), include the benefits of "the power of state agents to arrest, search, interrogate, carry weapons and use force and electronic surveillance, and gain access to otherwise protected information. Their legal liability may also be reduced or eliminated. The training, experience, skill, and backup support that public police can offer are other factors."

> Public police offer private security the power of interrogation, search, arrest and use of electronic surveillance. They may reduce or eliminate their legal liability, and they offer training, experience and backup.

In addition, Cassidy et al. (1993, p. 27) suggest: "Every private security company should act as a liaison with law enforcement agencies to procure crime statistics in its area. With this information, the security professional can better evaluate crime trends and adjust security budgets to fit needs."

The advantages of public police using private police, says Marx (1987, p. 183), include: "Information. Sworn agents cannot be everywhere and they face restrictions on access to private places. . . . But private agents, operating on private property and in contexts where persons appear voluntarily, are granted wide authority to carry out searches, to keep people under surveillance, and to collect and distribute extensive personal information." In addition: "Private police vastly extend surveillance and reduce demands on public police. In addition . . . they may offer public police a way to get things done that the former are prohibited from doing," such as interrogating without giving the Miranda warning and conducting searches and seizures without warrants. Private police are not bound by the **Exclusionary Rule,** which makes inadmissible any evidence obtained by means violating a person's constitutional rights.

> Private security officers offer the public police information, access to private places and extended surveillance and coverage. In addition, they are not bound by the Exclusionary Rule, so can question without giving the Miranda warning and can search without a warrant.

In fact, employees' obligations to their employees may sometimes allow public police greater freedom in their investigations. In *United States v. Dockery* (1984), for example, this was true.

A bank employee who was suspected of embezzlement submitted to questioning by FBI agents under instructions from her employer. Her attorney later argued that her confession should be barred. The U.S. Court of Appeals for the 8th Circuit disagreed. It observed that the statements had been made voluntarily, and the suspect had consented to the interview as part of her obligation to her employer.

Although not as rigidly controlled as public police, private security officers must still respect the rights of others. Failure to do so can and often does result in civil lawsuits, as discussed in the next chapter.

Areas Where Private Security Can Help Public Police

As noted by West (1993, p. 54): "State and local law enforcement authorities, confronted with rising costs and declining revenues, are being forced to find less costly ways to provide the necessary public safety services. The silver lining to this dark cloud is a growing market niche for private sector security providers." West gives as an example the extremely time-consuming law enforcement function of arresting shoplifters. Through an arrangement with the New York City Police Department, security personnel were provided authority to undertake surveillance, arrest and transport suspects, conduct record checks and enter the information into a computer terminal, greatly reducing the time the law enforcement officers needed to spend on the case. A similar situation existed in San Diego. After security personnel were given expanded authority to deal with shoplifters, the San Diego police officer's time involvement went from more than two hours to less than 30 minutes.

One area that police seem willing to let private security personnel handle is "economic crime." Crimes such as shoplifting, employee theft and pilferage, and credit card and check fraud are usually a low priority with public police and are usually well developed by the time the police are notified. In addition, management is usually more interested in the deterrent value of prosecution and in plea bargaining than in a conviction. Cunningham and Taylor (1985, p. 245) comment on this area: "Since employee theft is the largest single problem in business and institutions and is resolved largely through private justice systems, private security removes a tremendous burden from the public criminal justice system and contributes greatly to crime prevention, detection, and deterrence."

Bottom (1986, p. 13), reporting on the Hallcrest survey of police attitudes on transferring police responsibilities to private security companies, says: "In general, police executives said yes, police will be happy to yield burglar alarm response (57 percent); incident report completion for insurance purposes (68 percent); preliminary investigation (40 percent); and misdemeanor incident reports (45 percent)."

Trojanowicz and Bucqueroux (1990, p. 131) note the "dramatic and far-reaching change, for good or ill, taking place during this past decade . . . the continued and increasing privatization of public justice. . . . Almost invisibly, private for-profit and nonprofit corporations have been assuming roles that were once almost exclusively the province of the public criminal justice system."

An article, "Private Security Gets the Call" (1993, p. 3), reports:

> They will soon ride buses in Milwaukee County, Wis., to stem attacks on drivers. They will augment police patrols in a Chicago neighborhood where residents say street crime is on the rise and police are understaffed. And next month, they will provide protection for a New Jersey town that disbanded its four-officer police department last year after the police chief and another officer were implicated in drug-related misconduct.
>
> "They" are private security guards who are being drafted into service by localities seeking to increase the level of protection in their towns or simply trying to save a buck in fiscally austere times.

"Private security professionals are perfectly positioned to share the burdens of law enforcement" (Arbetter, 1994, p. 52).

Bocklet (1990, p. 54) identifies several areas in which private security officers can complement the efforts of the public police:

> [T]hey [private security officers] dispose of countless incidents meeting the statutory definition of crime that would otherwise inundate the police and criminal justice resources. Some areas of cooperation are burglar alarm response, investigation of internal theft and economic crimes, protecting VIPs and executives, terrorism countermeasures, moving hazardous materials, and crowd and traffic control for public events.

Another set of services is suggested by Hoffmann (1994, p. 320): "We have seen the recent use of private labs testing police seized evidence, private companies handling applicant screening, civilian fingerprint and handwriting experts and guards taking the place of commissioned law enforcement officers inside courthouses, government buildings and airports."

Cunningham et al. (1991, p. 2) list the following services as likely candidates for **privatization,** that is, duties normally performed by sworn personnel (e.g., police officers) being performed by others, often private security officers:

- Public building security;
- Parking enforcement;
- Patrolling of public parks;
- Animal control;
- Special event security;
- Funeral escorts;
- Court security;
- Prisoner transport;
- Public housing development patrol.

Mangan and Shanahan (1990, p. 18) suggest: "Private security has emerged as a major player in the safeguarding of Americans and their property."

Another area where private security has had an impact is in helping shelters for the homeless. According to Beattie (1994, p. 50): "Private security can play a role in helping shelters serve their intended purpose as safe havens, benefiting both the residents and those who must adjust to them as neighbors." Beattie describes examples of security professionals running secure, mostly crime-free lodging for the homeless such as The Housing Enterprises for the Less Privileged (HELP) Corporation's Morris Avenue and Crotona Park shelters in the New York Bronx. Beattie (p. 59) suggests: "Private security providers can make an important contribution by adapting their protection expertise to meet the unique demands of these necessary community facilities."

Yet another area in which private security is providing vital services is in the alarm industry. The false alarm problem is of immense proportions, with 98 percent of all responses or an expected 40 million false alarm responses per year expected by 1995 (Jones, 1991, p. 24). Such use of public police officers is ineffective and expensive. As noted by Jones (p. 24): "The alarm industry has focused on the wrong problem. The real problem is not 'false alarms': it is 'false alarm relay.' " Although considered synonymous for years, it is important to view them as two separate functions (Jones, p. 24):

- False alarms evolve from interaction between the customer premises and the monitoring station.
- False alarm relays evolve from interaction between the monitoring station and the emergency response services (ERS).

Many systems are available to reduce false alarm relays, including sound-activated listen-in systems allowing the monitoring station to listen to sounds from the protected site when an alarm has been received. Such a listen-in feature can provide valuable information such as if a weapon is being used or a hostage situation has developed.

The private policing upsurge affects not just the public police, but all areas of the criminal justice system. As noted by Trojanowicz and Bucqueroux (1990, p. 131):

> In addition to for-profit prisons that house adults, we are also seeing a tremendous surge in the number of private initiatives that handle juvenile offenders. . . . Litigants in civil suits can now choose to hire a private rent-a-judge-and-jury to settle claims, virtually bypassing the public court.

Although numerous areas are open to "privatization," the hesitancy expressed by Hamit (1994, p. 77) should be considered: "What troubles me is the question of whether or not security personnel should be assuming police duties, especially without proper compensation, training or authority."

In fact, in many instances a joint effort between private security and the public police is required to accomplish the desired result.

PARTNERSHIPS IN ACTION

As noted by Patterson (1995, p. 33):

> The relationship between private security and law enforcement has experienced a radical evolution that has taken form in public and private security initiatives. . . . Parallel objectives, commonality of threat, and crossover of professional career tracks have paved the road for alliance between private security and law enforcement.

Patterson cites several instances of "creative alliances." These include creating security teams to patrol major labor relations incidents, rescue victims of natural disasters, patrol churches, conduct government security-clearance background investigations and work with state and local governments and educational institutions to develop instructional programs such as certificate programs in security and corrections.

In Fresno, California, the police department was 338 officers below the level recommended by the California Peace Officers' Standards and Training Commission (**POST Commission**). They also had a big prostitution problem. To combat this problem, they enlisted the support of private security firms, with success. As suggested by West (1994, p. 88):

> At a time when crime is clearly escalating, most cities are struggling to find the answers to effectively impact it. Since it appears no additional revenue is forthcoming, government officials must seek alternative strategies if they ever hope to get a handle on crime. Police officials would be well served to explore the benefits of police-private security partnerships. The alliances forged in Fresno provide significant evidence that these arrangements can be an effective strategy in curbing crime.

Philadelphia's Security Watch, instituted in 1991, placed 3,000 security officers under the jurisdiction of the Central Police Division to be their eyes and ears. According to Zappile (1991, p. 23):

> With the cooperation and support of all those in the private security industry in central Philadelphia, tangible gains have been made in reducing violent crime, decreasing calls for service involving order-maintenance problems, and

identifying and eliminating repeat unfounded alarms. The private security sector and the Philadelphia Police Department have formed a true partnership to establish and maintain order in the Center City area.

Cooney (1991) describes a program in Tucson, Arizona, where 88-Crime stoppers has developed a working relationship between public law enforcement and the private sector. Their program consistently ranks as one of the top ten Crime Stoppers programs in the world, in large part because of the support of private security agencies such as Pinkerton's, whose support was described as "vital to the program" (p. 36).

Those communities that have instituted community policing are likely to be receptive to using the services of private security. As noted by Kolpacki (1994, p. 47):

> Community policing is public law enforcement's way of mirroring the private security industry. Like private security, community policing is proactive crime prevention that is accountable to the customer. The similar goal creates the opportunity for a cooperative program between the private and public sectors that would benefit both sectors as well as the community. Police forces, which are overburdened and understaffed, would be able to share some of their responsibilities with security officers, and the police department's resources would help the security professional better protect his or her client, as well as open up a new market.

Kolpacki (p. 49) describes several ways in which public and private police might work together and concludes:

> Realizing that the need for cooperative programs between the public and private sectors exists is the first step toward improved crime prevention and control. Toward this end, community policing programs should be expanded to include the resources of private security. Once this is done, responsibilities such as alarm response, workplace drugs, theft prevention, and disaster preparedness can be put into the hands of private security professionals for more effective handling.

Many segments of the population, including police chiefs, business managers and government officials, believe that services provided by the private sector are more efficient, more effective and less costly. Because of this, privatization of services is likely to continue to expand.

Patterson (1995, p. 35) notes: "Whether municipal or global, public and private security initiatives represent a win-win situation. . . . Public and private security initiatives will continue to be the leading edge of the industry well into the next decade.

SUMMARY

Private security officers and police officers have both similarities and differences. They both may wear uniforms and badges, are trained in compelling obedience and are apt to be sued. Both also seek to prevent crime and to apprehend criminals, with private security focusing efforts more on prevention than apprehension.

Private security officers differ from public police officers in that private security officers operate in a profit-oriented enterprise serving specific private clients to prevent crime, protect assets and reduce losses and to regulate noncriminal conduct not under the authority of law enforcement. They are given their authority by their private employers. Public police officers, in contrast, operate in a nonprofit, governmental enterprise serving the general public to combat crime, enforce laws and apprehend offenders. They have statutory authority.

The amount of authority and the restrictions placed on both also differ. For example, private security officers usually have no more powers than private citizens. As citizens, they have the power to arrest, to investigate, to carry weapons, to defend themselves and to defend their property or property entrusted to their care. They can deny access to unauthorized individuals into their employers' business or company, and they can enforce all rules and regulations established by their employers. They can also search employees and question them without giving the Miranda warning in most states.

Private security officers cannot invade another's privacy, electronically eavesdrop, trespass or, in some jurisdictions, wear a uniform or badge that closely resembles that of a public police officer.

There are now 2½ times as many people employed in private security as there are public police. Their roles are complementary. They may work together, may hire or delegate authority to each other or may move from one sector to the other. Public police offer private security the power of interrogation, search, arrest and use of electronic surveillance. They may reduce or eliminate their legal liability, and they offer training, experience and backup. Private security officers offer the public police information, access to private places and extended surveillance and coverage. In addition, they are not bound by the Exclusionary Rule, so can question without giving the Miranda warning and can search without a warrant.

✔ Application

1. The Metropolitan Transit Commission has decided to hire the Action Security Company to furnish private security officers on their buses because of frequent attacks on their drivers and the armed robbery of some of their riders. They need about 68 security officers to give the transit commission adequate policing. The officers of Action Security Company are reluctant to sign a contract unless it states that they will be sworn in as either city reserve police officers or as deputy sheriffs. What would be the advantages or disadvantages of the Action officers' request were it suitable to take this course of action? Would granting the company's request affect the officers' authority or power?

Discussion Questions

1. What are the advantages and disadvantages of private security officers not being restricted by the U.S. Constitution (not having to give the Miranda warning, for instance)?
2. How do private security officers assist public police officers in your community? Vice versa?
3. Should the private police be trained by the public police in some aspects of handling unruly individuals? Discuss both the positive and negative aspects of such training.
4. Do you feel police officers should be allowed to moonlight as private security providers? Why or why not?
5. Who do you feel has more status, private or public officers? Why? Do you foresee a change in status for either group in the future?

References

Arbetter, Lisa. "A Commitment to Cooperation." *Security Management,* January 1994, pp. 52–54.

Bayley, David H. "Foreword." In *Private Policing,* by Clifford D. Shearing and Philip C. Stenning, eds. Beverly Hills, CA: Sage Publications, 1987, pp. 6–8.

Beattie, Henry J. "Security's Helping Hand." *Security Management,* November 1994, pp. 50–59.

Bennett, Wayne W. and Hess, Kären M. *Management and Supervision in Law Enforcement.* 2nd ed. St. Paul, MN: West Publishing Company, 1996.

Bocklet, Richard. "Police-Private Security Cooperation." *Law and Order.* December 1990, pp. 54–59.

Bottom, Norman R., Jr. "Privatization: Lessons of the Hallcrest Report." *Law Enforcement News,* June 23, 1986, pp. 13, 15.

Burden, Ordway P. "Rent-a-Cop Business Is Booming." *Law and Order,* August 1989, pp. 92–94.

Cain, Candy M.; Drew, Edward J., Jr.; Guyet, Allan R.; and Maxwell, David A. "No Agency Is an Island." *Security Management,* December 1993, pp. 25–26.

Cassidy, Kevin A.; Brandes, Robert; and LeVeglia, Anthony J. "Finding Common Grounds." *Security Management,* December 1993, pp. 27–28.

Cooney, Caroline M. "Hotline to Preventing Crime." *Security Management,* September 1991, pp. 54–58.

Cunningham, William C.; Strauchs, John J.; and Van Meter, Clifford W. *Private Security: Patterns and Trends.* Washington, DC: National Institute of Justice Research in Brief, August 1991.

Cunningham, W. C. and Taylor, T. H. *The Hallcrest Report: Private Security and Police in America.* Portland, OR: Chancellor Press, 1985.

D'Addario, Francis. "The Cooperative Fight Against Violent Crime." *Security Management,* June 1992, pp. 57–60.

Hamit, Francis. "A Corporate Culture for Security." *Security Technology and Design,* September 1994, pp. 97–98.

Hamit, Francis. "Cops for Hire: Where Is the Line Between Private Enterprise and Government?" *Security Technology and Design,* October 1994, pp. 77–79.

Hertig, Christopher A. "What Course Should We Take?" *Security Management,* September 1991, pp. 216–218.

Hertig, Christopher A. "Who Are the Forgotten Soldiers?" *Security Management,* February 1993, pp. 95–96.

Hoffman, John W. "Court Says No to Private Police Force." *Law and Order,* January 1994, pp. 320–321.

Jones, Lee A. "The Alarm Industry: Friend or Foe to Police Officers?" *The Police Chief,* August 1991, pp. 24–28.

Kolpacki, Thomas A. "Neighborhood Watch." *Security Management,* November 1994, pp. 47–49.

"Local Police Just Aren't Enough." *Law Enforcement News,* November 30, 1991, p. 1, 14.

Mangan, Terence J. and Shanahan, Michael G. "Public Law Enforcement/Private Security: A New Partnership?" *FBI Law Enforcement Bulletin,* January 1990, pp. 18–22.

Marx, Gary T. "The Interweaving of Public and Private Police in Undercover Work." In *Private Policing,* by Clifford D. Shearing and Philip C. Stenning, eds. Beverly Hills, CA: Sage Publications, 1987, pp. 172–193.

Maxwell, David A. *Private Security Law: Case Studies.* Stoneham, MA: Butterworth-Heinemann, 1993.

Munk, Nina. "Rent-a-Cops." *Forbes,* October 10, 1994, pp. 104–106.

Patterson, Julien. "Forging Creative Alliances." *Security Management,* January 1995, pp. 33–35.

Private Security. Report of the Task Force on Private Security, National Advisory Commission on Criminal Justice Standards and Goals. Washington, DC: U.S. Government Printing Office, 1976.

"Private Security Gets the Call." *Law Enforcement News,* May 15, 1993, pp. 3, 10.

Reibstein, Larry. "The Prying Game Under New Rules." *Newsweek,* September 5, 1994, pp. 72–74.

Remesch, Kimberly A. "Shared Responsibility." *Police,* November 1989, pp. 32–35, 67.

Shearing, Clifford D.; Farnell, M.; and Stenning, Philip C. *Contract Security in Ontario.* University of Toronto: Centre for Criminology, 1980.

Shearing, Clifford D. and Stenning, Philip C. "Reframing Policing." In *Private Policing,* by Clifford D. Shearing and Philip C. Stenning, eds. Beverly Hills, CA: Sage Publications, 1987, pp. 9–18.

Shook, H. C. "Police and Private Security." *The Police Chief,* June 1978, p. 8.

Trojanowicz, Robert and Bucqueroux, Bonnie. "The Privatization of Public Justice: What Will It Mean to Police?" *The Police Chief,* October 1990, pp. 131–135.

United Way Strategic Institute. "Nine Forces Reshaping America." Bethesda, MD: World Future Society, 1989.

West, Marty L. "Get a Piece of the Privatization Pie." *Security Management,* March 1993, pp. 54–60.

West, Marty L. "Police and Private Security: Combined Efforts Can Decrease Crime." *Law and Order,* July 1994, pp. 86–88.

Zappile, R. "Philadelphia Implements Security Watch." *The Police Chief,* August 1991, pp. 22–23.

Cases

Bowman v. State, 468 N.E.2d 1064 (Ind. App. 1984)

City of Hialeah v. Weber, 491 So.2d 1204 (Fla. App. 1986)

Mount Sinai Hosp. v. City of Miami Beach, 523 So.2d 722 (Fla. App. 1988)

National Labor Relations Board v. St. Vincent's Hosp., 729 F.2d 730 (1984)

United States v. Dockery, 736 F.2d 1232 (1984)

CHAPTER 4

LEGAL LIABILITY

DO YOU KNOW

- How laws may be classified?
- How a crime differs from a tort?
- What a tort is?
- What a nondelegable duty is?
- How civil law is further categorized?
- What the elements of negligent liability are?
- For what actions security officers are most frequently sued?
- What Section 1983 of the United States Code, Title 43, the Civil Rights Act, establishes and how it might affect private security?
- How civil liability can be reduced?
- What the Six-Layered Liability Protection System includes?

CAN YOU DEFINE THESE TERMS?

armed personnel
assault
battery
civil liability
civil offense
collective deep pocket
crime
criminal offense
defamation
deposition
excessive force
false imprisonment
foreseeable danger
intentional infliction of emotional distress
intentional wrong
interrogatories
invasion of privacy
negligence
nondelegable duty
plaintiff
precedents
proximate result
punitive damages
reasonable care
respondent superior
restitution
Section 1983
strict liability
substantive damages
tort
vicarious liability

INTRODUCTION

Before looking at specific goals and responsibilities of the private security professional, it is important to understand the restrictions under which security personnel must function. They must know what civil lawsuits to protect themselves against and how to do so most effectively.

Civil liability has become of increasing concern in the private security profession. As noted in the Hallcrest Report II (Cunningham et al., 1990, pp. 33–34):

> Perhaps the largest indirect cost of economic crime has been the increase in civil litigation and damage awards over the past 20 years. This litigation usually claims inadequate or improperly used security to protect customers, employees, tenants, and the public from crimes and injuries. Most often these cases involve inadequate security at apartments and condominiums; shopping malls, convenience and other retail stores; hotels, motels, and restaurants; health care and education institutions; office buildings; and the premises of other business or government facilities.

One expert has estimated that U.S. corporations pay in excess of $20 billion annually to litigation lawyers (Allison, 1990, p. 166). The Hallcrest Report II goes on to note (p. 36): "All indications point to more security-related lawsuits and more $11 million-plus awards than ever before." In addition, the report says:

> Growing concern over lawsuits was expressed by virtually all of the corporate and contract security managers in the Hallcrest 1989 reconnaissance interviews. . . . [The concern was] manifest in a variety of security management issues such as hiring, training, equipment (armed vs. unarmed), personnel deployment, crime incident response, supervision, and security systems (locking, lighting, fencing, access control, etc.).

Schnabolk (1983) suggests not only that lawsuits have increased, but that judicial and legislative sanctions against the security industry have increased as well. He gives several reasons for this increase:

- The exceptional growth of the industry.
- The rising expectations of the public.
- The quality of security services.
- The increase in the number of new laws and lawyers.
- The availability of liability insurance.
- The increased sophistication of individuals regarding legal matters and their rights.

Taitz (1990, pp. 126) suggests additional reasons for the dramatic increase in lawsuits involving private security:

- The significant rise in the number of persons working in the security field and the increase in the variety of jobs performed by security personnel resulting in an increase in both the frequency of security/citizen contacts and the potential for negative security/citizen interactions.
- The tendency to hold security personnel more responsible for their behavior than the average individual. Unlike civilians, security officers are presumed and expected to know the law, to understand its provisions, and good intentions notwithstanding, to behave accordingly.

This chapter begins with a discussion of the types of law and liability governing all citizens, including private security personnel. Next the elements of negligent liability and the most commonly encountered lawsuits are discussed.

This is followed by a discussion of how liability might be reduced, including tightening hiring practices, providing effective training, establishing clear procedures for the use of force and the use of firearms, using clear contracts and carrying adequate insurance. The chapter concludes with some common defenses against charges and a brief discussion of how to survive a lawsuit.

LAW AND LIABILITY IN THE UNITED STATES

The colonists brought with them from England the common law, which remains the basis of law in the United States. This was unwritten law which eventually evolved into written laws. Laws are also classified by the offense committed, that is, criminal or civil. A **criminal offense** is an offense against the state or a public offense; a **civil offense** is an offense against a private party. Finally, law can be classified by where it originates: constitutional law from the numerous state constitutions and the federal Constitution; statutory law, referring to laws passed by federal or state legislatures and case law, originating in specific cases that serve as **precedents.** Oran (1985, p. 323) defines a precedent as:

> A court decision on a question of law that gives authority or direction on how to decide a similar question of law in a later case with similar facts. The American court system is based on judges making decisions supported by past precedent rather than by unsupported logic.

Laws may be classified in the following ways:

- Type—written or common law
- Source—constitution, statutory, case
- Parties involved—public, private
- Offense—criminal, civil

The most common distinction, however, is between criminal and civil law.

Criminal law deals with offenses against the public, called *crimes,* and fixes punishments for them. Civil law, in contrast, deals with offenses against individuals, called *torts*. It seeks **restitution** for the victim of the crime, that is, payment of some form.

A **crime** is a wrong against the public which the state prosecutes and which seeks punishment. Criminal intent is required. A **tort** is a private wrong where an individual sues seeking restitution. Intent is not necessary.

An offense may be both a crime and a tort. For example, if one person strikes another person, the assailant can be charged with the crime of assault and also sued for the tort of assault.

Security officers may be called upon to investigate crimes, as discussed later. They may also be charged with crimes if they break the law.

The focus of this chapter is on the **civil liability** of security officers, their agencies and their employers.

Civil actions may be brought against any private security personnel who commit an unlawful action against another person. Often, the officer's employer is sued as well as the officer.

In *Granite Construction Corp. v. Superior Court of Fresno* (1983), for example, a California court held that the term *person* includes corporations and that therefore a corporation *can* be prosecuted for manslaughter.

In addition, as noted by Schnabolk (1983), a "revolutionary theory" affecting private security is the "concept of a nondelegable duty":

> Under the principles of agency law, an independent contractor relationship relieves the one who hired the independent contractors of liability because no control is exercised over the activities of the contractor. Thus, a motel owner, for example, could employ a security agency to protect the motel. If an incident occurred that resulted in an injury, the motel owner would claim he/she was not responsible for the injury because the duty to provide protection had been given to the guard service. Under the concept of a nondelegable duty, however, the motel owner would remain liable. Some duties rightfully belong to certain individuals, according to the courts, and the law will not permit these individuals to escape liability by delegating the duty to someone else. The law allows a delegation of authority, but not of responsibility for the performance of a legal duty.

> A **nondelegable duty** is one for which authority can be given to another person, but responsibility cannot. Civil liability remains with the person who has the legal duty to act.

Closely related to nondelegable duty is the concept of vicarious liability.

Vicarious Liability

Oran (1985, p. 319) defines **vicarious liability** as "the legal responsibility for the acts of another person because of some relationship with that person, for example, the liability of an employer for the acts of an employee."

Using the authority of vicarious liability, it has become common for individuals to sue not only individual security officers, but their supervisors and the institution for which they work. Suing everyone remotely associated with the case creates what is often referred to as a **collective deep pocket** from which can be extracted astronomical judgments.

Categories of Civil Offenses

> Civil law is further divided into three categories: strict liability, intentional wrongs and negligence.

Strict liability refers to instances when the person is held liable to the injured party even though the person may not have knowingly done anything wrong. Strict liability, also called liability without fault, usually involves ultra-hazardous activities such as using explosives or keeping wild animals as pets. Although this area is seldom a problem for private security, it may become more so as high-tech equipment is used to compel compliance with orders. Any injuries resulting from such high-tech equipment might fall into this category.

Intentional wrong, as the name implies, is an illegal act committed on purpose. Remember that the same illegal act might be both a criminal and a civil offense. Intentional civil wrongs (torts) include assault, battery, false imprisonment, false arrest, malicious prosecution, intentional infliction of emotional distress, trespass, illegal electronic surveillance, invasion of privacy and defamation.

Negligence, the third category of civil charges, is the most frequently brought charge. Basically, negligence is a failure to use due care to prevent foreseeable injury that results in damages. Civil negligence torts include negligence in hiring/selection, training, supervising, retraining; negligence in operating a motor vehicle; failure to protect; use of force.

The basic ingredients required for a civil lawsuit, according to Meadows (1991, p. 60), are as follows: "To establish a claim for inadequate security, the plaintiff must prove that the business had a duty or standard of care to protect, that there was a breach of this duty and a failure to exercise care, and that harm was caused by such failure."

Elements of Negligent Liability

Although specific state statutes regarding negligent liability may vary from state to state, five basic elements are well established.

The elements of negligent liability include:

- Existence of some duty owed.
- Foreseeable likelihood of the incident occurring.
- Failure to meet a reasonable standard of care.
- Proximate results—the injury resulted from the failure to protect.
- Damages.

Duty to Protect or Duty Owed

Employers have a "duty to protect" their employees and the public. If an employer hires an employee who injures others, the employer and the company may be sued for negligent hiring and/or negligent retention. As noted by Ingber (1993, p. 63): "Employer liability flows from the established legal doctrine of master/servant liability, also known as **respondent superior,** which holds the employer liable for wrongful acts or negligence by an employee acting within the scope of his or her duties or in the employer's interest."

Respondent superior is a concept that implies that premises owners can't delegate their responsibility. Simply because an employer hires a security officer does not relieve the employer of responsibility.

In fact, according to Dunn (1991, p. 67): "common law holds that employers owed their employees a duty to provide a safe place in which to work."

This concept of duty owed is illustrated in *Brown v. Jewel Companies, Inc.* (1988), described by Maxwell (1993, pp. 2–4). This case involved a combination grocery and drug store in a mall in Iowa. The owners hired security guards to protect against shoplifting. On April 7, 1987, a woman was leaving this store when a suspected shoplifter fleeing from a guard knocked her through a door and onto the sidewalk. As she lay there, the pursuing guard kicked or stepped on her foot, further injuring her. The injured woman, the **plaintiff,** sued on the grounds that the defendants were negligent and violated their duty to protect because the security guard:

- Failed to restrain the suspect;
- Failed to block the suspect's path to the exit;
- Pursued the suspect when he knew or should have known that customers would thereby be endangered;
- Failed to avoid plaintiff's foot;
- Failed to apprehend the suspect at a place where her flight would not jeopardize other persons on the store premises.

In addition, the defendants failed to properly train their security guard in the restraint and pursuit of suspected shoplifters.

The court ruled that the guard did not err in pursuing the suspect and that to have a policy against such pursuit would encourage shoplifting. Where the guard did fail to take due care was in causing further injury to the plaintiff.

Foreseeable Danger

Foreseeable danger refers to knowing a problem is likely to occur. For example, if a number of attacks have taken place in a certain parking lot, it is foreseeable that more might occur. Steps must be taken to reduce the likelihood, or the owner and security officers responsible for the area may be sued if another incident occurs. In some instances a plaintiff's attorney has won a suit by citing crime statistics about the area in question.

Because foreseeable danger is important to prove in any civil liability case, as noted by Somerson (1991, p. 45): "Contract security companies also have a moral and ethical obligation to provide their clients with written warnings of dangerous situations."

Reasonable Standard of Care

Reasonable care, according to Oran (1985, p. 254), is "that degree of care a person of ordinary prudence would exercise in similar circumstances." This has also been called standard of care. Some would say it could be called using simple common sense. Taitz (1990, p. 127) lists several questions that might indicate if reasonable care *has* been taken:

- How would other people view your behavior, your maintenance, your security programs, the number of guards you have, the number of rooms and acreage covered?
- What kinds of programs do you have?
- How well are your guards trained?
- What kind of communication system do you have?

In some industries, standards have been established that can provide guidance as to what would constitute reasonable care.

Proximate Result

Proximate result means the injury must have been the result of the negligence or failure in the duty to protect. During the 34th Annual American Society for Industrial Security Seminar held in Boston in 1988, the speaker, Mark Rosen, explained that if a store is sued for false arrest and the arrest was made by one of the store's employees, obviously the offense, the arrest, was the result of the employee's actions. If, on the other hand, a police officer happened to be on the premises and he arrested someone who was shopping in the store, it would be hard to prove a connection between any injury suffered from that arrest and the store's responsibility.

Damages

The plaintiff must also prove actual damages suffered, either physical, emotional or financial, or that he or she incurred medical expenses. It is this area that determines the amount of any settlement made. Damages are of two types: substantive and punitive. **Substantive damages** relate to actual damages a judge or jury feels the plaintiff is entitled to. **Punitive damages,** on the other hand, are awards made to punish a defendant who is deemed to have behaved in such an abhorrent manner that an example must be made to keep others from acting in a similar way. These awards are often astronomical.

Security managers and those they employ must be aware of those actions that are most likely to put them at risk of a civil lawsuit or criminal charges.

Common Civil Lawsuits Brought against Private Security

> The most common civil suits brought against private security are for assault, battery, false imprisonment, defamation, intentional infliction of emotional distress, invasion of privacy and negligence.

Assault is an intentional act causing reasonable apprehension of physical harm in the mind of another. An example is threatening someone, with or without a weapon, into obeying your demands.

Battery is the unconsented, offensive touching of another person, either directly or indirectly. An example is touching a person or his/her clothing in an angry or rude manner. Use of bodily force should be avoided whenever possible. At times, however, security officers may have to use force to defend themselves or others from serious bodily harm.

False imprisonment is unreasonably restraining another person using physical or psychological means to deny that person freedom of movement. An example is requiring someone to remain in a room while the police are being called. If a person *is* detained, there must be reasonable grounds to believe that a crime was committed and that the person being detained actually committed it. *Mere suspicion is not enough*.

Defamation is injuring a person's reputation, such as by falsely inferring, by either words or conduct, in front of a third disinterested party, that a person committed a crime. An example is to falsely accuse someone of shoplifting in front of friends or to falsely accuse an employee of pilferage in front of co-workers or visitors.

Intentional infliction of emotional distress refers to outrageous or grossly reckless conduct intended to and highly likely to cause a severe emotional reaction. An example is to threaten to have an employee fired because he/she is suspected of stealing.

Invasion of privacy refers to an unreasonable, unconsented intrusion into the personal affairs or property of a person. An example would be searching an employee's personal property outside of search guidelines established by the employer.

Negligence occurs when a person has a duty to act reasonably but fails to do so and, as a result, someone is injured. An example is failing to correct a dangerous situation on the premises or failing to give assistance to an employee in distress.

Negligence suits are common, as illustrated in the following cases. These early cases have been, and in many cases continue to be, significant to the private security profession by providing early indications and direction as to how the courts would perceive private security's expanding role and responsibilities as well as the general standards to which the profession would likely be held and judged. It is too early to judge the significance of more recent cases in providing general direction for avoiding liability. More recent cases will be presented, however, throughout the remainder of this text.

Taylor v. Centennial Bowl, Inc. (1966). The plaintiff was attacked in a bowling alley's parking lot. Earlier in the evening, while she was in a cocktail lounge on the premises, a man had been bothering her, and she had asked the bouncer to keep him away from her. When the business closed for the evening, the bouncer warned her not to go out to her car because the man was in the parking lot. The plaintiff left anyway and was attacked by the man. The court held that the proprietor's knowledge of a threat of harm gave rise to a duty to take positive action to prevent the attack. A warning alone was not sufficient.

Kline v. 1500 Massachusetts Avenue Corp. (1970). The plaintiff was assaulted and robbed in the hallway outside her apartment. The premises had been the site of an increasing number of criminal attacks during the years of the plaintiff's residency, but despite this clear trend, the owner/landlord made no effort to maintain or continue the security devices that had been in place when the tenant moved in. The court found the landlord liable for the injuries suffered in the criminal attack.

Picco v. Ford's Diner, Inc. (1971). The plaintiff in this case presented no evidence of prior criminal acts on the premises. The plaintiff, a customer at the diner, was assaulted in an unlighted parking lot at the diner's rear. The court held that it is common knowledge that lighting an area during nighttime hours deters criminal activity. Therefore, the proprietor was found liable, even though no prior criminal acts had occurred on the premises.

Atamian v. Supermarkets General Corp. (1976). Three men raped the plaintiff in a grocery store parking lot. Prior to the rape, five assaults had occurred on the premises, and the store had employed a security guard. However, the court reasoned that where a proprietor has knowledge of previous criminal attacks on its premises, a security guard might not be enough. The proprietor has the duty to ensure adequate lighting and other preventive measures to protect customers from criminal assaults. Trying to give content to the nebulous standard of "reasonable care" is, at best, difficult and often impossible.

Trentacost, Florence v. Brussel, Dr. Nathan T. (1980). A tenant was robbed and beaten in the unlocked hallway of her apartment. The court held that the landlord/tenant relationship carries with it an implied warranty that the premises will be safe, even without requiring proof of notice of dangerous neighborhood conditions.

Sorichetti v. City of New York (1984). A New York Court of Appeals held that the failure to provide adequate police protection by a government unit *is* a basis for liability. The defendants had a reasonable duty to provide adequate protection, especially because the plaintiff had notified them she had been threatened and assaulted. The court awarded the plaintiff $2 million in damages.

Meyers v. Ramada Inn of Columbus (1984). An Ohio court held that hotel owners *can* be held liable for any injuries a guest suffers as a result of a criminal assault. However, the court stated that the guest must first demonstrate that the defendant should have anticipated the assault.

Pittard v. Four Seasons Motor Inn Inc. (1984). A New Mexico court held that a hotel *can* be held liable if one of its employees assaults a guest, provided the injured party could demonstrate that the hotel had notice of similar past conduct by the employee in question.

Kolosky v. Winn Dixie Stores, Inc. (1985). A Florida court awarded $80,000 to a woman who was knocked to the floor while at a supermarket and injured by an unruly customer. The court observed that a supermarket has an obligation to take all necessary steps to ensure the security and safety of its customers.

THE CIVIL RIGHTS ACT—SECTION 1983

In 1871, following the Civil War, the United States passed United States Code, Title 42, Section 1983, the Civil Rights Act, which states:

> Every person who, under color of any statute, ordinance, regulation, custom, or usage, of any State or Territory, subjects or causes to be subjected any citizens of the United States or other person within the jurisdiction thereof to the deprivation of any rights, privileges, or immunities secured by the Constitution and laws, shall be liable to the party injured in an action at law, suit in equity, or other proper proceeding for redress.

Section 1983 of the United States Code, Title 42, the Civil Rights Act, says that anyone acting under the authority of local or state law who violates another person's constitutional rights—even though they are upholding a law—can be sued.

According to Rosen (1988): "The courts have been holding fairly consistently until recently that private entities, i.e., shopping centers, retail stores . . . are not legitimate defendants in a 1983 action. There is a case on this issue as to whether or not a private entity, in this case, a retailer, whose security personnel are commissioned as special police officers can be sued under section 1983."

Note the use of the phrase "until recently." This is being challenged in several instances and should be recognized by those officers granted limited police powers while working in partnerships with the public police, as discussed in the last chapter.

The Use of Force

Security officers are sometimes required to use force to fulfill their responsibilities—for example, ejecting a disorderly intoxicated person from the premises. The amount of force allowable is restricted by the amount of resistance encountered and can be envisioned as being on a continuum. Connor (1991, p. 30) suggests that this continuum includes three varieties of force:

- No force—used with a cooperative person.
- Ordinary force—used with a person who resists.
- Extra-ordinary force—used with a person who is assaultive.

Figure 4–1 illustrates the use of force continuum.

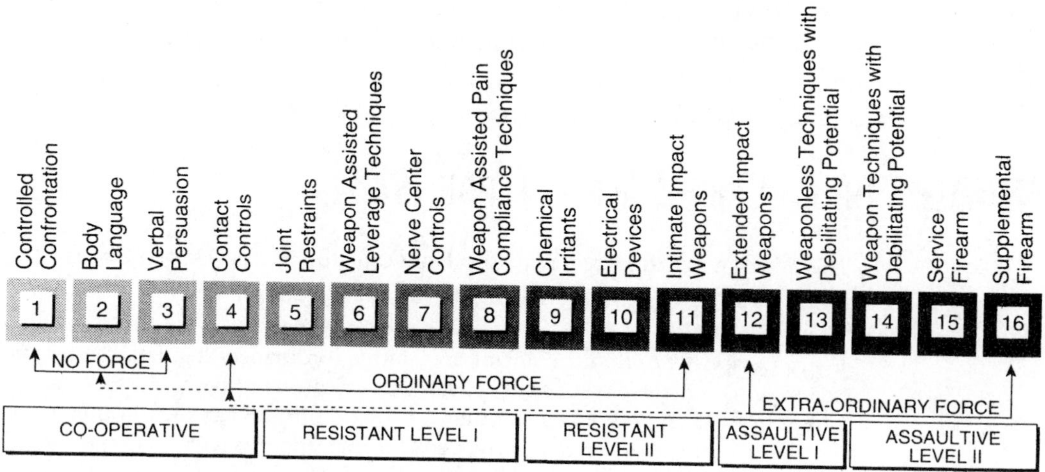

Figure 4–1. Use of Force Continuum

SOURCE: Adapted from G. Connor. "Use of Force Continuum: Phase II." *Law and Order*, March 1991: 30. Reprinted by permission.

This use of force continuum helps answer the question as to when handcuffs should be used. If a person is not resisting being detained, handcuffs might be deemed as unreasonable or **excessive force** by the court. As noted by Kouri (1994, p. 225):

> Security officers must realize that, unlike police officers, they are not permitted to escalate the amount of physical force they use against an attacker. . . .
>
> Once trained to recognize the different levels of resistance, the officer can be taught the correct response, be it a simple pressure point technique or a combination of moves. . . .
>
> Well-trained officers will be less inclined to rely on impact or chemical weapons when faced with a violent situation. The reduced use of force will greatly benefit the officer and the employer in the quest for a safe, crime-free workplace.

Should Security Personnel Be Armed?

As private officers are being called upon to provide services in an increasingly violent society, the question arises as to whether these officers should be armed. Many contract security officer companies refuse to arm their officers because of the financial liability. Other companies limit the number of contracts they will accept requiring **armed personnel.** As noted by Lang (1993, p. 86): "The private security industry may have to establish a larger gap between armed and unarmed officers, showing well-defined differences in the standards for each."

Because of the liability issues surrounding the use of firearms, many agencies are turning to nonlethal weapons to enhance security. According to the

Bureau of Justice Statistics, 52 percent of sheriff's departments nationwide were authorized to carry chemical weapons and 25 percent were authorized to carry electronic weapons; 51 percent of local police departments were authorized to carry chemical weapons; and 17 percent were authorized to carry electronic weapons ("Alternative Weapons," 1994, p. 1). Although no statistics on the use of alternative weapons by private security officers are available, according to manufacturers thousands of security officers nationwide are using electronic stunning devices, chemicals and pepper spray.

Reducing Liability

One extremely important way to reduce liability is to hire trustworthy, qualified individuals, whether they be proprietary or contractual. The following cases, although not pertaining specifically to private security employees, illustrate clearly the serious consequences of not hiring carefully.

Tolbert v. Martin Marietta Corp. (1985). A federal court allowed a secretary to sue her aerospace company for hiring a janitor who abducted her and raped her on company premises while she was walking to lunch. The janitor had a criminal record.

Cramer v. Housing Opportunities Commission (1985). Maryland's highest court ruled that a nighttime break-in and a rape of a public housing tenant *was* caused by the housing agency's earlier decision to hire the rapist as a building inspector. A new trial was ordered.

Malorney v. B & L Motor Freight, Inc. (1986). The Illinois Appellate Court ruled that because B & L should have known that "truckers" are prone to give rides to hitchhikers despite rules against such actions, the general duty to hire competent employees could be extended to checking for criminal convictions.

Sheerin v. Holin Co. (1986). The Iowa Supreme Court ruled that the estate of a waitress stabbed to death by a cook could sue the motel-restaurant that employed them, where the murder took place during working hours.

Gallagher (1990, p. 18) suggests that liability might be lessened by setting minimum standards, establishing clear policies and providing effective basic training. He suggests the following (p. 26):

> Consider undertaking a liability assessment—a comprehensive review of all policies, procedures, rules, regulations, operations, records and training—with an eye to uncovering the potential areas of liability and finding ways to decrease that liability. . . .
>
> Whatever is done to decrease liability simultaneously increases professionalism.

> Civil liability might be reduced by hiring wisely, setting minimum standards for job performance, establishing clear policies and providing effective training and supervision, using clear contracts and carrying insurance.

Gallagher (1990, p. 40) has developed a Six-Layered Liability Protection System based on an analysis of the major causes of lawsuits. Although developed for public police administrators, it applies equally to private security management.

> The Six-Layered Liability Protection System includes:
> - Policies and procedures.
> - Training.
> - Supervision.
> - Discipline.
> - Review and revision.
> - Legal support and services.

Hiring

Olick (1994, p. 19) cautions: "Lax hiring policies, especially for employees in a position of trust, could leave you open to liability risks. Also keep in the back of your mind that today's laws tend to favor the employee more than not and push the majority of responsibilities on the employer."

Training

Brown (1994, p. 42) stresses: "While security students need not become lawyers, they should learn the basics of contracts, torts, criminal law, civil rights, and regulatory requirements relating to the field." He (p. 43) also suggests:

> Officers need to thoroughly understand torts and liability issues such as those involving discrimination, slander, public humiliation, wrongful battery, false arrest and imprisonment, negligence, and failure to provide adequate security.

In addition to providing thorough training, these efforts need to be carefully documented. Chuda (1995, p. 59) notes:

> Accurate training records become vital if an organization or business is sued because of an officer's actions. All organizations are vulnerable to those who claim that security was either improper or inadequate, and the issue of poor training almost always comes into play.
>
> Training records, program or course outlines, attendance sheets, examinations, procedural manuals, and policy statements are all subject to subpoena. Adequate documentation of effective training and education could

> help to absolve the company of legal responsibility. . . . Security managers who take the initiative to implement quality training can avoid being put on the defensive when an incident leads to legal action or when the government mandates a standard security officer training program.

Some employers are reluctant to train their employees because of the high cost of training and the high turnover rate, believing that once their officers are well trained they will leave for "greener pastures." But as motivational guru Zig Ziglar is fond of saying, "I'd rather train an employee and lose him than not train him and keep him."

Ways that security officers might minimize civil lawsuits include the following (Hess and Wrobleski, 1993, p. 152):

- Know and follow their department's guidelines.
- Stay in the scope of their duties.
- Always act professionally.
- Know and respect their constituents' rights.
- If in doubt, seek advice.
- Carefully document their activities.
- Maintain good community relations.
- Keep up to date on civil and criminal liability cases.

Laws regarding civil liability vary from state to state. Nonetheless, certain guidelines will usually help reduce civil liability of on-line security personnel:

DO

- Consistently and fairly enforce policies and procedures regarding all security matters and employee safety.
- Know and understand your duties and responsibilities.
- Always identify yourself as a security officer before taking any actions involving an employee or visitor.
- Know the limits of your authority and recognize the authority of others. If you do not have authority to act, go to someone who does.
- Ask for help if you are unsure and do not feel confident to handle a problem.
- Maintain a helpful, courteous attitude when assisting employees and visitors.
- Always be aware of and sensitive to individuals' privacy.
- Guide your behavior by the standard of *reasonableness*. Make every effort to act objectively and fairly in all situations.
- Maintain high visibility in common areas to deter crime.
- Be alert to and remedy any safety risks or potential safety hazards you observe.
- Remain calm at all times to perform your duties efficiently and safely.
- Cooperate fully in investigations or inquiries.
- Know who to call in emergencies and keep names and telephone numbers easily accessible.
- Consciously observe and promptly record your observations in a clear, concise, complete report.

- Following any incident, immediately record all information on an incident report form. Include all facts. Avoid conclusions and opinions.

DO NOT

- Forcefully detain someone.
- Cause an employee or visitor to believe that he or she is not free to leave, whether it be through physical restraint or words.
- Make physical contact either directly or indirectly with employees, visitors or intruders while questioning them or escorting them to an exit.
- Use unnecessary force.
- Search any person, purse, lunch box or toolbox unless the search is specifically authorized by management and the search guidelines have been communicated to all employees.
- Search employees or visitors selectively.
- Issue a statement or opinion or discuss any issue associated with your duties with any reporter.
- Question individual employees or visitors in front of others. If you must ask sensitive questions, ask the person to accompany you to a private area.
- Discuss sensitive information with people who do not have a genuine *right* or *need* to know.
- Accuse an employee or visitor of committing a crime.
- Deviate from actions authorized by your security manual.

Some good may come from civil lawsuits, as suggested by the Hallcrest Report II (Cunningham et al., 1990, p. 38):

> Perhaps during the 1990s, as a secondary outcome of litigation, we will see evaluative research into the crime prevention effectiveness of security guards, alarms, locks, cameras, lighting, and employee training. The litigation explosion may also be the catalyst for long overdue security standards and/or codes which should help reduce the claims of inadequate security and ultimately may improve security services and products.

A Liability Checklist

❑ Have potential liabilities been identified?
❑ Have ways to reduce these risks been implemented?
❑ Are there clear policies on:
  a. Detaining
  b. Searching
  c. Arresting
  d. Emergencies
  e. Using force
  f. Carrying a weapon
❑ Have all employees been trained in these areas?
❑ Has a record of such training been kept?
❑ Are there clear, stringent employment standards?
❑ Are employees evaluated periodically?

- ❑ Are supervisors adequately trained?
- ❑ Are employees properly supervised?
- ❑ Are all incidents having potential civil liability properly reported and investigated?
- ❑ Are all incidents resulting in civil liability investigated and remedial actions implemented?

Properly reporting all incidents is critical. Lawsuits can be filed several years after an incident. Information from reports can be critical to refreshing the memory of those involved or if those involved are no longer employed there.

Contracts

Most security officers work under some sort of contract. According to Rosen (1992, p. 67): "In today's legal environment it is imperative that contracts between vendors and consumers of guard services protect and aid all parties involved." Should any lawsuits be brought, the contract will be extremely important in settling the case.

Rosen (pp. 67–68) suggests several terms and conditions that should be included:

- Scope of work—specific services to be provided.
- Premises to be patrolled—location and type.
- Guard staffing—number of personnel required.
- Field supervisors—number and duties.
- Guard replacements—who decides when to replace a guard?
- Uniforms and equipment—what is required and who is to provide?
- Hours—specific times services are to be provided.
- Force majeure—factors out of the control of either party such as natural disasters or employee strikes.
- Rate of compensation—how, when, and how much is the vendor going to be paid?
- Termination—how is the contract ended?
- Insurance—who carries what types of insurance?
- Indemnification—where one party agrees by contract to stand in the shoes of another in the event of a claim or judgment.

Insurance

Insurance is important to any business. Unfortunately, as noted by Rosen (1988):

> It is ironic that the insurance industry treats the security industry so shabbily. Very few insurance companies want to write guard services and yet without guard services, there would be many, many more claims filed against the insurance industry. Certainly guard services protect billions of dollars or property and millions of lives and prevent a lot of claims from occurring. Nonetheless, the insurance industry, for the most part, wants little to do with the security guard industry. Obviously because of their tremendous liability exposure.

Many security agencies carry insurance against civil lawsuits, but in many instances coverage may be excluded in many areas. One area that is frequently excluded is punitive damages—compensation awarded by a court to a person who has been harmed in an especially malicious or willful way. This is meant to serve as a warning to anyone else thinking of behaving in a similar way.

COMMON DEFENSES AGAINST CIVIL LAWSUITS

The most common defenses used by security officers and those for whom they work are that:

- They didn't intend to deprive a plaintiff of a constitutional right.
- They acted in good faith.
- They acted with what was considered reasonable judgment at the time and with valid authority.

SURVIVING A LAWSUIT

Even with carefully selected and trained security officers, lawsuits may still occur. Should this happen, officers should know what to expect as defendants.

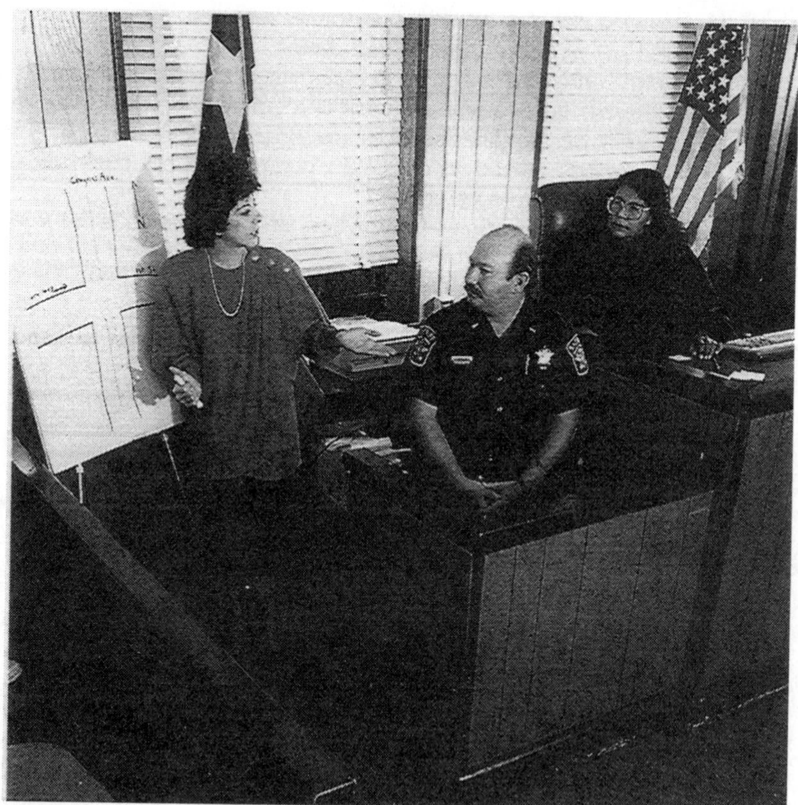

Testifying in court can be an ordeal unless the officer has acted professionally and documented what was done in a well-written report.

Lawsuits often involve **interrogatories,** written lists of questions to which the defendant is asked to respond. Interrogatories may be several pages long and may include questions attempting to obtain information that might be damaging to the defendant—for example, questions about financial or marital difficulties. The defendant need not answer each question, but any questions not answered must include an explanation for the omission.

The lawsuit may also involve a **deposition,** where attorneys for both sides ask questions of an individual involved in the lawsuit and the questions and answers are recorded verbatim by a stenographer or court reporter.

As noted by Dees (1994, p. 317): "The emotional toll of being a defendant in a civil lawsuit can be staggering." To survive this ordeal, Dees suggests:

> If you know that you are going to be subjected to a civil trial, plan ahead for it. See that you are relieved from duty during the proceedings so that you can devote your full energy to assisting with your defense. Put other matters aside to ensure that you are well-rested, and make an effort to exercise vigorously each day. The exertion will reduce your stress level harmlessly and allow you to think more clearly and realistically.

Summary

Although private security officers are given authority to enforce the rules and regulations of their employers, they must still be mindful of the rights of those with whom they interact. Laws may be classified in several ways: by type (written or common law), by source (constitutional, statutory, case), by the parties involved (public, private) or by the offense (criminal, civil).

A crime is a wrong against the public which the state prosecutes and which seeks punishment. Criminal intent is required. A tort is a private wrong where an individual sues seeking restitution. Intent is not necessary. In short, a tort is any civil wrong for which a person can be sued.

These laws may apply to individuals who are unaware that they are liable. One instance of this is the nondelegable duty. This is a duty for which authority can be given to another person, but responsibility cannot. Civil liability remains with the person who has the legal duty to act.

Civil law is further divided into three categories: strict liability, intentional wrongs and negligence. The elements of negligent liability include (1) the existence of some duty owed, (2) the incident occurring was foreseeable, (3) the defendant failed to meet a reasonable standard of care, (4) proximate results, that is, an injury resulted from the failure to protect and (5) damages. The most common civil suits brought against private security are for assault, battery, false imprisonment, defamation, intentional infliction of emotional distress, invasion of privacy and negligence.

Increasingly, private security is affected by Section 1983 of United States Code, Title 42—the Civil Rights Act—which says that anyone acting under the authority of local or state law who violates another person's constitutional rights—even though they are upholding a law—can be sued.

Civil liability might be reduced by hiring wisely, setting minimum standards for job performance, establishing clear policies, providing effective training and supervision, using clear contracts and carrying adequate insurance. The Six-Layered Liability Protection System includes policies and procedures, training, supervision, discipline, review and revision and legal support and services.

APPLICATION

On a Sunday in late November, James Stiles, a supervisor for the Mid-Atlantic Security Company, and Dean Duncan, security officer for the same company, were on duty at the Glass House Office complex. Their primary duty was to check tenants in and out. Both security officers had worked this assignment many times, and both were veterans in the security field.

About 5:00 P.M. on a Sunday, a female attorney, Estelle Grambling, came into the building to do some work in her office. Noting no one at the sign-in desk, she assumed that there was no security officer on duty, although she did see the sign-in book open on the counter. Without signing in, she went to the elevator and up to her office.

About 7:00 P.M. the security officers were approached by two public police officers who stated they were called by a woman to come to room 918 because she was accosted by an intruder, assaulted and robbed of her purse and credit cards. The two police officers and James Stiles, the supervisor, went up to 918 and found an hysterical victim, Estelle Grambling. After calming down, she stated that a man had struck her in the head while she was at her computer and stole her purse containing a considerable amount of money and credit cards. Before he left, he struck her in the face with his fist. Although dazed, she managed to dial 911 and summon the police. She had not tried to contact the front security desk, believing no one was on duty there.

This incident resulted in Estelle Grambling filing a lawsuit against the Pronto Management Company, which managed the building and hired the Mid-Atlantic Security Company, and the Mid-Atlantic Security Company for negligence of duty. She alleged that the private security officers were negligent in their duty, were careless in performing their patrol throughout the building and were completely oblivious to the fact that she was in the building. She was suing for one hundred thousand dollars in negligent damages and another one hundred thousand dollars in punitive damages.

1. Did the security guard owe a duty to the plaintiff to protect her while she worked in her office?

2. Did Grambling create a risk by not signing the log book even though the officers were not present when she entered the building?

3. What is your overall assessment of the situation, and what liability does the security company have, if any?

4. Evaluate the totality of the situation. What would you recommend to settle the damage claim?

DISCUSSION QUESTIONS

1. Liability is often used to refer to a person's failing to do something he or she should have. What does that really mean in general terms?
2. There is a continuous ravaging of the Old English common law principle that the master is not responsible for the criminal acts of his servants. Explain what this actually means as far as legal liability is concerned.
3. As a security officer, do you believe in the theory of foreseeable danger?
4. What is your understanding of punitive damages?
5. Why do the public police favor the private security sector handling economic crimes?

REFERENCES

Allison, John. "Five Ways to Keep Disputes Out of Court." *Harvard Business Review,* January–February 1990, p. 166.

"Alternative Weapons for a Lethal World." *Security Concepts,* July 1994, pp. 1, 17, 23.

Brown, Bill. "The Power of Preparation." *Security Management,* April 1994, pp. 42–44.

Chuda, Thomas T. "Taking Training Beyond the Basics." *Security Management,* February 1995, pp. 57–59.

Connor, G. "Use of Force Continuum: Phase II." *Law and Order,* March 1991, pp. 30–35.

Cunningham, William C.; Strauchs, John J.; and Van Meter, Clifford W. *Private Security Trends, 1970 to 2000: The Hallcrest Report II.* Stoneham, MA: Butterworth-Heinemann, 1990.

Dees, Timothy M. "Surviving a Lawsuit." *Law and Order,* January 1994, pp. 315–317.

Dunn, Patrick A. "Your Rights to References." *Security Management,* July 1991, pp. 67–68.

Gallagher, G. Patrick. "Management for Police Administrators." *The Police Chief,* June 1990, pp. 18–29.

Gallagher, G. Patrick. "The Six-Layered Liability Protection System for Police." *The Police Chief,* June 1990, pp. 40–44.

Hess, Kären M. and Wrobleski, Henry M. *Police Operations.* St. Paul, MN: West Publishing Company, 1993.

Ingber, Clifford J. "A Duty to Protect." *Security Management,* December 1993, pp. 63–67.

Kouri, James J. "Should Martial Arts Be Part of Security?" *Security Management,* September 1994, pp. 225–226.

Lang, William G. "To Arm or Not to Arm?" *Security Management,* November 1993, pp. 85–86.

Maxwell, David A. *Private Security Law: Case Studies.* Stoneham, MA: Butterworth-Heinemann, 1993.

Meadows, Robert J. "The Likelihood of Liability." *Security Management,* July 1991, pp. 58–66.

Olick, M. "Considerations when Hiring the Private Security Guard." *Security Concepts,* June 1994, pp. 19, 25.

Oran, Daniel. *Law Dictionary for Nonlawyers,* 2d ed. St. Paul, MN: West Publishing Company, 1985.

Rosen, Mark B. "Liability: Survival into the Nineties." Tape from the 34th Annual American Society for Industrial Security Seminar, Boston, MA, 1988.

Rosen, Mark B. "Trust but Verify." *Security Management,* November 1992, pp. 67–71.

Schnabolk, Charles. *Physical Security: Practices and Technology.* Woburn, MA: Butterworth Publishers, Inc., 1983.

Somerson, Ira S. "Avoiding the Pitfalls of Private Security." *Security Management,* April 1991, pp. 43–45.

Taitz, Sharyn, ed. *Getting a Job, Getting Ahead, and Staying Ahead in Security Management.* Port Washington, NY: Rusting Publications, 1990.

CASES

Atamian v. Supermarkets General Corp., 369 A.2d 38 (N.J. Super. 1976)
Brown v. Jewel Companies, Inc., 530 N.E.2d 57 (Ill. App. 1988)
Cramer v. Housing Opportunities Commission, 501 A.2d 35 (Md. 1985)
Florence Trentacost v. Dr. Nathan T. Brussel, 412 A.2d 436 (N.J. 1980)
Granite Construction Corp. v. Superior Court of Fresno, 197 Cal.Rptr. 3 (Cal. App. 1983)
Kline v. 1500 Massachusetts Ave. Apartment Corp., 439 Fed.2d 477 (1970)
Kolosky v. Winn Dixie Stores, Inc., 472 So.2d 891 (Fla. 1985)
Malorney v. B & L. Motor Freight, Inc., 496 N.E.2d 1086 (Ill. 1986)
Meyers v. Ramada Inn of Columbus, 471 N.E.2d 176 (Ohio 1984)
Picco v. Ford's Diner, Inc., 274 A.2d 301 (N.J. Super. 1971)
Pittard v. Four Seasons Motor Inn, Inc., 688 P.2d 333 (N.M. App. 1984)
Sheerin v. Holin Co., 380 N.W.2d 415 (Iowa 1986)
Sorichetti v. City of New York, 482 N.E.2d 70 (N.Y. 1985)
Taylor v. Centennial Bowl, Inc., 416 P.2d 793 (Cal. 1966)
Tolbert v. Martin Marietta Corp., 621 F.Supp. 1099 (Colo. 1985)

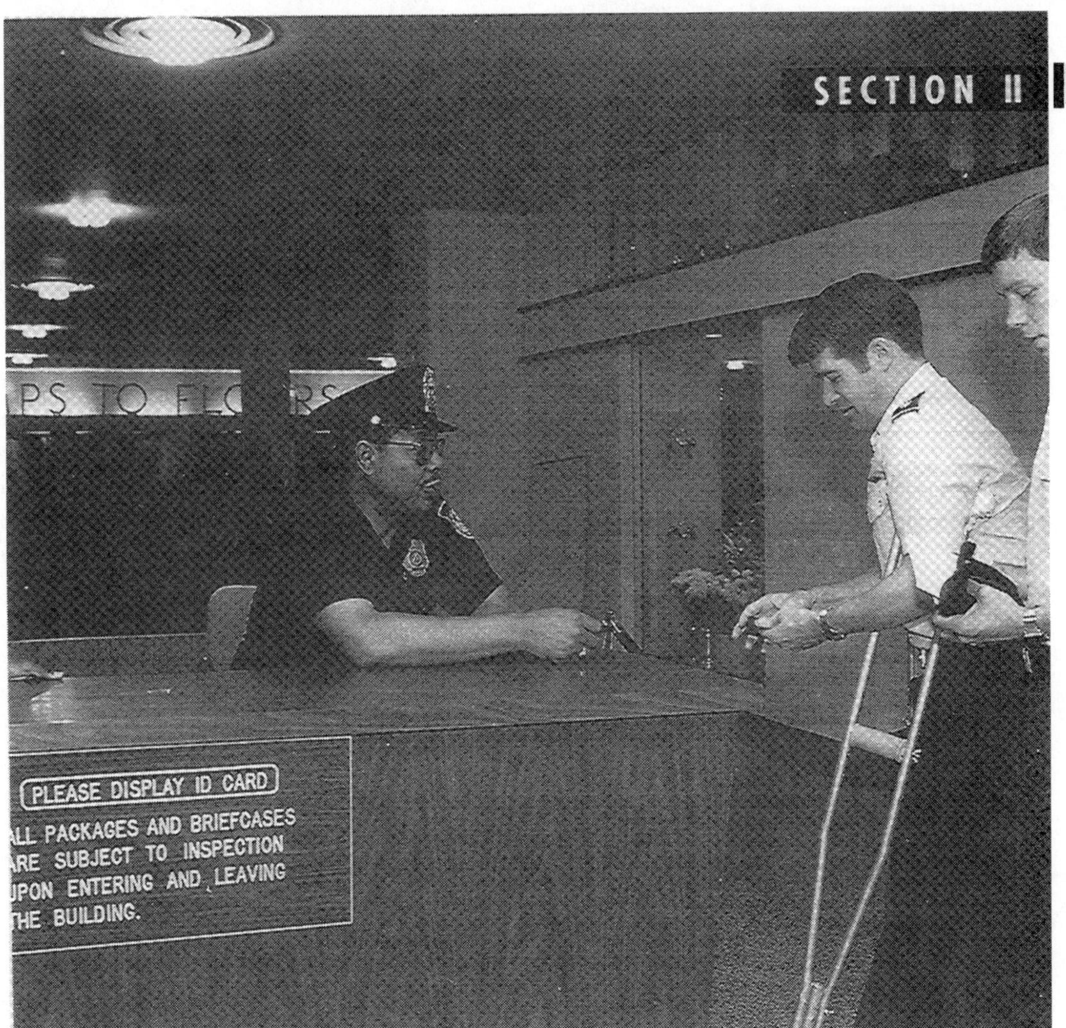

SECTION II
PLEASE DISPLAY ID CARD
ALL PACKAGES AND BRIEFCASES
ARE SUBJECT TO INSPECTION
UPON ENTERING AND LEAVING
THE BUILDING.

Basic Security Goals and Responsibilities

Security considerations affect every facet of a business or organization. Sometimes security measures are viewed as unnecessary expenses or even as impositions that lessen efficiency and lower the organization's public image. With careful planning and education, however, such negative effects can be avoided. Management, employees, customers and all who use the facility can be made to feel more comfortable, knowing they are being protected against intruders and/or harm from natural disasters.

Effective security involves all aspects of a facility, whether internal or external, whether occupied or not, as well as all individuals within the facility and all who might seek to gain illegal entrance.

One primary security responsibility is to prevent loss by ensuring physical and environmental controls (Chapter 5). But physical security in itself is rarely sufficient; the human factor must inevitably enter the picture. Therefore, security procedures are required to further prevent loss (Chapter 6). In combination, security personnel, equipment and procedures can be used to prevent or reduce losses resulting from accidents, natural disasters, violence and emergencies (Chapter 7) and those resulting from criminal actions (Chapter 8). They can also enhance computer security (Chapter 9). Finally, private security officers also play a vital role in any organization's public relations efforts (Chapter 10).

Although specific security goals and responsibilities will depend on the needs of the establishment, these basic responsibilities and alternatives to fulfill them are generally present in every establishment. Using analytic creativity, security managers can select and adapt those physical and procedural controls relevant to their individual situation. Possible applications in security systems for commercial, industrial and retail establishments, institutions and other special areas are discussed in Section IV.

CHAPTER 5

Enhancing Security through Physical Controls

Do You Know

- What four purposes are served by physical controls?
- What three lines of defense are important in physical security?
- How the perimeter of a facility can be made more secure? The building exterior? The interior?
- What the two common types of safes are and why the distinction is important?
- What constitutes basic security equipment?
- What kinds of locks are available? What type of key lock is recommended?
- What functions are performed by lighting?
- What the components of a total lighting system are?
- What types of alarms are available for the three lines of defense?
- Where alarms may be received?
- What factors must be balanced in selecting physical controls?
- What two factors are critical in establishing and maintaining physical controls?

Can You Define These Terms?

alarm systems
area alarms
biometric
capacity alarms
central station
central station alarms
concertina
crash bar
crime prevention through environmental design (CPTED)
cylindrical locks
dead bolts
defensible space
envelope (building)
exculpatory clauses
fail-safe locks
fail-secure locks
fenestration
fiber optic
header
keyway
local alarms
luminaire
panic bar
perimeter alarms
perimeter barriers
point alarms
police-connected alarm
proprietary alarms
razor ribbon
safe
slipping (a lock)
space alarms

spot alarms	top guard
spring-loaded bolts	vault
strike	warded locks
telephone dialer	watch clock

Introduction

Throughout the centuries, people have sought to protect themselves and their property by physical controls. Among other things, they have built their dwellings on poles, constructed high fences, rolled boulders in front of doors, buried money, tied gaggles of geese where an intruder would startle them, stationed lookouts, built fires to frighten away wild animals and the like. Although modern physical security controls are usually much more sophisticated, the intent is the same: to prevent any intruder from harming the owner or the owner's property.

The Hallcrest Report (Cunningham and Taylor, 1985, p. 41) says: "Physical security concerns the physical means used to (1) control and monitor the access of persons and vehicles; (2) prevent and detect unauthorized intrusions and surveillance; and (3) safeguard negotiable documents, proprietary information, merchandise, and buildings. . . . For certain entities, such as banks, the Defense Industry Security Program, and nuclear plants, the minimum standards of protection are mandated by a governing authority." Such standards may also enhance employee safety.

This chapter begins with a discussion of basic physical controls and the three basic lines of defense: the perimeter, the building exterior or shell and the interior. This is followed by an examination of basic security equipment: locks, lights and alarms. The chapter concludes with a discussion of surveillance systems, other types of security devices and how all the preceding can come together into an integrated physical security system.

Basic Physical Controls

Dingle (1993, p. 75) describes the concentric zone theory of asset protection, based on the premise that the more valuable an asset is, the more layers of protection it needs:

> Something extremely valuable may be in a safe (layer 1), in a locked office (layer 2), with an alarm system (layer 3), in a secured building (layer 4), with security patrols (layer 5), a perimeter fence (layer 6) and a perimeter alarm system (layer 7).

This concentric zone approach is illustrated in Figure 5–1.

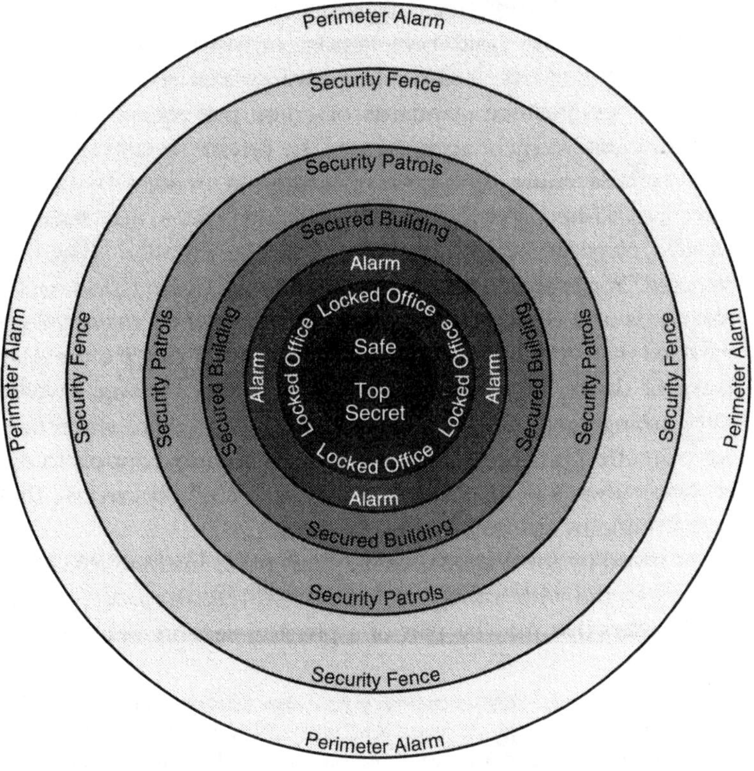

Figure 5–1. Concentric Layers of Physical Security

> Physical controls serve to reduce risk of loss by:
> - Denying unauthorized access.
> - Deterring or discouraging attempts to gain unauthorized access.
> - Delaying those who attempt to gain unauthorized access.
> - Detecting threats, both criminal and noncriminal.

Crime Prevention through Environmental Design (CPTED)

One important concept being used increasingly in security planning is that of **crime prevention through environmental design,** most commonly referred to as **CPTED.** According to Crowe (1991, p. 84):

> CPTED is based on the theory that the proper design and effective use of the built environment can reduce the incidence and fear of crime and make an improvement in the quality of life. This definition is a mouthful. Basically, it says that the better we manage our human and physical resources, the greater our profits and the lower our losses.

Use of CPTED in specific applications is discussed in Section IV.

As stated in the Task Force Report, *Private Security,* Standard 5.4 (p. 188): "Architects, builders, and/or their professional societies should continue to develop performance standards of crime prevention in design with advice from law enforcement agencies and the private security industry." Some cities now include crime prevention measures in existing building codes. Others have established specific building security codes that must be adhered to. Ideally, physical security controls would be included when a facility is constructed. For example, the National Advisory Commission on Criminal Justice Standards and Goals in a 1973 report, *Community Crime Prevention,* recommended that: "Careful considerations should be given to the design and placement of doors, windows, elevators and stairs, lighting, building height and size, arrangement of units, and exterior site design, since these factors can have an effect on crime." To add physical security controls to existing facilities is almost always more expensive; yet, such controls can pay for themselves in a short time by preventing loss of assets.

As noted by the National Crime Prevention Institute (NCPI) (1986, p. 57) in discussing the wide variety of natural and human-made physical and perceptual barriers that may be part of a physical security system:

> Security factors must compete with other functional and cost considerations. Inevitably in barrier design some sort of balance must be struck among the various needs for security, convenience, utility, illumination, access, climate control, and pleasing appearance. The objective is to design the barrier so that security features are compatible with all other considerations, are cost effective, and provide the needed degree of protection. . . .
>
> The primary functions of a barrier are to delay the intruder as much as possible and to force him to use methods of attack that are highly conspicuous or noisy. . . .
>
> As the value of the target increases, however, the strength of the barrier must increase proportionately. . . .
>
> The trade-off between delay time and detection time is perhaps the single most important consideration in designing a barrier.

The National Crime Prevention Institute (1986, pp. 59–60) also stresses "circles of protection" to create a **defensible space:**

> In security design, the concept of concentric barrier circles should be extended in depth as much as possible. Not only might there be an outer protective ring (such as a fence) at the property line and a second ring consisting of the building shell, but also within the building there might be one or more additional barriers to protect specific targets. . . .
>
> A single barrier ring (particularly in the case of commercial or industrial establishments) may be both ineffective and dangerous, because once an intruder penetrates it, he may be free to do as he wishes, screened from observation by the barrier that was intended to keep him out in the first place.

The three basic lines of physical defense are the perimeter of a facility, the building exterior and the interior.

Sometimes all three lines of defense are available, as in, for example, a manufacturing firm situated on its own acreage. Other times only one line of defense is available, for example, the interior of a small business occupying a single room in a large office complex. Although the office manager can bring pressure to bear on the office complex manager to ensure security, the individual office manager has very limited control.

THE PERIMETER

The location of a facility influences its security needs. When selecting a site for a new plant, managers should carefully consider security needs in the decision. Is the area a high-crime area? Is there ample public lighting? Do local law enforcement officers patrol there? If a facility has grounds around it, security measures can be used to protect this perimeter.

Perimeter barriers, according to the NCPI (1986, p. 62), are: "any obstacle which defines the physical limits of a controlled area and impedes or restricts entry into the area. It is the first line of defense against intrusion. . . . At a minimum, a good perimeter barrier should discourage an impulsive attacker. At the maximum, when used in conjunction with other security measures, it can halt even the most determined attack." The NCPI (1968, p. 60) stresses that:

> The growing weight of evidence, however, suggests that no boundary barrier can serve as anything more than a perceptual barrier, because it has been demonstrated that even the relatively unskilled attacker can go over, under or through any boundary barrier in a matter of seconds. Hence, fences, boundary walls, hedges, and other such obstacles are referred to by NCPI as *boundary markers* to make it clear that boundary marking is their major function. If boundary markers can also provide a degree of perceptual security, so much the better, but in no event should they be considered as physical security systems.

The perimeter can be physically controlled by fences, gates, locks, lighting, alarms, surveillance systems, signs, dogs and security personnel. Physical layout and neatness are other important factors.

Fences

Some facilities are protected by a natural barrier, such as the water surrounding Alcatraz. Usually, however, a barrier must be constructed as a physical and psychological deterrent to intruders.

Fencing can protect employees on an overpass and control their routes as well.

Vitch (1992, p. 50) suggests that although fences provide only minimal security, they do serve important functions in exterior perimeter protection, including the following:

- Define the site perimeter.
- Briefly delay an intruder.
- Channel employees and visitors to authorized gates.
- Keep honest people out.
- Serve as a sensor platform.

According to the NCPI (1986, p. 6), three types of boundary marker fencing are currently used: wood stockade fence, barbed wire and chain link. All provide about equal protection and cost less than concrete or masonry walls. The NCPI says chain link is the most commonly used and is "relatively attractive, low in maintenance cost, simple to erect and less of a safety hazard than barbed wire."

Fences should be straight, taut and securely fastened to metal poles; they must extend to the ground or below. Sometimes a **header** or **top guard** is used. This added protection consists of strands of barbed wire extending outward from the top of the fence at a forty-five-degree angle. A double top guard that extends both outward and inward is also available.

Chain-link fencing allows an unobstructed view both for security officers inside the perimeter and for private or public patrol cars passing on the outside. To provide adequate security, the chain link should be #11 gauge or heavier, with not larger than two-inch mesh, and the fence should be at least eight feet high. However, some building codes do not allow such tall fences in certain areas.

Objections are sometimes raised to the institutional look of chain-link fences. Such objections can be overcome by planting vines and/or bushes to conceal the fence, but the advantage of an unobstructed view is then negated. If a facility's appearance is high priority, masonry or brick walls are sometimes constructed. Such barriers are more attractive, but they obstruct the view and are often easy to climb. To thwart climbers, a barbed-wire top guard is sometimes used.

Other types of fences include wrought-iron fences, sometimes called "embassy fencing" because it is used where appearance is important, and "living" fences consisting of dense shrubs or hedges.

When appearance is not a concern, a barbed-wire fence is often used. Such fences are usually at least eight feet tall and have the strands of barbed wire no farther than six inches apart, and two inches apart at the bottom. Many types of barbed wire or barbed tape are available, including one very aptly named **"razor ribbon."** After a trucking firm in Phoenix, Arizona, installed barbed tape on top of its existing 10-foot chain-link fence, its severe losses from stolen parts and vandalism dropped to zero.

Concertina, rolls of barbed wire 50 feet long and 3 feet in diameter, provides the strongest barrier. Placing one roll on another creates a formidable six-foot-high barrier. Concertina is used primarily in emergencies when a fence, gate or building entrance is no longer secure.

Fences can also be electrified, but use of either an electrified fence or one with barbed tape has the potential for lawsuits from injury, especially if children are likely to be injured by the security devices.

As noted by Reynolds (1994, p. 35), **fiber optic** sensors can be fence mounted, and this "[n]ew fiber optic technology keeps false alarms and intruders at bay."

Fences should be inspected periodically. Attention should be paid to telephone poles, trees or other objects close enough to the fence to allow an intruder to use them in climbing the fence. Care should be taken so that vehicles cannot be driven beside a fence and used as an aid in climbing it.

A minimum number of entrances and exits should be used. Gates are usually locked with a post-locking bar and a padlock. If a gate is locked from the inside, a metal shield can be welded to the gate and the chain pulled through an opening in the shield and then locked on the inside. Although the shield offers greater security, it cannot be used if the gate has to be opened from the outside. Some businesses use electrically controlled gates operated by pushbuttons or a card-key. Pedestrian traffic can be controlled by turnstiles. In addition, a guard house located at major arteries can serve as a central security command post to monitor all entrances and exits.

For tight security, *all* perimeter openings must be secured, including not only gates, but also air-intake pipes, coal chutes, culverts, drain pipes, exhaust conduits, sewers, sidewalk elevators and utility tunnels. Perimeter openings that cannot be permanently sealed because they serve a function should be barred or screened if they are larger than 96 square inches.

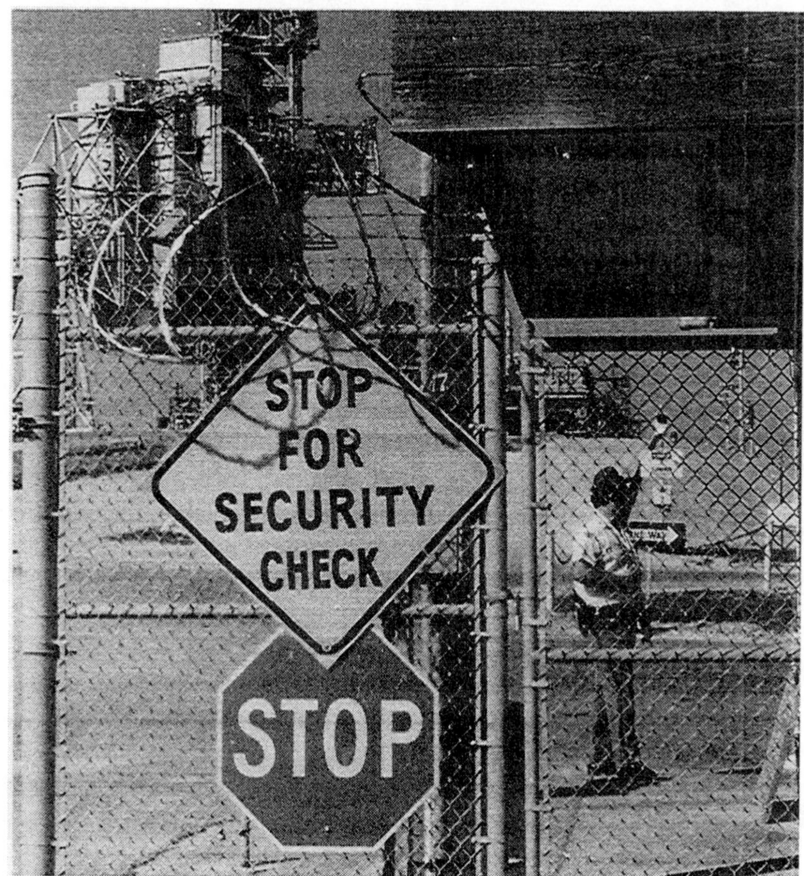

A security officer inspects the security fence. Note the header on the fence.

Often the fence, the gates and all perimeter openings are wired into an alarm system. They may also be monitored by a surveillance camera and may be patrolled by dogs or security personnel.

Perimeter Lighting

Adequate lighting on the perimeter is another prime consideration. An unobstructed view is of little consequence in complete darkness.

Four types of lights are commonly used:

- *Floodlights* form a beam of concentrated light for boundaries, fences and area buildings and, positioned correctly, produce a desired glare in the eyes of anyone attempting to see in.
- *Streetlights* cast a diffused, low-intensity light evenly over an area and are often used in parking lots and storage areas.
- *Fresnal units* provide a long, narrow, horizontal beam of light ideally suited for lighting boundaries without glare.
- *Searchlights,* both portable and fixed, provide a highly focused light beam that can be aimed in any direction and are ideal for emergencies requiring additional light in a specific area.

Boundary lighting is often provided by floodlights that create a barrier of light, allowing those inside to see out, but preventing anyone on the outside from seeing in. (See Figure 5–2.) Although the glare may deter intruders, it can also pose a traffic hazard or annoy neighbors; therefore, the technique is not always possible to use.

Inside the perimeter, lights are usually positioned 30 feet from the boundary, 50 feet apart and 30 feet high, depending, of course, on the size of the area to be lit. All storage areas, thoroughfares, entrances and exits, sides and corners of buildings, alleys and accessible windows should be adequately lit. A guideline for determining if the lighting is adequate is to see if enough light is available to read the subheads of a newspaper.

The illumination inside a guard house should be less than that outside so security personnel can see out, but others cannot see in. All electrical wires should be buried, if possible, to secure the source of power. The lights themselves should be protected with metal screens so the elements cannot be broken by vandals or intruders.

Security lighting is discussed in greater depth later in this chapter.

Physical Layout and Appearance

A clear zone of at least 20 feet on either side of the perimeter should be maintained when possible. Neatness is important not only for appearance, but also for security. Ladders and piles of debris or merchandise close to fences or buildings could easily be used to an intruder's advantage. Bushes and hedges should be no more than two feet tall and should be kept away from the boundary and buildings. Weeds should be cut, hedges and bushes trimmed and all discarded material or merchandise properly disposed of. Trash and boxes strewn around the premises not only are a safety hazard, but also can provide hiding places for intruders.

Buildings can be connected by tunnels or walkways, reducing the number of main entrances to be made secure. Tunnels, however, pose other security risks and should be used only after careful consideration. If tunnels are used, adequate lighting, surveillance cameras and perhaps patrol should be used to increase safety.

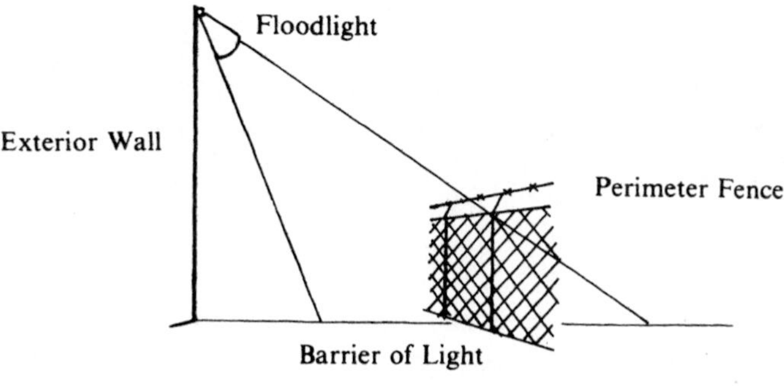

Figure 5–2. Barrier of Light

A utility building can centralize utilities, such as an emergency electric generator, emergency water tanks and pumps, gas valves and regulators, the main switch and power controls and the transformers. Whether in a separate building or located around the premises, all main-control valves, regulators and switches must be protected from vandalism, tampering and sabotage.

Parking lots often present a security problem. When possible, privately owned vehicles should be parked outside the perimeter in a parking lot with its own fence, gate and lights. Employees or visitors who park adjacent to a loading dock or warehouse doors present a security risk. Many thefts are committed by friends or family waiting in the parking area for an employee to get out of work. Some security managers feel that if employees and/or visitors must walk a long distance to their vehicles, the chances of theft are reduced. Others argue that a lengthy walk to a vehicle needlessly exposes people to the possibility of being the victim of an assault, robbery or rape.

When possible, all privately owned vehicles should be parked in a common parking lot on only one side of the building, thus reducing the number of common entrances to the building. Parking lots should have proper drainage and lighting, as well as appropriate marking and signing, including pedestrian crosswalks, if needed. Sometimes stickers or parking permits are used to identify vehicles with legitimate access to parking areas.

Additional ways to increase safety in parking lots and parking ramps are discussed in Chapter 19.

The Building Exterior

The first line of defense for some facilities is the building exterior, also called the building **envelope** or shell by some architects and security planners.

> Strong, locked doors and windows, limited entrances, secured openings (if larger than 96 square inches), alarms, surveillance and lighting help establish the physical security of a building's exterior.

In the majority of break-ins, entrance is gained through windows. The next most common method of entrance is through doors, followed by roof hatches, skylights, vents and transoms. A few break-ins have involved chopping or cutting holes through walls, floors and ceilings.

Doors

The vulnerable parts of a door are the lock, frame, hinges and panels. Not too many newer locks are picked, but many are pulled or "slipped," as discussed later.

The door frame should be heavy so it cannot be sprung with a crow-bar or jack. Experts recommend two-inch-thick solid wood or a frame covered with

16-gauge sheet steel if the wood is 1³⁄₈ inches or less. Strong frames thwart jamb-pulling (Figure 5–3).

The hinges should be inside, if possible. The pins should not be removable, but should be welded in (Figure 5–4, p. 106).

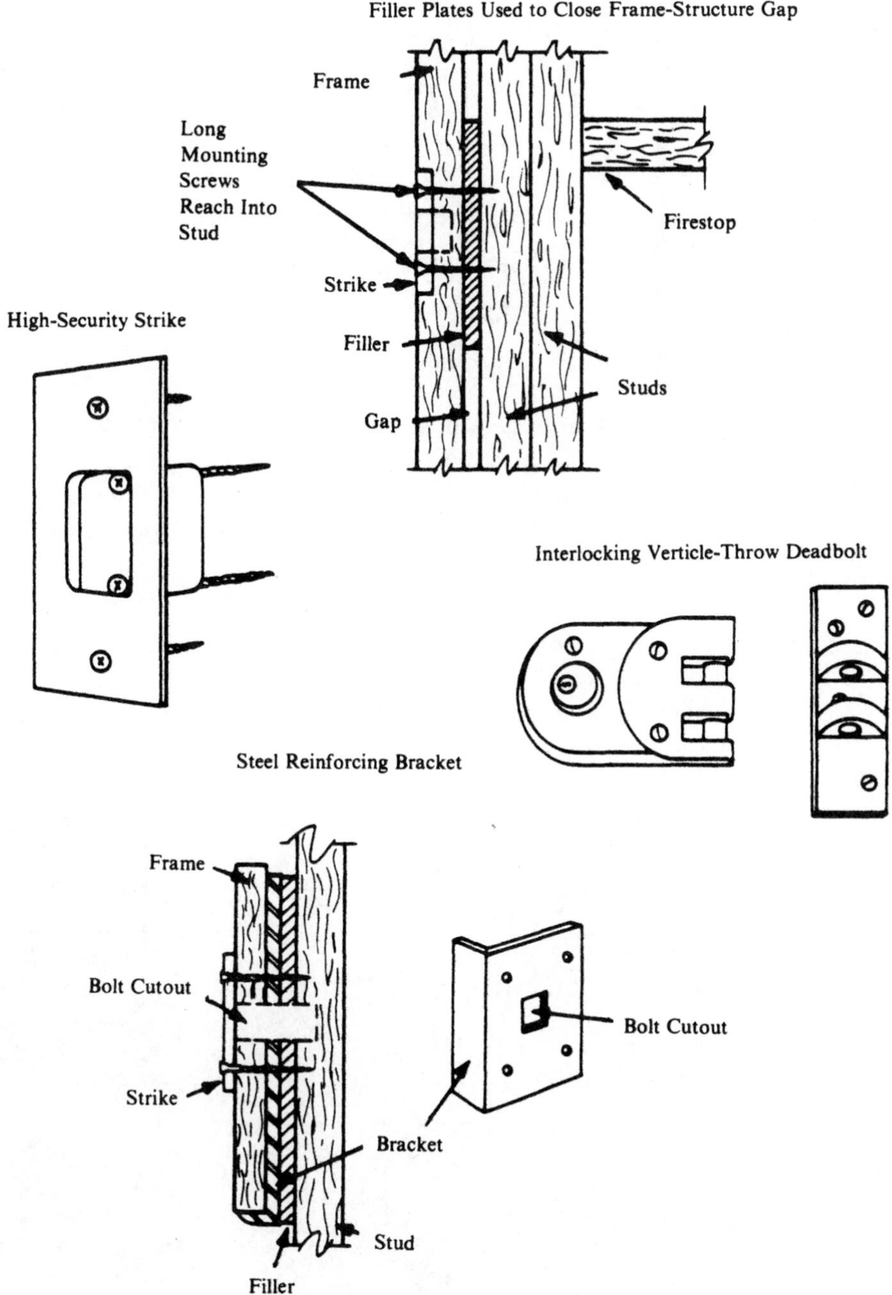

Figure 5–3. Measures Used to Protect Against Door Frame Spreading

SOURCE: "Understanding Crime Prevention," by the National Crime Prevention Institute. Reprinted by permission.

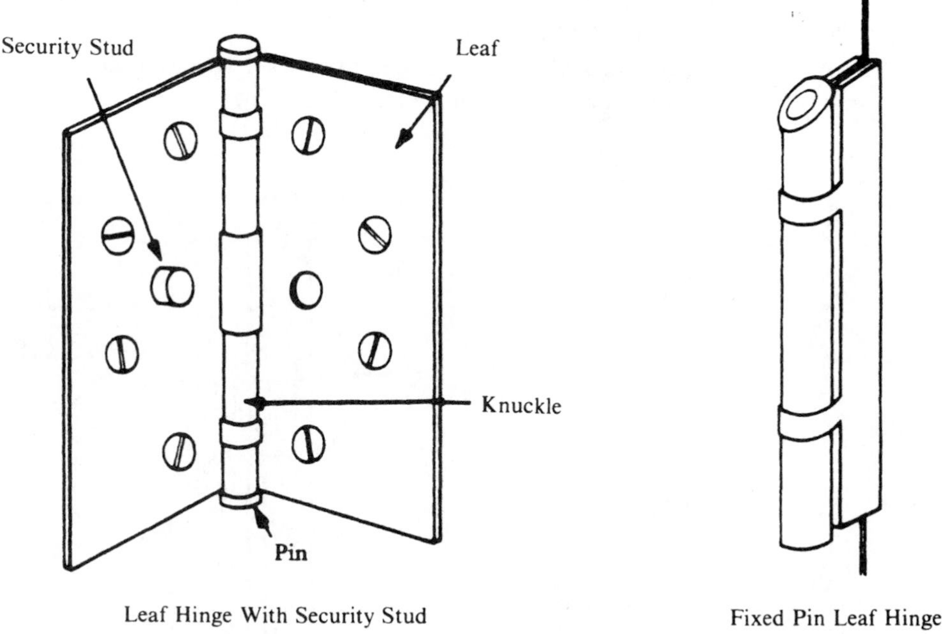

Figure 5–4. Standard Security Hinges
SOURCE: "Understanding Crime Prevention," by the National Crime Prevention Institute. Reprinted by permission.

The door panels should be solid, meeting the same specifications as the door frame stated above. If the panels are glass, they should be protected by bars or a screen on the inside. Often sheet metal is installed on the inside and outside of basement doors.

Door with security screen.

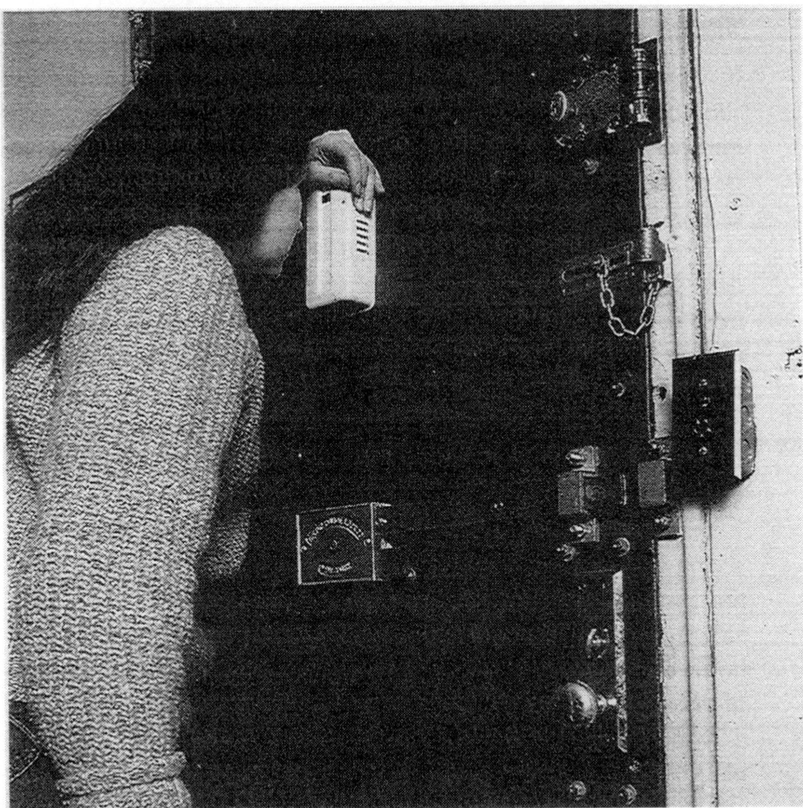

A heavily protected security door.

Doors should have a minimum of 60-watt illumination above them and should be wired into the alarm system to add further protection.

Although door transoms are seldom built into newer buildings, they exist in many older buildings. If they cannot be sealed because they are needed to provide ventilation, they should be fitted with locks on the inside and secured when the room is unoccupied.

Many facilities have installed hardware, for example, chains and padlocks, around the door exit bar that makes it impossible for a "hide-in" thief to exit the building after hours. However, some city ordinances prohibit such hardware, viewing it as a safety hazard.

The number of doors and their placement is extremely important to physical security. The number of personnel entrances should be limited to control access and to reduce thefts while the building is open. In some instances guards or receptionists are stationed at the entrance. All doors not required for efficient operation should be locked. If a door is required as an emergency exit, it can be equipped with emergency exit locking devices called **panic** or **crash bars.** The exterior of the door has no hardware. It can be opened only from the inside. Many emergency exit locking devices are equipped with an alarm that sounds if the door is opened. Some also have a lock so that if a key is used, the alarm does not sound.

Windows

If windows can be opened, they should be secured on the inside by a bolt, slide bar or crossbar with padlock. Window glass can be broken or cut by an intruder, so bars or steel grills should be installed inside the windows. However, the hazard this might present to employees should a fire occur must always be considered.

About 50 percent of all criminal intrusions are achieved by breaking window glass. Any opening larger than 96 square inches and less than 18 feet from the ground should be protected. If the window is not needed for ventilation, the panes can be replaced with glass block. If the likelihood is high of the glass being broken, security glass should be considered. This is especially applicable to display windows that are vulnerable to the "smash and grab" thief. Although security glass generally costs twice as much as regular glass, it can effectively thwart intruders.

Security glass meets the standards of the Underwriters Laboratories in resisting heat, flames, cold, hammers, picks and rocks. It is usually 200 to 300 times stronger than tempered or plate glass and is practically impenetrable, although it may crack. Older security glass usually consists of five or more layers of glass laminated to create a sheet 5⁄16-inch thick. Newer, synthetic types of glass are rapidly replacing these heavier, more expensive types of glass.

Window design, or **fenestration,** is also a security consideration. Security glass is available, as described by Harpole (1991, p. 121): "*Security glazing* refers to a wide range of glass products that share the common attribute of one or more interlayers of energy-absorbing, high-performance plastic." According to Harpole (p. 124), security glass is "one of the toughest building materials available":

> Indeed, an 8-in. thick, concrete-block wall can be breached with less than 10 blows of a sledgehammer, while a ½ in. laminated glass lite can resist dozens of blows from an identical tool.

Other Openings

Any accessible openings larger than 96 square inches should be protected the same way as windows. Utility tunnels, elevator shafts, ventilation openings, skylights and the like should all have protective screens or metal bars to prevent access to the building's interior. Such openings can also be connected to the alarm system.

Roof, Floor and Walls

The roof is a favorite entry point for many intruders. A building's roof is usually not lit, is not visible to passing patrols, is not strongly constructed, is not built into the alarm system and often has unsecured openings such as skylights or ventilation ducts. If no such openings exist, an intruder can often simply drill four holes arranged in a square and then saw out the square to gain access to the building. A facility in a row of buildings with connecting roofs is especially vulnerable. Roof intrusion can be deterred by a chain-link fence topped with a double barbed-wire header as long as zoning regulations allow this.

A common wall or floor between two buildings or establishments is also a potential entry point. An intruder may break into a nonsecure building having a common wall with a secure building and then break through the common wall with leisure. This same hazard exists when there are secure areas above and/or below nonsecure areas.

Fire escapes pose another problem. They often provide access to doors or windows that should be accessible only from the inside of the building. Counterbalanced fire escapes are preferable to stationary ones because the counterbalanced stairs are suspended until the weight of a person descending is on the last section.

Lighting

Lights should be mounted on the sides and corners of buildings, with the illumination cone directed downward and away from the structure to prevent shadows and glare. The alley, the rear of the building and all entry points should be lit. The lights can be turned on by an automatic timer if desired.

The Building Interior

Because no perimeter or building exterior can be 100-percent secure, internal physical controls are usually required as well.

> Interior physical controls include locked doors, desks and files; safes and vaults; internal alarms and detectors; lighting; mirrors; bolt-down equipment; dogs, security personnel; and communication and surveillance systems.

The physical layout of a building's interior directly affects its security. Secure areas should be separate from nonsecure areas and should be located deep within the interior so no windows, exterior doors or walls are in common with another building. Cashier offices, research laboratories, storage rooms and rooms containing classified documents or valuable property often require extra security.

The interior construction of the building is also important. The ceiling in many modern buildings is simply acoustical tile laid in place with a crawl space above it that provides access to any room on that floor. Older buildings are better constructed from this perspective, but they often have door transoms and inferior glass and locks.

Storing Assets

Assets requiring security include cash, stocks, inventory and records. The National Fire Protection Agency classifies business records into four classes: vital, important, useful and nonessential. Usually only 1 percent to 2 percent of an organization's records are classified as vital. Specific types of records to be protected and the means of doing so are discussed in Chapter 8. Generally, however, such records are kept in file cabinets with lock bars having combination padlocks. Sometimes they are kept in a **vault.** The National Fire Protection Association defines a vault as a "completely fire-resistive enclosure to be used exclusively for storage." Work should not be performed inside a vault. Because vaults are primarily for fire protection, many contain a burglar-resistant **safe.**

> Most safes are *either* fire resistant *or* burglar resistant, but *not* both.

A burglar-resistant safe must have an Underwriters Laboratories (UL) listed combination lock. It almost always has a very limited capacity, and it does not protect against fire. The UL classifies the fire resistance capacity of a safe as *A*, *B* or *C*. Safes with an *A* classification resist up to 2000°F for four hours; those classified as *B* resist up to 1850°F for two hours; those classified as *C* resist 1700°F for one hour. Alarms and time locks are often additional security precautions in safes.

Scheirer (1992, p. 37) advises: "The first and most fundamental step in buying a safe is to determine what items are to be protected—money, jewelry, irreplaceable documents, secret documents, guns, stamp collections, etc." The purpose of the safe will ultimately guide the buying decision.

According to Scheirer (1992, p. 38): "A number of resources are available to help a company determine the correct product, label, and classification for its needs. Any manufacturer or local safe and lock shop can get a company started on the path to making a safe selection."

According to Dunckel (1991, p. 70): "[A]fter more than 10 decades of variations on a theme, safe and lock manufacturers are making large, ambitious technical strides. . . . The shift to electronic safe locking has begun in earnest, and the security world is feeling the first drops of a deluge of change." Mechanical safe locks have presented numerous problems, including being difficult to operate and being vulnerable to drilling attacks. In addition, because the mechanical safe lock has only one combination, the more people who share it, the less control and accountability exist. The new electronic locks eliminate these problems. One new lock generates its own power internally to prevent being locked out in case of a power failure. It also eliminates the cumbersome "three to the left and four to the right" approach. The hundreds of thousands of safes with mechanical locks do not need to be scrapped. In most cases, the new electronic locks can replace the mechanical locks. According to Dunckel (p. 74): "In many cases retrofits involve removing and replacing fewer than 10 screws and then simply attaching a wire."

Some of the newer safes are what are referred to as smart safes, as described by Lorenzo (1993):

> Today's modern smart safe provides an effective addition to the loss prevention professional's arsenal of high-tech solutions. These safes are not the brainless steel cabinets of old but intelligent partners with watchful memories and sophisticated capabilities. . . . If a crime ends up in court, these safes are the prosecution's star witnesses in providing clear, unbiased, and factual evidence.

Smart safes have at least one of the following functions:

- Personalized access—through different combinations or electronic keys for each individual user.
- An audit trail—records and stores all transactions.
- Management features—allows control of who can do what in the safe and when.

In addition, according to Lorenzo (p. 55): "All smart safes also have one element in common—ease of use."

Although some controversy exists over whether a safe should be hidden or in clear view, most experts feel that hiding a safe just helps the burglar. It is better to have it located where it is plainly visible from the outside and clearly lit at all times. It should always be locked and the combination secured.

Basic Security Equipment

At all three lines of defense, perimeter, exterior and interior, certain basic equipment can add considerable security.

> Basic physical security equipment consists of locks, lights and alarms.

The degree of physical security required will determine which of the basic components is used. In some instances, locks may be all that are required. In other instances, lights and/or alarms may also be needed (Figure 5–5).

Locks

A beam across a door was one of the oldest security devices used for protection against an intruder. Locks were used in Egypt more than 4,000 years ago, and they have been important security devices ever since. Locks are, in fact, one of the oldest, most commonly used, cost-effective means to physically control access to an area, a building, a room or a container.

The primary function of a lock is to deter or deny access into a protected area. Although any lock can be opened by a determined, skilled person, locks are valuable because they increase the amount of time an intruder must spend gaining access, thereby increasing the probability of being detected. Additionally, locks frequently provide evidence of forced entrance, evidence that may be required to collect insurance.

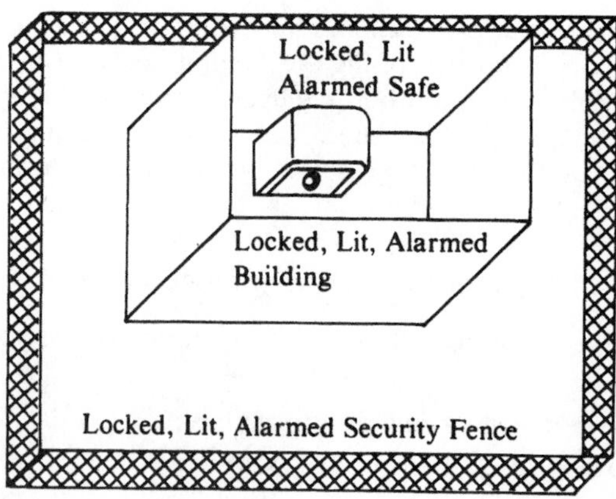

Figure 5–5. Basic Security Equipment at the Three Lines of Defense

The better the hardware's quality, the longer it will withstand physical abuse, and thus the more likely it will show signs of being forced.

Usually, with locks come locksmiths. As noted by Cunningham et al. (1990, p. 188): "Locksmiths primarily serve a security function. However, they generally operate outside of conventional security circles, with their own trade associations and journals." The Hallcrest staff estimates that revenues from the locksmith segment of security grew at an annual rate of 10 percent, with annual revenues by 1990 at $2.9 billion. The number of firms increased to 12,000, employing almost 70,000 people. Hallcrest projects that by 2000, revenues will increase at an average annual rate of 7 percent to $5.7 billion and that 17,000 lock shops will employ 88,000 people (p. 189).

Available types of locks include key operated, combination, card activated and electronically operated.

Key-Operated Locks

Key-operated locks are most frequently used and are simple to operate. A key is inserted into a **keyway** and turned to insert or withdraw a bolt from a **strike.** The keyway contains obstacles that must be bypassed to withdraw or insert the bolt. It can be housed in a doorknob or in the door itself. The key is notched so that when it is inserted into the keyway it either bypasses or arranges the tumblers (or other obstacles) so that it can be turned to insert or withdraw the bolt from the strike.

The keyway may be warded or cylindrical. **Warded locks,** commonly used up to the 1940s, have an open keyway (keyhole) that can easily be opened with a skeleton or pass key or picked with a wire. Warded locks also allow a view into the room's interior. Warded locks are often used on file boxes, suitcases and handcuffs.

Cylindrical locks may use disc tumblers or pin tumblers. Disc tumbler locks, commonly used in cars, desks, files and cabinets, are not too effective because they usually cause only a two- to four-minute delay in gaining access to the protected areas. Pin tumbler locks are usually preferred for business and industry because they can create up to a ten-minute delay in gaining access.

The lock's bolt can be either spring loaded or dead bolt (Figure 5–6). **Spring-loaded bolts** (sometimes called latches) automatically enter the strike when the door is closed. When locked, they can often be opened by inserting a plastic credit card or a thin screwdriver above the bolt and forcing it downward, releasing the spring. Such **slipping** can be deterred, however, by a latch guard, a metal plate extending from the strike area to the door frame.

Dead bolts are non-spring-loaded metal bars that are manually inserted into or withdrawn from a strike. Dead bolts are usually from 1/2 to 1 1/4 inches long and offer greater protection than spring-loaded bolts.

> A dead-bolt lock with a one-inch throw and an antiwrenching collar or a secondary dead bolt with a one-inch throw offers the best protection if a key-operated lock is used.

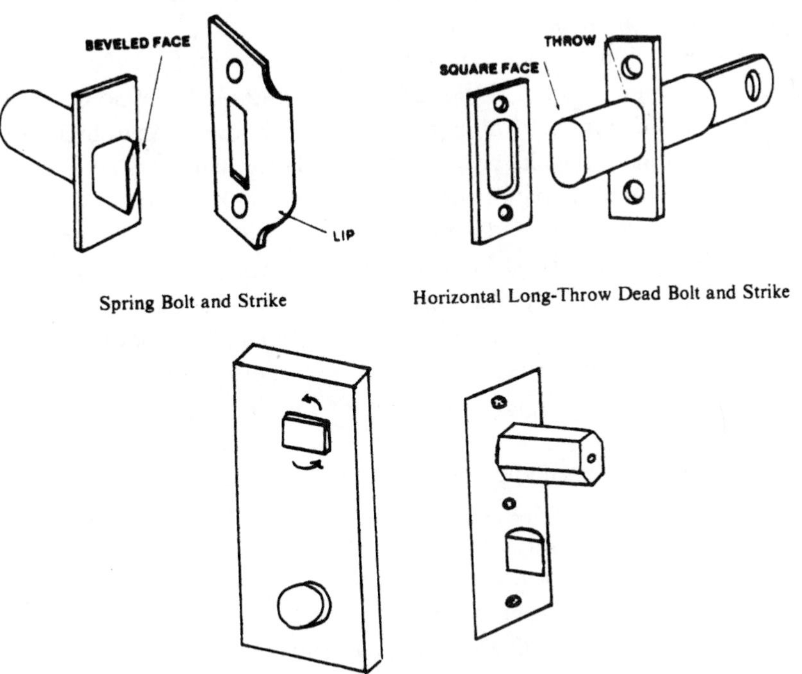

Figure 5–6. Basic Types of Bolt Mechanisms

SOURCE: "Understanding Crime Prevention," by the National Crime Prevention Institute. Reprinted by permission.

In a key-operated padlock, the same basic principles apply except that the bolt is replaced by a **shank** that can be secured or released by turning the appropriate key in the keyway.

The primary disadvantages of key-operated locks are that many locks can be picked, keys can be stolen or obtained by unauthorized people and keys may be duplicated. Another disadvantage is that some individuals may have to carry many keys, but this can be overcome by using a master keying system, discussed in the next chapter.

Whether keys should contain identification is debatable. Identified keys can be returned to the owner if they are lost, but they can also be used to gain unauthorized access. Key identification is an important management decision.

Combination Locks

Combination locks are often used on padlocks as well as on safe and vault doors. *Dial combination locks* usually have from two to six notched tumblers. Turning the dial to prespecified numbers aligns the notches to create a slot, allowing an arm to drop into it so that the locking bar can be withdrawn from the strike.

Some combination locks are operated by *pushbuttons* rather than dials. One or more buttons are pushed, either in sequence or simultaneously. Such locks are often used on individual rooms or on entrances to semiprivate rooms in large buildings.

Combination locks cannot be picked, and they use no keys that can be lost, duplicated, stolen or borrowed. The probability of someone randomly trying combinations and hitting on the correct one is extremely low. Nonetheless, combination locks are also vulnerable to unauthorized entry. A thief may obtain the combination from a disloyal employee or may even find it written down somewhere close to the combination itself. The combination to a lock should never be written down and kept in the same area as the lock. Combination locks should not be opened when unauthorized people might casually see what numbers are being dialed. If someone who knows the combination is fired or resigns, or if there is the slightest suspicion that the combination might be known to unauthorized people, the combination should be changed.

Padlocks, whether key or combination operated, should have a short shank to thwart prying and should be made of hardened steel to prevent cutting. The hasp through which the shank is inserted must also be strong and non-removable. An unlocked padlock is an open invitation to would-be intruders to substitute the padlock with one of their own. Consequently, padlocks should be distinctive so that any replacement can be easily detected.

Keypad Locks

Gillespie (1993, p. 12) notes: "Although the choice of keypads can be overwhelming to both installer and user, a little homework can help fit the right device to the application." Many keypads today rely on microcomputer technology and have great flexibility. For those who are hesitant to use keypads for access control, Gillespie (p. 13) notes:

> [T]here are dozens if not hundreds of ways you deal with a variety of keypads, many on a daily basis, including: telephone, vending machine, ATM, calculator, fax machine, computer, elevator, ticket machine, microwave oven, digital clock and VCR.

Card-operated Locks

Card-operated locks are inserted into a card reader installed near a restricted door or passageway. When an authorized card is inserted into the slot, a minicomputer activates the locking device, thereby opening the door, traffic control arm, gate or turnstile. Some card-operated locks are also equipped so that the identification of the person operating the lock and the time it was operated are automatically recorded.

The card itself is usually plastic and resembles an ordinary credit card. It is invisibly coded in a way that makes every card or group of cards identifiable, yet impossible to duplicate.

Card-operated locks are often used when areas are restricted to the general public, but accessible to large numbers of employees. In fact, a single card can be used to control access to parking, turnstiles, elevators, files, computer rooms, copy machines, fuel pumps, restrooms and executive offices. The same card could provide time and attendance reporting information. Card-operated systems can be easily programmed to reject cards that are no longer valid.

According to Naudts (1987, p. 169): "[In] 1000 BC the Chinese required servants at the Imperial Palace to wear rings engraved with unique and intricate designs identifying palace areas they were permitted to enter. Historians credit this method by the Chinese as the first comprehensive access control system."

Access control systems came into use in the early 1960s and have evolved into highly advanced, widely used security technology. Naudts (1987, p. 170) says that card manufacturers are producing systems that can control from eight card readers and one thousand cards up to several thousand readers and more than sixty thousand cards.

A typical system has the user insert, place or swipe a card into or by a reader. The reader determines if the card is valid and if access is to be granted. Many systems not only grant or deny access but also record information such as the card number, the door for which entry was requested, the time, the date and if entry was allowed.

Some systems can be programmed to lock and unlock doors at specific times of the day or specific days such as weekends or holidays.

Access Control Card Options. Mourey (1994, p. 42) suggests: "The access control card and reader market is dominated by wiegand, magnetic stripe and proximity. . . ."

According to Bordes (1994, p. 74): "The most dramatic changes in the card business have been in the field of proximity." Bordes explains that proximity cards are of two types, active and passive:

> The active technology card has an embedded lithium battery and transmits the signal; a passive card has no battery and relies on the strength of the receiver's signal to retransmit the encoded number.

Various options from which to choose are described by Naudts (1987, pp. 171–172). *Magnetic stripe cards* use a strip similar to those used on credit cards. Magnetic stripe cards can be encoded on site, but they can easily be copied or modified. *Watermark cards* also use a magnetic strip and can be encoded on site. They also have a permanently encoded number that cannot be changed or copied, making them more secure than magnetic stripe cards. *Barium ferrite cards* contain information encoded in a soft pliable magnetic material sandwiched between layers of plastic.

Wiegand cards have metallic rods or wires embedded in the card that are not visible to the unaided eye. *Infrared cards* use a pattern of shadows inside the card and a low-level infrared light in the reader to detect the pattern and determine if entry is to be granted. *Proximity cards* use radio frequency signals to gain entry.

Access control systems may also use a keyless system activated by a personal identification number (PIN), which allows access to individuals having the correct six- or seven-digit access number. Some automobiles have such a system as an option.

Electronic access control cards provide a vast array of potential uses for employers and security professionals, including time and attendance, purchases, inventory and after-hours entry records.

Electronic Locks

Electronic locks are frequently used in apartment buildings and in offices where strict physical security is required. For example, in an apartment building, the doorway between the foyer and the hallways to the apartment can be electronically locked. A person who has no key can gain an unforced entrance only by contacting someone within the building by a phone or buzzer system and then having that person unlock the door by pressing a button.

Electronic locks are also often used on gates as well as on doors where tight security is required—for example, computer rooms or the room in a bank containing safety deposit boxes or the cash.

Miehl (1993, p. 48) points out an important distinction in electromechanical locks:

- **Fail-safe locks** are locks that will remain unlocked when the power is off. Such locks are used on doors in the path of a fire exit.
- **Fail-secure locks** (also called intermittent-duty locks) remain locked with the power removed.

Dean (1994, p. 50) suggests: "When door hardware is electrified, it gains capabilities that take door security far beyond the basic locking function. Activities such as monitoring, alarming, time delays and remote access control can be customized to meet individual building needs."

Biometric Security Systems

Technological advances in security include **biometric** security systems that can recognize unique physical traits such as fingerprints, voices and even eyeballs. Says Hof (1988, p. 109): "Forget your key chain . . . computerized security guards are fast becoming the modern 'open sesame.' " Such systems are being used at the Los Alamos National Laboratory in New Mexico to protect high-security areas of the nuclear research lab, the wine cellar of the La Reserve Hotel in White Plains, New York, and a jewel vault in Dallas, Texas. According to Hof (1988, p. 129): "Beginning in 1991, fingerprint or retina readers will be used in a federal program to keep truckers with poor driving records from obtaining licenses in other states. . . . The microchip has made security machines smaller, cheaper, faster, and more reliable."

Miller (1991, p. 31) suggests: "[B]iometrics have begun to nudge their way into the impressive array of security applications throughout the world, from airport control towers to computer rooms, government facilities to college meal plans, prison lockups to sperm banks."

As noted by Murphy (1991, p. 37): "Biometric technology ranges from simple signature dynamics to the more sensational retina scanning."

According to Olick (1994, p. 6): "The most popular and readily accepted biometric access control system on the market today employs a technique of recognizing three-dimensional data about a person's hand, called 'hand geometry.' " Zunkel (1994, p. 87) also suggests: "Hand geometry is one of several biometric technologies that were once thought to belong only to the military and nuclear communities, but that now have found their way into everyday life."

Biometric systems are basically of two types: verification and recognition. A verification system requires that a person have some sort of identification such as a card with a personal identification number that is then matched with some physical characteristics of that person to verify the identification. According to Bowers (1994, p. 19): "[O]nly retinal scan systems have the practical capability of operating as a true recognition device, not requiring a personal identification number or code to corroborate the biometric search process."

Seidman (1994, p. 47) describes an innovation called the smart card, which is a credit-card-sized piece of plastic with an integrated circuit chip or microprocessor embedded in it. Seidman describes how organizers of the 1992 World Expo in Seville, Spain, used smart cards and biometrics to allow 100,000 season ticket holders to pass quickly through 52 turnstiles and 30,000 expo employees to do the same through 48 turnstiles. According to Seidman (p. 47): "the main selling feature of a smart card is its security. Over nearly twenty years of production and distribution, not one counterfeit smart card has been reported anywhere in the world."

Other Locks

In addition to the preceding types of locks, clamshell locks (such as those used on windows), bars, bolts, chains and time locks can also be used to provide additional security. Whatever type of lock is used, it will be only as secure as the material into which it is mounted and the integrity of the unlocking mechanism, be it a key, combination, code or card.

SECURITY LIGHTING

Zamengo (1994, p. 59) notes: "There is no question that light is the enemy of those who seek to perpetrate misdeeds . . . for those who would prevent such acts, security lighting is a powerful and economic tool." The importance of lighting the perimeter and the building's exterior has already been stressed.

> Adequate light inside as well as outside a building enhances safety, deters would-be intruders and makes detection of actual intruders more probable.

Intruders prefer the cover of darkness to conceal their actions. The majority of nonresidential burglaries occur at night. In fact, three out of four commercial burglaries are committed within buildings with little or no light.

Standard 5.2 of the Private Security Task Force Report (1976, p. 182) emphasizes adequate security lighting: "Where appropriate, property should be adequately lighted to discourage criminal activity and enhance public safety." The report presents evidence on relighting programs that have had significant success in reducing crime (p. 192):

> As a result of a relighting program, the City of Indianapolis, Ind., reported crime reductions of as much as 85 percent in specified neighborhood areas. An added plus accompanying the lowered incidence of crime was a reduction in accidents. A 40.9 percent reduction in crimes against persons, a 28 percent reduction in auto thefts, and a 12.8 percent reduction in burglaries were reported in St. Louis, Missouri, one year after the implementation of a new lighting system.

> A total lighting system includes four types of lighting:
> - *Continuous* on a regular schedule, for secure areas.
> - *Standby,* for occasions when more light is needed.
> - *Moveable,* for when light is needed in areas not usually lit.
> - *Emergency,* to be used as an alternate power source when the regular power source fails.

How much light is enough? Most authorities contend that adequate lighting should provide visibility and allow surveillance without creating excessive glare or shadows.* In our energy-conscious society, care must be taken not to

*The specific lighting needs for a facility can best be determined by contacting the Illuminating Engineering Society, which publishes *The American Standard Practice for Protective Lighting.* They can also suggest consultants to assist in planning for security lighting of a specific facility.

waste energy when using security lighting. The American Society of Industrial Security suggests that improving the efficiency of lighting systems can preserve lighting as a security aid. Use of high-efficiency fluorescent tubes can result in immediate energy and operating cost savings of 14 percent. An effective lighting system modification would be to install new, high-efficiency ballasts that can reduce energy consumption by as much as 7 percent without loss of light. High-efficiency lamp/ballast combinations can reduce energy consumption by as much as 20 percent without loss of light.

At the heart of any lighting system is the type of lamp selected. Often referred to as bulbs or tubes, lamps produce light. Six types of lamps are commonly used in lighting: incandescent, fluorescent, mercury vapor, high-pressure sodium, low-pressure sodium and metal halide. The oldest type of lamp is the incandescent lamp which produces light by heating an internal filament. As noted by Jefferson (1992, p. 63): "Almost 90 percent of the energy that goes to an incandescent lamp creates heat rather than light." Because they are relatively inexpensive, incandescent lamps are often used, but they are the least efficient and shortest lived, making them expensive in the long run.

Jefferson (1992, p. 63) suggests: "Security managers should compare each lamp's efficiency in terms of lumens (light output) per watt (power required to operate it)."

According to Zamengo (1994, p. 54): "The lamps most commonly used in security lighting systems use high-pressure sodium, low-pressure sodium, or metal halide technologies." The high-pressure sodium lamps are energy efficient and effectively illuminate detail. They are often used in streets or parking lots. Low-pressure sodium lamps are even more energy efficient, yielding much light from little power, but they provide limited visual acuity. The yellow light makes most things appear grey. They are also more subject to burnout.

Metal halide lamps are the most expensive type to install and maintain, but they give true colors. These lights are typically used in stadiums.

In addition to the lamps, the **luminaire** used is also an important consideration. The luminaire is what houses the lamp. It should be durable and tamperproof.

An interesting aspect of low-pressure sodium lamps is that, if they are the only light in the environment, everything loses color. As noted by Mele (1994, p. 25): "It looks horrible on human complexions. It literally makes human beings look like they ought to be laying on a slab in the morgue with a tag on their toe." He describes an instance where a neighborhood was experiencing problems with prostitutes. When the lighting was changed to low-pressure sodium lamps, the prostitutes, realizing they looked very unappealing in the new light, left.

Lighting can have the opposite effect, as described by Berube (1994, p. 31), who notes that metal halide lamps "give off a glowing white light that highlights colors . . . so [people] feel safer walking to their cars after hours."

ALARMS

McCullough (1994, p. 59) suggests: "Probably the fastest growing and most widely used means of adding security is the alarm system." And, as noted by

Chanter (1993, p. 18): "Alarm technology has evolved from mechanical to analog to digital, and now to microprocessor-based devices that are capable of handling sophisticated functions."

Alarm systems date back to at least 390 B.C., when squawking geese alerted the Romans to surprise attacks by the Gauls. Centuries later geese were used to protect the perimeter of the Ballantine Scotch distillery in Scotland. Many homeowners depend on their dog's sense of smell and hearing to detect intruders and to then warn them by barking. Alarms have always been an effective supplement to locks, especially if the locks do not stop a persistent intruder.

Lewin (1990, p. 69) cites a March 1990 study reporting that "monitoring alarm systems is now big business, an 'industry' that has grown an average of 17% per year since 1987." Recent studies indicate that a typical city of 25,000 to 40,000 population will have between 650 and 1,600 alarm installations that will generate 100 to 150 alarm calls per month (Lewin, 1990, p. 67).

Alarms are available for all three lines of defense:

- **Perimeter alarms** protect fences and gates, exterior doors, windows and other openings.
- **Area** or **space alarms** protect a portion of or the total interior of a room or building.
- **Point** or **spot alarms** protect specific items such as safes, cabinets, valuable articles or small areas.

Statistics indicate that alarm systems affect crime. For example, the burglary rate has been significantly reduced in communities where alarm systems are used extensively (*Private Security,* 1976, p. 135). Many federally insured institutions, such as banks, are required by law to install alarm systems. Additionally, many insurance companies offer lower premiums to businesses protected by alarm systems.

Alarms are used not only to detect intruders, but also to detect fires (to be discussed in Chapter 7), and, in some instances, many monitor physical conditions such as temperature, humidity, water flow, electrical power usage and machinery malfunction.

Trade magazines can provide current information on specific alarm systems' characteristics and capabilities. Standards for alarm systems are also issued by the Burglary Protective Department of the Underwriters Laboratories.*

*The following bulletins, available from the Underwriters Laboratories, describe the *minimum* standards for specific alarm systems:

#609, 610	Burglar Alarm Systems, Local
#611–1968	Burglar Alarm Systems, Central Station
#636	Hold-up Alarm Systems
#681	Installation, Classification, and Certification of Burglar Alarm Systems

Three Basic Parts of an Alarm System

Alarm systems consist of three basic parts:

- A *sensor,* a triggering device that detects a condition that exists or changes.
- A *circuit,* a communication channel activated by the sensor that provides the power, receives the information and transmits the required information.
- A *signal,* a visible or audible signal activated by the circuit that alerts a human to respond.

Sensors. Sensors in alarm systems range from simple magnetic switches to sophisticated ultrasonic Doppler and sound systems, as illustrated in Figure 5–7. The simplest sensors are electromechanical devices in which an electric circuit is broken or closed, including switches, window foil and screens. These sensors are also the easiest to thwart.

Some sensors are pressure devices that respond to the weight of a person, similar in principle to automatic door openers under mats. Taut wire detectors are often used on the top of fences. Any change in the tension of the wire activates the alarm. Photoelectric sensors are activated when a light beam is interrupted. Such sensors are frequently used in the entrance to establishments where a single clerk may leave the customer area unattended when no customers are present.

Other sensors detect sound, temperature, electrical capacitance, vibration or motion by using radio frequency transmissions or ultrasonic wave transmission.

An analogy can be drawn between sensor devices and the human senses. The sense of *touch* includes the more common electromechanical devices and a few electronic devices that function by breaking a conductor, moving an object, vibrating, applying pressure and sensing temperature. *Smell* includes those devices that sense ionized particles or products of combustion. *Hearing* covers those devices that use airborne sound in their sensing functions, including devices that transmit sound and listen for a reflected sound and those that simply receive the sounds. *Sight* includes devices that use electromagnetic radiation, regardless of frequency, including all photoelectric, microwave, electrical field and magnetic field devices.

The Circuit. The circuit is the communication channel that conveys the information from all sensors in the system to the signal by means of wire, radio waves, existing electrical circuits or a combination of these. Fiber-optic lines, dedicated leased lines and satellite dishes have also become popular means of conveying signals. The circuit is like the network of nerves that runs from the human senses to the brain and is usually the most vulnerable component of the alarm system. Power sources should be hidden, protected, checked and tested regularly.

According to Griffiths (1992, p. 46): "Innovative developments in fiber-optic technology make it ideal for intrusion detection above and below ground, as well as under water." Fiber-optic technology involves light being pulsed through a fine, strong strand of glass or other optical medium, much like electricity is carried along a wire. Advantages of fiber optics include the following (Griffiths, 1992, p. 46):

Magnetic contacts are attached to doors, windows, etc. so that when the door is opened the contacts are separated.

Pressure mats are usually placed under carpets and react to pressure from footsteps.

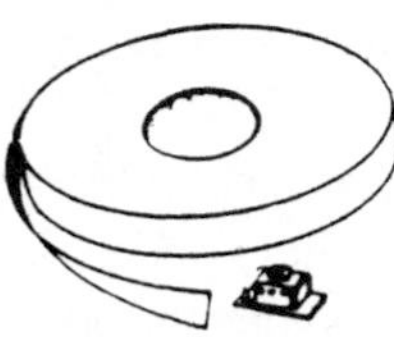

Foil is attached to glass or other surfaces and breaks when the surface is broken.

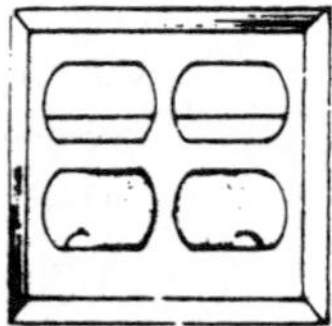

Photoelectric beams cast an invisible infrared light beam across doorways, etc. and react when the beam is interrupted.

Plunger contacts operate in the same way as the light switch on a refrigerator door.

Motion detectors transmit and receive patterns of ultrasonic or microwave radiation. The pattern is changed when a person enters it, causing the detector to react.

Electric and magnetic field devices create stable fields close to specific targets such as safes and react when a person or object enters the field.

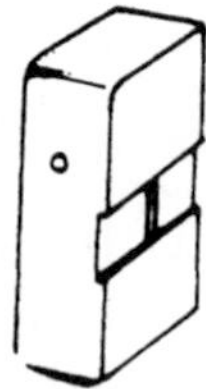

Vibration detectors are attached to surfaces and react to vibrations caused by attempts to break through the surface.

Figure 5–7. Typical Sensors

SOURCE: "Understanding Crime Prevention," by the National Crime Prevention Institute. Reprinted by permission.

- Optical fiber is immune to electrical interference from power supplies, generators, power cables, lights, lightning, radio frequencies, storms, or static in the air. This means fewer false alarms.
- Optical fiber is naturally safe in operation, making it ideal for explosives and other hazardous applications.
- Optical fiber is secure; it cannot be electrically bridged like an electric conductor.
- The drive circuits, light sources, and detectors required to operate fiber optics are low-power, long-life, and operationally reliable components that contribute to highly reliable systems.

As noted by Vitch (1993, p. 42): "[W]ireless transmission rapidly is becoming one of the most popular forms of transmitting alarm signals, both between individual sensors and their control units and between control units and the central monitoring stations." Such systems typically operate on batteries installed in the sensor or transmitter. Among the advantages of wireless alarms are ease of installation, low cost, ease of reconfiguration and immunity to wiring damage. Disadvantages include limited sensor and communications path supervision, radio frequency interference and range/signal path problems.

Some alarms have a fail-safe feature that activates the signal when the power line is cut. In fact, that is the principle behind **capacity alarms.** Such alarms are universally used for point protection of specific objects requiring a high degree of security. The protected object is part of the circuit's capacitance. If a change occurs in the region of the protected object, a change in the system's capacitance sets off the alarm.

Many alarm systems use an automatic **telephone dialer** that sends a recorded message or signal to a central station, the establishment's owner or manager or to the police station. Although this type of alarm is relatively inexpensive, it has several weaknesses. The dialer could call an answering service and be put on hold, allowing the tape to play itself out before the operator heard the message. Telephone lines can be cut. The telephone line of the person to receive the call may be busy, or the telephone line of the establishment where the sensor is located can be tied up by someone calling in.

The Signal. The actual alarm may be audible or silent, a bell, buzzer, phone ringing or a flashing light. Opinions vary as to which signal is more effective. An audible alarm may frighten intruders away, or it may simply hasten their activity. A silent alarm is unlikely to prevent a theft, but it is more likely that the thief can be apprehended while committing the crime.

Table 5–1 summarizes some of the most common kinds of detectors.

Other Considerations

No matter what type of system is used, periodic inspection is important. Vitch (1993, p. 34) suggests that the inspection include the equipment as well as the environment in which it operates. Inspections should also be conducted after any major changes to the system or any major repairs as well as if a deficiency is noted.

When selecting an alarm system, security managers should also pay careful attention to the contract and whether it contains a limitation of liability clause.

Table 5–1. Detectors—An Interior Space Protection Review

Device	Application	Operation	False-Alarm Potential	Advantages	Disadvantages
Contact Switches	Doors and windows to detect opening	Metallic contact held in place by magnet; removal of which causes spring to open contact, triggering an alarm. Mechanical contact switches operate on similar principle, but without magnet.	Basically stable Environmental conditions may cause gap between magnet and contact to widen	Wide variety of applications and types, i.e. plunger, recessed, leaf, wide gap, overhead door, mercury, tilt, tamper, reed.	Surface-mounted contacts subject to internal sabotage. Reed switches may "lock-up" if put on seldom-used door.
Shock Sensors	Mounted on surfaces subject to forced entry: doors and window frames, walls, safes, cabinets, roofs	Electronically analyzes shocks or vibrations in terms of frequency and intensity.	When sensitivity is improperly adjusted	Adaptable to various construction materials. Processor enables analysis of signal from sensor, ignoring ambient vibraGtions or shocks.	Relatively expensive.
Traps	Duct work, skylights, air conditioning sleeves, above false ceilings	A cord held under tension, when loosened, tightened or cut will open circuit.	Stable	Ideal for protection of unusual points of entry where other types of devices are impractical or ineffective.	When activated or tripped manual reset is required.
Foil	Mounted on glass, laced inside doors	Metallic tape, which carries current, is applied under tension to glass or wood. Forced entry severs tape and opens circuit.	Hostile environment like heavy traffic, temperature, wind may cause hairline cuts and intermittent opens	Reliable and stable. Visible deterrent. Low material cost.	Easily damaged in a hostile environment. Installation is labor intensive.
Glass Break Sensors (vibration)	Mounts directly on glass	Mechanically responds to the frequency of breaking glass.	When the sensitivity is improperly adjusted	Relatively inexpensive. Covers large area of continuous glass. Unit does not need power to operate.	Potential false alarms from ambient vibrations.
Audio Discriminators	Glass protection	Capable of detecting selected frequencies, such as the airborne sound of breaking glass.	When the sensitivity is improperly adjusted	Omni-directional and can protect several hundred square feet. Can protect several windows as well as multi-pane windows.	Many false alarms due to ambient sources.
Glass Break Sensors (piezoelectric)	Mounts directly on glass	Electronically detects the intermolecular noises of breaking glass.		Covers large area of continuous glass. Fairly stable device.	Unit needs power to operate. Relatively expensive when compared to other types of glass protection.
Vibration Contacts	Mounted on surfaces subject to forced entry: doors, window frames, walls, safes, and ceilings	Vibration/shock causes two touching pieces of metal to separate upon impact and open the circuit.	When the sensitivity is improperly adjusted	Inexpensive unit cost.	Limited sensitivity adjustment potential.

Table 5–1. Detectors—an Interior Space Protection Review (*continued*)

Device	Application	Operational Theory	Characteristics	Considerations
Ultrasonics	Volumetric coverage Warehouse Schools Municipal buildings	Transmits and receives sound waves. Transmitted sound waves, upon striking a moving object, return to the receiver at a different frequency. This frequency difference (or Doppler Shift) trips an alarm.	Easily contained; will not penetrate most materials, but may be absorbed. Sound waves will bounce off hard surfaces to fill protected area.	Avoid: Areas with air turbulence. Noisy areas, phones, machinery. Moving signs, displays, drapes, plants, etc; Severe humidity fluctuations. Changing configuration of area (moving stock or equipment) without a corresponding sensor adjustment.
Microwave	Volumetric coverage Large open areas Factories Warehouses	Radio waves transmission and reception; also works on the Doppler Shift principle.	Will penetrate most nonmetallic materials, but will be reflected off metal surfaces. Reflected waves may "leave" protected area. Can be mounted in false ceilings for covert detection or to protect unit from tampering.	Avoid: Aiming at vibrating or moving metal surfaces. Unwanted signal penetration. Fluorescent lighting (at least by 3 feet).
*System needs extensive walk-testing due to penetration potential.				
Passive Infrared	Pattern or array of beams Large open areas Hallways or aisles Offices	Receives only infrared energy or heat. Unit constantly looks for a relative rapid change in temperature between two separate zones. If intruder enters one zone, the relative change in temperature is sensed and an alarm occurs.	Infrared energy will not penetrate most materials. Needs a clear line of sight.	Avoid: Hot or cold drafts on unit. Pointing at areas where animals may move. Aiming at moving signs, plants. Hot environment, above 95°F. Moving stock, furniture or equipment that may block unit.
*Aim to force intruder to walk across zones.				
Photoelectric	Channel protection Main access areas or corridors Long hallways or warehouse aisles Long unobstructed walls or row windows	Transmission of a pulsed infrared light beam is focused on a receiver (photoconductive cell), causing current to flow. Interruption of this beam stops the current flow and causes an alarm.	Needs a clear line of sight. Range 300 to 800 feet. Use of mirror allows beam to go around corners.	Avoid: Moving objects that may cross beam. Areas where animals may move. Moving stock, furniture or equipment that may block beam.
*Alignment critical, use "guard rail" to protect unit.				
Mats	"Spot" protection Any place where intruder is likely to enter & walk: under windows, in front of safes, cabinets, doors and along corridors	When pressure is applied to two metal strips (or electrodes) separated by sponge rubber, they touch and short out the system and cause an alarm.	Inexpensive protection. Covert detection, used under carpets. Pressure sensitive.	Avoid: Moving furniture or equipment onto mats. Heavy traffic area. Wet or moisture prone areas.

Note: All devices should be mounted on stable, vibration-free surfaces.
SOURCE: *Security World*, Jan. 1985, pp. 44–45. Reprinted by permission.

According to Maxwell (1993, p. 16): "These exculpatory clauses, or disclaimers, have been for the most part valid and enforceable, and claims for the breach of these contracts have been dismissed." **Exculpatory clauses,** that is, clauses that limit liability, are reasonable in that alarms systems are not designed to guarantee that no loss will occur.

Alarm Respondents

An important decision facing a security manager who selects an alarm as one means of reducing risk is where the alarm should be received.

> Alarm systems may be local, proprietary, central station or police connected.

Local alarms sound on the premises and require that someone hears the alarm and calls the police. Such alarms are the least expensive but are also the least effective because no one may hear them; they may be heard but ignored; and they are easily disconnected by a knowledgeable intruder. In addition, they are extremely annoying to others in the area.

Proprietary alarms use a constantly manned alarm panel which may receive visible and/or audible signals to indicate exactly where the security break has occurred. Such systems are owned and operated by the owner of the property.

Central station alarms are similar to the proprietary system, except that observation of the control panel is external to the alarm's location and is usually under contract with an alarm agency. The **central station** can receive alarms from hundreds of different businesses. When the central station receives an alarm, it usually will dispatch its guard to the location of the alarm, notify the owner and notify the police.

Police-connected alarm systems direct the alarm via telephone wires to the nearest police department.

The False-Alarm Problem

Although alarm systems are important means of physical control, they also pose a very serious problem: false alarms. More than 90 percent of all intrusion-alarm signals are false alarms, resulting in needless expense, inappropriate responses and negative attitudes toward alarm systems.

A study conducted by the International Association of Chiefs of Police ("Study Estimates," 1994, p. 47) found that "police departments in the United States annually respond to as many as 15 million false alarms generated by private alarm systems in an increasing number of U.S. homes and businesses."

Because of this high percentage of false alarms, many cities prohibit alarms directly connected to the police apartment. Even with such restrictions, however, local law enforcement officers are usually called to respond to alarms received by central stations or proprietary centers. Department policy usually dictates that a burglary or robbery-in-progress call be treated as an emergency and that officers respond as rapidly as possible, presenting possible danger to the responding officers and any individuals along the route to the scene.

An additional hazard of the possible false alarm is that responding officers may not take the call seriously, may not respond as rapidly as they should and may not be on their guard when they approach the scene, leaving themselves exposed to a potentially dangerous situation.

The Hallcrest Report (Cunningham and Taylor, 1985, p. 269) states that studies by the National Burglar and Fire Alarm Association (NBFAA) and other groups studying false alarms indicate three major and several minor causes: "(1) between 40% and 60% are caused by customer (and their employees) misuse and abuse of their alarm system; (2) between 15% and 25% are caused by alarm company personnel in the installation and servicing of alarm systems; and (3) between 10% and 20% involve faulty equipment. Lesser causes of false alarms include telephone line problems and stormy weather conditions."

Lewin (1990, p. 67) suggests that most alarm systems now being installed are "so reliable and user-friendly that they cause less than one alarm annually." He also suggests that the number-one cause of false alarms is *people*. They either do not know their systems or they install systems that are far more sophisticated than they need.

No matter what the cause of false alarms, the end result is the same: great amounts of patrol time expended in responding to these calls.

However, alarm systems do deter and detect crimes. Burglary data, for instance, consistently indicates that three-fourths of burglaries involve forced entry—what alarm systems were designed to detect. Two police department studies of alarm system effectiveness found that homes with alarm systems were six times less likely to be burglarized than homes without such systems. Furthermore, one study found that the burglary rate for commercial establishments with alarm systems was half that of non-alarmed establishments. The Hallcrest Report (Cunningham and Taylor, 1985, p. 269) notes this success: "Studies by the NBFAA and the Western Burglar and Fire Alarm Association also indicate that alarm systems annually are responsible for the capture of tens of thousands of suspects, resulting in high conviction-to-arrest ratios, thus offsetting additional criminal justice expense and resolving a large number of other burglaries through 'clearance by arrest.' " The report goes on to note (p. 270):

> Efforts to control the false alarm problem have primarily involved enactment of alarm control ordinances and development of customer education and awareness programs by alarm companies. The NBFAA estimates over 2,000 communities with alarm control ordinances which generally have the following characteristics: (1) allowance for three to five false alarms per system per year, (2) punitive action in the form of graduating scales of fines, and ultimately nonresponse to problem locations, and (3) alarm system permits.

Some solutions to the false alarm problem being tried nationwide include the following ("Study Estimates," 1994, pp. 48–49):

- Alarm verification.
- User training.
- Installer training.
- Local ordinances and state laws.
- Permits.
- Non-response.
- Private response.
- Time-of-Day differentiation.
- Creation of standards.
- Codes.
- Repair and upgrading requirements.
- Equipment enhancements.

Hallcrest Systems surveyed two police departments on their opinions regarding the false-alarm problem and possible deterrents and found the most popular sanction was graduated subscriber fines.

Hallcrest's review of alarm control programs found that (p. 270): "The most effective programs appear to be those which were initially developed in conjunction with the alarm companies, and those which continue to involve the alarm companies in follow-up customer training."

SURVEILLANCE SYSTEMS

Some companies use surveillance systems in place of or to supplement security officers. These systems may be used at any of the three lines of defense: the perimeter, the entrance/exit to a building or a specific location within the building.

Convex mirror.

Interior surveillance.

Many forms of surveillance are available. One of the simplest and most commonly used is the convex mirror, which allows clerks to see areas that are not observable from a checkout station. More complex forms of surveillance include closed-circuit television and videotape and still, still sequence and motion picture cameras. Surveillance systems can operate continually or on demand. They can be monitored or unmonitored.

Closed-circuit television (CCTV) can be used in corridors, entrances and secured areas. Although expensive, it saves personal costs because one person can monitor several locations at one time. When combined with videotape capabilities, CCTV need not be continuously monitored because of its playback capabilities.

As noted by O'Brien (1992, p. 27A): "Closed-circuit surveillance systems used with other methods of access control . . . increase security officer efficiency and productivity, and the end result is a more secure facility."

Jacobson (1994, p. 30) describes the "old standby of CCTV systems—the pan and tilt drive":

> The basic function of a pan and tilt is simple: It swivels horizontally (panning) and vertically (tilting) in order to bring the camera to bear on a subject within its viewing area.

According to Major (1994, pp. 38, 41), pan and tilt technology has changed from "crude mechanisms to sophisticated high tech. . . . The devices are getting smaller, lighter and faster. . . . The resolution, sensitivity and overall quality of the cameras are increasing . . . as are the speed and mobility of the pan and tilt units containing them."

Inventor F. Jerry Gutierrez demonstrates one of his surveillance mannequins designed to watch for shoplifters. They are being photographed by the photographer shown on the TV monitor.

One important advancement in CCTV is digitization. According to Pappageorge (1993, p. 70): "Recent breakthroughs in closed-circuit video equipment (CCVE) provide security managers with options for greater programming flexibility and high-quality picture images required to identify suspects and win convictions. Among the more significant of these developments are the varied uses of digital-processing technology."

This view is shared by Newton (1994, p. 60): "Digitization opens up a world of capabilities for transmission and storage of video images." He suggests: "Digital video compression, in conjunction with modern low-cost, high-speed data communications, allows effective and viable remote surveillance at a cost that makes it accessible to all industries and applications."

Digitization has resulted in two significant advances: the QUAD and the video multiplexer. The QUAD compresses the images from four cameras into a single frame of VCR tape, allowing the operator to view all four cameras on a four-way split screen. The video multiplexer is a control system providing high-speed, full-frame recording from multiple cameras.

Digitization has also greatly enhanced storage capabilities, with one terabyte (one thousand gigabytes, which are one thousand million bytes) of hard disk storage representing about 120 conventional VHS tapes or a continuous recording of three to four months in the 24-hour mode (Newton, p. 62).

In some security systems, CCTV includes interactive video and audio (IAVA) capabilities. Norton (1992, p. 26A) describes how many convenience stores have used IAVA systems to deter robbery and increase employee safety.

Other systems have added color, enhancing recognition and identification of individuals, as noted by Parker (1992, p. 37):

> The difference between black-and-white and color is like day and night. Its biggest advantage is added differentiation. When you see something in color, it can be recognized for what it is faster. Color allows quicker and more accurate identification of people or objects—close up or at a distance.

If video surveillance is used without employees' knowledge, employers must be careful that they do not violate their employees' privacy rights, as will be discussed in Chapter 12.

An important addition to surveillance systems is the infrared (IR) camera which can be used for night surveillance. As noted by Frank (1991, p. 45):

> Once the exclusive domain of sophisticated aerospace and military imaging systems, high-quality IR focal plan arrays have been refined to give security professionals affordable see-in-the-dark technology. Designed to integrate into existing CCTV systems or operate alone, these new, high-resolution cameras are rugged, easy to operate, and portable.
>
> IR cameras can be put to work wherever poor visibility hampers the performance of visible CCTV cameras. With IR cameras in place, as much as 50 percent of a facility's night lighting costs can be eliminated for both interior and exterior surveillance.

IR cameras are ideally suited for parking lots, loading docks and remote locations. In addition, they are not hampered by rain, fog or snow as normal surveillance cameras are.

Although less expensive than CCTV, motion picture cameras are not as effective because they require light and almost always make noise. Infrared film can be used if night-only picture taking is anticipated. Sequence cameras can take still pictures at regular intervals or be activated to take pictures when a switch is thrown.

Each system has specific advantages and disadvantages, as illustrated in Table 5–2.

Security managers are cautioned to remember the restriction on surveillance and appropriate legal/privacy issues that might arise.

Other Means to Enhance Security through Physical Control

In addition to locks, lights, alarms and surveillance systems, numerous other alternatives are available to security managers to reduce losses through the use of physical controls.

Table 5–2. Selection and Application Guide to Fixed Surveillance Cameras—National Institute of Law Enforcement and Criminal Justice

	Still Demand Cameras			Still Sequence Cameras			Motion Picture Cameras (Demand)	TV Cameras	TV Camera and Videotape
	8mm	*16mm*	*35mm*	*8mm*	*16mm*	*35mm*			
EVIDENCE QUALITY	Fair	Good	High	Fair	Good	High	Variable	None	Poor
OPERATOR REQUIRED	Yes	Yes	Yes	No	No	No	No	Yes	No
CONTINUOUS COVERAGE	No	No	No	Partial	Partial	Partial	Yes	Yes	Yes
IMMEDIATE RESULTS	No	No	No	No	No	No	No	Yes	Yes
POSSIBLE PERSONNEL HAZARD	Yes	Yes	Yes	No	No	No	No	No	No
LIGHT VARIATION TOLERANCE	Low	Low	Low	Low	Low	Low	Low	High	High
LIGHT LEVEL REQUIRED (FC)	50–75	50–75	50–75	50–75	50–75	50–57	50–75	20	20
AGAINST BURGLARY	Poor	Poor	Poor	Fair	Good	High	High	None	Good
AGAINST ROBBERY	Fair	Good	High	Fair	Good	High	Variable	None	Poor
AGAINST EMPLOYEE THEFT	None	None	None	Good	High	High	None	None	High
AGAINST SHOPLIFTING	None	None	None	Poor	Fair	Good	None	Good	Good
AGAINST BAD CHECKS	High	High	High	High	High	High	High	None	Poor
EQUIPMENT FIRST COST	Very low	Low	Medium	Low	Medium	Medium	Medium	High	Very high
SUPPLIES COST	Very low	Very low	Very low	Very low	Low	Medium	Medium	None	Low
PERSONNEL COST	None	None	None	None	None	None	None	High	None

Quality of motion picture camera output will vary by film size, just as still cameras.
EVIDENCE QUALITY comparisons are based on prints from single frames.
LIGHT LEVEL REQUIRED is based on ASA 250 film exposed at 1/125 second, F2.8.
Effectiveness AGAINST BURGLARY comparisons assume use of available accessories including scanners on motion picture and TV cameras.
Effectiveness AGAINST SHOPLIFTING assumes that television monitors are constantly watched.
Effectiveness AGAINST BAD CHECKS assumes use of equipment to the passer with check in court.
All demand camera systems are assumed to be properly activated by some means, whether by personnel, sensors, or burglar alarm tie-in.
Note: Do not rely on the chart alone. Details are contained in the text.
Reprinted by permission.

New security devices are constantly being produced and marketed. Magazines such as *Security Management* and *Security World* can help security managers keep abreast of new developments in security hardware.

Other Security Devices

Other security devices available are paper shredders, used to make certain no classified information is improperly discarded; lock-down devices for office machines and other valuable equipment such as microscopes; mirrors in hallways to reveal if anyone is lurking around corners and in retail stores to detect shoplifting; metal detectors; electronic price tags and computerized telephone systems that automatically route outgoing calls over the least expensive lines and that detect and control long-distance phoning abuses and the like.

Other devices range from such basic items as bulletproof vests to such sophisticated items as bug detection systems that protect privacy during personal conversations in offices, hotels and at home; a bionic briefcase that contains a bomb and bug detector and is wired to prevent theft; and an electronic handkerchief that allows a person to disguise his or her voice over the telephone.

Signs

Signs can be used to provide instructions and warnings; for example, "Restricted Area," "No Unauthorized Personnel Beyond This Point," "No Admittance," "One Way," "This Building Protected by an Alarm," "Caution: Attack Dog," "All shoplifters will be prosecuted to the full extent of the law," "No Smoking" and so on can effectively improve safety and discourage crime. In most jurisdictions signs are a legal requirement for trespassing prosecutions.

Metal Detectors

Most people are familiar with the metal detectors used in airports, but such detectors are used in a wide variety of other settings, as described by Graham and Loveless (1994, p. 38):

> Metal detectors are used in a variety of venues for security purposes, including emergency rooms, gold mining operations, sporting events, government buildings, art exhibitions, and the lumber industry where environmental groups drive large metal spikes into trees marked for harvest.
>
> Other uses include archaeological displays, political conventions, protection of VIP and government officials, homeless shelters, inner city housing, and public transportation. Prisons were among the first institutions to recognize the efficacy of using metal detectors as a first line of security defense. In response to the escalating threat of violence, virtually all U.S. courts use detectors to screen those attending high profile trials.

Walk-through type metal detectors cost between $4,500 and $5,500 (McMicking, 1993, p. 54). Hand-held metal detectors are also available and cost considerably less, ranging from $20 to $200.

Often metal detectors are used in combination with x-ray machines, as is the case in most airports. According to McMicking (1993, pp. 54–55): "X-ray systems detect weapons, liquids, and explosives and are much more expensive than metal detectors—around $30,000 to $50,000."

Dogs

Security dogs may be classified as *patrol dogs* or *guard dogs*. *Sentry* or *patrol dogs* are usually leashed and make rounds with a security officer, providing companionship and protection. Because of their keen sense of smell and hearing, they can easily detect intruders. Sentry dogs, frequently German Shepherds or Doberman Pinschers, are the most expensive security dogs.

Guard dogs roam alone inside a perimeter or building to deter intruders. They may be alarm dogs whose growl and bark are intended to frighten intruders away, or they may be attack dogs, trained to physically restrain any intruders. Guard dogs are frequently used by the military, by some contract security firms, by car dealers, by junk dealers, by warehouse operators and in large stores. Often the dogs are leased from a security dog contractor. Such dogs usually respond to only one handler and therefore pose a potential risk, especially for police officers or fire fighters who might be called to the premises in an emergency.

Although security dogs are expensive and do present a potential risk for lawsuits, and although they can be shot, hit, anaesthetized or poisoned, they

Guard dogs are one effective way to deter trespassing.

remain a viable alternative for many establishments. According to Spurlock (1990, p. 94), the greatest expense is training. Budget reports for five small- to medium-sized police departments indicate that the highest annual maintenance cost was $800.

Security Officers

Many establishments depend on the presence of a uniformed security officer, perhaps armed, as a deterrent to most would-be offenders. In addition, security officers can perform the numerous functions discussed in Chapter 2, and they can ensure the effectiveness of security equipment.

Some establishments have their security patrols carry a **watch clock** on their rounds. Watch clocks are seven-day timepieces. Keys are located at various stations in a facility, and the security officer simply inserts the key into the watch clock at each station. A record is automatically made of the time the location was checked. Any stations not visited at the appropriate time can be monitored.

MacDonald and Clark (1991, p. 25A) note that for more than a century the mechanical watch clock has been the mainstay of security guards and patrols, ensuring that officers are making their rounds and documenting with irrefutable proof that security personnel are performing as expected. But the mechanical watch clock is being replaced.

> Now watchtour supervision has entered the era of computers and information management. New electronic systems collect, store, and retrieve tour data for

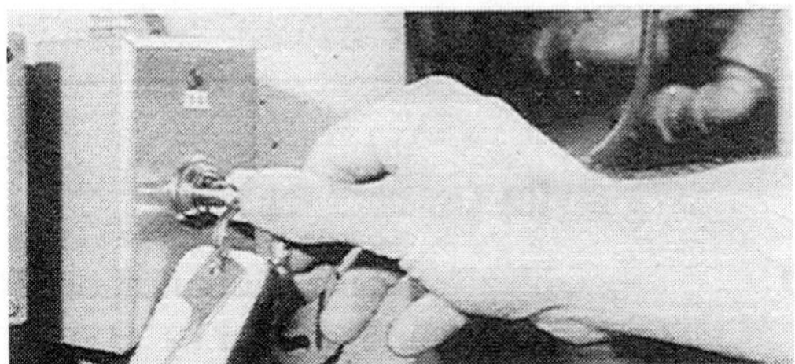

The traditional watch clock was carried by the security officer. Modern watch clocks operate by keys being inserted into them, which sends a record of when the check was made back to the central control panel.

> future analysis and verify security rounds on tape or from micro-processor storage. . . .
>
> Today security managers can select from a wide range of hardware and software, from simple bar code readers and recorders to sophisticated hand-held computers. One system records elapsed time between stations and informs officers of the location of the next checkpoint. Almost like a computer game, this unit is designed to keep guards on the go and on their toes.
>
> Another high-tech system uses telephones at each checkpoint. Officers record their stops by entering a digital code on the phone. In this telecommunications-age system, tour information is instantaneously transferred to a data base for future reporting.

Bar-coding devices now allow security personnel to check hazardous areas, inventory items, inspect fire equipment and produce neatly printed reports by simply attaching the bar-code wand to a desktop computer with a printer.

Some facilities have sophisticated automatic guard-monitoring systems that transmit a message to the central security office if a guard does not arrive at the appointed time. The central security office is thus alerted to any illness, accident or crime-related problems. One disadvantage of this system, however, is that an established patrol pattern can be learned by unauthorized people and used to their advantage.

Communication Systems

Numerous types of communications are available, including telephones, public address or loudspeaker systems, intercoms, radios or walkie-talkies, pagers, tape recorders and teletypes. Although means of communication are often taken for granted, they are vital in situations such as emergencies or natural disasters.

The Command Center

Ideally, the communication center should be linked to the security control center and should be in a controlled area. The communication center area might receive any alarm signals and might be the control for the switchboard, a closed-circuit television monitoring system and a public address system.

The Physical Security System

All too often, managers concentrate on appearance, efficiency and convenience to the neglect of security and safety.

> Aesthetic, operational, safety and security needs must be balanced.

The key factors in any physical security program are to identify risks and then to alleviate them when possible. A security survey allows managers to assess the vulnerability of assets as well as the criticality of their loss and then to select physical controls to meet the needs of their particular facility. Providing either more or less physical security than is needed is never desirable.

The security checklist in Figure 5–8 summarizes the key physical controls used to provide security.

PORTLAND POLICE BUREAU COMMERCIAL SECURITY SURVEY

Business Name ______________________ File No. __________

Address ______________________ Date __________

Name of Person Contacted ______________________ Position __________

Type of Premise ______________________ Phone No. __________

KEY: STND = STANDARD REC = RECOMMENDATION COMM = COMMENTS

1. BUILDING FRONT

	STND	REC	COMM
DOORS			
LOCKS			
WINDOWS			
LIGHTS			
VENTS			
MISC.			

2. BUILDING RIGHT SIDE

	STND	REC	COMM
DOORS			
LOCKS			
WINDOWS			
LIGHTS			
VENTS			
MISC.			

3. BUILDING REAR

	STND	REC	COMM
DOORS			
LOCKS			
WINDOWS			
LIGHTS			
VENTS			
MISC.			

4. BUILDING LEFT SIDE

	STND	REC	COMM
DOORS			
LOCKS			
WINDOWS			
LIGHTS			
VENTS			
MISC.			

5. BUILDING ROOF

	STND	REC	COMM
ROOF ACCESS			
ROOF			
SKYLIGHT			
ROOF			
VENTS			
MISC.			

6. LOADING DOORS

	STND	REC	COMM
OVER HEAD			
SLIDING			
SIDEWALK			
ELEVATOR			
ROLLER			

7. ALARMS

	STND	REC	COMM
AUDIBLE			
SILENT			
OTHER			

ALARM PERMIT # __________

8. SAFES

	STND	REC	COMM
ANCHORED			
SHIELDED			
DIAL			
VISIBLE			
LIGHTED			
MONEY CHEST			
FILE			

9. MISCELLANEOUS

	STND	REC	COMM
KEY CONTROL			
FENCING			
LIGHTING			
LANDSCAPING			
OFFICE EQUIPMENT ENGRAVED			

COMMENTS: ______________________

This report is advisory only and does not purport to list all hazards or the adequacy of present hazard controls.

OFFICER:	NO.	PREC/DIV:	DISTRICT:

PRECINCT

Figure 5–8. Security Checklist

SOURCE: Courtesy of the Portland Police Bureau.

It is common sense that a locked, well-lit building equipped with an alarm system will be less attractive to a thief than an unfenced, unlocked, unlit building with no alarm system. But locks, lights, alarms and other security equipment must be properly maintained and used to be effective.

> Common sense and attention to detail are critical factors in establishing and maintaining physical controls.

Because security hardware has become increasingly complex and sophisticated, the Private Security Task Force Report recommends that security consultants be used for specialized areas such as alarm systems, anti-burglary strategies, personnel control techniques and systems, security hardware for access points, security lighting techniques and special security needs such as those required for computers. This chapter has presented only an overview of the physical security control options available. Bobek and Thompson (1995, p. 6A) stress:

> Although traditionally viewed as separate concerns, security functions such as access control and fire safety can be integrated with nonsecurity facility operations such as lighting, and heating, ventilation, and air conditioning (HVAC). The key is linking multiple systems and pieces of equipment with a common interface. The interface allows information to be displayed in a single, common format and allows the method of controlling all equipment to be identical. This uniformity increases access to, and management of, the linked systems and equipment, in turn yielding quicker response times, reduced manpower and training, and more efficient use of resources.

Section IV presents integrated systems in practice in various types of establishments.

SUMMARY

One important responsibility of security managers is to provide security through physical controls. Physical controls serve to reduce risk of loss by denying unauthorized access, by deterring or delaying those who attempt to gain unauthorized access and by detecting threats, both criminal and noncriminal.

The three basic lines of physical defense are the perimeter of a facility, the building exterior and the interior. The perimeter can be physically controlled by fences, gates, locks, lighting, alarms, surveillance systems, signs, metal detectors, dogs and security personnel. Physical layout and neatness are other important factors.

The physical security of a building's exterior can be established by strong, locked doors and windows, limited entrances, secured openings (if larger than 96 square inches), alarms, surveillance and lighting. Interior physical controls include locked doors, desks and files; safes and vaults; internal alarms and detectors; lighting; mirrors; bolt-down equipment; dogs; security personnel; and communication and surveillance systems. Most safes are either fire resistant or burglar resistant, but not both.

From the preceding, it can be seen that basic security equipment at any of the three lines of defense includes locks, lights and alarms. Available locks include key operated, combination, card activated and electronically operated. If a key-operated lock is used, the best protection is offered by a dead-bolt lock with a one-inch throw and an antiwrenching collar, or a secondary dead bolt with a one-inch throw.

Adequate light inside as well as outside a building enhances safety, deters would-be intruders and makes detection of actual intruders more probable. A total lighting system includes four types of lighting: (1) continuous—on a regular schedule for secure areas, (2) standby—for occasions when more light is needed, (3) moveable—for when light is needed in areas not usually lit and (4) emergency—to be used as an alternate power source when the regular power source fails.

Alarms are also available for all three lines of defense: perimeter alarms, to protect fences, gates, exterior doors, windows and other openings; area or space alarms, to protect a portion of or the total interior of a room or building; and point or spot alarms, to protect specific items such as safes, cabinets, valuable articles or small areas. Alarm systems may be local, proprietary, central station or police connected.

When selecting physical controls to reduce losses from recognized risks, security managers must balance aesthetic, operational, safety and security needs. Once physical controls have been selected and installed, common sense and attention to detail are critical factors in establishing and maintaining the physical controls.

APPLICATION

1. The Ace Industrial Company is faced with the problem of saving on lighting to conserve energy without sacrificing its security. The company's president instructs the security manager to research the problem. If you were in this manager's position, what suggestions might you make to reduce the cost of lighting, conserve energy and yet maintain security?

2. Design a 50-foot-by-100-foot storage building that will contain heavy equipment, parts and a repair area for the equipment. Include locks, lighting and alarms that would be appropriate and justify each installation you recommend.

3. Obtain from several police departments statistical data regarding responses to false alarms in the community. Also obtain a copy of the community's false-alarm ordinance, if available, and bring it to class for a discussion and analysis of the ordinance's effectiveness in bringing the consumer, the law

enforcement agency and the alarm company together to curb the false-alarm problem.

CRITICAL THINKING EXERCISE

Read the following exercise carefully and then select the best answer. The exercise is based on information presented by Maxwell (1993, pp. 161–164).

A contract between NBK Company manufacturing jewelers and the D&W Central Station Alarm Company, Inc., states:

> The parties agree that the alarm system is not designed or guaranteed to prevent loss by burglary, theft, or other illegal acts of third parties, or loss by fire. If, notwithstanding the terms of this agreement, there should arise any liability on the part of the lessor, as a result of burglary, theft, hold-up, equipment failure, fire, smoke, or any cause whatsoever, regardless of whether or not such loss, damage or personal injury was caused by or contributed to by lessor's negligent performance or failure to perform any obligation under this agreement, such liability shall be limited to an amount equal to six (6) times the monthly payment by lessee at the time such liability is fixed, or to the sum of $250.00, whichever is greater.

FACTS OF THE CASE

Sometime between the evening of December 26 and the morning of December 27, NBK's plant was burglarized. D&W had received an alarm signal from NBK at 10:47 P.M. and another alarm at 12:30 A.M. A guard dispatched from D&W arrived at NBK at 1:54 but left without investigating because he could not get into the building. When he called D&W to tell them this, he was told to "forget that assignment and go on another guard run."

The record also showed that North Atlantic Security Alarm, Inc., which monitored NBK on CCTV, saw the burglars on camera at about 4:44 A.M. on December 27 and notified the police who arrived at 5:03. The burglars had left the scene. NBK's losses were reported as $243,000.

ISSUES AND QUESTIONS

1. Will the disclaimer of liability contained in the contract stand up in court in these circumstances?

- **a.** Yes, because it plainly states that D&W is not responsible for losses caused by burglaries.
- **b.** Yes, because a guard was dispatched and the police were called.
- **c.** No, because D&W failed to notify the police and told the guard to ignore the assignment, both grossly negligent acts that preclude exemption from liability.
- **d.** No, because such a disclaimer is not legally binding.
- **e.** Yes, D&W signed the contract in good faith.

Discussion Questions

1. Most adults have several keys in their possession. How many keys are in your possession? What types of locks do they fit? Compare the different types of keys that others have with your own.
2. Local communities frequently pass ordinances to curtail false-alarm responses by the public police. From the user's standpoint, is this an advantage or a disadvantage?
3. Despite the numerous advantages offered by a reliable surveillance system, what disadvantages might be expected?
4. Security managers frequently overcompensate in protecting areas with fencing. List some guidelines you would consider before recommending any type of outside security fencing.
5. In providing for security needs, why are aesthetics important to the security manager?

References

Berube, Henri. "New Notions of Night Light." *Security Management,* December 1994, pp. 29–33.

Bobek, John and Thompson, Steve. "Unification Theory: Putting All the Pieces Together." *Security Management,* March 1995, pp. 6A–9A.

Bordes, Roy N. "Pick a Card, Any Card." *Security Management,* November 1994, pp. 74–77.

Bowers, Kim. "Premises Security without Keys, Codes, Cards or Combinations." *Security Concepts,* December 1994, pp. 19, 22.

Chanter, N. "Control/Communicator Technology Is the Heart and Brains of Alarm Systems." *Security Technology and Design,* November/December 1993, pp. 18–20.

Crowe, Timothy D. "Safer Schools by Design." *Security Management,* September 1991, pp. 81–86.

Cunningham, W. C. and Taylor, T. H. *The Hallcrest Report: Private Security and Police in America.* Portland, OR: Chancellor Press, 1985.

Cunningham, William C.; Strauchs, John J.; and Van Meter, Clifford W. *Private Security Trends, 1970 to 2000: The Hallcrest Report II.* Stoneham, MA: Butterworth-Heinemann, 1990.

Dean, S. Carl. "Electrified Door Hardware and Keypads." *Security Technology and Design,* June/July 1994, pp. 50–55.

Dingle, Jeff. "Back to the Basics." *Security Technology and Design,* November/December 1993, p. 65.

Dunckel, Kenneth. "Electronic Safe Locks: A New Current." *Security Management,* November 1991, pp. 70–74.

Frank, Jeff. "Out of the Darkness." *Security Management,* 1991, pp. 45–47.

Gillespie, Tom. "Keypad Technology Matches Needs of End-Users." *Security Technology and Design,* May/June 1993, pp. 12–14.

Graham, Richard K. and Loveless, David G. "The Steely Eye of the Metal Detector." *Security Management,* June 1994, pp. 38–40.

Griffiths, Barry. "Detecting Intrusion with Fiber Optics." *Security Management,* July 1992, pp. 46–49.

Harpole, Tom. "Panes that Pay." *Security Management,* September 1991, pp. 121–125.

Hof, Robert D. "Forget the I.D.—Let's See Your Eyeball." *Business Week,* November 21, 1988, pp. 109–112.

Jacobson, Jerry L. "Pan and Tilt Technology in 1994." *Security Technology and Design,* October 1994, pp. 30–36.

Jefferson, Bob. "Shedding Light on Security Problems." *Security Management,* December 1992, pp. 63–66.

Lewin, Thomas M. "Plagued by False Alarms?" *Law and Order,* December 1990, pp. 67–69.

Lorenzo, Ray. "Getting Smart about Safes." *Security Management,* December 1993, pp. 55–57.

MacDonald, Robert R. and Clark, Bill. "High-Tech Touring." *Security Management Special Supplement: Priming Your Personnel,* March 1991, p. 25A.

Major, Michael J. "Pan and Tilt: Evolving Toward High-Tech Sophistication." *Security Technology and Design,* October 1994, pp. 38–41.

Maxwell, David A. *Private Security Law: Case Studies.* Stoneham, MA: Butterworth-Heinemann, 1993.

McCullough, Joseph B. "Prepared to Be Alarmed." *Security Management,* March 1994, pp. 59–62.

McMicking, Lawrence. "The Right Machine for the Job." *Security Management,* February 1993, pp. 54–56.

Mele, Joe A. "Security Lighting: 'You Move Me.'" *Security Concepts,* April 1994, p. 25.

Miehl, Fred. "The Ins and Outs of Door Locks." *Security Management,* February 1993, pp. 48–53.

Miller, Ben. "The Nuts and Bolts of Biometrics." *Security Management,* September 1991, pp. 31–35.

Mourey, Richard. "Wiegand Card Technology Remains a Secure Investment." *Security Technology and Design,* August 1994, pp. 42–44.

Murphy, Joan H. "Is Business Embracing Biometrics?" *Security Management,* September 1991, pp. 37–41.

National Advisory Commission on Criminal Justice Standards and Goals, Programs for Reduction of Criminal Opportunity. *Community Crime Prevention.* Law Enforcement Assistance Administration, Washington, DC: U.S. Government Printing Office, 1973.

National Crime Prevention Institute. *Understanding Crime Prevention.* Stoneham, MA: Butterworth Publishers, 1986.

Naudts, John. "Access Control: It's In the Cards." *Security Management,* September 1987, pp. 169–173.

Newton, Mike. "Picturing the Future of CCTV." *Security Management,* November 1994, pp. 60–63.

Norton, Kelly. "Cashing in on CCTV Technology." *Security Management,* March 1992, pp. 26A–29A.

O'Brien, Jim. "CCTV Watches the World Go By." *Security Management,* June 1992, pp.27A–30A.

Olick, M. "Biometrics: A Show of Hands." *Security Concepts,* June 1994, pp. 6, 24.

Pappageorge, Tom. "The Secrets of CCTV." *Security Management,* August 1993, pp. 70–72.

Parker, Eugene. "Color CCTV System: Jail Surveillance Out of the Shadows." *Law Enforcement Technology,* June 1992, pp. 36–37.

Private Security. Report of the Task Force on Private Security, National Advisory Committee on Criminal Justice Standards and Goals. Washington, DC: U.S. Government Printing Office, 1976.

Reynolds, Sandra. "Taking the Nuisance Out of Intrusion Detection." *Security Management,* August 1994, pp. 35–37.

Scheirer, S. Robin. "Sound Advice for Safe Storage." *Security Management,* May 1992, pp. 37–38.

Seidman, Stephan. "TVs to Toll Booths: Smart Card Capabilities." *Security Management,* April 1994, pp. 47–52.

Spurlock, James C. "K-9." *Law and Order,* March 1990, pp. 91–96.

"Study Estimates Police Respond to 15M False Alarms Annually from Burglar Alarms." *The Minnesota Police Journal,* October 1994, pp. 47–49.

Vitch, Martin L. "Sensing Your Way to Security." *Security Management,* July 1992, pp. 50–54.

Vitch, Martin L. "The Importance of IDS Inspection." *Security Management,* March 1993, pp. 34–37.

Vitch, Martin L. "Wireless Alarm Transmission Is Rapidly Becoming a Standard." *Security Technology and Design,* May/June 1993, pp. 42–46.

Zamengo, Edward. "White Nights." *Security Management,* October 1994, pp. 53–59.

Zunkel, Richard L. "Palm Reading for Protection." *Security Management,* November 1994, pp. 87–90.

CHAPTER 6

Enhancing Security through Procedural Controls

Do You Know

- What shrinkage is?
- What hiring procedures can help reduce shrinkage and negligence lawsuits?
- What educational measures can help promote security?
- How most procedural controls seek to prevent loss?
- What specific procedures can be used to control access to an area?
- What characterizes an effective employee badge or pass?
- What constitutes effective key control?
- What an effective closing procedure ensures?
- When opening and closing is a two-person operation?
- What areas are particularly vulnerable to theft?
- What accounting procedures can help prevent shrinkage?
- What procedures can help detect theft or pilferage?
- When searches of lockers, vehicles, packages and persons are acceptable?
- What procedures to use when transporting valuables?
- What additional protection against financial loss is available to owners/managers?

Can You Define These Terms?

blind receiving
change key
employment records
fidelity bonds
grand master key
integrity interview
master key
master keying system
neuter head blank
perpetual inventory
polygraph
shrinkage
sub-master key

Introduction

The BuildMore Construction Company has installed a sophisticated alarm system, the most modern security lighting and the best locks available. Management is confident that the facility is secure. It is unaware, however, that Employee A is taking small tools home in his lunch pail almost daily; Employee B is placing several lengthy personal long-distance calls a month; Employee C is loading extra lumber on his truck and using it to build his own garage; Employee D is falsifying her time card regularly; and Employee F is submitting false invoices to be paid to his wife under her maiden name. In addition, the typewriter repairer who just carried out a new electric typewriter is not really a technician but a thief.

Locks, lights and alarms cannot protect the BuildMore Construction Company from such losses. Physical controls must be complemented by procedural controls to establish security. The facility itself and the degree of security required will determine, of course, the extent of the physical and procedural controls. The following discussion presents general procedures that might apply in most facilities. Additional procedures frequently required in industrial, retail, commercial and other specific types of establishments are discussed in Section IV.

This chapter begins by discussing the problem of shrinkage and two of the main causes: employee dishonesty and alcohol/drug abuse in the workplace. Next the importance of the hiring process and employment practices in helping to reduce these problems is examined. This is followed by a discussion of controlling access to restricted areas as well as to vulnerable areas and equipment. The chapter concludes with discussions of accounting and receiving procedures for controlling shrinkage, transporting valuables, detecting employee theft and pilferage and insurance and bonding.

SHRINKAGE—A MAJOR PROBLEM AND CHALLENGE

Numerous books on private security differentiate between the "enemy from without"—the robber and burglar—and the "enemy from within"—the dishonest employee who systematically depletes a company's assets and causes **shrinkage.**

> *Shrinkage* refers to lost assets.

In reality, shrinkage is often a polite term for employee theft. Losses may be incurred due to employees actually stealing or because they are not doing the job as they should be.

Internal theft may account for up to 70 percent of all shrinkage. Such thefts may be of cash, merchandise, industrial tools and supplies, office supplies, time and/or vital information. Addis (1991, p. 116) cites the Department of Commerce as estimating that employees steal as much as $120 billion a year from their employers.

Draty (1995, p. 11) suggests: "The costs of dishonest employees are large enough to affect the Gross National Product, market competitiveness and your corporation." According to Draty:

> American business loses an estimated $150 billion per year to employee theft of tangible items, such as cash and merchandise, a figure growing by 15 percent per year. These are staggering statistics, but not as overwhelming as those relating to theft of intangibles, such as bogus sick days, long breaks, lack of productivity and false workers' compensation claims.

As noted by McClain (1995, p. 9): "It is well established that approximately one-third of all business failures annually in America are caused by employee theft including embezzlement." McClain also notes:

> We also know that substance abuse by employees goes hand-in-hand with theft from their employers. To afford the drugs, the employees must either "steal or deal." In addition, employee drug usage increases abuse of sick leave and medical benefits as well as absenteeism, safety violations and poor productivity.

According to Bartholomew (1991, p. 42), drug use while on the job presents "harrowing problems" for the employer: "Accidents, absenteeism, theft and insurance costs go up." Lisko (1994, p. 92) concurs: "The consequences of drug abuse in the workplace range from accidents and injuries to theft, bad decisions, and ruined lives."

Lasky and Steinberg (1994, p. 14) also note:

> The effects of drug use are well known. It increases absenteeism and decreases productivity. It raises the risk of injury to co-workers, members of the public and the drug user himself. Most importantly, drug use increases theft and pilferage.

Assets can also be lost because of employees who are absent or late, frequently the result of alcohol abuse. As noted by Stoller (1991, p. 127): "The costs of alcohol abuse in the workplace are enormous."

> The National Institute on Alcohol Abuse and Alcoholism estimates that alcohol and other drug abuse on the job costs the United States $102 billion each year through increased insurance rates, decreased productivity, and increased prices for goods and services.

Statistics from a Department of Labor report reflect the costly effects of workplace alcohol abuse:

> Employees who abuse alcohol and other drugs claim three times as many sickness benefits and five times as many workers' compensation claims.
>
> Workers who abuse alcohol are absent from the job 16 times more often than other employees. . . .
>
> Absenteeism, sick leave, overtime pay, tardiness, and insurance and workers' compensation claims are real, quantitative costs to American companies caused by alcohol abuse in the workplace.

The cost of abuse of alcohol and illicit drugs is also underscored by Martin and DeGrange (1993, p. 39):

> An average 10% to 20% of all employees abuse alcohol or use illicit drugs. Organizations lose an estimated $100 billion per year due to alcohol and drug abuse, resulting from poor performance, illness, absenteeism, injury, theft and product damage.

There is another problem with the "enemy from within." Many businesses are finding that they are legally liable for any misdeeds of their employees, particularly if they did not exercise "reasonable care" in their hiring procedures. For example, the owner of an apartment complex was sued by a tenant who had been sexually assaulted by the apartment manager (*Ponticas v. K.M.S. Investments*—Minn. 1983). The manager was on parole at the time he applied for the job and gave as his two references his mother and sister. The court ruled that the preemployment screening was insufficient given the responsibility associated with the job.

Such problems can often be greatly reduced by hiring wisely. As noted by McClain (1995, p. 9), employers can reduce the threats associated with employee theft and substance abuse by controlling three factors:

- The quality of people hired into the work force.
- The environment into which they are placed.
- The quality of supervision.

THE FIRST LINE OF DEFENSE—HIRING WELL

One way to reduce shrinkage and avoid negligence suits is to improve the quality of personnel hired. Kuhn (1990, p. 23A) notes that security and human resources personnel have several trends working against them:

- A shrinking pool of qualified workers.
- Diminished employee loyalty.
- Tougher legislation surrounding employee selection practices.
- Defamation of character suits brought against employers who provide references on ex-employees.
- Increasing workplace theft and drug use.
- Growing number of vicarious liability and negligent hiring suits.

Given these trends, effective preemployment screening is critical.

> Preemployment screening should include an application and resumé, intellectual and psychological tests, a thorough background check including references and a personal interview. It may include drug testing.

Beaudette (1992, p. 39) cautions: "[E]mployers cannot afford the losses that result from poor hiring decisions. Higher turnover rates, internal theft, insurance claims, loss of trade secrets, and losses due to employee-related litigation can sharply increase as a result of incomplete or ineffective screening." In addition, says Beaudette:

> The courts are increasingly upholding the Negligent Hiring and Retention Doctrine. They are taking the position that the employer should make every

effort to ensure that the employee selection process is a reasoned and useful exercise—not a process that culminates in an "intuitive guess."

Rosen (1993, p. 38) also cautions: "Employers have been held liable when they failed to investigate an employee's background adequately, where it was determined that an investigation could have discovered the risk. Employers, therefore, have a duty to investigate." Rosen (p. 39) lists the following elements of a cause of action for negligent hiring:

- The individual in question was an employee of the defendant.
- The employee was unfit for employment.
- The employer knew or should have known the employee was unfit for employment.
- The plaintiff was injured by the employee's acts during a contact with the employee that was connected to the employment.
- The employer owed a duty of care to the plaintiff.
- The hiring of the employee was the proximate cause of the injuries to the plaintiff.

Rosen also lists the elements for a cause of action involving negligent retention:

- The employee is hired.
- The employer becomes aware after the hiring that the employee is potentially dangerous.
- The employer retains the employee knowing of the danger.
- The plaintiff's contact with the potentially dangerous employee was connected in some way with the employment relationship.
- The plaintiff is harmed during that contact.

Nonetheless, as noted by Bequai (1991, p. 58): "[F]ederal and state privacy laws have made the task of screening job applicants more difficult and demanding, as well as fraught with legal pitfalls." He notes three key rights to privacy that job applicants have:

- The right not to be portrayed by a former or prospective employer in a false or misleading light.
- The right not to have a prospective employer make disclosure of private facts.
- The right to be free from unwarranted intrusions by a prospective employer.

In addition, job applicants are protected by the Civil Rights Act of 1964 which prohibits discrimination because of race, color, religion, sex or national origin in all employment practices, including hiring, promoting, compensating and firing.

They are also protected by the Americans with Disabilities Act (ADA) which prohibits asking questions related to medical history or disabilities until after a job has been offered, as described by Arnold and Thiemann (1994, p. 45):

> Along with its prohibition of requiring medical examinations prior to the job offer, the act also prohibits inquiries regarding disabilities at the applicant

stage. Test questions regarding mental and physical problems, such as whether a person becomes ill easily or has spent time in therapy, mandate that a test must be conducted only after tendering a conditional offer of employment.

In addition, as noted by Jayne (1994, p. 47): "[T]he Americans with Disabilities Act of 1990 confines an employer's preemployment inquiries concerning the use of illegal drugs to current or recent use."

Another reason hiring well is important is that, according to Mancebo (1992, p. 57), about one-fourth of all new hires are discharged for cause or quit their jobs at an estimated cost of $650 per employee. Another 20 percent work fewer than 30 days, at a cost of $400 each. Mancebo suggests that using the appropriate test can have dramatic results:

> Our research indicates it is possible to reduce turnover, cutting terminations for cause and job abandonment by 13 to 90 percent, and reduce the number of employees who work fewer than 30 days by 7 to 39 percent.
>
> Precision in hiring is particularly important for security firms because the product is people.

The Application and Resumé

As noted by Beaudette (1992, p. 63): "The resumé and application are the first chance to get a foot in the door, so naturally the applicant will put his or her best foot forward." He also suggests, however, that often what is put forward is not the truth: "The percentage of resumés and job applications that contain lies and exaggerations has been estimated at somewhere between 30 and 80 percent."

Schafer (1990, p. 17A) cautions: "One mistake in the hiring process can cost an employer millions in negligent hiring or retention lawsuits." Steps employers might take to avoid resumé fraud, according to Schafer, include the following:

- Establish and publish requirements within the company that background investigations must be completed on all new hires.
- Verify educational backgrounds.

Often those who make the best impression during a job interview are actually those who are the most skilled in lying.

The Integrity Test

Harris (1990, p. 21A) suggests that integrity tests are valuable tools but must be used "prudently and judiciously." Such tests are supposed to predict an individual's potential to commit job-related theft.

Paper-and-pencil tests are often very reliable. According to King and Dunston (1992, p. 61): "A special [American Psychological Association] task force, which reviewed more than 30 tests and 300 reports . . . concluded that preemployment tests are the best tool for identifying dishonest behavior as well as offering protection against claims of negligent hiring."

According to Inbau (1994, p. 36), however: "The research on integrity tests has not produced data that clearly supports or dismisses the assertion that these tests can predict dishonest behavior."

Psychological Tests

Such tests are also valuable and, according to Kuhn (1990, p. 23A), can be used to measure "various mental characteristics such as intelligence, aptitude, attitude, personality types, knowledge, and skills."

A wide range of other tests are available for preemployment screening, including tests that measure job aptitude, job abilities, emotional stability and mental health. A test should be *valid,* that is, it should measure attitudes or skills that are directly related to the position. Test publishers should supply such validity data. Some publishers, in fact, have compiled national norms that provide standards against which to compare applicants' scores.

A conscientious background and reference check should be made on every new employee for the best security. Although it is not permissible to ask a job applicant about prior arrest or prison records (Equal Employment Opportunity Commission ruling), gaps in employment history may indicate such records. Any unexplained time periods may be asked about.

Use of the Polygraph

Use of the **polygraph** as a preemployment tool has become severely restricted. In 1987, in *Texas State Employment Union v. Texas Department of Mental Health,* the Texas Supreme Court declared unconstitutional a state law requiring the state department of health's employees to take a polygraph test as a condition of employment. The court observed that polygraph tests constitute an unwarranted intrusion of privacy.

In 1988, the Employee Polygraph Protection Act (EPPA) was signed into law prohibiting employers from using lie detector tests for preemployment screening or during employment except in certain instances. One exception was prospective employees of private armored car, security alarm and security firms. Rea (1989, p. 51) cautions:

> There is not a blank exemption for security companies to administer lie detector tests. The exemption only applies to companies that derive 50 percent of their business from armored car, security alarm, and security guard business. Thus, a company that simply provides security services for its own use does not qualify to use lie detector tests for screening employees.

In 1989, in *Mest v. Federated Group, Inc.*, a California court awarded $12 million in damages to 15,000 job applicants who alleged that a retailer had violated their privacy rights by compelling them to take a polygraph. Although honest, reliable employees are desirable at all levels, the extensiveness of the personal background investigation will depend on the job and type of security required. Noncritical clearances may involve completion of an application form with name, address, telephone number, education, past work record and references. Even these noncritical clearances should be checked.

Critical clearance for positions involving large sums of cash, valuable merchandise or trade secrets goes further and may include a polygraph examination (where it is legal) and/or a psychological stress examination.

The Background Check

As noted by Beaudette (1992, p. 64): "The best predictor of a person's future behavior is his or her past behavior. . . . [I]t makes sense to check an applicant's criminal record, credit report, social security number, driving record, and workers' compensation record." Beaudette (p. 69) also suggests: "Other background checks that may be appropriate are earnings and employment records reported to the Social Security Administration, military records, professional licenses, civil litigation records, bankruptcy records, Uniform Commercial Code filings, and tax assessor files."

At least the last five years' employers and **employment records** and three references should be checked. It is often advisable to talk to neighbors as well, because most job applicants will list as references only those individuals who will speak favorably of them.

In *High Tech Gays v. Defense Industrial Clearance Office* (1990), the U.S. Ninth Circuit Court ruled that the U.S. Department of Defense did have the authority to conduct expanded background investigations of gay applicants who were candidates for secret and top secret clearance. The court observed that homosexuals are part of a "quasi-suspect" class that should receive heightened security.

The Interview

Jayne (1990, p. 18A) describes the **integrity interview** as a "face-to-face, nonaccusatory interview consisting of a series of questions that address issues such as significant thefts from prior employers, use of illegal drugs during work hours, participation in criminal activities, falsification of the application form, and similar job-related concerns." All questions asked must be job related and nondiscriminatory. Buckley (1993, p. 33) offers four basic rules for interviewing:

- Let the applicant do most of the talking throughout the interview.
- Introduce the question topic before asking the question.
- Assess the applicant's initial behavioral response to a question.
- Ask follow-up questions.

National Investigation Agencies

Hill (1990, p. 16A) contends:

> The need for thorough pre-employment screening is receiving more attention now that the courts have started to hold companies—and in some cases individuals—liable for negligent hiring procedures. To meet the screening demand, nationwide private investigation agencies have started using new approaches and the latest technology. These agencies provide background

investigation reports that are not only fast, accurate, and cost-effective but also viable to this modern-day employer problem. . . .

A national investigation agency specializing in employment screening provides services and benefits otherwise unobtainable:

- Quick turnaround.
- Legal accuracy.
- Thoroughness.
- Analysis—and experienced judgments.

Hill notes (p. 16A) that national private investigation agencies use computers and street investigators to search public records such as criminal records, federal records, workers' compensation records, driving records, credit records and quasi-public records such as medical and military records.

Any persons being considered for promotion into positions of trust should also be checked carefully from a security point of view. Despite careful screening and checking of job applicants, some dishonest people are likely to be hired.

The Second Line of Defense—Training and Supervising

Hire good people and then maintain the climate that will keep them honest. For example, an organization of fast-food restaurants was noted for its good employee relations. Management treated people fairly and displayed faith in their integrity and ability, but also provided uniforms without pockets. When the opportunity to steal is removed, half the battle is won. Nothing can substitute for rigid, well-implemented preventive measures.

Owners/managers should have a continuing program of investigation and training on ways to eliminate stock shortages and shrinkage. For example, one small retailer trained his employees to record each item, such as floor cleaner, taken out of stock for use in the store. Unless recorded, it was an inventory loss, even though it was a legitimate store expense. Management must let employees know that it is always aware and always cares.

Employees should be accountable for all assets entrusted to them.

> Educate all employees as to their responsibilities and restrictions. Establish reasonable rules and enforce them.

Make clear that certain areas are off-limits, that supplies are to be used only for job-related activities, that personal long-distance phone calls are not to be made on company phones, that periodic inspections will be held and that any thefts will be prosecuted.

Policies must not be stated as suggestions but rather as rules that are enforced. In addition, posters might be strategically placed emphasizing "Zero Shrinkage." A more negative but possibly effective poster might illustrate frequently pilfered items, a price tag attached to each and a caption reading, "Is your future worth more than this?"

Employee Awareness Programs

According to Hayes (1992, p. 153): "Employee awareness programs are vital to reducing loss in any company. To be effective, however, they must target resources to significant problems, employ a clear message, reward good efforts, and have the strong, visible support of senior management."

In addition, as noted by Maturi (1993, p. 12): "You can deter insider theft by encouraging staffers to report acts of dishonesty. According to a 1992 survey by the National Retail Security Federation, . . . co-workers tip-offs typically account for more than 43 percent of detected employee theft."

Of great significance is the climate established within a company, as noted by Turner and Stephenson (1994, p. 65):

> A company's corporate culture is a significant factor when determining the company's vulnerability to misuses and misappropriation. Corporate culture is an environment influenced by the prevalent morals, ethics, ideals, and standards for behavior as developed, implemented, and demonstrated by management: the company's conscience. By taking a preventive role in designing and implementing strategic loss control procedures, management can focus significant attention on the embezzlement problem.

The importance of total commitment is also emphasized by Adler (1993, p. 33) who suggests: "The loss prevention department's ability to provide a total deterrent program that involves management and staff will clearly demonstrate a team environment. Empowering employees to recognize the impact of employee theft will enhance loss prevention consciousness and give everyone a sense of responsibility."

THE THIRD LINE OF DEFENSE—ACCESS CONTROL

Many facilities require strict access control. In such cases they may require that all employees (including security), contractors and visitors sign in/out and may in addition require them to have identification badges. The only exceptions may be emergency service personnel such as fire, police and ambulance responding to a call for assistance.

The purpose of access control is to facilitate authorized entry and to prevent the unauthorized entry of those who might steal material or information, or might bring harmful devices onto the premises.

Most physical controls are aimed at limiting access to restricted areas, particularly during the time when an establishment is not conducting business, that is, after hours. During business hours, however, access cannot be completely limited, or the company could not function.

> Most procedural controls seek to prevent loss by limiting access to specific areas by unauthorized personnel.

Sometimes it is necessary to limit access to nonemployees only. Other times, however, even employees are denied access to certain areas of a facility. From a security standpoint, it is best to limit the number of people having access to cash, important documents, valuable merchandise and areas where these are stored.

Access control includes identifying, directing and/or limiting the movement of vehicles, employees, contractors, vendors and visitors.

> Procedural controls to limit access to specified areas include stationing guards, restricting vehicle traffic, requiring registration and sign-outs, requiring display of badges or passes, ensuring key control and using effective opening, closing and after-hours procedures.

Even in retail establishments where traffic flow is encouraged, certain areas are usually off-limits to nonemployees and perhaps even to some employees. A uniformed security guard, especially if armed, may be a psychological deterrent to a would-be thief, whether internal or external. Restricted areas and boundaries should be clearly specified and the restrictions unconditionally enforced.

Vehicle Control

Vehicle traffic can be restricted in several ways. The simplest way is to have only one gate, with a card-key system or a guard to check identities and allow or refuse admittance to drivers seeking entrance to the premises. Sometimes stickers on the bumper or windshield constitute the necessary identification for admittance.

Another method is to have two parking lots, both equipped with traffic control arms. Employees can gain entrance to their parking lot by use of a card-key. Visitors can gain entrance to their parking lot simply by driving in, but they cannot exit without a token obtained from the receptionist. This system is sometimes used at drive-in restaurants to prevent teenagers from cruising around the parking lot and not making a purchase. Without a purchase, the driver has no token and cannot exit without a confrontation with the manager.

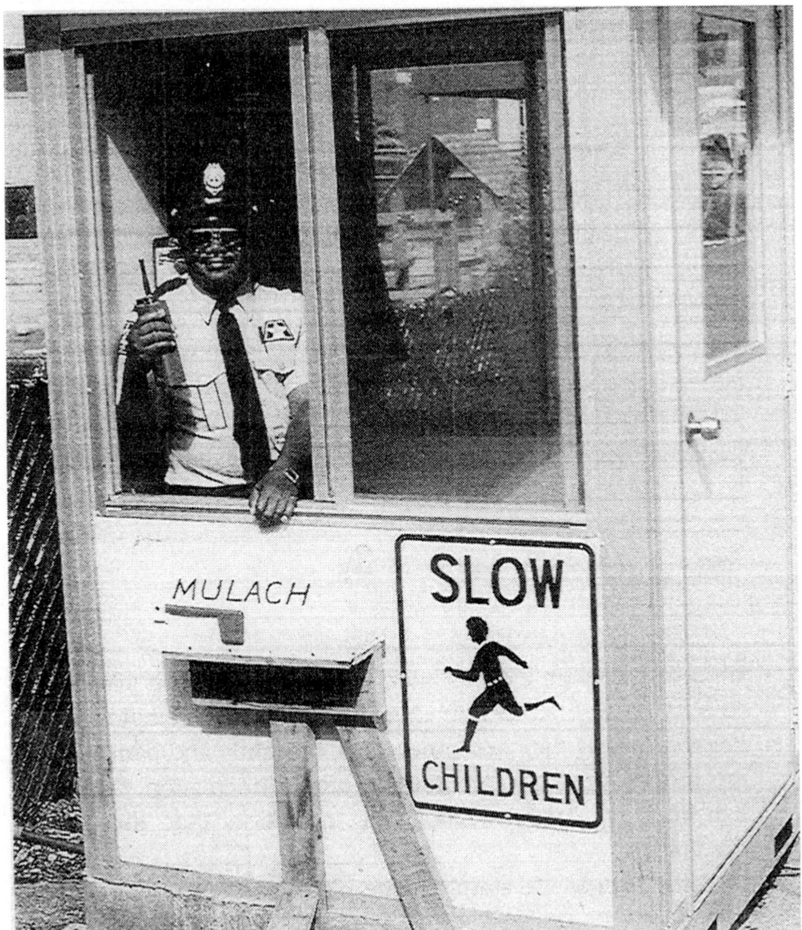

Controlling traffic into a facility may be accomplished by a guard stationed at the entrance.

Check-In/Out Register

A check-in/out register can be used with employees as well as with vendors, contractors and visitors. This system requires the person seeking entrance to sign in with a receptionist or security guard, present identification, state the purpose of the visit and sign out before leaving. The date, time of entrance and time of leaving are recorded. The person may then be directed to the desired location, may be given a badge or pass or may be met in the reception area by the person he or she is visiting. Either the business can be conducted there or the visitor can be escorted to an office. Sign-in/out logs such as that shown in Figure 6–1 (p. 156) are commonly used for after-hours entrance.

Badges and Passes

Sometimes supervisory personnel and/or security guards know all the employees, at least by sight, and the areas they are authorized to enter. Often,

Sign-In/Out Log

Please print

DATE ______________

POST ______________

SHEET NO. ______________

NAME	EMPLOYEE NO.	DEPT.	PHONE EXT.	TIME IN	TIME OUT

Figure 6–1. After-Hours Sign-In/Out Log

however, in large establishments, employees are required to wear badges or to carry passes that identify them. Although some employees object to wearing badges, feeling they are impersonal, unsightly and damaging to clothing, with the proper type of badge and the proper orientation, the badge can be established as a status symbol, an indication that the person is "part of the team."

Some badges are simply name plates and serve little security function.

Among the most common measures of access control are passes and a sign-in registry.

At minimum, effective employee badges and passes display the employee's name, employment number, signature and photograph as well as an authorizing signature. They are sturdy, tamper-proof and changed periodically.

Effective badges or passes should also use a distinctive, intricate background design difficult to reproduce; use a code denoting the area(s) for which the badge or pass is valid; contain an easily recognized serial number; be resistant to fumes inherent in the facility and have some secret characteristic known only to management.

The issuing of badges and passes should be carefully controlled. They should be issued only after the employee is cleared by the supervisor. Then the reason for the badge or pass and its importance to security must be carefully explained to the employee.

The system should specify when, where, how and to whom identification is displayed; what is to be done if the identification is lost or damaged and procedures to follow if an employee is terminated. Employees should be instructed to report lost or damaged passes or badges immediately. Temporary badges may be provided for employees who lose theirs or who forget them at home. Such passes should be valid for only one day and should be turned in at the end of the day. A log such as that shown in Figure 6–2 should be kept of these badges to maintain effective security.

Truncer and Magee (1995, p. 69) stress: "Badge reports should list all permanent employees who are assigned badges. The total number of permanent badges listed on this report should equal the number of people employed by the company. Any discrepancy between these figures signals a problem that must be investigated."

Temporary Badge Sign-In/Out Log

Please print DATE ____________

TEMP. BADGE NO.	NAME	EMPLOYEE NO.	PHONE EXT.	TIME IN	TIME OUT	APPROVED BY

Figure 6–2. Temporary Badge Sign-In/Out Log

Queeno (1994, p. 26) notes: "Today, the number of sophisticated card production systems on the market is rivaled only by the number of criminals trying to beat the technology." Queeno (p. 30) suggests that electronic ID card security can be enhanced by using the following design elements:

- Closely spaced diagonal lines.
- Difficult to reproduce photographic or pattern bit maps.
- A miniature, duplicate portrait next to the large one.
- A ghost image of the original portrait behind the text.
- Overlaying text or logos across the portrait's edge.
- Unique but readable text fonts.
- An authorization signature.
- Colored geometric shapes that logically appear based on certain database criteria.

Procedures for canceling and/or reissuing identification passes or badges must be clearly established. For example, if employees lose an ID badge, they must report the loss immediately to their supervisor, fill in a form authorizing a new badge to be issued and have that form approved and, perhaps, pay a fee for the replacement.

Security officers should be given a "hot sheet" of lost or stolen badges or passes, as well as those of terminated employees who have retained theirs. Security officers should also compare the photographs, signatures and descriptions with those of the wearer. They should *not* assume the pass or badge is valid, but should periodically check their "hot sheet."

Visitor badges or passes, often used for security purposes, should be distinct from employee badges and passes. If both employees and nonemployees are required to have a badge or pass, supervisors and security personnel can immediately ascertain whether a specific person is authorized to be in a specific location.

Visitors are often required to sign in, as previously described. If the visitor is issued a pass or badge, the number should be recorded in the check-in/out register. The visitor should return the badge or pass when signing out. If the visitor retains the pass, a serious breach in security is created. Visitor registration logs such as that shown in Figure 6-3 are used in many establishments.

If employees wish to have guests (relatives, children, friends) visit, some facilities require prior approval, using a form such as that shown in Figure 6–4.

Tour groups may present a special security problem in that a would-be thief, terrorist or industrial spy may join a tour group with the intention of slipping away and gaining access to a restricted area. Passes or badges can help prevent such illegal activity. Ideally, every member of a tour group should sign in with the receptionist or security guard and be issued a pass or badge that is clearly marked "Tour Group." The members should be required to stay together and be accompanied by a uniformed guard. When the tour is over, a head count should be done, all badges collected and all members signed out. Even though the tour will not be likely to go into restricted areas, these measures will deter anyone from leaving the group to gain access to restricted areas or will detect such illicit activity early.

VISITOR REGISTRATION LOG

Welcome To J&B Innovative Enterprises, Inc.

Please print

DATE	NAME	BADGE NO.	VEHICLE LICENSE	REPRESENTING	EMPLOYEE SPONSOR	TIME IN	TIME OUT

Figure 6–3. Visitor Registration Log

Contractors and vendors are frequently treated like visitors; that is, they sign in and receive a temporary badge or pass that identifies them as nonemployees and indicates the area(s) to which they have access.

Employees using contracted services often must arrange for badges to be issued to the individuals who will be providing the services. The form in Figure 6–5 serves this purpose.

NONBUSINESS VISITOR ACCESS REQUEST

Requests for any visit to the facility by individuals not conducting company business must be approved by your supervisor before the visit.

Visitors are not allowed in any restricted or hazardous area.

The host employee must maintain control and responsibility for visitors and their actions.

Employee Name ______________________________

Employee Number ______________ Phone Extension ______________

Date of Visit ______________

Guests' Names

______________ ______________

______________ ______________

______________ ______________

______________ ______________

Approximate Time ______________

Manager's Approval ______________________
Signature

Figure 6–4. Nonbusiness Visitor Access Request

CONTRACT EMPLOYEE ACCESS REQUEST

Complete this form if you want a contracted employee to be issued a badge. Allow three days for processing.

A contracted badge will be issued for the requested individual each day at the gate designated. They will sign in on the Visitor Register at that time. The badge must be returned at the end of the day.

Contract Company ____________________

Contact Company Telephone Number ____________________

Contact Employee(s) Name(s) ____________________

Dates of Contract Employment: from __________ to __________

Type of Employment ____________________

- ☐ Overload/Temporary Help
- ☐ Service/Maintenance
- ☐ Construction Work/Mover

Facility Required __________ Gates Required __________

Supervised by ____________________

Telephone Extension __________ Mail Station __________

Restrictions (if any) ____________________

Department Manager Authorization ____________________

Contrator badges are generally issued only during working hours unless other arrangements are made with the security office.

CONTRACTOR BADGE SIGN IN/OUT

DATE __________

NAME	BADGE NO.	REPRESENTING (COMPANY)	CALLING ON	TIME IN	TIME OUT

Figure 6–5. Contract Employee Access Request

Some regular contractors and vendors may be issued long-term passes, but caution should be exercised in using such passes. Holders of permanent passes should be required to use only one entry/exit, and the security guard should have a list of those with permanent passes, along with their signatures, to compare when they sign in. Contractors and vendors should be required to give their name, company, purpose, vehicle license number and badge number, and to sign in. The date, time in and time out should always be recorded. Such permanent passes should be reissued periodically, just like those of employees.

Key Control

Another procedure important in controlling access to restricted areas is adequate key control. As noted earlier, a lock is only as secure as the key or combination that operates it. Phelps (1995, p. 61) stresses: "One of the first goals of a company's security manager should be to develop a comprehensive key control program that tracks each key, who has it, and what it fits. No keys should be left unaccounted for or undocumented."

Having a key is often a status symbol. In small businesses, it is common for every employee to have a key, but from a security standpoint, this is unsound. The only reason for having a key should be *job necessity*. The greater the number of people having keys, the greater the security risk. A written record should be kept of all keys in use. The record might look like the one shown in Figure 6–6.

> A key control system limits the number of persons having keys, establishes a master list of all existing keys and to whom they are assigned, keeps all duplicate keys secure and requires a physical audit periodically.

To eliminate the inconvenience of a person having to carry several keys, perhaps even hundreds, a **master keying system** is sometimes used. Under this system, a **change key** opens only one specific door. A **sub-master key** opens the locks in a specific area. A **master key** opens the locks in the entire building. Sometimes the system extends even further if multiple buildings are concerned, with a **grand master key,** opening all locks in two or more buildings.

Name/Department	Exterior	Office	Store Room	Supply Room
H. King/Accounting		8/86		
S. Lewis/Administration	9/88	9/86		
B. Jones/Purchasing		5/85	5/85	8/85
T. Hall/Administration	1/84	1/84		
Etc.				

Figure 6–6. Sample Record of Keys in Use

Although master keying offers advantages to the user, it also is much less secure. If the master key falls into the wrong hands or is duplicated, the system poses a much greater security risk than a single key system. It is also much more costly to rekey an entire building should such a risk be discovered.

A checklist such as that illustrated in Figure 6–7 can help ensure effective key control. The same principles apply if a card-key system is used.

All keys, but especially master keys, should be stamped "Do Not Duplicate." This does not, however, guarantee that duplication is prevented. Some

Items with Locks	Number of Locks	Items with Locks	Number of Locks	Items with Locks	Number of Locks
Access Space		Dispensers		Mail Boxes	
Air Conditioning		Sanitary Napkin		Money Bags	
Alarms		Soap			
Athletic Supplies		Towel			
Automotive				Penthouse	
		Doors (Exterior)		Plan Case	
		Entrance			
Book Cases		Exit			
Bulletin Boards		Doors (Interior)		Refrigerators	
		Cafeteria		Rolling Grills	
		Classroom		Roof Vents	
Cabinets		Closet			
Electric		Connecting			
Filing		Elevator		Safe Compartments	
Instrument		Fan Room		Safe Deposit Boxes	
Key		Fire		Screens	
Medicine		Garage		Slop Sink Closet	
Storage		Office		Switch Key	
Supply					
Wardrobe					
		Drawers		Tabernacle	
		Bench		Tanks (Oil & Gas)	
		Cash		Thermostat	
		Drafting Room		Trailers	
		Lab. Table		Trap Doors	
Camera Cases		Safe		Trucks	
Cash Boxes		Tool		Trunks	
Cash Registers					
Chute Doors		Gasoline Pump			
Clocks		Gates		Valves	
				Vaults	
		Lockers			
		Gym			
Dark Rooms		Paint		Watchman's Box	
Desks		Student			
Display Cases		Teachers		X-Ray	

Figure 6–7. Key-Control Checklist

SOURCE: Courtesy of TelKee Inc., Subsidiary of Sunroc Corp., Glen Riddle, PA 19037.

security experts recommend scratching off the serial numbers on keys and padlocks because locksmiths can make duplicates if given the make and number.

Though marking keys "Do Not Duplicate" may seem futile, it will have some effect. The best way to hamper key copying, however, is to purchase locks that use restricted keys. These are particularly secure because lockmakers limit the distribution of restricted key blanks, even among reputable locksmiths.

Some security managers use an inexpensive method to reduce unauthorized key duplication by having keys made on a **neuter head blank.** These blanks have the same grooving as common blanks, but the heads have an unusual shape and contain no embossed stock numbers of coining marks, so a catalog cannot be used to identify the correct blank. This feature prevents the nonprofessional from duplicating the keys.

Keys should not be left lying around or left in desk drawers, in purses or in coat pockets. Such abuse is cause for revoking the key. Lending keys should also be strictly forbidden. Any employee found lending keys should lose the privilege of having a key. In rare instances when management loans a master key, care should be exercised that a duplicate is not made.

Do not give custodians keys, especially master keys. Because the turnover in custodial services is extremely high, it is preferable to have a guard or employee grant custodians entrance and exit. Otherwise, a custodian may have master keys to several buildings, have duplicates made and then several months later commit a series of burglaries. Likewise, do not give entrance keys to tenants of an office building. Establish procedures whereby they can be admitted by a security guard or receptionist.

When any employee having a master key leaves or is terminated, the locks should be changed, as should combinations of safes and/or vaults if the terminated individual knew them. It is also a good security practice to periodically change locks, even if no employee having a key has been terminated.

Dulcamaro (1994, p. 59) describes a total key system which includes a security key monitor (SKM) designed to electronically dispense and track keys:

> When a valid PIN code is entered, the electric strike in the SKM unit releases the latch on the door lock, allowing the door to open. After the door is pulled open, the door sensor will detect the open door, but will not alarm, because it is a proper entry. Different PIN codes will allow access to different key positions by turning on the light next to each authorized key position and releasing each set of keys that a particular person is allowed to use. Wherever a light is lit, the key in that lock can be turned and removed, thereby releasing the set of keys on that key ring. Everywhere a light is not lit, the keys in those locks will not turn, and therefore cannot be removed.
>
> All users in this type of system are given their own individual PIN code to accurately audit which key rings are used, by whom they are used, and when they are taken and returned.

In addition, periodic key audits should be conducted to ensure that those to whom keys have been issued still have the key(s) in their possession. Auditing key inventories requires physical verification that each assigned key is

A key depository is an important part of key control. Duplicate keys should be stored in a secure place, such as a safe or vault.

actually in the possession of the specified person. If it is discovered that a key to a critical area has been lost, the door should be immediately rekeyed.

Keys to internal areas of the building should be controlled in the same way as external keys. Only those who really need the keys should have them.

Opening, Closing and After-hours Procedures

Controlling access after hours is a critical part of any security system. Usually physical controls are heavily relied on, but certain procedures are required to ensure that these physical controls are effective.

> Effective closing procedures include checking all restrooms and areas where someone might be concealed, turning off all unnecessary lights and machinery, opening cash registers and placing money in the safe, locking the safe as well as all windows and interior doors, turning on security lighting, activating the alarm and securing all exterior doors.

Cash registers should be left empty and open to prevent costly damage caused by a burglar forcing the register open.

These procedures help ensure that no unauthorized persons remain on the premises and that all physical security measures are operative.

Opinions vary on whether blinds and/or shades should be drawn during closing procedures. Drawn blinds or shades do prevent intruders from seeing available "targets" inside, but they also give privacy to a successful intruder.

> In an establishment where the risk of burglary is high and no security guard is on night duty, opening and closing should be a two-person operation.

Opening and closing procedures with specific assigned responsibilities should be written out. Before someone opens an establishment, it is prudent to drive by the entrance at least once before parking. If anything looks suspicious, the police should be called. If everything looks normal, one person should unlock the exterior door that is most exposed to public view and traffic, enter, check the alarm and premises to ensure that everything is as it should be and then signal the person waiting some distance away from the premises. The time this takes is preestablished. The person outside waits until the "all clear" is given. If it is not given on schedule, the outside person notifies the police.

Periodically store management should be reminded to be alert to strangers in nonpublic areas immediately after opening or before closing.

The closing procedure is similar to the opening procedure, with one person waiting some distance away while another person makes a routine check of the premises, paying particular attention to areas where someone might hide, such as washrooms, perimeter stock areas, fitting rooms and the maintenance department. This person then checks and activates all security measures and joins the person waiting outside to lock up.

Procedures for admittance after hours should also be established and strictly enforced. The security officer should have a list of the individuals authorized to be in the building after hours, whether they stay late, arrive early or return after the building is closed. If an authorized person is in the building after hours, a record should be made of the reason for the person's being there, the time in and the time out. Employees who consistently arrive early or stay late with no good reason may be doing so to steal or to use company equipment without authorization.

Controlling Access to Vulnerable Areas and Equipment

> Particularly vulnerable to theft or employee pilferage are storage areas; areas where cash, valuables, records and forms are kept; mail rooms; supply rooms; duplicating rooms and computer rooms.

All these areas should have limited access and should be kept locked or have an authorized person in attendance at all times to monitor the activities of others present.

Warehouses and *stockrooms* are particularly vulnerable to theft, and there physical and procedural controls are especially important. Such areas should be locked or have an attendant on duty. In addition, high-value rooms or cages should be used for small, valuable items vulnerable to theft. Temporary help should work with a regular, full-time employee to prevent the temptation to steal.

Forklifts should be kept locked when not in use. In one warehouse burglary, the burglar gained access through the roof, but was unable to exit the same way. Alertly, he used the forklift that had been left with the key in the ignition to pry open the warehouse door. He then used the forklift to transport large quantities of merchandise to his pickup truck parked outside.

Limit access to important *documents* as well as to *business forms* such as purchase orders, checks, vouchers and receipts. Such forms, in the wrong hands, can cost a business thousands of dollars. Important papers and records that are no longer needed should not be discarded in the trash, but incinerated or shredded.

Mail rooms should have one person in charge to handle all incoming and outgoing mail. A postage meter eliminates the possibility of stamps being stolen. This meter should be kept locked when not in use. The practice of having routine outgoing mail unsealed, so that contents can be checked to ensure that the letter is indeed business related, can eliminate personal use of company postage. Of course, confidential or sensitive correspondence should be sealed and marked as such. Periodic checks should be made of unsealed letters and packages before they are sealed, stamped and sent.

Some mail rooms have a separate mailbox for the personal letters and packages of employees. Although the employees pay for their postage, they see this as a service provided by their employer.

Supply rooms are very susceptible to pilferage and, therefore, should be restricted to authorized personnel. One individual should be in charge of the supply room. Employees should obtain supplies by filling in a requisition, not by simply going to the supply room and helping themselves or asking for the supplies. An inventory should be taken regularly.

Copy machines may be a source of shrinkage if employees use them for making personal copies. Given that a single copy usually costs from three to ten cents depending on the system used, excessive personal use of copiers can cost an establishment hundreds, even thousands of dollars a year. Some establishments have attempted to alleviate the problem by having the copy machine locked and issuing keys to only a few authorized individuals. Others have machines installed that have an element bearing a coded number that must be inserted into the machine before it will run, or use a card-key system for access. In either case, the code and number of copies made are automatically recorded. Other companies have only one person authorized to run the copy machine and require that a work order or copy requisition be completed before copies can be made by the authorized person (see Figure 6–8).

Some companies recognize that being able to make copies of documents for personal use is appreciated by employees and, consequently, allow their employees to use the copy machine and pay for their copies. Such a practice is good public relations, but it can easily be abused if individuals are placed on the "honor system," as is frequently the case.

REPRODUCTION WORK ORDER

Name ____________________

Cost Center Code ____________________ Assembled ____________________

Date & Hour Received ____________________ Back to Back ___ Not Back to Back ___

Date & Hour Due ____________________ Total Number of Originals ____________________

Number of Copies ____________________ Other ____________________

Color of Paper/Card Stock ____________________ ____________________

Special Instructions:

Return to ____________________ Will pick up in duplicating ____________________

Secretary ____________________

Figure 6–8. Sample Reproduction Work Order

Computers can also be a source of shrinkage if employees use them for personal benefit, at substantial cost to the company. In some instances, employees have been discovered to have established their own sideline computer business, using the company's computer after hours and on weekends. One such employee rationalized the use by saying, "It was just sitting there, going to waste. I wasn't hurting anyone." Computer security is discussed in Chapter 9.

Property Control

Property control is of concern in most security systems. Control may be exercised over the employer's property as well as the property of individual employees, vendors, contractors or visitors.

Employer Property. Any property of the employer that is to be taken from a facility may require a pass such as that illustrated in Figure 6–9 (p. 168). Property passes play a major role in property control. A log such as that shown in Figure 6–10 (p. 169) should be kept of all property that is signed out.

Nonemployer Property. If employees, contractors, visitors or others bring personal property into a secured facility, they might be required to register it so that when they leave there is no question as to their legitimate right to remove the property. A form such as that in Figure 6–11 (p. 169) might be used for this purpose. Such passes are not usually necessary for briefcases, purses or lunch boxes.

Protecting Information

Frequently security personnel have access to trade secrets, product data and information that is proprietary and confidential. Specific action security managers might take to safeguard sensitive information and trade secrets include the following:

- Establish guidelines so all involved personnel can evaluate the sensitivity of information and classify it. Establish the specific protection required for each classification and ensure that classifications are clearly marked on documents.
- Use appropriate techniques to safeguard such information as passwords, coding and locking file cabinets.
- Keep records of who has received sensitive information and why.

____ **PROPERTY PASS**

PROPERTY PASSES ARE RETURNED TO THE APPROVING MANAGER FOR VERIFICATION OF ITEMS REMOVED FROM THE BUILDING.

MANAGER NAME
TELEPHONE EXT.

DESCRIPTION OF ITEMS TO BE TAKEN FROM THE BUILDING (INCLUDE MODEL, SERIAL AND TAG NUMBER)	TO BE RETURNED		DATE TO BE RETURNED
	YES	NO	

FROM (BUILDING)	TO (BUILDING OR HOME)	CHECKED EMPLOYEE NAME AGAINST BADGE OR I.D. ☐

EMPLOYEE (PRINT OR TYPE) AND SIGNATURE	EMPLOYEE NUMBER	RECEPTIONIST OR GUARD	DATE OUT
MANAGER SIGNATURE	RECEPTIONIST OR GUARD		DATE IN

FOLLOW-UP

☐ EQUIPMENT RETURNED
☐ EQUIPMENT NOT RETURNED

COMMENTS	
SIGNATURE	DATE

Figure 6–9. Property Pass

Property Sign-In/Out Log

PLEASE PRINT

NAME	PROPERTY	PASS NUMBER	DATE REMOVED	DATE RETURNED

Figure 6–10. Property Sign-In/Out Log

PERSONAL PROPERTY REGISTRATION

Complete this form if you wish to bring personal property into the building.

QUANTITY	DESCRIPTION OF MATERIAL

PLEASE PRINT

NAME	REPRESENTING	DEPARTMENT OR PERSON VISITED

I understand that items are to be removed from the plant only at the gate of entry, unless other arrangements are made at the gate of entry. This is not a property pass and applies only to people, vendors or employees who have a reason to bring in material.

SIGNATURE	GUARD SIGNATURE	TIME ENTERED	DATE

Figure 6–11. Personal Property Registration

- Share sensitive information only with individuals who have a genuine need to know. Make clear what security measures are expected.
- Establish procedures for disposing of sensitive information when no longer needed.

Using Seals

Seals can be used to indicate whether access has been breached. As noted by Heine (1994, p. 15): "Tamper-evident, tamper-indicating and tamper-resistant materials represent a family of indicative systems which can be used effectively as a visual deterrent to tampering and as a tool for streamlining internal security assessment." According to Heine, the seal with the greatest variety of applications is the tamper-indicating label seal. This is a hard-to-remove adhesive-backed seal applied across an opening. Under normal circumstances, gaining entry destroys the seal.

Restricting Use of Cameras or Video Equipment on Site

Many facilities do not allow cameras or video equipment to be brought into the facility without prior approval. This restriction may apply to all employees, contractors, visitors and even security personnel. A form such as that in Figure 6–12 might be used for this purpose. After the form is approved, the person authorized to take pictures or videos might be issued a pass such as that illustrated in Figure 6–13 (p. 172).

Accounting and Receiving Procedures to Control Access to Financial Assets

Security managers are not expected to be accountants, but they should be aware of where potential security problems exist within the accounting system and the receiving department. Temptation to steal can be reduced by following some basic procedures.

- Keep limited cash on hand.
- Establish strict procedures for obtaining petty cash.
- Keep purchasing, receiving and paying functions separate.
- Use prenumbered purchase orders in sequence.

The limited amount of cash that is kept should be secured in a safe at closing. People requesting petty cash should have an authorization and a signed voucher or request form before being given the cash. Strict records should account for every cent disbursed. Where possible, receipts should be provided by the person receiving the petty cash.

Whenever possible, purchasing, receiving and paying functions should be kept separate. Purchasing should be centralized, not only to minimize opportunity for unauthorized purchases, but also because buying in bulk is usually

REQUEST FOR AUTHORIZATION TO TAKE PICTURES

Date and time equipment will be used

Date (s) ________________ Time ________________

________________ ________________

Purpose of pictures ____

____

____

____

Location/Area pictures will be taken ______________________________

____

____

____

Person (s) taking pictures

Name	Company Name	Employee #
________________	________________	________
________________	________________	________
________________	________________	________

Requested By ____

Approved By ____

Figure 6–12. Request for Authorization to Take Pictures

less expensive. Purchase orders should be prenumbered and used in sequence. If more than one department does purchasing, each should be issued a purchase order book and made accountable for every number contained in the book before another is issued. Any purchase orders that are ruined should be marked void, *not* simply discarded. Copies of the purchase orders should be sent to the receiving and the paying department.

The receiving department should check the orders received against the purchase orders on file. Any missing or damaged items or extra items should be promptly reported. The supplier should be notified if a shipment is not received within a reasonable time; it may have been stolen or misrouted. It is usually best to have one central receiving area.

Merchandise should be received in a protected area such as a sheltered inside dock. Only suppliers' vehicles and company cars should be allowed in the receiving area. The receiving area should be physically separated from the shipping area. If a great security risk exists, the hours for receiving should be limited and a security guard assigned during this period. The doors should be

CAMERA PASS

________________ IS AUTHORIZED TO TAKE

PICTURES OF ____________________________

ON ________ , IN ______________________
(date) (plant)

____
(area)

COMPANY REPRESENTED ________________

ESCORT ____________________________

PURPOSE ___________________________

DEPT. MANAGER ______________________

SECURITY OFFICER ____________________

Figure 6–13. Camera Pass

kept closed and locked when not in use. A buzzer or bell can be used to alert personnel when a delivery is being attempted.

Suppliers should never leave merchandise unattended on the dock. If they do, the receiver is not legally responsible. Any supplier whose delivery agents simply unload merchandise on the dock and leave should be promptly notified of this break in security.

Train boxcars and truck trailers may use a numbered metal seal bar. In such cases, receivers should check the seal number with the bill of lading. If it appears to have been tampered with, the delivery should not be accepted.

Once a delivery is accepted, it should be unloaded and properly stored as soon as possible. If this cannot be done, the doors on the boxcar or truck trailer should be padlocked or nailed shut.

Receivers should not go by the packing slip (called **blind receiving)**, but should actually count the items delivered. Some purchasing departments omit the quantity on the copy of the purchase order sent to receiving, forcing the receiver to do a careful count. A hazard inherent in this procedure is that an incomplete shipment may be accepted. If a shipment is ordered by weight, the merchandise should be weighed when received. The accuracy of the scales should be checked periodically.

The paying department should issue checks for only those orders for which they have an authorized purchase order and authorized verification from the receiving department that the shipment has arrived as specified on the purchase order.

Keeping purchasing, receiving and paying functions separate will thwart such dishonest practices as writing purchase orders for nonexistent materials, writing double purchase orders or making payments for materials that were never ordered. Bill padding can be thwarted by insisting that competitive bids be obtained for any major purchases. Acceptance of gifts or gratuities from suppliers should be strictly forbidden, as this may foster doing special "favors" for each other.

Other Procedures to Enhance Security

In addition to effective hiring and employment practices and controlling access to restricted or vulnerable areas, other procedures can also help ensure safety/security, including drug testing, making rounds, taking precautions when transporting valuables and further protecting through insurance and bonding.

Drug Testing in the Workplace

Workers have challenged the employer's right to require drug tests, but usually that right is upheld if the employer has instituted a fair drug-testing program. For example in a Michigan case, *Baggs v. Eagle-Picher Industries* (1992), employees of an automobile trim manufacturing plant sued their employer for wrongful discharge after they had refused to submit to or failed a drug test. The Sixth District Court ruled in favor of the employer, and the decision was upheld on appeal.

Further, as noted by Martin and DeGrange (1993, p. 41): "Research demonstrates that implementing physical and psychological drug tests will improve job performance and reduce counterproductive behavior such as turnover and absenteeism."

Making Rounds

Often security personnel are responsible for *making rounds,* that is, for conducting a visual check of the facility to observe conditions. Security officers should be alert to hazards that might lead to an accident, such as water or grease on the floor, materials stacked too high, faulty railings and/or stairs, loose carpeting or rugs and inadequate lighting in walkways. They should also be alert to hazardous weather-related conditions such as slick sidewalks or ice or snow falling from roof and window ledges.

Security officers should also recognize and intervene in any employee behavior that might pose a safety hazard such as "goofing off," working without safety glasses and hard hats where designated, fighting, running or reckless driving in parking lots.

Being alert to fire hazards is also important. Security officers should note blocked aisles, stairway exits or fire doors. They should also note uncovered containers of solvent, oily rags, roof leaks, unusual odors or defective electrical wiring, as well as the operability of fire extinguishers and hoses.

Being alert to opportunities for theft is yet another responsibility of security officers as they make their rounds. They should check for evidence of illegal entry such as broken windows and locks, check that all doors that are to be locked have been and make certain safes and vaults are locked. They should also check to be sure that sensitive information is not being left out on desks or discarded in the trash.

Another function security officers often fulfill while making their rounds is that of energy conservation. They should be authorized to and responsible for turning off water left running and unneeded lights or equipment left on after hours, including copy machines, typewriters, desk lights and space heaters. Security officers should *not* turn off any computers or test equipment.

Yet another important function of security personnel making rounds is to ensure access control. They should question suspicious individuals. Suspicious behavior includes a person being in an unlighted area, being in a secured area without authorization, being at someone else's desk or going through someone else's desk drawers or file cabinets, going through wastebaskets and loitering near a card-controlled entry or a trash container. When security officers observe suspicious behavior, they should request identification from the individual, determine his or her purpose for being there and take appropriate action.

While making rounds, security officers are also usually responsible for checking monitoring devices for climate control and responding to any alarms. Last, but of utmost importance, security officers should be helpful and friendly to employees and all others they encounter while conducting their rounds.

If any risk-producing factors are encountered during rounds, security officers should promptly report them to the appropriate person and also make a written report. They should follow up to ensure that the risk has been eliminated.

Conducting Routine Searches

Individual facilities may adopt policies and procedures to allow searches to examine work areas, including lockers, desks and files, and items being brought into or removed from the facility, including packages, briefcases, purses and boxes. Searches are usually allowable if:

- All employees and visitors are notified about the program before it is implemented.
- The program itself is courteous, fair and nondiscriminatory, that is, it includes all employees/visitors.

Notices such as those in Figure 6–14 might be used to inform employees and visitors of a search policy.

Searches are extremely sensitive. Security personnel must be courteous and nonthreatening. Each inspection should be entered in the officer's daily log, including the person's name and time of the inspection. If the person refuses, policies should be in place as to whether the security officer confiscates the package, calls a supervisor or simply records the person's name and employee number or company represented and allows the person to leave. Security officers should not argue or forcefully attempt to conduct a search.

WORK AREA SEARCH NOTICE
TO ALL EMPLOYEES

Effective __________, 19__ we are establishing work area search procedures to improve security.

Work areas will be subject to search at our discretion. We will post the following notice in conspicuous places informing people of this policy.

WE RESERVE THE RIGHT TO INSPECT AND SEARCH EMPLOYEE LOCKERS, DESKS, FILES, BOXES, PACKAGES, BRIEFCASES, LUNCHBOXES, PURSES OR BAGS WITHIN THE WORK AREA.

Because this program will increase our work and work area security, we expect and appreciate your full cooperation. Failure to cooperate with this procedure will result in disciplinary action.

THE MANAGEMENT

ENTRANCE AND EXIT SEARCH NOTICE
TO ALL EMPLOYEES/VISITORS

Effective __________, 19__ we are establishing new entry and exit procedures to improve security.

People entering and leaving this facility may be subject to questions at our discretion. Packages, handbags, purses, briefcases, lunchboxes and other possessions may be subject to search.

The following notice will be posted in conspicuous places informing people of this policy.

WE RESERVE THE RIGHT TO QUESTION PEOPLE ENTERING OR LEAVING THE PROPERTY AND TO INSPECT ANY PACKAGE, HANDBAG, PURSE, BRIEFCASE, LUNCHBOX, OR OTHER POSSESSION CARRIED INTO OR OUT OF THE COMPANY PROPERTY.

Because this program will increase our work and work area security, we expect and appreciate your full cooperation. Failure to cooperate with this procedure will result in disciplinary action.

THE MANAGEMENT

Figure 6–14. Sample Search Notification

If security officers find during an exit search that a person has property that belongs to the facility, they should ask for a completed property pass authorizing removal of the property as discussed previously. If no pass has been filled in, it should be completed on the spot, or the person should write out an explanation as to why the property is being removed.

Likewise, if security officers find unauthorized property such as alcohol or illegal drugs during a routine search of a work area, such employees might be asked to submit to their manager a written explanation of why the property was in their possession.

TRANSPORTING VALUABLES

Procedures for transporting valuable goods and/or cash should be established and strictly adhered to.

> Maintain secrecy when transporting valuables. Vary times, routes, personnel and vehicles used.

All employees who are entrusted with transporting valuables should be thoroughly checked and perhaps bonded, as discussed later in the chapter. Large shipments might be divided into two or three different shipments. All vehicles used to transport valuables should be in good mechanical condition.

Many businesses prefer to use commercial firms for transferring valuable merchandise and cash. When armed courier services are used, employees should be instructed to always check the couriers' credentials carefully before handing over the cash or items to be transported.

DETECTING EMPLOYEE THEFT AND PILFERAGE

Accurate records help management discover when and where shrinkage is occurring.

> Some thefts can be detected by using a **perpetual inventory** and periodic internal and external audits.

Although keeping a perpetual inventory requires much time and effort, the benefits are worth it because the owner/manager has up-to-date information on existing supplies and stock and therefore is immediately alerted to inventory shrinkage. A perpetual inventory also serves as a psychological deterrent to theft. This is in contrast to the annual inventory system in which an employee may begin stealing shortly after completion of the inventory, knowing that the shortage will not be discovered until almost a year later.

When inventories are taken, care must be exercised not to be fooled by empty cartons or containers. Spot checks should be made to ensure that the merchandise is actually there. In one filling station, an attendant pocketed any cash received for oil and put the empty cans in the storeroom at the back of the shelf.

Careful, periodic internal and external audits also help detect shrinkage. An internal audit of accounting procedures can be conducted by intentionally introducing errors. For example, what does the purchasing department do if a purchase order is submitted without an authorized signature? What does the receiving department do if it is sent a shipment containing extra items? Is the error reported, do the extra items simply disappear or does the error go unnoticed? What does the paying department do with a bill for which there is no purchase order? Prompt reporting of shortages, losses and errors should be encouraged and positively reinforced. Periodic external audits are also important to security.

> Some thefts can be detected by *inspection* of lockers, packages, vehicles, persons and trash containers.

Although most employees and visitors are honest, security requires that periodic inspections be made to ensure that theft is not occurring.

Providing employees with *lockers* is a sound security practice because it helps employees keep their personal possessions safe. On the other hand, lockers are also a security risk because employees can conceal stolen property or goods in their lockers until an opportune time comes to remove them from the premises undetected. Employee lockers should be considered a privilege, not a right. They are not the employees' private property. Employees should not be allowed to use their own locks. They should be informed when they are given a locker that the locker is provided by the company as a convenience to the employee and that the company retains the right to inspect the locker at any time. Periodic inspections can and should then be made without fear of legal entanglements.

Packages brought into or taken from the premises may also be subject to inspection. Frequently people are required to check all packages before entering an area. College bookstores, for example, often require all books to be left in a rack before entering the store. Discount stores often require that packages brought into the store be checked. Some stores even require women to check their purses until they are ready to make their purchases. Such requirements may anger customers and/or visitors, but if the procedure is adequately explained, public relations may not suffer.

If people are allowed to take packages, briefcases or other containers into restricted areas, a receptionist or security guard frequently inspects the contents, lists what is being taken in and then reinspects the package or briefcase when the person leaves.

If a visitor, employee or repair worker takes a package or item from a secure area, the person authorizing the removal should sign a removal authorization, in ink, with all uncompleted lines on the form crossed out so the person receiving the authorization cannot add additional items to the pass. Persons authorizing such removals should sign their names in full. Initials can be easily forged.

Because thieves may pose as repair workers and simply walk out of an establishment with expensive recording equipment, televisions or office machines, strict security procedures should be followed. The person authorizing the removal should check the service person's credentials before signing the removal pass and should require the service person to sign a receipt for the items to be removed.

This removal pass system should also be used if it is company policy to lend tools and office machines to employees for personal use after hours or on weekends.

Inspections may also be made of lunch boxes, vehicle interiors and trunks and individuals, unless expressly prohibited in the labor contract.

> Inspections are acceptable if they are done democratically and if the procedure is clearly established and explained before the inspection.

Employees should not feel they are under suspicion or not trusted when a personal inspection is made. The chances of this are lessened if everyone is inspected or a systematic inspection is made (for example, every tenth person is inspected) and if everyone has been informed *prior* to employment that periodic personal inspections are part of the established security system. Likewise, visitors or customers should not be annoyed when their packages are inspected if a sign obviously displayed clearly states: "We reserve the right to inspect all packages," as discussed earlier.

Trash containers and trash removal procedures should be checked periodically. Dishonest employees can hide stolen items in the trash and later retrieve them, or items may be accidentally discarded. In some cases, employees/thieves have worked with trash collectors to steal vast quantities of merchandise.

Given that 70 percent of losses are caused by employees, probabilities are good that some dishonest employees will be caught stealing from the company.

> Usually an employee caught stealing from the company should be fired and prosecuted.

Frequently, however, such is not the case. Employees are given second, third and even fourth chances. Or, if they are dismissed, the reasons for the dismissal are kept secret. When the discharged person seeks employment elsewhere and the new potential employer makes a background check, the reason for the dismissal may be hidden. Such practices only encourage internal theft and should be discontinued.

Because there are degrees of seriousness of crimes and there may be mitigating circumstances, policies should exist setting forth actions to be taken for varying types of criminality, dollar amounts, safety considerations and the like, with punitive actions ranging from verbal reprimands to criminal prosecution.

An interesting type of justice system operating in the private sector is described in the Hallcrest Report (Cunningham and Taylor, 1985, p. 245):

> In responding to and resolving the criminal behavior of employees, organizations routinely choose options other than criminal prosecution, for example, suspension without pay, transfer, job reassignment, job redesign (elimination of some job duties), civil restitution, and dismissal. . . .
>
> While on the surface it appears that organizations can opt for less severe sanctions than would be imposed by the criminal justice system, in reality, the organizational sanctions may have greater impact on the employee-offender (e.g., loss of job, civil restitution, garnisheed wages). In addition, the private systems of criminal justice are not always subject to principles of exclusionary evidence, fairness, and defendant rights which characterize the public criminal justice systems. The level of position, the amount of power, and socio-economic standing of the employee in the company may greatly influence the formality and type of company sanctions. In general, private justice systems are characterized by informal negotiations and outcomes, and nonuniform standards and procedures among organization and crime types.

Firing *security* personnel who are discovered to be dishonest is a must. If the security profession is to grow and build respect, dishonest security personnel must be weeded out.

INSURANCE AND BONDING

Recall that one of the means to deal with risk is to *transfer* it. If the risk is still unacceptable after all measures to eliminate or reduce it are completed, insurance and bonding are viable alternatives.

> Insurance and bonding of specific employees may help reduce losses.

Most managers carry insurance on their buildings and on expensive equipment. If the risk is great that, despite effective physical and procedural controls, large value losses might be sustained by employee dishonesty or external crime, many security managers recommend that the company take out insurance and have individuals in key positions bonded. **Fidelity bonds** protect a company from losses suffered from dishonest employees. Most insurance companies require that all reasonable preventive measures be instituted before they will insure a company against crime. When such security devices and procedures exist, significant savings in insurance premiums often result—sometimes as high as a 70-percent reduction.

As noted by Maturi (1993, p. 10), a fidelity bond protects in two ways: (1) the surety company does a thorough background check before it bonds anyone, helping to eliminate individuals with questionable backgrounds and (2) once an employee is bonded, any losses suffered as a result of the employee's dishonest actions are covered by the bonding company.

"The most recent security development in the insurance industry," say Bottom and Kostanoski (1990, p. 54), "involved providing expanded risk assessment (survey) services for clients. Insurance employees visit clients, perform security surveys, and evaluate the data so that loss-control recommendations can be made. There is a growing number of security opportunities in today's insurance world."

SUMMARY

A prime responsibility of security is to prevent or reduce *shrinkage,* defined as lost assets. Good security can also help to prevent negligence lawsuits. An important first step is to screen all job applicants. Preemployment screening should include an application and resumé, intellectual and psychological tests and a thorough background check including references. All employees should then be educated as to their responsibilities and restrictions. Reasonable rules should be established and enforced.

Most procedural controls seek to prevent loss of shrinkage by limiting access to specific areas by unauthorized personnel. Procedural controls to limit access to specified areas include stationing guards, restricting vehicle traffic, requiring registration and sign-outs, requiring display of badges or passes, ensuring key control and using effective opening, closing and after-hours procedures. Effective employee badges and passes display the employee's name, employment number, signature and photograph as well as an authorizing signature. They should be sturdy, tamper-proof and changed periodically. An effective key control system limits the number of persons having keys, establishes a master list of all existing keys and to whom they are assigned, keeps all duplicate keys secure and requires a physical audit periodically.

Effective closing procedures include checking all restrooms and areas where someone might be concealed, turning off all unnecessary lights and machinery, opening cash registers, locking the safe, locking all windows and interior doors, turning on security lighting, activating the alarm and securing the exterior doors. In an establishment where the risk of burglary is high and no security guard is on night duty, opening and closing should be a two-person operation.

Particularly vulnerable to theft or employee pilferage are storage areas; areas where cash, valuables, records and forms are kept; mail rooms; supply rooms; duplicating rooms and computer rooms.

In addition to procedures for controlling access to certain areas, accounting and receiving procedures can help control shrinkage. A limited amount of cash should be kept on hand. Strict procedures for obtaining petty cash should be established. Purchasing, receiving and paying functions should be kept separate. Prenumbered purchase orders should be used in sequence.

When valuables are being transported, secrecy should be maintained and the times, routes, personnel and vehicles used should be varied.

Despite effective security procedures, thefts may still occur. Such thefts can be detected by using a perpetual inventory, periodic internal and external audits and periodic inspection of lockers, packages, vehicles, persons and trash containers. Inspections are better accepted if they are done democratically and if the procedure is clearly established and explained before the inspection. Insurance and/or bonding of specific employees may also help reduce financial losses.

✔ APPLICATION

Read the following rules from *Preventing Employee Pilferage* by S. D. Astor (1977, pp. 4–5):

> Company rules are important in setting up a strong loss-prevention program. Here are some rules which will help to insure against employee theft.
>
> - Make a dependable second check of incoming materials to rule out the possibility of collusive theft between drivers and employees who handle the receiving.
> - No truck shall approach the loading platform until it is ready to load or unload.
> - Drivers will not be allowed behind the receiving fence. (Discourage drivers from taking goods or materials from the platform by the following devices: heavy-gauge wire fencing between bays, with the mesh too fine to provide a toehold; closed-circuit television cameras, mounted overhead so as to sweep the entire platform; and locating the receiving supervisor's desk or office to afford him an unobstructed view of the entire platform.)
> - At the loading platform, drivers will not be permitted to load their own trucks, especially by taking goods from stock.
> - Every lunchbox, toolbox, bag, or package must be inspected by a supervisor or guard as employees leave the plant.
> - All padlocks must be snapped shut on hasps when not in use to prevent the switching of locks.
> - Keys to padlocks must be controlled. Never leave the key hanging on a nail near the lock where a crooked worker can "borrow" it and have a duplicate made while he is away from his work.
> - Trash must not be allowed to accumulate in, or be picked up from, an area near storage sites of valuable materials or finished goods.
> - Inspect disposal locations and rubbish trucks at irregular intervals for the presence of salable items when you have the slightest reason to suspect collusion between employees and trash collectors.

- Trash pickups must be supervised. (Companies have been systematically drained over long periods by alliances between crooked employees and trash collectors.)
- Rotate security guards. (Rotation discourages fraternizing with other employees who may turn out to be dishonest. Rotation also prevents monotony from reducing the alertness of guards.)
- Never assign two or more members of the same family to work in the same area. (You can expect blood to be thicker than company loyalty.)
- Key men will be kept informed about the activities and findings of the man who is in charge of security. (Thus weak points in security can be strengthened without delay.)
- Control receiving reports and shipping orders (preferably by numbers in sequence) to prevent duplicate or fraudulent payment of invoices and the padding or destruction of shipping orders.
- Receiving reports must be prepared immediately upon receiving a shipment. (Delay in making out such reports can be an invitation to theft or, at best, result in record keeping errors.)
- Employees who are caught stealing will be prosecuted. (Settling for restitution and an apology is inviting theft to continue.)

Green and Farber (1978, pp. 146–47) describe numerous types of employee dishonesty that account for between 7 and 10 percent of business failures annually. Read the list, keeping in mind the preceding rules to thwart pilferage.*

- Payroll and personnel employees collaborating to falsify records by the use of nonexistent employees or by retaining terminated employees on the payroll.
- Padding overtime reports, part of which extra unearned pay is kicked back to the authorizing supervisor.
- Pocketing unclaimed wages.
- Splitting increased payroll which has been raised on checks signed in blank for use in authorized signer's absence.

---

*Reprinted with permission of the publisher from Green and Farber, *Introduction to Security*, revised edition, Woburn, MA: Butterworth Publishers, Inc., 1978.

- Maintenance personnel and contract servicemen in collusion to steal and sell office equipment.
- Receiving clerks and truck drivers in collusion on falsification of merchandise count. Extra unaccounted merchandise is fenced.
- Purchasing agents in collusion with vendors to falsify purchase and payment documents. Purchasing agent issues authorization for payment on goods never shipped after forging receipt of shipment.
- Purchasing agent in collusion with vendor to pay inflated price. Split profit.
- Mailroom and supply personnel packing and mailing merchandise to themselves for resale.
- Accounts payable personnel paying fictitious bills to an account set up for their own use.

- Taking incoming cash without crediting the customer's account.
- Paying creditors twice and pocketing the second check.
- Appropriating checks made out to cash.
- Raising the amount of checks after voucher approval or raising the amount of vouchers after their approval.
- Pocketing small amounts from incoming payments and applying later payments on other accounts to cover shortages.
- Removal of equipment or merchandise with trash.
- Invoicing goods below regular price and getting a kickback from the purchaser.
- Under-ringing on a cash register.
- Issuing (and cashing) checks on returned merchandise not actually returned.
- Forging checks, destroying them when returned with statement from the bank, and changing books accordingly.

Which rules in the first selection might thwart specific dishonest practices in the second selection? What other rules might be required?

CRITICAL THINKING EXERCISE

ROUTINE INSPECTIONS

STATUTORY AND COMMON LAW

The operator or owner of a parking ramp has the duty to use reasonable care to deter criminal activity on its premises that may cause personal harm to customers. The care to be provided is that which a reasonably prudent owner or operator would provide. A security firm hired by an owner to patrol a parking ramp has a duty to use that degree of care which a reasonably prudent professional security firm would use. This duty extends to customers of the lessee of the ramp as well as customers of the owner.

FACTS OF THE CASE

For six months Ms. Garnet Erickson had been a monthly contract parker at the Curtis Ramp in downtown Minneapolis. The ramp is a self-serve, four-level parking facility with approximately 330 parking spaces. It is across the street from the Curtis Hotel and connected to the hotel by an enclosed skyway on the second level. For the past year the Curtis Investment Company had leased the ramp, reserving 142 spaces for its hotel guests and personnel plus some spaces rented to a car rental agency, Allright Parking, a wholly owned subsidiary of Allright Auto Parks, Inc., a foreign corporation. Although there had never been a report of a crime against a person in the ramp, Curtis had hired Leadens Investigation and Security, Inc., to provide services for the hotel and patrol the parking ramp also. If requested, the guards would escort women hotel employees and customers to their cars.

About 5:00 P.M. on December 7, Ms. Erickson left work and walked on the ground level to the parking ramp. She took the elevator to the second level and went to her car, a Chevette hatchback. The ramp was dimly lit, and she saw no security guards. The car was parked facing inward near the center of the ramp. As she attempted to start the car, a man opened the driver's side door and forced himself in. She screamed, and he attempted to silence her by putting his hand over her mouth and threatening her. Although she continued to struggle, she was unable to attract the attention of two or more people who entered the car next to hers, and they drove off. As the struggle continued, other cars drove off from nearby stalls even though twice she was able to honk the horn and scream for help.

The man finally forced her into the back seat, although she momentarily was able to open a back door and again screamed for help. There, in the back seat, the man raped her. The total time of the assault was about 25 minutes. After the man left, she cleaned herself up, restarted the car, defrosted the windows that had steamed up, and drove to the main entrance where she reported the assault to the booth attendant. The security guard on duty learned of the assault and wrote down the details at 5:27 P.M.

Allright Parking's manager claimed that he had walked through the ramp twice on the day of the assault. At 5:00 P.M. an Allright employee was in the exit booth on the ground level and the manager was in his office. Access to the ramp from street doors and the skyway could not be observed from the attendant's booth. The ramp did not have signs warning of security conditions or practices. The ramp was not equipped with television monitors.

According to Robert Buchan, the Leadens security guard at the time of the assault, he made two rounds through the parking ramp after coming on duty at 4:00 P.M. Standard procedure was to use a flashlight to look between the parked cars during each walk through, starting at the top level and finishing on the street level. Buchan's log showed that he made the second round from 5:08 to 5:24 P.M.

Police investigation later identified the assailant. Thomas Sabo, the alleged rapist, was on parole, having been released earlier that same day from the Minnesota Correctional Facility in Stillwater to the Nu-Way Halfway House. Sabo had an extensive history of criminal activity and drug abuse. He was intoxicated at the time of the assault.

Issues and Questions

1. Do Curtis, Allright Parking, Allright Auto Parks and Leadens owe a duty of care to deter criminal activity from a trespassing rapist?
   a. There is a genuine issue of material fact whether Leadens, the security firm, properly performed its security functions. The guard, making an hourly check of the ramp, should have noticed an assault in progress inside a customer's car. Additionally, Curtis and Allright Parking owe a duty to provide customers with a reasonably safe parking ramp, which this is not.
   b. Because Curtis did hire Leadens Investigation and Security, Inc., for services in both the hotel and the parking lot, and because hourly walks were documented, a duty of care was performed. Ms. Erickson had used the lot for half of a year and should have known that if requested the security guards would escort women to their cars in the ramp. It was her choice not to take the time to use this available security.

c. Tort law does not impose a duty on private citizens to provide their own police and law enforcement measures. There is a difference between a landowner's duty to sand a slippery step on his premises and his duty to contain a dangerous criminal. As there had never been a report of a crime against a person in the ramp prior to this Erickson assault, the security provided reasonable care; however, the state of Minnesota was negligent in supervising the parole of Sabo and in not warning area businesses that they could be in danger from a trespassing rapist.

d. Leadens was hired only by Curtis to patrol and provide security for hotel patrons. Only one security guard was hired for duty at the hotel. This guard was instructed to walk through the hotel complex once every hour and to include in his rounds a walk across the skyway to the Curtis ramp and a walk through the ramp from top to bottom, checking for break-ins and vandalism. Leadens did not increase the risk of harm, nor did Erickson contract to rely on Leadens' undertaking. Allright may be liable for not providing additional security.

e. The owner/operator of commercial properties does have a duty to provide security only when there is a special relationship where the customer has accepted that entrustment. If Erickson had been a contract parking customer, with a contractual clause stipulating guaranteed security, then the owner/operator would be liable for any damages or assault that may occur.

Discussion Questions

1. Why is curbing pilferage so important to a security manager?
2. What factual information should be obtained to make the decision to employ or not to employ an applicant?
3. What procedures can be used regarding employee coats, purses and packages to deter internal theft?
4. What are some rationales frequently given by employees for stealing from their employers?
5. What employee actions might lead security personnel to suspect dishonesty?

References

Addis, Karen K. "When Employees Beat the System." *Security Management,* September 1991, pp. 115–119.

Adler, Steven. "Selling Employees on Loss Prevention." *Security Management,* December 1993, pp. 30–33.

Arnold, David W. and Thiemann, Alan J. "Psychological Testing in ADA's Wake." *Security Management,* January 1994, pp. 43–45.

Astor, S. D. *Preventing Employee Pilferage.* Small Business Administration. Management Aids No. 209. Washington, DC: U.S. Government Printing Office, 1977.

Bartholomew, Douglas. "Say Yes to a Drug-Free Workplace . . . And As You Do, Protect Your Profits." *Your Company,* Summer 1991, pp. 42–48.

Beaudette, John P. "Hiring: Caveat Employer." *Security Management,* April 1992, pp. 63–70.

Beaudette, John P. "The Perils of Preemployment Screening." *Security Management,* November 1992, pp. 39–40.

Bequai, August. "What Can You Ask?" *Security Management,* November 1991, pp. 58–60.

Bottom, Norman R., Jr. and Kostanoski, John I. *Introduction to Security and Loss Control.* Englewood Cliffs, NJ: Prentice-Hall, 1990.

Buckley, David M. "Dealing with Artful Dodgers." *Security Management,* April 1993, pp. 32–35.

Cunningham, W. C. and Taylor, T. H. *The Hallcrest Report: Private Security and Police in America.* Portland, OR: Chancellor Press, 1985.

Draty, David. "Curbing the High Cost of Employee Theft." *Security Concepts,* January 1995, pp. 11, 34.

Dulcamaro, Sal. "Security Key Monitor: The Total Key Control System." *Reed's Security Reporter,* February 1994, pp. 59–64.

Green, G. and Farber, R. C. *Introduction to Security.* Los Angeles: Security World Publishing Company, 1978.

Harris, William G. "The Integrity Test." *Security Management: Special Supplement—The Ways and Means of Screening,* 1990, pp. 22A–23A.

Hayes, Read. "Battling Workplace Theft." *Security Management,* September 1992, pp. 150–154.

Heine, William D., Jr. "Using Tamper-Evident Label Seals." *Security Concepts,* August 1994, pp. 15, 19.

Hill, William T. "Getting Help from the Outside." *Security Management: Special Supplement—The Ways and Means of Screening,* 1990, pp. 15A–16A.

Inbau, Fred E. "Integrity Tests and the Law." *Security Management,* January 1994, pp. 34–41.

Jayne, Brian C. "The Interview." *Security Management: Special Supplement—The Ways and Means of Screening,* 1990, pp. 18A–19A.

Jayne, Brian C. "The Search for an Honest Work Force." *Security Management,* January 1994, pp. 47–50.

King, Carl E. and Dunston, Dain. "The Proof's on the Paper: Paper-and-Pencil Tests Prove to Be a Safe Alternative." *Security Management,* January 1992, p. 61.

Kuhn, Ryan A. "The Psychological Test." *Security Management: Special Supplement—The Ways and Means of Screening,* 1990, p. 23.

Lasky, Barry M. and Steinberg, Scott L. "Employment Practices Involving Drug Testing." *Security Concepts,* August 1994, p. 14.

Lisko, Richard F. "A Manager's Guide to Drug Testing." *Security Management,* August 1994, pp. 92–95.

Mancebo, Marty. "Selecting a Test to Get the Best." *Security Management,* January 1992, pp. 57–59.

Martin, Scott L. and DeGrange, Donna J. "How Effective Are Physical and Psychological Drug Tests?" *Security Technology and Design,* May/June 1993, pp. 38–41.

Maturi, Richard J. "To Catch a Thief: Protect Yourself Against Dishonest Employees." *Your Company,* Fall 1993, pp. 10–12.

McClain, Eddy L. "Defeating Employee Theft and Drug Abuse." *Security Concepts,* February 1995, pp. 9, 26.

Phelps, E. Floyd. "Getting a Lock on Key Control." *Security Management,* April 1995, pp. 61–63.

Queeno, Cameron L. "Designing Forgery Out of the ID Picture." *Security Management,* August 1994, pp. 26–32.

Rea, Kelly V. EPPA: "The Fine Print." *Security Management,* May 1989, pp. 49–55.

Rosen, Mark B. "Prescreen to Avoid Getting Burned." *Security Management,* April 1993, pp. 38–40.

Schafer, June P. "The Resumé."*Security Management: Special Supplement—The Ways and Means of Screening,* 1990, p. 17A.

Stoller, William H. "Sobering Up for Success." *Security Management,* September 1991, pp. 127–128.

Truncer, Earl and Magee, Maureen. "Setting Your Sites on Security." *Security Management,* January 1995, pp. 67–69.

Turner, Dana L. and Stephenson, Richard G. "A Plan to Prevent Pilfering." *Security Management,* June 1994, pp. 63–65.

CASES

Baggs v. Eagle-Picker Industries, 750 F.Supp. 264 or 957 F.2d 268 (1992)

High Tech Gays v. Defense Industrial Clearance Office, 895 F.2d 563 (1990)

Mest v. Federated Group, Inc., US Dist. Ct. Oakland, CA, No. 8129668-0, 6/89.

Ponticas v. K.M.S. Investments, 331 N.W.2d 907 (Minn. 1983)

Texas State Employment Union v. Texas Department of Mental Health, 746 S.W. 2d 203 (Tex. 1987)

CHAPTER 7

PREVENTING LOSSES FROM ACCIDENTS AND EMERGENCIES

DO YOU KNOW

- Why accident prevention is often a security responsibility?
- What OSHA is and how it relates to private security? What records it requires?
- What causes the vast majority of accidents? How they can be prevented or reduced?
- What security's role is during civil disturbances, riots and strikes?
- What the primary defenses against bombs are?
- How a bomb threat can be prepared for? Received? Acted on?
- What three elements are required for a fire to occur?
- How fires are classified?
- How fires can be prevented?
- What equipment can help protect lives and assets from fire?
- What types of fire detectors are available?
- When water or a Class A fire extinguisher should *not* be used?
- What procedures help protect against loss by fire?
- What the security manager's responsibilities are in the event of a fire?
- What natural disaster plans should be formulated?

CAN YOU DEFINE THESE TERMS?

fire triangle
fire-loading
ignition temperature
infrared detectors
ionization detectors
Occupational Safety and Health Act
Occupational Safety and Health Administration (OSHA)
photoelectric detectors
thermal detectors

INTRODUCTION

Preventing losses from accidents and emergencies is a critical responsibility of security managers. Despite the best efforts to reduce the possibility of accidents or emergencies occurring, they will happen. Security managers and personnel must be prepared to deal effectively with them. The simple fact that an accident or emergency happened might be the basis for a lawsuit. How the accident or emergency is dealt with might also be cause for civil action against security personnel and their employers.

Gardiner and Grassie (1994, p. 97) note: "Safe and secure work environments are rapidly becoming the industry standard as a result of legally imposed duty, court decisions regarding foreseeability, and the actions of workplace safety regulatory agencies."

> Security managers are often responsible for accident prevention programs as one means to prevent losses and protect assets.

It is only common sense to protect against accidents, but also federally mandated that such protection be provided.

This chapter begins by introducing the Occupational Safety and Health Act (OSHAct), which regulates much of the safety standards in business and industry. This is followed by a discussion of accident prevention. Next, general guidelines for dealing with emergencies are presented, including medical emergencies, hazardous materials incidents, civil disturbances, riots and strikes and bombs and bomb threats. The chapter concludes with a discussion of preventing and protecting against loss by fire and natural disasters.

The Occupational Safety and Health Act

Traditionally, loss prevention has focused on preventing and minimizing losses from internal and external crime. However, since the passage of the Occupational Safety and Health Act, the security function has gradually expanded to include specific safety responsibilities. Security managers involved in these safety programs often have titles such as Director of Loss Prevention, Director of Security and Prevention or Director of Safety and Security, reflecting the dual functions of security and safety.

Because of a disturbing pattern of increasing occupational injuries, in 1970 Congress enacted Public Law 91-596, the **Occupational Safety and Health Act.** The **Occupational Safety and Health Administration (OSHA),** a federal agency within the Department of Labor, was established to administer this act. The stated purpose of the act is "to assure so far as possible every working man and woman in the nation safe and healthful working conditions and to preserve our human resources." In essence, the act requires every employer covered by the act to furnish employees with a place of employment that is free from recognized hazards that cause or are likely to cause death or serious physical harm.

> OSHA, the Occupational Safety and Health Administration, was established to administer the Occupational Safety and Health Act, which seeks to ensure safe and healthful working conditions for every employee in the nation.

The act applies to every employer who is engaged in interstate commerce or whose business affects interstate commerce and who has at least one employee. The vast majority of employers in the nation are, therefore, under the jurisdiction of OSHA. The act excludes employees of federal, state and local governments and those protected under federal occupational safety and health laws, such as the Atomic Energy Act of 1954 or the Federal Coal Mine Safety and Health Act.

OSHA Standards

OSHA has established three types of standards: initial, emergency temporary and permanent.

Initial standards include the general rules for avoiding known hazards, such as having employees wear safety glasses, hard hats and face shields; having exits clearly marked and aisles and walkways to these exits free of obstacles or obstructions; providing an adequate supply of drinking water and adequate toilet facilities; and having fire protection and suppression equipment readily available and in good operating condition.

Emergency temporary standards are issued by the Department of Labor as needed when a new danger or hazard is recognized. These emergency temporary standards can remain in effect for six months, but they must then be either replaced by a permanent standard or rescinded.

Permanent standards include all new requirements since the initial set of standards was established. Many of these standards are quite controversial and are seen as unnecessarily restrictive. Given the current emphasis on deregulation, many OSHA standards may be modified or eliminated in the near future.

Employers can request a *variance* if a specific standard seems to be unnecessarily restrictive or impossible to comply with as specified. Four types of variances may be requested. A *permanent variance* may be obtained if an employer can prove that current conditions and processes are as healthful and safe as those established under a specific standard. A *temporary variance* may be obtained if the employer needs more time to comply with a standard, either because it is impossible to meet the requirements immediately or because the employer is financially incapable of making the required changes immediately. A temporary variance may be granted for up to two years. An *experimental variance* may be obtained if an employer wants to try out and validate new equipment or techniques. In rare cases, if the country's security is threatened, a *national defense variance* may be obtained.

Complying with OSHA Requirements

The act requires employers to post a notice informing employees of their protection under the act. In addition, all employees must have access to OSHA regulations and standards. Employees can request an OSHA inspection of their place of work, and they can request medical tests to determine if they are being exposed to unhealthy conditions.

To comply with OSHA requirements, security managers' responsibilities might include the following:

- Knowing the act and its initial standards and requirements.
- Understanding what OSHA standards apply to the specific facility.
- Keeping informed of and enforcing specific OSHA regulations.
- Posting all necessary notices.
- Keeping or supervising the retainment of all required OSHA records.
- Setting specific safety goals and measuring progress toward these goals.
- Conducting safety audits and surveys.
- Examining current unsafe or hazardous conditions and correcting them.
- Developing in-house safety programs and educating management and labor personnel.
- Dealing with OSHA representatives and inspectors.
- Seeing that OSHA violations are corrected.

> OSHA requires employers covered by the act to keep a log of all occupational injuries, accidents and illnesses, as well as an annual summary of the log's information.

The annual summary must be compiled and posted within one month after the close of the year and left up for 30 days. The act also requires employers to keep the detailed safety and health records for five years, subject to OSHA review at any time.

Inspections

To ensure that its requirements are fulfilled, the act stipulates that OSHA inspectors can investigate any facility subject to OSHA standards to see that they are in compliance. Inspectors can appear at any reasonable hour and should be allowed to inspect the facility. If they request an employee to accompany them, this request should also be honored.

Until recently, OSHA representatives and inspectors could enter an employer's premises without advance notice. These surprise visits were extremely unpopular and were viewed by some as a violation of their protection against unreasonable searches guaranteed by the Fourth Amendment of the United States Constitution.

In 1978, a small businessman refused to allow an OSHA inspector on his premises without a warrant, contesting such surprise inspections. In *Marshall v. Barlow's Inc.* (1978), the Supreme Court ruled, in a five-to-three decision, that government agents checking for safety and health hazards cannot make spot checks without a warrant. Such inspections, they contended, did amount to a violation of the Fourth Amendment, which protects not only private homes, but commercial premises as well. Certain establishments were held exempt from the warrant requirement, including those engaged in the production of liquor and firearms.

Unlike other search warrants, however, a warrant to check for safety and health hazards does *not* have to be based on the probable cause that unsafe conditions exist. Therefore, the surprise nature of the inspections, a necessary feature to avoid cosmetic changes, remains intact.

Representatives from management, employees or both have the right to accompany an OSHA inspector and to see the results of that inspection.

The U.S. Department of Labor is responsible for enforcing OSHA standards and proposing penalties for violators. The penalties apply *only* to the employer. Although the act requires employee compliance with all safety and health standards and regulations, the employer is responsible to see that the employees comply. For example, if a worker is seen without a hard hat in an area where such safety equipment is required, it is the employer, not the employee, who gets the citation.

Various types of violations might be found. They are usually classified as serious or nonserious, willful or nonwillful. An employer who is found to be in violation is cited and allowed a reasonable time to comply with a specific standard. The citation must be posted on the premises and corrective action taken. Failure to comply with a citation can carry a fine of $10,000 and/or a jail sentence of six months. Employers can also be fined up to $1,000 per day for serious violations of OSHA standards. If an imminent danger to workers is discovered, a facility can be shut down immediately.

Some companies have opted to simply accept financial penalties rather than make changes needed to meet standards, considering this one of the prices of doing business. Such an approach may no longer work since passage of the Omnibus Budget Rehabilitation Act of 1990, which increases maximum penalties for violations sevenfold. According to Roughton (1995, p. 41):

> Congress stated that the penalty increase has a three-fold purpose: to encourage compliance, deter wrongdoing, and reduce the federal deficit. OSHA penalties will be paid directly to the U.S. Treasury.
>
> Congress estimates that OSHA fines could increase from $30 million in 1990 to $180 million per year in the future. . . .

In 1994, OSHA conducted 42,377 inspections—32,822 for safety hazards; 9,555 for health investigations. The result was nearly $120 million in penalties ("OSHA Penalties," 1995, p. 1).

Additional information on OSHA and specific standards for a given type of facility can be obtained from the state labor departments or from the United States Labor Department in Washington, D.C.

In addition to OSHA inspectors, premises are often subject to safety and fire inspections by insurance underwriters and city and state inspectors.

Accident Prevention

As noted by Sunstrom (1994, p. 24): "No program has the potential to have such a positive or negative impact on the bottom line as the health and safety program." He notes that a single back injury can cost a company as much as $200,000.

The health and safety program should include a careful job analysis to determine where risks exist. It should also include training on personal hygiene, use of protective equipment and proper materials handling, including the handling of any hazardous materials. All such training should be documented because, as noted by Sunstrom (1994, p. 28): "Documentation is critical in showing OSHA that training was provided. If it isn't written down, it didn't happen."

Often safety hazards such as toxic chemicals and hydraulic presses, saws, grinders and punches are very apparent. Although accidents are commonly associated with heavy industry, the National Safety Council reports that more accidents occur in wholesale and retail businesses than in heavy industry. Accidents take an enormous human and economic toll each year. The National Safety Council also makes this statement:

> Ninety-five percent of all accidents (on or off the job) are caused by human error, especially lack of safety consciousness.

The vast majority of accidents result from carelessness, failure to have and/or follow safety rules and regulations or engaging in horseplay. The remaining 5 percent result from mechanical failures or natural disasters.

Careless accidents may result from improperly handling objects, slipping or falling, colliding with someone, being hit by a falling object, receiving an electric shock or being injured by machinery.

> Accidents can be prevented by removing hazards, using protective equipment, making employees aware of hazards that cannot be removed and following good housekeeping practices.

To prevent injuries from electric shock, employees should be alert to and report hazardous conditions such as frayed electric cords on office equipment or lighting; assume that wires and cables, whether indoors or outdoors, are "hot"; lock circuits when working on electric connections and wear rubber gloves when working on wires, circuits or electric lines.

Employees should be constantly aware of potential hazards when working around machinery. Safety equipment should be used when available. Employers should, for example, install hoods, canopies and/or ducts to exhaust noxious fumes and chemicals. They should install machine guards such as shields over grinding wheels and sweep arms that pull an operator's arms free from punch presses. Employees are also often required to wear personal protective equipment such as safety glasses or goggles, face shields, hard hats, safety shoes, rubber aprons and rubber gloves.

The government publication *Preventing Illness and Injury in the Workplace* (1985, p. 190) describes a "fundamentals program" in existence at Gray Tool Company, Houston, Texas, manufacturer of heavy machinery. This company trains its 800 workers and all supervisors in basic techniques to prevent injuries. The program emphasizes being aware of hazards and having each individual take responsibility for his or her own safety and that of fellow employees. The program is intended to help employees (1) perform the job while avoiding injury, (2) learn emergency procedures, (3) adopt proper hygiene and health care and (4) use protective devices and techniques. To accomplish the preceding, the health and safety staff instructs workers in proper lifting techniques, eye protection, use of respirators, hoist operating and sling inspection.

Accidents are more apt to occur in cluttered areas, so good housekeeping practices are essential. Trash and rubbish accumulations not only are unsightly, but also can block fire exits, extinguishers and alarm boxes. Neatness provides a safer working environment and usually increases efficiency as well.

When accidents or injuries do occur, they should be reported, recorded and investigated. An effective accident investigation determines why and how the accident happened and includes the date of the accident, the name and occupation of the person injured, details of the accident, identification of the hazard or cause and the corrective action taken.

Many managers use safety incentive plans such as cash or merchandise awards for employees with the best safety record. Trucking companies often provide awards for drivers who reach one hundred thousand miles without an accident.

Medical Emergencies

Kass (1994, p. 102) stresses: "The mishandling of illness and injuries that occur on a facility's premises is a major source of premises liability." According to Kass (1994, p. 101–102):

> Security is usually the first department that is notified when any type of emergency occurs at a facility. Medical emergencies are inevitable and all security departments must be prepared to deal with them. . . .
>
> At minimum, any security officer with public contact should be trained and certified in CPR and basic first aid. . . .
>
> All employees must know what number to call for help. Security officers or employee response teams should have preassigned responsibilities including caring for patients, controlling crowds, and escorting outside EMS personnel to the patient.

If the security personnel responding to a medical emergency have the necessary training, such as first aid or CPR, they should render aid. If they do not have such training, they should wait for trained personnel to arrive. Responding security personnel *must not* do more than they are trained to do. Any injured or seriously ill person should *not* be moved unless to leave them would put them in greater danger than if they were not moved. Improper moving can cause further injury or even death and could easily result in a civil lawsuit.

Facilities should have a wheelchair, stretcher and basic first-aid equipment readily available.

PROTECTING AGAINST AIDS AND HEPATITIS B

Kohr and Nobrega (1993, p. 36) make the observation: "Security is a contact sport. Security officers may serve as the front-line medical team in emergencies, or they may have to restrain or otherwise come in contact with potentially contagious individuals. In today's society, such contact can be life threatening if the proper precautions are not taken."

Care must be exercised by security personnel who deal with accident victims. Blood is frequently present, often in great quantity. Security personnel should take precautions because blood can transmit not only the deadly AIDS virus but also hepatitis B virus and tuberculosis.

A survey conducted by the Centers for Disease Control (CDC) from 1988 to 1991 indicates that 300,000 to one million Americans are infected with the AIDS virus ("U.S. AIDS Survey," 1993, p. 7A).

OSHA has issued rules to protect American workers from infection by AIDS or hepatitis (Epps, 1992, p. 14):

> Designed to prevent AIDS and hepatitis infections in workers who come into contact with blood or bodily fluids as part of their jobs, the mandatory rules require employers to provide workers with training and protective clothing, puncture proof receptacles for contaminated needles and other medical wastes, and vaccination against the hepatitis virus. . . .
>
> Scope. Covers all employees who could be "reasonably anticipated" as the result of performing their job duties to face contact with blood and other potentially infectious materials. Infectious materials include semen, vaginal secretions, cerebrospinal fluid, peritoneal fluid, amniotic fluid, saliva in dental procedures, any body fluid visibly contaminated with blood and all body fluids in situations where it is difficult or impossible to differentiate between body fluids.

The CDC has also compiled a list of other diseases serious enough to mandate notification requirements for emergency response employees (EREs), who may have been exposed to them (Kime, 1993, p. 12) including the airborne disease of infectious tuberculosis and such uncommon or rare diseases as diphtheria, hemorrhagic fever, meningococcal disease, plague and rabies.

"Scientific studies from around the world have shown that HIV is not spread through ordinary employee, client or public-client contact" ("AIDS," 1994, p. 3). It should also be noted that individuals with HIV/AIDS are protected by the federal Americans with Disabilities Act and cannot be discriminated against simply because of their disease.

The AIDS virus can survive at least 15 days at room temperature in dried and liquid blood. Those responsible for cleaning up any blood at an accident scene should be cautioned about the potential hazard and provided with appropriate protection such as gloves.

Accidents are not the only situation in which security personnel might have to deal with blood. Several other types of emergency situations and other security problems may also present this hazard.

HAZARDOUS MATERIALS INCIDENTS

Hazardous materials (H/M) incidents can cause serious, even life-threatening, problems and must be dealt with immediately. Contact with highly toxic chemical liquids, solids or gases or with highly corrosive materials requires extreme care. Hazardous materials emergencies may involve poor visibility, difficult breathing, fire, hysteria and lack of information about the substance causing the problem.

An estimated 1.5 to 2 billion workers or nearly two out of every three workers are exposed to chemicals in the workplace. Pesticides poison an estimated 3.5 to 5 million people yearly, killing more than 40,000 a year ("Chemicals in the Workplace," 1994, p. 17). In addition to pesticides, the following are considered dangerous chemicals:

- Heavy metals such as lead, cadmium, mercury and chromium.
- Carcinogens such as arsenic compounds, asbestos, benzene, benzidine, chromium, 2-naphtylamine and vinyl chloride.
- Organic solvents: halogenated hydrocarbons, ethers, alcohols, aromatic hydrocarbons, etc.
- Combustion products such as carbon monoxide and oxides of nitrogen.
- Commonly used gases such as chlorine, hydrogen fluoride, hydrogen cyanide, phosgene and ammonia.

In 1991, OSHA published a standard covering process safety management (PSM) of hazardous chemicals. Draty (May 1994, p. 5) notes: "More than three million United States workers (2.4 permanent and more than 650,000 contract employees) at nearly 25,000 worksites are exposed to chemicals covered by the OSHA rule."

Draty (February 1994, p. 2) cites Department of Transportation statistics indicating almost 10,000 hazardous waste incidents in 1992, resulting in 16 deaths, 594 injuries and $31,118,912 in damages.

Another hazard in the workplace is carbon monoxide (CO) often called the silent killer because it is difficult to detect and over time can be deadly. Olick (1994, p. 2) suggests: "[Carbon monoxide] is potentially more dangerous than a gun-wielding maniac demanding retribution for the downsizing that curtailed his career and destroyed his self-worth." Olick suggests:

> In the workplace, it's robbing employers of valuable man-hours when an employee calls in sick with the flu . . . and it's really some degree of CO poisoning that could have been avoided. In today's world, it's costing taxpayers, parents, employers, insurance companies and others millions upon millions each year.

This need not be the case. Residential carbon monoxide detectors are on the market and are relatively inexpensive. Many communities have passed ordinances mandating such detectors in homes, and a standard for such detectors is in development. Unfortunately, according to Olick (p. 26): "A commercial/industrial standard is not expected for quite some time." Therefore, security managers should research carefully before installing CO detectors in office buildings or in industrial settings.

OSHA mandates that training is required for all employees engaged in hazardous waste activities and that an emergency response plan be developed. According to Roughton (1992, p. 104): "Security officers' basic responsibilities before, during and after a hazardous waste emergency can be outlined as follows":

- Evaluate and document all possible hazards.
- Prevent hazards during containment and cleanup. Seal drains and remove other volatile materials.
- Identify the hazardous substance. Determine method of control.
- Establish communication between the central station and the security post.
- Ensure that people are protected, isolated, or evacuated from the area.
- Assist in implementing flow control procedures. Know locations of clean-up kits and breathing apparatuses.
- Maintain control of perimeter during spills, containment, and cleanup.
- Direct emergency vehicles and personnel to the proper location.

May (October 1990, p. 85) suggests several agencies that might assist in a hazardous material incident:

- State Fire Marshal's office.
- Local EMS system.
- U.S. Coast Guard.
- The shipping company.
- The manufacturer.
- CHEMTREC (1-800-424-9300).

Although writing for public patrol officers and their supervisors, May (October 1990, pp. 85–87) lists some key "dos" and "don'ts" for first responders that apply equally to security officers and supervisors:

- Report the incident as a possible hazardous material accident. Give exact location and approach route, and request assistance.
- Stay upwind and upgrade (if the hazard is outdoors).
- Clear the area of nonessential personnel.
- Avoid contact with liquids or fumes.
- Eliminate ignition sources. (Do not smoke or use flares.)
- Rescue the injured—only if prudent.
- Identify the material(s) involved and determine conditions.
- If necessary, initiate an evacuation.
- Establish a command post.

Additional steps if the hazard occurs indoors are to isolate and seal off the area by closing doors and to shut down the ventilation system for the area.

If hazardous materials are commonly present at a specific location, they should be clearly labeled as such. In addition, the security manager should consider having an H/M control team trained to respond to those materials that might cause a problem. In some instances special equipment such as chemical suits, gloves, boots and air packs should be available for emergency use.

GENERAL GUIDELINES FOR DEALING WITH EMERGENCIES

Cardwell (1994, p. 64) stresses: "Disasters ranging from fires and earthquakes to riots and terrorist bombings can have long-lasting ramifications for unprepared organizations. Businesses must be ready to minimize injuries and property damage during these emergencies."

Schmock (1991, p. 38) contends that a successful plan to be prepared for emergencies relies on seven factors:

- Management support.
- Identifying and addressing the catastrophes common to your location.
- A qualified emergency response team.
- Liaison with local emergency agencies.
- Communication.
- Proper equipment.
- Extensive training.

Turner (1994, p. 58) notes: "An appropriate response stabilizes critical functions first and then restores less important ones." Turner (p. 63) concludes:

> Developing an effective disaster recovery plan is one of the most prudent and cost-effective projects a company can undertake. Just as a ship without a rudder is at the mercy of the tides, a company without a plan is at the mercy of events.

As noted by Blake (1992, p. 71):

> Disaster recovery planning, catastrophe management, business resumption planning, emergency planning, contingency planning, business recovery planning—no matter what you call it, disaster recovery planning is important to corporate survival in the 1990s. Unfortunately, harried business executives concerned primarily with daily cash flow and sales projections frequently assign it a low corporate priority.

Foster (1993, p. 65) notes: "The Corrupt Foreign Practices Act makes corporate officers legally liable for ensuring the recoverability of business services following a disastrous event." Even without such legislation, however, disaster recovery planning makes good sense. According to Foster:

> Regardless of the name, it [disaster recovery planning] is business insurance—nothing more and nothing less. That insurance can take the form of redundant capabilities within a company, mutual agreements with other companies, or agreements with third parties called hot site vendors. . . .

> A hot site is a fully operational data processing facility configured to the user's specifications and available to the company within twenty-four hours. . . .
>
> Commercial hot site vendors have multiple remote data centers, with work space, air conditioning, security, storage space, and an uninterruptible power supply.

Security managers and their staff may be faced with a variety of emergencies including medical emergencies; civil disturbances, riots and strikes; bombs and bomb threats; fire and natural disasters. Every emergency presents a unique security challenge. Nevertheless, several guidelines can help ensure the most effective response possible.

Before the Emergency

- Be prepared. Be proactive. Anticipate the emergencies and the personnel needed to deal with them.
- Have written plans in place. Specify *in writing* who does what, how and when. The more common elements there are among the plans for different types of emergencies the better. This should include posting evacuation routes and emergency phone numbers for different types of emergencies. It should also include determining who will communicate with the media and what kind of information will be communicated.
- Identify the equipment and resources required and make certain they are either available or immediately accessible.
- Know how to use the emergency equipment: fire protection systems, first-aid equipment, hazardous material control equipment, communications systems.
- Inspect emergency equipment at least monthly. Check batteries in flashlights.
- Practice when possible.

During the Emergency

- Take time to assess the situation. Do not make the situation worse by acting without thinking.
- Keep the channels of communication open and the information flowing as required to those who need it.
- Keep as many options open as possible. Avoid "either/or" thinking.
- Do not get sidetracked by personal, individual requests for help, but rather focus on the "big picture," routing individual requests to the appropriate source of assistance.
- Involve key personnel as rapidly as possible. Do not hesitate to call for help from the police, fire department, medical centers and any other assistance that might be needed. When calling for help:
  - Speak slowly and clearly.
  - Give your name, position, company name, address and location of the emergency.

  - Answer any questions.
  - Do *not* hang up until directed to do so.
- Accept the fact that security cannot do everything. The security manager must prioritize and delegate responsibilities quickly. Mistakes probably will happen.
- Keep top executives fully informed of progress and problems.
- Ensure that someone is tending to "normal" security needs during the emergency.
- Maintain control of the media. Follow established procedures.

After the Emergency

- Get back to normal as soon as possible.
- *Document* everything that happened and was done. Accurate records are critical. (Expect that lawyers will get into it at some point.)
- Evaluate the response after the situation has returned to normal. Look at "mistakes" as the "least effective alternative" as well as learning opportunities. However, as May (March 1990, p. 99) cautions: "Nothing should be written down during these critiques that you wouldn't want to discuss in court if the material is subpoenaed."
- Modify any identified risks remaining and modify emergency-preparedness plans as needed based on what was learned.

Emergency procedures are designed to save lives; minimize injury, loss or damage and get back to normal as rapidly and safely as possible. In most instances the primary responsibility of security personnel is to respond rapidly and appropriately and to maintain control of the situation until support professionals such as police, fire fighters or medical specialists arrive.

Evacuation

If evacuation is required, an announcement such as the following should be made over the public address system:

> Attention. Please turn off all equipment and machines and leave the building through the nearest exit immediately. Move 200 feet away from the building. Stay there. Do not leave the premises unless directed to do so.

This message should be repeated at least three times. People should not leave the area so that a check can be made of all personnel to determine if anyone is still inside the building.

Civil Disturbances, Riots and Strikes

Some types of violence can also pose a threat to safety and property. As with other types of emergencies, the key to preventing or reducing losses is to *be prepared* with a written plan detailing who does what and when.

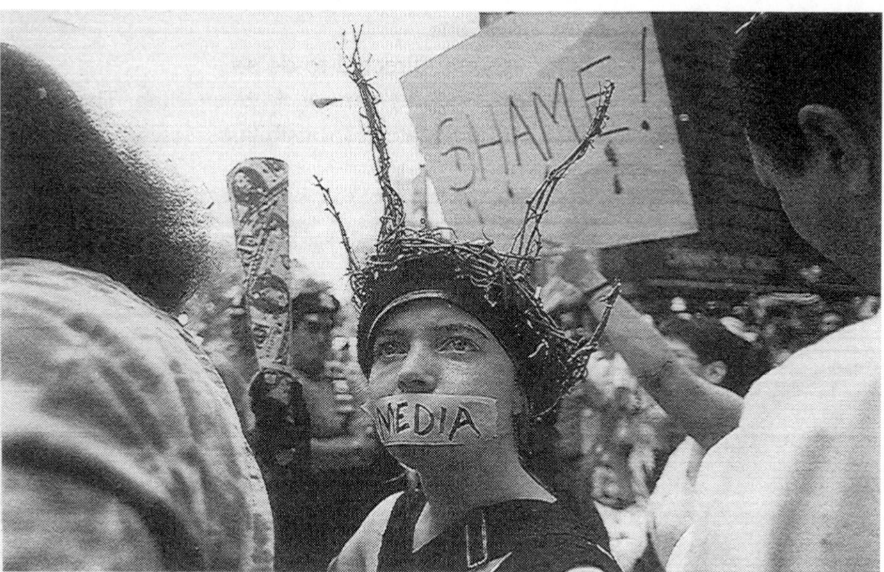

Anti-military rally/protest for Operation Desert Storm.

In the event of civil disturbances, riots or strikes, the security manager is responsible for maintaining order and protecting lives and assets.

Civil Disturbances

Protests, demonstrations, sit-ins, picket lines, blockades and confrontations can threaten the safety of employees and assets. Demonstrators often use abusive language and attempt to provoke security officers. Although nonviolent demonstrations are usually legal, a company may protect its rights, its personnel and its property. If demonstrators act illegally (for example, by destroying property), they should be charged and arrested. Often the assistance of the public police is requested in civil disturbances.

Riots

Some civil disturbances erupt into full-blown riots, causing tremendous destruction, as vividly demonstrated during the Watts riots of 1965, when 36 people were killed, 700 were injured and property losses estimated at half a billion dollars were incurred.

More recently, in April 1992, riots broke out in Los Angeles after jurors acquitted four white police officers charged with beating black motorist Rodney King. At least 37 people were killed, 1,419 were injured, nearly 4,400 were arrested and damage was put at $550 million ("L.A. Troops . . .," *Star Tribune,* May 2, 1992, p. 1A).

Retail stores are usually the hardest hit during riots, but wholesalers, manufacturers and institutions such as hospitals and colleges may also be involved.

Access control is critical in a riot situation. It is best to lock up and sit tight. Protecting personnel and assets becomes a proprietary responsibility because police and fire fighters are usually busy and cannot respond to private calls for assistance.

Management may seek to hire supplemental security forces, but often such forces are unavailable during a riot. Some establishments have paid a retainer to private contract security forces to ensure their availability in an emergency situation. Others have their own "auxiliary" security force.

If it is safe to do so, employees should be evacuated. The lights should be left on, and store windows and entrances should be barricaded. Some establishments keep rolls of concertina wire on hand for use during riots.

According to Oliver (1993, p. 27): "[B]usinesses found their civil disturbance plans totally inadequate. Companies such as Northrop Corporation's Aircraft Division, were forced to shut down for days, staffed only by emergency personnel." This corporation took steps to correct the situation, including many security upgrades: fences, gates, guard stations, lighting and a public address system. In addition, says Oliver (p. 27): "To fill the crisis management void, the company formed a new crisis management organization devoted to training building emergency leaders (BELs)."

The crisis management void was the result of 10,000 employees and 1,000 supervisors equaling 11,000 impressions of what was happening and what to do during the riot. To alleviate this situation, 27 senior managers were trained to serve as building emergency leaders. As noted by Oliver (1993, p. 28):

> The desired outcome during a disaster is to position all twenty-seven BELs to work together with the division general manager to ensure a coordinated response. They all share common training that enables them to make coordinated decisions, even in the event that one or more sites cannot communicate with the rest of the division.

Strikes

Almost one-fourth of the labor force in our country is now unionized. Though strikes are unpleasant even when nonviolent, they pose an especially difficult situation for security officers who belong to a union themselves. The situation can become next to impossible when labor contracts for employees and security personnel are not separate. As management's representatives, security officers are hired to protect the premises even though the employees are out on strike; they may have to cross picket lines.

Security officers must remain neutral and do the job they were hired to do. Picketing is legal as long as it remains nonviolent and there is no restraining order against the strike. Those who wish to cross the picket line to enter a picketed building must be allowed to do so. Any assaultive action should be prosecuted. As in any other potentially high-risk situation, management should have a preestablished strike plan, including what the consequences will be for security officers who honor the picket line.

Kouri (1992, p. 158), in describing the violence accompanying a labor dispute at the *New York Daily News,* notes: "Fire-bombings and arson, aggravated assaults, and physical and verbal abuse committed by workers on strike revealed the inability of the police and security forces to contain violence and maintain peace."

Kouri (p. 161) contends: "The most important point for security officers to remember is that they are not protecting a company from vicious criminals but guarding it against possible damage done in a fit of passion."

"A slight misunderstanding on either side may escalate into mob violence and retaliation by both sides" (p. 158). Kouri suggests that "[the] security force be thoroughly aware of what the strike involves. Familiarity with the objectives of both labor and management is paramount to the success of the peacekeeping."

Vance (1991, p. 46) describes outside, specialized strike teams which might be considered: "[A] good strike team should be able to document, correlate, and present in judicial form evidence of violations of law and court orders, unfair labor practices, and strike-related violence and damage." This is often done by videotaping. And, as noted by Vance (p. 46): "The power of the camera, both video and still, has often been shown to be a deterrent to violence and an effective way to document what actually occurred at a specific time, date, and place." He cautions, however, that such picture taking might be a "double-edged sword":

> In some instances, the courts have judged the filming of legal and peaceful picketing to be harassment, intimidation, and a violation of labor's legal rights.

Another hazard is that the video might show security personnel antagonizing picketers or using unnecessary force, causing the court to sympathize with the strikers.

Courts are increasingly granting large damage awards to victims of strike violence. Herman (1994, p. 1) describes the strike of an aluminum recycling plant by workers of the Oil Chemical & Atomic Workers Union in Cook County, Illinois. One striker had threatened to shoot any drivers who disregarded the strike and hauled aluminum for the recycling plant. The first day of the strike shots were fired at two company supervisors. Later, a 27-year-old truck driver hauling aluminum was shot and killed. A Cook County jury found the company negligent and awarded the driver's widow $2.25 million. The contract security company settled separately before the trial for $950,000. According to Herman (p. 1):

> The company was not found guilty of failing to take action to prevent the violent behavior and protect the potential victims; rather, it was found guilty of *failing to communicate* the danger to the parties that were specifically threatened, that is, the contract truck drivers.

The lesson in this, says Herman, is that communication is vital during any strike situation: "Everyone affiliated with the company and everyone who enters the company's facilities—employees, suppliers, and contract services—should be apprised from the outset of all relevant situational details, security procedures and special circumstances."

Dealing with Unruly People

Any group gathering near or in an establishment should be reported to the appropriate people and then observed. If the situation warrants, outside doors might be locked.

Any violent disturbance, especially if weapons are involved, is usually the responsibility of law enforcement. It is security's responsibility to protect people and property and to support the police responding to the scene.

Crowds might be classified into four general categories:

- Casual—at a shopping mall, at a concert, etc.
- Specific purpose—there for one purpose, e.g., accident, fight, fire, etc.
- Expressive—there for a religious, political or other cause.
- Aggressive—highly emotional, out to accomplish something.

Any of these types of crowds, especially if an emergency occurs, can turn into a mob—acting without reason, emotionally, sometimes hysterically. Mallory (1990, p. 85) suggests the following for dealing with unruly groups of people:

> - Have built-in plans, and exercise them periodically. The most important thing is to have a thought-out plan based on realistic capabilities.
> - Do not overcomplicate the paper plan. Fancy stuff may not work.
> - Use a phased response, and ask for more help before it is too late.
> - Conduct continual risk assessment during the incident, so decisions can be made promptly.
> - Always deal with equipment issues in advance. Do not wait until the equipment is needed, then start rounding it up.
> - Conduct annual training of your cadre.

The challenge of workplace violence is the topic of Chapter 20.

Bombs and Bomb Threats

McCarthy and Quigley (1992, p. 52) note: "Because security professionals in the United States rarely experience an actual explosion or confirm the existence of an improvised explosive device, they have been lulled to sleep when it comes to developing bomb threat and bombing response plans." The bombing of the World Trade Center should awaken such managers.

Jenkins (1991, p. 37) contends: "Nowadays bomb threats should be a major concern to management in both private businesses and the government. . . . Organizations that are highly visible as well as those involved in controversial enterprises must be especially cautious."

The bombing of the World Trade Center is a graphic example of the dangers posed by bombs. As described by Stedman (1994, p. 15): "In the blink of an eye, the blast shot through five underground floors in the garage beneath the twin towers, turning more than 200 cars, including 50 Secret Service vehicles, into toxically blazing torches."

The bombing of the World Trade Center shortly after noon on February 26, 1993, killed six people, injured 1,000 and caused $500 million in damage to the "Twin Towers" complex (Clark, 1994, p. 1). According to Stedman (1994, p. 14), the bombing also caused high-rise building owners and operators to rethink their security systems, but not to the degree one might expect:

> One study indicates that only 56% of the largest U.S. companies have improved or expanded their systems and procedures in response to the bombing. . . .
>
> Of the firms taking positive action, 43% are improving general security procedures; but only 38% are adding or improving systems and a mere 13% are increasing guard services.

Hamit (August 1994, p. 89) notes: "Office buildings are soft targets, and mushy."

The FBI moved quickly to find those responsible, but, according to Hamit (1994, p. 89): "[T]he truth is that they had tremendous luck, not only in the form of that mental giant who tried to get his deposit back on the truck rental, but also in the presence of a former Egyptian Army officer who decided that his duty to his new country was as great as it had been to his old one."

The February 1993 bombing of the World Trade Center in New York City alerted security managers to the dangers of explosives and fire, but, as noted by Draty (April 1994, p. 1): "What some people are not aware of is that explosions are almost a daily occurrence in the United States. Most of these explosions are caused by accidents because the proper safeguards were not employed."

More recently, the bombing of the Alfred Murrah Federal Building in Oklahoma City on April 19, 1995, again reminded all Americans of their vul-

The Alfred Murrah Federal Building in Oklahoma City following the bombing on April 19, 1995.

nerability. The bomb, apparently detonated by an anti-government militia group, killed 52 people and injured hundreds more, including children.

Seuter (1992, p. 48) notes that terrorists are not the only groups using bombs. Hard-core criminals may use explosives to gain access to buildings or to sterilize a crime scene. Explosives are often associated with drug deals. Interestingly, the most common motive for bombings is vandalism, followed by revenge.

Any business, industry or institution can be the victim of a bomb threat or an actual bombing. Despite the fact that 98 percent of telephoned bomb threats are hoaxes, such a threat is disruptive and disquieting. In addition, the response to the threat may be costly, emotionally charged and even dangerous. Bomb threats are a major security concern and are also a federal offense.

Several underground publications provide detailed instructions on making bombs. One common type of homemade bomb consists of a lead pipe filled with black powder, caps screwed on either end and a fuse. Another common type of bomb is made of sticks of dynamite taped together and set off by a timer or a trip wire. Incendiary bombs can consist of a container such as a glass bottle filled with a highly flammable substance, usually gasoline. The wick can be lit and the bomb thrown, or it can be attached to a timing device. Such bombs are frequently referred to as "Molotov cocktails."

Most bomb threats are telephoned and are hoaxes. The caller may simply want the day off if he or she is an employee, or the caller may want to disrupt the business. Few actual bombings are preceded by a warning. When such a warning is given, it is almost always to save lives. Most bombings occur at night for the same reason—to lessen the chance of killing someone.

Common victims of bombings and bomb threats are airlines, banks, hospitals, industrial complexes, utilities, educational institutions, government buildings and office buildings.

Preventing Bombings

Fay (1994, p. 12) suggests that to be prepared for a bombing incident, security managers should have a planning model with six sequential steps occurring in a cycle:

1. Assess the risk.
2. Decide policy.
3. Prepare a plan.
4. Prepare implementing procedure.
5. Test the plan and procedures.
6. Evaluate results.

This sixth step circles back to the first step. Fay (p. 12) concludes: "While it may not be possible to predict and plan specifically for all possible bomb threat scenarios, the security manager sets up general arrangements that, in the course of execution, can be adjusted to meet the needs of the situation."

> Access control, orderliness and regular inspections are the primary defenses against bombs.

Lock storerooms, equipment rooms and duplicating rooms. Provide adequate lighting. Control entrance into the facility. Conduct periodic inspections of lockers and have a procedure for checking packages and containers brought onto the premises.

Orderliness, keeping things in their proper places, will make it easier to detect unfamiliar objects that might be bombs. Employees should be instructed to be alert for any suspicious items they come across in their work area. Trash should be stored in metal containers outside the facility. Shipments of merchandise should be checked as soon as possible and then moved promptly to their appropriate locations. Fire doors should be kept shut at all times except for emergency use.

Responding to a Bomb Threat

A bomb threat is a frightening experience fraught with potential danger, and therefore a response plan must exist *before* such a call is received. Decisions made under the pressure of the moment should be based on previously established guidelines, so being prepared is vital.

> To be prepared for a bomb threat, teach personnel how to talk to a person making such a threat and whom to notify. Determine who makes the decision on whether to evacuate and, if an evacuation is necessary, how personnel are to be informed and what they are to do. Have a plan that specifies how to search for the bomb and what to do if one is found.

All personnel who answer the telephone should be taught to respond appropriately to a telephoned bomb threat. Some phones have tape recorders that can be activated to record the conversation. Others have phone traps that keep the line open until the *receiver* of the call hangs up, allowing the telephone company to trace the call. (Such traps do not work for long-distance calls.)

> The receiver of a bomb threat should:
>
> - Keep the caller talking as long as possible.
> - Try to learn as much as possible about the bomb, especially when it will go off and where it is located.
> - Try to determine the caller's sex, age, accent and speech pattern, and whether he or she is drunk or drugged.
> - Listen for any background noises.
> - Immediately notify the appropriate person(s) of the call.

Many organizations have a report form kept by the switchboard to record information on bomb threats (see Figure 7–1).

After the bomb threat is reported to the appropriate person, usually the chief administrator or manager, this individual decides who else is to be notified as well as whether the call is to be taken seriously. Evaluating the legit-

General Services Administration
Region 8
BOMB THREAT INFORMATION

Date: ____________

Time Call: Received ______ Ended ______

EXACT WORDS OF CALLER:

(Continue on reverse)

QUESTIONS TO ASK:

1. WHEN IS BOMB GOING TO EXPLODE?
2. WHERE IS BOMB RIGHT NOW?
3. WHAT KIND OF BOMB IS IT?
4. WHAT DOES IT LOOK LIKE?
5. WHY DID YOU PLACE BOMB?

DESCRIPTION OF CALLER'S VOICE:
☐ Male ☐ Female
☐ Young ☐ Middle-Aged ☐ Old

TONE OF VOICE

ACCENT

BACKGROUND NOISE

IS VOICE FAMILIAR?
☐ Yes. ☐ No.

IF "YES," WHO DID IT SOUND LIKE?

ADDITIONAL COMMENTS:

Name of Person Receiving Call

Organization & Location

Home Address

Office Phone

Home Phone

Figure 7–1. Sample Bomb Threat Form

SOURCE: Reprinted with permission of the publisher from Green and Farber, *Introduction to Security*, revised edition, Woburn, MA: Butterworth Publishers, 1978.

imacy of the bomb threat is important. Laughter in the background may indicate that it is a practical joke. Other indications are if the person receiving the call recognizes the voice or knows that the location where the caller claims the bomb is has been tightly secured and that no bomb could possibly have been planted there. Even if the decision is made that the call is a hoax, the police should be notified.

Because any bomb threat may be the real thing, many experts recommend that all such threats be treated as real. Assuming this, the decision must be made as to whether to evacuate. This decision is usually made by management, often in conjunction with the police. Although evacuation may seem the safest approach, this is not always true. Moving large groups of people may expose them to greater danger than not moving them. Evacuating may be exactly what the caller wanted and may prompt further calls. In addition, it is extremely costly.

Seuter (1992, p. 53) cautions: "Unnecessary evacuations are dangerous and expensive insurance policies. They provide no real protection from a bomb or the liability that may result from an improperly managed incident."

Nonetheless, sometimes the best alternative is to evacuate either the area where the bomb is suspected or the entire building. Total evacuation may cause panic and may expose more people to danger, especially if the bomber knows the evacuation plan. Sometimes it is thought that evacuation encourages or excites the caller. Planning carefully in advance should result in a safe, orderly evacuation.

Ideally, personnel are informed of a bomb threat over a central public address system rather than by an alarm. If an alarm is used, it should be different from that used for fire because the procedures to be followed are somewhat different. In a fire, windows and doors are closed; in a bomb threat situation, however, windows and doors are opened to vent any explosion.

In both fire and bomb threat evacuations, personnel should *walk* out of and away from the building until they are a block away and then wait until they are informed it is safe to return to the building.

The Bomb Search

Whether employees are evacuated or not, a search must be conducted if the threat is assumed to be real. A bomb search is an ultrahazardous task and is not to be undertaken lightly. It will be more effectively conducted by those familiar with the facility, so employees are often asked to search their own area before they evacuate.

Jenkins (1991, p. 41) suggests that if the caller does not say where the bomb is located, areas in the establishment should be checked in the following order:

1. The exterior of the facility.
2. Public access areas, such as lobbies, rest rooms, stairwells, and trash receptacles.
3. Physical plant spaces, such as custodial closets, lockers, and central heating and cooling areas.
4. Areas normally occupied by employees.
5. Record, storage, and mail rooms.

U.S. Capitol police officers inspect a van at a checkpoint near the U.S. Capitol grounds. Security was tight for the President's State of the Union address to Congress. Security officers assisted in the protective measures.

Areas that are usually unlocked and unwatched are the most common sites for bombs, for example, restrooms, lobbies, lunch rooms, elevators and stairs. Bombs can be hidden in lunch pails, briefcases, shopping bags, candy boxes and any number of other types of containers. The key is to look for anything out of place or foreign to the area, for example, a briefcase in the restroom.

A command post should be established as soon as the decision is made to treat the threat as real. The entire building should then be diagrammed and areas crossed off as they are searched. Some security managers have the searchers mark the doors of areas after they have been searched. If enough security guards are available, they should be positioned around the perimeter of the area in which a bomb may be planted to keep curious onlookers from endangering themselves.

A system of communicating among searchers must be established, but it must not involve the use of portable radios, as they may detonate the bomb. All searchers should be cautioned not to turn on lights, as this might also detonate the bomb. Searchers should move slowly and carefully, listening for any ticking sounds and watching for trip wires. Sometimes metal detectors or dogs are used to assist in the search.

> Do not touch or move any suspicious object found during a bomb search. Provide a clear zone of at least 300 feet around the device and call the nearest bomb disposal specialist or the police.

In addition, doors and windows should be opened to reduce shock waves, all fire extinguishers should be readied and highly flammable materials should be removed as should valuable documents, files and papers if time permits.

All procedures for dealing with bomb threats should be practiced, if possible. The operator may be called with a fake bomb threat to see the response. A suspicious container capable of concealing a bomb may be planted and a practice bomb search conducted. The evacuation plan may be practiced as well.

Explosives Received through the Mail

Some establishments are especially susceptible to explosives through the mail, including those that engage in animal testing, nuclear waste, abortion and the like. Sherwood (1994, p. 18) suggests the following tip-offs that an envelope or parcel might contain an explosive:

- An addressee's name misspelled or an incorrect title.
- Special instructions such as "personal" or "private" or other notations such as "rush" or "fragile" when such endorsements might be considered unusual.
- No return address or one that doesn't coincide with the postmark.
- A poorly handwritten address or one distorted by homemade labels or letters.
- Protruding wires, aluminum foil, oil stains or a peculiar odor.
- Excessive postage.
- Envelopes with rigid, lopsided appearance or poorly wrapped, irregular shaped packages with soft spots or bulges.
- Ticking, buzzing or sloshing sounds.
- Noticeable pressure or resistance when contents are being removed.

If the envelope or package is suspicious, security should contact the local law enforcement agency for assistance. Sherwood (p. 18) cautions that the envelope or package should not be submerged in water or put into an enclosed area.

The Institute of Makers of Explosives (IME) can assist in matters involving commercial explosives. This agency consists of 31 member companies and their subsidiaries which produce more than 85 percent of the commercial explosives used in the United States.

Preventing and Protecting Against Loss by Fire

Fire is probably the single greatest threat security must deal with. Studies show that three out of every five businesses struck by serious fires never open again. Security personnel should be continuously alert to the potential for fire. The ideal time to stop a fire is before it ever starts. Eliminating fire hazards is a prime responsibility of all security personnel and, indeed, of all personnel within a business, company or organization. Security managers can better prevent and protect against fire loss by understanding how fires occur, what frequently causes them and what equipment and procedures can help minimize losses.

Shaw (1992, p. 53) stresses: "Security personnel need to know how to use a fire extinguisher; they need to make certain all fire exits are unlocked; and they need to report fire hazards and get them corrected through cooperation with and education of company personnel."

Moore (1994, pp. 47–48) suggests that security managers consider their goals when designing fire protection. The fire protection plan will vary depending on whether the primary goal is to protect personal safety, property or the establishment's mission. He notes: "The fire protection goal most overlooked is mission protection, which asks the question: 'Will I still be in business after a major fire in my facility?' "

Knowing how fires burn helps one to understand potential fire hazards and how to control them.

> The **fire triangle** consists of three elements necessary for burning: *heat, fuel* and *oxygen.*

When a flammable substance is heated to a specific temperature, called its **ignition temperature,** it will ignite and burn as long as oxygen is present. Because oxygen and fuel are always present in business and industry, the potential for fire always exists. If any of the three elements is eliminated, the fire is extinguished. Remove oxygen by smothering, fuel by isolating and heat by cooling.

> The National Fire Protection Association has established four classifications of fires:
>
> - Class A fires involve ordinary combustible materials such as paper, packing boxes, wood and cloth.
> - Class B fires involve flammable liquids such as gasoline and oil.
> - Class C fires involve energized electrical installations, appliances and wiring.
> - Class D fires involve combustible metals such as magnesium, sodium and potassium. (Class D fires are sometimes called "exotic metals fires.")

Destruction and death are caused not only by flames, but by smoke, heat, gas and panic. Smoke can blind and choke. Carbon dioxide and carbon monoxide, by-products of burning, can poison and can cause buildings to explode. Intense heat can explode gases, ignite materials and expand air. Expanded air can exert tremendous pressure, shattering doors and windows. Because smoke, gas, heat and expanded air all rise, it is possible to determine safe and unsafe areas and to control the direction of a fire if building construction and preplanning are adequate.

Causes of Fires

The major sources of ignition in industrial fires are electrical circuits, overheating, sparking, friction, chemical reaction, flames and heat transfer.

Often fires result from carelessness or poor housekeeping practices, such as improperly storing or using flammable liquids; replacing electric fuses with ones having too high amperage or with coins, wires or nails; overloading electric circuits; carelessly discarding cigarette butts and/or matches; and allowing oily rags, rubbish or other materials to accumulate, resulting in spontaneous combustion. Fires have also been caused by faulty wiring and connections, ignition sparks from static electricity, lightning and arson.

An effective fire safety program has two parts: (1) preventing fires and (2) protecting against losses caused by fires that do occur.

Preventing Fire

Most fires can be prevented. The greatest single precipitant is carelessness. Factory Mutual estimated that 75 percent of the industrial fires were caused by human error and carelessness, and especially by deficiencies in housekeeping practices.

Although many modern buildings are built to be fire-resistive, a fireproof building does not exist. Despite the fact that an exterior of steel and concrete does not burn, the interior contains numerous flammable substances that can burn, causing the building to become like a furnace. Given sufficient heat, the structure can collapse.

> Fires can be prevented by reducing fire-loading, properly storing and handling flammable materials, enforcing no-smoking regulations, using proper wiring and following good housekeeping practices. Access controls can lessen the chance of arson.

Fire-loading refers to the amount of flammable material within an area, including flammable rugs, curtains, paper and liquids such as paints and solvents. To the extent possible, reduce fire-loading by using flame-resistant curtains and furniture.

When highly combustible chemicals, glues and the like are used, make sure ventilation is adequate. The main supply of such materials should be kept in protective containers stored in properly ventilated areas. Packing boxes containing excelsior and paper materials should be metal and should preferably be equipped with a lead link that causes the lid to drop into place if heat is generated in the metal box, reducing the oxygen supply and smothering a potential fire. Fire-preventive waste receptacles designed to smother a fire are also available. Never allow oily rags and other flammable materials to accumulate.

Good housekeeping is critical; keep areas free of trash and rubbish. Enforce no-smoking regulations. Check wiring periodically. Make employees aware of potential fire hazards and how to guard against them.

Among the most common fire hazards are violations of electrical codes including:

- Defective wiring.
- Use of long or wrong-size extension cords.
- Overloading outlets.
- Combustibles within three feet of an electrical access box.
- Coffee pots, hot plates and space heaters left on.
- Machinery left running.
- Typewriters and calculators left running.
- Soldering irons left on.

Materials that are a fire hazard include acids, oil, paint, solvents, explosives, flammable or combustible liquids, flammable gases and materials subject to spontaneous ignition.

Protecting against Losses from Fire

The best way to protect against loss from fire is to prevent fire from ever occurring. In spite of all efforts, however, the potential for a fire is always present. The best protection against loss from fire is to *be prepared*.

> Protection from fire losses is provided by detectors and alarms; properly marked and sufficient exits, fire doors and fire escapes; fire-resistive safes and vaults; and fire extinguishers, sprinkler systems and an adequate, accessible water supply.

Fire Detectors and Alarms. Fire detectors and alarms can provide advance notice of a fire, thereby allowing human life and assets to be protected as well as increasing the possibility of bringing the fire under control before it causes extensive damage.

Fire usually progresses through four stages:

- *Incipient stage*—Invisible products of combustion are given off. No smoke or flames are visible and there is no appreciable heat.
- *Smoldering stage*—Combustion products become visible as smoke, but there is no flame or appreciable heat.
- *Flame stage*—An actual fire exists. Flame and smoke are visible, but there is still no appreciable heat. Heat follows, however, almost instantly.
- *Heat stage*—Heat is uncontrollable and air expands rapidly.

Each stage of fire can be detected by specific types of detectors.

- Ionization detectors respond to invisible particles of combustion.
- Photoelectric detectors respond to smoke.
- Infrared detectors respond to flame.
- Thermal detectors respond to heat, usually temperatures in excess of 135°F.

Ionization detectors are most effective because they give the earliest warning, but they are too sensitive for most areas. Therefore, they are usually used only in such areas as computer rooms. **Photoelectric detectors,** also called smoke or early warning detectors, are commonly found in homes and in many office buildings. **Infrared detectors** have the disadvantage of responding to sun reflecting off glass or mirrors. **Thermal detectors** give the least amount of advance warning, but they are needed in areas such as boiler rooms, garages and manufacturing areas where smoke and flame are commonly present.

Smoke detectors are of two types: spot and line. According to Shalna (1994, p. 8):

> With "spot" detection, a detector is placed so that it protects an area or "spot," not unlike the area illuminated by a spotlight. A "line" detector protects an elongated path or line.

Once the detector is activated, an alarm is sounded, locally and/or at a central station. An alarm sounded in a very noisy area should also give a visible warning, for example, a flashing red light.

A typical fire alarm pull box.

Other types of alarms are activated by a person seeing a fire and manually activating a pull box that alerts the fire department. Such pull boxes carry labels reading "In Case of Fire, Pull" or "Break Glass."

One major advance in fire alarm systems is a combination of fire alarm and access control, as described by Hopkins (1993, p. 40): "The advent of the microprocessor-based fire alarm and access control system has brought the security industry a new combination: fire detection and access control in one control panel. This winning combination allows installation companies to provide a cost-effective fire alarm system with the added security of access control."

The National Fire Protection Association (NFPA), in May of 1993, consolidated all national fire alarm standards into one document, the National Fire Alarm Code, marking the "culmination of hundreds of man hours of effort" (Moore, May 1994, p. 53). This new NFPA 72 Code should be on the shelf of every security manager. (Copies can be obtained from the National Fire Protection Association, One Batterymarch Park, Quincy, MA 02269-9101; phone, 800-344-3555.)

Elevators and Exits. *Elevators* should be clearly labeled "In case of fire, do *not* use." An arrow should indicate where the nearest stairs are. Some establishments have their elevators controlled so that if a fire occurs the elevators return to the lobby level and are locked.

Fire escapes should be checked to be certain that they are safe and, if operated by a counterbalance, that they are in good working condition.

Exits should be unobstructed and clearly marked. Fire exit doors can be painted red, but often aesthetic considerations prevent this. Exit signs should be lighted and have emergency standby power. Routes to the exits should be well lit and free of obstructions. Building codes establish the minimum number of exits for a specific establishment and also require that provision be made for handicapped individuals. If access control dictates that some exterior doors be locked from the outside, they should be equipped with a crash bar so they can be opened in case of a fire.

Fire doors provide added protection and help contain a fire. They not only impede the spread of flame and smoke, but can also protect people trapped inside a burning building. Automatic fire doors are available that are held open by a pulley system. When there is combustion, the heat melts a fusible metal link that allows the counterbalanced door to automatically close.

Although fire doors are an essential component of many fire safety plans, such doors may work at cross purposes with building security. The NFPA code mandates that only one action be required to unlock a door with exit or fire exit hardware (Dean, 1993, p. 50). In addition, as noted by Olmstead (1994, p. 16):

> The National Fire Protection Association's NFPA 101 Life Safety Code and other national and local codes govern door construction, hardware components and integrity of the entire opening. Failure to consider the implications of these codes and concerns can lead to problems ranging from a fire inspector's demands for costly replacement of a nonconforming door

and hardware to disastrous property damage or even to loss of life. On the other hand, close adherence to code mandates and use of the options they provide will ensure that both security and life safety needs are met effectively.

Safes and Vaults. *Fire-resistive safes and vaults* can protect cash and records from being destroyed in a fire, as discussed in Chapter 5. Most such safes provide protection for paper that ignites at 350°F, but they do not usually provide adequate protection for computer tapes, which ignite at 150°.

Extinguishers, Water and Sprinkler Systems. *Fire extinguishers* should be located throughout the facility, be in good working order and be of the type appropriate for the kind of fire that might occur in the area.

It is important to know what type of fire is occurring (A, B, C or D) to select the appropriate extinguisher.

Portable fire extinguishers are pressurized cylinders containing materials to cool and/or smother a fire. Among the most common ingredients are the following:

- *Soda acid* uses water, bicarbonate of soda and acid. This type of extinguisher is operated by being turned upside down. Used on Class A fires.
- *Foam* smothers fire. Used on Class A and B fires.
- *Dry chemical* is usually clearly labeled to indicate what type of fire it will safety extinguish, usually Class B and C fires.
- *Carbon dioxide* cools and smothers. Used on Class B and C fires.

As noted by Purpura (1991, p. 259), fire extinguishers have special color-coded symbols to indicate the class of fire on which they can be used:

Class A	Green triangle (ordinary combustibles, e.g., wood, paper)
Class B	Red square (flammable liquids, e.g., gasoline, kerosene)
Class C	Blue circle (electrical)
Class D	Green star (metals, e.g., magnesium, titanium)

Multipurpose extinguishers have the label of each class of fires on which they may be used.

In addition, water, transported by hose or bucket, is effective on a Class A fire.

Water or a Class A extinguisher should never be used on energized electric equipment (Class C fires), because the electric charge can follow the water stream to the holder, causing instant electrocution. Water or a Class A extinguisher should not be used in a Class B fire, because it can splatter the burning oil or gasoline, spreading the fire to a larger area instead of extinguishing it.

The most common type of extinguisher is multi-purpose. Note the shapes around the letters showing the types of fires this extinguisher can handle.

ABC extinguishers are effective against all except Class D fires. Ideally, several ABC extinguishers should be placed in strategic locations and checked periodically. Employees should be instructed on their use. Unfortunately, many establishments rely almost exclusively on water and hoses or on type A fire extinguishers because they are cheaper and because Class A fires are the most common.

If fire extinguishers are used to fight a fire, they should be laid on the floor, *not* hung back up. They can then be collected and recharged.

Sprinkler systems also provide protection against loss from fire. Sprinkler systems use underground and overhead pipes that are activated by heat of a specific temperature, usually from 130 to 165°F. The heads of the sprinklers are plugged with a fusible metal that melts at a specific temperature, allowing water to flow and also activating an alarm. Many unheated establishments in southern states use a dry sprinkler system in which air holds the water pressure back until after the sprinkler head link is melted. A dry system prevents the water pipes from freezing, but it also causes a brief delay in getting the water to the fire.

Although water damage from sprinkler systems may result, the damage is usually considerably less than the damage a fire would cause. Frequently insurance companies give reduced fire insurance rates for establishments that have installed a sprinkler system. As with fire extinguishers and hoses, sprinkler systems should be periodically checked. The water supply must be adequate, and the pipes must be free of corrosion. In addition, nothing should be stacked closer than 18 inches to the sprinkler heads or the system will be ineffective.

Computer Rooms. Computer rooms present special fire hazards and require special fire precautions. They often are equipped with an ionization detector and/or a thermal rate of rise detector. They should *not* be equipped with a sprinkler system because steam and water can damage the computer tapes and because water should *not* be used on Class C fires, the type most commonly occurring in computer rooms. Carbon dioxide fire extinguishers can be used without damaging the hardware or the tapes, but the fumes may be hazardous to humans. Therefore, halon is often preferred. Carbon dioxide and halon should *not* be used together: a lethal condition results.

Seek professional advice from the fire department and/or the fire insurance company for special problems regarding fire prevention and protection.

The Montreal Protocol enacted in 1989, and signed by 52 countries including the United States, calls for production restrictions and a gradual phasing out of halon because it is believed to destroy ozone in the atmosphere. Certain establishments, however, are exempt from the prohibition against use of halon (Azano, 1993, p. 34):

> Companies with essential-use applications and many military applications are exempt from removing the agent from their fire prevention program. . . .
>
> Some examples of essential-use applications include protection of military aircraft; data processing equipment that is essential to a life safety function, such as an air traffic controller terminal; control rooms in nuclear facilities and some oil pipe lanes; switchgear rooms in which a period of downtime could have catastrophic results; telephone switchgear rooms and telecommunications centers that are vital to national defense; hospital control rooms and areas used for critical medical research; and some predetermined Department of Defense contract work areas.

Azano (p. 34) suggests that security managers contact their fire protection vendor to find out what is required for using halon properly and what alternatives exist.

Procedures for Protecting against Fire Loss

In addition to obtaining and maintaining equipment to help prevent fires, an effective fire safety program establishes specific procedures for protecting life and assets should a fire occur.

> Always call for help before attempting to extinguish a fire. Teach employees what to do in case of fire. Other procedures for protecting against fire loss include having and practicing a plan for evacuation, shutting doors and windows and using stairs rather than elevators.

Employees should know where the exits are and which they are to use, what kinds of fire extinguishers are available and how to use them, how to recognize fire hazards and report them and what to do if they cannot evacuate the premises.

Security personnel must recognize the different types of fires so they can select the correct method of putting it out if no extinguisher is available. Eliminating any one of the three components of the fire triangle should put a fire out. Table 7–1 summarizes how to extinguish common fires.

Doors and windows should be closed to reduce the oxygen supply and to confine the blaze. If the premises have central air-conditioning, this should be turned off because it will circulate the smoke throughout the building.

The *evacuation plan* should include how the employees will be alerted. Sometimes this is not by an alarm, but over the public address system. In some institutions a code word is used to indicate fire. For example, many hospitals have established a specific code to indicate that a fire is occurring and where. The use of the code reduces the probability of patients panicking. All employees should know the location of the nearest exit and how to get there *without* using the elevator. They should be instructed to close windows and doors, never to open a door without first touching it (opening a hot door can

Table 7–1. How to Extinguish Specific Types of Fires

Class	What Is Burning	How to Extinguish
A	Ordinary combustables, e.g., wood, paper	Quench or cool with water or water fog. Use soda acid, pump tank (water) or foam. (Smothering is ineffective.)
B	Flammable liquids, e.g., gasoline, kerosene	Blanket or smother. Use carbon dioxide (CO^2), dry chemicals or foam.
C	Electrical	Use dry chemicals, carbon dioxide (CO^2) or vaporizing liquid extinguishers.
D	Metals, e.g., magnesium, titanium	Use Class D extinguisher.

be deadly) and to *walk* out of the building and continue walking until at least a block away.

If evacuation is impossible, employees should know the following steps: (1) get as far away from the fire as possible, closing doors behind you; (2) if time permits, remove flammable objects from the room in which you seek shelter; (3) barricade the door; (4) open the window or, if necessary, break it to allow smoke and heat to escape and fresh air to enter; (5) hang something in the window to signal fire fighters and (6) stay low by the window.

When practical, fire drills should be conducted. Although such drills may be costly in time lost from the job, the practice may save lives should a fire occur. Fire drills in skyscrapers can be conducted weekly, one floor per week, to keep people abreast of how to evacuate and yet avoid disrupting the whole building.

Some establishments have established a fire brigade, but this should be a voluntary assignment. The security manager is usually in charge of such a brigade. The members of the brigade can be given specific responsibilities to assist security personnel.

The Security Manager's Responsibility in Case of Fire

All security personnel should know the location of fire extinguishers, fire-alarm boxes, sprinkler valve controls, escalator and elevator shutoffs, light control panels, emergency lights, wheelchairs, stretchers and first-aid equipment.

> Have a plan, take charge and stay calm. Take immediate action to protect lives first, assets second.

Panic can add to the danger and result in needless death. Security personnel might also assume any or all of the following responsibilities:

- Sound the alarm; alert the fire department.
- Attempt to control the blaze if it is not out of hand.
- Turn off the central air-conditioning and machinery, but leave lights on.
- Close all doors and windows.
- Ground all elevators.
- Provide traffic control.
- Direct fire fighters to the location of the fire.
- Time permitting, remove highly combustible stock and valuables.
- Cover expensive merchandise or equipment, such as computers, with a tarpaulin to prevent water damage.
- Move company cars, trucks and/or boxcars to a safe distance.
- Administer first aid.

Above all else, protect lives, including one's own.

Although some security managers dread fire inspections, in actuality they should be thoroughly prepared for and welcomed. DuBose (1993, p. 35) suggests:

A security manager should maintain a good relationship with the fire inspector and correct all violations to his or her satisfaction. Performing a periodic self-inspection of the fire safety program helps ensure fire code compliance and limits the risk of life and property losses from fire. The ultimate objective of any security manager is to protect lives and property. By being prepared to pass a fire inspection, that goal is achieved.

Among the areas to be checked are the following (DuBose, p. 35):

- General storage.
- Electrical equipment.
- Extinguishing system—test annually.
- Smoking—no-smoking areas enforced.
- Housekeeping practices.
- Extinguishing equipment.
- Life safety considerations—including periodic fire drills.
- Fire alarm system.
- Flammable material—safely stored.

Without an adequate fire protection plan, a fire can be more devastating than it need be. Platt (1992, pp. 51–52) describes the destruction caused by a fire in his office:

> Destruction is total. The fire burned or cooked every office and all of the furnishing, equipment, and business materials. Files, letters, company reference materials, personal effects, and any paper products left in the open are either burned or damaged beyond repair. Three computers and our telephones look like gummy models for a warped Salvador Dali painting. Office property damage is estimated at $150,000, plus $35,000 in losses in furnishing and office and personal effects.

Following this disaster, Platt examined what they had done wrong and discovered that "foremost in our embarrassing list of poor marks was our inattention to simple fire protection procedures." They had not periodically checked their smoke detector, which had failed to work. They had no safety lines or rope ladders. They had not invested in an effective surge protector for the computer—the cause of the fire. They had not secured vital or hard-to-replace records and documents. And they did not have adequate insurance. Hard lessons learned. Fortunately, no one was injured in this fire.

NATURAL DISASTERS

Papi (1994, p. 6) outlines a simple four-step approach to disaster planning:

- Step One: Risk assessment.
- Step Two: Prioritize risks.
- Step Three: Prepare for various scenarios.
- Step Four: Prepare a recovery plan.

This fourth step is becoming more critical, as noted by Coleman (1993, p. 61): "As PCs, workstations, and local area networks (LANs) have become more prevalent, industry has also begun to realize that data center recovery plans alone are not enough. A comprehensive, corporate-wide approach, known as *business recovery planning,* is required." As a first step security managers should identify natural disasters that might occur in their geographic location.

> Natural disasters necessitating a contingency plan might include floods, tornadoes, hurricanes and/or earthquakes.

As noted by Hamit (May 1994, p. 56): "Disaster planning is something that must be practiced and thought out if it is to work at zero hour." In looking at the L.A. earthquake, Hamit notes: "The Internet, designed to withstand a nuclear war, didn't even blink. E-Mail allowed people to find out about their loved ones when the phone companies blocked off the 818 area code." He suggests that this is a tremendous utility for emergency use.

Monday, August 24, 1992, Hurricane Andrew swept through South Florida leaving a 30-mile path of destruction. According to Harowitz (1992, p. 76): "Hurricane Andrew blew away trees, power lines, and many contingency plans":

> Security problems were exacerbated by the near total destruction of the area's infrastructure. Regular phone lines were down, and two-way communications were off because repeaters were blown down and cellular phones were gridlocked because of ongoing use.
>
> Getting around was also difficult. Road signs and other landmarks were gone, street lights were out, and roadways were blocked by fallen trees, live cable wire, and other debris.

Northridge earthquake January 17, 1994. Collapsed freeway—Highway 10.

A rescue worker and a dog, who is searching for bodies, look through the remains of what is left of a three-story building in the Marina District of San Francisco October 18, 1989 after an earthquake caused severe damage on October 17.

A plan to protect lives and assets in the event of a natural disaster should be developed, written out, distributed and practiced periodically. A good plan is logical, uncomplicated, yet comprehensive. It stipulates who does what and when, who is to be notified and what assistance is available. It should also include where a radio is available to be tuned to emergency frequencies.

As many elements as possible should be the same in plans for responding to different natural disasters. For example, procedures for evacuating in the event of a fire might be the same used in evacuating during a flood. In both instances elevators should *never* be used. This was tragically illustrated in the 1977 flood in Rochester, Minnesota, when three nursing home residents in wheelchairs were put into an elevator to be sent to higher floors. Unfortunately, the elevator shorted out, carrying them down into the water-filled lower level. All three drowned.

In some situations, however, evacuation is not the proper procedure, as in a tornado or hurricane alert. In such cases the alarm should be different from that used for fires. Employees should be directed to a clearly marked shelter within the facility, usually on the lowest level, in the center of the building, away from glass. The Civil Defense Department* can help security managers to determine the most appropriate locations and to develop effective plans for such disasters.

Two monitoring systems can assist security personnel by alerting them to impending hazardous weather conditions:

- A weather alert radio tuned exclusively to the weather bureau's frequency, left on continuously and activated by the weather bureau when conditions warrant.
- An AM radio for weather information.

According to Civil Defense authorities, the safest areas in the workplace during some natural disasters such as tornadoes are under office desks, under heavy tables or in specific shelter areas.

The difference between a *watch* and *warning* is important. A *watch* means that the weather conditions are right for a specific event to occur, for example, a tornado, blizzard or severe thunderstorm. A *warning* means such a condition has developed and will probably pose a problem for the area. Precautions should be implemented immediately, including a "take-cover" announcement such as the following if the emergency is a tornado or destructive winds warning:

> Attention. A tornado warning has been given for our area. Turn off all equipment, extinguish all flames, and take cover immediately under your desk, a heavy table or in our designated shelter areas. Do NOT go near windows, glass doors or outside. Stay under cover until the all clear is given.

Repeat this message at least three times.

First-aid equipment should be readily available, and emergency telephone numbers for ambulances, fire departments, police and other available assistance should be posted.

OTHER EMERGENCIES

Plans are needed for all other potential emergencies, such as power failures, water main or gas line breaks and toxic chemical leaks or explosions. The best emergency plans are simple. They specify *in writing* who does what, how and when. The more common elements there are among the plans for different types of emergencies, the better.

SUMMARY

Security managers are often responsible for accident prevention programs as one means to prevent losses and protect assets. OSHA, the Occupational Safety and Health Administration, was established to administer the Occupational

---

* Called Emergency Services and Disaster Agency in many areas.

Safety and Health Act, which seeks to ensure safe and healthful working conditions for every employee in the nation. OSHA requires employers covered by the act to keep a log of all occupational injuries, accidents and illnesses, as well as an annual summary of the log's information.

Ninety-five percent of all accidents are caused by human error, especially lack of safety consciousness. Accidents can be prevented by removing hazards, using protective equipment, making employees aware of hazards that cannot be removed and following good housekeeping practices.

In the event of civil disturbances, riots or strikes, the security manager is responsible for maintaining order and protecting lives and assets.

Bombs and bomb threats are a serious security concern. Access control, orderliness and regular inspections are the primary defenses against bombs. To be prepared for a bomb threat, teach personnel how to talk to a person making such a threat and whom to notify. Determine who makes the decision on whether to evacuate, and, if evacuation is necessary, how personnel are to be informed and what they are to do. Have a plan that specifies how to search for the bomb and what to do if one is found.

The receiver of a bomb threat should keep the caller talking as long as possible. Try to learn about the bomb, especially when it will go off and where it is located. Try to determine the caller's sex, age, accent and speech pattern, and whether he or she is possibly drunk or drugged. Listen for any background noises, and immediately notify the appropriate person(s) of the call.

Do not touch or move any suspicious object found during a bomb search. Provide a clear zone of 300 feet around the device and call the nearest bomb disposal specialist or the police.

Fire is a major threat to life and property. The fire triangle consists of three elements necessary for burning: heat, fuel and oxygen. The National Fire Protection Association has established four classifications of fires: Class A fires, which involve ordinary combustible materials such as paper, packing boxes, wood and cloth; Class B fires, which involve flammable liquids such as gasoline and oil; Class C fires, which involve energized electrical installations, appliances and wiring; and Class D fires, which involve combustible metals such as magnesium, sodium and potassium.

Fires can be prevented by reducing fire-loading, properly storing and handling flammable materials, enforcing no-smoking regulations, using proper wiring and following good housekeeping practices. Protection from fire losses is provided by detectors and alarms; properly marked and sufficient exits, fire doors and fire escapes; fire-resistive safes and vaults; and fire extinguishers, sprinkler systems and an adequate, accessible water supply.

Fires can be detected by ionization detectors that respond to invisible particles of combustion, photoelectric detectors that respond to smoke, infrared detectors that respond to flame and thermal detectors that respond to heat.

Water or a Class A extinguisher should never be used on energized electric equipment (Class C fires), because the electric charge can follow the water stream to the holder, causing instant electrocution. Water or a Class A extinguisher should not be used on a Class B fire, because it can splatter the burning oil or gasoline, spreading the fire to a larger area instead of extinguishing it.

Always call for help before attempting to extinguish a fire. Teach employees what to do in case of fire. Other procedures for protecting against fire loss include having and practicing a plan for evacuation and shutting doors and windows and using stairs rather than elevators during a fire. In case of fire, have a plan, take charge and stay calm. Take immediate action to protect lives first, assets second.

Natural disasters necessitating a contingency plan might include floods, tornadoes, hurricanes and/or earthquakes.

Application

Read the following emergency procedures established for a college faculty and evaluate their effectiveness.

EMERGENCY PROCEDURES FOR STAFF MEMBERS (separate procedures have been developed for administrators, switchboard operator and buildings and grounds workers)*

FIRE ALARM

1. All alarms should be treated as a real fire.
2. If a fire is spotted, the individual should find the nearest pull station and turn in the alarm.
3. Next, notify the switchboard operator as to the location of the fire.
4. Instructors should direct their students to leave quickly through the nearest safe exit in a safe and orderly manner, to a position at least 250 feet away from the buildings.
5. Instructors should be the last persons to leave their classrooms or other assigned space and should see that the lights are off, the lab gas is shut off and hazardous chemicals secured where possible. All doors should be shut.
6. No one should enter their car to leave the campus. This will affect the ability of fire fighting equipment to reach the scene of the fire.

POWER FAILURE

1. The switchboard operator should be notified so that Northern States Power can be contacted.
2. Call Northern States Power [phone #] when switchboard is closed.
3. All students and staff should remain in offices and classrooms unless told otherwise.
4. The maintenance staff will check each building to see if anyone needs assistance. They will also check the elevators.

TORNADO ALERT

1. The switchboard operator will immediately call the administrator on duty and tune to WCCO when the Civil Defense alarm sounds.
2. If the decision is made to take cover, the administrator in charge will make the appropriate announcement over the PA system. **Tornado announcement:** We are having a tornado emergency. Please go to the Commons lower level, LRC tunnel or the Activities tunnel. Please stay inside and away from all windows. Wait for the all clear to be given.

---

* *Staff Handbook of Policies and Procedures,* Normandale Community College, Bloomington, Minnesota. Reprinted by permission.

3. Once the alarm is sounded, all staff and students should take cover. No one should be in the following areas: gym, theatre, auditorium, LRC reading room and all areas with outside windows.

WATER MAIN BREAK

Day—switchboard open

1. Call switchboard—explain location and nature of break.
2. Move anything which could be damaged by water flow.

Night—switchboard closed

1. Call police emergency (911) and explain location and nature of break.
2. Meet emergency crew and direct them to area of break.
3. Notify [the administrator on duty].

GAS LINE BREAK

Day—switchboard open

1. Clear immediate area.
2. Call switchboard operator with location and extent of break.
3. If necessary, evacuate the area by pulling the fire alarm.

Night—switchboard closed

1. Call the fire department at [phone #]. Give location and extent of break.
2. Clear immediate area.
3. Notify [the administrator on duty].

MEDICAL EMERGENCY

1. The switchboard operator should be notified and given as much information as possible. The exact location of the individual needing assistance should be given and an individual sent to the closest main entrance to meet the emergency vehicles.
2. The switchboard operator will then notify the police.
3. When switchboard is closed, call the police at 911 and give them as much information as possible. One individual should stay with the person in need and another should meet the emergency vehicles at the nearest door.

STUDENT DISTURBANCES

1. The individual witnessing a major disturbance or disorder should notify the Dean of Students or the administrator on duty and give him/her all the important details. It will then be up to the administrator to decide what action is to be taken.
2. At times when an administrator is not present, a staff member should use his/her best judgment. Police can be reached at [phone #]. The incident should be reported to the Dean of Students on the next class day.

BOMB THREATS

1. Keep caller on the telephone as long as possible.
2. Try to get as much information as possible regarding the bomb. That is, the bomb's location, type of device, time of detonation and anything else that might be pertinent to the safety of the college and individuals inside.
3. Try to remember everything about the call, voice, accent, background noises. These items or anything else you might think of might help identify the caller.
4. Report the incident to the president or the administrator on duty.
5. The president or administrator on duty will make the final decision on what action is to be taken.
6. If the switchboard is closed, call the police at 911 and evacuate the buildings. If necessary, pull the fire alarm.

CRITICAL THINKING EXERCISE

Public Events

Statutory and Common Law

The owner or occupant of premises owes a duty to exercise ordinary care to keep and maintain the premises in a reasonably safe condition, and this duty requires the owner or occupant to exercise ordinary care to protect invited persons from injury inflicted by other persons present on the premises. If an owner or occupant fails to perform this duty and his negligence is the proximate cause of injuries inflicted upon an invited person by another person, the owner or occupant is liable to the invited person.

Facts of the Case

On the evening of May 29, Roy Masters attended a wrestling exhibition at the Raleigh County Armory. More than 4,000 people attended this event. The armory had been leased by Jim Crockett Promotions, Inc., for the exhibition, and Freedom Security and Detective Agency, Inc., was contracted to provide security for the evening. Fifteen security guards (up from the armory's request for 12) were on duty at the wrestling match. Stockholders of Freedom Security reported that it had traditionally been the case that the promoter used security personnel to "fill positions that the promoter wanted done." As a result, four security personnel were actually guarding the arena while 11 guards were selling and collecting tickets or guarding the fire doors to ensure that no one could enter without paying.

The final event of the wrestling exhibition featured a tag team match between "The Rock 'n' Roll Express" and "The Midnight Express." Stan Lane, known as "Sweet Stan," and Bobby Eaton, known as "Beautiful Bobby," were the two wrestlers on the "Midnight Express" tag team. They were managed by Jim Cornette.

The "Rock 'n' Roll Express" was declared the winner of the final match, and they were escorted from the ring to their dressing room by security personnel. "Sweet Stan" and "Beautiful Bobby" remained in the ring with their manager awaiting the return of the security personnel so that they could be escorted to their dressing room. During this waiting time, they were inciting the passions of the crowd and calling for a rematch in order to seek revenge (possibly part of their performance was to provoke the crowd). At this time the crowd began throwing such things as balled-up paper cups, coins and other objects into the ring.

While the spectators were demonstrating, one of them threw an aisle marker into the ring striking "Beautiful Bobby" on the neck and shoulder. "Sweet Stan," believing that he saw Roy Masters throw the aisle marker, jumped over the ropes and left the ring in pursuit of him. "Sweet Stan," who is 6′ tall and weighs approximately 255 pounds, struck Masters on the side of his face, fracturing the orbit of his left eye and other facial bones. Masters, who is a disabled coal miner in his mid-sixties, weighs about 145 pounds and is 5′6″ tall. He had to undergo surgery and was hospitalized for eight days.

Issues and Questions

1. Are the organizers, security providers or wrestlers liable for damages to Masters?
   a. Because "Sweet Stan" was not acting within the scope of his employment with Crockett Promotions, and because his assault on Masters was not foreseeable by either Crockett Promotions or Freedom Security, they cannot be held liable for damages to Masters. "Sweet Stan" acted impulsively; his act is the proximate cause of injury; and thus he alone can be held liable for damages.
   b. A total of 15 security guards may not be sufficient for the exercise of ordinary care and prevention of foreseeable problems that could reasonably be anticipated with a crowd of more than 4,000 spectators who are incited to become irate. The deployment of security personnel at fire doors to ensure that no one entered who had not paid and their use to sell and collect tickets are not appropriate. Therefore, the promoter is liable for all damages to Masters.
   c. Subcontractors (in this case Freedom Security) are responsible for the stipulations outlined in the contracts they sign. When a security agency contracts to provide security, it has a burden of duty to keep and maintain the premises in a reasonably safe condition. This duty requires them to exercise care to protect an invited person from injury inflicted by other persons present on the premises. Because Freedom Security failed to provide any security personnel in the arena area at the time of Masters' injury, they are liable for all damages.
   d. In no stretch of the imagination can "invited person" be interpreted to mean that a member of the audience is allowed to throw objects at entertainers during public events, even though these entertainers are supposedly provoking the crowd. Masters unfortunately suffered the consequence of his indiscretion, and his own health insurance must pay for his injuries. An older, frail person ought never become violent with a young athlete who may not know his own strength. "Sweet Stan" was simply sticking up for his teammate and teaching the crowd a lesson.
   e. Because it is reasonably foreseeable that there could be an altercation as a result of wrestlers and their manager provoking the crowd, and because insufficient security personnel were in the arena to control the crowd, both the promoter and the security agency are liable for damages to Masters. Additionally, "The Midnight Express" can also be held liable.

Discussion Questions

1. What alternatives are available to security managers in handling personnel conflicts? Are they the responsibility of the security manager?

2. What natural disasters are likely to occur in your geographic area, and how should a security manager prepare for an adequate response to them?
3. What resources would you contact to counter a series of bomb threats against your facility?
4. When a strike is certain to occur, what contingency plans should a security manager be concerned about?
5. If a security director notices OSHA violations and reports them to top management, and top management chooses to ignore the violations, what should the security director do?

References

"AIDS and State Employment." St. Paul, MN: Minnesota Department of Employee Relations, October 1994.

Azano, Harry J. "The Truth about Halon." *Security Management,* May 1993, p. 34.

Blake, William F. "Making Recovery a Priority." *Security Management,* April 1992, pp. 71–74.

Cardwell, Michael. "Survival Among the Ruins." *Security Management,* August 1994, pp. 64–68.

"Chemicals in the Workplace." *Security Concepts,* May 1994, pp. 17, 25.

Clark, Jacob R. "Crime in the 90's: It's a Blast. ATF Seeks Answers to Rise in Bombings." *Law Enforcement News,* March 15, 1994, pp. 1, 7.

Coleman, Randall. "Six Steps to Disaster Recovery." *Security Management,* February 1993, pp. 61–62.

Dean, S. Carl. "The Door to Fire Safety." *Security Management,* October 1993, pp. 50–59.

Draty, David. "Crisis Management: Fire Safety and Evacuation." *Security Concepts,* April 1994, pp. 1, 2, 25.

Draty, David. "Crisis Management Part II: Requirements for Chemicals and Gases." *Security Concepts,* May 1994, pp. 5, 26.

Draty, David. "The Ever-Present Danger—Hazardous Materials." *Security Concepts,* February 1994, pp. 2, 29.

DuBose, Michael J. "Taking the Heat off Fire Inspections." *Security Management,* May 1993, pp. 33–35.

Epps, Cheryl Anthony. "OSHA Issues Regs on AIDS and Hepatitis." *The Police Chief,* March 1992, p. 14.

Fay, John. "Getting Ready for the Bomb in Your Building." *Security Concepts,* August 1994, p. 12.

Foster, Al. "Hot News in Hot Site Selection." *Security Management,* April 1993, pp. 65–72.

Gardiner, Richard A. and Grassie, Richard P. "A Comprehensive Approach to Workplace Safety." *Security Management,* July 1994, pp. 97–102.

Hamit, Francis. "Blast Effect: The World Trade Center Bombing and the NRC." *Security Technology and Design,* August 1994, pp. 89–90.

Hamit, Francis. "L.A. After the Earthquake: Lessons Learned." *Security Technology and Design,* May 1994, pp. 56, 60.

Harowitz, Sherry L. "The Morning After." *Security Management,* December 1992, pp. 76–81.

Herman, Martin. "When Strikes Turn Violent, Somebody's Going to Pay." *Security Concepts,* October 1994, pp. 1, 27, 29.

Hopkins, Tricia. "Access Control and Fire Alarms: A Winning Combination." *Security Technology and Design,* July/August 1993, p. 40.

Jenkins, Alan B. "Bomb Threat Preparedness: Defusing an Explosive Situation." *Security Management,* November 1991, pp. 37–41.

Kass, Michael. "Are Emergency Medical Services a Priority?" *Security Management,* October 1994, pp. 101–102.

Kime, Roy Caldwell. "New Regulations Covering Emergency Response Employees." *The Police Chief,* February 1993, p. 12.

Kohr, Robert L. and Nobrega, Kathryn. "Safety First: An OSHA Primer." *Security Management,* August 1993, pp. 36–37.

Kouri, James J. "A System for Safe Strikes." *Security Management,* September 1992, pp. 158–161.

"L.A. Troops Gaining Upper Hand." (Minneapolis/St. Paul) *Star Tribune,* May 2, 1992, pp. 1A, 9A.

Mallory, Jim. "Demonstrations." *Law and Order,* September 1990, pp. 83–85.

May, William A., Jr. "Post-Traumatic Stress after Large-Scale Disasters." *Law and Order,* March 1990, pp. 97–99.

May, William A., Jr. "Responding to Hazardous Materials Incidents: Formulating a Basic Response Plan." *Law and Order,* October 1990, pp. 85–87.

McCarthy, William F. and Quigley, Robert C. "Don't Blow It." *Security Management,* March 1992, pp. 52–53.

Moore, Wayne D. "Design Your Detection System to Match Your Fire Protection Goals." *Security Technology and Design,* April 1994, p. 47–48.

Moore, Wayne D. "The National Fire Alarm Code Changes and Issues." *Security Technology and Design,* May 1994, pp. 53–55.

Olick, M. "Carbon Monoxide—The Silent Killer." *Security Concepts,* December 1994, pp. 2, 26.

Oliver, Carl R. "Building the BEL System." *Security Management,* May 1993, pp. 27–30.

Olmos, Ross A. "Is the Workplace No Longer Safe?" *Security Concepts,* April 1994, p. 9.

Olstead, Patrick R. "Getting a Handle on Door Safety." *Security Technology and Design,* May 1994, pp. 16–20.

"OSHA Penalties Hit Record Level in Fiscal '94." *Security Concepts,* January 1995, pp. 1, 26.

Papi, Vincent. "Planning Before Disaster Strikes." *Security Concepts,* February 1994, pp. 6, 19.

Platt, John. "Putting Out the Fire of Disaster." *Security Management,* January 1992, pp. 51–54.

Preventing Illness and Injury in the Workplace. Washington, DC: U.S. Congress, Office of Technology Assessment, OTA-H—256, April 1985.

Purpura, Philip. *The Security Handbook.* Albany, NY: Delmar Publishers Inc., 1991.

Roughton, James E. "Can You Handle Hazardous Waste?" *Security Management,* July 1992, p. 104.

Roughton, James E. "The OSHA Man Cometh." *Security Management,* February 1995, pp. 41–47.

Schmock, Leo F. "Are You Ready? We Are." *Security Management,* July 1991, pp. 38–39.

Seuter, Edward J. "Taking the Bang Out of Bomb Threats." *Security Management,* March 1992, pp. 47–51.

Shalna, Anthony J. "A Smoke Detector Primer, Part 1." *Security Concepts,* August 1994, p. 8.

Shaw, R. A. "Buck." "Carrying the Torch: A Quick Course in Fire Prevention." *Security Management,* January 1992, p. 53.

Sherwood, J. L. "What's in the Package?" *Security Concepts,* February 1994, pp. 9, 18.

Stedman, Michael J. "Limp Response to the Blast." *Security Technology and Design,* March 1994, pp. 14–20.

Sunstrom, Philip C. "Become the Company's OSHA Oracle." *Security Management,* March 1994, pp. 24–32.

Turner, Dana. "Resources for Disaster Recovery." *Security Management,* August 1994, pp. 57–63.

"U.S. AIDS Survey Says 300,000 to 1 Million Have Virus." (Minneapolis/St. Paul) *Star Tribune,* December 14, 1993, p. 7A.

Vance, Charles F. "Picture-Perfect Strike Protection." *Security Management,* November 1991, pp. 46–49.

Yearwood, Douglas L. "Law Enforcement and AIDS: Knowledge, Attitudes, and Fears in the Workplace." *American Journal of Police,* Vol. 11, No. 2, 1992, pp. 65–83.

CASE

Marshall v. Barlow's Inc. 436 U.S. 307, 98 S.Ct. 1816 (1978)

CHAPTER 8

Preventing Losses from Criminal Actions

Do You Know

- How criminal and civil offenses differ?
- What crimes are of major importance to private security?
- How the risk of these crimes can be reduced?
- How to differentiate among theft, burglary and robbery?
- What circumstances can indicate arson?
- What white-collar crime is?
- What pilferage is?
- What drugs are commonly abused in the workplace?
- What rights private security officers may be called on to enforce?
- When and how private security officers can make an arrest?
- When force or deadly force may be justified?
- When and how searches of suspects can be conducted?
- How interviewing differs from interrogating? How to make such questioning more effective?

Can You Define These Terms?

arson
assault
burglary
citizen's arrest
civil offenses
cocaine
corporate crime
crack
economic crime
embezzlement
felony
fraud
freebase
grand larceny
igniter
interrogation
interview
larceny/theft
marijuana
misdemeanor
petty larceny
pilferage
pyromaniac
robbery
torts
trailers
trespassing
Uniform Crime Reports (UCR)
unlawful taking
vandalism
white-collar crime

INTRODUCTION

Early Saturday morning, June 17, 1972, a private security patrol officer, Frank Wills, was walking his beat on a Washington, DC, street. He approached the entry door to the Watergate complex and tried the door to see if it was secure. Noticing that the latch had been taped open and that the door swung open freely, the officer immediately called the Washington police. Five men carrying photographic equipment and electronic gear were subsequently arrested for burglarizing the National Democratic Headquarters. Thus came about the most noted political upheaval in the history of our country—Watergate. Officer Wills' watchfulness and the quick actions of the Washington police led to the imprisonment of two top presidential aides, the incarceration of the United States attorney general and the resignation of the president of the United States.*

The primary role of private security in combating crime is to *prevent* its occurrence by reducing the opportunity for criminal activity. Criminal activity in business and industry takes many forms, ranging from simple property loss through shoplifting or pilfering to property loss by physical violence, as in armed robbery. The impact of burglary and robbery on the business community is substantial.

According to the Hallcrest Report (Cunningham and Taylor, 1985, p. 18), the most common ways of illegally taking money from a business have been robbery, burglary, larceny and embezzlement. However, more sophisticated, complicated forms of stealing have emerged, such as falsification of records, leading to payment for goods never received or hours never worked, sometimes to nonexistent employees. The American economy loses billions of dollars from employee "time theft"—excessive socializing, conducting personal business on employer time, late arrivals, abuse of sick leave, etc.

This chapter begins by looking at the seriousness of criminal actions, reviewing the difference between criminal and civil offenses and introducing those crimes of most concern to private security. This is followed by another look at alcohol and other drugs in the workplace as well as other crimes that might be encountered by security personnel. Next, actions that might be required in enforcing proprietary rights are discussed, including expelling, detaining and arresting; using force; investigating and searching; and interviewing and interrogating suspects. The chapter concludes with some recent court rulings and the trend toward the gradual transfer of police tasks to private security and the resulting restrictions.

THE SERIOUSNESS OF THE PROBLEM

According to Elig (1993, p. 1): "It has been estimated that businesses lost $128 billion to crime in 1991. This is approximately 69% of corporate America's after-tax profits."

*One reputable source states that Wills removed the tape the first time he saw it and that it was not until a subsequent round, when he noticed that it was retaped, that he called the police.

In addition to these direct losses, the Hallcrest Report also identifies three absorbers of indirect costs of economic crime against businesses: business, government and the public (p. 19).

Effects on BUSINESS include the following:

- Increased costs of insurance and security protection.
- Costs of internal audit activities to detect crime.
- Costs of investigation and prosecution of suspects measured in terms of lost time of security and management personnel.
- Reduced profits.
- Increased selling prices and weakened competitive standing.
- Loss of productivity.
- Loss of business reputation.
- Deterioration in quality of service.
- Threats to the survival of small business.

Effects on GOVERNMENT include the following:

- Costs of investigation and prosecution of suspects.
- Increased costs of prosecuting sophisticated (e.g., embezzlement) and technology-related (e.g., computer) crime.
- Costs of correctional programs to deal with economic crime offenders.
- Costs of crime prevention programs.
- Costs of crime reporting and mandated security programs.
- Loss of revenue (e.g., loss of sales tax, untaxed income of perpetrator, and tax deductions allowed businesses for crime-related losses).

Effects on the PUBLIC include the following:

- Increased costs of consumer goods and services to offset crime losses.
- Loss of investor equity.
- Increased taxes.
- Reduced employment due to business failures.

NOTE: These effects are concerned only with nonviolent business crime, but if the total crime environment of institutions (schools, hospitals, museums, etc.) were also considered, the effects on institutions would include the following:

- Declining enrollment, attendance, or occupancy due to crime-related incidents.
- Employee turnover and recruitment costs due to fear of crime incidents.
- Increased costs of service.
- Increased costs of insurance and security protection.

The crime problem in the United States is severe, as indicated by figures from the 1993 Uniform Crime Reports:

- One murder every 22 minutes.
- One forcible rape every 5 minutes.
- One robbery every 27 seconds.
- One aggravated assault every 28 seconds.

Security managers should carefully analyze the potential for crime in their establishments. What type of crime is likely to occur? At what rate? When? What method of attack is likely to be used? What is it likely to cost? If the risk is high, appropriate security measures should be taken to reduce, spread or shift the risks.

Thornton et al. (1991, p. 54) caution: "Crime must be evaluated in preparing a security program that meets the threat of existing levels of risk and deters foreseeable adverse criminal incidents." They (p. 56) suggest: "Foreseeability of crime, a factor in judging whether security is negligent, hinges almost exclusively on the use of official crime statistics to support the circumstances of the case."

Thornton et al. cite the 1974 civil litigation occurring after the attack on entertainer Connie Francis in her Long Island Howard Johnson motel room which yielded an award of $2.7 million. This case "opened the floodgate to third-party negligent liability" (p. 56).

When considering foreseeability of crime, the best indicator is the occurrence of past crimes in this particular location. Often cases are divided into no prior crime, one to a few prior crimes and several prior crimes. Even one prior crime, however, should lead to a careful examination of underlying causes and whether any changes in security are called for.

Keep one thing in mind when discussing the security officer's responsibilities regarding crimes. Although this chapter emphasizes the role of the security officer in dealing with potential and actual crimes, the majority of the security manager's time is spent dealing with noncriminal matters.

CRIMINAL AND CIVIL OFFENSES IN REVIEW

Our country's laws establish what actions constitute a crime. These laws include all the rules of conduct established and enforced by custom, authority or legislation of a city, state or federal government. In the United States, state and federal statutes define each crime, the elements involved and the penalty attached to each. The elements of the crime are the specific conditions and actions prescribed by law that must exist to constitute a specific crime. These elements vary from state to state.

Crimes and their punishments range in seriousness from pickpocketing to murder. They are classified according to their seriousness as a misdemeanor or a felony. A **misdemeanor** is a minor crime such as shoplifting or petty theft that is punishable by a fine and/or a relatively short jail sentence. In contrast, a **felony** is a serious crime, such as murder, robbery or burglary, that is punishable by death or by imprisonment in the state prison or penitentiary.

In addition to criminal offenses, security personnel may also have to deal with **civil offenses**—actions prohibited by law, but not classified as crimes. These actions, called **torts,** are governed by civil law and are not under the jurisdiction of public law enforcement, as discussed in Chapter 4. They include such offenses as libel, slander and negligence.

> A crime is an offense against the state for which punishment is sought. A tort is an offense against an individual for which restitution is sought.

CRIMES OF CONCERN TO PRIVATE SECURITY

> The crimes of most concern to private security are larceny/theft, burglary, robbery, trespassing, vandalism, assault, arson; white-collar crime, including embezzlement, bad checks and credit card fraud; and drugs in the workplace.

A major source of information on these crimes is the **Uniform Crime Reports (UCR)**.* These are annually compiled by the FBI, which serves as the national clearinghouse for crime-related statistical information. The Uniform Crime Reporting Program provides a yearly, nationwide summary of crime based on the cooperative submission of data by nearly 15,000 law enforcement agencies throughout the country. The data contained in these reports can be used by private security managers in making administrative, operational and management decisions. In addition to the Uniform Crime Reports, security managers should be familiar with their state statutes for the crimes they are most likely to have to deal with. They should be familiar with the elements that must be proven if they are to be of assistance in prosecuting perpetrators of crime. Definitions in the following discussions of specific crimes are based on those used in the Uniform Crime Reports.

Larceny/Theft†

Larceny/theft is (1) the unlawful taking (2) of the personal goods or property of another (3) valued above **(grand larceny)** or below **(petty larceny)** a specified amount, (4) with the intent to permanently deprive the owner of the property or goods. This crime includes shoplifting, to be discussed in Chapter 16, and employee pilferage, previously discussed in Chapter 6. It also includes such crimes as pickpocketing, purse-snatching, thefts from motor vehicles, thefts of motor vehicle parts and accessories and other thefts, where *no* use of force or violence occurs. The person simply takes something that does not belong to him or her.

The value of the property is usually determined by the actual value at the time of the theft or the cost of replacing it in a reasonable time. The value determines if the offense is grand or petty larceny. State statutes establish the dollar amount above which a theft is considered grand larceny, a felony, and below which a theft is considered petty larceny, a misdemeanor.

One form of larceny/theft of special concern to security managers is cargo theft, which costs the business sector billions of dollars annually. Four key

---

*These reports are entitled *Crime in the United States* and are published yearly.

†Larceny/theft is used here because the two terms are interchangeable. Some state statutes refer to larceny, others to theft. The Uniform Crime Reports use larceny/theft.

industries are affected: air, rail, truck and maritime. A federal study places the annual losses due to theft of air cargo at $400 million, rail cargo at $600 million, truck-related cargo at $1.2 billion and maritime cargo at $300 million. Such thefts frequently involve the cooperation of insiders.

These thefts can affect any mode of transportation and type of business. Because cargo thefts require organization and advance planning, organized crime syndicates often play a key role in both planning the theft and distributing the stolen merchandise. Stolen cargo can consist of valuable securities, drugs, precious metals and even cigarettes and shoes. Stolen cargo is a valuable commodity with a readily available market through a chain of fences. Furthermore, stolen merchandise is usually difficult to trace and identify. The cargo theft problem can involve carriers, shippers, insurers, labor unions, employers and employees, as discussed in Chapter 15.

Addis (1992, p. 36) notes: "If you are a security director for a company that manufactures or sells pharmaceuticals, computer chips, clothing, cosmetics, or anything else that is highly marketable, chances are employee theft is a big problem for your company."

According to Benny (1992, p. 40), 70 percent of an organization's employees would never steal from their employer no matter how much they needed money or how many opportunities presented themselves. Another 20 percent would steal only if the opportunity arose. The remaining 10 percent will always try to steal, not only from their employer but also from their fellow employees.

> To prevent or reduce losses from larceny/theft, limit access to assets and use basic security equipment and procedures to deter employee pilferage as well as theft by nonemployees.

Specific types of employee pilferage and nonemployee theft in various businesses are discussed in Section IV.

Burglary

Burglary is (1) entering a structure without the owner's consent (2) with the intent to commit a crime. Usually the crime is theft, but it may be another crime, such as rape or assault. Commercial burglaries are often committed in service stations, stores, schools, warehouses, office buildings, manufacturing plants and the like. Often burglars specialize in one type of facility.

Entrance can be made in any number of ways, but the most common method is prying open a door or window—the jimmy method. It can also be made by simply walking through an unlocked door, an open window, a tunnel or a ventilation shaft, or by remaining in a building after closing time. The smash-and-grab burglar breaks a display window and grabs whatever merchandise is available.

In many states, if a person is found in a structure and the person has no legal right to be there at that time, it is *presumed* the person intends to commit a crime, unless the suspect can prove otherwise.

Some states require an actual *breaking* into the structure—that is, a forced entry. Other states require that the structure be a *dwelling* or that the crime occur during the *nighttime*. It is provisions such as these that make it necessary for security managers to be familiar with the statutes of their own state to deal effectively with crimes that are attempted or actually committed.

These steps can prevent or reduce the risk of loss from burglary:

- Install and use good locks, adequate indoor and outdoor lighting and an alarm system. This may be supplemented with security patrols.
- Keep valuables in a burglar-resistant safe or vault.
- Keep a minimum amount of cash on hand.
- Leave cash registers open and empty at closing time.
- Be sure all security equipment is functional before leaving.

The security checklist in Figure 8–1 (p. 242) might be used in assessing a facility's protection against burglary.

Robbery

Robbery is (1) the unlawful taking of personal property (2) from the person or in the person's presence, (3) against the person's will by force or threat of force. The person from whom the property is taken need not be the owner of the property, but can be someone to whom the property has been entrusted. Usually "from the person or in the person's presence" means the victim actually sees the robber take the property, but this is not always the case. The robber may lock the victim in a room and then commit the robbery. This does not remove the crime "from the presence of the person" if the separation from the property is the direct result of force or threats of force used by the robber.

Most robberies are committed with a weapon or by indicating that a weapon is present and by a command suggesting that if the robber's demands are not met the victim will be harmed. The demands may be given orally or in a note; the threat may be against the victim, the victim's family or another person with the victim. The possibility of violence and/or a hostage situation must always be considered if a robbery occurs.

These steps can prevent or reduce losses from robbery:

- Train employees how to react if a robbery occurs.
- Do not build up cash. Used armed couriers to transport cash.
- Establish strict opening and closing procedures, and use extreme caution if someone seeks entrance to the facility after hours.

NAME: ______ PHONE: ______
ADDRESS: ______
PERSON INTERVIEWED: ______ OWNER ☐ OTHER ☐
CONSTRUCTION: WOOD ☐ METAL ☐ CONCRETE ☐ MASONRY ☐ OTHER ______
CONDITION: EXCELLENT ☐ GOOD ☐ FAIR ☐

DOORS	ADEQUATE		WOOD	METAL	GLASS	COMBINATION	NON-REMOVABLE HINGE PINS	
FRONT	☐ YES	NO ☐	☐	☐	☐	☐	YES ☐	NO ☐
REAR	☐ YES	NO ☐	☐	☐	☐	☐	YES ☐	NO ☐
SIDE	☐ YES	NO ☐	☐	☐	☐	☐	YES ☐	NO ☐
SIDE	☐ YES	NO ☐	☐	☐	☐	☐	YES ☐	NO ☐

LOCKS	ADEQUATE		DEAD BOLT	DROP BOLT	KEY IN KNOB	PADLOCK	SLIDE BOLT	OTHER
FRONT	☐ YES	NO ☐	☐	☐	☐	☐	☐	☐
REAR	☐ YES	NO ☐	☐	☐	☐	☐	☐	☐
SIDE	☐ YES	NO ☐	☐	☐	☐	☐	☐	☐
SIDE	☐ YES	NO ☐	☐	☐	☐	☐	☐	☐

LIGHTS	ADEQUATE		WEAK	NONE	LEFT ON		LOCATION	
INTERIOR	☐ YES	NO ☐	☐	☐	☐ YES	NO ☐	☐ GOOD	BAD ☐
EXTERIOR	☐ YES	NO ☐	☐	☐	☐ YES	NO ☐	☐ GOOD	BAD ☐
FRONT	☐ YES	NO ☐	☐	☐	☐ YES	NO ☐	☐ GOOD	BAD ☐
SIDE	☐ YES	NO ☐	☐	☐	☐ YES	NO ☐	☐ GOOD	BAD ☐
SIDE	☐ YES	NO ☐	☐	☐	☐ YES	NO ☐	☐ GOOD	BAD ☐
REAR	☐ YES	NO ☐	☐	☐	☐ YES	NO ☐	☐ GOOD	BAD ☐

WINDOWS	ADEQUATE		BARS	GATE	MESH	LOCKS	
FRONT	☐ YES	NO ☐	☐	☐	☐	☐ YES	NO ☐
REAR	☐ YES	NO ☐	☐	☐	☐	☐ YES	NO ☐
SIDE	☐ YES	NO ☐	☐	☐	☐	☐ YES	NO ☐
SIDE	☐ YES	NO ☐	☐	☐	☐	☐ YES	NO ☐

REMARKS:

ALARMS	DOORS			WINDOWS			CEILING			WALLS		
	Adequate	weak	none	Adequate	weak	none	Adequate	weak	none	Adequate	weak	none
LOCAL	☐	☐	☐	☐	☐	☐	☐	☐	☐	☐	☐	☐
CENTRAL	☐	☐	☐	☐	☐	☐	☐	☐	☐	☐	☐	☐
TELEPHONE	☐	☐	☐	☐	☐	☐	☐	☐	☐	☐	☐	☐

SAFE: VISIBLE FROM STREET ☐ YES NO ☐ ANCHORED ☐ YES NO ☐
LIGHTED ☐ YES NO ☐ ADEQUATE ☐ YES NO ☐
CASH REGISTER: VISIBLE FROM STREET ☐ YES NO ☐ ANCHORED ☐ YES NO ☐
LIGHTED ☐ YES NO ☐ ADEQUATE ☐ YES NO ☐

OVERALL EVALUATION: ☐ **EXCELLENT** ☐ **GOOD** ☐ **FAIR** ☐ **INADEQUATE**

To the storekeeper:
This is part of a program being conducted by your Fargo Police Department to help you protect yourself against burglars. If you follow the recommendations in this report, you will make it more difficult for a burglar to enter your business.

Investigating officer ______ Telephone number ______
Burglary Prevention Team

Recommendations: Compliance Date ______

Figure 8–1. Security Checklist
SOURCE: Courtesy of Fargo (ND) Police Department.

All employees who are in positions where they might be involved in a robbery should know what to do should that occur. It should be stressed that heroics are *not* expected and, in fact, could be a deadly mistake. Robbers are completely unpredictable, but employees should be taught to follow the guidelines below to reduce the risks involved should a robbery occur:

- Stay calm.
- Do exactly as you are told.
- Assure the robber that you will cooperate totally, but do not volunteer to do anything.
- Treat any firearm displayed as though it is real and loaded.
- Activate alarms only if you can do so undetected.
- Try to alert others if possible.

To assist in investigating the robbery, employees should mentally note the robber's appearance, clothing, voice and unique characteristics—anything distinctive. Some employers place a reference point on a wall or door frame to give employees who might face robbers something to use to estimate the robber's height.

Correctly Classifying "Unlawful Taking"

The preceding discussions illustrate several types of "unlawful taking" security managers may encounter. It is important to keep the basic distinctions among these types of stealing separate.

> *Larceny/theft* is the unlawful taking of the property of another without unlawful entrance or confrontation. *Burglary* includes unlawful taking *and* unlawful entry. *Robbery* includes unlawful taking *and* confrontation.

Private security is most often concerned with larceny/theft. However, the amount of losses sustained in a burglary or robbery may be significant if proper precautions are not followed. In addition, robbery carries with it the potential for violence.

Trespassing and Vandalism

Two frequently encountered problems of private security managers are trespassing and vandalism. **Trespassing** refers to the unlawful presence of a person on the property or inside the premises of someone else. The trespasser may mean no harm; in fact, the trespass may be unintentional if boundaries are not clearly marked and signs are not posted. Often, however, trespassers may smoke where it may be hazardous, or they may intend to steal or to damage property. Trespassing on railroad property can be extremely hazardous. According to an executive of the Association of American Railways in Washington, DC, some 500 to 600 trespassing deaths related to railways occur yearly.

Vandalism refers to the malicious or intentional damaging and/or destroying of public or private property. It is also called criminal damage to property or malicious destruction of property.

The gravity of this crime depends on the extent of property damage. In one sense, destruction of property is more serious than theft because it eliminates the possibility of recovering the property. Intent is always a factor in vandalism. School buildings, factories, warehouses, vehicles and homes are all vulnerable targets for the vandal. How much vandalism occurs internally in business and industry is not documented; however, it is likely to be a great amount. In some instances, vandalism may actually be sabotage. For example, assembly workers who become dissatisfied with their jobs may cause machinery breakdowns (to be discussed in Chapter 15).

> Trespassing and vandalism can be prevented or reduced by strict access controls, security lighting, signs and patrols.

"No Trespassing" signs can eliminate the excuse that the intruder's presence was "accidental."

Assault

Some private security managers must face the risks to their employees from verbal or physical assault, including sexual assault. **Assault** refers to an attack upon a person.* It may be committed to cause bodily injury or may result while committing another crime, such as robbery or rape. Establishments having night shifts and those employing large numbers of women are especially susceptible to this risk. Workplace violence is the focus of Chapter 20.

> Adequate lighting, patrols and communication systems are means to reduce the risk of assaults. Escort services may also be used.

The distance to parking lots is a key factor in employees' susceptibility to assault. When practical, this distance should be minimal. Parking areas should be well lit and fenced.

Arson

Arson is the willful, malicious burning of property. It can be committed for financial gain, to hide other crimes such as burglary or embezzlement, for revenge or as a form of terrorism.

Studies of arrested, institutionalized and paroled arsonists reveal distinct behavioral categories. The works of Columbia University psychiatrists Nolan Lewis and Helen Yarnell and sociologist James Inciardi, for example, have

*Some states distinguish between assault (threat) and battery (actual physical contact), but the UCR combines them into a single crime termed *assault*.

found that various offender types commit arson for various reasons (Inciardi and Binder, 1983, p. 77).*

1. *Revenge arsonists,* the most prevalent type, are persons who, as the result of arguments or feelings of jealousy or hatred, seek revenge by fire. The victims are typically family members and relatives, employers or lovers. In retaliation for real or imaginary wrongs, revenge arsonists set ablaze their victims' property or the premises in which they reside. These arsonists appear to be the most potentially dangerous of all types. They set occupied dwellings afire with little thought as to the safety of those within, thinking only of the revenge they must have on their specific victims. Furthermore, they are often intoxicated at the time of the offense. No elaborate incendiary devices are employed, typically only matches and gasoline. Although their crimes are premeditated, they take few steps to conceal their identities and are thus easily detected by alert investigators.
2. *Vandalism arsonists* include teenagers who willfully destroy property solely for purposes of fun and sport, although at times revenge motives may be partially present. As opposed to other arsonists, who work alone, vandalism arsonists usually have at least one accomplice. They tend to set fires at night in churches, school buildings and vacant structures.
3. *Crime-concealment arsonists* set fire to premises where they have committed other offenses. The crime is usually burglary but sometimes murder, and the arson is an attempt to cover the traces of the criminal or obliterate the proof that another crime has taken place. Such fires are usually set at night in unoccupied dwellings or places of business.
4. *Insurance-claim arsonists* include insolvent property owners, small-business owners, small-business operators and other individuals who, because of extreme financial pressure, incinerate their own property to collect the insurance on what has been destroyed. As a rule they do not set fire to occupied dwellings, and their offenses generally take place in the daytime.
5. *Excitement arsonists* set buildings ablaze for the thrill connected with fires. Some like setting or watching fires whereas others enjoy viewing the operations of fire fighters and fire equipment. (Occasionally a volunteer fire fighter is found among them.) Their offenses take place at night, they rarely set ablaze anything but uninhabited buildings, and they are usually intoxicated at the time of the offense.
6. *Pyromaniacs* are pathological firesetters. A **pyromaniac** seems to have no practical reason for setting fires and receives no material profit from them. The only motive seems to be some sort of sensual satisfaction, and the classic "irresistible impulse" is often a factor.

---

*Adapted with permission of The Free Press, a Division of Macmillan, Inc. from *Encyclopedia of Crime and Justice,* Sanford H. Kadish, Editor in Chief. Copyright© 1983 by The Free Press.

Arson is involved in approximately one-fourth of all fires in the United States. As noted by Woods and Wallace (1991, p. 80): "A security professional involved in a fire investigation that leads to a suspicion of arson should be aware that guidelines for investigations by government officials are different than those for private citizens. Knowing those differences can help the private security person conduct the investigation in a way that does not violate a suspect's constitutional rights." The bottom line, in most cases, is that (p. 84):

> . . . evidence obtained by a private arson investigator is admissible in a criminal prosecution provided there is no concerted activity with an official investigation.
>
> A security professional conducting an arson investigation as a private citizen is not bound by court guidelines regarding the Fourth Amendment. In addition, some states allow information obtained by a private investigator, acting alone, to be passed on to a government investigator.

Common sites for setting fires include the basement; stockrooms; duplicating, file and mail rooms and utility closets. Access control to such areas is critical to preventing arson.

Security managers might suspect arson in a fire where one of the three elements of the fire triangle is present in abnormal amounts. Greater than normal *oxygen* can come from opened windows, doors, pried-open vents or holes knocked in walls. Piled-up newspapers, excelsior or other combustible materials present at or brought to the scene can provide abnormal amounts of *fuel*. Excessive *heat* can be caused by accelerants, including gasoline (the most commonly used), kerosene, turpentine or paint remover.

Another indicator of arson is an **igniter,** including matches, candles, cigars, cigarettes, cigarette lighters, explosives and electrical, mechanical and chemical devices. Time fuses, shorted light switches, electrical devices left in the "on" position, kerosene-soaked papers in wastepaper baskets, magnifying glasses, matches tied around a lighted cigarette and numerous other igniters have been used to commit arson.

Yet another indication of arson is the presence of **trailers,** paths of paper or accelerants used to spread the fire from one location to another. Arsonists may also set multiple fires to ensure complete destruction, and they may disable the fire-fighting apparatus. Any of the preceding would be strong evidence of arson.

Security managers should suspect arson in fires that:

- Have more than one point of origin.
- Deviate from normal burning patterns.
- Show evidence of trailers.
- Show evidence of having been accelerated.
- Indicate an abnormal amount of air, fuel or heat present.
- Reveal evidence of incendiary igniters at the point of origin.
- Produce odors or smoke of a color associated with substances not normally present at the scene.

Other suspicious circumstances include goods being removed from the premises shortly before a fire occurs, over-insurance, economic difficulties of the owner, surplus out-of-date or damaged inventory or needed repairs—perhaps to comply with violations discovered by an OSHA inspector.

According to the UCR Program, arson is the fastest-growing crime in the United States today. In 1993, 102,000 cases of arson were reported.

Every fire, no matter how small, should be investigated and the cause determined so corrective steps can be taken to prevent a recurrence.

White-Collar Crime

The Chamber of Commerce of the United States has described **white-collar crimes** as "illegal acts characterized by guile, deceit, and concealment . . . not dependent upon the application of physical force or violence or threats thereof. They may be committed by individuals acting independently or by those who are part of a well-planned conspiracy. The objective may be to obtain money, property, or services; to avoid the payment or loss of money, property, or services; or to secure business or personal advantage." Such crimes are also referred to as **economic crime.**

> White-collar crime is business-related crime.

Included among white-collar crimes are bankruptcy fraud; bribery, kickbacks and payoffs; computer-related crime; consumer fraud; illegal competition and deceptive practices; credit card and check fraud; embezzlement and pilferage; insurance fraud; receiving stolen property; and securities thefts and frauds. Pilferage, a form of larceny/theft, is of prime concern.

According to the Chamber, the yearly cost of embezzlement and pilferage reportedly exceeds by several billion dollars the losses sustained throughout the nation from burglary and robbery.

Sharp (1994, p. 91) notes: "White-collar crime is on the rise—and it is costing citizens and businesses billions of dollars a year." According to Sharp, losses in the United States from four major credit cards—Visa, MasterCard, Discover and Optima—rose from $125 million in 1983 to $720 million in 1992. In addition, U.S. consumers are "bilked" out of about $100 billion a year, almost half attributed to telemarketing scams (Sharp, p. 91).

Turner and Stephenson (1993, p. 57) suggest: "White-collar crime probably costs U.S. businesses more than $40 billion each year." They note that the statistics are not all that reliable because many white-collar crimes are never reported.

Some notorious white-collar criminals have been in the headlines in recent years. Michael Milken, of Drexel Burnham & Lamber, for example, lost billions of dollars in questionable trades and yet will serve less than three years in prison. Patrick Finn, former chief financial officer of PHAR-MOR, pled guilty to participating in a $1-billion **fraud*** and **embezzlement†** scheme involving the discount-drug chain; he received a fine of $7,000 and 33 months in prison.

Elig (1993, p. 2) cautions:

> Don't assume that any sense of team loyalty will keep your employees honest! Don't believe that a long-time friend or employee would never steal from you! Don't be distracted by plausible excuses, find the facts! Remember, at this moment, there exists a greater than 50% chance that someone is committing a crime within your organization.

Elig suggests that **fidelity bonds** are one of the strongest protections against internal theft. These bonds are a form of insurance protecting employers from losses suffered from dishonest employees.

> **Pilferage,** or internal theft, is an important concern of private security managers.

Gordon (1990, p. 12) notes figures from the U.S. Department of Commerce stating that employees walk off with $40 billion in goods every year. Further, the American Management Association estimates that employee theft causes 20 percent of all business failures.

Gordon (p. 13) urges that the best way to avoid employee theft in the first place is to hire honest employees and maintain an environment that encourages honesty. She suggests that the single best deterrent is fear of being caught.

The Department of Labor says that employees suspected of theft are often involved in other types of misconduct such as unauthorized absences, chronic tardiness and violation of basic rules (Gordon, p. 13). Many businesses consider internal theft, by an embezzler or a pilferer, their number-one security problem. According to Braithwaite and Fisse (1987, p. 221), "Literature shows us that corporate crime is responsible for more property loss and more injuries to persons than is crime in the streets." They also note (pp. 240–41):

> Companies must be concerned not to put employees under so much pressure to achieve the economic goals of the organization that they cut corners with the law. The role of excessive performance pressures on middle managers in creating corporate crime has been frequently pointed to by the literature. . . .
>
> At one extreme are companies that calculatedly set goals for their managers that they know can only be achieved by breaking the law. Thus, the pharmaceutical chief executive may tell her regional medical director to do whatever he has to do to get a product approved for marketing in a Latin American country, when she knows this will mean paying a bribe. Likewise,

---

*Intentional deception to cause a person to give up property or some lawful right.

†Fraudulent appropriation of property by a person to whom it was entrusted.

> the coal mining executive may tell his mine manager to cut costs when he knows this will mean cutting corners on safety.
>
> The mentality of "Do what you have to do but don't tell me how you do it" is widespread in business.

Often computers are involved in white-collar crimes. Because this is such a serious problem for many establishments, the next chapter focuses on this relatively recent problem.

Businesses often investigate their own internal losses, and when they find someone to be guilty, they simply fire them. The police and the media often are not called. As noted by Sharp (1994, p. 95):

> Adverse publicity, which can be embarrassing to the company and possibly cause a loss in current or future clients, will be avoided through this process.
>
> Businesses don't want to be known as an easy target for theft or embezzlement, so avoid involving the police. Also, some employers do not want to confront their employees because they are afraid of retaliation, whether it be the destruction of company property or lawsuits.

Corporate crime is a type of white-collar crime whose distinctive feature is that the offense is committed primarily for the benefit of an ongoing legitimate business enterprise, rather than for the individual who carries out the offense. Benson et al. (1993, p. 1) define corporate crime as "a violation of a criminal statute either by a corporate entity or by its executives, employees, or agents acting on behalf of and for the benefit of the corporation, partnership, or other form of business entity." Such crimes include consumer fraud, securities fraud, insurance and tax fraud, environmental offenses, illegal payments and unfair trade practices.

Alcohol and Other Drugs in the Workplace

According to Carroll (1992, p. 54): "The epidemic nature of the drug problem in America has been underestimated. The effects of the problem are so far-reaching that all sectors of society have been contaminated; there are no safe sectors from which to draw drug-free employees."

Carroll (1992, p. 54), citing statistics provided by the National Institute on Drug Abuse (NIDA), notes the following:

- 10 to 23 percent of the work force in the United States use drugs while at work.
- Another 20 percent of workers use drugs so heavily the night before work that they are still impaired when they return to work.
- The result is that, on any given day, 20 to 33 percent of American workers are under the influence of illegal drugs or alcohol.

Although some drug users report that drugs such as cocaine increase their concentration and improve their performance on a variety of tasks, no concrete evidence supports such statements. Most drugs are short-acting, with the effects wearing off within an hour, leaving the user tired and depressed. In addition, users may steal to support their habit.

> Drugs commonly abused in the workplace include alcohol, marijuana and cocaine—snorted or smoked as freebase or crack.

Marijuana, according to Wrobleski and Hess (1993, pp. 435–436), "... is probably the most socially acceptable of the illegal drugs.... When smoked, marijuana enters the bloodstream quickly, causing rapid onset of symptoms. The effects of the drug on the user's mood and thinking vary widely, depending on the amount and strength of the marijuana as well as the social setting and the effects anticipated. The drug usually takes effect in about fifteen minutes and lasts from two to four hours. 'Social' doses of one or two cigarettes may cause an increased sense of well-being; initial restlessness and hilarity followed by a dreamy, carefree state of relaxation; alteration of sensory perceptions including expansion of space and time; and/or a more vivid sense of touch, sight, smell, taste, and sound; a feeling of hunger, especially craving for sweets; and subtle changes in thought formation and expression."

Cocaine is a white crystalline powder extracted from the South American coca plant. Until recently, most users "snorted" cocaine; that is, they inhaled the powdered mixture. The effects appear within minutes, including dilated pupils and increased blood pressure, heart rate, breathing rate and body temperature. The user initially feels a sense of well-being and may feel more energetic or alert, but within 30 minutes to an hour, is likely to feel down and depressed.

Another form of cocaine is **freebase,** which is made by chemically converting the street drug into a basic form that can be smoked. This is an extremely dangerous, yet popular, practice. Freebase is smoked in a water pipe and is more dangerous than snorting because the cocaine reaches the brain within seconds, producing a sudden, intense high. The symptoms of freebasing cocaine include weight loss, increased heart rate and blood pressure, depression, paranoia and hallucinations.

The most pressing concern in recent times has been the use of **crack,** the street name given to freebase cocaine that has been processed from cocaine hydrochloride to a base, using ammonia or baking soda and water and heating it to remove the hydrochloride. It resembles hard shavings like slivers of soap and is sold in small vials, folding papers or heavy aluminum foil. Like freebase, it is smoked in a pipe. Alarmingly, one or two doses of crack can be obtained for from five to ten dollars, making it available to almost everyone. In fact, it has been called the "poor-man's coke."

Bennett and Hess (1994, p. 624) stress that drug addicts frequently become unfit for employment as their mental, emotional and physical condition deteriorates. They list the following possible symptoms of drug abuse:

- Sudden and dramatic changes in discipline and job performance.
- Unusual degrees of activity or inactivity.
- Sudden and irrational flareups.
- Significant change in personal appearance for the worse.
- Dilated pupils or wearing sunglasses at inappropriate times or places.
- Needle marks or razor cuts, or long sleeves constantly worn to hide such marks.
- Sudden attempts to borrow money or to steal.
- Frequent association with known drug abusers or pushers.

The addict is generally an unkempt person, appears drowsy, does not feel well, has copious quantities of tears or mucous in eyes and nose and suffers from alternate chills and fever. Needle marks resembling tatoos may be present in the curve of the arm at the elbow or, after prolonged drug use, in other areas of the body. Table 8–1 summarizes the physical symptoms, signs and dangers of drug abuse.

As noted by Wrich (1988, p. 64):

> The National Institute on Drug Abuse (NIDA) and the National Institute of Alcohol Abuse and Alcoholism (NIAAA) estimate that at least 10 percent of the workforce is afflicted with alcoholism or drug addiction. Another 10 to 15 percent is affected by the substance abuse of an immediate family member. Still more bear the scars of having grown up with an addicted or alcoholic parent.
>
> All in all, even after eliminating duplicates, at least 25 percent of any given workforce suffers from substance abuse—their own or someone else's.

This is one out of every four employees—certainly of importance to employers. Wrich (p. 64) further notes Alcohol, Drug Abuse and Mental Health Administration figures indicating that alcohol and drug abusers together cost the country more than $140 billion annually, including $100 billion in lost productivity.

Further, in *Largo Corp. v. Crespin* (1986), a Colorado Supreme Court ruled that an employer or proprietor could be held liable for the conduct of an intoxicated employee or patron if the drinking occurred at work or at the place of business.

Drug Testing

Kahler (1991, p. 8D) reports on several studies dealing with drug testing in U.S. businesses:

- A 1989 study by the Bureau of Labor Statistics found that 43 percent of the nation's largest businesses, having more than one thousand employees, had drug-testing programs. But since 90 percent of U.S. businesses are small, the bureau estimated that only 3 percent of establishments overall had drug-testing programs.
- The Institute for Drug-Free Workplace says 80 percent of *Fortune* 500 companies require preemployment drug testing, although only a few require random testing of their entire work force.

Table 8–1. Common Symptoms, Signs and Dangers of Drug Abuse

Drug Used	Physical Symptoms	Look For	Dangers
ALCOHOL (beer, wine, liquor)	Intoxication, slurred speech, unsteady walk, relaxation, relaxed inhibitions, impaired coordination, slowed reflexes.	Smell of alcohol on clothes or breath, intoxicated behavior, hangover, glazed eyes.	Addiction, accidents as a result of impaired ability and judgment, overdose when mixed with other depressants, heart and liver damage.
COCAINE (coke, rock, crack, base)	Brief intense euphoria, elevated blood pressure & heart rate, restlessness, excitement, feeling of well-being followed by depression.	Glass vials, glass pipe, white crystalline powder, razor blades, syringes, needle marks.	Addiction, heart attack, seizures, lung damage, severe depression, paranoia (see Stimulants).
MARIJUANA (pot, dope, grass, weed, herb, hash, joint)	Altered perceptions, red eyes, dry mouth, reduced concentration and coordination, euphoria, laughing, hunger.	Rolling papers, pipes, dried plant material, odor of burnt hemp rope, roach clips.	Panic reaction, impaired short-term memory, addiction.
HALLUCINOGENS acid, LSD, PCP, MDMA, Ecstasy psilocybin mushrooms, peyote)	Altered mood and perceptions, focus on detail, anxiety, panic, nausea synaesthesia (ex: smell colors, see sounds).	Capsules, tablets, "microdots," blotter squares.	Unpredictable behavior, emotional instability, violent behavior (with PCP).
INHALANTS (gas, aerosols, glue, nitrites, Rush, White out)	Nausea, dizziness, headaches, lack of coordination and control.	Odor of substance on clothing and breath, intoxication, drowsiness, poor muscular control.	Unconsciousness, suffocation, nausea and vomiting, damage to brain and central nervous system, sudden death.
NARCOTICS (Heroin [junk, dope, Black tar, China white], Demerol, Dilaudid [D's], Morphine, Codeine)	Euphoria, drowsiness, insensitivity to pain, nausea, vomiting, watery eyes, runny nose (see Depressants).	Needle marks on arms, needles, syringes, spoons, pinpoint pupils, cold moist skin.	Addiction, lethargy, weight loss, contamination from unsterile needles (hepatitis, AIDS), accidental overdose.

Table 8–1. Common Symptoms, Signs and Dangers of Drug Abuse (*Continued*)

Drug Used	Physical Symptoms	Look For	Dangers
STIMULANTS (speed, uppers, crank, Bam, black beauties, crystal, dexies, caffeine, nicotine, cocaine, amphetamines)	Alertness, talkativeness, wakefulness, increased blood pressure, loss of appetite, mood elevation.	Pills and capsules, loss of sleep and appetite, irritability or anxiety, weight loss, hyperactivity.	Fatigue leading to exhaustion, addiction, paranoia, depression, confusion, possibly hallucinations.
DEPRESSANTS (Barbiturates, Sedatives, Tranquilizers, [downers, tranks, ludes, reds, Valium, yellow jackets, alcohol])	Depressed breathing and heartbeat, intoxication, drowsiness, uncoordinated movements.	Capsules and pills, confused behavior, longer periods of sleep, slurred speech.	Possible overdose, especially in combination w/ alcohol; muscle rigidity; addiction, withdrawal & overdose require medical treatment.

- The *Journal of the American Medical Association* (JAMA) reported in November 1990 on a two-year study of more than 25,000 postal workers that found that employees who tested positive for marijuana had 55 percent more industrial accidents, 85 percent more injuries, and 78 percent more absenteeism than those who were free of drugs.

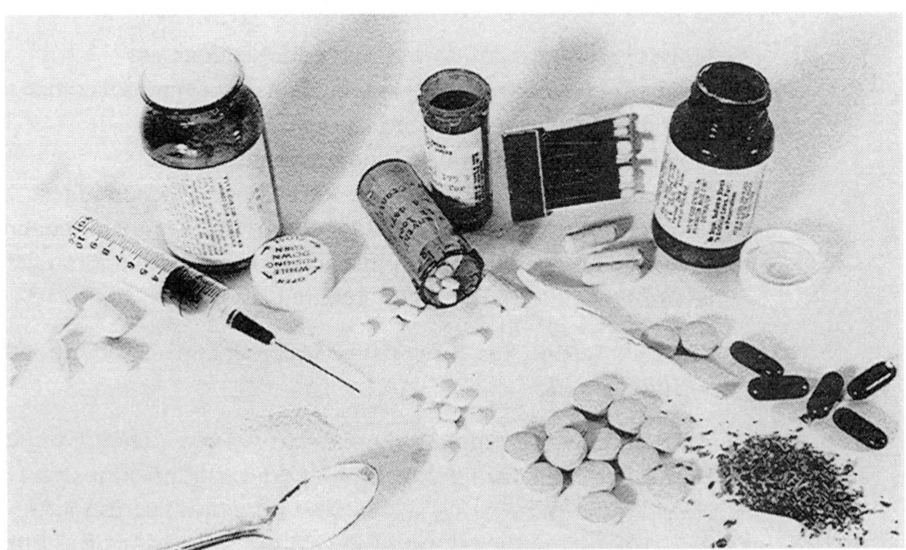

Commonly abused drugs and "tools" of the addict.

- Motorola will spend more than $1 million to implement the program in which every employee is tested for illicit drug use at least once every five years. For that investment, the company believes it will save more than $100 million in lost or unproductive employee time.

Lee Dogoloff, executive director of the American Council for Drug Education, says: "Drug testing has become a fact of life for anyone applying for a job in a major corporation. It's also a fact of life for anyone who holds a safety or security sensitive position in government" (Kahler, p. 8D).

According to King (1993, p. 22): "[A] drug-testing program can become a nightmare of bad feelings and legal entanglements. At its best, however, it can be a positive experience for everyone in the company and an important way to reduce a variety of workplace problems, from absenteeism to employee theft."

Carroll (1992, p. 56) stresses: "Leadership is the key word. Drug testing programs should be implemented at the top of the organization first and not at the bottom."

Most employees are in favor of such drug testing according to King (1993, p. 24):

> Study after study shows workers of all types giving employers the green light on drug and alcohol testing. A recent Gallup survey shows 97 percent of workers expressed favorable opinions about testing, and 26 percent said it was a necessity. . . .

Nearly 33 percent of the workers in the study said they knew of coworkers who used drugs; nearly 25 percent knew of substance abuse on the job.

To set up a drug-testing program, Wrich (1988, p. 66) suggests most employers do the following:

- Prepare a written policy and procedure statement.
- Train supervisors to recognize the signs and symptoms that would justify reasonable suspicion of drug use.
- Obtain and test a sample of the employee's urine.
- Confirm all positive tests with a second, more accurate test.
- Require testing without notice for those who complete treatment.
- Establish serious disciplinary measures, often termination, for those who test positive after undergoing treatment.

To make a drug-testing initiative (DTI) effective, Wrich (p. 68) says an organization should:

- Have an effective employee assistance program already in place.
- Familiarize itself with the technical and legal limitations of a DTI and consider the possible negative effect on employee relations.
- Place control and direction of the DTI in the hands of its human resource department with input from its legal department, not the other way around.

- Convince supervisors and employees of the need for drug testing and give them reason to trust and support the program.
- Require drug testing of everyone in the organization from the CEO on down.
- Establish criteria in advance for maintaining confidentiality and evaluating effectiveness.

King (p. 25) suggests that management announce that the drug-testing program will begin with new applicants immediately and that it will extend to current employees in 30 days. This gives present employees a chance to "clean up their act before the program goes into effect, which is exactly the desired effect. Prevention, not detection, is the objective."

Evans (1992, p. 48) states: "Drug testing decreases drug-related employee turnover and theft by helping to keep drug abusers out of the workplace." Evans (p. 53) concludes: "The use of drug testing is on the rise because it is proving its value. Simple, easy-to-use tests that provide an on-site capability expand an employer's ability to manage a healthy, productive, and profitable work force."

A Case Against Drug Testing. Bearman (1988, p. 67) makes a case against drug testing, saying:

> Employees have been known to smuggle in clean urine, . . . to drink large quantities of water to dilute their samples, and even to obtain prescriptions for legal drugs known to test positive. . . .
>
> The mere indication of the drug does not tell us whether the employee has used the drug once or a hundred times. . . .
>
> Ibuprofen, a painkiller found in Advil, Datril, Rufen, and other over-the-counter medications can cause a false positive for marijuana. Ephedrin, an ingredient of Nyquil, can test positive for amphetamines. Dextromathorphan, found in many cough suppressants, has tested positive for opiates. False positives may also result from laboratory errors such as mislabeling urine or transposing results, or from improperly cleaned equipment, incompetence, or out-and-out fraud. . . .
>
> In a litigious society, employers are well-advised to do two confirmatory tests. . . .
>
> Even without litigation, testing is expensive. Most tests range from $7.50 to $70 each and companies must add the costs of administration, supervision, and lost work time. Last but hardly least, the cost to employee morale cannot be measured.

In *James T. Hazlett v. Martin Chevrolet Inc.* (1987), an Ohio Supreme Court ruled that an employer did not violate the state's handicap laws by firing an employee addicted to drugs. But in *Glide Lumber Products Company v. Employment Division* (1987), an Oregon court of appeals ruled that a positive drug test, by itself, was not sufficient grounds to fire an employee. The employer must also show that the drug use negatively affected the employee's job performance.

In *National Treasury Employees Union v. Von Raab* (1989), the Court ruled that an employer, the U.S. Customs Service, could require job applicants applying for sensitive positions to undergo drug and alcohol testing. Such testing did not violate an employee's Fourth Amendment privacy rights.

An Alternative Method of Drug Testing. The Old Town Trolley in San Diego tests strictly for impairment using a 30-second computer examination that checks hand-eye coordination and psychomotor responses. The test detects motor impairment whether it is caused by drugs, alcohol, stress or fatigue. It is the impairment, not the cause, that is important. Every employee completes the test every morning.

Other Crimes

Several other crimes, such as shoplifting, bad-check writing, espionage and sabotage are discussed in following chapters, as they relate more specifically to certain types of establishments.

Enforcing Proprietary Rights

Not all crimes will be prevented. When they are not, security responsibilities change. According to the Rand Report (Kakalik and Wildhorn, 1977, p. 303):

> While many business organizations hire private policemen for the deterrence effect that results from their mere physical presence, they also expect their private security officers to take certain actions when confronted with disturbances, crimes, and threats to life and property. Therefore private security officers perform various law enforcement and protection functions, including arresting and detaining suspected shoplifters, ejecting persons from private property, quieting disturbances, and defending against potential attackers. These activities, akin to public police functions, may create a great risk of infringement upon the rights of innocent citizens. . . .
>
> In general the major contract agency will attempt to restrain the apprehension, search, and questioning activities of their personnel. . . . [W]henever possible all matters of arrest and search [are] turned over the local police authorities.

It is often not possible to simply leave the matter up to local authorities, however. Security managers are expected to *act* to protect the assets of their employers.

Security managers may be called on to enforce the following rights:

- Prevent trespassing.
- Control conduct of persons legally on premises.
- Defend self, others and property.
- Prevent the commission of a crime.

How these rights are enforced varies from establishment to establishment. Standards and procedures for arresting, searching and questioning persons should be clearly defined, because mistakes in these areas can result in either criminal or civil lawsuits, or both. Security managers should be thoroughly familiar with their state laws regarding the enforcement activities of private security. As in other areas of private security, common sense and reasonable actions are critical.

EXPELLING, DETAINING AND ARRESTING

To prevent trespassing or to control the conduct of persons legally on the premises, private security personnel may be used in retail establishments as plainclothes personnel to detect shoplifters; in industrial complexes as patrols to deter burglars; in offices as access control personnel or at sporting and entertainment events to expel gate-crashers and control or expel unruly spectators. Officers can use reasonable force to do so, if needed. Frequently, however, the person being expelled will consent to leave. In such cases, no force is justified.

In many states, private security personnel can do the following:

- Detain persons suspected of shoplifting.
- Make a citizen's arrest of persons who commit a misdemeanor in their presence.
- Make a citizen's arrest of persons who commit a felony if they have probable cause.

The report of the Task Force on Private Security (1976, p. 391) notes:

> The power of citizen's arrest is not a simple matter. The arrest power is complex and often ambiguous. It may be filled with legal pitfalls and may depend on a number of legal distinctions, such as the nature of the crime being committed, proof of actual presence, and the time and place of the incident.
>
> Because of these difficulties, the private security worker has to know the laws of the local jurisdiction. Improper action in making an arrest can expose the security worker and his employer to civil suits involving charges of false imprisonment, battery, assault, and malicious prosecution. An example of the seriousness of improper arrests by security personnel, as noted in *Security Systems Digest,* is the New York case in which a woman was awarded $1.1 million by the jury in a false arrest and wrongful detention civil suit.

Table 8–2 summarizes the statutory arrest authority of private citizens in the 30 states having such statutes.

Every citizen has the right to arrest a person who is committing or has committed a crime and to turn that person over to the local police. This is

Table 8–2. Statutory Arrest Authority of Private Citizens*

	Minor Offense											Major Offense												Certainty of Correct Arrest			
	Type							*Knowledge Required*				*Type*						*Knowledge Required*									
	Crime	Misdemeanor amounting to a breach of the peace	Breach of the peace	Public offense	Offense	Offense other than an ordinance	Indictable offense	Presence	Immediate knowledge	View	Upon reasonable grounds that it is being committed	Felony	Larceny	Petit larceny	Crime involving physical injury to another	Crime	Crime involving theft or destruction of property	Committed in presence	Information a felony has been committed	View	Reasonable grounds to believe being committed	That felony has been committed in fact	Is escaping or attempting	Summoned by peace officer to assist in arrest	Is in the act of committing	Reasonable grounds to believe person arrested committed	Probable cause
Alabama				X				X				X										X				X	
Alaska	X							X				X										X				X	
Arizona		X						X				X										X				X	
Arkansas												X									X					X	
California				X				X				X										X				X	
Colorado	X							X								X		X									
Georgia					X			X	X			X						X					X			X	
Hawaii	X							X								X		X							X		
Idaho				X				X				X										X				X	
Illinois						X					X	X									X						
Iowa				X				X				X										X				X	
Kentucky												X										X				X	
Louisiana												X										X					
Michigan												X						X				X		X			
Minnesota				X				X				X										X				X	
Mississippi			X				X	X				X										X				X	
Montana					X			X				X										X				X	
Nebraska												X		X								X				X	
Nevada				X				X				X										X				X	
New York					X			X				X										X					
N. Carolina**			X									X			X		X							X			X
N. Dakota				X				X				X										X				X	
Ohio												X									X	X				X	
Oklahoma				X				X				X										X				X	
Oregon	X							X					X			X		X									X
S. Carolina												X							X	X							
S. Dakota				X				X				X										X				X	
Tennessee				X				X				X										X				X	
Texas			X					X		X		X						X		X							
Utah				X				X				X										X				X	
Wyoming												X		X								X				X	

SOURCE: *Private Security*, Report of the Task Force on Private Security, National Advisory Committee on Criminal Justice Standards and Goals. Washington, DC: U.S. Government Printing Office, 1976.
*For specific authority see referenced state code. **Statute eliminates use of word "arrest" and replaces with "detention."

called a **citizen's arrest.** However, the extent and power of citizen's arrest authority varies from state to state. Arrest power often depends on whether the offense is a felony or a misdemeanor. In most states, citizens can make an arrest for a misdemeanor only if they actually see the crime committed. They can make an arrest for a felony if they know a felony has been committed and they are reasonably sure the person they arrest committed it.

A citizen's arrest is valid only if the person making the arrest intends to turn the suspect over to local law enforcement officers as soon as possible. The arrested person cannot be detained for questioning or to obtain a confession. Security officers can be sued for an unreasonable delay in turning a suspect over to the police.

In many states, exceptions to the preceding restrictions on arrests are made for instances involving shoplifting. Because most cases of shoplifting are misdemeanors and are not always witnessed by security officers, and because many cases of shoplifting are not prosecuted, several states stipulate that a person suspected of shoplifting can be *detained* for questioning and sometimes for searching. Detention differs from formal arrest in that arrest requires the suspect to be turned over to the authorities.

If an arrest is made, the arrested person must be told the reason for the arrest. Often a citizen's arrest certificate is completed by the arresting citizen (see Figure 8–2).

The Use of Force

> Force can be used only when and to the extent that it is necessary. Deadly force can be used only to protect human life.

What is "reasonable" force depends on the nature of the interest being protected, the kind of act being resisted and the specific facts in a given situation. Additionally, the amount of force allowed often depends on what right is being defended. If property rights are involved, a request for voluntary cooperation should precede any use of force. If only property is involved, the use of deadly force, a gun, for instance, is *not* permitted.

Use of deadly force to prevent a crime is usually allowed only if the crime threatens life and no other means can prevent the crime. However, some jurisdictions do allow use of deadly force to prevent some felonies.

Force in *self-defense* is limited to that which is necessary to protect against a threatened injury. It is not reasonable to use force calculated to inflict death or serious bodily harm unless a person believes he or she is in similar danger and there is no other safe means of defense.

The question of use of deadly force most frequently arises in instances when security officers have used a gun to fulfill their responsibilities. Security officers who are required to carry a gun should be thoroughly trained in its use. Standard 2.6 of the Private Security Task Force Report (1976, pp. 107–8)

CERTIFICATE AND DECLARATION OF ARREST BY PRIVATE PERSON AND DELIVERY OF PERSON SO ARRESTED TO PEACE OFFICER

DATE ______________________
TIME ______________________
PLACE ______________________

I, ____________, hereby declare and certify that I have arrested
(NAME) ______________________
(ADDRESS) ______________________
for the following reasons: ______________________________________

____

____

____

____

____

and do hereby request and demand that you, ____________, a peace officer, take and conduct this person whom I have arrested to the nearest magistrate, to be dealt with according to law; and if no magistrate can be contacted before tomorrow morning, then to conduct this person to jail for safe keeping until the required appearance can be arranged before such magistrate, at which time I shall be present, and I will then and there sign, under oath, the appropriate complaint against this person for the offense which this person has committed, and for which I made this arrest; and I will then and there, or thereafter as soon as this criminal action or cause can be heard, testify under oath of and concerning the facts and circumstances involved herein. I will save said officer harmless from any and all claim for damage of any kind, nature and description arising out of his or her acts at my direction.

Name of private person making this arrest

____

Address ______________________

Peace Officer Witnesses to this statement

____

____

____

Figure 8–2. Sample Citizen Arrest Form

stresses that "employees should not be allowed to carry firearms while performing private security duties unless they can demonstrate competency and proficiency in their use." Suggested training includes legal and policy restraints, firearms safety and care and shooting ability.

INVESTIGATING

According to the Private Security Task Force Report (1976, p. 24), investigative personnel are primarily concerned with obtaining information about any of the following:

- Crime or wrongs done or threatened.

- The identity, habits, conduct, movements, whereabouts, affiliations, associations, transactions, reputation, or character of any person, group of persons, association, organization, society, other groups or persons or partnership or corporation.
- Preemployment background check of personnel applicants.
- The conduct, honesty, efficiency, loyalty, or activities of employees, agents, contractors, and subcontractors.
- Incidents and illicit or illegal activities by persons against the employer or employer's property.
- Retail shoplifting.
- Internal theft by employees or other employee crime.
- The truth or falsity of any statement or representation.
- The location or recovery of lost or stolen property.
- The causes and origin of or responsibility for fires, libels or slanders, losses, accidents, damage, or injuries to real or personal property.
- The credibility of information, witnesses, or other persons.
- The securing of evidence to be used before investigating committees or boards of award or arbitration or in the trial of civil or criminal cases and the preparation thereof.

The Task Force Report (p. 9) notes that "investigative services may include preemployment investigation, surveillance, internal theft problems, undercover investigations, criminal investigations, polygraph examinations, and personal and property protection."

The Employee Polygraph Protection Act stipulates that a lie detector can be used in the context of an ongoing investigation if the following conditions are met:

- The employer's business suffers the loss of injury and the wrongdoing was intentional.
- The employee must have had access to the property.
- There must be reasonable suspicion that the employee was involved.
- The employee must be given a statement explaining these facts before the test.

The important responsibility of investigation is discussed in depth in Chapter 12. Investigations may involve searching as well as interviewing and interrogating.

SEARCHING

The law clearly establishes the right of an arresting officer to search a person legally taken into custody to determine if the arrested person has a weapon that could cause harm to the officer or others. Any person who has been apprehended for committing a serious crime (a felony) should be searched. Some agencies advise their security officers to treat persons arrested for a felony as though they would kill the officer if given the chance.

> Security officers usually have the authority to search a suspect's person and anything the person is carrying if the officers have a legitimate reason for detaining or arresting the suspect.

Most security searches do not involve arrests, however. They are conducted based on an established policy such as those discussed in Chapter 7 and involve cars, lunch boxes, lockers, purses, bags and boxes. According to the Rand Report (Kakalik and Wildhorn, 1977, p. 324):

> The law of searches in the private sector has simply not been developed as it has in the public-police sector.
>
> The common-law right of self-defense might justify reasonable searches for weapons, but only where there is reasonable ground to fear imminent attack by use of a concealed weapon. Under the common law, the arresting individual is empowered to search a suspect who is *already under arrest*. . . . However, this power is limited to cases of formal arrest (i.e. where the person will be turned over to the authorities), not mere detention. . . . Additionally some states authorize private citizens in arresting a person to search for incriminating evidence about the person.

Even without an arrest, the common-law privilege of reclaiming stolen property would tend to support searching persons suspected of stealing. It is preferable if consent for the search can be obtained.

> Any search must be conducted reasonably with the least possible use of force, intimidation or embarrassment.

Searches should be conducted in private, except in emergencies. It is best to have the person conducting the search be of the same sex as the suspect, or, if this is not possible, to have a person of the same sex as the suspect be a witness to the search. Any weapons or evidence found during the search should be turned over to the local authorities if the person is arrested by security personnel. Stolen property found during such a search may be reclaimed by the rightful owner if no prosecution is to be undertaken.

In *United States v. Tartaglia* (1989), the Supreme Court ruled that a railroad investigator and Drug Enforcement Administration (DEA) agents did not violate the defendant's Fourth Amendment rights when they acted on a tip about drugs being transported on an Amtrak train. The investigator and DEA agents located drugs in the defendant's suitcase with the assistance of drug-sniffing dogs.

INTERVIEWING AND INTERROGATING

Security personnel are frequently responsible for questioning witnesses to or persons suspected of crime.

> An **interview** is a controlled conversation with witnesses to or victims of a crime. An **interrogation** is a controlled conversation with persons suspected of direct or indirect involvement in a crime.

In actual practice, the difference between these two information-gathering processes is often blurred. What begins as an interview may end up as an interrogation. Security personnel should be instructed on how to make their questioning as efficient and effective as possible.

> Interviewing and interrogating will be more effective if you:
>
> - Prepare in advance.
> - Obtain the information as soon as possible.
> - Use a private setting and eliminate physical barriers.
> - Establish rapport.
> - Encourage conversation.
> - Ask simple questions one at a time.
> - Listen and observe.

Preparation

If circumstances allow, the interviewer should learn as much as possible about the incident under investigation, including what information is needed and what relationship the person to be questioned has to the incident. Is the person friendly or hostile? Emotionally involved or an objective outsider?

Random questioning is seldom successful because it lacks direction and can indicate to the person being questioned that the interviewer is not prepared or does not know much about the incident.

Timing

It is usually best to obtain information as soon as possible after an incident. People remember details better and also have less chance to fabricate a story or to think about the implications of becoming involved.

Sometimes, however, circumstances prevent immediate questioning. For example, it is best to delay questioning people who are emotionally upset. When emotions increase, memory decreases. Likewise, liquor, drugs or physical discomfort may hinder effective communication. Someone who is cold, sleepy, hungry or injured will usually be more concerned with his or her own condition than with answering questions.

Setting

Whenever possible, interviews and interrogations should be conducted in private. People who fear their statements may be overheard are frequently reluctant to talk. Interruptions can also break a person's train of thought. Any outside interference, such as telephones ringing, noises from traffic passing or office activity, detracts from the effectiveness of an inquiry.

Sometimes, however, the urgency of a situation requires that the questioning be done under adverse conditions. For example, private security officers may have to deal with a large crowd of people whose emotions are running high, with people shouting and contradicting one another. Obtaining accurate information under such circumstances is extremely difficult.

Physical barriers, such as a desk or counter, can also hinder effective communication and should be eliminated whenever possible.

Rapport

The first few minutes of the conversation are important in establishing a friendly relationship, or rapport. This is accomplished by showing a sincere interest in the person being questioned, respecting the person's opinions and reactions and trying to show the importance of cooperation. Frequently a person in a uniform with official credentials is seen as threatening. Some people fear or dislike authority and will not talk freely with officers of any kind. Others do not want to get involved. It takes skill to obtain information from such people.

Possible Restrictions on Interrogations

Public law enforcement officers are required to inform suspects of their constitutional rights *before* any interrogation occurs. The well-known Miranda decision (*Miranda v. State of Arizona,* 1967) has specifically protected these rights since that time. Many police officers carry a card containing the rights of citizens suspected of involvement in a crime (Figure 8–3).

Suspects can give up these rights (waive them), but if they do so, the waiver is usually obtained in writing to protect the officer.

Any statements or confessions resulting from police interrogation of a person in custody, under arrest or accused of a crime are not admissible as evidence unless the appropriate warnings *precede* the interrogation.

The courts have not clearly established whether the same restrictions apply to private security officers. Lower courts addressing the issue have not yet required security officers to precede interrogations with a recital of the suspect's Miranda rights.

MIRANDA WARNING

1) YOU HAVE THE RIGHT TO REMAIN SILENT.
2) IF YOU GIVE UP THE RIGHT TO REMAIN SILENT, ANYTHING YOU SAY CAN AND WILL BE USED AGAINST YOU IN A COURT OF LAW.
3) YOU HAVE THE RIGHT TO SPEAK WITH AN ATTORNEY AND TO HAVE THE ATTORNEY PRESENT DURING QUESTIONING.
4) IF YOU SO DESIRE AND CANNOT AFFORD ONE, AN ATTORNEY WILL BE APPOINTED FOR YOU WITHOUT CHARGE BEFORE QUESTIONING.

WAIVER

1) DO YOU UNDERSTAND EACH OF THESE RIGHTS I HAVE READ TO YOU?
2) HAVING THESE RIGHTS IN MIND, DO YOU WISH TO GIVE UP YOUR RIGHTS AS I HAVE EXPLAINED TO YOU AND TALK TO ME NOW?

Figure 8–3. Sample Card Listing Suspect's Rights—Miranda Warning

Some states have ruled that Miranda warnings do not apply to private security interviews because they are not done under the coercive threat of arrest by the police. In a California case (*In re Deborah C.*; 635 F.2d 446), a store detective placed a suspect under arrest without advising the suspect of her Miranda rights. The California Supreme Court held that Miranda warnings are not required because private security officers "don't enjoy the psychological advantage of official authority, which is a major tool of coercion." Employers, however, can use other forms of coercion, most notably the threat of terminating employment. On the other hand, businesses exist to make a profit and are not obligated to put the welfare of an employee above that of the company. A correlation often exists between the level of position, amount of power and socioeconomic standing of the employee in the company, and the subsequent amount of disciplinary action received. The higher a person's position in a company, the less disciplinary action is likely to be applied.

Despite the lack of an official ruling, many courts and judges require security officers to notify a suspect of these rights on the basis that they are, in reality, attempting to enforce the law, and in doing so must abide by public law enforcement standards. For example, in *People v. Haydel* (1973), the court ruled, in effect, that private store detectives used state law as authority and, therefore, were acting as agents of the state in the same manner as public police officers:

> The exclusionary rule is designed to deter illegal conduct by public officials, hence it is inoperative when the evidence is gained by a private citizen not acting as a public agent. The California Supreme Court has recognized, nevertheless, that the well trained and well financed private security forces of business establishments are heavily involved in law enforcement, that state laws such as Penal Code, Section 837, the citizen's arrest statute, blur the line between public and private law enforcement.

In *Wold v. State* (1989), a Minnesota court ruled that a confession given by a suspect under the influence of drugs or alcohol is admissible at trial.

Although this chapter has emphasized the role of the security officer in dealing with potential and actual crimes, remember that the majority of the security manager's time is spent dealing with noncriminal matters.

THE TREND TOWARD TRANSFERRING POLICE TASKS TO PRIVATE SECURITY

According to the National Institute of Justice, the number of security officers has increased by 50 percent over the last 10 years, and there are indications projecting an even further expansion. For example, there exists grave concern about the ability of many police departments to competently investigate the technical complexities of corporate crime, computer crime, commercial bribery and industrial espionage.

Maxwell (1993, p. 313) describes a case of particular interest to security managers: *People v. Stormer* (1987). This case involved a large resort hotel, the Sagamore, located on an island connected with the mainland only by a causeway. The Warren County Sheriff's Department had been informed that they need not patrol the resort area and that their presence was not needed unless requested. The hotel was experiencing a problem of thefts from guests' rooms, so security personnel planted $260 in a room assigned to the maid they suspected of the thefts. They observed her enter the room, and when she left and they checked the room, the money was gone. Members of the Sagamore security force then searched the defendant's car without her knowledge and found $260 in a paper bag. When they confronted the defendant, she denied stealing the money. She was detained by the security officers until the Warren County Sheriff's Department took her into custody. Her attorney claimed that the seizure of the money was the result of an illegal search and hence should be excluded from the trial.

The court agreed. It cited a relatively recent case ruled on by the California Supreme Court (*People v. Virginia Alvinia Zelinski*) in which the court stated:

> [I]n any case where private security personnel assert the power of the state to make an arrest or to detain another person for transfer to custody of the state, the state involvement is sufficient for the court to enforce the proper exercise of that power by excluding the fruits of illegal abuse thereof.

In the *Zelinski* case, security personnel turned a shoplifter over to local authorities rather than demanding return of the stolen merchandise and then releasing the shoplifter.

By analogy, according to Maxwell (1993, p. 314): "[T]he Sagamore's interest could have been vindicated by the confiscation of the $260.00 from the defendant and the termination of her services. By going further and detaining her for eventual criminal process the Sagamore's security personnel were promoting society's interest and, as such, the safeguards provided by the Fourth Amendment [against unreasonable searches and seizures] were activated."

Maxwell cautions that this ruling applies to only one county in the country but also suggests that it may be a "forerunner of things to come." As noted by Maxwell (p. 314):

> Security managers may want to determine if their security forces are solely in control and if therefore, routine police patrols are not necessary, if citizens'

privacy rights are increasingly jeopardized because their security staffs replace local law enforcement authorities, and if the security force is engaged in a public function.

SUMMARY

Security managers are responsible for preventing or reducing losses caused by criminal or civil offenses. A crime is an offense against the state for which punishment is sought. In contrast, a tort is an offense against an individual for which restitution is sought. A single action may be classified as both a crime and a tort.

The crimes of most concern to private security are larceny/theft, burglary, robbery, trespassing, vandalism, assault, arson; white-collar crime, including embezzlement, bad checks and credit card fraud; and drugs in the workplace.

Losses from larceny/theft might be prevented or reduced by using the basic security equipment and procedures to deter employee pilferage and theft by nonemployees. Loss from burglary might be prevented or reduced by installing and using good locks, adequate indoor and outdoor lighting and an alarm system, possibly supplemented with security patrols; keeping valuables in a burglar-resistant safe or vault; keeping a minimum amount of cash on hand; leaving cash registers open and empty at closing time and being sure that all security equipment is functional before leaving.

Losses from robbery might be prevented or reduced by training employees how to react if a robbery occurs; by not building up cash; by using armed couriers to transport cash; by establishing strict opening and closing procedures and by using extreme caution if someone seeks entrance to the facility after hours.

Larceny/theft, burglary and robbery are often confused. Larceny/theft is the unlawful taking of the property of another without unlawful entrance or confrontation. Burglary includes unlawful taking and unlawful entry. Robbery includes unlawful taking and confrontation, that is, force or the threat of force.

Trespassing and vandalism can be prevented or reduced by strict access controls, security lighting, signs and patrols. Assaults might be reduced by adequate lighting, patrols, communications systems and/or escort services.

Security managers should suspect arson in fires that have more than one point of origin; deviate from normal burning patterns; show evidence of trailers; show evidence of having been accelerated; indicate an abnormal amount of air, fuel or heat present; reveal evidence of incendiary igniters at the point of origin or produce odors or smoke of a color associated with substances not normally present at the scene.

White-collar crime is business-related crime. One prevalent type of white-collar crime of special concern to private security managers is pilferage, or internal theft, a form of larceny. Bad checks and credit card fraud are also white-collar crimes.

Drugs commonly abused in the workplace include alcohol, marijuana and cocaine—snorted or smoked as freebase or crack.

Not all crimes will be prevented. Security managers may be called on to enforce such rights as preventing trespassing, controlling the conduct of persons legally on the premises, defending lives or property or preventing the commission of a crime. In many states, private security personnel can detain persons suspected of shoplifting and make a citizen's arrest. Force can be used only when and to an extent that is reasonable and necessary. Deadly force can be used only to protect human life. Security officers also usually have the authority to search a suspect's person and anything the person is carrying if the officers have a legitimate reason for detaining or arresting the suspect. Any search must be conducted reasonably and with the least possible use of force, intimidation or embarrassment to the suspect.

Security personnel may also be called upon to question witnesses and/or suspects. An interview is a controlled conversation with witnesses to or victims of crimes. An interrogation is a controlled conversation with persons suspected of direct or indirect involvement in a crime.

Interviewing and interrogating will be more effective if the person doing the questioning prepares in advance, obtains the information as soon as possible, uses a private setting and eliminates physical barriers, establishes rapport, encourages conversation, asks simple questions one at a time, listens and observes.

✓ APPLICATION

1. While on patrol for the Smithtown Security Services, Kathy Ross pulls into the yard of a large warehouse where many semitrailer trucks are parked. As she patrols, her vehicle headlights shine on two juveniles hiding behind one of the tractor wheels. She also notices that the tire is going flat. As she orders the two juveniles to come out, she notices that one of them throws an instrument away. She has them retrieve it and, on inspection, sees it is an icepick. Further investigation reveals that two tires are flat, both having been punctured by what appears to be an icepick. Officer Ross arrests the juveniles and takes them to the police station. The youngsters, ages 12 and 13, have had extensive past contacts with police, all as the result of acts of vandalism.

   As manager of the Smithtown Security Services, how would you evaluate Officer Ross's actions?

2. The office manager of the Downtown Manufacturing Company states to the security manager that she has just apprehended Joe Myers, an employee, carrying an office typewriter out the side door of the building, and she is detaining him. The office manager demands that the security manager call the police and have Myers charged with robbery. If you were the security manager, how would you respond to this demand?

3. You are the security director called by the president of the Uptown Department Store to investigate the open, empty safe the president discovered

when he went into his office. How would you begin the investigation? What information would you need to obtain?

4. As a member of the Housing Authority Security Police, you are confronted with numerous investigations concerning a rash of arson fires. You are requested to prepare a presentation about what the statistics of the current FBI Uniform Crime Report reveal about the patterns, arrests and types of arson most frequently committed. Obtain from the library the latest FBI Uniform Crime Report and give a presentation to the class as if you were talking to the residents of a public housing complex.

CRITICAL THINKING EXERCISE

USE OF DEADLY FORCE

STATUTORY AND COMMON LAW

Private security guards hired to maintain order and protect business invitees have no obligation to retreat when acting in course of their employment but may meet deadly force with deadly force. To seek refuge under the doctrine of self-defense, security guards must establish that their own aggressive acts did not precipitate the conflict, that they entertained an honest belief at the time that they were in imminent danger of death or serious bodily harm and that their only recourse lay in physically repelling the attack.

FACTS OF THE CASE

On August 12, about 2:30 P.M., George Peaks, accompanied by a woman who had known him for several years, entered the Colonial Theater in Detroit to attend a movie. The Colonial is a 24-hour theater located near downtown where disturbances are not uncommon. At the concession stand in the lobby, Peaks ordered two bags of buttered popcorn. He asked the sales person, Gladys Campbell, for some salt. Campbell pointed to a red plastic container that looked like a catsup dispenser and said that the salt was in it. Peaks claimed that the container was not sanitary and he refused to use it. Even though Campbell explained that previous patrons had taken the other salt shakers and this one was the only shaker left, Peaks loudly demanded that he be given a regular salt shaker.

Hearing the disturbance, the manager, Frederick Kreger, came to try to settle the problem. For several minutes Kreger tried to explain and apologize for the salt shaker situation. Peaks did not stop shouting and would not let Kreger even finish a sentence. By this time a crowd of 15 to 20 people had gathered to observe the controversy. Kreger motioned for Joe Johnson, the security guard hired from the Gardner Security Agency, for help because Peaks was becoming increasingly aggressive.

Johnson attempted to find out from Peaks what was wrong and what could be done to satisfy him. Not knowing what could satisfy Peaks, Johnson asked Campbell to refund Peaks the price of the popcorn. Peaks did not pick up the money, so Johnson thrust it at him. They appeared to be shoving each other for several seconds. Peaks continually refused the money. He swore at Johnson and then jabbed at Johnson's face, hitting him on the side of his jaw. Peaks then reached into his coat pocket with his right hand, at which time Johnson pulled his gun. With his left arm, Peaks pushed at Johnson, and both of them seemed to lose their balance. While falling backward from the shove, Johnson discharged his gun, hitting Peaks once in the chest.

The bullet entered Peaks' chest, traveled upward, and lodged in the muscles of his neck. He was pronounced dead on arrival at the Municipal Hospital. The medical examiner reported that Peaks, at 6′4" and 175 pounds, was legally intoxicated at the time of his death. The woman who went with him to the theater said he always had been "strong as a bull" and did not easily change his mind. Peaks was found to be unarmed, and there were no traces of drugs on or in his body.

Joe Johnson, the security guard, weighed 139 pounds and was 5′4" tall.

Issues and Questions

1. Did the security guard, who was employed at a theater where noisy disturbances were common, exceed the bounds of law? Was the security guard possibly able to retreat or was it necessary that he use deadly force?

- **a.** Despite the fact that the security guard was dealing with a difficult situation, the decision to take a life can only be countenanced in the most extreme and compelling circumstances. There was nothing extreme or compelling in this case sufficient to justify use of deadly force. Neither a salt shaker nor the price of a bag of popcorn was worth a contest of wills. It is inexcusable for picking a fight with an inebriated customer in the first place. The security officer should have agreed with the man, apologized and offered to go out and buy him a salt shaker in a neighborhood store.
- **b.** The guard must provide three elements: (1) his own actions did not precipitate the conflict, (2) he believed he was in imminent danger of death or serious bodily harm and (3) his only recourse lay in physically repelling an attack. He obviously felt he was in danger. However, one out of three elements is not quite enough, and even that is doubted.
- **c.** A private security guard is always under a duty to retreat, when possible, to a safe haven when attacked on business premises. Joe Johnson made no effort to retreat and therefore failed in his duty to restrain from using deadly force, even though the firing of the shot was possibly accidental.
- **d.** If the security guard had attempted to flee when confronted with the threat of a deadly attack, the aggressor might have vented his anger on others nearby, and then the guard and his employer would have been held accountable for the havoc wreaked in his absence. A guard may use necessary and reasonable force to eject a person who refuses to

leave or persists in disorderly conduct. Although regrettable, the use of deadly force was probably accidental and thus not without reason.

e. To use deadly force against unproven although threatened acts of deadly force oversteps a security guard's lawful duty. A guard may request a disorderly patron to leave or may summon a police officer if force is necessary.

Discussion Questions

1. Private security officers are sometimes asked to arrest people. As a security director, what policies or guidelines would you adopt to cover these situations?
2. Discuss the advantages and disadvantages of private security officers carrying firearms.
3. What differences exist between interviewing a witness and interrogating a suspect?
4. Compare the statutory arrest authority of private citizens (Table 8–2) with those of public police officers in your state. How do the arrest powers of private security officers compare with those of public police officers in your state?
5. Why are some crimes divided into categories or degrees?

References

Addis, Karen K. "Company Crooks on the Line." *Security Management,* July 1992, pp. 36–42.

Bearman, David. "The Medical Case Against Drug Testing." *Security Management,* June 1988, p. 67.

Bennett, W. and Hess, K. M. *Criminal Investigation,* 4th ed. St. Paul, MN: West Publishing Company, 1994.

Benny, Daniel J. "Reducing the Threat of Internal Theft." *Security Management,* July 1992, p. 40.

Benson, Michael L.; Cullen, Francis T.; and Maakestad, William J. *Local Prosecutors and Corporate Crime.* Washington, DC: National Institute of Justice, Research in Brief, January 1993.

Braithwaite, John and Fisse, Brent. "Self-Regulation and the Control of Corporate Crime." *Private Policing,* by Clifford D. Shearing and Philip C. Stenning, eds. Beverly Hills, CA: Sage Publications, 1987, pp. 221–246.

Carroll, Charles R. "The Dilemma of Detoxing the Work Force." *Security Management,* May 1992, pp. 54–56.

Cunningham, W. C. and Taylor, T. H. *The Hallcrest Report: Private Security and Police in America.* Portland, OR: Chancellor Press, 1985.

Elig, Gene. "White-Collar Crime: The Silent Killer." *Security Concepts,* December 1993, pp. 1, 2.

Evans, David G. "A Dose of Drug Testing." *Security Management,* May 1992, pp. 48–53.

Gordon, Marsha. "Employee Theft." *IB (Independent Business),* July/August 1990, pp. 12–13.

Inciardi, J. A. and Binder, D. "Arson." In *Encyclopedia of Crime and Justice,* by Sanford H. Kadish, ed. New York: The Free Press, 1983, pp. 76–82.

Kahler, Kathryn. "Drug Testing Is No Longer Dreaded in the Workplace." (Minneapolis/ St. Paul) *Star Tribune,* January 20, 1991, p. 8D.

Kakalik, J. S. and Wildhorn, S. *The Private Police*. New York: Crane Russak, 1977 (The Rand Corporation).

King, Carl E. "Making Drug Testing a Positive Experience." *Security Management,* November 1993, pp. 22–26.

Maxwell, David A. *Private Security Law: Case Studies*. Stoneham, MA: Butterworth-Heinemann, 1993.

Private Security. Report of the Task Force on Private Security, National Advisory Committee on Criminal Justice Standards and Goals. Washington, DC: U.S. Government Printing Office, 1976.

Sharp, Arthur G. "White-Collar Crime: More Resources Needed to Combat Growing Trend." *Law and Order,* July 1994, pp. 91–96.

Thornton, William E.; McKinnon-Fowler, Ellen; and Kent, David R. "Stalking Security Statistics." *Security Management,* April 1991, pp. 54–58.

Turner, Dana L. and Stephenson, Richard G. "The Lure of White-Collar Crime." *Security Management,* February 1993, pp. 57–58.

Woods, Everett K. and Wallace, Donald H. "Investigating Arson: Coping with Constitutional Constraints." *Security Management,* November 1991, pp. 80–84.

Wrich, Manes T. "Beyond Testing: Coping with Drugs at Work." *Security Management,* June 1988, pp. 64–73.

Wrobleski, Henry M. and Hess, Kären M. *Introduction to Law Enforcement and Criminal Justice,* 4th ed. St. Paul, MN: West Publishing Company, 1993.

CASES

Glide Lumber Products Company v. Employment Division, 741 P.2d 907 (Or. App. 1987)
In re Deborah C., 635 P.2d 446 (Cal. 1981)
James T. Hazlett v. Martin Chevrolet, Inc., 1985 WL 9938 (Ohio App. 1985)
Largo Corp. v. Crespin, 727 P.2d 1098 (Colo. 1986)
Miranda v. State of Arizona, 384 U.S. 436, 86 S.Ct. 1602 (1966)
National Treasury Employees Union v. Von Raab, 489 U.S. 656, 109 S.Ct. 1384 (1989)
People v. Haydel, 109 Cal.Rptr. 222 (Cal. 1973)
People v. Stormer, 518 N.W.S.2d 351 (N.Y. 1987)
People v. Virginia Alvinia Zelinski, 594 P.2d 1000 (Cal. 1979)
United States v. Tartaglia, 864 F.2d 837 (1989)
Wold v. State, 430 N.W.2d 171 (Minn. 1988)

CHAPTER 9

ENHANCING INFORMATION/ COMPUTER SECURITY

DO YOU KNOW

- How valuable proprietary information may be obtained by competitors or criminals?
- Whether trash can be legally searched by others?
- What telecommunications security involves?
- What constitutes computer crime?
- How serious computer crime is?
- What the greatest threats to computer centers are?
- What legislation pertains to computer crime?
- What security measures can be taken to reduce losses from computer crime?
- What factors to consider when investigating a computer crime?
- Who the typical "electronic criminal" is?
- What the probability of detection of computer crimes and the risk of prosecution are?

CAN YOU DEFINE THESE TERMS?

check kiting
computer crime
computer virus
cyberspace
encryption
facsimile
faxpionage
hacker
industrial espionage
noncompete agreements
nondisclosure agreements
OPSEC
secrecy agreements
telecommunications
virtual corporation
virus

INTRODUCTION

Numerous security experts stress the importance of information:

- "[F]irst, information is an asset and, as such, it deserves protection" (Fay, 1994, p. 63).
- "Proprietary information—the lifeblood of the corporate body—must be immunized against outside agents for healthy profits" (Heffernan, 1992, p. 59).

- "Knowledge is no longer just power, it's money too. Big money" (Murray, 1992, p. 106).
- "Information is among the most costly and perishable of businesses' resources today" (Schweitzer, 1992, p. 53).
- "Information is now more important to success and survival of a business than access to capital" (Toffler, 1990, p. 3).
- "Business success in this high-tech world will belong to those who manage access to their corporate data" (Swartwood, 1993, p. 44).

This chapter begins by looking at the problem of information security and the specific threats that must be considered, including employees who divulge proprietary information, careless discarding of information and unsecured fax and telephone communications. This is followed by an in-depth discussion of computer security, including computer crime, the seriousness of the problem and the specific types of threats existing. Next, legislation related to computer crimes and security measures for computer systems are discussed. The chapter concludes with a brief discussion of investigating computer crime and prosecuting perpetrators of such crimes.

Problem of Information Security

According to Lukes (1994, p. 32): "[I]nformation theft has grown as rapidly as the technology to secure it. Some estimates place the cost of such theft as high as $500 billion per year for U.S. businesses alone."

Swartwood (1993, p. 42) cites the 1992 Proprietary and Technology Theft Survey, sponsored by the American Society for Industrial Security (ASIS), which found that 32 companies reported losses of $1.83 billion.

The ASIS's Standing Committee on Safeguarding Proprietary Information conducted a survey which found that 37 percent of those surveyed had experienced a theft or attempted theft of proprietary information (Heffernan, 1991, p. 39).

The scope of the problem of information security is summarized by Murray (1992, p. 106):

> Tapped phones. Bugged offices. Stolen papers. Covert recordings. Undercover employees. Phony repair people. Car phone monitors. Fax intercepts. Pretext calls. Dumpster divers. . . . Competitive intelligence professionals. Renegade employees. Foreign governments. The list goes on.

Competitive intelligence (CI) is a fact of life in the business world. In fact, those engaged in competitive intelligence have formed a professional association, the Society of Competitive Intelligence Professionals. They even have a code of ethics. However, as Littlejohn (1994, p. 134) cautions: "Problems arise when competitive intelligence activities cross the line and enter into industrial espionage, which is an everyday occurrence, due to the proliferation of former intelligence agents." According to Tanzer (1992, pp. 37–42):

> [CI] is a well-organized, well-educated, and abundantly resourceful worldwide army. What this means to the company as a whole and security managers specifically is simply this: The danger of losing business secrets and everything invested in them is greater than ever before.

Common targets of CI are research-and-development departments, marketing, manufacturing and production, and human resources. They may obtain their information from employees, facility tours, corporate publications, business associates, distributors, suppliers, maintenance workers—in fact, anyone associated with the business.

As noted by Fay (1994, p. 63): "The value that can be derived from information assets often is incalculable. The number of dollars can be enormous when viewed from the perspectives of what it costs to acquire information and the profits that can result from skillful use of that information."

Butler and Schultz (1993, p. 66) note:

> Corporate clients, wanting to know what their competition is up to, pay private investigators about $250 million every year. The competitive intelligence industry earns about $500 million annually. . . . [T]he Maryland Center for Business estimated U.S. business losses due to corporate espionage at more than $50 billion a year.

The threat of **industrial espionage** is not only a domestic threat, it is often a foreign threat as well, as noted by Scuro (1992, p. 78):

> [O]ur allies are aggressively conducting industrial espionage against American companies to gather economic information. This onslaught against industry only adds to the advantages held by many foreign countries in competing with American firms. . . .
>
> One of the most flagrant cases was by the French. French intelligence conducted a full-scale operation against the European offices of IBM, Texas Instruments, and other high-tech American companies. They planted spies in offices, intercepted communication, and used any other method they could to collect information about the companies.

Hansen (1992, p. 44) also describes the threats facing businesses following the end of the Cold War: "Businesses now face some experienced foes as Eastern European countries redirect the resources of their massive intelligence agencies from the political to the corporate spy arena." Hansen suggests that these are not the only threats:

> Equally formidable and more numerous threats exist at home where competitors, disgruntled employees, political terrorists, and blackmailers are ready to steal and use corporate information with potentially staggering consequences to their victims.

Specific Threats

> Specific threats to the security of proprietary information include employees, discarded information, unsecured telecommunication and acoustical surveillance.

Employees

Although most managers would agree that people are an organization's most important asset, they can also be their greatest liability.

According to Hansen (1992, p. 48): "Most information assets are lost through employee carelessness." This is an area security managers should focus on first. As noted by Syed and Totton (1992, p. 131): "Security starts with hiring the best personnel." In addition, employees must be made aware of what information is sensitive and not to be discussed with anyone. Many people who work with sensitive or secret material daily simply forget that not everyone knows what they know. They should not leave sensitive information lying around or dispose of it carelessly. Files should be kept locked as should offices in which employees using sensitive information work. Meeting rooms, likewise, should be kept locked when not in use to prevent their being "bugged." Employees should be instructed not to use cellular phones to discuss sensitive information.

Employees might also be asked to sign nondisclosure, noncompete and/or trade secrecy agreements. **Nondisclosure agreements** are usually requested of high-level executives, research-and-development personnel and other employees who have access to sensitive information. The agreements prohibit employees from disclosing sensitive information to outsiders. **Noncompete agreements** are designed to prevent employees from quitting and going to work for a competitor. **Secrecy agreements** are directed at individuals who come into contact with vital trade secrets of a business—for example, technicians called in to repair a vital piece of machinery. Such individuals may be asked to sign an agreement to keep such information confidential. As noted by Kochen (1994, p. 142):

> Incorporating the use of strict and enforceable nondisclosure, noncompete, and secrecy agreements as a normal course of business will strengthen a company's information security program. These legally binding contracts provide both a strong deterrent and, in the event of a breach, a tool for monetary compensation.

Vendors

Suppliers and distributors should also be included in the information security link. Those with access to what could be valuable information should be asked to sign nondisclosure agreements.

Visitors

Procedures to ensure that visitors do not obtain proprietary information were discussed in Chapter 5, including sign-in-and-out procedures, wearing badges, being escorted and being restricted to certain areas of a facility.

Discarded Information

Keough (1995, p. 24) cautions: "It is foolish to spend thousands of dollars on perimeter security guards and equipment just to hand over sensitive information to a waste paper or trash removal company."

All too often, sensitive or secret information is discarded in trash cans and then collected in plastic bags and put into a dumpster. Most dumpsters are in areas where the public has access to them. All people seeking information about a given company need to do is sort through the bags until they come across one with the envelopes bearing the name of their target and make off with that bag of trash.

This is perfectly legal in most states. The U.S. Supreme Court ruled in *California v. Greenwood et al.* (1988) that the Fourth Amendment protection against unreasonable searches does not apply to garbage left outside for collection.

> In most states, garbage in dumpsters can be legally searched.

Tanzer (1992, pp. 40–41) offers the story of a CI who approached a custodian working in a competitor's factory and offered to pay him to separate the trash from a specific area and turn it over to him. The custodian refused, explaining that he was already doing so for another competitor.

Keough (1995, p. 24) suggests that before documents are disposed of, it should be determined how sensitive the information is, how much information is involved and the medium—paper, magnetic or electronic. These factors will determine which disposal method is most appropriate: "trash disposal and recycling for nonsensitive materials; pulping, burning, shredding, grinding, and degaussing for more sensitive materials" (Keough, 1995, p. 24).

As government regulations become more strict regarding recycling, the disposal of sensitive documents may be even more problematic. As noted by Kornegay (1991, p. 96):

> [T]o refrain from destroying confidential or proprietary information before it is recycled is to ignore several potential risks: . . .
>
> - exposes the company to litigation.
> - breaches clients' confidence.
> - gives an unearned advantage to competitors or outside forces.

TELECOMMUNICATIONS

Telecommunications is the science of communicating by the transmission of electronic impulses, e.g., telegraph, telephone, fax, etc. Waltman (1994, p. 52) notes:

> In today's fast-paced and information-based business environment, companies communicate via cellular phones, faxes, and internal telephone systems, including private branch exchanges (PBXs) and voice mail systems (VMSs). Security managers must understand the inherent risks of these technologies to protect against the loss of proprietary information.

LeBeau (1994, p. 68) suggests: "The information superhighway has been billed as the road paved with opportunity for businesses and consumers alike, providing increased access to information and enabling new technologies to let you work better, smarter and faster. Unfortunately, it avails those same opportunities to hackers who make a living from cracking, stealing and selling access codes." LeBeau reports that toll fraud is a $2.3 billion business and that 70 percent of large telecommunications users have been victims of such fraud at a cost of almost $125,000 each.

Harowitz (1994, p. 54) cautions: "Before driving on the information superhighway, companies must make sure the trip will be a safe one." According to Harowitz, some seven million users in 70 countries are now linked by computers through 27,000 Internet networks, and it is estimated that by 1998 the user population will exceed 100 million.

Another caution is presented by Olick (1994, p. 12): "The 'information superhighway,' aka 'cyberspace,' that is paving the way for the rapid exchange of data to all connecting points may also be causing an increase in 'hackers' joy-riding their way right into your top-security computer systems."

Arneke (1994, p. 62) also notes: "More powerful communications systems are giving your adversaries a new route into your company's most sensitive information." He suggests (p. 63): "Digital encryption is the ultimate safety blanket for communicating information."

"Information," says Cullinane (1994, p. 36), "is transmitted across local area networks, wide area networks, the telephone system, cellular communications, satellite communications, radio frequency and soon by cable TV and even power companies. And we are still using the same physical protections we designed 15 years ago."

And, according to Kluepfel (1995, p. 40): "The old adage that the chain is only as strong as its weakest link has never been as true as it is today when applied to network security and integrity."

As noted by Wade (1993, p. 15A): "Polls indicate that an average of 60 percent of daily business communications is handled by telephone."

> Telecommunication security includes information communicated by voice, fax and computer using wirelines, microwave links, satellite systems and fiber-optic lines.

Unsecured Telephone Communications

Murray (1992, p. 113) contends:

> The telephone room is the most important room in most businesses. All phone conversations funnel through this room. It's a tapper's heaven and sabotage hell. . . . [T]he most vital room in business today probably doesn't even have a working lock on the door, a fire alarm, an intrusion detector, or even paint on the walls.

Wireless phones, intercoms and cellular phones pose a security risk in that others may intentionally or unintentionally hear messages that are transmitted. Satellite transmissions also are at risk, such as those used in teleconferencing. According to Heffernan (1992, p. 60): "With the right equipment, anyone within a satellite footprint—which could be a thousand miles across—can pick up the signal."

Unsecured Faxes

In the past few years, **facsimile** or fax machines have become common in most businesses, with an estimated 15 million stand-alone fax units and 15 million PC-based fax modems currently in use (Wenek, 1994, p. 57). Such machines make communication rapid and convenient, but also present a security risk. **Faxpionage**—unauthorized access to facsimile transmissions—is "one of the great hidden liabilities to the integrity of business operations" (Berry, 1991, p. 59). Berry gives as an example Donald Trump's withdrawal of a bid to buy American Airlines via fax in October 1989. When the withdrawal became known, stock plunged. Anyone who had access to Trump's fax line could have sold off his or her holdings while the prices were still high.

Wenek (1994, p. 57) notes: "Fax communication is the private sector's Achilles heel." Most fax machines are in nonsecured rooms. Faxes come in and can be read by anyone who happens to be in the room. Often they are stored to be read later—again by anyone who retrieves them. Wenek (1994, p. 57) suggests three features that can be added to fax machines to make basic fax communication more secure:

- Authentication—assuring the message is sent to the correct place, protecting against misdialing, switching errors and fax forgeries;
- Encryption—using code to prevent eavesdropping;
- Mailboxing—keeping received documents secure until they are retrieved by someone using a personal identification number (PIN).

Acoustical Surveillance

Chanaud (1993, p. 43) notes: "The amount of speech security needed is determined by the expected effort of the eavesdropper and several acoustical factors. These factors can be summarized in one sentence: Conversations are intelligible to the eavesdropper when the sound level of speech heard at the eavesdropping point is higher than the background sound level there." Chanaud (pp. 43–44) describes four levels of acoustical eavesdropping:

- Level I—a person passing by an open or partially open door accidently overhears sensitive information.
- Level II—an amateur using his or her ears or a simple listening device attempts to eavesdrop through an airduct, wall or ceiling.
- Level III—a professional surveillance person or company skilled in acoustical surveillance.
- Level IV—an eavesdropper from a government agency, domestic or foreign.

Monsanto Company has developed a metallized room-shielding material called Flectron which "is the best defense against the growing threat of corporate espionage," according to Moskowitz (1994, p. 58).

Other Threats

A unique security problem exists in safeguarding proprietary information within a **virtual corporation.** As noted by Englman (1993, p. 28): "In a virtual corporation, organizations form temporary partnerships in which each participating company brings to the table its core capabilities." The problem becomes, How can these partners work together and yet maintain their proprietary information and business secrets? As might be expected, one of the first measures is education of all employees at all levels. Englman (p. 30) gives the example of MCI's collaborative efforts and notes that its program theme "Don't Gamble with MCI's Future" was used throughout the organization to emphasize the importance of information protection. Employees also attended security awareness briefings.

Security Measures

Goodboe (1992, p. 53) stresses: "Managers must train their work forces to face industrial espionage and deal with it head-on." He presents a three-step strategy to combat information espionage:

- Security staff training.
- Work force training.
- Posttraining continuity.

Bird (1992, p. 46) offers the concept of security circles to guard sensitive information:

> To use the approach . . . first look at your business from afar in the context of its surroundings, then move progressively closer to the target—the company itself. In essence, you are pretending to be an industrial spy or a thief planning to fraudulently victimize your company. Thinking like the enemy reveals company vulnerabilities that are often not discovered through a conventional survey.

The largest circle in this approach is the entire surroundings of the building which might present a security problem. The circles become increasingly smaller until you are inside the building itself. Then the process is reversed, moving from the inside out, circling every known target of opportunity. Then draw another larger circle at the next point where individuals would be stopped and checked. If you cannot draw a second circle, you may lack adequate control.

Pavlicek (1992, p. 54) suggests developing a counterintelligence mind-set, noting that a majority of *Fortune* 500 companies now have full-time staff assigned to gather information on their competitors. Says Pavlicek:

> Intelligence collection is a fact of modern business life. Collection efforts pose a substantial risk to a company's operations despite the fact that they are legal and center mainly on open sources.
>
> Used effectively, intelligence methods can expose confidential strategies, identify important process changes, or provide a clearer picture of proprietary technologies. For the target company, this might translate into lost lead time, lower market share, and lower revenues.

Davis (1992, p. 50) suggests that businesses might adopt the approach used by government, known as **OPSEC**—Operations Security. He notes that OPSEC is a process to analyze business operations and identify potential intelligence indicators that competitors could use to gain a marketplace edge. More specifically, as noted by Swartwood (1993, p. 45): "Operations security (OPSEC) is a proven, systematic analytical process that uses an adversary's perspective to find vulnerabilities to critical information." Businesses seeking government contracts usually have to develop and implement an OPSEC plan before being awarded the contract. Jelen (1994, p. 67) outlines the five steps usually included in OPSEC:

1. Identification of critical information.
2. Analysis of the threat, including identifying adversaries, their goals, intentions, and capabilities.
3. A vulnerability analysis.
4. A risk assessment, estimating the potential effects of a vulnerability on the business and a cost-benefit analysis of corrective action.
5. Applying appropriate cost-effective countermeasures.

Somerson (1994, p. 61) suggests a similar approach using a value-added model: "An information security program's net present value is determined by measuring three factors: the predictable likelihood of a serious information loss, the cost of the information security program, and the total cost to the organization should an information loss occur."

Finally, Wade (1993, p. 6A) reminds security management:

> The revolution in information technology requires a similar revolution in providing security for the new information model. On one hand, security must become more technical in its design; at the same time, it must be easier to implement by users throughout the enterprise. Security safeguards must be incorporated in all aspects of information technology to provide seamless

> protection. The power of technology must be harnessed to provide protection safeguards commensurate with the risks to security that same technology has created.

For most businesses, computers are at the heart of their operations and their communications. Computer crime, including theft of information and fraud, is a serious security challenge.

COMPUTERS AND SECURITY

Dickey (1985, p. 29), in "Is Getting in Getting out of Control?" cites the example of two programmers responsible for maintaining computer files of all purchases made by an oil company plant. The programmers created a dummy supply company and then manipulated their company's database to show the fictitious vendor as a regular supplier to the plant. As a result, the computer registered receiving both materials and invoices from the dummy company. Dickey notes that "for two years, the plant bought its own inventory twice—embezzlement to the tune of several million dollars. The programmers were eventually caught by a fluke audit. The company decided not to prosecute because it did not want to call attention to how easily its database was invaded or how long it took to discover that invasion. Ironically, the two programmers were promoted—and put in charge of computer security."

In another instance, a computer support consulting firm offered diagnostic packs to troubleshoot problems with specific computer programs. While they were troubleshooting a particular program, they also made copies of the client's records. They then tried to sell these records to the client's competitors. In fact, the selling of stolen information was the primary source of income for this consulting firm; the diagnostic service was simply a cover to gain access to the records.

The invention of the microchip in 1976, leading to the development of the personal computer, has revolutionized our lives. By the year 2000, the total number of personal computers (PCs) should exceed two hundred million. In addition there has been a tremendous proliferation of modems (telephone devices that can connect one computer to another). Computers control the airplanes flying overhead and the subways running underfoot. They have changed the way teachers instruct students, physicians practice medicine, architects design buildings and corporations conduct business. They have made it possible for us to land astronauts on the moon and to begin exploration of outer space. The power of the personal computer to transform the world we live in is awesome. However, it also has spawned a new type of criminal and a new type of crime.

Computer security is an important example of the new frontiers opening up in the loss prevention field in response to social and technological changes. Electronic data processing personnel have responsibility as coordinators, analysts and security consultants. Coordinators work with conventional security departments and are responsible for implementing and maintaining computer security systems. An analyst usually is responsible for security inspections, surveys and reviewing any threats to the security system.

Computer Crime Defined

The definitions of **computer crime** are varied but generally include common elements.

> Computer crime includes accessing a computer's database without authorization or exceeding authorization for the purpose of sabotage or fraud. It includes theft or destruction of software and hardware as well.

In the nineteenth century, Thomas Carlyle observed: "Man is an animal who uses tools. Without tools, he is nothing, with tools he is all." Computers might be thought of as the ultimate tool, processing, transmitting, printing and storing information at lightning speed. Likewise, crimes can be committed using computers—crimes that are simple to commit and extremely difficult to detect. Because computer crime exists, computer security becomes mandatory for businesses and corporations. According to computer security consultant Bruce Goldstein of Total Assets Protection, Arlington, Texas, computer security is the protection of all assets, especially informational, from both humanmade and natural disasters. Computer security includes protecting data, telecommunications, personnel and the physical environment. It also includes formulating, implementing and testing a protection plan, and knowing when and how to seek additional expertise.

The Seriousness of the Problem

"The number of crimes involving computers is increasing dramatically throughout the country," say Manning and White (1990, p. 46). "There are documented offenses of every type—theft, fraud, burglary, prostitution, murder, child pornography—in which a computer was used in some way. Drug dealers and others involved in organized crime are using computers both to keep records and to facilitate the commission of other offenses."

Computer thieves steal billions of dollars every year. Some computer thefts involve astronomical figures. The Wells Fargo case, for example, used a computer to pull off a $21-million embezzlement.

> Computer crimes cost hundreds of millions of dollars annually. In fact computer crime or failure might destroy a business.

Many businesses rely extensively on electronic data processing (EDP) and could not function effectively for very long without their computer(s). Computer failure can destroy a company. Robert Huber, computer security expert with National Cash Register Company, suggests that a business that relies on computers will close its doors in three to five days if the computers fail. Yet computers are neither infallible nor invulnerable. Therefore, establishments that rely on computers cannot ignore the inherent risks involved in their use.

The computer is no longer mysterious, accessible to and usable by only an elite few. Grade school students are routinely taught to use computers. Computer use has become an accepted, integral part of our way of life, allowing tremendous advances in science, medicine, business and education. Unfortunately, many people in management do not take the computer as seriously as they should. This can have devastating consequences. Managers who do not understand computer technology have given up control over corporate information.

Computer crime has been called the "crime of the future" and home computers, the "burglar tool of the electronic age," reflecting concern for the rising rate of computer crime.

According to the Lipman Report (1988), the national direct cost to organizations of computer crime is estimated to be almost $560 million. However, the total direct and indirect costs of computer crime may be as much as $200 billion.

The National Center for Computer Crime Data has compiled data on the national costs of computer crime, as summarized in Table 9–1.

Many businesses rely heavily on computers as in this Prodigy newsroom.

Table 9–1. Summary of National Costs of Computer Crimes

Total Annual Person-Years Lost	930
Total Annual Computer-Years Lost	15.2
Average Annual Loss per Organization	$109,000
National Cost for Computer Crimes to Organizations	$555,000,000

SOURCE: Commitment to Security, Copyright National Center for Computer Crime Data, Santa Cruz, CA. Reprinted with permission.

According to the Hallcrest Report II (Cunningham et al., 1990, p. 75): "Management of computer security may be the greatest individual challenge facing private security managers over the next decade." As noted in the Hallcrest Report II (p. 64):

> Many security directors have little personal knowledge about computers or computer security. It is likely, however, that in the coming years security managers will be expected—perhaps required—to become increasingly knowledgeable about computer security. Moreover, as computer systems proliferate within security departments—both as management information tools and as a part of electronic systems—their systems, too, may become targets.

The Hallcrest Report II (p. 64) suggests that security managers must consider the following key factors:

- Electronic intrusion is currently a minimal threat that has the potential of growing to significant risk levels in the next years before it finally dissipates by the end of the decade.
- Most security managers are presently ill-equipped, personally and organizationally, to counter the computer security threat, particularly external, electronic intrusion.
- As security departments increasingly rely on computers, their vulnerability to electronic intrusion will commensurately increase.

Strandberg (1993, p. 22) notes: "New technologies traditionally present new opportunities for crime, and the seemingly harmless home computer is no exception. We all know that crime is strongly linked to opportunity, and the home computer offers an unprecedented opportunity to commit white collar crime to the over 10 million (conservative estimate) computer and modem users in the U.S. alone."

Conly and McEwen (1990, p. 3) define computer crime quite simply: "Computer crime today is any illegal act for which knowledge of computer technology is used to commit the offense." Table 9–2 presents the types of computer-related crimes currently seen at the state and local level.

Cyberspace is a term used to refer to the artificial world created on-line and between computer systems. According to Krott (1994, p. 1): "With over 20 million Americans on-line, the overnight growth of computer networks has created what sociologists are calling a 'virtual world.' " And, as in the real

Table 9–2. Categories of Computer Crime

Internal computer crimes
- Trojan horses
- Logic bombs
- Trap doors
- Viruses

Telecommunications crimes
- Phone phreaking
- Hacking
- Illegal bulletin boards
- Misuse of telephone systems

Computer manipulation crimes
- Embezzlements
- Frauds

Support of criminal enterprises
- Data bases to support drug distributions
- Data bases to keep records of client transactions
- Money laundering

Hardware/software thefts
- Software piracy
- Thefts of computers
- Thefts of microprocessor chips
- Thefts of trade secrets

SOURCE: Catherine H. Conly and J. Thomas McEwen. "Computer Crime." NIJ Reports. Washington, DC: National Institute of Justice, January/February 1994, p. 3.

world, a certain number of individuals will not obey the laws. Says Krott: "Cybercrime is real and happening. Data tampering, illegal data transfer, fraudulent transfer of funds, telephone fraud, sex crimes, and more, they all take place in Cyberspace."

As Kaplan (1995, p. 67) explains:

> Cyberspace, that unseen land through which information travels whenever it is e-mailed, is akin to the wild frontier of the American West. But, as in any dangerous neighborhood, there are ways to travel safely. With the pony express, a shotgun fended off attackers. Today, the defensive strategy is more subtle—protecting a package's contents with encryption.

According to Worthen (1992, p. 146): "Personal computer (PC) use in the 1990s has been explosive, with the desktop replacing the data center as the backbone of corporate data processing." Also problematic are laptop computers and notebook computers, as noted by Patterson (1993): "Sensitive information leaving the relative safety of the office presents a serious security risk, and that risk is deepened by the logistics of business travel." In addition, says Patterson: "A several-thousand-dollar notebook computer increases the attraction. Tack on a potentially priceless amount of data stored on that same six-pound package and the attraction takes a quantum leap upward."

Types of Threats to Computer Security

Computer-related crimes can involve the input data, the output data, the program itself or computer time. Adequate security requires not only physical security but at least a basic knowledge of how the computer works and how it can be used to commit crime. Input data can be altered (for example, a fictitious supplier can be entered into the billing system or figures can be changed or removed, leaving absolutely no trace). Output data can be obtained by unauthorized people through wiretapping, electromagnetic pickup or theft of data sheets or punch cards. The computer program itself might be tampered with to add costs to purchased items or to create double payments for particular accounts. Computer time also is sometimes used for personal use and/or profit. There are no dishonest computers, only dishonest employees, competitors and criminals.

A survey conducted by the Data Processing Management Association (DPMA), Park Ridge, Illinois, questioned one thousand data processing executives in *Fortune* 1000 companies. This survey found that the majority of computer abuses were rather mundane. Misuse of computer services made up nearly half of all incidents reported. Misuse included game-playing as well as using the computer for personal work, to divert funds or alter records. The next most prevalent area was program abuse, i.e., copying or changing programs. Third was data abuse—diverting information to unauthorized individuals, and fourth was hardware abuse, i.e., damaging or stealing computer equipment.

According to Steinbrecher (1987, p. 41): "The unintentional, improper use of data remains the largest, most basic security issue. . . . Incorrect data causes far greater losses than the more dramatic security problem of computer fraud and theft." He notes that the person entering the data may not understand what the data means, leading to errors. In addition, accurate data may be transmitted by one computer and be inaccurately received by a personal computer.

A somewhat different view is presented in the Hallcrest Report II (Cunningham et al., 1990, p. 60), which says: "Insider attacks by dishonest or disgruntled employees represent the greatest risk, accounting for up to 80% of incidents."

The National Center for Computer Crime Data (NCCCD) has categorized types of computer crimes and their incident rate, as summarized in Table 9–3. This center has also summarized data on computer crime victims, as shown in Table 9–4. Further, the center has summarized data on rates of computer crimes based on prosecution data, illustrated in Table 9–5.

> The greatest security threats to computer centers are theft by fraud or embezzlement, hackers, sabotage, employee carelessness or error and fire.

Theft by Fraud or Embezzlement

As noted by Martin (1993, p. 82): "The largest area of computer crime is telecommunications fraud—call-selling operations that usually work out of New

Table 9–3. Computer Threat Incident Rates

Category/Subcategory	Percent of Total/[Subtotal]
HUMAN INSIDER THREAT	70% to 80%
Human errors/accidents	55%
Dishonest employees	[15%]
Disgruntled employees	[10%]
NONHUMAN PHYSICAL THREATS	20%
Fire	[15%]
Water	[3%]
Earthquake, etc.	2%

SOURCE: Commitment to Security, Copyright National Center for Computer Crime Data, Santa Cruz, CA. Reprinted with permission.

York, L.A., or Miami." Such fraud was discussed earlier but is mentioned here to emphasize the role of computers in this crime.

Funds may be stolen by an outsider, using a telephone and the necessary passwords from a remote terminal to make an unauthorized transfer of millions of dollars to a designated account. Instances of such fraud include the Equity Funding Fraud of the late 1970s that resulted in losses of more than $100 million. In another such fraud, Jack Benny, Liza Minnelli and another individual lost $925,000.

Computerized banks are frequently the victims of **check kiting,** where a person makes simultaneous deposits and withdrawals using two or more banks to obtain credit before enough time has elapsed to clear the checks. Before the use of computers, bank personnel examined such transactions when they were made. Now, however, kiting can be detected only by using a special computer program to monitor unusually large transactions and continuous activity involving accounts with small running balances.

Funds can also be stolen by insiders, for example, employees who falsify claims in an insurance company, or the computer programmers with their fictitious supply company cited previously.

Table 9–4. Summary of Computer Crime Victims

Type of Organization	Percent of Attacks: 1986	Percent of Attacks: 1989
Commercial Organizations	37%	36%
Banks	18%	12%
Telecommunications Companies	16%	17%
Governmental Agencies	14%	17%
Individuals	11%	12%
Universities	4%	4%

SOURCE: Commitment to Security, Copyright National Center for Computer Crime Data, Santa Cruz, CA. Reprinted with permission.

Table 9–5. Summary of Rates of Computer Crimes (*based on prosecution data*)

Type of Computer Crime	Probability of Occurrence: 1986	Probability of Occurrence: 1989
Money Theft	45%	36%
Information Theft	16%	12%
Damage to Software	16%	2%
Malicious Alteration	6%	6%
Deceptive Alteration	6%	2%
Theft of Service	10%	34%
Harassment	0%	2%
Extortion	0%	4%

SOURCE: Commitment to Security, Copyright National Center for Computer Crime Data, Santa Cruz, CA. Reprinted with permission.

It is not always money that is stolen; sometimes the theft involves information or data. Computer data banks contain information worth billions of dollars, such as lists of customers, bank records, consumer records, trade secrets, business plans and the like. In addition, secrets regarding the manufacturing of computers are also sometimes the target of computer thieves. For example, in 1983, during an FBI sting operation, agents arrested employees of the Japanese firm Hitachi, Ltd., attempting to buy computer secrets from IBM. These employees plead guilty to conspiracy to commit theft, and Hitachi plead guilty and was fined $10,000 on federal charges of conspiring to transport secrets across state lines. The out-of-court settlement of a civil suit against Hitachi was reported as $300 million plus attorney fees.

The thefts need not involve huge sums of money or information. Theft of services is also a problem. Employees may use company computers to play games, run their own programs or, as in a few documented cases, even run their own businesses with their employers' computers and on their employers' time.

Hackers

Another serious threat to computer security is the **hacker**—the computer enthusiast who engages in electronic snooping, software piracy and other types of high-tech illegal activities. Sometimes the activities of such hackers are relatively harmless, as in the case of some computer students who electronically altered the Rose Bowl scoreboard to show Cal Tech playing MIT rather than UCLA playing Illinois. But it is not always harmless, as noted by Donn Parker: "There's an epidemic of malicious hacking going on across the country. Hackers consider breaking into computer systems an indoor sport, but there is a dark side."

This dark side is described by Folsom in *Security Management* (1986, pp. 92–93):

> Consider the case of a group of hackers known as the 414s. One June morning, Chen Chui, systems manager for the Sloan-Kettering Cancer Hospital in New York, made an alarming discovery. Sometime during the night the hospital's giant computer which monitors radiation treatments for the hospital's patients had failed. Chui discovered that someone had erased part of the computer's memory and that passwords had been issued to five unauthorized accounts. Hospital director Radhe Mohan was alarmed. He said, "If the files are altered, then a patient could get the wrong treatment."
>
> Baffled officials called the FBI and the New York City Police, who placed a tap on the phone lines to the computer. The mystery was solved after the FBI tracked down a group of Milwaukee area computer buffs who called themselves the 414s after the city's area code. Using home computers connected to ordinary phone lines, the group had been breaking into computers across the United States and Canada.

In addition to accessing computers without authorization, hackers also frequently engage in software piracy, costing computer companies millions of dollars in lost sales. Selling software is big business. Companies have tried many ways to stop the pirates. One video game maker hired full-time lawyers to sue the pirates. Other companies use special codes to prevent copying.

Cunningham et al. (1990, p. 66) say criminal hackers are "minuscule in number" and engage in such activities as "theft of telephone service, vandalism of computer systems and records, alteration of vital medical records, credit card fraud and manipulation of credit records." They caution that simple "modem hunting" computer programs can dial thousands of telephone numbers searching for "vulnerable modems" and that "hackers are successful only against the undefended and the careless. They remotely prey on the easiest victims they can find."

According to Draty (1994, p. 1), AT&T Global Business Communications Systems has created an antihacker investigative team whose "sole purpose is to monitor, track and catch phone-system hackers in the act of commiting toll fraud."

As noted by Arbetter (1994, p. 10): "Almost the entire investigation can be done remotely. After monitoring the system and identifying what appears to be hacker footprints, the investigators contact the customer and ask for cooperation in setting up a trap for the intruder."

Sabotage

Another risk to protect against is sabotage. Competitors, activists or dissatisfied employees might make the computer their target. Activists may see the computer room as the "vulnerable heart" of a business and make it the target of their attack. For example, one disgruntled programmer who thought he might be fired programmed the computer to destroy its database if it did not make up a salary check for him when the payroll was made up. Poor employee morale can greatly enhance the likelihood of computer sabotage.

Sabotage may be done by a **computer virus.** A **virus** is a "bug" entered into a computer program that can cause serious memory problems, destroying files or even entire programs. It can also spread from computer to computer.

It can lay dormant for weeks or months until activated by someone with access to the computer.

According to Forcht (1992, p. 134): "Virus programs usually consist of relatively few lines of programming code that can be easily hidden in software. Viruses can be created on any PC and transmitted via communications lines or an infected disk to other systems."

According to the *Washington Post* (1990, p. 7A), an advertisement such as the following might be placed by the U.S. Army:

> Wanted: Experienced computer hackers capable of breaking into enemy software systems and destroying secret files. Knowledge of computer viruses a must.

The Army is actually exploring using computer viruses, "a type of unwanted software program that can propagate undetected from one computer to another, thwarting the computer's normal functions and sometimes garbling data." According to the *Post:* "Incidents of computer sabotage have swept the country in recent months as hackers become increasingly efficient at breaking into the systems of businesses, universities, and research centers."

In *State v. Burleson* (1988), a Texas court found a defendant guilty of harmful access to a computer to sabotage its operations. The defendant had boasted to a fellow employee of how he had installed a computer virus in his company's computer system. This is thought to be the first computer virus prosecution in the country.

Perhaps the best-known virus is the Internet virus, developed by Robert T. Morris, Jr., and intended to be harmless. The program was introduced into the Internet on November 2, 1988, and as described by Forcht (p. 135):

> Within minutes the INTERNET network was devastated, and many computer centers had to shut down. These included NASA's Ames Laboratory, Lawrence Livermore Laboratory, MIT, and the Rand Corporation. . . .
>
> The total cost of recovery has been estimated at anywhere from $1 million to $186 million. Most agree $98 million was spent to get rid of the virus and return the network to normal.

Forcht also describes several other viruses including the notorious "Pakistani Brain Virus" which affected systems around the world, invading an estimated 100,000 PCs, and the "Israeli Virus" whose goal was to wipe out files on Friday, May 13, 1988. Notes Forcht (p. 135): "The virus had the potential to destroy important research findings, financial records, and other significant data. Fortunately, the virus was contained before it wreaked havoc." While working on this text we received the e-mail shown in Figure 9–1.

Access control is a key to preventing viruses. Effective software management can also protect against viruses. Not borrowing software and always purchasing from reliable vendors are important steps. All new disks should be checked. And, of utmost importance, is educating employees on how viruses can infect a computer and how to avoid this.

Time:10:47 AM
Date:4/20/95

FYI - better safe than sorry

Date: 4/20/95 10:08 AM

)READ IMMEDIATELY: Warning about a new computer virus
)
)** High Priority **
)
)*********************Forwarded Message****************
)
)There is a computer virus that is being sent across the Internet. If you
)receive an e-mail message with the subject line "Good Times", DO NOT
)read the message, DELETE it immediately. Please read the messages
)below.
)
)Some miscreant is sending e-mail under the title "good times"
)nation-wide. If you get anything like this, DON'T DOWNLOAD THE FILE! It
)has a virus that rewrites your hard drive, obliterating anything on it.
)Please be careful and forward this mail to anyone you care about—I have.
)**
)
)WARNING!!!!!!!!!: INTERNET VIRUS
)
)***
)
)The FCC released a warning last Wednesday concerning a matter of
)major importance to any regular user of the InterNet. Apparently, a new
)computer virus has been engineered by a user of America Online that is
)unparalleled in its destructive capability. Other, more well-known
)viruses such as Stoned, Airwolf, and Michaelangelo pale in comparison
)to the prospects of this newest creation by a warped mentality.
)
)What makes this virus so terrifying, said the FCC, is the fact that
)no program needs to be exchanged for a new computer to be infected.
)It can be spread through the existing e-mail systems of the InterNet.
)Once a computer is infected, one of several things can happen. If the
)computer contains a hard drive, that will most likely be destroyed.
)If the program is not stopped, the computer's processor will be placed in
)an nth-complexity infinite binary loop - which can severely damage the
)processor if left running that way too long. Unfortunately, most
)novice computer users will not realize what is happening until it is far
too late.
)
)Luckily, there is one sure means of detecting what is now known as
)the "Good Times" virus. It always travels to new computers the same
)way in a text e-mail message with the subject line reading simply "Good
)Times".
)
)Avoiding infection is easy once the file has been received - not
)reading it. The act of loading the file into the mail server's ASCII
buffer causes the "Good Times" mainline program to initialize and execute.

Figure 9–1. OFFICE MEMO Subject: FWD)Computer Virus

)The program is highly intelligent - it will send copies of itself to
)everyone
)whose e-mail address is contained in a received-mail file or a sent-mail
)file, if it can find one. It will then proceed to trash the
)computer it is running on.
)
)The bottom line here is - if you receive a file with the subject line "Good
)Times", delete it immediately! Do not read it! Rest assured that
)whoever's name was on the "From:" line was surely struck by the virus.
)
)Warn your friends and local system users of this newest threat to the
)InterNet! It could save them a lot of time and money.
)

Figure 9–1. OFFICE MEMO Subject: FWD)Computer Virus (*Continued*)

Other Threats

Employee carelessness and errors are also significant risks. Improperly stored computer tapes and disks can be damaged beyond use. Tapes wound too tightly can print through to the next layer. Excessive heat or humidity can destroy the tapes. A magnet closer than 12 cm might erase a computer tape or disk. And one transposed figure or one omitted zero or decimal point can cost a company millions of dollars.

In addition, according to the Hallcrest Report II (Cunningham et al., 1990, p. 63): "Any communications or computer network connected to telephone lines, microwave links, modems, facsimile machines, or similar apparatus is hypothetically vulnerable to external, electronic intrusion."

The threat of fire is another serious risk. The large number of electric wires and connections involved in computer installations, often located under a raised floor, and the fact that computer rooms are fire-loaded with large quantities of combustible materials make the risk of fire great. Even if a fire is detected early, the steam and humidity from extinguishing it may ruin the computer tapes.

Yet another problem is the controlled environment required for the computer to function correctly. Fluctuations in power can cause inaccuracies, so a continuous supply of unvarying power must be available. Air-conditioning must be maintained, or the computer can malfunction. Computers must also be protected against moisture; therefore, the location of water mains, air-conditioning pipes, sewer pipes and the like should be checked to ensure that they do not pose a threat to the computer should they break. If such pipes do exist, a drain should be installed in the computer room's floor. The computer and disks should be covered if construction or sandblasting is going on outside because the fine powder resulting from such activities can ruin a computer.

Legislation Related to Computer Crime

As computer crime has grown, states have passed legislation to deal with it. According to Nugent (1991, p. 1), 48 state legislatures and the U.S. Congress have passed some form of computer crime statutes. Among the most frequently used descriptions or titles of offenses are the following (Nugent, p. 6):

- Access to defraud.
- Access to obtain money.
- Computer fraud.
- Offenses against computer users.
- Offenses against intellectual property.
- Offenses against computer equipment and supplies.
- Unauthorized access.
- Unauthorized or unlawful computer use.

The laws aim at plugging loopholes in the criminal code, which prohibits traditional theft but does not include stealing electronic impulses from a computer. For example, in a 1976 case, *United States v. John DiGilio et al,* DiGilio copied investigative records during office time, with a government machine, on government paper and then sold them to the individuals who were the subjects of the investigation. The Third Circuit Court ruled that not only were government time and equipment illegally used, but also the contents of the documents themselves had been stolen.

Likewise, in a 1978 case, *United States v. Paul A. Lambert,* the defendant was convicted of stealing computer-stored information listing names of informants and the status of government drug investigations.

California has enacted a model computer crime code that includes the following specific violations:

- Publishing access codes through the use of a computer.
- Theft of computer data.
- Unauthorized interruption of computer service.
- Computer tampering.
- Unauthorized access to a computer system.

The Electronic Communications Privacy Act of 1986

On November 6, 1986, President Ronald Reagan signed into law the Electronic Communications Privacy Act, which amends Title 18, United States Code, by adding Chapter 121—Stored Wire and Electronic Communications and Transactional Records Access:

2701. Unlawful access to stored communications

(a) *Offense.*—Except as provided in subsection (c) of this section, whoever—(1) intentionally accesses without authorization a facility through which an electronic communication service is provided; or (2) intentionally exceeds an authorization to access that facility; and thereby obtains, alters, or prevents authorized access to a wire or electronic communication while it is in electronic storage in such system shall be punished as provided in subsection (b) of this section.

(b) *Punishment.*—The punishment for an offense under subsection (a) of this section is—(1) If the offense is committed for purposes of

commercial advantage, malicious destruction or damage, or private commercial gain—
(A) a fine of not more than $250,000 or imprisonment for not more than one year, or both, in the case of a first offense under this subparagraph; and
(B) a fine under this title or imprisonment for not more than two years, or both, for any subsequent offense under this subparagraph; and
(C) a fine of not more than $5,000 or imprisonment for not more than six months, or both, in any other case.

The Electronic Communications Privacy Act of 1986 makes it illegal to intentionally access, without authorization, a facility providing electronic communication services, or to intentionally exceed the authorization of access to such a facility.

The bill is intended to protect the privacy of high-tech communications such as electronic mail, video conference calls, conversations on cellular car phones and computer-to-computer transmissions.

The bill addresses the growing problem of unauthorized persons deliberately gaining access to, and often tampering with, electronic or wire communications that were intended to be private. If such access is for the purpose of commercial advantage, malicious destruction or damage or private commercial gain, the penalties are much more severe than for "other" types of access, which would include that of hackers. Although hackers may feel their actions are harmless, hacking is now illegal. In the view of most computer experts, it has always been unethical. Susan Myeum, computer law specialist from Palo Alto, California, explains why: "Even if a hacker's actions are not malicious, they can have serious consequences. Just getting into the system and messing around may accidentally alter or destroy valuable, vital information. Computer joyriding is also an invasion of privacy, and it fosters disrespect for the property of others."

Schools often fail to include the moral responsibilities of the computer user in their courses on computer programming. Such "ethical education" should be an integral part of a computer literacy program.

Security Measures for Computer Systems

The Hallcrest Report II (Cunningham et al., 1990, p. 61) suggests: "In a real-world sense, classified and restricted-access governmental and military computer systems are virtually impregnable, unless network operators have been negligent or there has been an 'insider' conspiracy."

According to the Hallcrest Report II (p. 62): "The technologies utilized to thwart electronic intrusion include: electromagnetic shielding and containment, optical disk storage, data encryption, local area network stations without local storage capabilities, computer-managed password software, audit trail software, increasingly sophisticated 'call-back' modems, fiber-optic cabling, enhanced call-tracing capabilities by telephone companies, call-in telephone number identification signals, biometric identification access to terminal hardware and many others."

Protecting computers and the information they use is a vital function of security personnel.

> Security measures for computer systems include logical controls, physical access controls, administrative controls, protecting against fire and maintaining a backup system.

Logical Controls

Logical controls are special programs written into the software. The most common are those that restrict access by requiring use of a password. That is, the user must type in a special password before the computer will follow any commands. The software might also determine what types of specific information a given user is allowed to access. Specific employees might be allowed into only certain parts of a file. Or they might be allowed to only read the data, but not make any changes in it.

Remote terminals must also be protected. When companies share time on a computer, care must be exercised to ensure that time-sharing customers are limited to their own database. Three ways to identify users wanting access to a computer by phone or terminal are a password (usually a word or phrase), a key or card and physical characteristics. Use of a password is most common, but because passwords can be overheard or given to unauthorized persons, they should be changed often.

Schwartau (1994, p. 60) stresses: "It cannot be overemphasized, passwords are an anemic way for a company to protect its information."

Key- or card-controlled systems must, of course, be protected by rigid key/card control procedures, as described earlier. The safest system of authorization and user identification is one that relies on physical characteristics (biometrics). However, such identification systems are expensive, and if voice identification is used, the system may deny access to authorized individuals whose voice characteristics have changed temporarily because of a cold or other illness.

Multilevel access capability makes a computer more flexible. Some access systems allow different operators to obtain different types of information, but only a limited number to have access to the total program.

Dickey (1985, p. 36) makes this suggestion: "For multiuser networked systems, most access-control software, which requires frequently changed passwords, guards against unauthorized access to systems and information resources. These programs log daily work activity, notify the system operator when unauthorized users attempt to access secured data and print reports of violations. Another security measure eliminates public telephone access to a network by implanting a block in the hardware architecture."

Another type of protection using logical controls is the call-back modem. Dickey describes it: "A user attempting to call into a system enters an identification code or password after dialing the computer; the modem scans its directory for the user's code and phone number and calls back. Only then is the user connected to the system."

One of the most effective types of logical controls is *data encryption,* in which an **encryption** device is placed between the host computer and a modem. The device puts the data into a code before it enters the transmission line. It is then decoded at the receiving end. The military uses sophisticated encryption systems that scramble messages to protect national security data.

Schwartau (1994, p. 60) cautions that security professionals should be aware of the various access points to their computers: "Locking one door and leaving the others wide open is nearly as bad as not locking them at all." At a minimum, the following entry points must be protected:

- Local workstations (the ultimate front door).
- Local area networks (the front door for many companies).
- Mainframes or other hosts.
- The Internet.

According to Schwartau: "The Internet is intolerably vulnerable to password compromises."

Even with logical controls, no system is 100 percent safe. If hackers can break into a cancer hospital for a lark, what might serious criminals or terrorists do?

Programs can be built into the computer that will detect fraud and embezzlement. Currently, however, most computer crimes are discovered by chance, not by audit, because there is no visible evidence of tampering—no erasures or doctored numbers. The crimes are committed by removals and changes that are done in seconds and leave no trace.

Physical Controls

Physical controls restrict access to computer terminals and other equipment and software.

Physical access control is critical to computer security. The practice of including computer centers in company tours to enhance public image has been discontinued by most establishments. Most computer centers are now in restricted areas with locked doors, alarm systems and supervisory personnel on duty whenever the computer is operating. Potential for access through air vents, windows and doors must be assessed. In computer centers where rigid access control is required, there is a single entrance/exit—ideally a riot door—then a corridor and a second (riot) door, both electronically controlled and guarded. Entrance may be obtained through use of an employee ID badge system, keys, key-cards or identification systems using physical characteristics such as fingerprints, palmprints or voice characteristics. In addition, various devices are available that lock computers to desktops.

Mele (1994, p. 71) suggests three steps to secure a vulnerable computer:

- Mark it.
- Secure it.
- Alarm it.

For users connected to a local area network (LAN), Bates (1995, p. 49) notes: "Surprisingly, a great percentage of the disasters and downtime on the LAN is directly attributable to cabling problems. Users accidently kick or bump connectors, causing disruptions to the network. Maintenance personnel in the building inadvertently sever wires." In addition, power should be protected by using surge suppressors and uninterruptible power systems.

The computer printouts and disks should also be safeguarded. When they are no longer needed, they should be run through a paper shredder. Company secrets can be obtained more easily through carelessly discarded printouts than through "bugging." Nonetheless, "bugging" must also be guarded against. Equipment is available that can indicate when a "bug" is in operation.

Computer tapes and disks should be stored in locked files. The computer-disk library should be protected against unauthorized access and should make use of a rigidly enforced sign-out/sign-in procedure.

Preston (1995, p. 30) cautions: "Leaving an index of the contents on a diskette is like leaving a roadmap for spies and thieves, making recovery of sensitive information considerably easier."

To minimize the threat of employee fraud or embezzlement and/or collusion, the functions of computer technicians, operators and programmers should be clearly separated. Programmers should not operate the computers except to try out new programs, and then only under supervision. A programmer should not be in the computer room unsupervised. And only authorized persons should be allowed to change programs. Sometimes such separation is not practical, but where it can be accomplished, it should be. It is also a good policy to rotate personnel working on various programs.

Administrative Controls

R. E. Johnston, director of data processing for Phoenix Mutual Life Insurance Company, makes this statement (Computer Security, 1986, p. 10):

> Administrative controls establish the practice and procedures for anyone wishing to gain access to data. These procedures include:
>
> - Having anyone who enters the building or a specified area sign an entry and exit log.
> - Having employees submit written requests before they can access certain data.
> - Reviewing the formal approval process periodically to ensure that it's being used properly.
>
> Administrative controls essentially establish accountability. Accountability establishes that *someone* is responsible for an act. Those who try to access

data are held accountable through a request form, roster or report produced by the system listing those who tried to gain access at any time.

Schweitzer (1993, pp. 60–61) offers eight rules for computer security:

1. All computer accounts must be based on some demonstrated business need.
2. Only the minimum privileges should be provided.
3. Business policy must assign the authority to establish and control computer accounts.
4. Effective control requires a coordinated effort by key company departments.
5. Adequate records of accounts must be maintained to allow rules 1, 2 and 3 to operate.
6. Accounts with special privileges must require special approvals and must have special restrictions.
7. All computer access authorizations and the records reflecting account activities should be frequently audited by disinterested parties.
8. Procedures should accommodate all cases.

Other administrative controls include making careful background checks on all employees and assuming responsibility for security, including stressing security during management meetings. Still other administrative security measures to protect against theft are periodic external audits as well as involving auditors in designing computer programs.

Administrative controls can also be used to reduce employee carelessness and ignorance. Employee carelessness and/or ignorance can result in tremendous losses for companies that rely on computers. All computer operators should be well qualified and should then be further trained on the specific hardware and software they will be using. Checklists and written instructions should be affixed to each machine and should delineate the procedures to be followed and any cautions to be taken. Detailed daily logs should be completed by each operator. Even the most skilled operators can make mistakes, however. Reporting of employee mistakes must be encouraged so the mistakes can be corrected rather than covered up, thereby creating even more serious problems than the original mistake may have caused. A system of error analysis should be established to reduce further errors. Clearly established rules and procedures as well as regular reviews and inspections will help reduce losses that result from employee carelessness or ignorance.

Recommendations for a Computer Security Program

In a report entitled "Computer Crime—Computer Security Techniques," the Bureau of Justice Statistics, U.S. Department of Justice, offers the following recommendations for a computer security program:

- Set up a system so that a user must get specific authorization to use it.
- Tightly control all after-hours processing.
- Carefully review and explain all computer shutdowns.
- Require that customer complaints about computer errors be investigated by a department other than the computer department.

- Control access to the computer operations center strictly.
- Commission independent consultants to audit the computer operations.
- Change passwords and security codes routinely as employees leave.
- Keep records of former employees' passwords and codes to trace the source of any subsequently discovered fraud.
- Staff and lock tape and disk libraries.
- Use scramblers and encryption devices for data transmission.
- Brief employees on security procedures frequently.
- Keep records of all unsuccessful attempts to access the computer system.
- Encourage employees to suggest security procedures that meet the company's specific needs.

Preventing Computer Crime

An additional helpful listing of "crime-stoppers" is offered by William E. Perry (1985):*

1) *Evaluating computer security*

- Is someone responsible for computer security in the central site?
- Have standards been developed for designing controls into financial systems?
- Has the confidentiality or sensitivity of each piece of information been identified?
- Have procedures been developed to define who can access the computer facility, as well as how and when that access can occur?
- Have procedures been developed to handle programs and data at remote sites?
- Is someone accountable for security at each remote site?
- Have security procedures been established for PCs?
- Has the ownership of microcomputer programs and data been defined by the firm?
- Is critical information that is transmitted over common-carrier lines protected (e.g., through cryptography)?
- Have provisions been made to destroy sensitive information controlled by office systems?

2) *Evaluating personnel issues*

- Are formal reports required for each reported instance of computer penetration?
- Is one individual accountable for each data processing resource?
- Does management understand the new threats posed by automated applications?
- Is management evaluated on its ability to maintain a secure computer facility?
- Are the activities of all non-employees in the computer center monitored?
- Do procedures restrict non-employees from gaining access to computer program listings and documentation (e.g., shredding the program listings rather than throwing them out in the trash)?
- Are employees instructed on how to deal with inquiries and requests originating from non-employees?

*From William E. Perry. "Management Strategies for Computer Security." © Butterworth, 1985. Reprinted with permission.

- Are errors made by the computer department categorized by type and frequency?
- Are records maintained on the frequency and type of errors incurred by users of data processing systems?

Steinbrecher (1987, p. 46) stresses: "A combination of controls and awareness of data integrity issues will help to safeguard your data—and possibly save your company from costly mistakes." He suggests the following error-reduction procedures:

- Use write/protect tabs on diskettes to prevent the accidental alteration of information.
- Erase files that are no longer needed.
- Establish logical file-naming rules.
- Label both the diskettes and the envelopes.
- Implement error-checking and correction procedures.

Individuals who deal with computer software should be familiar with the following guidelines:

- Avoid contact with recording surfaces of computer tapes and disks.
- Never write on labels on floppy disks with a ballpoint pen or pencil.
- Never use paper clips or rubber bands around computer disks.
- Store computer tapes and disks vertically at approximately 70 degrees Fahrenheit.
- Keep computer disks away from strong light, dust and magnetic fields.
- Do not store computer disks in plastic bags.

Preventing Losses by Fire

Although fire is a potential danger for any business, the hazard is greater for computer centers than for most other areas because of the higher probability of fire, the limitations on how such fires can be extinguished and the tremendous losses of hardware, software and data that could result.

Most computer centers have incorporated means to prevent fires—for example, not allowing smoking, using fire-resistant electric wiring and connectors and removing printout sheets (frequently tons of them) as soon as practical. Other common causes are careless cigarette smoking and faulty electrical wiring. However, many managers fail to recognize that the greatest threat is that of a fire that begins outside the computer center. Therefore, an important preventive measure is to decrease fire-loading of all adjacent areas, including not only the rooms that have common walls with the computer center, but those above and below it as well.

The fire detection systems in computer rooms are most frequently ionization-type detectors installed inside each computer or console cabinet, under the floor, in the ceiling and in the storage cabinets. Some detectors are also designed to shut off the electric power and all air-conditioning units. Many are connected to a visual display panel that shows the exact location of the fire.

Fire extinguishing systems are also important for adequate protection from fire losses. Three general alternatives are available. First is the automatic water sprinkler system which is the least expensive, is reliable and generally trouble-free and will continue to operate as long as the heat is above the designated temperature—usually 150 degrees Fahrenheit. This system also has important disadvantages, however. Recall that water and electricity do not mix and that water conducts electricity. Therefore, if such a system is used, it is imperative that it be connected so as to turn off all electrical power. Another important disadvantage is that water and heat cause steam and humidity, which can completely destroy the tapes and can also damage the computer itself. If the computer is not properly and thoroughly dried after a water sprinkler has been activated, it can rust and corrode. Further, if the fire originates in a computer cabinet, as is frequently the case, the water jets will not reach the fire.

The second type is the carbon dioxide extinguishing system. Although this system is more expensive than the water system, carbon dioxide does not conduct electricity or corrode the equipment, and the gas can penetrate computer cabinets. But this system, too, has serious disadvantages. It gives off a deadly gas, so all employees must be evacuated before it can be activated, thereby causing a delay that could result in greater losses. In addition, it is not continuous as is water, but rather shuts off when the gas has been expelled from the system. Carbon dioxide smothers rather than cooling like water does, so the chance of flareback is greater. Finally, carbon dioxide forms a cloud that can severely hinder fire-fighting efforts.

The third extinguishing system is Halon 1301 (freon). Like carbon dioxide, it is expensive, but unlike carbon dioxide, it is not lethal in the correct concentration and does not create a cloud. It is a nonconductor of electricity. However, it shares with carbon dioxide the disadvantages of expense and the possibility of a flareback because it is not continuous like water. (Outdoor halon systems are always dangerous.)

Although experts disagree on which type of extinguishing system is best for computer rooms, many prefer halon. They oppose the water system because of the danger of electrocution and the damage caused by water and steam, and they oppose the carbon dioxide system because of the lethal gas it produces. Nonetheless, many insurance companies require a water sprinkler system in computer centers before they will issue fire coverage. (Recall the discussion in Chapter 7.)

In addition to some type of automatic extinguishing system, computer rooms should also have portable carbon dioxide or halon extinguishers located throughout the area and floor pullers (handles with rubber suction cups on each end), which should be easily accessible to remove floor tiles should a fire originate under a floor housing the electrical wiring for the hardware.

Establishing a Backup System

Because establishments using EDP are so reliant upon computers, a backup system is usually mandatory. This includes backup power and air-conditioning, backup records and access to backup hardware. Some companies keep duplicate tapes of almost every file, whereas others make duplicates of only very important files. The criticality of the information and budgetary considerations will help determine which tapes should be copied. The copies should be kept in a secure location away from the facility that houses the computer center.

It is usually not economically feasible to have an "extra" computer in the center to serve as a backup. The common practice is for two establishments to enter into a "mutual aid" agreement whereby one company can use the other's computer during a breakdown. Sensible preplanning can greatly reduce losses. The contingency plan must ensure that adequate time will be available for the computer runs critical to the company's operation. For example, if a company's computer breaks down just before it is to run payroll, it is important that the payroll be issued. If a fire should damage the computer to such an extent that it must be replaced, it is important that the payroll be able to be run on a different computer. For such a "mutual aid" system to work, each must be sure that the computers' programs are compatible. This can most effectively be established through a trial run. Each should keep the other posted on any changes in hardware and/or scheduling requirements that occur. The initial trial run for compatibility should be periodically retested.

Computer centers should also be fully insured. The hardware and software represent a substantial investment and should be insured accordingly against all risks that may be present.

Before looking at investigating computer crimes, consider the suggestion of Olick (1994, p. 12): "Hacking is not just computers—it's about systems. Computers are just one part of an entire system that includes people, telephone lines, the building, and how your office interacts with the world. If you're thinking about security, you have to think about the entire system."

INVESTIGATING COMPUTER CRIME

As noted by Coutourie (1989, p. 18), challenges presented by computer crime include the fact that "computer criminals leave no traditional crime scene for investigators to photograph and examine. The victim is very likely to be a corporation, and the perpetrators may never be physically at the 'scene of the crime,' making it difficult to establish the relationship between the attacker and the victim."

Black (1986, p. 32) discusses some difficulties of the computer crime investigation: "The detective in a computer crime case may find himself in a totally unfamiliar environment, dealing with persons who communicate in a language he doesn't understand. . . . The amount of cooperation he receives may vary greatly as a result of the investigative requirements outlined by the detective at the initial interview, possibility of subsequent public embarrassment, loss of workhours, press coverage, outraged stockholders, or other unknown reasons. . . . The investigation of a computer crime in a hostile environment requires a much different approach than the friendly environment investigation. The victim must be approached in the same manner as a suspect. . . ."

> Factors to consider in investigating computer crime include the investigator's knowledge and whether outside expertise is required, the likelihood of the victim or an employee being involved and the difficulty in detecting such crimes.

In the survey previously mentioned conducted by the DPMA, it was found that only 2 percent of discovered and reported computer abuses were perpetrated by people outside the firm. The vast majority were committed by the firm's own employees.

This survey also found that the motivation for the internal abuse included ignorance of proper professional conduct (27 percent), misguided playfulness (26 percent), personal gain (25 percent) and maliciousness or revenge (22 percent). According to the survey, technical people such as programmers, systems analysts, machine operators, data entry clerks, etc., were the most common perpetrators.

According to Martin (1993, p. 83): "There's a widely-held belief that computer crimes are very difficult to investigate, or that it's beyond the ken of the average criminal investigator. Nothing could be further from the truth." With training, the proper equipment and a willingness to tackle the problem, investigators have a good chance of discovering the perpetrators of computer crime.

Folsom (1986, pp. 92–93) stresses that "pinpointing departments where computer crimes have a high probability of occurring is not difficult. The highest risks are found where the computer system generates negotiable instruments, transfers credit, processes loan applications or stores credit ratings. The potential for abuse is also high when access to computer centers is not regulated, after-hours use is not monitored, computer personnel are not carefully screened and unexplained lapses in computer operations go unexamined."

> The typical computer "criminal" is a young, middle-class technical person, highly educated, with no prior criminal record, employed by the firm reporting the crime.

Therefore, when investigating computer crimes, it is logical to start with a careful check of all employees having access to and knowledge of the computer and its programs. It will be necessary to know exactly how the security system was breached and what type of crime has been committed (altering of data, theft of data, etc.). Often it is necessary to know specifically what information was stolen to obtain a search warrant. Also, investigation of computer crimes often crosses several jurisdictional boundaries; consequently, security personnel usually do not handle investigation of such crimes alone. Often public enforcement agencies may also become involved. For example, the U.S. Secret Service is of great assistance in apprehending hackers.

Prosecuting Perpetrators of Computer Crimes

Only a small number of all computer crimes are detected. Of these only 12 percent are reported to the authorities and only 3 percent of offenders go to jail.

> The chance of a computer criminal being caught and going to jail is approximately one in twenty-seven thousand.

For a variety of reasons, the majority of computer crimes are not reported. The suspect may be an employee with a long record of trusted service; the employer may fear a tie-up of the computer system, fear that others will see how easy it is to access the system, fear criticism by stockholders or have numerous other reasons for not reporting the crime.

Even when computer crimes are reported, the majority are not prosecuted, often for the same reasons others do not even report them. In addition, prosecution is difficult because of lack of precedents and clear definitions. Frequently what has been stolen is information, which is intangible property and difficult to place a value on. In addition, as noted by Black (1986, p. 33), "the phrase, 'jury of your peers as trier of fact,' is probably a shade this side of impossible when applied to some of the more complex computer crimes . . . especially when the jury consists of people who believe that a floppy disk can be corrected by a good chiropractor." Nonetheless, to combat computer crime, a commitment to prosecution is vital in any security program.

Summary

Specific threats to the security of proprietary information include employees, discarded information, unsecured telecommunications and acoustical surveillance. Interestingly, in most states, garbage in dumpsters can be legally searched. Another vulnerable area is telecommunications. Telecommunication security includes information communicated by voice, fax and computer using wirelines, microwave links, satellite systems and fiber-optic lines.

Computer crime includes accessing a computer's database without authorization or exceeding authorization for the purpose of sabotage or fraud. It includes theft or destruction of software and hardware as well. Computer crimes cost hundreds of millions of dollars annually. In fact, computer crime or failure might destroy a business.

The greatest security threats to computer centers are theft by fraud or embezzlement, hackers, sabotage, employee carelessness or error and fire. The Electronic Communications Privacy Act of 1986 makes it illegal to intentionally access, without authorization, a facility providing electronic communication services, or to intentionally exceed the authorization of access to such a facility.

Security measures for computer systems include logical controls, physical access controls, administrative controls, protecting against fire and maintaining a backup system.

Factors to consider in investigating computer crime include the investigator's knowledge and whether outside expertise is required, the likelihood of the victim or an employee being involved and the difficulty in detecting such crimes. The typical computer "criminal" is a young, middle-class technical person, highly educated, with no prior criminal record, employed by the firm reporting the crime. The chance of such a criminal being caught and going to jail is approximately one in twenty-seven thousand.

APPLICATION

1. In the movie *War Games,* David, a bright young high-school student, is an adept hacker. Computers are his entire life, except for his girlfriend. Outwardly shy, he's totally different when he's with his computer. At first his hacking involves tapping into his school's computer and changing grades. Later, however, he accidently plugs into a secret Defense Department computer and is faced with the ultimate computer game—diverting thermonuclear war.

a. How likely is it that David could actually break into his school's computer and change his grades? What crime would be involved?

b. How likely is it that he could break into the Defense Department's secret computer? What crime would be involved?

2. A man named George Nickolson (spelled with a "k"), former sales manager of a Honda distributor, used his former position to tap into the credit records and social security number of George Nicholson (spelled with an "h"), a schoolteacher. Using the information obtained from the illegitimate inquiry, Nickolson obtained a $5,000 loan from a local bank, obtained a $7,500 loan from another local bank and charged purchases to American Express for more than $6,750.

Shortly thereafter, the banks began hounding Nicholson for payment on the debts which he obviously knew nothing about. He and his wife then went through three years described as a nightmare, being hounded by creditors. Ultimately, Nickolson was arrested and charged with incurring $26,750 in debts over the past three years.

a. What would the formal charge probably be?

b. How would investigators probably locate the suspect? What evidence would be required?

c. Could Nicholson sue Nickolson for the nightmarish three years?

CRITICAL THINKING EXERCISE

COMPUTER SABOTAGE

STATUTORY AND COMMON LAW

Government cybersleuths and computer law have lagged behind the skills and activities of computer hackers. Studies have shown that less than 5 percent of the intrusions into a computer system by an outsider are detected. Planting a virus is the equivalent of slashing tires, but it can also sabotage computer software and data. Illegal use of a telephone access device is punishable by up to 15 years in prison and a $250,000 fine. Computer fraud carries penalties of up to 20 years in prison and a $250,000 fine.

FACTS OF THE CASE

For more than two years, FBI agents sought a computer hack accused of a spree that included the theft of thousands of data files and at least 20,000 credit card numbers from computer systems around the nation. Authorities claimed that this computer hack had raided some of the most heavily protected corporate computer systems in the nation and took information worth more than one million dollars.

On December 25, Kevin Mitnick broke into the home computer of Tsutomu Shimomura, a computer security expert, and stole security programs Shimomura had written. Shimomura, a researcher at the San Diego Supercomputer Center, then made it his mission to track down the FBI's most-wanted hacker. Shimomura determined that the hacker was using a computer modem connected to a cellular telephone in the vicinity of Raleigh, North Carolina.

Sunday, February 12, Shimomura flew to Raleigh where he assisted telephone company technicians and federal investigators using cellular-frequency scanners to home in on Mitnick. On Wednesday at 2 A.M., Mitnick was arrested in his apartment.

Mitnick's therapist described him as a lonely man addicted to computers and pitifully obsessed with defeating their security systems. As a teenager Mitnick once broke into a top-secret military defense system. In 1989 Mitnick was convicted of breaking into MCI telephone computers and causing four million dollars of damage to the Digital Equipment Corporation. He was wanted in California for federal parole violation. Further investigation will look at his possible involvement in a spree of break-ins on the global Internet computer network.

The News & Observer in Raleigh, North Carolina, reported that Mitnick "broke into a computer because he could do it—like climbing Mount Everest—the challenge of doing it." His attorney who defended him in 1989 claimed his hacking was relatively benign because he "never planted a virus, never destroyed any information, never tried to make money off any of it."

His former therapist speculated that if he "had found a way to be accepted in the mainstream, he would have joined the mainstream."

Although some think that Mitnick is not an important case and it's laughable that he became public enemy number one, the guardians of databases do not take his case lightly. Evan Nosoff from the California Department of Motor Vehicles, which was allegedly infiltrated by Mitnick, said that "the security of our database is an ongoing effort; [infiltration] could be used to harass a person, to leverage credit files, to create false identities." Shimomura certainly thinks that hacking should not be taken lightly.

Issues and Questions

1. What is the most appropriate reaction to Mitnick's computer hacking?
   - **a.** Because Mitnick has repeatedly and obsessively stolen data files and credit card numbers and gained access to corporate trade secrets worth billions of dollars, he should receive a life sentence with no chance of parole. He has caused too much grief to ever be given another chance at freedom, for his next step would be to turn professional and burrow through several computers and across various phone lines and international boundaries to commit sabotage and espionage. Teach him and others like him a harsh lesson.
   - **b.** If convicted of computer fraud and illegal use of a telephone access device, Mitnick faces up to 35 years in prison and $500,000 in fines. The court also can set strict limits on Mitnick's jailhouse telephone privileges (meaning prison officials could dial and monitor all calls).
   - **c.** Mitnick's former therapist and others point out that Mitnick is not a dangerous person intent on committing sabotage or espionage. Because he was not a professional intent on major damage but was merely a benign "flamboyant sideshow, a noisy distraction from the stealthier, costlier threats to the world's computer networks," he should be committed for therapy but not imprisoned or fined.
   - **d.** Mitnick is a creative, egotistical showoff who steals for fun, not profit. As his defense attorney points out, "He never planted a virus, never destroyed any information, never tried to make money off any of it." So the best solution is to offer him a job under the tutelage of Shimomura so that he can be of benefit to society instead of being the most wanted computer criminal of the decade. What he probably needs is self-esteem, and with the increasing sophistication of computer hackers, we need computer security consultants who have Mitnick's abilities.
   - **e.** We have reacted with hysteria to Mitnick. Computer hacking should not be taken so seriously. Most cyber-dolts don't have a clue about what they are doing. Mitnick has benefited the computer security system by testing detection skills. We are fortunate to have had this experience with him because he was not malicious.

Discussion Questions

1. How familiar are you with computer systems? Which specific types?
2. Have there been recent computer crimes in your area? If so, what did they involve?
3. Do you know any computer hackers (or are you one yourself)? What types of activities are they most interested in? Do they perceive anything illegal about their activities?
4. How reliant is your local bank on a computer system?
5. Do you feel penalties for hackers should be as severe as they are under the Electronic Communications Privacy Act of 1986?

References

Arbetter, Lisa. "Hacker Trap." *Security Management,* November 1994, p. 10.

Arneke, David. "Securing the Information Superhighway." *Security Technology and Design,* September 1994, pp. 62–67.

Bates, Regis J. "Security Across the LAN." *Security Management,* January 1995, pp. 47–50.

Berry, S. L. "Faxpionage!" *Security Management,* April 1991, pp. 59–60.

Bird, Robert J. "Security Circles." *Security Management,* August 1992, pp. 46–49.

Black, J. K. "Taking a Byte Out of Crime." *Police Chief,* May 1986, pp. 31–33.

Butler, Charles W. and Schultz, Norman O. "Devising an Intelligence Collection Plan." *Security Management,* March 1993, pp. 66–68.

Chanaud, Robert C. "Keeping Conversations Confidential." *Security Management,* March 1993, pp. 43–48.

"Computer Crime—Computer Security Techniques." Bureau of Justice Statistics, U.S. Department of Justice.

"Computer Security: Protecting Information from Prying Eyes." *Executive Action Series,* #321, Waterford, CT: Bureau of Business Practice, Division of Simon and Schuster, November, 1986, pp. 9–11.

Conly, Catherine H. and McEwen, J. Thomas. "Computer Crime." NIJ Reports. Washington, DC: National Institute of Justice, January/February 1990, pp. 1–7.

Coutourie, Larry. "Preventing Computer-Related Crimes." *FBI Law Enforcement Bulletin,* September 1989, pp. 17–21.

Cullinane, David M. "Physical Security in a Distributed Computing Environment." *Security Technology and Design,* January/February 1994, pp. 36–39.

Cunningham, William C.; Strauchs, John J.; and Van Meter, Clifford W. *Private Security Trends, 1970 to 2000: The Hallcrest Report II.* Stoneham, MA: Butterworth-Heinemann, 1990.

Davis, Donald L. "OPSEC: Not for Government Use Only." *Security Management,* February 1992, pp. 50–52.

Dickey, S. "Is Getting in Getting Out of Control?" *Today's Office,* September 1985, pp. 29–36.

Draty, David. "Hackers Beware!" *Security Concepts,* September 1994, pp. 1, 18.

Englman, Steven. "Securing the Virtual Corporation." *Security Management,* November 1993, pp. 28–30.

Fay, John. "The Walled City Is No More." *Security Technology and Design,* April 1994, p. 63.

Folsom, W. B. "A Familiar Theme—with Variations." *Security Management,* July 1986, pp. 91–93.

Forcht, Karen. "Bolstering Your Computer's Immune System." *Security Management,* September 1992, pp. 134–40.

Goodboe, Michael E. "A Trained Eye Will See the Spy." *Security Management,* April 1992, pp. 49–53.

Hansen, Michael. "Counterespionage Techniques that Work." *Security Management,* September 1992, pp. 44–52.

Harowitz, Sherry L. "Building Security into Cyberspace." *Security Management,* June 1994, pp. 54–58.

Heffernan, Richard J. "And the SPI Survey Says . . . ." *Security Management,* October 1991, pp. 39–40.

Heffernan, Richard J. "Who's on the Line?" *Security Management,* September 1992, pp. 59–60.

Jelen, George F. "OPSEC for the Private Sector." *Security Management,* October 1994, pp. 67–68.

Kaplan, Jon. "Unscrambling the Secret of Encryption." *Security Management,* February 1995, pp. 67–70.

Keough, Patrick. "Talking Trash." *Security Management,* February 1995, pp. 24–27.

Kluepfel, Henry M. "A Recipe for Hacker Heartburn." *Security Management,* January 1995, pp. 40–44.

Kochen, William L. "Securing a Secret Trust." *Security Management,* September 1994, pp. 142–7.

Kornegay, Jennifer. "Security Goes Green." *Security Management,* August 1991, pp. 95–96.

Krott, Rob. "The New Crime Frontier: Surfing the Net with Cybercops, Phreakers and Hackers." *Security Concepts,* October 1994, pp. 1, 7.

LeBeau, Michael. "Protecting the Information Superhighway: How to Avoid Toll Fraud." *Security Technology and Design,* September 1994, pp. 68–71.

Lipman report. "Safeguarding Against Computer Crime." November 15, 1988.

Littlejohn, Robert F. "The Target Company." *Security Management,* September 1994, pp. 134–41.

Lukes, Beth. "Protecting 'Windows' of Information." *Security Technology and Design,* August 1994, p. 32.

Manning, Walt W. and White, Gary H. "Data Diddling, Salami Slicing, Trojan Horses . . . Can Your Agency Handle Computer Crimes?" *Police Chief,* April 1990, pp. 46–49.

Martin, Deirdre. "Fighting Computer Crime." *Law Enforcement Technology,* October 1993, pp. 82–84.

Mele, Joe A. "Protected Computer Security." *Security Technology and Design,* September 1994, p. 71.

Moskowitz, Carl. "Flectron Defends Against Corporate Espionage." *Security Technology and Design,* October 1994, pp. 58–60.

Murray, Kevin D. "Espionage 101 . . . and Much More." *Security Management,* July 1992, pp. 106–14.

Nugent, Hugh. *State Computer Crime Statutes.* Washington, DC: National Institute of Justice, Research in Action, November 1991.

Olick, M. "Joy-Riding in Cyberspace." *Security Concepts,* April 1994, pp. 12, 20.

Patterson, Tom. "Notebook Security in a Nutshell." *Security Management,* September 1993, pp. 93–96.

Pavlicek, Larry. "Developing a Counterintelligence Mind-set." *Security Management,* April 1992, pp. 54–56.

Perry, W. E. *Management Strategies for Computer Security.* Stoneham, MA: Butterworth Publishers, 1985.

Preston, Charles M. "The Data Dilemma." *Security Management,* February 1995, pp. 29–32.
Schwartau, Winn. "Low Cost Computer Security." *Security Management,* June 1994, pp. 59–60.
Schweitzer, James A. "Defining the Mission." *Security Management,* February 1992, pp. 53–54.
Schweitzer, James A. "Eight Rules of Computer Security." *Security Management,* May 1993, pp. 60–61.
Scuro, Daniel P. "Allies . . . or Enemies?" *Security Management,* January 1992, pp. 78–80.
Somerson, Ira S. "Information: What It Costs When It's Lost." *Security Management,* October 1994, pp. 61–65.
Steinbrecher, David. "Getting a Lock on Controlling Corporate Data." *Today's Office,* May 1987, pp. 40–46.
Strandberg, Keith W. "Chief Alfred Olson Pursues Crime in Cyberspace." *Law Enforcement Technology,* October 1993, pp. 22–23.
Swartwood, Dan T. "Is the Secret Out?" *Security Management,* June 1993, pp. 42–46.
Syed, Sohail A. and Totton, Mark S. "The Dos and Don'ts of DISE." *Security Management,* September 1992, pp. 131–32.
Tanzer, Marc. "Foiling the New Corporate Spy." *Security Management,* September 1992, pp. 38–42.
Toffler, Alvin. *Power Shift.* New York: Bantam Publishers, 1990.
Wade, Bob. "Encryption: A Primer." *Security Management,* March 1993, pp. 15A–20A.
Wade, James R. "Brave New World of Communications Technology." *Security Management,* March 1993, pp. 4A–6A.
Waltman, Jim. "Who's On the Line?" *Security Management,* May 1994, pp. 52–56.
Washington Post. "Army Looking for a Few Good Hackers to Disable Enemy Software." (Minneapolis/St. Paul) *Star Tribune,* Thursday, May 24, 1990, p. 7A.
Wenek, John R. "Fax Attack: Who's Getting the Message?" *Security Management,* May 1994, pp. 57–60.
Worthen, John D. "The P's and Q's of Protecting Your PCs." *Security Management,* September 1992, pp. 146–7.

CASES

California v. Greenwood, 486 U.S. 35, 108 S.Ct. 1625 (1988)
State v. Burleson, Dist. Ct., Tarrant City, TX: No. 0324930R, 1988.
United States of America v. John DiGilio et al., 538 F.2d 972 (1976)
United States of America v. Paul A. Lambert, 446 F.Supp. 890 (1978)

CHAPTER 10

ENHANCING PUBLIC RELATIONS

DO YOU KNOW

- What public relations is?
- What role security personnel have in public relations?
- What factors are important to effective public relations?
- What special populations security personnel must learn to interact with?
- What medical or other conditions can be mistaken for intoxication or being high on drugs?
- What balance security managers should strive for when dealing with the press and the media?
- How effective public relations affects security?

CAN YOU DEFINE THESE TERMS?

Alzheimer's disease (A.D.)
disability
epilepsy
public relations

INTRODUCTION

When you enter a business establishment and immediately encounter a uniformed security officer, how this officer acts toward you will greatly influence how you feel about the business itself. If the officer smiles, requests that you sign in with the receptionist and indicates exactly where the receptionist is, you are likely to feel welcomed and as though you have been helped. If, in contrast, the security officer bars your way and demands to know your business, you will have a completely different reaction. The image projected by security officers is critical to a business's or organization's public relations efforts.

This chapter begins by defining public relations and discussing the role of security personnel in public relations efforts, including the key factors involved. This is followed by a discussion of interaction with specific types of individuals such as the elderly, those with disabilities or impairing diseases, individuals who speak limited English, those who are homeless and those who are intoxicated or drug-impaired or just plain disorderly.

Next the importance of self-understanding and the image projected is examined, followed by a discussion of interacting and cooperating with the press, the media and the public police. The chapter concludes with an examination of how effective public relations can promote the entire security effort.

PUBLIC RELATIONS DEFINED

Public relations is a planned program of policies and conduct designed to increase the publics' confidence in and understanding of a business or organization. These publics may include customers, suppliers, creditors, competitors, employees, stockholders, members of the community or the government.

> Public relations includes all activities undertaken to enhance image and create goodwill.

Think for a moment about what makes for good interpersonal relations. How should people act toward one another if they want to establish solid, lasting friendships? Obviously, they will be considerate, open, honest, caring and the like. The same characteristics are important in building "public" relations. Most businesses and organizations are vitally concerned with how they are perceived by their many publics.

THE ROLE OF SECURITY PERSONNEL IN PUBLIC RELATIONS

Properly attired security officers who look professional and act professionally make a positive impression on those who come into contact with them. Such security officers, in fact, make a statement to employees and the public about how this particular company or organization does business, that is, that it takes itself, its business and it customers seriously. The importance of this function is noted by Brennan (1985, p. 32):

> In many cases, a security guard is the first employee with whom customers come into contact, and the importance of first impressions cannot be overstated. The significance of a properly uniformed guard is obvious and well recognized in the case of banks and other facilities that have large amounts of cash on hand and where public trust is essential. Still, the benefits of highly visible professional security officers can be substantial for nearly any type of company.

> Private security officers convey an image of their employer that can either promote or detract from public relations efforts. Promoting good public relations is a vital part of any security officer's job.

Brennan notes that before the Second World War most security was provided by night watchmen who made rounds with a flashlight. Because they worked when no one else was around, they dressed as they pleased, which was usually very casually. Unfortunately, this is the image many people still have of security officers: that of an untrained guard dressed like a bum, making rounds between snoozes. This image must be dispelled.

Hamit (1994, p. 79) provides the example of the security officers in the hotels/casinos in Las Vegas as exhibiting a high level of professionalism and self-esteem:

> [A]lthough they are uniformed and well armed, these officers could give many police officers pointers on how to deal with the public without losing their edge. They are generally a model for the ideal of being firm but courteous. In a hotel, of course, the safety of the guest is the highest order of business. The industry knows that one bad incident can hurt profits for years to come.

Factors Involved in Public Relations

To promote public relations, security personnel must be professional in every way.

> Good public relations require that security personnel:
> - Look professional;
> - Act professionally.

Appearance

One of the most important factors in a professional appearance is the uniform worn by the on-line officers. Brennan (1985, p. 32) warns: "Don't allow your guards to look like janitors and expect them to behave like professionals." He describes three types of uniforms currently in use: the military look, the security officer look and the soft look. Each has advantages and disadvantages.

The military uniform resembles that of police officers or officers in a branch of the military. It typically has a brimmed cap, a dark blue coat with matching pants, a white shirt, dark tie, black shoes and black socks. Such a uniform is often decorated with brass buttons, braids, stripes and epaulets. The badge is likely to be metal. Advantages to the military look include the sense of authority it conveys, as well as its aura of professionalism. Such uniforms also have disadvantages, however, including the fact that they are frequently cumbersome and bulky and that they are relatively expensive—to buy and to maintain. In addition, care must be taken that they do not too closely resemble the community's public police officers' uniforms. Brennan suggests that the military look is perhaps best suited for "stationary security officer positions where a highly visible security presence is desired."

The security officer uniform is less "official"-looking. Many security companies have established their own identities and reflect these identities in the uniforms provided their officers. Such uniforms frequently are of a color different from the traditional "police blue"—for example, brown, light blue or

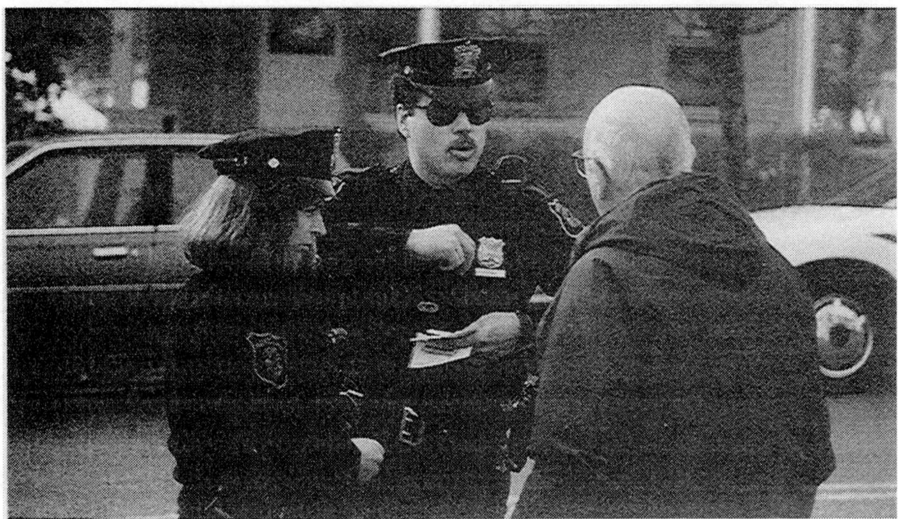

Military-type uniform.

forest green. Fabrics and styles are more functional, durable and easy to keep up. The jackets are usually shorter than the military-type jackets, are lighter and are water-repellent. They are not as heavily "decorated" as the military-style uniforms, and the badges are likely to be fabric rather than metal. Many do not have jackets. Such uniforms have the advantages of being clearly distinguishable from those of law enforcement officers, of being less bulky and cumbersome and of being relatively less expensive—to buy and to maintain. Brennan cites the comments of Rick Massimei, vice president of Metro Security Systems, Inc., in Tampa, Florida, in support of the security officer-type uniforms:

> We want our guards to be distinguishable as legitimate security officers. . . . A properly uniformed guard who looks and acts professionally will deter would-be criminals just as effectively as a guard whose uniform closely mimics the police. . . . They can be even more effective, because their presence tells criminals they are assigned solely to the location they patrol, rather than being mistaken for police officers who just happen to be in the area.

The soft look uniform is much more casual than either the military or the security officer-type uniform. It usually consists of a blazer with a cloth badge and contrasting slacks, frequently gray or blue. These uniforms are most often used by officers who work exclusively indoors, usually in office buildings or institutions such as museums, libraries and hospitals. The soft look is very low key and will blend in well with a corporate or office environment where an emphasis on security is deemed to be intimidating.

The style of uniform is not the only factor important in a security officer's appearance. Equally important is that it be clean and well pressed, and that the officer also be neatly groomed. Shirts should be clean, shoes should be shined, hair should be clean and combed and a smile should be present, under

Security officer-type uniform.

normal circumstances. An officer in uniform is a "walking advertisement for the company he works for" (Hamit, 1994, p. 98).

For security officers who drive company vehicles, the appearance of the vehicle and its condition are important. Frequently it is all a citizen sees, so it makes a major impression. It should be washed regularly, and the interior should be kept free of debris. In addition, how officers drive their vehicles will reflect on their professionalism. Rudeness, impatience and illegal driving should be scrupulously avoided.

Actions

Looking professional is not enough. Security officers must also act professionally. To do so, they must have a positive attitude toward their work. Zaleski (1986, p. 136), security supervisor at the corporate headquarters of Aetna Life Insurance Company, emphasizes this: "We should make sure they have the proper attitude and what I consider to be the three most important assets any security officer can have: a sense of humor, a sense of compassion, and good, old-fashioned common sense." Security officers should see themselves as providers of service and assistance, not as simply enforcers of company rules and policies. They should be perceived of as friend rather than enemy. When they encounter situations where they must intervene in an "enforcing" way, their actions should be objective, unemotional and understandable. For example, if a visitor is in an unauthorized area, the security officer should calmly explain the situation and escort the visitor out of the area. There is no need to be rude. A clear explanation and a firm request for action of some sort is generally all that will be required.

If security officers are to act professionally, they must fully understand what they are protecting and why it must be secure. They need to understand the company's policies as well as its goals and mission. They must understand what is expected of them and be trained to do it. And they must feel that they are supported. Zaleski (p. 135) notes the importance of this support:

> In many companies it is a firm policy that a direction given to an employee by a security officer carries the same force as a direction given by the employee's supervisor, as long as the security officer is acting within the bounds of his or her authority. Word of that type of support may spread quickly through your security department, and your officers will come to understand that if they act within the boundaries of their authority, they will always be supported, an especially important consideration when unpleasant situations occur on the job. . . . Security people like to feel their job is unique, and it does take a unique individual to be a good security officer. The fact of the matter is that security is not a nine-to-five job, and it is not for everyone. It takes a very special breed of person to be a security officer, to work seven days a week, rotating shifts in some cases, to work weekends and holidays, and to give up time with family and friends. There is a lot more than money at stake when a person decides to enter security as a career.

Security officers who have this positive self-image and are supported will do much to enhance their employer's image. In addition, although security officers are not usually thought of as part of management, they represent management when they enforce company rules. Hertig (1985, p. 85) suggests that, as a result of representing management, security officers "must be skilled in many of the same techniques required for management personnel, such as interviewing and assessment methods, written communication skills, and interpersonal communication techniques. In addition, security officers are frequently called on to instruct groups of people. . . . An officer's ability to communicate well is important to his or her job performance."

In addition to greeting people in a friendly manner and answering their questions politely, security personnel should know their facility so they can guide and direct people as requested. And they should be skilled at handling telephone conversations properly, an important way to build a positive image. The sound of a voice makes a profound impression on the caller. It should be firm yet friendly, and loud enough to be heard easily. If the officer is assigned to answer a phone, it should be done promptly—within three rings when possible. The officer should state his or her name and title, and ask what information or assistance is required. Seldom should a caller be asked to "hold." It is extremely exasperating to a caller to be put on hold.

INTERACTION WITH INDIVIDUALS

The most significant interaction security personnel have is one-on-one, be it with employees, visitors or clients/customers. As our society becomes more diverse, security personnel must understand the individual differences they are likely to encounter. Some differences such as age, sex, socioeconomic conditions and educational levels have been recognized and dealt with in public relations programs.

One such difference becoming of increasing concern is the elderly population. Other differences are less commonly known and are often much more difficult for security personnel to deal with. These differences include people with disabilities, people newly arrived in the United States who speak little English and the homeless.

> Security personnel may need to interact with the elderly, the disabled, non-English-speaking individuals and those who are homeless.

The Elderly

In the past decade the number of Americans age 65 years and older has increased by approximately 23 percent (Exter, 1989). According to Manning and Proctor (1989, p. 1D), the first wave of "baby boomers" will turn 50 in 1996, beginning a "senior boom" in the United States. By 2010 one-fourth of our population will be 55 or older.

One problem often accompanying advancing years is **Alzheimer's disease (A.D.).** Some 2.5 million American citizens have Alzheimer's. According to the Alzheimer's Disease and Related Disorders Association (1987, p. 5), the symptoms of Alzheimer's disease include the following:

> Gradual memory loss, impairment of judgment, disorientation, personality change, decline in ability to perform routine tasks, behavior change, difficulty in learning, loss of language skills and a decline in intellectual function.

Alzheimer's disease can cause several behavior problems that might bring the person into contact with security officers.

Wandering is common. A.D. victims may become hopelessly lost. They may not remember where they live or where they were going. They may become confused, uncooperative or even combative when questioned.

Indecent exposure is sometimes the result of the tendency of Alzheimer victims to fidget and to repeat behaviors. As noted by the A.D. Association (1987): "The A.D. victim who zips and unzips his pants or unbuttons her blouse in public may simply be fidgeting." They also have limited impulse control, and if clothing is too warm or is uncomfortable, they may simply take it off.

Shoplifting may occur as the result of simply forgetting to pay for an item. In addition, A.D. victims may misplace their purses or billfolds while shopping and then accuse store personnel of stealing from them. They may forget how much money they have or how much they have spent.

Poor driving and *auto accidents* are also problems. A.D. victims may lose their cars, forget that they drove somewhere and report their cars stolen, or have an accident and leave, actually forgetting that the accident happened or simply driving off.

The *appearance of intoxication* may bring A.D. sufferers to the attention of security personnel. Their wandering, confusion, inability to answer questions or driving behavior may be mistakenly interpreted as intoxication.

> Individuals with Alzheimer's disease may appear to be intoxicated.

Security personnel should be familiar with the symptoms of A.D. and have strategies for dealing with A.D. victims whom they encounter. The following suggestions are offered by the A.D. Association:

- Look for an ID bracelet or other identification.
- Avoid lectures or confrontation. They will not work with these people, and they are likely to make things worse.
- Keep communication simple. Speak softly and slowly.
- Identify yourself and explain what you are or will be doing, even if it is obvious.
- Use distraction to end inappropriate behavior. Sometimes just your presence will accomplish that.
- Maintain eye contact when speaking.
- Try to maintain a calm atmosphere. A.D. patients are prone to "catastrophic reactions" which you want to avoid.
- During a catastrophic reaction, A.D. patients often lash out, verbally and/or physically, at people who try to help them.
- Avoid restraints if possible. Physical restraints are almost certain to cause a catastrophic reaction.

The elderly may also have vision or hearing problems, or both.

Individuals with Disabilities or Impairing Diseases

A **disability** is any physical or mental impairment that substantially limits one or more major life activities of an individual.

Some 43 million Americans have some sort of disability, making them the largest minority group in the country. Recent legislation has made it illegal to discriminate against such individuals. The Americans with Disabilities Act (ADA), enacted in 1990, states:

> No individual shall be discriminated against on the basis of disability in the full and equal enjoyment of the goods, services, facilities, privileges, advantages, or accommodations of any place of public accommodation.

If charged and found guilty of violating the ADA, defendants face damages of up to $50,000 for the first violation and $100,000 for any subsequent violations.

As noted by Weiland (1995, p. 33): "The ADA was ground-breaking legislation. There's no question of that." For security managers who function in "public" facilities, the implications of this act are profound. Wheelchair ramps, wider doorways, accessible drinking fountains, elevators—the list of physical requirements is extensive. In addition, Cushing (1992, p. 19A) suggests:

> Just as the Americans with Disabilities Act requires us to build ramps, let our own commitment to inclusive communities require us to build attitudinal ramps. We can't really fight attitudes of discrimination and exclusion unless we do an end-run against ingrained beliefs.
>
> Perhaps individuals with disabilities will eventually serve as the unifiers of society. People with disabilities come from all races, socioeconomic groups and religions. The smartest and the strongest can be laid low as easily as all others.
>
> Perhaps if we begin to look at a disability as an equalizer, we'll understand that the greatest disability is what we do to our nation by preventing others from achieving their potential.

Also of importance to security officers and managers who are likely to deal with individuals with disabilities is the "politically" correct terminology. According to the "People with Disabilities Terminology Guide," (1992) using terms and definitions from the President's Committee on Employment of People with Disabilities," the following guidelines apply:

> General Guidelines
>
> - Put the person before the disability. For example, use "people with disabilities" as opposed to "disabled people" or "the disabled."
> - Do not use phrases such as "confined to a wheelchair," "crippled," "afflicted," "victim of" or "suffers from a disorder." These references diminish the individual's dignity and magnify the disability. Instead, refer to "the person who uses a wheelchair" or "the person with an emotional disorder."
> - Avoid portraying people with disabilities as superhuman, courageous, poor or unfortunate. Remember, people with disabilities do not want to be, nor should they be, measured against a separate set of expectations.
> - Avoid using trendy euphemisms to describe people with disabilities. Expressions such as "physically challenged," "special" and "handi-capable" generally are regarded by the disability community as patronizing and inaccurate. Stick with simple language, such as "people with disabilities" or "the person who is deaf."
>
> Guidelines on Specific Terminology
>
> It is probably unnecessary to mention a person's disability. If a person's disability is not in any way relevant to the story or the issue, leave it out.
>
> However, if a person's disability *is* relevant to a story or issue, it is important to understand the difference between impairment, disability and handicap.
>
> - *Impairment* is used to characterize a physical, mental or physiological loss, abnormality or injury that causes a limitation in one or more major life

functions. For example, "The loss of her right arm was only a slight impairment to her ability to drive."

- *Disability* refers to a functional limitation that affects an individual's ability to perform certain functions. For example, it is correct to say, "Despite his disability, he still was able to maintain employment."
- *Handicap* describes a barrier or problem created by society or the environment. For example, "The teacher's negative attitude was a handicap to her." Or, "The stairs leading to the stage were a handicap to him."

When necessary to refer to a person's disability, use the following list as a guide:

- *Deaf* refers to profound hearing loss. *Hearing impaired* may be used to describe any degree of hearing loss, from slight to profound. Use hearing impaired instead of antiquated terms such as "hard of hearing."
- *Blind* most frequently is used to describe a severe vision loss. Either blind or visually impaired are acceptable terms to describe all degrees of vision loss.
- *Developmental disability* is any severe mental and/or physical disorder that began before age 22 and continues indefinitely. Individuals with mental retardation, autism, cerebral palsy, epilepsy and other similar long-term disabilities may be considered to have developmental disabilities.
- *Mental illness* is a term describing many forms of illnesses such as schizophrenia, depression and emotional disorders. Use "person with a mental disability" rather than referring to an individual as "deranged" or "deviant." Clinical terms such as "neurotic" and "psychotic" should be used only for clinical writing. Other terms such as "demented," "insane," "abnormal," "deranged" and "mad" often are used incorrectly and should be avoided.
- *Nondisabled* is the correct way to refer to people without disabilities. Do not use "normal," "able-bodied" or "healthy" to describe people without disabilities, as these words imply a person with a disability isn't normal.

Table 10–1 (p. 322) summarizes the appropriate language to use when referring to disabilities.

Some physical disabilities are very obvious. Other disabilities, however, are not immediately apparent. Likewise, most impairing diseases are not immediately apparent and may be mistaken for intoxication, including Alzheimer's disease, as already discussed.

The visually impaired consist of over 11.5 million individuals according to the National Society to Prevent Blindness (Zehring, 1990, p. 33). When interacting with people who are blind, security officers should not only identify themselves, but also offer to let the person feel their badge or patch as a means of confirming their official capacity.

The hearing impaired are among those with "invisible" handicaps. Security personnel will interact more effectively with people who are hearing impaired if they understand that most deaf people are not good lip-readers.

> In addition, the speech of individuals who have been deaf since birth may sound garbled and even unintelligible. It has been mistaken for intoxication.

Table 10–1. Disability Language for the '90s

Acceptable	Substandard	Derogatory
People who are:		
blind, visually impaired	the blind, the visually impaired	those in darkness
deaf, hearing impaired	the deaf, the hearing impaired	deaf-mute, deaf and dumb
disabled	handicapped	abnormal
physically disabled	physically challenged	crippled, lame
mentally retarded	the retarded	moron, idiot, simple, retard
Persons with or who have:		
a disability	a handicap	a defect
cerebral palsy	afflicted with (stricken with, suffering from) cerebral palsy	spastic
mental illness	the mentally ill	crazy, psycho, lunatic
paraplegia, quadriplegia	confined to a wheelchair, wheelchair bound	trapped in a wheelchair, invalid, shut in
epilepsy, seizure disorder	victims of epilepsy	epileptic
a specific learning disorder	the learning disabled	slow learner

King (1990, pp. 98–100), director of deaf education at the University of Southern Mississippi, states: "Deaf people communicate differently, depending on the age at which the person became deaf, the type of deafness, language skills, speech and speech-reading abilities, intelligence, personality and educational background." He notes that, for officers who find themselves in a situation in which they need to communicate with a deaf individual, the key is to determine how that particular person communicates and use whatever combination of techniques is needed to help communication. He offers the following suggestions:

1. Get the person's attention. Gently tap a shoulder, wave, or call out loudly yet respectfully.
2. Make sure the person understands the topic of discussion.
3. Speak slowly and clearly, but do not overenunciate or overexaggerate words. This makes lip-reading difficult, if not impossible. Speak in short sentences.
4. Look directly at the person.
5. Do not place anything in your mouth when speaking. Pencil chewing or smoking make lip-reading more difficult.
6. Maintain eye contact. This conveys the feeling of direct communication.
7. Avoid standing in front of a light source.
8. Do not hesitate to communicate by paper and pencil. Keep the message simple.
9. Use pantomime, body language, and facial expressions.
10. If possible, learn sign language. Even basic signing can overcome barriers.

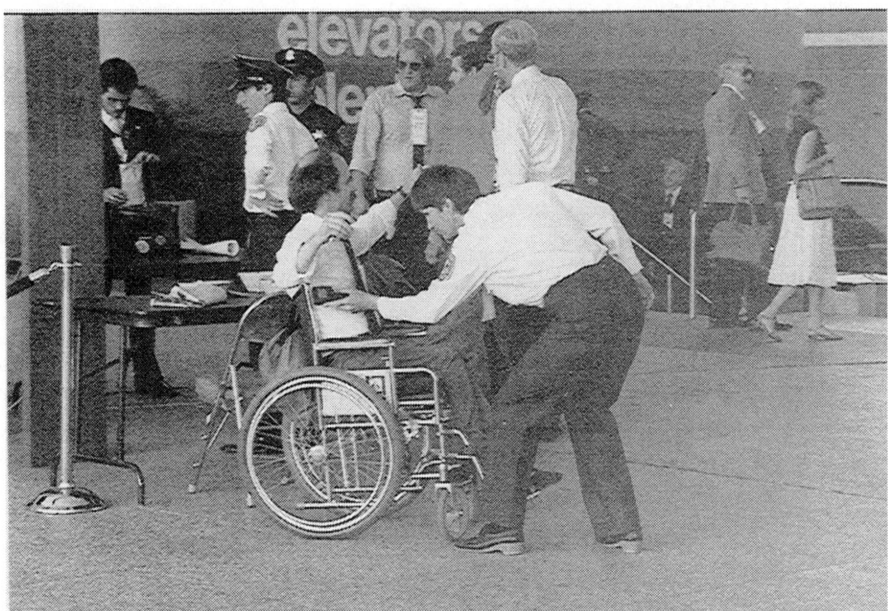

Going through security at a democratic national convention.

11. Do not assume the message has been understood just because the person nods.

People with Epilepsy

Epilepsy is a disorder that security officers should be familiar with. The Epilepsy Foundation of the University of Minnesota's educational program, "Epilepsy: A Positive ID," contains information all security personnel should know. The following discussion is based on information from that program.

Epilepsy is a disorder of the central nervous system in which a person tends to have recurrent seizures. It is:

- Chronic. (There is no cure. Medication or surgery is needed to control the seizures.)
- Episodic. (Seizures occur sometimes.)
- Sudden and unpredictable. (Seizures may occur at the most inopportune times—even when a person faithfully takes medication.)
- A disorder—*not* a disease. It is *not* contagious.

An important thing to know about seizures is that not all are convulsive. A seizure is not always a stiffening and jerking of the body. Seizures may alter behavior, level of consciousness, perception and/or the senses of individuals with epilepsy (*not* epileptics).

Absence seizures (formerly called petit mal) are often mistaken for daydreaming or staring and can occur up to 100 times a day or more.

Simple partial seizures consist of changes in motor function or sensations *without* accompanying alteration of consciousness. They may be characterized by stiffening or jerking in just one or more extremities, a strange feeling in the stomach, tingling or an alteration of taste or smell.

Complex partial seizures involve impairment of consciousness and may last from a few seconds to several minutes. The following behaviors may occur:

- Incoherent speech.
- Glassy-eyed staring.
- Aimless wandering.
- Chewing/lip-smacking motions.
- Picking at clothing.

The individual may be confused or need to rest after a seizure. This type of seizure may be mistaken for a drug or alcohol-induced stupor. A person having a complex partial seizure will have a fairly prompt return (several minutes) of his or her faculties, whereas a drunk or high person will not.

An epileptic seizure can look like street drugs or alcohol at work.

Table 10–2 summarizes the differences between an epileptic seizure and drug/alcohol abuse symptoms.

Epilepsy Education of the University of Minnesota suggests the following *assistance* for someone having a complex partial seizure:

- If possible, guide the person to a safe place to sit and let the seizure run its course.
- Keep the person calm.

Table 10–2. Epileptic Seizure or Drug/Alcohol Abuse?

Complex Partial Seizure Symptoms	Drug/Alcohol Abuse Symptoms
Chewing, lip smacking motions	Not likely
Picking at clothes	Not likely
Should regain consciousness in 30 seconds to 3 minutes, except in the rare case of a complex partial status (when seizure continues)	A drunk/high person will not recover in 3 minutes or less
No breath odor	A drunk will smell like alcohol
Possibly wearing an epilepsy I.D. bracelet/tag	Not likely

Symptoms common to both

- Impaired consciousness • Incoherent speech
- Glassy-eyed staring • Aimless wandering

SOURCE: Reprinted with permission of Epilepsy Education Program, University of Minnesota.

- Do not restrain the person in any fashion. He or she may resist.
- To determine level of consciousness, ask:
  - What is your name?
  - Where are you?
  - What day is it?
- Check for medical alert bracelet or tag.
- Smell breath for alcohol.
- Do not leave a confused person alone.

Generalized tonic (stiffening) *clonic* (jerking) *seizures* (formerly called grand mal) are what most people commonly associate with epilepsy. These seizures may last a few seconds to several minutes and may result in the following behaviors:

- Loss of consciousness.
- Falling.
- Stiffening and jerking (hence, the name tonic clonic).
- Tongue biting—sometimes.
- Drooling.
- Loss of bowel and bladder control—sometimes.

Epilepsy Education suggests the following *assistance* for a person experiencing a generalized tonic clonic seizure:

- Cushion head.
- Remove glasses.
- Loosen tie, collar.
- Clear the area of any hard objects the person may hit.
- Look for medical alert bracelet or tag.
- Do not put anything in the person's mouth (e.g., finger, pencil, tongue blade). This may damage the teeth or jaw.
- When seizure has subsided, turn person on his or her side and allow saliva to flow from mouth and keep the airway open.
- To determine level of consciousness, ask:
  - What is your name?
  - Where are you?
  - What day is it?
- If you arrive after the seizure, ask onlookers what they witnessed.
- Call for an ambulance if:
  - The person has hit head.
  - You suspect injury.
  - The seizure lasts more than 10 minutes.
  - The seizures occur one after another. This is a life-threatening situation requiring immediate action.

Epilepsy Education stresses that first responders need to be able to recognize seizures, administer the proper procedures and be responsive to the sensitivities and pride of people with epilepsy. The incorrect handling of a seizure can be embarrassing for the person having the seizure and can make the first responder potentially liable.

Non-English-Speaking Individuals

Thousands of immigrants and millions of foreign visitors arrive in our country annually. With such numbers, it is likely that security personnel will have encounters with individuals who speak no English or very limited English.

One obvious step toward effectively interacting with non-English-speaking individuals is to hire security personnel who speak other languages likely to be encountered within a given business or establishment.

Security personnel should recognize when a language barrier exists and be creative in finding ways to communicate. Often gestures are useful. If, for example, a security officer wants a non-English-speaking person to sign in, the officer could point to his or her name plate and imitate signing in. Many of the strategies useful with individuals having hearing impairments will work equally well with non-English-speaking individuals.

If management deems the language barrier to be a significant security/public relations problem, it might consider subscribing to the *language line*. This translation service offered by AT&T provides direct interpretations for police and other emergency service units that respond to calls. According to *Law Enforcement News* ("Parlez-Vous . . ." 1990, p. 3), the service is capable of providing translation for more than 140 languages from Swahili to Sanskrit. Subscribers are given cards that list all the languages the service can translate, written so non-English speakers can read the name of their language in their native script and point to it so the subscriber can connect with the right translator. Subscribers who encounter communication problems can call a toll-free number from almost any type of telephone and request the language needed on a 24-hour-a-day basis.

The Homeless

Studies indicate that 25 to 35 percent of the people living on the streets are alcoholics and that about 30 percent of all homeless people suffer from severe mental disorders (Glensor and Peak, 1994, p. 101). Dealing with individuals who are homeless may be the responsibility of security personnel who are assigned to bus depots, airports or any other type of structure where homeless people might seek temporary shelter.

According to Lamar (1988), more than two million people will be homeless sometimes during the year, one-third of whom will be families with children and one-fourth of whom will have jobs—the working poor. Lamar also says that one-third of the homeless are mentally ill.

The change in public attitudes toward the homeless is illustrated in three major cities that have toughened regulations on panhandling, sleeping in public places and other behavior associated with the homeless. As noted in *Insight* ("The New Drift . . ." 1990, p. 22): "While the plight of the homeless remains at the top of the nation's urban agenda, the public's sense of guilt appears to be giving way to exasperation. Responding to an unmistakable shift in public attitudes, officials in San Francisco, New York, and Washington, three of the most staunchly liberal cities in the nation, have adopted policies that now are

Security officers may need to deal with homeless people during their rounds.

as much attuned to the concerns of the average voter as to the demands of the homeless advocacy groups."

In New York City police are enforcing new regulations prohibiting lying down on floors or benches in Pennsylvania Station or Grand Central Terminal, panhandling, fighting or disrobing and urinating or defecating outside toilet facilities. In San Francisco new laws have displaced as many as 350 homeless who formerly camped in the Civic Center Plaza. In Washington, DC, the city council overturned a 1984 "right-to-shelter law" that was costing the city $40 million a year.

Security officers must walk a fine line between being compassionate with those who are homeless and protecting the employer's property and assets. Many security departments have been assigned the responsibility to keep the homeless off the property and to not allow them to use restrooms or come in out of inclimate weather. Handling such situations improperly or inhumanely can result in negative public attention from the media or advocate groups.

Security personnel should be aware of what kinds of assistance are available for the homeless and make this information known, including helping them to obtain services.

Intoxicated or Drug-Impaired Individuals

Recognizing intoxicated or drug-impaired individuals was discussed in Chapter 8. Security personnel who encounter individuals who appear to be under the influence of drugs or alcohol should identify themselves as "security" and should determine whether the individual is an employee. If the person is an employee, in most instances, that person's manager should be notified immediately and asked to deal with the situation. If the person is not an employee and the person's behavior is disruptive, security personnel should politely but firmly ask the person to leave the premises. In either case, an incident report should be completed.

Disorderly Individuals

Security personnel should usually follow the same procedures used for persons suspected to be under the influence of illegal drugs or alcohol. They should report disorderly individuals to their managers. After identifying themselves as "security," they should politely but firmly inform disorderly nonemployees that their behavior is unacceptable and they must leave the premises. In either instance, an incident report should be written.

Understanding Self and The Image Projected

In addition to being sensitive to the individual differences of those with whom they interact, security personnel should also be aware of their own beliefs, possible prejudices, insecurities in dealing with certain types of individuals and the image they are presenting to coworkers and the public.

As noted by Hamit (1994, p. 97): "The security industry, especially its human component, suffers from a lack of self-esteem. Generally, we are viewed as low-status, low-skilled individuals who are not really essential to the mission of the organizations we protect." This might be countered by following these suggestions for improving the one-on-one citizen contact, adapted from suggestions given by the International Association of Chiefs of Police (Training Key 94):

- Use a polite, unexcited or calm reasoning approach whenever possible. Try to be impersonal from two points of view: (1) remember the authority you wield is that of your employer, not yours personally, and (2) try to remain detached and not take as a personal insult or affront people's reaction to your authority.
- Be businesslike and self-assured; do not show anger, impatience, contempt, dislike, sarcasm and similar attitudes.
- Size things up as accurately as possible before making the contact. Be open-minded in evaluating the facts.
- Once you have the straight story, make your decision based on the policies and procedures under which you work and take decisive action.
- Offer explanations where advisable, but do not be trapped into arguing.
- Be civil and courteous.
- Show by your demeanor that you are not looking for and you do not expect any trouble.
- Try to avoid giving the impression that your presence constitutes a threat—either physical or psychological.

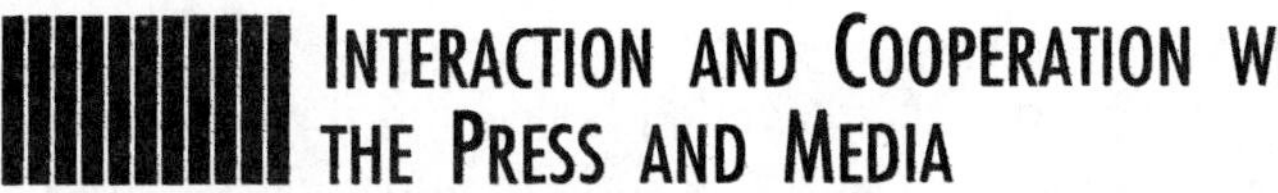

Interaction and Cooperation with the Press and Media

Garner (1989, p. 34) offers advice to police administrators that might be equally applicable to security administrators: "A police administrator can gain as much benefit from the media as they can from you. What they have to offer, in many instances, is publicity for your agency and to a lesser extent, yourself. With a little understanding, that publicity can be positive and make your organization look good. The secret to success is honesty and approachability." Other keys to success in dealing with the media include the following:

- Have a clear policy on what information is to be released to the press and what is not.
- Treat all reporters fairly.
- Be as sensitive to the need for privacy of employees, victims and witnesses as to the need of the public to know what is going on.

Some larger establishments have a public relations department which is the only one authorized to release information to the media.

> Security managers should balance the public's "right to know" and the reporters' First Amendment right to publish what they know with their employers' needs to withhold certain information and to protect their privacy.

Cawood (1995, p. 5) offers the following suggestions for managing the media:

- Keep cool.
- Be honest.—Never say "no comment."
- Don't volunteer information.
- Keep it simple.
- Stay in charge. Don't be afraid to call a time-out.
- Be prepared.

Cawood notes that sometimes workplace violence or disaster incidents end up in litigation. He cautions: "Make sure that any statements are clear and cannot be misconstrued as implying corporate wrongdoing." He also suggests leaving room for the unexpected by using phrases such as "as far as we know now" or "our investigation at this early point indicates."

Cooperation with Public Police

The importance of public police and private security personnel working together was discussed in Chapter 3. As noted by Bocklet (1990, p. 54): "The study [Hallcrest Report II] recommended that private security resources could contribute to cooperative, community-based crime prevention and security awareness programs. . . . The study recommended police and private security share crime prevention materials, specialized security equipment, expertise, and personnel."

How well public and private security agencies work together will depend in large part on how well they can communicate with each other and on how well the goals of each can be complementary rather than competing.

Public Relations and the Promotion of Security

Looking professional and acting professionally does much more than enhance public relations.

> A security officer who looks and acts like a professional will have a greater likelihood of preventing crime, the primary purpose for being hired initially.

Brennan (p. 34) suggests that, as a rule, "Professionally equipped, properly attired guards deliver a higher level of security." He quotes James Dunbar, CPP, president of the Loughlin Security Agency in Baltimore:

> There's no doubt that proper equipment and professional uniforms play a part in maintaining guards' security awareness, so they *do* react properly when the need arises. But the greatest value comes from deterrence—the number of crimes *not* attempted because of the presence of a uniformed guard. This is where we [contract guard companies] provide our greatest service to our customers—crimes that never happen because one of our guards was on the scene, looking and acting in a professional way.

> Good public relations can also promote the security program and its safety and protection objectives.

As noted by Shea (1987, p. 97):

> Every security department could benefit from using proven public relations methods to plan and develop its protection plan.
>
> Your security program will be more successful if you can encourage employees to comply with security procedures voluntarily. . . . A velvet-glove approach—not an authoritarian one—is best suited to achieving security compliance.

Shea describes several principles emphasized by Bernard Posner, public relations specialist, that cannot guarantee success, but whose absence generally cause failure:

- Define the objectives of your program early.
- Research the nature of the audience you are attempting to reach.
- Identify specific groups in that audience.
- Identify the trendsetters in each of these groups.
- Select the proper medium for communicating with each group.
- Develop a theme or slogan for your campaign.
- Pace the campaign to suit the environment in which it will be presented.
- Time specific aspects of the campaign for moments when they will make the greatest impression.
- Cooperate with other groups.
- Collect feedback from the target audience.

Objectives should be specific, measurable and in line with the overall philosophy and mission of the establishment. The audiences to be reached should also be very specific. In a retail establishment, for example, the audiences might include sales personnel, custodial staff, management and the public. Identifying trendsetters from among internal audiences is important because they can be approached to lend their support to the security objectives being introduced.

The medium to be used can vary from audience to audience and objective to objective and might include posters, signs, newsletters, additions to policy manuals, memos, announcements, meetings, orientation programs and in-service training sessions.

Timing and pacing can fit with state or national "drives" such as fire prevention week or accident prevention week. Cooperating with other groups would involve finding out what sort of personal, social and professional groups employees might belong to. For example, in a university setting, instructors may belong to a faculty association which could serve as a means of promoting security objectives.

After specific security measures have been in place for a prespecified amount of time, their effectiveness should be evaluated by getting feedback from a representative random sample of those involved. Purpura (1991, p. 62) notes:

> Too often in security and loss prevention texts and in practice attention is given to public relations while internal relations are ignored. Many experts state that the greatest threat to business or an organization is from within and employees throughout an organization can be recruited to aid loss prevention efforts.

According to Purpura (p. 63) several considerations are involved in effective human relations on the job, which he feels at their most basic level is simply getting along with others:

1. Make getting along with all employees as well as possible a conscious goal. Cooperation increases productivity.
2. Say hello to as many employees as possible, even if you do not know them.
3. Smile.
4. Think before you speak.

5. Be aware that nonverbal communication such as body language, facial expression, and tone of voice may reveal messages not included in your oral statements.
6. Listen carefully.
7. Maintain a sense of humor.
8. Try to look at each person as an individual. Avoid stereotyping (applying an inaccurate image of a group to an individual member of a group).
9. Personalities vary from one person to another.
10. People who are quiet may be shy, and these people should not be interpreted as being aloof.
11. Carefully consider rumors and those who gossip. Such information is often inaccurate.
12. Remember that when you speak about another person your comments are often repeated.
13. If possible, avoid people with negative attitudes. A positive attitude increases the quality of human relations and has an impact on many other activities (e.g., opportunity for advancement).
14. Do not flaunt your background.
15. Everybody makes mistakes. Maintain a positive attitude and learn from mistakes.

The importance to security programs of a good public relations program, going well beyond smiling and being friendly, is stressed by Shea (1987, p. 99):

> Friendly faces are pleasant to look at, but they don't communicate the need for specific security programs. Smiling security officers alone cannot persuade your target audience to comply with your security program. A successful security manager must know how to put a public relations program in gear. The successful application of proven public relations principles can increase a security department's ability to provide a safe and secure environment in which employees can work.

The benefits of a good internal and external public relations program are numerous:

- Builds respect among personnel and for the objectives of the organization.
- Reinforces compliance within the organization with policies and procedures to serve the public.
- Fosters assistance with the agency's activities and programs.
- Provides a united front with the general public against vulnerabilities which, in turn, creates lower losses.
- Assists in educating the employees, employers and community residents.
- Improves the understanding of the security function and the complex security problems involved.
- Reduces rumors and false information.
- Stimulates consciousness-raising of security measures.
- Makes for a more compatible environment.

Although this chapter is brief, its message is extremely important. Every action a security officer takes, or does not take, will affect not only his or her own image but that of the employer/business/company/institution as well.

Good public relations never stops. Look and act like a professional at all times.

SUMMARY

Public relations includes all activities undertaken to enhance image and create goodwill. Private security officers convey an image of their employer that can either promote or detract from public relations efforts. Promoting good public relations is a vital part of any security officer's job. Good public relations requires that security personnel look professional and act professionally as they deal with groups and with individuals.

Security personnel may need to interact with the elderly, the disabled, non-English-speaking individuals and those who are homeless. Individuals with Alzheimer's disease may appear to be intoxicated. Likewise, the speech of individuals who have been deaf since birth may sound garbled and even unintelligible and has been mistaken for intoxication. An epileptic seizure can look like street drugs or alcohol at work.

Security personnel may also interact with members of the media and the press. Security managers should balance the public's "right to know" and the reporters' First Amendment right to publish what they know with their employers' needs to withhold certain information and to protect their privacy.

Security officers who look professional and act professionally will have a greater likelihood of preventing crime. Good public relations can also promote the security program and its safety and protection objectives.

APPLICATION

Following is a list of public relations efforts a business or organization might engage in. Check those in which security personnel might play a role.

_____ Open house
_____ Reception
_____ Tour of the establishment
_____ Newsletter
_____ Speaking to local schools

CRITICAL THINKING EXERCISE

LEGAL LIABILITY

STATUTORY AND COMMON LAW

A security guard is liable whether his or her failure to act in a reasonable manner contributes to the cause of a person's injury. A security guard will not be held liable for failure to control the conduct of third persons; however, liability may arise where a guard stands in some special relationship to a victim of foreseeable injury.

Facts of the Case

In mid-summer, the Jack-In-The-Box fast food restaurant on East Vista Way in Vista, California, signed a contract with Royal Investigation and Patrol, Inc., to provide security in accordance with guidelines drafted by Foodmaker, Inc., the owner of Jack-In-The-Box. In the contract Royal agreed to minimize vandalism and parking lot problems to maximize customer volume. Guards were to patrol the parking lot and make "citizen's arrests, if the need arises and it is absolutely necessary for the protection of property and safety of employees and customers upon the premises." Royal prescribed that guards would not stress physical action. They preferred to attempt to handle incidents that arose by preempting any possible violent or explosive situation before it reached a critical stage. The Foodmaker guidelines required security guards to prevent loitering, request unruly persons to leave the premises and "detain anyone who creates damage to property or endangers lives for local law enforcement officers." If detention was not possible, they were to "obtain all pertinent information about the individual or incident" for law enforcement officers.

On September 8, Jim Prince and Derek Miller were assigned security guard duty. Their training program had consisted mainly of what they learned "on the job." About 11:30 P.M., Terry Hunt entered the restaurant. He was wearing dirty and bloody clothes, and there were smears of blood on his face and hands. Prince followed him into the restroom and after a short discussion asked him to leave the premises. Hunt left the building but stayed in the parking lot where Steve Gracelli joined him.

Twenty minutes later Hunt and Gracelli began to vandalize nearby Dean's Photo Service with a baseball bat. Dean's kiosk was located on the edge of the Jack-In-The-Box parking lot about 75 feet from the restaurant's drive-up window. A Jack-In-The-Box employee witnessed the vandalism and telephoned the sheriff's office. He then informed Prince and Miller about what was happening. Both security guards went to investigate.

Kevin Marios and Bruce Stingle were in their car waiting for their order when the vandalism began. Stingle got out of the car and approached Hunt and Gracelli. Marios followed, and when he saw them turn aggressively on Stingle, Marios armed himself with a beer bottle. Hunt grabbed the baseball bat and charged Marios. Marios dropped the bottle and tried to retreat. At this point Prince and Miller tried to tell Hunt to stop, but despite their efforts Hunt struck Marios with the bat. This assault occurred within several feet of the drive-up window.

Hunt and Gracelli then fled in a car they had parked on the other side of the lot. Prince and Miller took written notes on the make and license number of the car, which they turned over to the sheriff when he arrived moments later. They also told other employees to call for paramedics to assist Marios.

Marios later successfully sued Hunt and Gracelli for assault and battery. He also sued Foodmaker, Inc., for negligence.

ISSUES AND QUESTIONS

1. Would Marios have a case against Royal Investigation and Patrol as well as Prince and Miller?
   a. Hunt originally had cooperated with Prince and left the restaurant. Up to and including the time when the vandalism occurred, the security guards saw no risk of physical injury to anyone. The sheriff's office had been called. Prince and Miller tried to verbally restrain Hunt. When detention became impossible, they obtained all pertinent information and gave it to the sheriff. Thus they fulfilled their duty and neither they nor Royal can be viewed as negligent.
   b. Both Stingle and Marios voluntarily inserted themselves into a scene where vandalism was happening; they are responsible for their injuries. Because Marios threatened Hunt by arming himself with a beer bottle, he was attacked. The security guards owed them no duty to act affirmatively to prevent the assault; they did all they could by trying to talk Hunt out of attacking. This is a situation of nonfeasance as opposed to misfeasance.
   c. A generally recognized exception to the rule of negligence (where a security guard is liable whenever his failure to act in a reasonable manner contributes to the cause of a person's injury) is that a security guard will not be held liable for failure to control the conduct of third persons. As a matter of law, the events leading up to Marios' injury were unforeseeable. No reasonable duty or liability can thus be imposed.
   d. The security guards did not ensure that Hunt left not only the restaurant but also the parking lot. They did not physically intervene to prevent vandalism at Dean's, nor did they then detain or effect a citizen's arrest. Prince and Miller were already negligent before Stingle and Marios got out of their car. It takes no sophisticated philosophical analysis to know that a man smashing property with a baseball bat presents a foreseeable danger. These facts alone make for negligence of duty.
   e. After Hunt and Gracelli attacked Stingle, the risk of injury made it reasonable for Prince and Miller to take affirmative action to protect customers who were on the business's premises. When Hunt took the baseball bat and charged Marios, the threat of serious physical harm compelled the guards to do more than merely verbally try to persuade Hunt to stop. Because they did not react reasonably to this threat, they failed in their duty and they as well as Royal Investigation and Patrol can be held liable for damages.

DISCUSSION QUESTIONS

1. What type of uniform would you prefer to wear and why?
2. In what types of businesses is public relations most important?
3. Why is a sense of humor important for security personnel?
4. Why are communication skills important for security personnel?

5. What activities might a security officer volunteer to do to promote public relations?

REFERENCES

Alzheimer's Disease and Related Disorders Association. *Victim, Not Criminal: The Alzheimer Sufferer*. Chicago, IL, 1987.

Bocklet, Richard. "Police-Private Security Cooperation." *Law and Order,* December 1990, pp. 54–59.

Brennan, J. "Outfitting Your Guard Force." *Security Management,* June 1985, pp. 32–35.

Cawood, Gil. "Managing the Media." *ASIS Dynamics,* March/April 1995, p. 5.

Cushing, Loretto. "Attitudes about the Disabled Need Repair, Along with Buildings." (Minneapolis/St. Paul) *Star Tribune,* October 10, 1992, p. 19A.

Epilepsy Education. *Epilepsy: A Positive ID*. Minneapolis, MN: University of Minnesota, 1990.

Exter, Thomas. "Demographic Forecasts—On to Retirement." *American Demographics,* April 1989.

Garner, Gerald. "Working with the Media: Winning at the Interview Game." *Law and Order,* May 1989, pp. 34–37.

Glensor, Ronald W. and Peak, Ken. "Policing the Homeless: A Problem-Oriented Response." *The Police Chief,* October 1994, pp. 101–3.

Hamit, Francis. "A Corporate Culture for Security." *Security Technology and Design,* September 1994, pp. 97–98.

Hamit, Francis. "Cops for Hire: Where Is the Line Between Private Enterprise and Government?" *Security Technology and Design,* October 1994, pp. 77–79.

Hertig, C. A. "A Holistic Approach to Security Training." *Security Management,* March 1985, pp. 84–86.

"Improving the Officer/Citizen Contact." Training Key 94. International Association of Chiefs of Police.

King, J. Freeman. "The Law Officer and the Deaf." *Police Chief,* October 1990, pp. 98–100.

Lamar, Jacob V. "The Homeless: Brick by Brick." *Time,* October 24, 1988, pp. 34–38.

Manning, Anita and Proctor, David. "Senior Boom: The Future's New Wrinkle." *USA Today,* January 31, 1989, p. 1D.

"The New Drift in Homeless Policy." *Insight,* August 6, 1990, pp. 22–24.

"Parlez-Vous Miranda Warnings? Language Line Gives Police Gift of Gab." *Law Enforcement News,* September 30, 1990, p. 3.

"People with Disabilities Terminology Guide." Bethesda, MD: Good Will Industries of America, Inc., 1992.

Purpura, Philip. *Security and Loss Prevention: An Introduction,* 2d ed. Stoneham, MA: Butterworth-Heinemann, 1991.

Shea, John B. "More Than a Happy Face." *Security Management,* May 1987, pp. 97–99.

Weiland, Ross. "Equal Rights." *Successful Meetings,* January 1995, pp. 31–35.

Zaleski, J. E., Jr. "Should You Remake Your Security Image?" *Security Management,* August 1986, pp. 135–6.

Zehring, Timothy. "New Insights for the Visually Impaired." *Law and Order,* December 1990, pp. 33–35.

SECTION III

When Prevention Fails

The preceding section looked at ways to prevent losses and to ensure a safe, productive workplace. Despite security's best efforts, however, prevention does not always work. When accidents occur or crimes are committed, it is the function of security to investigate, sometimes singly, sometimes in cooperation with government officials or the public police (Chapter 11). A key to effective investigation is good communication skills to obtain the needed information and the ability to write professional reports that convey this information to others (Chapter 12). In addition, security officers and managers may be called upon to testify in civil or criminal matters in which their employers become involved (Chapter 13).

CHAPTER 11

The Investigative Function

Do You Know

- What a primary characteristic of an effective investigator is?
- What the primary responsibilities of an investigator are?
- What questions investigators must seek answers to?
- What the single most important factor is in the successful disposition of an incident?
- What makes sexual harassment illegal?
- What must be present before security officers can begin a criminal investigation?
- What crimes security personnel are likely to be asked to investigate?

Can You Define These Terms?

cybercop
investigate
predication

Introduction

Investigation means to trace or track mentally, to examine and take evidence, to find out by careful inquiry. The word **investigate** comes from the Latin word *vestigare,* which means "to track or trace." Investigative skills are important to those involved in security at all levels. The same skills discussed in this chapter will be of importance when conducting security surveys and risk assessments, the focus of Chapter 14. Whether working for a detective agency or as general security officers or managers, contract or proprietary, security personnel require certain basic investigative skills.

This chapter begins with a discussion of the characteristics of an effective investigator and the responsibilities involved. This is followed by information on investigating accidents, fires and sexual harassment allegations. Next, specific investigative background and investigative questions for specific crimes are provided. The chapter concludes with a brief discussion of avoiding lawsuits resulting from improper investigations.

Characteristics of an Effective Investigator

Effective investigators are able to obtain and retain information. They must be familiar with investigative equipment available and be knowledgeable of the balance between the rights of employers and the rights of employees. They must be observant, inquisitive, discerning, objective and logical.

A primary characteristic of an effective investigator is objectivity.

As noted by Wells (1992, p. 31): "Investigation is a tough, demanding business. What separates good investigators from bad investigators is attitude. A good investigator wants to get the facts; a bad investigator wants to get someone." This is mindful of the defense's claim in the O.J. Simpson trial that investigators made a "rush to judgment." Objectivity and an open mind are critical to effective investigation.

In addition, effective investigators know the laws and are able to conduct effective interviews and interrogations, as will be discussed later. As noted by Bennett and Hess (1994, p. 10): "Successful investigation involves a balance between the scientific knowledge of the investigative process acquired by study and experience and the skills acquired by the artful application of learned techniques."

Knowledgeable of Resources

As stressed by Wells (1992, p. 29): "Investigators should be intimately familiar with what is available for the asking: real estate records, mortgages, voter registrations, liens and judgments, deeds, birth and death certificates, criminal convictions—and the list goes on."

Pankau (1993, pp. 37–40) presents an extensive list of resources available for the "consummate investigator":

Law enforcement and intelligence sources include:

- The National Crime Information Center (NCIC) whose database includes criminal arrests, conviction, and intelligence on wanted suspects.
- The International Criminal Police Organization (INTERPOL), whose database includes location of suspects, fugitives, and witnesses; criminal history checks; prevention of terrorism; stolen artwork; weapons, motor vehicle, and license plate traces; and driver's license checks.
- El Paso Intelligence Center (EPIC), a database of U.S. Customs providing information on foreign travel.
- Financial Crimes Enforcement Network (FinCEN), a database of the U.S. Department of the Treasury, which includes information on case transactions and real property.

In addition, public records and credit bureaus may be of assistance in providing valuable information.

Garrett (1994, p. 71) notes that the amount of investigative information available through commercial on-line and CD-ROM databases is extensive and growing rapidly. Garrett (p. 73) provides the following "rules to search by":

- First, computers and databases do not replace the investigative thought process. They simply add a new dimension to it that investigators must learn to understand and use.
- Second, an investigator should never log on to any on-line service without a detailed search strategy prepared in advance.

- The on-line researcher should also try to avoid wild goose chase searches based on a possible lead that flashes across the screen.

Garrett suggests that on-line and CD-ROM database searches are especially helpful to locate, verify and identify investigations; to obtain background information and in financial investigations.

RESPONSIBILITIES OF INVESTIGATORS

Investigators have several responsibilities that will vary depending on the focus of the investigation. In most investigations, some or all of the following are responsibilities of security:

- Providing emergency assistance as a first priority.
- Securing the scene, to preserve evidence and to protect the safety of any injured people.
- Photographing, videotaping and sketching.
- Taking detailed notes.
- Searching for and collecting physical evidence.
- Obtaining information by interviewing witnesses to or victims of accidents or crimes.
- Interrogating suspects.
- Writing reports.
- Testifying in court.

> Primary responsibilities of investigators are to provide emergency assistance, secure the area of an incident, gather evidence and information, record information in notes and reports and testify about civil and criminal incidents in court.

According to Nemeth (1992, p. 7), investigation serves many purposes in both the civil and the criminal justice system, including the following:

1. To determine if there is sufficient factual evidence to support or defeat each element of a cause of action.
2. To accumulate the necessary factual evidence to prove or defeat a case at trial or to form the basis for a settlement.
3. To locate leads to additional evidence.
4. To locate persons or property.
5. To find evidence that might be used to discredit (impeach) a witness or the opponent.

> An investigation seeks answers to the questions: who, what, where, when, how and why?

Ricks et al. (1988, pp. 173–4) note the following areas in which investigations may be needed:

- Crime or wrongs committed or threatened;
- The identity, habits, conduct, movements, whereabouts, affiliations, associations, transactions, reputation, or character of any person, group of persons, association or organization, society, other group of persons or partnership or corporation;
- Preemployment background checks of personnel applicants;
- The conduct, honesty, efficiency, loyalty, or activities of employees, agents, contractors, and subcontractors;
- Incidents and illicit or illegal activities by persons against the employer or employer's property;
- Retail shoplifting;
- Internal theft by employees or other employee crime;
- The truth or falsity of any statement or representation;
- The whereabouts of missing persons;
- The location or recovery of lost or stolen property;
- The causes and origin of or responsibility for fires, libels or slanders, losses, accidents, damage, or injuries to property;
- The credibility of informants, witnesses, or other persons; and
- The securing of evidence to be used before investigating committees, boards of award or arbitration, or in the trial of civil or criminal cases and the preparation thereof.

No matter what the investigation involves, the information gathered by the security officer at the time is critical. As noted by Stokes et al. (1993, p. 51):

> "The single most important factor in determining the successful disposition of an incident is the information gathered by the security officer at the time of the initial report."

Surveillance

Sometimes investigators use surveillance to ascertain if safety violations or crimes are occurring. According to Wells (1992, p. 29): "In general, surveillance is legal as long as the reasonable expectation of privacy is not violated. Surveillance in a public place, for example, is generally permissible."

A caution when using video surveillance: do not violate an employee's right to privacy. As noted by Groussman (1995, p. 72): "Private sector employees who believe that their privacy rights have been violated when their employer uses hidden video cameras may challenge the employer's conduct in court."

Groussman describes a case where an employer, acting on a tip that drug deals were being made in the locker room, used a hidden video camera to investigate. When an employee noticed the camera, management stopped using it. Twenty employees filed a lawsuit against the employer for violating their right to privacy and for emotional distress. In this case, *Anderson et al. v. Monongahela Power Company and The Allegheny Power System Inc.* (1994),

School police gather information at a crime scene on Venice Boulevard in Los Angeles where a gang taking revenge left two dead.

the court ruled in favor of the plaintiffs, saying that other less intrusive alternatives were available to the defendants. As noted by Groussman (p. 72):

> The ruling of the court in this case implies that the use of covert video surveillance of employees cannot be based simply on the employer's suspicions. Surveillance must be based on a thorough preliminary investigation and a legitimate employer interest. Security managers should determine whether covert video surveillance is the least intrusive investigative technique available and whether there are reasonable alternatives.

Investigation and the Polygraph

The Employee Polygraph Protection Act stipulates that a lie detector can be used in the context of an ongoing investigation if the following conditions are met:

- The employer's business suffers the loss or injury, and the wrongdoing was intentional.
- The employee must have had access to the property.
- There must be reasonable suspicion that the employee was involved.
- The employee must be given a statement explaining these facts before the test.

INVESTIGATING ACCIDENTS

It's an old adage: "Accidents will happen." Sunstrom (1994, p. 32) describes the 300–30–1 accident ratio which basically says that for every 331 times a safety rule is violated, in 300 cases no injuries will result, in 30 instances a minor injury will result and in 1 instance a serious injury will result. When accidents happen, it is security's responsibility to determine why the accident happened and to take steps to assure that it will not happen again.

It is easy to say that the "cause" of an accident was that the employee was careless and didn't follow the safety precautions. But this will not eliminate future accidents of a similar nature. According to Sunstrom (1994, p. 32), when an accident happens, two reasons are often given:

- The money has not been budgeted for safety equipment.
- The task had to be done quickly.

According to Sunstrom: "Both reasons are excuses. They are both a way of saying, 'I didn't plan properly.' " Sunstrom explains how to deal effectively with accidents:

> When an accident occurs involving injury to an employee, it is important that senior management get involved immediately. The general manager should be on the scene quickly, asking questions, ensuring that the employee is properly cared for, and gathering facts. There is no better way of demonstrating that the company cares. . . . The general manager also makes it a point to get involved early and stay involved until the cause is identified.
>
> The next step is to identify specific preventive action. A completion date must be established, and security must follow up to ensure that the prevention recommendations were carried out.
>
> An accident investigation report should be completed and the lessons learned distributed to all employees in the organization. . . .

Improper lifting technique is a common cause of back injury.

Dealing with occupation health and safety issues is not easy. Like other security matters, it requires time, patience, and a willingness to learn new tasks. It also offers new opportunities for security practitioners who must find ways to enhance security's value to the corporation.

INVESTIGATING FIRES

The role of security should a fire occur is vital. Stokes et al.* (1993, pp. 56–57) suggest the following:

> Unconfined smoke and/or flames must be dealt with immediately. The first step is to call the fire department.
>
> - Sound the alarm; alert the fire department.
> - Cordon off the area.
> - Attempt to control the blaze if it is not out of hand.
> - Turn off the central air-conditioning and machinery, but leave lights on.
> - Close all doors and windows.
> - Ground all elevators.
> - Provide traffic control.
> - Direct firefighters to the location of the fire.
> - Time permitting, remove highly combustible stock and valuables.
> - Cover expensive merchandise or equipment, such as computers, with a tarpaulin to prevent water damage.
> - Administer first aid.
> - Record times/persons at the scene and around the scene.
> - Consider immediate photos/videotape.
> - Talk to witnesses.
> - Determine what started the fire.
> - Assess the damage caused.
> - Determine what can be done to prevent further damage.
> - Notify insurance company if appropriate.

INVESTIGATING COMPLAINTS OF SEXUAL HARASSMENT

Several high-profile incidents of alleged sexual harassment have focused attention on this issue. The Anita Hill/Clarence Thomas Senate hearings, the Navy Tailhook scandal and other incidents have heightened awareness of this problem.

The Equal Employment Opportunity Commission (EEOC) defines sexual harassment as "unwelcome sexual advances, requests for sexual favors, and other verbal or physical contact of a sexual nature" made implicitly or explicitly as a condition of employment (Morgan, 1993, p. 156). Sexual harassment has two conditions. First, it must occur in the workplace or an extension of

---

*The bulleted lists that follow are from a pocket-size *Outline Guide for Private Security* available from Innovative Systems, Publishers, P.O. Box 97, Blue Lake, CA 95525-0097.

the workplace. Second, it must be of a sexual nature that does not include romance.

Sexual harassment is illegal based on Title VII of the Civil Rights Act of 1964 and amendments in 1972 and 1991, as well as state and local laws.

Litchford (1994, p. 8) provides the following definitions of the two categories of behavior included in sexual harassment:

> *Quid pro quo sexual harassment.* This type of harassment occurs when submission to, or rejection of, unwelcome sexual conduct is used as the basis for employment decisions affecting the individual, or when some term of employment is either expressly or implicitly conditioned on participation in unwelcome sexual conduct.
>
> *Hostile work environment sexual harassment.* This type of harassment contains each of the following elements:
>
> - the conduct is unwelcome;
> - the conduct is sufficiently severe or pervasive to alter the conditions of the victim's employment and create an abusive working environment;
> - the conduct is perceived by the victim as hostile or abusive; and
> - the conduct creates an environment that a reasonable person would find hostile or abusive.

Sexual harassment includes sex-oriented comments or humor, subtle or overt pressure for sexual activity, physical contact such as patting or brushing against another person's body, demands for sexual favors that affect an individual's position or salary, posting sexually graphic materials and having different expectations for men and women.

Jacobs (1993, p. 34) cautions: "The 1991 Civil Rights Act, which, among other things, greatly expanded the remedies available to victims of sex discrimination, has upped the ante for lawsuit-prone employees." Jacobs notes that previously sexual discrimination or harassment cases were decided by a judge but that new law permits jury trials, which tend to favor the complainant.

Head and Veich (1994, p. 43) note that the number of harassment complaints filed with the EEOC has increased 71 percent and is likely to continue. They note:

> While individuals perpetrate sexual harassment, the EEOC holds the employer responsible for its prevention, and the courts consequently hold the employer liable for its occurrence. The direct costs to the organization can be staggering. Aside from the legal fees for defense and employee time lost, punitive and compensatory damages may be awarded to the victim.
>
> The organization may have to pay indirect costs as well. When sexual harassment occurs, employee morale drops significantly. This morale problem can lead to higher rates of absenteeism and turnover, job apathy, and a decrease in productivity.

Managers, including security managers, should be knowledgeable of sexual harassment and have policies in place to deal with it should it occur. All employees should have copies of the policy and should know the procedure to file a complaint. Managers must also know how to avoid harassment in their own behavior. The American Management Association (Head and Veich, 1994, p. 43) suggests that managers ask the following questions:

- Would you say it in front of your spouse, parent, or child?
- Would you say it if you were going to be quoted on the front page of the newspaper?
- Would you behave that way toward a member of your own sex?
- Why does it need to be said at all? What business is it furthering?

Jacobs (1993, p. 36) notes that the "first line of defense" against sexual harassment is to educate yourself about the issues and to act in a way that makes it clear what type of behavior is expected of others.

Morgan (1993, p. 156) notes: "Investigating sexual harassment is a relatively new responsibility. The process cannot be compared to criminal investigations, since it is not legally necessary to prove sexual harassment beyond a reasonable doubt. Hearsay evidence is acceptable. Companies must understand the law and then apply investigative techniques to document the findings."

Jayne (1993, p. 36) lists the following questions to ask someone who is making a sexual harassment complaint:

- What happened?
- How often has this occurred?
- What was the sequence of events?
- Did you in any way consent to the behavior?
- How have you responded to the person who harassed you?
- Did anyone else see or hear what happened to you?
- Has [the accused] punished you in any way?
- Have you told anybody about your problems with [the accused]?
- Have any other employees mentioned to you that they have experienced a similar problem with [the accused]?
- Are there any documents or other evidence involved?
- How does this conduct make you feel?
- What effect, if any, has this behavior had on your ability to do your job?

Jayne (1993, p. 36) cautions: "With few exceptions, business owners are liable for sexual harassment committed by company supervisors, clients and suppliers, even if the owners didn't know about the conduct."

Most sexual harassment complaints involve one person's word against another's. Therefore, the investigator's role is to determine who is being truthful. Jayne (1994, p. 37) suggests five goals for the investigator during interviews involving allegations of sexual harassment:

- Advise the employee of the sexual harassment allegation that was filed.
- Seek admissions or explanations concerning the allegation.
- Advise the employee of company policy concerning sexual harassment.
- Caution the employee about any retaliation against the victim.

- Advise the employee that a thorough and impartial investigation will be conducted and that he or she will be notified of its results.

Interviewers should avoid asking questions that directly address the allegations, focusing instead on the general interaction.

Webb (1993, pp. 96–97) suggests the following steps to properly investigate a sexual harassment complaint:

1. Interview the person complaining.
2. Interview the accused person.
3. Search for paperwork clues.
4. Assess the incidents.
5. If warranted, discipline the harasser.

Stokes et al. (1993, pp. 57–58) offer the following suggestions for investigating a sexual harassment complaint:

- Call the personnel officer if company policy requires.
- Determine the relationship of the victim and the suspect.
- Determine the exact nature of the harassment; was it verbal, physical, or both?
- Determine how long the harassment has been occurring.
- Determine if there have been witnesses to the harassment.
- Determine if other complaints of harassment have been made against the suspect.
- Obtain the suspect's version of the harassment.
- Refer the incident to the appropriate person or agency.

As noted by Morgan (1993, p. 157): "Treating a sexual harassment charge as a serious policy infraction and providing the appropriate investigative resources can encourage complainants to view court as an unnecessary last resort. This approach will also provide companies with the basis for a sound defense should formal charges be filed."

INVESTIGATING CRIMES

As noted by Stokes et al.: "It is recognized that most incidents uncovered occur on private property, and management has certain rights and obligations to decide what actions should be taken. In many instances, private action is more expedient, less expensive, and less embarrassing to the company. In addition, fear of lawsuits or a desire to protect the offender from a criminal record may be important."

According to Wells (1992, pp. 28–29), about 33 percent of allegations of criminal actions come from tips and complaints. About 20 percent come from management reviews or audits. The remaining 47 percent come from various sources.

Criminal investigations conducted by security officers are usually quite different than those conducted by public police. As noted by Wells (1992, p. 27): "Investigations in corporations involve employees, not hardened criminals.

Most of these employees have no history of criminal activity. And employees have rights criminals do not have." Wells (p. 28) cautions:

> Investigators in the private sector have less latitude conducting investigations. They must be much more sensitive to privacy issues—and for good reason. In an increasingly litigious society, investigators get sued for poking their noses into the business of others. As a result, investigators should open inquiries only on adequate predication.

> "Investigations by security personnel should be based on adequate **predication,** that is, the total set of circumstances that would lead a reasonable, prudent and professionally trained person to believe that an offense has occurred, is occurring or will occur" (*Fraud Examiners Manual*).

Predication is not as strong as the probable cause required for public police officers to arrest someone, but it must be more than mere suspicion.

Wrobleski and Hess (1993, p. 307) suggest that effective investigations require that officers: "(1) [T]ake their time, (2) use an organized approach that is efficient and methodical, because this may be their only chance to observe the scene, (3) recognize the issues and find the facts to settle these issues and (4) determine if a crime has been committed, and, if so, by whom and how."

The Hallcrest Report suggests that private security plays an important role in investigating both civil and criminal complaints, including the following:

arson
bankruptcy fraud
burglary
cargo theft
check fraud
commercial bribery
computer-related crime
credit-card fraud
drug abuse
embezzlement
extortion
industrial espionage
insurance fraud
pilferage/employee theft
receiving stolen property
robbery
securities/theft and fraud
shoplifting
terrorism
vandalism

Because fraud and embezzlement often involve altered documents, security personnel should know when to call in forensic document examiners (FDEs). As described by Hayes and Lettieri (1993, p. 76):

> An FDE examines, compares, and analyzes documents to determine entry authenticity and accuracy. In doing so, examiners decipher alterations, obliterations, additions, and deletions, showing authorship through the examination of handwriting or handprinting or by the source of typewriting, other impressions, marks, or evidence.

Hayes and Lettieri (p. 77) suggest that security managers institute policies to make an FDE's work easier and to aid in investigations. They note that one essential policy is to obtain handwriting standards from all employees to have on file. Handwriting exemplar forms are available from most FDEs.

Technology can be of great assistance in some types of investigations. For example, Anthem Corporation has released a PC software program to help detect and prove contract and procurement fraud:

> The Financial Crime Investigator uses expert systems technology to guide an investigator through a complicated fraud or corruption case in a fraction of the time previously required. The system uses artificial intelligence techniques to identify contract fraud indicators, convert them to possible schemes, identify the various remedies and suggest the steps necessary to conclude the case ("Attack on White Collar Crime," 1995, p. 10).

> Among the most common crimes security personnel will be asked to investigate are assault, breach of peace/disturbing the peace/disorderly conduct, burglary/unlawful entry/breaking and entering, theft, trespassing and vandalism.

Specific Crimes and Investigative Responsibilities

The following investigative background, responsibilities and tips are reprinted by permission from *Outline Guide for Private Security* (Stokes et al., 1993, pp. 52–61).

ASSAULT

In most states, assault is defined as an unlawful attempt, coupled with the present ability, to commit a violent injury to another person.

The degrees and forms of assault vary widely from state to state. For example, assault can vary in degree from simple assault or assault with a deadly weapon or assault with great bodily injury. It can vary in form from simple assault of another to spousal abuse, child abuse, or elder abuse. For demonstration purposes, only the simplest degree and form are discussed in this section.

Responsibilities

- Call the police if company policy requires.
- Interview victim for complete details of event.
- Note injuries to victim. Obtain photos, medical release, emergency room information, treatment.
- If weapon involved, consider photographing in place.
- Obtain complete description of suspect, vehicle, weapon, etc.
- Obtain complete details of the incident: was there provocation, escalation, etc.
- Separate and interview witnesses.
- Locate and interview suspect. Note any alibis. Photograph if appropriate.

Tips

- Denial or self-defense are common defenses.

- In spousal abuse incidents, evidence of "fresh complaint" (that is, what the victim said to the first person he or she told about the assault) can prove important.
- Determine if anyone was under the influence of alcohol or drugs.

BREACH OF PEACE/DISTURBING THE PEACE/DISORDERLY CONDUCT

This refers to any conduct that puts fear into employees or citizens when committed, whether in public or private.

Responsibilities

- Call the police if company policy requires.
- Note time you became involved in the incident.
- Assess any damages, property or personal, that may have occurred.
- Seek out witnesses.
- Interview witnesses when possible.
- Determine if additional assistance should be obtained.
- If people are injured, see to it that they receive medical assistance.
- Seek out cause of incident.
- Determine disposition.

BURGLARY/UNLAWFUL ENTRY/BREAKING AND ENTERING

The unauthorized or unlawful entry into a room or building by force or other means. The opening of a closed door or window will suffice whether it is locked or not. Anything that has been relied on to prevent intrusion constitutes a violation.

Responsibilities

- Call the police if company policy requires.
- Note time you were made aware of the incident.
- Determine how entry was made.
- Determine who discovered the entry.
- Obtain description of losses, including amount, brand names, manufacturers, model numbers, serial numbers, color, sizes, personal identifiers, unique marks, estimated value.
- Secure/protect the scene if necessary.
- Attempt to determine point of entry and point of exit. Thoroughly determine and examine those areas for physical evidence.
- Attempt to locate witnesses.
- Interview witnesses if possible.
- Mark any physical evidence that may be found at the scene.
- Photograph and diagram scene if possible.
- Determine appropriate disposition.

THEFT

Theft is taking the personal property of another with the intent to permanently deprive that person of the property. Theft includes shoplifting, purse snatching, and pickpocketing.

Responsibilities

- Call the police if company policy requires.
- Interview victim. Obtain a complete statement, including when the property was last seen, when it was discovered missing, and what the conditions were when the loss occurred.

- Obtain complete description of property loss, including amount, brand names, manufacturer's number, model number, serial numbers, color, sizes, personal identifiers, unique marks, estimated value.
- Secure/protect the scene if appropriate.
- Conduct thorough scene investigation including search for fingerprints, trace evidence, etc.
- Photograph/diagram scene if necessary.
- Search area for footprints, tireprints, other physical evidence.
- Attempt to locate witnesses.
- Interview all witnesses separately.
- If you have a suspect, interview and obtain a statement, including alibis.
- Contact insurance company if appropriate.

TRESPASS OF PROPERTY

To invade the property of another without permission. In most incidents an individual is on the private property of another person without permission.

Responsibilities

- Call the police if company policy requires.
- Note time you first observed the trespass.
- Note what called the person to your attention (actions, clothing, etc.).
- Determine if the person has any equipment with him such as a portable radio, beeper, or arson materials.
- Describe how you confronted the individual and the actions you took.
- Take statements from any witnesses.
- Determine appropriate disposition.

VANDALISM/CRIMINAL MISCHIEF/CRIMINAL DAMAGE TO PROPERTY

Vandalism is defined as a harmful act whereby the usefulness or value of property is considerably diminished or destroyed. It includes vending machines, windows, motor vehicles, telephone coin boxes, fixtures, signs, construction equipment, walls, restrooms, etc. Graffiti is included in vandalism.

Responsibilities

- Call the police if company policy requires.
- Note time you received the call or found the damage.
- Secure scene if necessary.
- Seek out witnesses or individuals having knowledge of incident.
- Conduct thorough scene investigation.
- Photograph scene if appropriate.
- Search for physical evidence.
- If you have a suspect, interview for possible admissions.

COMPUTER-RELATED CRIMES

McEwan (1995, p. 93) describes **cybercops** as investigators involved in the new field of computer forensics. He cautions: "[C]yberspace can be a confusing and challenging location to those in the tradition-laden field of law enforcement." Nonetheless, computer crimes are increasing rapidly, and law enforcement agencies must gear up to meet this challenge. He offers the following suggestions for dealing with computer-related crimes (pp. 93–94):

1. Prior to executing a search warrant, use intelligence sources to determine the likelihood of encountering computers at the scene.
2. To secure the site, remove all persons from the computers and prevent further access.
3. Immediately evaluate any possible evidence displayed on the monitor. If possible, photograph the screen and then unplug the system from the wall. Unplug any phone lines leading to the computer. NEVER use the toggle switch to turn off the machine, always unplug from the wall.
4. Photograph the rear of the machine to record the cabling configuration.
5. Label the cabling system (using masking tape and pen) before disconnecting any cables. Label all ports and slots so the proper reconstruction can be done later.
6. If more than one system is seized, keep the components separate.
7. Collect all operating manuals and software found at the scene, including collections of floppy disks and peripheral components, such as printers and keyboards. Pay attention to scraps of paper nearby that may note passwords.
8. In boxing the system for transport avoid static charges. Do not wrap the unit in plastic, and keep the unit away from electromagnetic sources such as the radio transmitter in the trunk of your car.
9. The property room should be temperature and climate controlled. Again, keep the unit away from magnetic sources such as stereo speakers.

Avoiding Lawsuits

Wells (1992, p. 28) suggests that security officers can avoid being sued by doing the following:

- Make sure there is predication to conduct an investigation.
- Respect the privacy and other rights of persons involved.
- Confine the investigation to questions.
- Refrain from making unnecessary comments or opinions.

Summary

A primary characteristic of an effective investigator is objectivity. Primary responsibilities of investigators are to provide emergency assistance, secure the area of an incident, gather evidence and information, record information in notes and reports and testify about civil and criminal incidents in court. The single most important factor in determining the successful disposition of an incident is the information gathered by the security officer at the time of the initial report.

One important area of investigation is that of claims of sexual harassment. Sexual harassment is illegal based on Title VII of the Civil Rights Act of 1964 and amendments in 1972 and 1991, as well as state and local laws. Security personnel also may become involved in investigating criminal acts. Investigations by security personnel should be based on adequate predication, that is, the total set of circumstances that would lead a reasonable, prudent and professionally trained person to believe that an offense has occurred, is occurring or will occur. Among the most common crimes security personnel will be asked to investigate are assault, breach of peace/disturbing the peace/disorderly conduct, burglary/unlawful entry/breaking and entering, theft, trespassing and vandalism.

Application

Bart Gibson, a security officer for the M. C. Auto Parts distribution center, has been told that the latest inventory indicates that many boxes of spark plugs have been unaccounted for and the losses are mounting. It is his job to find out what is happening and how these losses can be curtailed.

After considerable investigation and interviewing of personnel in the distribution center, Gibson is told that some employees throw parts out of the window at lunchtime into the bushes that surround the complex. After completing their shifts for the day, they then retrieve the stolen items and leave the premises. He also has heard rumors that there is a garage in the vicinity that is purchasing these stolen spark plugs at a very reduced price.

On Gibson's first surveillance of the window that abuts the shrubbery, where, according to his sources, some of the items are leaving the plant, he notices that several branches are moving as if someone has thrown something into the bushes. After the lunch hour, he makes a cursory search of the area where he observed the branch movement and finds one box of spark plugs, a water pump and a box of PCV valves.

He stakes out the site, and at 4:30 P.M., at the end of the shift, he notices Gary Schmitz go into the shrubbery area and come out with the described items. He lets Schmitz get into his car and drive off. He then stops Schmitz five blocks from the distribution center, confiscates the stolen items and brings Schmitz back to the plant security officer. There he notifies the security chief and begins to interview Schmitz about his activities.

Schmitz is somewhat cooperative but reluctant to tell the security officers about the thefts. The officers continue to verbally pressure Schmitz and threaten to prosecute him to the fullest extent of the law and to recommend jail time if he is convicted. Schmitz consents to tell all if the security officers will make a deal. He wants no prosecution because he would lose his job. However, he knows just about everything that is going on as far as parts thefts are concerned, and he knows who else is doing it.

This poses a problem for the security officers because they would like to show their bosses that they have done a good job and have broken up a theft ring within the plant. You are the decision maker.

- Under the circumstances, how far are you willing to concede to Schmitz's demands in order to stop further thefts?
- Should you deal with him at all?
- Do you think you can trust him?
- Will he lead you to the purchaser of the stolen parts?
- Is it ethical to make a deal with him?
- What will be the effect on the other employees?

It's your decision. What are you going to recommend?

CRITICAL THINKING EXERCISE

MALL SECURITY

STATUTORY AND COMMON LAW

"Whoever, with intent to commit a crime, does an act which is a substantial step toward, and more than preparation for, the commission of the crime is guilty of an attempt to commit that crime," according to Minnesota statutes. Anyone who assaults another person with a dangerous weapon may be sentenced to imprisonment for assault in the second degree. And if someone assaults a peace officer when that officer is effecting a lawful arrest or is executing any other duty and inflicts demonstrable bodily harm, then that person is guilty of a felony.

FACTS OF THE CASE

When the Mall of America in Bloomington, Minnesota, opened for business, security staff members were given security training, such as first aid, CPR and defusing tense crowd situations. Each carried handcuffs, pepper-spray canisters and batons, and they were in uniform.

On February 11 two security officers spotted Guillermo Garza-Herrera and two juvenile boys acting suspiciously near the transit station where about 100 persons were gathered waiting for busses. Police had previously informed security that illegal activity had occurred in the restrooms by the transit station. So about five minutes after observing Garza-Herrera and the juveniles go into the restroom, the two security officers decided to go in and check on what was going on. Garza-Herrera was standing with his hands in his pockets. When one of the guards asked him to take his hands out of his pockets, he at first hesitated but then did take his hands out. As a guard approached him, he stepped back, put his hand back into a pocket and pulled out a pistol. Garza-Herrera pointed the gun at the guard furthest from him and then aimed the gun at the head of the nearer guard and said "how 'bout this." The gun was about two feet away when the guard head a loud click. He said that the sound was what he "knows to be the sound of a gun trigger being pulled."

The gun did not discharge, but observers saw Garza-Herrera attempting to put another bullet into the pistol. The two security guards ran out of the restroom and called for armed transit police for assistance. When Garza-Herrera came out of the restroom, transit police officers with the assistance of the two security guards wrestled him to the ground without his putting up much resistance. A 17-year-old juvenile who was with Garza-Herrera, however, unsuccessfully attempted to intervene and free him. This juvenile, along with the other juvenile companion who attempted to escape, were arrested by the officers.

In Garza-Herrera's pocket, police officers found a second loaded clip for the pistol. A witness who observed the incident gave officers an unfired bullet that had been found on the restroom floor. Police later identified the pistol as a Colt .45 semiautomatic.

When questioned by police, Garza-Herrera denied that he attempted to shoot the security guard. One of the juveniles, however, told police that Garza-Herrera pointed the pistol at the security guard and pulled the trigger.

Garza-Herrera was taken to the Hennepin County Jail on $100,000 bail.

Issues and Questions

1. Did the security guards act appropriately and what charges should be brought against the gunman?
   - **a.** The security guards were acting within their duty by investigating suspicious behavior in an area where known illegal activities had occurred. Attempted murder charges in addition to second degree assault charges will be filed against Garza-Herrera.
   - **b.** Garza-Herrera may be held on a $100,000 bail, but because it is his word against the word of security guards, attempted murder charges should not be filed. Furthermore, a semiautomatic pistol could have a clip with more than one defective round in it. So Garza-Herrera was obviously not intending to commit murder; he was only bluffing. Second degree assault charges can be filed because they are clearly substantiated by observers who witnessed the incident.
   - **c.** The security guards were within their rights to investigate suspicious activities. They also acted appropriately in retreating in the face of threatened deadly force. Their retreat probably helped to avoid possible disaster. Once outside the restroom and confronted by police officers, Garza-Herrera did not assault anyone or cause further incident. He may be charged with attempted murder, but second degree assault charges are redundant and inappropriate.
   - **d.** The security guards had no warrant for arrest or right to invade the personal privacy of an individual in a restroom. Without a clear and probable cause of bodily harm to other patrons, the guards should not have assumed an aggressive attitude toward Garza-Herrera (who could, as a matter of fact, sue them for harassment). And even if they did have probable cause, their retreat in the face of deadly force leaves other patrons vulnerable, which is clearly a breach of their duty.
   - **e.** The security guards did not have probable cause for detaining or inspecting Garza-Herrera or his friends. As their advances and demands would alarm anyone, it is reasonable for someone to act in self-defense. Because no person suffered injury, no charges should be brought against Garza-Herrera or his companions.

Discussion Questions

1. How would you go about obtaining the basic skills needed to become an effective investigator?
2. What resources would you use if you were involved in a financial investigation?

3. What do you feel is the most important factor in determining the successful disposition of an incident you investigated?
4. What is the best way to curtail sexual harassment in a plant or office?
5. What is your understanding of the word *predication* as it applies to private security?

REFERENCES

"Attack on White Collar Crime." *Law Enforcement Technology,* March 1995, p. 10.

Bennett, Wayne W. and Hess, Kären M. *Criminal Investigation,* 4th ed. St. Paul, MN: West Publishing Company, 1994.

Garrett, Glen R. "In-House Investigations in the Information Age." *Security Management,* October 1994, pp. 71–73.

Groussman, Jon D. "Video Surveillance: Balancing Employee Privacy Rights." *Security Management,* January 1995, p. 72.

Hayes, James L. and Lettieri, Linda. "Reading Between the Lines." *Security Management,* September 1993, pp. 74–79.

Head, Thomas and Veich, Mickey. "Would You Say That in Front of Your Mother?" *Security Management,* February 1994, p. 43.

Jacobs, Deborah L. "Sexual Harassment: What You Don't Know Can Destroy Your Firm." *Your Company,* Spring 1993, pp. 34–39.

Jayne, Brian C. "Interviewing Strategies that Defeat Deceit." *Security Management,* February 1994, pp. 37–42.

Litchford, Jody M. "Preventing Sexual Harassment Liability in the Law Enforcement Workplace." *The Police Chief,* August 1994, pp. 8, 10.

McEwan, Tom. "Cybercops: Court-Defensible Evidence from Computer Forensics." *Law and Order,* March 1995, pp. 93–94.

Morgan, Lynn H. "Investigating Sexual Harassment: Procedures for Appropriate Management." *Security Management,* September 1993, pp. 156–7.

Pankau, Edmund J. "The Consummate Investigator." *Security Management,* February 1993, pp. 37–41.

Ricks, T.; Tilett, B.; and Van Meter, C. *Principles of Security.* Cincinnati, OH: Anderson Publishing Company, 1988.

Stokes, Floyd D.; Hess, Kären M.; and Wrobleski, Henry M. *Outline Guide for Private Security.* Blue Lake, CA: Innovative Systems, 1993.

Sunstrom, Philip C. "Become the Company's OSHA Oracle." *Security Management,* March 1994, pp. 24–32.

Webb, Susan L. "Handling a Problem: What to Do When an Employee Is Being Sexually Harassed." *Successful Meetings,* May 1993, pp. 96–97.

Wells, Joseph T. "What Inquiring Minds Need to Know: Why, When, and How to Conduct an Investigation." *Security Management,* November 1992, pp. 27–31.

Wrobleski, Henry M. and Hess, Kären M. *Introduction to Law Enforcement and Criminal Justice,* 4th ed. St. Paul, MN: West Publishing Company, 1993.

CASE

Anderson et al. v. Monongahela Power Company and The Allegheny Power System Inc., Cir.Ct., Monongalia County, West Virginia, No. 92–C–483, 1994.

CHAPTER 12

OBTAINING AND PROVIDING INFORMATION

DO YOU KNOW

- What the communication process involves?
- What the average speaking speed is? Listening or "word processing" speed?
- What nonverbal communication includes? Written nonverbal communication?
- What the lines of communication are?
- How to take notes?
- What the characteristics of effective notes are?
- What are the two basic types of reports security officers write?
- Why reports are so important?
- The characteristics of a well-written report?

CAN YOU DEFINE THESE TERMS?

administrative reports
calibrating
communication
conclusionary language
connotative words
denotative words
empathy
facts
feedback
grapevine
inferences
judgments
military time
nonverbal communication
operational reports
opinion
reports
24-hour clock

INTRODUCTION

One of the most basic jobs of security personnel is to obtain information and then provide it to others, usually in the form of a report.

Security managers are also in the communications business. Of all the skills needed to be an effective manager, skill in communicating is the most vital. In addition, a large part of security work at all levels involves some form of communication.

Effective communication can produce several positive outcomes. It can be used to inform, guide, reassure, persuade, motivate, negotiate or diffuse. In contrast, ineffective communication can result in confusion, false expectations, wrong conclusions, negative stereotypes, frustrations, anger, hostility, aggression and even physical confrontations.

Security managers and on-line officers routinely communicate in every facet of their jobs, not only in their interactions with those for whom they work and their employees, but also in their interactions with the public and with professionals in other fields. Communication is all around us. We are continuously bombarded by spoken and written messages, yet most people give little thought to what the communication process consists of, nor are they trained in communicating effectively.

This chapter begins by describing the communication process, including listening and nonverbal communication. This is followed by a look at barriers to communication and the lines of communication commonly found in the workplace. Next, general guidelines for facilitating communication and specific interviewing and interrogating techniques are introduced.

After the factors involved in obtaining information are discussed, the focus turns to providing this information to others, usually in the form of a written report. The basis for most reports is careful notes, described in detail in this chapter. This is followed by a discussion of the process of writing reports and characteristics of effective reports. The chapter concludes with some tips on writing more effectively, advice on structuring the narrative of the report and some specific phrases that might be used in investigative reports of specific incidents.

The Communication Process

The communication process, on the surface, is rather simple, but when all the variations in each component of the process are considered, it is exceedingly complex.

Communication is the process through which information is transferred from one person to another through common symbols. It is sometimes explained as having a sender, a message, a channel and a receiver. The message may be spoken or written, verbal or nonverbal. The channel can be a memo, letter or report. It may be a phone call, a conversation or a video. It may even be a shrug or a shove.

> The communication process involves a sender, a message, a channel and a receiver. It may also include feedback.

Successful communication occurs only if:

- The sender can correctly code the message.
- The channel is free of distortion.
- The receiver can correctly decode the message.

How messages can get lost in translation is apparent in going from one language to another. For example, a computer that translated Russian into English and vice versa translated the familiar phrase "Out of sight, out of mind" as "invisible idiot." In Mexico, an "H" on the water faucet means helado—cold. A "C" means caliente—hot. For the unsuspecting, the result can be surprising.

Messages do, indeed, often get lost in translation, be it from one language to another, or simply from one human mind to another. Effective communication, written or spoken, takes into consideration not only the message and channel but also the sender and receiver of that message.

The Sender

Many variables must be considered when looking at the sender of the message, including age, sex, intelligence, education, biases, past experience, vocation and purpose for communicating.

When security managers and on-line officers communicate, it is important to understand *why* they send the messages they do. They may be attempting to establish rapport, or they may be trying to calm a hysterical victim of a bloody accident. Other times they may be trying to extract information from a hostile person. The purpose behind the communication should be clearly understood if the communication is to be effective.

The Message

The message can be written or spoken, verbal or nonverbal. Most messages consist of some form of words surrounded by other nonverbal factors. The message should be in simple, standard English, avoiding jargon and evasive or "impressive" language. All too often speakers and writers seek to *impress* rather than to *express*.

Security personnel must be aware of ethnic, cultural and sexual differences in language and avoid using terms that might be viewed as derogatory, such as calling a woman "girl." Messages must be clear and must avoid faulty thinking if they are to communicate well.

Spoken messages are common in security work. Security officers give directions, ask questions and relay information over their radios. Sometimes these spoken messages are conveyed amid confusion and a multitude of distractions. Noise levels may be high, and distances may be involved.

Written messages are also common in security work. On-line officers take notes, primarily as reminders to themselves of information they obtain. They write reports based on these notes to communicate the facts of an incident to others. Security managers may also write letters, memos and other types of messages for a variety of purposes. Effective written communication is discussed later in the chapter.

The Channel

Having efficient channels to communicate is essential to security work both during routine functions as well as during emergencies. Specific methods of communication include telephone, paging and public address paging, two-way radio, closed-circuit television, conversations, reports, letters and memos.

Portable radios are a vital link in the private security communications system.

Information conveyed using any of these methods should be brief, objective, courteous and professional.

On-line officers are often expected to answer telephones, take messages, provide information and page individuals if an emergency exists. Many businesses have a policy prohibiting use of the telephone for personal use. Some even have phones that record, measure and count the calls made. Pagers allow immediate one-way contact with others as does a public paging system. Such systems can be invaluable in emergencies for getting information to all personnel immediately. Two-way radios also provide for immediate communication, but the message can be heard by anyone in the immediate area.

Written channels of communication include policies and procedures, letters, memos, proposals and reports as well as many of the forms previously introduced in Chapter 6.

The Receiver

The same variables that influence the sender of messages influence those who receive the messages, including age, sex, intelligence, education, biases, past experience, vocation and purpose for listening.

If the message is spoken, the receiver of the message must be a good listener. Yet many people, including security personnel, lack this skill. They hear, but they do not actively listen. Consequently, many messages are misinterpreted or not received at all.

LISTENING

Says communications expert Elaine Thomas (1987, p. 99): "Of all the communication skills we use daily, we spend the most time listening." Research has shown that 45 percent of the total time devoted to communication is spent in listening, 30 percent in speaking, 16 percent in reading and 9 percent in writing.

According to Montgomery (1981, p. 65): "We listen more than we do any other human activity except breathe." He goes on to note, however, that "listening is the most neglected and the least understood of the communications arts."

Too often people simply hear, but they do not listen. Why? A large part of the problem is the difference between the speed at which people speak and that at which they can mentally process information.

> People can speak about 150 words per minute. People can listen to more than 450 words per minute.

Further, people can probably think at least 1,000 words per minute. That lag time can be devastating to listening effectiveness. It allows the mind to wander, to daydream, to formulate arguments and to attend to the person rather than the message being conveyed.

This hazard was recognized by listening expert Dr. Ralph Nichols (1957) almost 40 years ago when he said: "Not capitalizing on thought speed is our greatest single handicap. The differential between thought speed and speech speed breeds false feelings of security and mental tangents. Yet, through listening training, this same differential can be readily converted into our greatest asset."

Guidelines for Better Listening

The following guidelines can improve listening:

Attitudinal

- Be interested in the person and the message. Be empathetic. Show you care.
- Be less self-centered.
- Resist distractions.
- Do not let personal biases turn you off.
- Prepare to listen. Clear your mind of other things.

Behavioral

- Be responsive to demeanor, posture and facial expressions.
- Offer encouragement.
- Look at the other person.
- Do not interrupt.
- Take notes. Adjust your note taking to the speaker.

Mental

- Ask questions (preferably open-ended ones).
- Do not change the subject.
- Listen for ideas, not just facts. Separate facts from opinions.
- Attend to content, not delivery. Look for main points.
- Listen optimistically.
- Avoid jumping to conclusions. Stay with the speaker; try not to jump ahead. Draw only tentative conclusions.
- Concentrate. Work at listening, especially when the material is difficult or complex.
- Use excess listening time to summarize the speaker's main ideas. But do *not* plan your response.
- Keep your mind open and your emotions in check. Do not judge.
- Exercise your mind.
- Periodically clarify what has been said.
- Pay attention to body language (nonverbal factors).

Listening is a skill, just as speaking, reading and writing are. Listening can be improved by practicing. It should never be taken for granted. Neither should it be taken for granted that what is heard will be remembered. If the information received is important, it should be written down.

Understanding

Simply because a message has been sent, either written or spoken, does not mean that it has been understood. One way to illustrate this is to think of the sender of the message as having a "blue" outlook on the world and the receiver as having a "yellow" outlook on the world. The message is not likely to be either blue or yellow, but a shade of green. That is why one-way communication can be extremely dangerous.

One-Way vs. Two-Way Communication

Most written messages are one way, that is, the sender writes the message, and it is relayed in some manner to the reader who reads it. If the reader of the message communicates back to the sender, this is two-way communication because **feedback** has taken place.

Feedback is critical to effective communication; it is an indication that a message is or is not understood. In a face-to-face conversation, this can take the form of an affirmative nodding of the head (message understood) or a puzzled look (message not understood). Security managers and officers should watch for such feedback when they talk with people, and they should also provide such feedback to those with whom they talk. Much feedback is nonverbal. Indeed, much communication is nonverbal.

NONVERBAL COMMUNICATION

A security manager's physical appearance—a suit and tie or an attractive dress—conveys a message of professionalism. Likewise, on-line officers' physical appearance—the uniform and badge, sometimes a gun—conveys a message of authority before they ever say a word. This can be intimidating to many people. A harsh look can add to the intimidation; a smile can weaken or even dispel it. Security officers should be aware of the nonverbal messages they send and use them to their advantage.

Likewise, effective communicators are alert to the nonverbal messages conveyed by those with whom they communicate.

> **Nonverbal communication** includes eye movements, facial expressions, posture, gestures, clothing, tone of voice, proximity and touch.

The *eyes* are very expressive. They can reveal if someone is happy, sad, excited, interested, tired, confused, sick and perhaps lying. An entire science has sprung up around eye movements and what they can tell about individuals. People usually have very little control over the messages sent by their eyes.

Facial expressions, such as smiles, frowns, grimaces, scowls, pouts or raised eyebrows, convey messages as do flushed cheeks and perspiration. *Posture* also conveys messages. A person standing erectly with arms folded and feet apart conveys authority. A person slouching conveys a different message. *Hand gestures* can confirm or contradict what a person is saying, or they can even take the place of words. For example, a hand held out in protest or a finger to the lips can stop someone from speaking further. A hand behind the ear can cause a speaker to increase volume.

Clothing conveys messages, too, but must be very carefully interpreted. Millionaires have been known to dress as bums. Generally, however, it is accepted that clothes make a definite statement.

Tone of voice as well as pitch and rate can tell much about the person speaking. A high pitch and rapid rate can reveal nervousness or anxiety. *Proximity* can reveal if a person feels comfortable or threatened. In the United States we tend to stand 18 to 24 inches away when talking. Standing closer is usually perceived as either intimate or threatening (perhaps both). Standing farther away than about four feet usually shows lack of interest or concern for the other person. In some cultures, however, the comfortable zone is much

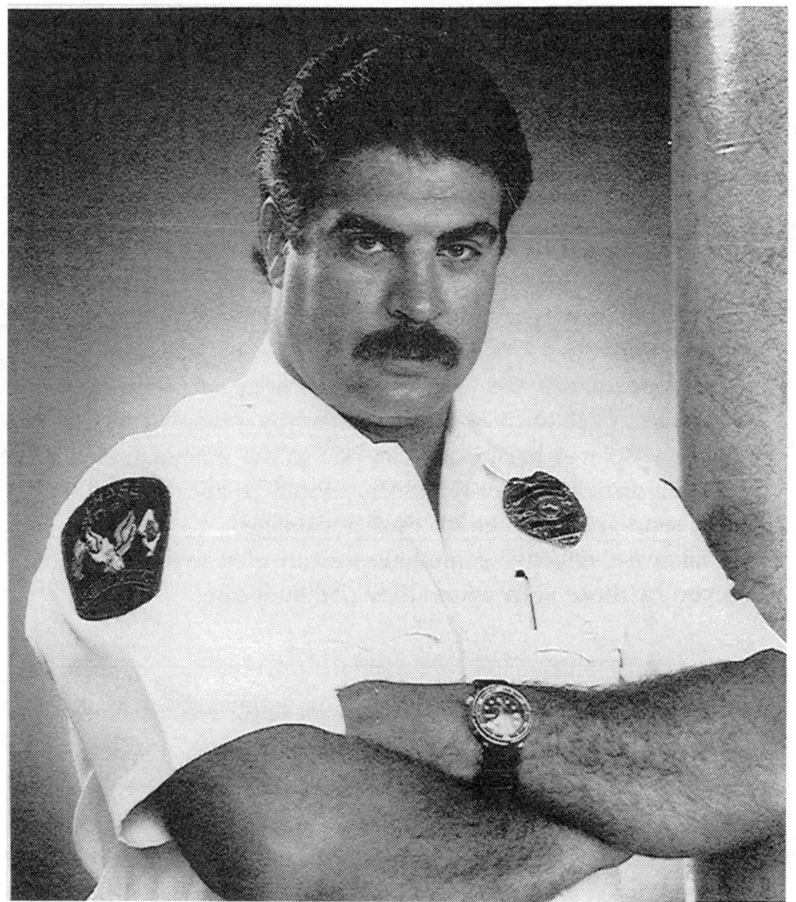

What nonverbal messages do you "hear"?

smaller, a fact security officers should be aware of when talking with individuals who are not Americans.

Touch in our culture also conveys messages, although not as much as in many other cultures. A handshake, a pat on the back, an arm around a shoulder can show personal care and concern. Touch can also lead to a sexual harassment lawsuit.

In *written communication,* messages are conveyed by appearance and neatness (or lack of it), the quality of the copy and paper and the like. A poorly reproduced copy with a coffee stain on it conveys one message. A laser-printed original placed in a plastic carrier conveys quite another. Certainly a message written on a scrap of paper or on a page torn from a spiral notebook does not convey the image of professionalism desired by the security industry.

> Written communication includes neatness, paper quality, copy quality, binding and the like.

BARRIERS TO COMMUNICATION

Time is important to everyone, including security personnel. Communication systems have greatly enhanced the ability to pass information from one person or organization to another. On the other hand, computers, fax machines, copiers and many other communications devices have deluged line staff and managers alike with information of many forms and types. The sheer volume of information can be overwhelming. Other barriers to communication include the following:

- Being preoccupied so the message is not heard.
- Being too emotionally involved to correctly interpret the message.
- Being defensive because of previous interchanges with a specific individual.
- Tending to hear what you want to hear.
- Noise—interference of any kind, physical or mental.
- Excessive repetition.
- Complex language.
- Lack of interest.
- Bad timing.

LINES OF COMMUNICATION

Most businesses and organizations have established lines of communication.

> Communication lines may be downward, upward (vertical) or lateral (horizontal). They may also be internal or external.

Downward communication includes directives, policies and procedures, either spoken or written, from managers and supervisors. When time is limited or an emergency exists, communication often must flow downward and be one way.

Upward communication includes incident reports as well as requests from subordinates to their superiors. It may also include a security survey being presented to the CEO or the board of directors. Security managers should ensure that all upward communications are in terms those unfamiliar with security will understand. Security risks can sometimes be better explained using photographs and charts. Probabilities of such risks and the potential loss in dollars might be best presented through graphs and charts, quite easily developed if the manager has access to a desktop publishing setup.

Lateral communication refers to communication between managers on the same level of the hierarchy and between subordinates on the same level. This would include on-line security officers talking to each other via two-way radios while making rounds.

Informal channels of communication also exist within most organizations. Sometimes referred to as the **grapevine** or the *rumor mill,* such channels tend to be unreliable but can cause great harm. Usually the grapevine is strongest in organizations in which information is not openly shared. Employees begin to guess and speculate about what they do not know—hence the rumors. Communicating with subordinates is an essential managerial responsibility because it is through these line officers that the security goals will be met. Officers who are told about their employer are more apt to be supportive. The more direct, personal communication that exists between management and employees, the greater the employee identification with management and the organization.

Internal Communication

Security managers rely heavily on information provided by on-line officers. Much of this information may be relayed via radio or telephone rather than face-to-face, necessitating careful pronunciation and lots of feedback.

Accuracy is critical in security work, so officers should spell any words that might be misunderstood or spelled incorrectly, especially names and addresses. Such spelling is most effective if done in the phonetic alphabet adopted by most police departments and the military:

A	Adam	N	Nora
B	Boy	O	Ocean
C	Charles	P	Paul
D	David	Q	Queen
E	Edward	R	Robert
F	Frank	S	Sam
G	George	T	Tom
H	Henry	U	Union
I	Ida	V	Victor
J	John	W	William
K	King	X	X-ray
L	Lincoln	Y	Young
M	Mary	Z	Zebra

If the spelling of a name is the "normal" spelling, this can be stated, for example, "Smith, normal spelling." But if the name is spelled *Smythe,* it should be spelled out.

Another way to enhance clarity of communication is to use the **24-hour clock** rather than A.M. and P.M.. This is also referred to as **military time.** It begins at midnight with 0000. The first two digits refer to the hour and the last two digits refer to the minutes. Usually the word *hours* follows the time designation. For example, ten minutes after midnight would be 0010 hours. Three fifteen in the morning would be 0315 hours. Noon is 1200 hours. From that point on, 12 is added to each hour. One o'clock in the afternoon is 1300 hours. It continues full circle this way, with midnight also being called 2400 hours, depending on department policy.

24-Hour Clock			
Morning		Afternoon	
Midnight	= 0000	1 P.M.	= 1300
1 A.M.	= 0100	2 P.M.	= 1400
2 A.M.	= 0200	3 P.M.	= 1500
3 A.M.	= 0300	4 P.M.	= 1600
4 A.M.	= 0400	5 P.M.	= 1700
5 A.M.	= 0500	6 P.M.	= 1800
6 A.M.	= 0600	7 P.M.	= 1900
7 A.M.	= 0700	8 P.M.	= 2000
8 A.M.	= 0800	9 P.M.	= 2100
9 A.M.	= 0900	10 P.M.	= 2200
10 A.M.	= 1000	11 P.M.	= 2300
11 A.M.	= 1100	Midnight	= 2400
noon	= 1200		

Internal communication is also often in the form of activity logs and incident reports, to be discussed shortly.

General Guidelines for Effective Communication

A key to effective communication is to have **empathy** for the person with whom you are communicating. This is not the same as sympathy. Empathy means understanding where the other person is coming from, whether you agree with it or not. Parker et al. (1989, p. 81) suggest: "Empathizing with another means communicating both verbally and nonverbally, and appreciating where the other person is at. It means letting that person know that you are able to 'hear' what he or she is really saying." They describe three levels of empathy (p. 83):

- *Low Empathy*—The communicator shows little or no understanding of the most basic part of what the other has communicated, seems out of touch with what the other has said, and responds only from her or his own frame of reference. In *Low Empathy* the first person *subtracts* from the interpersonal encounter.
- *Moderate Empathy*—The communicator grasps at least the essential part of the message, and sends a message that fits well with what the other is saying and is essentially interchangeable. The communicator shares with the other an understanding of at least the surface feelings and main content of the message. This communicator has not completely missed the point as in *Low Empathy,* where there may not be even the slightest acknowledgement of what the person has communicated.
- *High Empathy*—In deep [high] empathy there is a consistent communication on the part of the communicator that indicates that she or he not only hears the surface message, but is able to sense the underlying feelings and concerns that are barely hinted at in the overt communication of the second person. In *High Empathy,* the communicator's responses are *additive* or expand on what the person has stated, and thus allow the second person to explore his or her feelings. In deep empathy, the recipient has a feeling of

> being able to elaborate on the discussion, and feels truly understood. Communication is opened up; there is an air of excitement about really being heard by the other. This is most important when the police officer . . . must communicate with distressed persons, as they are often required to do in their daily work.

Parker et al. (p. 86) give the following example of the difference between low and high empathy:

Barricaded Man: I haven't done a damn thing wrong. You get the hell out of here and get off my property before I blast you off!

(Low Empathy) First Officer (angrily and in a demanding tone): Now look, you better cool it and come out, before we have to drag you out.

Barricaded Man: I told you to get the hell out of here and I mean it; you make a move to come in here and you'll regret it.

(Low Empathy) First Officer: Look, you've got to come out sooner or later, and if it isn't pretty damn quick, I'm going to have to come in and force you out.

Barricaded Man: Shove it!

(High Empathy) Second Officer (in a tentative tone): It sounds to me like you're pretty angry about this whole mess, but I'm also hearing that you're a bit frightened about what's happening. Can we talk about it?

Other components of effective communication include openness, concreteness, immediacy and positive regard or respect for the other person.

INTERVIEWING AND INTERROGATING TECHNIQUES

Interviewing and interrogating were introduced briefly in Chapter 8. According to Wells (1992, p. 33), up to 90 percent of interviews are routine. Most individuals will cooperate and provide the needed information. It's that other 10 percent that take special skills. He suggests that most people who are hostile become so for one of two reasons: "They feel threatened, or they have close emotional ties to someone who has a reason to feel threatened." If an interviewee is likely to be hostile, it is best to conduct the interview unannounced so the individual does not have time to become angry about it. In addition, the technique of beginning an interview with small talk to observe how the individual responds to questions—called **calibrating** a witness—is not likely to work with hostile witnesses. In fact, suggests Wells (p. 34): "To the contrary, it agitates them more."

An individual who is pressured to give information may become antagonistic and refuse to cooperate. The following procedures suggested by Hess and Wrobleski (1991, pp. 37–38) may make the interview more productive:

- Prepare for each interview in advance if time permits. Know what questions you need to have answered.
- Obtain your information as soon after the incident as possible. A delay may result in the subject's not remembering important details.
- Be considerate of the subject's feelings. If someone has just been robbed, or seen an assault, or been attacked, the individual may be understandably

upset and emotional. Allow time for the person to calm down before asking too many questions. Remember that when emotions increase, memory decreases.

- Be friendly. Try to establish rapport with the subject before asking questions. Use the person's name; look at the person as you ask questions; respond to the answers.
- Use a private setting if possible. Eliminate as many distractions as you can, so that the subject can devote full attention to the questions you ask.
- Eliminate physical barriers. Talking across a desk or counter, or through a car window, does not encourage conversation.
- Sit rather than stand. This will make the subject more comfortable and probably more willing to engage in conversation.
- Encourage conversation. Keep the subject talking by:
  - Keeping your own talking to a minimum.
  - Using open-ended questions, such as "Tell me what you saw."
  - Avoiding questions that call for only a "yes" or "no" answer.
  - Allowing long pauses. Pauses in the conversation should not be uncomfortable. Remember that the subject needs time to think and organize his thoughts. Give the subject all the time needed.
- Ask simple questions. Do not use law enforcement terminology when you ask your questions. Keep your language simple and direct.
- Ask one question at a time. Allow the subject to answer one question completely before going to the next question.
- Listen to what is said, and how it is said.
- Watch for indications of tension, nervousness, surprise, embarrassment, anger, fear or guilt.
- Establish the reliability of the subject by asking some questions to which you already know the answers.
- Be objective and controlled. Recognize that many persons are reluctant to give information to the police. Among the several reasons for this reluctance are fear or hatred of police, fear of reprisal, lack of memory or unwillingness to become involved. Keep control of yourself and your situation. Do not antagonize the subject, use profanity or obscenity, lose your temper or use physical force. Remain calm, objective and professional.

Tables 12–1 (pp. 370–371) and 12–2 (p. 372) summarize interviewing techniques and the kinds of questions that might be asked.

Nationally known clinical psychologist Dr. Stanton Samenow ("Some Considerations in Interviewing," n.d.) offers the following considerations when interviewing hostile and resistant clients:*

1. Do not put a premium on getting the client to "like" you; rather you must try to earn his (her) respect;
2. Do not think that you must manipulate or do things that are contrived to court the client's favor; for example, use street language, dress a certain way;
3. Avoid the twin pitfalls of gullibility and cynicism;
4. Be alert to problems of semantics; that is, a client may use a regular everyday English word and mean something totally different from your interpretation of it;

---

*Reprinted by permission from Stanton E. Samenow, Ph.D., author of *Inside the Criminal Mind* (Times Book, 1984) and *Before It's Too Late: Why Some Kids Get Into Trouble and What Parents Can Do About It* (Time Books, 1989).

5. Be prepared to terminate interviews when anger stands in the way of receptivity, disclosure, and a dialogue and most certainly if the client is directly threatening or intimidating;
6. If you use a confrontive style, be sure to be direct and firm but *without* being provocative and forcing the client into a corner where an attack is his only way out;
7. Expect to have to repeat the same point in different ways;
8. Do not be totally consumed by whether the client is currently telling the truth; that is, playing "detective" (if overdone) can stand in the way of what you are doing;
9. Take the position in counseling such a client that it is his life, whether he is sincere and truthful will be born out over time;
10. Avoid ridicule, anger, or sarcasm;
11. Ask yourself before each interview, "What do I expect to accomplish?" Then ask yourself if this is realistic;
12. You must try to control the interview politely and firmly rather than utilize a nondirective approach; being nondirective or basically silent is seen as weakness.

Table 12–1. Interviewing Subjects

Types of Individuals	Police Interviewing Behavior
Hostile Witness	Relieve anxiety and stress. Indicate what can and cannot be said. State the purpose of the interview. Exert control (nonthreatening). Develop trust and cooperativeness. Indicate potential outcomes of noninvolvement or silent behavior.
Nonhostile Witness	Listen closely to disclosures. Double-check all observations and perceptions. Avoid angering, confusing, frustrating, or silencing the interviewee. Record all descriptions. Seek specific details.
Victims	Check their mental and physical health. Conduct the interview when the victim has stabilized from shock or trauma. Be patient. Forgotten or confused recall may be brought out with careful questions. Reassure, calm, relax, protect victim. Seek appropriate help where necessary. Keep initial questions to a minimum. Encourage cooperation.
Indirectly Involved or Uninvolved Subject	Be polite, patient, understanding. Thoroughly canvas frequented locales. Listen carefully. Be perceptive. Observe nonverbal signals. Avoid antagonizing the general public. Persuade reticent individuals to disclose.

Table 12–1. Interviewing Subjects (*Continued*)

Types of Individuals	Police Interviewing Behavior
Suspects	Safety first. Monitor the suspect's behavior and likelihood of possessing a weapon. Gather information; avoid initial interrogation. Inform a suspect of appropriate rights. Avoid forming prejudgments. Avoid giving a suspect cause for alarm. Avoid signaling nervousness or anxiety. Be honest. Do not make false promises. Do not bully or ridicule. Never underestimate a suspect's behavior or testimony.
Angry Witness	Assess the interviewee's mental stability. Check for weapon. Call for assistance where necessary. Gain control of the interview. Demonstrate neutrality. Never argue or disagree. Defuse anger with questions. Do not allow a shouting match to develop.
Excessively Verbal Subject	Redirect the interviewee's responses. Remind interviewee of the interview's purpose. Interrupt and ask closed-ended questions. Indicate specific topic areas for discussion.
Reticent Interviewee	Establish rapport. Compliment the interviewee. Reassure, reduce anxiety. Establish pleasant demeanor. Encourage talk. Avoid limiting response choices.
Uncooperative Interviewee	Exercise control. Remind interviewee of penalty for noncooperation. Reduce apprehension. Clarify unfounded fears. Provide incentives for disclosing.
Anxious and Stressed Interviewee	Direct stressed interviewee, when necessary, to professional counseling. Release tension in face and body. Establish a conversational climate. Clarify the nature of the interview. Allow opportunity for thinking. Do not rush responses. Double-check responses.
Interviewee of Different Race, Culture, Sex, or Ethnic Background	Be cognizant of how others communicate in interview situations. Understand the unique or specific verbal and nonverbal behaviors of people who differ from yourself. Repeat, reiterate, re-explain. Translate your meanings into the language of the interviewee.

SOURCE: T. R. Cheatham and K. V. Erickson. *The Police Officer's Guide to Better Communication.* Copyright © 1984. Reprinted by permission of the authors.

Table 12–2. Interview Questions

Type of Question	Purpose	Characteristics	Example
Open-Ended	To elicit a variety of responses To provide interviewee response choices To break the ice To reduce apprehension	No set response expected of interviewee No specific topic Found in nondirected interviews Interviewee centered Nonthreatening	"How is the weather today?" "How have you been?" "Will it be a good football year?" "Life treating you well?" "What do you think of politics?" "How is the economy affecting you?"
Closed-Ended	To limit interviewee response choices To gather specific information from subject To facilitate use of time	One- to three-word replies Specific answers sought Authoritarian Frequently appears in a series of closed-ended questions Brusque	"What did he say?" "Did you do it?" "What is your name? "Where do you work?" "What time is it?" "What did she wear?" "Was it red or green?"
Probing	To force replies Explanation Clarification Elaboration Confrontation Repetition	Seeks additional information Requires respondent to be responsive to interviewer Clears up misunderstandings Reveals sensitive/ disguised information	"Explain what you mean." "Tell me again what you said." "How is that possible?" "You don't believe that do you?" "Why did you do that?" "More details, please."
Mirror	To keep interviewee talking Clarification Explanation	Repeats or paraphrases interviewee's remarks Places burden of talk on interviewee	"So, you took the bike, huh?" "And then you left town?" "You say you like it?" "Which job are you talking about?"
Leading	To lead interviewee to particular response To reveal discrepancies in testimony To facilitate admissions To force a stand	Suggests or implies an appropriate answer Places words in respondent's mouth Leaves little room for interviewee explanation of responses Placed in a series of questions	"You didn't like her, did you?" "Do you think that was right?" "Can you really say that was the correct thing to do?" "You won't act like that again, will you?"

SOURCE: T. R. Cheatham and K. V. Erickson. *The Police Officer's Guide to Better Communication*. Copyright © 1984. Reprinted by permission of the authors.

Jayne and Buckley (1992, p. 65) cite three primary objectives of most interrogations:

- To ascertain the probability that the suspect is or is not the offender.
- To eliminate the innocent by eliciting information, evidence, or behavior symptoms indicative of that fact.
- To obtain a confession from the guilty or information from him or her regarding the involvement of other persons.

However, as Wells (1992, p. 31) cautions: "One of the worst mistakes made by inexperienced interrogators is to promise that criminal charges will not be filed if the person confesses. In many instances, this is not up to the investigator, but the authorities."

Detecting Signs of Deception

A skilled interviewer or interrogator is adept at recognizing deception. Evans (1990, p. 94) presents the following reliable indicators of lying:*

> Deceptive subjects often hesitate in order to gain more time to develop a lie. They use con words, such as "I swear to God," "Honestly," and "Believe me," to make their lies sound more believable.
>
> Deceptive subjects are more likely to challenge minute details of factual information, such as the difference in a few minutes of time. People tend to look more while listening than speaking, and research shows that men engage in less eye contact than women. Still, a person will generally not look you in the eyes when making a deceptive response.
>
> Truthful subjects, on the other hand, usually identify with the issue under investigation, respond without hesitation and are not afraid to discuss motive. Truthful subjects usually name individuals who might be guilty and eliminate others from suspicion. They tend to suggest harsher punishment than their deceptive counterparts.
>
> Be conscious of body language. Body movements, gestures, facial expressions and eye contact can all be interpreted during the course of an interview to help determine whether or not a person is being truthful. Normally, lying causes anxiety and stress. To reduce anxiety, the body reacts by releasing energy through the shifting of body posture, bringing hands to the face or picking lint from clothing.
>
> Learn to evaluate body language—and to consciously look for it. You will find it useful during an interview to note when the body language reinforces and when it contradicts the feelings that are communicated verbally.
>
> Remember, no single verbal statement or nonverbal behavior automatically means a person is lying or telling the truth. Each behavior must be considered in the context of the environment, the intensity of the setting and

---

*Reprinted by permission of *Law and Order* magazine.

in comparison to the subject's normal behavior patterns. An assessment of a subject's truthfulness should be based on clusters of behavioral characteristics, not on a single observation.

PROVIDING INFORMATION

External communications may occur with the general public, with the media or with the courts. It includes all interactions with agencies and individuals outside the employing agency. These communications are critical to effectively conducting business as well as to a sound public relations program, discussed in Chapter 10.

Most security managers have a policy that on-line officers are not to issue statements or opinions about any activities or conditions related to their duties to any newspaper reporters or members of the press, radio or television media. Such requests are to be referred to the security manager who, in turn, may refer them to the public relations department.

One form of external communication most security managers and on-line personnel dread is having to testify in court, the focus of Chapter 13. Most communication will be internal.

All incidents are to be reported in writing. Some facilities use an incident report log such as in Figure 12–1. This log contains a detailed, chronological description of everything the security officer saw and did during the shift—for example, opening or locking doors, observing minor water leaks or mechanical malfunctions, receiving special requests, escorting individuals to specific locations, receiving phone messages, delivering packages and noting any significant incidents that occur.

In addition, officers may complete incident **reports** for any potential, suspected or actual security risks. A form such as in Figure 12–2 (p. 376) might be used. Most such reports will deal with a situation that requires a corrective action to be taken. When the corrective action has been taken, a follow-up report is written on a form such as the one in Figure 12–3 (p. 377). If no follow-up or report is needed, that should be stated in the incident report.

Information in such reports should be kept confidential, and the reports themselves should be protected from access by unauthorized people. Before looking at how to write effective reports, consider the basis for most such reports—effective notes.

TAKING NOTES

Notes are a permanent aid to memory. Good notes help security personnel remember conditions or incidents they observe, actions they take and actions others take. They form the basis for official reports and may be of great assistance should a court appearance be required.

Security Services Daily Activity Log

Officer	Badge #	Shift Time	Date
Assigned Area			

Time	Detailed Activities

Be Sure All Information is Detailed and Accurate

This report has been read and approved by ______________________ Date ______

Figure 12–1. Incident Report Log

> Record all relevant information legibly, in ink, in a notebook.

Several procedures should be followed in taking notes. Common sense provides the reasons behind these procedures. First, information is recorded in a notebook, not on scraps of paper that can be easily lost. The notebook should be easy to carry (3¾ by 6¾ is a good size). A loose-leaf notebook is best because it is easy to organize, pages can be removed or added and it looks professional. It should be kept full of blank paper and well organized.

Corporate Incident Report

File # __________

Today's date ________________ Date incident occurred ____________________

Incident summary ____

____

____

Complete details of event (date, time, individuals, places, situations) _____________

____

____

____

____

____

____

____

(continue on extra sheet of paper if required)

External involvement (describe location, individual statements, contacts, include law enforcement contacts, etc.) ____

____

____

Estimated loss ________________ (dollars, assets, etc.) Estimated recovery ________________

Planned action to resolve incident ______________________________________

____

____

Individual responsible for follow-up ____________________________________

Reported by __________________________ Phone (____) ______________

Name (s) of managers notified ____

Describe and attach any additional explanations and supporting documents.

Incident Information Should Be Protected and Held in Strict Confidence

Figure 12–2. Incident Report Form

Index tabs are helpful to separate sections: observations, incidents and the like. The notes should be removed and filed when they have served their purpose. Because notes frequently become part of the permanent record of a case, they should be recorded in ink rather than in pencil, which can become blurred and smudged. Felt-tip or ballpoint pens are acceptable.

The notes must be legible. Security staff do not want to waste time later trying to decipher what they have written or, worse, to lose important information because it cannot be read.

Corporate Incident Report Follow-up

Original Incident Report file # ______________

Today's date ____________________ Date of original report ____________________

This incident was reported and investigated by (include dates) ____________________

Have or will any discipinary actions take place as a result of this incident? __________

Explain: ____________________

Describe any involvement by external organization/law enforcement agencies ________

What resources, assets, or revenues were lost/recovered? ____________________

Describe any personal injury, actual or threatened, relating to this incident __________

What lessons have been learned/or recommendations made as a result of this incident? __

List any other actions that have been or will be taken as a result of this incident. ______

Comments: ____________________

Attach copies of investigations, supporting documentation, or other information pertinent to this incident.

Figure 12–3. Incident Report Follow-Up Form

Each page of notes should be identified with the officer's name, the date and the type of information contained on the page. Because officers work in several different areas on any given shift, it is important to identify which notes belong to which incident.

All relevant facts should be recorded as they are obtained, if possible. If an officer is called to deal with a personal injury, obviously, administering first aid would take precedence over taking notes. As soon as anything of an

Officer recording information received from a concerned citizen.

emergency nature is attended to, however, the information should be recorded. Officers should not wait until later to write down information because they may forget some important details. Not everything that is said is recorded, but officers should make note of anything that might be important. A good rule of thumb is: "When in doubt, write it down."

All spellings, numbers and dates should be verified as they are recorded. This can be done by simply repeating the information aloud as it is written and getting verification from the person providing the information.

Effective notes are:

- Accurate
- Brief
- Clear/complete

The ABCs of effective notes are accuracy, brevity, clarity and completeness. Accuracy is ensured by repeating information back, spelling names and verifying numbers. Brevity is accomplished by omitting the articles, *a, an* and *the;* by omitting all other unnecessary words and by using common abbreviations. Commonly used abbreviations in security notes are summarized in Table 12–3.

Good notes should be clear, complete, concise, accurate and objective. They are the foundation for a good report.

WRITING REPORTS

Most people enter private security for the activity and excitement. They often do not realize the amount of paperwork involved. For almost every action

Table 12–3. Common Abbreviations Used in the Security Profession

A&A	Assisted and advised	Off.	Officer
AKA	Also known as (alias)	Rec'd.	Received
Asst.	Assistant	R/F	Right front
Att.	Attempt	R/O	Reporting officer
Dept.	Department	R/R	Right rear
Dist.	District	S/B	Southbound
DOB	Date of birth	Subj.	Subject
DOT	Direction of travel	Sup.	Supervisor
E/B	Eastbound	Susp.	Suspect
GOA	Gone on arrival	S/W	Stationwagon
Hdqtrs.	Headquarters	UNK	Unknown
Hwy.	Highway	UTL	Unable to locate
I.D.	Identification	V.	Victim
L/F	Left front	Viol.	Violation
Lic.	License	W/B	Westbound
L/R	Left rear	Wit.	Witness
Memo	Memorandum	WFA*	White female adult
N/A	Not applicable	WFJ	White female juvenile
NFD	No further description	WMA*	White male adult
NMN	No middle name	WMJ	White male juvenile
N/B	Northbound		

*The "W" indicates the race. It is appropriate to substitute "B" for black, "O" for Oriental, "H" for Hispanic and "NA" for Native American.

private security officers take, they must write a report. Security managers, too, write much.

> Two major types of reports are administrative and operational.

Administrative reports deal with the routine functioning of the security department. They include such things as reports on proper uniform, reporting procedures, policies and procedures, security surveys, evaluation reports and performance reports.

Operational reports deal with the actions taken by security officers. Most agencies have their own forms and procedures for completing operational reports, but many of the forms have common elements. For example, most have a series of boxes to be completed at the top, as in the form used at Canterbury Downs race track, illustrated in Figure 12–4. The specific information requested is not important in the illustration. What is noteworthy is that basic information is requested for every crime or incident involving a security officer.

If the department uses report forms that include boxes and blanks to be filled in, they should *all be filled in,* using "N/A" if information is not applicable or "Unknown" if the information is unknown. After the basic information is recorded, the officer must write a narrative account of the incident in the space following the boxes.

CANTERBURY DOWNS SECURITY REPORT

DATE	
ICR #	

CLASSIFICATION - TYPE of CRIME or INCIDENT | OFFICERS NAME

TIME of INCIDENT	PERSON REPORTING	ADDRESS	PHONE #	TIME REPORTED

SUBJECT

NAME - LAST -FIRST - MIDDLE (AKA)								M.R.C. # YEAR
SEX	RACE	D.O.B.	AGE	HEIGHT	WEIGHT	HAIR	EYES	SOCIAL SECURITY #
EMPLOYER		BARN # & TACK ROOM			OCCUPATION		RES. PHONE	BUS. PHONE
RESIDENCE ADDRESS ——— CITY — STATE — ZIP								

SUSPECTS
NAME & ADDRESS OF SUSPECT (S)
(1) ______
(2) ______

WITNESSES
NAME & ADDRESS OF WITNESSES
(1) ______
(2) ______

DETAILS: ______

PAGE ______ of ______

OFFICERS SIGNATURE ______ BADGE NUMBER ______

Figure 12–4. Canterbury Downs Report Form
SOURCE: Courtesy of Canterbury Downs.

> A report is a permanent written record that communicates important facts to be used in the future.

Security officers' reports are *used,* not simply filed away. If they were not needed for the efficient operation of businesses' or agencies' activities, they would not be required. Reports are permanent records of all the important facts of an incident, a stockpile of information drawn on by several other individuals. They may be an aid to other security officers, supervisors, administrators and, when necessary, the courts, law enforcement agencies and other governmental agencies interested in safety and loss prevention.

Characteristics of a Well-Written Report

Because reports are so important in the security profession, it is vital that private security officers develop skill in writing effective reports. Such reports will not only communicate information better, but also reflect positively on the officer's education, competence and professionalism.

> A well-written report is factual, accurate, objective, complete, concise, clear, correct, in standard English, legible and on time.

Factual

The basic purpose of any operational report is to record the **facts.** A fact is a statement that can be proven. (It may be proven false, but the statement is still classified as a fact.) For example, the man is wearing a black leather jacket that has a bulge in the pocket. Facts need to be distinguished from two other types of statements: inferences and opinions. **Inferences** (sometimes called **judgments**) are statements about the unknown based on the known—they use logic. For example, the bulge in the man's pocket is a gun. Notice that this inference will become a fact IF the matter is pursued, that is, if the person wearing the black leather jacket is frisked and a gun is, in fact, discovered—or not. Any inferences in official reports should be clearly identified as such.

The third type of statement is **opinion.** An opinion is a statement of personal belief. For example, people who wear black leather jackets are hoodlums. Opinions have no place in official reports.

Facts and inferences can be discussed and debated logically and reasonably and brought to some degree of agreement. Opinions, however, reflect personal beliefs on which there is seldom agreement. How do you resolve, for example, who has the best-looking spouse? You can't, as attested to by the adage, "Beauty is in the eye of the beholder."

Incident reports must not contain assumptions or **conclusionary language.** Among the most common problems here are making statements about what someone can or cannot do. For example, it is a conclusion to write in an incident report, "The man *could not* answer my questions." The factual report would instead say, "The man *did not* answer my questions." Even clearer, however, would be to say, "The man shrugged and said nothing."

Another common problem is the phrase "signed by" as in, "The camera pass authorization was signed by John Doe." Unless the report writer saw John Doe sign the authorization, the report should read, "The camera pass authorization was signed John Doe." The little word *by* can get an officer into a lot of trouble on the witness stand.

Other problems arise when officers write about someone's state of mind, for example, saying a person is *nervous, frightened, uncooperative, belligerent.* These are all conclusions on the officer's part. The report should contain facts that lead to the conclusions. For example, rather than saying a person is nervous, describe the person's appearance and actions: "The man began to tremble, he began to perspire heavily and his voice wavered. He repeatedly glanced over his shoulder at the door."

> A well-written report is factual. It contains no opinions.

Inferences, on the other hand, are valuable in a report, provided they are identified as such and are based on sufficient evidence. Sometimes it is hard to distinguish between facts and inferences. One way to tell them apart is to ask the question: "Can the statement be simply proven true or false, or are other facts needed to prove it?"

For example, to verify the statement "The man is a good driver," you would need to supply several facts to support the inference. One such fact might be that he had never received a traffic ticket. But is that sufficient support to prove that he is a good driver? Perhaps he was simply lucky and never got caught driving carelessly. Or imagine you see a teenager staggering down an alley. You might infer she is drunk or high on drugs, but she might, in fact, be ill. An inference is not really "true" or "false"; it is "sound" or "unsound." And what makes an inference sound (believable) are facts to support it.

Accurate

To be useful, facts must be accurate. A license number recorded wrong may result in the loss of a witness or suspect—or in a lawsuit for wrongful detention. Inaccurate measurements or recording of the time of an incident may cause problems in a later investigation of the incident. An effective report accurately records the correct time and date, correct names of all persons involved, correct phone numbers and addresses and exact descriptions of property, vehicles and suspects. Security officers should have people spell their names and should then repeat spellings and numbers for verification.

> A well-written report is accurate; it is specific.

To be accurate, you must be specific. For example, it is better to say, "The female suspect had a pearl necklace, a gold watch and a small diamond pin in her skirt pocket," than to say, "The shoplifter had several items of jewelry in her pocket." It is more accurate to describe a suspect as "approximately 5 feet tall" than as "short."

Objective

Reports must be not only factual and accurate, but also objective. It is possible to include only factual statements in a report and still not be objective. Objective means nonopinionated, fair and impartial. Lack of objectivity can result from two things: poor word choice and omission of specific facts.

> A well-written report is objective, impartial.

Objectivity is attained by keeping to the facts, using words with nonemotional overtones and including both sides of the account. The importance of sticking to the facts and leaving out personal opinions has already been discussed. The next means of achieving objectivity is through the words used. Word choice is extremely important in objective writing. A reader would react to the following three sentences very differently:

The man cried. The man wept. The man blubbered.

"The man cried" is an objective statement; "the man wept" is slanted positively; "the man blubbered" is slanted negatively. Although writers want to be specific, they must also be aware of the effect of the words chosen. Words that have little emotional effect, for example, *cried,* are called **denotative words.** The denotative meaning of a word is its objective meaning. In contrast, words that have an emotional effect are called **connotative words,** for example, *wept* and *blubbered.* The connotative meaning of a word includes its positive or negative overtones. The term *rent-a-cop* is a clear example of how word choice affects meaning.

Slanting can also make a report nonobjective. A good report includes both sides of an incident. Even when some facts tend to go against an officer's theory about what happened, the officer is obligated to include these facts. Omitting important facts is not being objective.

Complete

Information kept in the reporting security officer's head is of no value to anyone else. An effective incident report contains answers to at least six basic questions:

WHO? WHAT? WHEN? WHERE? WHY? HOW?

As noted, all applicable blanks at the top of a report form should be filled in. If a blank is not applicable, N/A is recorded in the blank so anyone reading the report will not erroneously conclude that information is missing. All relevant details should also be included in the narrative portion of the report. It is inconsiderate of the reader to begin a narrative: "On the above date, at the above-specified time, the above-named suspect. . . ." The narrative should be able to stand alone. For example, the same narrative might begin like this: "On December 12, 1995, at 2200 hours, the suspect, Jack Jones, was. . . ."

The narrative will not include everything from the boxes at the top of the report form or from the notes taken regarding the incident. But the report as a whole, including both boxed information and narrative portion, must be complete.

> A well-written report is complete.

Each specific incident requires different information. The "who," "what," "when" and "where" questions should be answered by factual statements. The "how" and "why" statements may require inferences. When this is the case, as already noted, the statements should be clearly labeled as inferences. This is especially true when answering the question of causes. To avoid slanting a report, officers must record all possible causes reported to them, no matter how implausible they may seem at the time.

Concise

To be concise is to make every word count. No one wants to read a wordy report. Length does *not* necessarily indicate quality. Some reports can be written in half a page; others may require 10 pages. No exact length can be specified. Reports will be effective if they include *all* relevant information in as few words as possible. This does not mean, however, omitting important details, or leaving out words such as *a, an* and *the*.

> A well-written report is concise.

Wordiness can be reduced in two basic ways: (1) leaving out unnecessary information and (2) using as few words as possible to record the necessary facts. In the following (taken from an actual report), notice what information is not necessary:

> I arrived within a minute of the call. I noticed upon my arrival numerous people standing around. I bent over to spit a bug out that flew into my mouth, and this male party came over and asked for help. . . . Once at the hospital I found myself assisting the doctors in emergency with this victim as two doctors and two nurses were not enough to get everything done and hold her at the same time. . . . I was thanked for my jumping in at the emergency room by both doctors and the family of the injured girl. I then cleared the hospital at 1800 hours.

It is not necessary to include the fact that a bug flew into the officer's mouth, that two doctors and two nurses were not enough personnel to care for the victim or that the officer was thanked. Such details are superfluous.

Another way to be concise is to omit "empty words." For example, in the phrase "blue in color" the words "in color" are empty—blue *is* a color. Following are some wordy phrases and their more concise counterparts:

Wordy	Concise
in view of the fact that	because
with reference to	about
made note of the fact that	noted
for the purpose of	for
subsequent to	after
along the lines of	like
for the reason that	because
comes into conflict with	conflicts with
square in shape	square
in the event that	if
despite the fact that	although
in the amount of	for
is of the opinion	thinks
attempt to ascertain	determine
month of April	April
state of California	California

Make every word count.

Clear

Statements in a report should have only one interpretation. There should be no chance of two people reading the report and coming up with a different picture. For example, "The man was tall" is open to interpretation, but the statement, "The man was 6′11″" is not. Or consider this statement: "The security officer saw the intruder on the elevator and he fired." WHO fired—the officer or the intruder? The sentence is not clear.

> A well-written report is clear.

Sometimes unclear writing produces unintentional humor. Consider the following examples:

- She found a book of matches on the car seat that was not hers.
- Three cars were reported stolen by ABC Security yesterday.
- Here are some suggestions for handling obscene phone calls from the security manager.
- As the unauthorized person came toward me in the dark hallway, I hit him with my flashlight.
- Guilt, vengeance and bitterness can be emotionally destructive to line staff. You must get rid of them.

- Changing the color of our shirts to navy blue will make the officers look more professional, less costly and easier to launder.

To write clearly, keep descriptive words and phrases close to the words they describe. For example, lack of clarity is seen in this statement: "He placed the gun into the holster which he had just fired." It was not the holster he had just fired, it was the gun. It would be clearer to say, "He placed the gun which he had just fired into the holster."

Another way to achieve clarity is to avoid uncommon abbreviations. Confusion can result if two people have different interpretations of an abbreviation. For example, to most people, S.O.B. has negative connotations, but for people in health-related fields, it simply means "short of breath." In contrast, some abbreviations are so common that they can be used in reports, for example, Mr., Dr., Ave., St., Feb., N.W. and the like. Other abbreviations are commonly used in private security, but not by the general public, for example, A & A (assisted and advised), DOB (date of birth), DOT (direction of travel), L/F (left front), N/B (northbound), NFD (no further description) and NMN (no middle name). Such abbreviations can be used in notes (see Table 12–3 on p. 379), but they should not be used in reports.

Yet another way to achieve clarity in writing is to use short sentences, organized into short paragraphs. Sentences that are not too long are easier to read. Likewise, paragraphs should be relatively short, usually five to ten sentences. The reports should be logically organized. Most reports commonly begin with "when" and "where" and then tell "who" and "what." The "what" should be in chronological order, that is, going from the beginning to the end without skipping back and forth. Each question to be answered in the report should be contained in its own paragraph. It is also "reader friendly" to skip a line between paragraphs.

Mechanically Correct

Specific rules of English must be followed when notes (or the spoken word) are transferred into a written report. These include rules for spelling, capitalization and punctuation.

> A well-written report is mechanically correct.

If you were to hear the words, "Your chances of being promoted are good if you can write effective reports," you would not be aware of mistakes that could be contained in the written statement: "Yur chanses of bein promotid are gud if you kin rite effectiv riports." This sentence appears to have been written by a young child or by an illiterate adult. The mechanics involved in translating ideas and spoken words into written words are complex, but important, and must be mastered. Several good English grammar handbooks are available.

If spelling is a problem, writers should use a dictionary or a speller/divider. Speller/dividers are easier to use in that they contain on one page what a dictionary would require 10 to 15 pages to include. No matter which resource is used, when you look up a word, make a tally mark in the margin (assuming the dictionary or speller/divider is your own). You will quickly see that you are looking up the same words over and over. Write these words in the back cover of your spelling reference—or *learn* to spell them.

Of special importance is correct use of *homonyms,* those troublesome words that sound alike but have different meanings and different spellings. They are usually taught in second grade. Writers who have not mastered their use will appear very uneducated. Table 12–4 (p. 388) contains some of the more common homonyms.

In Standard English

People often disagree about what "standard English" is. And the standards between spoken and written English differ. For example, people often drop the "g" in the "-ing" ending when they talk. Listen for it. Even very well-educated people might say: "I'm goin' home." But they would *not* write it that way.

Just as there are rules for spelling, capitalization and punctuation, there are rules for what words are used when. For example, it is "standard" to say "he doesn't" rather than "he don't," or "I saw it," rather than "I seen it."

A well-written report is written in standard English.

Experience with English is needed to know what is "standard" and what is not—especially for people raised in surroundings in which a standard English was not used. People who speak standard English, however, usually also write in standard English.

Legible and on Time

It does little good to learn to write well if no one can read it or if the report is turned in after the need for it is gone.

A well-written report is legible. It must also be on time.

Ideally, reports are typed or done on a word processor. Often, however, this is not practical. And sometimes a poorly typed report is as difficult to read as an illegible one. Security officers who know they have poor handwriting should print their reports. Although this is slower than writing in long-hand (cursive), it will be a benefit to the reader.

Table 12–4. Common Homonyms

Word	Meaning	Use in a Sentence
accept	to take, receive, agree to	I *accept* that alibi.
except	to exclude, leave out	It is sound *except* for one point.
affect	to influence (verb)	How will that *affect* me?
effect	result (noun)	The *effect* is devastating.
ascent	motion upward	His *ascent* to the top was swift.
assent	consent, agree	Do you *assent* to the conditions?
brake	device for stopping motion	Did the trolley *brake* fail?
break	fracture, interrupt	How did you *break* your arm?
capital	money, seat of government	How much *capital* is involved?
capitol	government building	Turn left at the *capitol*.
cite	quote, summon to appear in court	He *cited* the Fifth Amendment.
sight	act of seeing, perception	The *sight* was ghastly.
site	location	He reached the *site* at noon.
council	an assembly	The *council* was in agreement.
counsel	an attorney, advice	His *counsel* gave him *counsel*.
decent	proper, suitable, right	It's the *decent* thing to do.
descent	motion downward	The *descent* from the top was rapid.
dissent	disagreement	The *dissent* caused a strike.
desert	forsake, abandon	I will not *desert* my post.
dessert	course at end of meal	He had pie for *dessert*.
forth	onward or forward	He came *forth* on command.
fourth	numerically number 4	He was *fourth* in line.
hear	perceive by ear, listen to	Did you *hear* him leave?
here	this place	We got *here* too late to save him.
its	owned by "it"	The car lost *its* wheel.
it's	contraction of *it is*	*It's* time for us to go.
knew	past tense of *to know*	Dan *knew* the suspect was guilty.
new	modern, fresh	The *new* car gets good mileage.
lead	a metal	He was hit by a *lead* pipe.
led	past tense of *to lead*	He *led* the procession.
meat	food	I eat *meat* once a day.
meet	encounter, come together	I will *meet* you on the corner.
principal	chief, money, head of a school	He is the *principal* witness.
principle	rule, a fundamental truth	It is a matter of *principle*.
precede	to come before	A *precedes* B in the alphabet.
proceed	to continue, to go on	The investigation will *proceed*.
right	correct, privilege	He was *right* to go first.
rite	ceremony	It was a religious *rite*.
write	to inscribe by hand	Can you *write* the note?
their	belonging to "they"	It is *their* car.
there	in that place	I went *there* yesterday.
they're	contraction of *they are*	*They're* late, as usual.
threw	past tense of *to throw*	He *threw* the brick through the door.
through	from end to end	He drove *through* the tunnel.

Table 12–4. Common Homonyms (*Continued*)

Word	Meaning	Use in a Sentence
to	toward, in the direction of	He went *to* the store.
too	more than enough; also	I have *too* many, *too*.
two	number 2	I have *two* cars.
vary	to change	His story did not *vary*.
very	extremely, much	He is *very* tired.
whose	belonging to "who"	*Whose* car is this?
who's	contraction of *who is*	*Who's* going to drive it home?
your	belonging to "you"	*Your* car has been stolen.
you're	contraction of *you are*	*You're* going to walk home.

Checklist

A checklist such as that in Figure 12–5 (p. 390) might be used to evaluate reports.

The following tips for writing more effectively, advice on structuring the narrative and suggested phrases to include in specific types of incidents are from Stokes et al. (1993, pp. 47–61):*

TIPS FOR WRITING MORE EFFECTIVELY

Effective writing is based upon proper time management, rapid and accurate incident assessment, proper structuring of the report, and the ability to create a favorable impression in the mind of the reader toward the writer. Consider the following:

One of the major problems faced by security officers is proper time management, especially in large establishments where much activity is continuous. How much time do you devote to a particular incident? Is it a "go nowhere" incident or a "go somewhere" incident? How much "paper" do you need to write?

As the sole source of "unbiased" information in many events which involve safety and security, the security officer has a strong obligation to conduct a thorough investigation—when such an investigation is needed—and to provide a complete report of the investigation. For many officers, the problem lies in knowing when to put forth the effort.

As any good attorney will tell you, the secret to success when dealing with incidents is the ability to determine the most important "issue" involved in each incident. For the security officer, this case assessment ability needs to be "fine tuned" until it can be done quickly, but accurately.

TIP: Learn to quickly, but accurately, assess each incident for the most important "issue."

Another major problem faced by security officers is rapid structuring of the report. Officers who have become skilled at good time management when responding to requests for assistance are those who begin writing the report in their mind as they approach the scene and as they first begin receiving information.

---

*Reprinted by permission of Innovative Systems.

Evaluation Checklist for Reports

- Is the report:
  - factual?
  - accurate?
  - objective?
  - complete?
  - concise?
  - clear?
  - legible?
- Does the report use:
  - first person?
  - active voice?
  - correct modification?
  - correct pronoun reference?
  - parallel sentence structure?
- Are the sentences effective with:
  - no fragments?
  - no run-on sentences?
  - similar ideas combined into single sentences?
- Are the sentences mechanically correct in terms of:
  - spelling?
  - use of apostrophes?
  - abbreviations?
  - numbers?
  - capitalization?
  - punctuation?
- Are the sentences gramatically correct in terms of:
  - correct use of pronouns?
  - agreement of subject and verb?
  - correct use of adjectives and adverbs?
  - correct use of negation?
  - correct use of articles?
- Does the report allow the reader to visualize what happened?

Figure 12–5. Evaluation Checklist for Reports

SOURCE: From *For the Record: Report Writing in Private Security*. Kären M. Hess and Henry Wrobleski. Institute for Professional Development, 1991. Reprinted by permission.

TIP: Start writing the report in your mind as soon as you have assessed the incident and determined the "issue."

Skilled security officers are also those who have learned to quickly determine if an incident is a "go nowhere" (except to a file folder) or a "go somewhere" (likely to end up in court) case. Those security officers devote very little time (and a very short report) to the "go nowhere" cases. By so doing, they can afford to spend more time where it's needed—on those incidents which will likely end up in a courtroom.

TIP: Learn to quickly determine if it is a "go nowhere" or "go somewhere" incident and devote your time accordingly.

Most security officers who write effectively have learned a very important rule: write to the reader, not to yourself. Who are the most critical readers of security reports? Supervisors and employers—that's who. They are interested in the facts. Write to express those facts, not to impress your reader with all the security jargon you know. Write a report that shows you handled the incident professionally.

TIP: Write to the reader, not yourself. Ensure the reader clearly understands you handled the incident thoroughly and impartially.

You can be assured that the reader's perception of you, the writer, matters greatly. Your goal should be to enhance that perception—without distorting your report. You can do this by using "key" words and phrases which tend to leave a positive impression about how you handled an incident. "Key" words and phrases include: "I thoroughly . . ., I carefully . . ., The cause of the fire appeared to be . . ., I collected (rather than seized) the following items of evidence: . . ., I concluded. . . ." Words and phrases like these tend to make the reader feel more comfortable about what you were doing, and they result in the perception that you are objective and thorough.

TIP: Use "key" words and phrases to enhance the reader's perception of you, the writer.

STRUCTURING THE NARRATIVE

The security narrative is essentially a technical report structured in chronological order describing a sequence of events. These events are:

1. You, the reporting officer, receive information by either viewing something or by being told something, e.g., seeing someone violating a safety rule or being told that someone is violating a safety rule.
2. You act on the information you receive, e.g., by talking to individuals who know about the safety rules and observing whether the rules are being violated.
3. Your actions cause you to receive additional information, e.g., you see other people breaking additional rules.
4. You act on the new information you receive.

This process continues until you have all the information you need to handle the situation effectively.

The narrative should set the stage, giving time, date, and how you came to be involved in the incident. For example:

> On 11-11-93 at 0930 hours I received an assignment to investigate reported safety rule violations in the manufacturing area. Upon arriving in that area I spoke with the supervisor, Mary Brown.

The narrative should next explain what information you received. For example:

> Brown told me that Johnson, a welding machine operator, was not wearing safety glasses as required by OSHA. She had spoken to him several times, but he ignored her requests. Brown wanted a formal report of these violations made.

The narrative should then explain what you did about the information you received. For example:

> I asked Brown where Johnson worked, and she pointed him out to me. I saw that he was wearing glasses, but not the required safety glasses. I then approached Johnson and asked him why he wasn't wearing his safety glasses. He said he had to wear his prescription glasses to see and he couldn't wear them and the safety glasses at the same time. He also said that Brown had it in for him and wouldn't order him prescription safety glasses as she had done for several other employees.

The narrative should explain what you did with this new information.

> I returned to Brown's office and asked about the policy for providing employees with prescription safety glasses. Brown said it was the policy to provide them for those employees who requested them, but that Johnson had never made such a request.

Finally, the narrative should explain the disposition of the incident.

> I suggested that Brown get the request in writing from Johnson and that the prescription safety glasses be ordered immediately. I also advised Brown that Johnson should be reassigned until he could comply with the OSHA safety requirements.

The completed narrative should look like this:

> On 11-11-93 at 0930 hours I received an assignment to investigate reported safety rule violations in the manufacturing area. Upon arriving in that area I spoke with the supervisor, Mary Brown.
>
> Brown told me that Johnson, a welding machine operator, was not wearing safety glasses as required by OSHA. She had spoken to him several times, but he ignored her requests. Brown wanted a formal report of these violations made.
>
> I asked Brown where Johnson worked, and she pointed him out to me. I saw that he was wearing glasses, but not the required safety glasses. I then approached Johnson and asked him why he wasn't wearing his safety glasses. He said he had to wear his prescription glasses to see and he couldn't wear them and the safety glasses at the same time. He also said that Brown had it in for him and wouldn't order him prescription safety glasses as she had done for several other employees.
>
> I returned to Brown's office and asked about the policy for providing employees with prescription safety glasses. Brown said it was the policy to provide them for those employees who requested them, but that Johnson had never made such a request.
>
> I suggested that Brown get the request in writing from Johnson and that the prescription safety glasses be ordered immediately. I also advised Brown that Johnson should be reassigned until he could comply with the OSHA safety requirements.

KEY PHRASES OR SENTENCES TO WRITE FOR SPECIFIC INCIDENTS

—Fire

On (date) at (time) I discovered a fire at (location).

I sounded the alarm, called the fire department, and (other immediate actions).

I took the following emergency measures (turning off air-conditioning and machinery, closing doors and windows, grounding elevator): . . .

I took the following protective measures (moving or covering expensive property): . . .

I talked to a witness, (name), who told me the following: . . .

I determined the likely cause of the fire to be . . .

The estimated amount of damage was (amount).

Future fires might be prevented by (recommended preventive steps to be taken): . . .

—Sexual Harassment Complaint

On (date) at (time) I was dispatched to investigate a report of (actual complaint).

I talked to the victim, (name), who told me the following: . . .

I talked to a witness, (name), who told me the following: . . .

I talked to the suspect, (name), who told me the following: . . .

Because of the sensitivity of this incident, it has been referred to (name of agency).

—Assault

On (date) at about (time), I was dispatched to (location) regarding the report of a (type of assault).

Upon arrival at about (time) I talked to the victim, (name), who told me the following:

I photographed the victim.

I searched . . .

I located and collected (items of evidence).

I interviewed the witness, (name), who told me the following: . . .

I interviewed the suspect, (name), who told me the following: . . .

—Breach of Peace/Disorderly Conduct

On (date) at about (time), I was dispatched/notified/observed at (location) a (type of incident).

Upon investigation and inquiry I received the following information: . . .

I talked to witnesses and the participants, and they told me the following: . . .

Evidence has been obtained and is being held according to policy and procedure.

I am forwarding this report to: . . .

—Burglary

On (date) at about (time), I was dispatched/informed/noticed an (incident) at (location).

I interviewed a witness, (name), who told me the following: . . .

Missing was . . . valued at . . .

I searched . . .

I photographed . . .

I discovered the probable point of entry was (location) and the probable point of exit was (location).

A suspect in the incident was (name).

The incident has been turned over to (person or agency).

—Theft

On (date) at about (time), I was dispatched/discovered/notified to (location) regarding the report of a theft.

Upon arrival, I talked to the reporting party/victim, (name), who told me the following: . . .

Missing was . . . valued at . . .

I searched for . . .

I talked to a witness, (name), who told me the following: . . .

—Trespass

On (date) at (time) I observed at (location) the following suspicious persons: . . .

Upon investigation and inquiry I obtained the following information: . . .

I talked to a witness, (name), who told me the following: . . .

I contacted (person) to escort the individuals from the premises.

—Vandalism

At (time) on (date) I was dispatched/discovered (type of vandalism).

I talked to (name) who told me the following: . . .

I photographed (object vandalized).

I talked to a witness, (name), who told me the following: . . .

A Reminder: Communications as Public Relations

Every contact with employees and the public is a public relations contact. All members of the security force, especially those in positions of authority, must present a positive image and communicate effectively.

Effective communication—downward, upward, lateral, formal and informal, internal and external—is the lifeblood of the security department. Effective communication also establishes the image security will have as well as the amount of cooperation security will receive from those they work with.

Summary

Communication skills are essential both for managing and for accomplishing loss prevention goals. The communication process involves a sender, a message, a channel and a receiver. It may also include feedback. The weakest communication skill for most people is listening. This is partly because people can speak about 150 words per minute but can listen to more than 450 words per minute, leaving lag time that can be devastating.

Nonverbal communication includes eye movements, facial expressions, posture, gestures, clothing, tone of voice, proximity and touch. Written nonverbal communication includes neatness, paper quality, copy quality, binding and the like.

Communication lines may be downward, upward (vertical) or lateral (horizontal). They may also be internal or external.

Recording and communicating information is an important part of any security professional's job. Officers should record all relevant information legibly in ink, in a notebook. Effective notes are accurate, brief, clear and complete. This information can then be used as the basis for reports.

Security reports are usually one of two types: administrative or operational. Such reports are important because they are permanent written records that communicate important facts to be used in the future. A well-written report is factual, accurate, objective, complete, concise, clear, mechanically correct, written in standard English, legible and on time.

APPLICATION

Read and evaluate the following report written by a security guard at a racetrack. Determine if it is acceptable in the following ways:

___ Factual
___ Accurate
___ Objective
___ Complete
___ Concise
___ Clear
___ Correct
___ In Standard English

Mark any instances of ineffective writing and, if you can, make needed corrections.

> While on stable patrol on 02/05/95, at 2120, right after coffee break, a Mexican-American approached me. He identified hisself as Jose Martinez, DOB 01/04/39. Mr. Martinez is a groom whose employed by a Mr. Andrew C. Wallace. Martinez complained of being robbed, which occurred between the hours of 1100 and 2100 hours, this day, 02-05-95. He was robbed from his tackroom, #C in Barn 3. Items taken was a insulated lite-wait jacket, cream in color, four pears of wool slacks, gray in color, and one pair of black shoes. Martinez stated the tackroom was unlocked cuz other grooms had to get in to get there gear. I seen that Martinez's bed was torn apart like someone searched the place real good. While swearing profusely about getting ripped off, I asked Martinez if he seen anyone hanging around the barn or the tackroom area, but he didn't. I suspect its an inside job done by someone who knows the area. No leads at this time. Case pending.

CRITICAL THINKING EXERCISE

USE OF FORCE

STATUTORY AND COMMON LAW

In Delaware, Minnesota, South Dakota and Wisconsin, a merchant may detain a suspect for the sole purpose of delivering him or her to a law enforcement officer. Minnesota statutes provide that a merchant or shopkeeper may be immune from liability for detention of a suspected shoplifter if the merchant's action in detaining a suspect is based upon reasonable cause. Detention must be for the purpose of delivering without delay a suspect to a law enforcement officer and then immediately making a charge against the suspect. The detained suspect must be promptly informed of the purpose of the detention and not subjected to unnecessary or unreasonable force. The detained suspect cannot be interrogated against his or her will.

FACTS OF THE CASE

In the early afternoon of October 31, Godfrey Alderman entered a Knox Lumber Company store in St. Paul, Minnesota. Allen Burger, a 28-year-old weight lifter and bodybuilding coach employed by Knox as a plainclothes security officer, was on duty at the time. One of the checkout clerks called Alderman to his attention; she said Alderman was acting strangely. Burger spotted Alderman at a utility blades display where he took a package of utility blades off the shelf and scraped off the price tag with a utility knife he took out of his pocket. Alderman took another package off the shelf, began to scrape the price tag off, but then cut the package open and put the blades in his pocket. Alderman dropped the package on the floor and pushed it with his foot against the edge of the display case. After Alderman left the display area, Burger retrieved the empty package and continued to follow Alderman. Burger was unable to observe Alderman pocket any other items, although he saw him attempt to alter the price tag on at least one other item.

About an hour later Alderman went to the checkout counter and purchased items totaling $64. He walked out into the front parking lot where he was confronted by Burger and Steve Boman, another Knox employee. There Burger told Alderman he was under arrest for stealing the utility blades and defacing price markings. Alderman was led back into the store and taken to a seminar training room.

Burger read Alderman his rights and asked him to sign a confession form. Alderman said he understood but refused to sign the form. He tried to explain that he brought his knife and blades from home to compare them with those in the store, because "all blades are not exactly the same." He took the knife out of his pocket as he was making this explanation. Burger told him to place the knife on the table because he considered it a weapon. Alderman said it was his knife and tried to put it back in his pocket. Burger grabbed Alderman's arm, took the knife and placed it on the table. Burger asked to see a driver's license so he could complete the confession form. Alderman produced a license, but Burger could not read it because it was covered with tar stains. At that point Burger asked Boman to call the police because Alderman was being uncooperative.

As Burger continued to fill out the confession form, Alderman grabbed the knife and held it in his lap. Burger got up and put his arms around Alderman, pinning Alderman's arms to his sides. As Alderman attempted to get up several times, his arms were twisted and lifted, and he started screaming and shouting for someone to call the police. He said he was 73 years old and had a heart condition. Burger released his hold on Alderman four minutes later when a law enforcement officer arrived.

Alderman was not examined or treated by a physician after this incident; however, he claimed that for several days his shoulders and arms were stiff and ached. He took aspirin for the pain and "a small dose of valium" because he was upset. He reported that he had nightmares about the incident and having his arms twisted. Alderman regularly took medication for a heart condition and high blood pressure.

Burger said that he initially intended to "simply arrest him, have him sign a form, and kick him loose." Knox has a policy that allows its employees to release suspected shoplifters without calling the police under circumstances where the theft involves a small sum and the suspect cooperates fully. The suspect is asked to sign a confession before being released.

Issues and Questions

1. Does the evidence reasonably support a finding that Burger used unnecessary force in detaining Alderman and that there was unnecessary delay in delivering him to a law enforcement officer?
   - **a.** Because he will be unable to convince a judge of his innocence, Alderman will be charged with petty theft and convicted after a bench trial. This fact will negate any claim of false imprisonment or assault and battery that he might try to bring against Burger and Knox Lumber Company.
   - **b.** A merchant can escape liability in Minnesota only if he detains a suspect for the sole purpose of delivering him to a peace officer. The evidence in Alderman's case shows that Burger failed to deliver him without unnecessary delay and that unreasonable force was used in detaining the suspect. There may be an award to Alderman of compensative and punitive damages for assault and battery.
   - **c.** Although it is regrettable that Alderman suffered some pain and emotional distress, he did not seek medical treatment and so did not suffer monetary loss. He thus has no basis for bringing an action against Knox for assault and battery and false imprisonment. Knox could apologize for the rough treatment he received, but his uncooperative behavior brought on any painful results. If anything, it is good common sense for him to realize that the mental anguish he experienced is deserved.
   - **d.** Alderman should write a letter absolving Knox of all liability and thanking the company for not attempting to convict him of petty theft. As an employee of Knox, Burger merely intended to have him sign a form and then release him. Knox has a policy of not pressing charges when the suspect's innocence is established, when the suspect is a young child or when the theft involves a small sum and the suspect cooperates fully.
   - **e.** There is insufficient proof to convict Alderman of petty theft. Because he is 73 years old and he did purchase $64 worth of materials, it is possible that he simply overlooked the blades in his pocket and forgot to pay for them. He might be slightly senile and should be given the benefit of the doubt, especially in the case of such a small item as a single package of blades. The unreasonable force used by a muscular 23-year-old security officer who does not follow Minnesota statutes can

result in an award of $2,000 in compensatory damages and $10,000 in punitive damages.

Discussion Questions

1. Which basic communication skill—speaking, listening, reading, writing—do you have most difficulty with? Why?
2. How can security managers encourage upward communication from their officers?
3. What are the most significant barriers to communication in security work?
4. How can you improve your skills in note taking? In report writing?
5. How do internal and external lines of communication differ? What must be taken into account in each? Is one more important than the other?

References

Evans, D. D. "10 Ways to Sharpen Your Interviewing Skills." *Law and Order,* August 1990, pp. 90–95.

Hess, Kären M. and Wrobleski, Henry M. *For the Record: Report Writing in Private Security.* Eureka, CA: Innovative Publications Company, 1991.

Jayne, Brian C. and Buckley, Joseph P. III. "Criminal Interrogation Techniques on Trial." *Security Management,* October 1992, pp. 64–72.

Montgomery, Robert L. "Are You a Good Listener?" *Nation's Business,* October 1981, pp. 65–68.

Nichols, Ralph G. "Listening Is a 10-Part Skill." *Nation's Business,* July 1957.

Parker, L. C., Jr.; Meier, R. D.; and Monahan, L. H. *Interpersonal Psychology for Criminal Justice,* 2d ed. St. Paul, MN: West Publishing Company, 1989.

Samenow, Stanton E. "Some Considerations in Interviewing Hostile and Resistant Clients." Seminar handout (Clinical Psychology, 4921 Seminary Rd., Suite 104, Alexandria, VA 22311). No publisher or date.

Stokes, Floyd D.; Hess, Kären M.; and Wrobleski, Henry M. *Outline Guide for Private Security.* Blue Lake, CA: Innovative Systems, 1993.

Thomas, Elaine. "Listen Well and Profits Will Tell." *Successful Meetings,* May 1987, pp. 99–100.

Wells, Joseph T. "Getting a Handle on a Hostile Interview." *Security Management,* July 1992, pp. 33–35.

Wells, Joseph T. "What Inquiring Minds Need to Know: Why, When, and How to Conduct an Investigation." *Security Management,* November 1992, pp. 27–31.

CHAPTER 13

TESTIFYING IN COURT

DO YOU KNOW

- What is important in testifying in court?
- What the usual sequence in a criminal trial is?
- What direct examination is? What cross-examination is?
- What kinds of statements are inadmissible in court?
- How to testify most effectively?
- When to use notes while testifying?
- What nonverbal elements can influence courtroom testimony positively and negatively?
- What strategies can make testifying in court more effective?
- What defense attorney tactics to anticipate?

CAN YOU DEFINE THESE TERMS?

cross-examination
direct examination
impeaching

INTRODUCTION

The importance of effective investigations and professional-quality reports is highlighted when an incident ends up in court. The case may be a civil matter with the employer and possibly security personnel as defendants. Or it may be a criminal trial where security personnel testify on the side of the prosecution. In either event, it is critical that security personnel be well prepared.

Taitz (1990, p. 136) notes that security officers should have answers to the following questions about their personal legal liability:

- Does the company provide liability coverage for security personnel?
- If so, how much?
- If sued, will the company provide an attorney for security personnel?

As noted by Purpura (1991, p. 194): "Most private-sector investigations do not result in judicial activity. But when a private-sector investigator appears in court, well-prepared testimony is important."

One attorney has observed that a jury trial is like a crap shoot. He'd much rather face a judge than a jury. The reality of this situation is also noted by Taitz (1990, p. 139):

> "It's regrettable, but very true, that the outcome of trials is not related to evidence—it's more related to witnesses on both sides," says a leading security consultant. "The jury tends to be swayed by witnesses, and if they

> like the witness, they will believe him. And they tend to like or dislike a witness depending on what they see or hear. That's our natural experience. People will say, 'I don't like that person,' but they just don't like his looks or how he acts. That's where the weight of the evidence comes in. The jurors are looking at who they think is credible," he adds.

Therefore, security personnel testimony *must* be professional.

This chapter begins by presenting an overview of testifying in court. This is followed by an examination of what happens before the trial and then an in-depth examination of the trial itself. Next, numerous tips for excelling in the courtroom are presented, followed by a discussion of how security personnel might qualify themselves as expert witnesses. The chapter ends with a brief look at trends in court decisions and settlements.

TESTIFYING IN COURT—AN OVERVIEW

Although the vast majority of information that security personnel communicate to others will be through written reports, they may also be called on to testify in court. This can be a rather frightening experience, but it need not be if they know what to expect. Ideally, all security personnel should attend a few court trials in which they are *not* involved to get a feel for what happens.

> To effectively testify in court, be prepared, look professional and act professionally.

Thorough *preparation* is essential. It should begin with a review of all notes and reports related to the case, going over the main facts and checking their accuracy. Be aware of anything that might discredit the testimony. If possible, discuss the case with the prosecutor beforehand and anticipate any problems that might arise with the testimony.

Appearance is also very important. In most instances security managers appear at trials in business clothes, whereas officers appear in their uniforms. These should be clean and well pressed. A careless appearance might suggest to a jury that an officer is also careless about his or her job. Security personnel should be well groomed and should not wear dark glasses. They should have good posture, carry themselves erect without being stiff and maintain eye contact with the attorneys, the judge and the jurors. They should not exhibit signs of nervousness, such as constantly shifting in the chair, staring at the ceiling or off into space or drumming their fingers on the railing. They should not smoke, chew gum or wear a hat in the courtroom.

Behavior and attitude are critical in effective testimony. Security personnel should not appear to "know it all" or take the process personally. They should speak clearly, without mumbling, and loudly enough so that everyone in the courtroom can hear the testimony. They should address individuals by the appropriate title, for example, "Your honor" and "sir."

Many courthouses are large, bustling buildings that can be intimidating.

The defense attorney will make every effort to discredit the testimony—that is the attorney's job. Discrediting testimony is technically known as "**impeaching** the witness."

It is not quite so difficult when the security officer is on the side of the prosecution, having important information about some crime that has been committed. It is much more difficult if the security manager or officer is the defendant, being sued for some action.

BEFORE THE TRIAL

Recall that, before a trial, interrogatories and/or depositions may be used. The interrogatories are a series of questions to which a defendant is asked to respond. A deposition is like a mini-trial where the statements of a defendant are recorded verbatim. Taitz (1990, p. 141) notes that a person giving a deposition has the following rights:

- The right to not incriminate yourself.
- The right to be personally served with a subpoena before testifying at a deposition.
- The right to bring to the deposition notes or other materials that may help you testify.
- The right to read your deposition after it is transcribed and to change your answers if you feel they were wrong or incomplete. Those changes can be added as an addendum. "Too often," says one expert, "even lawyers mistakenly tell witnesses they may correct for typos and misspellings only."

Taitz (p. 141) cautions: "Be aware, however, that it is possible to inadvertently waive some of your rights." The example given is that if you begin to talk about something you and your lawyer discussed regarding the case, you have waived the attorney-client privilege.

THE TRIAL*

The main participants in the trial are the judge, jury members, attorneys, the defendant and witnesses. The *judge* presides over the trial, rules on the admissibility of the evidence and procedures, keeps order in the court, interprets the law for the jurors and passes sentence if the defendant is found guilty.

The *jurors* hear and weigh the testimony of all witnesses. Jurors consider many factors other than the words spoken. The attitude and behavior of witnesses, suspects and attorneys are constantly under the jury's scrutiny. Jurors notice how witnesses respond to questions and their attitudes toward the prosecution and the defense. They reach their verdict based on what they see, hear and feel during the trial. Typical jurors will have had limited or no experience with the criminal justice system outside of what they have read in the newspaper and seen on television.

Legal counsel presents the prosecution and defense evidence before the court and jury. Lawyers act as checks against each other and present the case as required by court procedure and the rulings of the presiding judge.

Defendants may or may not take the witness stand. If they do so, they must answer all questions put to them. They may not use the Fifth Amendment as a reason for not answering.

Witnesses present the facts personally known to them.

Sequence of a Criminal Trial

The trial begins with the case being called from the court docket. If both the prosecution and the defense are ready, the case is presented before the court.

The sequence in a criminal trial is as follows:

- Jury selection.
- Opening statements by the prosecution and the defense.
- Presentation of the prosecution's case.
- Presentation of the defense's case.
- Closing statements by the prosecution and the defense.
- Instructions to the jury.
- Jury deliberation to reach a verdict.
- Reading of the verdict.
- Acquittal or passing of sentence.

If the trial is before a judge *without a jury,* the prosecution and the defense make their opening statements directly to the court. The opening statements are brief summaries of what the prosecution plans to prove against the defen-

*The description of the trial is adapted from *Criminal Investigation,* 4th ed., pp. 702–704, by Wayne M. Bennett and Kären M. Hess, St. Paul, MN: West Publishing Company, 1994. Reprinted by permission.

It is common for civil cases to be heard by a judge rather than by a jury.

dant and what the defense plans to do to challenge the prosecution's allegations. In a *jury trial,* the jury is selected and then the opening statements are made by both counsels before the judge and jury.

The prosecution presents its case first. Witnesses for the prosecution are sworn in by the court, and the testimony of each is taken by direct examination through questions asked by the prosecuting attorney. At the conclusion of each witness's testimony, the defense attorney may cross-examine the witness. After the cross-examination, the prosecuting attorney may re-direct examine, and the defense attorney may re-cross-examine.

> **Direct examination** is the initial questions of a witness or defendant by the lawyer who is using the person's testimony to further his or her case. **Cross-examination** is questioning by the opposing side for the purpose of assessing the validity of the testimony.

After the prosecutor has completed direct examination of all prosecution witnesses, the defense presents its case. After the direct examination of each defense witness, the prosecutor may cross-examine, the defense counsel may re-direct examine, and the prosecutor may re-cross-examine.

After each side has presented its regular witnesses, both sides may present *rebuttal* and *surrebuttal* witnesses. When the entire case has been presented, prosecution and defense counsel present their closing arguments to the jury. In these arguments, the lawyers review the trial evidence of both sides and then tell the jury why the defendant should be convicted or acquitted. Sometimes the lawyers also make recommendations for penalty.

The judge instructs the jurors on the laws applicable to the case and on how they are to arrive at a decision. The jury then retires to the jury room to deliberate and arrive at a verdict. When the verdict is reached, court is reconvened and the verdict is read. If the verdict is for acquittal, the defendant is released. If the verdict is guilty, the judge passes sentence or sets a time and date for sentencing.

Testifying under Direct Examination

> You are on trial, too—your credibility, your professionalism, your knowledge, your competence, your judgment, your conduct in the field, your use of force, your adherence to official policies, your observance of the defendant's rights—they're all on trial.—Devallis Rutledge

First impressions are critical. Know what you are doing when you enter the courtroom. Go to the courtroom ahead of time and familiarize yourself with the layout of the room.

When your name is called, answer "Here" or "Present" and move directly to the front of the courtroom. Do not go between the prosecutor and the judge; go behind the attorneys. Walk confidently; the jurors are there to hear the facts from you. If your investigation has been thorough and properly conducted, the jury will give a great deal of weight to your testimony.

If you have notes or a report, have them contained in a clean manila file folder carried in your left hand so your right hand is free for taking the oath. Stand straight and face the clerk of court, holding the palm of your hand toward the clerk. Use a clear, firm voice to answer "I do" to the question: "Do you promise to tell the truth, the whole truth, and nothing but the truth, so help you God?" Do not look at the judge, either legal counsel or the jury. Do not raise your hand and take your oath on the way from your seat in the courtroom. Wait until you are directly in front of the clerk.

Sit with your back straight but in a comfortable position, usually with your hands folded in your lap or held on the arms of the chair. Do not move the chair around or fidget in the chair because this distracts from your testimony. The witness chair in all courtrooms is positioned so that you can turn to face the judge, legal counsel, jury or the audience, depending on to whom your answers are directed. Hold notes and other reports in your lap.

The prosecutor will ask you to state your name and position. As you respond to these questions, keep in mind the types of statements that are not admissible.

Inadmissible statements include:

- Opinion (unless the witness is qualified as an expert).
- Hearsay.
- Privileged communication.
- Statements about character and reputation, including the defendant's past criminal record.

Testify only to what you actually saw, heard or did, not what you believe, heard from others or were told about. You can testify to what a defendant told you directly, but any other statements must be testified to by the person making them. Opinions and conclusions also are inadmissible unless you are qualified as an expert. You cannot testify about criminal offenses the defendant committed before the present case.

Proper preparation is the key to being a good witness. After a review of your personal notes and all relevant reports, you will be familiar with the case and can "tell it like it is," which will come across well to the jury and establish your credibility. Vail (1992, p. 96) stresses: "Testifying in court is as important as using a weapon: you don't do it often, but when you do, you had better be correct and accurate."

Guidelines for effective testimony:

- Speak clearly, firmly and with expression.
- Answer questions directly. Do not volunteer information.
- Pause briefly before answering.
- Refer to your notes if you do not recall exact details.
- Admit calmly when you do not know an answer.
- Admit any mistakes you make in testifying.
- Avoid jargon, sarcasm and humor.
- Tell the complete truth as you know it.

How you speak is often as important as what you say. Talk slowly, deliberately and loudly enough to be heard by everyone. Never use obscenity or vulgarity unless the court requests a suspect or victim's exact words and they include it. In such cases, inform the court that the answer requested includes obscenity or vulgarity. Vail points out (p. 96): "It is said that an audience remembers 7 percent of what you say, 38 percent of how you sound, and 55 percent of how you look. In other words, 93 percent of the strength of your testimony lies in your presentation—how you sound and look."

Ignore the courtroom's atmosphere. Devote your entire attention to giving truthful answers to questions. Answer all questions directly and politely with "Yes" or "No," unless asked to relate an action taken, an observation made or information told to you directly by the defendant. Refer to the judge as "Your honor" and to the defendant as "the defendant." Do not volunteer information. Instead, let the prosecution decide whether to go into a particular line of questioning.

Take a few seconds after hearing the question to form your answer. If the counsel or the court objects to a question, wait until instructed to proceed. If it takes some time for the objection to be ruled on, ask to have the question repeated.

Refer to your notes if you are uncertain of specific facts, but do not rely on them excessively.

Reviewing the case thoroughly before your courtroom appearance does not mean you should memorize specific dates, addresses or spellings of names and places. Memorization can lead to confusion. Instead, use notes to help avoid contradictions and inconsistencies in testimony. An extemporaneous answer is better received by the judge and jury than one that sounds pat. Mogil (1989, p. 9) cautions against scripted responses: "Nothing, and I mean nothing, will turn off a jury faster than their perception that the officer is being coached with a specific script of testimony."

Using notes too much detracts from your testimony, weakens the strength of your presentation and gives the impression that you have not adequately prepared for the case. It can also lead to having your notes introduced into the record. If as you refer to your notes you discover that you have given erroneous testimony such as an incorrect date or time, notify the court immediately. Do not try to cover up the discrepancy. Everyone makes mistakes; if they are professionally admitted, little harm results. Do not hesitate to admit that you do not know the answer to a question or that you do not understand a question. Never bluff or attempt to fake your way through an answer.

Mogil (1989, p. 8) also suggests that officers should be aware of and avoid certain "trigger words" that lead jury members to believe that "a response is less than definitive. For example, instead of answering a question with a clear 'Yes,' the witness begins with 'I believe,' or 'I'll try to explain,' or 'To the best of my recollection.' "

Do not argue or use sarcasm, witticism or smart answers. Be direct, firm and positive in your answers. Be courteous whether the question is from the prosecutor, the defense attorney or the judge. Do not hesitate to give information favorable to the defendant. Your primary responsibility is to state what you know about the case.

Nonverbal Factors. Vail (1992, p. 99) states: "In order to win cases in court, you must always appear to be self-confident and in control of yourself and the situation."

> Important nonverbal elements include dress, eye contact, posture, gestures, distance, mannerisms, rate of speech and tone of voice.

Some nonverbal messages such as dress, posture, rate of speech and tone of voice have already been stressed. How you appear *is* crucial.

Strategies for Excelling as a Witness

Hope (1992, pp. 56–60) has compiled the following "Ten Commandments of Courtroom Testimony":

I. Relax and be yourself.
II. Answer only questions that are before you.

III. Refer to your report only when allowed.
IV. Paint the scene just as it was.
V. Be ready to explain why you are remembering details in court if they are not in your report.
VI. Avoid jargon or unduly difficult language.
VII. Avoid sarcasm.
VIII. Maintain your detachment.
IX. You don't need to explain the law.
X. Explanation of what you said is possible on rebuttal.

The quotation at the beginning of the previous section is by Devallis Rutledge, a former police officer, presently a prosecutor. His book *Courtroom Survival: The Officer's Guide to Better Testimony* (1987) contains more than 180 pages of practical, common-sense, vital advice for courtroom testimony and many examples of courtroom dialogue.

> Rutledge's strategies for testifying in court include the following: (1) set yourself up, (2) provoke the defense into giving you a chance to explain, (3) be unconditional and (4) don't stall.

- Get into the habit of thinking ahead to the trial while you're still out in the field. What if they ask me this in court?
- The rules of court severely restrict you in answering questions. No defense attorney in his right mind is ever going to give you a chance to explain anything. So, if you're ever going to get the chance to explain yourself before the jury's impression of you gets set in their heads, you've got to know how to provoke the defense attorney into giving you a chance to explain. Some of these provokers are: *definitely; certainly; certainly not; naturally; naturally not;* and one that always does the trick: *Yes, and no.*
- Be unconditional. Some cops seem to like the sound of the conditional word *would*. When I'm prosecuting a case, I cringe at the sound of it. It's too indefinite:
  Example:
  Q: Who was your partner?
  A: That would be Officer Hill.
- Don't stall. Don't repeat the question back to the attorney.
  Example:
  Q: Were you holding a flashlight?
  A: Was I holding a flashlight? Yes, I was.

Testifying under Cross-examination

Cross-examination is usually the most difficult part of testifying. The defense attorney will attempt to cast doubt on your direct testimony in an effort to win an acquittal for the defendant. Know the methods of attack for cross-examination to avoid being trapped.

During cross-examination the defense attorney might:

- Be disarmingly friendly or intimidatingly rude.
- Attack your credibility and impartiality.
- Attack your investigative skill.
- Attempt to force contradictions or inconsistencies.
- Ask leading questions or deliberately misquote you.
- Ask for a simple answer to a complex question.
- Use rapid-fire questioning.
- Use the silent treatment.

The defense attorney can be extremely friendly, hoping to put you off-guard by making the questioning appear to be nothing more than a friendly chat. The attorney might praise your skill in investigation and lead you into boasting or a show of self-glorification that will leave a very bad impression on the jury. The friendly defense attorney might also try to lead you into giving testimony about evidence of which you have no personal knowledge. This error will be immediately exposed and your testimony tainted, if not completely discredited.

At the opposite extreme is the defense attorney who appears outraged by statements you make and goes on the attack immediately. This kind of attorney appears very excited and acts as though a travesty of justice is being presented in the courtroom. A natural reaction to such an approach is to overreact by exaggerating your testimony or by losing your temper, which is exactly what the defense attorney wants. If you show anger, the jury might believe you are too concerned about the case and are more interested in obtaining a conviction than in determining the truth. It is often hard for a jury to believe that the well-dressed, meek-appearing defendant in court is the person who was armed with a gun and robbed a store. Maintain dignity and impartiality, and show concern only for the facts.

The credibility of your testimony can be attacked in many ways. The defense may attempt to show that you are prejudiced, have poor character or are interested only in seeing your arrest stick. If asked, "Do you want to see the defendant convicted?" reply that you are there to present the facts you know.

The defense may also try to show that your testimony itself is erroneous because you are incompetent, lack information, are confused, have forgotten facts or could not have had personal knowledge of the facts testified to. Do not respond to such criticism. Let your testimony speak for itself. If the defense criticizes your reference to notes, state that you simply want to be completely accurate. Be patient. If the defense counsel becomes excessively offensive, the prosecutor will intervene. Alternatively, the prosecutor may see that the defense is hurting its own case by such behavior and will allow the defense attorney to proceed.

The defense attorney may also try to force contradictions or inconsistencies by incessantly repeating questions using slightly different wording. Repeat your previous answer. If the defense claims that your testimony does not agree with that of other officers, do not change your testimony. Whether your testimony is alike or different is irrelevant. The defense will attack it either way. If it is exactly alike, the defense will allege collusion. If it is slightly different, the defense will exaggerate this in an attempt to make the jury believe the differences are so great that the officers are not even testifying about the same circumstances.

The defense counsel may use an accusatory tone in asking whether you talked with others about the case and what they told you about how to testify. To inexperienced officers, such accusations may produce guilt because the officers know they have talked about the case with many people. Because the accusing tone implies this was legally incorrect, the officers may reply that they talked to no one. Such a response is a mistake because there is nothing wrong with discussing the case before testifying. Simply state that you have discussed the case with several persons in an official capacity, but that none of them has told you how to testify.

If defense counsel asks whether you have refreshed your memory before testifying, do not hesitate to say "yes." You would be a poor witness if you had not done so. Discussions with the prosecution and witnesses and a review of notes and reports are entirely proper. They assist you in telling the truth, the main purpose of testimony.

Another defense tactic is to use leading questions. For example, defense counsel may ask, "When did you first strike the defendant?" This assumes you did, in fact, strike the defendant. Defense attorneys also like to ask questions that presume you have already testified to something when in fact you may have said no such thing. If you are misquoted, call it to the counsel's attention and then repeat the facts you testified to. If you do not remember your exact testimony, have it read from the court record.

In addition, defense counsel may ask complicated questions and then say, "Please answer 'yes' or 'no.' " Obviously, some questions cannot be answered that simply. Ask to have the question broken down. No rule requires a specific answer. If the court does not grant the request, answer the question as directed and let the prosecutor bring out the information through re-direct examination.

Yet another tactic used by defense attorneys is rapid-fire questioning in the hope of provoking unconsidered answers. Do not let the attorney's pace rush you. Take time to consider your responses.

Do not be taken in by the "silent treatment." The defense attorney may remain silent for what seems like many seconds after you answer a question. If you have given a complete answer, wait patiently. Do *not* attempt to fill the silence by saying things such as, "At least that's how I remember it," or "It was something very close to that."

Another tactic frequently used by defense attorneys is to intentionally mispronounce officers' names in an attempt to cause the officer to lose concentration.

Regardless of how your testimony is attacked, treat the defense counsel as respectfully as you do the prosecutor. Do not regard the defense counsel as your enemy. You are in court to state the facts and tell the truth. There should be no personal prejudice or animosity in your testimony, no reason to become excited or provoked at the defense counsel. Be professional. Table 13–1 (p. 410) summarizes the common tactics used during cross-examination.

Table 13–1. Brief Review of Common Tactics of Cross-Examination

Counsel's Tactic	Example	Purpose	Officer's Response
Rapid-fire questions	One question after another with little time to answer.	To confuse you; an attempt to force inconsistent answers.	Take time to consider the question; be deliberate in answering; ask to have the question repeated; remain calm.
Condescending counsel	Benevolent in approach, oversympathetic in questions to the point of ridicule.	To give the impression that you are inept, lack confidence or may not be a reliable witness.	Firm decisive answers, asking for the questions to be repeated if improperly phrased.
Friendly counsel	Very courteous, polite; questions tend to take you into his confidence.	To lull you into a false sense of security, where you will give answers in favor of the defense.	Stay alert; bear in mind that purpose of defense is to discredit or diminish the effect of your testimony.
Badgering, belligerent	Counsel staring you right in the face, shouts, "That is so, isn't it, officer?"	To make you angry, so that you lose the sense of logic and calmness. Generally, rapid questions will also be included in this approach.	Stay calm, speak in a deliberate voice, giving prosecutor time to make appropriate objections.
Mispronouncing officer's name; using wrong rank	Your name is Jansen; counsel calls you Johnson.	To draw your attention to the error in pronunciation rather than enabling you to concentrate on the question asked, so that you will make inadvertent errors in testimony.	Ignore the mispronunciation and concentrate on the questions counsel is asking.
Suggestive question (tends to be a leading question allowable on cross-examination)	"Was the color of the car blue?"	To suggest an answer to his or her question in an attempt to confuse or to lead you.	Concentrate carefully on the facts, disregard the suggestion. Answer the question.
Demanding a yes or no answer to a question that needs explanation	"Did you strike the defendant with your club?"	To prevent all pertinent and mitigating details from being considered by the jury.	Explain the answer to the question; if stopped by counsel demanding a yes or no answer, pause until the court instructs you to answer in your own words.
Reversing witness's words	You answer, "The accident occurred 27 feet from the intersection." Counsel says, "You say the accident occurred 72 feet from the intersection?"	To confuse you and demonstrate a lack of confidence in you.	Listen intently whenever counsel repeats back something you have said. If counsel makes an error, correct him or her.
Repetitious questions	The same question asked several times slightly rephrased.	To obtain inconsistent or conflicting answers from you.	Listen carefully to the question and state, "I have just answered that question."
Conflicting answers	"But, Officer Smith, Detective Brown just said . . ."	To show inconsistency in the investigation. This tactic is normally used on measurements, times and so forth.	Remain calm. Conflicting statements have a tendency to make a witness extremely nervous. Be guarded in your answers on measurements, times and so forth. Unless you have exact knowledge, use the term "approximately." Refer to your notes.
Staring	After you have answered, counsel stares as though there were more to come.	To have a long pause that one normally feels must be filled, thus saying more than necessary. To provoke you into offering more than the question called for.	Wait for the next question.

SOURCE: Reprinted from "Officer in Court" Training Key # 248, published by the International Association of Chiefs of Police, Alexandria, Virginia. (The Training Key is a police training publication of IACP designed for individual study and agencywide training programs. For detailed information, contact IACP.)

The best testimony is accurate, truthful and in accordance with the facts. Every word an officer says is recorded and may be played back or used by the defense.

Handling Objections. Rutledge (1987, pp. 99–115) gives the following suggestions for handling objections:

> There are at least 44 standard trial objections in most states. We're only going to talk about the two that account for upwards of 90 percent of the problems a testifying officer will have: that your answer is a conclusion, or that it is non-responsive.
>
> - How to avoid conclusions. One way is to listen to the form of the question. You know the attorney is asking you to speculate when he starts his questions with these loaded phrases:
>   Would you assume . . .?
>   Do you suppose . . .?
>   Don't you think that . . .?
>   Couldn't it be that . . .?
>   Do you imagine . . .?
>   Wouldn't it be fair to presume . . .?
>   Isn't it strange that . . .?
>   And the one you're likely to hear most often:
>   Isn't it possible that . . .?
> - Another major area of conclusionary testimony is what I call mindreading. You can't get inside someone else's brain. That means you don't know for a fact—so you can't testify—as to what someone else sees, hears, feels, thinks or wants; and you don't know for a fact what somebody is trying to do, or is able to do, or whether he is nervous, excited, angry, scared, happy, upset, disturbed, or in any of the other emotional states that can only be labeled with a conclusion.
> - How to give "responsive" answers. You have to answer just the question that you're asked—no more, no less. That means you have to pay attention to how the question is framed. You answer a yes-or-no question with a "yes" or "no."

Avoid conclusions and nonresponsive answers. Answer yes-or-no questions with "yes" or "no."

> The defense lawyer's most important task is to destroy your credibility—to make you look like you're either an incompetent bungler, or a liar, or both. How does he do that? He attacks you. He tricks you. He outsmarts you. He confuses you. He frustrates you. He annoys you. He probes for your most vulnerable characteristics.

Willingham (1993, p. 48) suggests the following:

> The formula for successful courtroom testimony is: be brief, politely; be aggressive, smilingly; be emphatic, pleasantly; be positive, diplomatically; and be right, graciously.

Former L.A.P.D. detective Mark Fuhrman testifying during the O. J. Simpson trial.

Concluding Your Testimony

Do not leave the stand until instructed to do so by the counsel or the court. As you leave the stand, do not pay special attention to the prosecution, defense counsel, defendant or jury. Return immediately to your seat in the courtroom or leave the room if you have been sequestered. If you are told you may be needed for further testimony, remain available. If told you are no longer needed, leave the courtroom and resume your normal activities. To remain gives the impression you have a special interest in the case.

If you are in the courtroom at the time of the verdict, show neither approval nor disapproval at the outcome.

Tips for Success

Taitz (1990, p. 139) offers the following tips for success once in the court:*

- When arriving in court, make yourself known to counsel on each side and follow your own counsel's instructions.
- Sit in the rear and be as inconspicuous as possible. If you must sit at the counsel's table be aware that you are in public view. Sit upright, hands clasped on the table, in a professional manner.
- If you have to communicate with counsel, do not whisper. Instead, write a note and gently pass the paper to the attorney. This is accepted courtroom practice—but only if absolutely necessary. In short, don't be a distraction.

*Reprinted by permission.

- Grooming and posture are also important. Dress in a business suit in good taste. When called, walk, with good posture, toward the stand. Face the clerk of the court and raise your hand to accept the oath. After the oath is administered, say clearly and convincingly "I do," so that everyone can hear. Do not mumble.
- When you take the stand, adjust the microphone, if there is one, and sit upright with hands clasped and ankles crossed. When the clerk of the court asks you to state your name, look directly at the recorder, state your full name clearly, and spell out your last name.
- Then, make eye contact with the jury so that the jurists may sense, albeit subtly, that you recognize their presence and that they are the ones who are going to make the decisions.
- Under cross-examination, expect to be tested by the plaintiff's attorney, who will try to intimidate you or cast doubt on your training and/or your program.
- Beware of a question that starts "Isn't it a fact that . . .?" This is often a signal for "here comes a challenge to your credibility."
- Answer questions in as few words as possible, without elaboration. Be polite. Never frown or get angry, clever, or excited. And never answer a question with a question.
- "If the attorney races or pressures you, take all the time you need to think through your answer," says our consultant. "And if you don't know the answer or understand the question, say so."
- Always tell the truth—even though the truth may hurt. "A key issue is that, at times, the answers you have to give won't be what you want to give, but sometimes you have to give the attorney a point. Some answers you just have to give up or you will be made a fool. It does get hairy when a lawyer tries to intimidate you, but it's just a matter of keeping cool and not getting rattled, and telling the truth."
- When you are finished testifying and are excused by the judge, say "Thank you, your honor" and immediately leave the courtroom. Remaining to watch the remainder of the proceedings demonstrates an interest that is not warranted. "If you stay, you look curious, and that's not professional," notes our consultant, adding that "you can't look like you have a personal axe to grind."

Expert Testimony

Officers who qualify as experts in an area are allowed to give opinions and conclusions, but the prosecution must qualify the officer as an expert on the stand. It must be established that the person has special knowledge that persons of moderate education or experience in the same field do not possess. To qualify as an expert witness, one must have:

- Present or prior employment in the specific field;
- Active membership in a professional group in the field;
- Research work in the field;
- An educational degree directly related to the field;
- Direct experience with the subject if not employed in the field;
- Papers, treatises or books published on the subject or teaching experience in it.

According to the American Society for Industrial Security (ASIS, 1993), several factors enter into qualifying someone as an expert in security:

- Experience.
- Formal education.
- Professional certification, e.g., Certified Protection Professional (CPP), Certified Protection Officer (CPO), certified by the International Association for Hospital Security or certified by the Academy of Security Educators and Trainers.
- Speeches delivered and articles or textbooks written.
- Prior testimony as an expert.

The ASIS suggests that a security officer discuss any weaknesses in background with his or her attorney. The ASIS also suggests that a security officer balance cases between plaintiffs and defendants so as not to appear like a "hired gun." When security personnel qualified as experts take the witness stand, they might expect three types of questions: (1) those based on their personal knowledge, (2) those based on the facts of the case and (3) those based on hypothetical questions. All hypothetical questions must be based on facts already admitted into testimony or likely to be admitted. Finally, the ASIS suggests that security personnel should not be embarrassed about getting paid to testify if such is the case. They should simply state the facts.

Trends in Decisions and Settlements

Using the hotel industry as a typical example, Taitz (1990, pp. 136–137*) notes that in cases where the hotel came out on top, it was able to show the following:

- It was truly concerned with the well-being of its guests.
- It paid attention to criminal occurrences in the area and on the property.
- Within financial limitations, it took steps to provide the best security it could and was able to document this.
- When the crime was reported, its people immediately went to the aid of that victim, called police, sought to catch the perpetrator or conducted a thorough investigation.
- It was supportive of the victim's feelings and needs both psychological and medical.

In the cases where the hotel was the loser, some factors contributing to its defeat included the following:

- Insufficient screening and reference checking of new employees.
- A history of robberies and break-ins.
- A history of not implementing recommendations of its own security people.

Reprinted with permission from *Getting a Job, Getting Ahead, and Staying Ahead in Security Management,* © 1990, Rusting Publications, Port Washington, NY.

- Not enough security personnel (or communications and surveillance equipment) for the size and area of the property.
- Poor key control and failure to replace missing master keys.
- No formal written security policy or instructions for employees on security, not just security guards.
- Inadequate lighting especially in hallways and parking lots.
- Placing female guests in rooms remote from the office.
- No deadbolt locks.
- No warning to guests to double lock their doors and not open them for anyone.
- Failure to respond promptly to a call for help.
- Failure to train employees in security or otherwise from the time of employment.
- Failure to prepare, file and review written incident reports.
- Poor exit control.
- Poor perimeter definition of the property.
- Unclear perimeter protection policies.

Although drawn from the hotel industry, most of these deficiencies also would be detrimental to any facility where security is important.

SUMMARY

To effectively testify in court, be prepared, look professional and act professionally. The sequence in a criminal trial is as follows: jury selection, opening statements by the prosecution and the defense, presentation of the prosecution's case, presentation of the defense's case, closing statements by the prosecution and the defense, instructions to the jury, jury deliberation to reach a verdict, reading of the verdict and acquittal or passing of sentence.

Direct examination is the initial questioning of a witness or defendant by the lawyer who is using the person's testimony to further his or her case. Cross-examination is questioning by the opposing side for the purpose of assessing the validity of the testimony. Important nonverbal elements include dress, eye contact, posture, gestures, distance, mannerisms, rate of speech and tone of voice.

When testifying, security personnel must avoid making inadmissable statements, including opinion (unless the witness is qualified as an expert), hearsay, privileged communication and statements about character and reputation, including the defendant's past criminal record.

Guidelines for effective testimony include the following:

- Speak clearly, firmly and with expression.
- Answer questions directly. Do not volunteer information.
- Pause briefly before answering.
- Refer to your notes if you do not recall exact details.
- Admit calmly when you do not know an answer.
- Admit any mistakes you make in testifying.
- Avoid jargon, sarcasm and humor.
- Tell the truth as you know it.

In addition, refer to your notes if you are uncertain of specific facts, but do not rely on them excessively.

Strategies for testifying in court include (1) setting yourself up, (2) provoking the defense into giving you a chance to explain, (3) being unconditional and (4) not stalling.

Anticipate the tactics commonly used by defense attorneys during cross-examination. They may be disarmingly friendly or intimidatingly rude; attack your credibility and impartiality; attack your investigative skill; attempt to force contradictions or inconsistencies; ask leading questions or deliberately misquote you; request a "yes" or "no" answer to complex questions; use rapid-fire questioning or use the "silent treatment."

Avoid conclusions and nonresponsive answers. Answer yes-or-no questions with "yes" or "no."

If you are well prepared, know the facts and present them truthfully and professionally, you have done your part in furthering the cause of justice. The disposition of a case should be made known to the complainant.

Application

You are a supervisor with the Allen Security Company, and one of your security officers approaches you about an upcoming court appearance in a civil case. Security Officer McDuff has never had the experience of testifying in court and asks you to suggest ways that he can present a professional image. What suggestions would you make to Officer McDuff to assure that he presents a good image?

Critical Thinking Exercise

Testifying

Statutory and Common Law

Any person who, having taken an oath that he will testify, declare, depose or certify truly before any competent tribunal, officer or person, in any of the cases in which such an oath may by law be administered, intentionally and contrary to such oath, states any material matter that he knows to be false, is guilty of perjury.

Facts of the Case

On January 7, at the McDonald's restaurant at 2410 Cuming Street in Omaha, Nebraska, Carol Barr, a cook, was taking out the trash as the restaurant was closing. When she turned away from the trash container, a man with a ski mask over his head came alongside her and asked her who was in the restaurant. She told him the crew, a manager and the security guard. He asked if the security guard was black or white. When she said he was white, the man told her to act busy and get the manager to come to the back area. At that time she noticed he held a gun in his right hand.

As Barr proceeded to call the manager, she met Eric Howard, another cook. The man with a covered head pushed Howard against a door, pointed the gun at his head and said, "Don't say anything." Ronald Parker, the manager, appeared. The man told everyone else to move to the front of the restaurant, but he told the manager to give him the restaurant's money. Rose Stennis, a cashier, heard Charlotte Moore, an assistant manager, say, "Don't shoot; take everything; just don't hurt nobody."

The man collected the money from the cash register drawers and then went to the security guard (McWaters), stuck the gun in his side and removed his gun, watch and wallet. As he left, he said, "Nobody move; don't nobody move."

During the next two days, the employees were shown a mug book containing more than 200 photographs, and Barr, Parker, Howard, Stennis and Moore all identified Lawrence Atwater. From a police lineup on January 9, they all identified Atwater as the robber.

In court testimony, Barr described the robber as wearing a dark blue ski mask with white trim, a brown leather jacket and work gloves. She also said he had large bloodshot eyes and a full mustache. Parker said he remembered the large eyes and lips because they were wider than normal. Howard said that the robber seemed to have a large nose and lips and that his eyes were nervous. Stennis said the robber had a bush mustache and buggy eyes. Moore said he had big eyes and a heavy mustache.

McWaters had given no resistance during the holdup but attempted to make close observations while the robber was standing within a foot of him while taking his possessions. In his testimony he said that the robber was a black male about 5′ 10″ tall and about 190 pounds. He wore gloves and a blue ski mask, but McWaters could see the robber's eyes which were large and protruded such that one would call them "bulgy-type" eyes. The robber had a heavy mustache, extremely dark complexion and a chipped upper middle tooth. McWaters also saw a skin deformity or scar just below the robber's right eye.

Issues and Questions

1. Evaluate the action and testimony of the security guard, McWaters.
   a. McWaters should have acted to prevent the holdup. He did not have his gun taken away until after the robber collected money from the cash register drawers. McWaters' testimony reveals that his presence as a security guard was ineffective, and the fragmentary observations he was able to make are insufficient to convict beyond a reasonable doubt.
   b. If Officer Richard Swircinski, who supervised the police lineup, would testify that "Atwater's brother has the same physical description as Atwater," and that "McWaters' gun had been recovered from a location near where Atwater's brother was arrested on February 16," then the testimony given by McWaters would not be sufficient to convict beyond a reasonable doubt. Otherwise, the action and testimony would be sufficient.
   c. In this case a conviction would be possible only if McWaters had made some attempt to resist the progress of the attempted robbery and if he

could give testimony that his wallet (which was in fact returned) and gun had been found in Lawrence Atwater's residence. Also, McWaters should testify about a pawnshop ticket found at Atwater's residence that listed one Gruen watch, a match to the one taken along with the gun and wallet.

d. Although McWaters was appropriate in his actions, he should have observed more completely and in detail everything the robber wore, giving exact details about his shoes, pants, jacket, gloves and ski mask. These precise facts must be noted in a written report that includes the eyewitness reports of all who were there. Without a much more complete and detailed report, the differences in courtroom testimony will be torn apart by defense counsel and there will be no possibility of gaining a conviction with the meager testimony given by McWaters and others.

e. McWaters' lack of resistance was appropriate, given that the robber threatened people with a gun, and his testimony is sufficiently specific to convict.

Discussion Questions

1. What is one of the most important documents a security officer can bring to court?
2. What does an attorney look for from the security officer when the officer testifies?
3. Why is there so much emphasis on keeping good notes?
4. How should a security officer on the witness stand deal with an attorney who is trying to confuse him or her with rapid-fire questioning so that the answers the officer gives might be inconsistent?
5. How do most attorneys attempt to attack security officers' credibility before the jury?

References

ASIS 34th Annual Seminar, recorded September 26–29, 1990 in Boston, MA. From the telecommunications security program: "Your Role in Litigation—Part 2: Trials, Expert Witnessing, Who Is an Expert?"

Hope, George. "Ten Commandments of Courtroom Testimony." *Minnesota Police Journal,* April 1992, pp. 55–60.

Mogil, B. Marc. "Maximizing Your Courtroom Testimony." *FBI Law Enforcement Bulletin,* May 1989, pp. 7–9.

Purpura, Philip. *Security and Loss Prevention: An Introduction,* 2d ed. Stoneham, MA: Butterworth-Heinemann, 1991.

Rutledge, Devallis. *Courtroom Survival: The Officer's Guide to Better Testimony.* Sacramento, CA: Custom Publishing Company, 1987.

Taitz, Sharyn, ed. *Getting a Job, Getting Ahead, and Staying Ahead in Security Management.* Port Washington, NY: Rusting Publications, 1990.

Vail, Christopher. "Presenting Winning Testimony in Court." *Law and Order,* June 1992, pp. 96–99.

Willingham, Mark. "The Importance of Being an Impressive Witness." *Law and Order,* February 1993, pp. 45–48.

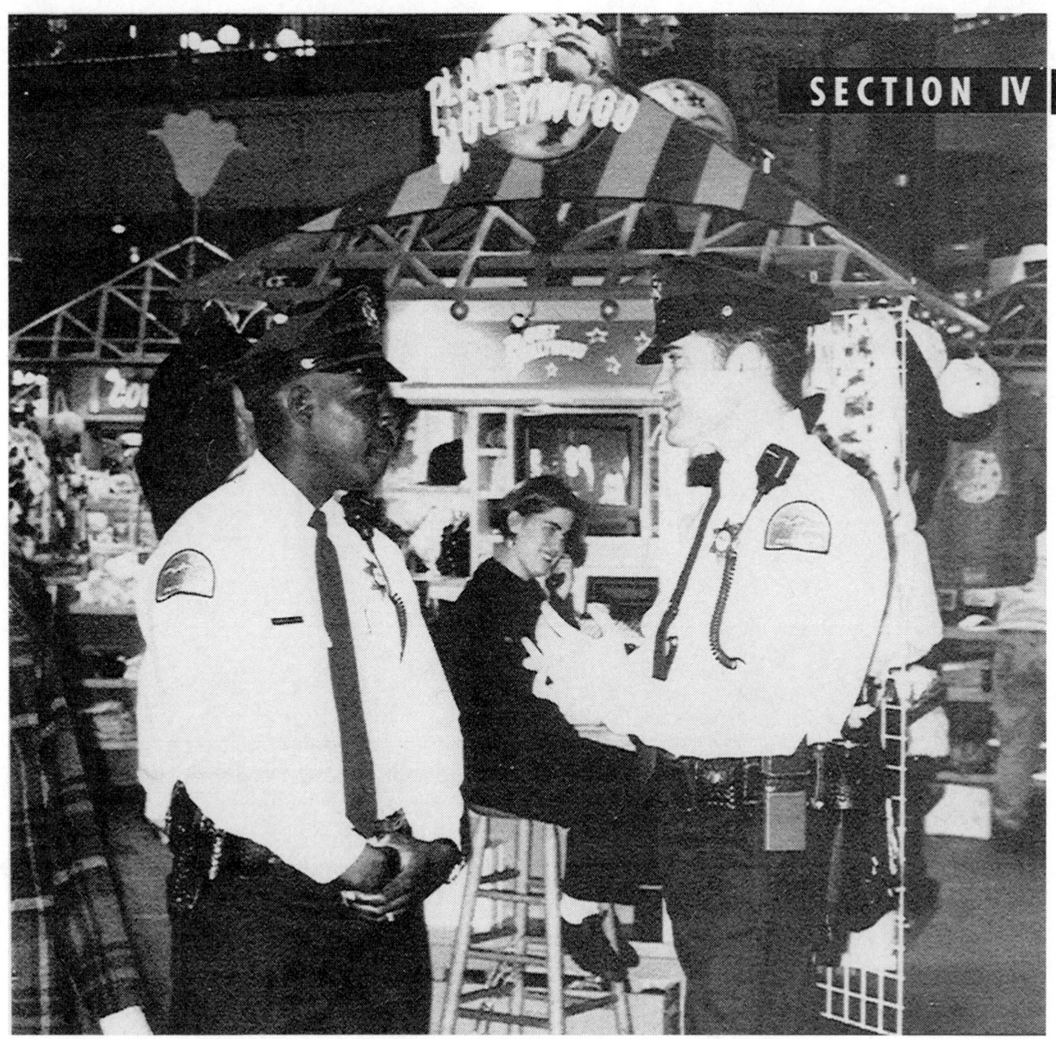

SECTION IV

Security Systems at Work: Putting It All Together

The basic security responsibilities discussed in Section II can be adapted to fit specific security systems. The criteria for determining the amount of security needed are based primarily on the relative criticality and vulnerability of the establishment, as well as on management's perceived need for and commitment to achieving a reasonable degree of security.

Security equipment, procedures and personnel can be used singly or in combination to prevent losses. Where all three interact, the greatest security is provided (see Figure IV–1 p. 420).

Although security measures add costs, they can also result in considerable savings. The National Crime Prevention Institute cites several fundamental

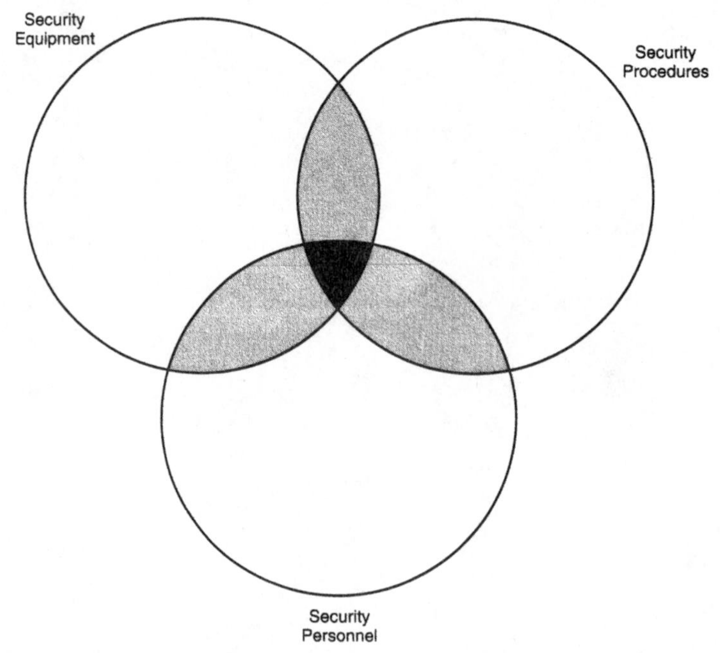

Figure IV–1. The Interaction of Security Equipment, Procedures and Personnel

conditions that must exist before an effective security program can be implemented and more profits realized:*

- **M**anagement support of security from the top level.
- **O**rganizational structure allowing security access to top management.
- **R**ecognize and establish sound physical and procedural controls.
- **E**ducate employees to follow established procedures.
- **P**ost and impartially enforce all procedures.
- **R**ecord all incidents of procedural violations.
- **O**rganize operational procedures to avoid conflict of interest.
- **F**idelity bonds utilized and implications explained to employees.
- **I**nformation given to all employees regarding pure risk potential in job.
- **T**rain all employees to react properly to pure risk confrontation.
- **S**et example by refusing to violate rules at all management levels.

This section begins with a discussion of risk management and its importance to any business or industry (Chapter 14). The following chapters examine how security functions in specific settings and some of the specific problems encountered and the security systems developed for industrial security (Chapter 15), retail security (Chapter 16), commercial security (Chapter 17) and institutional security (Chapter 18). The section concludes with a chapter focusing on special areas of concern such as parking lot security and executive protection (Chapter 19).

---

*"Understanding Crime Prevention" by the National Crime Prevention Institute. Reprinted by permission.

CHAPTER 14

Loss Prevention through Risk Management

Do You Know

- The difference between pure and dynamic risk?
- What risk management is?
- What is included in a systematic approach to preventing loss through risk management?
- Whether risk management is a moral or a legal responsibility?
- What three factors are considered in risk analysis?
- What a security survey is?
- How the information needed for a security survey is obtained?
- What alternatives exist for handling risks?
- When components of the security system should be evaluated?

Can You Define These Terms?

criticality
dynamic risk
probability
pure risk
risk
risk acceptance
risk elimination
risk management
risk reduction
risk spreading
risk transfer
security survey
vulnerability

Introduction

When the contract security operations manager for a 500-room hotel in the Midwest was informed that one of two grand master keys for the hotel was missing, it was a crisis. Security was doubled until the entire hotel could be re-keyed, a process that cost $500,000. The hotel manager responsible for the key's security lost his job. That single, lost key created an extreme risk that had to be dealt with immediately.

Risk management, however, is much more than dealing with crises. In fact, effective risk management should greatly reduce such crises. The purpose of risk management is to make an organization's environment secure, yet consistent with its operations and philosophy. Consequently, risk managers must consider not only the possible targets of attack and existing security measures as they relate to profits, but also the aesthetic and operational needs of the enterprise. Efficiency, convenience, appearance and profit are all important factors as security systems are planned.

Effective risk management should provide an integrated, comprehensive approach to a secure environment. Unfortunately, this is often not the case, as noted by Kohr (1994, p. 64):

> In today's corporate environment, security staffs and budgets are smaller, but the expectations for services and programs remain the same. As a result, many companies have abandoned their preventive security and safety efforts and now target limited resources to putting fires out. That approach is misguided and will prove costly over the longer term.

Eberhart (1994, p. 12) also cautions: "The results can be disastrous when systems are integrated in a piecemeal fashion without advance planning."

This chapter begins by defining risks and risk management and presenting an overview of the factors involved. This is followed by a discussion of risk analysis and the role of the security survey. Next, alternatives to deal with identified risks are discussed. The chapter concludes with suggestions for reporting the results of the risk analysis, implementing the recommendations and evaluating the security system.

Risks and Risk Management Defined

The concept of risk is familiar to most people. A **risk** is a known threat that has effects that are not predictable in either their timing or their extent. The effects can include actual losses, interruption of production cycles, reduction of sales opportunities, injury to persons, liability claims and property damage.

Golsby (1992, p. 55) defines risk using a formula: risk = intention + capability + opportunity. The National Crime Prevention Institute (NCPI) identifies two types of risks existing in any enterprise: pure risk and dynamic risk.

> **Pure risk** is the potential for injury, damage or loss with no possible benefits. **Dynamic risk,** in contrast, has the potential for both benefits and losses.

Pure risks include crimes and natural disasters. These offer no benefit to management—only added cost. Also included within the category of pure risks is the employer's liability to protect employees, customers and visitors. People have a right to be reasonably safe when on the property of businesses or organizations. Several years ago a popular nightclub entertainer was assaulted, raped and robbed in a hotel where she was staying during her singing engagement. The singer sued the hotel for negligence and won the case. Lawsuits based on inadequate security have increased.

In contrast to pure risks, dynamic risks result from a management decision and may result in both benefits and losses. For example, management personnel decide to accept checks because doing so stimulates business. At the same time, they recognize that some losses may occur from the pure risk of check fraud. Or, they decide to hire security personnel. They are then liable for the actions of such personnel. Among charges sometimes brought against security personnel are improper detention or search, false arrest, injury resulting from excessive force, slander and the like, as discussed in Chapter 4.

Both pure and dynamic risks must be recognized and dealt with in a systematic approach to private security.

Although many small businesses may not feel the need for a security system, as noted by McDonough (1992, p. 74): "More and more small and medium-sized firms are finding that risk management programs are essential if they are to survive and prosper in a more competitive economy." McDonough cites two reasons this is occurring:

- Tangled Web of Risks. The web of risks that can snare a small or midsize company has multiplied tenfold in recent years.
- Litigation Avalanche. Small and midsize companies have also been buried under an avalanche of federal and state regulations that can make doing business a costly nightmare.

Kahn (1994, p. 61) suggests: "Companies cannot avoid getting sued, but security managers can limit potential losses."

Risk should not be viewed as all negative. Change necessitates taking risks. As knowledge proliferates and organizations restructure, security managers must deal with the inevitable uncertainty that results from change. They should not be bound by tradition, but rather be willing to take some risks. Security managers who fail to take risks have a rigid, inflexible approach, perceiving change as a threat. Such security managers tend to seek stable, unchanging environments in which they feel safe, but also in which obsolescence and stagnation are found.

> **Risk management** is anticipating, recognizing and analyzing risks; taking steps to reduce or prevent such risks and evaluating the results.

Risk management is sometimes referred to as loss prevention or loss prevention management. The following discussion provides an overview of risk management. What is important at this point is the overall security system and how it is developed. Specific risks and alternatives to eliminating or reducing them are the focus of Sections II and III.

Risk Management: The Total Picture*

Risk management is a complex challenge to security managers. In the market economy a company must take risks; this situation has always existed. But given our sophisticated technology and the demand for high production, even

*Adapted from Statsföretag AB, Skandia Insurance Co. and Skandia Risk Management Ltd., Stockholm, Sweden. Reprinted by permission.

a minor disturbance can cause a substantial economic setback. Consequently, security managers must define and analyze all risks companies may encounter to make it possible to restrict the number and the scope of such disturbances. Risk management is a comprehensive system of measures aimed at achieving that end.

The Risk Management Circle

In Figure 14–1, the outer area shows a company's risk environment—all the risks that affect the company. These will vary, of course, from business to business. The second circle shows the various components of the protection a company can include. The third circle shows the positions involved in a company's protection plan and each individual's areas of responsibility. At the center of the risk management circle is the coordinator, the person who manages the entire security effort and all its components. Plante (1993, p. 49) stresses: "An effective, overall security plan should consider all stakeholders in the facility."

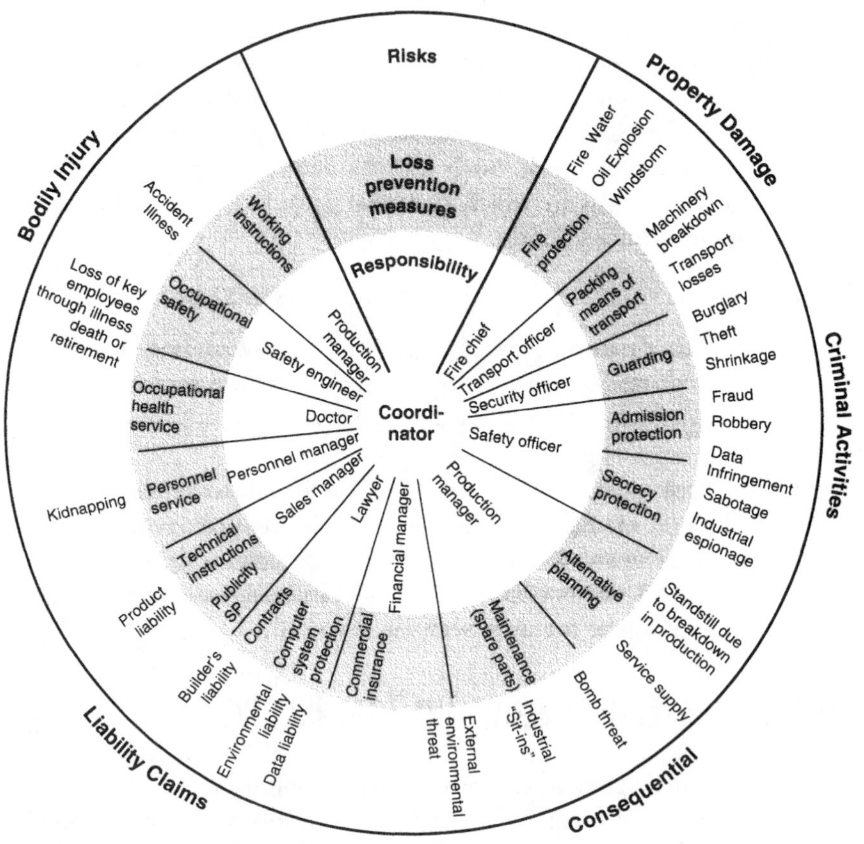

Figure 14–1. The Risk Management Circle
SOURCE: Adapted from Statsföretag AB, Skandia Insurance Co. and Skandia Risk Management Ltd., Stockholm, Sweden. Reprinted by permission.

An important part of asset valuation is an inventory. Computers have greatly simplified this task.

Kohr (1994, p. 65) describes stakeholders as the CEO, directors, stockholders, employees, visitors and the community itself.

The Joint Security Commission (*Security Concepts,* June 1994, pp. 8, 23) describes the risk management process as a five-step procedure:

1. Asset valuation and judgment about consequences of loss. We determine what is to be protected and appraise its value.
2. Identification and characterization of the threats to specific assets. Intelligence assessments must address threats to the asset in as much detail as possible, based on the needs of the customer.
3. Identification and characterization of the vulnerability of specific assets.
4. Identification of countermeasures, costs, and tradeoffs.
5. Risk assessment. Asset valuation, threat analysis, and vulnerability assessments are considered, along with the acceptable level of risk and any uncertainties, to decide how great is the risk and what countermeasures to apply.

Figure 14–2 (p. 426) illustrates this risk management process.

The Risk Cycle

An efficient, effective, non-crisis-oriented security system does not just happen. Developing such a system involves critical observations and judgments.

> A systematic approach to preventing loss through risk management includes risk analysis, policy formulation, specification of a protection plan and follow-up.

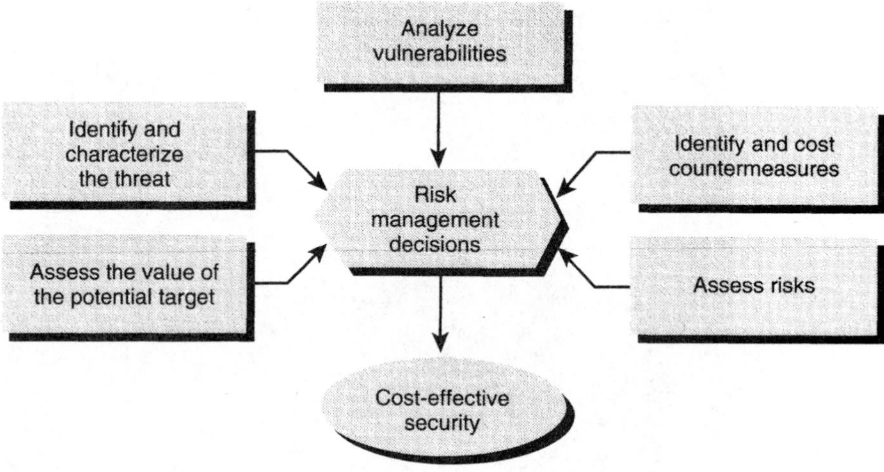

Figure 14–2. The Risk Management Process
SOURCE: Joint Security Commission. "Redefining Security. Part I—Approaching the Next Century." *Security Concepts*, July 1994, p. 23. Reprinted by permission.

The purpose of the *risk analysis* is to create an awareness within a company of any risks and to determine as far as possible their potential influence on the business.

After the risk analysis is completed, *policy* is formulated. The necessary security measures are arranged in order of importance, the cost of such measures is computed and management determines the level of protection the company should choose.

Next a *protection plan* is specified that includes which risks are to be eliminated and how; the degree of need for loss prevention and loss limitation, for protective company health care and for training in company protection; risks to be insured; and allocation of responsibility, management and coordination.

Follow-up should insure a reasonable balance between the risks with which the company has to live and the protection against these risks. New risks can rapidly materialize (e.g., as a result of a kidnapping threat). Other risks may become less serious. The risk cycle might be diagrammed as in Figure 14–3.

The Risk Balance

Risk management seeks to establish a cost-efficient protection system. The higher the protection costs, the lower the costs for loss and damage. But as can be seen in Figure 14–4, there is a point in the protection cost curve that should not be passed, i.e., the point where the lowest total cost is obtained. In addition, the protection must be organized so that the requirements prescribed in state law are fulfilled. It is not always possible to calculate the cost of these requirements.

A well-functioning company protection system means that few disturbances will arise and thus the operations can be carried on according to plan.

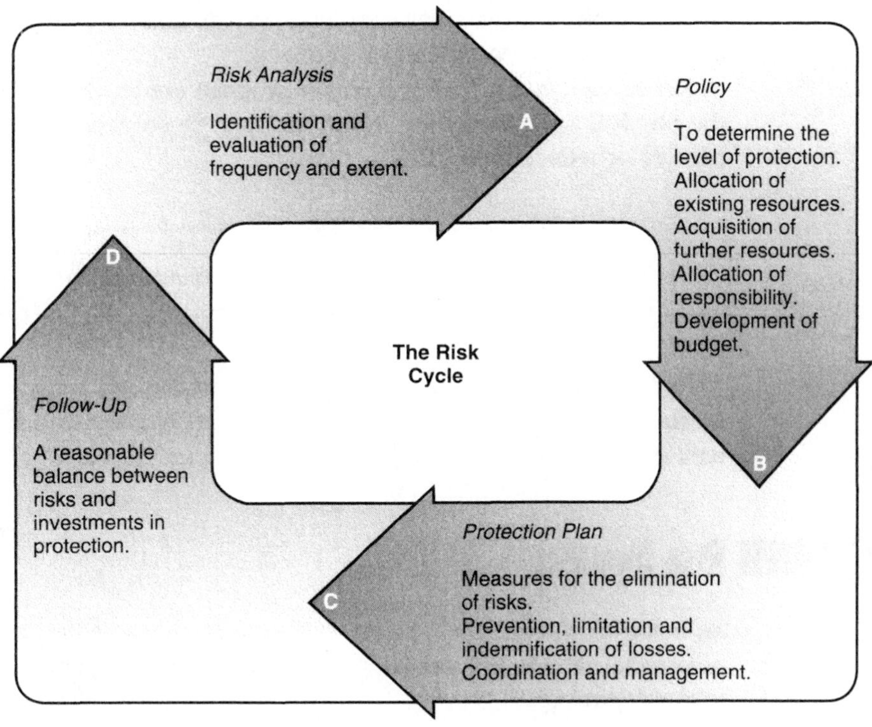

Figure 14–3. The Risk Cycle

SOURCE: Adapted from Statsföretag AB, Skandia Insurance Co. and Skandia Risk Management Ltd., Stockholm, Sweden. Reprinted by permission.

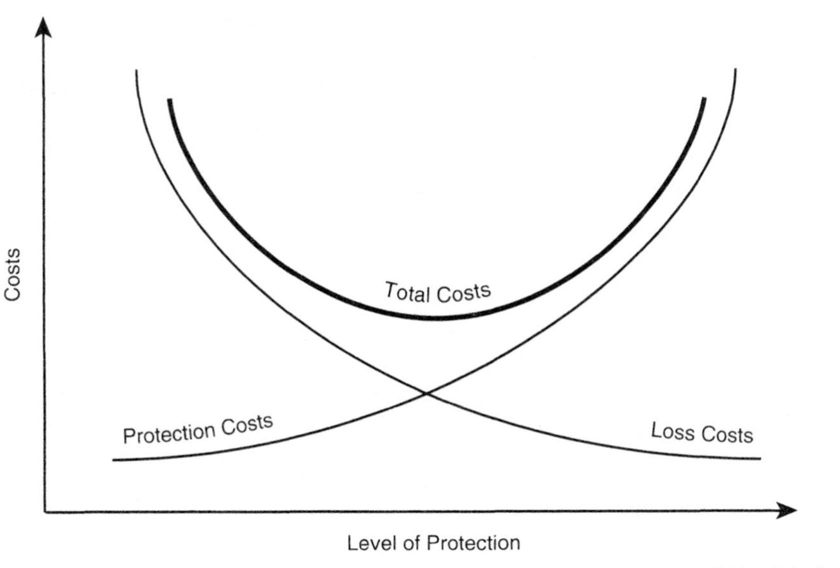

Figure 14–4. Cost vs. Level of Protection

SOURCE: Adapted from Statsföretag AB, Skandia Insurance Co. and Skandia Risk Management Ltd., Stockholm, Sweden. Reprinted by permission.

Consequently, management can devote more time to proper working tasks. Investment in such protection is profitable.

Key factors in any loss prevention program are to identify risks, including the physical opportunity for crime, and then to prepare recommendations to prevent or reduce these risks.

> Risk management is both a moral and a legal responsibility.

Organizations that do not have a comprehensive risk management program in place leave themselves open to disgruntled employees and customers as well as to potential civil liability, as discussed in Chapter 4.

Risk Analysis

As noted by Green (1987, p. 115): "If security is not to be one-dimensional, piecemeal, reactive, or pre-packaged, it must be based upon analysis of the total risk potential."

> Three factors to consider in risk analysis are (1) vulnerability, (2) probability and (3) criticality.

Establishing **vulnerability** involves identifying threats. Where could losses occur? How? What types of thefts might occur? What safety hazards exist? Security managers should consider their vulnerability to such risks as accidents, arson, assault, auto theft, bombs, burglary, fraud (including credit-card and check fraud), kidnapping, larceny/theft (both internal and external), robbery, sabotage, sex crimes, shoplifting and vandalism. They should also consider their vulnerability to natural disasters such as earthquakes, floods, tornadoes, fires and the like.

Establishing **probability** involves analyzing the factors that favor loss. Is the establishment located in a high- or low-crime area? How tight is existing physical security? Records of past losses help establish probability. Where is a shrinkage occurring? Is it primarily due to internal or external causes? Where is it most likely to occur? Are OSHA* requirements being met? How likely are civil disturbances in the area? Would the establishment be a probable target?

*Occupational Safety and Health Administration, discussed in Chapter 7.

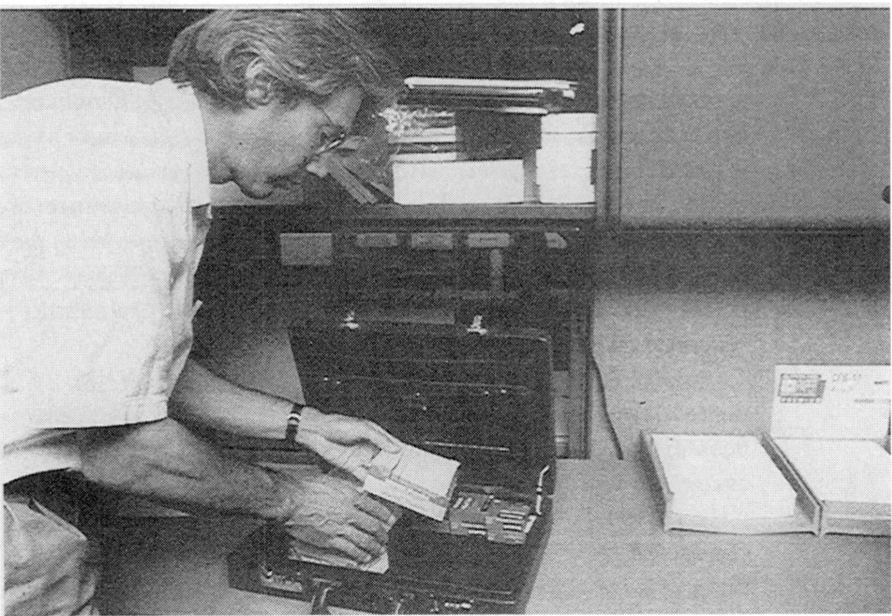

This employee may feel his pilfering will be inconsequential to his employer, but over time, if several employees pilfer, the losses can be more costly than those resulting from a burglary.

Establishing **criticality** involves deciding whether a loss, if it occurs, would be of minimum or maximum consequence. How serious would it be? Pilferage may appear to be of negligible seriousness, but if it is continuous and engaged in by many employees, it may be more costly than a robbery or burglary. According to Green (1987, pp. 117–18), criticality "has been defined to mean the impact of a loss as measured in dollars." He cautions: "The dollar loss is not simply the cost of the items lost." It also includes:

- Replacement cost (including delivery and installation costs).
- Temporary replacement (for example, if a main computer goes down and must be temporarily replaced until new equipment can be bought and installed).
- "Down time" (including not being able to continue doing business and having employees idled).
- Insurance rate increases.

Of course, when considerations such as human life or the national security are involved, cost becomes secondary.

Management makes the preliminary decisions on the degree of security desired or required. Common sense plus the establishment's past history are key ingredients in stating security objectives. Security measures should neither obstruct operations nor be neglected; rather, they should be an integrated part of the establishment's operations.

To determine what risks exist and what approach to use in dealing with them, security managers frequently rely on conducting a security survey.

THE SECURITY SURVEY

A **security survey** is an objective but critical on-site examination and analysis of a business, industrial plant, public or private institution or home. Its purpose is to determine existing security, to identify deficiencies, to determine the protection needed and to recommend improvements to enhance overall security. As noted by Golsby (1992, p. 53): "The security review is one of the most important tools in the security professional's repertoire." Kovacich (1993, p. 111) also suggests: "A survey is an excellent way to identify weak links in security and save jobs."

According to Floyd (1991, p. 51): "[T]he survey is one of the basic and necessary tools of loss prevention. The survey not only points out the weaknesses in physical security and internal controls but also serves as an effective awareness tool."

Leo (1994, p. 11) notes: "A site security survey is similar to a physical exam conducted by a doctor, in that he/she is attempting to discern what, if anything, is wrong with the patient before prescribing any course of treatment." A comprehensive listing of Leo's 137 specific questions that might be included in a site security evaluation is contained in Appendix A.

Golsby (1992, p. 57) offers the following "compelling reasons" for a company to conduct a security review:

- Obligation to protect personnel and visitors.
- Necessity to protect property.
- Necessity to protect information.
- Legal obligations.
- Contractual obligations.
- Threat of litigation.
- Threat of industrial disputation.
- Insurance company requirements.
- Moral obligations.
- Professional integrity.

Golsby observes that all the preceding reasons might be reduced to one basic reason: financial expense. He notes that such expense might take any of the following forms:

- Replacement cost of equipment.
- Repair cost to equipment.
- Repair cost to buildings.
- Cost of rebuilding.
- Loss of revenue due to loss of market edge as a result of information or data loss.
- Loss of contracts.
- Awarding of damages.
- Cost of loss of company time due to industrial disputation.
- Increased insurance costs.
- Loss of insurance coverage.
- Damage to professional reputation or loss of accreditation.

Further, as noted by Roll (1994, p. 65): "Using basic risk management principles during an internal security survey can help a company document, identify, abate, and monitor problems, therefore protecting itself against loss and liability." Roll (p. 66) concludes: "The tremendous increases in security litigation make a method of documentation that shows an attempt to identify problems, abate the problems, and monitor the outcome essential for a successful defense."

"A security survey," says Green (1987, p. 122), "is essentially an exhaustive physical examination of the premises and a thorough inspection of all operational systems and procedures. Such an examination or survey has as its overall objective the analysis of a facility to determine the existing state of its security, to locate weaknesses in its defenses, to determine the degree of protection required, and, ultimately, to lead to recommendations establishing a total security program."

Risk analysis involves developing (or adapting) the security survey, conducting the survey and assessing the results.

Developing the Security Survey

Kingsbury (1973, pp. 27–28) outlines the following topics to consider in developing a security survey:*

A) Planning (purpose): What and how much security?—Degree
1) Physical security (property, etc.)
2) Personnel (background, etc.)
3) Information (files, records, etc.)
4) Security survey/consultant

B) Responsibilities: Who?
1) Administrative authority (Vice-President level, etc.)—Security organization
2) Budget/scheduling

C) Area (duties): Where will the security emphasis be placed?
1) Parking
2) Visitor control
3) Hazards (man-made and environmental)
4) Employee pilferage
5) Outside losses
6) Disaster planning/civil disturbance
7) Fire/safety responsibility
8) Special events

D) Issues (policy—procedure): When? Why?
1) Legal basis
2) Education/training
3) Manuals (general/specific)
4) Intelligence gathering

---

*From A. A. Kingsbury, *Introduction to Security and Crime Prevention Surveys,* 1973. Courtesy of Charles C. Thomas, Publisher, Springfield, Illinois.

5) Contract guard vs. in-house
6) Side arms vs. none
7) Extra chores (escort, lock-up, room checks, protect transfer of monies)
8) Guard force vs. hardware
9) Uniform vs. nonuniform
10) Contract with local law enforcement
11) Security cadets
12) Consultant (outside)
13) Consultant (staff member)—contract guard

The actual survey can be in the form of a checklist, prepared with adequate space between entries for detailed notes. Often aerial maps or diagrams of the facility are included with the security survey. The amount of detail in the survey will vary depending on the degree of security required. A thorough security survey would include the general area, as well as all roads and/or streets leading to the facility; the perimeter, including fencing, warning signs and No Parking signs; the buildings, including construction and possible points of unauthorized entry, entrances and exits, entry control, locks and keys, alarm systems and lighting; identification of restricted areas, including computer rooms; procedures to control theft or pilferage of property or information; employee safety, including fire protection and emergency plans; security personnel required, including needed training and responsibilities; and security indoctrination of all employees.

All potential targets of attack should be identified and the means for eliminating or reducing the risk to these targets specified. Pure risks should also be identified. For example, is the facility susceptible to accidents, arson, auto theft, bombs, burglary, fraud, kidnapping, larceny, sabotage, theft or vandalism? For each pure risk identified, appropriate security measures should be recommended.

> The security survey (audit) is a critical, objective, on-site analysis of the total security system.

The survey lists the components of the security system to be observed and evaluated. Many such surveys exist. Figure 14–5 (p. 433) illustrates a security survey.

The Mecklenburg County Police Department has developed a graphic checklist for security measures to prevent burglary (Figure 14–6 p. 434). They also have developed a checklist to assess vulnerability to crime that could be adapted to suit a given establishment (Figure 14–7 p. 435).

Floyd (1991) has developed a detailed checklist for manufacturing on which specific areas are evaluated as to the probability of risk (see Table 14–1 p. 436). A score of 1 indicates that risk is "virtually certain," whereas a score of 4 indicates that it is improbable.

J&B Innovative Enterprises, Inc.
123 South Street, Anywhere, U.S.A.
HOLIDAY/WEEKEND SECURITY CHECKLIST

Instructions: Check all items, ensure each area has been inspected for general safety, see GENERAL SAFETY checklist.** **DO NOT leave this facility unattended if ANY of the *Bold items on this checklist cannot be checked.** Refer to the emergency personnel list at the receptionist desk, contact one of the persons on the list for further instructions. Minor problems that can be resolved the next working day should be logged under comments. This checklist must be submitted to the plant manager the next working day.

**GENERAL SAFETY (check each area)

- ☐* ***All cigarettes extinguished***
- ☐* ***All roof access doors locked***
- ☐* ***All water faucets closed***
- ☐* ***Flammable spills which may ignite***
- ☐* ***Obvious frayed/defective wiring***
- ☐* ***All fire doors secured***
- ☐ Floors' condition okay
- ☐ Aisles clear
- ☐ Stairways clear
- ☐ Lights (no burned-out bulbs)
- ☐ First aid kits visible & stocked
- ☐ Fire extinguishers visible & charged

PRODUCTION AREA (Do not power down any equipment, unless specified)

- ☐* ***Windows secured***
- ☐* ***Compressor off, relief valve open***
- ☐* ***Fans & machinery off***
- ☐ Compressor room locked
- ☐ Air hose service lines bled
- ☐ Rest rooms empty
- ☐ Lights off/night lights on

SHIPPING & RECEIVING AREA

- ☐* ***Fans & machinery off***
- ☐* ***Garage doors secure***
- ☐* ***Battery chargers turned off***
- ☐ Rest rooms empty
- ☐ Forklift secure
- ☐ Windows secure
- ☐ Lights off/night lights on

STOCK/CRIB ROOM

- ☐* ***Stock room locked***
- ☐* ***Crib window locked***
- ☐ Rest room empty
- ☐ Lights off/night lights on

OFFICE AREA (Do not power down any equipment including computers)

- ☐* ***Safe locked***
- ☐* ***File cabinets locked***
- ☐ All office doors closed
- ☐ Lights off/night lights on

BUILDING EXTERIOR

- ☐* ***All external doors & windows locked***
- ☐ Outside lights timer set
- ☐ Parking lot empty
- ☐ Gates in parking area locked

COMPUTER ROOM (Do not power down any equipment)

- ☐* ***Door locked, alarm set***

CHECKLIST COMPLETED (minor problems logged under comments)

- ☐* ***Plant secured***
- ☐* ***Security alarm tested & armed***

I understand and have completed the preceding checklist. It will be submitted to the plant manager the next working day.

Name ____________________
Time ____________ Date ____________

Comments: ____
____

Figure 14–5. Basic Security Survey

SOURCE: Courtesy of J & B Innovative Enterprises, Inc.

Prevention can be best achieved by:

1. Recognition of security risks.
2. Initiation of corrective action to remove it.

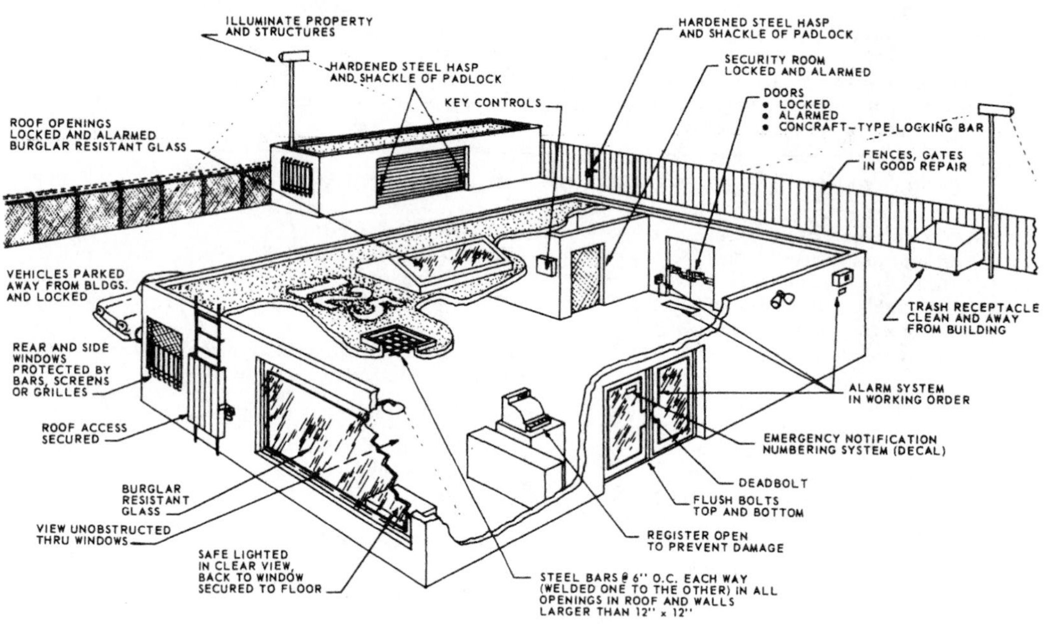

Figure 14–6. Illustrated Checklist of Security Measures
SOURCE: Courtesy of Mecklenburg County Police Department, Charlotte, N.C.

Businesses and industries that work for the federal government *must* meet certain security standards and do self-audits. Skurecki (1992, p. 59) notes that such organizations must conform to the guidelines outlined in the *Industrial Security Manual (ISM)* which establishes minimum requirements of the government's information security program. According to this manual:

> Contractors shall establish a self-inspection program for the purpose of evaluating all security procedures applicable to the facility's operations. Contractors shall review their security system on a continuous basis and shall also conduct a formal self-inspection to occur between inspections conducted by the Defensive Investigative Service (DIS), Cognizant Security Office (CSO). . . .
>
> Self-inspection shall consist of an audit of all the facility's operations in light of its Standard Practice Procedures and the requirements of the ISM. Deficiencies identified as a result of self-inspection shall be corrected promptly.

Skurecki (1992, p. 64) suggests: "Sound, quality, self-inspection security programs can be the present and future tool for reaching the ultimate goal of security excellence in all programs."

How Vulnerable Is Your Business?

- Are you and your employees careful and alert when opening and closing your place of business?
- Do you keep a record of equipment and merchandise serial numbers?
- Are your employees thoroughly screened before hiring?
- Do you keep more than a minimum amount of money on hand?
- Is your alarm system checked regularly?
- Do you have a key control system?
- Are locks re-keyed after an employee leaves your employment?
- Is your safe combination changed periodically?
- Are any company vehicles parked where they block the view of doors and windows, or can be used for climbing onto the roof?
- Do you vary your route and schedule of banking?
- Are your employees trained in procedures for a robbery, burglary, shoplifter, short change, check, and credit card artist?
- Have you participated in Operation Identification?

Figure 14–7. Sample Security Survey

SOURCE: Courtesy of Mecklenburg County Police Department, Charlotte, N.C.

Conducting the Security Survey

After the survey is developed, someone should physically walk through the establishment, observing and talking to personnel to obtain the required information. Usually the survey is conducted by the security director, but it may be conducted by an outside consulting firm.

> The information needed for a security survey is obtained by observing and by talking to personnel.

All those in positions of responsibility for assets should be interviewed, taking care that the interview be nonthreatening.

Table 14–1. Detailed Security Checklist for Manufacturing Companies

Areas Evaluated and Grading Factors	Possible/Assigned Raw Score		Comments
1. Fences/barriers			
a. Gates secured and access controlled	4		
b. Routinely inspected	4		
c. Good state of repair	4		
d. Top guards/bottom rails	4		
e. Appropriate height	4		
	20	—	
2. Building protection			
a. Windows protected	5		
b. Doors protected	5		
c. Unusual openings protected	5		
d. Hinge pins sealed	5		
	20	—	
3. Security officers/alarms			
a. Officers are assigned or intrusion alarm system is installed	5		
b. Officer orders and procedures are in writing and adequately describe duties and system	5		
c. Clock rounds are made by officers; sprinkler alarm monitored by outside agency	5		
d. Officer training; alarms tested	5		
	20	—	
4. Locking system/key control			
a. Key control records	3		
b. Distribution appropriate	3		
c. Master key system	2		
d. Changed as needed	2		
e. Lock type appropriate	2		
f. Key control officer	2		
g. Spare key protection	2		
h. Markings obliterated	2		
i. Good working order	2		
	20	—	
5. Access controls			
a. Entry/exits designated	4		
b. Employees access monitored	4		
c. Visitors controlled	4		
d. Contractors/vendors/service employees controlled			
e. Employee ID cards	4		
	4		
	20	—	
6. Outside material storage			
a. Property protected and access controlled	5		
b. Stored or stacked	5		
c. Clear zones	5		
	15	—	
7. Scrap/trash controls			
a. Contracts exist	3		
b. Supervision in effect	3		
c. Storage/staging adequate	3		
d. Inspections made	3		
e. Access controlled	3		
	15	—	
8. Vehicle controls			
a. Away from buildings	3		
b. Out of dock areas	3		
c. Clear firelanes	3		
d. Employee parking adequate	3		
e. Access controlled	3		
	15	—	

Table 14–1. Detailed Security Checklist for Manufacturing Companies (*Continued*)

Areas Evaluated and Grading Factors	Possible/ Assigned Raw Score		Comments
9. Exterior lighting			
a. Dock areas	2		
b. Parking lots	2		
c. Building perimeter	2		
d. Employee entrances	2		
e. Maintenance checks	2	___	
	10		
10. Control signs			
a. Access points/perimeter	2		
b. Parking	2		
c. No trespassing signs	2		
d. Safety/security	2		
e. Restricted areas	2	___	
	10		
11. Employee screening/verification			
a. Credit	3		
b. Criminal record check	3		
c. Previous employer	3		
d. Reference checks	3		
e. Other screening	3	___	
	15		
12. Package/material control			
a. Written procedures in effect	3		
b. Forms adequate and controlled	3		
c. Authorizations defined	3		
d. Inspections made	3		
e. Accountability/verification	3	___	
	15		
13. Security awareness			
a. Management attitude	9		
b. Program orientation	3		
c. Bulletins/newsletters	3	___	
	15		
14. Proprietary information protection			
a. Designated and marked	2		
b. Filed and protected	2		
c. Formulas and microfiche protected	2		
d. Computers/computer software	2		
e. Destruction and disposal	2	___	
	10		
15. General office security			
a. Funds (petty cash, etc.)	2		
b. Purchasing	2		
c. Payroll	2		
d. Negotiables	2		
e. Portable office equipment	2		
f. Prenumbered forms accounted for and protected	2	___	
	12		
16. Shipping/receiving controls			
a. Double checks made	4		
b. Forms accountability/protection	3		
c. Seal accountability/protection	3		
d. Dock access restricted	3		
e. Drivers controlled	3		
f. Housekeeping	2		
g. Raw material protection	2	___	
	20		

Table 14–1. Detailed Security Checklist for Manufacturing Companies (*Continued*)

Areas Evaluated and Grading Factors	Possible/ Assigned Raw Score		Comments
17. Tractor trailer theft prevention			
a. Kingpin locks used	5		
b. Loaded trailers sealed	5		
c. Trailers locked	5		
	15	—	
18. Emergency planning/response			
a. Sprinkler system maintained	3		
b. Extinguisher equipment adequate	3		
c. Emergency plans implemented	3		
	9	—	
19. Utility protection			
a. Water/steam	2		
b. Gas/electricity	2		
c. Generators/boilers	2		
d. Telephone equipment	2		
	8	—	
20. Demographic/risk assessment*			
a. Burglary	5		
b. Robbery	5		
c. Auto/vehicle theft	5		
d. Violent crime	5		
	20	—	

*Risk probability is virtually certain—1; highly probable—2; moderately probable—3; improbable—4; unknown—5

SOURCE: William R. Floyd. "A Quantitative Tool." *Security Management*, April 1991, p. 53.

Evaluation may be inherently threatening to employees. No one wants to be found responsible for a breach in security. But employees must be honest in their responses if the results of the survey are to be valid. Therefore, the correct climate must be established so that employees will cooperate and answer questions honestly. Of utmost importance is explaining the purpose of the survey to those from whom information is requested. Without such an explanation, the people interviewed may feel they are "under suspicion" for their actions. Many of the interviewing techniques discussed in Chapter 12 are applicable when conducting a security survey.

Selecting Alternatives to Handle Identified Risks

Once risks are identified, alternatives are selected to reduce vulnerability to them. Inherent in risk management is a logical, systematic approach to deal with the recognized hazards.

Alternatives for risk handling include the following:

- **Risk elimination**
- **Risk reduction**
- **Risk spreading**
- **Risk transfer**
- **Risk acceptance**

Risk Elimination

The best alternative, if realistic, is to eliminate the risk entirely. For example, the risk of losses from bad checks or credit-card fraud can be avoided if the business does not accept checks or credit cards. The risk of employees till tapping is eliminated if they are denied access to the cash register. Dynamic risks can be avoided or eliminated. They exist because of a management decision and can be eliminated by a change in management decision.

Risk Reduction

Pure risks will always exist and cannot be completely eliminated, and some dynamic risks cannot be avoided without incurring some other type of loss. Frequently, the best alternative is to establish procedures and use physical hardware to reduce or minimize the risk. For example, establishing and implementing check-cashing policies can reduce the risk of loss from bad checks. Installing locks, security lighting and alarm systems can reduce the risk of loss from burglary by helping delay and/or detect intruders. If the assets at risk are of high value, such risk-reducing methods should be considered.

Burglars often operate under cover of darkness. Lighting and alarms may deter a burglar.

Risk Spreading

Closely related to risk reduction is the practice of risk spreading. This approach uses methods that ensure that the potential loss in any single incident is reduced (for example, placing expensive jewelry in separate display cases). Such risk spreading further reduces exposure to threats after risk-avoidance and risk-reduction measures have been instituted.

Risk Transfer

If risk elimination, risk reduction and risk spreading do not bring the risk to an acceptable level, the risk may be transferred either by taking out insurance or by raising prices. Most establishments carry insurance against fires and other types of natural disasters, as well as liability insurance in case an employee or other person is injured on the premises. Bonding employees is another alternative.

Rising insurance costs, however, can drastically affect reliance on insurance as a way to guard against unforeseen business losses. In addition, some losses are virtually impossible to insure against, for example, loss of customer confidence, lowered employee morale and loss of reputation.

Clearly, insurance can never be a substitute for a security program. Another alternative to effective risk reduction is price raising, which also has obvious drawbacks. Most retail establishments raise prices to cover shoplifting losses. The key element of this method is the absorption of the loss by a third party.

Risk Acceptance

As noted by Eberhart (1994, p. 8): "If the value of the assets is low, the cost of recovering from an incident is low and the threat is low, you may choose to accept the risk of having little or no protection."

It is never cost-effective, practical or, indeed, possible to provide 100-percent security for an establishment. Risks can never be entirely eliminated. Some must simply be accepted. If the security survey has been completely conducted and the results competently analyzed, the greatest risks will be identified and dealt with by the appropriate alternative or combination of alternatives. The remaining risks will be accepted as part of the "cost of doing business."

Combination

Usually a combination of alternatives provides the best risk management.

Several constraints on security systems are noted by Betts (1992, p. 16A), including technical constraints such as environmental considerations and non-technical constraints such as operational requirements and political and economic considerations.

REPORTING THE RESULTS

Once the survey is conducted, the risk analysis is completed and the alternatives for handling the risks are selected, the information must be communicated to individuals who can act on the findings. The information should be written into a comprehensive report that includes, at minimum, the following sections:

I. Introduction—a brief summary of the purpose of the survey, the anticipated risks and the identified needs and objectives of the total security system; also, a description of the survey developed and conducted to assess the system. Include a copy of the survey in an appendix at the end of the report.

II. A discussion of the risk analysis.
   A. Strengths of the system—what is working well.
   B. Weaknesses of the system—areas of vulnerability and potential risk, arranged in order of priority.

III. Recommendations for alternatives for managing the risks, including the estimated cost and savings and who should be responsible for making the changes.

Kovacich (1993, p. 112) advises: "Recommendations should be listed with projected savings, cost-benefits, and value-added information."

The professional security manager must devote as much time to quantifying and qualifying security initiatives as any other department within an organization to justify resource allocations and expenditures. The completed security survey, the security report and any copies of these documents should be treated as *confidential* documents.

IMPLEMENTING THE RECOMMENDATIONS

Implementing the recommended changes is management's responsibility. Changes might include modifying procedures, improving or upgrading security equipment or adding security equipment or personnel.

Budgeting is always an important consideration in implementing any recommended changes. Budgeting efforts may be facilitated by dividing costs into specific categories, as illustrated in Table 14–2 (p. 442). Budget requirements may limit somewhat the extent of implementation. Some changes may not be made for weeks or months, but a schedule should be established so that high-priority changes are made first.

Implementing the recommendations also frequently requires tact and diplomacy. Security managers must recognize their establishment's overall plan, goals and needs. The security system does not operate in a vacuum, but relies on the understanding and support of all persons involved in the business or industry. Consequently, security managers must build acceptance and trust,

Table 14–2. Example of a Budget for Security

	Investment		Operating Costs		
	Prevention	*Loss Limitation*	*Prevention*	*Loss Limitation*	*Insurance*
Work Protection					
Common equipment	x		x		
Individual equipment	x		x		
Surveillance					
Identity card			x		
Personnel			x		
Technical	x		x		
Fencing, locks	x				
Fire Service					
Prevention	x		x		
Extinguishing		x	x		
Company Health Care					
Sick care	x	x	x	x	
Insurance					
Company insurance					x
Personal insurance					x
Products liability					x
Labor market no-fault					x
Liability insurance					
Reserve Equipment				x	
Training and Information in Company Protection Questions			x	x	
Total Sum					

SOURCE: Statsföretag AB, Skandia Insurance Co. and Skandia Risk Management Ltd., Stockholm, Sweden. Reprinted by permission.

and they must act as professionals who understand and respect the needs and wants of others.

EVALUATING THE SECURITY SYSTEM

Evaluation of security should be ongoing. The effects of any changes made as a result of the security survey should be studied. For example, if a need for personnel training is identified and a program instituted, the effectiveness of that training should be assessed. Periodic, unannounced audits should be conducted of security procedures, such as cash handling or check cashing.

> Each component of the security system should be periodically evaluated and changes made as needed.

Some aspects of the security system, such as closing procedures, are checked daily. Other components should have a regular schedule of inspection.

The needs and objectives of the entire security system should be reevaluated annually. Security needs change as an establishment grows or as the neighborhood changes. If the city installs street lights or provides routine patrol by local police, the establishment may need less of its own external security. However, if the neighborhood deteriorates and vandalism and crime increase, it may need more security.

Figure 14–8 (p. 444) illustrates a typical audit process. Such a process serves several functions according to Kohr (1994, p. 68):

> Auditing affirms top management's concern over the importance of security in the day-to-day operations of a company. It also helps front-line employees meet management goals and adapt to changing regulation and risks. It is the key to management effectiveness and stakeholder assurances regarding a company's ability to meet security challenges and protect personnel, assets, and profits.

SUMMARY

Private security managers must recognize and deal with both pure risks—risks with the potential for injury, damage or loss with no possible benefits—and dynamic risks—risks that have the potential for both benefits and losses. They do so through risk management: anticipating, recognizing and analyzing risks; taking steps to reduce or prevent such risks and evaluating the results.

A systematic approach to preventing loss through risk management includes risk analysis, policy formulation, specification of a protection plan and follow-up. Risk management is both a moral and a legal responsibility. Risk analysis focuses on three factors: vulnerability, probability and criticality. A key tool in risk analysis is the security survey. The security survey is a critical, objective, on-site analysis of the total security system. The information needed for a security survey is obtained by observing and by talking to personnel.

Once risks are identified, alternatives to handle these risks must be selected. Alternatives for risk handling include risk elimination, risk reduction, risk spreading, risk transfer and risk acceptance.

In addition to the comprehensive security survey that may be conducted yearly or at even more lengthy time intervals, periodic audits should be made of each component of the security system, and changes should be made as needed.

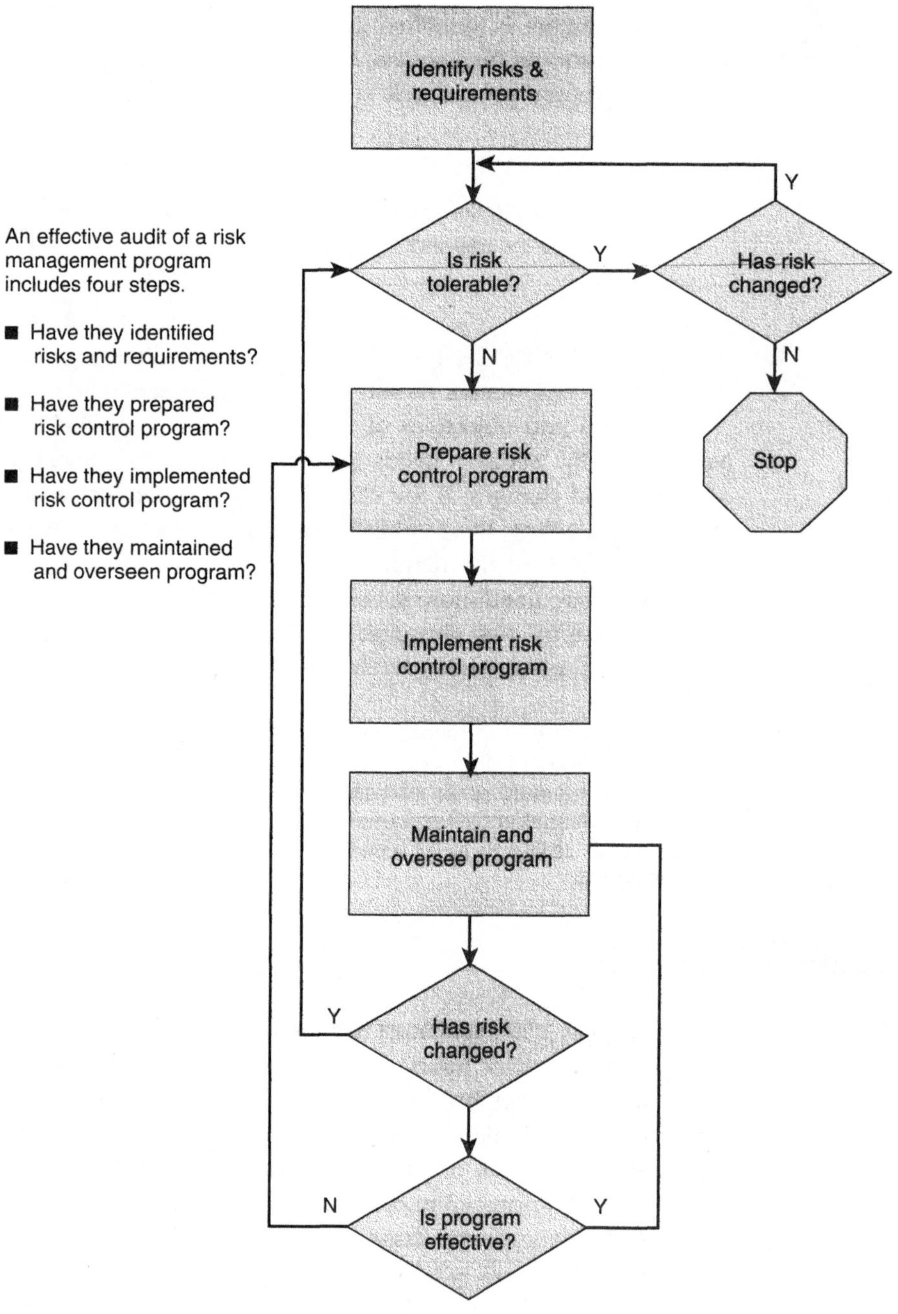

Figure 14–8. The Security Audit Process

SOURCE: Arthur D. Little, Inc. "Put Security to the Test." *Security Management,* December 1994, p. 66. Reprinted by permission.

APPLICATION

1. List the pure and dynamic risks in your own daily life. Then indicate whether you have taken steps to reduce these risks and, if so, list the actions you have taken.

2. As the security manager for a local hotel, list the dynamic and pure risks that could affect the operation and rank them in order of priority.

3. As security manager in charge of organizing company protection, list the statutes in your state that affect a cost-effective security program, e.g., licensing, bonding, training requirements and the like.

CRITICAL THINKING EXERCISE

Risk Management

Statutory and Common Law

Affirmative duties are not placed on private citizens who do not have a special relation between parties. Police officers and others with police authority have a duty to investigate crimes that they are informed of or that they witness. If security guards have authority to arrest, they have a duty to arrest law violators on the premises they are guarding. The source of this duty is based on actual control. The duty of one who takes charge of a person whom he or she knows or should know to be likely to cause harm to others, if not controlled, is the duty to exercise reasonable care to prevent the person from doing harm.

Facts of the Case

About 1:45 A.M. in mid March, Thunder Corporation security guards, providing security for Southwest Indian Polytechnic Institute, observed Frank Lopez driving slowly on one of the Institute's streets. His car lights were not on. He came to a stop and got out of the car with a can of beer in his hand. Kasey Teller, one of the guards, called out to him to stop where he was, but Lopez staggered away mumbling that he had to urinate. Teller called out again demanding that he leave the area, but Lopez slurred abuses back at him. At that point Garfield Katerly joined Teller, and the two of them took hold of Lopez and led him back to his car. By the smell of his breath and the way he slurred his speech, they could tell that he was intoxicated. There were a number of empty beer cans on the floor of the car by the passenger's seat. They said that unless he left the Institute's grounds they would call the state police. (Lopez was neither an employee nor a student at the Institute.)

Lopez got in the car, started the ignition and drove off, still with his headlights off. Leaving the Institute's grounds, he ran a stop sign and headed into the wrong lane of the divided highway that fronts the Institute. Within 15 seconds he ran into a motorcycle driven by Raymond Korbalson. The accident severed Korbalson's left leg.

Korbalson sued Thunder Corporation. He argued that danger to the public by intoxicated drivers operating automobiles on public highways is foreseeable, and that the guards had a responsibility to detain a drunken driver they had stopped and not redirect him back onto a public roadway.

The record of Southwest Indian Polytechnic Institute reads that when an "individual is found on the campus with liquor," the guards are to "place the individual in protective custody." If the individual appears to be intoxicated, the guard is to call the sheriff's department, and the guard is to take reasonable steps to detain the individual until the sheriff arrives. These measures may include closing the campus gate or confiscating car keys.

In order to perform their duty, Thunder Corporation guards are issued cards from the sheriff's office. Kasey Teller had received no training and had not received a card, so he did not feel commissioned to exercise full authority in terms of detaining an individual or confiscating anything. Garfield Katerly did have a commission card, but because he arrived late on the scene, he did not feel that he should countermand Teller.

Issue and Questions

1. Are Thunder guards under a duty to detain a drunken driver or at least not to direct a drunken driver they had stopped on campus back onto the highway; and if they do, can they be held liable as the proximate cause of an injury?
   - **a.** Security guards clearly do not have the authority to patrol streets and highways outside the premises of the grounds that they are hired to protect. If and only if Lopez had committed some crime while on campus, they could have arrested or detained him. Because he did not commit a crime on campus, they had no authority over him other than to ask him to leave the campus.
   - **b.** The Thunder guards are not responsible for the injury to Korbalson. Lopez had successfully driven to their site; he was able to walk and talk; and the guards had no way to test the degree to which he was affected by his supposed consumption of alcohol. They had no reasonable way of foreseeing that Lopez would drive off without turning on his headlights, run through a stop sign, turn down the wrong way on a divided highway and hit a motorcyclist.
   - **c.** The campus security guards had neither the authority to arrest a person from the community, even if such a person did commit a crime, nor did they have the authority to control him. They are not public police officers; they did not have the right to physically control Lopez. Thus they did not and could not be expected to have a duty of care for Lopez.
   - **d.** The Thunder guards were wearing uniforms and had an official appearance which imparts an air of authority. Given the fact that Lopez did assume that they had authority, they should have persuaded him to obey laws, but they had no legal coercive power to restrain him. Although they should have made an attempt to send him on his way with the headlights on, they are not responsible for what happened to him some time after he left their premises.
   - **e.** Because the guards had the authority to arrest or at least detain, they then had a duty to do so. And even if they did not have such authority, but exercised actual control over Lopez, they had a duty of reasonable care. It is common knowledge that a drunken driver is a serious danger to the public if he or she is allowed or encouraged to drive on public

highways. This duty was breached, and thus the guards (and Thunder Corporation) can be held liable.

Discussion Questions

1. What types of programs would you implement to eliminate pure risks in a company?
2. How much responsibility and authority should be placed at the security supervisory level to cope with dynamic risks?
3. What could cause the needs and objectives of a security system to change? Elaborate.
4. In developing a security survey, what areas should receive high priority?
5. Is it better for security managers to develop their own security survey or to use one developed by someone else?

References

Betts, Curt. P. "What You Say Is What You Get." *Security Management,* November 1992, pp. 12A–16A.

Eberhart, Jon A. "Planning a Security System." *Security Technology and Design,* June/July 1994, pp. 6–12.

Floyd, William R. "A Quantitative Tool." *Security Management,* April 1991, pp. 51–53.

Golsby, Mark. "Four Steps to Success." *Security Management,* August 1992, pp. 53–57.

Green, Gion. *Introduction to Security,* 4th ed. Revised by Robert J. Fisher. Stoneham, MA: Butterworth Publishers, 1987.

Joint Security Commission. "Redefining Security. Part I—Approaching the Next Century." *Security Concepts,* July 1994, pp. 8, 23.

Kahn, James R. "The Premise Behind Premises Liability." *Security Management,* February 1994, pp. 61–63.

Kingsbury, A. A. *Introduction to Security and Crime Prevention Surveys.* Springfield, IL: Charles C. Thomas, 1973.

Kohr, Robert L. "Put Security to the Test." *Security Management,* December 1994, pp. 64–68.

Kovacich, Gerald L. "Six Secrets of a Successful Survey." *Security Management,* September 1993, pp. 111–12.

Leo, Thomas W. "Site Security Evaluation." *Security Concepts,* September 1994, pp. 11, 23, 30.

McDonough, Thomas. "Risk Management for Small Business." *Security Management,* October 1992, pp. 74–76.

Plante, William. "The Art of Planning." *Security Management,* March 1993, pp. 49–53.

Roll, Fredrick G. "Simple Survey Saves the Day." *Security Management,* March 1994, pp. 65–66.

Skurecki, Michael H. "The Service of Surveys." *Security Management,* August 1992, pp. 59–64.

CHAPTER 15

Industrial Security

Do You Know

- What types of losses are usually specific to industry?
- How to protect against loss of tools?
- What special problems must be considered in industrial security?
- What sabotage and espionage are?
- How to protect against industrial espionage?
- What areas are most vulnerable to theft?
- What cargoes are most frequently stolen from trucks?
- What security measures have been used by the trucking industry?
- What the primary security problems of the railroad industry are?
- What security measures have been taken by railroads?
- What security problems exist at utility companies?
- How to protect against a utility company's losses?

Can You Define These Terms?

espionage
sabotage

Introduction

Effective security can affect all aspects of industry, from selection of employees to distribution of finished products. Security is inseparable from good management and profits, and profits are vital to the national economy. Manufacturing includes a range of primary products, such as those related to food processing, textiles, transportation, metals, machinery, electrical products and heavy durable goods.

Security officers were first used in manufacturing plants on a large scale prior to World War I because of concern about sabotage and espionage. During World War II many manufacturing plants established proprietary security forces. More than two hundred thousand of these plant security officers were granted the status of auxiliary military police because their primary duties were to protect war goods and products, supplies, equipment and personnel. After the war, many larger manufacturers continued to maintain proprietary security forces, but more recently, as such programs have become more expensive, many plants have begun using contractual security officers. Sometimes the contract security officers are supervised by a small proprietary security force.

As in any other type of establishment, the criteria for determining the expense and effort to be expended to protect a particular plant are based largely on the plant's importance and vulnerability. Especially vulnerable are plants whose products are small, valuable or particularly desirable, such as watches, calculators, small transistor radios, television sets and jewelry. The incidence of theft is usually high in general merchandising warehouses and factories that manufacture such valuable articles. The incidence of theft is usually lower in heavy industrial plants, such as steel mills or furniture factories.

In addition, security needs generally increase as the size of the plant increases. Some plants cover many acres and have many buildings, such as Minnesota Mining and Manufacturing (3M) which, during the day, has more employees present than the population of many cities. When employees number in the thousands, it is extremely difficult to deter those who steal company property or break company rules.

This chapter begins with a discussion of industrial security responsibilities and the types of industrial losses to protect against. This is followed by a discussion of sabotage and espionage and areas that are vulnerable not only to these threats but to theft as well. Next, security problems involved in transporting goods by truck, rail and ship are explored. The chapter concludes with a discussion of the special security problems faced by the utilities industry.

INDUSTRIAL SECURITY RESPONSIBILITIES*

Industrial security personnel may use any of the physical or procedural controls discussed in Section II. Fences, locks, lighting, alarms, access control through passes or badges, inspections, package pass systems and vehicle control are all very appropriate for industrial security. The Task Force Report (*Private Security,* 1976, p. 52) explains some industrial security responsibilities:

> The responsibilities of security [officers] in manufacturing plants often include the monitoring of electrical utility systems for failure or malfunction of automated machinery, fire prevention, and inspections for Occupational Health and Safety Act (OSHA) violations. These responsibilities, coupled with crime prevention and detection functions, essentially comprise manufacturing security, which is often referred to as "plant protection."
>
> A major emphasis of plant security programs is the regulation and screening of visitors; service, repair, delivery, and maintenance personnel; vendors; truck drivers; and employees.

Plant security personnel coordinate their efforts with local, county and state law enforcement agencies in investigating internal theft and criminal incidents that occur on the premises. Defense-industry security personnel maintain liaison with the FBI and the Defense Investigative Service, Office of Industrial

*Further information on specific kinds of industrial security problems may be obtained by contacting the American Society for Industrial Security, 1655 North Fort Myer Drive, Suite 1200, Arlington, VA 22209; (703) 522-5800; FAX 703/243-4954.

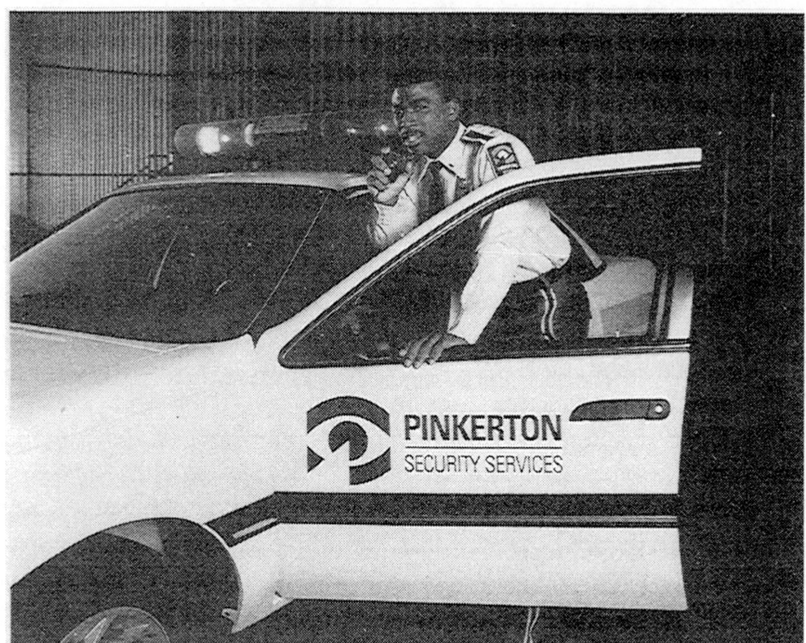

Many industrial complexes use security patrols as an integral part of plant protection.

Security, and must report all security violations, theft of classified materials and/or products to the Defense Supply Agency.

The security linkage between the Department of Defense (D.O.D.) and the industrial sector in the United States is not only massive, but also complex. Strict regulations are spelled out in the D.O.D.'s *Industrial Security Manual* as well as in other security requirements specified by the military branches, NASA, the Atomic Energy Commission and the like. As noted by Gallati (1983, pp. 201–2):

> The Department of Defense supplies governmental security employees and nongovernmental security personnel with rules and regulations that must be carried out to the letter.
>
> Security personnel, both military and civilian, must have clearances for access to classified documents and materials as well as buildings, parts of buildings, and spaces and locations. . . .
>
> D.O.D. regulations are very specific about the types of storage for classified materials. Some of these files, locking devices, safes, and vaults are extremely expensive and would not normally be used in most security operations. Likewise, classified areas are protected by specific physical electronic and guard protections, usually far in excess of the installations found in non-D.O.D. security systems. Most security directors envy their colleagues in D.O.D. facilities for the ease with which they can obtain budget support for the ultimate in security resources. On the other hand, there are threats involved that are more acute, and hazards that are of international consequence—sabotage, espionage, theft of top-secret documents, and so on that justify these security expenditures.

Murphree (1992, p. 61) notes: "For years, fire safety marshals and government defense contractors have sat on opposite sides of the fence. . . . Both sides have valid concerns, yet they are diametrically opposed." The basic issue is safety versus security. Advanced security technology may be the answer. As noted by Murphree (p. 62): "The future for combining security and safety in the defense industry looks bright. . . . Security systems for the '90s and beyond will be challenged to ensure that they meet not only the most rigid security requirements but also the most sensitive life safety regulations."

Since the ending of the Cold War, the Defense Industrial Security Program (DISP) and its Defense Investigative Service (DIS) have been reevaluating their roles. As noted by Donnelly (1994, p. 187): "To prepare for the future DIS is taking steps to modernize its objectives and procedures." Four objectives have been established:

- Cut red tape.
- Improve customer service.
- Endorse empowerment.
- Streamline management control.

Anderson (1994, p. 67) describes the efforts of the Joint Security Commission, formed in June 1993 at the request of the director of the CIA to reexamine the government's security policies in light of post-Cold-War threats:

> The commission found that the amount of physical security provided to protect classified information in facilities within the United States is excessive. At the same time, information security may be lacking. . . .
>
> According to Smith [chair of the Joint Security Commission], the focus needs to be shifted in other ways, as well. "There is far too much time, money, and effort spent on physical security and not enough on personnel security. . . ." Resources should, instead, be focused on more probable risks such as disgruntled employees and computer theft.

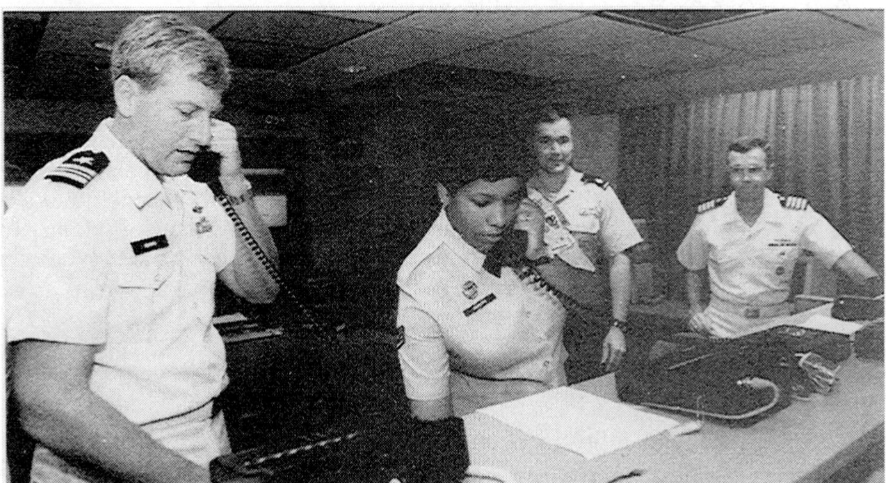

The Rwanda crisis center at the Pentagon, equipped with computers and a handful of officers to handle Rwanda aid.

A new industrial security responsibility is that arising from the introduction of robots into the workplace. Dr. Ted S. Ferry, author of "Safety Management Planning," cites four high-tech developments in industry that will cause new protection and insurance needs:

- CAD—computer-assisted design
- CAM—computer-assisted manufacturing
- CIM—computer-integrated manufacturing
- CAE—computer-aided engineering

The increasing interaction between robots and people will cause accidents more costly than those in the past. Ferry suggests that "the exorbitant costs will put an increased burden on security professionals responsible for loss control and planning."

List (1993, p. 34) describes a new approach to security efforts at Houston-based Star Enterprise, the sixth largest retail gasoline marketer in the United States. Following a security survey, action teams were developed to identify, prioritize and develop specific security programs for their marketing regions. Says List (p. 35): "Throughout the organization, management and employees began to see security as an innovative, proactive group of service-oriented security professionals focused on helping management solve security-related problems. This new view replaced the old concept of security as a reactive, primarily investigative resource."

The "new security landscape" at Caterpillar Inc. is described by Blackwell (1995, p. 19A):

> Advancements in security technologies have led many companies to reassess and upgrade their security systems. Such was the case with Caterpillar Inc., which recently went on-line with a new proprietary central station in Peoria, Illinois. This new central station monitors and controls the security and fire alarm systems in Caterpillar's fifteen administrative and manufacturing facilities in and around Peoria, the company's world headquarters.
>
> Also under the central station's purview are facilities in Tennessee, South Carolina, and Nevada. Soon facilities in North Carolina and Florida will be incorporated into the system. Caterpillar plans to link all of its facilities to this system eventually. . . .
>
> The security consultant found that all of the access control systems needed to be completely replaced by a new state-of-the-art system; none of the existing equipment could be adequately upgraded and integrated into a new system. Further, much of the other security equipment was becoming obsolete and had to be replaced. For example, old black-and-white tube cameras needed to be replaced by color solid-state cameras.

Types of Industrial Losses

Although industry is susceptible to the same types of internal theft as any business, as well as to burglary and/or robbery, certain types of losses are more frequently encountered in industry than in other businesses.

Industrial losses frequently include tools, materials, supplies, products, pallets, hand trucks, valuable scrap, uniforms, side-products, time and vital information.

The Task Force Report (p. 52) elaborates on this:

> Internal theft by employees is a major contributor to manufacturing crime losses. The items most frequently stolen include tools; electronic components; assembly parts; consumable items such as cleaning supplies, oils and greases, paints, wire, and the like; plumbing and electrical supplies; and manufactured products, including consumer products that can be readily used by employees. External theft losses include not only cartons and containers of finished products but also raw materials in usable form, silver, gold, and other precious metals, small machinery and power tools, and office equipment from administrative offices located at production facilities.

Reported instances of internal theft from employees within the manufacturing sector include:

- Taking raw materials.
- Taking company tools and equipment.
- Getting paid for more hours than worked.
- Getting excess expense reimbursement.
- Taking finished products.
- Taking precious metals.

Some employees engage in three or four of these types of internal theft. The categories are *not* mutually exclusive.

In many types of industry, side-product control is important. Such items as metal shavings, wood scraps and reclaimable oil may be recovered and sold as salvage. Food scraps may be sold as hog feed. Employees, however, may mistakenly believe that such side-products are of little value to their employer and may take them for their own use. Employees should be told of any side-products having potential value. Then, the weighing, loading and disposing of valuable salvage should be carefully supervised.

A manufacturing company that provides uniforms should caution employees that personnel are expected to care for their uniforms and not take them for personal use. Pallets and hand trucks are also sometimes taken for personal use and never returned. In addition, these should be kept secured because burglars can transport stolen goods on pallets and hand trucks. Security officers should also be aware that intruders might use the company's own acetylene torches to open safes and that prybars, cutting tools, ladders and forklifts should be secured so as not to make the task of a would-be thief easier.

Maintenance supplies such as cleaning liquids, paper towels, soap and even toilet paper are often stolen by employees and, consequently, should be kept secure. Proprietary gas pumps, too, may be used for personal vehicles and must be kept secured. Records should be kept of company vehicles' gas and oil use and mileage to further ensure that such supplies are not being transferred to personal vehicles.

Finally, employees who are allowed to use company products or who are given discounts when purchasing products may abuse this privilege by making purchases for friends or for selling such products at a profit, resulting in considerable loss to the employer.

Security problems faced by industry are typified by those encountered in the building and timber industry. Burton (1983, p. 65) discusses losses in this industry: "By conservative estimate, two-thirds of losses in the building and timber industry were sustained as a result of internal theft by employees conniving with visiting customers. The remaining third was made up of goods that never made it from the distributors to the lumber or brick yards and goods stolen by customers who were able to help themselves because of the firm's lax security systems." Burton (p. 66) outlines the types of theft common in a lumber yard:

> The most common theft in lumber yards is giving customers extra goods at the loading dock in hopes of receiving a tip. Other tricks include:
>
> - Keeping a supply of damaged and broken goods—plasterboard, cement, damaged timber—hidden from the foreman (unless he's in the shareout). If no legitimately damaged goods are available, the thieves damage the goods themselves and are then able to acquire them at a reduced price.
> - Stealing tickets, used and unused, so the thieves can write out bogus customer receipts.
> - Hiding produce in dustbins or garbage cans and leaving them outside to be taken away by the "trash collectors."
> - Signing nonexistent goods in for truck drivers and turning the delivery tickets in to management for payment.
> - Befriending the security officer by offering him bathroom facilities at certain times of the day so illegal customers can go in and out. Talking to the security officer to find out whether he has product knowledge before smuggling merchandise past him.
>
> If an employee wanted to steal from the company, he would work exceptionally hard, smiling on those above him and frowning on those below. He would be polite to management, want to work lots of overtime, and not want to take holidays. Someone in this position could hide copper tube inside plastic piping, conceal extra fittings inside baths, or put extra goods in boxes sealed with security tape. Eventually he would try to get the best job of all—that of local delivery driver. This position can be a license to print money in some of the following ways:
>
> - Under-delivering. Stealing damaged goods from the lumber yard and re-delivering them so corrupt customers can get credit.
> - Trying to persuade management to let him take the vehicle home at night so he can use it for theft and other jobs.
> - Submitting fraudulent bills for diesel petrol fuel, antifreeze, tires, wipers, etc.

Burton continues (p. 66): "To attack the theft situation in the building and timber trades successfully, an investigator or security consultant must have product knowledge. . . . Different grades of timber, importation marks, and the colored ends of timber, which indicate the origin of soft and hard woods, are a recognized part of training for investigators in the building trades. The different types of bricks, materials, and trade jargon must also be understood if the investigator is to break into the magic circle of theft."

Another "big ticket" industrial security problem is theft of heavy equipment and machinery. Rubin (1992, p. 85) notes that some pieces of heavy equipment such as crawler tractors cost as much as $1 million. Thefts of heavy equipment typically occur between 5:00 P.M. on Friday evening and 6:00 A.M. on Sunday. Rubin (p. 86) suggests that owners of heavy equipment install inexpensive, commercially available antitheft devices such as fuel, hydraulic and electrical cutoffs, and that they not park their equipment along roadways or other easily accessible areas.

Tools

Tools constitute one of the most serious areas of industrial loss. Losses can result either from the improper use of tools or from actual theft. Proper maintenance not only lengthens a tool's life, but also avoids merchandise damage and production slowdowns.

Hand power tools, drills, wrenches, hammers and pliers are highly susceptible to theft, especially if employees use their own tools as well as those belonging to the plant. All company tools should be checked into a tool room or a tool crib at the end of each shift.

> Reduce tool loss by having a tool room or tool crib with an attendant, a check-in/out procedure, distinctive markings on the tools, periodic inspections and inventories, metal detectors at gates and possibly a system for lending tools for personal use after hours.

Tools should be locked up when not in use. If possible and practical, a single check-out and service point should be used. The tool rooms should be kept neat and attractive to impress on employees that tools are important. Tool room attendants should know about tools and be able to keep them in good condition. They should have the necessary equipment to maintain the tools (for example, equipment for sharpening cutting tools), and they should be able to make minor repairs.

A check-in/out procedure should be established and followed. In addition, a procedure for lost, broken or damaged tools should be clearly specified. Any broken or damaged tool should be turned in and the employee required to complete a brief report describing how the loss occurred. If such procedures are not followed and the tool does not have to be turned in, the employee might report a tool broken when it was actually taken for personal use.

Expensive tools are often identified with a serial number. Some companies paint the handles of their tools a bright color such as red or orange to make identification easy. Some companies, having experienced severe tool loss, have combated the problem by installing a metal detector at the gate.

Metals

According to Gates and Readhimer (1992, p. 57):

> Metal theft—a multimillion dollar windfall for criminals and a multi-billion dollar business for the scrap metal industry—is sweeping the nation. . . . [It is] a phenomenon that has reached epidemic proportions across the United States.

Knight (1991, p. 67) cites as examples thieves cutting open three large transformers at a remote electrical substation and removing $70,000 in copper windings and thieves removing vital support braces from an aluminum electric-power transmission tower causing it to collapse, resulting in $100,000 in losses. Says Knight: "These are not isolated cases. Copper, aluminum, brass, and other metals are vital components for many industries in such uses as electric power delivery, communication equipment, and support structures. Each year utilities, mining companies, and other businesses attribute millions of dollars in losses to the theft of those metals."

Metal theft is one area where the mutual efforts of public police officers and private security officers might have great payoff (Gates and Readhimer, 1992, p. 58):

> The benefits of mutual understanding and cooperation between law enforcement and private industry are increasingly evident. Law enforcement/private industry "summits" are held regularly with members of the Scrap Metal Deals Association. Joint committees from this association meet with legislators and other key people to address common metal theft problems. All work together to develop strategies that successfully attack the metal theft problem.
>
> The interaction has become a model for joint public-private sector efforts in the metal industry.

Sabotage and Espionage

Although security measures were originally introduced into manufacturing companies to protect against sabotage and espionage during wartime, these two threats remain very real even during peacetime. They can be committed by competitors or by dissatisfied employees.

> Two special concerns of industry are sabotage and espionage.

Sabotage

The word **sabotage** originated in France during the Industrial Revolution when disgruntled factory workers threw their wooden shoes (sabots) into the machinery, thereby halting production.

> Sabotage is the intentional destruction of machinery or goods, or the intentional obstruction of production.

In April 1985, almost 80 percent of the United Auto Workers (UAW) at the American Motors Corporation (AMC) Jeep plant in Toledo, Ohio, were sent home without pay because of extensive vandalism occurring on the assembly line. The UAW's Jeep unit chairman, Danny Wilson, reported "major damage to at least 65% of the unfinished Jeeps in early April." The destruction began when AMC cut the employees' investment plan payments to a few hundred dollars rather than the several thousand the workers were expecting. The most serious damage was done in the body and paint departments. As noted by a UAW spokesperson, "In the body shop people have hammers in their hands. They took pick hammers and literally caved in quarter panels on cars and welded car doors shut."

Chamberlain (1985, p. 19) stresses that "preventing internal destruction of company property is always more difficult than protection against outsiders. Fences, guard stations, alarms and other protective devices are almost useless against deliberate internal attacks. More importantly, this type of crime cannot be prevented by the security department alone. It requires a concerted effort from all levels of management." Chamberlain goes on to make this suggestion:

> Response to internal vandalism should include plans for closing the operation on a moment's notice because even an hour's delay can result in thousands of dollars in damage. Alternate delivery and maintenance operations also should be developed. Employees are often aware of which suppliers and deliveries are most vital to production. In low-tech machinery operations alternate facilities or sub-contracting should be considered.
>
> Most importantly, other methods to control internal sabotage should be discussed. Like the instances at AMC, most vandalism is caused by employees with a real or perceived grievance against the employer. Strong company policies, well publicized and uniformly enforced, are usually the best prevention. . . .
>
> Modern technology has sped up production faster than ever before. But the human factor is the backbone of every plant, no matter how automated. The satisfied employee increases production. The angry, vengeful employee throws a "sabot" in the works.

Methods of sabotage may be chemical, electrical, explosive, mechanical or psychological (strikes, riots and boycotts). Psychological sabotage has become more frequent in the last decade. For example, in Minnesota, protestors against electrical power lines running through privately owned fields have toppled several of the huge powerline towers, each at a cost of hundreds of thousands of dollars. These costs were passed on to the consumer in higher energy rates. Access control and inspections are two means to prevent sabotage.

Espionage

Traditionally **espionage** is associated with spying, especially spying to obtain military secrets. More recently the term has broadened considerably in meaning.

> Industrial espionage is the theft of trade secrets or confidential information.

Some well-intentioned executives may claim they are not concerned with espionage, that they have no secrets to hide. However, it is well known that competition is the "fuel" of the American economy. Nowhere is this manifested more clearly than in industries that are trying to reach the market with improvements on an established item. All too often there are some executives who delay until competition has driven them to near bankruptcy before they will acknowledge the need for protecting secrets, as discussed in Chapter 9.

Competition is the heart of the free enterprise system. As noted, most manufacturers have information they want to conceal from their competitors because "lead time" is so critical. Confidentiality of information buys time to "get a jump" on the market. In other instances, secret formulas are a company's primary source of profits. Although many products can be protected by patents, some cannot. Trade secrets such as formulas are much harder to protect than real property because, if they are stolen, the rightful owner still has possession, but not exclusive possession, thereby greatly diminishing the value of the formula. Sometimes, in fact, the rightful owner may never realize the formula has been stolen.

Other types of information that may be stolen include new product research, production costs, sales figures, profit breakdowns, markups, salaries, reports on problems, merger plans, blueprints and the like. The minutes of executive committee meetings often contain such information and should be carefully guarded.

The FBI is investigating a case of espionage in California ("Suspected Spy Ring Found in Silicon Valley," April 5, 1995, p. 3D). According to an affidavit filed in the U.S. District Court in San Jose, California, Silicon Valley firms or their outside contractors have supplied copies of top-secret technical drawings of parts to a small San Carlos, California, company:

> Gary Weiss, an attorney representing Applied Materials, said the company believed its losses from the scheme "could be well into the millions of dollars. . . ."

> "Any company which could steal the OEM's [original equipment manufacturer] drawings and vendor information, and use it to have a part made, could eliminate both the research and development costs and the delay in bringing a product to market, gaining great advantage," the affidavit said.

The FBI went through the dumpster of the company suspected of stealing the information and found many drawings of parts, several of which had borders including the Applied Materials name and logo.

> Trade secrets should be identified as such, be secured and be made known to the fewest people possible.

Confidential information should be stamped "Confidential" or "Secret." Some companies place a warning on the front of confidential material which states: "This document is the sole property of Company X and may not be reproduced or duplicated." Each classified document should be numbered. If more than one copy exists, it should be identified by copy number, for example, Document 187, Copy 3 of 4. The original and all copies should be kept in a locked file or vault and should be signed in and out, with precautions taken to ensure that copies or photographs are not made while the materials are checked out. Some highly confidential material may be marked "Eyes Only," meaning that the originator of the document must hand-carry it to the individuals who are to read it and must wait while they do so. Therefore, the document never leaves the sight of the originator.

Confidential information should be known by as few people as possible. The adage, "Once you share a secret with a friend it is no longer a secret," holds true of trade secrets; the fewer people knowing a trade secret, the better. A good example is the formula for Worcestershire sauce. It has been kept secret for more than one hundred years because only two company officials know it at any one time.

Business secrets can fall into the wrong hands either through carelessness or through theft. Leaks can result from scientists who boast or who share ideas with other professionals, from spouses who know trade secrets and inadvertently let information slip, from mail-room personnel or secretaries who read confidential information, from janitors who see confidential information lying around, from consultants who obtain information while working for a firm or from ex-employees.

> Prevent espionage through careful screening of personnel, document control and clear guidelines for personnel.

Thorough background checks should be made of employees who will be working with confidential materials. Sometimes security clearances are required before a person can work in a given area, especially in government production plants. Employees should know what things are not to be discussed with anyone, including spouses. Some companies require new employees who will be working with confidential material to sign an agreement against unauthorized disclosure of trade secrets. Courts will usually uphold such agreements, as discussed in Chapter 9.

Engineering and scientific personnel should be provided with clear guidelines for security and should know what they "own" of what they invent. Of great concern is the scientist or inventor who leaves one company to join another. When scientific or engineering personnel are terminated, they should have a termination interview and sign an agreement that specifies precisely what information is not to be disclosed to the new employer. They should also turn in all confidential files, records and keys. An even greater threat is an employee who moonlights for a competitor and shares the secrets of the full-time employer with this competitor.

Employers should be suspicious of a break in security if competitors are consistently ahead of them, if they lose bids more often than usual or if their competition is hiring away key people.

Manufacturing firms working under Department of Defense contracts must protect classified information and materials and follow prescribed governmental regulations for safeguarding classified defense information, documents, materials, end products and storage and work areas. The security programs and policies at these manufacturing plants are mandated by Department of Defense regulations, and the plants can be inspected at any time by the Office of Industrial Security of the U.S. Defense Supply Agency.

VULNERABLE AREAS

A study conducted by the Office of Transportation Security, U.S. Department of Transportation, showed that most cargo thefts occurred in warehouses, loading docks, shipping and receiving areas and distribution centers during normal operating hours. Most of these thefts were accomplished by people and with vehicles that were authorized to be in the area, indicating a considerable degree of collusion between employees and outside individuals.

> The areas most vulnerable to theft are tool rooms or tool cribs, warehouses, loading docks, shipping and receiving areas and distribution centers.

Warehouses and stockrooms should be kept orderly and should have an attendant on duty. Appropriate lighting and locks should be used, along with alarms, if necessary. Rotating the stock and keeping a perpetual inventory will also help to reduce losses. Packing crates should be randomly opened and checked. In one instance, the person taking inventory of refrigerators in a warehouse simply pushed against the cartons to ensure that they were as heavy as they should be. It was later discovered that several of the cartons were empty and had been nailed to the floor.

Dumps should be fenced and kept locked. Trash containers and/or dumpsters should be inspected periodically. If possible, trash should be compacted so that discarded, defective merchandise is not recovered by employees and turned in for a refund.

Losses also occur frequently during shipping. To avoid this type of shrinkage, instruct transporters to carefully count merchandise, use factory-sealed cartons, seal the truck trailer doors, make sure the delivery trucks are kept secure, make nonstop hauls and send trucks in convoys when possible.

It is best not to pre-load trucks,* but if this cannot be avoided, the loaded trucks should be parked back to back.

Railroad spur lines are also highly vulnerable. Ideally, the area around railroad spurs should be fenced, locked and kept lit at night. Railroad cars should be unloaded immediately. If this is not possible, they should be sealed until they can be unloaded.

Transporting Goods by Truck, Rail and Ship†

Our national economy depends on the movement of goods and merchandise by our transportation system, one of the largest industries in the United States. Manufacturing and industrial enterprises depend on the transportation system to supply them with raw materials for production and to then distribute the finished merchandise to customers. Most materials and goods are transported by common carrier rather than by company-owned transportation fleets.

For this discussion *cargo* refers to anything that enters and is moved by the nation's transportation system, beginning at the shipper's loading platform and ending at a consignee's receiving dock. *Cargo theft* may involve entire shipments, containers and cartons, or pilferage of smaller amounts of merchandise.

Commodities such as clothing, electrical appliances, automotive parts, food products, hardware, jewelry, tobacco products, scientific instruments and alcoholic beverages make up about 80 percent of the total national losses.

Most security staffs have developed effective countermeasures against cargo theft, but common denominators can be seen. Measures that can be equally effective in all types of transportation to protect both shippers and carriers from losses due to theft and vandalism include personnel security, physical security, procedures for accepting cargo, secure packaging, documenting movement and delivery, periodic review of security procedures and prosecution of offenses.

Agencies that may assist with investigating cargo crime include the local police department, the United States Bureau of Customs and the FBI. Liaison with other carriers should be maintained to ensure mutual cooperation in all

*Loading several hours prior to the scheduled departure time.

†Transportation Security—See *Private Security,* pp. 58–59.

areas related to cargo security. Prosecution is of vital importance in deterring future thefts.

The Trucking Industry*

Virtually all cargo moves by truck at least once during shipment. Cargo theft can occur at any point in the distribution system: warehouses, receiving and shipping platforms, storage areas, depots, distribution centers, terminals and piers. Direct financial loss to the transportation industry due to cargo theft is estimated at from $1 to $2 billion annually.

The Office of Transportation Security, United States Department of Transportation, estimates that cargo theft losses were the result of hijacking (5 percent), breaking and entering and external theft (10 percent), and internal theft, collusive theft and unexplained shortages (85 percent). Although hijackings receive national publicity, they account for only a small portion of losses. As noted by the Department of Transportation, 85 percent of the goods and materials stolen go out the front gate, and those transporting these items have authorization to be in the cargo handling area.

> The cargoes most frequently stolen from trucks include clothing and textiles, electrical and electronic supplies and components, foods, tobacco and liquor, appliances, automotive and other vehicle parts and paper, plastic and rubber products.

Organized crime activities account for 15 to 20 percent of the *value* of all cargo thefts, with the remainder resulting from employee collusion either

The trucking industry is a vital part of our transportation system.

*Cargo Theft—See *Private Security,* pp. 58–60.

among themselves or with people outside the transportation system and fences, organized along geographic areas and/or product lines.

> Security measures in the trucking industry include use of proprietary and/or contract guards in shipping, receiving and storage areas; access control systems and perimeter fencing and lighting; CCTV systems and alarms; and special security seals and alarms on trucks.

The seal system is adapted from that initiated by the railroads several years ago. Under this system a numbered metal band is used to seal the door. Careful records should be kept of all seals. It is a federal crime for a nonauthorized person to break the seal on any interstate shipment. Therefore, if a seal is broken, the FBI and local police should be called to investigate.

Tichenor notes that "thieves can work the rivets off the locking bars [of trucks] with a crow bar and pull the vertical locking bars out. Then they install a new carriage bolt and spray paint the area to cover their tracks" ("Trucking Cargo Security," 1995, p. 30). Tichenor suggests the following:

- Install cam locks on all containers.
- Install cable between vertical locking bars.
- Don't tell drivers what is in their containers.
- Warn drivers to be wary of hijacking the first few miles after they leave their pick-up point.
- Stop only when necessary—cargo at rest is cargo at risk.

Bordes (1992, p. 44A) cautions: "There is still too much dependence on seals and locks to protect cargo and not enough demand made on the electronics industry to assist with these problems." Bordes believes: "Access control systems in the freight and shipping portion of the transportation industry have basically no limit from a technology standpoint."

Some high-value shipments are monitored by transmitters on the vehicle or by a directional monitoring receiver in a helicopter. In addition, most of the security measures discussed in Chapter 5 regarding safeguarding shipments are also applicable to common carriers.

Because employee theft accounts for such a large percentage of loss, a system of accountability with proper documentation from the purchase order to invoice and receiving slip is necessary. Although truckers have no control over the issuing of such documentation, drivers are responsible for carefully checking shipments as they are loaded and unloaded.

Another safeguard for trucking security is the new law requiring drug and alcohol testing of drivers. According to Nianiatus (1995, p. 2): "Federally mandated drug and alcohol testing for company drivers is now a reality for larger firms [50 commercially licensed drivers or more] this year." Firms with fewer than 50 drivers will have to comply after January 1, 1996. The law requires that each year 50 percent of potential drivers be tested for controlled substances and 25 percent be tested for alcohol. All such tests are to be strictly random.

Railroad Security*

Railroad security is provided by the oldest, perhaps most highly organized segment of the private security industry, the railroad police. The country's 3,500 railroad police work closely with local, state and federal law enforcement agencies. Although the railroad police are paid with corporate funds, at least 40 states have given them broad police powers. In these states, the railroad police have a dual responsibility to the rail industry and the public.

The Police and Security Section of the Association of American Railroads describes the basic objectives of the railroad police as protecting life and property; preventing and suppressing crime; investigating criminal acts committed on or against the railroad, patrons, or employees; arresting criminal offenders; supervising conduct on railroad property; and performing certain nonpolice services such as accident and claims investigation and safety management.

Theft of railroad cargo may occur on any point along a quarter million miles of track. It is one of the most important concerns of the railroad police.

> The primary security problems of the railroad industry are cargo theft, vandalism and theft of metals.

Approximately 400,000 miles of railroad are impossible to adequately secure. Sturdy boxcars, locks and seals help improve security.

---

*Railroad Security—See *Private Security,* pp. 54–55.

Total losses incurred by these crimes cost railroad carriers millions of dollars every year. The security problems faced by railroads are immense (*Private Security,* p. 54):

- A freight car loaded at one part of the country may move over several different railroads to its final destination in another part of the nation. The cargo is not examined unless an exception to a seal is noted during the movement or the car is listed on a special bulletin as a high-value load.
- Many railroads pass through the most crime-ridden areas of our largest cities.
- It is impossible to fence or adequately patrol the approximately 400,000 miles of railroad right-of-ways.
- Most criminals causing major problems are not railroad employees; therefore, internal controls do not suffice.
- Many thefts occur in large rail yards which are difficult to monitor with conventional hardware.
- The number and size of rail yards also make them difficult to cover by saturation of manpower.
- Metals belonging to the railroads are easily stolen and fenced. Examples are copper communication wire, brass rail car bearings, and steel track material.
- The physical nature of railroads makes them vulnerable to acts of vandalism by trespassers, especially by juveniles.

The deliberate derailment of Amtrak's Sunset Limited in the Arizona desert in the fall of 1995 illustrates the vulnerability to terrorism of our 110,425-mile national railway system.

> Security measures used by railroads include patrol, surveillance, undercover operations, CCTV monitoring, locking devices and gate controls and seals.

Railroad police prevent and control crime and enhance security by using such security measures as radio-equipped foot and vehicle patrol, canine patrol, and fixed-wing aircraft and helicopter patrol; fixed-surveillance stakeouts; undercover operations; exchange of intelligence information with public law enforcement agencies; employee security-consciousness programs; criminal investigations aimed at prosecuting persons found responsible for crimes against the railroads; task forces moving many railroad police officers into a specific problem area to perform a tactical mission; public relations and education programs aimed at community awareness and support of railroad police activities; and installation protection, including CCTV, electronic security and sophisticated locking devices and gate controls.

Most railroad security administrators believe engineering improvements to cars and trailers would help prevent cargo theft and vandalism, including improved door construction of boxcars and trailers, container locking mechanisms, boxcar and trailer locking devices and cable seals. They also suggest that further research is needed in other areas, such as:

- Night lighting (portable and permanent) for operational surveillance;

- Helicopter patrol for theft and vandalism surveillance;
- Canine units for trailer terminals and rail yard patrol;
- CCTV in trailer terminal operations;
- Photographic methods for trailer terminal operations;
- Sensor devices used on rail car and trailer shipments;
- Use of computers for determining claim and theft patterns;
- Use of screened rail cars to protect auto shipments from vandalism and theft.

Seaport Security

Rubin (1992, p. 58) describes how at shipping docks in Los Angeles, Long Beach and San Pedro, cranes lift large sealed containers off the ships and set them onto wheels. A tractor hooks up and drives away with the container containing valuable cargo such as 540 cartons of tennis shoes valued at $650,000. Rubin (p. 60) notes: "Cargo thieves maintain their own intelligence network of informers. Port workers who have access to ship manifests sometimes pass on information that makes it possible to pinpoint containers with valuable loads."

Confusion and masses of materials make cargo security at seaports especially difficult, as unauthorized vehicles may carry out thousands of dollars of cargo at a time. Imported cars are especially a problem at seaports. Most cars are stored in areas with no perimeter fencing, with inadequate lighting facilities and without proper guard protection. The result is that many vehicles are stolen and vandalized.

Cargo security at seaports poses extra challenges as shipments valued at thousands of dollars are loaded onto docks awaiting further transportation. Here a container ship is being unloaded at Newark Port.

The American Society for Industrial Security Subcommittee on Seaports and Harbors (1992, p. 19A) notes:

> Vessels in a seaport seek more than to discharge and load passengers and cargo. They need a safe haven; they need to be protected from the maritime security threats that face all vessels today—theft, drug smuggling, sabotage, piracy, hijacking, and stowaways.
>
> A seaport must also be concerned about its own security—its buildings, storage areas (including tank farms), equipment, and so on. The seaport's security responsibilities, therefore, are first to the ships that call at the port, second to the cargo, and third to the seaport itself. The secret to successfully meeting all these responsibilities is proper access control.

Special Problems in the Utilities Industry

Everyone has contact with utility companies—water, gas, electric companies. We are heavily dependent on them daily. Higgins (1985, p. 79) notes that the accessibility of utilities makes them "subject to a variety of crimes, from trespassing to vandalism, from robberies to terrorism, and leaves them vulnerable at many points." He goes on to note the primary problems facing the security director for a utility company.

> Primary problems at utility companies include loss of tools, loss of stored items, trespassers and vandals at substations and distribution centers, security at construction sites, access control for office buildings, protection of collection centers from theft and robbery, plans for emergencies and detection of resource diversion.

Utility service trucks are heavily equipped with supplies and tools that remain in the vehicles even when they are not in use. These are highly vulnerable to theft. To counter this problem, inventory control and strict check-in/out procedures are needed. In addition, when the vehicles are at a service location, crew members often must leave the vehicle unattended—and, again, vulnerable.

Another problem is encountered in utility companies' numerous unstaffed substations, frequently secured with chain-link fences and security lighting. Despite these measures, trespassers and vandals may pose serious problems. Higgins cites additional problems with crews using the substations for beer parties, gambling and an "occasional prostitution fling"; homeless individuals taking over the buildings; and contractors moving mobile homes onto a site and hooking up to the substation's electricity and water. Solutions to such problems might include alarms, guard dogs or roving patrols.

Construction of major generating facilities presents additional security problems. According to Higgins, such sites can be valued at more than $1 billion and can incur losses of 10 to 30 percent of this total value. He suggests that the major key to solving construction site theft is "not allowing tools and materials to leave the site" and continues, "All personal vehicles should be parked off site and all employees or contractors must wear badges and enter the site at controlled points."

Like any other business, utility companies also have valuable records: subscriber credit histories, financial data and the like, often stored on computer. Controlling access to this information is the same as for any other business and might include locks, alarms, sign-in/out procedures and guards.

In addition to records and information, utility companies also handle large amounts of cash. Money at collection sites must be protected from internal theft as well as from robbery. For cash-handling problems, Higgins suggests that "utilities would be wise to adopt the proven methods used by banks and even retail stores in the periodic removal of excess cash from the teller booths." They might also consider having panic alarms and CCTV cameras installed and training employees who handle cash in responding to a robbery.

Yet another area of concern is that of emergencies. Although utility companies are particularly accustomed to dealing with emergencies, emergencies must still be built into the overall security plan. Included are fires, bombs and bomb threats. As for any other type of establishment, procedures for evacuation should be determined and practiced.

Another area of concern, which lacks the high visibility of emergencies, is that of diversion of the resource provided by the utility, whether gas, electricity or water. The most usual means of diverting the resource is bypassing the meter that measures its use. Higgins cites the example of a large restaurant with an all-electric kitchen whose owner "allegedly paid a utility employee to bypass the electric meter. One light bulb was connected to the meter to show some usage. This ploy was discovered when a new employee of the restaurant had an electrical problem and called the utility. A utility repairman not included discovered the diversion." Such losses might be reduced by monitoring monthly usage and comparing it with predetermined norms.

> A utility company's losses can be reduced by careful access controls to tools and supplies, careful check-in/out procedures, alarms and surveillance cameras at substations, attention to cash-handling procedures and establishment of emergency plans.

Other measures that might be employed will vary from utility to utility. The following list of risks and responsibilities facing utility security professionals, compiled by Higgins (p. 80), should indicate what other types of security measures might be appropriate.

- No corporate security policy oriented toward utilities
- Executive protection
- Terrorism—bomb threats, etc.
- Physical security
- Emergency operations/procedures
- Access controls
- Employee entry controls/visitor badging and controls
- Operations center security
- Warehouse security
- Distribution center security
- Substation security
- Transmission line security
- Diversion of assets and electric power diversion
- Guard dogs and incident reports
- Records maintenance
- Position descriptions for security personnel
- Lost/found procedures
- Security meetings
- Key and lock control procedures
- Construction site security
- Fire safety
- Patrols and surveillance
- Trespass procedures
- Cash-handling—holdup procedures
- Parcel pass procedures
- Screening and investigation of applicants
- Guard contracts
- Alarm station contracts
- Alarm equipment evaluations
- Communications
- Employee theft
- Computer security
- Office building security
- Plant security
- Parking lots
- Lighting standards

Hinman (1993, pp. 22–23) describes the security efforts at Alabama Power Company where security oversees 8,000 employees and one million customers in a service area consisting of 55 of Alabama's 67 counties. Security is provided by a proprietary force of 150 officers with a budget of $1.5 million or about $1.10 per customer. At Alabama Power Company, corporate security has the following missions (p. 22):

- Protect corporate assets, including property and personnel at headquarters and in the field.
- Develop preventive programs wherever a service or property is subjected to criminal activity, internal or external.
- Act as liaison to the criminal justice structure at the state, federal, and local levels.
- Assist in the company's emergency restoration efforts.
- Represent the utility in all criminal matters in which the company is a party at interest, including investigative assistance where appropriate.

Two incidents in 1993, the intrusion by an unidentified person into the controlled area of the Three Mile Island Nuclear Generating Station and the bombing at the World Trade Center, resulted in congressional committee hearings in March of 1993. Following these hearings, the Nuclear Regulatory Commission (NRC) began examining nuclear plant security. As noted by Stapleton (1994, p. 62):

> In the development of its physical protection programs, NRC uses the concept of a design basis threat to assure adequate protection. The design basis threat is a hypothetical situation against which facilities must design protection measures. The approach has three main purposes: it provides a standard with which to measure changes in the real threat environment; it is used to develop regulatory requirements; it provides a standard for evaluation of implemented safeguards programs.

SUMMARY

Industrial losses frequently include tools, materials, supplies, products, pallets, hand trucks, valuable scrap, uniforms, side-products, time and vital information. Of special concern is tool loss, which can be minimized by having a tool room or tool crib with an attendant, a check-in/out procedure, distinctive markings on the tools, periodic inspections and inventories, metal detectors at gates and possibly a system for lending tools for personal use after hours.

Two special concerns of industry are sabotage and espionage. Sabotage is the intentional destruction of machinery or goods, or the intentional obstruction of production. Industrial espionage is the theft of trade secrets or confidential information. Trade secrets should be identified as such, be secured and be made known to the fewest people possible. In addition, espionage can be prevented by careful screening of personnel, document control and clear guidelines for personnel. The areas most vulnerable to theft are tool rooms or tool cribs, warehouses, loading docks, shipping and receiving areas and distribution centers.

The transportation industry also relies heavily on security for carriers such as trucks and railroads. The cargoes most frequently stolen from trucks include clothing and textiles, electrical and electronic supplies and components, foods, tobacco and liquor, appliances, automotive and other vehicle parts and paper, plastic and rubber products. Security measures in the trucking industry include use of proprietary and/or contract guards in shipping, receiving and storage areas; access control systems and perimeter fencing and lighting; CCTV systems and alarms; and special security seals and alarms on trucks.

The primary security problems of the railroad industry are cargo theft, vandalism and theft of metals. Security measures used by railroads include patrol, surveillance, undercover operations, CCTV monitoring, locking devices and gate controls and seals.

Primary problems at utility companies include loss of tools, loss of stored items, trespassers and vandals at substations and distribution centers, security at construction sites, access control for office buildings, protection of collection centers from theft and robbery, plans for emergencies and detection of resource diversion. A utility company's losses can be reduced by careful access controls to tools and supplies, careful check-in/out procedures, alarms and surveillance cameras at substations, attention to cash-handling procedures and establishment of emergency plans.

APPLICATION

As security director of a manufacturing company, if you were informed that an employee was engaging in the theft of company trade secrets, what steps would you take to investigate the charge? If the charge was well founded, what steps would you take? What resources would you use?

CRITICAL THINKING EXERCISE

COMMERCIAL LIABILITY

STATUTORY AND COMMON LAW

Implied in every contract for work or service is a duty to perform it skillfully, carefully, diligently and in a workmanlike manner. The purpose of a contract entered into between a security agency and a property owner is for protection of property from theft. Oklahoma law states that "a master or other principal who is under a duty to provide protection for or to have care used to protect others or their property and who confides the performance of such duty to a servant or other person is subject to liability to such other persons for harm caused to them by the failure of such agent to perform the duty."

FACTS OF THE CASE

Oklahoma Gas and Electric Company contracted with ABC Security for protection of its property at its Post Road facility. ABC Security assigned employees to shifts around the clock, and security guard Ritter was assigned to guard duty between 4:15 P.M. and midnight six days a week. He served in this capacity for a number of years.

In November Ritter was discovered stealing copper wire belonging to Oklahoma Gas and Electric Company and stored at the Post Road location. In his confession Ritter admitted to having stolen wire for five years during working hours when he was on security guard duty. The total estimated value of the stolen wire was $110,849.

Ritter was prosecuted criminally, and Oklahoma Gas and Electric Company filed a civil action against ABC Security to recover the value of the stolen copper wire. The company argued that when the purpose of a contract is protection of property from theft, the contracting company (ABC Security) is liable for the thefts by a security guard employee, especially because the thefts occurred while the security guard employee was assigned to be on duty to guard the property.

Issues and Questions

1. Is a security company that furnishes a security guard to protect the property of another company liable for losses resulting from theft by the security guard assigned to the site?
   a. The doctrine of supervening impossibility of performance allows for a contract to be dissolved and the parties excused from performing it when conditions essential to the fulfillment of the contract cease to exist. In this case ABC Security had no control or responsibility for the criminal activity of Ritter who acted outside his assigned duty and contrary to his employer's instructions. Due to these changed conditions, ABC Security is absolved from liability.
   b. Tort and contract law requires that "unless one has directed a specified tortious act or result, or has been negligent, he is normally not responsible for the conduct of others." So ABC Security is liable only to that degree that its training or instructions might be insufficient or confusing to an employee. Possibly it could be held 50 percent responsible for damages.
   c. ABC Security is liable not for the felonies of its employee, but for its failure to provide the protection contracted for. Oklahoma Gas and Electric Company contracted for a security service to protect its property, but instead it received a thief. Common sense tells us the contract would never have been signed if it expressly disclaimed responsibility for larceny by its own security guard employees.
   d. When larceny was committed with such sophistication that it continually went undetected for five years, it was unreasonable to expect ABC Security to detect or prevent it, nor in all probability could any security guard have detected or prevented this theft. Ritter alone is liable.
   e. ABC Security is responsible for the felonies of its employees, for by contract a company is responsible for harm caused by the conduct of one's agents or employees. The clear duty assumed by ABC Security was protection of property from theft. And if theft is committed while the employee is on duty to guard the property, the contracting company is strictly liable. So ABC Security can be assessed a penalty and asked to pay all damages.

Discussion Questions

1. What are some preventive measures a security director might apply to guard against espionage in a computer manufacturing company?
2. Name several effective ways to protect vital documents and records from destruction or theft.
3. What methods might espionage agents use to undermine a competitor?
4. What are some reasons employees engage in sabotage?
5. What security measures are effective in minimizing the possibility of cargo theft from trucks? Railroad cars?

REFERENCES

Anderson, Teresa. "Rechanneling Security Toward Changing Threats." *Security Management,* June 1994, pp. 67–69.

ASIS Subcommittee on Seaports and Harbors. "Securing the World's Seaports." *Security Management,* June 1992, pp. 19A–21A.

Blackwell, Ray. "Caterpillar Creates a New Security Landscape." Special Supplement to *Security Management,* March 1995, pp. 19A–22A.

Bordes, Roy N. "Tracking the Trucking Industry." *Security Management,* June 1992, pp. 43A–44A.

Burton, P. J. "Theft in the Lumber Industry." *Security Management,* August 1983, pp. 65–67.

Chamberlain, C. S. "Internal Vandalism Presents a Problem That Demands Both Prevention and Response." *Security World,* June 1985, p. 19.

Donnelly, John F. "DIS Procedures Adapt for the Future." *Security Management,* September 1994, pp. 187–89.

Gallati, Robert J. *Introduction to Private Security.* Englewood Cliffs, NJ: Prentice-Hall, 1983.

Gates, Daryl and Readhimer, Robert. "Metal Theft: A Growing Concern." *The Police Chief,* January 1992, pp. 57–58.

Higgins, C. E. "Shedding Light on Utility Security." *Security Management,* May 1985, pp. 79–82.

Hinman, David B. "Security at the Power Source." *Security Management,* June 1993, pp. 22–26.

Knight, George. "Making a Dent in Metals Theft." *Security Management,* April 1991, pp. 67–68.

List, Bruce C. "Powering Up Energy Security." *Security Management,* December 1993, pp. 34–38.

Murphree, Gary. "Satisfying Uncle Sam." *Security Management,* February 1992, pp. 61–62.

Nianiatus, George. "Companies Now Required to Do Drug, Alcohol Testing for Commercial Drivers." *Security Concepts,* March 1995, p. 2.

Private Security. Report of the Task Force on Private Security, National Advisory Committee on Criminal Justice Standards and Goals. Washington, DC.: U.S. Government Printing Office, 1976.

Rubin, Hal. "Cargo Cats." *Law and Order,* June 1992, pp. 58–60.

Rubin, Hal. "Heavy Equipment Theft." *Law and Order,* May 1992, pp. 85–86.

Stapleton, Bernard. "Maximize the Margin for Sabotage Safety." *Security Management,* September 1994, pp. 62–67.

"Suspected Spy Ring Found in Silicon Valley." (Minneapolis/St. Paul) *Star Tribune,* April 5, 1995, p. 3D.

"Trucking Cargo Security." *Security Concepts,* March 1995, p. 30.

CHAPTER 16

Retail Security

Do You Know

- What crimes are most frequently committed against retail establishments?
- What legally constitutes shoplifting?
- How shoplifters are classified?
- What methods are commonly used to shoplift?
- What preventive methods can be taken to curtail shoplifting?
- What basic difference exists between security officers and floorwalkers?
- What merchandising techniques, procedures and physical controls can be used to deter shoplifting?
- When and how to apprehend individuals suspected of shoplifting?
- What factors influence when prosecution is advisable?
- How to deter losses from bad checks?
- Which types of checks are considered high-risk checks?
- What the most common types of bad checks are?
- How checks should be examined?
- What identification to require?
- How to deter losses from credit cards?
- What types of employee theft frequently occur in retail establishments and what preventive measures can be taken?
- What honesty shopping is?
- What the two primary objectives of shopping center security are?

Can You Define These Terms?

booster box
floor release limit
floorwalkers
honesty shopping
kleptomaniac
prima facie evidence
probable cause
reasonable cause
shoplifting
shopping service
sliding
zero floor release limit

Introduction

It is a Friday evening. In the X Supermarket, a woman buys a dozen rolls from the bakery department. The rolls are placed in a white sack with the price marked on the outside. To this sack, the woman adds a pen and three cigarette lighters. She hurriedly pays the cashier the correct amount for the rolls in change and leaves without waiting for a receipt. The cashier pockets the money. At the next counter a man is cashing a stolen government check. Across the street, the corner gas station is being held up. Farther down the street, in a large department store, some teenagers are palming small objects as an initiation into the local gang, a woman is in a fitting booth putting her street clothes on over an expensive bathing suit, another woman is switching prices on jewelry and an employee is marking down prices on items she is purchasing for herself.

Hourly, across the country, such actions result in tremendous losses to retailers. Retail establishments include general merchandise department stores, specialty and clothing stores, food and drug stores, appliance and furniture stores, radio and television stores, hardware stores, lumberyards, restaurants, fast-food shops, automobile dealers and gasoline service stations. Retail businesses that absorb the greatest losses are general merchandise and clothing stores, food stores and drug stores, in that order.

A modern phenomenon is the large shopping mall, centralizing a large number of retail, entertainment, professional and business operations into one location that provides ample parking and easy access for thousands of customers. Shopping center management has become such a specialized field that the International Council of Shopping Centers (ICSC) has begun to certify the qualifications of managers for shopping centers. Different combinations of local law enforcement personnel and proprietary and/or contractual guard forces provide security for these shopping centers. Some of the larger centers are assigned local law enforcement officers. In others, shopping center security personnel are given limited police powers through local ordinances. Most larger shopping centers have a director of security, a proprietary security force, closed-circuit television (CCTV), a communications system and mobile patrols for parking lots.

Whether located in a shopping mall, in a downtown business district or in isolation from other businesses, retailers face many common problems.

Retail parking lots often require added security which may be contracted for.

Managers of such establishments often use security measures to protect their assets.*

The highest-loss items in department stores are junior sportswear and high-fashion clothing, jewelry, leathers, furs, cosmetics, compact discs and tapes and small electronic items. Losses from drug stores include cosmetics, costume jewelry, candy, toys, drugs and tapes. Careful records on high-loss items are necessary to plan appropriate security measures.

> Reported crimes committed against all types of retail establishments are shoplifting, burglary, vandalism, bad checks, fraudulent credit cards, employee theft and robbery.

The physical and procedural controls discussed in Section II are the most effective means of deterring robbery, burglary and vandalism in retail establishments. Proper lighting, locks, alarm systems and other measures are also appropriate in retail establishments. Of equal or greater importance, however, is safeguarding against losses from shoplifting, bad checks, fraudulently used credit cards and employee theft, the focus of this chapter.

This chapter begins with a discussion of shrinkage and of one of the most serious retail security concerns: shoplifting. Next, preventing losses from bad checks and fraudulent credit cards is discussed. This is followed by a look at retail employee theft, shopping center security and how assistance in retail security might be obtained. The chapter concludes with a brief discussion of retail security in the future.

SHRINKAGE

The problem of shrinkage has been discussed in previous chapters. Recall that shrinkage is the loss of assets. The 1994 National Retail Security Survey (Hollinger and Dabney, 1995) found that retail shrinkage was the highest it had been in four years. It equaled 1.95 percent of total retail sales—or more than $20 billion ("Retail Shrinkage," 1995, p. 1). The major sources of shrinkage are illustrated in Figure 16–1.

SHOPLIFTING

Shoplifting is often considered the most widespread crime affecting retail stores. It is also generally considered to be a security problem rather than a law enforcement problem.

---

*Retail Security—See *Private Security,* pp. 55–58. Shopping Center Security—See *Private Security,* p. 44.

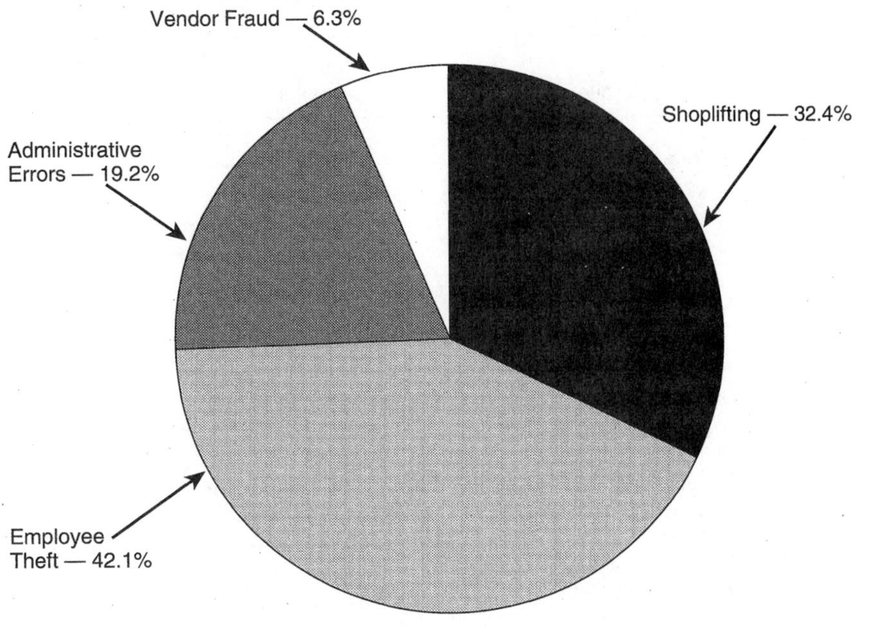

Figure 16–1. Sources of Retail Shrinkage
SOURCE: Security Research Project, University of Florida, Gainesville, Florida. Reprinted by permission.

> Shoplifting* is the theft of retail merchandise by a person lawfully on the premises. Concealment of merchandise is **prima facie evidence**† of intent to shoplift. In many states price changing is also considered shoplifting.

Statistics from the U.S. Department of Justice indicate that shoplifting is the fastest-growing crime in the larceny-theft category—up 22 percent between 1986 and 1990—and that more than one million arrests have been reported each year since 1989 (McNamara, 1993, p. 90). In addition, notes McNamara: "[S]ome experts speculate that for every shoplifter caught, as many as 10 to 20 others go undetected." Fenker (1993, p. 94) notes: "Statistics indicate that about one out of every 100 customers entering a store will try to remove an item without paying for it."

Adler (1993, p. 61) compares shoplifting to the common cold: "Like the common cold, shoplifting strikes indiscriminately and, left untreated, can prove deadly. But before retailers seek a cure, they must examine the community and the store to avoid an incorrect diagnosis of the underlying cause."

---

*Some states call shoplifting "retail theft."

†Evidence established by law. Also called "direct evidence." For example, 0.1 percent ethanol in the blood is prima facie evidence of intoxication in some states.

Table 16–1. Inventory Shrinkage as a Percentage of Retail Sales

Type of Retailers	Percentage 0	1	2	3	4	5
Auto Parts & Tires						
Books & Magazines						
Cameras & Photo						
Cards, Gifts & Novelties						
Catalog Showrooms						
Consumer Electronics						
Convenience Store						
Department Store						
Discount Store						
Drug Store						
Furniture						
Homecenter/Hardware						
Household Furnishings						
Jewelry						
Liquor/Wine/Beer						
Office Supplies						
Optical						
Recorded Music/Video						
Shoes						
Specialty Men's Apparel						
Specialty Women's Apparel						
Specialty Other Apparel						
Sporting Goods						
Supermarket/Grocery						
Toy & Hobbies						
Other						
OVERALL						

SOURCE: Security Research Project, University of Florida, Gainesville, Florida. Reprinted by permission.

Shoplifting is a form of larceny costing billions of dollars annually. Compounding the problem is public apathy. Most people have shoplifted at one time in their lives, and many have very little sympathy for big business. Thus, the responsibility for preventing shoplifting losses falls almost entirely on retail management.

The problem has many facets. Sales and security personnel must be familiar with the various types of shoplifters, methods they commonly use, signs indicative of shoplifting activity and means to prevent the crime. They must also be knowledgeable of the establishment's policies and procedures for apprehending, arresting, interrogating and deciding whether to prosecute offenders.

Types of Shoplifters

Although anyone can be a shoplifter, it is helpful to recognize the most common types of shoplifters.

> Shoplifters can be classified as amateurs—students, housewives, vagrants, alcoholics, drug addicts and kleptomaniacs—or as professionals—those who steal for resale of merchandise.

The great majority of shoplifting is done by amateurs—ordinary customers who give in to temptation. Most shoplifting incidences are impulsive. Shoplifting is often called a "crime of the young." Many studies indicate that juveniles are involved in at least half of shoplifting incidents. Juveniles seldom steal from true need, but rather for "kicks," as a dare or to be initiated into a club. They often enter stores in groups and "rip off" the merchant. Some steal items they have been given money to purchase and then use the money to purchase drugs or alcohol.

Housewives are the next most common category of shoplifters. This may be partly because they frequently do most of the family's shopping and, therefore, are exposed to temptation more often than other individuals. They may also be trying to stretch their budget. Vagrants and alcoholics frequently are truly in need of food or liquor and steal to meet these needs. They are often easy to detect because they are clumsy and obvious in their actions. Drug addicts, because of their desperation, pose a very direct threat to the safety of store personnel and should always be approached cautiously. A **kleptomaniac** (compulsive thief) seldom needs the items stolen, but simply cannot resist. There are very few true kleptomaniacs.

Professional shoplifters are much more difficult to detect. For them shoplifting is a way of life, often their sole source of income. They usually steal to resell the items, either to a fence or on the black market. This not only results in a direct loss to the store, but also sets up competition for the victim—with the victim's own merchandise. Many professional shoplifters steal "on order."

A survey conducted by Loss Prevention Specialists, Inc., the 1993 Retail Theft Trends Report, presents the following statistics on shoplifters and their activities based on more than 80,000 actual shoplifting apprehensions ("Survey Reports . . .," 1993, p. 9):

- Baby boomers, age 31–55 account for 43.15% of all shoplifting.
- December is the busiest month for shoplifting, September the lowest.
- More than 24.5% were apprehended between noon and 3:00 P.M. and an additional 29.3% apprehended between 3:00 P.M. and 6:00 P.M.. Only 9% of all apprehension occurred between 6:00 A.M. and noon.
- Weekends account for more than a quarter of all incidents, with Saturday the busiest day of the weekend.
- True pros often make more than $100,000 a year, tax free, from their shoplifting activities. They also often work in teams.

In a study conducted using 1,935 apprehended shoplifters, some interesting facts emerged (Carolin, 1992, pp. 11A–11B):

- 72 percent said they stole merchandise because they liked it and couldn't pay for it.
- 28 percent indicated an economic need—they were on a mission to steal.
- 35 percent said they would steal from any store.
- Three-fourths of the women and two-thirds of the men believed stealing is wrong.
- One-third had suggestions on deterring shoplifting.

Among the suggestions for deterring shoplifting were the following (p. 12A): "More sales personnel on the sales floor, fitting room service or controls, lower prices on the merchandise, and having sales personnel approach them."

Common Methods of Shoplifting

Shoplifters usually prefer crowded first floors, large sales and self-service establishments where they are less apt to be detected. Most shoplifting thefts are simple and direct. Items are simply picked up and put into a pocket or purse. Professional shoplifters, on the other hand, may use sophisticated methods and devices. Adults may have children unknowingly carry out merchandise that has not been paid for. Some professional shoplifters have claimed items in the layaway areas having only a small amount left due, paid the small balance and taken the item. Some are even bold enough to stand behind an unattended register and sell merchandise to customers, pocketing the money.

> Shoplifting methods include palming objects, dropping articles into a receptacle, placing items inside clothing, wearing items out of the store and switching price tags.

Palming articles is a frequent method. This practice is often aided by using packages, newspapers, coats, gloves and the like. Items may be knocked off counters into packages, shopping bags or umbrellas.

Some shoplifters have specially tailored clothing that aids in their thefts. They may have coats and capes with hidden pockets and slits or zippered hiding places. Some coats have special hooks or belts inside on which to hang articles. Aprons and undergarments may be designed to hold articles; for example, "shoplifter bloomers" have elastic waistbands so the thief can stuff all manner of articles into them and they will not fall out. Others may wear bulky clothing and place articles between their legs, walking in the "shoplifter's shuffle" from the store.

A favorite device of professional shoplifters is the **booster box,** a box whose top, bottom or end is hinged so that articles can be placed inside without actually opening the box.

Articles may also be worn out of the store, either under street clothing or in place of clothing that was worn upon entering. Jewelry, hats, purses, cam-

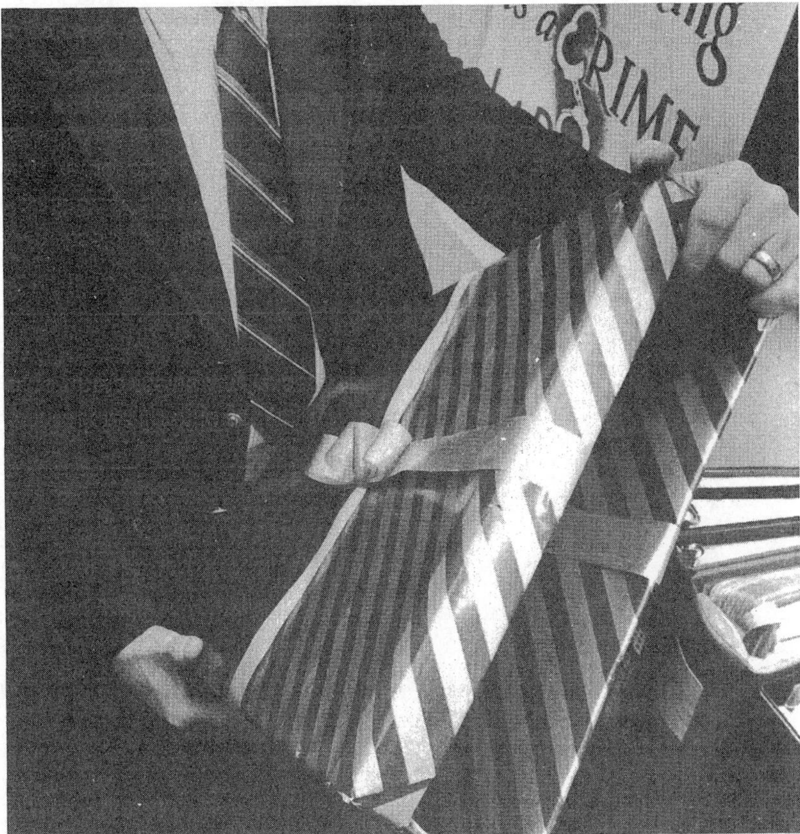

This booster box looks like a gift-wrapped package, but has a hinged lid allowing a shoplifter to put merchandise into it. The spring-loaded lid snaps shut giving an innocent appearance.

eras and sunglasses may all be worn so as to imply that they are the personal possessions of the shoplifter.

Items may also be dropped down the neck of clothing or placed into socks. A customer who frequently adjusts her hair may be concealing articles either in her hair or by dropping them down the back of her dress.

Frequently, professional shoplifters work in teams, with one diverting the clerk while the other, who is "just waiting," steals merchandise. Another common ploy is to send the clerk away for another size or color and then to shoplift while the clerk is gone.

Indicators of Possible Shoplifting

Knowing how shoplifters operate can be of great value in spotting the potential or actual shoplifter. Personnel can be trained to watch for certain characteristics and actions commonly associated with shoplifting.

Actions. Actions that might be indicative of shoplifting include:

- Picking up and putting down items.
- Comparing two identical items.

- Frequently opening and closing a purse.
- Adjusting hair and clothing.
- Continuously looking around.
- Walking in an unusual way.
- Reaching into display counters.
- Walking behind sales counters.
- Showing disinterest in articles asked about.
- Roaming while waiting for someone else to shop.
- Walking aimlessly around the store.
- Appearing nervous, flush-faced or dry-lipped, or perspiring heavily.
- Keeping one hand constantly in an outer pocket.
- Frequently using elevators and/or restrooms.
- Sending clerks to get merchandise from back rooms.
- Making rapid purchases and leaving the area hastily.
- Changing packages with someone else.

Clothing. Clothing, too, might be indicative of shoplifting, including bulky clothing in warm weather, a coat over an arm, a full skirt or a large hat.

Receptacles. Individuals who carry many bags or boxes; carry briefcases, newspapers or umbrellas; or have an arm in a sling might be using these items to conceal shoplifted merchandise.

Although any one or two of the preceding indicators could be very normal (for example, having a briefcase and carrying a topcoat over the arm), a combination of several of the indicators may be regarded as suspicious.

Deterring Shoplifting

Numerous approaches to deter shoplifting are open to management. Commonly used preventive measures include training personnel, implementing antishoplifting merchandising techniques and using physical and procedural controls. Such deterrents discourage borderline thieves and help trap bold ones.

The 1994 National Retail Security Survey identified four main ways to detect shoplifters, summarized in Table 16–2.

> The single most effective deterrent to shoplifting is surveillance by an alert, trained sales force. This may be supplemented by security officers or **floorwalkers.**

People are "key" to detecting shoplifting, with employees detecting 84.1 percent of shoplifters according to the 1994 National Retail Security Survey (Table 16–2).

Grevenites (1992, p. 80) advises: " 'Hi, may I help you?' are the last words a criminal [shoplifter] wants to hear." Clerical attention to customers may be

Table 16–2. Methods of Detecting Shoplifters

Method of Detection	Mean %
Floor Employees	55.5
Security Employees	28.6
Article Surveillance	10.4
Customer Tip-Offs	3.6
Other Detection	1.9

SOURCE: Security Research Project, University of Florida, Gainesville, Florida. Reprinted by permission.

the single most important factor in deterring shoplifting. Self-service establishments that save in personnel costs may simply be trading such savings for increased losses from shoplifting.

Sales personnel should be trained in the characteristics that may indicate shoplifting as well as in the common methods of shoplifting. This can be done by films, demonstrations, talks, pamphlets, posters and conferences. It is important, however, not to teach personnel how to shoplift themselves. In some instances, employees have become intrigued with the ingenuity of various shoplifting methods and have attempted the same methods themselves.

In addition to being alert and observant, sales personnel should be trained to serve all customers promptly. Fast, efficient service will usually deter shoplifting, especially that committed by youths. True customers will appreciate this promptness; shoplifters will be aware that they are noticed. If the salesperson is busy with one customer when another enters, the salesperson should tell the customer, "I'll be with you in a minute." Salespeople should not turn their backs on customers, if possible. They should keep an eye on people who are "just looking" or wandering aimlessly around the store and should never leave the assigned area unattended.

Sales personnel may be supplemented by security officers or floorwalkers, at least during peak sales periods.

> Security officers are prevention oriented, seeking to deter crime by their presence. In contrast, floorwalkers are apprehension oriented, seeking to arrest and prosecute shoplifters.

Security officers, usually in uniform, may be positioned at entrances and/or exits and may also "float" around in a retail establishment, making their presence very obvious. Floorwalkers, on the other hand, pose as customers and seek to remain unnoticed so that they can catch shoplifters "in the act." Thus, the goals of trained salespeople and those of floorwalkers are often in direct conflict. Salespeople who approach customers, believing they may be about to shoplift, thwart the objectives of the floorwalker. Whether the focus should be on prevention or on apprehension is a critical management decision. Whatever approach is selected, working hours of personnel should be scheduled with floor coverage in mind.

Other deterrents to shoplifting that require little expense but that can result in great savings include merchandising techniques that thwart the would-be thief. Although modern merchandising rests on the premise that customers should be able to examine items, this also makes these items more susceptible to theft.

> Merchandising techniques to deter shoplifting include keeping displays orderly and not stacking merchandise too high; returning to the display any item looked at and not bought; keeping small, valuable items locked in display cases; placing identifying tags on all merchandise; displaying only one of a pair; not displaying expensive merchandise near exits and having small, easily stolen items located by the checkout.

Merchandise should be displayed in an orderly way so that any losses are very obvious. Counters piled high with merchandise or counters arranged in a haphazard fashion make it easier for the shoplifter to operate undetected.

Coat racks with expensive clothing should not be near a door because a thief may simply reach in and grab an armload of clothing. To discourage such acts, some stores alternate coat hangers, with every other one facing the opposite direction, making snatching an armload of clothing virtually impossible.

Small, easily stolen items such as razor blades, pens, film, gum, candy and the like are frequently displayed close to the checkout. Additionally, all merchandise should be clearly identified as store property.

Procedural controls are another inexpensive way to counter shoplifting losses. Although retail establishments vary tremendously in size and merchandise, they all share one common need: an effective point of sale (POS) system. Brooks (1992, p. 50) notes:

> All POS systems collect information, such as inventory levels, total sales, tendering media, and cashier activity. . . .
>
> A POS system's ability to secure specific report information, particularly when coupled with exception handling, provides a powerful tool to authenticate operations.

> Procedures such as keeping unused checkout lanes closed, locking the back door, having package checks, carefully checking price tags and bar codes, maintaining tight controls on fitting rooms and restrooms, issuing receipts, controlling refunds and establishing a communication system are important in deterring shoplifting.

Checkout Lanes. Requiring that customers pass by a checkout before leaving a store is a good deterrent to shoplifting. Unused checkout lanes should be chained or blocked off.

Package Inspections. All packages brought into a store should be inspected and stapled closed or checked. If a package inspection policy is clearly posted, customers should have no objection to having packages examined. Some stores require all packages to be checked before customers are allowed to enter the merchandise areas.

Price Tag Checks. Salesclerks should be alert to price tags that look as though they have been altered or to prices that seem too low for the article. Prices that are stapled to items may use a specific staple pattern recognizable to the clerk. Prices marked in ink will deter price changing, and prices fastened with strong plastic string will deter price switching. Other price tags are available that fall apart when they are removed. These are commonly used in liquor stores. Extreme care must be exercised if a clerk suspects price changing or switching, as such changes are almost impossible to prove unless the acts are actually observed. In fact, the price may have been changed by a customer who intended to shoplift the article and who then thought better of it. An innocent person may then have recognized the bargain and selected the item, with no intent to steal from the merchant.

Clerks should also be alert to possible instances of carton switching or instances of smaller items being concealed within larger items being purchased.

Bar Codes. Bar codes can also be tampered with. In one case a Florida couple used sophisticated equipment to produce false price codes—for example, changing a bar code from $129.00 to $12.90. Working with an organization specializing in such crimes, the couple would then obtain a receipt for the merchandise from the organization and return it to the store for full price. This type of fraud could net $6,000 to $7,000 a day.

Fitting Rooms. Fitting rooms pose a particular problem for security. Some clothing stores shorten the doors on their fitting rooms so that the legs and head of the average person are visible. One simple procedure to deter someone from shoplifting while in a fitting room is to limit the number of people allowed in the rooms and the number of items a person may take in. Many clothing stores have sales personnel stationed at the fitting room entrance to issue a color-coded marker or a number indicating the number of garments taken into the fitting room and to then check the number of items brought back out. Frequently fitting rooms are kept locked when not in use, requiring customers to ask a salesperson for the key to enter. Sales personnel should watch to see that old clothes are not replaced by new clothes and that price tags have not been altered. They should check fitting rooms for discarded price tags (sometimes stuck behind mirrors) or for empty hangers, indicators that shoplifting has occurred. Packages should never be allowed into fitting rooms.

Receipts. All purchases made should be accompanied by a receipt. If this policy is followed without exception, a person having an article from the store and no receipt can be assumed not to have paid for it. Closely related to this policy, however, is the potential problem presented by receipts lying around that another customer can pick up and use as proof of purchase. If the customer does not take the receipt, as is often the case with cash register tapes, the salesclerk should immediately discard the receipt. Some establishments counter this problem by stapling the receipt to the bag or by placing it inside the bag rather than handling it to the customer or placing it on the checkout counter.

Refund Procedures. A refund procedure should be established and followed to prevent shoplifters from stealing merchandise and then returning it for cash. Many establishments require the original sales slip before a refund will be given. Others give no refunds but will allow credit toward other purchases. In any event, the refund system should require written documentation of the name, address and telephone number of the person receiving the refund, the reason for the return and the amount refunded. The identification of the returner should also be verified. Periodic audits of the refund vouchers will indicate if one person is making a suspiciously large number of returns.

Communication System. A communication system is also important in deterring shoplifting, especially in larger stores having many departments. Sales personnel who notice someone acting suspiciously can alert a security officer or floorwalker to take up surveillance or can warn other sales personnel if the person is heading for their department. Close cooperation is needed. A warning system should exist to alert all sales personnel when the presence of a shoplifter is suspected. In smaller stores, this might simply be a code word.

Although they require some capital outlay, physical controls often pay for themselves in preventing shoplifting losses.

> Physical controls to deter shoplifting include changing the actual store layout, posting signs, installing locks and alarms and installing surveillance equipment such as convex mirrors and/or CCTV.

Physical Layout. The physical arrangement of a store can aid or hamper the would-be thief. The physical layout can be changed to eliminate too many entrances and exits, merchandise too close to doors, crowded aisles, display counters that obstruct the salesperson's view and incorrect placement of the cash register. Low counters in orderly rows are a good deterrent to shoplifters, as is adequate lighting. The checkout counter should be positioned so that sales personnel can view the display area. The cash register and phone should be located so that the checkout person does not need to turn away from the display area while ringing up sales or taking phone calls.

Some stores locate the office and accounting department on a balcony that offers a view of the entire floor below. All back exits should be locked if fire regulations permit. Otherwise they should be alarmed.

Signs. Signs stating "Shoplifters will be prosecuted" may deter shoplifting, but as indicated in at least one study, such signs may plant the idea in the mind of someone who had not thought of it before. The signs may also cause the store to be selected as a target by juvenile shoplifters because they see it as posing a greater risk and challenge.

Locks. Locks are also effective. Display cabinets can be locked, as can valuable items such as stereos and televisions. Furs may be locked to hangers that are not removable. Such locks are often supplemented by alarms. For example, a rack alarm may be activated if someone attempts to remove permanent hangers. Display case lock alarms may go off if the case is not locked. The weight of the salesperson on the mat by the lock overrides the alarms.

Alarms. Loop alarms, coaxial cables that form a closed electric circuit, may be looped through handles of expensive items such as televisions and photographic equipment; if the cable is cut or broken, the alarm sounds. Cable alarms, coaxial cables with a pad that is attached to merchandise, may be used with merchandise that has no holes or handles, such as computers and fax machines.

Other alarms are operated by pressure. For example, a wafer switch alarm can be set under an object. If the object is lifted, the alarm goes off. The removal of as little as one ounce of pressure may activate the alarm. In contrast, the ribbon switch alarm is activated when pressure is applied. Such alarms are often used on furniture or large appliances. Anyone attempting to lift such items will set off the alarm. Plug alarms are simple devices used for calculators, typewriters, stereo equipment and televisions. When such merchandise is unplugged, the alarm sounds. Art dealers often use a special type of canvas painting alarm that is sensitive to any vibration, such as that caused by a thief attempting to remove the painting from its frame.

Electronically activated price tags are being used more and more. Such tags set off an alarm if the item is taken from the store with the price tag still on. These tags may be wafers, pellets or long plastic strips which are removed with a special instrument by sales personnel. Anyone attempting to remove the tags without the instrument will damage the article. There is a real danger, however, if sales personnel are not meticulous about removing the tags. Should a tag be left on carelessly, an innocent customer will set off the alarm. Lawsuits may result. For example, in *Dent v. May Department Stores Company (1982),* a customer at one of the defendant's stores was stopped by a security guard as she was about to leave the store. A skirt she had purchased at the store had activated a buzzer because the cashier had failed to remove a magnetized surveillance device designed to detect shoplifters. The customer filed an action for false arrest and imprisonment, and the case made its way to the

District of Columbia Court of Appeals. The court ruled in favor of the store, observing that the guard had probable cause to detain the customer when the alarm sounded. Also, because the guard allowed the customer to leave once the tag was removed, the customer was *not* illegally detained.

Such electronic article surveillance (EAS) is a cost-effective weapon against shoplifting. Lottes (1992, p. 20A) notes: "Close to 60 percent of the retailers surveyed cited EAS as the most effective technique in fighting theft." Lottes describes the three predominant technologies currently used by EAS:

- Microwave—the oldest form, typically found in apparel stores protecting clothing with a highly visible hard tag.
- Magnetic—initially used in libraries to protect books from theft.
- RF—radio frequency tags or labels contain a paper-thin, RF-printed circuit which activates an alarm when it passes between sensors. These tags or labels can be integrated in the POS scanners so that they are deactivated when scanned for price.

Klein (1991, p. 58) describes the latest development in EAS—source tagging:

> In source tagging, the security circuit is embedded in a product or in product packaging at the point of manufacture. Shoplifters will no longer be able to determine which products are protected.

Surveillance Devices. Surveillance devices are also commonly used in retail establishments. Wide-angle (convex) mirrors are one inexpensive, effective surveillance device. Sometimes called detection mirrors, they are often used in fitting room aisles, in difficult-to-see areas of an establishment and above book racks and displays of merchandise likely to be stolen. Some security experts, however, feel that such mirrors enhance safety more than they deter shoplifting because they distort the image. It is critical that salespersons, guards or floorwalkers see the stolen object clearly. Flat mirrors in hard-to-see areas are perhaps more satisfactory in this respect because they do not distort the image.

Many stores use CCTV, with the cameras very obviously mounted to act as a deterrent. Some even have signs such as "Smile, You're on Camera," and phony cameras interspersed with functional cameras, giving the impression of greater coverage. CCTV cameras can pan the entire display area, but they must be continuously monitored to be effective. Videotape recording (VTR) equipment is sometimes preferred because it is a permanent record, can "replay" an incident and does not have to be watched continually. Some stores use a combination of CCTV and VTR equipment. As noted by Tyska and Fennelly (1987, pp. 262–63), by the year 2000:

> In-house protection of stock will continue to use the principles of electronic article surveillance, closed circuit television and two-way radio communication. But a strong likelihood exists that physical protection in the form of locks, bolts and bars, etc., will be far more dominant than it is in the 1980's.
>
> Article surveillance tags will serve a dual purpose to their present primary function. They will also bear pure merchandising information such as stock codes and selling prices.

> By the year 2000, closed circuit television within retail outlets, probably linked with a two-way sound facility, will be far more widespread and flexible, in color and accepted as being an effective tool of management in fields other than pure security. Fiber optics will be considered as the normal means of picture communication.

Peepholes, two-way mirrors and CCTV in dressing rooms may present legal problems for merchants. State statutes regarding such surveillance should be checked carefully before such procedures are used.

Many other deterrents to shoplifting have been implemented in retail establishments. Some stores have an employee incentive program that rewards personnel who assist in deterring or apprehending shoplifters. Others have encouraged customers to help in the detection of shoplifting. For example, the General Mills Honesty Patrol encourages supermarket customers to report retail theft. Customers are given "Honesty Patrol" buttons and can report any retail thefts anonymously. They do not have to confront the suspect. Educational programs in the schools can also help deter shoplifting.

In addition, a careful system of inventory control so that the magnitude of the problem can be recognized and a careful record of shoplifters detained (whether prosecuted or not) can help combat shoplifting. Such a list can be circulated to other merchants, provided it is marked "Confidential." Many cities have established a merchants' protective association to assist in maintaining and circulating a central list of shoplifters and bad-check passers.

Keep in mind, however, that all the preceding procedures and devices are supplemental to an alert, trained sales force—the first line of defense against shoplifting.

Other Ways of Deterring Shoplifting

One innovative approach to deterring shoplifting is to use cardboard cutouts of police officers. A study in New Zealand showed that toy retailers could make up the cost of a year's rental of a cardboard cutout of a police officer within three days through reduced shoplifting ("Cardboard Cutouts Reduce Shoplifting and Speed," 1993, p. 161).

Another innovative approach is to enclose with floor-to-ceiling glass high-risk departments such as those with teenagers' trendy clothing—a frequent target of shoplifters—and provide only one entry/exit into the rest of the store.

Atlas (1992, p. 33A) cautions: "When business security is lax, profits can slip all too easily out the back door. This is particularly true in a retail setting." To address this problem of lax business security, Atlas suggests:

> One approach to crime prevention is through environmental design, often referred to as CPTED. Environmental designers consider three questions: What is the designated purpose of the business, and how will the building be used? How well is the space defined physically, socially, legally, and culturally? How well does the physical design support the intended function of the space and the desired or accepted behavior?

Atlas (p. 34A) gives examples of using the environment to advantage by placing unsafe activities in safe areas and vice versa. That is, vulnerable activities such as parking and cash machines should be in open spaces close to the building and visible from inside the building. Safe activities such as sidewalk sales and craft shows can be placed in parking lots that are usually empty.

Finally, the 1994 National Retail Security Survey ("Retail Shrinkage," 1995, p. 31) found that those companies with management or salesperson compensation levels equal to those paid by their competitors experienced lower shrinkage rates:

> Companies that believe their low wage scales are saving them money may want to reconsider that line of logic. . . . The money invested in bringing quality employees into the fold can have a measurable impact on the bottom line through lower shrinkage.

Jewelry Thefts

Wilson (1993, p. 61): contends that "most jewelry store thefts are committed by highly mobile, organized, and sophisticated gangs that know what they are looking for and know how to turn their bounty into quick cash."

As Frank and Serpico (1995, p. 51) note: "As retail jewelry operations have fortified their stores with alarms and CCTVs, those who sell jewelry to these outlets have become the 'soft' targets." They also note:

> A typical TJS [traveling jewelry salesperson] carries from $50,000 to $1 million worth of jewelry during daily visits to jewelry retailers. Usually forced to travel with bulky sample cases or bags needed to transport the jewelry, referred to in the industry as the "line," and dressed to impress customers in an industry that deals in some of the most beautiful baubles in the world, the TJS is easily targeted by cunning predators.

The Jewelers' Security Alliance (JSA) has developed a computer program called Polygon, a unique network for jewelers. Approximately 1,000 jewelers subscribe to Polygon, using the network to "publicize information on wanted criminals, send out advisories and alerts about frauds and scams, provide crime prevention tips, and distribute guidelines on topics such as remaining safe during an armed robbery" ("Criminal-Catching Computer," 1994, p. 16). Polygon is viewed as the "information superhighway for jewelers."

Another program to combat jewel thieves is a joint effort of Zale jewelry stores and the FBI, called JAG—the Jewelry and Gem Initiative. George Slicho, the Zale's vice president for loss prevention, inherited a reactionary-type security program and turned it around, saying (Wilson, 1993, p. 64): "My background in retailing taught me that you need to focus at least 50 percent of your energy on prevention, because if you don't, if you simply react, you'll be running in circles." The JAG program focuses on employee training, teaching them such techniques as asking for and holding a customer's driver's license while they are looking at expensive items. Another technique is to physically touch each item in the store valued at more than $500 at least twice a day to verify inventory.

Apprehension of Shoplifters

It is critical to distinguish the thief from the absent-minded shopper who simply walks out of a department or store carelessly, but not fraudulently, without paying for an article. Recall the earlier discussion of individuals with Alzheimer's disease. Shoplifters should be apprehended so that stolen merchandise can be recovered. This is a basic purpose of private security—to protect assets.

> To apprehend a suspect for shoplifting, someone must actually see the item being taken and concealed or be reasonably certain an item has been taken, and the suspect must be kept under *continuous* observation until apprehension is made. This may occur on the premises or outside the premises, depending on state statute.

Mere suspicion is not enough. There must be evidence of an intent to steal, including such actions as leaving the department or floor without paying, concealing the property, taking off price tags or having no money to pay for items.

Watch for all actions that make you suspicious, such as a person entering a fitting room with six dresses and coming out with only one, a fitting room with empty hangers and price tags lying all over, a person who goes into a fitting room with a relatively empty shopping bag and comes out with it bulging and the like. In such instances, a merchant or the merchant's employee can detain the person *if* reasonable grounds exist for believing shoplifting has occurred. In Minnesota, for example, state statute 629.366 states:

> "A merchant or merchant's employee who has reasonable cause for believing that a person has taken, or is in the act of taking, any article of value without paying therefor, from the possession of the merchant in his place of business or from any vehicle or premises under his control, with the intent to wrongfully deprive the merchant of his property or the use and benefit thereof or to appropriate the same to the use of the taker or any other person, may detain such person for the sole purpose of delivering him to a peace officer without unnecessary delay and then and there making a charge against such person to the peace officer. The person detained shall be informed promptly of the purpose of the detention and shall not be subject to unnecessary or unreasonable force, nor to interrogation against his will."

The key phrase in the preceding statute is **reasonable cause.** This is interpreted in the same way as **probable cause** by the courts. The United States Supreme Court has defined probable cause as "facts and circumstances within their knowledge and of which they had reasonable trustworthy information [that] were sufficient in themselves to warrant a man of reasonable caution in the belief that the suspect had committed a crime" (*Carroll v. United States,* 1925).

In many states, concealment is prima facie evidence of the intent to permanently deprive. In addition to seeing the item being taken, salespeople must provide continuous surveillance; otherwise, the suspect may pass the stolen merchandise to a confederate or simply get rid of it. The result would be "no case" and the risk of a false imprisonment suit.

A set procedure should be established for apprehending shoplifters. In most states it is no longer necessary for the shoplifter to leave the store, although prosecution is easier if the person has left the premises. In addition, an apprehension outside the store causes less commotion and interference with the store's operation. However, if the merchandise is valuable and the thief may get away if allowed to leave the premises, the suspect should be apprehended inside the store.

Usually salespeople do *not* apprehend shoplifters. Rather, they notify the manager, security officer or floorwalker. It takes courage and confidence to confront a shoplifter and a strong personality able to withstand verbal and sometimes even physical abuse. The person who does the apprehending should first seek assistance because the suspect may have an accomplice to come to the rescue. The apprehending employees should never call the suspect a "thief" or use the word "steal," nor should they touch the suspect unless absolutely necessary.

The usual procedure is for the person making the apprehension to identify himself, instruct the person to give up the merchandise, describe it specifically and state where it was taken from and then ask for the sales slip. If the suspect cannot product a receipt, he or she is taken to the office. Force can be used if necessary. Courts have repeatedly ruled that requiring a suspected shoplifter to return to a store once outside constitutes an arrest, even if no physical force is used.

Managers, security officers, floorwalkers or sales personnel may make a citizen's arrest, but must use extreme caution. It is usually better not to arrest until after questioning is completed.

Case law has upheld the right of management to search suspected shoplifters and to recover stolen property by force, if necessary. However, recent California Supreme Court rulings may preclude such practices in the future. In *People v. Virginia Alvinia Zelinski*, the California Supreme Court ruled that the Exclusionary Rule applies to private security officials when acting in a "public" capacity. In this case two detectives in Zody's Department Store observed a suspect put a blouse in her purse. They stopped Virginia Zelinski outside the store and returned her to the security office, where they opened her purse and retrieved the blouse as well as a vial later determined to contain heroin. She was subsequently charged with heroin possession. The trial judge allowed the evidence to be presented, stating that store detectives were not governed by the prohibition against unreasonable searches. On appeal, the California Supreme Court reversed this decision.

Historically, courts have allowed such evidence to be presented. In the Zelinski case, however, the judges viewed the actions differently, an important precedent.

A witness should be present when questioning a shoplifting suspect to avoid the charge that undue pressure was applied. Any involuntary confession is inadmissible, as is any confession given after prolonged questioning. The suspect should be treated courteously. If the suspect confesses, obtain a written confession to avoid civil lawsuits.

Detention has at least four very specific purposes (Hayes, 1992, p. 30A):

- To recover stolen merchandise.
- To identify the suspect.
- To learn the reasons for his or her actions.
- To decide whether to take criminal or civil action against the subject.

Persons detained on suspicion of shoplifting are often asked to sign a standard release form such as the following:

> I hereby release the person(s) who detained me in connection with this incident and his or her employees, superiors, principals and customers from any claim or demand arising out of or in connection with the incident.

Such waivers often are not upheld in court, however. If items are taken from the suspect, they should be marked with the initials of the person obtaining the evidence, as well as the place and date. Careful records should be kept of all persons apprehended, whether prosecuted or not.

Prosecution

Existing state statutes and the severity of punishment may be factors in whether prosecution is undertaken. In some states, punishment depends on the value of the item and how many times the person has been caught for a similar offense. Shoplifters may receive a fine and/or a jail sentence. In some states a civil suit can also be brought. Procedures for prosecuting juveniles must be especially well defined. In some states, such as California and Illinois, parents of minors are held civilly responsible for shoplifting offenses of their children.

The type of retailer most likely to prosecute, according to the National Retail Survey of 1994, was office supplies retailers (75.6%) followed by homecenter/hardware establishments (64.5%) and department stores (63.9%). The prosecution rates for shoplifting and for employee theft, discussed later in the chapter, are summarized in Table 16–3 (p. 494).

Some managers feel that all shoplifters should be prosecuted and that failure to prosecute even "first offenders" encourages shoplifting. They hold that the person who steals will also lie and may very well have shoplifted before but gotten away with it. Prosecution will serve as a deterrent to others, these managers argue. It will also help avoid false arrest suits and will improve security staff morale. Other managers, however, feel that criminal prosecution is a law enforcement objective that does not meet security (prevention) objectives.

Table 16–3. Prosecution Rates (in percents)

Type of Retailer	Employee Theft	Shoplifting
Auto Parts & Tires	36.8	56.7
Books & Magazines	24.2	41.5
Cameras & Photo	0.0	33.3
Cards, Gifts & Novelties	27.3	37.4
Catalog Showrooms	50.8	45.0
Consumer Electronics	73.9	15.0
Convenience Store	40.0	57.2
Department Store	58.4	63.9
Discount Store	43.9	51.0
Drug Store	21.0	28.3
Furniture	62.5	0.0
Homecenter/Hardware	32.3	64.5
Household Furnishings	22.9	5.6
Jewelry	25.0	52.5
Liquor/Wine/Beer	18.3	25.0
Office Supplies	0.0	75.6
Optical	7.9	10.7
Recorded Music/Video	20.7	46.4
Shoes	46.3	28.3
Specialty Men's Apparel	46.8	36.3
Specialty Women's Apparel	33.0	32.1
Specialty Other Apparel	26.3	56.6
Sporting Goods	41.7	48.5
Supermarket/Grocery	31.7	50.8
Toys & Hobbies	0.0	46.1
Other	40.5	0.0
OVERALL	35.2	44.9

SOURCE: Security Research Project, University of Florida, Gainesville, Florida. Reprinted by permission.

Even if a person has admitted guilt, the store does not always prosecute. There are many reasons for nonprosecution, including the fear of losing a good customer, the fear of damaging the store's reputation, the loss of time and the expense of testifying and the leniency of the courts to first offenders. Additionally, while security or sales personnel are in court testifying, the establishment is more vulnerable to other losses from shoplifting. Obviously, not all shoplifters will be prosecuted. Again, management must decide on goals and establish guidelines.

> Establish reasonable guidelines for prosecuting shoplifters. Consider the value of the article, along with the person's age, number of offenses and attitude. Guard against illegal detention, malicious prosecution and slander suits.

Factors to consider in establishing a policy on prosecuting shoplifters include the following:

- *Age*—Those 12 and under usually have their parents called and then are released to them. Those 13 to 16 are treated as juvenile offenders.
- *Monetary value*—Taking a 50¢ package of gum (a misdemeanor) differs from taking an $850 camera (a felony).
- *Past history*—A person with a past record of shoplifting is more likely to be prosecuted.
- *Attitude*—Is the suspect repentant and sorry or belligerent and hostile?
- *Strength of the case*—Are there witnesses, a confession, recovered property?

One primary reason for not prosecuting shoplifters is the time involved in going to court. Experiments in shoplifting courts may be a solution to this problem. In 1973 Cook County, Illinois, initiated the first shoplifting court system. This system used existing municipal courts to hear 100 or more cases each afternoon. Illinois also has the stiffest penalties for shoplifting convictions. Yet there is no evidence that the special courts or the stiff penalties have deterred shoplifting.

All personnel, and especially security personnel, should know how to avoid being sued for malicious prosecution.

Malicious Prosecution

According to Maxwell (1993, pp. 66–67): "Malicious prosecution . . . deals with the liability of persons who initiate prosecution for purposes other than enforcing the criminal law or bringing an offender to justice." In this tort the person making the accusation does not believe the accused is guilty but makes the charges out of spite, hostility or ill will to obtain an advantage over the person or to force the payment of money or the transfer of property. Says Maxwell: "Malice can be inferred from a lack or want of probable cause, circumstances surrounding the prosecution, or the motives of the accuser or instigator."

In the case of *Eastman v. Time Saver Stores, Inc.* (1983), a clerk, Mrs. Alice P. Eastman, brought a malicious prosecution action against her employer, Time Saver Stores, Inc. Eastman was employed on the 3:00 P.M. to 11:00 P.M. shift, and during this time there were repeated cash shortages. Eastman's supervisor and a member of the Time Saver security department helped another employee climb into an air-conditioning vent above the cash registers where he could observe Eastman. He saw Eastman put a handful of quarters, a $20 bill from the customer and a $20 bill from a special envelope into her pocket. Store employees closed the business and called the police. Eastman's explanation was that she was just holding the money temporarily and fully intended to put the funds in their proper place. In the case the judge ruled:

> Plaintiff's testimony explaining why she had store money on her person at the time of her arrest seems implausible. The fact that she even carried property

> on her person was suspicious in and of itself. The explanation by plaintiff does not overcome the other circumstances which led Time Saver to have her arrested. The store employees observing her testified she acted suspiciously when pocketing the money. There had been systematic cash shortages in the store which always coincided with her shift regardless of whom she worked with.

In this instance the business won. One alternative that might have saved the company the time and anxiety of a criminal trial would have been to seek civil recovery from the individual accused of theft.

Civil Recovery in Shoplifting Cases

One approach to dealing with apprehended shoplifters is to collect civil damages. As noted by Hayes (1992, p. 31A): "When a customer or employee steals from a company, that action is both a crime and a civil tort. In either action, a third party with legal expertise is needed." He suggests (p. 30A):

> Retailers may collect damages from shoplifters in addition to, or instead of, criminal prosecution in 42 states. Retailers can use "civil demand" laws to demand money from shoplifters without taking them to court, freeing retailers from costly court cases. . . .
>
> The idea is to pass the high cost of theft on to thieves instead of consumers. When the civil demand process is handled properly, merchants can significantly offset their annual security budgets. They also will discover that the civil penalty is an effective deterrent to both shoplifting and employee theft.

According to Hayes, most civil demand service companies charge a fee of 30 percent of the money collected.

Bad Checks

Most checks are cashed not in banks, but in retail stores. Some estimate that as many as 80 percent of all checks are cashed in retail stores. In essence, as a service to customers, retailers substitute for banks as the major supplier of cash. Providing this service, however, creates the risk of loss through bad checks. One-third of check losses are sustained by supermarkets, 30 percent by department stores and the next greatest amount by liquor stores and gas stations.

To reduce losses from bad checks, retailers should do the following:

- Teach personnel to recognize the different types of checks and the common types of bad checks.
- Establish a check-cashing policy and adhere to it.
- Train personnel to examine checks and identification.
- Record relevant information on the backs of all checks cashed.
- Reconcile identity documents with check passers' characteristics.

Types of Checks

Retail sales personnel are likely to encounter seven types of checks:

1. A *personal check* is written and signed by the individual offering it made out to the firm. This is the most commonly encountered check in retail establishments.
2. A *two-party check* is issued by one person to a second person who endorses it so that it may be cashed by a third person. This type of check is most susceptible to fraud because, for one thing, the maker can stop payment at the bank.
3. A *payroll check* is issued to an employee for services performed. Usually the name of the employer is printed on it, and it has a number and is signed. In most instances, "payroll" is also printed on the check. The employee's name is printed by a check-writing machine or typed. In metropolitan areas, you should not cash a payroll check that is handwritten, rubber stamped or typewritten as a payroll check, even if it appears to be issued by a local business and drawn on a local bank. It may be a different story in a small community where you know the company officials and the employee personally.
4. A *government check* can be issued by the federal government, a state, a county or a local government. Such checks cover salaries, tax refunds, pensions, welfare allotments and veterans' benefits, to mention a few examples. You should be particularly cautious with government checks. Often they are stolen, and the endorsement has been forged. In some areas, such thievery is so great that some banks refuse to cash Social Security, welfare, relief or income tax checks, unless the customer is known by or has an account with the bank. You should follow this procedure also. In short, know your endorser.
5. A *blank check,* sometimes known as a *universal check,* is no longer acceptable to most banks due to the Federal Reserve Board regulations that prohibit standard processing without the encoded characters. This check may be used. However, it requires a special collection process on the part of the bank, and, therefore, the bank incurs a special cost.
6. A *counter check* is still used by a few banks and is issued to depositors when they are withdrawing funds from their accounts. It is not good anywhere else. Sometimes a store has its own counter checks for the convenience of its customers. A counter check is *not* negotiable and is so marked. You should check local bank practices on blank checks and counter checks because of the coded magnetic tape imprints that many banks use for computer processing. Personal printed checks often have the individual's bank account number in magnetic code.
7. A *traveler's check* is a check sold with a preprinted amount (usually in round figures) to travelers who do not want to carry large amounts of cash. The traveler signs the checks at the time of purchase and should countersign them only in the presence of the person who cashes them.

In addition, a *money order* can be passed as a check. However, a money order is usually bought to send in the mail. Most stores should not accept money orders in face-to-face transactions. Some small stores sell money orders. If yours does, never accept a personal check in payment for money orders. Purchasers having a valid checking account do not need money orders. They can send a check in the mail.

High-risk checks include second-party checks, counter checks, illegible checks, post-dated checks and out-of-town checks.

Types of Bad Checks

Writing a "bad" check is a crime. It may be either forgery or fraud, depending on the type of check written. In either event, bad checks are of major concern to businesses. Often forged traveler's checks and other such drafts that on their face are valid will not be paid to the company if they have been fraudulently passed. That is, traveler's checks are as good as cash for the purchaser, but many issuing banks treat a forged traveler's check just like any other forged check and will refuse to pay the party who cashes it.

The most common types of bad checks are forged or altered checks, no-account checks and nonsufficient funds checks.

Forged checks include stolen checks bearing a forged endorsement on the back, deliberately altered third-party checks such as Social Security or government checks or payroll checks endorsed to a retail merchant. The amount of the check may also be raised or the name of the payee changed. Counterfeit checks may be printed to resemble payroll or government checks.

No such account (NSA) checks are those drawn on an account that never existed or that has since been closed. Although sometimes such checks are honest mistakes, they often are written by a person who deposits money to obtain checks and then closes the account, writing several checks over a weekend before the fraud can be detected.

Nonsufficient funds (NSF) checks are drawn against an account that exists but does not contain enough money to cover the check. The majority of such checks are honest mistakes caused by such things as mathematical errors in the check ledger, failure to record checks written or two people having checkbooks for the same account and not keeping careful records. Most NSF checks will be cashed when they are deposited a second time, but often with a hefty fee attached.

Incorrectly written checks are also often returned by the bank unpaid. Mistakes can include an incorrect date, a discrepancy between the amount in figures and that written in words or a questionable signature.

Only a small percentage of money lost through bad checks is recovered, so *prevention* is the key to reducing losses from bad checks.

Establishing Check-Cashing Policies

Every retail establishment should establish a check-cashing policy and post it. Customers will therefore not feel they are being treated unfairly, and employees will be constantly reminded to enforce the policies. The following check-cashing policies are among those often established by retailers:

- No checks cashed.
- No checks cashed above the amount of purchase.
- Checks cashed for only $X over the amount of purchase.
- No out-of-town checks.
- No two-party checks.
- No government checks.
- No checks cashed unless registered with the store.
- No checks cashed unless registered with a check verification system.
- No checks cashed without proper identification.
- No checks cashed without two pieces of identification.
- All checks over $X must be authorized by the supervisor.
- All checks over $X must be verified by the bank.
- No checks cashed that are numbered lower than 300.

Although the first policy is the simplest and safest, it also may result in losing many customers who do all their purchasing by check and do not carry much cash.

Examining Checks

Personnel who cash checks should be taught how to examine all checks presented to them.

> Checks should be carefully examined. Look at the printed name and address, check number, date, payee, numerical and written amount, bank and address and signature (or endorsement). Accept no checks that are illegible, that are not written in ink or that contain erasures or written-over dates or amounts.

The name of the person holding the account, the address and often the phone number are usually printed in the upper left corner of the check. These should be compared with identification presented. The address and/or phone number can also be verified in a local phone directory. The number on a personal check should be examined. Most banks begin their numbering sequence with 101 and continue in sequence. Experience shows that more personal checks under 300 are returned than are those over this number. Bad-check passers, however, may be aware of this and request that their numbering begin with a number over 300.

The date should be correct. A check with no date, a date later than the actual date (post-dated) or a date more than 30 days ago should not be accepted.

The dollar amount in digits and the amount in words should be identical. If the amount of the check is over the amount of the purchase, many establishments record the actual amount of purchase at the top of the check. Personnel authorized to cash checks should be aware that most bad-check passers write checks for between $25 and $30, assuming that retailers will be less suspicious than if they wrote the check for a greater amount. Checks over a certain amount frequently require authorization by a supervisor.

The check should also indicate the name of the bank and its address. Extra care should be used in examining a check drawn on a nonlocal bank.

Finally, the signature or endorsement should be checked and compared with the identification required. Be wary of checks in which the maker's name is preceded by a title (Mr., Mrs., Ms., Dr., etc.) or extends past the allotted space.

Examining Identification

Many establishments require at least two pieces of identification before a check may be cashed. However, a person who steals checks may also steal identification.

> Persons presenting checks to cash should be required to produce identification containing a physical description (preferably a photograph) and a signature. The description should be compared with the person; the signature should be compared with the signature on the check.

Owens (1990, p. 18) suggests these measures to reduce losses from bad checks:

- Collect as much information as possible: driver's license number, bank check guarantee card, place of employment and employer's phone number.
- Examine the check and customer's ID carefully for signs of alteration. Checks without perforation marks, for example, may be forged duplicates. Also check the signature against another piece of signed identification, and be sure the photo on a photo ID matches the person presenting the check. If the check is large—and you have the time—call the bank or the employer for verification.

Acceptable forms of identification include driver's licenses, military or government IDs and national credit cards. Always check the date on the identification to be sure it is current.

The following should *not* be used as identification:

bank books
birth certificates
business cards
club or organization cards
customer's duplicate cards
initial jewelry
insurance cards
learner's permits
letters
library cards
Social Security cards
unsigned credit cards
voter's registration cards
work permits

In addition, some stores use photo-identity cameras that take a picture of the person writing the check, the check itself and the identification presented. If a check is returned, the specific section of film bearing that check number can be developed and used in attempting to identify the bad-check passer.

Some establishments also make use of a thumbprint made without ink on the back of the check as a means of identification.

Recording Information

The identification presented should be recorded on the back of the check. Many establishments use a stamp such as the one shown in Figure 16–2 (p. 502). In addition, the person who accepts the check should initial it, in the event that later identification of the person writing the check is required. If a supervisor is called to authorize the check, the supervisor should also initial the check.

A list of all returned checks should be kept at each checkout, and sales personnel should compare checks presented against this list. Some merchants tape bad checks to the register, an embarrassing situation for a local bad-check passer. The list of bad checks can also be circulated among retailers in a city.* Such cooperation can help to minimize bad-check losses. All check law violators should be reported to the local authorities. Merchants should know their state laws regarding bad checks and should prosecute when possible.

Refusing Checks

Retailers do *not* have to accept checks if they are suspicious of the person presenting the check, even if the person presents the required identification. Checks should not be accepted if they have the word *hold* written on them or if the person presenting the check is intoxicated or acting suspiciously. Sometimes bad-check passers will wave to someone in the store, often another employee, drop names of people who work there or claim to be "old customers." Such actions should never cause the sales personnel to ignore established check-cashing policies.

---

*Posting/circulation practices may be illegal in some locations.

PRINT

Salesperson—Name and No.

Auth. Signature

Customer's Address

Home Phone Business Phone

Ident. No. 1

Ident. No. 2

Dept. No. Amount of Sale

Take Send COD Will Call

Figure 16–2. Check-Cashing Information Stamp

FRAUDULENT CREDIT CARDS

Use of credit cards is a way of life for many Americans. Gardner (1985, p. 327) states that the average adult in our country carries five to six credit cards, with almost 550 million such cards in use: "With the increased use of credit cards as part of everyday life, the possibilities for fraud will continue to exist." He describes precautions being taken to deter such fraud, including hiring more investigators, making careful checks before credit is extended and verifying shipments of cards that are sent out to make sure the true cardholder has placed the order. Even though fraud constitutes a small fraction of total credit-card sales, Gardner contends that "yearly losses in the United States are estimated between $100 and $300 million in credit card fraud."

Gardner suggests that burglars, robbers and thieves have many and varied methods of obtaining credit cards for fraudulent use, including picking pockets and snatching purses. Or a prostitute might decide that stealing credit cards is more profitable than "turning tricks." Restaurant, retail store or gas station employees might simply keep a card after completing a transaction. Or the cards might be stolen from the mail or during a burglary. In some instances credit card applications have been stolen from the mail or retrieved from a trash can, completed by another person, and submitted using the intended applicant's name but the thief's address and signature. They can also be counterfeited or altered, or obtained through corrupting credit-card manufacturer employees or postal employees.

According to Gardner, it is also easy to obtain credit-card numbers. He cites as an example a woman who asked a drugstore to save the used carbons from credit-card purchases for her child to do a school project. The store complied, setting aside bundles of carbons for her. The woman then used these numbers to make unauthorized charges at other stores. The same care that is exercised in accepting checks should be used in accepting credit cards. The signature should be compared with that on the sales charge slip. The expiration date should be examined. Frequently, stores have a **floor release limit,** meaning that any charge above a certain amount must be cleared through the credit-card company. Some stores have a **zero floor release limit,** meaning that all charges are cleared with the credit-card issuer.

> Protect against losses from fraudulent use of credit cards by comparing the signature on the card with that on the sales slip, checking the card's expiration date and establishing a reasonable floor release limit.

In addition to the various types of theft of credit cards or numbers, other fraudulent uses of credit cards include the following (Gardner, 1985, p. 328):

- Knowingly receiving stolen credit cards.
- Use of a credit card without the cardholder's consent.
- Use of a revoked or canceled credit card.
- Knowing use of a counterfeit or altered card.
- Illegal use of a credit card number (or use of the pretended number of a fictitious card).
- Use of an illegally possessed card to negotiate a check.
- Receiving or possession of an illegally obtained card with intent to defraud.
- Delivery or sale of an illegally obtained credit card.

Illegal use of credit-card numbers to make long distance phone calls is a major concern. Gardner gives as examples a Michigan labor union that received a phone bill for approximately $321,000 and a New York woman who received a bill for $109,500. He suggests, because the calls are often global and the practice is persistent, that much of the fraud is committed by organized narcotic and other criminal groups wanting to avoid detection by law enforcement officials or the IRS.

The illegal use of a credit-card number (rather than the card itself) *is* fraud, as established in the case of *United States v. Bice-Bey* (1983), in which the Fourth Circuit Court of Appeals held that "the core element of a credit card is the account number, not the piece of plastic."

RETAIL EMPLOYEE THEFT

"Employee theft is the primary cause of shrinkage to any retailer" (Bridges, 1994, p. 22A). The 1994 National Retail Security Survey found that 42.1 percent of annual shrinkage losses were due to employee theft (32.4 percent were due to shoplifting, 19.2 percent were due to administrative error and 6.3 percent were due to vendor fraud). Addis (1991, p. 115) says: "According to the Department of Commerce, employees steal as much as $120 billion a year from their employers. A third of all employees steal from their companies in some form." Further, as Chapman (1994, p. 26) notes, the FBI has estimated that three of every five business bankruptcies are primarily due to internal theft.

Many losses assumed to be the result of customer shoplifting may actually have been caused by employees. Employees have an easier time shoplifting because they know what security measures exist, and they may frequently be in a department alone. In addition, turnover in personnel may be high, and extra personnel may be added during peak seasons when the risk of theft is known to be higher than usual.

Security measures previously discussed have special relevance to curbing retail losses. First, have effective preemployment screening so that honest employees are hired. Next, establish the proper climate for honesty. Employees who are treated fairly and paid fairly are less likely to steal from their employers. A "zero shortage" attitude should be adopted, maintained and rewarded.

Just as people are key to detecting shoplifting, so people are key to detecting employee theft, with coworker tip-offs responsible for 39.5 percent of employee dishonesty detection (as shown in Table 16–4). Incentives to reduce employee theft include the following:

- Make certain each person is matched to his or her job.
- Set reasonable rules and enforce them rigidly.
- Set clear lines of authority and responsibility.
- Give employees the resources they need to achieve success.
- Be fair in rewarding outstanding performance.
- Remove the temptation to steal.

In addition, physical and procedural controls are essential. Limiting the number of employee exits, keeping storerooms locked and allowing entrance only by authorized personnel, checking lockers and packages, flattening trash and restricting access to assets, as feasible, should all be part of the retail security plan.

CCTV can be an effective deterrent against internal theft (Tesorero, 1993, p. 34):

Table 16–4. Methods of Detecting Employee Dishonesty

Method of Detection	Mean %
Coworker Tip-Offs	39.5
Exception Reports	18.2
Security Audits	16.1
Electronic Surveillance	11.7
Other Detection	8.1
Shopping Service	6.5

SOURCE: Security Research Project, University of Florida, Gainesville, Florida. Reprinted by permission.

Always a deterrent for external crime, sophisticated CCTV systems are also effective against employee theft, particularly in cash-based fast-food operations, such as Hardee's. . . .

Reviewing and reacting to the information on the videotapes is crucial to the success of the system.

Special employee security problems in retail establishments include access to merchandise and cash. Specific pricing procedures, cash-handling procedures and refund procedures are essential. Personnel should be rotated periodically, and responsibilities should be separated.

Pricing

One major cause of inventory shrinkage is loosely controlled pricing procedures. Price switching or price altering can be done either by employees or by customers. The pricing procedures suggested earlier should thwart such actions.

To deter employee theft by price alterations:

- Allow only authorized employees to set prices and mark merchandise.
- Mark merchandise by machine or rubber stamp, never pencil.
- Conduct periodic audits of prices recorded and prices changed.
- Check on the "popular" salesperson.

A special risk is the salesperson who adds extra items to a customer's purchases to win the favor of that customer or who undercharges friends or relatives. Clerks who sell articles to friends and/or relatives at lower cost (called **sliding**) will find that once they start, they cannot stop without losing friends. Although the "popular" salesperson is certainly an asset to an establishment, his or her popularity should be for the right reasons. In one instance customers stood in line to wait for one saleswoman, refusing to be served by anyone else. Investigation revealed that she switched tickets for many "special" customers, giving them substantial markdowns. Store losses amounted to about $300 a week, not including the $25 a week in increased commissions for the dishonest saleswoman. Pay special attention to salespeople who are visited by too many personal friends. To discourage such socialization, some retailers hire employees who live outside the store's vicinity.

Employees who are allowed to make purchases at a discount may abuse the privilege and buy for friends and relatives, or sometimes even for resale at a profit, setting themselves up in direct competition with their employer. To thwart such actions, a manager or supervisor should make all employee sales and should keep a record to see that the cumulative amount is reasonable

In addition, employees should not shop until the end of the day and should leave the premises after their shopping is completed.

Other methods of cheating employers include picking out expensive clothes and putting them on layby or lay away* under a fictitious name. Then, when the clothes are out of season and are put on sale, the employee purchases them at a considerable savings.

In restaurants, unauthorized consumption of food and drink can result in tremendous losses. Policies establishing what employees can and cannot eat or drink while on the job should be clearly established.

Cash Handling

Cash is particularly vulnerable to theft. The customer who hurriedly lays the correct change on the counter and leaves without waiting for a receipt presents an especially tempting situation for cash-handling personnel. All cash-handling personnel should be properly trained, supervised and rewarded for efficiency and honesty.

To reduce losses of cash:

- Establish strict cash-handling procedures.
- Use a tamper-proof recording system.
- Have each clerk responsible for his or her own receipts.
- Have cash receipts balanced by someone else.
- Perform unannounced audits.
- Use honesty shoppers.

Cash receipts can be handled in many ways. One of the most common is the *cash register system* in which each transaction is recorded on a tape. When this system is used, each clerk should have his or her own register and be responsible for the receipts, but someone other than the clerk should balance it. When the sale is made, the clerk should call back the price of each item, the total amount of the sale and the amount of money tendered, and then count back the change. The customer should always be given a receipt. Failure to do so is usually indicative of poor supervision. The cash drawer should be closed after each transaction.

Several methods may be used to steal money from the cash register, often called "till tapping." Clerks may fail to ring up a sale and simply pocket the money. They may purposely shortchange people. They may deliberately under-ring a purchase and then "catch" the error, adding the charge manually

*Putting money "down" on an item so that the store will save it for the customer until the full payment has been made.

to the customer's receipt and receiving the full price from the customer. The added amount would not show on the tape, and the clerk would be free to pocket the money. Clerks may also enter an over-ring, as though to correct an error, when they are actually pocketing the money. Supervisors should make periodic checks of the registers to ensure they balance. A clerk who is consistently over or under the correct amount should probably be given a job that does not involve handling money.

In one instance a clerk in a pharmacy stole $5,000 from her employer during the year. It was a policy of the store that all customers receive a written receipt to be used for income tax purposes. The clerk used this receipt to cover her dishonest actions. She gave the customer the receipt and kept the payment. If the payment was by check, she put the check in the drawer and took out a comparable amount of cash. An audit eventually revealed five checks totaling $96.41 that were not recorded on the register tape.

In addition to audits, other ways to prevent such thefts are available; for example, a *validating cash register* uses a process in which each check is inserted into the register with the amount rung up printed on the check. Another safeguard is to have registers that display a readout of the transaction on the customer's side, so the customer and store supervisory personnel can observe the amount easily.

A second frequently used system is the *written sales slip system,* in which each salesclerk has a sales book. In such a system, all sales slips should be numbered in sequence and duplicate slips kept in the book. Periodic audits of cash in the register and amounts shown in the sales book should be made.

A third commonly used system of handling cash is the *autographic register system,* which uses a locked box into which the audit copy of the sales ticket is cranked when the customer's copy is removed. Again, such forms should be prenumbered. Key control is also essential when such a system is used.

Figure 16–3 (p. 508) illustrates one way to separate the functions of employees who deal with cash and how to trace transactions.

The cashier position in most retail establishments is an entry-level position with low pay and high turnover. Consequently, many managers do not invest much in training their cashiers. This can be a costly mistake. As Phelps (1992, p. 47) insists: "Management can prevent some of the losses through proper training, supervision, explanation of expectations, and a compensatory reward system."

> **Honesty shopping,** or a **shopping service,** tests the honesty of sales personnel who handle cash.

Retailers frequently hire personnel from security firms who offer shopping services, that is, professional shoppers who pose as customers and who then check for violations of cash-handling procedures. Such services are often used in retail stores, bars, restaurants and other sales establishments.

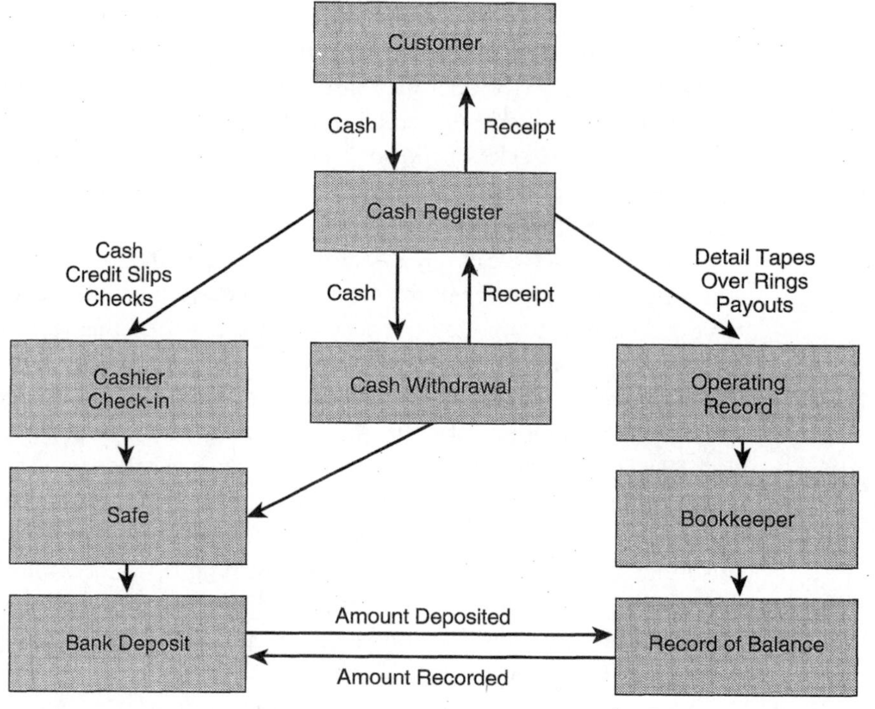

Figure 16–3. Retail Cash and Cash Flow Records
SOURCE: From the National Crime Prevention Institute. Reprinted by permission.

Typically, the honesty shopper makes a purchase using the correct change and leaves hurriedly (called a *put down*), the ideal situation for the till-tapping clerk. A second honesty shopper may observe whether the clerk rings up the sale, or the register tape may later be examined to see if that sale was recorded. Some honesty shoppers also use marked money. Remember, however, that employees may make an honest mistake, get busy and forget to ring up a sale. However, if it *is* an honest mistake, there will be an overage for that amount at the end of the day.

Honesty shopping is an effective means of discovering salespeople who are stealing cash. It can be used on a large scale and be repeated often. When employees are informed that such a system is used, it will also act as a psychological deterrent to potentially dishonest employees.

Honesty shopping may also be used to check on the sales personnel's efficiency and courtesy, information that is helpful for management. Some security experts feel that one person cannot effectively perform both types of evaluation at the same time and recommend that the store have two separate operations, an honesty shopper and a service shopper.

The fast-food industry faces some unique problems, including minimum wage employees and rapid turnover of employees. In addition, as Tesorero (1995, p. 64) notes: "The food service industry has seen a steady increase in liability claims brought by customers over the past several years." He cites as an example the high-profile case in which a fast-food restaurant was sued when several people died of food poisoning after eating the restaurant's hamburgers tainted with a deadly strain of E-coli bacteria. He notes that customers also complain to fast-food establishments about breaking their teeth while eating or finding foreign objects in the food or beverage. Determining the legitimacy of such complaints is often a challenge.

Security has much to offer fast-food establishments, as noted by D'Addario (1993, p. 30):

> Loss prevention practitioners, still ribbed with labels including "hamburger police" and "chicken cops," are earning the look and credibility of sophisticated profit centers. Security managers in the fast-food industry now contribute to policy design, loss reporting management and analysis, investigation, fraud detection, prevention technology development, capital investment recommendations, employee screening, and executive protection.

Refunds

It is easier for employees to abuse the return/refund system than it is for customers. Therefore, the same policies regarding refunds discussed previously should be rigidly applied to employees as well.

> Require all employees to comply with the return/refund policy. Keep tight control of all credit documents, and match items to the return vouchers. Conduct periodic audits of return vouchers.

Employees are often given first chance to buy damaged merchandise. Some may even intentionally damage merchandise to get the markdown. Often, however, an employee will purchase "as is" merchandise and then attempt to return it for a full refund. The merchandise should be inspected by someone other than the person who made the sale. Returned items should be carefully matched to the return vouchers and then returned to stock as quickly as possible.

Other times employees may report phony customer returns and refunds, simply pocketing the money. They may keep receipts left by customers and use the receipts to cover shortages. Periodic audits of refund vouchers should be made. Several people who presumably have received refunds should be called to verify that they actually did receive a refund and that the amount recorded was correct.

Employees who are found guilty of stealing from their employer usually should be fired. They also may be prosecuted either criminally or civilly. In many instances an employee who is terminated is asked to sign a statement such as the one shown in Figure 16–4 (p. 510).

MYTOWN RETAIL SALES CO.

STATEMENT

Date: ______________ Time: ______________ Page: ______________

I, ______________ Age, ______________ Date of birth, ______

Marital status, ______________ Address, ______________

Phone, ______________ Department, ______________

have been advised of my rights according to the company personnel rules and regulations, and herewith give this statement of my own free will and voluntarily to ______________ whom I know to be a security officer of the Mytown Retail Sales Co. No threats or acts of force have been made against me, nor have any promises of any kind been made to me. I understand that this statement will contain only facts for which I am responsible, and I wish to clear myself of other suspicions and do admit to the following:

____

____

____

____

____

____

____

____

____

____

____

____

Witness: Signature ______________

This is a true statement to the best of my knowledge.

____

____

Receipt

I have written and/or read the above statement consisting of ______ pages and have signed each page of ______ copies and have received one copy of this statement from ______ at ______ a.m./p.m.

Date: ______________ Signature for receipt ______________

Figure 16–4. Sample Employee Termination Statement

SHOPPING CENTER/MALL SECURITY

Shopping centers and malls are found throughout the country and pose special problems for security officers. The goal of these centers, like that of the individual establishments located within them, is profit. Because security represents a cost rather than a profit, it must make its contribution felt in other ways.

> The primary objectives of shopping center security are loss prevention and public relations.

Wilson (1992, p. 41) suggests: "Malls must balance the need to be easily accessible public places with the need to keep out the dangerous elements that such places attract." She also notes: "Security directors face some compelling challenges as shopping malls become America's new town centers." Wilson cites the results of a 1990 International Council of Shopping Centers Gallup Survey on Shopping Centers which indicated that people do feel safe in most shopping centers: "Eighty-six percent of respondents felt that shopping centers were safe places for their families to visit; 84 percent felt that security at a shopping center was better or the same as in a downtown area."

Nonetheless, problems are ever present, as described by Story and Black (1991, p. 76): "Stolen vehicles, burglaries from vehicles, shoplifting, credit card fraud, loitering youths, assaults—all of these and more, constitute the kinds of criminal offenses that occur at retail shopping centers."

Security officers providing services at shopping centers and malls might consider the following "quick tips for being seen" offered by Hively (1994, p. 20):

- White uniform shirts are more readily observed from a distance.
- Uniform hats also help officers to be viewed at a distance.
- The police-type uniform is more readily observed, than the blazer, more subdued look.
- Officers on foot patrol (interior) should walk more to the center of the aisle, rather than against the store fronts.

Such efforts are not, in themselves, sufficient, however, as pointed out by Durham (1994, p. 59):

> In an effort to counter negative customer perceptions, malls have tended to focus on gimmicks and techniques such as making security officers look more like police, making officers more visible, and distributing marketing materials on how to avoid crime. Security professionals should instead direct their efforts toward improving the underlying quality of the security force. The key is written operating procedures, detailed reports, proper treatment and training of the staff, and regular performance evaluations. The security director must also properly select and nurture leaders within the ranks who can handle the front-line supervisory responsibilities.

The predominant area of loss prevention is that of losses resulting from criminal activity—primarily theft. Potter (1984, p. 34) suggests that "effective shopping center security programs prevent criminal activity in three ways:

> *Deterrence.* Security must provide a highly visible, effective deterrent to criminal activity. Adequate lighting, alert and aggressive patrols, and appropriate physical security measures such as controlling access to nonpublic areas are all effective deterrents in a shopping center environment.
>
> *Detection.* No retail facility can deter all criminal activity and remain in business. However, an effective security program must be able to detect criminal activity, through the use of closed circuit television and intrusion alarm systems, for example, and then generate an appropriate response.

> *Limitation of loss*. The response to any threatened or actual criminal activity must be designed to prevent loss of life and limit or eliminate property losses and potential liability.

Losses from criminal actions are not the only type of losses for which security personnel are responsible. They should be observant and watch for any fire or safety hazards that could ultimately result in a loss.

The second primary objective of shopping center security is to promote good public relations. Potter emphasizes this (1984, p. 35): "To the shopping public, the uniformed security officer is shopping center management, and a sharply uniformed, courteous officer is a tremendous asset. Many shopping centers enhance this image by allowing officers on patrol in parking areas to assist customers by jump-starting cars with dead batteries, opening cars locked with the keys inside and even changing flat tires. Such tasks detract little or nothing from the officer's visibility and generate invaluable customer loyalty to the mall."

Some shopping centers have experimented with having their officers wear blazers and slacks rather than the more traditional, military-type uniforms. This does foster public relations, but research also shows that much of the deterrent effect of the highly visible, uniformed officer is lost.

Cosper (1993, p. 33) describes a new approach being used at Fashion Island, a 1.2-million-square-foot open-air shopping center in Newport Beach, California, and at North Star Mall, a 2.5-million-square-foot enclosed mall in San Antonio, Texas—bike patrol:

> Bike officers are involved in a preventive program. They assist in risk management by reporting or eliminating physical dangers or hazards for customers, be it from a spilled ice-cream cone, a pothole, or a suspicious person. Bike officers have a physical perspective of the property not available either to foot patrol officers or to officers in vehicles. . . .
>
> [T]he officers are also able to assist shoppers who have misplaced their keys, to give directions, to help lost children, and to assist individual merchants in improving their own in-store security.

Cosper (p. 34) reports that a study indicated that the bike patrol resulted in a 69 percent decrease in crime at Fashion Island and a 40 percent decrease at North Star Mall.

The Mall of America, in Bloomington, Minnesota, has 4.2-million square feet containing 400 retail stores, 30 restaurants, 14 theaters, eight nightclubs, an 18-hole miniature golf course and a seven-acre amusement park, Knotts Camp Snoopy (Cernock, 1993, p. 43). In addition to the millions of shoppers and sightseers, security must be concerned with more than 12,000 employees. Mall of America shoppers' security is assisted by 120 CCTV cameras, 125 emergency phones, 32 evacuation posts and a written emergency plan. Cernock (p. 45) also notes that security at the mall has "proved to be a lesson in cooperation between public and private security."

> The Mall of America project is one that will not soon be forgotten by those who took part in it. It exemplifies what instructors and authors have been

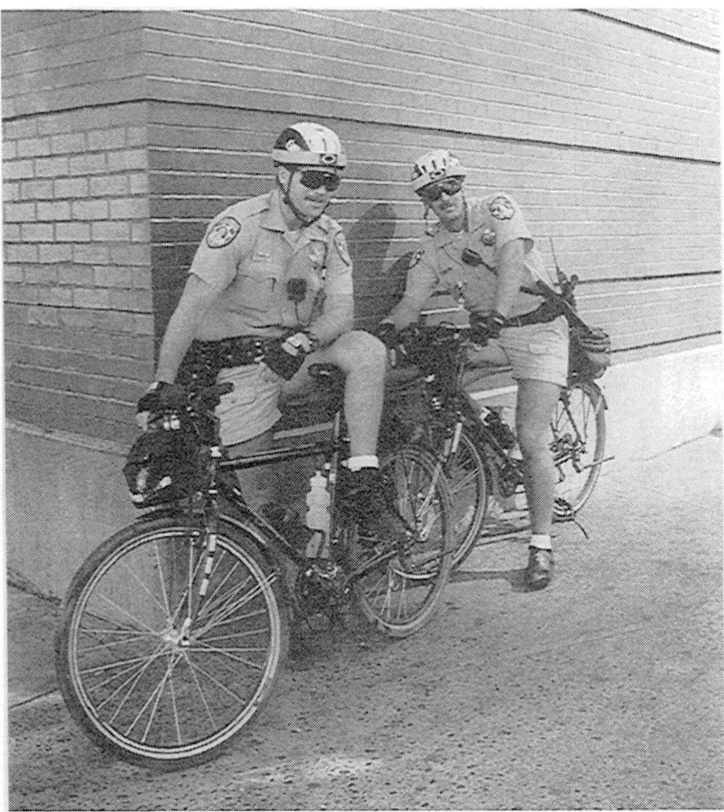

Bicycle patrols add another dimension to the security surrounding retail establishments and shopping centers/malls.

saying for years—cooperation between security and law enforcement can lead to success.

Another mall where the public and private security forces cooperate to provide improved safety is the Sawgrass Mills Mall in Sunrise, Florida, which typically has more than 50,000 shoppers and 3,000 employees each day. According to Perry (1992, p. 48):

> The Sunrise police maintain an office at the mall, and a police officer is stationed there when the mall is open. Should an incident occur, unarmed Sawgrass Mills security officers detain the suspect while a Sunrise police officer makes the arrest and detains the suspect in one of four on-site holding cells. The city has also placed emergency medical technicians on mall property.

Not all security experts favor the employment of public police at shopping centers and malls. According to Durham (1994, p. 63):

> The employment of police officers has obvious attractions, but there are negatives. The mall is already paying for police protection through its sizable contribution to the local tax coffers and the hourly pay rate for off-duty police

Security officers at the Mall of America practice good public relations when interacting with shoppers.

officers is high. In most markets, an hour of police time equates to about two security officer hours.

Additionally, managing police employees puts the security manager in a difficult position. Public safety support is important to a mall. When police officers double as mall employees, directing them or reprimanding them for conduct that is less than desirable is a delicate undertaking. Management can avoid these complications with a top quality private security staff.

Assistance in Enhancing Retail Security

Retail security requires that merchandise and cash be protected from internal (employee) and external (customer, burglar or robber) theft. Advice, assistance and information on retail security can be obtained from merchant's protection associations, retail credit bureaus, better business bureaus, police departments and/or district attorneys' offices. In addition, a retail security checklist such as that shown in Figure 16–5 might be used to identify areas of weakness in the security system.

Retail Security in the Future

Tyska and Fennelly (1987, p. 260) suggest: "The older type of multi-floored department or chain store will be a thing of the past. . . . Overall technological progress will be principally electronic with the micro-chip and micro-processor playing an even greater role than it does at present." They further suggest (1987, p. 261):

The application of security or loss control measures will have to be very clearly defined and positively enforced.

Although the general level of security staffing in retail establishments will be similar to today, the caliber of personnel involved will be much higher, far more retail management orientated. The actual job descriptions will be substantially upgraded. The days of second career security operatives will be long gone and career prospects will have to be offered to direct entry specialist security employees. Professional security associations and institutions will play a far greater and wider role in personal and general security education in retail communities.

Page 1 CRIME PREVENTION SURVEY COMPLAINT NUMBER
REQUEST ______ RETAIL BUSINESS ______ ____________
ROUTINE ______ RESIDENTIAL ______

Business Name ______________ Address ______________
Manager's Name ______________ Business Phone ______ Home Phone ______
Survey Date(s) ______________ Officer(s) ______________
Type of Goods ______________ Survey Based On ______________

		1 2 3			1 2 3
I. SAFE	a. Anchored	___	VI. BLDG (front)	a. Doors	___
	b. Visible	___		b. Locks	___
	c. Lighted	___		c. Windows	___
	d. Decals	___		d. Vents	___
	e. Locks operable	___		e. Lighting	___
II. CASH DEPOSIT	a. Excess in safe	___	VII. BLDG (left side)	a. Doors	___
	b. Excess in register	___		b. Locks	___
	c. Other locations	___		c. Windows	___
	d. Armored car	___		d. Vents	___
	e. Employee(s)	___		e. Lighting	___
III. EMPLOYEE TRAINING	a. Shoplifting	___	VIII. BLDG (rear)	a. Doors	___
	b. Robbery	___		b. Locks	___
	c. Till tap	___		c. Windows	___
	d. Short change	___		d. Vents	___
	e. Checks	___		e. Lighting	___
IV. EMPLOYEE SCREENING	a. Previous employers	___	IX. BLDG (right side)	a. Doors	___
	b. Neighbors	___		b. Locks	___
	c. Fingerprints	___		c. Windows	___
	d. Police record	___		d. Vents	___
	e. Polygraph	___		e. Lighting	___
V. EMPLOYEE ACCESS CNTRL	a. No. exterior keys	___	X. BLDG (roof)	a. Doors	___
	b. No. ex-emp. w/keys	___		b. Locks	___
	c. Date comb. changed	___		c. Skylights	___
	d. Date locks changed	___		d. Vents & ducts	___
	e. No. emp. opening and closing	___		e. Lighting	___

ADDITIONAL COMMENTS ______________________________

NOTE: 1–Adequate 2–Inadequate 3–Comments

Figure 16–5. Retail Security Checklist

SOURCE: Courtesy of Chattanooga Police Department.

Page 2 COMPLAINT NUMBER ____________

Emergency Call List:

NAME	POSITION	ADDRESS	PHONE

BURGLAR ALARM

	Yes	No	Comments:
A. Intrusion			
1. front	____	____	____
2. left side	____	____	____
3. rear	____	____	____
4. right side	____	____	____
5. roof	____	____	____
6. traps	____	____	____
7. safe	____	____	____
B. Robbery	____	____	____
C. Fire	____	____	____
D. Audible	____	____	____
E. Central Station	____	____	____
F. Police Dept.	____	____	____
G. Other (describe)	____	____	____
H. System last treated on:			____

Name and address of installing and maintenance alarm company:

NAME ____________ ADDRESS ____________

PHONE NUMBER ____________

ITEM NO.		ITEM NO.	

Figure 16–5. Retail Security Checklist *(continued)*

The 1994 National Retail Security Survey found that retailers projected an increase of use in honesty shoppers (20.6%), live CCTV (18.7%) and POS/CCTV interface (17.5%), as summarized in Table 16–5.

Tyska and Fennelly (1987, p. 263) stress: "One thing stands out. Full cognizance will have to be taken by management of loss control on a basis of

Table 16–5. Anticipated Change in the Use of Loss Prevention Systems

Loss Prevention System	% Projected Increase of Use
Honesty Shoppers	20.6
Live CCTV	18.7
POS/CCTV Interface	17.5
Electronic Anti-Shoplifting Tags	16.3
Vendor/Source Tagging	10.1
Plain Clothes Detectives	7.7
Secured Displays	7.7
Ink/Dye Tags	7.7
Simulated CCTV	7.4
Observation Mirrors	7.1
Merchandise Alarm	6.1
Cable, Locks & Chains	5.8
Uniformed Guards	4.3
Fitting Room Attendants	2.8
Observation Booths	2.1
Merchandise Destruction Tags	1.8
Subliminal Messages	0.6

SOURCE: Security Research Project, University of Florida, Gainesville, Florida. Reprinted by permission.

the widest possible meaning of the expression. Those who fail to assess fully and react appropriately will stand every chance of not surviving."

SUMMARY

Reported crimes committed against all types of retail establishments in order of frequency are shoplifting, burglary, vandalism, bad checks, fraudulent use of credit cards, employee theft and robbery. The focus of this chapter is on shoplifting, bad checks and employee theft.

Shoplifting is the theft of retail merchandise by someone lawfully on the premises. Concealment of merchandise is prima facie evidence of intent to shoplift. In many states price changing is also considered shoplifting.

Shoplifters can be classified as amateurs—students, housewives, vagrants, alcoholics, drug addicts and kleptomaniacs—or as professionals—those who steal for resale of merchandise. Shoplifting methods include palming objects, dropping articles into a receptacle, placing items inside clothing, wearing items out of the store and switching price tags.

The single most effective deterrent to shoplifting is surveillance by an alert, trained sales force. This may be supplemented by security officers or floorwalkers. Security officers are prevention oriented, seeking to deter crime by their presence. In contrast, floorwalkers are apprehension oriented, seeking to arrest and prosecute shoplifters.

Merchandising techniques to deter shoplifting include keeping displays orderly and not stacking merchandise too high; returning to the display any item looked at and not bought; keeping small, valuable items locked in display cases; placing identifying tags on all merchandise; displaying only one of a pair; not displaying expensive merchandise near exits and having small, easily stolen items located by the checkout.

Procedures to deter shoplifting include having unused checkout lanes closed, locking the back door, having package checks, carefully checking price tags, maintaining tight controls on fitting rooms and restrooms, issuing receipts, controlling refunds and establishing a communication system.

Physical controls to deter shoplifting include changing the actual store layout, posting signs, installing locks and alarms and installing surveillance equipment such as convex mirrors and/or CCTV.

To apprehend a suspect for shoplifting, someone must actually see the item being taken and concealed or be reasonably certain an item has been taken; and the suspect must be kept under *continuous* observation until apprehension is made. This may occur on the premises or outside, depending on state statutes. Reasonable guidelines for when to prosecute shoplifters should be established, taking into consideration the value of the article as well as the suspect's age, number of offenses and attitude. Illegal detention, malicious prosecution and slander suits must be guarded against.

Losses from bad checks are a second major concern of retail establishments. To reduce losses from bad checks, retailers should teach personnel to recognize the different types of checks and the common types of bad checks, establish a check-cashing policy and adhere to it, train personnel to examine checks and identification, record relevant information on the back of all checks cashed and reconcile identity documents with check passers' characteristics. High-risk checks include second-party checks, counter checks, illegible checks, post-dated checks and out-of-town checks. The most common types of bad checks are forged or altered checks, no-account checks and nonsufficient funds checks.

All checks should be carefully examined, including the printed name and address, check number, date, payee, numerical and written amount, bank and address and signature (or endorsement). No checks should be accepted that are illegible, that are not written in ink or that contain erasures or written-over dates or amounts.

Persons presenting checks to cash should be required to produce identification containing a physical description (preferably a photograph) and a signature. The description should be compared with the person; the signature should be compared with the signature on the check.

Protect against losses from fraudulent use of credit cards by comparing the signature on the card with that on the sales slip, checking the card's expiration date and establishing a reasonable floor release limit.

Another retail security problem is employee theft. Special risks in retail establishments include easy employee access to merchandise and cash. Specific pricing procedures, cash-handling procedures and refund procedures are essential. Personnel should be rotated periodically, and responsibilities should be separated.

To deter employee theft by price alterations, allow only authorized employees to set prices and mark merchandise, mark merchandise by machine or rubber stamp, conduct periodic audits of prices recorded and prices charged and check on the "popular" salesperson. To reduce losses of cash, establish strict cash-handling procedures, use a tamper-proof recording system, have each clerk responsible for his or her own cash receipts, have cash receipts balanced by someone else, perform unannounced audits and use honesty shoppers. Honesty shopping, or a shopping service, tests the honesty of sales personnel who handle cash.

In addition, require all employees to comply with the return/refund policy. Keep tight control of all credit documents, and match items to the return vouchers. Conduct periodic audits of return vouchers.

The primary objectives of shopping center security are loss prevention and public relations.

✔ APPLICATION

1. Terry Benson, a private security officer, is working in a liquor store to prevent armed robberies and the purchase of liquor by juveniles. The manager of the store has taken into custody a man who presented a check for payment of liquor. On being asked for identification, he ran out of the store with his purchase. The manager has caught him and brought him back to Officer Benson. What actions should Officer Benson now take?

2. The Riteway Department Store is being sued by a shoplifting suspect for destruction of his property. The suit is the result of the actions of a private security officer, Donald Clough, who saw the suspect, a white male about 24 years old, palm a watch and put it in his jacket pocket. When Officer Clough approached the suspect to make inquiry, the suspect ran from the store to the parking lot, where he entered his car and then closed and locked the doors. Officer Clough ordered the suspect to open the car door. When he refused, Officer Clough broke the window and arrested the suspect. A search of the car revealed the stolen watch under the car's front seat.

   As security director for Riteway, would you recommend that management try to settle out of court or that it fight the charges? Why?

3. Evaluate the completeness of the retail security checklist in Figure 16–5. Are any important areas missing? If so, which ones?

4. As the security manager for the Mytown Retail Sales Company, you are asked to develop a form to use when dismissing dishonest employees and attempting to recover any losses. What would you add to the form in Figure 16–4 to further protect the company from any civil litigation?

CRITICAL THINKING EXERCISE

Retail Security

Statutory and Common Law

Nebraska holds that a landlord is under a duty to exercise reasonable care to protect his patrons. Such care may require giving a warning or providing greater protection where there is a likelihood that third persons will endanger the safety of patrons. A possessor of land who holds it open to the public for entry for his business purposes is subject to liability to members of the public while they are upon the land for such a purpose, for physical harm caused by the accidental, negligent or intentionally harmful acts of third persons or animals and by the failure of the possessor to exercise reasonable care to (a) discover that such acts are being done or are likely to be done or (b) give a warning adequate to enable the visitors to avoid the harm, or otherwise to protect them against it.

Facts of the Case

On July 28, at 6:00 A.M., Janis L. Erichsen went shopping at No-Frills Supermarket in Harold's Square Shopping Center in Omaha. She parked her car in the No-Frills' parking lot and entered the store to purchase groceries. Half an hour later, with several bags of groceries, she attempted to return to her vehicle. Thirty feet from the exit door she was assaulted and robbed of her purse by an assailant. Erichsen resisted the assailant with the result that she dropped her bags of groceries, was beaten and in the process of trying to retain her purse was pulled toward the assailant's car. As the assailant attempted to flee in his car with her purse, Erichsen reached through the car's passenger-side window in an attempt to grab her purse. Unfortunately her arm became caught in the seat belt. As a result Erichsen was dragged about a mile and a half down Blondo Street and severely injured before she broke loose and tumbled into the roadside curb.

Erichsen later brought suit against No-Frills Supermarkets of Omaha, Inc., a Nebraska Corporation, and Harold Cooperman, owner of the property that was being leased by the supermarket. Testimony during the trial revealed that within the previous year and a half before the incident there had been at least 10 other crimes such as theft, robbery and purse snatching in the No-Frills parking lot or in nearby properties. It also was revealed that the management of No-Frills knew about these crimes in the area, and although it added lighting to the parking lot after the third incident, it did nothing to warn customers about the condition and did not tell employees to assist customers to their vehicles. Management stated that No-Frills was a low-cost, economy operation that could not afford to provide additional services, and that was the way it advertised in the community. Janis Erichsen is a resident of the community and knows the character and services that the store offers. She is a regular customer of the store and knows that its low prices are due to its attempt to conserve on costs.

Issues and Questions

1. Do both No-Frills Supermarkets and Harold Cooperman owe a duty of care to Janis Erichsen?
   a. Both the supermarket and the property owner have a duty to foresee the type of criminal activity of which Erichsen was a victim, and they should have taken steps to guard her against the possible harm or at least warned her of the possible risk. Because they did not, they are both liable for damages.
   b. Because the assault occurred suddenly and unexpectedly within a few feet of the well-lit exit to the supermarket (no previous assaults occurred in that exact area), the supermarket and the property owner are not to be held liable for this unfortunate incident.
   c. Although the alleged attempted purse-snatching incident began in the supermarket parking lot, the severe injuries were sustained at a distance from the supermarket's parking lot. As a result of the location of the injuries, Harold Cooperman, the property owner, is not liable even though the supermarket can be held liable for a minor portion of the damages.
   d. The property owner has a duty of care because many of the criminal incidents occurred on neighboring properties. He must warn persons of the risk in areas where criminal actions have repeatedly occurred. But in July by 6:30 A.M., a parking lot is well lit and this is not a time of day when such criminal acts could be anticipated. Thus the supermarket is not to be held liable.
   e. The significant injuries Erichsen experienced were due to her resistance and attempt to regain her purse by reaching into the get-away car. Furthermore, she was shopping at No-Frills because it advertised low prices in return for minimal service. She was a resident of the community and thus already knew the reputation and character of this location. Because she chose to take the action that caused her injuries, neither the supermarket nor the property owner are liable.

Discussion Questions

1. What are the advantages and disadvantages of prosecuting juvenile shoplifters? Adult shoplifters?
2. What type of system would aid retail stores in combatting bad-check artists?
3. How can retail stores aid one another in preventing shoplifting? What is done in your area?
4. What considerations should be evaluated when a private security officer notices that an employee is stealing?

5. What training devices might be used in conducting a shoplifting reduction seminar?

REFERENCES

Addis, Karen K. "When Employees Beat the System." *Security Management,* September 1991, pp. 115–19.

Adler, Steven. "Has Your Store Had a Check-Up?" *Security Management,* April 1993, pp. 61–70.

Atlas, Randall. "Righting the Wrongs in Retail Security." *Security Management,* November 1992, pp. 33A–34A.

Bridges, Curtis. "A Pound of Prevention for a Ton of Merchandise." *Security Management,* July 1994, pp. 22A–23A.

Brooks, C. M. "The Pros of Your POS." *Security Management,* June 1992, pp. 50–51.

"Cardboard Cutouts Reduce Shoplifting and Speed." *Law and Order,* September 1993, p. 161.

Carolin, P. James. "Survey of Shoplifters." *Security Management,* March 1992, pp. 11A–12A.

Cernock, Thomas W. "The Mall of America." *Security Management,* February 1993, pp. 43–47.

Chapman, William E. "Retail Loss Prevention Corner." *Security Concepts,* April 1994, p. 26.

Cosper, George W. "A Bicycle Built for Security." *Security Management,* June 1993, pp. 32–34.

"Criminal-Catching Computer." *Security Management,* October 1994, p. 16.

D'Addario, Francis. "Security Turns a Profit at Hardee's." *Security Management,* February 1993, pp. 30–33.

Durham, N. C. "Training Boosts Security's Retail Value." *Security Management,* December 1994, pp. 59–63.

Fenker, Lisa. "Combating Retail Theft: Seattle's Problem-Solving Approach." *The Police Chief,* October 1993, pp. 94–99.

Frank, Robert W. and Serpico, Philip. "All that Glitters Becomes a Target." *Security Management,* April 1995, pp. 51–54.

Gardner, T. J. *Criminal Law: Principles and Cases,* 3d ed. St. Paul, MN: West Publishing Company, 1985.

Grevenites, Jim. "Making Criminals Feel Unwanted." *Security Management,* August 1992, pp. 80–83.

Hayes, Read. "The Civil Recovery Side of Shoplifting." *Security Management,* March 1992, pp. 30A–31A.

Hively, Jeff. "Shopping Center/Mall Security: The Art of Seeing and Being Seen." *Security Concepts,* March 1994, pp. 20, 31.

Hollinger, Richard C. and Dabney, Dean A. 1994 National Retail Security, Security Research Project, Gainesville, University of Florida, 1995.

Klein, Gerald. "The Hidden Benefits of EAS." *Security Management,* June 1991, pp. 57–60.

Lottes, Steve. "What's in Store with EAS." *Security Management,* March 1992, pp. 20A–21A.

Maxwell, David A. *Private Security Law: Case Studies.* Stoneham, MA: Butterworth-Heinemann, 1993.

McNamara, John. "Helping Merchants Mind the Store." *The Police Chief,* October 1993, pp. 90–92.

Owens, Thomas. "Bum Checks." *IB (Independent Business),* July/August 1990, pp. 14–18.

Perry, Mary E. B. "Safe Shopping at the Mall: What's New and Improved in Mall Security." *Security Management,* June 1992, pp. 47–48.

Phelps, E. Floyd. "Checking Out Cash Register Theft." *Security Management,* November 1992, pp. 47–49.

Potter, A. N. "Shopping Center Security." *Security Management,* December 1984, pp. 34–35.

Private Security. Report on the Task Force on Private Security, National Advisory Committee on Criminal Justice Standards and Goals. Washington, DC: U.S. Government Printing Office, 1976.

"Retail Shrinkage Highest in Four Years." *Security Concepts,* February 1995, pp. 1, 31.

Story, Donald W. and Black, Michael A. "Shopping Center Security: A Tactical Problem." *Law and Order,* April 1991, pp. 76–80.

"Survey Reports Baby Boomers as Nation's Leading Shoplifters." *Security Concepts,* November 1993, p. 9.

Tesorero, Francis X. "Centralized Security: A Chain Reaction." *Security Management,* February 1995, pp. 60–65.

Tesorero, Francis X. "Tune In to Turn Off Employee Theft." *Security Management,* February 1993, p. 34.

Tyska, Louis A. and Fennelly, Lawrence J. "Retail Security in the Year 2000." In *Security in the Year 2000 and Beyond,* by Louis A. Tyska and Lawrence J. Fennelly, eds. Palm Springs, CA: ETC Publications, 1987, pp. 259–64.

Wilson, Caroline. "Ganging Up on Jewel Thieves." *Security Management,* August 1993, pp. 61–68.

Wilson, Caroline. "Securing America's New Town Centers." *Security Management,* June 1992, pp. 41–48.

CASES

Caroll v. United States, 267 U.S. 132, 45 S.Ct. 280, 69 L.Ed.2d 543 (1925)

Dent v. May Dept. Stores Co., 459 A.2d 1042 (1982)

Eastman v. Time Saver Stores, Inc., 428 So.2d 1163 (La. App. 1983)

The People v. Virginia Alvinia Zelinski, 594 P.2d 1000 (Cal. 1979)

United States v. Bice-Bey, 701 F.2d 1086 (1983)

COMMERCIAL SECURITY

DO YOU KNOW

- What commercial enterprises rely heavily on private security?
- What specific security problems are encountered in each type of enterprise?
- What targets are most common in each?
- What special security precautions are implemented to protect the assets of each?
- What is required by the Bank Protection Act?
- What agency regulates security of airports and airlines?

CAN YOU DEFINE THESE TERMS?

backstretch area
bait money
core concept
Dram Shop Acts
skips

INTRODUCTION

Several types of security systems besides those already examined are important. These systems are in place in businesses most people consider to be public. Because of this, they pose special problems. Of course, these public places should follow the basic lines of defense against internal and external crime and against threats to safety that apply to the types of facilities already discussed. It is assumed that a facility's physical vulnerability has been minimized by adequate lighting, fencing, locks and alarms as appropriate and that basic procedural security controls have been established to minimize risk.

> Financial institutions, office buildings, public and private housing, hotels and motels, facilities housing large public gatherings, racetracks, recreational parks, airports and airlines, mass transit and cruise lines are now making use of private security concepts, equipment, procedures and personnel on an ever-increasing scale.

This chapter begins with a discussion of security systems and challenges found in financial institutions, office buildings, housing developments and hotels/motels. This is followed by a discussion of security at public gatherings, movie theaters, recreational parks and racetracks. The chapter concludes with an examination of security at airports, in mass transit systems and aboard cruise ships.

FINANCIAL INSTITUTION SECURITY*

According to the Private Security Task Force Report (1976, p. 46): "The security and stability of the Nation's financial institutions (commercial banks, savings and loan associations, credit unions, loan companies, and brokerage houses) are critical to a lasting and healthy economy. In contrast to the many indirect losses sustained by other businesses, most losses in the financial community are direct financial losses. . . ."

Financial institutions are highly attractive to robbers, burglars, embezzlers and other types of thieves. In addition, enormous losses are incurred yearly through fraudulent use of credit cards and checks. Added to these losses are an estimated $40 million in stock certificates and $25 million in government bonds that are lost or stolen annually.

Security Problems in Financial Institutions

Marketing techniques such as electronic fund transfer systems, remote tellers, automatic bank machines and telephone transferring have had a major impact on security problems of financial institutions.

> The movement to make banking activities more accessible to citizens makes security more difficult. In addition, the large amounts of financial assets centralized in one location are extremely attractive to thieves. The most frequent losses involve theft of cash or stocks and bonds, check and credit-card fraud and embezzlement of funds.

A bank's security program is not limited to areas where money and valuables are exchanged or stored, but rather is closely related to all aspects of the business operation. For example, embezzlement may account for more losses than burglary and robbery combined.

A survey completed by more than 100 senior financial institution security professionals produced the following results (Harowitz and Murphy, 1994,p. 6A):

- Robbery (22%) and fraud (19%) topped their major security concerns.
- ATM crime, credit card fraud, forgeries, internal theft, internal investigations, and disaster management evenly split about 36% with 6% each.

This survey found that typically bank security departments were responsible for physical security, crime prevention, guard force management, fraud investigations, loss prevention, alarm monitoring (sometimes through a third party), executive protection, safety, fire prevention and disaster management.

---

*Financial Institutions—See *Private Security,* pp. 46–48.

Banks with many branches face additional security challenges. Wessells (1994, p. 26) describes how the First National Bank of Ohio's "centralized security system monitors downtown and all branch offices 24 hours a day with sophisticated integrated philosophy." In-house security staff monitors the system 24 hours a day from a 150,000-square-foot building containing the security control center.

One of the largest problems remaining within the financial transactions taking place in the banking industry is the use of the automated clearinghouse (ACH) which processes all transactions at the end of the business day. McClure (1994, p. 24A) provides the example of a communications breakdown resulting in substantial risk for the bank. At the start of a business day, an account has $5 million dollars. The customer requests that the bank wire out $2 million (leaving $3 million in the bank account). Then the bank automatically settles ACH payroll for $4 million, leaving the bank $1 million short. The customer requests another $2 million to be wired out, and the bank, unaware that the payroll was funded, complies, leaving the bank short $3 million. This was the direct result of the wire service and ACH being unable to communicate with each other, leaving the bank very vulnerable.

Security Measures in Financial Institutions

Great vulnerability existed in the amount and type of security measures used in financial institutions before 1968. This vulnerability was of concern to the government agencies that regulated federally insured financial institutions. FBI investigations of bank robberies revealed that many banks had totally inadequate protective and preventive measures against robbery. These findings were confirmed in a survey conducted between 1967 and 1969 by the Federal Home Loan Bank Board, whose survey of 194 banks showed fewer than 50 percent having alarm systems, only 17 percent using cameras and just over 10 percent having security guards.

Significant increases in bank robberies, larcenies and burglaries, and the obvious absence of adequate protective measures, moved Congress to enact the Bank Protection Act in 1968.

The *Bank Protection Act (1968)* requires all federally insured banks, savings and loan institutions and credit unions to:

- Designate a security officer.
- Cooperate with and seek security advice from the FBI and other law enforcement agencies.
- Develop comprehensive security programs and implement protective measures to meet or exceed federal standards.
- Maintain **bait money.***
- Periodically remove excess cash from tellers' windows and bank premises.
- Develop security-conscious opening and closing procedures and stringent security inspections.

---

*Bait money is currency whose serial numbers have been recorded. Sometimes this money is placed so that picking it up sets off a silent alarm.

By February of 1970 each federally insured financial institution was to develop a written security plan that met federal standards, appoint a security officer, file a formal report on current security measures at the facility and install and maintain required security equipment.

In addition to developing and implementing a formal, written security plan and appointing a security officer, federally insured financial institutions must install and maintain vault area lighting systems, tamper-resistant exterior doors and window locks, cameras and alarm systems.

Unfortunately, many small-town banks installed poor-quality cameras that use fast film and have poor resolution. Consequently, the resulting pictures are often worthless. In addition, the cameras are sometimes installed at a six-foot level, making them susceptible to being blacked out with spray paint or shaving foam. According to Green (1987, p. 30), banks have "a heavy reliance upon electronic technology and physical security rather than large numbers of personnel."

Chovanes (1994, p. 115) cautions:

> None of the existing regulatory requirements recognize the indirect cost from financial crime. None requires that appropriate and prudent methods be developed and implemented to minimize losses from other than financial crime. The institution that does not recognize this, opting instead for mere compliance, falls far short of its moral and ethical responsibility to provide a total approach to asset protection. . . .
>
> [I]f a bank's security program relies solely on absolute compliance with the above primary regulatory influence, it may be perhaps 40 percent effective in addressing the potential losses of the corporation. . . .
>
> Financial institutions must find a way to reorient themselves away from a compliance perspective and toward total preventive security.

In addition, many banks' alarm systems are outdated, leaving the institution vulnerable. As noted by Barron (1993, p. 33): "An iron safe under the stagecoach seat kept robbery losses low in the last century. Today, an alarm upgrade cuts losses from emergency repairs by 82 percent. Recurring costs can be reduced by $1.5 million."

Another area in which banks may be dated is in the use of signature cards to verify identification. Such cards take time and are highly unreliable. Bordes (1994, p. 71) suggests: "Computerized signature and photo records can enhance service while providing better access control."

Further, the open design of many banks leaves the tellers exposed and makes the patrons' transactions quite public. Bordes suggests that the teller's area be protected by a standard door enclosed to the ceiling and controlled by a card reader. The area should be designed to prevent those standing in line from being able to listen to the transactions occurring in front of them or to watch as someone receives a large amount of cash.

Yet another area that might be improved is the entrance/exit of the bank. Foyle (1995, p. 62) describes the Melon Bank Corporation's reaction to a number of armed takeover-style bank robberies. It installed access control metal-detecting units:

> The access control unit is a sophisticated system that controls entry into branches. It consists of an entry and exit portal with double interlocking doors, level one bullet-resistant glass, and a weapon detection device. Weight-sensitive floor mats and interlocking doors limit branch entry to one person at a time, and individuals must pass the weapon detection device to gain entry to the branch itself.
>
> An intercom system allows employees to communicate with people in the units and guide them through the process if a problem occurs.

Although the bank was initially concerned about the public's reaction to this technology, customers at the pilot sites gave a 90-percent approval rating.

Automatic Teller Machines

Of special concern is the problem of the automatic teller machine (ATM). According to Wipprecht and Barron (1994, p. 30): "ATMs have become the symbol of customer convenience, but also a security headache for many bank security managers." They note that the ATMs have come a long way since they were first introduced by International Business Machines Corporation (IBM) in 1972:

> At a full-service ATM today, one can purchase stamps and bus tickets, buy and sell mutual funds, transfer money between accounts and, most recently, obtain a mini-statement listing recent check cashing transactions to help you balance your checkbook.

In 1992 the Association of Trial Lawyers of America identified ATM attacks as one of five major growth areas for litigation in America (Schreiber, 1994, p. 18A). Available data suggest that the rate of attacks on ATM customers is about one in every 3.5 million transactions ("ATM Security Legislation," 1995, p. 2). As noted by Schreiber (1994, p. 18A): "To expect America's 87,000 ATMs [completing some 7.2 billion ATM transactions] to be oases free of crime in a crime-ridden nation is unreasonable." However, Schreiber (p. 21A) notes: "[F]ar in excess of 99 percent of the tens of billions of ATM transactions that will take place [during the rest of this century] will occur conveniently, accurately, and safely."

Surveys conducted by the Bank Administration Institute (BAI) and the American's Bankers Association (ABA) report the following (Schreiber, 1992, p. 29):

- Ninety-six percent of the crimes involve a single ATM customer victim.
- About 50 percent of the crimes occur between 7:00 P.M. and 12:00 A.M.
- Most of the crimes began as the customer was using the ATM (54%) or leaving the ATM (33%).
- Customers were injured in about 14 percent of the crimes.

ATMs may be located inside or outside a building. Those outside pose the greatest danger.

The American Society for Industrial Security (ASIS) Standing Committee on Banking & Finance, in "Keeping the Lid on the Cookie Jar," describes the six categories of criminal activity involving ATMs: unauthorized card use, fraudulent card use, insider manipulation, embezzlement, robbery and mugging and physical attack on the ATM itself.

Unauthorized Card Use. The Electronic Funds Transfer Act (the Federal Reserve Board's Regulation E) defines an unauthorized electronic funds transfer as ". . . a transfer from a consumer's account initiated by a person other than the consumer without actual authority to initiate such transfer and from which the consumer receives no benefit." These unauthorized transfers can be initiated through ATM access cards. Typically unscrupulous users obtain these cards by stealing the holder's purse or wallet. Because many customers keep a written record of their personal identification number (PIN) with their card (although all financial institutions advise against it), access to the customer's account becomes all too simple.

Fraudulent Card Use. Fraudulent card use can occur in many ways. Customers can defraud financial institutions by withdrawing more money than is actually in their accounts or by depositing worthless checks and then withdrawing the money before the scam can be stopped. Collusion is another way in which a customer can defraud a financial institution. In this case, ATM card holders dispute a transaction after knowingly giving their card and PIN to someone else and allowing that person to make a withdrawal from the account.

Insider Manipulation. Bank employees can also be involved in fraudulent card use. Employees may establish fictitious accounts and order ATM cards for these accounts, or they may have access to legitimate cards and PINs through undelivered mail that is returned to the bank. An employee could also order a duplicate card for a customer and then have the card and the PIN sent to an address other than the one supplied by the customer. A similar problem can exist when the financial institution uses customer-generated PINs. Employees can watch a customer select a PIN and then order a duplicate card for themselves, thereby gaining access to the customer's account.

Embezzlement. Employees are also responsible for this category of ATM crime. Although the misappropriation of funds by an employee is nothing new to financial institutions, the advent of the ATM has provided another source of funds for dishonest workers. The money in the machine itself can be taken either by bank employees or by personnel who service the machines. Also, funds deposited through the ATM are vulnerable to embezzlement and manipulation by employees who process these deposits.

Robbery and Mugging. Service personnel who replenish the ATM cash supply or repair breakdowns are susceptible to robbery at ATM sites, particularly after normal banking hours. In addition, customers not only have been robbed while making withdrawals, but also have been forced by thieves to return to the ATM and withdraw additional funds. A recent staff commentary by the Federal Reserve Board held that such robberies of customers at ATMs constitute an unauthorized transfer as defined under Regulation E; consequently the customer's liability in these situations is limited.

Physical Attack. Finally, the ATM itself is subject to attack. In some cases, vandalism is the problem. But in others, professional burglars attempt to break into the machine and obtain the cash supply. Thieves have been known to drill into the machines, burn through them, pull the cash dispenser out of the wall and even blow them apart with dynamite.

Security Measures. Adequate lighting is critical for ATMs because they may be used at any time, day or night. How much light is enough? Goetzke (1994, p. 58) suggests that a person ask: "Would a reasonable person feel comfortable on these premises during the hours of darkness?" Goetzke (p. 60) stresses: "Planning for adequate lighting and illumination of the ATM or branch site will provide the safest environment for bank customers and employees. Good security planning can deny the night to the criminal element."

New technologies include a 911 button on the machines that can be used to summon the police immediately and a "Customer Awareness Monitor" which is placed above an ATM and allows the users to see the area behind them. High-resolution, wide-angle transaction and surveillance cameras, which are date and time stamped, are also used.

According to Schreiber (1992, p. 30): "ATM security camera photos have been dramatically helpful in apprehending ATM robbers." Schreiber (p. 31) suggests that a majority of ATM robbers may be under the influence of drugs.

Servicing. Fahed (1991, p. 63) cautions: "Because ATM servicers are most vulnerable to attack during daily servicing, security is extremely important." Fahed stresses the importance of stringent, written servicing procedures covering dual control, cash transport and handling deposits. Included in the procedures should be three *don't evers* (pp. 63–64):

Don't Ever

- Transport currency alone. Instead, use at least two people, one to carry and one to look out.
- Transport currency through the lobby when it is open to the public.
- Transport currency openly to a detached ATM site.

OFFICE BUILDING SECURITY*

The United States once had more blue-collar (production) workers than white-collar workers, but this situation has reversed. Increasing mechanization in manufacturing has caused a decrease in the number of blue-collar workers needed. As the number of white-collar employees increases, so does the incidence of white-collar crime. Additionally, offices are more often the targets of thieves.

Many contractual and proprietary security forces perform guard, alarm and armored car/courier services at thousands of office buildings throughout the country as corporations seek to protect company assets as well as the lives and personal property of their employees.

Some companies establish specific levels of security in their offices or buildings to meet requirements stipulated in government contracts. Others feel their corporation's work is highly sensitive, involving, for example, trade secrets, and thus view security as essential. In yet other instances, private developers build, own and manage inner-city office buildings and/or commercial industrial parks (frequently suburban office complexes that include nonmanufacturing businesses such as research laboratories, sales facilities, medical buildings and other professional offices situated along the front of the building with warehouses behind). These private developers may either provide security for the buildings and tenants in the complex or assign this responsibility to the prime tenant, the tenant who is leasing the most space in a particular building. Most private developers use the services of contract security firms to protect the entire complex.

Security Problems of Office Buildings

"Open for Business" means open to the public. Most offices have a steady stream of outsiders. Among them may be persons intent on committing such open-hour crimes as robbery or larceny. In addition, a would-be thief may "case" a particular office during business hours with the intent of returning for an after-hours burglary. Custodial personnel and tenants having keys to the building pose another after-hours threat. Further, employees can pilfer office supplies and/or petty cash during or after business hours.

- *The major security problems* in office buildings include after-hours burglaries and theft; theft from a tenant by another tenant's employees; theft by service, maintenance and custodial employees; assaults, rapes and other crimes against persons; regulation and control of visitor traffic; bomb threats; protection of executive offices and personnel and fire watch.
- *The items most frequently stolen* from office buildings include small office equipment such as typewriters, calculators, duplicating and photocopying machines and computers and peripherals; office furnishings; securities and valuable documents; blank payroll checks and check-writing machines.

*Office Building Security—See *Private Security,* pp. 43–44.

Other corporate valuables that are often burglary targets include blank (unissued) stock certificates, the corporate seal, corporate minutes, office art and decorations and books. Many larger corporations maintain extensive professional libraries containing thousands of dollars worth of books, yet they often provide little or no control over access to them. And, as in any other type of business, office supplies and petty cash present another potential area for loss.

An additional problem in office security is that frequently some tenants do not perceive a need for security, thereby increasing the risk for other tenants in the same building who have security needs. As noted earlier, a nonsecure area adjacent to an area seeking security provides a vulnerable area for the "secure" office. Further, fire loading one office may pose a direct threat to other tenants, who may be completely unaware of such a threat. Compounding the problem is the fact that in office buildings having many different tenants, it is usually impossible to conduct fire or bomb evacuation drills.

A study conducted by the Security Industry Association (SIA) in 1994 found that among commercial enterprises, suites in office parks faced the highest risk of burglary ("Understanding Commercial Burglaries," 1994, p. 13). Office suites accounted for 46.5 percent of all commercial burglaries perhaps because they are "new and attractive; offices within them have newer equipment that is more easily fenced; and the parks in which the offices are located are large and secluded." The study also found that most commercial burglars (51 percent) enter through the front door.

High-rise office buildings present extreme challenges, as noted by Witkowski (1994, p. 14): "The responsibility for the protection of millions, if not billions of dollars in people and assets calls for utmost care in the selection process." Witkowski suggests that the job description include the need for agility skills such as climbing stairs. In addition:

> [T]he first round of the shift after personnel have departed for the day is the most critical. This is the ideal time to find potentially hazardous conditions that may have been left behind (i.e., equipment and machinery left on, charred coffee pots still on the heater, materials and chemicals improperly stored, etc.).

Security Measures in Office Buildings

The amount of security devices and personnel required in an office building depends on the size and location of the building, the number and nature of tenant businesses and the crime rate of the area.

> Primary security measures in office buildings are access control, proper authorization and documentation of the use of corporate assets by employees and periodic fire inspections and fire drills.

Usually office or tenant space is protected primarily through access control: master key systems, card-key readers, closed circuit television (CCTV) and security officers. Many new office buildings are constructed using the **core concept,** which has all elevators, restrooms, lobbies and service facilities located at the building's center, thus allowing more effective control of "public" areas while also permitting more flexible use of office space. Extra security measures to protect these public areas include CCTV, receptionists to monitor a visitor pass system and security officers. Some security firms have successfully controlled access by training their security guards to recognize potential thieves.

Elevators can be programmed to allow only authorized personnel to operate the elevators or to obtain access to specified floors after hours. Fire stairwells are often a key security concern for many high-rise office buildings because local fire codes may require that the stairwell doors be left unlocked. Installing crash-bars with alarms may overcome this security problem.

In addition to access control, many offices use security officers for patrol, generally following programmed watch-clock stations. Many newer, larger office buildings have central consoles to monitor access along with heating, ventilating and air-conditioning systems. These central consoles reduce personnel requirements, increase monitoring and detecting efficiency and allow faster response by security personnel.

Corporate assets such as records, stocks, securities and cash are usually stored in vaults, which are frequently equipped with CCTV or time-lapse cameras. Additionally, many companies keep vital information on computers, which poses another security problem. Protecting a computer processing center's remote terminals and the information contained in the machine was discussed in Chapter 9.

Recording the serial numbers on office machines is an important security procedure. If these machines are stolen, the numbers can be reported to police, greatly increasing the chances of recovering the stolen property. For

Multi-image closed circuit TV allows security personnel to observe several areas at once.

example, California has established a successful recovery program to trace stolen electric typewriters through the joint efforts of the Department of Justice and IBM. State law requires dealers to report by serial number all used business machines bought, traded, repaired and received. Investigators can then match the serial numbers with their list of stolen items and relay the information to local police for recovery of the stolen item.

Internal losses can be minimized by requiring authorization and proper documentation of the use of company assets. For example, supplies should be obtainable only by requisition. The requisition forms should be checked periodically to ensure that the usage is reasonable. Petty cash is an easy target for internal loss unless a system of authorization and documentation is established. Vouchers should be required for all petty cash disbursed (see Figure 17–1). The person responsible for disbursing petty cash might alter the amount on a voucher; for example, a voucher for $5 might be changed to read $35, with the person in charge pocketing $30. Therefore, vouchers should be periodically routed to the person signing for the cash to ensure that such changes have not occurred. Vouchers should be canceled after they are recorded to prevent their reuse. In addition, unannounced audits of vouchers and petty cash ledgers should be made.

Libraries should have a book checkout system similar to that used in public libraries. All books in the library should be clearly marked as company property.

The mail room is another target for loss. Losses may occur because stamps are stolen or because mail-room personnel are not taught to weigh packages correctly or to determine the best postal rate and may be sending everything first class when third class or book rate might be more appropriate. Such practices, over time, can involve considerable financial loss for a business.

HOUSING*

Although private security is usually thought to be solely involved with business and industry, it is becoming more important in residential units, where it is

DATE: ____________

AMOUNT: ____________

FOR: ____

____

BY: ____

RECEIVED PAYMENT: ______________________ (Signature)

DISBURSED PAYMENT: ______________________ (Signature)

Figure 17–1. Sample Petty Cash Voucher

*Housing—See *Private Security,* pp. 50–51.

also needed. Burglaries of residential dwellings now account for hundreds of millions in property losses annually, and this figure is probably underreported. In addition, muggings and vandalism create problems for homeowners and renters.

> Security problems of residential units include theft, vandalism and assaults, particularly muggings. Security consultants address these problems.

Although it would seem logical that expensive homes in exclusive neighborhoods would be the targets of thieves, often such is not the case. Studies by the U.S. Department of Housing and Urban Development indicate that crime is considerably higher in public housing with low- and medium-income residents and with senior citizen residents than in other residential areas. In fact, crime rates in some public housing projects are two to four times higher, with higher rates of victimization per household or dwelling unit and substantially higher rates of multiple victimization of the same dwelling—that is, a large number of residences experiencing more than one burglary.

Anyone who has come home to find that his/her house or apartment has been burglarized may feel indignation, anger, rage and desire for revenge. It is, indeed, one of the most traumatic experiences a person can have. Knowing some stranger has gone through your most private possessions has an impact surpassed only by a personal assault or rape.

Some steps individuals can take to deter burglars are given in a security checklist with the acronym Stop Thief, shown in Figure 17–2 (p. 536).

Security consultants and firms advise homeowners on security measures they might take (see Figure 17–3 p. 537). Many also offer around-the-clock monitoring of security systems installed within private homes. Such systems may include fire alarms connected directly with the fire department as well as sensors that will detect if the temperature drops below freezing.

Contractual security services may be hired to patrol neighborhoods and to protect public housing units, high-rise apartments and exclusive residential developments.

> Access control, patrol by security officers and the provision of youth programs help to reduce residential losses.

Increasing numbers of homeowners are installing special locks, floodlights and less expensive burglar alarms and/or buying safes and large dogs to protect their homes, valuables and families. Some homeowners' associations and exclusive residential developers hire security personnel to perform patrol services and to monitor central-gate entrances.

The rapid increase in the rate of burglaries and muggings has also resulted in increased security measures in private high-rise apartment and condominium complexes, with emphasis on limiting the access of nonresidents.

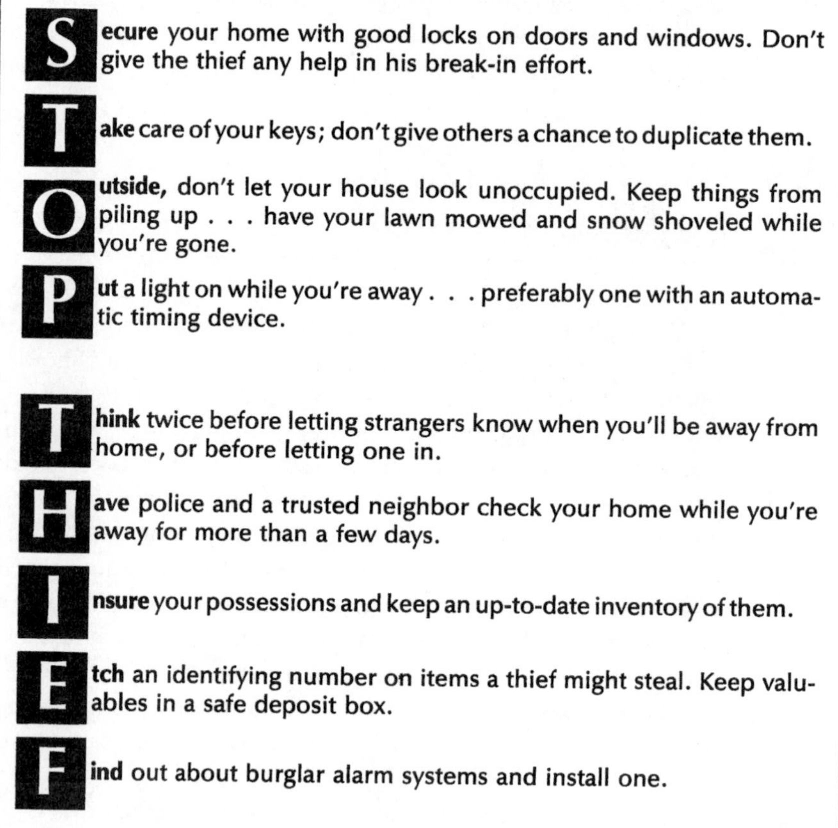

Figure 17–2. Stop Thief

SOURCE Reprinted with permission from State Farm Fire and Casualty Co.

According to Green (1987, p. 29): "The future of security in high-rise apartment buildings and housing complexes offers great potential for the security professional because of the growing emphasis on the concept of total environmental protection." Access control measures include doorkeepers in vestibules, external door locks to interior hallways that tenants activate by remote control and monitoring of entrances with CCTV, sometimes connected so that tenants can view visitors seeking admittance. Some newer high-income apartment and condominium complexes have installed extensive alarm, monitoring and access control systems monitored around the clock by a central console operator.

Many public housing authorities are implementing the same protective measures used by private apartment buildings in their high-rise complexes, including CCTV monitoring and access control. Housing authorities in some large cities with many housing projects maintain armed proprietary or quasi-public security forces with limited or full police powers. Smaller housing authorities often organize tenant patrols or hire contract security firms to provide services. Although the inherent dangers in using tenant patrols must be ac-

Home Security Is Good Housekeeping

Crime Prevention can be best achieved by:

1. Recognition of Security Risks
2. Initiation of corrective action to remove them

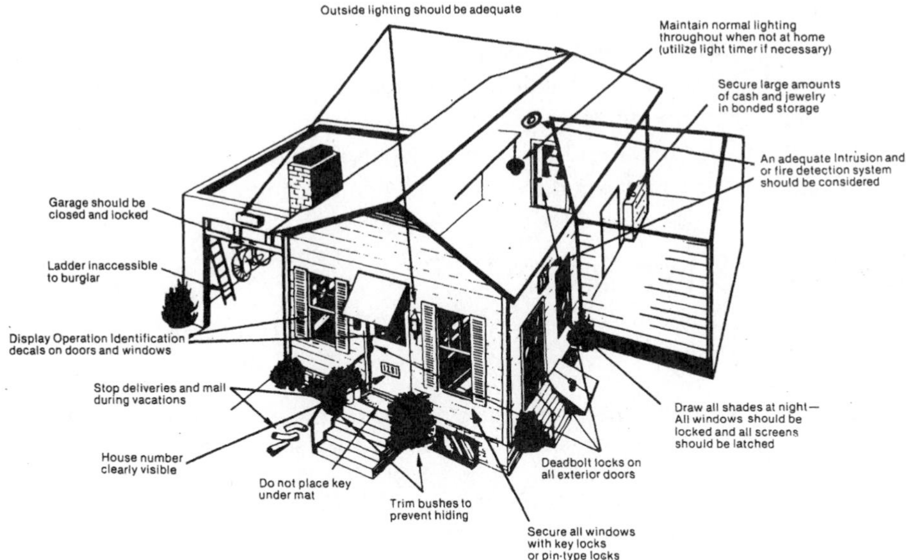

Outside lighting should be adequate
Maintain normal lighting throughout when not at home (utilize light timer if necessary)
Secure large amounts of cash and jewelry in bonded storage
An adequate Intrusion and/ or fire detection system should be considered
Garage should be closed and locked
Ladder inaccessible to burglar
Display Operation Identification decals on doors and windows
Stop deliveries and mail during vacations
House number clearly visible
Do not place key under mat
Trim bushes to prevent hiding
Secure all windows with key locks or pin-type locks
Deadbolt locks on all exterior doors
Draw all shades at night— All windows should be locked and all screens should be latched

These are a few of the security measures that you can institute to help reduce criminal opportunity.

Remember, Your home should always give the appearance that it's occupied.

Home Security Tips

- Make sure locks are locked
- Never admit strangers inside
- Do not broadcast your travel plans
- Do not leave notes indicating your absence
- Do not keep valuables out in the open
- Join Operation Identification
- Join Neighborhood Watch

Before Going on a Vacation or Week-end Trip . . .

☑ PRE-VACATION HOME SECURITY
☐ Property has been marked under "OPERATION IDENTIFICATION"
☐ Neighbors have been instructed to watch my home
☐ Arrangements have been made to have my lawn mowed
☐ Deliveries have been stopped, or someone will pick up delivered items
☐ Automatic timers are in use for lights and radio
☐ Shades and blinds are in normal positions
☐ My home will have that "lived in" look
☐ Police have been notified to watch my home

Figure 17–3. Home Security Educational Materials

SOURCE: Courtesy of the Mecklenberg County Police Department. Reprinted by permission.

knowledged, they frequently do provide a good deal of security for residents in the building. Many public housing authorities have also established recreation programs and youth activities programs in an attempt to reduce the incidence of vandalism and crimes committed by juveniles.

As in business and industry, there is an architectural emphasis in designing neighborhoods and buildings that seeks to create safer environments that will minimize opportunities for the commission of crimes. Demonstration projects indicate that architectural features, lighting, building, and neighborhood layout and site design can reduce the incidence of crime.

HOTEL/MOTEL SECURITY*

According to Ronan (1993, p. 38):

> Owners and general managers of lodging facilities, regardless of the property size, have a responsibility to ensure that guests are provided with safe and secure accommodations. No less important is the protection of the employees at each site, as well as the security of their personal property and, of course, the company's assets.

As noted by Aiken (1993, p. 37):

> In the hospitality industry service provided to guests is of paramount importance. Quality service extends beyond a color television and clean sheets to a reasonable expectation of security. Although preventive measures help keep the hotel secure, disasters and accidents where loss of life, injury, and property damage occur cannot always be prevented. By developing and documenting an ERT [emergency response team] program, the facility will be in a more favorable position to protect patrons who stay at the hotel and to prove that it prepared for such situations if challenged in court.

Crime in lodging establishments has climbed to dangerous heights, both in terms of the number of incidents and the severity of the incidents, as have lawsuits against hotels and motels. There has been an unprecedented increase in civil filings against these establishments, charging that security negligence resulted in harm to a guest or an employee. In many cases, a new innkeeper's case law is developing as the hotels appeal adverse court decisions.

Says Green (1987, p. 29): "The hotel and motel industry has been characterized in the past by serious neglect of many security responsibilities, an attitude that has only slowly been changing in spite of a number of very large awards by the courts in recent years against hotels or motels charged with negligent security, particularly in the area of protecting guests. However, this neglect, coupled with court-mandated responsibility, has created opportunity for security professionals."

Koentopp (1992, p. 55) notes: "Security has assumed an increasingly important role in the hotel business. The larger the facility and the more diverse

---

*Hotel/Motel Security—See *Private Security,* pp. 49–50.

the features, services, and amenities, the more demanding the need for comprehensive security management."

Security Problems in Hotels/Motels

In its efforts to make hotels and motels more convenient for guests, management has increased the vulnerability to theft, vandalism and assault. Elevators and parking garages provide outside thieves, employees and guests with greater access to unprotected areas and less probability of detection while committing crimes.

- *Major security problems* of the hotel/motel industry include both internal and external theft, vandalism, vice and fire.
- *Items most frequently stolen* from hotels and motels include money, credit cards, jewelry, linens, silver, food, liquor and other easily concealed articles.

The most significant internal theft losses result from inadequate procedures for cash handling, housekeeping activities, receiving and storing supplies, laundry services and restaurant/bar services. Many employees of hotels and motels must have master or submaster keys to perform their jobs. Therefore, they have access to secured hotel/motel property as well as to the personal property of guests.

Guests are vulnerable to theft not only by hotel/motel employees, but also by professional thieves and burglars who obtain master keys and loot rooms while the guests are away. Hotels and motels in resort areas encounter additional security problems because most guests are occupied with recreation or sightseeing and spend much time away from their rooms, often leaving large sums of cash, plane tickets, sporting equipment, cameras, credit cards, jewelry and expensive clothing in their rooms. Likewise, hotels and motels hosting large conventions and conferences face special security problems because the guests' schedules are easily predetermined and the times when rooms will be empty anticipated.

Guests are not always the victims, however. Sometimes guests are the criminals, whether they consider their actions "criminal" or not. The American Hotel and Motel Association estimates that millions of dollars worth of property are lost each year because guests take items such as ashtrays and towels as souvenirs. Millions of dollars more are lost as the result of carelessness with hotel property and furnishings, as well as by intentional vandalism. Conventions pose an additional problem in that conventioneers can be extremely unruly. Further, some guests do not pay their bills, or they pay them with bad checks or invalid credit cards.

In addition to these losses, the hotel/motel industry must deal with problems such as prostitution and gambling, which frequently occur in semipublic establishments. The emphasis placed on this problem is determined by management.

One extremely important security hazard is fire. The *Statistical Abstract of the United States* for 1994 reported approximately 6,000 hotel/motel fires in 1992 resulting in over $56 million in property loss. According to Thompson (1991, p. 86): "Fewer than half of all U.S. hotel rooms have fire sprinklers. Surprisingly, only five states—Connecticut, Florida, Hawaii, Massachusetts, and Nevada (and Puerto Rico)—require sprinklers in hotel rooms."

In the fall of 1990, however, the Hotel-Motel Fire Safety Act (HR94) was passed. This law, which will be phased in over six years, requires federal employees who stay or meet in hotels or motels of three stories or more to use facilities that have sprinkler systems.

Another safety hazard exists in facilities with indoor swimming pools: carbon monoxide poisoning. This deadly gas is given off by the pool's heater. Adequate ventilation is a necessity to prevent such hazards.

Even freak accidents must be anticipated. For example, in New Carrollton, Maryland, a woman was electrocuted after putting her key card in the hotel-room door. She was barefoot and soaking wet when she tried to enter her room. Police did not think the electronic key used in more than 1 million hotel and motel rooms worldwide was to blame. This view was also held by a spokeswoman for the American Hotel & Motel Association who stated: "This appears to be a freakish, isolated but very tragic incident" (Associated Press, June 28, 1995, p. 9A).

Budget motels face many different challenges (Kohr, 1991, p. 33):

- Exterior entrances to rooms, some with sliding glass doors.
- Numerous remote entrances and exits.
- Parking right outside each room's door.
- Limited staff—usually no security personnel.
- Little or no physical security.
- Limited capital resources.

Security Measures in Hotels/Motels

Providing free movement and open facilities to guests must be balanced with implementing procedures to minimize criminal opportunities. Sound security measures not only increase the guests' safety, but also raise the profitability of the establishment. With huge losses sustained from employee theft and the growing frequency of guest-room theft and attacks on guests, more and more hotel and motel operators are turning to private security to reduce their losses. The security practices of a particular hotel or motel are usually the responsibility of the individual owner or the franchise holder. Large, nationwide lodging chains often have corporate security staffs to provide support and guidance to the franchise owners. The corporate security staff conducts security surveys; investigates specific losses; establishes guidelines for security policies and staffing; makes recommendations on cash-handling procedures, preemployment screening and emergency plans; and maintains liaison with local law enforcement agencies.

> Security measures in hotels/motels include stringent key control and frequent re-keying, careful preemployment screening, monitoring systems and use of unmarked towels and ashtrays.

At the heart of the hotel/motel security system is adequate key control, which is a difficult procedure given the large number of employees and guests who have keys. As noted by Sunstrom (1992, p. 59):

> Lack of security of guest room keys is the most serious problem faced by lodging security professionals. The front desk clerks have access to keys. Room attendants frequently find guest room keys when cleaning the rooms. Bellpersons, maintenance personnel, and most other employees find guest room keys from time to time.

This problem is compounded by the fact that the base population in most lodging establishments turns over 100 percent or more in a week (Sunstrom).

A procedure for ensuring that keys are not duplicated and that departing guests and terminated employees turn in their keys is required. Frequent re-keying is often part of the key control system.

One advance in the key control area is the use of an electronic lock using a plastic card that bears no room number. (Of course, guests must make a point of remembering that number.) Little (1993, p. 27) describes the ultra-compact Front Desk Controller (FDC) which measures less than 7 inches by 9 inches but has a 10,000-room capacity. It can encode key cards, store 4,000 transactions and audit locks.

In addition, as noted by May (1994, p. 11): "In recent years two central problems have plagued the hospitality industry—fire prevention and alcohol server liability." The first problem, that of fire prevention, is emphasized by the more than 10,000 fires per year experienced by this industry over the past decade.

May cites the example of the MGM Grand in Las Vegas, Nevada, as the most publicized hotel fire in recent years with 84 dead, 600 injured and 900 lawsuits claiming billions of dollars worth of negligence. He notes that 78 of the 84 deaths were caused by breathing toxic and poisonous gases and that about 60 percent of the hotel's furnishing contained polyvinyl chloride or PVC.

Other factors contributing to losses from fire in the hotel industry include the following (May, pp. 11, 18):

- Delayed discovery.
- Failure to notify the fire department.
- Failure to notify the guests.
- Use of highly combustible materials in decorating or design.
- Improper or lack of training of employees.
- Failure to comply with existing codes.
- Failure to have sufficient personnel on duty to provide services.

The checklist in Figure 17–4 (p. 542) can be used to assess fire as well as pool safety in hotels and motels.

CHECKLIST FOR FIRE AND POOL SAFETY

Here is a checklist of basics for evaluating hotel safety. Each group is different. If you have elderly or handicapped attendees, be sure to consider their special safety needs.

FIRE

- ☐ Do all areas of the hotel have sprinklers and fire alarms?
- ☐ Are fire-alarm systems regularly tested?
- ☐ Does the hotel have a *written* emergency plan?
- ☐ Does the plan include meeting and dining areas?
- ☐ Has the hotel staff been trained in evacuation procedures?
- ☐ Are there alarm switches on each floor?
- ☐ Do fire alarms alert the fire department directly?
- ☐ Are all exits clearly marked and unobstructed?
- ☐ Do all exit doors open in the direction of travel?
- ☐ Are stairwells open to ground and roof?
- ☐ Do meeting rooms have at least two exits? (or more, if the room is large)?
- ☐ Does the hotel have emergency lighting?
- ☐ How far away is the fire department?
- ☐ When was the hotel last inspected by the fire department?
- ☐ What is the fire department's phone number?
- ☐ What is the hotel's security police phone number?
- ☐ Where are fire extinguishers located?
- ☐ Is the hotel in compliance with local fire codes?
- ☐ Are there any outstanding fire code violations?
- ☐ Are stairways and exits obstructed in any way?
- ☐ Are exits clearly marked with an exit sign?
- ☐ Are diagrams of emergency exits, stairways, and fire extinguisher locations posted in each room?

POOLS

- ☐ If pools are enclosed in hotel atriums, do rooms have a window that can be opened for ventilation?
- ☐ Are any of the rooms adjacent to the pool heating system?
- ☐ What codes or inspections apply to the pool heating system?
- ☐ Has the pool heating system been inspected and certified as safe?

Figure 17–4. Checklist for Fire and Pool Safety

SOURCE: Reprinted with permission from *SUCCESSFUL MEETINGS Magazine.* Copyright © 1991, Bill Communications, Inc.

Thompson (1991, p. 897) stresses: "Having safety plans in writing is central to a strong legal position. This goes way beyond just keeping a file of checklists. It means documentation and contracts." This would include contracts and warranties with those supplying fire safety equipment as well as an accurate record of the dates on which smoke detectors, fire extinguishers and sprinkler systems are checked. It would also include documentation of all training conducted for staff and guests. Educating guests is particularly important. Some facilities do more than simply post the location of fire exits. For example, the Red Lion Hotels and Inns have a "fire safety and survival guide" in every room described by Thompson (p. 86):

> The one-page sheet, illustrated so that children can readily grasp the basics, counsels guests to find two exits; learn the layout of their room; keep a key nearby as they sleep; act, not investigate, if they hear a fire alarm; leave the room, if possible, but stay in if the door is hot; crawl low in smoke; and avoid elevators.

In addition to the preceding essential components of adequate protection against loss from fire, many motels and hotels have flashlights, first-aid kits, oxygen and wheelchairs on each floor.

Hotel/motel executives and security directors generally agree that security should be given a greater emphasis in the training of managers, owners and franchise holders. Specifically, degree programs in hotel and restaurant management should require courses in security, including civil liability issues.

Concerning the problem of alcohol server liability, May (1995, p. 9) notes: "A number of lawsuits are being filed in various states against hotels, motels, bars and restaurants that allegedly served intoxicated persons who later caused injury to third parties." Many states have enacted **Dram Shop Acts** making bartenders who continue to serve an obviously intoxicated patron liable for any harm that individual might do to others.

The National Licensed Beverage Association (NLBA) recommends a program known as Techniques of Alcohol Management (TAM) as described by May (1995, p. 27):

> The standard operating procedures used in this program is called SIR:
>
> **S** . . . Size them up (referring to body size—small person—1–2 drinks/hr.; medium size person—2–3 drinks/hr.; large person—3–4 drinks/hr.).
>
> **I** . . . Interview them (watching for signs of intoxication such as slurred speech, confusion).
>
> **R** . . . Rate them (using the concept of a traffic light):
>
> Green = Go. All's normal.
>
> Yellow = Caution. Pay careful attention to next drink order.
>
> Red = Stop. Serve no more alcohol.

In addition, as noted by Kohr (1994, p. 26): "Hotels and motels are microcosms of our society, in that they reflect society's ills and benefits. . . . Theft, domestic disputes and violent crime occur in hotels just as in society at large."

The increase in the number of armed robberies at motels has prompted many to follow the lead of hotels and install CCTV monitoring systems in lobby and cashier areas. Increasingly, hotels and motels are using monitoring systems in parking areas, ancillary lobbies and elevators. They have also begun to use central access-control systems for guest rooms.

Motels have generally avoided one problem that has traditionally plagued the hotel industry: **skips** or nonpaying guests. Most motels require guests to pay in advance or to establish valid credit. In most hotels, on the other hand, room charges and other costs incurred are accumulated and paid at checkout time. Guests may check out before all charges have been posted to the bill or, in some cases, not check out at all.

Although security usually requires the identification of items, an exception to this is the practice of identifying towels, ashtrays and any other items that tempt guests to "take" them as souvenirs. Unmarked towels and ashtrays have little sentimental value to travelers.

The American Automobile Association (AAA) rates 19,000 of the 28,000 U.S. hotels each year. One of its recommendations for establishments seeking a four-diamond rating is that they have in-room safes (Straub, 1992, p. 51). The AAA set forth new standards in 1995 (Kohr, 1994, p. 28):

> The new security requirements include guest room entry doors which automatically lock when the guest leaves, deadbolts which cannot be opened except with an emergency master key, and peepholes. In addition, sliding doors and room connecting doors must have an effective locking device and deadbolt, respectively.

No matter what security hardware is instituted, the bottom line still boils down to people. As noted by Yule, director of security for New York's Hotel Millenium (Selwitz, 1993, p. 23):

> My real emphasis is people patrol. Electronics is fine for record keeping and creating an atmosphere that encourages people to honestly do their jobs. But we depend on our staff to be a real presence, particularly in the lobby where they keep a watch out for luggage boosters, or for keeping undesirable people who want to enter out of the hotel.

People are every bit as important in the economy hotels and motels. And although economy hotels and motels may have limited capital resources, Kohr urges: "With the volume of litigation against motels today, owners and operators can't afford *not* to upgrade facilities." Among the relatively inexpensive steps motel managers might take are the following (p. 34):

- Step 1. Manage by walking around. Get out there and see what's happening.
- Step 2. Conduct background checks on all employees.
- Step 3. Involve employees in security through training.
- Step 4. Establish a liaison with local law enforcement.
- Step 5. Designate or hire a security person to patrol the property.

Court Cases

Court cases related to hotel/motel security include the following:

De Lema v. Waldorf Astoria Hotel, Inc., 1984. A federal court held that a hotel *is* liable for the theft of a guest's property, provided it has first accepted responsibility for safeguarding a guest's property.

Meyers v. Ramada Inn of Columbus, 1984. An Ohio court held that hotel owners *can* be held liable for any injuries a guest suffers as a result of a criminal assault. However, the court stated that the guest must first demonstrate that the defendant should have anticipated the assault.

Pittard v. Four Seasons Motor Inn, Inc. 1984. A New Mexico court held that a hotel *can* be held liable if one of its employees assaults a guest, provided the injured party can demonstrate that the hotel had notice of similar past conduct by the employee in question.

Some cases deal not with liability, but rather with constitutional issues related to searches of hotel/motel guests' rooms.

United States v. Lyons, 1983. A U.S. Court of Appeals held that a guest in a hotel room *is* entitled to constitutional safeguards against unreasonable searches and seizures. However, the court did observe that the privacy to which hotel guests are entitled is not comparable to that of owners or tenants of a house.

State v. Weiss, 1984. A Florida court held that the search of a guest's suitcase by a hotel employee did *not* constitute an illegal search and seizure unless the employee was following police instructions.

Maxwell (1993, p. 362) describes the case of *Ramada Inns, Inc. v. Sharp* (1985), which involved the questions of compensatory and punitive damages against a motel and its security guard because the guard allegedly pushed an escort service employee down a flight of stairs. The motel contended that punitive damages could not be assessed against an employer for an employee's act unless the employer authorized the act or approved the act, commonly known as the complicity theory. The victim disagreed, claiming that through vicarious liability the employer was liable. The court agreed. Compensatory damages of $15,000 and punitive damages of $10,000 were awarded to the victim. This $25,000 award might have been avoided had there been closer supervision and less latitude allowed the security officer.

Exemplary Security Systems

Orlando, Florida, is the number-one tourist destination in the country, with 75,000 hotel rooms. The Orlando convention and visitor's bureau has developed a Tourist Employees Against Crime program to educate all tourist-industry employees in crime prevention. According to Channell (1994, p. 35):

> Posters and payroll stuffers are used to inform employees about the different types of crimes that can occur on their property and what they can do to prevent it.
>
> With this type of multifaceted approach to hotel security in place on a day-to-day basis, Orlando area hotels are well prepared for VIP visits, major events such as the World Cup Soccer games, and the many major golf tournaments hosted in Orlando year-round. Orlando's network of security and law enforcement professionals plays a vital role in making the area the world's number one vacation destination.

Bock (1994, p. 63) describes the security at the Little Nell Hotel, a first-class ski lodge in Aspen Mountain, Colorado: "Guests who stay at the Little Nell can ski down Aspen Mountain into the secure environment the hotel offers, which includes effective key control, CCTV, and employee security awareness." This hotel received the American Automobile Association's Five-Diamond Award in 1992 and 1993.

Likewise, security at the Las Vegas Mirage Hotel is on the cutting edge. Major (1994, p. 25) says of the Mirage: "To keep order in the casino, the hotel relies on its 250-person security force, larger than that found in many cities." In the casinos many problems result when people get wrapped up in the game and forget about their personal belongings, purses, cameras and the like at their feet. The biggest problem, however, is people cheating at the games.

This is also a problem encountered at Foxwoods Casino and Resort in Connecticut. According to Azano (1994, p. 43): "With an average take of $1.5 million per day, it is probably one of the most profitable casinos in the world." Azano (p. 44) notes: "Security officers are taught everything from how to recognize the various forms of scams used in casinos to CPR."

The Mystic Lake Casino in Prior Lake, Minnesota, and The Showboat Casino in Atlantic City, use cameras to enhance security. As noted by Draty (1993, p. 6): "More than 150 ceiling-mounted cameras provide video surveillance of roulette wheels, blackjack tables, slot machines, and other gaming areas throughout the casinos." The digital, high-resolution cameras capture extremely detailed video pictures.

Public Gatherings and Special Events*

Private security plays a significant role in maintaining order and controlling traffic at large public gatherings such as conventions, entertainment events, festivals, parades, political rallies, rock concerts, sporting events and trade shows. Many cities have built large, multipurpose facilities which they lease to organizations, such as a professional football or baseball franchises on a long-term seasonal basis, or for events such as auto, boat and home shows or concerts on a short-term basis.

According to Werth (1994, p. 32): "Organizations spend millions of dollars every year on special events, meetings, and conventions. While corporations regularly use special events and meetings to gain recognition, they fail to consider the potential risks associated with these events. An untimely accident, criminal incident, or unanticipated emergency can cast gloom over an entire event, undoing all the goodwill it might have generated."

> Security problems at public gatherings include maintaining order, preventing admission of nonpaying people, preventing internal and external theft, providing first aid for injuries and regulating pedestrian and vehicle traffic.

Most multipurpose facilities and stadiums maintain a small security force and then require the lessee or promoter of an event to provide additional security as the circumstances dictate. The number of patrons at a special event can vary considerably. For example, a stadium may host a football game attracting eighty thousand people one night and a rock concert attracting only one thousand people the next night. Security directors estimate the number

---

*Special Events—See *Private Security,* p. 58.

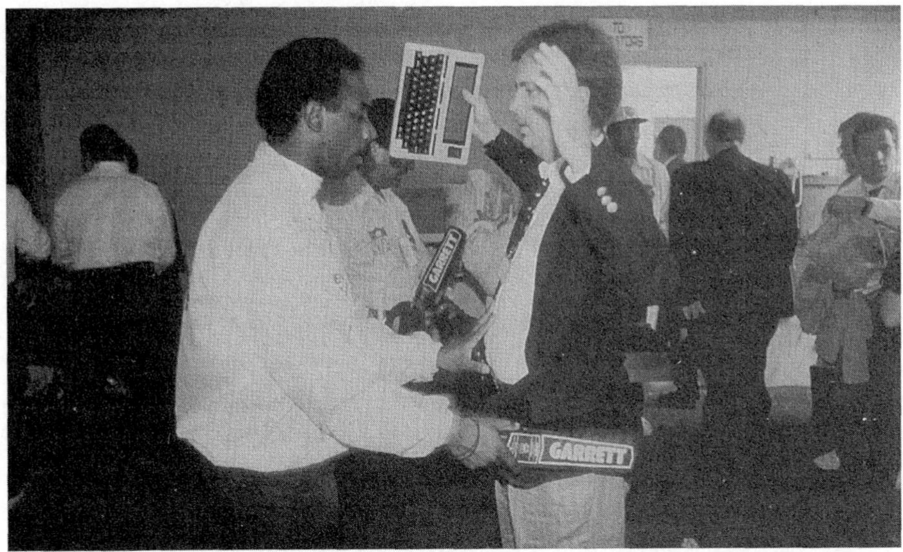

Security was especially tight during Superbowl XXV due to increased worries of a terrorist attack as a result of the Gulf War.

of patrons by keeping a careful watch on advance ticket sales and then use those figures to determine the amount of security required.

Multipurpose convention centers such as the Crown Center, Kansas City's largest convention and tourist destination, also present enormous security challenges. As Potoski (1993, p. 66) describes, this center has grown to include 11 office buildings, 110 garden apartments, 135 high-rise condominiums, a three-level retail shopping and entertainment center, 5,000 parking spaces and the Hyatt and Westin hotels. When it redesigned its security dispatch center, it installed bulletproof glass windows and an upgraded uninterrupted power supply to run for 30 minutes after any power failure. This also became one of the first locations to integrate security for parking, businesses, shopping and entertainment facilities, according to Potoski (p. 71).

The major problems at exhibitions and trade shows are protecting high-value merchandise and exhibits from theft and vandalism and maintaining access control. When exhibits are dismantled, special precautions must be taken to avoid theft by people posing as truckers or exhibitors.

As noted by Thompson (1993, p. 57): "Whether a provider of contract security or part of in-house security, security personnel can help prevent theft, damage, or spying at trade shows by taking a few precautions." Thompson divides trade show security into four areas:

- Cooperation between exhibitors and security personnel.
- Preparation for the show.
- Application of appropriate systems.
- Execution of security measures.

Thompson (1993, p. 58) suggests: "The most vulnerable periods for exhibitors are during setup and teardown." In addition, Thompson states (p. 62):

"Strictly controlled access is the most effective measure security can take." Thompson concludes: "Cooperative efforts and meticulous preparation will generate appropriate choices in security systems and produce an effective plan of execution to prevent loss at trade shows."

> Security personnel are the primary means of reducing problems at public gatherings.

Security personnel often work closely with local law enforcement agencies to control traffic and to reduce problems such as pickpocketing and disorderly or abusive behavior. Some cities require local law enforcement officers to be present at public gatherings. Other cities hire off-duty law enforcement officers to supplement security personnel, a highly controversial practice.

The specific problems to be anticipated depend partly on the type of function. For example, sports spectators tend to be unruly, and they often get caught up in the emotion, competition and aggressiveness of the game. Spectators often try to bring alcoholic beverages into a stadium, and some stadiums sell beer. In either case, drunken sports fans may have to be ejected from the stadium. Spectators may also attempt to get onto the playing field or to get to players for autographs.

Security is needed at even minor sporting events. Arbetter (1994, p. 42) describes the security used at Cashman Field in Las Vegas for the city's minor-league baseball team. This system is considered in terms of points of conflict, with this field having four such points: parking, gates, giveaway nights and seating. This is where security is concentrated.

On a much larger scale is the security needed at a facility such as New Orlean's Superdome, the largest indoor exhibition center in the country, covering 52 acres. In this area, "Everything has a security angle, even the lighting and the sound" (Anderson, 1994, p. 24A). The Superdome uses 28 full-time security officers during major events as well as CCTV monitors.

On an even grander scale is the security needed for the XXVI Olympiad to be held in Atlanta in 1996. To protect the 14,000 athletes and officials, the 50,000 volunteers and the expected two million visitors is an enormous task. Lang (1994, p. 19A) says the security plan has expanded to more than 600 tasks to be completed. As always, planning is an absolute MUST.

Rock concerts pose a different type of problem. The spectators for such events are often emotionally excited young people who may be on drugs. The concerts are often sold out in advance, and people without tickets often mill about outside, hoping to see the rock stars and causing disturbances. They may attempt to crash the gate en masse, a dangerous action—vividly evident at a Who rock concert when eight people were trampled to death.

Sharp (1992, p. 149) recalls the 1991 Guns N' Roses concert in Maryland Heights, Missouri, where lead singer Axl Rose dove into the crowd to stop attendees from taking pictures and a riot broke out. He cites problems of congestion, noise, disturbances, drinking, narcotics, large numbers of people and traffic congestion as factors that should be considered.

More recently, as reported on the on-line computer service Prodigy ("Hundreds Riot at Rock Concert," July 3, 1995):

> More than 1,000 ticketless Grateful Dead fans rioted outside a concert at the Deer Creek Music Center [in Nobelsville, Indiana]. Police used tear gas to break up the crowd. Three thousand to 4,000 fans in the parking lot stormed the gates behind the stage and tore them down. Thirty-eight were arrested for drug offenses and resisting law officers. Some 200 officers at the scene were injured.

Shirley (1987, pp. 251–52) cites several incidents that "illustrate the recent negative trends in crowd behavior":

- Eleven were killed in a panic at a rock concert.
- A security officer was thrown head first over the rail by football fans.
- A riot occurred in a stadium after a rock group failed to perform in the rain. Many police officers and spectators were injured.
- Fans stormed the stage at a concert causing injuries to police and security officers.

Shirley (p. 256) suggests that such incidents occur because "raw emotions surface in individuals during a crowded situation where one often feels a mask of anonymity is worn."

Large public gatherings usually pose security problems in four specific time frames and locations:

- *Parking lots*—before and after the event (with theft and vandalism a threat during the event).
- *Ticket windows*—before the event—sometimes hours or even days.
- *Gates and turnstiles into the facility*—primarily before the event.
- *Inside the facility itself*—during the event.

Parking Lots

Shirley (1987, p. 253), although speaking of sporting events, offers suggestions that fit most large public gatherings. He notes that in parking areas, crimes on the rise are "auto thefts, rapes, robberies, ticket scalping, assaults, and even murder." He notes: "Good parking lot security has a profound influence on the fans prior to entering" and "diverse techniques are essential" with observation, lighting and communication being major concerns. Included in the security might be helicopters, mounted horse patrols and motorized golf carts, supplemented by stationary cameras and observation towers. Some facilities hosting large public gatherings are planning to have parking lots farther away and make use of rapid transit systems, including computerized trains and people movers.

Shirley suggests that parking lots may soon have "computerized machines [that] will receive the money and make the necessary change. As the drivers proceed through the parking lot, computerized machinery will direct the driver to a designated space. Proper surveillance of such vast facilities can only be successfully achieved through the use of mounted cameras freely moving on cables stretched above all areas. In addition, the sophisticated 'eyes' will include night vision, zoom lenses and a public announcement system."

Ticket Windows

Another security problem is ticket windows, especially if fans begin lining up hours before the windows open. Among the problems are "sanitation, pickpockets, placement in line, and general panic" (Shirley, 1987, p. 254). Crowd control can be maintained by creating a buffer zone between the ticket window and the fans. Shirley suggests creating a 50-foot to 75-foot buffer zone using crowd control stands or sawhorses. He suggests that soon "computerized automation will be necessary to provide the most convenient means of ticket sales. As the fan approaches the ticket window, available seating will be listed on a computerized screen. After the customer has selected and paid for the requested seats, the computer will dispense the tickets." Security personnel will still be needed, however, to monitor the ticket window and ensure crowd control.

Gate and Turnstile

To keep crowd control, the facility must have enough entrances to avoid pushing and shoving. Shirley (1987, p. 255) says: "Efficient ticket takers, uniformed security personnel, clearly stated policies on posted signs, and gates in good working order are all matters to be considered currently when handling gate security." He again suggests that in the future gates and turnstiles will be computerized and that "mechanically controlled gates will be encased with emergency lighting, panic bars, P.A. systems, cameras, and automatic locking devices."

Inside the Facility

As with gate control, having a large, well-trained, uniformed security force, often supplemented by public police, can maintain crowd control. Shirley (1987, p. 256) stresses: "Procedures incorporating video taping of unruly spectators, emergency lighting, and emergency evacuation should already be in practice. . . . Much emphasis should be placed on the public relations aspect as well. It is a proven fact that a well-trained, uniformed security person who is courteous and helpful will encourage fans to visit the facility again."

Many of the security concerns that are common to public gatherings and public events may also be encountered by the movie industry when controversial or inflammatory movies are involved.

MOVIE INDUSTRY

When *Boyz 'N the Hood* opened in 1991, 11 people were wounded by gunfire in southern California. According to Graham (1992, p. 43):

> Properly planned security measures at theaters screening urban action films can reduce or eliminate the danger of violent incidents and show reasonable care to protect against civil litigation. Recognizing the potential for danger early on and planning to reduce the threat of third party assaults are essential in areas where gang members or other violence-prone individuals may be drawn to theaters showing urban action films. . . .

Although the owner or operator of the theater is not an insurer of a patron's safety, he or she has a duty to supervise patrons and prevent injuries where the risk of those injuries is known or, by the exercise of reasonable care, should be known. The standard is one of ordinary care exercises under the circumstances.

RECREATIONAL PARKS

According to Chuvala and Peterson (1994, p. 84): "Park security is a growing concern for county boards, city commissioners, and city officials who recognize that a lack of safety may be costly both in terms of assets and reputation. As a result, cities around the country are turning to security consultants for guidance."

Of equal concern are the major theme parks, which attract millions of visitors yearly. Large crowds are common at theme parks throughout the country: Disney Land, Marine Land, Knotts Berry Farm, and the like. Disney World offers one example of security at its finest. According to Shearing and Stenning (1987, p. 317): "[The Disney order] is a designed-in feature that provides—to the eye that is looking for it, but not to the casual visitor—an exemplar of modern private corporate policing. Along with the rest of the scenery of which it forms a discreet part, it too is recognizable as a design for the future." Shearing and Stenning (p. 319) say Disney World is able to have such order because: "Potential trouble is anticipated and prevented. Opportunities for disorder are minimized by constant instruction, by physical barriers which severely limit the choice of action available and by the surveillance of omnipresent employees who detect and rectify the slightest deviation. . . . Control strategies are embedded in both environmental features and structural relations. . . . Control is pervasive."

But most people never notice it. What visitors notice is the sense of security, the orderliness, the cleanliness and the ever-present, helpful, smiling employees. As noted by Arbetter (1992, p. 80): "It takes more than magic to keep Mickey and the gang safe." Security director Jim Chaffee pays special attention to his staff. When he came on the job, he changed the title from security guard to security host to remove any stigma associated with the former term. He changed the hosts' uniforms from the military type to the softer blazer type, and he set up a recognition program for staff who did outstanding jobs. Arbetter (p. 82) describes how staff is made central:

> Hosts learn about everything from first aid, crisis management, and fire prevention and suppression, to corporate culture. . . .
>
> The professionalism of the security personnel is further fostered by the fact that all hosts work full time and receive full benefits. . . .

"That's the key to a great security outfit," Chaffee says. "Treat your people well, and you're going to get payback 10 times."

Universal Studios in Orlando also has an emphasis on security. According to Ohlhausen (1991, p. 147): "In a setting like this, it's no surprise that Brauner [manager of security] describes the work of his security officers ('studio guards' they're called) as 85 percent public relations." Security is enhanced through patrol, using cars, golf carts and bicycles. In addition, CCTV cameras cover the parking lot and grounds.

RACETRACKS

Ohlhausen (1986, pp. 51–55) suggests that "security at a racetrack is a microcosm of security in industry generally. . . . In particular, horses need to be protected from tampering by their owners or their opponents. Patrons need to be protected from con artists, pickpockets, and other, feistier patrons. Drivers need to be protected from patrons who bet on other drivers. Parking, gambling, drinking, large crowds, and the excitement of racing add up to a lot of fun for patrons, a lot of money for the track, and a lot of work for the security department."

> Security problems at a racetrack include access control, crowd control, parking security, vault security, alcohol control and fraud detection.

The aim of racetrack security is to protect the patrons, horses, jockeys/drivers, owners and grooms and to help the track meet the standards set forth by the various state racing commissions.

Some tracks use proprietary security guards in the **backstretch area**—the area where the horses, drivers and grooms are quartered. This is the most problematic area of the racetrack, with drinking, fighting and stealing being the major security problems.

The public areas of the racetrack such as the grandstand are usually protected by contract security officers who play an important public relations role as well as handle brawls and drunken patrons, personal injuries and protection of the big winners. They also frequently provide parking lot security.

Other services provided by security personnel include guarding the vault and the runners conveying cash to and from the betting area, providing travel information, paging and handling lost-and-found articles.

An additional responsibility is determining who has a legitimate phone call to make within one hour of post time. All public pay phones at the track are disconnected an hour before post time by order of the racing commission (to discourage bookmaking). It is the responsibility of the security officer at security headquarters to determine if a patron's need to place an outside phone call is, indeed, urgent.

> Security problems at a racetrack can best be met by adequate access control and by the presence of well-qualified, well-trained security personnel.

As noted by Ohlhausen:

> Racetracks throughout the country usually have minimum selection standards for security officers selected to work at the racetracks. These are usually set out by the racing commissions of the states affected and consist of:
>
> - Applicant must be a citizen of the U.S.
> - Complete a comprehensive written application
> - Submit to a thorough background check
> - Not have been convicted of a felony or a pari-mutuel horseracing or gambling crime
> - Provide a set of fingerprints
> - Undergo a thorough medical and psychological examination
> - Pass an oral examination conducted by the appointing authority

Minnesota has what according to Ohlhausen "is believed to be the only comprehensive additional requirement to be eligible for a race track security officer's position": a 40-hour program developed jointly by Normandale Community College (the largest community college in Minnesota) in conjunction with the Canterbury Downs Race Track, which began operations in 1985, and approved by the Minnesota Racing Commission. That program consists of the following:

Criminal Procedure (14 hours). Selected Minnesota Statutes. Differentiation of the public peace officer's and private peace officer's applications of criminal procedure as they apply in the public and private sectors.

- Constitutional law
- Laws of arrest, search and seizure
- Use of excessive force; laws regarding force
- Civil liability
- Searching arrested persons
- Other related operational procedures necessary for the officer to function in an effective and efficient manner

Report Writing (12 hours). Report writing, of which two hours are devoted to evaluation of written reports used in a simulated civil or criminal case.

- Introduction to reports and report writing
- Characteristics of a well-written report
- Principles of clear writing
- Clear and understandable narrative reports
- Evaluating reports

Human Relations (8 hours).

- Handling stressful and emotional complaints
- Gathering information from people

- Crowd control
- The security officer and stress
- Behavior modification
- Crisis situations—personal power vs. position power
- Other subjects related to human relations

Health (4 hours). A modified first-aid course plus CPR to familiarize the security officer with the various types of calls for medical assistance he or she may be asked to respond to. Course covers recognition and symptoms of diabetes and asthma attacks, strokes, heart attacks, trauma, heat exhaustion and other relevant medical problems.

Defensive Tactics (2 hours). A course designed to instruct security officers how to protect themselves without the use of a baton, club, nightstick or gun.

On completing the 40-hour course, participants receive four continuing education credits and a certificate.

AIRPORT AND AIRLINE SECURITY*

Skyjackings of commercial aircraft, bombings, bomb threats and extortion attempts involving aircraft and hostages have made the need for airport and airline security obvious. Terrorist groups have increasingly used such means to advance their causes, making some people afraid to travel by air because of these perceived dangers. Bomb threats can result in air traffic delays and in evacuation of entire sections of a terminal. Actual explosions result in serious injuries, deaths and extensive property damage.

> Security problems of airports and airlines include skyjackings; bombs and bomb threats; air cargo theft; theft of passenger baggage, airline tickets, credit cards, merchandise from airport retail shops and items from vehicles in parking lots; crowd control; VIP escorts; traffic control and the potential for large-scale disasters.

Although skyjackings and bombings receive the most publicity, other serious security problems exist in airports. Losses from air cargo theft are estimated to be in excess of $100 million annually and are especially serious at the airports infiltrated by organized crime. Air cargo is different from other types of cargo because most is coordinated with passenger schedules. Also much air cargo is small and highly valuable, making it especially vulnerable to theft. In addition, because of the great number of people using airports, the maintenance of order and crowd control, VIP escorts and traffic control must be provided by airline and airport security personnel.

---

*Airport Security—See *Private Security,* pp. 41–43.

A unique problem of airports and airlines is the potential for a large-scale disaster caused by a plane crash. Response to such a disaster requires close cooperation among fire, medical, law enforcement, private security and airport personnel.

By 1972 the increasing frequency of skyjackings and bomb threats prompted the Federal Aviation Authority (FAA) to require certain security measures.

The FAA requires:

- Screening of all persons and carry-on baggage before entering an airport's departure area.
- The availability of a sworn law enforcement officer at the screening point within three to five minutes.
- Development by both scheduled airline carriers and airport managers of security programs for FAA approval.
- Development of an airport disaster plan.

According to Jenkins (1993, p. 20): "Federal Aviation Administration FAR 107.14 mandates the upgrading of access control identification and security systems at all major commercial airports in the U.S. Such systems must ensure that only authorized personnel can enter restricted areas."

The responsibility for screening passengers and baggage rests with the air carriers. In most major airports, this is done by a contract security firm with a sworn law enforcement officer within minutes of the screening point to

Security at Denver International Airport is tight but attempts to keep passengers moving along.

apprehend anyone who makes threats or tries to carry a dangerous weapon into the departure area. Although employees of contract security firms usually conduct the passenger checks, they maintain close cooperation with law enforcement agencies and airline and airport security personnel. Overall airport security is usually provided by law enforcement officers.

The importance of such access control is stressed by Stedman (1993, p. 15), who suggests: "The key to airport security is access control, particularly passenger screening at checkpoints where individuals are required to pass through a metal detector. But the checkpoints are only as effective as the people and equipment used to maintain them." And, as Stedman notes (p. 18): "To keep traffic moving at airports, detection equipment only has four to six seconds to check a piece of luggage or a passenger during check-in procedures."

One problem with the predeparture screeners is the high turnover rate, which is more than 100 percent in some airports because of the near-minimum wages paid (Cantor, 1994, p. 61). And as Cantor notes: "Screening can be the most effective weapon you have, but it also is the weakest link because that's where the human element comes in." He further notes (p. 65): "The effectiveness of security technology, such as X-rays, CCTV and metal detectors, is limited by the performance of the equipment and, just as important, by the people who operate it."

Miller (p. 58) stresses: "The key to good security is alert employees. Having people who are technically trained does not guarantee effective security. It is the alert person, the one who is conscious of his or her duty to monitor the machines, to pay attention to the regular and routine events rather than just the idiosyncratic and unusual ones, who really guards the safety of the airport."

As noted by Libby (1992, p. 11A): "Screening requires tact, professionalism, discretion, and adherence to the rules." It is sometimes difficult to tell if a cast that sets off the metal detector is really harmless.

According to Demoulpied (1992, p. 53): "Weapons and explosives detection at airports continues to be a top priority, yet the majority of X-ray systems at airport carry-on checkpoints use older technology." Ideally, they should be using enhanced x-ray systems built into the check-in counters to screen bags as they are checked.

In addition, as pointed out by Stedman (p. 15): "Only about 15% of the weapons go through the metal detector; many are thrown over the fence, some are brought in by people posing as airline personnel and some by authorized personnel."

Another area where security is being improved is the entry to the jetways. As described by Dalrymple (1994, p. 54):

> Exit devices with electric latch retraction, known as El devices, are popular in jetways to allow free egress from the jetway into the terminal. The electric latch retraction feature makes it possible to control entry into the jetway, and the door can be opened by a standard pull handle when the latch is retracted. At other times, the door is locked from the terminal side but allows safe egress from the jetway.

Boynton (1992, p. 22A) notes: "Today's airline security is enhanced by state-of-the-art access control technology." In addition, notes Boynton (p. 26A), technology is being used to harden the aircraft so it can withstand a minimum-level explosion. Development of baggage containers that can withstand explosive devices is also underway.

Miller (1993, p. 58) recommends several actions that can improve security:

- Ask questions.
- Inform passengers.
- Inform airport authorities.
- Address the boredom.
- Follow the rules.

Security is not inexpensive. To meet the increased expense of adding security, some airlines, such as United, have added a security surcharge on passenger tickets. Currently about 2 percent of a passenger's ticket price pays for security (Addis, 1991, p. 28).

Green (1987, p. 28) says of airport security:

> The field is relatively new, mushrooming especially since the hijacking scares which began in the late 1960s (and continue today, even with increased security standards). It seems clear that, with mandated security requirements including physical security and access controls, baggage screening, 100% screening of air passengers and carry-on luggage, cargo security, and other controls, the demand for personnel to fill these needs will continue to rise.

The Gulf War placed additional emphasis on airport security as the threat of terrorism became even greater. One of the first actions taken as the threat of war became a reality was to tighten airport security.

Recently, a new type of hijacking has come upon the scene, as described by Corbett (1993, p. 124):

> A new threat, or rather the resurgence of an old threat, faces commercial aviation—escape hijacking. . . . [E]scape hijackings are carried out by the disenfranchised, disgruntled, and those seeking better economic conditions.

Corporate Airlines

Also at risk are private corporate planes. As Pizer and Sloan (1993, p. 69) caution: "Corporate aviation personnel must also be sensitive to the danger that their aircraft may be used as airborne 'mules' for drug trafficking." Benny (1993, p. 71) also notes: "Drug traffickers and thieves will continue to target corporate aircraft."

MASS TRANSIT SECURITY*

Millions of Americans depend on public transit systems for transportation. Our public transit system developed at the beginning of the nineteenth century as the need for moving large numbers of people within congested major cities

*Mass Transit Security—See *Private Security,* pp. 60–61.

became apparent. The first mass transit systems were horse-drawn streetcars. They were eventually replaced by cable and electric cars, buses and finally the rapid transit systems of today, including such systems as New York's subway, Chicago's El and San Francisco's BART. The early transit systems were not immune from the crime problems of the congested urban environment in which they operated. By the early 1900s, thieves, vandals, roving gangs of youths and pickpockets caused several states to authorize transit companies to establish security forces, some with full police authority. As crime increased nationally, it also increased at comparable levels in transit systems. As a result, most transit systems have established full-time security forces with full or limited police powers.

> The major security problems faced by mass transit systems are robberies and assaults of operators, passengers and fare collectors; rapes and murders and theft of vehicles or their contents in park-and-ride areas.

Such crimes occur most often in the mass transit systems located in or near high-crime areas. People are most often victimized while waiting for transit vehicles, especially on platforms and in the rapid transit stations. Crime also occurs at station entrances and exits, stairwells, ramps and tunnels, and on the vehicles themselves.

As noted by Arko (1992, p. 31): "Crime, threats to the public's safety, and the well-being of patrons are growing concerns for the transit industry, especially in major metropolitan areas." He further notes (p. 26): "[M]ass transit systems face the same economic pressures as public corporations and privately owned business."

In addition, as Backler (1992, p. 31A) notes: "Collectively, these industries [land transportation] lose millions of dollars every year from vandalism done to parked vehicles and theft of vehicle content."

An additional problem making rapid transit transportation unattractive to riders is the antisocial behavior of some riders—for example, drunkenness and the use of abusive conduct and language.

In the energy-conscious 1990s, a concerted national effort to promote use of rapid transit systems depends heavily on making such systems safe and attractive to the general public.

> Security measures for rapid transit include security guards, CCTV in waiting areas and on vehicles, telephones and other emergency communications devices for riders, unbreakable glass as see-through barriers and high-intensity lighting.

Installing such security equipment is expensive because of the large number of stations and vehicles in any given system, as well as the susceptibility of the equipment to vandalism. In addition, CCTV must be continuously monitored if it is to be effective, requiring more personnel than may be available.

Arko (1992, p. 31) suggests: "The use of contract security can decrease liability and bolster the bottom line." According to Arko (p. 28), corporate security can be used for a number of security functions:

- Station patrols.
- Revenue pickup.
- Parking areas.
- Yards and buildings.
- Monitoring security hardware.
- Miscellaneous security areas.

The Long Island Rail Road is the busiest commuter rail system in the country. It was on this railroad on December 7, 1993, that Colin Ferguson opened fire on passengers, shooting 23, six fatally. This incident received national attention and heightened awareness of the need for better security on mass transit systems. According to Obremski (1994, p. 45): "Rail system security must balance the need for accessibility with the need to provide enhanced protection, thereby increasing customer use and revenue for the corporation." On this particular line, says Obremski (p. 44): "The corporate security department has targeted its resources toward three goals: tightening access control, improving security awareness, and maximizing external networking."

Cruise Ship Security

Cruise ships carry more than four million passengers a year (Henrickson, 1994, p. 43). Such cruises are usually associated with sun and fun and relaxing, but danger also exists here. Henrickson recalls: "The seminal event was the 1985 high-profile hijacking of the Italian liner *Achille Lauro* by four armed men."

In 1986 the International Maritime Organization (IMO) published "Measures to Prevent Unlawful Acts Against Passengers and Crews on Board Ships." As noted by Robbins (1992, p. 14A):

> The IMO recommendations include conducting a comprehensive security survey; establishing specific responsibility for security; designating restricted areas; using barriers, lighting, alarms, and communications equipment; and using access control and personal identification.

Many of these same recommendations found their way into the Coast Guard's Notice of Proposed Rule Making, published in March 1994, setting forth new standards and security requirements to prevent acts of terrorism against passenger vessels (Henrickson, pp. 43–44):

- Designation of security officers.
- Use of standardized, descriptive crew and passenger photo ID cards.
- Implementation of screening procedures to prevent the introduction of weapons and explosives on board in either carry-on luggage or baggage in the hold.
- Designation and control of certain restricted areas on board ships and at terminals, including use of intrusion detection systems.

- Establishment of adequate communication and coordination between ship terminals.
- Training of crews in handling security responsibilities.
- Use of periodic security surveys.
- Development of security plans.
- Installation of adequate barrier fencing and lighting.
- Reporting of unlawful acts and threats.

As Robbins (1992, p. 16A) concludes: "A minimum level of security is no longer a luxury. When considering the world situation and how fast it is changing, security professionals owe the users of the maritime transportation system a reasonable level of security."

SUMMARY

Commercial enterprises that rely heavily on private security include financial institutions, office buildings, public and private housing, hotels and motels, facilities housing large public gatherings, racetracks, recreational parks, airports and airlines and mass transit.

Financial institutions face unique security problems. The movement to make banking activities more accessible to citizens makes security more difficult. In addition, the large amounts of financial assets centralized in one location are extremely attractive to thieves. The most frequent losses in financial institutions involve theft of cash or stocks and bonds, check and credit-card fraud and embezzlement of funds.

The Bank Protection Act (1968) requires that all federally insured banks, savings and loan institutions and credit unions designate a security officer; cooperate with and seek security advice from the FBI and other law enforcement agencies; develop comprehensive security programs and implement protective measures to meet or exceed federal standards; maintain "bait" money; periodically remove excess cash from tellers' windows and bank premises; and develop security-conscious opening and closing procedures and stringent security inspections. In addition, federally insured financial institutions must install and maintain vault area lighting systems, tamper-resistant exterior doors and window locks, cameras and alarm systems.

Major security problems in office buildings include after-hours burglaries and theft; theft from a tenant by another tenant's employees; theft by service, maintenance and custodial employees; assaults, rapes and other crimes against persons; regulation and control of visitor traffic; bomb threats; protection of executive offices and personnel and fire watch. The items most frequently stolen from office buildings include small office equipment such as typewriters, calculators, duplicating and photocopying machines and computers and peripherals; office furnishings; securities and valuable documents; blank payroll checks and check-writing machines. Primary security measures in office buildings are access control, proper authorization and documentation of the use of corporate assets by employees and periodic fire inspections.

Security problems of residential units include theft, vandalism and assaults, particularly muggings. Access control, patrol by security officers and the provision of youth programs help to reduce these residential problems.

Major security problems of the hotel/motel industry include both internal and external theft, vandalism, vice and fire. The items most frequently stolen from hotels and motels include money, credit cards, jewelry, linens, silver, food, liquor and other easily concealed articles. Security measures include stringent key control and frequent re-keying, careful preemployment screening, monitoring systems and use of unmarked towels and ashtrays.

Security problems at public gatherings include maintaining order, preventing admission of nonpaying people, preventing internal and external theft, providing first aid for injuries and regulating pedestrian and vehicle traffic. Security personnel are the primary means of reducing these problems.

Security problems at a racetrack include access control, crowd control, parking security, vault security, alcohol control and fraud detection. Such problems can best be met by adequate access control and by the presence of well-qualified, well-trained security personnel.

Security problems of airports and airlines include skyjackings; bombs and bomb threats; air cargo theft; theft of passenger baggage, airline tickets, credit cards, merchandise from airport retail shops and items from vehicles in parking lots; crowd control; VIP escorts; traffic control and the potential for large-scale disasters. The Federal Aviation Authority (FAA), which regulates airport and airline security, requires screening of all persons and carry-on baggage before entering an airport's departure area; the availability of a sworn law enforcement officer within three to five minutes of the screening point; development by both scheduled airline carriers and airport managers of security programs for FAA approval and development of an airport disaster plan.

The major security problems faced by mass transit systems are robberies and assaults of operators, passengers and fare collectors; rapes and murders and theft of vehicles or their contents at park-and-ride areas. Security measures include security guards, CCTV in waiting areas and on vehicles, telephones and other emergency communications devices for riders, unbreakable glass as see-through barriers and high-intensity lighting.

✔ APPLICATION

1. Develop a security checklist for three of the types of facilities discussed in this chapter.

2. Evaluate the burglary prevention materials shown in Chapter 14, Figures 14–5 and 14–6, in relation to commercial establishments.

CRITICAL THINKING EXERCISE

COMMERCIAL SECURITY

STATUTORY AND COMMON LAW

Minnesota statutes declare it unlawful for persons to permit minors to engage in sexual performances. Additionally there is a common-law duty to protect known trespassers from foreseeable criminal acts of third parties occurring on one's premises.

FACTS OF THE CASE

In August the annual Quaker State Northstar National race takes place at the Brainerd International Raceway (BIR) on the west side of Brainerd, Minnesota. This event lasts several days and has a reputation for somewhat unruly crowds, especially for events such as the wet T-shirt contest. The BIR each year contracts the services of North Country Security, Inc. (NCS) to provide security for all its events. As part of the agreement, BIR provides some equipment to NCS, such as radios, flashlights and handcuffs. However, BIR does not allow NCS to use the public address system without advance permission.

A wet T-shirt contest, similar to one held the previous year, was planned by persons other than management or employees of BIR or NCS, although both BIR and NCS were aware of these plans. Posters advertising the event were in obvious locations on the grounds, and a stage was constructed for the event. Organizers collected "contributions" at the gate from those who wanted to observe the event. Organizers did obtain permission from BIR to go ahead with the contest when the agreement was made that no one of minor age would be allowed on the grounds, and NCS was informed (even though prevention of the contest had been part of the agreed security plan).

The previous year's event involved nudity but no sexual contact between contestants and viewers in the crowd or contestant organizers. Security personnel, however, said that they did not want to venture into the area where the wet T-shirt contest was held; they called this area the "zoo." Several violent acts had occurred in the "zoo" area, and the crowds had been extraordinarily raucous and uncontrolled.

Attendance at this year's T-shirt contest was greater than in previous years. The number in the crowd was estimated at close to 3,000—mainly younger men. With the number of people trying to get in, it was difficult for security to screen and keep all minors out. Jane Doe, a 16-year-old runaway, who had previously participated in another wet T-shirt contest, entered the contest. She admitted entering the BIR grounds by using identity cards borrowed from another person. She also admitted using drugs and drinking alcohol that had been given to her by some of the men who attended the event.

The wet T-shirt contest began with pouring water on the contestants' T-shirts and clothes. The music, dancing and shouts from the crowd gradually encouraged the contest to escalate into a striptease. As some of the contestants became nude, the male organizers of the event who were on stage began fondling breasts and lifting the girls into the air. Jane Doe was one of the contestants who was sexually molested. The entire contest lasted for almost an hour.

Shortly after the incident Jane Doe brought suit in trial court against Brainerd International Raceway, Inc., and North Country Security, Inc., for damages of $50,000.

NCS testified that three officers had been assigned to provide security for the "zoo" area. One of these officers testified he knew nothing about the contest until it was over. A second said that when he noticed the size and temperament of the crowd he tried to call additional security by means of his phone, but others said they never received or heard such a call. By the time some additional security personnel did arrive at the scene, the contest was over.

Issues and Questions

1. Do BIR and NCS have a duty of care toward Doe?
   a. Neither BIR nor NCS have a duty of care toward Doe because she entered the contest voluntarily having previously experienced what wet T-shirt contests involve and can lead to. She is the sole person responsible for what happened to her because she is old enough to know better than to striptease down to nudity.
   b. BIR does not have a duty of care to Doe because of the contract made with NCS that no minors would be allowed in the area. NCS had a duty to check passes and identification cards. However, NCS is not liable because Doe, a minor, knowingly used deception to avoid security.
   c. Only the male organizers of the contest can be liable because they were the only ones to profit from the contest, they were on stage and responsible for running the contest and they were the ones who initiated sexual interaction (in contrast with how the contest was run in previous years).
   d. BIR does not have a duty of care to Doe who after all was a trespasser on the property; however, NCS is liable because it was responsible for security which must provide for both statutory and common-law rights.
   e. BIR has a duty of care toward Doe. BIR is vicariously liable for the negligence of NCS because it has a duty to prevent foreseeable criminal acts of third parties occurring on its premises. Previous rambunctiousness imposed a heightened degree of responsibility on both property owners and providers of security.

2. What would sufficiently alter the duty of care that either BIR or NCS have toward Doe?
   a. BIR would become liable only if it had known that in the previous year there was a case involving the rape of a 13-year-old girl during the wet T-shirt event and that for every five adults there would be two minors gaining entrance to the area.
   b. NCS would be liable if they had been informed in writing that they must prevent a wet T-shirt contest from taking place. Without such notification, they cannot be held responsible for degenerate actions by supposedly responsible third parties.
   c. If BIR had given NCS use of the public address system and total control of the security plan, then BIR would not be liable but NCS would be.
   d. If Jane Doe had a clear knowledge of the risk, an appreciation of the risk's consequences and the choice to avoid the risk but voluntarily chose to chance the risk, these elements would affect the primary assumption of risk.

e. NCS would become liable if the organizers of the wet T-shirt contest had contracted with them for security, and NCS would be liable if they were the managing organizers of the wet T-shirt contest.

Discussion Questions

1. Why is a properly trained security staff an asset to the hotel/motel business?
2. What are some legal requirements of hotels/motels that guests of the establishments should know?
3. What areas of security does the Bank Protection Act ignore?
4. Which types of security discussed in this chapter seem most important to you? Why?
5. What public gatherings in your area might pose a security problem?

References

Addis, Karen K. "Securing the Friendly Skies." *Security Management,* July 1991, pp. 27–31.

Aiken, Kevin A. "Checking in with Security." *Security Management,* August 1993, pp. 30–37.

Anderson, Teresa. "Security Sports a Winning Strategy." *Security Management,* July 1994, pp. 24A–26A.

Arbetter, Lisa. "Major League Security Hits the Minors." *Security Management,* August 1994, pp. 40–50.

Arbetter, Lisa. "Protecting Disney's Wonderful World." *Security Management,* October 1992, pp. 80–82.

Arko, Robert L. "Contract Security Rolls into the Transit Industry." *Security Management,* July 1992, pp. 26–31.

ASIS Standing Committee on Banking & Finance 1984–85. "Keeping the Lid on the Cookie Jar." *Security Management,* September 1985, pp. 57–61.

Associated Press. "Woman Electrocuted After Placing Key Card in Hotel-Room Door." *Star Tribune* (Minneapolis/St. Paul), June 28, 1995.

"ATM Security Legislation Provides Opportunity for Bank Security Technology Vendors." *Security Concepts,* March 1995, p. 2.

Azano, Harry J. "Making Security a Sure Bet." *Security Management,* November 1994, p. 43.

Backler, Michael A. "One by Land, Two by Air." *Security Management,* June 1992, pp. 31A–38A.

Barron, Ted P. "Anatomy of a Redesign." *Security Management,* March 1993, pp. 25–33.

Benny, Daniel J. "Corporate Aircraft Security Takes Off." *Security Management,* October 1993, p. 71.

Bock, Peter E., Jr. "Securing the Little Nell." *Security Management,* May 1994, pp. 63–65.

Bordes, Roy N. "Security Measures that Earn Interest." *Security Management,* June 1994, pp. 71–72.

Boynton, Homer A. "An Eye on Airline Security Technology." *Security Management,* June 1992, pp. 22A–26A.

Cantor, Michael B. "Aviation Security: The Human Factor." *Security Technology and Design,* August 1994, pp. 60–65.

Channell, Warren T. "Fun, Sun, and Security." *Security Management,* September 1994, pp. 52–55.

Chovanes, Michael H. "Does Regulatory Compliance Provide Serious Security?" *Security Management,* May 1994, pp. 115–16.

Chuvala, John and Peterson, Raymond L. "Learning to Love Leisure." *Security Management,* September 1994, pp. 84–87.

Corbett, William T. "Are Hijackings a Returning Threat?" *Security Management,* July 1993, pp. 124–45.

Dalrymple, John. "Closing the Door on Airport Security." *Security Technology and Design,* August 1994, pp. 54–59.

Demoulpied, David S. "Effective Screening for Airport Checkpoints." *Security Management,* October 1992, pp. 53–54.

Draty, David. "SpeedDome Keeps a Watchful Eye on Casinos." *Security Concepts,* November 1993, pp. 6, 33.

Fahed, Joseph M. "Armoring ATMs Against Attack." *Security Management,* November 1991, pp. 63–64.

Foyle, Michael P. "Closing the Door to Easy Money." *Security Management,* January 1995, pp. 61–64.

Goetzke, Richard. "Shedding New Light on ATM Security." *Security Management,* September 1994, pp. 57–60.

Graham, James P. "Making the Cinema Safe at Showtime." *Security Management,* August 1992, pp. 43–44.

Green, Gion. *Introduction to Security,* 4th ed. Revised by Robert J. Fischer. Stoneham, MA: Butterworth Publishers, 1987.

Harowitz, Sherry L. and Murphy, Joan H. "Examining 1993 Changes and 1994 Challenges." *Security Management,* March 1994, pp. 5A–6A.

Henrickson, David E. "Plotting a Course for Seaworthy Security." *Security Management,* June 1994, pp. 43–45.

"Hundreds Riot at Rock Concert." Prodigy, July 3, 1995.

Jenkins, Joe. "Airport Security Systems: Where to Begin?" *Security Technology and Design,* July/August 1993, pp. 20–22.

Koentopp, Juli. "The Mirage Concerning Hotel Security." *Security Management,* December 1992, pp. 54–60.

Kohr, Robert L. "Assessing the State of Hotel Security in the '90s." *Security Technology and Design,* May 1994, pp. 26–31.

Kohr, Robert L. "Mastering the Challenge of Securing a Budget Motel." *Security Management,* December 1991, pp. 33–40.

Lang, Robert F. "Gold Medal Security for 1996." *Security Management,* June 1994, pp. 13A–21A.

Libby, Don. "The Challenge of Screening Passengers." *Security Management,* June 1992, pp. 11A–12A.

Little, Stephen. "The Evolution of Hotel Security." *Security Technology and Design,* May/June 1993, p. 27.

Major, Michael J. "The Name of the Game Is Security." *Security Technology and Design,* May 1994, pp. 22–25.

Maxwell, David A. *Private Security Law: Case Studies.* Stoneham, MA: Butterworth-Heinemann, 1993.

May, Johnny R. "Hotel Liability: Dealing with Fire Prevention and Alcohol Server Liability." *Security Concepts,* December 1994, pp. 11, 18.

May, Johnny R. "Hotel Liability: Dealing with Fire Prevention and Alcohol Server Liability—Part II." *Security Concepts,* January 1995, pp. 9, 27.

McClure, Leslie. "Taking the Risk Out of Transactions." *Security Management,* March 1994, pp. 23A–24A.

Miller, R. Reuben. "The People Problem." *Security Management,* June 1993, pp. 49–50, 58.

Obremski, Frank. "Workin' on the Railroad." *Security Management,* October 1994, pp. 43–46.

Ohlhausen, P. "Racetrck Security." *Security Management,* October 1986, pp. 51–55.

Ohlhausen, Peter. "Silver Screen Security." *Security Management,* September 1991, pp. 146–52.

Pizer, Harry and Sloan, Stephen. "Danger on the Runway." *Security Management,* October 1993, pp. 69–70.

Potoski, Jim. "Security's Crowning Glory." *Security Management,* September 1993, pp. 66–72.

Private Security. Report of the Task Force on Private Security, National Advisory Committee on Criminal Justice Standards and Goals. Washington, DC: U.S. Government Printing Office, 1976.

Robbins, Clyde E. "Making Security a Port of Call." *Security Management,* July 1992, pp. 14A–16A.

Ronan, Thomas O. "The Hospitality of Hotel Security." *Security Management,* August 1993, pp. 38–40.

Schreiber, F. Barry. "The Future of ATM Security." *Security Management,* March 1994, pp. 18A–21A.

Schreiber, F. Barry. "Tough Trends for ATMs." *Security Management,* April 1992, pp. 27–31.

Selwitz, Robert. "Security Is Job One at New York's Hotel Millenium." *Security Technology and Design,* May/June 1993, pp. 20–23.

Sharp, Arthur G. "Rock Concerts." *Law and Order,* October 1992, pp. 149–54.

Shearing, Clifford D. and Stenning, Philip C. "Say 'CHEESE!': The Disney Order That Is Not So Mickey Mouse." In *Private Policing,* by Clifford D. Shearing and Philip C. Stenning, eds. Beverly Hills, CA: Sage Publications, 1987.

Shirley, Joe. "Sporting Event Security in the Year 2000." In *Security in the Year 2000 and Beyond,* by Louis A. Tyska and Lawrence J. Fennelly, eds. Palm Springs, CA: ETC Publications, 1987.

Statistical Abstract of the United States 1994. Washington, DC: U.S. Department of Commerce, Bureau of the Census, September 1994.

Stedman, Michael J. "Airport Security Pratfall: Is the FAA Falling Down?" *Security Technology and Design,* July/August 1993, pp. 14–18.

Straub, Joanne. "A Safe Solution for Hotel Rooms." *Security Management,* December 1992, pp. 51–52.

Sunstrom, Phil. "Unlock the Secret to Key Control." *Security Management,* November 1992, pp. 59–61.

Thompson, Pamela Kleibrink. "Don't Let Others Steal the Show." *Security Management,* September 1993, pp. 57–62.

Thompson, Richard. "False Security." *Successful Meetings,* February 1991, pp. 82–87.

"Understanding Commercial Burglaries." *Security Management,* June 1994, pp. 13–14.

Werth, Richard P. "The Special Needs of Special Event Security." *Security Management,* January 1994, pp. 32–33.

Wessells, Fred P. "Diebold and the First National Bank of Ohio Lock Up Security." *Security Technology and Design,* January/February 1994, pp. 26–29.

Wipprecht, William R. and Barron, Ted P. "Principles and Planning for ATM Security." *Security Technology and Design,* January/February 1994, pp. 30–33.

Witkowski, Michael J. "The Fire Role of Security Officers." *Security Concepts,* October 1994, pp. 14, 24.

CASES

De Lema v. Waldorf Astoria Hotel, Inc., 588 F.Supp. 19 (D.C.N.Y. 1984)
Meyers v. Ramada Inn of Columbus, 471 N.E.2d 176 (Ohio 1984)
Pittard v. Four Seasons Motor Inn, Inc., 688 P.2d 333 (N.M. App. 1984)
Ramada Inns, Inc. v. Sharp, 711 P.2d 1 (Nev. 1985)
State v. Weiss, 449 So.2d 915 (Fla. App. 1984)
United States v. Lyons, W.L.Rept. Vol. III, No. 114 (1983)

CHAPTER 18

INSTITUTIONAL SECURITY

DO YOU KNOW

- What institutions may require special security?
- What security problems exist at health care facilities?
- Educational facilities?
- Libraries?
- Museums and art galleries?
- Religious facilities?
- What security measures can be taken to avoid or reduce these problems?

CAN YOU DEFINE THESE TERMS?

ARTCENTRAL	INTERPOL
ethnoviolence	photogrammetry

INTRODUCTION

Like most commercial establishments, many of the institutions discussed in this chapter are considered "open to the public." Each has its own unique security problems and challenges.

> Institutions that may require special security include hospitals and other health care facilities, educational institutions, libraries, museums and art galleries and even religious facilities.

This chapter focuses on institutions, traditionally considered "safe havens," free from crime and violence. It begins with a discussion of security in hospitals and other health care facilities. This is followed by a look at security in educational institutions, including K–12 schools and colleges and universities. Next security in libraries and in museums and art galleries is examined. The chapter concludes with a discussion of security in religious facilities.

HOSPITALS AND OTHER HEALTH CARE FACILITIES*

The United States has well over thirty thousand health care facilities, including publicly and privately owned hospitals, clinics, nursing homes, outpatient

*Health Care Facilities—See *Private Security,* pp. 48–49.

centers and physicians' office complexes. In fact, health care is the fifth largest industry in the country. Of the health care facilities, hospitals have the most serious security problems. They must maintain a safe environment for patients, visitors and employees, as well as protect physical assets such as medical equipment, supplies, buildings and personal property.

Hospitals are big businesses, facing all the problems of restaurants, hotel/motels, offices and retail stores. They are often spread over large areas, causing even greater security problems. One industry source estimates that theft losses amount to $1,000 per hospital bed annually. In addition, providing protection from violent crime to hospital users and employees is a major security problem. Little wonder that hospital security is one of the fastest growing fields in the industry.

Nonetheless, many hospital administrators are unaware of their security risks or, if they are aware of such risks, think that they are of low priority. The risks should be obvious, however. Hospitals have a stressful atmosphere for most patients, many staff members and most visitors. And they have a reputation as being a "magnet" for criminals, drug addicts and employee thieves.

Security officers who work in hospitals and health care facilities must be able to interact with the medical staff—physicians, nurses, therapists—the clerical staff, the administration, as well as patients and visitors—frequently under emergency conditions. Public relations skills are vital in this position.

Draty (1994, p. 12) notes: "Hospital security has progressed a long way since the beginning of the century." For the first 50 years, security was barely mentioned in connection with hospitals other than in a fire prevention role. During the fifties and sixties, the emphasis shifted from fire watch to law enforcement. Then, in the late sixties and into the seventies, security departments were created, expanding the function into the area of safety.

According to Bagley (1993, p. 98): "The Joint Commission for Accreditation of Healthcare Organizations, the nongovernment agency that surveys and accredits hospitals based on certain criteria and standards, has for the first time included minimum standards for security in hospitals."

Problems

Most hospitals are very open, have few locked doors and cover large areas. They often include coffee shops, gift shops, flower shops, laundries, pharmacies and doctors' offices. The openness of most health care institutions makes access control more difficult. Any access controls must fit the institution's medical care objectives and its public relations program. Security restrictions that impede the primary goal of life preservation are unacceptable to administrative and medical staffs. For example, rigid procedures for checking out surgical equipment or supplies may hinder prompt medical treatment.

Security problems of hospitals include the heavy daily flow of people, including patients, visitors, medical personnel, other employees and vehicle traffic; a substantial number of female employees; a high percentage of professional staff who often ignore security procedures and large quantities of consumable items such as drugs, linens, food, medical supplies and equipment, making property inventory and accountability extremely difficult.

> The major security problems of health care facilities are emergency room security, visitor control, internal and external theft and the potential for fire.

Visitor control is a formidable security problem. Yet most hospitals encourage visitors because the patients usually benefit from such visits. This policy can also create problems, however, because often visitors are emotionally upset, do not know their way around the hospital, smoke in no-smoking areas or steal. Most hospitals establish visiting hours in an attempt to control access during the hours when the hospital is not fully staffed and the corridors are not as well lit as usual. Some hospitals issue color-coded visitor passes that indicate the ward the wearer is authorized to visit. However, this system can cause lineups at the beginning of visiting hours and annoy visitors. To have to wait in line to visit someone who may be gravely ill could understandably cause anger and hostility.

Many hospitals also use an employee identification badge system, color coded to indicate the person's position—for example, nurse, volunteer, secretary. Employees and staff may be restricted to certain exits, and package inspections may be required. What can be locked should be (see Figure 18–1 p. 570).

Significant losses can result by not controlling services, cash and supplies. Services and supplies are especially difficult to monitor because of the emergency nature of many situations. Medications and services may be administered and never recorded or not charged to the appropriate patient. Not documenting medication given can also result in the loss of accreditation by a hospital and endanger government funding as well for failure to comply with regulations on certain listed drugs.

Theft from cars, especially physicians' cars, is another major problem. Most hospitals encourage physicians to lock their medical bags in their cars' trunks.

Crimes against persons, including simple assaults as well as violent crimes such as rape and aggravated assaults on patients, nurses and visitors, are also frequently committed in and around medical centers. Historically, hospitals have attracted peeping Toms and sex criminals. Therefore, many hospitals provide escort services for women.

A survey conducted by the International Association for Healthcare Security and Safety (IAHSS) found that nonsexual assaults decreased in 1991 but that sexual assaults rose ("Hospital Crime Survey," 1993, p. 15). This survey also suggests that hospital employees were three times as likely to be victims of assault than any other group. Hospital patients, on the other hand, while least likely to be victims, were most likely to commit the assaults.

Hospitals and health care facilities must tightly control access to medications and sensitive areas such as intensive care units in spite of the numbers of patients, visitors and staff that pass through the facility daily ("Security Management Systems Tailored for Healthcare," 1994, pp. 1, 26).

Items with Locks	Number of Locks	Items with Locks	Number of Locks	Items with Locks	Number of Locks
Access Space		Dispensers		Mail Boxes	
Air Conditioning		Sanitary Napkin		Money Bags	
Alarms		Soap			
Automotive		Towel			
				Penthouse	
		Doors (Exterior)			
Book Cases		Entrance			
Blood Bank		Exit			
Bulletin Boards		Doors (Interior)		Refrigerators	
		Closet			
		Connecting			
		Elevator		Roof Vents	
Cabinets		Entrance			
Electric		Fire			
Filing		Office		Safe Compartments	
Instrument		Storage Room		Safe Deposit Boxes	
Key				Screens	
Kitchen				Slop Sink Closet	
Medicine				Switch Key	
Narcotics					
Storage		Drawers			
Supply		Bench		Tabernacle	
Suture		Cash		Tanks (Oil & Gas)	
Tool		Lab. Table		Thermostat	
Ward Room		Safe		Trap Doors	
		Tool			
		Gas Pump		Valves	
Cash Boxes		Gates		Vaults	
Cash Register					
Chute Doors					
Clocks		Lockers		Watchman's Box	
		Employee			
Dark Rooms		Patients			
Desks		Physicians		X-Ray	

Figure 18–1. Key and Lock Survey for Hospital Administration
SOURCE: Reprinted with permission from TelKee Inc., Subsidiary of Sunroc Corp., Glen Riddle, PA 19037.

Bagley (1993, p. 98) says: "As criminal acts grow annually, medical facilities can no longer be considered safe havens, free from attack and violence. This reality hit home when three physicians were gunned down at the county medical center in Los Angeles in February [1993]."

Sherwood (1994, p. 2) notes: "On any given day, major hard narcotics and other illegal substances that can carry up to $7 million on the street are kept within the confines of our walls."

Hazardous wastes in hospitals and health care facilities pose another security problem to be addressed. An extremely important risk to guard against is the hazard of fire or explosions. Hospitals have large quantities of flammable chemicals, paper and oxygen, making them fire-loaded. Patients, some under sedation, may smoke in bed or in chairs. In an actual fire, many patients would not be ambulatory and would need to be evacuated on stretchers or litters, and those patients who could walk might be under sedation. Few patients or visitors know where the nearest stairs are because they customarily use the elevator.

Emergency Room

Hospital emergency rooms, especially in county hospitals, pose a serious problem for security. Patients admitted to the emergency room are frequently drunk, disorderly and very combative. Some are victims of gunshot or knife wounds or of muggings. At times both the victim and the assailant are brought to the emergency room, posing a great threat to the security of other patients and hospital personnel. Most county hospitals have a security officer on duty around the clock in the emergency room.

According to Kramer (1993, p. 14A): "On any given day the action in the emergency room may resemble that of a mobile army surgical hospital (MASH) unit. Added to the normal anxiety and disorder, the fear of crime in this setting can affect the hospital's ability to recruit and retain valuable people."

Jackson and Flinn (1994, p. 25) also emphasize the hazards present in hospital emergency rooms:

> Emergency department staffs find themselves in harm's way as acts of aggression follow the patient to the hospital. The magnitude of the problem was highlighted in a survey reported in the June 1992 article, "Violence in the Emergency Room," which appeared in *Topics in Emergency Medicine*. Forty-three percent of the hospitals responding reported at least one physical attack per month on a medical staff member. Seven percent said a violent incident that occurred in the emergency department had resulted in death.

In another study conducted by the University of Louisville School of Medicine, Department of Medicine, the following results were reported (Jackson and Flinn, 1994, p. 26):

- 32 percent received at least one verbal threat daily.
- 18 percent observed weapons displayed as a threat to staff at least once a month.
- 43 percent reported frequency of physical attacks on medical staff of one or more per month.
- 70 percent described an act of violence in the last five years resulting in a death.
- 46 percent said weapons were confiscated at least once a month.

As the gang problem escalates in our country, the impact is often felt in hospital emergency rooms. As noted by Jackson and Flinn (1994, p. 26): "Frequently, rival gangs pursue the injured to the medical facility for revenge."

Closely related to hospital security is the problem of violence at family planning clinics, as evidenced by the fatal shooting of Dr. David Gunn by an antiabortion activist. According to Surette (1993, p. 55): "For clients and employees, safe access into the facility was a major concern. Persons parking vehicles up against doors, jamming locks, and chaining themselves to vehicles in the driveway were not uncommon occurrences, and all had to be considered."

A second major problem is internal theft. The items most frequently stolen are, in order, linens, patients' cash and personal effects, office supplies and equipment, food, radios and television sets and drugs. To reduce such losses, inventory controls must be established so that administration can identify problems and determine the significance of each.

Reducing the Problems

> Hospital security problems can be reduced through recognition of the risks, careful inventory control, access control, training in fire prevention and evacuation procedures and surveillance.

Samson (1994, p. 22) suggests that security planning should begin with a concise mission statement such as the following: "The goal is to provide a safe and secure environment so the mission of the hospital can be carried out."

Lombardi (1991, p. 56) stresses that an important part of any security program is information on the current situation, including compiling statistics on the frequency and type of criminal incidents occurring around and within the hospital. This is crucial in addressing the issue of foreseeability, a key in most liability suits.

Photo ID badges to control access may be used, and metal detectors might be used in emergency rooms. Hall (1994, p. 29) suggests that badging could provide access control to patient areas. Access control is also critical in the distribution of narcotics and in nurseries. Hall suggests using sensor tagging technology to stop infant and child abductions. Emergency telephones might be installed in elevators and parking lots. Alarms might be installed on all perimeter doors.

Duress buttons and closed circuit television (CCTV) cameras may be located in highly sensitive areas such as the nursery and pharmacy. These buttons may be tied into the access control system, allowing staff members to instantly alert a security guard in case of an emergency. The system can also alert security if a monitored door is open anywhere in the hospital ("Hospital Patient, Personnel Safety," 1994, p. 22).

Another problem noted by Dean (1992, p. 148) is that federal "no restraints" legislation as well as liability and safety concerns have forced hospitals and nursing homes to reevaluate how they manage patients who wander.

> Generally, wanderer control systems consist of a tag worn by the patient that activates an exit alarm. Both active and passive systems are available. Passive tags react to a generic signal from the hardware at the exit. Active tags are transponders that send back an intelligent signal to a radio frequency emitted at the exit.
>
> Passive tags are usually larger than active ones and can require bulky hardware at the exit. Active systems often resemble a wristwatch in size, shape, and weight and can operate with hidden antennae that cover the entire exit periphery.

Many hospitals have elaborate surveillance systems established to monitor patients from the nurses' stations. These same systems may also be used to increase security. In addition, security officers stationed in the main lobby area as well as security officers on patrol, equipped with radios, can do much to increase security.

To lessen the risk of fire, smoking should be restricted to designated areas. All recommendations in Chapter 7 regarding preventing and extinguishing fires should be carefully adhered to. To avoid patient and visitor panic, a code word should be established to alert the staff to the existence of a fire if one occurs.

Chuda (1994, p. 35) describes the reaction of a hospital employee to a 69-year-old patient who set her bed on fire.

> [The clerk] automatically pulled an alarm and cut off the oxygen to the room. Sprinklers in the patient's room kept the fire under control while security officers used fire extinguishers and nurses evacuated the patients safely to other floors.

Chuda stresses: "Evacuation cannot be the first response, and the fight-in-place attitude must be stressed."

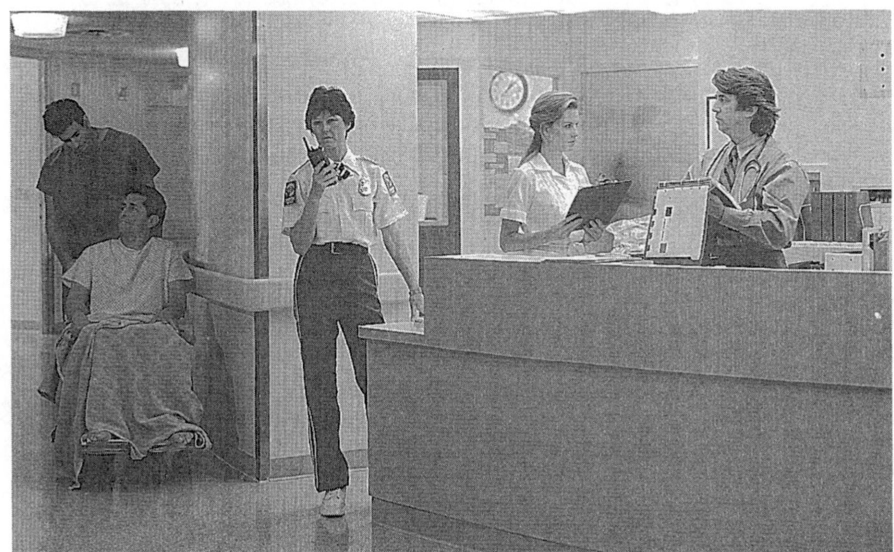

Security officers equipped with radios can do much to increase hospital security. They also serve an important public relations function.

Campbell (1995, p. 49) underscores the threat posed by fire: "A fire in a hospital, ambulatory care center, or nursing home poses one of the most potentially tragic scenarios. Patients, many of whom are heavily medicated, dangerously ill, or physically or mentally handicapped are extremely vulnerable." According to Campbell, most hospitals train their employees to use a fire response system called RACE (p. 49):

R = Removing people from danger.

A = Activating a fire alarm.

C = Closing doors and windows.

E = Extinguishing and escaping.

At Robert Wood Johnson University Hospital in New Brunswick, New Jersey, employees are given training beyond the RACE system, moving through a 45-minute session with six specific demonstrations (Campbell, 1995, pp. 49–51):

Station One: Discussion of the flammability of common patient care accessories, e.g., patient gowns, scrub suits, blankets, sheets.

Station Two: Exposure to smoke in a smoke chamber and how to stay low and cover mouth with wet towel.

Station Three: Demonstration of door safety and importance of doors during a fire.

Station Four: Demonstration in putting out a bed fire with a patient in it.

Station Five: Review of procedures and demonstration of how various substances burn.

Station Six: Hands-on experience using three types of fire extinguishers—water, carbon dioxide and multipurpose dry chemical.

In addition to the extreme danger presented by the potential for fire, the existence of hazardous wastes in hospitals must also be dealt with. Graves (1991, p. 43) identifies five categories of hazardous wastes commonly found in hospitals and health care facilities: chemical, infectious, physically hazardous, radioactive and cytotoxic waste. Guidelines for accumulating, storing and on-site managing of hazardous wastes are available. In addition, according to Graves (p. 46), three waste reduction techniques should be considered:

- Source reduction (using good housekeeping practices, using new product materials, and substitution).
- Recycling (on-site and off-site).
- Treatment (neutralization, precipitation, filtration, evaporation and incineration).

Graves (1991, p. 46) cautions:

Your liability continues as long as the waste is out there, even after it has been taken away by a waste disposal agency. That is why you file an EPA

> waste manifest, so it can be traced back to you. This responsibility makes operations like incineration or recycling especially attractive.
>
> Managing your hazardous waste program is an important responsibility.

Another approach to reducing problems is to be proactive, anticipating problems that might occur with patients or their families due to extreme emotional or psychiatric problems. In one hospital, as noted by Dawson (1992, p. 34): "Whenever a potentially dangerous situation is identified, a social worker is assigned to assess the family or patient and to ascertain the level of risk to other patients, staff, visitors, and property." Dawson describes the change in role that has evolved:

> Previously, security was used only to defuse a volatile situation immediately and provide bulk strength. Security was never involved in planning and was never consulted on a potentially dangerous situation before it went out of control. But security's role has expanded and now the staff is directly involved with patient care.

"The latest trend in hospital security," says Bagley (1993, p. 97), "is the use of K-9s."

Exemplary Programs

The security program at Children's National Medical Center in Washington, DC, serves some 58,000 children each year. As noted by Harowitz (1993, p. 43): "Children's Hospital is protected by state-of-the-art electronic security, including ninety-six access card readers and fifty cameras. . . . Security staff members are all commissioned as special police officers with authority to make arrests." At Children's Hospital, fitness is stressed for all security personnel. Officers must be able to climb 11 flights of stairs and move a patient in three minutes. Extensive fire brigade practices are conducted, and infection control training is included. The hospital has a helipad equipped with fire cannons and back-up hoses that can cover the area with 24 inches of protective foam. Harowitz (p. 44) notes: "High visibility and quick response timep are continually emphasized by the department. This philosophy is applied to everything from a serious emergency call to a minor flat tire repair."

Another example of an effective hospital security system is that in place at New England Baptist Hospital. At this facility, according to Stedman (1994, p. 30): "Equipment and procedure updates, along with the integration of fire and security systems, provides a hospital with a clean bill of health." Hospital staff are given a metal key with a PIN-embedded smart chip. These smart keys record traffic in and out of extremely critical areas such as the pharmacy, doctors' offices, radiology labs, medical records and the like.

Additional security problems are encountered when hospitals admit criminals or celebrities and must ensure their safety. For example, the security to protect the Shah of Iran when he was hospitalized in New York City Hospital was the maximum possible (Kmet, 1980, pp. 22–36). Security was made more difficult by the fact that New York City Hospital, the oldest in the city and one of the largest in the world, has 9,200 doors, 6 miles of corridors and 20 miles of air ducts. It has 1,400 beds, 5,500 employees and 80 clinics serving 10,000 patients a day, in addition to 2,500 employees at the adjoining Cornell Medical College and Hospital.

Security at the hospital is provided by a staff of 100 security officers, with 25 to 30 officers on three shift patrols covering 30 different posts. Three of the officers are sergeant/investigators who have been granted special police powers and the power of arrest. This security team has at its disposal sophisticated security hardware, including 30 CCTV cameras which cover the main entrances, the cashiers' offices and the tunnels. The CCTV also has videotape capability. The hospital requires all employees to be photographed and fingerprinted upon employment and to wear ID badges when working. It also requires passes for all packages that leave the building.

When the Shah was admitted, the security director chose to have his own security officers work overtime rather than hire outside officers. The 100 officers of the hospital put in 4,000 hours of overtime during the Shah's stay. All employees who had any contact with the Shah were cleared by the Secret Service. The security officers screened all mail, flowers and gifts sent to the Shah. Although the Shah refused to allow CCTV in his room, the corridor was monitored. The officers who guarded the Shah's ward wore helmets, batons and bulletproof vests. The most difficult aspect of security was providing protection when the Shah had to be moved for surgery and treatments. Routes were carefully secured before each move, were changed frequently and were heavily guarded. A minimal number of people knew when or by what route the move would occur. The tight security provided the Shah ensured his safety while at the hospital.

The Contribution of Security Systems

As noted by Bagley (1993, p. 97): "Facilities will be liable for failing to act. Investing in more qualified personnel and up-to-date equipment for the hospital security program may involve increased expenses that will be difficult to absorb at first, but the cost of inaction will be much greater." This message is also stressed by Saenz (1992, p. 68):

> [S]ecurity is often thought to contribute to neither the healing nor the profit-generating process. Security is generally viewed as an expense, a service that is required solely for insurance purposes and for its presumed public image value.
>
> That fallacy is being laid to rest by enlightened health care administrators around the world. They understand that security is cost-effective. Security not only decreases liability but also, in a modern, nontraditional health care facility, directly supports both healing and profit.

Educational Institutions*

Educational institutions are responsible for providing a safe learning environment for staff and students, yet they are also subject to the same risks faced

*Educational Institutions—See *Private Security,* pp. 44–46.

by business and industry. Employees and students from the elementary through the college level may be victims or perpetrators of crimes.

Bias (1994, p. 49) suggests: "The ideal school would have open and free entry into the learning environment. Security, however, means access control. In a public school, the two objectives are balanced. Entry is managed but it is not necessarily restricted."

> The major security problems of educational institutions are safety of students and staff, violence, vandalism and theft, including burglary.

K–12 Programs

Security needs of schools vary tremendously, depending on the size of the school system and the location of the facilities. For example, the New York City Public School System has 1,000 schools and 400 auxiliary buildings which cover more than one hundred million square feet. Problems faced by systems such as New York's will be more complex than those faced by small, rural schools. Nonetheless, crime in schools is not limited to the large school systems. It has increased substantially in both suburban and rural school systems. Some school administrators place the blame on the open school concept, which they contend encourages an influx of idlers and dropouts who disrupt academic functions.

Problems

Vandalism is a serious problem for the vast majority of schools, compounded by general public apathy. People who live close to a school may see vandalism occurring at night, on weekends or during holidays, yet do nothing and notify no one. One solution to this problem has been to use the school for community functions after school hours. This not only decreases the opportunity for undetected vandalism, but also improves community interest in protecting its facilities.

Court-ordered desegregation of school systems has also created serious problems, including the constant threat of violence. Crimes of violence in general are a significant problem in schools.

Increased violence, along with increases in burglaries, arson and vandalism coupled with the school's civil liability for its students' safety, has caused many school systems to develop a comprehensive security program, including intrusion-detection systems and nonbreakable windows. Some schools are even constructed without windows. The primary objectives of most school security programs are to protect staff and students and their personal property and to protect the school's facilities and equipment.

A national crime victimization survey (Bastian and Taylor, 1991, p. 1) reported that an estimated 9 percent of students ages 12 to 19 were crime victims in or around their school over a six-month period. Bias (1994, p. 51) suggests:

"The high-risk period for school facilities occurs at night. A trespasser can quickly become an arsonist, destroying millions of dollars of school property."

Blauvelt (1991, p. 89) notes two relatively new problems facing schools—crack and gangs:

> At one time, only major urban school districts had to be concerned with crack cocaine and youth gangs. Unfortunately, school districts across the country now are having to develop plans, policies and strategies for coping with these issues and the resulting increase in fights, assaults, homicides, drive-by shootings, and general disruption of previously quiet schools.

Reducing the Problems

> Access control, lighting and security personnel are means to reduce risks at educational institutions.

School systems use varying combinations of contract and proprietary personnel to establish security programs. In some states county and local ordinances give police powers to school security personnel. Many of these personnel have primary jurisdiction over criminal incidents that occur in the schools. Alarm systems are commonly used. For example, 70 percent of New York's public schools have some sort of alarm system. Other schools require all students to carry ID cards so that if they are involved in an incident, they can be easily identified. Educational programs are a key component of most school security programs.

According to Bias (1994, p. 50): "Only schools located in communities with serious crime problems rely on CCTV and other more restrictive electronic access control devices."

Texas public school districts are legislatively empowered to establish their own police departments separate from municipal or county forces.

Crowe (1991, p. 81) notes: "Crime prevention through environmental design (CPTED) is being used successfully in schools and communities to improve the management of human space." Crowe describes the three major school designs that have evolved during the past 30 years. Up to the 1950s, most schools followed the traditional classroom design. During the 1950s and '60s, schools began to organize around departments, with teachers moving "home base" out of the classroom and into offices. Classrooms became multipurpose rooms with no one having "ownership." In the 1970s, the open school became popular, resulting in many "schools without walls." Security in such schools presents a formidable challenge because no one is a "proprietor" of the internal space.

As noted by Crowe (1991, p. 84): "The underlying objective of CPTED is to help school administrators attain their primary goal of student achievement and a positive environment with the added byproduct of improved security and loss prevention." Crowe explains that an example of a CPTED strategy is to relocate gathering areas to locations with natural surveillance and access control or to locations out of view of would-be offenders. Crowe (p. 86) concludes:

> At first, CPTED may appear to be the proverbial 2,000 pound marshmallow—you think it's going to be good, but you don't know where to start chewing. Most school administrators have an inherent understanding of these basic concepts. It is perhaps the most important tool school officials can use in ensuring a safe educational environment.
>
> CPTED is a powerful concept that may be used to improve the productive use of school space. Code of conduct violations can be reduced, and environmental design may be used to improve the ability of school administrators to operate safe and secure schools. The potential value to the school and community is worth the time and effort it takes to implement crime reduction through environmental design.

The National School Safety Center (1988, p. 25) publication *Gangs in Schools: Breaking Up Is Hard to Do* suggests: "A positive, consistent approach to discipline and conflict prevention can achieve long-term and far-reaching results and improve the overall school climate." The center suggests several prevention and intervention strategies to reduce problems with gangs and gang members.*

Behavior codes should be established and firmly and consistently enforced. These codes may include dress codes and bans on showing gang colors or using hand signals. On the positive side, schools should promote and reward friendliness and cooperation.

Graffiti removal should occur in schools immediately. Graffiti is not only unattractive, it enables gang members to advertise their turf and authority. In some instances photographs of the graffiti may aid certain police investigations. School officials should give remaining paint cans and paint brushes that might be used as evidence to the police. As an alternative to graffiti, students might be encouraged to design and paint murals in locations where graffiti is most likely to occur.

Conflict prevention strategies are also important to address the problem of gangs in school. Teachers should be trained to recognize and deal with gang members in nonconfrontational ways. Staff should identify all known gang members. Staff must try to build self-esteem and promote academic success for all students, including gang members.

Crisis management is another important part of dealing with gangs. The police department and school officials should have a plan in place for dealing with crises that might arise. Included in the plan should be means for communicating with the authorities, parents and the public. The center (pp. 33–34) recommends the following actions in a school crisis:

- Have a media policy worked out in advance. Spell out who will be the media spokesperson, and make it clear no one else should speak *officially* for the school or agency.
- Route all media inquiries to one person or, at least, to one office.
- Prepare an official statement responding to the particular crisis situation. Read from or distribute this statement when media inquiries are made. This will maintain consistency.
- Anticipate media questions and prepare and rehearse answers.
- Don't be afraid to say, "I don't know." This is better than lying or responding with the offensive phrase, "No comment." Volunteer to get the answer and follow up within a specified time.
- Start a rumor control center, if the situation warrants. Publish a number for media representatives to call if they hear a rumor or need information.
- Provide the news media with updates as events unfold, even after the initial crisis is handled.
- Keep calm and maintain a professional manner. Once calm has returned, it is imperative to begin work that will prevent a recurrence of the crisis.

Community involvement is also needed to effectively reduce and prevent gang activity. Parents and the general public should be made aware of gangs operating in the community, as well as of popular heavy metal and punk bands. They should be encouraged to apply pressure to television and radio stations and to book stores and video stores to ban material that promotes use of alcohol, drugs, promiscuity or devil worship.

COLLEGES AND UNIVERSITIES

"The future of campus security is guided by its past," notes Collins (1992, p. 27). "Only by understanding where it has been and where it is now can campus security determine where it needs to go." Sloan (1992, p. 89) provides a typology of the evolution of campus police systems, as shown in Table 18–1. In a study of campus police conducted at 10 large universities in the Midwest and Southeast, Sloan (p. 100) found:

> [C]ampus police agencies in the sample bear a strong resemblance to municipal police agencies. They call themselves "university *police* departments." They have specialization among personnel. They are autonomous from other law enforcement agencies in the area and have wide jurisdictional boundaries. They also use the same kind of "authority symbols" associated with municipal police. In addition, campus police departments and municipal departments are similar in terms of job requirements for new officers.

As noted by Warrington and Kaufer (1994, p. 36): "Whether driven by potential litigation, regulations, increased public awareness or a combination of each, campus communities not only accept security—they demand it." Warrington and Kaufer (p. 37) suggest that administrators want campus security that:

Table 18–1. Typology of Evolution of Campus Police Systems

System	Organizational Ties	Major Functions
"Watchman" (1894–1950)	Maintenance/Physical Plant	Protect College Property Detect Fire Hazards Check Boilers Preventive Maintenance
"Pseudo-Police" (1950–1965)	Dean of Students/Physical Plant	Preventive Maintenance Protect Evidence Detain Suspects Report Crimes to Local Police In Loco Parentis Regulate Student Conduct
"Modern Campus Police" (1965–)	Campus Police Department (Paramilitary Structure)	Formal Police Powers Carry Authority Symbols Enforce Law on Campus Maintain Order on Campus Service to Campus Community

SOURCE: John J. Sloan. "The Modern Campus Police: An Analysis of their Evolution, Structure, and Function." *American Journal of Police,* Vol 11, No. 2, 1992, p. 89. Reprinted by permission.

- Meets legal and moral obligations to provide a safe campus.
- Is seen by the community as effective and satisfactory.
- Is supportive of the institution's mission.
- Avoids major problems, claims and litigation.

They suggest that students, faculty and staff also have expectations of a security system, including the following:

- A safe and welcoming campus.
- An open and free environment.
- Good security service if needed.
- Knowledge of where to get help and what services are available.
- Security officers who are competent and comfortable in relating to students and campus life.
- Security procedures and systems that do what they are supposed to do and are easy to live with.

"The mission of University police," says Utz (1990, p. 104), "is to protect and to support the educational responsibility of the institution of higher learning."

Utz (1990, p. 104) advises that in addition to providing a secure campus, university police serve other important functions as well:

> Such services can range from transporting female students from dark parking lots to their dormitories all the way to unlocking an office door for an

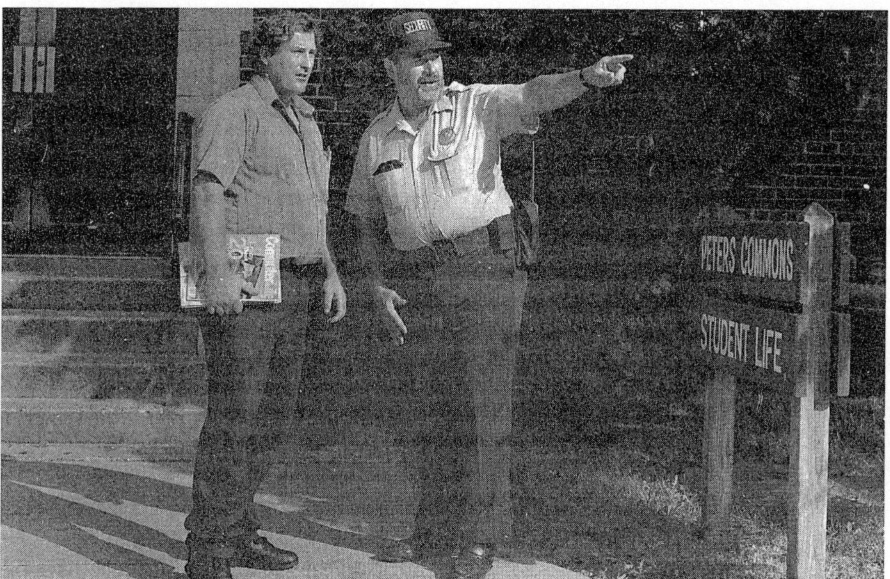

Campus security officers can provide assistance to students seeking directions as well as help to ensure a safe, welcoming campus.

absentminded professor. While some may not consider these activities to be police work, they are essential services that university officers provide to their community.

Problems

The security problems of colleges and universities are somewhat different from those of secondary school systems. A major difference is that some college and university facilities are used almost continuously (except at community colleges which typically close by midnight). The 24-hour access to areas such as student unions that are heavily trafficked and usually have several entrances and exits is a major constraint in using electronic security. However, CCTV and alarm systems are often installed in bursars' and cashiers' offices, and in the areas that serve as central collection points for all cash from campus facilities such as student unions and cafeterias.

Phelps (1993, p. 19A) cautions: "Failing to realize the great importance of access control makes campuses vulnerable to lawsuits." According to Phelps (1992, p. 86): "The major problem is not break-ins but unauthorized key duplication."

College campuses sustain significant losses from theft of college property. The items most frequently stolen are audiovisual and laboratory equipment, typewriters, calculators, computers and educational materials such as books and art objects. Theft of examinations is also a major concern at colleges and universities, as is protecting the computer system, particularly against grade changing.

The large numbers of residential housing units for students and staff create a densely populated community. Some campuses are larger than many towns.

These campuses have the same problems as cities, particularly crime, including rapes, assaults, student robberies, muggings and theft of college or university property, as well as the problem of nonpaying dormitory users.

Population density in high-rise dormitories makes it difficult to protect students and their personal property. The high concentration of students makes it impossible for them to know all the other residents of the dormitory; therefore, an intruder can easily pose as a student. Many colleges have installed extensive locking and access control systems to restrict access to student housing areas.

The 1984 standards established by the Building Officials Conference of America (BOCA) recommended that all dorms be fitted with interconnected smoke detectors in public areas, such as halls, stairs and dining rooms (Salamone, 1991, p. 70).

A constant challenge of security is to provide access control while assuring ease of exiting a building in an emergency. Dowling (1994, p. 47) describes a common problem on college campuses—students propping fire doors open for convenience: "Many times the doors are closer to the parking area and, in inclement weather or at night, provide a quick entrance into the resident hall. Other times the doors are used for pizza delivery people or to bypass guest registration."

Besides dense population, the physical size of the campus may pose security problems. For example, the University of Houston campus covers 390 acres. Large campuses frequently provide motorcycle patrols and/or foot patrols equipped with portable radios and emergency call boxes along pedestrian walkways.

The need for organized, well-trained security personnel at colleges and universities was dramatically demonstrated in the late 1960s by campus demonstrations, student strikes, forceful occupation of school buildings by students and violent riots. Local and/or state law enforcement agencies were frequently called in such situations, but their intervention was viewed negatively by many students, faculty members and administrators. Increasingly, however, both students and staff are supporting comprehensive security programs.

A primary concern is safety of individuals. Armed robberies, assaults, muggings and rapes at college campuses have increased dramatically throughout the country. On some campuses, students have organized rape crisis centers to counsel and assist rape victims. On other campuses, male students have formed protective night escort services for female students.

Drinking and use of illegal drugs are major problems on some campuses. For example, in 1986 19-year-old Jeanne Clery was brutally raped and murdered in her dormitory room by a male student. Her parents founded Security on Campus Inc. to bring the issue of campus crime to the forefront. According to Mr. Cleary ("Coming Clean on Campus Crime," 1991, p. 10), it is important for college and university administrators to enforce laws regarding illegal drug use and underage drinking: " 'That's important,' says Cleary, because alcohol use is 'the chief motivator in campus crimes, particularly rape. Students commit 70 percent of the felonies and violent crimes on college campuses and underage drinking is behind 80 percent to 90 percent of all violent student crimes.' "

Nielsen (1990, p. 136) describes a new type of crime occurring on campuses—**ethnoviolence:**

> Ethnoviolence is just a new word for an old behavior that is once again on the rise. . . . Across the nation, campuses are experiencing a resurgence of prejudicial insensitivity and related behavior. Acts motivated by racial, religious and ethnic prejudice have included such unfortunate incidents as physical assaults, cross burnings, racially offensive posters and fliers, hate mail, anonymous telephone threats and other forms of misconduct.

Hinkle and Jones (1991, p. 142) call attention to an often unrealized problem:

> The innocence of students is legendary. They trust everybody, particularly those of their own age group. They leave their doors unlocked while they sleep, they leave their valuables unattended while they shower, they give their telephone charge numbers to casual acquaintances, they get drunk with total strangers and not infrequently go to bed with them. They loan their cars, money and clothing to fellow students they hardly know, they actively resist the controls put in place for their own safety—and when their infinite faith in the goodness of man is shattered, they blame somebody else, generally one or more grownups.

Special events on campus also challenge security. Many of the problems discussed in Chapter 17 are also present on campuses. According to Arbetter (1994, p. 44): "The types of problems that occur at the various events differ with the crowds they attract. For example, certain musical groups attract gang members or heavy drinkers while boxing matches, which attract people who carry large amounts of cash, beckon pickpockets." Alcohol seems to be a problem existing at most special events.

Haynes (1991, p. 55) describes the problems that may occur at scholastic sporting events:

> In addition to fights and other violence, thefts from cars, vandalism, muggings, and the like can ruin what would otherwise be an enjoyable time for those attending.

Reducing the Problems

The Crime Awareness and Campus Security Act of 1990 and the Student Right-to-Know Act require institutions of higher education to gather and publish at least annual campus crime statistics. These figures must be available to all students and parents, faculty and current and prospective employees ("Coming Clean on Campus Crime," 1991, p. 1). Statistics are to be gathered on the following crimes: assault, burglary, criminal homicide, drug-abuse violations, forcible rape, liquor-law violations, motor vehicle theft, robbery and weapon possession. These figures are included in the FBI Uniform Crime Reports (UCR).

However, as noted by Hinkle (1992, p. 28), the figures in the UCR may represent only the "tip of the iceberg" due to manipulation of the figures by university officials:

> College and universities use this deception because they have a powerful financial interest in their good name. . . .
>
> The motivation of schools to downplay their crime stats and to stonewall outside investigations include not only threats of decreased enrollment but liability lawsuits (inadequate security, negligence, etc.), loss of fraternity house charters, disqualification of star athletes for fraud or sexual transgressions, and a possible reduction in gifts and endowments.

Phelps (1992, p. 86) also stresses: "A record-keeping system that tracks all criminal and violent acts on campus must be established." These acts might be geographically located on a pin map or analyzed by computer.

Like secondary schools, higher education institutions use a combination of contractual and proprietary security personnel and security hardware to protect their campuses, students and employees.

Green (1987, p. 29) suggests: "Unlike many areas of modern security, campus security has generally been evolving from a low visibility operation in the direction of a highly visible, police-oriented image in response to rising crime problems of the 1980s."

As noted by Powell (1981, p. 3) more than a decade ago: "The growth and trend towards the professionalism of campus security has been the most rapid in the private security field in recent years." That trend has continued. Powell traces the origins of campus security to Yale University and the late 1800s when a "Town-Gown ad hoc committee" was formed to address the problem of the bloody riots that often occurred between the townspeople and the students. Their solution was to assign two New Haven police officers to Yale University to "protect students, their property, and University property." In 1894 Yale hired the officers away from the city, establishing the Yale Campus Police. The campus police retained their full police authority, a situation that still exists today.

In 1958 the National Association of College and University Traffic and Security Directors was formed. This organization changed its name to the International Association of Campus Law Enforcement Administrators in 1967, during the period of student dissent which, according to Powell (p. 5), "provided campus security with its greatest impetus toward professionalism." Following this period (pp. 5–7):

> Physical changes also took place. Campus security emerged from the basements and boiler houses where, for the most part, they had utilized office equipment and lockers discarded by other departments. They were relocated into attractive, well-equipped, businesslike office space with lockers and squad rooms for the officers. New, unmarked police vehicles were purchased for patrol purposes and equipped with two-way mobile radios. . . .
>
> Truly professional departments emerged that could relate to all segments of the campus community. *Service* and *prevention* were the watchwords. . . .
>
> The advent of the 1990s will present new challenges to campus security, such as escalating crime, threats to personal safety, and possible acts of terrorism. Campus administrators must more and more face up to the fact that a well-trained, professional campus security department is an absolute necessity in order to insure the safety and well-being of students, faculty, and staff.

The trend is to establish proprietary security forces and appoint directors of security for colleges and universities. Approximately 40 states have legislation providing police authority for proprietary security personnel on campus. Most restrict such police powers to public institutions of higher education, but some states also make these powers available to private institutions.

At some larger institutions, security personnel are responsible for comprehensive law enforcement, traffic and fire safety and loss prevention functions. For example, the University of Connecticut Public Safety Division not only serves a police function, but also maintains a fire department, a mounted patrol, locksmith and key controls, an ambulance service and a campus transportation system.

Another trend in campus security is the active involvement of students in crime prevention. On some campuses, students informally assist in crowd control and traffic direction at large public events such as sporting events. Other campuses have a more formal organization of student patrol or student marshal programs. At Syracuse University, students equipped with two-way radios and identified by arm patches as "student security services" patrol parking areas and general residence halls. The University of Georgia campus security department consists entirely of students with undergraduate degrees who are taking graduate programs in police science or criminal justice. Other universities offer incentives such as free tuition or tuition assistance to campus security workers.

Among the crime prevention programs used in many colleges to reduce criminal activity are Operation Identification, Neighborhood Watch, security surveys, working with architects, rape awareness programs, office security, key control, escort services and orientation programs. These programs and any other crime prevention strategies for college campuses should involve students, employees and staff.

Locks and effective key control can significantly reduce such losses. Figure 18–2 is a checklist that could be used to enhance key and lock security.

Major (1994, p. 32) suggests that electronic access control for colleges and universities may be a way to achieve security efficiently and effectively:

> ID cards can be programmed in and out as many times as you need without changing the locks on the doors. You can monitor what's happening at the doors, and don't need a special person to open or close buildings.

The installation of electronic sensor detection devices in libraries has significantly reduced the number of stolen library books. Installation of photocopy equipment has likewise reduced the number of mutilated books and periodicals.

Improved lighting has also proved to be a sound security measure. Installing mercury vapor lamps, removing bushes and shrubs and adding a number of direct-ring emergency phones along all major walkways provide "corridors of security." The improved lighting acts as a psychological deterrent, allows people to see farther and thus to avoid would-be attackers, allows campus police to see potential trouble and, if a crime should occur, makes identification of the perpetrator easier. To meet energy conservation needs, after high-

Items with Locks	Number of Locks	Items with Locks	Number of Locks	Items with Locks	Number of Locks
Access Space		Dispensers		Mail Bags	
Air Conditioning		Sanitary Napkins		Mail Boxes	
Alarms		Soap		Money Bags	
Automotive		Towel			
		Doors (Exterior)		Penthouse	
Bulletin Boards		Entrance		Plan Case	
		Exit			
		Doors (Interior)			
		Cafeteria		Refrigerators	
		Closet		Rolling Grills	
		Connecting		Roof Vents	
Cabinets		Elevator			
Electric		Elevator Corridor			
Filing		Fan Room		Safe Compartments	
Key		Fire		Safe Deposit Boxes	
Medicine		Garage		Screens	
Storage		Office		Stop Sink Closet	
Supply				Switch Key	
Tool					
Wardrobe					
		Drawers		Tanks (Oil & Gas)	
		Cash		Thermostat	
		Lab. Table		Trucks & Trailers	
		Safe		Trucks	
		Tool & Bench			
Cash Boxes					
Cash Registers					
Chute Doors		Gas Pump		Valves	
Clocks		Gates		Vaults	
		Lockers		Watchman's Box	
Dark Rooms		Employee			
Desks		Paint			
Display Cases		Tool Room			

Figure 18–2. Key and Lock Survey for Education

SOURCE: Reprinted with permission from Telkee Inc., Subsidiary of Sunroc Corp., Glen Riddle, PA 19037.

traffic periods are over, every other light is turned out for the remainder of the night.

Communications is vital to a campus security system. As noted by Arbetter (1994, p. 42): "Like a savvy advertiser, campus security uses mixed media to deliver its message." This might include publishing the Right-to-Know statistics monthly, publishing articles on safety in the campus newspaper or posting security alerts over e-mail.

According to Thomas (1992, p. 33): "The view of a security system as a management information system is an important concept that more colleges and universities are beginning to adopt, and technology is available to achieve that goal."

Phelps (1993, p. 44) advises security personnel to become knowledgeable of the fads on their campuses. He cites as an example an incident at Southern Methodist University in the fall of 1992 where two students fell down an elevator shaft. One student was killed, the other seriously injured. According to Phelps: "Security was shocked to learn that the students had intentionally entered the shaft as part of a new fad known as elevator surfing. No one at Southern Methodist had heard of the game prior to that night." Phelps (p. 48) stresses:

> A preventive approach to potential problems is essential. The first step is for security personnel and university officials to stay abreast of trends. The next step is to examine preventive strategies based on the special characteristics of the campus. The third step is to educate students regarding their responsibility to protect themselves. They must be made aware of potential dangers and helped to realize their own exposure to dangerous situations.

Security on campuses fits well with the community policing philosophy being adopted by many police departments throughout the country. According to Jackson (1992, p. 63):

> Campus police agencies have an excellent environment in which to operate in a community-oriented manner. In fact, the campus environment demands it and successful agencies have realized that. The challenge now, for all departments, is to find ways to address problems that breed criminal activity. Conventional thinking, on or off campus, does not seem to be effective.

Jackson compares three contemporary policing models being used in the United States in the 1990s: traditional law enforcement, community policing and campus policing (Table 18–2). The similarities between community policing and campus policing are striking.

Increasingly, universities are instituting bicycle patrols. They are less expensive and more mobile than vehicles, are environmentally acceptable, fulfill community policing goals and provide a more efficient deterrent to crime on campus.

Two court cases of relevance to individuals involved with security in educational institutions are *In re T.L.O.* and *Kuehn v. Renton School District No. 403*. In *In re T.L.O.* (1983), the Supreme Court of New Jersey held that school officials and teachers must have reasonable grounds before they can conduct a search. In *Kuehn v. Renton School District No. 403* (1985), the Supreme Court of Washington held that the search of a student's luggage by school officials *does* constitute a violation of the Fourth Amendment if school officials are acting under the authority or on the behalf of state authorities.

Hinkle and Jones (1991, p. 146) urge colleges and universities to protect themselves by having the following security goals, which match the public's expectations for security:

Table 18–2. A Comparative Analysis of Contemporary Police Models

Philosophy	Traditional Law Enforcement	Community Policing	Campus Policing
1. *Police Mandate*	Control of crime: response, deterrence, apprehension	Crime control as a means to community order, peace and security	Law enforcement and disciplinary action as means of control to ensure campus order, peace and security
	Law enforcement Crisis response	Preventive as well as reactive policing	Preventive as well as reactive policing
2. *Police Authority*	Authority from law	Authority from society, community granted through law	Authority primarily from faculty, staff and students; granted through regulations and law
	Agency of the criminal justice system	Agency of municipal government and community	Agency of the university administration and community
3. *Police Role*	Legally defined/limited by law Distinct and separate Law enforcement officers/professional crime fighters Addresses crime only	Socially defined, expanded role Legal and social agencies One of a number of agencies of order Addresses crime and social problems that affect crime	Environmentally defined Legal, educational and social agencies Peacekeeping/educational professionals Addresses crime and environmental problems that affect crime
4. *Community-Police Relationship*	Passive role Supportive, adjunct to police	Active role; policy making Shared responsibility for crime and social order Community as client	Active role; policy making Shared responsibility for crime and social order Community member, community as client
5. *Politics*	Apolitical	Political: mediate interests	Political: mediate interests, take advocacy role
	Police and political issues separate	Responsible to community and political representatives	Responsible to community and governing board
	Fiscal accountability only	Policy and operational accounting	Totally accountable

SOURCE: Reprinted from *The Police Chief* magazine, Vol LIX, No. 12, page 64, 1992 Copyright held by The International Association of Chiefs of Police, Inc., 515 N. Washington St, Alexandria, VA 22314, U S A Further reproduction without express written permission from IACP is strictly prohibited

- A numerically adequate police force trained and equipped to state-mandated standards, including computerized dispatch centers.
- Security devices that include physical barriers such as self-locking doors, electronic warning systems, emergency telephones, and crime-deterrent landscaping and architecture.
- Pre- and post-incident counseling by trained professionals both within and without the police department.
- Crime prevention tactics such as neighborhood watch and escort services.
- Up-to-date risk assessment analyses.

Exemplary Program

According to Borchert (1993, p. 40): "Access control at the University of Southern California rates an A-Plus. USC's is the largest monitoring system of its kind in the U.S. with more than 105 locations campus-wide." This system has Sanyo cameras positioned at 80 locations on campus and three residential monitoring centers. In addition, Durado system card readers are installed at more than 170 locations.

LIBRARIES*

The value of certain library holdings, such as special collections, rare books and out-of-print or irreplaceable books, magazines and manuscripts, cannot be estimated accurately. Usually valuable books and periodicals are kept in closed stacks, and their use is restricted and closely supervised. Libraries frequently use security personnel to deter disorderly behavior and vandalism during the hours they are open and to provide fire and security protection at night.

- The major losses in libraries result from theft of or damage to books, CDs and videos.
- Library losses can be reduced by the electronic marking of books and by providing photocopy equipment.

Using electronic markings on books and detection sensors at main exits can significantly reduce book theft. Book mutilation can be minimized by providing photocopying machines so that material can be reproduced rather than torn from the books or periodicals. Some libraries have also instituted an annual or semiannual "amnesty" period during which overdue books can be returned without a fine.

In 1993 3M introduced a Self-Check System that integrates library security with automated circulation systems ("3M Introduces Self-Check System," 1993, p. 13):

---

*Libraries—See *Private Security,* p. 54.

> Operating much like a bank's Automatic Teller Machine, the 3M Self-Check System features a color monitor and easy-to-follow screen prompts. The system allows library patrons to independently check out, renew and potentially check in materials. . . .
>
> If a patron is not an approved borrower or there is some other problem or information to convey—such as fines owed or materials on hold—the screen directs the patron to the circulation desk for further information.

MUSEUMS AND ART GALLERIES*

According to Bracalente (1993, p. 4A): "Possibly spurred by the speculative auction prices, the biggest art thefts ever to besiege American institutions have occurred in the last five years."

Konicek (1993, p. 36) says: "Theft and vandalism are an art museum's arch nemeses, with potential costs in the millions of dollars each year." According to Gates and Martin (1990, p. 60): "Art theft has become the second most important international criminal activity after drug trafficking."

The severity of the "artnapping" problem is also underscored by Kissane and Burns (1992, p. 52):

> In this decade, we could see the worst plunder of the world's art treasures since the fall of Rome. Targeted by increasingly sophisticated organized crime groups with access to high-tech methodology, our artistic heritage could disappear into the black market and secret, private collections forever. Just a few years ago, masterpieces valued at approximately $100 million were stolen from Boston's Gardener Museum. Unfortunately, this was not an isolated incident.

Erickson (1994, p. 48) observes that unlike banks, museums cannot lock up their valuables but must put them on public display. Consequently, "Museum security professionals must continue to find creative ways to balance viewing considerations with their responsibility to preserve and protect priceless and irreplaceable collections."

Problems

Criminal problems most frequently encountered by museums and art galleries are theft of collection pieces and the inadvertent purchase of works of art fraudulently presented as authentic or that have been stolen. Museums also experience order-maintenance and vandalism problems, but the trend toward charging admission fees has reduced these problems.

> Major security problems of museums and art galleries include theft, fraud, vandalism and arson.

---

*Museums—See *Private Security,* pp. 53–54.

Erickson (1994, p. 45) puts it this way: "Trafficking in stolen and smuggled art has become a major industry. It is sometimes easier to cut out and roll up a Van Gogh and hide it under a coat than it is to rob a bank. In addition, museum collections are at risk from vandalism, fire, and environmental damage."

Many objects in museums are priceless and irreplaceable. Most frequently stolen are small items that can be easily concealed and sold for cash. Such items are often stolen while the museum is open to the public, but more valuable items are generally stolen at night. Sometimes precious metals and gems are removed from artifacts, reset and then sold. The primary areas of concern are vaults, reserve collections, study collections and public exhibition sections.

Public exhibition sections are particularly vulnerable if a controversial exhibit is on display. For example, a Russian cultural or art exhibit on loan to U.S. museums or galleries could be threatened by activist groups.

In addition, as noted by Keller (1993, p. 51): "Because museums and other institutional clients are traditionally poor, security is inadequate." Keller also suggests: "Museums used to look like museums: The exteriors were classical, and the interiors decorative. They were generally built of solid masonry with windows and skylights, often protected by bars or shutters." But modern museums have changed all that, greatly increasing security problems and challenges. Unfortunately, security is seldom considered in the designing and construction stages of new museums. Keller (1993, p. 54) contends: "The security manager has always been a stepchild in the building process." For maximum security, this situation should change; security managers should be involved in all phases of the designing of new facilities. He notes (p. 59): "Museums, for example, with high-security needs sharing space with theaters and community centers, rarely have good security at a good price unless planned."

Reducing the Problems

Burrows (1992, p. 34) suggests that when designing museum security, a common-sense three-step approach be used:

1. List what to protect. Careful cataloging is a key.
2. Consider what is likely to happen to it. Include theft, vandalism, publicity-seeking, fire, and water damage.
3. Consider action to counter the threat.

The American Society for Industrial Security (ASIS) Standing Committee on Museum, Library and Cultural Properties provides a listing of minimum security standards in its "Suggested Guidelines in Museum Security," published in 1989. The guidelines include general directives as well as specific recommendations (Keller, 1994, p. 104):

- Every museum shall have a written protection program and policies.

- The security manager shall report to a high ranking official in the organization. Ideally, the person responsible for security should report directly to a deputy director or higher.
- All exterior windows shall have magnetic switches or other sensing devices that alert the monitor when a window is opened or left open.
- The method of electronic communication between the premises alarm system and the remote monitoring facility shall comply with Underwriters' Laboratories (UL) Standard 1610.

Museums and galleries can reduce losses by:

- Establishing a basic security system, including locks, alarms and security officers at stations and on patrol.
- Maintaining detailed inventories.
- Having each object professionally appraised and authenticated.
- Positively identifying and registering each item.

Recall that alarm systems can provide three types of protection: (1) *perimetric,* to control access to the building, (2) *volumetric,* to detect motion and entry into a showcase or room and (3) *fixed-point,* to protect individual pieces. Whether to use an alarm for an individual object depends on several factors, including its history of loss or damage, the alarm's compatibility with the overall system, exhibition procedures and budget. Alarms on objects, however, are the last line of defense.

Several years ago the president of the International Association of Art Security, T. P. Kissane (1977), stressed the importance of identification: "Perhaps the most important defense against well-organized art theft is having a central recording location with a computerized record of the unique characteristics of all valuable works; and a reporting point of all art works stolen. . . . Lack of positive identification of most objects—documented visual evidence of the existence and condition of the work—is a critical factor in the soaring art theft statistics" (pp. 7–8).

Such a system, called **ARTCENTRAL,** has been developed in New York by the International Association of Art Security. This organization registers works of art using computer-oriented **photogrammetry,** a process comparable to fingerprinting. Photogrammetry provides a permanent, exact identification of works of art that is impossible to duplicate. It can identify two-dimensional works such as paintings, lithographs, wall hangings and tapestries, as well as three-dimensional works such as artifacts, antiques, silverware, porcelains and sculptures.

All identified works are visibly and invisibly labeled, indicating that they are on file with **INTERPOL** (International Criminal Police Organization). A central file is located in New York, another at INTERPOL and a third at a secret, heavily guarded location. If a work registered with ARTCENTRAL is stolen, the theft is reported to INTERPOL, which in turn notifies state and local authorities as well as the FBI because it is assumed that interstate transportation of stolen goods will be involved.

This system is a deterrent to theft because the stolen objects are less marketable. It also greatly aids in recovery of stolen objects and their return to the rightful owner.

ARTCENTRAL is also available to individuals and to corporations. It is important for security directors of businesses and corporations to be aware of this because many corporations are now acquiring art collections. Such security managers may need to become familiar with the procedures for safeguarding artwork, including access control, CCTV and security patrols.

The importance of protecting our country's museum treasures is apparent from the federal funds available for renovating, developing and expanding protection programs. The following areas may qualify for federal support: organizing and using guard forces; physical security, including windows and doors, security hardware and locks and storage facilities; fire safety plans; fire alarm systems; intrusion detection systems; surveillance, including lighting and CCTV and communications. Loss prevention is vital because once an art treasure is stolen, chance of recovery is less than 5 percent.

Bracalente (1993, p. 4A) describes an innovation in museum security:

> A recent development for the protection of vulnerable displays is the use of an active infrared (AIR) sensor to create a security curtain. Unlike the commonly used passive infrared (PIR) sensors that detect intrusion by temperature, AIR uses a laser light, which detects intrusion when the beam of light is interrupted.
>
> Magnetic tape applied to the floor around the area to be segregated maintains the laser beam within the security curtain and provides a fairly narrow protective field. This application allows the public to stand at a comfortable viewing distance from each work of art, while providing a protective barrier without stanchions. . . .
>
> An audible alarm attached to a relay gently reminds the public to keep a distance from the paintings, while signaling the officers on gallery post and at the central station.

Bordes (1993, p. 11A) describes the major impact computerized access control systems have had on protecting art:

> Alarm-oriented software has the ability to provide computer-based monitoring of subsystem technologies, such as intrusion detection equipment, and interface with other systems, such as CCTV. The functions are designed to assist the security console officer and the response teams in being more efficient and more effective. . . .
>
> The monitoring of alarms and subsystem interface using special software applications is a major access control feature available today.

Bracalente (1993, p. 6A) stresses: "While technology and good policies are critical to any successful security program, hiring honest, professional staff members is the first step. The IUAM's [Indiana University Art Museum] security officers are in plain view of the public. They assist with crowd control for the more than 300 public school tours that visit the museum annually. In each of the exhibition galleries, officers help visitors while maintaining a constant vigilance over the collections."

Exemplary Programs

Erickson (1994, p. 45) describes the security at the Philadelphia Museum of Art, the third largest in the country with collections worth in excess of $5 billion and a security department of about 120 people: "The museum's hidden cameras, infrared motion detectors, and lasers allow visitors free movement through the galleries while unobtrusively protecting exhibits." Other important aspects of the security system include inventory control, fire prevention efforts, vandalism prevention programs and a network with other galleries and museums throughout the country.

McDaniel (1994, p. 6a) describes the security to protect an open-air museum, Colonial Williamsburg, consisting of 88 original eighteenth-century buildings scattered over the 174-acre site. This museum has 3,500 employees and is visited by more than three million people annually. Security officers are not sworn officers and are not armed. McDaniel notes (p. 10A): "A high profile security presence is unacceptable in an open-air museum like Colonial Williamsburg." Instead their approach is one of "meet and greet" visitors. Security includes a central alarm monitoring computer and a CCTV system with 35 cameras as well as officers on foot patrol and bicycle patrol.

Alpert and McInerney (1992) describe the security involved in the national tour exhibiting our Bill of Rights in December 1991:

> Incorporating state-of-the-art security equipment, scientific technology, architecture and design, the exhibit established new precedents in cooperation between private enterprise, public safety and special event security.
>
> The project called for the creation of an environment that was both secure and reverential, providing visitors with an inviting, entertaining and educational experience.

Alpert and McInerney (p. 49) list the three fundamental principles on which security was based:

- The Bill of Rights is an irreplaceable document.
- Although security must be absolute, all aspects of the exhibit, including personnel, must be pleasant and welcoming to the public.
- The positive corporate image of the sponsor and its subsidiaries must be maintained and enhanced.

The security provided began by removing the National Archives' system and turning it on its side. The Bill of Rights remained sealed in a "specially built, nitrogen-filled, climate-controlled capsule" and was placed on a "railroad track" which transported it to the Secure Transport Vehicle (STV). As described by Alpert and McInerney (p. 51):

> The STV, a custom-built prototype vehicle used for the secure transport of the Bill of Rights, also served as a vault for the document during normal non-exhibition hours. The vehicle's body was heavily armored with quarter-inch steel and lightweight Kevlar armor materials. The steel was coated inside with a spall shield to prevent shrapnel from reaching the document if the vault's walls were breached by an explosion.
>
> The exterior shell of the STV was surrounded by the insulation materials used by NASA on space shuttles for protection from excessive heat when passing through the earth's atmosphere. For this project, the purpose of the insulation was the same—to protect the document from heat if the STV were threatened by fire.
>
> To avoid detection, the vehicle did not travel on the open road but was transported with a standard unmarked 48-foot semi-truck. Finally, through satellite tracing and communications technology, the location of the truck carrying the document was constantly monitored via a satellite communications link. This system provided precise location information, within 100 feet, to three land-based sites in the United States.

In the viewing position, the public could view the document from as close as two feet. The capsule was continuously monitored by security agents present in the viewing room or an agent monitoring it from command post cameras.

Archives Security

Another area of concern for many museums is archival material. Stoks (1992, p. 126) notes: "Threats to the long-term preservation of archival material include moisture and vermin, as well as careless handling." One way to combat the careless handling problem is to restrict access to valuable documents. Stoks (p. 126) suggests dividing the facility into four zones and color coding them:

- Public (free access).
- Semi-public (limited supervision).
- Private (staff areas only).
- Restricted (off-limits to the public and some staff.)

He notes: "Good defense-in-depth requires at least two access control points between a public area and a restricted area." In addition, fire protection should include fire-resistant construction, fire compartment isolation, fire detections systems and fire suppression systems. Further, air-conditioning, heating and ventilation should be considered as they relate to documents. Flooding should always be protected against. Some measures might include keeping collections out of basements and off floors, installing floor drains, not storing collections under water pipes, installing moisture detectors and conducting regular inspections. Stoks (p. 130) concludes:

> Finally, the public should not be overlooked for its role in security management. The total atmosphere of the facility is an important factor in

shaping the attitudes of the public to the archives. Protective measures must be managed sensitively and must not be unnecessarily restrictive. The archive should not bristle with technology; this approach creates resentment. A strong emphasis should be placed on public relations.

A protective services program for an archives is a careful balance of intrinsic protection by design, judicious use of security technology, and, above all, a sensitive and comprehensive security management system.

National Parks

Closely related to problems in museum and archive security are problems involved with security in our national parks. As noted by Layne (1994, p. 67): "Valuable artifacts have been systematically excavated and looted from national parks by professional thieves, amateur explorers, and overzealous collectors through the years. The losses are stagggering, and the threat to many of the nation's cultural resources is extreme."

Problems in these parks range from insufficient personnel, lack of training, lack of staff awareness and incorrect use of electronic countermeasures. Among the security measures to be considered are fire prevention, adequate lighting, perimeter protection and a communication system. Ongoing security awareness training should be provided for all park personnel.

RELIGIOUS FACILITIES

"[L]aw enforcement officials, insurance executives and others attempting to track the number of incidents say religious institutions are no longer off-limits to criminals. Most say the problem has become sufficiently widespread that few churches can leave their doors open, as was common in days past" ("Churches Offer Tempting Targets," 1994, p. 5). The result is that churches can no longer provide the sanctuary they traditionally provided. In fact, churches are the scene of violence just like other institutions in our society. In Bridgeport, Connecticut, a former mayor, a priest and another person were critically wounded in a shooting as they stood on the steps of a church. In other instances, entire church services have been held up at gunpoint, and drive-by shootings through sanctuary doors have occurred ("Churches Offer," p. 11).

Problems

Churches, synagogues, temples and other places of worship are in need of security. Fey (1986, p. 115) emphasizes this: "Both the news media and police officials report dramatic increases in crimes against religious property and personnel in recent years. . . . Burglary, robbery, assault, vandalism, and arson have shown the greatest increases in spite of the fact that, according to police, many of these crimes go unreported. The Metropolitan Police Department of Washington, DC, estimates only one-third of church, synagogue, and temple crime is reported."

Historically, the church was considered relatively immune from criminal actions because of its special status in the community. Such is no longer the case. To hard-core criminals and even to many juvenile delinquents, the church has no special status. In fact, as businesses and private homes tighten their security, churches are perceived as an easy mark.

In addition, according to Story (1987, p. 81): "Ritualistic crimes are occurring with greater frequency in America." Such crimes may involve religious articles stolen from churches. Further, hate groups such as the Skinheads may become involved in desecrating synagogues.

> Security problems faced by religious institutions include the desire for easy accessibility at all times, their attractiveness to indigents and mental patients and the individuals included in their social outreach programs.

Many churches still pride themselves on being there for people 24 hours a day, seven days a week, including all holidays. Many churches have valuable religious relics, statues, money boxes and the like completely unprotected in their sanctuaries.

Fey points out a further complication (1986, pp. 115–20): "These institutions are opening their doors to a wider segment of the community than ever before. Even where the institutions themselves have not taken the initiative, many new clients in need have come calling. For example, one growing group seeking help from religious institutions is mental patients who are being discharged as soon as possible from institutions where the federal government is paying the bills. Homeless former patients come to houses of worship in search of shelter, food, and other help."

In addition to such individuals, numerous other individuals from the disadvantaged segments of society are attracted by the religious institutions' social outreach programs—for example, soup lines, shelters for the homeless and food and clothing distribution outlets. Fey warns that "a small number of vocal and mentally unbalanced clients, some with violent tendencies, often appear for help. Over the long run one or more career criminals are likely to find their way into a program."

Another security problem presents itself when the religious institutions open their doors for use by outside groups, either free of charge or for a fee. A religious institution seldom has control over what these groups do within its facility.

Reducing the Problems

Because religious institutions vary so greatly in size, basic philosophy regarding security measures and actual vulnerability, no one security system is applicable to all. Nonetheless, most might benefit from certain common-sense procedures.

Security measures for religious institutions include perimeter protection, including lighting and fencing; safeguarding of valuables by such means as lighting, locks and alarms and contingency plans for handling disruptive individuals.

If cemeteries are being vandalized, security measures might include improved lighting and decorative fencing, particularly protecting any historically significant graves.

An additional area of concern is to take precautions when money is being collected at special events, concerts, fundraisers and the like. Purse-snatchers and pickpockets may also be in attendance.

Fey also notes that "works of art and historically valuable objects in religious institutions require security techniques similar to those used by museums." Spot alarms might be used, such as a pressure-sensitive pad or a strip that is set under an object. If the object is lifted, an alarm sounds.

SUMMARY

Institutions that may require special security include hospitals and other health care facilities, educational institutions, libraries, museums and art galleries and even religious facilities.

The major security problems of health care facilities are emergency room security, visitor control, internal and external theft and the potential for fire. These problems can be reduced through recognition of the risks, careful inventory control, training in fire prevention and evacuation procedures and surveillance.

Major security problems of educational institutions are safety of students and staff, violence, vandalism and theft, including burglary. Access control, lighting and security personnel are means to reduce these risks.

The major losses in libraries result from theft of or damage to books. Such losses can be reduced by the electronic marking of books and by providing photocopy equipment.

The major security problems of museums and art galleries include theft, fraud, vandalism and arson. These can be reduced by establishing a basic security system, which includes locks, alarms and security officers at stations and on patrol; maintaining detailed inventories; having each object professionally appraised and authenticated; and positively identifying and registering each item.

Security problems faced by religious institutions include the desire for easy accessibility at all times, their attractiveness to indigents and mental patients and the individuals included in their social outreach programs. Security measures for religious institutions include perimeter protection, including lighting and fencing; safeguarding of valuables by such means as lighting, locks and alarms and contingency plans for handling disruptive individuals.

APPLICATION

1. Develop a security checklist for three of the types of facilities discussed in this chapter.

2. Evaluate the burglary prevention materials in Figures 14–5 and 14–6 in relation to institutional security.

CRITICAL THINKING EXERCISE

INSTITUTIONAL LIABILITY

STATUTORY AND COMMON LAW

The state is liable for the torts committed by its employees acting within the scope of their employment. Also, the state has the burden to prove it is immune from liability under discretionary acts. Generally, however, one has no duty to protect another from actions of a third party unless a special relationship exists or foreseeable risk is involved. A landowner has no duty to protect entrants on its land from a third party's criminal activities, because a criminal act committed by another person is not an activity of the owner and does not constitute a condition of the land.

FACTS OF THE CASE

For the past five years, the Southeast Asian Club at Lakeside Community College has sponsored an annual festival called Southeast Asian Days. Each year between 1,500 and 2,000 people attend the two-day festival. This event is held on Lakeside's college property. The club is encouraged to hold this event because it builds good relationships with the community and helps to promote enrollment by Southeast Asian students.

Several weeks before the festival, four violent incidents occurred in neighboring cities between rival Southeast Asian gang members. Local police departments heard a report that there might be another incident at the soccer tournament during the festival, but college officials were not notified of this rumor. William Nesbit, the dean of students, did not know of any gang-related retaliatory incidents in the area, and although he and the advisor of the Southeast Asian Club heard of vague rumors, they did not believe there would be any trouble on the college campus. In fact, although similar vague rumors were heard in previous years, no incidents were reported.

In past years the college had hired uniformed, off-duty police officers to provide security for the festival. In addition, a Southeast Asian police officer from another community volunteered his services to help with security. So this year Lakeside Community College contacted Lieutenant James Putnum of the local police department to obtain security for the festival. Nesbit offered to hire off-duty police officers to provide security, but Putnum said two on-duty uniformed officers would be supplied at no charge. Putnum said he would work from 11:00 A.M. until 3:00 P.M. as one of the officers and would bring the police bus and as many reserves as would volunteer with him. At 3:00 P.M. two other uniformed officers would relieve Putnum and his partner and stay until the festival ended. Nesbit did say that he thought the number of officers to be supplied for security was "ridiculously low," and he requested that officers "pay more attention to Lakeside's special needs." Manpower limitations, however, limited Nesbit's ability to assign additional officers to the festival, and the college's limited financial resources (along with concern for maintaining good relations with the local police department) mitigated against hiring additional security personnel.

On the first afternoon of the festival, the Mankato State University soccer team arrived at Lakeside to participate in the soccer tournament. About 2:10 P.M., while the teams were warming up for their match, several gunshots were fired by gangs that began a fight near the sidelines of the playing field. Phedra Rasibone, a player on the Mankato team, was hit in the stomach by one of the shots. He did not know who fired the shot that hit him, and he did not think he was intentionally hit.

Immediately after the shooting incident, Nesbit canceled the remainder of the festival. He asked security officers to clear the area and requested that they continue to patrol the area for the remainder of the day and throughout the next day.

Rasibone sued the college for not canceling the festival in light of the threatened violence, for not warning the members of the Mankato team about the possibility of violence and for not providing sufficient security to prevent gang encounters leading to violence. He also sued James Putnum as the person who took responsibility for providing security for the festival.

ISSUES AND QUESTIONS

1. Does the college as a landowner, or other person as a security official, have a duty to protect the public from possible violence as in this case?
   a. Because Putnum took on the responsibility to provide security, and he volunteered to provide sufficient officers or obtain additional volunteers at no charge to the college, he personally will be held responsible for the fact that security was insufficient to prevent violence. After all, he was the person who had received reports of possible gang violence, and he knew of four previous incidents between rival gangs. The college, on the other hand, is protected by the doctrine of discretionary immunity.
   b. Because the dean of students attempted to secure additional security and expressed the opinion that what was offered was "ridiculously low," the college will not be held liable for damages. The agency providing security, in this case the White Bear Lake Police Department (and the local municipality), can be held responsible for insufficient security (insufficient both in numbers of officers made available for duty and insufficient in tactics employed for surveillance). After all, neither an

individual officer nor a poorly funded college (let alone a club advisor) could afford to recompense damages.

c. The college must warn all persons attending a public festival on its grounds that possible violence could occur. Only when a public warning is clearly and repeatedly given so that all who attend are aware of possible danger, and can thus chose to leave or stay and risk the chance of injury, will the college (and its officers) be immune from liability.

d. Because a landowner is required to use reasonable care in carrying on activities and to maintain security by ensuring entrants that they are not exposed to danger, the college must exercise greater care when there is a report of possible violence during a public assemblage. Given that security was insufficient to prevent violence, the college has failed in its duty to protect and is therefore liable for injuries sustained.

e. The college's decision not to hire additional security for the festival even in light of threatened violence was protected by discretionary immunity. The decision by the dean of students to rely on the local police department to provide security involved balancing a number of policy considerations including public safety, confidence in the effectiveness of the police department, whether obtaining additional security would damage the college's relationship with the police and whether the college's limited budget should be used to obtain additional security.

Discussion Questions

1. Which types of security discussed in this chapter seem most important to you? Why?
2. How can security directors enhance the public relations of a health care facility?
3. What kind of security is provided at your campus?
4. Do you have art galleries or museums in your community that might be at risk? If so, what kind of security do they have?
5. Have there been instances of crimes committed against any religious facilities in your community?

References

Alpert, David and McInerney, Robert. "Securing the Bill of Rights." *The Police Chief,* July 1992, pp. 49–51.

Arbetter, Lisa. "A Textbook Case of Campus Security." *Security Management,* September 1994, pp. 40–46.

Bagley, Gerald L. "How Can Hospitals Operate Safely?" *Security Management,* December 1993, pp. 97–98.

Bastian, Lisa D. and Taylor, Bruce M. *School Crime: A National Crime Victimization Survey Report.* Washington, DC: Bureau of Justice Statistics, September 1991.

Bias, Bronson S. "Welcome Tools to Education." *Security Management,* September 1994, pp. 49–51.

Blauvelt, Peter D. "The Ultimate Test." *Security Management,* September 1991, pp. 89–93.

Borchert, Don. "Access Control at the University of Southern California Rates an A-Plus." *Security Technology and Design,* November/December 1993, pp. 40–47.

Bordes, Roy N. "Protecting Pablo and Associates." *Security Management,* June 1993, pp. 11A–12A.

Bracalente, Anita. "The Fine Art of Museum Security." *Security Management,* June 1993, pp. 4A–6A.

Burrows, Robin. "Artful Protection from Down Under." *Security Management,* February 1992, pp. 34–38.

Campbell, Douglas A. "Hospital Fire Training Heats Up." *Security Management,* February 1995, pp. 49–54.

Chuda, Thomas J. "Fanning the Flames of Fire Safety." *Security Management,* July 1994, pp. 35–37.

"Churches Offer Tempting Targets for Crime." *Law Enforcement News,* November 30, 1994, pp. 5, 11.

Collins, Pam. "Big Plan on Campus." *Security Management,* March 1992, pp. 27–30.

"Coming Clean on Campus Crime." *Law Enforcement News,* October 15, 1991, pp. 1, 10.

Crowe, Timothy D. "Safer Schools by Design." *Security Management,* September 1991, pp. 81–86.

Dawson, Donald F. "A New Chapter in Hospital Security." *Security Management,* June 1992, pp. 34–38.

Dean, Edward T. "Solving the Patient Protection Problem." *Security Management,* September 1992, p. 148.

Dowling, Jack F. "Secure Dorms: An Open and Shut Case." *Security Management,* September 1994, p. 47.

Draty, David. "Hospital Security through the 20th Century." *Security Concepts,* June 1994, p. 12.

Erickson, John. "A Systems Approach to Museum Security." *Security Management,* February 1994, pp. 45–48.

Fey, T. M. "The Holy War." *Security Management,* October 1986, pp. 115–20.

Gates, Daryl F. and Martin, William E. "Art Theft—A Need for Specialization." *The Police Chief,* March 1990, pp. 60–62.

Graves, C. Ray. "Treating Hazardous Waste." *Security Management,* May 1991, pp. 43–45.

Green, Gion. *Introduction to Security,* 4th ed. Revised by Robert J. Fisher. Stoneham, MA: Butterworth Publishers, 1987.

Hall, Stephen J. "Healing with Access Control." *Security Management,* April 1994, p. 29.

Harowitz, Sherry L. "Healthy Security at Children's Hospital." *Security Management,* August 1993, pp. 42–48.

Haynes, Richard A. "Scoring a Touchdown for Security." *Security Management,* November 1991, pp. 55–61.

Hinkle, Douglas P. "Campus Crime Investigations: How to Avoid Being Stonewalled." *Security Technology and Design,* June 1992, pp. 28–30.

Hinkle, Douglas P. and Jones, Theodore S. "Security Guards or Real Cops? How Some Major Universities Are Facing the Nineties." *Law and Order,* September 1991, pp. 141–46.

"Hospital Crime Survey." *Security Management,* November 1993, p. 15.

"Hospital Patient, Personnel Safety." *Security Concepts,* July 1994, p. 22.

Jackson, Eric. "Campus Police Embrace Community-Based Approach." *The Police Chief,* December 1992, pp. 63–64.

Jackson, Fred J. and Flinn, Rick J. "The Emergency Room View on Violence." *Security Management,* April 1994, pp. 25–30.

Keller, Steven R. "Framing Security for the Future." *Security Management,* April 1993, pp. 51–60.

Keller, Steven R. "How Much Security Is Enough?" *Security Management,* February 1994, pp. 103–4.

Kissane, T. P. "Protecting Works of Art from Theft and Fraud." *Security Management,* May 1977, pp. 6–9.

Kissane, Thomas and Burns, Kenneth. " 'Artnapping': The Need for More Sophisticated Training." *The Police Chief,* September 1992, pp. 52–54.

Kmet, M. A. "Handling a Hot Potato—The Shah in NYC." *Security Management,* March 1980, pp. 22–36.

Konicek, Joel. "Security Takes Shape in Sculpture Garden." *Security Management,* May 1993, pp. 36–38.

Kramer, Tom. "A Prescription for Security." *Security Management,* June 1993, pp. 14A–18A.

Layne, Stevan P. "Halting History's Disappearance." *Security Management,* May 1994, pp. 67–70.

Lombardi, John H. "Prescription for Prevention." *Security Management,* August 1991, pp. 55–56.

Major, Michael J. "Ease of Application, Ease of Use . . . Campus Security at University of Oregon." *Security Technology and Design,* April 1994, pp. 32–35.

McDaniel, Danny. "Safeguarding Virginia's Colonial Past." *Security Management,* July 1994, pp. 6A–12A.

National School Safety Center. *Gangs in Schools: Breaking Up Is Hard to Do.* Malibu: Pepperdine University Press, 1988.

Nielsen, Robert C. "Videos Help Police Fight Campus Crime." *The Police Chief,* October 1990, pp. 136–39.

Phelps, E. Floyd. "Coping with Crisis on Campus." *Security Management,* April 1993, pp. 44–48.

Phelps, E. Floyd. "Physical Education for Campus Security." *Security Management,* October 1992, pp. 86–88.

Phelps, E. Floyd. "Signing Up for Security 101." *Security Management,* June 1993, pp. 19A–20A.

Powell, John W. *Campus Security and Law Enforcement.* Woburn, MA: Butterworth Publishers, 1981.

Private Security. Report of the Task Force on Private Security, National Advisory Committee on Criminal Justice Standards and Goals. Washington, DC: U.S. Government Printing Office, 1976.

Saenz, Paul. "A Tonic for Hospital Security." *Security Management,* February 1992, pp. 68–69.

Salamone, Robert. "Safeguarding Our Students." *Security Management,* April 1991, pp. 70–74.

Samson, Andrea. "Securing a Healthcare Facility Ensures Business as Usual." *Security Technology and Design,* March 1994, pp. 22–29.

"Security Management Systems Tailored for Healthcare and Corporate Environments." *Security Concepts,* July 1994, pp. 22, 26.

Sherwood, J. L. "Beyond the Call of Duty: Hospital Security in the '90s." *Security Concepts,* March 1994, pp. 1–2.

Sloan, John J. "The Modern Campus Police: An Analysis of their Evolution, Structure, and Function." *American Journal of Police,* Vol. 11, No. 2, 1992, pp. 85–104.

Stedman, Michael J. "Corrective Surgery at New England Baptist." *Security Technology and Design,* March 1994, pp. 30–35.

Stoks, Francis G. "A Gallery of Security." *Security Management,* September 1992, pp. 126–30.

Story, Donald W. "Ritualistic Crime: A New Challenge to Law Enforcement." *Law and Order,* September 1987, pp. 41–42.

Surette, Kevin J. "A Clinical Approach to Security." *Security Management,* August 1993, pp. 55–60.

Thomas, Ronald C. "Universal Security at the University." *Security Management,* March 1992, pp. 33–34.

"3M Introduces Self-Check System." *Security Concepts,* November 1993, p. 13.

Utz, Thomas E. "The Challenge of University Policing." *Law and Order,* July 1990, p. 104.

Warrington, Mark and Kaufer, Steve. "Designing and Implementing Physical Security in the Campus Environment." *Security Technology and Design,* April 1994, pp. 36–39.

CASES

Kuehn v. Rento School Dist. No. 403, 694 P.2d 1078, (Wash. 1985)

State in Interest of T.L.O., 463 A.2d 934, (N.J. 1983)

Other Applications of Security at Work

Do You Know

- In what other areas security systems are frequently in place?
- What security problems exist in parking lots and ramps? How these problems might be reduced?
- What security problems exist in the courtroom? How such problems might be reduced?
- What security problems exist in protecting VIPs, corporate executives and political candidates? How these problems might be reduced?
- What problems exist in businesses located abroad? How such problems might be reduced?

Can You Define These Terms?

choke points
preincident indicators

Introduction

Certain applications of security at work do not fit neatly into any of the preceding chapters, but they are important areas that security professionals should be knowledgeable about.

> Other areas in which security measures are important include parking lots and garages; courtrooms across the country; instances involving VIPs, corporate executives and political candidates; and businesses located abroad.

This chapter begins with what may appear to be a rather mundane subject—parking lot and parking garage security. This is followed by a look at providing security in courtrooms across the country. Next, strategies for safeguarding VIPs, corporate executives and political candidates are discussed. The chapter concludes with a brief discussion of protecting American business interests abroad.

Parking Lot and Parking Garage Security

Everyone is familiar with the multitude of parking lots and parking garages associated with industry, commerce and institutions. Most people have probably felt vulnerable in such areas at one time or another. As noted by Konicek (1992, p. 50): "The shadowy, open spaces of parking lots have long served as the perfect cover for criminal activities. Crimes ranging from car theft to assault, robbery, and rape occur in parking lots day and night."

In addition, as noted by Viau (1994, p. 63): "Parking garages always have been a favorite movie setting for car chases, assaults and kidnapping. With dim or no lighting, along with many blind spots and hiding places, parking garages can be reminiscent of dark alleys. It's no wonder people have felt uneasy about walking late at night through garages to their cars."

Establishments that own or lease parking lots or garages have a responsibility to protect those who park there or face costly litigation. Konicek (1992, p. 50) states: "In recent years, the courts have found parking lot owners liable when security measures that could have been taken to deter a crime were ignored."

Nonetheless, according to Church (1991, p. 43): "The average security manager avoids the issue of parking because it usually brings nothing but heartache and bad press. But, a properly managed parking program can be a boon to a security department."

Problems

Most of the security problems encountered in parking lots and garages are apparent. Patrons are exposed to assault, robbery, theft, kidnapping and vandalism of their vehicles. In addition, the parking garages themselves may be the target of vandals.

> Problems presented by parking lots and garages include assault, robbery, theft, kidnapping and vandalism.

Reducing the Problems

As with any other area presenting security problems, the first step is to carefully assess the situation. Where might problems occur? How likely is it that a problem will occur? How costly would it be in terms of liability? What can be done to prevent or at least lessen the probability of the problem occurring?

Konicek (1992, p. 50) suggests that vulnerable areas within parking lots or garages might include stairways, elevators, poorly lit areas and isolated areas.

Adequate lighting in parking lots is one important physical security measure.

> Among the measures to reduce problems in parking lots and garages are adequate lighting; surveillance via closed circuit television (CCTV) cameras or patrol; communications such as intercoms, telephones or call buttons; and patron awareness programs.

Lighting is essential, especially in isolated areas. Surveillance cameras will be of little use if the lighting is inadequate. Surveillance via CCTV not only provides continuous, visible monitoring of activity in the area, but also may provide evidence of crimes committed. In addition, such cameras can be integrated with the communications system so that if a call for help is initiated, the camera pans to that immediate area, monitoring and recording simultaneously.

As noted by Viau (1994, p. 63): "Usually the most costly method is patrols using vehicles, foot patrols, bicycles or even canine units." Although such human presence is likely to serve as a deterrent, this approach also has inherent weaknesses. The most important weakness is that a single patrol can be in only one area at a time. A person intent on committing a crime might simply wait until the security guard has passed and then proceed with the criminal act. In addition, the possibility exists that a patrol could go past a car in which a crime is being committed and be completely unaware of the illegal activity.

Viau suggests: "As crime increases, the trend in security is toward more electronic equipment and more surveillance. . . . Improved technology and decreasing costs are contributing to the addition of video and audio systems in garages."

Security in a parking lot or garage is enhanced if only one entrance and one exit are available. If this decision is made, it should be weighed against the need for emergency personnel to have rapid access to parking. Konicek (1992, p. 56) cautions: "Consider, for example, situations where immediate and unhampered access into a building can be an essential element of a person's job. Paramedics and police officers, for instance, have to be able to get onto the premises where they work at a moment's notice."

Church (1991, p. 43) takes a somewhat different approach to parking management, suggesting two focuses: service to the customer and protection of rights.

Church tells the story of his first venture into security as manager at a health care center. He instituted a parking system requiring permits and enforced it vigorously, averaging 60 to 90 citations a day. One day at a meeting an outspoken manager asked Church what Church would do if a flying saucer lit in the parking lot. Church asked if the saucer had an employee permit and received "no" for an answer. Church's response was that he'd give it a ticket. This brought an uproar of laughter and a realization to Church that rather than focusing on enforcement, security should focus on customer service and protecting rights.

According to Church (p. 43): "Citations, for example, are viewed by most people as forms of punishment. . . . Yet, citations are a service to those who park in the proper area and to a facility's customers." Among the strategies Church (1991, pp. 43–44) recommends for parking management are the following:

- Vehicle registration: The foundation of a successful program is the quantity and quality of information about those who park there.
- Citations: When given, information should be kept about the license number, date, time and who issued the citation.
- Services: Again, information should be recorded about all services provided, when they were provided, where, and by whom.
- Assigned parking: Parking can be assigned by a parking space number or a title/name.
- Towing records: Vehicles may be towed to enforce parking regulations or to remove abandoned vehicles.
- Wheel locks: These are an effective form of enforcement because they require an offender to report to the security department.

Church (p. 44) concludes: "The two major driving forces of business in the 90s continue to be quality and service. How well you do what you do and how fast and pleasantly you do it make the difference. Both measures of performance will make or break your department. Developing a parking program improves the quality and speed of one of your major operations."

COURTROOM SECURITY

"Assaults on the judiciary and violence in the courtrooms of America are at an all-time high," says McMicking (1993, p. 31A). He continues: "The killing of a federal appellate judge by a pipe bomb in Alabama, the bombing and maiming of a county judge in Maryland, and the shootings of judges and lawyers inside courtrooms in Florida and Texas are all evidence of the seriousness of the situation."

Maintaining order and security in courtrooms across the country is usually the responsibility of court security officers who supplement the local marshal's staff. According to Muller (1993, p. 48), court security officers must have police training and three years of experience as police officers. Although they usually are considered contract personnel, they work directly with the local marshal's service personnel. Muller notes:

> The court security officers' main functions are securing the court building or court space in a multitenant federal building, responding to duress alarm situations, and maintaining order in the court areas. These officers are deputized and have full police authority while on duty.

Across the country, security officers help keep order in our courts.

As noted by Lesce (1994, p. 84): "Court security has to meet two conflicting requirements by being both effective and inoffensive. Officers have to be vigilant against threats to the security of the court, but on the other hand, most visitors are not threatening."

In addition to keeping order in the court, security officers also are responsible for assuring that prohibited items are not brought into the courtroom. Such items might include weapons of any sort, cameras and recording equipment.

As noted by Lesce (p. 86), court security officers should be trained in prisoner control, weapon control, records and evidence, judges' security and witness security. Other topics he suggests are prisoner movement, weak links in the custodial process, use of restraining devices, escape types and timing, disruptive conduct, emergency situations and a physical security survey. Finally, he encourages court security officers to be adept at screening incoming packages, recognizing bomb threats and handling a bomb threat caller.

Problems

Although the usual perception of a courtroom is one of orderly dignity, violence can and does occur. Judges, prosecutors, defense attorneys, witnesses and even security officers are assaulted each year. Spectators may become unruly. Defendants may attempt to escape. And demonstrations might occur outside the courthouse.

> Security problems that might occur in courtrooms include threats, including bomb threats; assaults; unruly spectators; escape attempts and demonstrations outside the courtroom.

Lesce (1994, p. 84) notes: "Experience has shown that 90% of courtroom disturbances and security problems involve males. Teenagers and young adults cause the most disruptions, but offenders between the ages of 30 and 45 cause the most serious incidents." Lesce also notes: "A surprising finding was that 30% of those causing disruptions had law enforcement or security training, and 47% had knowledge of guns."

Reducing the Problems

As noted by Muller (1993, p. 47): "The U.S. Marshals Service has always maintained that drug-related trials require a higher level of security and are more complex than other categories of criminal offenses." As with the challenge of establishing a security system in most other areas, the first step is to assess the risks involved, determine the probability of them occurring and then select appropriate preventive measures.

Most of the physical, procedural and personnel strategies discussed in Section II are appropriate for courtroom security.

> Courtroom security problems might be reduced by effective access control including screening of people and packages using metal detectors and x-ray machines; surveillance equipment; security glass in vulnerable areas; locks on doors; duress alarms and a plan on how to react in emergencies such as a duress alarm, an escape or a bomb threat.

Muller (1993, p. 47) stresses: "An effective security program depends on the proper integration of security personnel and equipment." Muller (p. 49) emphasizes the importance of the entry screening in any court security program but cautions that it is not a cure-all. Reliable systems to alert the security force to problems must be installed.

McMicking (1993, p. 31A) notes that retail security managers have found that using CCTV cameras provides a psychological deterrent to shoplifters. He suggests: "Ninety percent of the security battle may be won in courthouse security if the same psychology is used around the courthouse grounds, including adding signs that advertise the use of such cameras."

Vulnerable areas such as the judges' chambers, clerk of court's office, cashier's office and the court's probation, parole and pretrial offices should be equipped with security glass, surveillance systems and duress alarms. McMicking (1993, p. 37A) recommends: "Judges' benches in courtrooms should be equipped with duress alarms and ballistic-resistant material capable of withstanding a projectile from a .357 caliber weapon." He further recommends (p. 38A):

> Audiovisual equipment should be available in case a defendant becomes unruly and is removed to his or her holding cell to hear and see the trial on a video monitor. The courtroom should be equipped with a defendant's chair that is bolted to the floor and is equipped with chain loops to anchor the defendant to the chair if he or she becomes unruly.

An additional recommendation from McMicking (p. 38A) is that one elevator should be reserved for the judge's exclusive use and that it should be key or card operated. He concludes: "By focusing on these access control concerns, both exterior and interior, courthouse security managers can fulfill their goal —to protect the people and assets of the courts of law and work to prevent potential violence perpetrated on the judiciary and innocent bystanders."

PROTECTING VIPS, CORPORATE EXECUTIVES AND POLITICAL CANDIDATES

As Hildreth (1991, p. 66) writes: "No one can imagine just how much work it is to provide protection in a free society to someone that may need it."

Most VIPs require a team for protection as they travel around the country. Hildreth (1991, p. 70) suggests: "There's no substitute for people who have been there and done it before, who've had the training. Select your people with this in mind. Pick those in whom you have the fullest confidence, even in times of high stress."

Corporate executives usually do not require a team for protection but offer other challenges. As noted by Olick (1995, p. 1): "Terrorism is on the rise in this country as well as abroad and powerful executives, regardless of their exact role in business, are very often targeted by terrorists . . . merely because of the authority they hold. They represent the elite, the strongest among the Western civilization."

Security for corporate executives is usually provided by a "bodyguard" who must be intimately familiar with the executive and must also be concerned about the executive's family. Heine (1994, p. 57) notes: "Contrary to popular belief, the best bodyguards are those who would rather not hurt anyone if possible. Macho bodyguards are more likely to get themselves or their clients killed by trying to prove how tough they are." This same perspective is set forth by Olick (1995, p. 23):

> This is 1995, and the game has changed. The stakes are higher and out of the most primitive, basic concept of a "bodyguard," a new age of protection has evolved.
>
> Highly skilled, polished executive protection agents are the end result of years at work. These individuals will blend with the life-style of the person they are protecting . . . they will fit a mold that has been tailor-made by the client to meet aesthetic requirements. Internally, the executive protection agent possesses an arsenal of knowledge, cunning and foresight carefully nurtured to thwart even the deadliest of intentions.

Heine futher suggests (p. 58):

> A bodyguard should have good moral character, good hearing and eyesight, patience, and thoroughness. He or she should have no history of drug or alcohol addiction, and no criminal record.
>
> A bodyguard should also be a team player, with first-aid and CPR certification or paramedic training. Physical fitness and the ability to work long hours in uncomfortable environments are important, as is a basic knowledge of explosives and terrorist weapons. The bodyguard also needs excellent communication skills to be effective.
>
> The bodyguard must be able to blend in with the life style of the person he or she is protecting.

It is obvious that not everyone is suited to this line of work.

The third category of high-profile individuals who may need the services of private security specialists is political candidates. Kochis (1994, p. 27) notes: "Protecting a political candidate, his or her campaign staff, and family members provides a unique security challenge." He suggests: "The level of security required to protect a specific candidate is determined by the type of office sought, the candidate's public image and reputation, the attitude of the voters, the mode and direction of the campaign, and the campaign issues surrounding that office." At one level, a bodyguard may be the appropriate protection. At another level a security team may be required.

Unique challenges presented by protecting political candidates include the need for security to adapt to schedules revised on short notice and the candidate's disappearing from view while intermingling with large crowds (Kochis, 1994, pp. 28, 29). Security risks also may be heightened by any of the following factors (Kochis, p. 33):

- The size and population of the campaign territory.
- The sensitivity of the issues.
- The extent to which the office is heavily contested.
- The level of rhetoric being used by opponents.
- The socioeconomic character of the voters.
- The manner in which the media presents issues.
- The candidate's demeanor when dealing with the press and public.

As with protecting corporate executives, protecting a political candidate is a "family affair." The candidate's spouse, children and even grandchildren must be considered vulnerable to attack. Kochis (1994, p. 33) advises: "[C]ampaigns are hectic affairs and providing security in such an atmosphere is at times difficult. The security director should be prepared to accept change as the only constant."

Dermaut (1993, p. 3) notes: "[N]o matter the amount of agents nor the quality of protection, terrorists, killers, and fanatics will continue to try to eliminate the people who they perceive as their enemies." Further, says Dermaut: "These days CEOs, directors, diplomats, judges and law enforcement officials are all potential victims of terrorists, kidnappers, and just plain killers."

The following discussion of problems and ways to reduce them may sometimes include suggestions regarding one specific type of personal protection, but usually such suggestions will apply to the other types of personal protection as well. Before exploring the problems and potential approaches to reducing them, consider the recommendation of the International Network of Protection Specialists (INPS) which recommends that protection specialists be proficient in 12 main subjects (Dermaut, 1993, pp. 29–30):

1. Terrorism-Crime.
2. Explosives.
3. Kidnapping.
4. Advance work.
5. Hardware.
6. First aid.
7. Personal [protection].
8. Protective security procedures.
9. Simulation exercises.
10. Case analysis.
11. Electronic security.
12. Shooting skills.

Consider, now, why such skills might be required of protection specialists.

Problems

Most high-profile individuals who require personal protection travel extensively, and many do not perceive the risks they face. And the risks are many, including criminals, disgruntled employees, politically motivated groups or individuals and even well-meaning groups such as environmentalists.

According to Mason (1992, p. 63): "Criminals prey on executives in a number of ways. Extortions are among the most common." They also may be victims of blackmail, harassment or assault. Mason (p. 64) also notes: "Threats can emanate from inside a company, too. The wave of recessionary layoffs has stimulated a flurry of activity from disgruntled employees." In addition, Mason notes: "Climbing the corporate ladder also triggers internal discontent."

> Security problems involved in providing personal security include the principal's mobility and lack of concern, and the potential for threats, assaults, blackmail, harassment or kidnapping.

Reducing the Problems

Specialized strategies are required to reduce the security threats inherent in personal protection. Most depend on the skills of the security professional rather than on equipment.

> Security problems associated with providing personal protection may be reduced by heightening the principal's awareness of the risk, watching for preincident indicators, checking out choke points, using advance work prior to any travel and avoiding routines.

One of the first steps to take in a personal protection plan is awareness. As noted by Flores and Nudell (1993, p. 39): "Accepting responsibility for one's own safety is the first step toward achieving greater executive protection." They also suggest (p. 40): "One objective of security awareness training is to bridge the gap between the executive and the corporate security professional." In addition, say Flores and Nudell: "Of equal importance, exposing family members and employees to this type of training can help to place security in a perspective that makes it less intrusive and, therefore, more acceptable."

According to Heine (1994, p. 58): "The effectiveness of executive protection depends on the willingness and ability of executives and their families to maintain a low profile." Duress signals should be established and practiced by all members of the family.

Mason (1992, pp. 65–66) suggests that those individuals needing protection should follow five basic preventive measures:

- Be aware and suspicious.
- Be methodical.
- Avoid routines.

- Develop good communications.
- Take initiative and use common sense.

Awareness of and alertness to preincident indicators is another important means to prevent problems from developing. **Preincident indicators** are any signals that an attack on an individual is being planned or is about to occur. Scotti (1992, p. 42) notes that most terrorists will put their intended target under surveillance and will work out an elaborate plan to carry out their intentions: "In the process of surveillance, however, terrorists often inadvertently give signals that they are organizing an attack."

He gives as an example the indicators of surveillance that were ignored in the assassination of German businessman Alfred Herrhausen on November 30, 1989. From October 1 to October 18, the terrorists posed as construction workers, positing less than 500 yards from Herrhausen's home. But no one thought to call the city to check them out. Herrhausen left for work as usual, in an armored car, with bodyguards in a lead car and a follow car. He was killed when his car broke a light beam coming from a photoelectric cell triggering a bomb, packed to look like a child's knapsack affixed to a child's bicycle left along the roadside. As noted by Scotti (p. 42):

> No amount of driver training and no armored car would have saved Herrhausen. Despite the use of bodyguards and extra vehicles, his best protection would have been surveillance detection.
>
> The bicycle was an important part of the ambush. . . . The terrorists left the bicycle there for more than a week, then took it away, and then put it back again. They did this until the bicycle became part of the environment. Again, no one questioned why an expensive bicycle was left along the road for days, how it got there, or who was the owner.

Scotti (p. 43) stresses the importance of checking out **choke points**—locations a person must go through to get to his or her intended destination. Such a choke point is often the location of an ambush, as was the case in the killing of Herrhausen. In most instances, someone should go through such choke points in advance of the person being guarded, looking for any signs of an ambush. As noted by Scotti (p. 44):

> A surveillance detection program may be the most important security precaution taken. A basic surveillance detection program consists of several steps.
>
> Step 1. Someone who knows the environment needs to determine what is normal around the home, office and choke points.
>
> Step 2. Once the environment around the home, office, and choke points is determined, constant observation of these areas is required. If in a foreign country, the people who perform this task must be nationals.
>
> Step 3. What is found in step 1 is compared to what is found in step 2. This is easily done with a computer.

Step 4. If a change in the normal environment occurs, a system needs to be developed that immediately indicates what that change is.

Step 5. Once the surveillance information has been collected and analyzed, it needs to go out to those in the field.

Another key component to comprehensive personal protection is advance work—physically preceding the person being protected to check out the situation in its entirety, including means of transportation, lodging, restaurants, meetings and offices to be visited. Dermaut (1993, p. 29) believes: "Probably the most important factor after good intelligence is advance work." The advance person should visit all airports included in the trip. He or she also should meet with the security director of the hotel in which the principal is staying and request a tour, which includes the room assigned to the principal. In addition, suggest Blennerhassett and Glazebrook (1992, p. 50):

> The advance work for business visits to offices should include the contact person and phone number, a crime index reading of the area, the closest hospital with trauma unit, security in the building (armed or unarmed), entry requirements for employers and visitors to the building, and hours of access.

They stress (p. 51): "A football team cannot win with only one player; an advance person cannot succeed without help from others."

According to Blennerhassett and Glazebrook (1992, p. 47): "The time required to perform an advance successfully depends on such factors as trip distance and duration; whether travel is for business, pleasure, or both; whether the itinerary is complex; and the number of principals involved." They also note (p. 51): "[T]he advance person must be meticulous and possess enormous self-discipline, since he or she is generally working alone with ample opportunity to take shortcuts."

Before the advance work is undertaken, however, important pre-advance work should be completed. One important step is to review the records of previous trips to determine what went well and what went not-so-well. Newspapers from the area to be visited should be read to determine any potential violence likely to be encountered.

Also important to those who provide personal protection is a knowledge of how to respond to illnesses, accidents or injuries. In addition, as noted by Zimmerman (1992, p. 46), those who provide personal protection should know where the best and the closest medical facilities are located when traveling. He suggests (p. 47) that the personal protection professional have a basic trauma box containing bandages, splints, cold packs, adhesive bandages, antiseptic, blood-pressure cuff, stethoscope, scissors, tweezers, pen-sized flashlight and, if permitted, common drugs such as intravenous solutions for trauma situations, Benadryl tablets, nitroglycerin tablets, dextrose or any drugs the client may need daily.

Mason (1992, p. 67) concludes: "Crimes committed against executives [and VIPs and political candidates] will continue to be a fact of life. No protective measure will ever entirely eliminate the psychological or bodily threats confronting the corporate elite. . . . However, proactive planning is an effective means of stymieing attempts as well as maintaining damage control."

Protecting Individuals and Business Interests Abroad

Many companies have offices abroad. In most cases, security is even more critical in such branches than in the United States because cultural factors influencing security may not be known.

Problems

The security problems in protecting people and businesses in foreign countries are compounded by lack of experience with the traditions of the country and language barriers.

> The primary problem when providing security abroad is unfamiliarity with the language, local customs and expectations.

Boim and Smith (1994, pp. 50–53) list the following "weak links in executive armor":

- Communications.
- Information control (especially fax messages).
- Lack of awareness.
- Lack of adequate intelligence.

They give as an example of lack of awareness the following actual incident (p. 53) involving executives arriving via commercial carrier who were to be met by a limousine, but because the flight was three hours late, the limousine was no longer there:

> An airport employee instructs them to simply take a taxi and arranges for a vehicle to pick them up. The taxi driver, however, is collaborating with a local criminal gang. The men are driven to an isolated area and robbed at gunpoint. Since in many countries law enforcement officials collaborate with criminals, a call to the police department may simply provide the adversary with assistance.

Reducing the Problems

McKennan (1994, p. 35) notes: "U.S. companies with overseas operations need a way to prevent adversaries from obtaining proprietary information about executives, procedures, and plans. The key is to identify, control, and protect corporate vulnerabilities."

Corporate and business security problems can be reduced by following the same procedures that would be followed in a hostile surrounding in the United States. Threats to personal safety can be reduced by following the procedures suggested for personal protection. In addition, the more that is known of the language, the culture and the political atmosphere, the greater the likelihood that the security plan will be effective.

In addition, according to Blennerhassett and Glazebrook, for those security professionals charged with protecting individuals traveling abroad (p. 49):

> The research to be completed during the pre-advance stage should include information about the destination, such as climate, terrain, type of government, and primary religion; necessary passports, visas, or shots; U.S. embassy and consulate phone numbers; currency and conversion rates; customs restrictions; terrorist organizations operating in the area; official holidays; State Department background notes; phone numbers for lodging and airlines; and car service contacts.

Heine (1994, p. 58) makes the following additions: "Before beginning a foreign trip, the bodyguard should become thoroughly familiar with the country's customs, laws, and culture. During a stay in a foreign country, executives should remember to maintain a low profile at all times."

One of the greatest threats to security when abroad is the domestic help if they are not properly screened and trained. McKennan (1994, pp. 38, 40) advises that domestic employees be given the following instructions, written in their native language:

- Keep exterior doors closed and locked during the day.
- Close and lock all exterior doors at night.
- Close and lock windows and shutters and roll down window coverings at night.
- Do not admit strangers, peddlers, inspectors, survey or census takers, or investigators you do not know, even if they are in uniform or display credentials. Tell them to call your employer or contact the company office.
- Do not admit repair people unless you have been told by your employer to expect them.
- Do not accept packages unless you have been told by your employer to expect such a delivery.
- Do not give information of any kind about the family on the telephone unless you are absolutely certain the caller is a friend. Do not identify the family's street address or telephone number to unknown callers.
- If you receive any anonymous calls or threats, or if you observe anything unusual or suspicious in the vicinity of the house, report it to your employer.

- Make a note of the license number of any suspicious vehicle parked near the house and give the information to your employer.
- If any strange objects or packages are discovered in the house or yard, leave them alone and inform your employer at once. If your employer is not available, call the police.

McKennan (1994, p. 41) concludes: "Managers should make sure that the company shares its security concerns and experiences with U.S. embassies to help embassy staff stay current regarding existing local threats. The security director should also check with the embassy where the company is located for specific details about measures that should be taken to protect business [and individuals] in that part of the world."

SUMMARY

Other areas in which security measures are important include parking lots and garages; courtrooms across the country; instances involving VIPs, corporate executives and political candidates; and businesses located abroad.

Problems presented by parking lots and garages include assault, robbery, theft, kidnapping and vandalism. Among the measures to reduce problems in parking lots and garages are adequate lighting; surveillance via CCTV cameras or patrol; communications such as intercoms, telephones or call buttons and patron awareness programs.

Security problems that might occur in courtrooms include assaults, unruly spectators, escape attempts and demonstrations outside the courtroom. Courtroom security problems might be reduced by effective access control including screening of people and packages using metal detectors and x-ray machines; surveillance equipment; security glass in vulnerable areas; locks on doors; duress alarms and a plan on how to react in emergencies such as a duress alarm, an escape or a bomb threat.

Security problems involved in providing personal security include the principal's mobility and lack of concern, and the potential for threats, assaults, blackmail, harassment or kidnapping. Security problems associated with providing personal protection may be reduced by heightening the principal's awareness of the risk, watching for preincident indicators, checking out choke points, using advance work prior to any travel and avoiding routines.

The primary problem when providing security abroad is unfamiliarity with the language, local customs and expectations. Corporate and business security problems can be reduced by following the same procedures that would be followed in a hostile surrounding in the United States. Threats to personal safety can be reduced by following the procedures suggested for personal protection. In addition, the more that is known of the language, the culture and the political atmosphere, the greater the likelihood that the security plan will be effective.

✔ APPLICATION

The Quality Private Security Services Company has assigned you to the Interstate Parking lot of the Interstate Manufacturing Company to assist in the flow of traffic and parking. At the end of the day, you are somewhat exhausted because of the sheer volume of paperwork and forms you were required to fill out, but also during the tour of duty you had to assist three employees by jump starting their cars, you assisted in changing two flat tires, you helped another two people who had locked their keys in their cars and you gave another person a ride to the bus stop because his car had a leaky radiator.

You do not think that all these services you performed were part of your instructions to keep the flow of traffic and parking orderly. You complain to your supervisor about all this responsibility. What do you think your supervisor would say to you about parking lot management?

CRITICAL THINKING EXERCISE

COMPUTER CRIME

STATUTORY AND COMMON LAW

Absent exigent circumstances, an officer must obtain an arrest warrant before entering a suspect's home to make an arrest. If, however, a police officer discovers probable cause to arrest while executing a lawful warrant to search a suspect's home, the suspect may be immediately arrested.

FACTS OF THE CASE

On May 12 Raymond Mahlberg submitted his resignation, to be effective May 31, as a security guard for the University of Nebraska at Lincoln. On May 18 materials were reported missing from the University Love Library. Mahlberg was suspected of rigging the situation so that it would look like there had been a break-in. He was informed that his effective resignation would be May 19, and he was given severance pay for the balance of the month.

On May 26 computer hardware and software were reported missing from the University College of Engineering. Dr. Goddard, a member of the engineering faculty, informed Edward Mentzer, the security investigator working on both cases, that Mahlberg made an unauthorized copy of their Autocad program. Mentzer called the Autodesk Company and was told that such copying would be illegal.

After several weeks of investigation, Mentzer obtained a warrant from the Lancaster County attorney to search Mahlberg's home. The warrant listed the serial numbers of two Autocad programs.

On July 1 Mentzer and another law enforcement officer executed the search warrant. Mahlberg's wife was home at the time and directed the officers to the basement where Mahlberg kept his computer equipment and software. After Mentzer and the officer had searched unsuccessfully for the Autocad programs for several hours, Mahlberg came home. Mentzer explained what they were looking for and they continued searching through hundreds of computer disks. Finally Mahlberg led the officers to some boxes under the stairs and he said, "I think what we are looking for is in here." Some of the disks in these boxes were marked "Autocad." Dr. Goddard had warned Mentzer that Mahlberg might try to "booby-trap" the programs to erase evidence if they were examined on Mahlberg's home computer. Because Mentzer did not know exactly which disks contained the Autocad programs, he decided to seize all the disks for review at a later time away from Mahlberg's residence.

Mentzer eventually took 160 computer disks, several instruction manuals, a three-ring "Horizon Seed" binder with a computer printout of a directory listing Autocad, a Lotus 1-2-3 program and manual found in a box labeled "University of Nebraska–Lincoln Metals Lab," and two library books labeled "Property of the University of Nebraska Love Library." Mentzer gave Mahlberg a receipt for these items.

Mentzer placed Mahlberg under arrest, and Mahlberg was later charged with two counts of felony theft.

Issues and Questions

1. Does the investigating officer have probable cause to arrest, or has he violated Mahlberg's Fourth Amendment rights of privacy?
   - **a.** Mentzer plainly had probable cause when Mahlberg pointed out the location of materials and disks marked Autocad and said, "I think what we are looking for is in here."
   - **b.** Even without finding Autocad materials, the discovery of library materials and other computer equipment and software reported missing from the University would be sufficient for an arrest. Mahlberg, as a matter of record, was under suspicion for theft of numerous items from the University. He was asked to resign early because he was suspected of illegal activity. The seized items prove his guilt of criminal activity.
   - **c.** Mentzer had probable cause to arrest with the materials he seized, but he first should have obtained an arrest warrant. The mere fact that he had a search warrant was insufficient to make an immediate arrest. There was no reason to assume that Mahlberg would flee; it was unreasonable to act hastily and do anything more than confiscate property for closer examination and then obtain a proper arrest warrant.
   - **d.** Mentzer lacked probable cause to arrest because he could not be sure, before actually examining the content of the disks, that Mahlberg had in fact stolen the Autocad program. And Mentzer was not required to accept what Mahlberg voluntarily told him as sufficient evidence on which to make an arrest. Therefore, Mentzer had neither an arrest warrant nor exigent circumstances to justify arresting Mahlberg in his home.

e. Although Mentzer believed he had reason to assume that the computer manuals, library books and items other than the numbered Autocad programs that he seized were connected to criminal activity, these items were not listed in the search warrant. Mentzer was in violation of Mahlberg's Fourth Amendment rights in seizing items not listed on the search warrant. Mentzer's actions were clearly an invasion of privacy and in violation of Nebraska law, and thus the fruits of Mentzer's search must be suppressed.

Discussion Questions

1. In your experience with parking lots and ramps, do you find that most have taken some measures to provide security?
2. What are some security problems American businesspeople confront when in a foreign country?
3. Review the Critical Thinking Exercise regarding the University of Nebraska case. Mahlberg was a proprietary security officer, hired by and working for the University of Nebraska. Do you think that if the University had used a private security agency for its security personnel this would have happened?
4. In the case of the terrorist assassination of German businessman Alfred Herrhausen, what would have been Herrhausen's best protection according to the experts?
5. Why do people feel uneasy about walking late at night through parking garages or ramps?

References

Blennerhassett, Charles H. and Glazebrook, Jerome H. "On the Road Again." *Security Management,* October 1992, pp. 47–51.

Boim, Israel and Smith, Karen. "Detecting Weak Links in Executive Armor." *Security Management,* February 1994, pp. 50–55.

Church, Wayne. "The Key to Parking Management." *Security Management,* June 1991, pp. 43–44.

Dermaut, John M. "Executive Protection." *Security Concepts,* December 1993, pp. 3, 29.

Flores, Thomas V. and Nudell, Mayer. "Executive, Protect Thyself." *Security Management,* January 1993, pp. 39–41.

Heine, Kimberly. "Body Double: Protecting Company Executives." *Security Management,* February 1994, pp. 57–58.

Hildreth, Reed. "VIP Security: Planning Ahead." *Law and Order,* May 1991, pp. 66–70.

Kochis, Joseph A. "Campaign Security Hits the Hustings." *Security Management,* November 1994, pp. 27–33.

Konicek, Joel. "Reserve Space for Parking Lot Security." *Security Management,* November 1992, pp. 50–57.

Lesce, Tony. "Economical Courtroom Security." *Law and Order,* October 1994, pp. 83–86.

Mason, Marcy. "Protecting a Tempting Target." *Security Management,* February 1992, pp. 63–67.

McKennan, John. "Protecting Overseas Business Operations." *Security Management,* November 1994, pp. 35–41.

McMicking, Lawrence. "Security Found Not Guilty." *Security Management,* June 1993, pp. 31A–38A.

Muller, Michael G. "Keeping the Peace on Judgment Day." *Security Management,* May 1993, pp. 47–49.

Olick, M. "From Primal to Polished . . . A New Age in Executive Protection." *Security Concepts,* January 1995, pp. 1, 23.

Scotti, Anthony J. "On the Lookout for Suspicious Signals." *Security Management,* May 1992, pp. 42–45.

Viau, Bryan. "Parking Garage Security." *Security Technology and Design,* June/July 1994, p. 63.

Zimmerman, David H. "Taking a Pulse on Protection." *Security Management,* May 1992, pp. 46–47.

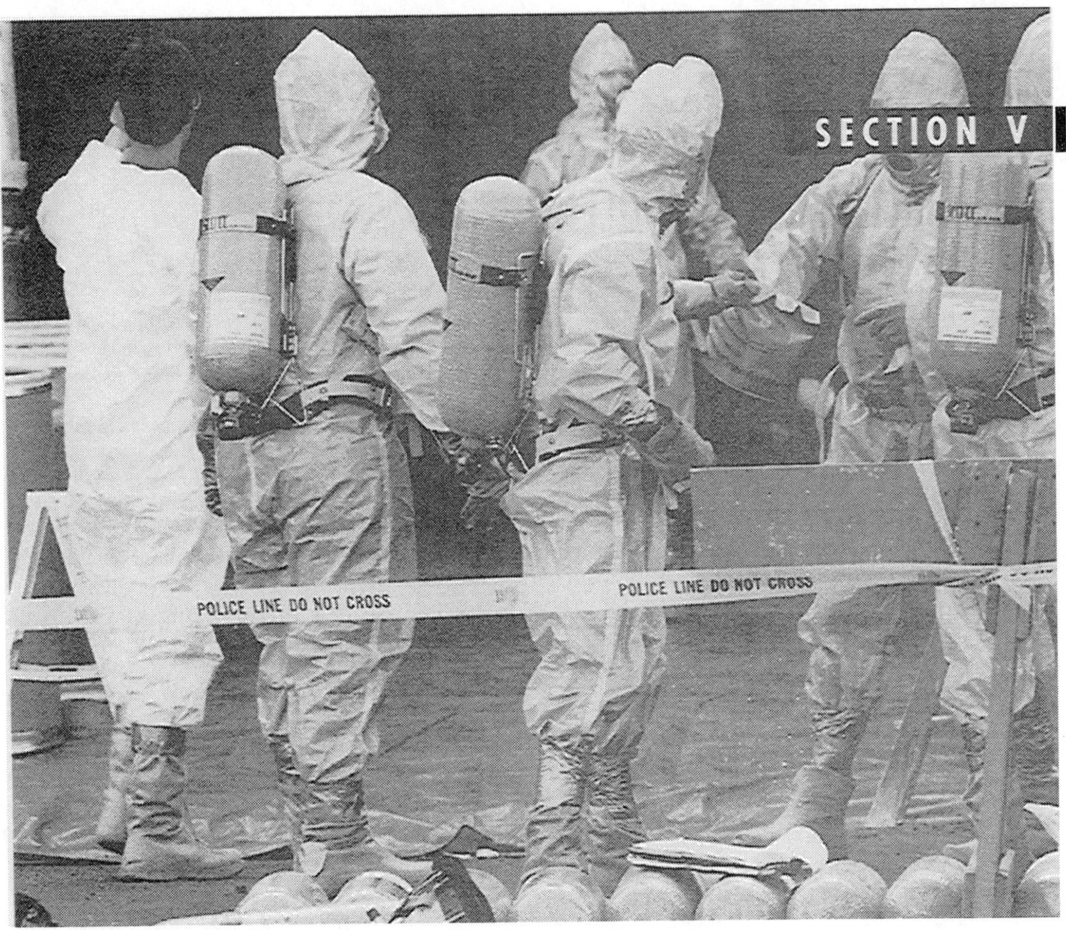

CHALLENGES FACING THE SECURITY PROFESSION IN THE 1990s AND BEYOND

To this point you have learned about the evolution of private security from its early beginnings to its present form in the 1990s, considered the public/private interface and been exposed to the legal liabilities involved with the profession. You have looked at the specific goals and responsibilities of private security and how physical controls, procedural controls and the efforts of personnel combine to reduce accidents and emergencies, prevent criminal actions, protect information and enhance public relations. You also have looked at what functions must be performed if preventive efforts fail. Finally, you have seen how the various components of security have been put together in numerous settings.

This final section focuses on two extremely important challenges facing the security profession: violence in the workplace (Chapter 20) and ethical conduct (Chapter 21). The section then discusses the security profession as it appears in the 1990s and the numerous challenges and responsibilities of security professionals (Chapter 22). The section concludes with a look at several experts' views of the challenges ahead and what the future might hold for the security profession (Chapter 23).

CHAPTER 20

THE CHALLENGES OF VIOLENCE IN THE WORKPLACE

DO YOU KNOW

- How extensive workplace violence is?
- What forms violence in the workplace may take?
- What are potential causes of such violence?
- What are characteristics of the typical perpetrator of workplace violence?
- What might be predictors of workplace violence?
- What factors might increase a worker's risk of being a victim of violence?
- What steps might be taken to prevent workplace violence?
- What should be done if workplace violence occurs?

CAN YOU DEFINE THIS TERM?

toxic work environment

INTRODUCTION

Violence in the workplace is a major challenge facing the security professional. In its most extreme form, such violence has turned deadly ("Murder in the Workplace on the Rise," 1992, pp. 76–77):

> 3-31-86. California State Employment Department, Garden Grove, California: An employee, who was upset with his supervisor and wanted a transfer, shot and killed the supervisor and himself.
>
> 8-20-86. Edmond, Oklahoma, post office: A disgruntled employee killed 14 co-workers and wounded six, then killed himself.
>
> 12-7-87. Pacific Southwest Airlines, in-flight between San Diego and San Francisco: A laid-off employee, who still had his identification card, smuggled a gun aboard the flight, and shot and killed his supervisor and the members of the flight crew, causing the plane to crash. All 43 people aboard were killed.
>
> 2-16-88. ESL, Sunnyvale, California: A former employee killed seven co-workers and wounded five others. The killings came after the employee had sent more than 100 increasingly threatening letters to a former co-worker during a four-year period. The employee also had made threats against his bosses during conversations with other former co-workers.
>
> 6-18-91. General Motors Acceptance Corp., Jacksonville, Florida: Eight employees were killed and five wounded by a gunman who was upset because the company had repossessed his car. The man used a .30 semiautomatic rifle, which he then turned on himself.

> 9-23-91. Unnamed children's clothing store, Cushing, Oklahoma: A man with a 12-gauge shotgun attempted to kill his wife, an employee at the store. He killed himself after she escaped.

More recently, on March 10, 1995 a day after gunning down Mario Ruggero, a Northwestern University faculty member who was his boss eight years ago when he worked at the University of Minnesota, John Costalupes showed up at the University's May building in the office of the dean of the medical school, Shelly Chou. Although Chou was not at the University when Costalupes left under a cloud of suspicion, Costalupes intended to kill the dean as well. But he never got the chance due to the quick actions of a plainclothes University police officer who thwarted his attempt. Ultimately, Costalupes put his revolver in his mouth and fired once, dying instantly (Broderick, 1995, pp. 1–2).

A month later, in Corpus Christi, Texas, a gunman killed five people and then himself. According to the Associated Press release (April 1995):

> James Simpson, 28, a former worker at Walter Rossler Co., entered through the front door and shot five people with a 9mm semiautomatic pistol and a .32-caliber revolver before leaving through the back door, police said. He then shot himself behind the business. . . .
>
> Police said that Simpson worked at Walter Rossler Co. until September 1994 but that they did not know why he left.

And the list goes on. Not all violence in the workplace ends in death, but violence in any form can be destructive to the morale of all employees of an establishment.

This chapter begins by looking at the extent of the problem of violence in the workplace and the various forms it can take. This is followed by a discussion of possible causes, specific indicators to be aware of, a profile of the typical perpetrator of workplace violence and risk factors to consider. Next, means of preventing workplace violence and what steps to take when prevention fails and violence does occur are discussed. The chapter concludes with a look at the legal implications of workplace violence.

The Extent of the Problem

According to Brandt and Brennan (1994, p. 25): "Workplace violence has established its mark on corporate America. During the year ending July of 1993, 2.2 million Americans were physically assaulted in the workplace. Another 6.3 million workers were victims of some type of harassment."

A national crime victimization survey, "Violence and Theft in the Workplace" (Bachman, 1994, p. 1), reports that each year nearly one million individuals become victims of violent crime while working or on duty, resulting in almost 16,000 injuries (see Table 20–1, p. 628). According to the survey:

- Crime victimizations occurring in the workplace cost about half a million employees 1,751,100 days of work each year, an average of 3.5 days per

Table 20–1. Violence in the Workplace (Annually, 1987–1992)*

	Average Annual Number	
Type of Violent Crime	*Victimizations*	*Injuries*
	971,517	159,094
Rape†	13,068	3,438
Robbery	79,109	17,904
Aggravated assault	264,174	48,180
Simple assault	615,160	89,572

* Nearly 1 million violent victimizations occurred while victims were working or on duty. These victimizations resulted in almost 160,000 injuries.
† Injuries are those in addition to the rape.

SOURCE: Bureau of Justice Statistics, U.S. Department of Justice. "Violence and Theft in the Workplace," by Ronet Bachman, 1994.

crime. This missed work resulted in over $55 million in lost wages annually, not including days covered by sick and annual leave.
- Among only those persons injured by a crime victimization at work, an estimated 876,800 workdays were lost annually, costing employees over $16 million in wages, not including days covered by sick and annual leave.
- Over half of all victimizations sustained at work were not reported to police.
- An estimated 200 fatalities, half of them homicides, occurred in parking lots or garages.

Another study conducted by Northwestern National Life Insurance Company (1993) found that more than two million Americans came under physical attack at work during the past year. In addition, another six million workers were threatened and 16 million were harassed. The project director of this study notes: "We like to think that the workplace is safe and that hostile behavior is random and rare. The reality is that violence in America is spilling out of the back streets and into the workplace. The safety, productivity and health of American workers are at risk." Other findings of this study included the following:

- Customers were twice as likely as co-workers to do physical harm to people in the workplace. Almost 45 percent of all attackers were customers, clients and patients, 20 percent came from co-workers and 7 percent came from bosses.
- About 15 percent said they had been attacked on the job at least once in their lives.
- Twenty-six percent said their attacks were motivated by irrational behavior; 19 percent said the attacks stemmed from dissatisfaction with service; 15 percent said the attacks were the result of interpersonal conflict.
- Twenty-one percent said a co-worker had been threatened during the past year.
- Nearly one attack in six involved a lethal weapon.
- Six out of 10 incidents of workplace violence occurred in private companies.

> Workplace violence has been called "epidemic" with estimates ranging from one million to two million workers experiencing violent victimization every year.

Murder in the workplace is the fastest-growing type of homicide in this country. Fox and Levin (1994) suggest that homicides of supervisors and co-workers by disgruntled employees have grown at a disturbing rate in the American workplace. Such homicides often are referred to as employer-directed homicides.

Supplemental homicide reports compiled by the FBI in conjunction with their Uniform Crime Reporting Program indicate that the incidence of murders on the job involving employers/employees has doubled over the last 10 years. On average, two such murders occur each month. Further, assaults and violent acts account for 43 percent of women's workplace fatalities, as shown in Figure 20-1 (p. 630).

Olmos (1994, p. 9) reports that each year America experiences at least 11,000 incidents of workplace violence that result in serious injury—at an annual cost of more than $2,750,000,000!

According to Broderick (1995, p. 2): "Ultimately, of course, violence in the workplace is a reflection of American society—the most violent in the industrial world. Endemic stress, access to deadly weapons, a glorification of violence in the media and popular entertainment . . . all contribute to a climate where hostility can flourish."

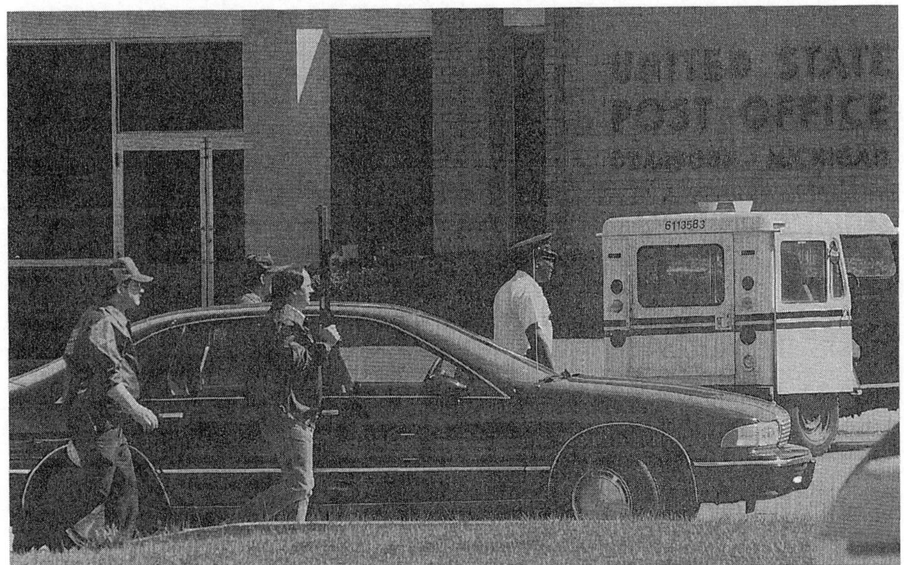

Police at the scene of the Dearborn, Michigan post office following a shooting inside. An employee walked into the post office and began shooting, killing at least one person and wounding another (May 6, 1993).

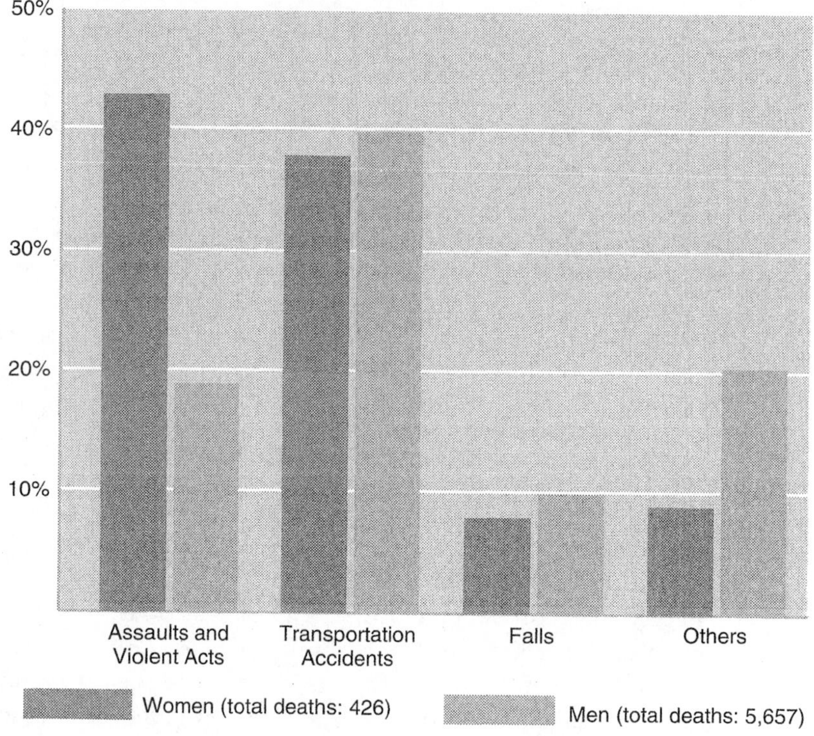

Figure 20–1. Fatalities of Women in the Workplace
First appeared in *WORKING WOMAN* in August 1994. SOURCE: Bureau of Labor Statistics. Reprinted with the permission of *WORKING WOMAN* Magazine. Copyright ©1994 by WORKING WOMAN, Inc.

FORMS OF WORKPLACE VIOLENCE

Johnson et al. (1994, p. 26) separate workplace violence into four categories:

- Robbery and other commercial crimes.
- Domestic and misdirected affection cases.
- Employer-directed situations.
- Terrorism and hate crimes.

The violence resulting during strikes and demonstrations might constitute a fifth category that should be anticipated.

> Workplace violence may occur during robbery and other commercial crimes, during domestic and misdirected affection cases, in employer-directed situations, as a result of terrorism or hate or during a strike or demonstration.

Terrorism is an unrecognized threat for many employers. This threat was brought to the country's attention when terrorists bombed the World Trade Center in 1993. As noted by Krott (1994, p. 1): "The bombing of the World Trade Center, the symbolic heart of business in America, was not only an attack on America, but on corporate America as well. The terrorists demonstrated that it's all too easy to strike a major target in the United States." Terrorism is a global problem because terrorists are not confined by geographic boundaries or languages ("Is the War on Terrorism Over?" 1991, p. 21).

This chapter focuses on employer-directed violence.

CAUSES

Olmos (1994, p. 9) cites the following reasons for the increase in workplace violence:

- The workplace environment merely reflects society in general.
- Our country has always had a love affair with violence.
- Our criminal justice system appears to be in total disarray and incapable of effectively dealing with crime in America. For the first time in our history, the police are openly admitting that they cannot effectively protect us.
- The sluggish performance of our economy has created large scale disruption in employment and financial security.
- Americans have a passion for firearms. Using a gun is infinitely easier than hands, knives, or clubs when committing acts of violence.

Krott (1994, p. 27) cites the following societal factors as being partially responsible for the increase in workplace violence:

- Societal pressures and the importance placed on the role of occupation and the workplace in American society.
- A poor economy triggering layoffs combined with employee resentment.
- Availability of firearms to the average employee.
- Loss of self-worth when an employee loses his job, because society tends to define people by their occupation.
- Increased stress level of employees, both on the job and at home. A decrease in leisure time and an increase of job responsibilities combine to induce high levels of stress.
- Personality conflicts between employees and supervisors exacerbated by a refusal by many people in our society to accept responsibility for their actions and shoulder the blame when something is their fault.

> Among the commonly cited causes of workplace violence are downsizing of companies, uncaring working environment, the availability of guns, personality conflicts, resentment and high levels of stress on the job.

Dr. Dennis Johnson, a leading expert in workplace violence, suggests that a culture steeped in violence, growing economic pressures, "toxic" working conditions and the decline of personal responsibility have created an epidemic of violence in our workplaces (Draty, 1994, p. 9).

Johnson et al. (1994, p. 28) explain the concept of **toxic work environment:** "Indicators of a toxic work environment include highly authoritarian management styles, supervision that is changeable and unpredictable, management methods that are invasive of privacy, and extreme secrecy."

Another list of causes for workplace violence is set forth by security consultant Anthony Baron (Hodges, 1995, p. 1D):

- Failure to acknowledge and/or deal with corporate problems.
- Preferential treatment based on title/responsibility.
- Employees viewed as tools.
- Senior managers don't do what they say.
- Unclear rules for success.
- Lack of mutual respect among departments/employees.
- Dishonest, indirect communication.
- Increased workload, decreased responsibility.
- Repetitive, monotonous, unfulfilling work atmosphere.
- Inconsistently applied rules.
- Autocratic management style.
- Ineffective grievance procedure.
- Blame orientation in labor/management relations.
- Insufficient attention to physical environment/security needs.

Job frustrations can increase employee aggression, so much so as to result in extreme violence. The first type is long-term, cumulative frustration such as repeated failures in an employee's career. The employee fails to get the expected raise, promotion or recognition he feels he deserves.

Loss of a job may also result in violence. Studies at the University of California–Berkeley report that laid-off workers often become "walking time bombs" who are six times more likely to commit violent acts than the average employed worker (Krott, 1994, p. 29).

PROFILE OF THE PERPETRATOR OF VIOLENCE

According to Brandt and Brennan (1994, p. 11), certain characteristics and behaviors constitute the profile of most avengers and should trigger a "red flag":

- Male between 35 and 55 years old.
- Mid-life transition, dissatisfied with life.
- Loner without a true support system.
- Low self-esteem.
- Generally works in jobs with high turn-over.
- History of being disgruntled during employment.
- Tends to project his own shortcomings to others.
- History of intimidating co-workers and supervisors.
- Feels persecuted and views efforts to help with suspicion.
- Watches others for violations and may keep records.
- Interested in weapons, may be a collector or marksman.
- Probably does not have a police record.

Graham (1992, p. 83) suggests: "Traits to look for include substance abuse, which has a disinhibiting effect on the individual; lack of impulse control under pressure; a history of violent episodes or criminal acts; paranoia; and narcissistic personality disorders."

Fox and Levine (1993) used statistics from the FBI's Supplementary Homicide Reports from 1976 to 1992 to identify characteristics of murders of employers by employees.

> The typical perpetrator of workplace violence is a disgruntled, middle-aged white male who is a loner, who either has been or is about to be fired and who is a gun enthusiast. One in four is suicidal.

Walton (1993, p. 84) states: "The potentially violent individual is usually depressed, a loner who intimidates those around him or her, and abuses drugs or alcohol. This person is often paranoid, a constant complainer, with a history of violence, or someone whose only source of self-worth seems to be his or her job."

The great majority of violent employees, 93 percent, are men. Campbell (1993) notes that men often regard violence as a way to establish or maintain control whereas women may view it as a loss of control.

Often the perpetrator is distraught over his perceived inability to capture the American Dream. He feels entitled to a financially secure future and is deeply resentful if it is threatened. He may be resentful of others who still have jobs or of those who have passed him by in promotions. He may view a gun as the "great equalizer" and use it to get his revenge. Almost one-third of victimizations in the workplace involve a weapon, as shown in Table 20–2 (p. 634).

Krott (1994, p. 1) describes the following incidents:

> El Cajon, CA—A gunman walks into a San Diego County health club and opens fire with a 12-gauge shotgun, killing four people before committing suicide. . . . [T]hree days later at Fort Knox, Kentucky, a man kills three civilian government employees in an office on the Army base and wounds two others. . . . Kenosha, Wisconsin, 8/11/93, three patrons are killed in a shooting spree in a McDonald's restaurant. . . . [T]he list could go on and on.

According to Krott: "The perpetrators of such shooting spree crimes have become known as 'avengers' or 'workplace revenge killers,' also known in some circles as suffering from 'the postal-employee syndrome,' because 36 U.S. Postal Service employees have been killed by co-workers since 1986." Krott (p. 27) suggests that many shooting-spree killers exhibit much interest in weaponry and may be avid collectors and shooters. He cites the following example:

> [O]n July 31, 1993, in San Francisco, Gian Luigi Ferri walked into the law offices of Pettit and Martin at about 3 P.M. carrying an attache case full of

Table 20–2. Victims of Violence at Work Were Less Likely to Be Injured than Persons Victimized While Not Working, 1987–92

	Percent of Violent Victimizations, by Activity of Victim	
Characteristic	*Working*	*Not Working*
Offender was armed		
No	62%	56%
Yes	32	35
Not ascertained	6	9
Sustained injuries		
No	84%	69%
Yes	16	31
Required medical care	10	16
Lost worktime because of injuries	6	5
Incident reported to police		
No	56%	52%
Yes	43	47
Not ascertained	1	1

SOURCE. *Violence and Theft in the Workplace,* by Ronet Bachman, July 1994. Crime Data Brief from the Bureau of Justice Statistics.

ammunition and armed with a .45 caliber automatic pistol and two altered TEC-9 "machine" pistols (carried on a shoulder strap rig). He fired between 50 and 100 rounds (reports differ), killing eight and wounding six before killing himself. Ferri was a failed businessman and former client of Pettit and Martin who blamed the law firm for his problems.

INDICATORS

Johnson et al. (1994, p. 27) recommend that supervisors learn to recognize relevant behavioral changes in an employee, including increased absenteeism, abrupt departures from work, erratic work patterns, progressive disciplinary problems, dramatic changes in personal appearance, unwarranted anger or difficulty accepting criticism.

The majority of those who commit violent acts against co-workers or management have made threats beforehand. Fox and Levin (1994) cite the example of Paul Calden who vowed he would be back when he was fired from his job at Fireman's Fund Insurance Company in Tampa, Florida. Eight months later he did return, approached three of his former supervisors having lunch in the company cafeteria and announced while taking aim: "This is what you get for firing me." He not only killed the three former managers, he wounded two other employees. Then he turned the gun on himself.

Indicators of impending violent behavior include depression, paranoia, erratic behavior, fixation on a co-worker and threats.

Contrary to popular belief, most violent workers do not simply snap. They coldly and methodically plan and carry out their attacks. Their actions are deliberate rather than spontaneous in most instances. Workplace killers may be depressed, despondent, disillusioned or high on drugs, and they generally are not deranged. As noted by Kinney and Johnson (1993, p. 42), only 11 of 125 workplace killers had histories of mental health treatment.

The widely publicized mass killing in 1986 by letter carrier Patrick Sherrill of Edmond, Oklahoma, illustrates care in planning. Two days after being reprimanded for poor job performance, Sherrill arrived early at the post office, armed to the teeth. But he did his shooting long before the post office opened so that no customers would be injured. He also made certain the one co-worker he liked would not be at work at the time and that the supervisor who had threatened his job would be. Although many of the postal workers who were wounded or killed had nothing to do with his poor job rating, they represented the post office. Such actions have been termed "murder by proxy." This phenomenon is seen when a man who kills his wife also kills the children as an extension of her.

Several of the characteristics identified in the discussion of the profile of a person likely to commit violent acts also serve as indicators of an employee's potential to commit murder by proxy.

Risk Factors

Herman (1992, p. 34) notes several "trigger situations" that are likely to incite violence, including disciplinary actions, terminations, strikes and closures. Certain establishments also face the risk of violence occurring from demonstrators.

The National Institute of Occupational Safety and Health (NIOSH, 1993) has identified several factors that place workers at greater risk of being murdered on the job.

> Working alone or in small numbers, exchanging money with the public, working at night or early in the morning, guarding property or valuable possessions and working in high-crime areas increase the risk of victimization.

NIOSH also suggests that certain occupations present a greater risk of being a murder victim. In the following two lists, the number following the workplace indicates the number of murders committed in 1993 per 100,000 workers:

Cab driver/chauffeur	15.1
Police officer	9.3
Hotel clerk	5.1
Gas-station worker	4.5

Cab drivers and chauffeurs are at greatest risk of being killed on the job. Their risk is five times greater than that of a security officer.

Security guard	3.6
Stock handler/bagger	3.1
Store owner/manager	2.8
Bartender	2.1

In addition, NIOSH has identified several workplaces that present more risk than usual:

Taxicabs/dispatch offices	26.9
Liquor stores	8.0
Gas stations	5.6
Detective/guard/protective agencies	5.0
Courthouses, prisons, police departments, fire departments	3.4
Grocery stores	3.2
Hotels/motels	1.5
Restaurants/bars	1.5

Preventing Workplace Violence

A concern for workplace violence must start at the very top of any organization or institution. A prime example of this is the United States Postal Service, where Marvin Runyon, Postmaster General, has declared:

> Let the word go out. America is united on this issue and we will not stand by and let violence terrorize our workplaces. . . .
>
> America as a nation is suffering from a disease called violence. Every few minutes, a violent act takes place somewhere in this country. We are all victims of these crimes. . . .
>
> We cannot solve this problem by ourselves. It's a national epidemic, not a postal one ("USPS Moves to Prevent Violence," 1995, p. 18).

In 1993 the Postal Service convened a ground-breaking day-long symposium on workplace violence. The third such symposium will be conducted in 1996.

As noted by Herman (1992, p. 37): "Violence is irrational and unpredictable. It can strike at any time or place. Adequate preparation is the only way that a company can ensure that it will not fall victim to an employee who has gone beyond the breaking point, and if it does fall victim to such an employee, that the effects are minimized and tragedy is averted."

Walton (1993, p. 84) notes: "Nothing can be done to guarantee a violent incident will not take place on company property, but much can be done to reduce the chances of it happening. The security manager should play an active and major role in reducing these possibilities."

According to Brandt and Brennan (1994, p. 11): "Human resources can play a significant role in spotting and disarming potentially dangerous employees. Being prepared and vigilant is the best way to avoid a crisis situation."

Herman also stresses the importance of communicating with employees (1992, p. 37): "The first rule is never to keep employees in the dark. . . . Keeping employees abreast of the situation is the best way to earn and keep their trust and to ally their fears. Open, confidential lines of communication are essential to facilitate employee cooperations."

Johnson (1994, p. 81) describes the three options open to employees at Florida Power and Light:

- Report threats to a 24-hour security hot line.
- Make a direct contact with the threat management committee chairperson (the manager of corporate security).
- Report through the chain of command.

According to Lindsey (1994, p. 69): "A truly preventive approach to workplace violence requires the recognition that the acting out is the end result of an invisible process that goes on inside the mind of the potentially violent individual who perceives that he or she has been treated unfairly, discriminated against, harassed, or purposely exposed to stress by a supervisor."

Walton (1993, pp. 81–82) recommends a three-step approach to reduce outbreaks of employee violence:

- Criminal, education, and employment background checks on potential employees are essential.
- A drug testing policy is essential.
- The establishment of a firm nonharassment policy is a must.

Walton (p. 82) stresses:

> Most of those who have committed acts of violence in the workplace have been described by co-workers and supervisors as intimidators. A zero-tolerance policy [should state] that threats, intimidation, harassment, or acts of violence will not be tolerated by the company. . . . New and current employees should be required to read and sign an acknowledgement of this policy.

> Preventive measures include preemployment screening, drug testing, employee education, a "zero tolerance" for any type of violence, a nontoxic workplace, open communication and humane termination procedures.

Jack Jones, licensed industrial psychologist, suggests several steps that might minimize employees' risk of being a victim of workplace violence ("Steps That Can Reduce Workplace Violence," 1995, pp. 1, 27):

- Implement pre-employment screening.
- Implement drug screening.
- Create anti-harassment policies to be followed by all employees. Promote a workplace culture with "zero tolerance" for any form of violence.
- Train managers in recognizing high-risk employees.
- Establish a threat and incident management team.

Another way to promote a safer working environment is through employee training in such areas as stress management, conflict resolution, how to handle confrontations and drug and alcohol abuse awareness.

Managers also need specialized training in such areas as perpetrator profiles, employee risk factors, warning signs and indicators, the sequence of violence, workplace dynamics, sexual harassment and fair treatment of others (Johnson, 1994, pp. 81–82).

Johnson et al. (1994, p. 27) recommend that managers and supervisors track employees' behavior. If the frequency, intensity or duration of inappropriate behavior is noted, the employee should be interviewed to determine what the problem is. This can result in a win-win situation with the employee feeling cared about and correcting the behavior and the employer getting appropriate output from the employee. As noted by Johnson et al.: "When properly implemented in a progressive, nonpunitive manner, a behavioral observation system creates a win-win situation."

One important area that is likely to directly affect the probability of violent retaliation is the termination process. Employees who do not understand why they are being terminated, who are surprised by the termination and who are offered no support may be resentful and act accordingly. Brandt and Brennan (1994, p. 11) suggest: "Employers may consider providing employees who are being terminated with such assistance as outplacement services, psychological counseling, severance benefits, skills development, and training and educational assistance."

Brandt and Brennan (1994, p. 25) recommend that several postemployment practices can reduce the potential for the terminated worker to pose a threat:

> This phase [postemployment] includes all aspects: from security canceling ID badges and changing access codes, human resources alerting payroll and other related groups that the individual has had his employment terminated, information systems blocking access to computer systems and exit interviews with particular attention paid to what is said by the exiting employee, and appropriate follow-up in all instances. Most importantly, treating the departing employee with dignity, respect and professionalism may prevent a horrible event from taking place.

If the terminated individual has shown unstable emotional or mental behavior in the past or during the exit interview and is believed to pose a threat, the security force should be alerted and warning notices posted at building entrances.

Olmos (1994, p. 9) suggests that the workplace violence prevention proceed along two parallel tracks: physical access and management awareness. Access control is vital to curbing workplace violence. In addition, management must take the threat seriously. Olmos notes: "Most employers pay little attention to this type of threat." In a recent survey of nearly 100 medium-sized work sites, Olmos found that nearly 90 percent had no access control during normal working hours and none had internal surveillance systems.

Draty (1994, p. 3) also stresses the need for management awareness of the problem, quoting Eric Greenbert, the American Management Association's director of management studies:

> No organization waits for a fire to break out before running a fire drill. But many are waiting for something to happen before they organize a response to workplace violence. . . . What we have is management being reactive as opposed to proactive. . . .
>
> One-fourth of the respondents reporting violent incidents said that early warning signs were ignored by the eventual victim, and 29 percent said such signs were ignored by others within the organization.

Krott (1994, p. 29) lists the following 10 steps for security managers:

1. Background investigation and personal interviews during pre-employment screening to determine if there are violent incidents in a prospective employee's past.
2. Check the company's history of violence to focus on problem areas and main concerns. If it led to violence in the past, it may do so again.
3. Evaluate facilities, programs, and policies related to the company's security and assess possible threats to property and personnel. Initiate interviews with management, supervisors, and employees to identify and assess possible threats.
4. Ensure that company policy properly addresses such topics as: workplace violence, drug abuse, sexual harassment, equal opportunity employment, and fair treatment of others.
5. Institute an "early warning system" by confidentially interviewing employees about their thoughts and perceptions on the company's

policies and practices. Attempt to identify changes and trends in employee attitudes and behavior.

6. Attempt to involve employees in formulating company policy and procedure.
7. Termination and layoff methods should be safe and appropriate. Employee discipline must be equitable, fair, and should follow company policy.
8. Organize and train a threat management team to help develop security oriented policies and identify threats.
9. Train supervisors to recognize possible threats and to be observant of human behavior in the workplace, noting changes in behavior, and indicators of stress, violence, and substance abuse. Insure they report instances of aggression, substance abuse, and stress.
10. Make sure there is a procedure for an immediate response following any violent incident or confrontation at work. It should include interviews with participants and their supervisors, counseling (if necessary), and follow-up. Review the response of supervisors and employees to the incident.

Preemployment screening is advocated by most security experts when discussing ways to prevent workplace violence. Among the tools available are some recently developed tests designed to identify predictors of violence in the workplace: The Hilson Safety/Security Risk Inventory and the Inwald Survey 8. According to Inwald (1994, p. 19):

> The theory behind these inventories is that a person with the characteristics of expressed anger/low frustration tolerance and risk-taking/disregard for safety regulations is more likely than other employees to lose control when under pressure or stress in the workplace. Using scales such as Risk-Taking Patterns, Firearms Interest, Lack of Anger Control, Reckless Driving/Safety Patterns and Work Difficulties, these tests have been designed to aid in the identification of individuals at high risk for acting on violent impulses.

Olmos recommends the following if an employee is threatened (p. 9):

- Provide proper counseling and advice to the intended victim.
- File complaints with the police.
- Take advantage of stalking laws, orders of protection and the like.
- Refer the employee to the proper employee assistance program.
- Notify the offender in writing regarding trespassing.
- Take swift legal action against the offender if he or she should come to the work site.

Anyone who is threatened should be interviewed and the following information obtained (Cawood, 1991, p. 132):

- The exact statement made.
- The circumstances in which the statement was made.
- Any knowledge the person has of the person who made the statement.
- The relationship between the person who made the statement and the person who reported it.
- The names of any others who may have witnessed the incident, who have personal knowledge of other threats or odd behavior by the same person,

or who might have detailed knowledge of the person who made the statements.

In addition, as noted by Walton (1993, p. 84): "One should not overlook the importance of physical security surveys in this matter. Much can be accomplished at little cost. Limiting and controlling access, rearranging offices and furniture, security awareness briefings and training, and security hardware can all contribute to reducing employee vulnerability to angry co-workers."

When dealing with threats to an employee made by a co-worker, management must maintain a balance between the rights of the accused and the duty of the employer.

In addition to reducing the risk of violence occurring on the job, having a proactive approach to avoiding such violence sends a strong message to the work force that management cares about its people and considers them its most valuable resource. Other ways to make employees feel needed and valued include the following (Brandt and Brennan, 1994, p. 11):

- Wellness programs including stress management.
- An employee assistance program.
- Fair compensation and promotional practices.
- Reasonable sick leave and vacation policies.
- Adequate internal training and support.

Stalkers

Gargan (1994, p. 32) describes stalkers as being from dysfunctional families and having a need to control and intimidate. The stalking usually takes the form of annoying, threatening or obscene telephone calls. When an employee is being stalked, co-workers also may feel threatened. In some instances they refuse to work in the same area as the threatened employee.

Gargan (1994, p. 32) outlines several security options once security officers become aware than an employee is being stalked:

- Check with police.
- Protect the target. (Change the victim's work number, take his or her name out of the directory, conceal the target's vehicle, have all inquiries regarding him or her forwarded to the security console.)
- Involve the victim. (Request that the victim use an answering machine at home and record calls, keep all letters, and get the name and address of any witnesses to the stalking.)

In addition, Gargan (p. 34) suggests: "All security officers should not only be aware of the severity of the case but also should know the stalker's description, type of vehicles he or she may be using, and each vehicle's license plate number."

Preventing Violence during Demonstrations

Graves (1995, p. 37) stresses that, before any demonstration, planning is essential. A meeting should be held to discuss priorities: "Items of discussion

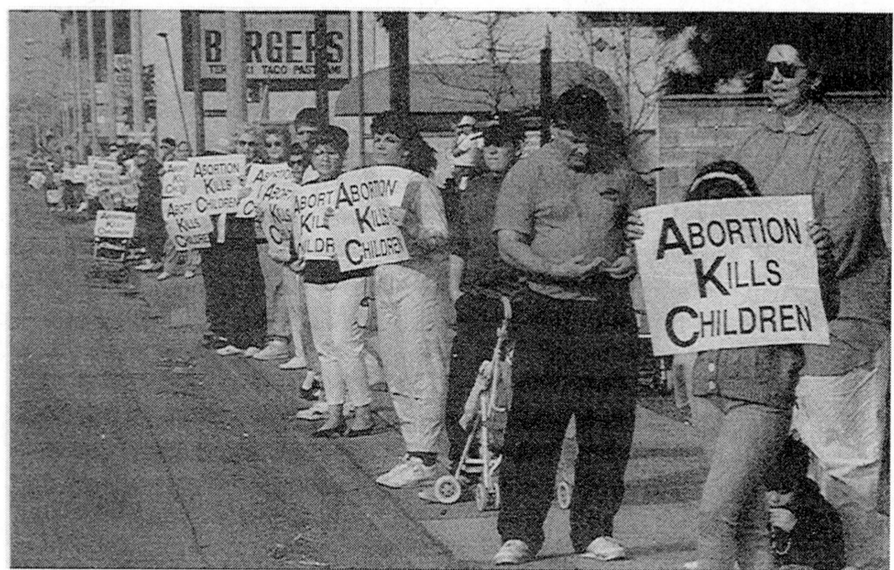

Certain establishments also face the risk of violence occurring from demonstrations.

should include press releases, use of cellular phones, barricading, police liaison, activity cancellation, staffing, access control, patient protection and visitor management."

Preventing Violence during Strikes

Workers do have a right to strike, but they cannot prevent others from entering an establishment and they cannot be violent. Herman (1995, p. 35) recommends the following:

- Implement security. Put adequate security in place immediately.
- Maintain communications.
- Document activities.
- Seek injunctive relief if violence occurs.

Herman stresses: "A strike is costly enough without the added fear of liability lawsuits and extravagant jury awards. Following these steps will help ensure that when the courts make awards to the victims of strike violence, your company does not get handed the bill."

DEALING WITH VIOLENCE THAT OCCURS

Franklin (1991, p. 144) cautions: "After violence punctuates the lives of the employee and his or her co-workers, what follows may be a situation that debilitates morale, productivity, and overall function. It is during this period of post event management that the security professional's responsibility is the greatest and his or her recommendations the most criticized."

Security professionals may want to have a threat and incident management team trained in how to deal with violence on the job. The team should include at least three elements: security, human resources and legal counsel. Among the responsibilities of this team would be treating injured employees and traumatized observers and providing employee counseling.

> If violence should occur, be prepared by having specific tasks identified. Keep communication with employees and clients open. Record exactly what happened, investigate the possible reasons and take corrective steps if needed.

Brandt and Brennan (1994, p. 11) list the following critical tasks that must be performed should violence occur:

- Alerting the police.
- Attending injured employees.
- Contacting victims' families.
- Dealing with upset employees.
- Organizing professional counseling services.
- Cleaning up the premises.
- Arranging for additional temporary security.
- Communicating with the organization's clients.
- Handling members of the press.

Legal Implications

Herman (1992, p. 33) notes: "From a legal standpoint, companies that have failed to take adequate measures to counter a threat have been found liable in court for injuries caused by out-of-control employees."

As noted by Olmos (1994, p. 9): "Aside from the human tragedy, violence induced injury carries serious financial implications as well. Any employer who has knowledge of a potential risk and fails to act can be held liable for a court action arising from a workplace assault." Further:

> There is a growing body of case law which clearly indicates that the courts are willing to go beyond the indemnification restrictions of workers' compensation for damages resulting from criminal acts. Negligence in hiring and/or negligence in exercising due diligence to prevent a violent incident provides the legal framework for assault related lawsuits by employees against corporations.

Cawood (1991, p. 130) also suggests: "The cost of violence in the workplace is high, not only in legal fees and possible punitive damages but also in the loss of employee confidence, morale, and productivity. Lawsuits over negligent security, which normally follow violent incidents, are on the rise. These suits involve not just employers but also landlords and property management companies that operate the buildings where such incidents occur."

Johnson (1994, p. 73) cautions that employers have been legally required to provide a safe, healthy work environment since the passage of the Occupational Safety and Health Act of 1970. Johnson explains that the general duty clause of that law has been interpreted to mean that employers have an obligation to respond to threats. He stresses: "Recent verdicts and judicial rulings are now creating case law to lend cement to that interpretation, and there are numerous regulations from governmental entities (far beyond OSHA) that mirror that philosophy. Workplace safety requirements have been codified everywhere from state worker's compensation laws to rules issued under the authority of the Americans with Disabilities Act."

Olmos (1994, p. 9) concludes: "While it is true that an employer cannot guarantee absolute safety, it is also true that there is a legal and moral responsibility to provide a good faith effort to make the workplace as safe as possible."

SUMMARY

Workplace violence has been called "epidemic" with estimates ranging from one million to two million workers experiencing violent victimization each year. Workplace violence may occur during robbery and other commercial crimes, during domestic and misdirected affection cases, in employer-directed situations, as a result of terrorism or hate, or during a strike or demonstration.

Among the commonly cited causes of workplace violence are downsizing of companies, uncaring working environment, the availability of guns, personality conflicts, resentment and high levels of stress on the job.

The typical perpetrator of workplace violence is a disgruntled, middle-aged white male who is a loner, who either has been or is about to be fired and who is a gun enthusiast. One in four is suicidal. Indicators of impending violent behavior include depression, paranoia, erratic behavior, fixation on a coworker and threats.

Employees who work alone or in small numbers, exchange money with the public, work at night or early in the morning, guard property or valuable possessions or work in high-crime areas are at an increased risk of victimization.

Preventive measures include preemployment screening, drug testing, employee education, a "zero tolerance" for any type of violence, a nontoxic workplace and open communication. If violence should occur, be prepared by having specific tasks identified. Keep communication with employees and clients open. Record exactly what happened, investigate the possible reasons and take corrective steps if needed.

APPLICATION

As a security officer for the Gopher Security Company, you have been instructed by your supervisor to admit into the manufacturing plant only individuals who have proper photo identification and presumably are employees.

Keith Wilson comes through your station, presents credentials that appear valid and enters the plant. As he places the identification back into his pocket, you notice he is carrying a concealed gun. No one else notices this, and you are somewhat traumatized by the observation. You are in a dilemma and feel you have to take some kind of action. You have a number of alternatives. Which do you feel is appropriate for this particular incident:

1. Confront Keith Wilson and make him give up his gun.

2. Call the public police and have them seize the weapon.

3. Do nothing because you were never trained or instructed in what to do in this type of situation.

4. Notify your supervisor.

5. Notify the company management.

CRITICAL THINKING EXERCISE

WORKPLACE VIOLENCE

STATUTORY AND COMMON LAW

Whether duty exists sufficient to give rise to a claim of negligence depends upon two factors: (1) the existence of a special relationship between a security guard and a third person where there is a duty to control, or between the security guard and the other which gives the other the right to protection and (2) foreseeability of harm.

FACTS OF THE CASE

The General Services Administration (GSA) hired Echelon Service Company to provide security for federal employees working in the Crystal Mall complex in Arlington. The security contract stipulated that Echelon would provide patrolling and controlled access to the building and would "[protect] occupying personnel against fire, injury, theft, destruction, molestation and vandalism."

On the evening of November 29, a few minutes after 6:00 P.M., security guard Warren Jowett saw a "flash in the elevator corridor." He thought it looked like someone had run "from the down elevator to the up elevator." The down elevators connect the underground garage and public concourse to the lobby where Jowett was patrolling. The up elevators connect the lobby to the higher floors where various federal offices are located. Jowett called out, but no one answered. He did not pursue the individual, assuming it was another employee.

At 6:18 P.M. security guard Joseph Thrasher, also on duty in the lobby of the building, received a telephone call from the 11th floor that someone there was screaming for help. He sent Jowett to investigate. In the hallway of the

11th floor, Jowett saw a man holding a bloody pair of long scissors in his hand. The man dropped the scissors and ran. The door to room 1101 was open, and Jowett heard strange sounds coming from the room. Inside he found Linda Billings, an Environmental Protection Agency employee, with blood on her shirt. She was gasping and said to "stop that man; he's got my credit cards." Jowett called this information down to Thrasher, and within three minutes they succeeded in apprehending Michael Johnson in the lobby. Johnson was the only unauthorized person found in the building at the time of the assault. Some traces of fresh blood were found on his hands, and he had credit cards belonging to Linda Billings in his pocket.

Meanwhile, Billings was able to get into an elevator and went down to the lobby. Another employee found her there, attempted to help her and called 911 for medical assistance. An emergency medical unit arrived about 10 minutes later, and as Billings' vital signs began to fail, the emergency medical personnel gave her CPR. She was then taken to a nearby hospital where she underwent emergency heart repair surgery. The surgery was not successful, and she died later that evening.

Co-administrators of her estate filed a motion for judgment under the Wrongful Death Statute alleging that Echelon was liable for the death of Linda Billings. They argued that Billings was a third party beneficiary of Echelon's contract to provide security services to the GSA and that Echelon's breach of that contract was a proximate cause of Billings' death.

Issues and Questions

1. Is there credible evidence to allow a jury to find that the Echelon guard's failure to pursue an unidentified person was the proximate cause of Billings' death?

   a. In this case there is sufficient evidence for a jury to conclude that the individual who was seen and called to by the security guard was the perpetrator who gained access to the building at that point. The guard's failure to pursue and detain the individual can be seen as a proximate cause of Billings' death.

   b. In order for the security guard to be found in breach of the contract and thus responsible as the proximate cause of Billings' death, there would have to be proof beyond a reasonable doubt that the perpetrator entered the building through the negligence of security.

   c. The inference that the "flash" of motion Jowett saw was caused by Michael Johnson is the product of mere conjecture, surmise or speculation. It is not credible evidence from which to judge the guard as failing to provide a duty of care, let alone be a proximate cause of Billings' death.

   d. The Echelon guards are not in breach of contract for the fact that someone entered the building from either the garage or the public access level, but Jowett is in breach of contract for leaving Linda Billings alone in room 1101. He has a duty of care to assist her before running after her suspected assailant even though she said "stop that man." After all, the other security guard would be able to stop Johnson once he reached the lobby, which in fact is what did happen. But the proximate cause of Billings' death is actually the fact that she attempted to go down to the lobby, which resulted in her loss of consciousness and eventual death.

e. The only person who can be reasonably accused of being the proximate cause of Billings' death is Michael Johnson. An indistinguishable "flash" of motion is insufficient to blame security guards, and one would be completely without common sense to think Linda Billings' actions are the proximate cause of her own death.

Discussion Questions

1. Statistics released by the U.S. Department of Justice on violence in the workplace indicate that more than half of all workplace victimizations were never reported to the police. Discuss why this occurs.
2. Do you think that security officers working in highly emotionally charged areas should undertake preventive measures in the interest of employee safety? What should their role be?
3. Recently a University of Iowa doctoral student who had lost a cherished dissertation prize stated just before killing five people that the gun was a "great equalizer." What comments do you have about a person who takes such forceful measures to show his feelings?
4. Is it possible to screen prospective employees for violence proneness?
5. Whose responsibility do you think it is to see that violence prevention policies are established?

References

Associated Press. "Gunman Kills 5, Self in Corpus Christi. He Was Ex-Employee of Company." (Minneapolis/St. Paul) *Star Tribune,* April 4, 1995, p. 7A.

Bachman, Ronet. "Violence and Theft in the Workplace: National Crime Victimization Survey." *Crime Data Brief.* Washington, DC: U.S. Department of Justice, July 1994.

Brandt, Gerald T. and Brennan, Joseph M. "Workplace Time Bombs Can Be Defused." *Security Concepts,* March 1994, pp. 11, 31.

Broderick, Richard. "Breaking Point." *University of Minnesota Update.* July 1995, pp. 1–3.

Campbell, Anne. *Men, Women, and Aggression.* New York: Basic Books, 1993.

Cawood, James S. "On the Edge: Assessing the Violent Employee." *Security Management,* September 1991, pp. 130–36.

Draty, David. "Crisis Management III: Workplace Violence Incidents Are Common." *Security Concepts,* June 1994, pp. 3, 18.

Draty, David. "Workplace Violence: The Victims." *Security Concepts,* December 1994, pp. 9, 23.

Fox, James Alan and Levin, Jack. "Employee Dismissal: Justice at Work." *The Annals of the American Academy of Political and Social Science,* November 1994, p. 40.

Fox, James Alan and Levin, Jack. "Postal Violence: Cycle of Despair Turns Tragic." *USA Today,* May 12, 1993.

Franklin, Forrest P. "Over the Edge: Managing Violent Episodes." *Security Management,* September 1991, pp. 138–44.

Gargan, Joseph P. "Stop Stalkers Before They Strike." *Security Management,* February 1994, pp. 31–34.

Graham, James P. "Disgruntled Employees—Ticking Time Bombs?" *Security Management,* January 1992, pp. 83–85.

Graves, C. Ray. "Domestic Extremists: Dealing with Demonstrators." *Security Management,* March 1995, pp. 37–39.

Herman, Martin B. "Planning for the Unpredictable." *Security Management,* November 1992, pp. 33–37.

Herman, Martin B. "When Strikes Turn Violent." *Security Management,* March 1995, pp. 32–35.

Hodges, Jill. "Workplace Violence." (Minneapolis/St. Paul) *Star Tribune,* February 17, 1995, pp. 1D–2D.

Inwald, Robin E. "New Tests for Identifying Predictors of Violence in the Workplace." *Security Concepts,* June 1994, p. 18.

"Is the War on Terrorism Over?" *Dynamics,* July/August 1991, pp. 21–24.

Johnson, Dennis L. "A Team Approach to Threat Assessment." *Security Management,* September 1994, pp. 73–83.

Johnson, Dennis L.; Klehbauch, John B.; and Kinney, Joseph A. "Break the Cycle of Violence." *Security Management,* February 1994, pp. 24–28.

Kinney, Joseph K. and Johnson, Dennis L. *Breaking Point: The Workplace Violence Epidemic and What to Do About It.* Chicago: National Safe Workplace Institute, 1993.

Krott, Rob. "Corporate Threat: Muslim Extremist Terrorism in the 90's." *Security Concepts,* September 1994, pp. 1, 27.

Krott, Rob. "Reaching the Breaking Point: Workplace Avengers." *Security Concepts,* September 1994, pp. 1, 27, 29.

Lindsey, Dennis. "Of Sound Mind? Evaluating the Workforce." *Security Management,* September 1994, pp. 69–71.

"Murder in the Workplace on the Rise." *Personnel Journal,* February 1992, pp. 76–77.

National Institute of Occupational Safety and Health. *Preventing Homicide in the Workplace.* Washington, DC: Department of Health and Human Services, 1993.

Northwestern National Life Insurance Company. *Fear and Violence in the Workplace.* Minneapolis, MN: Northwestern National Life Insurance, 1993.

Olmos, Ross A. "Is the Workplace No Longer Safe?" *Security Concepts,* April 1994, p. 9.

"Steps That Can Reduce Workplace Violence." *Security Concepts,* March 1995, pp. 1, 27.

"USPS Moves to Prevent Violence." *Security Concepts,* May 1995, pp. 18, 30.

Walton, J. Branch. "Dealing with Dangerous Employees." *Security Management,* September 1993, pp. 81–84.

CHAPTER 21

Practicing and Promoting Ethical Conduct

Do You Know

- What the term "ethics" refers to?
- What three personal ethics-check questions are?
- What five principles underlie individual ethical power?
- What three organizational ethics-check questions are?
- What purpose is served by a code of ethics for security professionals?
- How to promote an ethical organization?
- How ethics can relate to problem solving?

Can You Define These Terms?

code of ethics	ethics
ethical behavior	moral

Introduction

The importance of the topic of this chapter is clearly stated by Simonsen (1992, p. 224):

> As a security professional, I have grown increasingly concerned about something we seem to have lost sight of in America. It has been the mortar between the bricks of our national character and our industrial strength, and it is represented by one small word, a word that encompasses the best qualities we have always expected of ourselves, our peers, and our leaders—*ETHICS.*

Ethics has become a "hot" topic in the 1990s with numerous workshops and seminars about business ethics being conducted throughout corporate America. Himelfarb (1995, p. 24) suggests several reasons for this increased attention to ethics in management and organizational development:

- Growing public cynicism about public institutions.
- Increased public demands for participation in decision making and accountability.
- Increased visibility of incidents, in part because of the evolution of communications technology.
- The rapid rate of social change and increasing diversity, which seem to make ethical decision making more problematic than in the past.
- Reduced resources, which raise questions about the cost effectiveness of reactive, control-oriented approaches and oversight.

Himelfarb (p. 24) concludes: "The environment of rapid change, diversity, restraint and shifting public demands and expectations provides a challenge, as well as an opportunity to revisit and revitalize our understanding of ethics."

This chapter begins by defining ethics and what they involve. This is followed by a discussion of how to develop one's own personal ethics and then how to promote ethical behavior throughout an organization. It concludes with a look at ethical (and unethical) practices in the 1990s.

ETHICS DEFINED

Most people have a general idea of what the term "ethics" refers to. Oran (1985, p. 114) defines ethics as "standards of fair and honest conduct." In reality, the term has several definitions:

- Principles of right or good conduct.
- A system of moral principles or values.
- Rules or standards governing the conduct of a profession.
- Accepted standards of right and wrong.

> **Ethics** deal with questions of right and wrong, of moral and immoral behavior.

Wasserman and Moore (1988, p. 1) define ethics as the discipline dealing with what is right and with moral duty and obligation, as a set of moral values, or as the principles of conduct governing an individual or group. McArney and Moore (1994, p. 2) cite a Gallup Poll showing that car salesmen and politicians were rated poorly for their honesty and ethical standards (see Table 21–1). Unfortunately, security officers were not included in the survey, but their public counterpart was rated highly, right up there with the professionals. McArney and Moore also note the public's "rather dim view of business ethics" as being reinforced by a survey conducted by *Business Month* ("An Ethical Double Standard," 1989, p. 7) which ranked five corporate offenses as follows:

- Taking credit for someone else's accomplishment was picked by 57% as being the most egregious infraction.
- Playing dirty tricks on a competitor was chosen by 27% as the number-one offense.
- Cheating on an expense report was selected by 23% as the primary offense.
- Lying to protect a friend was picked by 15%.
- Paying bribes in a country where it is the accepted custom was the least offense, with 14% selecting it.

Ethical behavior refers to actions that are considered right and moral, such as being honest, being considerate of others, keeping promises. Unethical behavior, in contrast, is behavior that is considered immoral, corrupt and against

Table 21–1. Honesty and Ethics: 1994 Poll

	Very High	High	Average	Low	Very Low	No Opinion	1994 Rank	1993 Rank
Druggists, pharmacists	13%	48%	33%	4%	1%	1%	1	1
Clergy	14	40	34	9	1	2	2	2
Dentists	9	42	41	6	1	1	3	6
College teachers	9	41	39	8	1	2	4	3
Engineers	9	40	42	4	1	4	5	7
Medical doctors	10	37	40	10	2	1	6	4
Policemen	9	37	41	9	3	1	7	5
Funeral directors	6	25	51	11	3	4	8	8
Public opinion pollsters	6	21	54	13	3	3	9	NA**
Bankers	3	24	56	13	3	1	10	10
Business executives	3	19	57	18	2	1	11	13
TV reporters, commentators	3	19	42	27	8	1	12	9
Journalists	3	17	50	24	5	1	13	11
Local officeholders	2	16	56	20	5	1	14	15
Building contractors	3	14	57	20	4	2	15	14
Newspaper reporters	2	15	47	27	8	1	16	12
Lawyers	3	14	36	31	15	1	17	17
Stockbrokers	3	12	59	18	4	4	18	23
Real estate agents	1	13	57	23	4	2	19	19
Labor union leaders	2	12	41	33	10	2	20	20
State officeholders	2	10	55	27	5	1	21	22
Advertising practitioners	2	10	49	29	7	3	22	25
Senators	2	10	48	32	7	1	23	16
Insurance salesmen	2	7	43	36	10	2	24	24
Congressmen	1	9	46	34	10	•	25	21
Car salesmen	2	4	32	43	18	1	26	26

Note: Rank based on "very high" and "high" combined; 1994 based on pre-rounded figures
• Less than 0.5%
**Replaces TV talk show hosts
SOURCE: *The Gallup Poll Monthly*, October 1994. Reprinted by permission.

accepted standards, such as lying, taking advantage of others and reneging on promises.

The difficulty with ethical behavior is that it varies from individual to individual, group to group and even country to country. At the heart of ethical behavior is what is considered **moral**—that is, right or virtuous. Moral standards may be:

- Constructed by an individual.
- Set forth by a particular society or culture.
- Laid down by a religious body or doctrine.

The Ten Commandments are an example of religious doctrine. They would seem to be very clear—for example, "Thou shalt not kill." But this commandment is at the heart of the heated debates involving abortion and capital punishment. Opinions do differ! Questions of morality often involve what people commonly refer to as their "conscience."

A common ethical question is whether security officers should accept free coffee. Most would say no. The person providing the free coffee may expect special favors in the future. Accepting gifts of any kind gives the appearance of unethical behavior.

Philosophers such as Epicures and Thomas Hobbes believed that the good of the individual is the ultimate factor. In contrast, such philosophers as Jeremy Bentham and James Mill believed that the ethical criterion is the greatest good for the greatest number. Who decides what is good? The individual? The corporation? The state? A certain group? Again, opinions differ.

Simonsen (1992, p. 226) states: "What is considered right or wrong can be placed on a behavior continuum. The continuum ranges from prescribed or encouraged to proscribed or discouraged behavior. The balance point is not constant. It changes at different times in different societies." Simonsen cites as examples our changing standards as to what constitutes pornography and our views on the consumption of alcohol.

Simonsen (p. 224) notes: "The private security professional is often encouraged by less ethical colleagues in the organization to 'go along to get along.' " This may involve compromising personal or professional standards or even engaging in illegal behavior.

Hyams (1991, p. 130) describes noted researcher and philosopher Lawrence Kohlberg's six stages in the development of morals:

> In the earliest stages, usually first noted in children, adherence to standards is the result of a fear of punishment and pervasive self-interest. Very little self-awareness or ability to examine one's own motives is present. At the higher stages, adherence to standards is based upon principles and a deep respect for the rights of others. The ability for critical introspection is present.

> Unfortunately, most people "freeze" at some stage of moral development, and very few reach the higher stages. . . .
>
> Occupying Kohlberg's middle stage of development is the conventional level, where "right" behavior is determined by what is expected by the group. To be accepted, one must conform to the group's norms, often without regard to prior beliefs or other standards.

Many individuals think that the younger generation is lacking in values and morals. The director of education for the Ethics Resource Center in Washington, DC, Frederick Close, contends: "The fundamental tragedy of American education is not that we are turning out ignoramuses but that we are turning out savages" (Elam et al., 1994, p. 49).

A professor at Boston University, Kevin Ryan, notes that public schools have "bent over backwards not to offend anyone about anything. In their efforts to make themselves inoffensive and studiously neutral, they have all but cleansed the curriculum of religious and ethical content." He says that schools are "morally dangerous places for children" (Elam et al., 1994, p. 49).

The 26th annual Phi Delta Kappa/Gallup Poll of the Public's Attitudes Toward the Public Schools (Elam et al., 1994, p. 49) asked if character education should be part of the curriculum or left to parents and/or churches. Forty-nine percent thought that it should be left to the schools; 39 percent thought that it should be left to parents and/or churches; 12 percent thought that schools, parents and/or churches should teach it. The poll also asked about specific personal traits or "virtues" that might be included in such education. Topping the list was respect for others, as seen in Table 21–2 (p. 654).

Your ethical principles will guide your thinking as a manager.

DEVELOPING PERSONAL ETHICS

Blanchard and Peale (1988) provide direction for developing personal ethics. At the heart of their philosophy is the simple statement (p. 9): "There is no right way to do a wrong thing." They suggest (p. 20) three questions that can serve as personal "ethics checks."

Three ethics-check questions are:

- Is it legal?
- Is it balanced?
- How does it make me feel about myself?

Obviously individuals entrusted with the safety and security of an establishment's assets and personnel must always act legally. The question of balance deals with whether the decision or action is fair to all parties involved. Does it create a win-win situation or are there losers? The third question is often referred to as a "gut check." To answer it honestly, ask yourself such questions

Table 21–2. 1994 Survey Respondents' Opinions of What Character Traits Should Be Taught in Public Schools*

Should Be Taught	National Totals %	No Children in School %	Public School Parents %	Nonpublic School Parents %
Respect for others	94	94	93	91
Industry or hard work	93	93	93	95
Persistence or the ability to follow through	93	92	94	94
Fairness in dealing with others	92	93	92	90
Compassion for others	91	91	91	89
Civility, politeness	91	91	90	91
Self-esteem	90	90	92	80
High expectations for oneself	87	87	88	82
Thrift	74	73	74	71

*In the 1993 poll, a different list of character traits (some better described as attitudes) was offered, with the following results: honesty, 97%; democracy, 93%; acceptance of people of different races and ethnic backgrounds, 93%; patriotism or love of country, 91%; caring for friends and family members, 91%; moral courage, 91%; the golden rule, 90%; acceptance of people who hold different religious beliefs, 87%; acceptance of people who hold unpopular or controversial political or social views, 73%; sexual abstinence outside of marriage, 66%; acceptance of the right of a woman to choose abortion, 56%; acceptance of people with different sexual orientations (i.e., homosexuals or bisexuals), 51%.

SOURCE: Stanley M. Elam et al. "The 26th Annual Phi Delta Kappa/Gallup Poll of the Public's Attitudes Toward the Public Schools." *Phi Delta Kappan*, September 1994, p. 50. © 1994, Phi Delta Kappan, Inc. Reprinted by permission.

as "Would I feel good if my family knew about this decision or action?" "Would I mind seeing this decision or action as a headline in the local newspaper?"

Sometimes an action may involve both legal and ethical issues. The article "Your Ethics Quotient" (1993, p. 47) gives the following example, as conceived by Nan DeMars, president of Executive Services, who gives ethics seminars around the country:

> A colleague is being sexually harassed. You've witnessed her superior's unwelcome advances. She asks you to come forward and state what you've seen when she reports the problem to the Human Resources Department. You:
>
> **a.** Tell her she's on her own. You don't want to lose your job.
> **b.** Come forth and report what you've witnessed.
> **c.** Tell her you're willing to help, but pretend to be too busy whenever she makes an appointment with Human Resources.
>
> Answers DeMars: b. You needn't wait until she asks. You should report incidents of sexual harassment anyway. Under the federal sexual harassment law, if you witness sexual harassment and don't report it, you can be named in a lawsuit. Human resources is obligated to protect your identity.

Blanchard and Peale (p. 79) also list five principles of ethical power for individuals:

1. *Purpose:* I see myself as being an ethically sound person. I let my conscience be my guide. No matter what happens, I am always able to face the mirror, look myself straight in the eye, and feel good about myself.
2. *Pride:* I feel good about myself. I don't need the acceptance of other people to feel important. A balanced self-esteem keeps my ego and my desire to be accepted from influencing my decisions.
3. *Patience:* I believe that things will eventually work out well. I don't need everything to happen right now. I am at peace with what comes my way.
4. *Persistence:* I stick to my purpose, especially when it seems inconvenient to do so. My behavior is consistent with my intentions. As Churchill said, "Never! Never! Never! Never give up!"
5. *Perspective:* I take time to enter each day quietly in a mood of reflection. This helps me to get myself focused and allows me to listen to my inner self and to see things more clearly.

> Five principles underlying individual ethical power are purpose, pride, patience, persistence and perspective.

In addition to developing personal ethics, security professionals also should seek to promote ethics throughout the organization.

PROMOTING AN ETHICAL ORGANIZATION

Wasserman and Moore (1988, p. 2) note that high-performance organizations share one thing in common: "They operate with a core set of values that guides conduct throughout the organization."

Ethical behavior is critical for those involved with security, as explained in "Is Peer Pressure the Answer?" (1991, p. 98):

> Unlike those employed in other professions, people who work in security have access to confidential information and are routinely faced with opportunities to commit unethical behavior such as theft. With the exception of law enforcement, ethics is more important in the industry than in any other. Consequently, the principles that foster ethical behavior must be more deeply ingrained in security personnel. . . .
>
> Because there is no greater authority in the field than that which comes from peer pressure, a system of formalized peer sanctions within the industry could be the most devastating consequences for violators of a code of ethics.

This article concludes (p. 100): "Managers in the security industry must bring ethics to the surface and be ready to ingrain in their employees a sensitivity to ethical conduct. For the benefit of the public and the industry, managers also have the responsibility to lead by example."

Carey (1993, p. 6) suggests: "You can use an ethics program to build a company's positive image, improve quality and raise morale." Carey also notes:

> The most common ethical dilemmas are minor ones, and they are therefore often overlooked. The challenges most of us face include whether to cut corners, take responsibility for our own actions, deliver what we promised or give customers what they deserve.

Just as personal ethics can be checked by asking specific questions, the ethics of an organization can also be checked by asking three questions (Carey, 1993, p. 7).

Three organizational ethic-check questions are:
- Are we delivering what we promise in terms of quality and customer service?
- Are we selling a product or service that is harmful to society?
- Are we honest in the way we do business?

One starting point in developing an ethical organization is with a clear vision statement and goals as to how this vision is to become a reality. Wackenhut (1994), for example, has stated its corporate vision and the operating and financial goals to accomplish the vision (Figure 21–1).

In addition, as noted by Cunningham et al. (1990, p. 49): "Usually, corporations with strong values and ethical statements have a more proactive attitude toward workplace security and asset protection. Management and employee support for ethical behavior, security awareness, and loss prevention is most frequently found in organizations where top management and boards of directors have established corporate codes of ethical principles and practices."

CODE OF ETHICS

Even without legislative guidance from the state level, private security directors can set their own standards for conduct and service to increase the professionalism of the field. Both those hired and those hiring should adhere to a code of ethics similar to that guiding professionals. In fact, a self-enforcing code of ethics is required to meet the definition of a true profession. As noted by Simonsen (1992, p. 226), one of the accepted tests of qualifying as a profession is having a code of ethics—"specific standards and a code of ethics and conduct that govern the actions of the members of that profession."

A **code of ethics** sets forth self-enforcing moral and professional guidelines for behavior in a given field.

Corporate Vision:

By the year 2000, The Wackenhut Corporation will be recognized throughout the world as a uniquely diversified, superior performing and profitable protective and support services company.

Operating and Financial Goals

The Wackenhut Corporation will:

- Conduct all Corporate relationships according to the highest moral and ethical standards.
- Increase earnings per share and shareholder value on a continuing basis.
- Attract and retain a skilled work force, using only the highest standards in the recruitment and selection of personnel.
- Increase the productivity and professionalism of personnel at all levels within the organization, by emphasizing sound initial and ongoing training.
- Respect the dignity, rights and contributions of its employees.
- Maintain Return on Equity (ROE) at consistently high levels.
- Develop and retain a prestigious client base, including companies listed on the Fortune 500 and important agencies within federal, state and local governments.
- Seek long term relationships with our clients, based upon quality of service, not lowest price.
- Establish and maintain a mechanism for identifying and satisfying real customer needs through a total Corporate quality improvement program.
- Continue to improve the quality of Corporate services, to internal as well as external customers.
- Develop and achieve meaningful market share goals for each Business Unit.
- Continue to diversify into areas that will maximize profits and cash flow, and/or improve market penetration.
- Develop a balanced plan of short, medium and long-term interests while achieving sustained, profitable growth.

Figure 21–1. **The Corporate Vision and Operating and Financial Goals of The Wackenhut Corporation**

SOURCE: *Wackenhut 1993 Annual Report,* Palm Beach Gardens, Florida. © The Wackenhut Corporation. 1994, p. 28. Reprinted by permission.

Just as physicians take the Hippocratic Oath, private security personnel and management should agree on guidelines to achieve the desired goals. Codes of ethics have been developed and adopted by numerous organizations, including the American Society for Industrial Security (ASIS), the Council of International Investigators, the National Council of Investigation and Security Services, the National Burglar and Fire Alarm Association, Inc., the World Association of Detectives, Inc. and the Law Enforcement/Private Security Relationship Committee of the Private Security Advisory Council. The ASIS has established a code of ethics for its membership (Figure 21–2), for security officers (Figure 21–3, p. 662) and for security managers (Figure 21–4, p. 663).

Private security directors may want to obtain copies of additional codes of ethics and draw from them those guidelines that seem most relevant to their particular situations.

> Ethics can be promoted throughout the organization by the security manager serving as a role model, by having a clear vision statement and by having a code of ethics. Prescreening potential employees and ongoing inservice training can help promote ethical behavior as well.

Cunningham et al. (p. 49) stress:

> The best security people in the world can't be effective if they have to function in a climate where integrity and honesty are the exception rather than the rule. It's up to management to establish the highest ethical standards for business conduct and to see that those standards are adopted throughout the company.

Ethics and Decision Making

Fair and Pilcher (1991, p. 25) suggest considering the following three values when making decisions:

> *Rights*—this includes both the human rights that we all have and also any special rights that we have because of some special relations, such as being the recipient of a promise.
>
> *Excuses*—one place to look for a good excuse is how the people involved in the decision will be affected—not just in the short term, but after they have had time to think. The happier they are, the easier it will be to explain the action; the more miserable and unhappy they are, the harder it will be to justify what was done.
>
> *Human flourishing*—not just how people feel should be considered, but also how the decision will affect values needed for human beings to flourish as human beings.

With these values clearly in mind, Fair and Pilcher (pp. 25–27) recommend a five-step process for ethical problem solving in the workplace:

ASIS Security Code Of Ethics

PREAMBLE

Aware that the quality of professional security activity ultimately depends upon the willingness of practitioners to observe special standards of conduct and to manifest good faith in professional relationships, the American Society for Industrial Security adopts the following Code of Ethics and mandates its conscientious observance as a binding condition of membership in or affiliation with the Society:

ARTICLE I

A member shall perform professional duties in accordance with the law and the highest moral principles.

Ethical Considerations

I-1 A member shall abide by the law of the land in which the services are rendered and perform all duties in an honorable manner.

I-2 A member shall not knowingly become associated in responsibility for work with colleagues who do not conform to the law and these ethical standards.

I-3 A member shall be just and respect the rights of others in performing professional responsibilities.

ARTICLE II

A member shall observe the precepts of truthfulness, honesty and integrity.

Ethical Considerations

II-1 A member shall disclose all relevant information to those having a right to know.

II-2 A right to know is a legally enforceable claim or demand by a person for disclosure of information by a member. Such a right does not depend upon prior knowledge by the person of the existence of the information to be disclosed.

II-3 A member shall not knowingly release misleading information, nor encourage or otherwise participate in the release of such information.

Figure 21–2. The American Society for Industrial Security Code of Ethics for Members
SOURCE: Reprinted by permission from the American Society for Industrial Security, 1655 North Fort Myer Drive, Arlington, VA 22209.

ARTICLE III

A member shall be faithful and diligent in discharging professional responsibilities.

Ethical Considerations

III-1 A member is faithful when fair and steadfast in adherence to promises and commitments.
III-2 A member is diligent when employing best efforts in an assignment.
III-3 A member shall not act in matters involving conflicts of interest without appropriate disclosure and approval.
III-4 A member shall represent services or products fairly and truthfully.

ARTICLE IV

A member shall be competent in discharging professional responsibilities.

Ethical Considerations

IV-1 A member is competent who possesses and applies the skills and knowledge required for the task.
IV-2 A member shall not accept a task beyond the member's competence nor shall competence be claimed when not possessed.

ARTICLE V

A member shall safeguard confidential information and exercise due care to prevent its improper disclosure.

Ethical Considerations

V-1 Confidential information is nonpublic information the disclosure of which is restricted.
V-2 Due care requires that the professional must not knowingly reveal confidential information or use a confidence to the disadvantage of the principal or to the advantage of the member or a third person unless the principal consents after full disclosure of all the facts. This confidentiality continues after the business relationship between the member and his principal has terminated.
V-3 A member who receives information and has not agreed to be bound by confidentiality is not bound from disclosing it. A member is not bound by confidential disclosures made of acts or omissions which constitute a violation of law.
V-4 Confidential disclosures made by a principal to a member are not recognized by law as privileged in a legal proceeding. The member may be required to testify in a legal proceeding to information received in confidence from his principal over the objection of his principal's counsel.
V-5 A member shall not disclose confidential information for personal gain without appropriate authorization.

Figure 21–2. The American Society for Industrial Security Code of Ethics for Members *(continued)*

ARTICLE VI

A member shall not maliciously injure the professional reputation or practice of colleagues, clients or employers.

Ethical Considerations

VI-1 A member shall not comment falsely and with malice concerning a colleague's competence, performance, or professional capabilities.
VI-2 A member who knows, or has reasonable grounds to believe, that another member has failed to conform to the Society's Code of Ethics shall present such information to the Ethical Standards Committee in accordance with Article XIV of the Society's Bylaws.

Figure 21–2. The American Society for Industrial Security Code of Ethics for Members *(continued)*

1. Recognizing that a problem exists—the first, absolutely essential step and one that can be particularly difficult in ethics.
2. Problem identification—thinking and data gathering to understand just exactly what the problem is.
3. Creating alternatives—part of making the problem more specific is to create an array of alternative responses.
4. Evaluate the alternatives.
5. Public justifiability of each of the alternatives—address the issue of whether the alternatives are the kinds of actions that a person could defend publicly.

Values and a strong sense of ethics should be the core of the decision-making/problem-solving process.

Brown (1991, p. 8) stresses: "Ethical standards should be in the form of clear, unambiguous, written policies, disseminated to all personnel. Supervision and training are essential to ensure that the department's ethical principles are positively reinforced."

Although referring to police departments, the suggestions of Braunstein and Tyre (1992, p. 30) apply equally to the security profession:

> Ethically sound police officers are most likely to be found in an atmosphere that clearly gives high priority to ethical behavior and integrates ethics into every part of the department. . . . Ethical behavior must be seen as a primary goal of the administration and the department. If we are to expect officers to *behave* ethically, we must *treat* them—and the citizens they serve—ethically.

Finally, as Simonsen (1992, p. 224) urges: "Security professionals must make management realize that the long-term costs of unethical shortcuts in security

Code of Ethics for Private Security Employees

In recognition of the significant contribution of private security to crime prevention and reduction, as a private security employee, I pledge:

I To accept the responsibilities and fulfill the obligations of my role: protecting life and property; preventing and reducing crimes against my employer's business, or other organizations and institutions to which I am assigned; upholding the law; and respecting the constitutional rights of all persons.

II To conduct myself with honesty and integrity and to adhere to the highest moral principles in the performance of my security duties.

III To be faithful, diligent, and dependable in discharging my duties, and to uphold at all times the laws, policies, and procedures that protect the rights of others.

IV To observe the precepts of truth, accuracy and prudence, without allowing personal feelings, prejudices, animosities or friendships to influence my judgements.

V To report to my superiors, without hesitation, any violation of the law or of my employer's or client's regulations.

VI To respect and protect the confidential and privileged information of my employer or client beyond the term of my employment, except where their interests are contrary to law or to this Code of Ethics.

VII To cooperate with all recognized and responsible law enforcement and government agencies in matters within their jurisdiction.

VIII To accept no compensation, commission, gratuity, or other advantage without the knowledge and consent of my employer.

IX To conduct myself professionally at all times, and to perform my duties in a manner that reflects credit upon myself, my employer, and private security.

X To strive continually to improve my performance by seeking training and educational opportunities that will better prepare me for my private security duties.

Figure 21–3. The American Society for Industrial Security Code of Ethics for Security Officers

SOURCE: From *Private Security: Report of the Task Force on Private Security,* National Advisory Committee on Criminal Justice Standards and Goals, Washington, DC, 1976.

practices will outpace the short-term savings once litigation awards are considered." His conclusion:

> The cost to American industry as a result of unethical behavior by employees is in the billions. In the government, this cost is passed on to the taxpayer; in business, it is passed on to the consumer. Those who report unethical or illegal behavior are called whistle-blowers. Unfortunately, whistle-blowing often results in harder treatment of the informant than of the violators.
>
> The apparent corporate and government tolerance of violators makes an individual think several times before taking action. While the security professional may feel that whistle-blowing will not enhance his or her career, always remember that the security person is the one charged with blowing the whistle.

PRIVATE SECURITY CODE OF ETHICS
Code of Ethics for Private Security Management

As managers of private security functions and employees, we pledge:

I To recognize that our principal responsibilities are, in the service of our organizations and clients, to protect life and property as well as to prevent and reduce crime against our business, industry, or other organizations and institutions; and in the public interest, to uphold the law and to respect the constitutional rights of all persons.

II To be guided by a sense of integrity, honor, justice and morality in the conduct of business; in all personnel matters; in relationships with government agencies, clients, and employers; and in responsibilities to the general public.

III To strive faithfully to render security services of the highest quality and to work continuously to improve our knowledge and skills and thereby improve the overall effectiveness of private security.

IV To uphold the trust of our employers, our clients, and the public by performing our functions within the law, not ordering or condoning violations of law, and ensuring that our security personnel conduct their assigned duties lawfully and with proper regard for the rights of others.

V To respect the reputation and practice of others in private security, but to expose to the proper authorities any conduct that is unethical or unlawful.

VI To apply uniform and equitable standards of employment in recruiting and selecting personnel regardless of race, creed, color, sex, or age, and in providing salaries commensurate with job responsibilities and with training, education, and experience.

VII To cooperate with recognized and responsible law enforcement and other criminal justice agencies; to comply with security licensing and registration laws and other statutory requirements that pertain to our business.

VIII To respect and protect the confidential and privileged information of employers and clients beyond the term of our employment, except where their interests are contrary to law or to this Code of Ethics.

IX To maintain a professional posture in all business relationships with employers and clients, with others in the private security field, and with members of other professions; and to insist that our personnel adhere to the highest standards of professional conduct.

X To encourage the professional advancement of our personnel by assisting them to acquire appropriate security knowledge, education, and training.

Figure 21–4. The American Society for Industrial Security Code of Ethics for Security Managers

SOURCE: From *Private Security: Report of the Task Force on Private Security,* National Advisory Committee on Criminal Justice Standards and Goals, Washington, DC, 1976.

ETHICS IN PRACTICE

Roberts (1991, p. 96) asks: "What do you do if the man or woman you report to, the person who rates your performance and possibly directs your daily activities, is involved in illegal activities affecting your corporation?" What if you have absolute proof of your boss's illegal activity? This person is a trusted official of the company, a family person, a churchgoer and a volunteer for the Boy Scouts. Would this be a nightmare or a secret wish? Roberts notes:

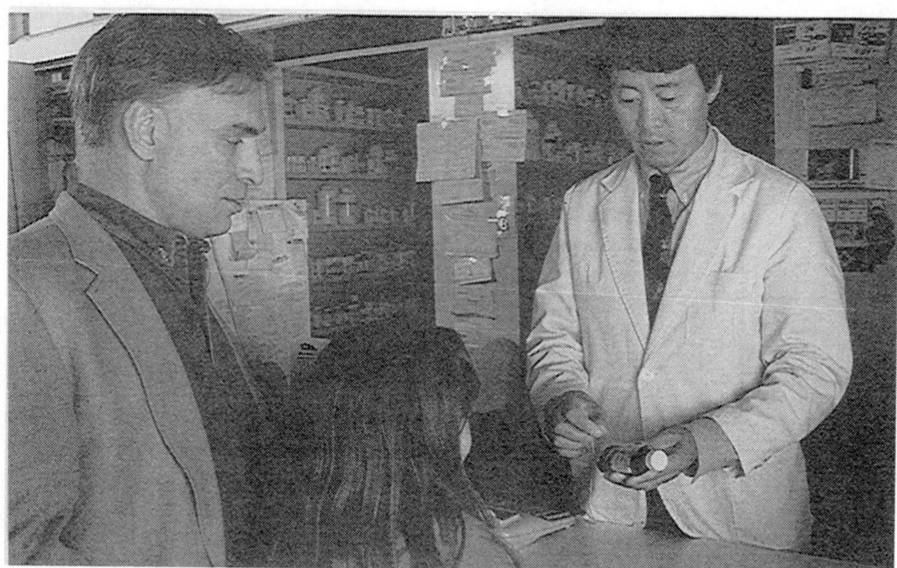

In the 1993 and 1994 Gallup Poll, pharmacists ranked highest in honesty and ethics. What might account for this?

> To many security professionals, this situation may be one to relish. It's a chance to blow the whistle loudly and clearly on the one who has been giving you fits over your budget, your assignment of subordinates, and your policies. Payback time is here!
>
> To other security professionals, this situation is a nightmare—a true-life, full-blown moral dilemma. A trusted associate, a valuable and cherished mentor, a friend is implicated in criminal activity.

Roberts does not provide an answer but suggests that the reader should act ethically and then live with the consequences.

A second example presented by Roberts involves an American working in a Middle Eastern country as director of fire and safety for the start-up of a large military hospital. He is confronted by the city manager of the company-owned and -maintained city where all hospital employees live and is told that from now on he is to report to the city manager. The security director responds that his contract calls for him to report to the project director. But the city manager persists. A few weeks later the security director learns that the city manager has been illegally diverting project funds and was involved in kick-backs. What should the security director do? Confront the boss with the evidence and warn him that if he does not stop, he will report him to the project director and the local authorities? Hand him over to the local authorities in a country where punishment for theft is severe, one of the penalties being loss of the right hand? Or inform the project director?

He chose to inform the project director, and within two hours the city manager had lost his job. As for the city manager, he was probably thankful that he was going home in disgrace rather than being subjected to Islamic law.

The final example helps to differentiate between what is illegal and what is unethical. This case, described by Maxwell (1993, pp. 208–11) involved a General Motors employee, Jerry Turner, Sr., who brought suit against the chief security officer at the plant where he was employed and against General Motors. In this case, *Turner v. General Motors Corp.* (1988), Turner was working the second shift and was to be picked up by his son after work. His son arrived, drove into the company parking lot and waited for his father. Surveillance cameras, installed as protection against theft and vandalism and their presence clearly posted, taped Turner's son in an act of masturbation. The next day the security director and other security guards showed the videotape of Turner's son to many employees. As a result, Turner was ridiculed, humiliated and insulted for several months. He began to experience chest pains, stomach upset and sleeplessness and required a physician's care. Turner sued for negligent infliction of emotional distress.

Turner was awarded actual and punitive damages in a jury verdict, which General Motors appealed. In reviewing this appeal, the court noted that a basic requirement of any tort is:

> . . . the infringement of a legally cognizable right and the corresponding breach of a legally recognized duty. The existence of a cause of action presupposes the presence as a matter of law as a right and corresponding duty as elements of a justifiable claim.
>
> Those rights which are recognized and protected by the law encompass property rights, including contractual and business relations, and personal rights, including the right to enjoyment of one's reputation and the right to privacy. Plaintiff's claim that General Motors owed him a duty not to cause emotional distress does not involve any of these rights or interests.
>
> We emphasize, however, that there is no necessary nexus between a legal right or duty and a moral or humane right or duty. The former are the accepted bases for an action in tort. The latter are principles which are dictated by good morals and conscience but are not necessarily within the boundaries of the law.

The court described the showing of the videotape as "devoid of any semblance of good judgment," as "callous, cruel and contemptible," as "reprehensible." However, it was not illegal:

> As tasteless as I find the conduct of defendants to be, I find no legal basis for imposing upon them, or anyone else, an obligation to keep secret, information which is true and not covered by the tort of invasion of privacy.

In commenting on this case, Maxwell (p. 211) notes that although the jury's award of actual and punitive damages was overturned, General Motors was probably still the loser due to loss of employee productivity while viewing the tape and the time and expense of the trial. Says Maxwell: "The very idea of security is to prevent loss, not perpetrate it."

SUMMARY

Ethics deal with questions of right and wrong, of moral and immoral behavior. Three personal ethics-check questions are: (1) Is it legal? (2) Is it balanced? and (3) How does it make me feel about myself? Five principles underlying individual ethical power are purpose, pride, patience, persistence and perspective.

In addition to practicing ethical behavior individually, security managers also should promote ethical conduct throughout the organization. Three organizational ethic-check questions are:

1. Are we delivering what we promise in terms of quality and customer service?
2. Are we selling a product or service that is harmful to society?
3. Are we honest in the way we do business?

A code of ethics sets forth self-enforcing moral and professional guidelines for behavior in a given field. Ethics can be promoted throughout the organization by the security manager serving as a role model, by having a clear vision statement and by having a code of ethics. Prescreening potential employees and ongoing in-service training can help promote ethical behavior as well. Values and a strong sense of ethics should be the core of the decision-making/problem-solving process.

✔ Application

Johnny Abrams, a supervisor for the Seymour Private Security Agency, was making his inspection of personnel under his supervision. He entered the men's room of the Mainline Corporation and came upon subordinate security officer Hynes and an employee talking. Officer Hynes had come upon George Simon as Simon was snorting cocaine. Simon was crying, begging the security officer not to turn him in to management because he would lose his job. He was desperate economically, and his wife was about to have their third child. Simon said he would do anything to get out of the situation so the company would not fire him. Officer Hymes lectured him and warned him that if it happened again, he would be reported.

It is unfortunate that Johnny Abrams as a person being paid to supervise and advise subordinates does not offer Officer Hynes any suggestions as to what he should do. The fact that Officer Hynes let George Simon off with a verbal warning may indicate two things: that the officer had no experience in handling this type of situation and he did not realize that sending him back to his job under the influence of a drug may have been devastating to other employees, particularly if Simon was working with highly volatile chemicals, machinery or any type of work that could lead to a disaster.

It may have been a fair decision in Officer Hynes' mind, but it seems that he took the easy way out. It definitely was not a good decision from any aspect—the security officer, his supervisor, George Simon, his supervisor and the company.

The actions of Johnny Abrams, the supervisor and Officer Hynes undoubtedly perpetuated the use of cocaine by George Simon. Had the private security officers notified Simon's immediate supervisor at the time of the incident, he could have been placed into a drug rehabilitation program that the company sponsored.

Evaluate how this incident was handled.

1. Was this a fair decision by Officer Hynes?

2. Do you think it was a good decision?

3. Should the supervisor have been more assertive in handling the situation?

4. Should Officer Hynes have called the public police?

5. Four days later Simon was picked up by the public police for possession of cocaine. Do you think the actions of the security officers perpetuated Simon's use of cocaine?

CRITICAL THINKING EXERCISE

ETHICS

STATUTORY AND COMMON LAW

A defendant is liable only for consequences that are reasonably foreseeable at the time when a contract is entered into. Damages shall be those arising naturally from the breach of a contract, or such as may fairly and reasonably be supposed to have been in the contemplation of the parties to the contract at the time it was made. They must be reasonably certain and definite consequences of the breach, as distinguished from mere quantitative uncertainty.

FACTS OF THE CASE

For more than a decade, Sandvik, Inc., had attempted to control or limit inventory theft by use of its own personnel and procedures. These attempts, however, did not succeed. In an attempt to solve the problem, the company contracted with Statewide Security Systems, a division of Statewide Guard Services, Inc., in June with services to begin in July. Statewide is a licensed private detective agency. The purpose of this contract was to "help abolish inventory loss," and for this service Sandvik agreed to pay a yearly charge of $24,000.

Three years later William Miles was hired by Statewide and assigned to guard the plant on the midnight to 8:00 A.M. shift. The personnel managers claimed that his application for a position as a security guard was "as clean as any application" they had ever seen, and there was "no way in the world that we could have found anything wrong with this guy." Unfortunately, however, the personnel office could not find his file with the original job application papers and letters of reference in it. Miles was apparently not given any intelligence test or personality evaluation. Statewide Security Systems did not offer an ethics training session, nor did they have any program to encourage honesty or to alert employees to potential embezzlers. Miles was assigned to guard the plant. He was not informed as to the exact value of the tungsten carbide powder he was to guard, and he was not informed about the exact nature of the previous internal theft problem.

In the first several months of guard duty, Miles made several friends among plant workers. He would sometimes do favors for them and they would occasionally do favors for him or give him gifts. The following January several individuals approached Miles with a tempting offer. If he would deliver a note to a location outside the premises of Sandvik, they would give him the contents of an envelope. When Miles opened the envelope to consider this offer, he saw 10 one-hundred-dollar bills. He estimated that it would take him no more than a half hour to deliver the note, and although he recognized that this was an extraordinary offer, it appeared to be a quick and easy way to pay for some expenses that he was unable to cover out of his minimum salary as a security guard. He accepted the offer, took the envelope and left the premises at 4:00 A.M. to deliver the note. Thirty minutes later Miles was back on duty at his assigned guard post.

Later investigation discovered that during Miles' absence, 4,205 kilograms of tungsten carbide powder worth $118,000 were stolen from the plant.

Issues and Questions

1. Should the security service be held liable for the total amount of inventory loss because a contractual obligation was breached, and should Miles be indicted and convicted on charges of embezzlement because he accepted a bribe?
   a. Miles may be naive, but he is not criminal. He neither planned nor executed the theft of inventory. He had no accurate knowledge that the inventory was of extraordinary value. Because his personnel record purportedly did not show any previous unethical behavior, not to mention any illegal record, he should not receive a more severe judgment than a letter of reprimand and be reassigned to a different security position that involves less strategic inventory.
   b. If, and only if, as a result of his testimony, Miles is able to assist in the conviction of those responsible for the theft of inventory and in the recovery of much or all of the inventory, he should be given a reward (minimally the amount of the bribe).
   c. Miles' deliberate 30-minute absence from his guard duty station supports the finding that Statewide Security Systems' contractual obligation was breached. Thus, the security system is liable to the full extent of the value of stolen inventory. In addition, Miles can be indicted and convicted on charges of embezzlement.
   d. Miles' unethical and wrongful behavior will result in his being charged with embezzlement, because he in effect is an accessory to a felony. But because Miles left the site of his employment, his employer is not liable for his breach of duty, because an employer is not answerable for the acts of an employee outside the scope of his employment. In other words, when Miles left the premises, he no longer was engaged in the furtherance of the security company's business, and thus there should be no civil liability against Statewide Security Systems.

e. The circumstance of the missing file weighs heavily against Statewide Security because it has the burden of proof to demonstrate that Miles was a capable, ethical and well-trained security agent. Without proof of a psychological evaluation to determine Miles' character, and lacking a program to encourage honesty or to alert the employer to potential embezzlers, Statewide is liable to the extent of a portion of its annual contract price—in this case one-twelfth ($2,000). Miles should be given a second chance; he has learned his lesson and does not deserve to lose more than the bribe (which he did not totally understand to be such in the first place).

Discussion Questions

1. Security personnel, whether guards, supervisors or managers, frequently are in a position to obtain information that could prove embarrassing to a company that relies on the contractual or the proprietary services to see that the business is creating a good image and that all violators of unethical conduct are handled in a manner conducive to good company business. To uphold this philosophy, as a security supervisor or manager, how would you proceed?
2. Which is more serious—unethical behavior by a business or unethical behavior by the contractual agency that the business hired?
3. Johnny McGuire, a security officer at the Glenview Nursing Home, during the hours of midnight to 8:00 A.M., makes coffee during the course of his shift without the knowledge of the complex managers and periodically has a cup to stay awake. What is your opinion of this unsupervised activity?
4. Do you believe ethics are only for those who are vulnerable?
5. What are the additional benefits of adopting and enforcing a code of ethics?

References

"An Ethical Double Standard." *Business Month,* December 1989, p. 7.

Blanchard, Kenneth and Peale, Norman Vincent. *The Power of Ethical Management.* New York: Fawcett Crest, 1988.

Braunstein, Susan and Tyre, Mitchell. "Building a More Ethical Police Department." *The Police Chief,* January 1992, pp. 30–35.

Brown, Lee P. "Values and Ethical Standards Must Flow from the Chief." *The Police Chief,* January 1991, p. 8.

Carey, Patricia. "Do the Right Things: An Ethics Program Can Strengthen Your Firm." *Your Company,* Winter 1993, pp. 6–7.

Cunningham, William C.; Strauchs, John J.; and Van Meter, Clifford W. *Private Security Trends–1970–2000: The Hallcrest Report II.* Stoneham, MA: Butterworth-Heinemann, 1990.

Elam, Stanley M.; Rose, Lowell C.; and Gallup, Alec M. "The 26th Annual Phi Delta Kappa/Gallup Poll of the Public's Attitudes Toward the Public Schools." *Phi Delta Kappan,* September 1994, pp. 41–56.

Fair, Frank K. and Pilcher, Wayland D. "Morality on the Line: The Role of Ethics in Police Decision-Making." *American Journal of Police,* Vol. 10, No. 2, 1991, pp. 23–37.

Himelfarb, Frum. "Rediscovering Ethics." *The Police Chief,* February 1995. pp. 24–25.

Hyams, Michael T. "Communicating the Ethical Standard." *The Police Chief,* October 1991, pp. 127–33.

"Is Peer Pressure the Answer?" *Security Management,* April 1991, pp. 98–100.

Kohlberg, Lawrence. *The Philosophy of Moral Development.* San Francisco, CA: Harper and Row, 1981.

Maxwell, David A. *Private Security Law: Case Studies.* Stoneham, MA: Butterworth-Heineman, 1993.

McArney, Leslie and Moore, David W. "Annual Honesty and Ethics Poll: Congress and Media Sink in Public Esteem." *The Gallup Poll Monthly,* October 1994.

Oran, Daniel. *Law Dictionary for Nonlawyers,* 2d ed. St. Paul, MN: West Publishing Company, 1985.

Roberts, Kenneth M. "When Your Boss Is a Crook." *Security Management,* November 1991, pp. 96–98.

Simonsen, Clifford E. "What Value Do Ethics Have in the Corporate World?" *Security Management,* September 1992, pp. 224, 226.

Wackenhut 1993 Annual Report. Palm Beach Gardens, FL: The Wackenhut Corporation, 1994.

Wasserman, Robert and Moore, Mark. "Values in Policing." *Perspectives in Policing.* Washington, DC: National Institute of Justice, November 1988.

"Your Ethics Quotient." *Successful Meetings,* February 1993, p. 47.

CASE

Turner v. General Motors Corp., 750 S.W.2d 76 (Mo. App. 1988)

CHAPTER 22

THE PRIVATE SECURITY PROFESSIONAL AND PROFESSION

DO YOU KNOW

- Where in an establishment's organizational structure private security fits?
- What roles a security director fills?
- What administrative, investigative and managerial responsibilities a security director has?
- What the primary goal of a private security system is?
- What a SMART objective is?
- How employees and management can be educated about the security/ safety system?
- What the basic investigative skills are?
- What areas security directors are responsible for investigating?
- What the managerial responsibilities of security directors are?
- What preemployment qualifications should be met by private security personnel?
- What constitutes adequate preemployment screening?
- How effective job performance of security officers can be increased?
- When training of security officers should occur?
- What progressive discipline is?

CAN YOU DEFINE THESE TERMS?

affirmative action
agenda
andragogy
authoritarian
authority
bureaucratic
delegation
democratic
dictatorial
discipline
Equal Employment Opportunity Commission (EEOC)
firearm
goals
grievance
hierarchy
hierarchy of needs
job description
management
management by objectives (MBO)
manager
mentor
morale
motivate
Occupational Safety and Health Act of 1970 (OSHAct)
on-line personnel
pedagogy

performance appraisal
permissive
SMART objectives
span of management (or control)
supervisor
unity of command

INTRODUCTION

"Security," states Wainwright (1984, p. 295), "is the most exciting profession in industry today. The practitioner is required to focus on the entire spectrum of corporate activity as well as on the environment in which corporations operate. While both conflict and opportunity can be found in the security field, it is safe to say there is more opportunity than conflict. Security professionals must not only capitalize on the opportunities of today, but also identify, understand, and manage the opportunities that will arise in the future."

The security professional is responsible for protecting corporate/organizational assets, predicting where they are at risk and taking steps to reduce these risks. Security professionals must keep within budget. They must also ensure that the organization has the most qualified and efficient services at the best price. Whether the services are proprietary or contracted, staff must meet the highest standards.

Security managers must also be able to deal in liability-prone areas in ways that are not only correct, but also documented and defensible. If they fail to do so, insurance may rise, legal fees may escalate and the organization's reputation may be damaged.

Security managers must also be aware of what is going on within the organization—who has the power, who gets things done and who the troublemakers are. They should avoid getting involved in the politics of the organization, but they must be politically aware, nonetheless, of what is happening. The position of security professional has taken on increased importance in the past decade. Some reasons for this are:

- The increasing size of both contractual and proprietary security organizations.
- The demand for specialization, such as patrol officers, investigators, equipment installers, computer technicians and consultants, and the need to coordinate the efforts of these specialists.
- The growing emphasis on private security because of fiscal problems in many cities.

The net effect of these changes has been to place even greater emphasis on the intangible elements of management, particularly the ability to work with and through people. Although *management* is a commonly used term with relatively broad agreement on its meaning, managers may perhaps be seen most appropriately as those who have the responsibility of getting things done through other people. This may happen through a three-tier system consisting of the manager, supervisor and on-line workers. In small organizations the same person may function in all three capacities.

This chapter begins with a discussion of the responsibilities of the security professional and that individual's place in the organizational structure. This is followed by a review of the specific responsibilities of most security professionals: loss prevention, administration, investigation and management/supervision. The chapter concludes with a brief discussion on becoming a security professional.

The Place of Private Security in the Organizational Structure

In many establishments the security function evolved from simple reliance on locks and alarms to a complex, comprehensive system that grew primarily in response to losses that occurred. This reactive response often resulted in a disorganized security approach rather than in an integrated service department. The need for a security system as an integral component of the organizational structure has been recognized by growing numbers of establishments. Usually such departments are headed by a specialist in security.

Effective management practices are integral to private security, whether it is proprietary or contractual, and regulated by the state or not. It is management that decides what money is spent where, what rules and procedures are established *and* enforced and who has specific responsibilities for given assignments. Finally, it is management that is responsible for ensuring security. If an organization has a security problem, it has a management problem.

> Private security should be a priority concern of top-level management of businesses, industries and institutions.

Those in charge of security must be given the necessary authority to fulfill their responsibilities and must have access to top-level management. Lines of communication must be kept open. Planning, evaluating and updating must be continuous to ensure the full benefits of private security equipment, procedures and personnel.

Heads of security departments have varying titles, including Chief of Security, Director of Security, Executive Security Officer, Security Director, Security Manager and Security Supervisor. Whatever their title, to be effective, security directors must have a position of authority within the organization, and they must have the support of top management. Whether this is the president or a vice president will depend on the availability of these executives. Although ideally the security director would report directly to the president, in large organizations the president may be too busy to effectively communicate security needs and concerns to the security director. In such organizations, a vice president may be designated the responsibility and, in fact, may do a better job than the president.

> Security directors must be given authority and have access to top management. They must communicate with and coordinate the security efforts of all departments within the organization.

As noted by Gallati (1983, p. 46):

> The enormous importance of appropriate role and status for the security manager is highlighted by the fact that the morale of all the security manager's subordinates will undoubtedly be directly affected, constructively or destructively, by the status accorded their superior. Also the quality, cost-effectiveness, and ultimate success of the security operation, and perhaps, the success of the company itself, will depend upon the role and status accorded to the security manager.

If security is to be effective, the cooperation of all departments is essential. This can best be accomplished by private security directors who are not only knowledgeable in their field, but also innovative, who can deal forcefully yet tactfully, objectively yet imaginatively, flexibly yet systematically with people and with security problems.

RESPONSIBILITIES OF THE SECURITY DIRECTOR

Sopsic (1977, p. 66) almost 20 years ago envisioned the function served by today's private security professional:

> The security manager of today and tomorrow must possess those qualities and characteristics of an upper management executive with the ability to relate to all levels of employees. He must bridge the gap between law enforcement and functional security methodology yet complement the organizational image and corporate profile.
>
> The time for molding a new concept of the security function and for building acceptance of the security profession will never be better. It is, however, the emphasis on program management, a systematic approach to problem solving, that security and safety management must embrace.

Whether proprietary or contractual, security managers have a vast array of responsibilities to meet:

- Develop security guidelines and standards.
- Develop short-range and long-range plans.
- Develop and periodically review goals and objectives, policies and procedures.
- Develop emergency contingency plans.
- Conduct risk analysis.
- Establish an annual budget.
- Develop job descriptions and hiring guidelines.
- Hire and train security personnel.

- Evaluate security personnel.
- Conduct investigations.
- Conduct inspections, audits and evaluations.
- Procure needed security hardware; install and inspect it regularly.
- Educate all members of the business/organization about the security program and their responsibilities in it.
- Attend designated meetings.
- Prepare required reports.
- Establish working relationships with other departments.
- Provide liaison with other managers, the CEO, union representatives, auditors, personnel department, engineers and architects, city inspectors, local police, the fire department, health officials, insurance companies and the press, as needed.

Security directors must establish rapport with top management and with other departments, enlisting their cooperation by helping each meet their own objectives. A positive attitude toward the budgetary and personnel problems of each department helps foster such rapport.

Because private security is a rapidly changing field, it is important to communicate with others in the field, to read professional journals, to join professional associations and to maintain outside contacts with other private security professionals.

Security directors must also understand and function not only within the formal structure depicted in the corporate organizational chart, but also within the informal organization that exists in any establishment.

> A security director's primary roles are those of loss prevention specialist, administrator, investigator and manager.

Loss Prevention Specialist Responsibilities

The appropriate physical and procedural controls discussed throughout this book are selected by security directors in conjunction with top management. Because no individual security director can be knowledgeable in every aspect of private security, and because the expenditures involved are sometimes large, consultants are often used in such areas as electronic or audio surveillance, protective lighting, protective fencing, alarm systems, locking systems, master keying and key control and security training. As private security becomes more specialized, use of security consultants is likely to increase.

Once the appropriate physical and procedural controls have been established, security directors delegate responsibility for maintaining the controls to each department and maintain liaison with each department to ensure that the controls are properly used. The loss prevention responsibility is the focus of the entire text, so will not be expanded on here.

ADMINISTRATIVE RESPONSIBILITIES

Security directors are responsible for security goals; policies, procedures and daily orders; financial controls and budgets; educational programs and the image of security within the organization.

Establishing Goals

Management's philosophy and the desired overall atmosphere greatly influence the security **goals** that are established. Some managements strive for a very open environment; others, for a very rigid one. Security goals are easier to set if a proper balance is maintained between openness and rigidity.

The ultimate goal of private security is loss prevention—resulting in maximum return on investment.

As emphasized throughout this book, security measures are aimed at deterring crime, reducing risks and making the establishment less attractive to would-be criminals. Different establishments obviously have different needs that must be discussed with top management before specific security goals can be established.

The goals should be measurable—for example, reducing shrinkage by a certain percent, or eliminating a certain number of risks identified during a security survey. Once the goals are stated, specific steps to accomplish the goals can be listed, ranked in order of priority and set into a time frame. According to Blanchard (1988, p. 14), **SMART objectives** can ensure that goals are met.

SMART objectives are:

- **S**pecific.
- **M**easurable.
- **A**ttainable.
- **R**elevant.
- **T**rackable.

To establish an objective of eliminating *all* accidents on the job is probably not realistic. To establish an objective of reducing accidents by 50 percent might be.

Establishing Policies, Procedures and Daily Orders

Managers also use three kinds of instructions: policies, procedures and daily orders.

Policies are general guidelines or underlying philosophies of the organization. They help ensure that an organization runs efficiently and effectively and meets its goals and objectives. They are the basic rules of the organization and are seldom changed without a basic change in organizational philosophy. For example: All visitors must check in at the reception area.

Procedures are the general instructions detailing how employees are to conduct various aspects of their job. Most procedures are aimed at achieving a reasonable, acceptable level of security as unobtrusively and cost-effectively as possible. For example: When visitors check in at the reception area, they will sign in, including who they are representing, who they are visiting and the time. They will be given badges. The person they are visiting will be called to escort them to his or her office. Visitors will be instructed to return the badges and sign out at the conclusion of the visit.

Daily orders are temporary instructions or informational items. They are usually dated and last for only a few days. For example: A list may be provided to the receptionist indicating specific individuals who may be allowed to go directly to the person they are visiting without an escort on a specific day or days.

Establishing Financial Controls and Budgets

One of the most difficult administrative responsibilities is establishing a budget, including costs of equipment, equipment maintenance and security personnel. Cost for security personnel should be carefully considered.

Ideally, security directors are allowed to prepare their own budgets for management's consideration. Justifying expenses for security is extremely difficult if results cannot be proven. Ironically, if security efforts are effective, nothing happens. This may lead top management to the erroneous conclusion that security efforts are no longer critical. Baseline data illustrating what existed before specific security measures were instituted will help to justify security expenses.

Security directors must also be realistic in their budget preparations. Security is one department among many, all vying for limited resources. Priorities must be set because everything cannot be accomplished at once. Rather, an effective security system is built logically and systematically as resources become available.

Establishing Educational Programs

People are many companies' most important assets, but they also can be great threats to the companies' other assets. Educational programs to promote safety, to implement security procedures and to reduce losses from internal theft are critical to an effective security system.

A security system is not established or operated in a vacuum. It requires the informed cooperation of management and all employees. Security directors are often directly or indirectly involved in such education. Sometimes they are given the responsibility to educate personnel on security equipment and procedures. At other times, especially in large companies, training departments are responsible for educating employees. Even in such instances, however, security directors may provide valuable assistance.

Education can enhance the image of private security by showing management and employees that the primary function of security is to ensure a safe place to work and to protect the company's assets so all can benefit. Losses from internal or external theft make raises and/or other benefits less likely. Safety programs can serve a positive public relations function as well. A cardiopulmonary resuscitation (CPR) program, for example, can make employees feel secure and prepared. Such a program can make them feel they are of value to the company and to one another. If someone does have a heart attack, those in the best position to help will be prepared.

Visitors and the public can also be educated as restrictions and safety procedures to be followed are explained. Effective educational programs can change the image that some people have of security officers from negative to positive.

> Personnel can be educated about the security/safety system through posters, signs, manuals, training sessions, drills and the suggestions and examples of security officers.

Signs and posters can be an effective educational tool and can also heighten awareness. Although permanent signs are cost-effective, they lose their impact after a time; therefore, they should be used only to give directions rather than to educate. Educational posters and displays should be bright, attractive and changed frequently.

Training manuals are helpful because management is forced to put the procedures into writing, which usually requires careful consideration of what is important. Although preparing a security/safety manual is a good idea, it is *not* sufficient by itself. Employees may not read it; they may not understand it; not wanting to appear ignorant, they may not ask questions or ask for clarification. The manual might also be simply put away and forgotten. Another hazard inherent in training manuals is that frequently they are not kept current.

Training programs or workshops are excellent means of educating. However, it is often hard to get the employees together at one time. In addition, turnover may leave some employees without needed training until the next training session is conducted.

Employee Awareness Programs

The Department of Defense is a leader in mandatory security awareness programs to safeguard national energy and industrial secrets. Security managers in other areas should follow this lead, using such mechanisms as videotapes, newsletters, posters and safety/crime prevention activities to accomplish the following:

- Explain important security programs and help gain their acceptance.
- Stimulate employees to be aware of security measures directly in their control.
- Give the security department the additional eyes and ears needed to combat crime.
- Help reduce problems in high-crime areas such as computer rooms, parking areas, storage rooms or docks.

Information about "intellectual property" and property information security to preserve trade secrets should be an integral part of a security awareness program.

Establishing Image

Security directors also establish the image of the security department. Many security directors are retired police, FBI or military officers who once served in an apprehension function; that is, they were primarily reactive rather than preventive in their responsibilities. This difference in purpose and authority has posed problems for some security directors, making it difficult for them to become an integral, accepted part of the organization. An authoritarian image will perhaps deter a few dishonest employees, but it is also likely to make other employees resentful and uncooperative. The influence of security should be pervasive, but not suffocating. Security directors can set this tone by example.

Decisions must also be made as to whether security officers will be uniformed and whether they will be armed. Factors influencing these decisions include the product produced or sold, the type of security interest involved, the number and type of employees and the area in which the establishment is located. Other important considerations are the availability of local police, past experience and hazards inherent in foreign locations. If security officers are armed, strict regulations regarding the issuing, use and care of weapons must be established and enforced.

Grady (1991, p. 11A) suggests that personnel professionalization needs to extend beyond managers to the uniformed security officer force:

> It needs the dignity and respect that we as managers possess. We must provide it with the proper leadership so that security officers can become security professionals as well. This can be done by:
>
> - Forming effective policies and procedures for the security department.

- Ensuring that our training concepts, programs, and approaches are realistic and reliable.
- Sensitizing and educating nonsecurity employees and the public on the value of our security personnel.

We must reach out beyond our own departments and make our professionalism and training known to our colleagues and superiors. We must prove our value and win the authority, respect, and support of our organizations. This can be done by making the value of security real, personal, and valuable to nonsecurity employees and by taking an active rather than reactive approach to loss prevention in serving organizational needs.

Investigative Responsibilities

Although investigative responsibilities and skills were discussed in depth in Chapter 12, they are important enough to briefly review in this chapter.

Investigation is both a science and an art, requiring very specific skills. Proficiency comes through practice and experience. The primary activity of investigators is to acquire information, so it is logical that the ability to elicit or obtain such information is critical to a successful investigation.

> The basic investigative skills are communication skills and surveillance capabilities.

Effective investigators are able to elicit information from all types of people, including those who are uncooperative and belligerent. They must also be able to communicate effectively in writing. Their investigative reports must be accurate, clear and readable. In addition, investigators are often called on to follow and observe persons and activities inconspicuously, so they must develop skill in surveillance techniques.

> Security directors are responsible for investigating the potential for loss (risk analysis), for investigating actual occurrences of loss and for conducting background checks and periodic audits.

Conducting Security Surveys

The foundation of a security system is the security survey and resultant risk analysis, discussed in Chapter 14. To determine existing and potential problems, security directors survey the physical facility, the procedures used in each department and the internal and external traffic patterns during open and closed periods.They may need to know basic principles of accounting and computer operations in some instances. They must also understand and have access to company statistics, computer operations, personnel department operations and records and the operations of every other department, including accounting (petty cash, cash handling, refund procedures, check cashing, accounts receivable, accounts payable, payroll, etc.), purchasing, shipping and receiving.

Security directors should be involved in top-management discussions and decisions in any area that might affect security and safety, especially any building or remodeling plans, *before* final decisions are made.

Investigating Losses

Any losses or accidents that occur should be thoroughly investigated. This sometimes involves cooperation with local authorities, with police and fire departments and with representatives of the Occupational Safety and Health Administration. Careful records of losses should be kept so that problems can be more easily identified. Security files should be well organized and current. Internal data on losses can be used to develop, improve and evaluate the security system.

Conducting Background Checks and Audits

Security directors may also conduct employee security clearances, either before employment or when employees are being considered for promotion to sensitive positions or positions with access to valuable assets. Conducting a background check on a long-time employee is a sensitive but important responsibility that requires tact and diplomacy.

Investigation often requires coordinating security investigations with investigations conducted by the public police.

Security directors also conduct or assign someone else to conduct periodic, unannounced audits to verify cash-handling, refund, check-cashing, accounting, shipping and receiving procedures.

THE SECURITY DIRECTOR AS MANAGER

Management is a complex relationship among employees of different levels, ranks, authority and responsibilities. It is often a person-to-person relationship, working within the organizational framework.

Security directors must support the development of *individual* responsibility, encouraging all personnel to achieve maximum individuality and potential while simultaneously supporting the organization's needs. The sum total of individual energy is transformed into organizational energy needed for success.

Because management is an area in which many private security professionals have limited experience, a brief summary of the language it uses follows before specific managerial responsibilities are discussed.

The Language of Management

In addition to being expert and current in all areas of loss prevention/asset protection, security managers must also be familiar with the language of business management if they are to effectively interact with other business executives and overcome the stereotypical image of the "company cop." Most security managers must vie with other top executives for personnel and budget. To successfully compete, they must be familiar with "management jargon" such as the following:

- **Affirmative action**—actions to eliminate current effects of past discrimination.
- **Agenda**—items to be accomplished, usually during a meeting.
- **Authoritarian**—describes a manager who uses strong control over personnel; this type of manager also is called autocratic.
- **Authority**—right to give orders.
- **Bureaucratic**—reliance on rules and regulations.
- **Delegation**—assigning tasks to others.
- **Democratic**—describes a manager who involves personnel in decision making.
- **Dictatorial**—describes a manager who is close-minded and uses threats with personnel.
- **Discipline**—actions taken to get personnel to follow rules and regulations.
- **Equal Employment Opportunity Commission (EEOC)**—commission set up to enforce laws against discrimination in the workplace.
- **Goal**—end result desired.
- **Grievance**—a complaint, usually written, made to one's supervisor.
- **Hierarchy**—levels; management hierarchy goes from the CEO to vice presidents (managers) to supervisors to on-line personnel.

- **Hierarchy of needs**—human needs identified by psychologists, placed in order from lower-level needs (food, shelter, etc.) to higher-level needs (self-actualization).
- **Job description**—statement of duties and responsibilities for a specific position.
- **Management**—the "bosses" in an organization.
- **Management by Objectives (MBO)**—management and staff set goals and time lines within which to accomplish the goals.
- **Manager**—one who accomplishes things through others.
- **Mentor**—teacher, role model.
- **Morale**—how a person feels; the general mood of an organization or company (e.g., morale is high/low).
- **Motivate**—encourage, inspire.
- **Occupational Safety and Health Act of 1970 (OSHAct)**—makes employers responsible for providing a safe workplace.
- **On-line personnel**—those who do the work (e.g., security guards and patrols).
- **Performance appraisal**—evaluation of an employee's work.
- **Permissive**—describes a manager who has or exercises little control over personnel.
- **Span of management (or control)**—number of people for whom a manager is responsible.
- **Supervisor**—directly oversees the work of on-line personnel; usually reports to a manager.
- **Unity of command**—people have only one supervisor.

Managerial Responsibilities

> Security directors are responsible for hiring, writing job descriptions, training, issuing equipment, scheduling, supervising, conducting inspections, taking corrective action and evaluating security personnel.

Hiring Security Personnel

When security directors are responsible for hiring security officers, they should keep in mind the vicious circle shown in Figure 22–1 (p. 685).

The first step in breaking this vicious circle is to hire qualified people who will perform effectively and who will make private security their career.

LeDoux (1995, p. 38) suggests: "The turnover rate of contract personnel is directly related to wage rates, benefits and working conditions. . . . [I]f contract personnel are treated properly, paid appropriately, and provided clear standards and expectations, they will identify with their workplace, regardless of employer, and perform exceptionally."

This view is shared by Dodson (1991, p. 6A) who suggests that a first step in "beating the high cost of turnover" is to recruit security officer candidates who will do well and stay with the job. To do so, managers should seek candidates with the following characteristics: reliability, pride, orientation to detail and alertness. Dodson also suggests that turnover might be reduced by providing salary raises every six months. But he cautions that money isn't the whole answer to the turnover problem: "In a survey of 2,200 security officers, good wages ranked fifth in a list of job-related considerations. Full appreciation of a job well done won first place as the most important factor in job satisfaction."

Private security personnel should meet the following minimum preemployment standards:

- Minimum age of 18.
- High-school diploma or equivalent written examination.
- Written examination to determine the ability to understand and perform the duties assigned.
- No record of conviction (of a serious crime).
- Minimum physical standards:
  - Armed personnel—vision correctable to 20/20 (Snellen) in each eye; capable of hearing ordinary conversation at a distance of 10 feet with each ear without benefit of a hearing aid.
  - Others—no physical defects that would hinder job performance (*Private Security*, 1976, p. 82).

These are minimum requirements. Others may be established depending on the position to be filled.

Age. Police departments have traditionally required that applicants be 21 years of age, a restrictive requirement that need not apply to private security. A mature 18-year-old, given proper training, can function effectively as a security officer, as evidenced by the military services, which have used people under age 21 for years. The age requirement should be low enough that qualified applicants can enter the field before they are committed to other careers. By the time a person is 21, he or she usually has made a career decision that is not readily changed.

Education. Applicants should demonstrate that they have mastered the basic skills taught in high school, either by having a high-school diploma or by having passed an equivalent written examination (GED). Additionally, a valid test should be given to assess the applicant's ability to learn the information required to effectively fill the role of security officer.

Conviction Record. Because security officers are in a position of extreme trust, they should have a clean record. This means that criminal history records should

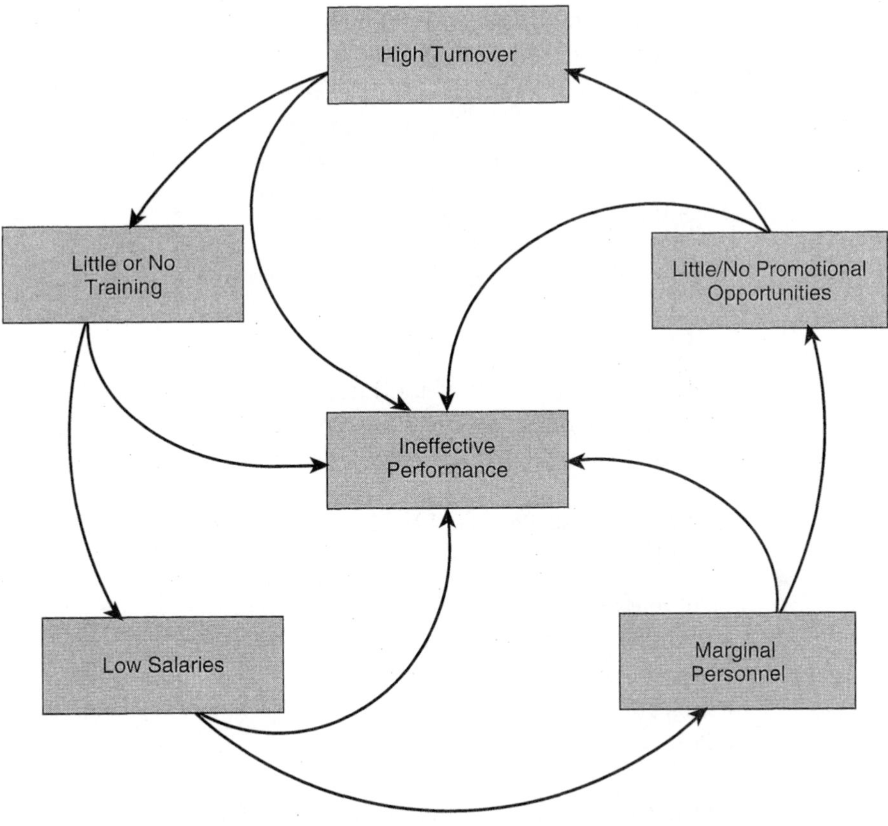

Figure 22–1. Private Security Vicious Circle

be available to employers of private security officers, a key issue in many states today. Current rules and regulations do not authorize dissemination of nonconviction data to private security personnel, but do authorize release of conviction data. Additionally, criminal history record information, including arrest data on an individual currently being processed through the criminal justice system, may be restricted. It is up to individual states whether to allow other than criminal justice agencies to have access to such records. Therefore, private security professionals should encourage their state officials to specifically allow private security employers access to nonconviction data to assist in screening potential employees.

An arrest or conviction record does not necessarily mean the person should not be hired, but the employer should be provided this information so an informed decision can be made.

Physical Requirements. Physical requirements should be based on the specific type of job the person is expected to perform. Height and weight are often relevant, and vision and hearing are almost always relevant, especially if the person will be armed.

State Requirements. Different states have different personal qualifications for licensing private security personnel. The same requirements might be considered for each individual security officer being considered for a position.

> Applicants for security positions should complete an application and should be carefully screened using such methods as an interview, a background check and other tests as appropriate to the job.

Unfortunately, because of the high turnover rate in security personnel, management is sometimes unwilling to invest much time or money in screening security personnel. This decision can accelerate the "vicious circle."

Application. All applicants should complete a form that contains, at minimum, the following information:

- Full name
- Current address and phone number
- Date of birth
- Education
- Previous employment
- Military record, if any
- Physical conditions as they relate to the job
- Personal references
- Fingerprints*

The application should contain a statement to the effect that incorrect information can be used as the basis for dismissal from employment. The form should be signed by the applicant.

Background Check. The information on the application should be verified. This is particularly true if the person was formerly employed in a security position. If employers would cooperate in exchanging information on the previous work of their employees, the overall personnel quality would improve substantially. Because the movement of individuals from one employer to another in the security field is extremely high, cooperation among employers helps eliminate unqualified, untrustworthy personnel. Records waivers should be obtained from all applicants. Personal references listed by the applicants should be contacted and interviewed.

Interview. Personal interviews with the applicant can help clarify any missing or vague information on the application form and can provide an opportunity

---

*Local fingerprint and police checks should be made because national agency checks often overlook important data.

to observe the applicant's appearance and demeanor. Questions can be geared to probe the applicant's honesty, dependability, judgment and initiative. For example, applicants might be asked why they want the job, what their goals are, why they left their last job, etc. When permitted by law, information on such items as arrest record, use of drugs and/or alcohol, credit and interpersonal relations with fellow workers should be obtained. Psychological stress interviews are sometimes used, but their value is controversial.

Other Tests. Other job-related tests, psychological tests and detection of deception (honesty) tests are sometimes used by employers when they hire security personnel. Where permitted by law, polygraph examinations are sometimes required. Use of such examinations is highly controversial.

> To increase effective job performance, security directors should provide security personnel with a job description, basic training, a security manual or handbook and the necessary equipment.

Job Descriptions

Because private security is a complex, diverse field, personnel are assigned to many kinds of security functions. Carefully prepared job descriptions help ensure that each function is properly carried out. The job description can also help in the selection process, increase productivity and promotability and ensure that training programs are job related.

Most job descriptions specify the type of work involved and the type of employee who would be best suited for this work. The description should include a summary of the major functions of the job; a description of the training, experience, skills and equipment needed; physical requirements, if any; a specific listing of the activities performed and the relationship of this job to other jobs in the department. Many job descriptions also include the normal working hours, the pay range and the name of the supervisor.

In addition, new personnel need an orientation to the company—its philosophy, organization, goals and operating procedures and policies. They should know the location of all stairways and where they lead, all emergency exits, fire alarm boxes, fire fighting equipment, telephones, emergency switches, water sources and the like. They should be taught the operation of any security equipment for which they may be responsible.

Training

As with screening, management is frequently unwilling to devote much time or expense to training security personnel because of the high turnover rate. Untrained security officers are not only a waste of money, but also may be a direct threat to themselves and to the company.

Both basic preassignment training and ongoing training should be provided.

Preassignment Training. The preassignment training will depend on the type of job to be performed and the existing level of training of the applicant. As soon as possible, new employees should receive training in the following areas:

- *Access control*—employee IDs, visitor IDs, contractors, surveillance cameras, sign-in/out log, after-hours access.
- *Alarms*—operation, controls, panels, actions to take for each alarm state.
- *Communications*—telephones (directory of critical numbers, professional answering), walkie-talkies, radios, cellular phone, computer.
- *Package control*—what to accept, procedures for accepting, what to allow out, procedures for packages leaving premises.
- *Passes*—property passes, camera passes.
- *Emergency procedures*—bomb threats, weather emergencies, earthquake.
- *Parking*—security, permits, traffic control.

Each security employee should have a policy and procedures manual and become thoroughly familiar with it. The manual should be kept current.

Ongoing Training. In addition to preassignment training, security directors should provide security personnel with continuous training, the content of which would depend on the specific company and the job. Such ongoing training can keep personnel informed on things such as issues, changes in company policies, updates in criminal and civil law and technological improvements in the system. This ongoing training is not classroom-oriented like the preassignment training, but rather is individualized and job related. Job descriptions are

Ongoing security personnel training is a vital management function.

often the basis for ongoing training. These steps are necessary to establish an ongoing, individualized, job-related training program:

1. Analyze job descriptions and identify the specific skills/knowledge needed to perform effectively. Determine the frequency and importance of each skill identified. Establish priorities and a timeline.
2. Write objectives to be met and how each will be evaluated.
3. Implement the training. This may be through audiovisual resources, practical exercises, case studies, roll-call sessions, training bulletins and the like.
4. Evaluate the results. Job performance, not test performance, should determine the effectiveness of the training.

Any discussion of on-the-job training should distinguish between **pedagogy,** or youth learning, and **andragogy,** or adult learning, a term coined by Malcome Knowles, nationally recognized expert in adult education. Goodboe (1995, p. 65) suggests that andragogy is based on four "fundamental tenets of adult education":

- Adults prefer to be self-directed, rather than instructor-directed.
- Adults have unique life experiences that they bring with them to the learning situations.
- Adult readiness to learn is linked to what adults consider relevant.
- Adults want an immediate application of knowledge rather than the postponed application indicative of youth learning.

In essence, says Goodboe: "Andragogy challenges instructors to think of themselves as facilitators—not teachers—of adult learning." The training requirements of individual states are summarized in Appendix B.

Training is critical to avoid charges of negligent training and negligent entrustment. Maxwell (1993, p. 15) cautions: "The failure of a security company to adequately train employees in the use of dangerous instrumentalities issued to them exposes the company to liability." He gives as an example the case of *Gonzales v. Southwest Security and Protection Agency, Inc.* (1983).

In this case Gonzales sued for damages resulting from false imprisonment, battery and negligent hiring, training, supervision and retention of certain personnel. The plaintiff was awarded $15,000. The case began at a wrestling match where Southwest Security and Protection Agency provided security guards. Gonzales sustained a broken jaw and lost four teeth in a beating he claimed was administered by the security guards even though he had done nothing wrong. The court found the following:

- Southwest Security did not adequately investigate the background and character of the defendants before hiring them.
- Southwest Security did not adequately supervise their guards in general and in particular on the evening of the incident.
- Southwest Security failed to adequately train the guards in using the weapons, such as clubs and handcuffs, with which they were provided.
- Southwest Security failed to adequately instruct its employees in proper methods to restrain and arrest individuals.

- At least one prior beating by Southwest guards had occurred at a wrestling match where Southwest was providing security.
- The negligence of Southwest Security proximately caused the damages to the plaintiff.

Issuing Equipment

After basic preassignment training is completed, security directors should give security officers the necessary equipment to perform their job. This might include a watch clock, flashlight, pocket pager or two-way radio, nightstick, pen and pad, handcuffs and, in some instances, a weapon. If a weapon is issued, appropriate training must be provided.

Firearms Training. A **firearm** refers to a pistol, revolver, other handgun, rifle, shotgun or other such weapon capable of firing a missile. The serious consequences for both employers and employees when untrained security officers are assigned to take jobs that require firearms include:

- Self-injury because of the mishandling of the weapon.
- Injury to others, often innocent bystanders, because of the lack of skill when firing the weapon.
- Criminal and/or civil suits against both employers and employees resulting from the above actions.

To reduce such consequences:

> All armed private security personnel, including those presently employed and part-time personnel, should:
>
> **1.** Be required to successfully complete a 24-hour firearms course that includes legal and policy requirements—or submit evidence of competence and proficiency—prior to assignment to a job that requires a firearm;
>
> **2.** Be required to requalify at least once every 12 months with the firearm(s) they carry while performing private security duties (the requalification should cover legal and policy requirements).

A second case described by Maxwell focused on negligent entrustment. According to Maxwell (1993, p. 18): "Liability may extend to the person or company that entrusts a dangerous object to a person who lacks competency and skill in handling the object." Maxwell urges: "[M]anagers should see that those entrusted with firearms are competent, fit, skilled, experienced, mature, trained and licensed, if required. Conditions that may signal fitness or competency problems relative to the entrustment of firearms include aggressiveness, violent disposition, recklessness, quickness of temper, physical or mental handicap, or substance abuse."

The case of *Horn v. I.B.I. Security Service of Florida, Inc.* (1975) involved a wrongful death suit. The defendant, I.B.I. Security Service, employed George Lowe and Cecil Westfall as security guards. Lowe was "entrusted" with a revolver to use on the job. While off the job and playing "quick draw," Lowe shot and killed Westfall with that revolver or with another revolver missing from the job. The court ruled: "For the owner of a firearm to be liable for injury negligently caused by the person to whom he has entrusted the gun, he need only be negligent in the entrustment of that firearm."

Scheduling

Security directors are also responsible for determining where personnel are to be assigned—for example, a fixed post, patrol or reserve. They must also decide whether to change assignments and rotate responsibilities. Such changes can keep personnel from getting too familiar with the people with whom they work, and thereby decrease the possibility of corruption. But there is a disadvantage in that they must then learn a new position.

Scheduling personnel is time consuming, yet critical to accomplishing goals and objectives. Scheduling is usually done according to the following priorities:

1. Cover the shift; ensure that competent staff is available and trained to provide an acceptable level of security at each post.
2. Provide this coverage in the most cost-effective way (avoiding overtime when possible).
3. Use personnel effectively and fairly.
4. Train and assign personnel to achieve the best balance of capability and desire.

Efficient scheduling begins with a permanent schedule showing all employees when and where they will be working. In some instances employees might be designated as on "standby" in case of illness or other reasons assigned employees cannot fulfill their assignment.

Effective managers are sensitive to the needs of regular part-time employees who are likely to be working under the demands of another regular part-time commitment such as school or another job. Once part-time employees are trained, retaining them is important. They allow managers to have additional personnel on hand when the need is there. They also make scheduling more flexible.

Security directors may also direct undercover operations within the organization to detect internal thefts and rule violations. Or they may hire honesty shoppers to perform the same functions.

Supervising

In larger organizations and companies, the security director/manager may have several supervisors to directly oversee security personnel. In smaller organizations, the security director may also function as the supervisor. The basic differences between the executive security director/manager and the security supervisor are as follows:

Manager	Supervisor
Goal oriented	Task oriented
Long-term planner	Short-term planner
Mission oriented	Program oriented
Works in future	Works in present
Represents whole	Represents unit
Concept oriented	Data oriented
Establishes policies and procedures	Enforces policies and procedures
Internal and external politics	Internal politics

In either case, supervisors must have a basic knowledge of the facility and of the duties of all personnel under their supervision. They must also know the basic policies and procedures of the security department. One primary responsibility of security supervisors is to conduct inspections.

Inspections

Random inspections of individual facilities and officers during regular shift assignments might include the following:

- Presence of all required personnel and equipment.
- Personal appearance and behavior of security personnel.
- Orderly appearance of site.
- Operability of equipment.
- Assessment of potential problems or hazardous situations.
- Preparation of reports of inspections.

The objective of such inspections is to ensure that time, equipment and personnel are being used as effectively and efficiently as possible.

Taking Corrective Action

If security personnel are not performing as expected, corrective action must be taken. In most instances, security directors or supervisors use *progressive discipline,* going from the mildest reprimand to the most severe—termination.

> *Progressive discipline* goes from the least severe reprimand, a warning, to the most severe, termination.

Progressive discipline usually involves the following actions:

1. *Warning*—This may be verbal or written, formal or informal. It should always be given in private and should always be documented.
2. *Reprimand*—This is a formal, written statement of an unacceptable behavior, the time line for correcting it and perhaps an offer of assistance.

Random inspections of security equipment and procedures is a vital management responsibility.

3. *Suspension*—This should be preceded by a reprimand in all but the most serious problems. Review and appeal procedures should be available.
4. *Demotion or termination*—This should be a last resort. The reasons and previous corrective actions taken should be carefully documented.

In most instances, managers who are skilled at effectively giving warnings will need go no further. They will accomplish the desired behavior change if they fit the warning to the individual and the situation. The purpose should be to change behavior, not to embarrass the person.

Evaluating Security Personnel

Security directors evaluate their personnel, provide feedback on how well they are performing and determine what is being done well and what can be improved. They provide nonthreatening evaluation, recognize accomplishments and recommend pay raises and promotions.

Factors managers might use in performance evaluations of security personnel include the following:

- Quality of work/technical skills

- Quantity of work
- Attendance/punctuality
- Organization
- Cooperation
- Problem-solving ability
- Communication skills
- Initiative
- Attitude

Guidelines for Effective Management

To manage effectively and to obtain the most from a security staff, security directors must:

- Create a good work environment—safe, pleasant.
- Be open to suggestions and input.
- Give credit to others when deserved.
- Keep employees informed—let them know what is expected, when it is or is not accomplished; let them know of changes, etc.
- Be fair and impartial.
- Act when necessary, but know your authority.
- Set a good example.

Occasionally, security directors might review the management code of ethics (see p. 18).

On Becoming a Security Professional

The future for private security professionals is bright, filled with opportunities for growth and advancement, along with increasing professional acceptance. However, Wainwright (1984, p. 295) cautions that this growth will involve many changes.

> The transition from smokestack industries to an information economy will require security practitioners to relate to a new kind of organization in the future. The information age, with its associated technologies, is causing the creation of more decentralized organizations with integrated networks. As a result, the security practitioner will need to understand the formal and informal movement of security programs through complex organizations. Training in intuitive management and a global view of the organization's environment will be necessary. Security practitioners will need to establish the link between the security function and various business and environmental issues that affect the organization. . . . The challenge is clear: we must measure the impact of technology and develop our own alternative security futures. Futuristics methodology is a good way to approach the complexity caused by technological and social change.

Knowledge and skills beyond those associated with the security field are clearly needed and involve communications, critical thinking and problem solving and intuitive management. Security professionals who acquire such additional skills will find ample opportunities in this exciting field. As noted by Green (1987, p. 24):

> Positive considerations for the future not only of jobs in security but also the potential for advancement or growth include the following:
>
> - The increasing professionalism of security is reflected in higher standards of educational criteria and experience and correspondingly higher salaries, especially at the management level.
> - The rapidity of the growth of the loss-preventive function has created a shortage of qualified personnel with management potential, meaning less competition and greater opportunities for advancement for those who are qualified.
> - The shift in emphasis to programs of prevention and service, rather than control or law enforcement, has broadened the security function within the typical organization.
> - The acceleration of both two-year and four-year degree programs in criminal justice and/or security at the college level is creating at the corporate management level a new awareness of a rising generation of trained security personnel. Many companies, especially the larger corporations, are actively emphasizing the degree approach in hiring.

Appendix C contains a listing of college and university programs in security available in the United States.

A fair number of security professionals make well in excess of $150,000 per year, although security directors have an average income of $63,000 ("Security/Loss Prevention Can Pay Well," 1994, p. 9). Langer (1994, p. 46) notes: "Security professionals with policy-making responsibility make an average 54 percent more than those without such responsibility." Level of education is an important factor, notes Langer (p. 48), with security directors with a graduate degree making 37 percent more ($71,789) than those with only an associate degree ($52,541).

According to Taitz (1990, p. 3), executive placement consultants say "the demand for security professionals is growing." To ensure upward mobility, Taitz suggests:

- Get a good criminal justice background—a baptism by fire—through working with an investigative agency, whether private or governmental.
- Educate yourself about as many aspects of the field as possible, and learn as much as you can about such subjects as access control, CCTV cameras, security surveys, and so on.
- Stay with your strengths. Skills may be transferable from one industry to another, but according to one management recruiter, corporations tend to prefer security executives who are knowledgeable and experienced in their particular industry.
- Be able to interface with all levels of management, including top management.
- Develop good rapport with the people who work in the field and those who would work for you.
- Strive to become the "ideal security management candidate," which another executive placement consultant defines as "a strong technical individual who, hopefully, has a college degree, has excellent communications skills, understands business principles, and is not rigid in approach."

The security field in the 1990s is a challenging, high-tech profession aimed at preventing losses in every way possible.

SUMMARY

Private security has come into its own during the past decade. Security directors must be given authority to act and have access to top management. They must communicate with and coordinate the security efforts of all departments within the organization. Their primary roles are those of loss prevention specialist (the focus of the entire book), administrator, investigator and manager.

As administrators, security directors are responsible for security goals; policies, procedures and daily orders; financial controls and budgets; educational programs and the image of security within the organization. The ultimate goal of private security systems is loss prevention—thereby maximizing return on investment. One way to achieve this goal is through SMART objectives, objectives that are specific, measurable, attainable, relevant and trackable.

Other employees and staff can be educated about the security/safety system through posters, signs, manuals, training sessions, drills and the suggestions and examples of security officers.

Security directors are responsible for investigating the potential for loss (risk analysis), for investigating the actual occurrences of loss and for conducting background checks and periodic audits. The basic investigative skills are communication skills and surveillance capabilities.

As managers, security directors are responsible for hiring, writing job descriptions, training, issuing equipment, scheduling, supervising, conducting inspections, taking corrective action and evaluating security personnel.

If the vicious circle leading to high rates of turnover is to be broken, private security personnel selected for employment should meet minimum employment standards, including being at least 18 years old, having a high-school diploma or equivalent written examination, passing a written examination to determine the ability to understand and perform the duties assigned, having no criminal record and meeting minimum physical standards. All applicants for security positions should complete an application and should be carefully screened using such methods as an interview, a background check and other tests appropriate to the job to be performed.

To increase effective job performance, security directors should provide security personnel with a job description, training, a security manual or handbook and the necessary equipment. Both preassignment training and ongoing training should be provided. If personnel do not perform up to standards, progressive discipline should be used. Progressive discipline goes from the least severe reprimand, a warning, to the most severe, termination.

APPLICATION

1. As a security supervisor, you are aware that the security director is considering arming his proprietary security force. List the advantages and disadvantages of having armed proprietary security officers.

2. List as many factors as you can that contribute to the image of a private security officer.

3. Write a job description for a private security supervisor.

CRITICAL THINKING EXERCISE

Civil Liability

Statutory and Common Law

In defense of property, the use of force is privileged when an invader takes property from another's possession and it appears that the invader is about to remove the property from the possessor's premises. The privilege allows only for the use of reasonable force. In an action for assault and battery, on the other hand, provocation cannot be considered in mitigation of damages. In awarding damages, a jury is entitled to determine what portion of claimed injury is proximately caused by an incident and what portion of medical bills is reasonably required.

Facts of the Case

In April Milo P. Vacanti's wife delivered a JVC compact disc (CD) player to Master Electronics Corporation for repair. On November 21 of that same year (seven months later), Vacanti went to Master Electronics to pick up the CD player. The CD player had been a Christmas gift from their daughter the previous December. She had purchased the player five weeks earlier. Vacanti thought that they should have the player when their daughter returned home for Thanksgiving vacation. He also was under the impression that the repairs would be covered by warranty. Vacanti was told by a Master Electronics employee, Arthur W. Hull, that the player had been repaired but that Vacanti would have to pay $70.07 (charges for material and labor) before he could take the CD player home. A verbal argument about the bill ensued, and Vacanti began using profanities and threatening Hull. At that point Hull called Robert A. Dolezal, the security guard who was on duty. As Dolezal approached, Vacanti grabbed the CD player and attempted to leave the premises. Both Hull and Dolezal attempted to stop Vacanti, and after a brief struggle they succeeded in taking the CD player from him.

Vacanti brought a civil assault and battery action against Master Electronics Corporation in which he claimed that as a result of being "attacked by three Master employees" he had suffered a "torn hand," a "muscle separation on a rib," several "torn ligaments" and injury to his "neck musculature and lip." He testified that one person grabbed him around the neck, choking him, another grabbed his legs and a third bit his finger and jerked the CD player away from his hands. At trial Vacanti presented medical bill statements totaling $3,150.00. Vacanti testified that he was still experiencing back pain almost half a year after the incident. However, under cross-examination, he admitted that before this incident he had been treated for back pain caused by his work as a bricklayer. Six months after the incident he went to the Mayo Clinic in Scottsdale, Arizona, and was examined by Dr. Michael A. Covalciuc. The doctor's medical report detailed Vacanti's examination and included numerous test results as well as a bill for services.

The defendants (Master Electronics Corporation) asserted that Vacanti made an inquiry about whether they could repair his CD player without mentioning the existence of a warranty and that, after leaving the CD player at their place of business for more than seven months without communicating with them, he abruptly entered the shop, demanded the CD player without paying for the costs and became abusive. When Master's employees tried to stop Vacanti from removing the CD player without paying, he became violent and thus provoked the incident where he received minor injuries as the CD player was wrested from his grasp. But it was Vacanti who dragged Hull outside the building and pushed him against a brick wall. Dolezal testified that he took the CD player away from Vacanti but otherwise did not grab him and that no other person was involved. Lois Fernald, another Master employee, confirmed Dolezal's testimony.

Master Electronics Corporation further argued that in accordance with Nebraska statutes they had a lien on the subject CD player to the extent of its reasonable or agreed charges for the work done and was legally entitled to retain possession of the CD unit until such charges were paid.

Issues and Questions

1. Does Vacanti have a valid tort action against Master Electronics Corporation?

a. In a defense-of-property case, the use of force is privileged when an invader takes property from another's possession and it appears that the invader is about to remove the property from the possessor's premises. Therefore, Master Electronics is not liable for any of Vacanti's damages, and he is not entitled to his CD player without paying for it.

b. The defense-of-property privilege allows only for the use of reasonable force. Master Electronics will thus be liable for Vacanti's proven injuries, but not for remote pain documented only by hearsay evidence (the report from Covalciuc).

c. Vacanti admitted that due to his work as a bricklayer he had been treated for back pain before this incident. He saw a doctor at that time for back pain that developed into numbness on his right side. It is not possible for him to recover damages from Master because it is impossible for him to establish sufficient evidence that this incident caused all his current physical problems.

d. Whenever there is conflicting testimony concerning crucial evidence, credibility will be granted to the defense because the person bringing the action has the burden to establish by a preponderance of the evidence the allegations made. Thus Master Electronics cannot be held liable in this particular tort action.

e. Employees and private security officers are responsible for their actions and damages they may cause. Both Vacanti's injuries are directly related to Hull and Dolezal physically detaining Vacanti and forcefully grabbing the CD player from him, they have committed a criminal act and Master Electronics is liable for all claimed damages. Furthermore, the total of Vacanti's medical bills, only $3,150, is hardly an exorbitant amount considering the extent and probably duration of his pain and suffering (not to mention the embarrassment to him and his family).

Discussion Questions

1. How can private security directors enhance the image of the private security officer?
2. List the resources one might use to obtain qualified people to hire as security officers.
3. What are three characteristics of a good training program?
4. What are the minimum requirements for an effective security officer?
5. What additional qualifications are required for a security supervisor? A security director?

References

Blanchard, Kenneth. "Getting Back to Basics." *Today's Office,* January 1988, pp. 14, 19.

Dodson, Minot. "Beating the High Cost of Turnover." *Security Management Special Supplement: Priming Your Personnel,* March 1991, pp. 6A, 8A.

Gallati, Robert J. *Introduction to Private Security*. Englewood Cliffs, NJ: Prentice-Hall, 1983.

Goodboe, Michael E. "Should Security Practice Andragogy?" *Security Management,* April 1995, pp. 65–67.

Grady, John C. "Personnel Professionalization." *Security Management Special Supplement: Priming Your Personnel,* March 1991, p. 11A.

Green, Gion. *Introduction to Security,* 4th ed. Revised by Robert J. Fischer, Stoneham, MA: Butterworth Publishers, 1987.

Langer, Steven. "A Window on Wages." *Security Management,* June 1994, pp. 46–48.

LeDoux, Darryl T. "Exploding the Myths of Contract Security." *Security Management,* January 1995, pp. 37–39.

Maxwell, David A. *Private Security Law: Case Studies*. Stoneham, MA: Butterworth-Heinemann, 1993.

Private Security. Report of the Task Force on Private Security, National Advisory Committee on Criminal Justice Standards and Goals. Washington, DC: U.S. Government Printing Office, 1976.

"Security/Loss Prevention Can Pay Well." *Security Concepts,* July 1994, p. 9.

Sopsic, J. P. "Security in Its Proper Management Perspective." *Security Management,* May 1977, p. 66.

Taitz, Sharyn, ed. *Getting a Job, Getting Ahead, and Staying Ahead in Security Management*. Port Washington, NY: Rusting Publications, 1990.

Wainwright, O. O. "Security Management of the Future." *Security Management,* March 1984, pp. 47–51, 295.

Cases

Gonzales v. Southwest Security and Protection Agency, Inc., 665 P.2d 810 (N.M. App. 1983)

Horn v. I.B.I. Security Service of Florida, Inc., 317 So. 2d 444 (Fla. App. 1975)

CHAPTER 23

A Look to the Future

Do You Know

- How to view change?
- What experts say regarding the challenges ahead and what the future of the security profession holds?

Can You Define This Term?

outsourcing

Introduction

Change is inevitable. No person or organization can stop it. Managers must accept that the only constant is change. Whether that change is positive or negative is characterized by Enright (1984) in this way:

> . . . a branch floats peacefully down a river whose waters are high with the spring run-off. Although the branch is floating rapidly and occasionally bumps gently into a rock, it is almost effortlessly motionless in relation to the water it floats in. A similar branch has become wedged between some rocks, and is thus resisting the swift flow of water around it. This branch is buffeted, whipped, and battered by the water and debris floating past it, and will soon be broken by the pressures against it [unless it dislodges and "goes with the flow"]. If branches could experience, the one wedged into the rocks would be experiencing change with intense pain and distress; the floating one would experience ease and, paradoxically, comfortable stability even in the midst of rapid motion.

> Change is inevitable. View it as opportunity.

Using an analogy similar to Enright, Band (1995, p. 22) advises:

> Perhaps the greatest challenge for any change catalyst is dealing with the inevitable proponents for the status quo. No matter how well motivated and activated, radical change exposes status quo agents who cannot be converted. Their interests are directly threatened. For them, yielding to the pressure to change is much less attractive than resisting.
>
> The wave of motivation and excitement created by successful change during the initial phases of the change process can be dashed on the rocks of this submerged resistance.

This chapter provides a look towards the future through a wide array of comments and predictions by security professionals from greatly diverse backgrounds. The contributions by Minot B. Dodson, executive vice president of Pinkertons, and Michael E. Goodboe, vice president of training for Wackenhut Training Institute, were prepared specifically for this text.

As you read the comments and observations of the numerous security professionals included in this section, certain themes and trends will become apparent.

> Trends in the security profession include growth, outsourcing, privatization, globalization and an emphasis on training and professionalization of the field, including a professional image.

WHAT THE FUTURE HOLDS FOR SPECIFIC AREAS OF THE SECURITY PROFESSION

Sherwood (1994, p. 2) comments on the future for *hospital security*:

> So what does the future hold? When I first came into the industry, security was seen as a profit drain. Through various methods, professionalism and expansion of services and functions, we now see that security departments create additional profit by decreasing inappropriate activities, by limiting the potential for theft as well as decreasing the potential for lawsuits. . . . By reducing employee theft, workman compensation accidents and . . . substance abuse, they are in fact making money for that company, or in this case [health care facilities]. Private security is viewed as the growth industry of the 90s and in a field of business where every dollar counts because of the tightening of purse strings by the government and business managers, security directors and their departments will play a big role in achieving profitability goals.

Kohr (1994, p. 31) speaks of *hotel/motel security* in the future:

> Hotel and motel security will continue to evolve around technology; current security technology will be used more in renovation and new construction. The challenges in hotel security will not change; litigation still will be the driving force. However, if voluntary nationwide standards are adopted, and more states pass hotel and motel security laws, technology will remain in the forefront of hotel security.
>
> The future will need to rely even more on technology to assist in deterring the ever increasing exposures to crime. The lodging industry cannot be expected to correct social ills, but they are charged with the responsibility of providing reasonable levels of security for guests and employees.
>
> The key to the future for manufacturers and suppliers of security equipment is developing cost-effective systems; for the lodging industry it remains continued education of the public and lodging operators on the need for adequate security.

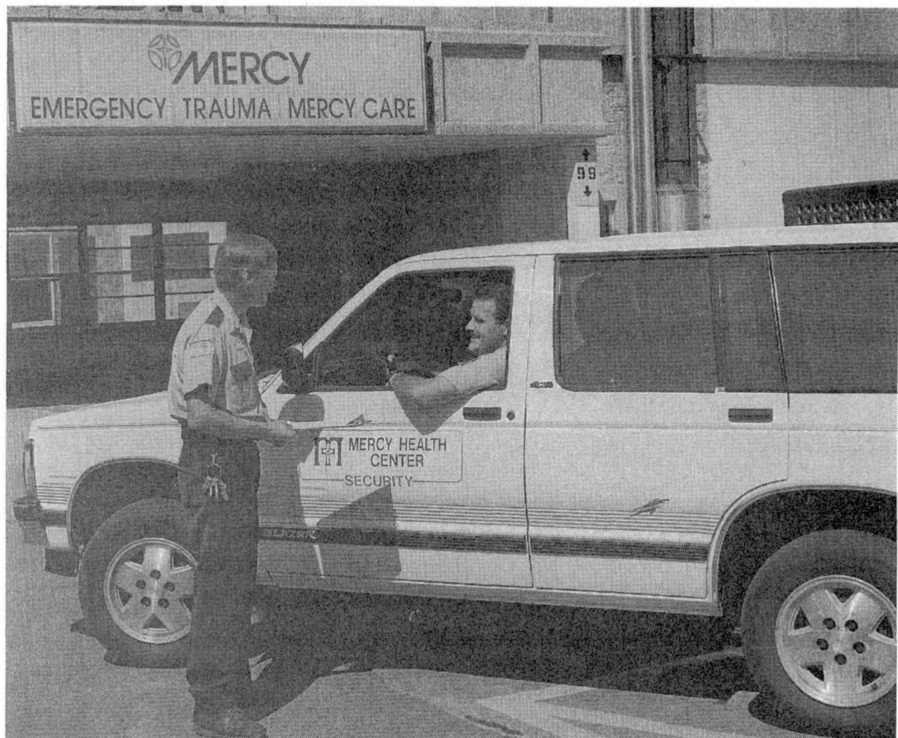

Hospital security departments can create additional profit rather than being viewed as a profit drain.

Robert L. Arko, president of Arko Executive Services Inc. (1992, p. 31), speaks on the future of the *transit industry*:

> The new direction of the transit industry is through the logical division of services and a working partnership between the public and private sectors, both seeking the same level of excellence. Tomorrow's successes in corporate America will result from today's efforts to deal with the nation's fiscal

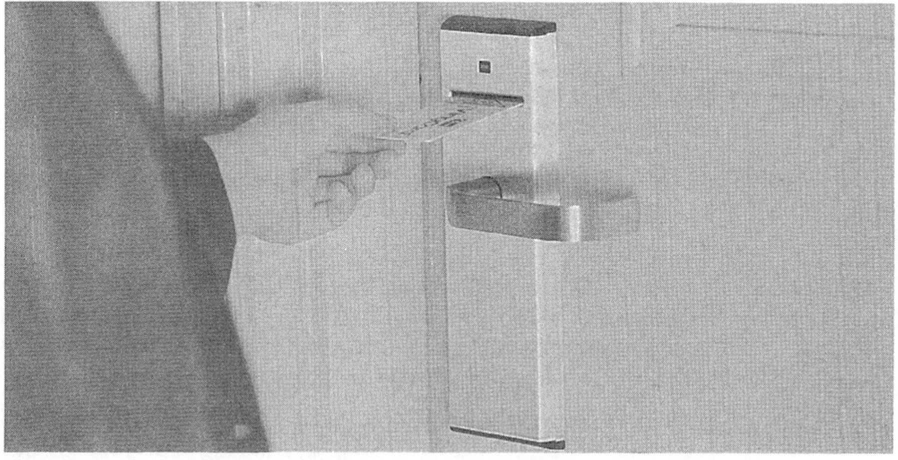

The future of hotel security lies in changing technology.

> problems. The old way is no longer appropriate. The new way still requires creativity and innovation.

Pam Collins (1992), coordinator of security and loss prevention at Eastern Kentucky University, Richmond, Kentucky, comments on the future of *campus security*:

> Campus security should focus on internal issues and becoming a more effective support service to the campus community. Success in the future depends on the development of sound policies and procedures for providing a high quality of service that results in a safe and secure college environment. Campus security should be viewed as a requisite component of American higher education and an integral part of the campus infrastructure.

COMMENTS FROM A ROUND TABLE OF EXPERTS

In a round-table discussion reported by Goldberg (1994, pp. 40–44), president of Management Development Systems, Inc., challenges facing security managers and their views of the future were among the topics. Participants included Daniel A. Conger, security manager at Merck & Co., Inc.; John F. Mallon, security director at Johnson & Johnson; Louis A. Tyska, former director for Revlon and currently an independent consultant; Robert L. Pearson, senior vice president at First Fidelity Bancorporation and James T. Christian, manager of security operations, Sandoz Pharmaceutical Corp. Following are their observations:*

Goldberg: *What do you think is the greatest challenge facing security managers today?*

Conger: The greatest challenge, I think, is trying to fulfill our functional and operational responsibilities with reduced resources. Though I sometimes feel like I have to justify my department's existence, I also know and understand that we are in an era of corporate downsizing, and everyone is being asked to make sacrifices. We have to be flexible and do our best to get the most from our people. We also have to do more ourselves, expanding the traditional role of the security manager.

Christian: The challenge is to use our resources in the most effective, productive way possible, and we can't be afraid to say "no" to a request if it will result in those resources being spread too thin. We have to prioritize as well as we can.

Pearson: The security manager has to be more of a business manager than ever before, so for me, the challenge is dealing effectively with that expanded role. We have to be much more business-oriented, looking at the bottom line and devising ways to improve our operational efficiencies.

Mallon: The global economy will continue to have an impact on the corporations for which we work and that impact will affect our departmental budgets and our staffing. We therefore have to take a global perspective, doing things to contribute to corporate profitability.

Tyska: We need to find the key to unlock the door to marketing what our discipline can bring to the party—letting people know that our expertise can be useful in many ways.

Goldberg: *What new trends, operational, technological, or management-related, do you see coming in the next few years?*

Pearson: More outsourcing of security functions, which would have been taboo because of political sensitivities and confidentiality issues. The determining factor will be the scope and quality of services that are available to us.

Christian: The use of technology to save recurring costs. We will be making capital investments to realize long-term savings. Some examples of these investments include: robotic patrols, optical disks to supply pictures to all checkpoints, motion detectors linked with alarms and CCTV, and other new technology. The need for individual security officers will be reduced through capital investment in new technology.

Mallon: We will be using state-of-the-art telephones, video conferences, and satellites. The "techies" should be thinking more about security issues, and the security industry should provide training on issues like risk avoidance for the technical people. Cost reduction, though, will continue to be an overriding theme.

Conger: Outsourcing and the use of new technologies will certainly be predominant trends, but I also think that security departments will be more involved with other company operations. More than ever, security departments will work cooperatively with other groups, designing and implementing initiatives to conduct building management activities and other similar tasks. Security departments can do a lot more, and the coming years should see greater realization of that potential.

Tyska: Gee-whiz technological improvements will help us to concentrate our resources more productively. These technological advances should be accompanied, though, by a concerted effort to elevate the standing of our industry, our discipline, both inside and outside the boardrooms of America.

Goldberg: *What are you doing to deal with the increasingly prevalent problem of workplace violence?*

Conger: Merck screens its candidates for employment very carefully, and if employees are having personal problems, there is a range of employee assistance options offered by the company. Merck has a security council that is assessing this issue, but we will also be looking to OSHA, which may mandate that companies protect employees against violence. This will certainly represent another challenge for security and human resources departments in the 90s and beyond.

Pearson: At First Fidelity, the Human Resources, Legal, and Corporate Security Departments work in concert with our Employee Assistance Program (EAP) to develop and, if necessary, implement a coordinated response to address issues of this nature.

Goldberg: *Another of today's key issues is the impact of the information superhighway on workplace operations. What impact has the superhighway had on your department?*

Pearson: Management Information Systems offer tremendous opportunity to enhance efficiencies in the analysis of security-related activities and the development of strategies derived from that analysis. Standardized reporting formats, transmission and receiving technologies, and report-generation capabilities are resources that security managers should evaluate in the continuing development of the security function.

Conger: The information superhighway has yet to be determined for us, but the promised available data should be an asset to security operations at Merck. The current networks and highways, such as e-mail, already enhance communications about security issues. Of course, the superhighway will bring some risks regarding data security and privacy with it, and these risks must be calculated and analyzed.

VIEWS FROM THE JOINT SECURITY COMMISSION

The Joint Security Commission ("Redefining Security," June 1994, p. 8) makes the following key points:

- Managers must make tradeoffs during the decision phase between cost and risk, balancing the cost in dollars, manpower, and decreased flow of needed information against possible asset compromise or loss.
- As the twentieth century nears its end, events require that the United States assess the basic assumptions and goals that guide the protection of government, information, facilities, and people.
- The Commission believes that the complexity and cost of current security practices and procedures are symptoms of the underlying fragmentation and cannot be alleviated without addressing it.
- The problems are many and the mandate for change is strong, but change must be guided by clear goals and principles.
- We can and must provide a rational, cost-effective, and enduring framework using risk management as the underlying basis for security decision making.

OTHER EXPERTS LOOK TO THE FUTURE

Ted P. Barron (1993, p. 33), vice president and security project manager for Wells Fargo Bank in San Francisco, states:

> The future holds great promise for innovations in the security field. In the coming years improvements will occur in diagnostics, encryption, and product performance. Computer languages will readily allow integration of many types of alarm systems into a single processor. Each advance will make it easier for security directors to bring these systems into a single, vendor-operated, central station or to establish their own proprietary alarm system.

This security robot from Denning Robotics, Inc., can sense heartbeats through walls using microwaves, uses infrared detectors to sense temperature and changes in motion and can detect fire and flooding.

Darryl T. LeDoux (1995, p. 39), security services manager for Syntex, Inc. and American Society for Industrial Security (ASIS) Region II vice president, comments on change in the security profession:

> Unfortunately, too many people see change as a burden rather than an opportunity for improvement. Security managers must fight that tendency as they look for ways to meet expanding responsibilities with shrinking budgets. Those with proprietary forces who have rejected outsourcing as a poor-quality alternative should take a new look at this option—and how managing the change can ensure success.

Edward A. Sundberg (1994, p. 133), president of ConsultAmerica, offers this view of technology:

> No technology improvements are going to solve all the industry's woes at one time, but technology is now available to truly create differentiation among the many competing guard companies. The companies that will prosper in the future will use this technology to shift towards customer service with better risk management practices at the customer's facility.

Tyska ("APEC II Goes West," 1991, p. 14), former director of security for Revlon, Inc., noted: "Security managers of the future will have to deal with a work force that is older and includes more women and flex- and part-time workers." Other factors Tyska sees in the future are that the work force of 2000 will include more individuals working out of their homes and a dramatic increase in the use of robotics and computers. In addition: "Tomorrow's security manager has got to think globally, internationally." Finally, Tyska believes the public should be prepared for massive civil unrest and disorder by the year 2000.

Mallon, 1995 ASIS president and security director for Johnson and Johnson, interviewed by Longmore-Etheridge, offered the following opinions on current trends and his vision of private security's future (Longmore-Etheridge, 1995, p. 58):

- An increase in external consultants and outsourced security forces.
- "As information systems continue to mature, there are going to be benefits to the security business in record keeping, in statistic gathering, in developing models that can provide trend analysis so you can determine where it is you want to place your resources."
- "I see the day when people will use their employee identification card—through perhaps holograms or some other type of microchip implanted in it—to serve as everything from your passport to your medical records."

"To get somewhere, you need to see beyond where you are, and that takes vision," Mallon says. His vision includes "unparalleled educational programs, a greater international role, and a closer relationship with other security associations and law enforcement organizations to strengthen the Society's [ASIS] role as the industry's leadership force into the twenty-first century."

The following text is from an article by Sherry Harowitz (1993), senior editor of *Security Management.**

To survive, security managers are changing both the services they deliver and the methods they use. The new functions may be related, like safety and fire, or they may be totally separate, like managing the company's fleet of cars. Some of these new responsibilities, such as facility management, get their impetus from new technology. Others are a response to the downsizing and consolidation occurring in the corporate world.

The new job of the security director will be to know where the expertise is.

In this new environment, the security manager's ability to be an administrator, to plan, to budget, to find ways to generate revenue, and to communicate with senior management in financial terms will be more important than a knowledge of specifics, such as alarm systems. This new manager will preside over a loose affiliation of consultants that comprise what might be called the virtual security department.

Fay [John Fay, CPP, director of security at British Petroleum Exploration in Houston and editor of *The Encyclopedia of Security Management: Techniques and Technologies*] notes that he has seen other companies merging security with internal auditing, the legal department, human resources, or a department called health, safety, and the environment.

"Many security departments in the future are going to be one-man operations," says Fay. How can one person handle security? Call it the virtual security department. It may involve a security manager who has had some or all of his or her in-house staff stripped away; it could involve a company that merged security with another department such as human resources, which lacks security expertise; or it could involve a mid-sized company that did not previously have security.

In each case, much of what the in-house person does is interconnected with what outsiders do; together they form a security department that does not consist primarily of full-time company personnel. The consultants may do everything from designing to carrying out the security program, and their relationships may exceed traditional boundaries.

Partnering. Horn [John Horn, CPP, managing director of Kroll Associates in New York City] calls them strong relationships. Others call them partnerships. This strategy is an extension of a general business trend toward temporary alliances, which is finding its way into the security industry. As James G. Spencer, vice president of marketing for Casi Rusco, explains, "You can treat outsourcing purely as a contract or as partnering like the virtual corporation."

Companies using this combination of inside and outside resources are still in the minority, but Strauchs [John Strauchs, CPP, president of Systech Group, Inc. in Reston, Virginia], who calls the practice hybridization, says that it's the industry's fastest growing trend. Even so, he adds, "It goes without saying that the management side is going to be the proprietary side."

Maybe not. . . . Meet Bill Nesbitt, CPP, security manager for hire. Nesbitt is principal of the Nesbitt Group, based in Thousand Oaks, California. He serves as the virtual security manager for clients that cannot justify the cost of a full-time, in-house professional. "I come in, develop policies and standards, and monitor the operation," he explains. An in-house supervisor handles the day-to-day operations. Security officers report to the in-house supervisor, but security reports go to Nesbitt and the company's senior management.

Nesbitt's group is itself a virtual corporation. He is loosely affiliated with other people to meet client needs that fall outside of his own expertise.

"The need to have specialists on site is [becoming] obsolete," says Dow Corning's Haywood. "Corporations no longer can afford to have people on staff waiting for something to happen," agrees James Royer, CPP, director of corporate security for FMC Corporation in Chicago.

The evolving corporate structure is also changing the risks security managers must address. Business is global; assets, such as information, must be allowed to flow; and work forces are leaner, not as closely supervised, perhaps less loyal as the result of downsizing, and often temporary or contractual.

Awareness. Employee awareness programs will become increasingly essential as companies operate in teams with less supervision.

Training and awareness are also seen as the best ways to tackle workplace violence, a growing concern. "We are training the human resource people and first-line supervisors and managers for early identification of stresses and referrals to the employee assistance program for intervention," says Royer.

Prescreening. Businesses are also placing more value on prescreening new employees in response to workplace violence, negligent hiring cases, substance abuse, and other problems.

Integrated systems are becoming the norm, with increasing emphasis on what is known as open architecture. Open architecture refers to computer operating systems and software programs that use standard computer language and formats. The use of standardized formats gives the security manager and his or her company the ability to integrate various vendors' products and to upgrade the systems more easily.

Improvements in signal processing and video motion detection, as well as the downsizing of computer chips, are cited as significant developments by many consultants. The simultaneous growth of multimedia systems is opening up new possibilities for moving images, such as digitized photo IDs, over networks rather than coaxial cable. It may even get to the point where a roving security officer can essentially carry the control room on patrol in the form of a hand-held multimedia response terminal, says Chandler [Edmonds H. Chandler, Jr., CPP, chairman of Security By Design in Walnut Creek, California].

CCTV is more efficient, smaller, and less expensive. Advances are being made in color monitors and low-light level cameras. The next hot development will be digital cameras that allow the user to switch cameras by computer without large switching boards, says Bordes [Roy Bordes, president of the Bordes Group in Orlando, Florida].

He notes also that computer software is getting better and is more targeted to security management. Incident tracking and report analysis software is becoming a must as senior management places more pressure on security managers to plan and to justify budget dollars in specific terms, says Grassie [Richard Grassie, CPP, principal of Techmark Security Integration Services in Hanover, Massachusetts].

Looking farther down the road, most security consultants and directors remain skeptical of cutting-edge technologies, although biometrics and smart cards are gaining acceptance on a limited basis. Strauchs, however, sees revolutionary changes on the horizon that will affect both the security technologies that will dominate in the future and the companies that will be delivering those products.

New Players. "Up until now the industry leaders were comparatively small," says Strauchs. "I believe with certainty in the next few years that's going to change, probably dramatically."

Security companies have already been consolidating, and that will continue, but Strauchs is referring to the entrance of new players—mega-corporations the size of IBM. On the positive side, this sea change could drive the industry to a higher plateau in terms of research spending and revenues, but on the downside, he notes that many small companies could be driven out of the business.

Revolutionary Changes. With regard to new technology, "access control and how it's accomplished is going to radically change in the next few years," says Strauchs. "By having some device on your person," he explains, "you will walk up to the building, walk in through some access control device, and go to work. Meanwhile, the system will have tracked you on a square foot by square foot basis."

The technology will also be used to track inventories, a big issue for business. Theft is one concern. In addition, "most large corporations spend huge sums each year buying things they own but can't find," explains Strauchs. Such warehouse management and monitoring is another potential revenue enhancing service that security departments can offer.

All of this type of access control and tracking will be done with what is called radio frequency identification or remote sensing identification systems with per unit costs no higher than today's access control systems. To those who scoff at this futuristic vision, Strauchs says, "The technology is already here. We are waiting for beta tests, second and third generations."

Security managers will benefit from these developments as they struggle with expanding responsibilities and shrinking staffs. They must, however, keep senior management from focusing on technology as the end, rather than the means. That's a constant battle, but the chances of success are improving as security directors are being given more access to corporate decision makers. "Security has made inroads in getting the lines of reporting changed," says Kaufer [Steve C. Kaufer, CPP, president of Inter/Action Associates, Inc., in Palm Springs, California]. The media's focus on security problems has helped. Part of the change may also be due to an emphasis on selling security within the corporation in financial terms. "We've been pounding on the boardroom door for years," says Royer. "It's finally opening, because we are talking their language."

The following text is from an article by Francis Hamit (1994), security and safety consultant, who envisions the future of private security as follows:*

The security officer of the future still will patrol the property he or she protects. Officers will be more capable because of policy decisions that will force better pay, more training and higher standards to become a security officer. Hopefully, people will realize that the term "rent-a-cop" is both a misnomer and a misperception.

Since the beancounters steadfastly resist any attempt to raise these standards, there will be governmental mandates that force them to nationwide. Security officers will have to be classroom trained in fire protection and report writing, their primary functions. They will have to know fire-life safety codes, basic criminal laws and even a bit about investigative techniques (if for no

---

*From Francis Hamit, "The Human-Machine Interface: A New Paradigm." *Security Technology and Design,* June/July 1994. Reprinted by permission.

other reason than that they often are the first at a crime scene and must protect it from contamination).

They also will learn to use a new generation of security technology. Each officer will carry a personal digital communicator, a cellular telephone and a dispatch radio system, perhaps all in the same box. This PDA will be able to read barcodes and/or holograms on key stops, employee ID cards and vehicle passes. The PDA will have resident data entry forms for personnel and truck logs, daily and incident reports, etc.

Officers will enter data either by writing on a screen with a pen stylus or by using an auxiliary keyboard. Daily reports also may be kept vocally, using voice-recognition technology which will convert them to text and also keep an audio record for a limited time.

The closed-circuit TV will continue to extend the officer's range of vision. Night vision technology will turn night into day. The officer will wear a special see-through visor that will relay images gathered by video cameras to a special screen. The images will be high-definition, full-color and recorded by a client server network for review. Patrolling officers will be able to carry the images with them. They will be transmitted to a beltpack receiver by wireless radio using video/data compression. Officers will be able to pan, tilt, rotate and zoom individual images by use of imaging technology that can split a fisheye lens (or any other lens) into four discreet images, flatten the curves and use algorithms instead of servomechanisms to provide full coverage of a scene.

Officers also will be able to talk to each other and to their central dispatch and immediate superiors, either immediately or by leaving voice mail on a multi-layer radio dispatch system. The cellular phone option will be used to summon emergency services such as fire and police. To prevent abuse, most other numbers will be blocked out.

Officers will be able to use cards to hold data and transfer it to workstations, which will be linked by telephone lines to other facilities and to the home office. Special news services and training materials (full multi-media presentations with audio and video) will be played on these terminals. These workstations also will contain work schedules, payroll information, post orders, access codes and lists and as much other information as an officer can use.

Officers also will carry beltpack video recorders and lapel-button video cameras to help them record unexpected events and confrontations. The lenses for these devices will be fixed wide angles that collect a lot of information. Night vision technology will strip away the mask of night. The officer's visor also will display data feeds from the PDA, the security monitoring systems and emergency messages relayed through the radio dispatch/telephone component of the officer's on-body electronics. The PDA may be worn on a wrist cuff so that data can be typed in with the other hand.

Intrusion alarms, motion detectors, card access devices and all other systems that go into a modern building will be monitored, with artificial intelligence decision-making software that will advise an officer when to call for assistance. Buildings will become "intelligent," in that their systems will be integrated and self-monitoring. Security officers, working in their traditional "observe and report" role, will be able to know when to call an operating engineer about a faulty boiler or HVAC system. Emergency plans would be integrated into the system.

Virtual reality computer graphic representations will allow officers to locate the exact place that a fire or other emergency is occurring, and software intelligent assistants will guide their responses, telling them how to handle the immediate emergency while the emergency services are enroute.

Large facilities will use both computer mapping and global positioning systems technology to track officers and vehicles on their rounds. Private services will become part of a larger whole that will provide mutual assistance and intelligence regardless of individual ownership and assigned territories.

The addition of new technologies will not replace security officers, but will empower them and make them valued professionals. It will be a community and a profession rather than just a job. Some will dismiss this as science fiction, but none of these technologies is beyond our reach. In fact, the individual components are currently available. What remains to be done is the creation of standards that will allow them to be integrated into an efficient whole.

Change is hard to manage, and everything seems to be changing very rapidly. Culture shocks are constant, but can be absorbed. Unfortunately, technological sophistication has not been this industry's hallmark, but it now must become our watchword.

Part of the solution is cultural; part is political. We must view government licensing not as unwarranted interference in our business, but as a way to elevate standards. Or we must create a strong association that will endorse and enforce standards, so those who fail or refuse to adhere fail to prosper.

We must raise expectations of the security officers in the field, not just their expectations for a more rewarding job, but our expectations for a higher level of expertise and performance.

Some call this a paradigm shift, because it means change and doing things differently than they have been done. That doesn't mean throwing out what we have, but simply building something new and very powerful.

Putting the technology together is the easy part. The attitudes are really going to need some work. Tell the beancounters that you are using technology to make your people more efficient and to meet a higher standard. They love that kind of thing. When you get the money for the new equipment and the training programs and increased pay, use it to make it happen.

The following view of the future is from an article titled "The Next Generation" by Ira S. Somerson (1995), president of Loss Management Consultants and a member of the ASIS Standing Committee on Safeguarding Proprietary Information.*

[P]rivate industry is changing and security practitioners must change with it. In the future, security practitioners will need to develop more business expertise. Law enforcement skills will still be strategic to security's mission, but most management positions in the security industry will go to highly skilled business executives.

Security professionals must be equally ready to initiate and adapt to change based on the larger forces shaping the future of business. With that in mind, security practitioners should first look at what futurists are saying business will be like in the next twenty years. Here is a brief overview of trends the experts have cited:

- The most obvious trend will be the expansion of global markets. "As companies expand globally, production will continue twenty-four hours a day," wrote John Naisbitt in the September 1992 *Journal of the Conference Board* article "A Brief History of the Future."
- Twenty-first-century business managers will have to adapt to a multinational, multicultural work force. As explained by S. M. Jameel Hasan in the Winter 1992 *Journal of Human Resource Management,* "Instead of making people fit the system, the system must adapt to fit the work force."
- Companies will continue to downsize. Employees must be prepared to integrate within their industry or migrate to different industries to survive.
- Technology is changing how and where people work. As Naisbitt wrote in his 1992 article on the future, "A technological revolution is propelling the world into the Telehumanic Age of the twenty-first century. In the Telehumanic Age, telephones, facsimiles, televisions, and personal computers will merge into multimedia telecenters, which will link households and businesses into a seamless global network."
- A qualified work force will be in scarce supply, forcing companies to look for nontraditional solutions. One result will be an increased need for human resource personnel to find ways to improve the productivity of an aging work force, reconcile the competing demands of work and family, and improve workers' education and skills.
- Small groups of religious extremists will become more prevalent as the year 2000 approaches.
- Biotechnology will become a powerful presence in society and its social and ethical implications will have to be addressed.

What do these trends mean for security executives for the next twenty years?

Global Markets. Security managers can expect their companies to enter markets in many countries around the world, creating the need to secure property, personnel, and information across diverse cultures and circumstances. Conducting a vulnerability analysis to determine the likelihood and impact of various risks is always challenging; the difficulties are multiplied when the study must be conducted globally. The ethics, mores, and political system an organization must deal with change drastically at each international border. The security team must understand each culture and the risks associated with it.

Security personnel must also carefully assess and constantly monitor the changing risks to executives traveling abroad.

Security executives must be able to provide company employees with a wide range of up-to-date and accurate details about the risks in various countries. Quantifying these many risks and offering practical approaches to minimizing them without curtailing overseas business activities will pose a significant challenge.

Staff Reductions. The current business trend is to "rightsize" by combining one staff function with another. This trend will grow significantly in the future. To survive the next twenty years, the security department must absorb other staff functions such as health and safety and facilities management. Otherwise other small business units will gladly absorb the security function.

With that goal in mind, today's security executives must expand their educational and management skills to prepare for other staff or management functions. The broader their business skills and educational background, the better their chances of surviving a "rightsizing."

Workplace Violence. To employees without a psychological support system—family, close friends, or religion—the workplace may serve that purpose for them. The sudden removal of the support system is one of the many suspected causes of violence in the workplace.

Cultural Diversity. Security managers and their staff must learn to interact with diverse cultures in both the company and its client base. Ignorance of different values and mores can cause considerable problems. For example, a security supervisor may think a new employee is being disrespectful because he or she never looks the supervisor in the eye. But if this employee is from a Pacific Rim nation, quite the contrary is probably true, as it is disrespectful in certain Pacific Rim cultures to look directly into the eyes of a person in authority.

Technology. Technology improves the way labor works. It has also raised the skill levels security practitioners need to succeed in their field. Security professionals of the future must be able to work with computers, on which will reside software programs for management tasks and security functions. For example, integrated software packages will control alarms, access, and badges, while management programs will facilitate incident tracking, key control, and accounting. Access to dial up services for research, investigations, and other information needs will also become commonplace in the security manager's office. Future security managers will need to rely on hard data, not intuition.

Home-Based Employment. This new phenomenon, brought about through technological advancement, will also become a major security issue. Home-based employment presents a clear challenge to coping with information security and a whole host of other security risks. It isolates employees from the workplace culture. It could further erode loyalty to the company and complicate attempts to encourage employee attitudes of ownership in corporate objectives. Making employees partners in the security department's mission is difficult in the best of circumstances. Put employees in a vacuum and the challenge increases significantly. Other complications can also result from home-based employment.

The Next Century. It is difficult to study the next century's security issues without looking at trends in religious, ethical, and philosophical thought. As Naisbitt and Patricia Aburdene note in their *Megatrends 2000,* "Religious belief is intensifying worldwide under the gravitational pull of the year 2000."

What impact will this historic influence have on religious and political fanaticism as it relates to security risks in business? Many predict that religion will change dramatically. On the wane during the second half of the twentieth century, religion is having a rebirth, mostly at an orthodox level of adherence. Fundamentalism often leads to terrorism and violence. If fundamentalism increases with the approach of the millennium, terrorism and violence will likely follow.

Ethics programs in business have proven to be effective in reducing incidents of fraud, the abuse of intellectual property, and other corporate crime. To be effective however, these ethics programs must be strongly supported by senior management and implemented in such a way that they become part of the decision-making process.

If the security profession is to make dramatic improvements in the years ahead, security practitioners must reach out to the business community. Security management as a curriculum must be taught as part of a business program. Every resource to make this happen should be expended. The business leaders of tomorrow must hear today what security management is, and how it can positively affect the future of business. Security executives must be knowledgeable not only in security management but also in marketing, computer science, business administration, and related fields.

Security executives of today must also become better risk takers. Too many refuse to push for change. They become comfortable with the status quo and their membership in a unique and exclusive network. This clique is comfortable, but detrimental. Isolation from mainstream business thinking has been the demise of many security departments throughout corporate America.

Companies will face a host of new threats as the future unfolds. Not all of these risks will develop as anticipated, but security practitioners who expand their knowledge and skills, as well as the network of associates with whom they can exchange information, will be best prepared to meet the challenges that lie ahead.

The Perspective of Minot B. Dodson, CCP

The following comments were written exclusively for this textbook by Minot B. Dodson, CCP, executive vice president of operations and training, Pinkerton Security and Investigation Services, and a member of the ASIS Standing Committee on Physical Security.*

*Reprinted by permission.

General. Private security consists of those individuals, organizations and services other than public law enforcement and regulatory agencies that are engaged primarily in preventing and investigating crime, loss or harm to specific individuals, organizations or facilities.

Currently private security is provided in three forms: contract, proprietary and hybrid. Contract security refers to situations where clients/users of guard services hire a guard company to furnish guard services plus administering the guard force. Proprietary security refers to situations where clients/users of guard services hire their own guards and administer the guard force. A clear distinction between these types of security might be out-house versus in-house. Hybrid security services combine contract and proprietary security.

Image. In the security industry, we have an image problem to overcome. We need to point out that the image has changed. We used to call ourselves watchmen, then guards and now security officers—a much better term that fits the situation today.

Many people have the image of the old Rand Report. They have not read or even heard of the Hallcrest Reports published by Bill Cunningham of Hallcrest Systems in 1983 and 1990. The 1973 version of a security officer is an aging male, average age between 45 and 55, with very little education beyond the ninth grade and a few years of experience in security. The reality today, however, is a young person, a high-school graduate with probable college who has met at least minimum training standards. The median age is 31 to 35.

Growth of Security. Twelve years ago the market had become 57 percent larger than public law enforcement (federal, state and local) in terms of annual expenditures. In 1990, a national study addressed the years 1970 through 2000. It confirmed the trends and forecast that they would continue at least another decade.

Private security is now clearly the nation's primary protection resource, outspending public law enforcement by 73 percent ($64 billion versus $35 billion) and employing nearly three times the people, that is 1.6 million versus 625,000. By the year 2000, we expect private security will reach $103 billion and law enforcement $44 billion.

The annual growth rate will be 8 percent for private security, double that of public law enforcement. Private security employment is growing at twice the rate of national employment for many reasons, but probably the two primary causes are (1) loss prevention becomes more important when companies are facing reduced profit margins and (2) the possibility of financial failure. Studies have suggested that as many as one out of three small businesses fail because of employee theft.

Table 23–1 compares the growth and projected growth of the number of contract and proprietary security employees over two decades. The growth will mean that security managers will be expected to have more education

Table 23–1. Growth and Projected Growth of Number of Contract and Proprietary Security Employees

Year	Contract Security Employees	Proprietary Security Employees	Total
1980	556,000	420,000	976,000
1990	965,000	528,000	1,493,000
1993	1,101,000	506,000	1,607,000
2000	1,473,000	410,000	1,883,000

than in the past. Most positions will require Certified Protection Professionals. Relevant bachelor degrees will be mandatory. Holders of master degrees will receive premium opportunities. Degreed security managers with formal education in business will be in demand.

$64-billion Business. As mentioned, private security for 1993 is a $64-billion business. Table 23–2 shows where these revenues are expended. By the year 2000 we expect this to be $103 billion. The figure does not include equipment for 1993 which was at $15 billion and estimated to be $24 billion in 2000.

In Summary. The security industry is not only a fast-growing business—it is *big* business.

The U.S. security industry, as a whole, continues to be one of the fastest growing sectors of the economy with more than 10,000 guard companies and 1.6 million security officers. Adding the related work areas of alarms, investigations and the like results in a 64-billion-dollar industry.

Table 23–2. Private Security Revenues/Expenditures, 1993

Segment	Annual Revenue/Expenditure
Armored car	$ 848,500,000
Alarm companies	6,204,400,000
Contract guard	12,761,300,000
Private investigators	3,065,500,000
Consultants/Engineers	478,700,000
Locksmiths	3,673,500,000
Manufacturers and distributors	18,960,500,000
Other	4,456,300,000
Proprietary security	13,970,500,000
Total	$64,419,200,000

The Perspective of Michael E. Goodboe, CCP

This perspective was also written exclusively for this textbook by Michael E. Goodboe, Vice President of Training, Wackenhut Training Institute, member of the State of Florida Investigations, Recovery and Private Security Council and associate member of the National Association of Security and Investigative Regulators.*

The security industry is changing in many regards (Freedonia Group, 1994). It is far more professional than it was even five years ago. Many entry-level security officers come to us with college degrees. They also come to us with an expectation that they will be put in responsible positions and held accountable. In my own tenure as head of Wackenhut training which spans more than 11 years, I find that they increasingly expect more from training and from their leadership. None of this should come as a surprise. In contrast, a very high percentage of applicants come to us poorly educated, even though they have high school diplomas. The real problem is that they lack basic skills. This, too, impacts any number of variables linked to the industry. The issue of training will be discussed in greater depth later.

Carnevale (1991), Peters (1992) and others have documented a monumental shift of jobs to the service sector. Indeed, *The Hallcrest Report II* (Cunningham, Strauchs and Van Meter, 1990) projects that, in terms of sheer numbers of employees, private security will outnumber law enforcement by a ratio of three to one as we move into the next millennium. We feel the impact of change not only from a standpoint of demographics but from technology as well. Certainly, the old days of the *night watchman* are gone forever.

As private security grows and evolves professionally, a number of concerns make their presence felt: growth, privatization, globalization, diversity, change and training.

Growth. The private security industry is experiencing exponential growth. The Freedonia Group (1994) projects worldwide increase of more than 8 percent per year through 1998. The Wackenhut Corporation, one of the four major players in the guard industry (Freedonia, 1994), is celebrating its 40th anniversary this year. In a relatively small number of years, Wackenhut has grown to employ some 50,000 people worldwide.

New opportunities are emerging in unexpected places such as the former Soviet Union, where Wackenhut has opened offices, and in the Peoples Republic of China. This demand is fueled by a number of factors such as a perceived or actual increase in crime, reduced budgets for traditional law enforcement, increasing acceptance of the security industry by the public and technological advances such as satellite tracking of cargo movements, a service provided by security companies.

---

*Reprinted by permission.

Privatization. There is a decided trend in the United States and abroad to privatize former government domains such as prisons, security at military and governmental installations and even local police forces (Freedonia, 1994; Cunningham et al., 1990). Just recently, Wackenhut Corrections Corporation opened its 22nd detention facility. The corrections business represents an expansion into new areas for private security.

Globalization of the Security Market. The very things that propel an increase in the need for private security in the United States correspondingly prompt a similar increase abroad. As this is happening, the world is becoming smaller. Thus, the security market is largely becoming a global one. Wackenhut, for example, has affiliates in 54 nations of the world.

Diversity. Numerous studies indicate that the U.S. work force will become highly diverse in the future. Clearly, there are signs of increasing diversity now. Carnevale (1992) and the American Society for Training and Development tell us that the work force of the future in the U.S. services sector, hence in private security, will most likely be composed of older men, immigrants and females. The average age of the American worker is approaching 40 (Johnston and Packer, 1987). As you conjure up an image of the typical "security officer," this should certainly challenge your imagination. Diversity is a strength; nevertheless, it does not come without challenge. Most notably, there is ample indication that the entry-level worker will be foreign born.

Change. Peters (1992) characterizes the coming world market as one replete with change. Organizations that will survive are those that are able to adapt to recurring change. There is ample indication that some industries, private security among them, are ill-equipped to do this precisely because of their conservative nature (Barr and Barr, 1989; Bridges, 1992). Therefore, a major challenge for the future will be predicting and dealing with change—in any number of contexts. The history of The Wackenhut Corporation, however, suggests that the company deals well, though predictably uncomfortably, with change (Minahan, 1994).

Training. As stated, there is a decided need to improve the education and skills of security providers, particularly at the entry level, a condition we share with industry in general. The security industry is just beginning to recognize this need, though Wackenhut as a company has long recognized it. We currently are researching learning styles of security officers and their supervisors in an effort to design better and more effective programs for them. (This research is unparalleled in the industry though long overdue.) Additionally, we have developed self-directed learning programs that enhance the generic training common to the industry. For example:

- *The Wackenhut Leadership Manual* is a survey course in basic management interpreted within the context of industrial security. Participants in this program are all volunteers who get continuing education units (CEUs) or continuing professional education (CPE) credits from the University of Maryland University College.

- *The Professional Development Program* is available for security officers and supervisors. This employs our 84 workbooks and 56 lesson plans which are available to any team member for study or reference. These programs also earn CEUs or CPEs from UM/UC.
- The Wackenhut Corporate Library is a vast collection of security-related books, videotapes, audiotapes and learning programs available to company trainers, most of whom are certified through our instructor certification process.
- Wackenhut is currently using the Myers-Briggs Type Indicator (MBTI) model to assess and address individual training needs at corporate group training sessions. The MBTI is ideal for assessing any number of training-related issues (McCaulley and Natter, 1980; Hammer, 1993). The MBTI is widely used in the *Fortune* 1000 group though it is my impression that we are the only security company using it.

Training is an issue closely linked to the integrity, survival and growth of the security industry over the long term.

> The future is not a result of choices among alternative paths offered by the present, but a place that is created—created first in mind and will, created next in activity.
>
> The future is not some place we are going to, but one we are creating. The paths are not to be found, but made, and the activity of making them changes both the maker and the destination.
>
> —John Schaar

Security professionals must learn to move with the flow of society's needs and constantly improve services. Going against the tide will result in adversity, conflict and frustration. Continual buffeting leads to emotional, mental and physical stress, and ultimately to personal and organizational breakdowns.

SUMMARY

Change is inevitable. View it as opportunity. Trends in the security profession include growth, outsourcing, privatization, globalization and an emphasis on training and professionalization of the field, including a professional image.

APPLICATION

You are giving a lecture at the local university to a class of students interested in pursuing a career in private security. How would you answer the following questions the students have written down and handed to you before your lecture?

1. What are some of the forecasts of the future for private security?

2. What public police tasks will be relegated to private security in the future?

3. What is the future of the alarm industry?

DISCUSSION QUESTIONS

1. What skills and knowledge would an individual need to find opportunities in the private security field?
2. To ensure upward mobility in a private security agency, what characteristics and experiences should be acquired?
3. What is your understanding of the word *outsourcing*?
4. What dramatic changes in society will affect the nature of private security?
5. The private security experts are predicting that "new players" will enter the field of private security in the future. Who are they talking about?

REFERENCES

"APEC II Goes West." *Dynamics,* September/October 1991, pp. 14–15.

Arko, Robert L. "Contract Security Rolls into the Transit Industry." *Security Management,* July 1992, pp. 26–31.

Band, William A. "Making Peace with Change." *Security Management,* March 1995, pp. 21–22.

Barr, L. and Barr, N. *The Leadership Equation*. Austin, TX: Eakin Press, 1989.

Barron, Ted P. "Anatomy of a Redesign." *Security Management,* March 1993, pp. 25–33.

Bridges, W. *Character of Organizations*. Palo Alto, CA: Consulting Psychologists Press, Inc., 1992.

Carnevale, A. P. *America and the New Security*. Washington, DC: Employment and Training Administration, U.S. Department of Labor, 1991.

Collins, Pam. "Big Plan on Campus." *Security Management,* March 1992, pp. 27–30.

Cunningham, William C., Strauchs, John J., and Van Meter, Clifford W. *Private Security Trends–1970–2000: The Hallcrest Report II.* Stoneham, MA: Butterworth-Heinemann, 1990.

Enright, John. "Change and Resilience." In *The Leader Manager,* Eden Prairie, MN: Wilson Learning Corporation, 1984, pp. 59–73.

Freedonia Group. *Freedonia Study #608: World Security Services.* Cleveland, OH: Freedonia Group, 1994.

Goldberg, Joel A. "Security's Challenges: A Roundtable Discussion." *Security Management,* July 1994, pp. 40–44.

Hamit, Francis. "The Human-Machine Interface: A New Paradigm." *Security Technology and Design,* June/July 1994, pp. 82–83.

Hammer, A. *Introduction to Type and Careers.* Palo Alto, CA: Consulting Psychologists Press, Inc., 1993.

Harowitz, Sherry L. "Reengineering Security's Role." *Security Management,* November 1993, pp. 37–45.

Johnston, W. and Packer, A. *Workforce 2000.* Indianapolis, IN: Hudson Institute, 1987.

Joint Security Commission. "Redefining Security. Part I—Approaching the Next Century." *Security Concepts,* July 1994, pp. 8, 23.

Kohr, Robert L. "Assessing the State of Hotel Security in the '90s." *Security Technology and Design,* May 1994, pp. 26–31.

LeDoux, Darryl T. "Exploding the Myths of Contract Security." *Security Management,* January 1995, pp. 37–39.

Longmore-Etheridge, Ann. "A Life of Learning: A Conversation with the 1995 ASIS President." *Security Management,* January 1995, pp. 55–58.

McCaulley, M. and Natter, F. *Psychological (Myers-Briggs) Type Differences in Education.* Gainesville, FL: Center for Applications of Psychological Type, Inc., 1980.

Minahan, J. *The Quiet American: A Biography of George R. Wackenhut.* Westport, CT: International Publishing Group, 1994.

Peters, T. *Liberation Management.* New York: Alfred A. Knopf, 1992.

"Security/Loss Prevention Can Pay Well." *Security Concepts,* July 1994, p. 9.

Sherwood, J. L. "Beyond the Call of Duty: Hospital Security in the '90s." *Security Concepts,* March 1994, pp. 1–2.

Somerson, Ira. S. "The Next Generation." *Security Management,* January 1995, pp. 28–30.

Sundberg, Edward A. "Is the Security Guard Industry Ready for Its Future?" *Security Management,* August 1994, pp. 132–33.

APPENDIX A

SITE SECURITY EVALUATION*

A site security survey is similar to a physical exam conducted by a doctor, in that he/she is attempting to discern what, if anything, is wrong with the patient before prescribing any course of treatment or medicine. The survey form that follows is by no means the work of a single individual, the questions posed having come from a multitude of sources over a period in excess of fifteen years. This is not to say the form is old, because it is reviewed on a regular basis, questions added as new areas, such as violence in the workplace, surface and impact the Security Profession.

Administrative/General Data

1. Site:
Function:
Address:
Telephone No.:
Manager:
Assistant Manager:
Human Resources Superintendent:
Control Superintendent:
Number of Employees:
Area covered (acres):
Operating hours:
Products Manufactured:

2. Review last finance department audit of this site for any exceptions relating to security. What action(s) has been taken relative to these exceptions?

3. Since the last survey has the site terminated anyone for theft, fraud, etc., or drug related activities?

4. Relative to the preceding, have any investigations been conducted on the site since the last survey?

5. Survey should include review of theft reports prepared by this site for an appropriate period of time. Where appropriate, has corrective action been taken? Do theft reports reflect patterns, trends, or particular problems at this location?

---

*SOURCE: Thomas W. Leo, "Site Security Evaluation." *Security Concepts,* September 1994, pp. 11, 23, 30. Thomas W. Leo, CPP, formerly a member of the Corporate Security staff of DuPont in Wilmington, DE, is a member of the board of directors of The American Society for Industrial Security. Reprinted by permission.

6. What does site management regard as the most prevalent or serious security problem?

7. Has the person responsible for day-to-day site security received any formal training in the subject; and if so, what?

8. What are the site's most theft attractive assets?

9. Have you under your control (including in your manufacturing process) any precious metals, controlled substances, precursor chemicals, or anything else readily convertible to cash on the illicit market?

10. Does the site have the latest revision of the Precursor Chemical List?

11. Identify off-site locations which should be included in survey, to include warehouses, river pumping stations, outflow lines, well-heads, purchase power substations, magazines, etc.

12. Does the site have a security committee? Who are the members, do they rotate, and how often do they meet?

13. Is the site properly posted with respect to search and trespass?

14. What police agency has jurisdiction over the site? Does the plant have a dedicated phone line to this agency? Has management established a continuing relationship with this agency? Have they been called for in the recent past; and if so, what has been their response? Do they normally include any of our perimeter in their patrols? If requested, would they?

15. Are police emergency numbers readily available to plant security personnel?

16. Is information readily available on how to reach the proper agency for assistance with illegal narcotics, bomb threats, obscene calls, etc.?

17. Do you have a policy of reporting identifiable items of stolen property to the local police?

18. Does your law enforcement agency have a Crime Prevention Unit qualified to speak on such topics as drug usage, personal and residential security and highway safety?

Comments

External Security

Lighting Evaluation

19. Is the manufacturing/operations area perimeter adequately lighted?

20. Is site exterior lighting checked on a regular basis to be certain it is functioning properly? How frequently and by whom?

21. Is lighting compatible with CCTV?

22. Is power supply adequately protected?

23. Is lighting properly maintained and cleaned?

24. Are sensitive areas (parking lots, computer areas, stores, tool rooms, shipping/receiving areas) adequately lighted?

Comments

Security Force

25. Proprietary or Contract? If contract, name of agency and telephone number. If proprietary, how are personnel selected? Security Officer pay rate? Site billing rate?

26. Are posts rotated; what is the frequency?

27. How many officers per shift?

28a. What type of training and supervision do officers receive?

28b. Where a solitary security officer is on duty after normal business hours, is there a procedure in place requiring that individual to call, or be called, to verify his/her well-being?

28c. Do security officers possess any type of defensive weapons such as mace, nightsticks, etc.? If so, is there a written policy in effect governing their use? Have officers received training in their use? Company policy prohibits lethal weapons except on specific authorization of Director of Corporate Security.

29. Are security facilities adequate and are unauthorized people kept out of the gatehouse(s)?

30. Is a current list of authorized signatures (for passes, etc.) maintained at the gatehouse? Who monitors property passes for returnable items?

31. Is an incident log maintained?

32. Is the log reviewed daily and by whom?

33. Are security personnel utilized for non-security related duties?

34. Does site utilize photo I.D. cards? Who administers it? Are all employees required to show a photo I.D. card to security personnel upon entry? Is duplicate copy kept in security file?

35. Does facility have on-site parking? Are vehicles registered? Can an individual reach a vehicle without passing a guard?

36. If needed, does the security force have a properly equipped and maintained patrol vehicle?

37. Does the site have a receptionist in place at all times? Are visitors required to sign in? Are they provided with an identifying badge, and if non-employees, escorted while on site? Is visitor identification verified, e.g., vending company I.D., etc.?

Comments

Perimeter Protection

38. Is the site completely fenced? Describe type of fencing.

39. Is it secure against the ground especially on uneven terrain? Are there rivers, ponds, trees, buildings or other structures on the perimeter that can be utilized to achieve unauthorized entry? Are articles susceptible to theft stored close to the fence?

40. Is a 10′ clear zone maintained around the entire perimeter, on each side of the fence, where physically possible?

41. If outside building walls form part of the perimeter, are all doors and windows secured against surreptitious entry? Can entry be achieved via the roof? Can hinge pins be removed from doors? Are all entry/egress points manned when opened? Is fence line patrolled? If so, how often? By vehicle or on foot?

Comments

Internal Security

Lock/Key Control

42. With whom does physical and administrative key control rest?

43. Describe control of keys, including issuance to non-personnel.

44. Is a master key system in use? How many grandmasters/master keys have been issued?

45. Is a cross control system (name versus key number) in use? What type of numbering system is in use? Is the entire system, including blanks, inventoried on a regular basis?

46. Are the keys stamped "Do Not Duplicate"?

47. What level of management authorization is required for issuance of keys?

48. Are plant keys, particularly masters, permitted to be taken home? Are keys signed in/out in a daily log?

49. Are locks rotated?

50. How long has the present lock/key system been in use?

51. Have keys been reported lost?

52. Is a record of locations of safes and their combinations maintained?

53. How frequently are combinations changed?

Comments

Alarms and Electronics

54. Is an electronic security alarm system in use here?

55. Is a card access system in use here?

56. Do alarms terminate on the site or at an outside central station?

57. Who responds to alarms? Has service/response been satisfactory?

58. Does the site have a radio network? Separate frequency for security? Battery back-up?

59. Are portable radios, chargers and cellular phones properly secured when not in use?

Comments

Theft Control Procedures

60. Does this location have a program of pedestrian inspections?

61. What is the frequency of these inspections?

62. Does this location have a vehicular inspection program? If so, briefly describe procedures.

63. Does this location have a locker inspection program? If so, briefly describe procedures.

64. Does the site have a policy of marking theft sensitive items (TSI) (such as PCs, VCRs, electronic scales and hand tools) as company property? Describe the program. Is someone responsible for accountability of all TSI at the end of the day? Who maintains the list of theft sensitive items?

65. Are serial numbers of all items recorded?

66. In the event of theft, is this information furnished to the police for identification purposes in the event of subsequent recovery?

67. Are items susceptible to theft left out in the open (e.g., unfenced laydown areas)?

68. Are trash receptacles periodically inspected by supervision to determine whether items of value may be removed from the site via them?

69. Can the trash receptacles be locked at night?

70. Is the trash truck followed to the dump on a random basis? Is what is dumped checked to be certain that nothing of value, including documents, is deposited, possibly for later pickup?

71. Is scrap metal segregated by type? Does the site have a salvage removal program? Are printer sequentially numbered scrap passes utilized? Does security inspect scrap items versus the pass?

72. Describe the site's toolcrib system.

73. What is the procedure during off hours?

74. Are all stores attended when open? What is the procedure for admittance when no attendant is present?

75. Is access to telephone switching equipment (frame room) restricted?

76. Are shipping/receiving functions performed from the same dock?

77. Does that area have secure facilities (lockable cages) for high value items?

78. Are these high value items checked/inventoried regularly?

79. Are other than shipping/receiving personnel permitted in the area?

80. Has a restricted waiting area been designated for drivers?

81. Are seals used?

82. Is documentation for Federal Express and UPS shipments spot checked, audited?

83. Is there a truck or railroad scale on site? Is it operable or accessible to non-company personnel? How is the operation supervised?

84. Do you utilize printer sequentially numbered weight tickets?

85. Who performs custodial services?

86. Are they bonded?

87. Are they required to wear ID badges?

88. Which areas are serviced?

89. Are they inspected by guards as they leave? Are the janitors' vehicles inspected on the way off the site?

90. Do the janitors have access to restricted or sensitive areas (shipping/receiving, stores, tools, computers)?

91. Are the janitors permitted to take keys off the site with them?

92. How much cash is kept on site? Describe cashier's operation.

93. Where are checks held?

94. Considering the products you manufacture, the required raw materials or intermediates, the neighborhood the site is located in, and the amount of cash on site, how do you assess your vulnerability to robbery?

95. Is there a monitoring procedure for fuel consumption? Gasoline and diesel?

96. Is fuel stored on site? If so, can unauthorized people access it?

Comments

Proprietary Information

97a. Is there proprietary data on site; and if so, in what form?

97b. Has critical information been identified?

97c. How vulnerable is this information to unauthorized access and reproduction?

97d. Have the owners, custodians, or security people identified any potential threat or possible adversaries vis-a-vis this information?

98. Describe site's PIP (Proprietary Information Protection) program.

99. Does the site have a PIP Committee?

100. Are PIP posters in evidence?

101a. Is copying equipment controlled and locked after hours, or can anyone use it?

101b. Are facsimile machines located behind lockable doors so messages received after hours are not available to unauthorized persons?

101c. If you have reproducing blackboards (whiteboards), are they the type that store information in memory and copy from that memory, or do they copy on command and then automatically erase? If they copy from memory, does someone ascertain that the memory has been cleared when that information is no longer needed?

102. Are PIP inspections made during off hours?

103a. Do you have a specific method for destroying sensitive proprietary information? If so, what is it?

103b. Is anyone at this site involved in the acquisition of competitive intelligence? If so, who?

104a. Does the site have a clean desk policy?

104b. What method do you use to disseminate the company's nondisclosure (PIP) policy to employees? To contractors?

104c. How does the site destroy proprietary, confidential documents? If a contractor is used, has the firm been investigated to determine that they actually do what they advertise they do? Has their truck been followed to verify this?

Comments

Personnel Security

105. Are background checks conducted prior to employment?

106. Are previous employment dates verified?

107. Are personnel and medical records properly safeguarded?

108. Is security included in the new hire orientation?

109. Is company property (credit cards, I.D., keys, PCs) retrieved during exit interviews?

Comments

Emergency Procedures

110. Do you have a current bomb threat procedure?

111. Who implements it (searches area)?

112. Does the procedure include a checklist for the switchboard operator?

113. Is there a contingency plan for acts of violence?

114. Does the site have an up-to-date strike plan?

115. If personnel are required to work alone, are they periodically checked?

116a. Identify the most critical areas on the site, the disruption of which could cause the plant to shut down.

116b. Have any steps been taken to protect or at least alarm these areas against unauthorized entry or trespass?

117. Has an individual been identified whose job it will be to interface with the media in an emergency/disaster situation?

Comments

Electronic Information/Date Security

118. Has the site received a copy of Electronic Information Security (ELIS) standards? Are you working toward complete implementation?

119. Does a member of management review computer audit trails for evidence of hacking attempts and/or improper use of DP facilities by employees? Has anyone been terminated for abuse/improper use of data processing function/systems since the last survey?

120. Are records kept that will ensure that a person cannot clear a site (transfer, etc.) with company property (PC, etc.) in his/her possession?

121a. Are site employees aware of rules/limitations relative to reproducing copyrighted or licensed software?

121b. Have you reviewed all PCs to insure all software is covered by appropriate licenses?

121c. Are all personnel aware of the prohibition against introducing outside (possibly contaminated) software into company systems?

122. Is physical access to the data center restricted? Locked when not in use? Visited by patrolling guards?

123a. Are terminated employees immediately separated from electronic information?

123b. Are their passwords/access ability invalidated?

124. Is tape library maintained physically separate from machine room?

125. Are laptop PCs locked in cabinets/closets when not in use? Are they branded/marked?

126. Are users aware of good electronic information security practices and the ramifications of not following them? Do users know where to go for help?

127. Are passwords checked for conformity with ELIS Standards regarding structure, minimum length, and expiration? Do users write down their passwords or share them with other users?

128. Have all critical applications been included in a disaster recovery plan and has that plan been tested? Do PC owners back up their data on a regular basis consistent with the value of their data?

129. Do users leave their terminals/PCs "in session" while they are out of the office? Is there confidential information left on the screen?

130. Do travelers leave portable PCs unattended in their hotel rooms? Is confidential information displayed on the screen of portable PCs in public locations?

131. Do application programmers (those who maintain/change an application's source code) have the system access to install revised code in a production environment?

132. Do users of cellular phones discuss confidential information on them? Do users access their voice mail via cellular phone?

133. Are requests for E-mail accounts on company computers for non-employees evaluated for suitability of MCI mail instead? Are accounts for non-employees on company computers documented using ELIS Form 0002?

134. Are computer rooms, telecom rooms, wiring closets, PBX [private branch exchange] rooms, etc., locked at all times? Are desktop computing systems protected from physical removal?

135. Are all electronic documents older than three years destroyed? Are documents classified other than for "Internal Use Only" marked with the proper classification?

Comments

136. What overall security improvements do you feel could be made at this location? What would you like to see done here to enhance security?

137. What can we in corporate security do to help you in the security field?

APPENDIX B

TRAINING REQUIREMENTS STATE BY STATE*

Since there are no federal requirements for security officer training, some states have taken the initiative in instituting their own. Certain states, such as North Dakota and Oklahoma, have taken the responsibility quite seriously; others have not. Have a look and see if your state is aiding in—or neglecting—the professionalization of today's security officers. The following training requirements are reprinted with permission from *The Security Letter Source Book, 1990–1991*. The *Source Book* is published by *Security Letter* and distributed by Butterworth-Heinemann, 80 Montvale Ave., Stoneham, MA 02180. The list was compiled by Robert McCrie, CPP, publisher/editor; Diane Botnick, associate editor; and Fulvia Madia, editorial assistant.

Note: No data is available for Alabama, Colorado, Idaho, Kansas, Mississippi, Missouri, Nebraska, Oregon, Puerto Rico, South Dakota, Washington, and Wyoming.

Alaska

Armed and unarmed: eight-hour preassignment training on duties for temporary permit; additional 40 hours of in-service training within six months of hiring on relevant laws, fire prevention, first aid, and patrol techniques. Annual eight-hour refresher course on these topics. Armed: eight-hour preassignment training in weapons use and pertinent laws.

Arizona

No fixed number of hours. Guard firms' training curricula must be approved for agency license.

Arkansas

Armed and unarmed: eight-hour training course and exam on legal authority, act, and field note taking and report writing; renewal two-hour refresher course on act, two-hour course on legal authority, and exam within 60 days of expiration. Armed: four hours of firearms training on legal limitations, weapons safety, marksmanship, and range firing; minimum score of 60 percent on range. Yearly renewal—firearms training and qualification requirements as specified.

*© 1991 American Society for Industrial Security, 1655 N. Fort Myer Drive, Suite 1200, Arlington, VA 22209. Reprinted with permission from the March 1991 issue of *Security Management* Magazine.

California

Armed and unarmed: 20-hour course on powers of arrest, 100 percent score on open-book exam. Armed: 14 hours of firearms training; 85 percent minimum score on written test; eight-hour range instruction.

Connecticut

Armed: seven hours of state police course and certified course for firearm permit ($25 fee for five-year permit).

Delaware

None required for unarmed. Armed: Guards must be certified by a certified instructor.

District of Columbia

Armed: four hours of classroom preassignment training; range qualification.

Florida

Armed: 16 hours of basic training at approved school. Must pass course exam with 70 percent score. Regulations detail topics, hours, and classroom space/student.

Georgia

Minimum eight hours of classroom instruction covering duties, functions, legal authority, fire prevention and control, familiarity with act, regulations, and first aid. Armed: minimum 12 hours of classroom instruction; eight hours of basic program (above) and one hour each in laws of arrest, search and seizure, mechanics of arrest, and misdemeanors and felonies. Classroom instruction on weapons use, firearm range instruction, and familiarization course for special weapons.

Hawaii

Armed: eight hours of preassignment training.

Illinois

Armed and unarmed: minimum 20 hours of basic classroom training; employer must verify successful completion. Armed: 20 hours of firearms training with practice firing on range, firearms qualification course.

Indiana

None required.

Iowa

Armed: Four-hour firearms course through county sheriff's office. On-campus requirements: successfully complete approved firearms training program, possess weapons permit, and have sworn affidavit from employer stating duties and justification. Sheriff can require additional firearms training.

Kentucky

(Special law enforcement officer only.) Eighty hours of approved program on related laws or minimum one-year, full-time employment as sworn public peace officer or successfully completed, approved exams on related subject matter. Must demonstrate proficiency in firearms safety and use and first aid. Exam fee $15; firearms exam fee $20; "reasonable fee" to cover training costs of program.

Louisiana

Armed and unarmed: eight hours of classroom instruction within 30 days of hiring on rules, regulations, law, legal powers, first aid, general duties, and report writing. Additional eight hours within six months in approved program taught by certified instructor. Exams given after each eight-hour segment. Armed: additional eight hours of preassignment firearm course on handgun safety and firing and firing range qualification with annual four-hour refresher courses, firearms instruction, and marksmanship qualification. Must score 60 percent to qualify, 150/250 to pass course. (Detailed basic and armed training manuals available.)

Maine

None required.

Maryland

None required for unarmed. Armed: eight hours of preassignment training.

Massachusetts

None required.

Michigan

None required despite legislative attempts.

Minnesota

Bill introduced in 1989 state legislature addressed training for armed and unarmed guards and proprietary employees. No action to date.

Montana

None required for unarmed. Armed: training by approved instructor. Minimum 10 hours of training on safety, handling, liability, and statutes. Seventy percent score on firearms safety and proficiency test—written exam and combat shooting course with authorized firearm. Demonstration of reasonable competence in firearm skill as determined by certified instructor. Registration based on satisfactory completion of certified combat shooting course annually.

Nevada

None required for unarmed. Armed: six hours of classroom instruction, exam; firing range, shooting minimum of 50 rounds with 70 minimum score.

New Hampshire

None required for unarmed. Armed: four hours of classroom and range qualification; instruction to include firearms techniques, safety, and laws on use of deadly force. Minimum qualification score of 75 percent for practical police course or tactical revolver course, shotgun familiarization course if used.

New Jersey

None required for unarmed. Armed: number of hours of training not specified.

New Mexico

None required for unarmed. Armed: Minimum 20 hours—four hours of classroom training related to legal aspects of use of deadly force, 16 hours on the range. Additional four-hour shotgun qualification course if shotgun carried. Ten-hour yearly requalification course—two hours of classroom and eight hours of range instruction program specified.

New York

None required. Bills now in committee would require training for armed and unarmed guards.

North Carolina

None for unarmed guards. Armed: four hours of classroom training by certified trainer on legal limits on handgun use, knowledge of act, range firing, and procedure and safety. Must fire 70 percent score on approved target course. Annual renewal includes complete refresher course and requalification on prescribed range firing. Guard agencies or in-house departments may qualify as training institutions if programs include required courses taught by approved instructors.

North Dakota

Three levels:

Apprentice: Minimum 16 hours of classroom instruction on security services, first aid, and other training employer deems necessary for assignment. Minimum 16 hours of field training under supervision of qualified security officer before working unsupervised.

Security officer: After 1,000 hours and before 2,000 hours as active apprentice, individual applies for registration as private security officer that is contingent on training—32 hours of classroom instruction, which includes required curriculum and other training employer deems necessary.

Commissioned security officer: Requires 4,000 hours of active service as security officer and additional 80 hours of classroom instruction based on suggested curricula.

Ohio

None required for unarmed guards. Armed: as of 1986, must satisfactorily complete firearms basic training program, including 20 hours of handgun training and five hours of training in use of other firearms if used or authorized equivalent training or former peace officer training. Must requalify annually on firearms range.

Oklahoma

Private security division's motto: "Professionalism Through Training." Second only to North Dakota in length of training. Three courses of instruction:

I. Basic, 22 hours of instruction related to general private security tasks.

II. Security guard, 18 hours of instruction related to tasks of unarmed guards.

IV. Firearms, phases I and II, plus 24 hours of training in care, handling, and firing of revolvers and shotguns (eight hours of classroom, 16 hours of range).

Armed: I, II, IV—64 hours for Armed Security Guard Training Course at approved schools. Specifies student-instructor ratios of 30:1 (5:1 for range) and instructor qualifications and facilities standards (for example, 10 sq. ft./student). During phase IV, must take Minnesota Multiphasic Personality Inventory or approved equivalent given by qualified person and evaluated by licensed psychologist chosen and paid for by student.

Pennsylvania

Armed: 40-hour basic training course; eight hours of additional training required for five-year license renewal.

Rhode Island

None required for unarmed. Armed: range test required with minimum score of 195/300.

South Carolina

Unarmed: eight hours of instruction. Armed: 12 hours of preassignment instruction, including classroom instruction.

Tennessee

Completed within 30 days of employment, basic four-hour course on general training by certified trainer. Armed: eight more hours of classroom firearm training—four hours on range and marksmanship training—with 75 percent score on silhouette target course. Renewal: four-hour refresher training, requalification in firearm use with minimum 75 percent score. Requirements given for certified trainers—contractor proprietary employee.

Texas

None required for unarmed. Armed: 30-hour basic training program, including minimum five hours on firearms.

Utah

Model programs provided in rules. Unarmed: 12 hours of training prior to application—minimum six hours of classroom instruction, six hours of on-the-job training working unarmed and accompanied by licensed guard. Armed: 12 hours of preassignment training as for unarmed guard. Twelve hours of firearms instruction with certificate as proof: four hours of classroom, eight hours of range experience with weapon to be used on duty. Must pass range test with 70 percent score. Renewal: eight hours of in-service training and same firearm instruction as required for original license.

Vermont

None required for unarmed. Armed: 16 hours of preassignment classroom instruction program to stress safe and proper use and handling of firearms and dogs, legal responsibility for improper or negligent use of either. NRA-approved police combat or security firing course using silhouette targets. Dog handlers: 16 hours of classroom and practical exercise training, additional four hours of firearm training if armed. Training waived with proof of equivalent training elsewhere.

Virginia

At agent's discretion for unarmed guards; none required. Armed: training certification of firearm classroom training and range firing for specific weapon; two-year firearm certification $50; renewal $15. Must carry registration card while on duty.

West Virginia

None required.

Wisconsin

None required for unarmed. Armed: Wisconsin Department of Justice course prescribed with certified trainer; annual recertification.

Academic Programs in Security and Loss Prevention*

State	Institution	City	Offerings
ALABAMA	Athens State College	Athens	Course(s)
	Auburn University	Auburn	BS/MS
	Chattahoochee Valley Community College	Phenix City	AAS
	Community College of the Air Force	Maxwell AFB, Montgomery	AA
	Jacksonville State University	Jacksonville	Course(s)
	Jefferson State Junior College	Birmingham	Course(s)
	Samford University	Birmingham	Course(s)
	Troy State University	Troy	Course(s)
	Troy State University—Dothan	Dothan	Course(s)
	University of Alabama	University	Course(s)
	University of Alabama at Birmingham	Birmingham	Course(s)
	University of Alabama in Huntsville	Huntsville	Course(s)
	University of Alabama	Mobile	Course(s)
	University of North Alabama	Florence	Course(s)
	University of South Alabama	Mobile	Course(s)
	Wallace State Community College	Henceville	Course(s)
ALASKA	University of Alaska	Fairbanks	BS
ARIZONA	Cochise College	Douglas	Course(s)
	Maricopa Technical Community College	Phoenix	Course(s)
	Northern Arizona University	Flagstaff	BS/MS
	Phoenix College	Phoenix	Course(s)
	Scottsdale Community College	Scottsdale	Course(s)
ARKANSAS	Arkansas Technical University	Russellville	Course(s)
	University of Arkansas at Fayetteville	Fayetteville	Course(s)
	University of Arkansas at Pine Bluff	Pine Bluff	Course(s)
CALIFORNIA	Antelope Valley College	Lancaster	Course(s)
	Barstow College	Barstow	Cert.
	Cabrillo College	Aptos	Course(s)

*This list of colleges and universities that offer academic programs undoubtedly contains errors and omissions. Please report any needed corrections to the authors. Those corrections will be incorporated into later editions of this text.

SOURCE: *Introduction to Private Security,* by H. W. Timm and K. E. Christian. Copyright © 1991 by Wadsworth, Inc. Reprinted by permission of Brooks/Cole Publishing Company, Pacific Grove, CA 93950.

State	Institution	City	Offerings
	California State College	Bakersfield	University
	California State University, Fresno	Fresno	Course(s)
	California State University, Long Beach	Long Beach	BS/MS
	California State University, Los Angeles	Los Angeles	Course(s)
	California State University, Sacramento	Sacramento	Course(s)
	California State University, San Bernadino	San Bernadino	Course(s)
	Cerritos College	Norwalk	Cert./AA
	Chabot College	Hayward	Cert.
	Coleman College	La Mesa	Course(s)
	College of Marin	Kentfield	AS
	College of the Canyons	Valencia	Cert./AA
	College of the Sequoias	Visalia	Course(s)
	De Anza College	Cupertino	AA
	East Los Angeles College	Monterey Park	Cert.
	El Camino College	Torrance	AA
	Fresno City College	Fresno	Course(s)
	Fullerton College	Fullerton	Course(s)
	Golden Gate University	San Francisco	BS
	Golden West College	Huntington Beach	Course(s)
	Grossmont College	El Cajon	Cert.
	Hartnell College	Salinas	AA
	Lake Tahoe Community College	South Lake Tahoe	Course(s)
	Lassen College	Susanville	Course(s)
	Long Beach City College	Long Beach	Course(s)
	Los Angeles Southwest College	Los Angeles	Course(s)
	Los Angeles Valley College	Van Nuys	Course(s)
	Merritt College	Oakland	Course(s)
	Monterey Peninsula College	Monterey	Cert./AA/AS
	Mount San Antonio College	Walnut	BS
	Napa Valley College	Napa	AA/AS
	Ohlone College	Freemont	Course(s)
	Palomar College	San Marcos	AA
	Rio Hondo College	Whittier	AA
	San Diego Miramar College	San Diego	AS
	San Joaquin Delta College	Stockton	Course(s)
	San Jose State University	San Jose	Course(s)
	Sierra College	Rocklin	Course(s)
	Sonoma State University	Rohnert Park	BS
	Ventura College	Ventura	AA/AS
COLORADO	Arapahoe Community College	Littleton	Cert.
	Colorado Mountain College	Breckenridge	Course(s)
	Community College of Denver	Denver	Course(s)
	Metropolitan State College	Denver	Course(s)
	Pikes Peak Community College	Colorado Springs	Cert./AS
	Red Community College	Golden	Cert.
	Trinidad State Junior College	Trinidad	Course(s)
CONNECTICUT	Eastern Connecticut State University	Willimantic	Course(s)
	Housatonic Regional Community College	Bridgeport	AA
	Mattatuck Community College	Waterbury	Course(s)

State	Institution	City	Offerings
	Northwestern Connecticut Community College	Winsted	Course(s)
	Norwalk Community College	Norwalk	Course(s)
	Sacred Heart University	Bridgeport	BS
	Tunxis Community College	Farmington	Cert.
	University of New Haven	West Haven	BS/MS
	Western Connecticut State University	Danbury	Course(s)
DELAWARE	Delaware Technical and Community College	Newark	AS
DISTRICT OF COLUMBIA	George Washington University	Washington, DC	MA
	University of the District of Columbia	Washington, DC	Course(s)
FLORIDA	Broward Community College	Ft. Lauderdale	Course(s)
	Daytona Beach Community College	Daytona Beach	Course(s)
	Florida State University	Tallahassee	Course(s)
	Gulf Coast Community College	Panama City	Course(s)
	Lake–Sumter Community College	Leesburg	Course(s)
	Manatee Junior College	Bradenton	AS
	Miami–Dade Community College	Miami	AS
	Miami–Dade Community College—South	Miami	AA/AS
	Nova Southeastern University	Miami	Course(s)
	St. Thomas University	Miami	Course(s)
	Tallahassee Community College	Tallahassee	Course(s)
	University of Central Florida	Orlando	Course(s)
	University of North Florida	Jacksonville	Course(s)
	University of South Florida—Bayboro	St. Petersburg	Course(s)
	University of South Florida—St. Petersburg	St. Petersburg	Course(s)
GEORGIA	Albany State College	Albany	Course(s)
	Armstrong State College	Savannah	Course(s)
	Brenau Professional College	Gainesville	BA/BS
	Brunswick Junior College	Brunswick	Cert.
	Columbus College	Columbus	Course(s)
	Fort Valley State College	Fort Valley	Course(s)
	Georgia Southern College	Statesboro	Course(s)
	Valdosta State College	Valdosta	Course(s)
HAWAII	Hawaii Community College	Hilo	Course(s)
	Honolulu Community College	Honolulu	Course(s)
	Maui Community College	Kahului	Course(s)
IDAHO	Lewis–Clark State College	Lewiston	Course(s)
ILLINOIS	Belleville Area College	Belleville	Cert./AA
	Carl Sandburg College	Galesburg	Course(s)
	City Colleges of Chicago, Harry S. Truman College	Chicago	Course(s)
	City Colleges of Chicago, Loop College	Chicago	Cert./AS
	College of DuPage	Glen Ellyn	Course(s)
	College of Lake County	Grayslake	Cert./AA
	Frontier Community College (EPE)	Fairfield	Course(s)
	Illinois Central College	East Peoria	AAS

State	Institution	City	Offerings
	John A. Logan College	Carterville	Course(s)
	Joliet Junior College	Joliet	Cert./AS
	Kankakee Community College	Kankakee	Course(s)
	Lake Land College	Mattoon	Course(s)
	Lewis and Clark Community College	Godfrey	Cert./AAS
	Lincoln Land Community College	Springfield	Cert.
	McHenry County College	Crystal Lake	Course(s)
	McKendree College	Lebanon	Course(s)
	Moraine Valley Community College	Palos Hills	Cert./AAS
	Oakton Community College	Des Plaines	Course(s)
	Parkland College	Champaign	Course(s)
	Rend Lake College	Ina	AAS
	Rock Valley College	Rockford	Cert./AA
	Saint Xavier College	Chicago	Course(s)
	Sangamon State University	Springfield	Course(s)
	Southeastern Illinois College	Harrisburg	Course(s)
	Southern Illinois University	Carbondale	BS/MS
	Spoon River College	Canton	Course(s)
	State Community College of East St. Louis	East St. Louis	AS
	Triton College	River Grove	Course(s)
	University of Illinois	Chicago	Course(s)
	Waubonsee Community College	Sugar Grove	Course(s)
	Western Illinois University	Macomb	BS
	William Rainey Harper College	Palatine	Cert.
INDIANA	Indiana Northern Graduate School of Professional Management	Marion	MPM
	Indiana State University	Terre Haute	BS/MS
	Indiana Vocational Technical College	Indianapolis	Cert./AS
	University of Evansville	Evansville	Course(s)
IOWA	Des Moines Area Community College	Ankeny	Course(s)
	Ellsworth Community College	Iowa Falls	AA
	Hawkeye Institute of Technology	Waterloo	AA
	Indian Hills Community College	Ottumwa	AAS
	Mount Mercy College	Cedar Rapids	Course(s)
	Saint Ambrose College	Davenport	BA
	Southeastern Community College	West Burlington	AA
	Wartburg College	Waverly	BA
KANSAS	Butler County Community College	El Dorado	Course(s)
	Garden City Community College	Garden City	AA/AA
	Johnson County Community College	Overland Park	Course(s)
	Washburn University	Topeka	Course(s)
	Wichita State University	Wichita	BS
KENTUCKY	Eastern Kentucky University	Richmond	AA/BS
	Franklin College	Paducah	Course(s)
	Kentucky State University	Frankfort	BS
	Murray State University	Murray	Course(s)
	Thomas More College	Crestview Hills	BA
	University of Louisville	Louisville	Course(s)
LOUISIANA	Grambling State University	Grambling	Course(s)

State	Institution	City	Offerings
	Louisiana State University at Eunice	Eunice	AS
	Louisiana State University in Shreveport	Shreveport	Course(s)
	McNeese State University	Lake Charles	Course(s)
	Northeast Louisiana University	Monroe	Course(s)
MAINE	Bangor Community College—Orono	Bangor	BA
	Southern Maine Vocational Technical Institute	South Portland	Course(s)
	University of Maine	Augusta	Course(s)
MARYLAND	Anne Arundel Community College	Arnold	Cert.
	Catonsville Community College	Catonsville	AA
	Chesapeake College	Wye Mills	Course(s)
	Community College of Baltimore—Harbor Campus	Baltimore	AA
	Coppin State College	Baltimore	BS
	Essex Community College	Baltimore	Cert.
	Hagerstown Junior College	Hagerstown	Course(s)
	Harford Community College	Bel Air	Course(s)
	Montgomery College	Rockville	AA
	Prince George's Community College	Largo	AA
	University of Maryland	College Park	BA
MASSACHUSETTS	American International College	Springfield	Course(s)
	Bristol Community College	Fall River	Cert.
	Bunker Hill Community College	Charlestown	Course(s)
	Cape Cod Community College	West Barnstable	Course(s)
	Dean Junior College	Franklin	Course(s)
	Greenfield Community College	Greenfield	Course(s)
	Holyoke Community College	Holyoke	Course(s)
	Middlesex Community College	Bedford	AA
	Mt. Wachusett Community College	Gardner	Course(s)
	Northeastern University	Boston	BS/MS
	Northern Essex Community College	Haverhill	Cert.
	Quinsigamond Community College	Worcester	Course(s)
	University of Lowell	Lowell	Course(s)
	Westfield State College	Westfield	Course(s)
MICHIGAN	Central Michigan University	Mount Pleasant	MS
	Delta College	University Center	AA
	Detroit College of Business Administration	Dearborn	Course(s)
	Ferris State College	Big Rapids	BS
	Grand Valley State University	Allendale	BS
	Henry Ford Community College	Dearborn	AA
	Jackson Community College	Jackson	Cert./AA
	Kalamazoo Valley Community College	Kalamazoo	AA
	Lake Superior State College	Sault Ste. Marie	BS
	Lansing Community College	Lansing	AA
	Macomb County Community College—Center Campus	Mt. Clemens	AA
	Madonna College	Livonia	AS/BS
	Mercy College of Detroit	Detroit	AA/BA
	Michigan State University	East Lansing	BS/MS

State	Institution	City	Offerings
	Muskegon Community College	Muskegon	AA
	Northern Michigan University	Marquette	BS
	Northwestern Michigan College	Traverse City	Course(s)
	Oakland Community College	Bloomfield Hills	Cert./AS
	Saginaw Valley State College	University Center	Course(s)
	St. Clair County Community College	Port Huron	Course(s)
	Schoolcraft College	Livonia	Cert./AS
	Suomi College	Hancock	Course(s)
	University of Detroit	Detroit	BS/MS
	Wayne State University	Detroit	Course(s)
MINNESOTA	Bemidji State University	Bemidji	Course(s)
	Inver Hills Community College	Inver Grove Heights	AA
	Metropolitan State University	St. Paul	Course(s)
	Normandale Community College	Bloomington	Cert.
	North Hennepin Community College	Minneapolis	Course(s)
	St. Cloud State University	St. Cloud	BA/MS
	University of Minnesota Duluth	Duluth	Course(s)
MISSISSIPPI	University of Southern Mississippi	Hattiesburg	Course(s)
MISSOURI	Central Missouri State University	Warrensburg	BS/MS
	Drury College	Springfield	AS
	Missouri Southern State College	Joplin	BS
	Penn Valley Community College	Kansas City	Course(s)
	St. Louis Community College at Florissant Valley	St. Louis	Course(s)
	St. Louis Community College at Forest Park	St. Louis	Course(s)
	St. Louis Community College at Meramec	St. Louis	Course(s)
	Tarkio College	Tarkio	BS
MONTANA	Dawson Community College	Glendive	Course(s)
NEBRASKA	Kearney State College	Kearney	BS
	Metropolitan Technical Community College	Omaha	AAS
	Northeast Technical Community College	Norfolk	AA
	Wayne State College	Wayne	BS
NEVADA	Clark County Community College	North Las Vegas	AAS
	Truckee Meadows Community College	Reno	AAS
	University of Nevada	Las Vegas	Course(s)
NEW HAMPSHIRE	Hesser College	Manchester	AA
	Keene State College (Safety Studies)	Keene	Course(s)
NEW JERSEY	Atlantic Community College	Mays Landing	Course(s)
	Bergen Community College	Paramus	Cert./AAS
	Brookdale Community College	Lincroft	Course(s)
	County College of Morris	Randolph	Course(s)
	Essex County College	Newark	AA
	Fairleigh Dickinson University	Rutherford	Course(s)
	Glassboro State College	Glassboro	Course(s)
	Gloucester County College	Sewell	Cert.

State	Institution	City	Offerings
	Jersey City State College	Jersey City	BS/MS
	Mercer County Community College	Trenton	Course(s)
	Monmouth College	West Long Branch	BS
	Passaic County Community College	Paterson	AA
	Rutgers University	Newark	Course(s)
	Rutgers University	New Brunswick	Course(s)
	Thomas A. Edison State College	Trenton	Course(s)
	Union College	Cranford	AA
	Upsala College—Wirths	Sussex	Course(s)
NEW MEXICO	Eastern New Mexico University	Clovis	Course(s)
	New Mexico State University	Las Cruces	BS
	Northern New Mexico Community College	Espanola	AAS
	Western New Mexico University	Silver City	Course(s)
NEW YORK	Adirondack Community College	Glens Falls	Course(s)
	Broome Community College	Binghamton	Course(s)
	Clinton Community College	Plattsburgh	Course(s)
	Columbia—Greene Community College	Hudson	Course(s)
	Erie Community College–City Campus	Buffalo	Course(s)
	Erie Community College	Williamsville	AA
	Erie Community College —North Campus	Amherst	Course(s)
	Herkimer County Community College	Herkimer	AA
	Hilbert College	Hamburg	AA
	Hudson Valley Community College	Troy	AA
	Iona College	New Rochelle	BS
	Jamestown Community College	Jamestown	Course(s)
	Jefferson Community College	Watertown	Course(s)
	John Jay College of Criminal Justice, SUNY	New York	AA/BS/MS
	Long Island University—Brooklyn	Brooklyn	BS/MS
	Long Island University—C. W. Post Center	Brookville	BS/MS
	Mercy College	Dobbs Ferry	AS/BS
	Monroe Community College	Rochester	AAS
	Nassau Community College	Garden City	AA
	New York Institute of Technology	Old Westbury	BS
	Niagara University	Niagara University	BS
	Onondaga Community College	Syracuse	Course(s)
	Orange County Community College	Middletown	Course(s)
	Rochester Institute of Technology	Rochester	BS
	Rockland Community College	Suffern	AAS
	Russell Sage College	Troy	Course(s)
	St. John's University, St. Vincent's College	Jamaica	BS
	St. John's University, St. Vincent's College	Staten Island	BS
	Schenectady County Community College	Schenectady	Course(s)
	State University of New York at Albany	Albany	Course(s)
	State University of New York College at Brockport	Brockport	BS

State	Institution	City	Offerings
	SUNY	Farmingdale	Cert./AAS
	Westchester Community College	Valhalla	Course(s)
NORTH CAROLINA	Alamance Community College	Haw River	AA
	Appalachian State University	Boone	Course(s)
	Bladen Technical College	Dublin	Course(s)
	Cape Fear Technical Institute	Wilmington	Course(s)
	Central Piedmont Community College	Charlotte	AAS
	Cleveland Technical College	Shelby	AAS
	East Carolina University	Greenville	Course(s)
	Edgecombe Technical College	Tarboro	AAS
	Fayetteville Technical Institute	Fayetteville	AA
	Gaston College	Dallas	Course(s)
	Haywood Technical College	Clyde	AA
	Martin Community College	Williamston	Course(s)
	Maryland Technical College	Spruce Pine	AAS
	Nash Technical Institute	Rocky Mount	AAS
	Pfeiffer College	Misenheimer	BA
	Piedmont Technical College	Roxboro	AAS
	Surry Community College	Dobson	AAS
	Western Carolina University	Cullowhee	Course(s)
	Western Piedmont Community College	Morganton	Course(s)
	Wilkes Community College	Wilkesboro	Course(s)
NORTH DAKOTA	Bismarck Junior College	Bismarck	AA
OHIO	Bowling Green State University	Bowling Green	BS
	Case Western Reserve University	Cleveland	Course(s)
	Cincinnati Technical College	Cincinnati	AA
	Columbus Technical Institute	Columbus	AAS
	Cuyahoga Community College	Cleveland	Course(s)
	Hocking Technical College	Nelsonville	Cert./AAS
	Jefferson Technical College	Steubenville	AAS
	Kent State University	Kent	Course(s)
	Kent State University	Tuscarawas	AA
	Lakeland Community College	Steubenville	AS
	Lorain County Community College	Elyria	AAS
	Michael J. Owens Technical College	Toledo	AAS
	North Central Technical College	Mansfield	Course(s)
	Ohio University	Chillicothe	AAS
	Sawyer College of Business	Cleveland	AA
	Sinclair Community College	Dayton	AAS
	University of Akron	Akron	Cert./AA
	University of Dayton	Dayton	Course(s)
	University of Toledo	Toledo	Course(s)
	Youngstown State University	Youngstown	BS/MS
OKLAHOMA	Cameron University	Lawton	Course(s)
	Connors State College	Warner	Course(s)
	Eastern Oklahoma State College	Wilburton	Course(s)
	Oklahoma City Community College	Oklahoma City	AA
	Oklahoma City University	Oklahoma City	Course(s)

State	Institution	City	Offerings
	Oklahoma State University	Stillwater	Course(s)
	South Oklahoma City Junior College	Oklahoma City	
OREGON	Lane Community College	Eugene	AS
	Portland Community College	Portland	Cert.
	Southern Oregon State College	Ashland	Course(s)
PENNSYLVANIA	Allentown College of St. Francis de Sales	Center Valley	Course(s)
	Alvernia	Reading	BA
	Bucks County Community College	Newton	Course(s)
	Community College of Allegheny County	Monroeville	AS
	East Stroudsburg University of Pennsylvania	East Stroudsburg	Course(s)
	Edinboro University of Pennsylvania	Edinboro	Course(s)
	Harrisburg Area Community College	Harrisburg	AA
	Indiana University of Pennsylvania	Indiana	Course(s)
	King's College	Wilkes-Barre	Course(s)
	Lehigh County Community College	Schnecksville	Cert./AA/AS
	Luzerne County Community College	Nanticoke	AAS
	Mansfield University of Pennsylvania	Mansfield	Course(s)
	Mercyhurst College	Erie	BS
	Mercyhurst College	Glenwood Hills	AS/BA
	Pennsylvania State University—Harrisburg Capital College	Middletown	Special BA
	Pennsylvania State University—University Park	University Park	Course(s)
	St. Joseph's University	Philadelphia	Course(s)
	Shippensburg University of Pennsylvania	Shippensburg	Course(s)
	Temple University	Philadelphia	Course(s)
	Triangle Tech	Pittsburgh	Cert.
	University of Pittsburgh	Pittsburgh	BA/MA
	Villanova University	Villanova	Special BA
	West Chester University	West Chester	Course(s)
	Westmoreland County Community College	Youngwood	Course(s)
	York College of Pennsylvania	York	Course(s)
RHODE ISLAND	Salve Regina—The Newport College	Newport	Course(s)
SOUTH CAROLINA	Beaufort Technical College	Beaufort	Course(s)
	Denmark Technical College	Denmark	Course(s)
	Florence—Darlington Technical College	Florence	Course(s)
	Horry—Georgetown Technical College	Conway	Cert.
	Midlands Technical College	Columbia	Course(s)
	Orangeburg—Calhoun Technical College	Orangeburg	Cert.
	Sumter Area Technical College	Sumter	Course(s)
	Tri-County Technical College	Pendleton	Course(s)
	University of South Carolina	Columbia	Course(s)
TENNESSEE	Aquinas Junior College	Nashville	Course(s)
	Cleveland State Community College	Cleveland	AS

State	Institution	City	Offerings
	Dyersburg State Community College	Dyersburg	Course(s)
	East Tennessee State University	Johnson City	Course(s)
	Memphis State University	Memphis	Course(s)
	Middle Tennessee State University	Murfreesboro	BS
	Shelby State Community College	Memphis	Cert.
	University of Tennessee at Chattanooga	Chattanooga	Course(s)
	University of Tennessee at Martin	Martin	Course(s)
	Walters State Community College	Morristown	AS
TEXAS	American Technological University	Killeen	Course(s)
	College of the Mainland	Texas City	Cert.
	Dallas Baptist College	Dallas	Course(s)
	Houston Community College System	Houston	AA/AS
	Lee College	Baytown	AA
	McLennan Community College	Waco	AA
	Odessa College	Odessa	Cert.
	Pan American University	Edinburg	Course(s)
	Sam Houston State University	Huntsville	Course(s)
	San Jacinto College	Pasadena	AA/AS
	Southwest Texas State University	San Marcos	Course(s)
	Stephen F. Austin State University	Nacogdoches	BA
	Texarkana Community College	Texarkana	Course(s)
	University of Houston—Downtown	Houston	BS
	University of Texas at Arlington	Arlington	Course(s)
	University of Texas at San Antonio	San Antonio	BA
	Victoria College	Victoria	Course(s)
UTAH	Southern Utah State College	Cedar City	AAS
	Weber State College	Ogden	AA
VERMONT	Castleton State College	Castleton	Course(s)
	Southern Vermont College	Bennington	Course(s)
VIRGINIA	Blue Ridge Community College	Weyers Cave	Course(s)
	Central Virginia Community College	Lynchburg	AA
	Germanna Community College	Locust Grove	Course(s)
	J. Sargeant Reynold Community College	Richmond	AA
	Liberty University	Lynchburg	Course(s)
	Northern Virginia Community College	Annandale	AA
	Northern Virginia Community College—Alexandria	Alexandria	AAS
	Northern Virginia Community College—Manassas	Manassas	AAS
	Northern Virginia Community College—Woodbridge	Woodbridge	AA
	Old Dominion University	Norfolk	Course(s)
	Paul D. Camp Community College	Franklin	Course(s)
	Piedmont Virginia Community College	Charlottesville	Course(s)
	Radford University	Radford	Course(s)
	Virginia Commonwealth University	Richmond	BS
	Virginia Western Community College	Roanoke	Course(s)
WASHINGTON	Clark College	Vancouver	Course(s)
	Eastern Washington University	Cheney	BS
	Everett Community College	Everett	AA/AS

State	Institution	City	Offerings
	Fort Steilacoom Community College	Tacoma	Cert.
	Olympic College	Bremerton	Course(s)
	Shoreline Community College	Seattle	AA
WEST VIRGINIA	Fairmont State College	Fairmont	BS
	Marshall University	Huntington	Course(s)
	Parkersburg Community College	Parkersburg	Course(s)
	Salem College	Salem	BA
	West Virginia Northern Community College	Wheeling	AS
	West Virginia State College	Institute	Course(s)
WISCONSIN	District One Technical Institute	Eau Claire	Course(s)
	Fox Valley Technical Institute	Appleton	AA
	Gateway Technical Institute	Kenosha	Course(s)
	Milwaukee Area Technical College	Milwaukee	Course(s)
	Northeast Wisconsin Technical Institute	Green Bay	Course(s)
	University of Wisconsin—Platteville	Platteville	AA/BS
	University of Wisconsin—Whitewater (Safety Studies)	Whitewater	Course(s)
	Waukesha County Technical Institute	Pewaukee	Course(s)
WYOMING	Casper College	Casper	Course(s)
	Sheridan College	Sheridan	Course(s)
CANADA	Algonquin College	Ottawa, Ontario	BS
	College of Trades & Technology	St. Johns, Newfoundland	Cert.
	Concordia University	Montreal, Quebec	Cert.
	Fanshawe College	London, Ontario	Course(s)
	Humber College	Toronto, Ontario	AA
	Lethbridge Community College	Lethbridge, Alberta	Cert.
	Mohawk College	Hamilton, Ontario	Cert.
	Mount Royal College	Calgary, Alberta	AA
	Sheridan College	Brampton, Ontario	LSA
	Sir Stanford Fleming College	Petersborough, Ontario	Dip.
	University of Alberta	Calgary, Alberta	Cert.
ENGLAND	College of Technology	Letchworth, Herts	Course(s)
	Twickenham College of Technology	Middlesex	Course(s)

Glossary

Items preceded by * are adapted from the glossary of *Private Security,* Report of the Task Force on Private Security, National Advisory Committee on Criminal Justice Standards and Goals, Washington, DC: U.S. Government Printing Office, 1976.

administrative reports Reports that deal with the routine functioning of the business or agency. (12)

affirmative action Actions to eliminate current effects of past discrimination. (22)

agenda Items to be accomplished, usually during a meeting. (22)

*****alarm respondent*** Person employed by an organization to answer an alarm condition at a client's protected site, to inspect the protected site to determine the nature of the alarm, to protect or secure the client's facility until alarm system integrity can be restored and to assist law enforcement according to local arrangement. The alarm respondent may be armed and also may be a servicer. (2)

*****alarm systems*** Devices that, on detection of an intrusion, transmit and articulate messages for help. An alarm system is composed of three fundamental parts: (1) *sensor*—detects or senses a condition that exists or changes, be it authorized or unauthorized; related directly to the senses of touch, hearing, sight, smell and taste; (2) *control*—provides power, receives information from the sensors, evaluates the information and transmits the required information to the annunciation function; (3) *annunciation*—alerts a human to initiate a response that will result in investigating the sensor environment. Could be a bell, buzzer, light flashing, etc. (5)

Alzheimer's disease A condition affecting the elderly and causing such symptoms as gradual memory loss, impairment of judgment, disorientation, personality change, decline in ability to perform routine tasks, behavior change, difficulty in learning, loss of language skills and a decline in intellectual function. Individuals with Alzheimer's disease may appear to be intoxicated. (10)

andragogy Adult learning. (22)

area alarms Alarms that protect a portion of or the total interior of a room or building. Also called *space alarms.* (5)

*****armed courier services*** Companies that provide armed protection and transportation, from one place to another, of money, currency, coins, bullion, securities, bonds, jewelry or other articles of value; transportation is provided by means other than specially constructed, bullet-resistant armored vehicles. (2)

armed personnel Persons, uniformed or nonuniformed, who carry at any time any form of firearm. (4)

armored car services Companies that provide protection, safek and secured transportation of money, currency, coins, bullion, sec bonds, jewelry or other items of value by means of specially const bullet-resistant armored vehicles and vaults under armed guard. (2)

arrest Taking into custody, in a manner authorized by law, a persor taken before a magistrate. (3)

arson The willful, malicious burning of a building or property. (8)

ARTCENTRAL An organization in New York that registers works of ar computer-oriented photogrammetry, comparable to fingerprinting. (

assault An attack on a person. (4, 8)

assize of arms A provision of the Statute of Westminster requiring male between ages 15 and 60 to keep a weapon in his home as a "t to keep the peace." (1)

authoritarian Manager who uses strong control over personnel. Al scribed as *autocratic*. (3, 22)

authority Right to give orders. (3, 22)

backstretch area The area of a racetrack where the horses, drive grooms are quartered. (17)

bait money Money in a bank, placed in such a way that when it is up an alarm sounds. (17)

battery The unconsented, offensive touching of another person, eitl rectly or indirectly. (4)

biometric System that uses physical traits such as fingerprints, voic even eyeballs to identify individuals. (5)

blind receiving Going by the packing slip rather than actually cour received shipment. (6)

booster box A box whose top, bottom or end is hinged so that articl be placed inside without actually opening the box. Apparatus of a lifter. (16)

Bow Street Runners The first detective unit; established in London by Fielding in 1750. (1)

bureaucratic Reliance on rules and regulations. (22)

burglary Entering a structure (1) without the owner's consent (2) w intent to commit a crime. (8)

calibrating The technique of beginning an interview with small talk serve how the individual responds to questions. (12)

capacity alarms An alarm in which a protected object is part of the c capacitance. If a change occurs in the region of the protected ob change in the system's capacitance sets off the alarm. (5)

****central station*** A control center to which alarm systems in subsc premises are connected, where circuits are supervised and personı maintained continuously to record and investigate alarm or trouble s Facilities are provided for reporting alarms to police and fire depar or to other outside agencies. (5)

central station alarms Systems in which the secured area is directly connected to an alarm panel in a centrally located alarm receiving station via a pair of leased telephone wires. (5)

Certified Protection Professional (CPP) Program of the American Society for Industrial Security that provides certification for individuals who meet specific experience and educational requirements and pass a common knowledge examination as well as an examination in four specialty subjects. (2)

change key A key that opens only one specific door. (6)

check kiting A person makes simultaneous deposits and withdrawals using two or more banks to obtain credit before enough time has elapsed to clear the checks. (9)

choke points Locations a person must go through to get to his or her intended destination. Are often the location of an ambush. (19)

citizen's arrest The right of every citizen to arrest someone who is committing or has committed a crime, to be turned over to local authorities. (8)

civil liability An offense against an individual for which restitution is sought, in contrast to criminal liability. (4)

civil offenses Actions prohibited by law, but not classified as crimes. (4)

cocaine A white crystalline powder extracted from the South American coca plant; a narcotic. (8)

code of ethics Self-enforcing moral and professional guidelines for behavior in a given field. (21)

collective deep pocket A case where everyone even remotely involved with the case is sued, resulting in astronomical judgments. (4)

communication Involves a sender, a message, a channel and a receiver. It may also include feedback. (12)

computer crime Accessing a computer's database without authorization or exceeding authorization, for the purpose of sabotage or fraud. It includes theft or destruction of software and hardware as well. (9)

computer virus An unwanted software program that can cause serious memory problems, destroying files or even entire programs. It can spread undetected from one computer to another, thwarting the computer's normal functions and often garbling data. (9)

concertina Rolls of barbed wire 50 feet long and 3 feet in diameter. (5)

conclusionary language Assumptions or opinions, nonfactual. (12)

connotative words Words with strong emotional overtones. (12)

contract services Outside firms or individuals who provide security services for a fee. (2)

core concept A style of building design in which all elevators, rest rooms, lobbies and service facilities are located at the building's center, allowing more effective control of public areas while also permitting more flexible use of office space. (17)

corporate crime A type of white-collar crime whose distinctive feature is that the offense is committed primarily for the benefit of an ongoing legitimate business enterprise, rather than for the individual who carries out the offense. (8)

***courier** An armed person assisting in the secured transportation and protection of items of value. (2)

crack Freebase cocaine processed to remove the hydrochloride. Like freebase, it is smoked in a pipe. Because it can be obtained for from five to ten dollars, it is often called "poor man's coke." (8)

crash bar An emergency exit locking device. The door can be opened only from the inside, and if it is, an alarm sounds. Also called a *panic bar.* (5)

crime An action that is harmful to another person and/or to society and that is punishable by law. (4)

Crime Prevention Through Environmental Design (CPTED) A theory proposing that the proper design and effective use of the built environment can reduce the incidence and fear of crime and make an improvement in the quality of life. (5)

criminal offense An offense against the state, a public crime for which punishment is sought, as opposed to a civil offense. (4)

criticality Level of importance or seriousness of consequences. (14)

cross-examination Questioning by the opposing side for the purpose of assessing the validity of the testimony. (13)

cybercop An investigator involved in the new field of computer forensics. (11)

cyberspace The artificial world created on-line in and between computer systems. (9)

cylindrical locks Locks that use disk tumblers or pin tumblers. (5)

dead bolts Non-spring-loaded metal bars manually inserted into or withdrawn from a strike. (5)

defamation Injuring a person's reputation, such as by falsely inferring, by either words or conduct, in front of a third disinterested party, that a person committed a crime. (4)

***defensible space** The name of a hypothesis developed by Oscar Newman holding that building designs that hinder crime give occupants a sense of security, thus encouraging them to guard themselves and their property. (5)

delegation Assigning tasks to others. (22)

democratic Describes a manager who involves personnel in decision making. (22)

denotative words Objective, nonemotional words. (12)

deposition Where attorneys for both sides ask questions of an individual involved in a lawsuit and the questions and answers are recorded verbatim by a stenographer or court reporter. (4)

dictatorial Describes a manager who is closed-minded and uses threats with personnel. (22)

direct examination The initial questioning of a witness or defendant by the lawyer who is using the person's testimony to further his or her case. (13)

disability Any physical or mental impairment that substantially limits one or more major life activities of an individual. (10)

discipline Actions taken to get personnel to follow rules and regulations. (22)

Dram Shop Acts Make bartenders who continue to serve an obviously intoxicated patron liable for any harm that the individual might do to others. (17)

dynamic risk Risk with the potential for both benefits and losses, e.g., extending credit or accepting checks. (14)

economic crime Crimes such as shoplifting, employee theft, pilferage, credit-card fraud and check fraud. (8)

embezzlement Fraudulent appropriation of property by a person to whom it has been entrusted. (8)

empathy Understanding where another person is coming from, whether you agree with it or not. (12)

****employment records*** Normal business information, including employment application, health records, job performance records and other records maintained on an employee. (6)

encryption The coding of a message. Used to thwart computer crime. (9)

envelope A building's exterior; the first line of defense. (5)

epilepsy A disorder of the central nervous system in which a person tends to have recurrent seizures. These seizures may look like street drugs or alcohol at work. (10)

Equal Employment Opportunity Commission (EEOC) Commission set up to enforce laws against discrimination in the workplace. (22)

espionage, industrial Theft of trade secrets or confidential information. (15)

ethical behavior Refers to behavior considered to be right and moral, such as being honest, being considerate of others and keeping promises. (21)

ethics Deals with questions of right and wrong, of moral and immoral behavior. (21)

ethnoviolence Violent acts motivated by racial, religious and ethnic prejudice. (18)

excessive force More force than is reasonable to counteract the amount of resistance encountered. (4)

Exclusionary Rule Makes inadmissable any evidence obtained by means violating a person's constitutional rights. (3)

exculpatory clauses Clauses in a contract that limit liability, a disclaimer. (5)

facsimile or ***fax*** An exact copy transmitted by wire or radio for reproduction. (9)

fact A statement that can be proven true or false. (12)

fail-safe locks Locks that will remain unlocked when the power is off. (5)

fail-secure locks Locks that remain locked when the power is off. Also called intermittent-duty locks. (5)

false imprisonment Unreasonably restraining another person using physical or psychological means to deny that person freedom of movement. (4)

faxpionage Unauthorized access to facsimile transmissions. (9)

feedback An indication that a message has or has not been understood. (12)

felony A serious crime such as murder, robbery or burglary that is punishable by death or by imprisonment in a state prison or penitentiary. (8)

fenestration Window design. (5)

feudalism A form of government whereby peasants (serfs) labored for a nobleman who answered to the king. (1)

fiber optic Light transmitted through very fine, flexible glass rods by internal reflection. (5)

fidelity bonds Insurance protecting employers from losses suffered from dishonest employees. (6)

fire triangle The three elements necessary for burning: heat, fuel and oxygen. (7)

****firearm*** A pistol, revolver, other handgun, rifle, shotgun or other such weapon capable of firing a missile. (22)

fire-loading The amount of flammable materials within an area. (7)

floor release limit A value limit that cannot be exceeded with a check or credit card unless the clerk clears it with the central office. (16)

floorwalkers Employees who pose as customers and seek to remain unnoticed so as to catch shoplifters "in the act." (16)

foreseeable danger When it is known that a problem is likely to occur. (4)

Frankpledge system The Normans' modification of the Tithing system: the king demanded that all free Englishmen swear to maintain the peace. (1)

fraud Intentional deception to cause a person to give up property or some lawful right. (8)

freebase A form of cocaine made by chemically converting the street drug into a basic form that can be smoked. (8)

goals End results desired. (22)

grand larceny Larceny that is classified as a felony, based on the value of the property stolen. (8)

grand master key A key that opens all locks in two or more buildings. (6)

grapevine Informal channels of communication. Sometimes called the rumor mill. (12)

grievance A complaint, usually written, made to one's supervisor. (22)

****guard*** A person paid a fee, wage or salary to perform one or more of the following functions: (a) prevent or detect intrusion, unauthorized entry or activity, vandalism or trespass on private property; (b) prevent or detect theft, loss, embezzlement, misappropriation or concealment of merchandise, money, bonds, stocks, notes or other valuable documents or papers; (c) control, regulate or direct the flow or movements of the public, whether by vehicle or otherwise, to ensure the protection of property; (d) protect individuals from bodily harm and (e) enforce rules, regulations and policies related to crime reduction. (2)

hacker A computer enthusiast who engages in electronic snooping, software piracy and other types of high-tech illegal activities. (9)

header A barrier made of strands of barbed wire extending outward from the top of the fence at a 45-degree angle; also called a *top guard*. (5)

hierarchy Levels. Management hierarchy goes from on-line personnel (lowest level), to supervisors, to managers, to the chief executive officer (highest level). (22)

hierarchy of needs Human needs identified by psychologists, placed in order from lower level (food, shelter, etc.) to higher level (self-actualization); most well-known psychologist using this theory is Maslow. (22)

honesty shopping A procedure in which an individual, often a security officer, is hired to shop in such a way that will test the honesty of sales personnel who handle cash. Also called a *shopping service*. (16)

hue and cry The Anglo-Saxon practice whereby if anyone resisted the watchman's arrest, the watchman cried out and all citizens chased the fugitive and assisted in capturing him. (1)

hybrid services Combine proprietary services and contract services. (2)

igniter Device to start a fire; includes matches, candles, cigarettes, explosives and the like. (8)

ignition temperature The specific temperature at which a substance will ignite and burn as long as oxygen is present. (7)

impeaching Discrediting a witness's testimony. (13)

industrial espionage Theft of trade secrets or confidential information. (9)

inferences Statements about the unknown based on the known; deductions, using logic. Sometimes referred to as *judgments.* (12)

infrared detectors Fire detectors that respond to flame. (7)

integrity interview A face-to-face, nonaccusatory interview consisting of a series of questions addressing issues such as significant thefts from prior employers, use of illegal drugs during work hours, participation in criminal activities, falsification of the application form and similar job-related concerns. (6)

intentional infliction of emotional distress Outrageous or grossly reckless conduct intended to and highly likely to cause a severe emotional reaction. (4)

intentional wrong An illegal act committed on purpose. (4)

INTERPOL International Criminal Police Organization. (18)

interrogation A controlled conversation with persons suspected of direct or indirect involvement in a crime. (8)

interrogatories Written lists of questions to which the defendant is asked to respond in writing. May be several pages long and may include questions attempting to obtain information that might be damaging to the defendant. (4)

interview A controlled conversation with witnesses to or victims of a crime. (8)

invasion of privacy Unreasonable, unconsented intrusion into the personal affairs or property of a person. (4)

investigate To trace or track mentally, to examine and take evidence, to find out by careful inquiry. (11)

ionization detectors Fire detectors that respond to invisible particles of combustion. (7)

job description Statement of duties and responsibilities for a specific position. (22)

judgments Statements about the unknown based on the known; deductions using logic. Also called *inferences.* (12)

keyway A passage containing obstacles through which a key must pass to unlock a lock. (5)

kleptomaniac A compulsive thief. (16)

larceny/theft The (1) unlawful taking (2) of the personal goods or property of another (3) valued above (grand larceny) or below (petty larceny) a specified amount, (4) with the intent to permanently deprive the owner of the property or goods. (8)

licensing Permission from a competent authority to carry out the business of providing security services on a contractual basis. (2)

local alarms Alarms that sound on the premises and require that someone hears them and calls the police. (5)

luminaire What houses a lamp. (5)

Magna Charta A decisive document in the development of constitutional government in England that checked royal power (King John) and placed the king under the law. Similar to our Bill of Rights, it gave Englishmen "due process" of law (1215). Also known as *Magna Carta.* (1)

management The "bosses" in an organization. (22)

management by objectives (MBO) Management and staff set goals and timelines within which to accomplish the goals. (22)

manager One who accomplishes things through others. (22)

marijuana The most socially acceptable of the illegal drugs, made from the cannabis plant and usually smoked. (8)

master key A key that opens the locks in an entire building. (6)

master keying system Under this system, a change key opens only one specific door; a sub-master key opens the locks in a specific area; a master key opens the locks in the entire building; and, if multiple buildings are involved, a grand master key may open all locks in two or more buildings. (6)

mentor Teacher, role model. (22)

military time Uses the 24-hour clock rather than A.M. and P.M. (12)

misdemeanor A minor crime punishable by a fine and/or a relatively short jail sentence. (8)

moral That which is right or virtuous. (21)

morale How a person feels; the general mood of an organization or company, e.g., morale is high/low. (22)

motivate Encourage, inspire. (22)

negligence Occurs when a person has a duty to act reasonably but fails to do so and, as a result, someone is injured. (4)

neuter head blank A key blank that has an unusual shape and contains no embossed stock numbers or coining marks, so that it cannot be identified using a catalog. (6)

noncompete agreements Agreements preventing employees from quitting and going to work for competitors. (9)

nondelegable duty One for which authority can be given to another person, but responsibility for it cannot. Civil liability remains with the person who has the legal duty to act. (4)

nondisclosure agreements Agreements prohibiting employees from revealing sensitive information to outsiders. (9)

nonverbal communication Includes the eyes, facial expressions, posture, gestures, clothes, tone of voice, proximity and touch. In writing, it includes neatness, paper quality, copy quality, binding and the like. (12)

Occupational Safety and Health Act of 1970 (OSHAct) Makes employers responsible for providing a safe workplace. (12)

Occupational Safety and Health Administration (OSHA) Enforces the Occupational Safety and Health Act of 1970. (7, 22)

on-line personnel Those who do the work, e.g., security guards and patrols. (22)

operational reports Reports that deal with the activities taken by private security officers. (12)

opinion A statement of personal belief, e.g., chocolate is better than strawberry. (12)

OPSEC Operations security—a process to analyze business operations from an adversary's perspective to identify vulnerabilities. (9)

OSHA The Occupational Safety and Health Administration. (7)

outsourcing Contracting of security services by private corporations and government agencies. (23)

panic bar An emergency exit locking device that can be opened only from the inside; if it is opened, an alarm sounds. Also called a *crash bar.* (5)

parish A geographical area defined by the congregation of a particular church; the local unit of government in rural areas of England. (1)

pedagogy Youth learning. (22)

performance appraisal Evaluation of an employee's work. (22)

perimeter alarms Alarms that protect fences and gates, exterior doors, windows and other openings. (5)

perimeter barriers Any obstacle defining the physical limits of a controlled area and impeding or restricting entry into that area. (5)

permissive Describes a manager who has or exercises little control over personnel. (22)

perpetual inventory A policy of keeping track of supplies/merchandise on hand almost daily; this is in contrast to an annual inventory, i.e., taking stock only once a year. (6)

petty (petit) larceny Theft classified as a misdemeanor, based on the value of the property stolen. (8)

photoelectric detectors Fire detectors that respond to smoke. (7)

photogrammetry A process comparable to fingerprinting; provides a permanent, exact identification of works of art which is impossible to duplicate. (18)

pilferage Internal theft, an important concern of private security. (8)

plaintiff An individual who has been wronged and who files suit against the person committing the offense. (4)

point alarms Alarms that protect specific items such as safes, cabinets, valuable articles and small areas. Also called *spot alarms.* (5)

police-connected alarm An electronic system that directs an alarm via telephone wires to the nearest police department. (5)

polygraph A lie detector; scientifically measures respiration and depth of breathing, changes in the skin's electrical resistance and blood pressure and pulse. (6)

POST Commission Peace Officers' Standards and Training Commission established in each state to oversee the quality of law enforcement training. (3)

power The force that can be used to carry out one's authority. (3)

precedents A court decision on a question of law that gives authority or direction on how to decide a similar question of law in a later case with similar facts. (4)

predication The total set of circumstances that would lead a reasonable, prudent and professionally trained person to believe that an offense has occurred, is occurring or will occur. (11)

preincident indicators Any signals that an attack on an individual is being planned or is about to occur. (19)

prima facie evidence Evidence that establishes a fact if not contested, e.g., the specific blood alcohol level for intoxication is stated in state laws. (16)

private security A profit-oriented industry that provides personnel, equipment and/or procedures to *prevent* losses caused by human error, emergencies, disasters or criminal actions. (1)

private security services May be proprietary, contract or hybrid. Include guards, patrols, investigators, armed couriers, central alarm respondents and consultants. (2)

privatization Duties normally performed by sworn personnel (for example, police officers) are performed by others, often private security officers. (3)

probability The likelihood of something occurring. (14)

probable cause The situation in which individuals have facts and circumstances within their knowledge and of which they have reasonable trustworthy information that are sufficient in themselves to warrant a person of reasonable caution in the belief that the suspect has committed a crime *(Carroll v. United States)*. (16)

proprietary alarms Alarms that use a constantly monitored alarm panel that may receive visible and/or audible signals to indicate exactly where a security break has occurred. (5)

proprietary services In-house security services, directly hired and controlled by the company or organization, usually for a salary rather than a fee. (2)

proximate result An injury is caused by the negligence or failure in the duty to protect. (4)

public relations A planned program of policies and conduct designed to build confidence in and increase the understanding of a business or organization; includes all activities undertaken to bolster image and create good will. (10)

punitive damages Award made to punish a defendant who is deemed to have behaved in such an abhorrent manner that an example must be made to keep others from acting in a similar way. (4)

pure risk Risk with the potential for injury, damage or loss with no possible benefits, e.g., crimes and natural disasters. (14)

pyromaniac A pathological firesetter. (8)

razor ribbon Barbed tape. (5)

reasonable care "That degree of care a person of ordinary prudence would exercise in similar circumstances" (Oran). (4)

reasonable cause Facts and circumstances within a person's knowledge and of which he or she had reasonable trustworthy information that were sufficient in themselves to warrant a man of reasonable caution in the belief that the suspect had committed a crime. The same as probable cause. (16)

registration Permission from a state authority before being employed as an investigator or detective, guard, courier, alarm system installer or repairer, or alarm respondent. (2)

reports Permanent written records that communicate important facts to be used in the future. (12)

respondent superior A concept that implies that employers are held liable for wrongful acts or negligence by an employee acting within the scope of his or her duties or in the employer's interest. (4)

restitution Making up for a crime, a payment of some form. (4)

risk A known threat that has effects that are not predictable in either their timing or their extent. (14)

risk acceptance The recognition that some losses are likely to occur and that 100 percent security is virtually impossible. (14)

risk elimination Adopting a practice that does away with a risk, e.g., not accepting checks. (14)

risk management Anticipating, recognizing and appraising a risk and initiating some action to remove the risk or reduce the potential loss from it to an acceptable level (NCPI). (14)

risk reduction Taking steps to minimize a risk, e.g., installing alarms. (14)

risk spreading Ensuring that potential loss in any single incident is minimized, e.g., placing expensive jewelry in separate display cases; closely related to *risk reduction*. (14)

risk transfer Putting the risk elsewhere, e.g., taking out insurance or raising prices to cover losses. (14)

robbery (1) The unlawful taking of personal property (2) from a person or in the person's presence, (3) against the person's will by force or threat of force. (8)

sabotage The intentional destruction of machinery or goods, or the intentional obstruction of production. (15)

safe A semiportable strongbox with combination lock. (5)

secrecy agreements Agreements directed at individuals who come into contact with vital trade secrets of a business—for example, technicians called in to repair a vital piece of machinery. Such individuals may be asked to sign an agreement to keep such information confidential. (9)

Section 1983 Part of the Civil Rights Act which says that anyone acting under the authority of local or state law who violates another person's constitutional rights—even though they are upholding a law—can be sued. (4)

****security services*** Those means, including guards, detectives or investigators, couriers and alarm system installers, repairers or respondents, that are provided on a contractual basis to deter, detect and prevent criminal activities. (2)

security survey An objective, critical, on-site examination and analysis of a business, industrial plant, public or private institution or dwelling to determine its existing security, to identify deficiencies, to determine the protection needed and to recommend improvements to enhance overall security. (14)

shoplifting The theft of retail merchandise while lawfully on the premises. Concealment of merchandise is prima facie evidence of intent to shoplift. In many states, price changing is also considered shoplifting. (16)

shopping service See *honesty shopping*. (16)

shrinkage Loss of assets. (6)

skips Nonpaying hotel or motel guests. (17)

sliding The practice in which a clerk sells articles to friends or relatives at lower cost. (16)

slipping a lock The insertion of a plastic credit card or thin screwdriver above the bolt of a lock, thereby forcing it downward and releasing the spring. (5)

SMART objectives Objectives that are specific, measurable, attainable, relevant and trackable. (22)

space alarms Alarms that protect a portion of the total interior of a room or building. Also called *area alarms*. (5)

span of management (or control) Number of people a manager is responsible for. (22)

spot alarms Alarms that protect specific items such as safes, cabinets, valuable articles and small areas. Also called *point alarms*. (5)

spring-loaded bolts Bolts that automatically enter the strike when the door is closed. Also called *latches*. (5)

Statute of Westminster A law issued by Kind Edward I that formalized England's system of criminal justice and apprehension. Established the *watch and ward, hue and cry* and *assize of arms* (1285). (1)

strict liability Refers to instances when the person is held liable to the injured party even though the person may not have knowingly done anything wrong—for example, using explosives or keeping wild animals as pets. Also called liability without fault. (4)

strike The part of a locking system into which the bolt is extended. (5)

sub-master key A key that opens all locks in a specific area. (6)

substantive damages Refer to actual damages a judge or jury feels the plaintiff is entitled to. (4)

supervisor Directly oversees the work of on-line personnel. Usually reports to a manager. (22)

telecommunications The science of communication by the transmission of electronic impulses—for example, telegraph, telephone, fax. (9)

telephone dialer An alarm system that automatically sends a recorded message or signal to a central station, the establishment's owner or manager or the police station. (5)

theft See *larceny/theft*. (8)

thermal detectors Fire detectors that respond to heat, usually temperatures in excess of 135 degrees Fahrenheit. (7)

tithings In Anglo-Saxon England, a unit of civil administration consisting of 10 families; established the principle of collective responsibility for maintaining law and order. (1)

top guard A barrier made of strands of barbed wire extending outward from the top of a fence at a 45-degree angle; also called a *header.* (5)

torts Civil wrongs for which the court seeks a remedy in the form of damages to be paid. (4)

toxic work environment A hostile workplace. Indicators of such an environment include highly authoritarian management styles, supervision that is changeable and unpredictable, management methods that are invasive of privacy and extreme secrecy. (20)

trailers Paths of paper or accelerant that spread fire from one location to another. (8)

trespassing The unlawful presence of a person on a property or inside the premises of someone else. (8)

24-hour clock Begins at midnight and does *not* start over in numbering at noon; it adds 12 to each hour in the afternoon, for example, 1:00 P.M. is 1300 hours. Also called *military time.* (12)

Uniform Crime Reports (UCR) Statistics on crime, compiled annually by the FBI. (8)

unity of command People have only one supervisor. (22)

unlawful taking A category of crime that includes *larceny/theft, burglary* and *robbery. (8)*

vandalism The malicious or intentional damaging and/or destroying of public or private property. Also called *criminal damage to property* or *malicious destruction of property.* (8)

vault A completely fire-resistive enclosure used exclusively for storage. (5)

vicarious liability The legal responsibility for the acts of another person because of some relationship with that person—for example, the liability of an employer for the acts of an employee. (4)

virtual corporation Results when several organizations form temporary partnerships in which each participating company brings to the table its core capabilities. (9)

virus See *computer virus.* (9)

vulnerability An organization's susceptibility to risks. (14)

warded locks Locks that have an open keyway; commonly used up to the 1940s. (5)

watch and ward A custom that provided town watchmen to patrol the city during the night and the ward to patrol the city during the day. (In Middle Engligh, *Wardien* meant to keep watch.) (1)

watch clock A seven-day timepiece. Keys are located at various stations in a facility; the security officer simply inserts the key into the watch clock at each station, and a record is automatically made of the time the location has been checked. (5)

white-collar crime Business-related crime, such as embezzlement, bribery and receiving kickbacks. (8)

zero floor release limit All charges are cleared with the credit-card issuer. (16)

Answers to Critical Thinking Exercises

Chapter 5 The court considered the alarm company's failure to respond to multiple alarm signals, its failure to notify the police and the advice to "forget the assignment" and found these to be grossly negligent acts. [Answer is C.]

Chapter 6 There appear to be conflicting inferences on whether the guard should have noticed an assault in progress inside Erickson's car. A security firm hired to patrol a ramp has a duty to use that degree of care that a reasonably prudent professional security firm would use, and this duty extends to customers of the ramp as well as to customers of the hotel. The owner/operator of a parking ramp facility has a duty to use reasonable care to deter criminal activity on its premises that may cause personal harm to customers. [Answer is A.]

Chapter 7 The organizer, sponsor and promoter of a wrestling exhibition is required to anticipate foreseeable problems and to use care to prevent injury to patrons. This duty included arranging for a sufficient number of security personnel to control the crowd. The security firm has a duty to exercise ordinary care by ensuring that there are adequate security guards stationed in the arena to control the crowd and prevent any injuries. When they fail to perform this duty and their negligence is the proximate cause of injuries inflicted upon an invited person by another person, they are liable along with the one who actually delivers the blow. [Answer is E.]

Chapter 8 Private security guards hired to maintain order and protect business invitees have no obligation to retreat when acting in the course of their employment but may meet deadly force with deadly force. It is not reasonable for them to retreat to safety when their job requires them to be present and maintain order to provide security for business invitees. [Answer is D.]

Chapter 9 Illegal use of a telephoned access device is punishable by up to 15 years in prison and a $250,000 fine. Computer fraud carries potential penalties of 20 years in prison and a $250,000 fine. Charges in connection with the Internet spree could be in addition to these. [Answer is B.]

Chapter 10 When a security company signs a contract with a business to provide security services, a special relationship is created between the security provider and the business's customers. This relationship is sufficient to obligate the security officers to act affirmatively to protect customers while they are on the business premises. [Answer is E.]

Chapter 11 The security guards acted in accordance with their duty to investigate suspicious activity, and their retreat in the face of deadly force was reasonable. There is demonstrable evidence that Garza-Herrera can be accused of committing assault in the second degree. And his act of pointing a pistol at a security guard and pulling the trigger is sufficient for him to be charged with attempted murder. [Answer is A.]

Chapter 12 There is sufficient proof to convict Alderman of petty theft. However, a merchant can escape liability in Minnesota only if he detains a suspect for the sole purpose of delivering him to a peace officer. Use of unreasonable force precludes immunity for false imprisonment regarding detention of suspected shoplifters by merchants or for citizen's arrest. Intentional torts frequently support an award of punitive damages; malice is inferred from such conduct. [Answer is B.]

Chapter 13 Property loss is less serious than the possibility of personal injury or death, so McWaters acted appropriately in being nonconfrontational. His courtroom testimony was sufficiently specific in essential ways to accurately identify and convict Lawrence Atwater of a felony. McWaters should not give testimony on anything other (hearsay evidence) than the facts he observed. [Answer is E.]

Chapter 14 The degree of control the guards possessed is the crucial factor. Based on their employer-employee relationship, they have a duty to exercise reasonable care. Lopez created the necessary relationship by driving onto the campus in their presence in an intoxicated condition. The guards did take control of Lopez by returning him to his car and removing him from the campus, despite campus policy that states that anyone "found on campus with liquor" is to be placed in "protective custody." [Answer is E.]

Chapter 15 A security agency is liable to a landowner for theft by the security agency's guard while the security guard is on duty. It is not necessary to determine whether the guard was acting within the scope of his employment at the time of the theft. In this case all that the ABC Security guard had to do to prevent theft was exactly what the contract called for: guard the property and not steal it. [Answer is C.]

Chapter 16 The occurrence of numerous occasions of similar criminal activity in one fairly contiguous area in a limited time span makes further criminal acts reasonably foreseeable. The supermarket and land owner have a duty to take steps to guard patrons from harm or at least warn them of the risk. [Answer is A.]

Chapter 17 A landowner may be liable for injuries to a known trespasser caused by criminal acts of third parties when the landowner is aware of the high risk of criminal activity. Minnesota statutes impose a duty of care not to permit minors to engage in a sexual performance. Violation of the statute imposes absolute liability. [Answer for 1 is E.]

The elements of primary assumption of risk are whether a person had (1) knowledge of the risk, (2) an appreciation of the risk and (3) a choice to avoid the risk but voluntarily chose to chance the risk. [Answer for 2 is D.]

Chapter 18 Decisions of a college not to cancel an event and not to hire additional security for an event are policy decisions protected by the doctrine of discretionary immunity. A college has no duty to warn an entrant onto its property of the danger of a third party's criminal acts when those actions are not foreseeable. [Answer is E.]

Chapter 19 The officers were lawfully in Mahlberg's residence to conduct a search. Mahlberg was present when the search produced evidence of theft. An officer is not required to first obtain a separate arrest warrant but can arrest a suspect immediately in his home. [Answer is A.]

Chapter 20 Proximate cause need not be established with such certainty as to exclude all other possible means of entry and access to the 11th floor. Because the Echelon contract called for protecting employees from injury, the company can be held liable as the proximate cause of Billings' death. [Answer is A.]

Chapter 21 When the employee of a security guard service is retained by a manufacturer, but he is bribed to leave his post and during his absence theft occurs, the guard service has breached its contract and its liability extends to the total amount of inventory loss, especially because the service knew that the manufacturer had internal theft problems and that the purpose of hiring was to help abolish inventory loss. Because Miles was deliberately absent from the premises, the contractual obligation was breached. [Answer is C.]

Chapter 22 The medical report of Covalciuc can be properly excluded as inadmissible hearsay, but a jury could conclude that Vacanti's back pain was caused by the incident. The use of force sufficient to cause this injury can be interpreted to go beyond the exercise of reasonable force. Thus, Master Electronics can be held liable for provable damages. [Answer is B.]

AUTHOR INDEX

A

Adam, H.L., 14
Addis, Karen K., 145, 240, 504, 557
Adler, Steven, 153, 477
Aiken, Kevin A., 538
Allison, John, 73
Alpert, David, 595, 596
Anderson, Teresa, 451, 548
Arbetter, Lisa, 65, 290, 548, 551, 584, 587
Arko, Robert L., 558, 559, 702
Arneke, David, 278
Arnold, David W., 148
Arscott, Robert D., 40
Astor, S.D., 181
Atlas, Randall, 489
Azano, Harry J., 220, 546

B

Bachman, Ronet, 627
Backler, Michael A., 558
Bagley, Gerald L., 568, 570, 575, 576
Bailey, F. Lee, 37
Band, William A., 700
Barr, L., 719
Barr, N., 719
Barron, Ted P., 527, 528, 705
Bartholomew, Douglas, 146
Bastian, Lisa D., 577
Bates, Regis J., 298
Bayley, David H., 51
Bearman, David, 255
Beattie, Henry J., 66
Beaudette, John P., 147, 149, 151
Bennett, Wayne W., 52, 250, 339
Benny, Daniel J., 240, 557
Benson, Michael L., 249
Bequai, August, 148
Berry, S.L., 279
Berube, Henri, 119
Betts, Curt P., 440
Bias, Bronson S., 577, 578
Binder, D., 245
Bird, Robert J., 280
Black, J.K., 303, 305
Black, Michael A., 511
Blackwell, Ray, 452
Blake, William F., 199
Blanchard, Kenneth, 653, 654, 676
Blauvelt, Peter D., 578
Blennerhassett, Charles H., 617, 619
Bobek, John, 138
Bock, Peter E., Jr., 545
Bocklet, Richard, 58, 61, 65, 329
Boim, Israel, 618
Borchert, Don, 590
Bordes, Roy N., 115, 463, 527, 594
Bottom, Norman R., Jr., 65, 180
Bowers, Kim, 117
Boynton, Homer A., 556
Bracalente, Anita, 591, 594
Braithwaite, John, 248
Brandes, Robert, 63
Brandt, Gerald T., 627, 632, 637, 638, 639, 641, 643
Braunstein, Susan, 661
Brennan, J., 313, 314, 315, 330
Brennan, Joseph M., 627, 632, 637, 638, 639, 641, 643
Bridges, Curtis, 503
Bridges, W., 719
Broderick, Richard, 627, 629
Brooks, C.M., 484
Brown, Bill, 84
Brown, Lee P., 661
Buckley, David M., 151
Buckley, Joseph P. III, 373
Bucqueroux, Bonnie, 65, 66
Burden, Ordway P., 62
Burns, Kenneth, 591
Burrows, Robin, 592
Burton, P.J., 454
Butler, Charles W., 275

C

Cain, Candy M., 56
Campbell, Anne, 633
Campbell, Douglas A., 574
Cantor, Michael B., 556
Cardwell, Michael, 199

Carey, Patricia, 656
Carnevale, A.P., 718, 719
Carolin, P. James, 479
Carroll, Charles R., 249, 254
Cassidy, Kevin A., 63
Cawood, Gil, 329
Cawood, James S., 640, 643
Cernock, Thomas W., 512
Chamberlain, C.S., 457
Chanaud, Robert C., 279, 280
Channell, Warren T., 545
Chanter, M., 120
Chapman, William E., 504
Chovanes, Michael H., 527
Chuda, Thomas, 84, 573
Church, Wayne, 607, 609
Chuvala, John, 551
Clark, Bill, 135
Clark, Jacob R., 206
Coleman, Randall, 223
Collins, Pam, 580, 703
Conly, Catherine H., 285
Connor, G., 81
Cooney, Caroline M., 68
Corbett, William T., 557
Cosper, George W., 512
Coutourie, Larry, 303
Critchley, T.A., 7, 8, 10, 12
Crowe, Timothy D., 97, 578, 579
Cullen, Francis T., 249
Cullinane, David M., 278
Cunningham, William C., 24, 31, 40, 56, 59, 65, 66, 73, 86, 96, 112, 127, 179, 236, 285, 287, 290, 293, 295, 656, 658, 718, 719
Cushing, Loretto, 320

D

Dabney, Dean A., 476
D'Addario, Francis, 60, 509
Dalrymple, John, 556
Davis, Donald L., 281
Dawson, Donald F., 575
Dean, Edward T., 572
Dean, S. Carl, 116, 217
Dees, Timothy M., 89
DeGrange, Donna J., 146, 173
Demoulpied, David S., 556
Dermaut, John M., 614, 617
Dewhurst, H.S., 17
Dickey, S., 282, 296, 297
Dingle, Jeff, 29, 96
Dodson, Minot, 683, 684
Donnelly, John F., 451
Dowling, Jack F., 583
Draty, David, 145, 197, 206, 290, 546, 568, 632, 639
Drew, Edward J., Jr., 56
DuBose, Michael J., 222, 223
Dulcamaro, Sal, 163
Dunckel, Kenneth, 110
Dunn, Patrick A., 77
Dunston, Dain, 149
Durham, N.C., 511, 513

E

Eberhart, Jon A., 422, 440
Elam, Stanley M., 653
Elig, Gene, 236, 248
Englman, Steven, 280
Enright, John, 700
Epps, Cheryl Anthony, 196
Erickson, John, 591, 592, 595
Evans, D.D., 373
Evans, David G., 255
Exter, Thomas, 318

F

Fahed, Joseph M., 530
Fair, Frank K., 658
Farber, R.C., 182
Farnell, M., 51
Fay, John, 207, 273, 275
Fenker, Lisa, 477
Fennelly, Lawrence J., 488, 514, 516
Fey, T.M., 597, 598, 599
Fischer, Robert J., 11
Fisse, Brent, 248
Flinn, Rick J., 571
Flores, Thomas V., 615
Floyd, William R., 430, 432
Folley, Vern, 5
Folsom, W.B., 289, 304
Forcht, Karen, 291
Foster, Al, 199
Fox, James Alan, 629, 633, 634
Foyle, Michael P., 528
Frank, Jeff, 131
Frank, Robert W., 490
Franklin, Forrest P., 642

G

Gallagher, G. Patrick, 83, 84
Gallati, Robert J., 450, 674
Gallup, Alec M., 653

Gardiner, Richard A., 190
Gardner, T.J., 502, 503
Gargan, Joseph P., 641
Garner, Gerald, 329
Garrett, Glen R., 339, 340
Gates, Daryl, 456, 591
Gillespie, Tom, 114, 115
Glazebrook, Jerome H., 617, 619
Glensor, Ronald W., 326
Goetzke, Richard, 530
Goldberg, Joel A., 703
Golsby, Mark, 422, 430
Goodboe, Michael E., 280, 689
Gordon, Marsha, 248
Gough, T.W., 16, 18
Grady, John C., 679
Graham, James P., 550, 633
Graham, Richard K., 133
Grassie, Richard P., 190
Graves, C. Ray, 574, 641
Green G., 182
Green, Gion, 11, 428, 429, 431, 527, 536, 538, 557, 585, 695
Grevenites, Jim, 482
Griffiths, Barry, 121, 122
Groussman, Jon D., 341, 342
Guyet, Allan R., 56

H

Hall, J., 7, 20
Hall, Stephen J., 572
Hamit, Francis, 38, 54, 63, 67, 206, 224, 314, 316, 328, 710
Hammer, A., 720
Hansen, Michael, 275, 276
Harowitz, Sherry L., 224, 278, 525, 575, 707
Harpole, Tom, 108
Harris, William G., 149
Hayes, James L., 348
Hayes, Read, 153, 493, 496
Haynes, Richard A., 584
Head, Thomas, 345, 346
Healy, R.J., 3, 4
Heffernan, Richard J., 273, 279
Heine, Kimberly, 613, 615, 619
Heine, William D., Jr., 170
Henrickson, David E., 559
Herman, Martin B., 204, 635, 637, 642, 643
Hertig, Christopher A., 29, 57, 61, 317
Hess, Kären M., 52, 85, 250, 339, 341, 344, 347, 348, 349, 368, 389
Higgins, C.E., 467, 468
Hildreth, Reed, 612, 613
Hill, William T., 151, 152
Himelfarb, Frum, 649, 650
Hinkle, Douglas P., 584, 588
Hinman, David B., 469
Hively, Jeff, 511
Hodges, Jill, 632
Hof, Robert D., 117
Hoffman, John W., 65
Hollinger, Richard C., 476
Hope, George, 406
Hopkins, Tricia, 217
Hyams, Michael T., 652

I

Inbau, Fred E., 150
Inciardi, J.A., 245
Ingber, Clifford J., 76
Inwald, Robin E., 640

J

Jackson, Eric, 588
Jackson, Fred J., 571
Jacobs, Deborah L., 345, 346
Jacobson, Jerry L., 129
Jayne, Brian C., 149, 151, 346, 373
Jefferson, Bob, 119
Jeffery, C.Ray, 23
Jelen, George F., 281
Jenkins, Alan B., 205, 210
Jenkins, Joe, 555
Johnson, Dennis L., 630, 632, 634, 635, 637, 638, 644
Johnston, W., 719
Jones, Lee A., 66
Jones, Theodore S., 584, 588

K

Kahler, Kathryn, 251, 254
Kahn, James R., 423
Kakalik, J.S., 29, 256, 262
Kaplan, Jon, 286
Kass, Michael, 195
Kaufer, Steve, 580, 581
Kaye, Michael S., 19, 20
Keller, Steven R., 592
Kent, David R., 36, 238
Keough, Patrick, 277
Kime, Roy Caldwell, 196
King, Carl E., 149, 254, 255
King, J. Freeman, 322

Kingsbury, A.A., 431
Kinney, Joseph K., 630, 632, 634, 635, 638
Kissane, Thomas P., 591, 593
Klehbauch, John B., 630, 632, 634, 638
Klein, Gerald, 488
Kluepfel, Henry M., 278
Kmet, M.A., 575
Knight, George, 456
Kochen, William L., 276
Kochis, Joseph A., 613, 614
Koentopp, Juli, 538
Kohr, Robert L., 196, 422, 425, 443, 540, 543, 544, 701
Kolpacki, Thomas A., 68
Konicek, Joel, 591, 607, 609
Kornegay, Jennifer, 277
Kostanoski, John I., 180
Kouri, James J., 82, 203, 204
Kovacich, Gerald L., 430, 441
Kramer, Tom, 571
Krott, Rob, 285, 286, 631, 632, 633, 639
Kuhn, Ryan A., 147, 150

L

Lamar, Jacob V., 326
Lambert, Marc P., 40
Lang, Robert F., 548
Lang, William G., 82
Langer, Steven, 695
LaRatta, Robert, 34
Lasky, Barry M., 146
Lavine, S.A., 18
Layne, Stevan, 597
LeBeau, Michael, 278
LeDoux, Darryl T., 39, 683, 706
Leo, Thomas W., 430
Lesce, Tony, 611
Lettieri, Linda, 348
LeVeglia, Anthony J., 63
Levin, Jack, 629, 633, 634
Lewin, Thomas M., 120, 127
Libby, Don, 556
Lindsey, Dennis, 637
Lisko, Richard F., 146
List, Bruce C., 452
Litchford, Jody M., 345
Little, Stephen, 541
Littlejohn, Robert F., 274
Lombardi, John H., 572
Longmore-Etheridge, Ann, 707
Lorenzo, Ray, 110, 111
Lottes, Steve, 488
Loveless, David G., 133
Lukes, Beth, 274

M

Maakestad, William J., 249
MacDonald, Robert R., 135
Magee, Maureen, 157
Major, Michael J., 129, 545, 586
Mallory, Jim, 205
Mancebo, Marty, 149
Mangan, Terence J., 24, 56, 66
Manning, Anita, 318
Manning, Walt W., 283
Martin, Deirdre, 287, 304
Martin, Scott L., 146, 173
Martin, William E., 591
Marx, Gary T., 52, 61, 62, 63
Mason, Marcy, 615, 617
Maturi, Richard J., 153, 180
Maxwell, David A., 56, 62, 77, 126, 140, 266, 495, 545, 664, 665, 689, 690
May, Johnny R., 541, 543
May, William A., Jr., 198, 201
McArney, Leslie, 650
McCarthy, William F., 205
McCaulley, M., 720
McClain, Eddy L., 146, 147
McClure, Leslie, 526
McCullough, Joseph B., 119
McDaniel, Danny, 595
McDonough, Thomas, 423
McEwan, Tom, 351
McEwen, J. Thomas, 285
McGuffey, Jim, 35
McInerney, Robert, 595, 596
McKennan, John, 618, 619, 620
McKinnon-Fowler, Ellen, 36, 238
McMicking, Lawrence, 133, 134, 610, 612
McNamara, John, 477
Meadows, Robert G., 76
Meier, R.D., 367, 368
Mele, Joe A., 119, 298
Miehl, Fred, 116
Miller, Ben, 117
Miller, R. Reuben, 556, 557
Minahan, J., 719
Mogil, B. Marc, 406
Monahan, L.H., 367, 368
Montgomery, Robert L., 361
Moore, David W., 650
Moore, Mark, 650, 655
Moore, Wayne D., 213, 217
Morgan, Lynn H., 344, 346, 347

Moskowitz, Carl, 280
Mourey, Richard, 115
Muller, Michael G., 610, 611, 612
Munk, Nina, 32, 60
Muntz, Alan M., 39
Murphree, Gary, 451
Murphy, Joan H., 117, 525
Murray, Kevin D., 274, 279

N

Natter, F., 720
Naudts, John, 115, 116
Newton, Mike, 130, 131
Nianiatus, George, 463
Nichols, Ralph G., 361
Nielsen, Robert C., 584
Nobrega, Kathryn, 196
Norton, Kelly, 131
Nudell, Mayer, 615
Nugent, High, 293, 294

O

Obremski, Frank, 559
O'Brien, Jim, 129
Ohlhausen, Peter, 552, 553
Olick, M., 40, 84, 117, 197, 198, 278, 303, 613
Oliver, Carl R., 203
Olmos, Ross A., 629, 631, 639, 640, 643, 644
Olmstead, Patrick R., 217
Oran, Daniel, 74, 75, 77, 650
Owens, Thomas, 500

P

Packer, A., 719
Paine, D., 30
Pankau, Edmund J., 339
Papi, Vincent, 223
Pappageorge, Tom, 130
Parker, Eugene, 131
Parker, L.C., Jr., 367, 368
Patterson, Julien, 67, 68
Patterson, Tom, 286
Pavlicek, Larry, 281
Peak, Ken, 326
Peale, Norman Vincent, 653, 654
Perry, Mary E.B., 513
Perry, William E., 300
Peters, T., 718, 719
Peterson, Raymond L., 551
Phelps, E. Floyd, 161, 507, 582, 585, 588
Pierce, Kenneth R., 37
Pilcher, Wayland D., 658
Pizer, Harry, 557
Plante, William, 424
Platt, John, 223
Potoski, Jim, 547
Potter, A.N., 511, 512
Powell, John W., 585
Preston, Charles M., 298
Proctor, David, 318
Purpura, Philip, 218, 331, 399

Q

Queeno, Cameron L., 158
Quigley, Robert C., 205

R

Ramsdell, Edward A., 40
Rea, Kelly V., 150
Readhimer, Robert, 456
Reibstein, Larry, 56, 60
Reith, C., 2, 3, 5, 11, 13, 19
Remesch, Kimberly A., 56
Revis, Sharon W., 40
Reynolds, Sandra, 101
Ricks, T., 341
Robbins, Clyde E., 559, 560
Roberts, Kenneth M., 663, 664
Roll, Fredrick G., 431
Romilly, S., 10
Ronan, Thomas O., 538
Rose, Lowell C., 653
Rosen, Mark B., 81, 87, 148
Roughton, James E., 193, 198
Rubin, Hal, 455, 466
Rutledge, Devallis, 404, 407, 411

S

Saenz, Paul, 576
Salamone, Robert, 583
Samson, Andrea, 572
Schafer, June P., 149
Scheirer, S. Robin, 110
Schmock, Leo F., 199
Schnabolk, Charles, 73, 75
Schreiber, F. Barry, 528, 530
Schultz, Norman O., 275
Schwartau, Winn, 296, 297

Schweitzer, James A., 274, 299
Scotti, Anthony J., 616
Scuro, Daniel P., 275
Seidman, Stephan, 117
Selwitz, Robert, 544
Serpico, Philip, 490
Seuter, Edward J., 207, 210
Shalna, Anothny J., 216
Shanahan, Michael G., 24, 56, 66
Sharp, Arthur G., 247, 249, 548
Shaw, R.A. "Buck," 213
Shea, John B., 330, 332
Shearing, Clifford D., 23, 51, 551
Sherwood, J.L., 212, 570, 701
Shirley, Joe, 549, 550
Shook, H.C., 59
Simonsen, Clifford E., 649, 652, 658, 661, 662
Skurecki, Michael H., 434
Sloan, John J., 580
Sloan, Stephen, 557
Smith, Karen, 618
Somerson, Ira S., 77, 281
Sopsic, J.P., 674
South, Nigel, 9
Spurlock, James C., 135
Stapleton, Bernard, 470
Stedman, Michael J., 205, 206, 556, 575
Steinberg, Scott L., 146
Steinbrecher, David, 287, 301
Stenning, Philip C., 23, 51, 551
Stephenson, Richard G., 153, 247
Stokes, Floyd D., 341, 344, 347, 349, 389
Stoks, Francis G., 596
Stoller, William H., 146
Story, Donald W., 511, 598
Strandberg, Keith W., 285
Straub, Joanne, 544
Strauchs, John J., 24, 31, 40, 56, 66, 73, 86, 112, 285, 287, 290, 293, 295, 656, 658, 718, 719
Sundberg, Edward A., 706
Sunstrom, Philip C., 193, 194, 342, 343, 541
Surette, Kevin J., 572
Sutherland, Garrell E., 29
Swartwood, Dan T., 274, 281
Syed, Sohail A., 276

T

Taitz, Sharyn, 73, 77, 399, 401, 412, 414, 695
Tanzer, Marc, 275, 277
Taylor, Bruce M., 577
Taylor, T.H., 31, 59, 65, 96, 127, 179, 236
Tesorero, Francis X., 504, 508, 509
Tharp, David O., 40
Thiemann, Alan J., 148
Thomas, Elaine, 361
Thomas, Ronald C., 588
Thompson, Pamela Kleibrink, 547, 548
Thompson, Richard, 540, 542
Thompson, Steve, 138
Thornton, William E., 36, 238
Tilett, B., 341
Toffler, Alvin, 274
Totton, Mark S., 276
Tozer, E., 20
Trojanowicz, Robert, 65, 66
Truncer, Earl, 157
Turner, Dana L., 153, 199, 247
Tyre, Mitchell, 661
Tyska, Louis A., 488, 514, 516, 706, 707

U

Utz, Thomas E., 581

V

Vail, Christopher, 405, 406
Van Meter, Clifford W., 24, 31, 40, 56, 66, 73, 86, 112, 285, 287, 290, 293, 295, 341, 656, 658, 718, 719
Vance, Charles F., 204
Vassell, William C., 40
Veich, Mickey, 345, 346
Viau, Bryan, 607, 608, 609
Vitch, Martin L., 100, 123

W

Wade, Bob, 278
Wade, James R., 281
Wainwright, O.O., 672, 694
Wallace, Donald H., 246
Waltman, Jim, 278
Walton, J. Branch, 633, 637, 638, 641
Warrington, Mark, 580, 581
Wasserman, Robert, 650, 655
Webb, Susan L., 347
Weiland, Ross, 320
Weiss, Robert P., 22
Wells, Joseph T., 339, 341, 347, 348, 352, 368, 373
Wenek, John R., 279

Werth, Richard P., 546
Wessells, Fred P., 526
West, Marty L., 64, 67
White, Gary H., 283
Wildhorn, S., 29, 256, 262
Willingham, Mark, 411
Wilson, Caroline, 490, 511
Wipprecht, William R., 528
Witkowski, Michael J., 532
Woods, Everett K., 246
Worthen, John D., 286
Wrich, Manes T., 251, 254
Wrobleski, Henry M., 85, 250, 341, 344, 347, 348, 349, 368, 389

Z

Zaleski, J.E., Jr., 316, 317
Zamengo, Edward, 118, 119
Zappile, R., 67
Zehring, Timothy, 321
Zimmerman, David H., 617
Zuckerman, Roger E., 37
Zunkel, Richard L., 117

Subject Index

A

AAA standards for hotels/motels, 544
abbreviations in security, common, 379
ABC fire extinguishers, 219
absence seizures, 323
acceptance of risk, 440
access control, 115–116, 153–173, 203, 217, 458, 532–534, 535–536, 556, 568, 569–570, 572, 582, 586, 594, 612, 639
  accounting procedures, 170–173
  after hours, 156
  airline, 556
  badges, 155–161
  business forms, 166
  camera use restrictions, 170, 171, 172
  cards, 115–116
  check in/out procedures, 155, 156
  colleges and universities, 582
  computerized, 594
  computers, 167
  contractors, 159–161
  copy machine, 166
  courts, 612
  documents, 166
  electronic, 586
  equipment, 165–167
  financial assets, 170–173
  fire alarm, 217
  forklifts, 166
  hospitals, 568, 569–570, 572
  housing complexes, 535–536
  key control, 161–164
  mail rooms, 166
  office buildings, 532–534
  passes, 155–161
  property control, 167
  protecting information, 167–168, 170
  purpose of, 153
  receiving procedures, 170–173
  riots, 203
  seals, 170
  stock rooms, 165–166
  supply rooms, 166
  system, 115
  tour groups, 158
  vehicle, 154
  vendors, 159–161
  video equipment use restrictions, 170
  visitors, 158, 159
  vulnerable areas, 165–167
  warehouses, 165–166
  workplace violence, 639
accident prevention, 193–195
  OSHA, 194
accidents, 189–234, 342–344
  investigating, 342–344
  preventing losses from, 189–234
accounting procedures, 170–173
accurate notes, 378
accurate reports, 382
Achille Lauro, 559
acoustical surveillance, 279–280
  four levels of, 280
actions and public relations, 316–317
administrative controls for computer security, 298–299
administrative reports, 379
administrative responsibilities, 676–680
  budgets, 677
  daily orders, 677
  educational programs, 677–678
  employee awareness programs, 679
  financial controls, 677
  goals, 676
  image, 679–680
  policies, 677
  procedures, 677
  SMART objectives, 676
advance security technology, 451
advance work, 617
affirmative action, 682
after-hours procedures, 156, 164–165
age requirements, 684
agenda, 682
agreements, 276
AIDS, protecting against, 196–197
air cargo, theft of, 240, 554
airport-airline security, 554–557
  access control, 556
  bombings, 554, 555, 557

cargo theft, 554
corporate, 557
drug trafficking, 557
escape hijacking, 557
screening passengers and baggage, 555
skyjacking, 554, 555
terrorism, 557
alarm dogs, 134
alarm respondents, 35–36, 126
alarm services, 31
alarms, 19–20, 66, 119–128, 133, 215–217, 487–488, 527, 578, 582, 593
area, 120
banks, 527
basic parts, 121–123
cable, 487
canvas painting, 487
capacity, 123
central station, 126
circuits, 121–123
electronically activated price tags, 133, 487–488
false, 66, 126–128
fire, 19, 120, 215–217
listen-in systems, 66
local, 126
loop, 487
monitored, 120
museums, 593
perimeter, 120
plug, 487
point, 120
police-connected, 126
proprietary, 126
pull boxes, 217
respondents, 126
ribbon switch, 487
schools, 578
sensors, 121, 122
signal, 121
space, 120
spot, 120
telephone dialers, 123
wafer switch, 487
wireless, 123
alcohol abuse, workplace, 146, 249–256
alcohol server liability, 543
Alfred P. Murrah Federal Building bombing, 206–207
alternative weapons, 83
alternatives to handling risks, 438–440
Alzheimer's disease (A.D.), 318, 491
American Automobile Association (AAA) standards for hotels/motels, 544
American Banking Association, 21, 528
American District Telegraph Company (ADT), 20, 36
American Express, 16
American Society for Industrial Security (ASIS), 44–45, 46, 528, 659–661, 662, 663
code of ethics, 659–661, 662, 663
Americans with Disabilities Act (ADA), 148–149, 196, 319–320
ancient times, 3–6
Anderson et al. v. Monongahela Power Company and the Allegheny Power System, Inc., 341–342
andragogy, 689
Anglo Saxon times, 6
animal control, 66
annual inventory system, 176–177
antiabortion activists, violence by, 572
appearance and public relations, 314–316
appearance of premises, physical, 103–104
application, 149, 686
apprehension of shoplifters, 491–493
architecture, open, 709
archives security, 596–597
area alarms, 120
armed couriers, 35, 38, 176
armed security personnel, 82–83
armored car services, 20, 31, 35, 38
arrest, 54, 56, 63, 257–260, 491–493
citizens, 257–260, 492
power of, 54, 56, 63
shoplifters, 259–260, 491–493
arson, 244–247
common sites for, 246
defined, 244
evidence of, 246
igniter, 246
offender types, 245
trailer, 246
art galleries (*see also* museums), 591–597
art theft, 591
ARTCENTRAL, 593–594
ASIS, 44–45, 46, 528, 659–661, 662, 663
assault, 55, 79, 244, 349–350, 393, 569
report, 393
assets, storing, 109–111
assize of arms, 8
Association of American Railroads, 16
assumptions, 381
Atamian v. Supermarkets General Corp., 80

attack dogs, 134
audio discriminators, 124
audits, 163–164, 176–177, 299, 434, 444, 681–682
  conducting, 681–682
  external, 176–177, 299
  internal, 176–177
  key, 163–164
  self, 434
  typical process, 444
Augustus, Emperor, 4–6
authoritarian, 682
authority, 51, 54–56, 682
  defined, 51
  legal, 54–56
authorization to take pictures, request for, 171
autocratic, 682
autographic register system, 507
automated clearinghouse (ACH), 526
automatic guard-monitoring systems, 136
automatic teller machine (ATM), 525, 528–530
  embezzlement, 530
  fraudulent card use at, 529
  insider manipulation of, 529
  muggings, 530
  physical attack of, 530
  robbery, 530
  security measures at, 530
  servicing, 530
  unauthorized card use at, 529
  vandalism of, 530
automobile accidents, 319
avoiding lawsuits, 147, 352

B

background investigations, 34, 148, 149, 150, 151, 299, 459, 681–682, 686
backstretch area, 552
backup (computer), 302–303
bad checks (*see also* checks), 496–501
  types of, 498–499
badges and passes, 155–161, 569
  contractors, 159–161
  employee, 569
  permanent, 160–161
  sign-in/out log, 157
  temporary, 157
  tour groups, 158
  vendors, 159–161
  visitors, 158, 159
baggage security, 555
Baggs v. Eagle-Picher Industries, 173
bait money, 526
ballasts, 119
Bank Administration Institute (BAI), 528
Bank Protection Act of 1968, 526
bank security department responsibilities, 525
bank security officers (*see also* financial institutions), 56
bank vaults, 19
bar codes, 485
barbed wire fence, 100, 101
bar-coding devices, 136
barium ferrite cards, 116
barrier of light, 103
barriers, 98, 99, 365, 618
  functions of, 98
  language, 618
  perimeter, 99
  to communication, 365
basic lines of defense, 99–111
  exterior, 104–109
  interior, 109–111
  perimeter, 99–104
basic physical controls, 96–99
basic security equipment, 111–131
basic security survey, 433
battery, 79
becoming a security professional, 694–696
behavior codes, 579
behavior requirements for CPP, 45
bike patrol, 512, 588
biometric security system, 117, 296, 709
bionic briefcase, 133
blank check, 497
blind individuals, interacting with, 321
blind receiving, 172
body language, 373–374
bodyguard services, 31, 32, 613–614
bolt mechanisms, 112–114
bomb detectors, 133, 212
bombs and bomb threats, 205–212, 554, 555, 557
  airlines, 554, 555, 557
  common sites for, 211
  common victims of, 207
  communication among searchers, 211
  evacuation, 210
  homemade, 207
  incendiary, 207
  Institute of Makers of Explosives (IME), 212
  mail, 212
  Molotov cocktails, 207

motives for, 207
preventing, 207–208
receiver of threat, 208
recent attacks, 205–207
response to, 208–210
sample form, 209
search, 210–212
telephone operator's response, 208–210
bonded couriers, 20
bonding, 179–180
bonds, fidelity, 180
booster box, 480
boundary lighting, 103
boundary markers, 99, 100–101
Bow Street Runners, 12, 13–14
Bowman v. State, 54
boxcars, 172
breach of peace, 350, 393
breaking and entering, 350
brevity (notes), 378
briefcase inspection, 177–178
Brink, Washington Perry, 20
Brink's, 20–21, 38
Brown v. Jewel Companies, Inc., 77
budget, security, 442, 677
establishing, 677
example, 442
budget motels, security of, 540
bug detection systems, 133
bugging, 298
building codes, 98
building exterior, 104–109
doors, 104–107
floors, 108–109
lighting, 109
other openings, 108
roof, 108–109
walls, 108–109
windows, 108
building industry, theft from, 454
building interior, 109–111
physical layout, 109
bulletproof vests, 133
bureaucratic, 682
burglar alarms, 19, 22, 65
central, 19
devices, 22
electric, 19
response to, 65
systems, 22
burglarproof safes, 18
burglar-resistant safe, 110
burglary, 110, 118, 240–241, 243, 350, 393, 535
checklist, 242
defense against, 241
defined, 240
report, 393
residential dwellings, 535
resistant files, safes and vaults, 110
"smash and grab," 240
steps individuals can take to deter, 535
unlawful taking, 243
Burglary Protection Council, 22
Burns, William J., 21, 38
Burns' Detective Agency, 21, 38
bushes, 101, 103
business form protection, 166
business records, 109–111
business recovery planning, 224

C

cable alarms, 487
calibrating a witness, 368
California v. Greenwood et al., 277
call-back modem, 297
cameras, 129–131, 132, 170, 171, 172, 501, 527, 608
authorization to use, 171
pass, 172
photo-identity, 501
restrictions on use of, 170
campus security (*see* colleges and universities, educational institutions)
Canterbury Downs report form, 380
canvas painting alarm, 487
capacity alarms, 123
carbon dioxide fire extinguishers, 218, 220, 302
carbon monoxide, 197–198, 540
detectors, 198
in hotels/motels, 540
cardboard cutouts, 489
card-key, 162, 541
card-operated locks, 115–116, 541
carelessness, 194
cargo security, 170, 172, 239–240, 460, 461, 554, 557
agencies assisting with investigations, 461
hijacking, 557
seals, 170, 172
theft, 239–240, 460, 461, 554
Carroll v. United States, 491
case law, 74
cash, 164, 170, 506–509, 534
handling, 164, 506–509

petty, 170, 534
procedural controls, 164
cash flow records, 508
cash registers, 164, 506–507
autographic, 507
theft from, 506–507
validating, 507
Cashman Field, 548
categories of civil offenses, 75–76
CCTV, 129–131, 132, 488–489, 504–505, 516, 608, 709, 711
CD-ROM databases, 339–340
cellular phones, 276, 279, 295
cemeteries, 599
central alarm respondents, 35–36
central burglar alarm services, 19
central role of security personnel, 37
central station alarm systems, 35–36, 126
Certified Protection Professional (CPP), 44–46
behaviors, 45
Code of Professional Responsibility, 45
education, 45
endorsement, 45
examinations, 45–46
experience, 45
chain-link fence, 100–101, 108
challenges facing security managers, 703–704
change in private security, future, 719
change key, 161
channels of communication, 358, 359–360
characteristics of a well-written report, 381–394
accurate, 382
checklist, 389, 390
clear, 385–386
complete, 383–384
concise, 384–385
factual, 381–382
in standard English, 387
key phrases for specific incidents, 392–394
legible, 387
mechanically correct, 386–387
objective, 383
on time, 387
structuring the narrative, 391–392
tips for writing more effectively, 389–391
characteristics of an effective investigator, 338–340
check fraud, 65
check kiting, 288
check-cashing information stamp, 502
check-in/out procedures, 155, 156
checklists, 162, 242, 390, 434, 435, 436–438, 443, 515–516, 542
burglary, 242
fire and pool safety, 542
key control, 162
manufacturing security, 436–438
reports, 390
retail security, 515–516
risk management, 435, 436–438
security, 434, 443
vulnerability, 435
checkout lanes, 485
checks, 65, 288, 496–502, 525
acceptable forms of identification, 500
bad, 496–501
blank, 497
cashing policies, 499
counter, 497, 498
examination of, 499–500
forged, 498
fraud, 65, 525
government, 497
high-risk, 498
identification, 500–501
illegible, 498
incorrectly written, 498
information stamp, sample, 501, 502
kiting, 288
money order, 497–498
no such account (NSA), 498
nonsufficient funds (NSF), 498
out-of-town, 498
payroll, 497
personal, 497
post-dated, 498
recording information, 501
refusing, 501
second-party, 498
traveler's, 497, 498
two-party, 497
types of, 497–498
unacceptable forms of identification, 501
universal, 497
chemical weapons, 83
chemicals, dangerous, 197
CHEMTREC, 198
Children's National Medical Center, 575
choke points, 616–617
circles of protection, 98
circuit, 121–123
citizen's arrest, 257–260, 492
certificate, 259

sample form, 260
statutory arrest authority by state, 258
City of Hialeah v. Weber, 62
civil disturbances, 201–202
civil lawsuits, 78–81
assault, 79
battery, 79
commonly brought against private security, 78–81
defamation, 79
false imprisonment, 79
intentional inflection of emotional distress, 79
invasion of privacy, 79
negligence, 79
civil liability, 55, 75, 85–86, 697–699
critical thinking exercise, 697–699
laws regarding, 85–86
civil litigation matters, 34
civil offenses, 74, 75–76, 238
categories of, 75–76
review, 238
civil recovery in shoplifting cases, 496
Civil Rights Act, 81–83, 148
armed security personnel, 82–83
use of force, 81–82
clamshell locks, 117
clarity (notes), 378
clear reports, 385–386
clearance, security, 150–151, 459–460
cliff dwellings, 3, 4
climate control, 174
clocks, watch, 135–136
closed circuit television (CCTV), 129–131, 132, 488–489, 504–505, 516, 578, 608, 709, 711
closing procedures, 164–165
clothing, 363
Coast Guard's Notice of Proposed Rule Making, 559
cocaine, 250
code of ethics, 656–662, 663
ASIS, 659–661, 662, 663
manager, 663
officer, 662
organizations with, 658
Code of Professional Responsibility, CPP, 45
collective deep pocket, 75
collective responsibility, 15
collective security, 2
colleges and universities, security of, 580–590, 703
access control, 582
alarm systems, 582
communications, 587
community policing philosophy, 588
dormitories, 583
drug use, 583
electronic access control, 586
ethnoviolence, 584
evolution of campus police systems, 581
exemplary program, 590
fads, 588
future of, 703
items most frequently stolen, 582
policing models, comparison of, 589
problems, 582–584
reducing problems, 584–590
special events, 584
statistics, 584–585
student patrol programs, 586
underage drinking, 583
Colonial Williamsburg, 595
Colquhoun, Patrick, 12–13
combination locks, 110, 114
command center, 136
commercial crimes, 630
commercial liability, 471–472
commercial security, 524–566
airport and airlines, 554–557
critical thinking exercise, 561–564
cruise ships, 559–560
financial institutions, 525–530
hotels/motels, 538–546
housing, 534–538
mass transit, 557–559
movie industry, 550–551
office buildings, 531–534
public gatherings, 546–550
racetracks, 552–554
recreational parks, 551–552
special events, 546–550
common abbreviations used, 379
common civil lawsuits brought against private security, 78–81
common defenses against civil lawsuits, 88
common law, 74
common tactics of cross-examination, 410
communication, 136, 358–368, 394, 486, 680
barriers to, 365
channels, 358, 359–360
defined, 358
downward, 365
general guidelines for effective, 367–368

informal, 366
internal, 366–367
lateral, 365
lines of, 365–367
listening, 361–363
message, 358, 359
methods of, 359
nonverbal, 363–364
one-way vs. two-way, 362–363
process of, 358–361
public relations, 394
receiver, 358, 360–361
sender, 358, 359
skills, 680
successful, 358
systems, 136, 486
upward, 365
written, 364
communications systems, 136, 486, 587
community involvement, 580
community policing, 68, 588, 589
comparative analysis of policing models, 589
Community Service Representatives (CSRs), 61
competition between private and public officers, 56
competitive intelligence (CI), 274–275
common targets of, 275
complaints of sexual harassment, investigating, 344–347
complementary roles of private and public officers, 58–64
complete reports, 383–384
completeness (notes), 378
complex partial seizures, 324
complying with OSHA requirements, 191–192
computer crime (*see also* computer security), 249, 282–305, 307–309, 351–352, 621–623
categories of, 286
computer programs, 287
computer time, 287
cost of, 284, 285
critical thinking exercise, 621–623
defined, 283
embezzlement, 249, 287–289
fraud, 287–289
hackers, 289–290, 304
Hallcrest Report II, 285, 293, 295–296
input data, 287
investigating, 303–304
output data, 287
preventing, 300–301
prosecuting, 305
rates of, 289
sabotage, 290–291, 307–309
software piracy, 289–290
types of, 287
typical computer criminal, 304
victims of, 287, 288
white-collar, 249
computer programs, 287
computer security (*see also* computer crime), 167, 220, 249, 282–305, 533
access control, 167, 296–298
administrative controls, 298–299
backup systems, 302–303
biometrics, 296
call-back modem, 297
computer programs, loss via, 287
computer time, loss via, 287
disks, 298
encryption, 286, 297
fire protection, 220, 293, 301–302
hackers, 289–290, 304
Hallcrest Report II, 285, 293, 295–296
input data, loss via, 287
investigating computer crime, 303–304
legislation, 293–295
logical controls, 296–297
magnets, 293
output data, loss via, 287
passwords, 296, 297
physical controls, 297–298
preventing problems and crime, 300–301
printouts, 298
rates of crime, 289
recommendations for security programs, 299–300
rules for, 299
security measures, 295–303
seriousness of problem, 283–286
software piracy, 289–290
threat incident rates, 288
threat to, 287–293
typical computer criminal, 304
viruses, 290–291, 292–293
white-collar crime, 249
computer time, 287
computerized telephone systems, 133
computers used in security, 707, 709
concentric barrier circles, 98
concentric layers of physical security, 97
concentric zone theory of asset protection, 96, 97
concertina, 101
concerts, rock, 548–549

concise reports, 384–385
conclusionary language, 381
condominiums, security of, 535–536
conduct of private security officers, laws governing, 55–56
conducting routine searches, 174–176
conducting security surveys, 435, 438
confessions, 264, 265
confidential information, 459
conflict prevention strategies, 579
connotative words, 383
consolidation of security companies, 709
constables, 16
constitutional law, 74
consultants, security, 31, 36–37, 707
containers, security (*see* files, safes, vaults)
contemporary police models, comparative analysis of, 589
contemporary private security, 23–24
continuous lighting, 118
contract employee access request, 160
contract guards, 31
contract security forces, 17
contract security services (*see also* guards), 23, 37–41, 531, 717
  advantages of, 39
  commonly provided, 38
  compared to proprietary, 37–41
  disadvantages of, 39
  growth of, 717
  image of, 38–39
contractors, 159–161
contracts, 87
controls, physical, 95–143
controls, procedural, 144–188
conventions, 539
convex mirrors, 129, 488
conviction record, 684–685
cooperation between private and public officers, promoting, 58–59, 512–513
copy machine security, 166
core concept, 533
corporate airlines, 557
corporate assets, 533
corporate crime (*see also* white-collar crime), 249
corporate executives, protecting, 612–618
corporate vision of Wackenhut Corporation, 657
corrective action, taking, 692–693
Corrupt Foreign Practices Plan, 199
cost vs. level of protection, 427
counter check, 497, 498
courier services, 38, 176
couriers, armed, 35, 176
court, testifying in, 399–418
court security, 66, 610–612
  access control, 612
  entry screening, 612
  equipment, 612
  problems, 611
  reducing problems, 611–612
  vulnerable areas, 612
CPTED, 97–99, 489–490, 578–579
crack, 250, 578
Cramer v. Housing Opportunities Commission, 83
crash bars, 107
credit cards, 65, 502–503, 525
  fraud, 65, 502–503, 525
  long distance phone calls, 503
  release limit, 503
crime (*see also* criminal actions), 11, 74, 237–249, 282–305, 347–352
  computer, 282–305, 351–352
  concerning private security, 239–249
  corporate, 249
  defined, 74
  economic, 237–247
  foreseeability of, 238
  investigating, 347–352
  prevention, 11, 300–301
  Uniform Crime Reports (UCR), 239
  white-collar, 247–249
Crime Awareness and Campus Security Act of 1990, 584
Crime Prevention Through Environmental Design (CPTED), 23, 97–99, 489–490, 578–579
Crime Stoppers, 68
crime-concealment arsonists, 245
criminal actions, 55, 64, 65, 235–272, 347–352, 630–631
  arson, 244–247
  assault, 55, 244, 349–350
  bad checks, 65
  burglary, 240–241, 243
  cargo theft, 239–240
  credit card fraud, 65
  drug use, 249–256
  felony, 238
  internal theft, 64, 65
  investigating, 347–352
  larceny/theft, 239–240, 243
  misdemeanor, 238
  robbery, 241–243
  seriousness of, 236–238
  shoplifting, 64
  trespassing, 243–244

unlawful taking, 243
vandalism, 243–244
white-collar crime, 247–249
workplace violence, 630–631
criminal damage to property, 351
criminal intent, 74
criminal laws, 55
criminal mischief, 351
criminal offense (*see also* crime, criminal actions), 74, 238
crisis management, 579–580
critical thinking exercises, 140, 184–186, 230–231, 269–271, 307–309, 333–335, 354–355, 395–398, 416–418, 445–447, 471–472, 520–521, 561–564, 600–602, 621–623, 645–647, 667–669, 697–699
civil liability, 697–699
commercial liability, 471–472
commercial security, 561–564
computer crime, 621–623
computer sabotage, 307–309
ethics, 667–669
institutional liability, 600–602
legal liability, 333–335
mall security, 354–355
physical controls, 140
public events, 230–231
retail security, 520–521
risk management, 445–447
routine inspections, 184–186
testifying, 416–418
use of deadly force, 269–271
use of force, 395–398
workplace violence, 645–647
criticality, 429
cross-examination, 403, 407–411
common tactics used during, 409, 410
defined, 403
testifying under, 407–411
crowd control, 205, 546–550
Crown Center, 547
cruise ship security, 559–560
cultural diversity, 714
cybercops, 351
cybercrime, 286
cyberspace, 285–286
cylindrical locks, 113

D

daily orders, 677
damages, 78, 88
danger, foreseeable, 77
dangerous chemicals, 197
data encryption, 286, 297
dead bolt locks, 113
deadly force, use of, 259
deaf individuals, interacting with, 321
dealing with unruly people, 205
Deborah C., In re, 265
debris, 103
deception, detecting signs of, 373–374
deep empathy, 367–368
defamation, 79
defense, physical, 99–111
defense, three lines of, 99–111, 112
exterior, 104–109
interior, 109–111
perimeter, 99–104
Defense Industrial Security Program (DISP), 451
Defense Investigative Service (DIS), 451
delegation, 682
De Lema v. Waldorf Astoria Hotel, Inc. 544
delivery services, 20
democratic, 682
demonstrations, 630, 641–642
demotion, 693
denotative words, 383
Dent v. May Department Stores Company, 487–488
deposition, 89
Depression, the, 21–23
deputized, 55
desegregation, 577
detaining, 257–259, 493
detecting deception, 373–374
detecting employee dishonesty, 504
detecting employee theft/pilferage, 176–179
detecting shoplifters, 483
detection devices, 19–20
detective, private (*see* investigator)
detective agency, first, 12
detectors, 124–125, 198, 215–217
carbon monoxide, 198
fire, 215–217
smoke, 216
detention, purposes of, 493
deterring shoplifting, 480, 482–490
alarms, 487–488
bar codes, 485
cardboard cutouts, 489
checkout lanes, 485
communication system, 486
CPTED, 489–490
floor-to-ceiling glass, 489
floorwalkers, 482–484

fitting rooms, 485
locks, 487
merchandising techniques, 484
package inspections, 485
physical controls, 486–489
physical layout, 486–487
point of sale (POS) system, 484
price tag checks, 485
procedural controls, 486–489
receipts, 486
refund procedures, 486
signs, 487
surveillance devices, 488–489
developing personal ethics, 653–655
developing security surveys, 431–434
developmental disability, 321
dial combination locks, 114
Dickens, Charles, 14
dictatorial, 682
differences between private and public officers, 53–54
digitization, 130–131
direct examination, 403, 404–406
defined, 403
testifying under, 404–406
director, security, 674–675, 682–694
as manager, 682–694
responsibilities of, 674–675
disabilities, individuals with, 319–323
appropriate language to use with, 321, 322
disability, 319, 321, 322
disasters (*see* emergencies, emergency planning)
discarded information, 277
discipline, 682, 692–693
progressive, 692–693
disease, protecting against, 196–197
diseases, individuals with impairing, 319–323
Disney World, 551
disorderly conduct, 350, 393
disorderly individuals, 328
distribution centers, 460
disturbances, civil, 201–202
disturbing the peace, 350
diversity, 719
docks, 172, 460
leaving merchandise on, 172
document protection, 166
Dodson, Minot B., 715–717
dogs, 120, 134–135, 211
domestic employees, using abroad, 619–620
domestic violence, 630
door frame spreading, 105
doors, 104–107, 217
crash bar, 107
fire, 217
frame, 104–105
hardware, 107
hinges, 105, 106
illumination of, 107
number of, 107
panels, 106
panic bar, 107
transoms, 107
dormitories, 583
downsizing, 713
downward communication, 365
Dram Shop Acts, 543
drawbridges, 4
dressing rooms, 485, 489
surveillance in, 489
drug testing, 147, 173, 251–256, 463–464
alternative method of, 256
businesses doing, 251
case against, 255–256
initiative (DTI), 254–255
preemployment, 251
random, 251, 463–464
setting up a program, 254
drug trafficking, 557
drug use, 146, 249–256, 324, 583
symptoms of abuse, 250–251, 252–253
vs. epileptic seizures, 324
drug-impaired persons, 324, 327–328
drugs, 250
dry chemical fire extinguishers, 218
dry sprinkler system, 220
due process, 7
dumps, 461
dumpsters, searching, 277
duty, nondelegable, 75
duty owed, 76–77
duty to protect, 76–77
dynamic risk, 422–423

E

Eastman v. Time Saver Stores, Inc., 495
economic crime, 64–65, 237, 247
education, alleviating friction through, 57–58
education of employees, 695, 716–717, 718
education requirements, 684
educational institutions, security of, 576–590, 703

alarm systems, 578, 582
behavior codes, 579
colleges and universities, 580–590
community involvement, 580
conflict prevention strategies, 579
CPTED, 578–579
crisis management, 579–580
dealing with the media, 579–580
dormitories, 583
ethnoviolence, 584
exemplary program, 590
future of, 703
gangs, 578, 579–580
graffiti removal, 579
ID cards, 578
K-12 programs, 577–580
key and lock survey, 587
reducing problems, 578–580, 584–590
searches, 588
security problems, 577–578
educational programs, 677–678
educational requirements of CPP, 45
Edward, King, 7
effective investigator, characteristics of, 338–340
effective management, guidelines for, 694
eighteenth century, 9–13
El Paso Intelligence Center (EPIC), 339
elderly individuals, interacting with, 318–319
electric burglar alarm systems, 19
electric shock, 194
electrified fences, 101
electromechanical alarms, 121
electromechanical locks, 116
electronic access control cards, 116, 586
electronic article surveillance (EAS), 488
Electronic Communication Privacy Act of 1986, 294–295
Electronic Funds Transfer Act, 529
electronic funds transfer system, 525
electronic handkerchief, 133
electronic ID card security, 158
electronic locks, 110, 116
electronic mail (e-mail), 295
electronic stunning devices, 83
electronic surveillance (*see also* CCTV), 63
electronic weapons, 83
electronically activated price tags, 133, 487–488
elements of negligent liability, 76–78
elevators, 108, 217, 533
fire, 217
shafts, 108
elimination of risk, 439
embezzlement (*see also* internal theft), 146, 247–248, 287–289, 525, 530
using computers for, 287–289
emergencies, preventing losses from, 189–234
bombs and bomb threats, 205–212
civil disturbances, 201–202
Corrupt Foreign Practices Plan, 199
factors of a successful plan, 199
fire, 212–223
guidelines for, 199–201
hazardous materials incidents, 197–199
medical, 195–196
natural disasters, 223–226
Occupational Safety and Health Act, 190–193
riots, 202–203
strikes, 203–204
unruly people, 205
emergency exits, 107, 217
emergency lighting, 118
emergency planning, 199–201
after the emergency, 201
before the emergency, 200
documentation, 201
during the emergency, 200–201
evacuation, 201
hot site vendors, 199–200
emergency response plan, 198
emergency room security, 571–572
gangs, 571
emergency temporary standards, 191
emotional distress, intentional infliction of, 79
empathy, 367–368
employee awareness programs (EAP), 153, 679, 708
employee identification badge system, 569
employee incentive program, 489
Employee Polygraph Protection Act (EPPA), 36–37, 150, 261, 342
employee screening (*see* background investigations)
employee termination statement, 510
employee theft (*see also* internal theft), 64, 65, 145–147, 153, 176–179, 239, 248–249, 503–509, 713
cash handling, 506–509
food service industry, 508–509
honesty shopping, 507–508
incentives to reduce, 504
pricing, 505–506

retail, 503–509
sliding, 505
employees as threats to security, 276, 619–620
in foreign countries, 619–620
employer property, 167, 168, 169
employer-directed homicide, 629, 630
employment, estimates of private security, 40, 42, 57, 716
employment records, 150, 151
encryption, 286, 297
endorsement requirements of CPP, 45
energy conservation, 174
enforcing proprietary rights, 256–257
England, nineteenth century, 13–15
English, standard (reports), 387
enhancing information/computer security, 273–311
enhancing public relations, 312–336
enhancing security through physical controls, 95–143
Enigma, 22
envelope, building, 104–109
environmental design, crime prevention through, 23, 97–99
epilepsy, individuals with, 323–325
epileptic seizure, 323–325
Equal Employment Opportunity Commission (EEOC), 682
equipment, 111–131, 133–134, 165–167, 690–691
alarms, 119–128
basic, 111–131
controlling access to, 165–167
issuing, 690–691
lights, 118–119
lock-down devices, 133
locks, 111–118
metal detectors, 133–134
mirrors, 129, 133
paper shredders, 133
surveillance systems, 128–131
escape hijacking, 557
escapes, fire, 217
escort service, 31
espionage, industrial, 274–275, 456, 458–460
defined, 458
preventing, 459–460
types of information stolen, 458
establishing security goals, 676
ethical conduct, 649–670
check questions, 653, 656
corporate offenses, 650
developing personal ethics, 653–655
five principles of ethical power, 654–655
moral, 651
philosophers, 652
problem solving, 658, 661–662
promoting, 655–656, 658
public perception of various occupations, 651
teaching in school, 654
vision statement, 656
ethics, 649–670, 715
check questions, 653, 656
code of, 656–663
critical thinking exercise, 667–669
decision making, 658, 661–662
defined, 650–653
developing personal, 653–655
honesty and, 651
in practice, 663–665
program, 656
promoting, 655–656
seminars, 654
teaching in school, 654
Ethics Resource Center, 653
ethnoviolence, 584
evacuation, 201, 210, 221–222
in bomb threats, 210
in fire, 221–222
evaluating personnel, 693–694
evaluating security systems, 442–443
evaluation checklist for reports, 390
evolution of campus police systems, 581
evolution of private security, 2–27
ancient times, 3–6
eighteenth century, 9–13
in the United States, 15–24
middle ages, 6–9
nineteenth-century England, 13–15
other security advances, 19–21
examination to become a CPP, 45–46
mandatory subjects, 45–46
specialty subjects, 46
excessive force, 82
exchange of personnel, 62
excitement arsonists, 245
Exclusionary Rule, 64, 492
exculpatory clauses, 126
executive kidnappings, 31
executives, protecting corporate, 612–618
exemplary security programs, 575–576, 590, 595–596
hospitals, 575–576
schools, 590
museums, 595–596
exemplary security systems, 545–546

exhibitions, 547
expelling, 257–259
expenditures, private security, 717
experience requirements of CPP, 45
experimental variance, 191
expert testimony, 413–414
experts, comments from security, 703–720
  Dodson, Minot B., 715–717
  Goodboe, Michael E., 718–720
  Joint Security Commission, 705
explosives (*see* bombs and bomb threats)
express delivery services, 20
exterior defenses, 101–102, 104–109
  crash bars, 107
  doors, 104–107
  floors, 108–109
  gates, 101–102
  lighting, 109
  other openings, 108
  panic bars, 107
  roof, 108–109
  walls, 108–109
  windows, 108
external audit, 176–177
extinguishers, 218–220
eye movements, 363
eyeballs, 117

F

facial expressions, 363
facsimile, 279
fact, 381–382
factual report, 381–382
fail-safe locks, 116
fail-secure locks, 116
false alarms, 66, 126–128
  causes of, 127
  solutions to, 127–128
false imprisonment, 79
Fashion Island, 512
fatalities of women in the workplace, 630
Father of Police Administration, 15
faxes, unsecured, 279
faxpionage, 279
Federal Bureau of Investigations (FBI), 21, 22, 23
Federal Home Loan Bank Board, 526
federal laws regulating private security, 55–56
feedback, 362–363, 366
felony, 238
fences, 99–102
  alarms, 102
  barbed wire, 100, 101
  boundary marker, 100–101
  chain link, 100–101
  concertina, 101
  electrified, 101
  fiber-optic sensors, 101
  gates, 101–102
  header, 100
  living, 101
  patrolling, 102
  razor ribbon, 101
  top guard, 100
  turnstiles, 101
  wood stockade, 100
  wrought iron, 101
fenestration, 108
feudalism, 6, 9
fiber-optic lines, 121–123
fiber-optic sensors, 101
fidelity bonds, 180, 248
Fielding, Henry, 10–12
Fifth Amendment, 402
file cabinets, 110
financial controls, 170–173, 677
Financial Crimes Enforcement Network (FinCEN), 339
financial institution security, 525–530
  automatic teller machines (ATMs), 528–530
  bait money, 526
  Bank Protection Act, 526
  security measures, 526–528
  security problems, 525–526
financial liability, 82
fingerprints, 117
fire, 19, 173–174, 212–223, 244–247, 293, 301–302, 344, 392, 512, 533, 540, 541–543, 571, 573–574
  access control, 217
  alarms, 215–217
  areas to be checked, 223
  arson, 244–247
  causes of, 214
  checklist, 542
  classes of, 213
  computer rooms, 220, 293, 301–302
  detectors, 215–217
  doors, 217, 221–222
  drills, 222
  elevator use, 217–218
  escapes, 217
  evacuation procedures, 221–222
  exits, emergency, 217–218

extinguishers, 218–220, 302
hazards, 173–174, 215, 512
hospitals, 571, 573–574
hotels/motels, 540, 541–543
how to extinguish different types of, 221
ignition temperature, 213
investigating, 344
prevention of, 214–215
procedures for protecting against loss from, 221–222
protecting against losses from, 215–222
protection plan, 213
pull boxes, 217
RACE, 574
reports, 392
safes, 218
safety program, 214
security manager's responsibilities, 222–223
sensors, 19
sprinkler systems, 218–220
stages of, 215
stairwells, 533
triangle, 213
types of, 221
vaults, 218
water, use of, 218–220
windows, 221–222
fire escapes, 109, 217
fire extinguishers, 218–220, 302
ABC, 219
carbon dioxide, 218, 220, 302
dry chemical, 218
foam, 218
halon, 220, 302
ingredients in, 218
multipurpose, 218
portable, 218
soda acid, 218
water, 218–219, 302
fire safety checklist, 542
firearms, 55, 82–83, 260, 679, 690–691
image, 679
training, 260, 690–691
fire-loading, 214
fire-resistant files, safes and vaults, 110, 218
fitting rooms, 485, 489
surveillance in, 489
fixed surveillance cameras, 132
flame stage (fire), 215
floodlights, 102, 103
floor release limit, 503
floors, 108–109
floor-to-ceiling glass, 489
floorwalkers, 482–484
Florence Trentacost v. Dr. Nathan T. Brussel, 80
fluorescent lamps, 119
fluorescent tubes, 119
foam fire extinguishers, 218
foil detectors, 124
food service industry, 508–509
force, use of, 81–82, 259–260, 269–271, 395–398
continuum, 81–82
critical thinking exercise, 269–271, 395–398
deadly, 259, 269–271
excessive, 82
self-defense, 259
forensic document examiner (FDE), 348–349
foreseeable danger, 77
forged checks, 498
forgery, 525
forklifts, 166
formulas, secret, 458
Fourth Amendment rights, 192, 256, 262, 277
Foxwoods Casino and Resort, 546
Frankpledge system, 6
fraud, 149, 247, 248, 278, 287–289, 525
using computers for, 287–289
fraudulent ATM card use, 529
freebase, 250
fresnal units, 102
friction between private and public officers, 56–58
Front Desk Controller (FDC), 541
funeral escort, 66
future of private security, 700–722
campus security, 703
change, 719
cultural diversity, 714, 719
experts' views, 703–720
global markets, 713–714, 719
growth, 718
home-based employment, 714–715
hospital security, 701
hotel/motel security, 701
information superhighway, 705
joint security commission views, 705
new players, 709
outsourcing, 704
partnering, 708–709
privatization, 719
revolutionary changes, 710
staff reductions, 714

technology, 710–713, 714
transit security, 702–703
workplace violence, 704, 714

G

gangs, 571, 578, 579–580
garage security, 607–609
garbage, searching, 277
gates, 3, 101–102, 550
security, 3, 101–102
gathering information on individuals, 55
geese as alarms, 120
general guidelines for dealing with emergencies, 199–201
General Mills Honesty Patrol, 489
generalized tonic clonic seizures, 325
glass, security, 108
glass breaking sensors, 124
glazing, security, 108
Glide Lumber Products Company v. Employment Division, 255
global markets, 713–714, 719
goals, 676, 682
establishing, 676
Gonzales v. Southwest Security and Protection Agency, Inc., 689–690
Goodboe, Michael E., 719–720
Gordon Riots, 12
government check, 497
graffiti removal, 579
grand larceny, 239
grand master key, 161
grandstand, 552
Granite Construction Corp. v. Superior Court of Fresno, 75
grapevine, 366
Great Wall of China, 4
grievance, 682
growth of security services, 716, 717, 718
guard dogs, 134
guard house, 103
guards, 31–32, 37–41
contract, 31, 37–41
proprietary, 37–41
guidelines for better listening, 361–362
guidelines for effective communication, 367–368
guidelines for effective management, 694
guidelines for effective testimony, 405

H

hackers (computers), 289–290, 295, 304
Hallcrest Report, 24, 31, 59, 65, 96, 112, 127, 179, 236, 237, 348
Hallcrest Report II, 24, 31, 40–41, 73, 86, 285, 287, 293, 295–296, 329, 718
halon fire extinguishers, 220, 302
hand geometry, 117
hand gestures, 363
hand trucks, theft of, 453
hand-held metal detectors, 133
handicap, 321
handling risks, alternatives to, 438–440
harassment, investigating sexual, 344–347, 392–393
hate crimes, 630
hazardous materials incident, 197–199
CHEMTREC, 198
do's and don'ts for first responders, 198
process safety management (PSM), 197
security officers' responsibilities, 198
hazardous waste, 571, 574–575
hazards, safety, 194
James T. Hazlett v. Martin Chevrolet, Inc., 255
header, 100, 109
health and safety program, 193–194
health care facilities security (*see also* hospital security), 567–576
antiabortion activists, 572
family planning clinics, 572
key survey, 570
hearing impaired individuals, interacting with, 321
heat sensors, 19
heat stage (fire), 215
heavy equipment, theft of, 455
hedges, 101, 103
Hepatitis B, protecting against, 196–197
hierarchy, 682, 683
of needs (Maslow's), 683
high empathy, 367–368
High Tech Gays v. Defense Industrial Clearance Office, 151
high-efficiency ballasts, 119
high-efficiency fluorescent tubes, 119
high-pressure sodium lamps, 119
high-rise apartments, security of, 535–536
high-risk checks, 498
hijacking (*see also* cargo security), 557
Hilson Safety/Security Risk Inventory, 640
hinges, security, 105, 106
hiring, 76–77, 84, 147–152, 683–687, 709
age requirements, 684
application, 149, 686
background check, 151, 686
conviction record, 684–685

education requirements, 684
integrity test, 149–150, 687
interview, 151, 686–687
national investigation agencies, 151–152
negligent, 76–77, 147–149, 709
physical requirements, 685
polygraph, 150–151, 687
preemployment standards, 684–687
psychological tests, 150, 687
references, 686
resume, 149
security personnel, 683–687
state requirements, 686
wisely, 147–152
historical friction between private and public officers, 56–58
history of private security (*see also* evolution of private security), 2–27
Holmes, Edwin, 19
home security educational materials, 537
home-based employment, 714–715
homeless individuals, 326–327
homeless shelters, 66
homemade bombs, 207
homonyms, 387, 388–389
homosexuals, 151
honesty patrol, 489
honesty shopping, 507–508, 516
honesty tests, 687
Horn v. I.B.I. Security Service of Florida, Inc., 690–691
hospital security, 567–576, 701
access control, 568, 572
assault, 569
controlling cash, 569
controlling services, 569
controlling supplies, 569
crimes against persons, 569
documenting medication given, 569
drug room, 570
emergency room, 571–572
exemplary programs, 575–576
fire prevention and protection, 571, 573–574
future of, 701
gangs, 571
hazardous wastes, 571, 574–575
internal theft, 572
items frequently stolen, 572
key and lock survey, 570
major security problems, 568–571
reducing problems, 572–575
security systems, 576
theft from cars, 569
use of K-9s, 575
visitor control, 569
hostage situation, 31
hostile work environment sexual harassment, 345
hot site vendors, 199–200
Hotel-Motel Fire Safety Act, 540
hotel security, 538–546, 701
AAA standards, 544
alcohol server liability, 543
carbon monoxide poisoning, 540
conventions, 539
court cases, 544–545
exemplary security systems, 545–546
fire hazards, 540, 541–543
future of, 701
gambling, 539
items frequently stolen, 539
key control, 541
lawsuits, 538
prostitution, 539
safes in rooms, 544
search and seizure, 544–545
security measures, 540–544
security problems, 539–540
skips, 543
Housing Enterprises for the Less Privileged (HELP) shelters, 66
housing security, 534–538
educational materials, 537
Stop Thief, 536
hue and cry, 7–8
hybrid security services, 37, 708, 716
hybridization, 708

I

ID card, 158, 578
electronic, 158
identification, 114, 500–501
check cashing, 500–501
keys, 114
igniter, 246
ignition temperature, 213
illegible check, 498
image of private security, 328, 679–680, 716
impairing diseases, individuals with, 318–321
impairment, 320–321
impeaching a witness, 401
impersonating public police officials, 55
implementing recommendations of security surveys, 441–442

imprisonment, false, 79
In re Deborah C., 265
State in interest of T.L.O., 588
inadmissible statements, 404
incandescent lamps, 119
incendiary bombs, 207
incident report, 374–377
  follow-up form, 374–377
  form, 376
  log, 374, 375
incipient stage, 215
income of security professionals, 695
incorrectly written checks, 498
indecent exposure, 318
industrial espionage, 274–275
Industrial Revolution, 9
industrial security, 23, 448–473
  espionage, 456, 458–460
  items most frequently stolen, 453
  metals, 456
  responsibilities, 449–452
  robots, 452
  sabotage, 456–458
  side product control, 453
  tools, 455–456
  transportation, 461–467
  types of losses, 452–456
  utilities, 467–470
  vulnerable areas, 460–461
Industrial Security Manual (ISM), 434
industry, 23
inferences, 381–382
informal communication, 366
information, obtaining and providing, 357–398
  barriers to communication, 365
  communication process, 358–361
  guidelines for effective communication, 367–368
  interviewing and interrogating techniques, 368–374
  lines of communication, 365–367
  listening, 361–363
  nonverbal communication, 363–364
  taking notes, 374–379
  writing reports, 378–394
information protection/security, 167–168, 170, 273–311, 459
  disposal methods, 277
  industrial espionage, 274–275
  problem of, 274–275
  security measures, 280–282
  specific threats, 276–277
  telecommunications, 278–280
information superhighway, 705
infrared (IR) cameras, 131
infrared cards, 116
infrared flame detectors, 216
initial standards, 191
input data, 287
insider manipulation (ATMs), 529
inspections, 177–178, 184–186, 191, 192–193, 458, 692
  briefcases, 177–178
  lockers, 177
  OSHA, 191, 192–193
  packages, 177–178
  purses, 177
  removal authorization, 178
  trash containers, 178
  vehicles, 178
  violations found during, 193
Institute of Makers of Explosives (IME), 212
institutional liability, 600–602
institutional security, 567–605
  archives security, 596–597
  art galleries, 591–597
  colleges and universities, 580–590
  educational institutions, 576–590
  hospitals and health care facilities, 567–576
  K-12 programs, 577–580
  libraries, 590–591
  museums, 591–597
  national parks, 597
  religious facilities, 597–599
insurance, 87–88, 179–180, 440
insurance-claim arsonists, 245
integrity interview, 151
integrity testing, 149–150, 687
intent, 74
intentional infliction of emotional distress, 79
intentional wrongs, 76
interaction of security equipment, procedures and personnel, 420
interaction with individuals, 318–328
interaction with the press/media, 329
interactive video and audio (IAVA), 131
intercoms, 279
interior defenses, 109–111
internal audit, 176–177
internal communication, 366–367
internal theft (*see also* embezzlement, employee theft, pilferage, shrinkage), 64, 65, 145–147, 153, 176–179, 248–249, 453, 572
International Criminal Police Organization (INTERPOL), 339

International Maritime Organization (IMO), 559
International Network of Protection Specialists (INPS), 614
Internet virus, 292–293
INTERPOL, 339, 593–594
interrogating (*see also* interviewing), 63, 263–265, 368–374
  detecting deception, 373–374
  Miranda warning, 264–265
  objectives of, 373
  restrictions on, 264–265
  techniques, 368–374
interrogatories, 89
interview, 151, 263–264, 368–374, 686–687
  calibrating a witness, 368
  defined, 263
  detecting deception, 373–374
  integrity, 151
  making more productive, 368–369
  preparation, 263
  questions, 372
  rapport, 264
  setting, 264
  subjects, 370–371
  techniques, 368–374
  timing, 263–264
interviewing, basic rules for, 263–265
intoxicated individuals, interacting with, 327–328
intoxication, appearance of (Alzheimer's disease), 319
intrusion detection systems, 35
invasion of privacy, 79
inventions, 460
inventories, tracking, 710
inventory, perpetual, 176–177
inventory control, 489
inventory shrinkage as a percent of retail sales, 478
investigate, 338
investigating, 260–261, 338–356, 681
  accidents, 342–344
  characteristics of an effective investigator, 338–340
  complaints of sexual harassment, 344–347
  crimes, 347–352
  fires, 344
  losses, 681
  polygraph, 342
  purpose of, 340
  surveillance, 341–342
investigation agencies, national, 151–152
investigative responsibilities, 340–352, 680–682
  audits, 681–682
  background checks, 681–682
  conducting security surveys, 680–681
  losses, 681
  specific crimes and, 349–352
investigative skills, 680
investigators, 31, 33–34, 38, 43–44, 338–342
  characteristics of effective, 338–340
  private, 31, 33–34, 38, 43–44
  responsibilities of, 340–342
Inwald Survey 8, 640
ionization detectors, 216
issuing equipment, 690–691

J

JAG, 490
James T. Hazlett v. Martin Chevrolet, Inc., 255
jetways, 556
Jewelers Security Alliance, 21
Jewelry and Gem Initiative (JAG), 490
jewelry thefts, 490
jewelry vaults, 19
job description, 683, 687, 688–689
John, King, 7
Joint Security Commission, 451, 705
judgments, 381

K

K-12 programs, 577–580
  problems, 577–578
key and lock survey, 570, 587
  hospitals, 570
  schools, 587
key phrases for specific incidents (reports), 392–394
key-operated locks, 112–114
  disadvantages of, 114
keypad locks, 114–115
keys (*see also* locks), 114, 161–164, 541, 586
  audits, 163–164
  card, 162
  change, 161
  checklist, 162
  control, 161–164, 541, 586
  grand master, 161
  identification, 114
  lending, 163
  master, 161–162
  neuter head blanks, 163

record of, 161
restricted, 163
security key monitor (SKM), 163
sub-master, 161
total system, 163
keyway, 112
Kidde, Walter, 38
kidnappings, 31
King Edward, 7
King John, 7
kleptomaniacs, 479
Kline v. 1500 Massachusetts Avenue, 80
Kolosky v. Winn Dixie Stores, Inc., 81
Kuehn v. Renton School District No. 403, 588

L

ladders, 103
lake dwellings, 3–4
lamps, types of, 119
language, 326, 373–374, 381, 618, 682–683
barriers, 618
body, 373–374
conclusionary, 381
line, 326
of management, 682–683
laptop computer, 286
larceny/theft (*see also* pilferage, shoplifting), 239–240, 243
cargo, 239–240
defined, 239
grand, 239
petty, 239
unlawful taking, 243
Largo Corp. v. Crespin, 251
Las Vegas Mirage Hotel, 545–546
lateral communication, 365
Law Enforcement Intelligence Unit (LEIU), 62
Law Enforcement Liaison Council, 58
laws, 2, 55–56, 74, 85–86
classification of, 74
governing conduct of private security officers, 55–56
need for, 2
regarding civil liability, 85–86
lawsuits, 73, 78–81, 88–89, 147, 257, 352, 487, 528, 538, 543, 544
against hotels and motels, 538
alcohol server liability, 543
avoiding, 147, 352
brought against private security, 78–81
defending against, 88
negligence, 147
surviving, 88–89
layout, physical, 103–104, 109, 486–487
leaks, 459
legal authority, 54–56
arrests, 54
restrictions on private security officers, 55–56
legal liability, 63, 72–92, 333–335, 399
critical thinking exercise, 333–335
personal, 399
reasons for increase in lawsuits, 73
legible reports, 387
legislation related to computer crime, 293–295
lending keys, 163
level of protection v. cost, 427
liability, 40, 55, 63, 72–92, 147, 238, 333–335, 399, 471–472, 544–545, 600–602, 643–644, 689, 697–699
checklist, 86–87
civil, 55, 75, 85–86, 697–699
commercial, 471–472
contracts, 87
critical thinking exercise, 333–335, 471–472, 697–699
financial, 82
hiring, 84
hotel/motel, 544–545
institutional, 600–602
insurance, 87–88
issues, 82–83
legal, 63, 72–92, 333–335, 399
negligent, 76–78, 238, 689
personal, 399
reducing, 83–88
Six-Layered Protection System, 84
strict, 76
training, 84–87
vicarious, 75
without fault, 76
workplace violence, 643–644
library security, 534, 586, 590–591
major losses, 590
self-check system, 590–591
licensing, 43, 56
lie detector (*see* polygraph)
lighting, 102–103, 109, 118–119, 586–587, 608
boundary, 103
efficiency of, 119
exterior, 109
guard house, 103

lamp types, 118
luminaire, 119
parking areas, 608
perimeter, 102–103
position of, 103
types of, 118
line smoke detectors, 216
lines of communication, 365–367
listening, 361–363
feedback, 362–363
guidelines for better, 361–362
one-way vs. two-way communication, 362–363
understanding, 362
litigation avalanche, 423, 528, 544
Little Nell Hotel, 545
living fences, 101
loading docks, 460
local alarms, 126
lock-down devices, 133
locker inspection, 177
locks, 110, 111–118, 487, 570, 586, 587
biometric security systems, 117
bolts, 113
card-operated, 115–116
clamshell, 117
combination, 110, 114
cylindrical, 113
dead bolts, 113
electromechanical, 116
electronic, 110, 116
fail-safe, 116
fail-secure, 116
function of, 111
key-operated, 112–114
keypad, 114–115
mechanical, 110
other, 117–118
padlocks, 114
shank, 114
spring-loaded bolts, 113
survey of educational institutions, 587
survey of health care facilities, 570
time, 117
warded, 112
locksmiths, 31, 112
logical controls for computer security, 296–297
London Metropolitan Police, 15
Loomis, 38
loop alarm, 487
loss prevention, 421–447, 517, 675
specialist responsibilities, 675
systems, 517
through risk management, 421–447
losses, 452–456, 681
industrial, 452–456
investigating, 681
low empathy, 367, 368
low-pressure sodium lamp, 119
lumber yard, theft from, 454
luminaire, 119
lunch box inspection, 178
lying, indicators of, 373

M

machinery, theft of, 455
Magna Charta, 7
magnetic stripe cards, 116
magnetic switch (sensor), 121
magnetic tags and labels, 488
mail bombs, 212
mail rooms, 166, 534
maintenance supplies, theft of, 453
making rounds, 173–174
malicious prosecution, 495–496
Mall of America, 512–513
mall security, 354–355, 510–514
Malorney v. B & L Motor Freight, Inc., 83
management, 421–447, 682–694, 703–704, 705
by objectives (MBO), 683
greatest challenge facing, 703–704
guidelines for effective, 694
information system (MIS), 705
language of, 682–683
responsibilities, 683–694
risk, 421–447
management by objectives (MBO), 683
manager, 682–694
difference between supervisor and, 691–692
security director as, 682–694
managerial responsibilities, 683–694
evaluating security personnel, 693–694
hiring security personnel, 683–687
inspections, 692
issuing equipment, 690–691
job descriptions, 687, 688–689
scheduling, 691
supervising, 691–692
taking corrective action, 692–693
training, 687–690
manufacturing security (*see* industrial security)
marijuana, 250
maritime cargo, theft of, 240
Marshall v. Barlow's Inc., 192

Maslow's hierarchy of needs, 683
mass transit security, 557–559
master keying system, 161–162
mats (detectors), 125
mechanical locks, 110
mechanical watch clocks, 135
mechanically correct reports, 386–387
media, working with, 329
medical emergencies, 195–196
medical tests, 191
mental illness, 321
mentor, 683
merchandising techniques to deter shoplifting, 484
merchants' protective association, 489
mercury vapor lamps, 119
message, 358, 359
Mest v. Federated Group, Inc., 150
metal detectors, 133–134, 211, 455–456
metal halide lamps, 119
metal seal bar, 172
metals, theft of, 456
Metropolitan Police Act of 1829, 8, 12, 15
Metropolitan Police of London, 15
Meyers v. Ramada Inn of Columbus, 80, 544
microwave detectors, 125
microwave tags and labels, 488
Middle Ages, 3, 6–9
Middlesex Justice Bill, 12
military time, 366–367
military uniform, 314
minimum preemployment standards, 684–687
Miranda v. State of Arizona, 264
Miranda warning, 54–55, 64, 264–265
  sample card, 265
mirrors, 129, 133, 488
misdemeanor, 238
moderate empathy, 367
modern private security, 28–49
Molotov cocktails, 207
money order, 497–498
monitored alarm systems, 120
Montreal Protocol, 220
moonlighting, 55, 62–63
  potential problems with, 62–63
moral, 651
morale, 683
motel security (*see also* hotel security), 538–546
motion picture cameras, 129, 132
motivate, 683
motives for bombings, 207
Mount Sinai Hospital v. City of Miami Beach, 62–63
moveable lighting, 118
movie industry, security issues involving, 550–551
muggings at ATMs, 530
multicultural work force, 713
multipurpose extinguishers, 218
murder, 629, 633, 635
  by proxy, 635
  in the workplace, 629, 633, 635
museum security, 591–597
  access control, 594
  alarm systems, 593
  ARTCENTRAL, 593–594
  exemplary programs, 595–596
  INTERPOL, 593–594
  major problems, 591–592
  photogrammetry, 593
  reducing problems, 592–595
mutual advantages for private and public officers, 63
Myers-Briggs Type Indicator (MBTI), 720
Mystic Lake Casino, 546

N

narrative, structuring the (reports), 391–392
National Auto Theft Bureau, 62
National Center for Computer Crime Data (NCCCD), 284, 287
national costs of computer crimes, 285
National Crime Information Center (NCIC), 339
National Crime Prevention Institute (NCPI), 23
national defense variance, 191
National Fire Alarm Code, 217
National Fire Protection Association (NFPA), 217
national investigation agencies, 151–152
National Labor Relations Act, 55
National Labor Relations Board v. St. Vincent's Hospital, 55
National Licensed Beverage Association (NLBA), 543
national parks security, 597
National Recovery Act of 1933, 22
National Treasury Employees Union v. Von Raab, 256
natural disasters, 223–226
  approach to planning for, 223
  difference between watch and warning, 226
need for rules and laws, 2

negligence, 76, 79, 238
negligence lawsuits, 79, 147
negligent entrustment, 689, 690
negligent hiring, 76–77, 147–149, 709
  elements for a cause of action for, 148
Negligent Hiring and Retention Doctrine, 147–148
negligent liability, elements of, 76–78, 147–149, 238
  damages, 78
  duty owed, 76–77
  duty to protect, 76–77
  foreseeable danger, 77
  plaintiff, 77
  proximate result, 78
  reasonable care, 77–78
  respondent superior, 76–77
negligent retention, 76–77, 148
  elements for a cause of action for, 148
negligent training, 689
Neighborhood Watch, 586
neuter head blanks, 163
New England Baptist Hospital, 575
New York City Hospital, 575–576
night surveillance, 131
night town watchmen, 16
nineteenth century England, 13–15
no such account (NSA) checks, 498
nobleman, 6
nonbusiness visitor access request, 159
noncompete agreements, 276
nondelegable duty, 75
nondisabled, 321
nondisclosure agreements, 276
nonemployer property, 167, 169
non-English speaking individuals, interacting with, 326
nonlethal weapons, 82–83
nonsufficient funds (NSF) checks, 498
nonverbal communication, 363–364
Norman Conquest, 6, 8
North Star Mall, 512
notebook computers, 286
notes, 374–379
  abbreviations, 379
  effective, 378
  taking, 374–378
nuclear facility officers, 56

O

objective reports, 383
objectives, SMART, 676
obtaining and providing information, 357–398
Occupational Safety and Health Act of 1970, 190–193, 644, 683
Occupational Safety and Health Administration (OSHA), 190–193, 194
  annual summary, 192
  documentation of training, 194
  inspections, 191, 192–193
  requirements of, 191–192
  standards, types of, 191
occupations at greater risk of workplace violence, 635–636
office building security, 531–534
  access control, 532–534
  core concept, 533
  high-rises, 532
  items frequently stolen, 531
  major problems, 531
  office parks, 532
  office suites, 532
  security measures, 532–534
  security problems, 531–532
officers, private v. public, 50–71
  complementary roles, 58–64
  differences between, 53–54
  interdependence, 61–62
  similarities between, 52–53
Omnibus Budget Rehabilitation Act of 1990, 193
on time (reports), 387
one-way vs. two-way communication, 362–363
ongoing training, 688–690
on-line databases, 339–340
on-line personnel, 683
open architecture, 709
opening procedures, 164–165
openings, exterior, 108
openings, perimeter, 101–102
Operation Identification, 586
operational reports, 379
Operations Security, 281
opinions, 381–382
OPSEC, 281
Orlando, Florida's exemplary security systems, 545
OSHA, 190–193
OSHAct, 190–193
  purpose of, 190
out-of-town check, 498
output data, 287
outsourcing, 704, 707

P

package inspections, 177–178, 485
padlocks, 114
pallets, theft of, 453
pan and tilt cameras, 129–130
panic bars, 107
paper shredders, 133
paper-and-pencil tests, 149
parish, 9
parking areas, 66, 104, 549–550, 552, 607–609
  enforcement in, 66
  lighting, 608
  management strategies, 609
  patrols, 608–609
  problems, 607
  reducing problems, 607–609
  surveillance cameras, 608
parks, 66, 551–552, 597
  national, 597
  patrolling, 66
  theme, 551–552
partnering, 708–709
partnerships, private and public, 67–68
passenger screening, 555
passes, 155–161, 167, 168, 569
  contractors, 159–161
  property, 167, 168
  tour groups, 158
  vendors, 159–161
  visitors, 158, 159, 569
passive infrared detectors, 125
password, 296, 297
patents, 458
patrol dogs, 134
patrol officers, private, 32–33
patrols (*see* guards)
pay phones, 552
paying department, 172–173
payroll check, 497
Peace Officers' Standards and Training (POST) Commission, 67
pedagogy, 689
Peel, Sir Robert, 12, 13, 14–15
People v. Haydel, 265
People v. Stormer, 266
People v. Virginia Alvinia Zelinski, 266, 492
pepper spray, 83
performance appraisal, 683
perimeter alarm, 120
perimeter defenses, 99–104, 120
  alarms, 102, 120
  appearance, 103–104
  fences, 99–102
  gates, 101–102
  layout, 103–104
  lighting, 102–103
  openings, 101–102
permanent passes, 160–161
permanent standards, 191
permanent variance, 191
permissive, 683
perpetrator of workplace violence, profile of, 632–634
perpetual inventory, 176–177
personal check, 497
personal computer (PC), 286
personal identification number (PIN), 116
personal legal liability, 399
personal property registration, 167, 169
personal references, 686
personnel, security, 31–37, 44–46
  armed couriers, 35
  central alarm respondents, 35–36
  central role of, 37
  Certified Protection Professional (CPP), 44–46
  consultants, 36–37
  private investigators, 33–34
  private patrol officers, 32–33
  private security guards, 31–32
pesticides, 197
petty cash, 170, 534
  sample voucher, 534
petty larceny, 239
Philadelphia's Museum of Art, 595
Philadelphia's Security Watch, 67
photoelectric detectors, 125
photoelectric sensors, 121
photoelectric smoke detectors, 216
photogrammetry, 593
photo-identity cameras, 501
physical attack of ATM, 530
physical controls, 95–143, 297–298, 486–489
  basic, 96–99
  command center, 136
  communication systems, 136
  computer security, 297–298
  CPTED, 97–99
  deterring shoplifting, 486–489
  dogs, 134–135
  exterior, 104–109
  interior, 109–111
  metal detectors, 133–134
  other means of, 131–136
  perimeter, 99–104

signs, 133
physical defense, basic lines of, 99–111
physical layout, 103–104, 109, 486–487
physical requirements, 685
physical security, 3–4, 136–138
ancient times, 3–4
check-list, 137
system, 136–138
Picco v. Ford's Diner, Inc., 80
pickpocketing, 239
pictures, request for authorization to take, 171
pilferage, 64, 176–179, 239, 247, 248–249
Pinkerton, Allen, 17–19
Pinkerton National Detective Agency, 18, 38
Pinkerton's, 38, 68
Pitt, William, 12
Pittard v. Four Seasons Motor Inn, Inc., 80, 544
Pitts Reform Bill, 12, 14
plaintiff, 77
plant security (*see also* industrial security), 23
plug alarms, 487
point alarms, 120
point of sale (POS) system, 484, 516
police, cooperation with, 329–330, 512–513
police, railroad, 16–17
Police Chief, The, 59
police models, comparative analysis of contemporary, 589
police tasks, transferring to private security, 266–267
police-connected alarms, 126
police-fire integrated service, 5–6
policies, 677
policing, preventive, 12
political candidates, protecting, 612–618
family concerns, 614
unique challenges presented by, 614
Polygon, 490
polygraph examination, 36–37, 150–151, 261, 342, 687
Ponticas v. K.M.S. Investments, 147
pool safety checklist, 542
Pope, Augustus, 19
popular salesperson, 505
portable fire extinguishers, 218
POST Commission, 67
post-dated check, 498
posters, 678
posture, 363
power, defined, 51
Praetorian Guard, 5
preassignment training, 688
precedents, 74
precincts, 6
predication, 348
preemployment screening, 147, 640–641, 709
preemployment standards for security personnel, 684–687
preincident indicators, 616
press, working with, 329
pressure sensors, 121
preventing accidents, 193–195
preventing bombings, 207–208
preventing fires, 214–215
preventing workplace violence, 636–642
preventive philosophy, 23
preventive policing, 12
price changing, 477
price raising, 440
price tag checks, 485
price tags, electronic, 133, 487–488
pricing, 505–506
prima facie evidence, 477, 492
prisoner transport, 66
privacy, 50, 79, 148, 150, 256, 341–342
invasion of, 79
laws, 148
rights, 150, 256, 341–342
private detectives/investigators, 31, 33–34, 43–44
regulation of, 43–44
private hiring of public police, 61
private patrol officers, 32–33, 38
private security, 2–27, 28–49, 50–71, 512–513, 671–699, 700–722
compared to public, 50–71, 716
consumer of services, 30
contemporary, 23–24
defined, 29–30
employment estimates, 40, 42, 57, 716
evolution of, 2–27
functions of, 30
future of, 700–722
guards, 31–32
helping public police, 64–67, 512–513
legal authority, 54–56
modern, 28–49
objectives of, 30
partnership with public police, 67–68, 512–513
personnel, 31–37
place in the organizational structure, 673–674

profession, 671–699
proprietary vs. contract, 37–41
purpose of, 30
regulation of, 41–43
responsibilities of directors, 674–675
restrictions on, 55–56
spending, 57, 58, 716
types of services, 31–37
vicious circle, 685
private/public interdependence, 61–62
private/public interface, 50–71
privatization, 65–67, 68, 719
probability, 428
probable cause, 491
procedural controls, 144–188, 484–486
access control, 153–173
accounting, 170–173
after hours, 156, 164–165
badges, 155–161
bonding, 179–180
check-in/out register, 155, 156
closing, 164–165
detecting employee theft/pilferage, 176–179
deterring shoplifting, 484–486
drug testing, 173
hiring, 147–152
insurance, 179–180
key control, 161–164
making rounds, 173–174
opening, 164–165
passes, 155–161
receiving, 170–173
routine searches, 174–176
shrinkage, 145–147
supervising, 152–153
training, 152–153
transporting valuables, 176
vehicle control, 154
procedures, 677
process safety management (PSM) of hazardous chemicals, 197
Professional Development Program, 720
profile of the perpetrator of workplace violence, 632–634
progressive discipline, 692–693
promoting ethics, 655–656, 658
promotion of security, 330–333
property check-in/out log, 169
property control, 167
property pass, 167, 168
property registration, personal, 159
proprietary alarms, 126
proprietary gas pumps, theft from, 453–454
proprietary rights, enforcing, 256–257
proprietary security services, 23, 37–41, 717
compared to contract, 37–41
disadvantages of, 39
growth of, 717
prosecution of computer crime, 305
prosecution of shoplifting, 493–496
malicious, 495–496
policy factors, 495
reasons for nonprosecution, 494–495
type of retailer most likely to prosecute, 493
protecting against disease, 196–197
protecting business interests abroad, 618–620
protecting individuals, 612–620
abroad, 618–620
advance work, 617
choke points, 616–617
corporate executives, 612–618
political candidates, 612–618
preincident indicators, 616
preventive measures, 615–616
problems, 614–615, 618
reducing problems, 615–620
skills required for, 614
VIPs, 612–618
protecting information, 167–168, 170
protection, circles of, 98
protection plan, 426
protection specialists, skills required of, 614
protection vs. cost, 427
providing information, 374–394
proximate results, 78
proximity, 363–364
proximity cards, 115–116
psychological stress evaluation (PSE), 36
psychological tests, 150, 687
public building security, 66
public events, 230–231, 546–550
public gathering security, 546–550
exhibitions, 547
gates, 550
inside the facility, 550
parking lots, 549–550
rock concerts, 548–549
sporting events, 548
ticket windows, 550
trade shows, 547–548
turnstiles, 550
public hiring of private police, 61
public housing development patrol, 66
public housing security, 535–538

public parks, patrolling, 66
public pay phones, 552
public police, working with, 329–330, 512–513
public relations, 30, 312–336, 394, 512
  actions, 316–317
  appearance, 314–316
  benefits of programs, 332
  communications as, 394
  defined, 313
  factors involved in, 314–317
  image, 328
  interactions, 318–330
  media, 329
  promotion of security, 330–333
  public police, 329–330
  role of security personnel in, 313–314
public/private interdependence, 61–62
public/private interface, 50–71
  complimentary roles, 58–64
  differences between officers, 53–54
  historical friction, 56–58
  partnerships, 67–68
  similarities between officers, 52–53
pull boxes (fire), 217
punitive damages, 78, 88
purchase orders, 170–173
pure risk, 422–423, 432
purse inspections, 177
purse-snatching, 239
pushbutton locks, 114
pyromaniac, 245

Q

QUAD, 130
quid pro quo sexual harassment, 345

R

RACE, 574
racetracks, 552–554
  backstretch area, 552
  comprehensive security office training program, 553–554
  grandstand, 552
  public pay phones, 552
  vault, 552
radio frequency tags and labels, 488, 710
rail cargo, theft of, 240
railroad police, 16–17, 56, 464
  basic objective of, 464
railroad security, 16–17, 56, 464–466
  engineering improvements to cars and trailers, 465–466
railroad spur lines, 461
railways, 13
Ramada Inns, Inc. v. Sharp, 545
Rand Report, 256, 262
razor ribbon, 101
reasonable cause, 491
receipts, 486
receiver of communication, 358, 360–361
receiving, blind, 172
receiving department, 170–173
receiving procedures, 170–173
record of keys in use, sample, 161
records, business, 109–111
recreational parks, security, 66, 551–552
reducing liability, 83–88
reduction of risk, 439
reference checks, 150, 151, 686
refunds, 486, 509
registration, 43
regulation of private investigators, 43–44
regulation of private security, 41–43
release form, 493
release limits, 503
religion, 715
religious facilities, 597–599
  cemeteries, 599
  problems, 597–599
  reducing the problems, 598–599
  ritualistic crimes, 598
remote sensing identification systems, 710
remote tellers, 525
removal authorization, 178
rent-a-cop, 62
rent-a-judge-and-jury, 67
reporting results of security survey, 441
reports, 374–394
  administrative, 379
  characteristics of well-written, 381–394
  evaluation checklist, 390
  follow-up, 374, 377
  incident, 374–377
  operational, 379
  sample form, 376, 380
  taking notes, 374–379
  writing, 378–394
reprimand, 692
reproduction work order, sample, 167
request for authorization to take pictures, 171
requirements, OSHA, 191–192
requisition forms, 534

residential security, 534–538
  sample survey, 537
resources, investigative, 339–340
respondent superior, 76–77
respondents, central alarm, 35–36
responding to a bomb threat, 208–210
responsibilities of administration, 676–680
responsibilities of investigators, 340–342, 680–682
responsibilities of loss prevention specialists, 675
responsibilities of security directors, 674–675
responsibility, collective, 15
restitution, 74
restricted keys, 163
resume, 149
  fraud, 149
retail security, 474–523
  alarm systems, 487–488
  assistance in, 514
  bad checks, 496–501
  checklist, 514, 515–516
  credit cards, 502–503
  critical thinking exercise, 520–521
  employee theft, 503–509
  enhancing, 514
  floorwalkers, 482–484
  food service industry, 508–509
  future of, 514–517
  high-loss items, 476
  honesty shoppers, 507–508, 516
  loss prevention systems, 517
  refunds, 486, 509
  shoplifting, 476–496
  shopping centers, 510–514
  shopping malls, 510–514
  shopping services, 507–508
  shrinkage, 476, 477, 478
retention, negligent, 76–77, 148
retina scanning, 117
return/refund system, 509
revenge arsonists, 245
revenue, private security, 717
revocation of license, 43
ribbon switch alarms, 487
rights, 150, 256–257, 264–265, 341–342
  Miranda warning, 264–265
  privacy, 150, 256, 341–342
  proprietary, 256–257
  suspect's, 265
Riot Act, 9
riots, 202–203
risk, 422–423, 432
  defined, 422
  dynamic, 422–423
  pure, 422–423, 432
risk analysis, 426, 428–429
  factors to consider, 428–429
  purpose of, 426
risk balance, 426, 428
risk cycle, 425–426, 427
risk management, 421–447
  acceptance, 440
  alternatives, 438–440
  audit process, 444
  budget for security, 442
  circle, 424–425
  cost vs. level of protection, 427
  critical thinking exercise, 445–447
  criticality, 429
  defined, 423
  elimination, 439
  evaluating security systems, 442–443
  implementing recommendations, 441–442
  policy, 426
  probability, 428
  process, 426
  protection plan, 426
  reduction, 439
  reporting results of security surveys, 441
  security survey, 430–438
  spreading, 440
  transfer, 440
  vulnerability, 428, 435
ritualistic crimes, 598
robbery, 241–243, 525, 530, 630
  ATMs, 530
  defined, 241
  prevention, 241
  training in, 242–243
  unlawful taking, 243
robots, 452, 707
rock concerts, 548–549
Roman security, 4–5
roof, 108–109
rounds, making, 173–174
routine inspections, 184–186
routine searches, 174–176
rules, need for, 2
rumor mill, 366

S

sabotage, 290–291, 307–309, 456–458
  defined, 457

methods of, 457–458
preventing, 458
psychological, 457
response to, 457
using computers for, 290–291, 307–309
safes, 110–111, 114, 218, 544
burglar-resistant, 110
fire-resistant, 110, 218
hotel/motel, 544
purpose of, 110
selection, 110
smart, 110–111
safety, 193–195, 512
hazards, 194, 512
incentive plans, 195
violations, 193
satellite transmissions, 279
Sawgrass Mills Mall, 513
scheduling, 691
schools (*see* educational institutions)
screening, preemployment, 147
seal bar, 172
seal system, 463
seals, 170, 465
seaport security, 466–467
search notification, sample, 175
search warrants, 192–193, 304
searches, routine, 174–176
searches, unreasonable, 192, 277
searching, 63, 64, 261–262, 277, 304, 544–545, 588
hotels/motels, 544–545
schools, 588
searchlights, 102
second-party check, 498
secrecy agreements, 276
secret formula, 458
secrets, trade, 459
Section 1983, 81–83
armed security personnel, 82–83
use of force, 81–82
security, collective, 2
security advances, early, 19–20
security audit process, 444
security checklist, 137, 434, 436–438, 443
security circles, 280–281
security consultants, 31
security departments, heads of, 673
security director, 674–675, 682–694
as manager, 682–694
responsibilities of, 674–675
security dogs, 134–135
security equipment, 111–131
security glass, 108
security glazing, 108
security goals and responsibilities, 93–336
security hinges, 105
Security Industry Association (SIA), 532
security key monitor (SKM), 163
security landscape, 452
security lighting, 118–119
security officer uniform, 314–315
security officers, 135–136
security surveys, 430–438, 441–443, 586, 680–681
basic, 433
conducting, 435, 438, 680–681
defined, 430
developing, 431–434
evaluating the system, 442–443
implementing recommendations, 441–442
purpose of, 430
reasons to conduct, 430
reporting results, 441
samples, 433, 435
specific questions to include, 430
security systems, 117, 136–138, 442–443, 576
biometric, 117
evaluating, 442–443
hospitals, 576
physical, 136–138
selecting alternatives to handle identified risks, 438–440
self-audits, 434
Self-Check System (libraries), 590–591
self-defense, use of force in, 259
sender of communication, 358, 359
sensors, 19, 121, 122
sentry dogs, 134
sequence of criminal trial, 402–404
closing arguments, 403
cross-examination, 403
direct examination, 403
opening statements, 402–403
rebuttal, 403
verdict, 403–404
serf, 6
serial numbers of office machines, 533–534
sexual harassment, 344–347, 392–393
conditions of, 344–345
defined, 344
hostile work environment, 345
investigating complaints of, 344–347
quid pro quo, 345
report, 392–393
shank, 114

Sheerin v. Holin Co., 83
shelters, homeless, 66
ship security, 559–560
shipping-receiving department, 172, 460
shock sensors, 124
shopkeeper statutes, 55–56
shoplifter bloomers, 480
shoplifters (*see also* shoplifting), 478–480, 482, 483, 491–493
  amateurs, 479
  apprehension of, 491–493
  clothing worn by, 482
  kleptomaniacs, 479
  methods of detecting, 483
  professional, 479
  types of, 478–480
shoplifter's shuffle, 480
shoplifting, 64, 239, 259–260, 318, 476–496
  actions indicative of, 481–482
  arrests, 259–260
  booster box, 480
  civil recovery, 496
  clothing indicative of, 482
  defined, 477
  deterring, 480, 482–490
  floorwalkers, 482–484
  indicators of, 481–482
  jewelry thefts, 490
  malicious prosecution, 495–496
  merchandising techniques to deter, 484
  methods of, 480–481
  nonprosecution of, 494–495
  palming articles, 480
  physical controls, 486–489
  price changing, 488
  prima facie evidence, 477
  procedural controls, 484–486
  prosecution, 493–496
  receptacles indicative of, 482
  retailers most likely to prosecute, 493
shopping center security, 510–514
  primary objectives of, 511–512
shopping mall security, 354–355, 510–514
shopping services, 507–508
Showboat Casino, 546
shrinkage, 145–147, 476, 477, 478
shrubs, 101, 103
side product control, 453
signal (alarm), 121, 123
signature cards, 527
signs, 133, 487, 678
similarities between private and public officers, 52–53
simple partial seizures, 323–324
Sir Robert Peel, 12, 13, 14–15
Six-Layered Liability Protection System, 84
skills, investigative, 680
skips, 543
skyjacking, 554, 555
skylights, 108
sliding, 505
slipping (bolts), 113
smart card, 117
SMART objectives, 676
smart safes, 110–111
"smash and grab" thief, 240
smoke detectors, 216
smoldering stage (fire), 215
Societies for the Reformation of Manners, 16
Society for the Suppression of Vice and Encouragement of Religion, 16
Society of Competitive Intelligence Professionals, 274
soda acid fire extinguishers, 218
soft look uniform, 315
software piracy, 289–290
Sorichetti v. City of New York, 80
source tagging, 488
space alarms, 120
span of control, 683
span of management, 683
special event security (*see also* public gatherings), 66, 546–550
spending, private security, 57, 58, 716
spoken messages, 359
sporting events, 548
spot alarms, 120
spot smoke detectors, 216
spreading of risk, 440
spring-loaded bolts, 113
sprinkler systems, 220, 302
staff reductions, 714
stagecoaches, 16
stalkers, 641
standard of care, 77–78
standard release form, 493
standards, OSHA, 191
standby lighting, 118
State in Interest of T.L.O., 588
state requirements, 687
state statutes regulating private security, 55–56
State v. Burleson, 291
State v. Weiss, 545
statement, 264
statistics, 13
Statute of Westminster, 7–8

statutory arrest authority of private citizens, 258
statutory law, 74
still cameras, 129, 132
still sequence cameras, 129, 132
stockrooms, 165–166, 460
Stop Thief, 535, 536
storing assets, 109–111
strategies for testifying in court, 407
streetlights, 102
strict liability, 76
strike (locks), 112
strike team, 204
strikebreakers, 19
strikes, 203–204, 630, 642
structuring the narrative (reports), 391–392
student patrol, 586
Student Right-To-Know Act, 584
sub-master key, 162
substance abuse (*see also* alcohol abuse, drug use), 146
substantive damages, 78
Superdome, 548
supervising, 152–153, 691–692
supervisor, 683, 691–692
  difference between manager and, 691–692
supply room security, 166
surveillance, 55, 64, 279–280, 341–342, 488–489, 608, 680
  acoustical, 279–280
  devices, 488–489
  parking areas, 608
  privacy rights, 341–342
  techniques, 680
  video, 341
surveillance cameras, 129–131, 132, 341
surveillance systems, 128–131, 132, 341, 488–489, 504–505
  CCTV, 129–131, 132, 488–489, 504–505
  convex mirrors, 129, 488
  dressing rooms, 489
  employee incentive program, 489
  General Mills Honesty Patrol, 489
  infrared (IR) cameras, 131
  motion picture cameras, 129, 132
  still cameras, 129, 132
  still sequence cameras, 129, 132
  videotapes, 129, 132, 341, 488
surveys, security (*see* security surveys, risk analysis)
surviving a lawsuit, 88–89
suspect's rights, 265
suspension, 693

T

taking corrective action, 692–693
taking notes, 374–379
tangled web of risks, 423
Taylor v. Centennial Bowl, Inc., 79–80
Techniques of Alcohol Management (TAM), 543
technology, 710–713, 714
telecommunications, 278–280
  acoustical surveillance, 279–280
  unsecured, 279
telemarketing scams, 247
telephone communications, unsecured, 279
telephone dialers, 123
telephone systems, computerized, 133
telephone transferring, 525
temporary badge sign-in/out log, 157
temporary variance, 191
termination, 693
terrorism, 31, 557, 559, 613, 616, 630, 631, 715
testifying in court, 399–418
  appearance, 400
  attitude, 400
  before the trial, 401
  behavior, 400
  concluding your testimony, 412
  critical thinking exercise, 416–418
  cross-examination, 403, 407–411
  direct examination, 403, 404–406
  excelling as a witness, 406–407
  expert testimony, 413–414
  Fifth Amendment, 402
  guidelines for effective testimony, 405
  handling objections, 411
  impeaching a witness, 401
  inadmissible statements, 404
  nonverbal factors, 406
  overview, 400–401
  preparation for, 400
  referring to notes, 405–406
  sequence of criminal trial, 402–404
  strategies for, 407
  tips for success, 412–413
  trends in decisions and settlements, 414–415
  trial, 402–412
testing, drug, 147, 173, 251–256, 463–464
Texas State Employment Union v. Texas Department of Mental Health, 150
theft (*see also* shrinkage, pilferage), 64, 65, 145–147, 153, 176–179, 239–240, 248–249, 350–351, 393–394, 453,

460–461, 503–509, 525, 572, 591, 716
areas most vulnerable to, 460–461
art, 591
employee, 64, 65, 145–147, 153, 176–179, 248–249, 453, 503–509, 572, 716
from motor vehicles, 239
larceny/theft, 239–240
report, 393–394
theme parks, 551–552
thermal detectors, 216
threat and incident management team, 643
threat assessment (*see* risk analysis)
threats to information security, 276–277
ticket windows, 550
till tapping, 506–507
timber industry, theft from, 454
time locks, 117
tips for success in court, 412–413
tips for writing more effectively, 389–391
tithing system, 6
Tolbert v. Martin Marietta Corp., 83
toll fraud, 278
tone of voice, 363
tool room, 455
tools, 455–456
top guard, 100
tort law, 55
torts, 74, 238
touch, 364
tour groups, 158
town watchmen, 16
toxic work environment, 632
trade secrets, 459
trade shows, 547–548
traffic control (*see* vehicle control, visitor control)
trailers (arson), 246
trailers (truck), 172
training, 84–87, 152–153, 194, 678, 687–691, 710–711, 719–720
documentation of, 194
firearms, 690–691
manuals, 678
negligent, 689
ongoing, 688–690
preassignment, 688
programs, 678
state requirements, 689
trains (*see* railroad)
transfer of risk, 440
transferring police tasks to private security, 266–267
transportation security, 461–467, 554–559, 702–703
airport, 554–557
cargo, 461
future of, 702–703
mass transit, 557–559
railroad, 464–466
seaport, 466–467
trucking, 462–464
transporting valuables, 176
traps, 124
trash removal inspection, 178
traveler's check, 497, 498
Treatise on the Police of the Metropolis, 13
trends in the security profession, 701, 704, 713
Trentacost, Florence, v. Brussel, Dr. Nathan T., 80
trespass of property, 351, 394
trespassing, 243–244
trial, 401–412
before the, 401
jury, 403
participants, 402
sequence of criminal, 402–404
trucking industry, 240, 462–464
cargo theft, 240, 462
direct financial loss to, 462
drug and alcohol testing of drivers, 463
employee collusion, 462–463
organized crime, 462
seal system, 463
tuberculosis, 196
tunnels, 101, 103, 108
Turner v. General Motors Corp., 665
turnover of security personnel, 683–684
turnstiles, 101, 550
24-four hour clock, 366–367
two-party check, 497
two-way vs. one-way communication, 362–363

U

Ultra, 22
ultrasonic detectors, 125
ultrasonic Doppler (sensor), 121
unauthorized ATM card use, 529
underage drinking, 583
undercover investigations, 34
understanding, 328, 362
self, 328
Underwriters' Laboratories (UL), 22, 110

Uniform Crime Reports (UCR), 239, 584
uniforms, 314–316, 453, 679
  image, 679
  military, 314
  security officer, 314–315
  soft look, 315
  theft of, 453
United States, evolution of private security in, 15–24
United States Secret Service, 304
United States v. Bice-Bey, 503
United States v. John DiGilio et al, 294
United States v. Dockery, 64
United States v. Paul A. Lambert, 294
United States v. Lyons, 545
United States v. Tartaglia, 262
unity of command, 683
universal check, 497
Universal Studios in Orlando, 552
universities (*see* colleges and universities)
University of Southern California (USC), 590
unlawful entry, 350
unlawful taking, 243
unreasonable searches, 192
unruly individuals, dealing with, 205
unsecured faxes, 279
unsecured telephone communications, 279
upward communication, 365
Urban Cohorts, 5–6
use of force, 81–82, 259–260, 269–271, 395–398
  continuum, 81–82
  critical thinking exercise, 269–271, 395–398
  excessive, 82
utility company security, 467–470
  diversion of the resource, 468
  nuclear plants, 470
  primary problems, 467
  reducing losses, 468
  risks and responsibilities, 468–469
  service trucks, 467
utility tunnels, 101, 108

V

validating cash register, 507
valuables, transporting, 176
vandalism, 243–244, 351, 394, 578
  report, 394
  schools, 578
vandalism arsonists, 245
variances, 191
vaults, 19, 110–111, 114, 218, 552
vehicle control, 154
vehicle inspections, 178
vendors, 159–161, 276
  as security threats, 276
ventilation openings, 108
vibration contacts, 124
vicarious liability, 75
vicious circle, private security, 685
victims of bombings, common, 207
video equipment, restrictions on use of, 170
video multiplexer, 130
videotape cameras, 129, 132, 488
Vigiles, 5–6
violence, 578, 626–648, 704, 708, 709, 714
  dealing with, 642–643
  during demonstrations, 641–642
  during strikes, 642
  in schools, 578
  in the workplace, 626–648, 704, 708, 709, 714
  legal implications of, 643–644
VIPs, protecting, 612–618
virtual corporation, 280
virus, computer, 290–291, 292–293
vision statement, 656
visitor control, 158, 159, 277, 569
visitor register log, 159
visually impaired individuals, 321
voice, 117, 133
  disguising, 133
voice-recognition technology, 711
vulnerability, 428, 435
  checklist to assess, 435
vulnerable areas, 165–167, 460–461, 612
  controlling access to, 165–167
  courts, 612

W

Wackenhut, George E., 23
Wackenhut Corporate Library, 720
Wackenhut Corporation, 23, 38, 657, 718, 719, 720
  corporate vision and goals of, 657
Wackenhut Leadership Manual, 719–720
wafer switch alarm, 487
Wagner Act, 22
walk-through metal detectors, 133
walkways, 103
walls, 3, 4, 108–109

wandering, 318, 572–573
warded locks, 112
wards, 6
warehouse protection, 165–166
warehouses, 460
Warne, Kate, 18
warning (discipline), 692
warning (weather), 226
warrant to check for safety and health hazards, 192–193
warrantless search, 64
watch (weather), 226
watch and ward, 7–9
watch clocks, 135–136
watchmen, 16
water (fire), 218–220, 302
watermark cards, 116
Watkins, William, 19
weapons (*see also* firearms), 3, 8, 82–83, 679
  image, 679
Wells Fargo and Company, 16, 38
well-written reports, characteristics of, 381–394
Western Union, 20
white-collar crime, 34, 247–249
  types of, 247
wide-angle (convex) mirrors, 129, 488
Wiegand cards, 116
William J. Burns' Detective Agency, 21
William the Conqueror, 6
windows, 108
wireless alarms, 123
wireless phones, 279
wiretapping, 55
witness, excelling as in court, 406–407
Wold v. State, 265
wood stockade fence, 100
work forces, changes in, 713
workplace violence, 626–648, 704, 708, 709, 714
  access control, 639
  causes of, 631–632
  critical thinking exercise, 645–647
  dealing with, 642–643
  demonstrations, 641–642
  employer-directed homicide, 629
  extent of the problem, 627–629
  female fatalities, 630
  forms of, 630–631
  Hilson Safety/Security Risk Inventory, 640
  indicators, 634–635
  injuries, 634
  Inwald Survey 8, 640
  job frustration, 632
  legal implications, 643–644
  loss of a job, 632
  murder, 629
  occupations at greater risk of, 635–636
  postemployment practices, 639
  preemployment screening, 640–641
  preventing, 636–642
  profile of the perpetrator, 632–634
  societal factors, 631
  stalkers, 641
  statistics, 628
  strikes, 642
  threat and incident management team, 643
  training, 638
  victims, 634
  weapons, 633–634
World Trade Center bombing, 205–206
World War II, 22, 23
world wars, 21–23
writing security reports, 378–394
written communication, 360, 364
written messages, 359
written sales slip system, 507
wrongs, intentional, 76
wrought-iron fence, 101

X

x-ray machines, 134

Y

Yale Campus Police, 585

Z

zero floor release limit, 503

Photo Credits

1 *Jeroboam Inc./Emilio Mercado;* 4 *Chromosohm/Sohm/MCMXCII/Stock Boston;* 5 *Bachmann/Stock Boston;* 6 *Dallas and John Heaton/Stock Boston;* 8 *The Bettmann Archive;* 10 *Stock Montage;* 14 *Topham/The Image Works;* 17 *AP/Wide World Photos;* 17 *The Granger Collection;* 21 *Courtesy of Brinks Security;* 21 *AP/Wide World Photos;* 33 *© Scott Harr;* 34 *Monkmeyer/Conklin;* 35 *Dean Abramson/Stock Boston;* 53 *© Linda Miller;* 53 *Monkmeyer/Sidney;* 88 *Robert E. Daemmrich/Tony Stone Worldwide, ltd.;* 93 *C. Johnson/Gamma-Liaison;* 100 *Etienne De Malglaive/Liaison International;* 102 *The Bettmann Archive;* 106 *Mike Mazzaschi/Stock Boston;* 107 *Stock Boston;* 128 *Herb Snitzer/Stock Boston;* 129 *Monkmeyer/Goodwin;* 130 *Wide World Photos;* 134 *James L. Shaffer;* 135 *Irene Bayer/Monkmeyer Press Photo Service;* 155 *Monkmeyer/Dunn;* 156 *John Coletti/Stock Boston;* 164 *James L. Shaffer;* 202 *Monkmeyer/Kerbs;* 206 *Gamma Liaison Brad Markel;* 211 *UPI/Bettmann;* 217 *PhotoEdit/Terry Freeman;* 219 *Stock Boston/Stephen Frisch;* 224 *Stock Boston/© 1994 Joseph Sohm/Chromosohm;* 225 *UPI Bettmann;* 253 *Monkmeyer/Mensheenfreund;* 284 *Monkmeyer/Kerbs;* 315 *Monkmeyer/The Photo Works;* 316 *Courtesy of Pinkerton's, Inc.;* 323 *Cheryl A. Traendly/Jeroboam;* 327 *Robert Ullmann Design Conceptions;* 337 *Tom McCarthy/PhotoEdit;* 342 *Stock Boston;* 343 *Stock Boston Charles Gupton;* 360 *Monkmeyer/Sidney;* 364 *Courtesy of Chase Security Corp.;* 378 *Joel Gordon;* 401 *Stock Boston/ Mark Burnett;* 403 *Frank Fisher/Liaison International;* 412 *Pool Liaison;* 419 *© Linda Miller;* 425 *Cindy Charles/PhotoEdit;* 429 *Michael Newman/PhotoEdit;* 435 *David Young-Wolff/PhotoEdit;* 439 *Monkmeyer/Mimi Forsyth;* 450 *Courtesy of Pinkerton's, Inc.;* 451 *AP/Wide World Photos;* 462 *Marc C. Biggins/Liaison International;* 464 *Bill Morson/Liaison International;* 466 *Monkmeyer/Goodwin;* 475 *Courtesy of Chase Security Corp.;* 481 *AP/Wide World Photos;* 513 *Stock Boston/Amanda Merulle;* 514 *© Linda Miller;* 529 *Liaison International/Ron Coppock;* 529 *Stock Boston Sue Klemens;* 533 *Stock Boston John Coletti;* 547 *Jon Simon/Liaison;* 555 *David R. Frazier Photolibrary;* 573 *Courtesy of Pinkerton's, Inc.;* 582 *James L. Shaffer;* 608 *Bonnie Kamin/PhotoEdit;* 610 *David R. Frazier Photolibrary;* 625 *AP/Wide World Photos;* 629 *AP/Wide World Photos;* 636 *David R. Frazier Photolibrary;* 642 *Tony Freeman/PhotoEdit;* 652 *Jeff Greenberg/PhotoEdit;* 664 *Michael Newman/PhotoEdit;* 681 *Michael Newman/PhotoEdit;* 688 *Michael Newman/PhotoEdit;* 693 *Michael Newman/PhotoEdit;* 702 *Mary Kate Denny/PhotoEdit;* 702 *James L. Shaffer;* 706 *AP/Wide World Photos;* 720 *Micheal G. Bennett/Imagemakers International, Inc.*